MW00341445

Celebrity Rights

Celebrity Rights

Rights of Publicity and Related Rights in the United States and Abroad

David S. Welkowitz
PROFESSOR OF LAW
WHITTIER LAW SCHOOL

Tyler T. Ochoa
PROFESSOR OF LAW
SANTA CLARA UNIVERSITY SCHOOL OF LAW

CAROLINA ACADEMIC PRESS
Durham, North Carolina

ISBN 978-1-59460-657-1
LCCN: 2009939230

Carolina Academic Press
700 Kent Street
Durham, North Carolina 27701
Telephone (919) 489-7486
Fax (919) 493-5668
www.cap-press.com

Printed in the United States of America

Contents

Table of Illustrations

Table of Cases

Table of Secondary Authorities

Foreword

In our celebrity-obsessed culture, it cannot be denied that celebrities are big business. Sports stars such as Tiger Woods are paid millions of dollars to endorse a wide variety of products and services, and often earn more from their endorsements than they do from their sporting prowess. Actors, singers and other performers are paid millions of dollars to appear in films and on television, to make recordings, and to endorse products or services. Supermodels are paid millions of dollars to have their photographs taken and published in various states of dress and undress. Tabloid newspapers and gossip magazines pay millions of dollars for the right to publish photos of celebrities and celebrity offspring, while paparazzi make a living by stalking celebrities and taking candid photos which they sell to the highest bidder. Manufacturers make millions of dollars selling products—everything from t-shirts and posters to coffee mugs, dart boards and bobblehead dolls—adorned with celebrity likenesses. Even dead celebrities can earn millions of dollars annually when their heirs lend their fame to various commercial enterprises.

The legal foundation for all of this economic activity is the right of publicity. The right of publicity can be defined simply as "the inherent right of every human being to control the commercial use of his or her identity." J. Thomas McCarthy, THE RIGHTS OF PUBLICITY AND PRIVACY § 1:3 (2d ed. 2008). Technically speaking, however, there is not one right of publicity but many, since the right of publicity is protected in the United States only as a state-law right (although various aspects of the right of publicity may also be protected under federal trademark and unfair competition law, as we will see). These rights help insure that celebrities get paid for their labors in accumulating fame and bestowing the benefit of that fame upon various products and services.

As of 2008, at least 28 states recognize a right of publicity (10 states as a common-law right, 10 states as a statutory right, and 8 states as both). McCarthy, § 6:3. In addition, all states recognize a common-law or statutory right of privacy, which generally provides at least some protection against commercial appropriation of a celebrity's identity. And yet, despite widespread agreement that celebrities should be paid for their endorsements, rights of publicity are often shrouded in controversy. How far should rights of publicity extend? Should a tabloid newspaper be prohibited from featuring a celebrity on its cover without that celebrity's consent? Can a local television station show a clip of a performance at the county fair of a human cannonball without his consent? May an artist create and sell pictures of celebrities without their consent? To what extent should celebrity impersonators be permitted to imitate others in advertisements and performances? Should rights of publicity endure after the death of a celebrity; and if so, for how long?

Moreover, although courts in the United States may consider the right of publicity to be an inherent right, the same consensus is not necessarily shared in other countries of the world. As you will see, a number of countries protect celebrities from the use of their names and likenesses in situations that lawyers in the United States would recognize as similar, if not identical, to our "right of publicity." However, the rationales used in other countries differ significantly from our conception of the "right of publicity," which sometimes leads to differing results. Obviously, it is impossible to canvass all of the countries of the world to determine which ones grant such rights, and to what extent. However, these materials are designed to give you some idea of the range of issues contested in the United States, and a taste of how other countries address those issues.

The purpose of these materials, therefore, is twofold. First, these materials are designed to give you a thorough understanding of rights of publicity as they are understood in the United States. Therefore, each chapter begins with materials from courts and/or legislatures in the United States. Second, these materials allow you to compare the analysis and conclusions of courts and legislatures in the United States with those in other countries. Again, these comparisons are only selected samples of what is done elsewhere. Moreover, because of language issues, some of the material concerning other countries is presented via commentary from knowledgeable academics and practitioners.

Although any significant discussion of other legal systems is beyond the scope of these materials, you should understand that not all countries have legal systems that mirror the system in the United States. In the United Kingdom and in many countries in which British influence is strong, such as Canada and Australia, the common-law system of legal development through case law is an important aspect of the legal system. (As in the United States, however, those systems are also increasingly governed by statutory schemes. Moreover, because the United Kingdom is part of the European Union, there is now a strong European influence in many aspects of British law, particularly in intellectual property.) Other countries, such as France, are governed by a civil law tradition, in which civil codes set forth various rights and responsibilities. In these countries (at least in theory), it is the codes that govern civil wrongs, and relatively less importance is placed on case law. However, some of the provisions of those codes are relatively broad, which has allowed courts to interpret those provisions in ways that in many respects are similar to rights of publicity in the United States.

As you read the materials, do not just seek the results of the cases. You should attempt to develop a sense of the differences in the various legal systems and traditions that lead courts in different directions. Often courts in different countries may reach similar results, but they arrive at those results from very different premises. It is important that you recognize those differences as we go through the course. Consider for yourself how courts in other countries might decide some of the difficult issues faced by courts in the United States.

Celebrity Rights

Chapter I

Introduction: The Origins of Rights of Publicity

A. The Development of Rights of Publicity in the United States

Rights of publicity are rights of relatively recent vintage, having evolved from the right of privacy that was first recognized in the first decade of the 20th Century, and having received express recognition as a separate cause of action in 1953, only 57 years ago. The following cases illustrate how the right of privacy came to be recognized in the United States, and how those cases eventually led to the development of rights of publicity.

Roberson v. Rochester Folding Box Co.
171 N.Y. 538, 64 N.E. 442 (1902)

PARKER, C.J.:

The appellate division has certified that the following questions of law have arisen in this case, and ought to be reviewed by this court: (1) Does the complaint herein state a cause of action at law against the defendants, or either of them? (2) Does the complaint herein state a cause of action in equity against the defendants, or either of them? These questions are presented by a demurrer to the complaint, which is put upon the ground that the complaint does not state facts sufficient to constitute a cause of action....

The complaint alleges that the Franklin Mills Company, one of the defendants, was engaged in a general milling business and in the manufacture and sale of flour; that before the commencement of the action, without the knowledge or consent of plaintiff, defendants, knowing that they had no right or authority so to do, had obtained, made, printed, sold, and circulated about 25,000 lithographic prints, photographs, and likenesses of plaintiff ... ; that upon the paper upon which the likenesses were printed and above the portrait there were printed, in large, plain letters, the words, 'Flour of the Family,' and below the portrait, in large capital letters, 'Franklin Mills Flour,' and in the lower right-hand corner, in smaller capital letters, 'Rochester Folding Box Co., Rochester, N.Y.'; that upon the same sheet were other advertisements of the flour of the Franklin Mills Company; that those 25,000 likenesses of the plaintiff thus ornamented have been conspicuously posted and displayed in stores, warehouses, saloons, and other public places; that they have been recognized by friends of the plaintiff and other people, with the result that plaintiff has been greatly humiliated by the scoffs and jeers of persons who have recognized her face and picture on this advertisement, and her good name has been at-

Figure 1-1. From the Collection of The Public Library of Cincinnati and Hamilton County

tacked, causing her great distress and suffering, both in body and mind; that she was made sick, and suffered a severe nervous shock, was confined to her bed, and compelled to employ a physician, because of these facts; that defendants had continued to print, make, use, sell, and circulate the said lithographs, and that by reason of the foregoing facts plaintiff had suffered damages in the sum of $15,000. The complaint prays that defendants be enjoined from making, printing, publishing, circulating, or using in any manner any likenesses of plaintiff in any form whatever; ... and for damages.

It will be observed that there is no complaint made that plaintiff was libeled by this publication of her portrait. The likeness is said to be a very good one, and one that her friends and acquaintances were able to recognize. Indeed, her grievance is that a good portrait of her, and therefore one easily recognized, has been used to attract attention toward the paper upon which defendant mill company's advertisements appear. Such publicity, which some find agreeable, is to plaintiff very distasteful, and thus, because of defendants' impertinence in using her picture, without her consent, for their own business purposes, she has been caused to suffer mental distress where others would have appreciated the compliment to their beauty implied in the selection of the picture for such purposes; but, as it is distasteful to her, she seeks the aid of the courts to enjoin a further circulation of the lithographic prints containing her portrait made as alleged in the complaint, and, as an incident thereto, to reimburse her for the damages to her feelings, which the complaint fixes at the sum of $15,000.

There is no precedent for such an action to be found in the decisions of this court.... Nevertheless [the appellate] court reached the conclusion that plaintiff had a good cause of action against defendants, in that defendants had invaded what is called a 'right of privacy'; in other words, the right to be let alone. Mention of such a right is not to be found in Blackstone, Kent, or any other of the great commentators upon the law; nor, so far as the learning of counsel or the courts in this case have been able to discover, does its existence seem to have been asserted prior to about the year 1890, when it was presented with attractiveness, and no inconsiderable ability, in the Harvard Law Review.... [See Samuel D. Warren & Louis D. Brandeis, *The Right of Privacy*, 4 Harv. L. Rev. 193 (1890).]

The so-called 'right of privacy' is, as the phrase suggests, founded upon the claim that a man has the right to pass through this world, if he wills, without having his picture published, his business enterprises discussed, his successful experiments written up for the benefit of others, or his eccentricities commented upon either in handbills, circulars, catalogues, periodicals, or newspapers; and, necessarily, that the things which may not be written and published of him must not be spoken of him by his neighbors, whether the comment be favorable or otherwise. While most persons would much prefer to have a good likeness of themselves appear in a responsible periodical or leading newspaper rather than upon an advertising card or sheet, the doctrine which the courts are asked to create for this case would apply as well to the one publication as to the other, for the principle which a court of equity is asked to assert in support of a recovery in this action is that the right of privacy exists and is enforceable in equity, and that the publication of that which purports to be a portrait of another person, even if obtained upon the street by an impertinent individual with a camera, will be restrained in equity on the ground that an individual has the right to prevent his features from becoming known to those outside of his circle of friends and acquaintances.

If such a principle be incorporated into the body of the law through the instrumentality of a court of equity, the attempts to logically apply the principle will necessarily result not only in a vast amount of litigation, but in litigation bordering upon the absurd, for the right of privacy, once established as a legal doctrine, cannot be confined to the restraint of the publication of a likeness, but must necessarily embrace as well the publication of a word picture, a comment upon one's looks, conduct, domestic relations or habits. And, were the right of privacy once legally asserted, it would necessarily be held to include the same things if spoken instead of printed, for one, as well as the other, invades the right to be absolutely let alone. An insult would certainly be in violation of such a right, and with many persons would more seriously wound the feelings than would the publication of their picture. And so we might add to the list of things that are spoken and done day by day which seriously offend the sensibilities of good people to which the principle which the plaintiff seeks to have imbedded in the doctrine of the law would seem to apply. I have gone only far enough to barely suggest the vast field of litigation which would necessarily be opened up should this court hold that privacy exists as a legal right enforceable in equity by injunction, and by damages where they seem necessary to give complete relief.

The legislative body could very well interfere and arbitrarily provide that no one should be permitted for his own selfish purpose to use the picture or the name of another for advertising purposes without his consent. In such event no embarrassment would result to the general body of the law, for the rule would be applicable only to cases provided for by the statute. The courts, however, being without authority to legislate, are required to decide cases upon principle, and so are necessarily embarrassed by precedents created by an extreme, and therefore unjustifiable, application of an old principle....

It is undoubtedly true that in the early days of chancery jurisdiction in England the chancellors were accustomed to deliver their judgments without regard to principles or precedents, and in that way the process of building up the system of equity went on, the chancellor disregarding absolutely many established principles of the common law.... In their work the chancellors were guided not only by what they regarded as the eternal principles of absolute right, but also by their individual consciences; but after a time, when 'the period of infancy was passed, and an orderly system of equitable principles, doctrines, and rules began to be developed out of the increasing mass of precedents, this theory of a personal conscience was abandoned; and 'the conscience,' which is an element of the equitable jurisdiction, came to be regarded, and has so continued to the present day, as a metaphorical term, designating the common standard of civil right and expediency combined, based upon general principles, and limited by established doctrines to which the court appeals, and by which it tests the conduct and rights of suitors,—a juridical, and not a personal, conscience.' Pomeroy's Eq. Jur. § 57.

The importance of observing the spirit of this rule cannot be overestimated; for, while justice in a given case may be worked out by a decision of the court according to the notions of right which govern the individual judge or body of judges comprising the court, the mischief which will finally result may be almost incalculable under our system, which makes a decision in one case a precedent for decisions in all future cases which are akin to it in the essential facts.

So, in a case like the one before us, which is concededly new to this court, it is important that the court should have in mind the effect upon future litigation and upon the development of the law which would necessarily result from a step so far outside of the beaten paths of both common law and equity, assuming ... that the right of privacy, as a legal doctrine enforceable in equity, has not, down to this time, been established by decisions.

The history of the phrase 'right of privacy' in this country seems to have begun in 1890, in a clever article in the Harvard Law Review—already referred to—in which a number of English cases were analyzed, and, reasoning by analogy, the conclusion was reached that, notwithstanding the unanimity of the courts in resting their decisions upon property rights in cases where publication is prevented by injunction, in reality such prevention was due to the necessity of affording protection to thoughts and sentiments expressed through the medium of writing, printing, and the arts, which is like the right not to be assaulted or beaten; in other words, that the principle actually involved, though not always appreciated, was that of an inviolate personality, not that of private property.

This article brought forth a reply [*see* Herbert Spencer Hadley, *The Right to Privacy*, 3 Nw. L. Rev. 1 (1894)] ... urging that equity has no concern with the feelings of an individual, or with considerations of moral fitness, except as the inconvenience or discomfort which the person may suffer is connected with the possession or enjoyment of property, and that the English authorities cited are consistent with such view. Those authorities are now to be examined, in order that we may see whether they were intended to and did mark a departure from the established rule which had been enforced for generations; or, on the other hand, are entirely consistent with it.

The first case is *Prince Albert v. Strange*, [64 Eng. Rep. 293 (Ch. 1849)]. The queen and the prince, having made etchings and drawings for their own amusement, decided to have copies struck off from the etched plates for presentation to friends and for their own use. The workman employed, however, printed some copies on his own account, which afterwards came into the hands of Strange, who purposed exhibiting them, and published a descriptive catalogue. Prince Albert applied for an injunction as to both exhibition and catalogue, and the vice chancellor granted it, restraining defendant from publishing, 'at least by printing or writing, though not by copy or resemblance,' a description of the etchings. An examination of the opinion of the vice chancellor discloses that he found two reasons for granting the injunction, namely, that the property rights of Prince Albert had been infringed, and that there was a breach of trust by the workman in retaining some impressions for himself. The opinion contained no hint whatever of a right of privacy separate and distinct from the right of property.

Pollard v. Photographic Co., 40 Ch. Div. 345 [(1888)], is certainly not an authority for granting an injunction on the ground of threatened injury to the feelings, although it is true … that the court did say in the course of the discussion that the right to grant an injunction does not depend upon the existence of property; but the decision was, in fact, placed upon the ground that there was a breach of an implied contract. The facts, briefly stated, were that a photographer had been applied to by a woman to take her photograph, she ordering a certain number of copies, as is usual in such cases. The photographer made copies for himself, and undertook to exhibit them, and also sold copies to a stationer, who used them as Christmas cards. Their action was restrained by the court on the ground that there was an implied contract not to use the negative for any other purpose than to supply the sitter with copies of it for a price. During the argument of plaintiff's counsel the court asked this question: 'Do you dispute that, if the negative likeness were taken on the sly, the person who took it might exhibit copies?' Counsel replied, 'In that case there would be no consideration to support a contract.'…

In *Duke of Queensbury v. Shebbeare*, [28 Eng. Rep. 924 (Ch. 1758)], the Earl of Clarendon delivered to one Gwynne an original manuscript of his father's 'Lord Clarendon's History.' Gwynne's administrator afterwards sold it to Shebbeare, and the court, upon the application of the personal representatives of Lord Clarendon, restrained its publication on the ground that they had a property right in the manuscript which it was not intended that Gwynne should have the benefit of by multiplying the number of copies in print for profit.

In not one of these cases, therefore, was it the basis of the decision that the defendant could be restrained from performing the act he was doing or threatening to do on the ground that the feelings of the plaintiff would be thereby injured; but, on the contrary, each decision was rested either upon the ground of breach of trust, or that plaintiff had a property right in the subject of litigation which the court could protect.

A more recent English case, decided in 1898, is more nearly in point, and negatives the contention that plaintiff may restrain an unauthorized publication which is offensive to him,—namely, *Dockrell v. Dougall*, 78 Law T. (N. S.) 840 [(Q.B. 1898)]. In that case defendant, the owner of a medicine called 'Sallyco,' published the following substantially true but unauthorized statement about plaintiff: 'Dr. Morgan Dockrell, physician to St. John's Hospital, London, is prescribing Sallyco as an habitual drink. Dr. Dockrell says nothing has done his gout so much good.' In the course of the opinion the court said, in effect, that plaintiff claimed to be entitled to an injunction restraining defendant from using plaintiff's name in his advertisements on the ground that an injunction should be granted in every such case where it can be shown that the use of the plaintiff's name is unauthorized, and is calculated to injure him in his profession; and, after saying that he did not think that this was right, he stated the proper rule to be that, 'In order that an injunction may issue to restrain a defendant from using a plaintiff's name, the use of it must be such as to injure the plaintiff's reputation or property.'...

The case that seems to have been more relied upon than any other by the learned appellate division in reaching the conclusion that the complaint in this case states a cause of action is *Schuyler v. Curtis*, 147 N.Y. 434, 42 N.E. 22 [(1895)]. In that case certain persons attempted to erect a statue or bust of a woman no longer living, and one of her relatives commenced an action in equity to restrain such erection, alleging that his feelings and the feelings of other relatives of deceased would be injured thereby. At special term an injunction was granted on that ground. [15 N.Y. Supp. 787 (Sup. Ct. 1891).] The general term affirmed the decision. [19 N.Y. Supp. 264 (Sup. Ct. 1892).] This court reversed the judgment, Judge Peckham writing, and, so far as the decision is concerned, therefore, it is not authority for the existence of a right of privacy which entitles a party to restrain another from doing an act which, though not actionable at common law, occasions plaintiff mental distress. In the course of the argument, however, expressions were used which it is now claimed indicate that the court recognized the existence of such a right.... The question up for decision in the *Schuyler* case was whether the relatives could restrain the threatened action of defendants, and not whether Mrs. Schuyler could have restrained it had she been living. The latter question not being before the court, it was not called upon to decide it, and, as we read the opinion, there is no expression in it which indicates an intention either to decide it or to seriously consider it; but, rather, it proceeds upon the assumption that, if such a right did exist in Mrs. Schuyler, her relatives did not succeed to it upon her death....

There are two other cases in this state bearing upon this question: *Marks v. Jaffa*, 6 Misc. 290, 26 N.Y. Supp. 908 [(1893)], decided at Special Term, and *Murray v. Gast Lithographic & Engraving Co.*, 8 Misc. 36, 28 N.Y. Supp. 271 [(1894)], decided at an Equity Term of the Court of Common Pleas at New York. In the first case the relief prayed for was granted upon the authority of the decision of the General Term in the *Schuyler* case, which was subsequently reversed in this court. In the *Murray* case, in a well-reasoned opinion by Judge Bischoff, it is held that a parent cannot maintain an action to enjoin an unauthorized publication of the portrait of an infant child, and for damages for injuries to his sensibilities, caused by the invasion of his child's privacy, because 'the law takes no cognizance of a sentimental injury, independent of a wrong to person or property.' In the course of his opinion he quotes from the opinion of Lumpkin, J., in *Chapman v. Western Union Telegraph Co.*, 88 Ga. 763, 15 S.E. 901 [(1892)], as follows: 'The law protects the person and the purse. The person includes the reputation. The body, reputation, and property of the citizen are not to be invaded without responsibility in damages to the sufferer. But, outside these protected spheres, the law does not yet attempt to guard the peace of mind, the feelings, or the happiness of every one by giving recovery of damages for mental anguish produced by mere negligence. There is no right, capable of enforcement by process of law, to possess or maintain, without disturbance, any particular condition of feeling. The law leaves feeling to be helped and vindicated by the tremendous force of sympathy. The temperaments of individuals are various and variable, and the imagination exerts a powerful and incalculable influence in injuries of this kind. There are many moral obligations too delicate and subtle to be enforced in the rude way of giving money compensation for their violation. Perhaps the feelings find as full protection as it is possible to give in moral law and a responsive public opinion. The civil law is a practical business system, dealing with what is tangible, and does not undertake to redress psychological injuries.'...

An examination of the authorities leads us to the conclusion that the so-called 'right of privacy' has not as yet found an abiding place in our jurisprudence, and, as we view it, the doctrine cannot now be incorporated without doing violence to settled principles of law by which the profession and the public have long been guided.

I do not say that, even under the existing law, in every case of the character of the one before us, or, indeed, in this case, a party whose likeness is circulated against his will is without remedy. By section 242 of the Penal Code any malicious publication by picture, effigy, or sign, which exposes a person to contempt, ridicule, or obloquy, is a libel, and it would constitute such at common law. 'Malicious,' in this definition, means simply 'intentional and willful.' There are many articles, especially of medicine, whose character is such that using the picture of a person, particularly that of a woman, in connection with the advertisement of those articles, might justly be found by a jury to cast ridicule or obloquy on the person whose picture was thus published. The manner or posture in which the person is portrayed might readily have a like effect. In such cases both a civil action and a criminal prosecution could be maintained. But there is no allegation in the complaint before us that this was the tendency of the publication complained of, and the absence of such an allegation is fatal to the maintenance of the action, treating it as one of libel. This case differs from an action brought for libelous words. In such case the alleged libel is stated in the complaint, and, if the words are libelous *per se*, it is unnecessary to charge that their effect exposes the plaintiff to disgrace, ridicule, or obloquy. The law attributes to them that result. But where the libel is a picture, which does not appear in the record, to make it libelous there must be a proper allegation as to its character.

The judgment of the appellate division and of the special term should be reversed, and questions certified answered in the negative, without costs, and with leave to the plaintiff to serve an amended complaint within 20 days, also without costs.

Gray, J. (dissenting):

The question arises on the defendants' demurrer to the sufficiency of the complaint to state a cause of action.... [The factual allegations in the complaint] must be regarded as admitted, under the defendant's demurrer; as must all other facts which can be implied by reasonable and fair intendment. These defendants stand before the court, admitting that they have made, published, and circulated, without the knowledge or the authority of the plaintiff, 25,000 lithographic portraits of her, for the purpose of profit and gain to themselves; that these portraits have been conspicuously posted in stores, warehouses, and saloons in the vicinity of the plaintiff's residence, and throughout the United States, as advertisements of their goods; that the effect has been to humiliate her, and to render her ill; and yet claiming that she makes out no cause of action....

Our consideration of the question thus presented has not been foreclosed by the decision in *Schuyler v. Curtis*, 147 N. Y. 434, 42 N. E. 22 [(1895)]. In that case it appeared that the defendants were intending to make, and to exhibit at the Columbian Exposition of 1893, a statue of Mrs. Schuyler, formerly Miss Mary M. Hamilton and conspicuous in her lifetime for her philanthropic work, to typify 'Woman as the Philanthropist,' and, as a companion piece, a statue of Miss Susan B. Anthony, to typify the 'Representative Reformer.' The plaintiff, in behalf of himself, as the nephew of Mrs. Schuyler, and of other immediate relatives, sought by the action to restrain them from carrying out their intentions as to the statue of Mrs. Schuyler, upon the grounds, in substance, that they were proceeding without his consent (whose relationship was conceded to be such as to warrant such an action, if it were maintainable at all) or that of the other immediate members of the family; that their proceeding was disagreeable to him, because it would have been disagreeable and obnoxious to his aunt, if living, and that it was annoying to have Mrs. Schuyler's memory associated with principles which Miss Susan B. Anthony typified, and of which Mrs. Schuyler did not approve. His right to maintain the action was denied, and the denial was expressly placed upon the ground that he, as a relative, did not represent any right of privacy which Mrs. Schuyler possessed in her lifetime, and that, whatever her right had been in that respect, it died with her. The existence of the individual's right to be protected against the invasion of his privacy, if not actually affirmed in the opinion, was, very certainly, far from being denied. 'It may be admitted,' Judge Peckham observed, when delivering the opinion of the court, 'that courts have power, in some cases, to enjoin the doing of an act, where the nature or character of the act itself is well calculated to wound the sensibilities of an individual, and where the doing of the act is wholly unjustifiable, and is, in legal contemplation, a wrong, even though the existence of no 'property' as that term is usually used, is involved in the subject.'

That the individual has a right to privacy, which he can enforce, and which equity will protect against the invasion of, is a proposition which is not opposed by any decision in this court, and which, in my opinion, is within the field of accepted legal principles.... In the present case, we may not say that the plaintiff's complaint is fanciful, or that her alleged injury is purely a sentimental one. Her objection to the defendants' acts is not one born of caprice, nor is it based upon the defendants' act being merely 'distasteful' to her. We are bound to assume, and I find no difficulty in doing so, that the conspicuous display of her likeness in various public places has so humiliated her by the notoriety and by the public comments it has provoked as to cause her distress and suffering in body and mind, and to confine her to her bed with illness.

If it were necessary, to be entitled to equitable relief, that the plaintiff's sufferings by reason of the defendants' acts should be serious, and appreciable by a pecuniary standard, clearly, we might well say, under the allegations of the complaint, that they were of such degree of gravity. However, I am not of the opinion that the gravity of the injury need be such as to be capable of being estimated by such a standard. If the right of privacy exists, and this complaint makes out a case of its substantial violation, I think that the award of equitable relief by way of an injunction preventing the continuance of its invasion by the defendants will not depend upon the complainant's ability to prove substantial pecuniary damages, and, if the court finds the defendants' act to be without justification, and for selfish gain and purposes, and to be of such a character as is reasonably calculated to wound the feelings and to subject the plaintiff to the ridicule or to the contempt of others, that her right to the preventive relief of equity will follow, without considering how far her sufferings may be measurable by a pecuniary standard.

The right of privacy, or the right of the individual to be let alone, is a personal right, which is not without judicial recognition. It is the complement of the right to the immunity of one's person. The individual has always been entitled to be protected in the exclusive use and enjoyment of that which is his own. This common law regarded his person and property as inviolate, and he has the absolute right to be let alone. Cooley, Torts, p. 29. The principle is fundamental and essential in organized society that every one, in exercising a personal right and in the use of his property shall respect the rights and properties of others. He must so conduct himself, in the enjoyment of the rights and privileges which belong to him as a member of society, as that he shall prejudice no one in the possession and enjoyment of those which are exclusively his. When, as here, there is an alleged invasion of some personal right or privilege, the absence of exact precedent and the fact that early commentators upon the common law have no discussion upon the subject are of no material importance in awarding equitable relief.... In the social evolution, with the march of the arts and sciences and in the resultant effects upon organized society, it is quite intelligible that new conditions must arise in personal relations, which the rules of the common law, cast in the rigid mold of an earlier social status, were not designed to meet. It would be a reproach to equitable jurisprudence if equity were powerless to extend the application of the principles of common law or of natural justice in remedying a wrong, which, in the progress of civilization, has been made possible as the result of new social or commercial conditions.... Equity has neither fixed boundaries nor logical subdivisions, and its origin, both in Rome and in England, was that there was a wrong for which there was no remedy at law. *See* 1 Story, Eq. Jur. §§ 49, 50. It supplements the deficiencies of the common law by applying, where otherwise there would result a wrong, those principles of natural justice which are analogous to settled principles of the common law.... [T]hat the exercise of this peculiar preventive power of a court of equity is not found in some precisely analogous case, furnishes no valid objection at all to the assumption of jurisdiction if the particular circumstances of the case show the performance, or the threatened performance, of an act by a defendant, which is wrongful, because constituting an invasion, in some novel form, of a right to something which is, or should be conceded to be, the plaintiff's, and as to which the law provides no adequate remedy. It would be a justifiable exercise of power whether the principle of interference be rested upon analogy to some established common-law principle, or whether it is one of natural justice. In an article in the Harvard Law Review of December 15, 1890, which contains an impressive argument upon the subject of the 'right of privacy,' it was well said by the authors: 'That the individual shall have full protection in person and in property is a principle as old as the common law; but it has been found necessary from time to time to define anew the exact nature and extent of such protection.... The right to life has come to mean the right to enjoy life, — the right to be let alone; the right to liberty secures the exercise of extensive civil privileges; and the term 'property' has grown to comprise every form of possession, intangible as well as tangible.'

Instantaneous photography is a modern invention, and affords the means of securing a portraiture of an individual's face and form, *in invitum* their owner. While, so far forth as it merely does that, although a species of aggression, I concede it to be an irremediable and irrepressible feature of the social evolution. But if it is to be permitted that the portraiture may be put to commercial or other uses for gain by the publication of prints therefrom, then an act of invasion of the individual's privacy results, possibly more formidable and more painful in its consequences than an actual bodily assault might be. Security of person is as necessary as the security of property; and for that complete personal security which will result in the peaceful and wholesome enjoyment of one's privileges as a member of society there should be afforded protection, not only against the scandalous portraiture and display of one's features and person, but against the display and use thereof for another's commercial purposes or gain. The proposition is, to me, an inconceivable one that these defendants may, unauthorizedly, use the likeness of this young woman upon their advertisement as a method of attracting widespread public attention to their wares, and that she must submit to the mortifying notoriety, without right to invoke the exercise of the preventive power of a court of equity.

Such a view, as it seems to me, must have been unduly influenced by a failure to find precedents in analogous cases, or some declaration by the great commentators upon the law of a common-law principle which would precisely apply to and govern the action, without taking into consideration that in the existing state of society new conditions affecting the relations of persons demand the broader extension of those legal principles which underlie the immunity of one's person from attack. I think that such a view is unduly restricted, too, by a search for some property which has been invaded by the defendants' acts. Property is not, necessarily, the thing itself which is owned; it is the right of the owner in relation to it. The right to be protected in one's possession of a thing or in one's privileges, belonging to him as an individual, or secured to him as a member of the commonwealth, is property, and as such entitled to the protection of the law. The protective power of equity is not exercised upon the tangible thing, but upon the right to enjoy it; and so it is called forth for the protection of the right to that which is one's exclusive possession as a property right. It seems to me that the principle which is applicable is analogous to that upon which courts of equity have interfered to protect the right of privacy in cases of private writings, or of other unpublished products of the mind. The writer or the lecturer has been protected in his right to a literary property in a letter or a lecture, against its unauthorized publication, because it is property, to which the right of privacy attaches.... I think that this plaintiff has the same property in the right to be protected against the use of her face for defendant's commercial purposes as she would have if they were publishing her literary compositions. The right would be conceded if she had set for the photograph; but if her face or her portraiture has a value, the value is hers exclusively, until the use be granted away to the public. Any other principle of decision, in my opinion, is as repugnant to equity as it is shocking to reason....

The right to grant the injunction does not depend upon the existence of property which one has in some contractual form. It depends upon the existence of property in any right which belongs to a person.... It would be, in my opinion, an extraordinary view, which, while conceding the right of a person to be protected against the unauthorized circulation of an unpublished lecture, letter, drawing, or other ideal property, yet would deny the same protection to a person whose portrait was unauthorizedly obtained and made use of for commercial purposes. The injury to the plaintiff is irreparable, because she cannot be wholly compensated in damages for the various consequences entailed by defendants' acts. The only complete relief is an injunction restraining their continuance. Whether, as incidental to that equitable relief, she should be able to recover only nominal damages, is not material, for the issuance of the injunction does not, in such a case, depend upon the amount of the damages in dollars and cents.

A careful consideration of the question presented upon this appeal leads me to the conclusion that the judgment appealed from should be affirmed.

O'Brien, Cullen, and Werner, JJ., concur with Parker, C.J. Bartlett and Haight, JJ., concur with Gray, J.

Judgment reversed, etc.

————

Notes and Questions

1. Why did the court in *Roberson* reject a right of privacy, as proposed by Warren & Brandeis? Do the cases cited by Warren & Brandeis, and discussed by the court, support the recognition of a right of privacy? Why or why not? Would recognition of such a right entail the line-drawing problems foreseen by the majority? Assuming that a right of privacy is good public policy, should such a right be recognized or created by a court, or by the legislature?

2. The principal authority relied upon by the dissent in *Roberson* is *Schuyler v. Curtis*. Should a right of privacy be recognized in such a situation? Would it have made a difference if Mrs. Schuyler had been alive and had brought the action, instead of it being brought by her nephew after her death? Should any other distinction be drawn between *Schuyler* and *Roberson*?

3. The decision in *Roberson* provoked a storm of controversy. Less than one year later, the New York Legislature enacted a statute to overturn the decision. The statute made it a misdemeanor to use "for advertising purposes, or for purposes of trade, the name, portrait or picture of any living person without having first obtained the written consent of such person." Act of Apr. 6, 1903, ch. 132, § 1, 1903 N.Y. Laws 308. The statute also allowed the person depicted to obtain an injunction and damages for any violation of the prohibition. *Id.*, § 2. The current version of the 1903 statute is codified at N.Y. Civ. Rights L. §§ 50–51, and is contained in the statutory appendix at the end of the casebook.

4. The story of the *Roberson* case did not end there. In 1904, Chief Judge Alton B. Parker, who wrote the majority opinion in *Roberson*, was nominated by the Democratic Party to run for President against the Republican incumbent, Theodore Roosevelt. After Parker and his family were repeatedly harassed by photographers, he issued a press release demanding that they stop photographing him and his family. Abigail Roberson, the disappointed plaintiff, wrote an open letter to Judge Parker which was published on the front page of the *New York Times*:

> My Dear Sir: I read in The Associated Press dispatches yesterday afternoon that Mrs. Parker was obliged to leave home to avoid the annoyance of ubiquitous photographers, notwithstanding the warning given by you and reported in the same dispatches last Saturday morning in which it was announced that that would be the last day of promiscuous photographing of yourself and family, and wherein you are quoted as saying: 'I reserve the right to put my hands in my pockets and assume comfortable attitudes without being everlastingly afraid that I shall be snapped by some fellow with a camera.'

> I take this opportunity to remind you that you have no such right as that which you assert. I have very high authority for my statement, being nothing less than a decision of the Court of Appeals of this State where in you wrote the prevailing opinion. The action was one in which I was the plaintiff, ... [and] in an opinion sixteen pages long you arrived at the conclusion that I had no rights that could be protected by your tribunal....

> I am forced to the conclusion that this incident well illustrates the truth of the old saying that it makes a lot of difference whose ox is gored. I sympathize by Mrs. Parker in her annoyance, but I know of no reason why you or your family have any rights of the nature suggested which do not equally belong to me. Indeed, as between us, I submit that I was much more entitled to protection than you.

> I was a poor girl making my living by my daily efforts, and never had courted publicity in any manner. I had never appeared before the public in any capacity nor solicited any favor at its hands. You, on the other hand, are a candidate for the highest office in the gift of the people of the United States, and that fact makes you the legitimate centre of public interest. You are asking the suffrage of the American public, and the American public would seem to have some legitimate right of investigation. Your candidacy is something more than merely voluntary, and it may fairly be said that you have invited the curiosity which we have both found to be somewhat annoying.

> To this extent, at least, it would seem to me that the right which you denied me, but which you now assert for yourself, was stronger in my case than in yours.

Parker Taken to Task by an Indignant Woman, N.Y. Times, July 27, 1904.

5. Abigail Roberson went on to play piano in and to manage several silent movie theaters. She died in 1977 at the age of 94. For more information regarding Abigail Rober-

son and the influence of her case on the right of privacy, see Daniel J. Kornstein, *The Roberson Privacy Controversy*, in [2006] Hist. Soc'y of the Cts. Of the State of N.Y., Issue 4, at 3, available at *http://courts.state.ny.us/history/pdf/HSNLVol.4.pdf.*

Pavesich v. New England Life Ins. Co.
122 Ga. 190, 50 S.E. 68 (1905)

Paolo Pavesich brought an action against the New England Mutual Life Insurance Company, a nonresident corporation, Thomas B. Lumpkin, its general agent, and J. Q. Adams, a photographer, both residing in the city of Atlanta. The allegations of the petition were, in substance, as follows: In an issue of the Atlanta Constitution, a newspaper published in the city of Atlanta, there appeared a likeness of the plaintiff, which would be easily recognized by his friends and acquaintances, placed by the side of the likeness of an ill-dressed and sickly looking person. Above the likeness of the plaintiff were the words: "Do it now. The man who did." Above the likeness of the other person were the words: "Do it while you can. The man who didn't." Below the two pictures were the words: "These two pictures tell their own story." Under the plaintiff's picture the following appeared: "In my healthy and productive period of life I bought insurance in the New England Mutual Life Insurance Co., of Boston, Mass., and to-day my family is protected and I am drawing an annual dividend on my paid-up policies." Under the other person's picture was a statement to the effect that he had not taken insurance, and now realized his mistake. The statements were signed, "Thomas B. Lumpkin, General Agent." The picture of the plaintiff was taken from a negative obtained by the defendant Lumpkin, or some one by him authorized, from the defendant Adams, which was used with his consent, and with knowledge of the purpose for which it was to be used. The picture was made from the negative without the plaintiff's consent, at the instance of the defendant insurance company, through its agent, Lumpkin. Plaintiff is an artist by profession, and the publication is peculiarly offensive to him. The statement attributed to plaintiff in the publication is false and malicious. He never made any such statement, and has not, and never has had, a policy of life insurance with the defendant company. The publication is malicious, and tends to bring plaintiff into ridicule before the world, and especially with his friends and acquaintances, who know that he has no policy in the defendant company. The publication is a "trespass upon plaintiff's right of privacy, and was caused by breach of confidence and trust reposed" in the defendant Adams. The prayer was for damages in the sum of $25,000. The petition was demurred to generally, and specially on the grounds that there was a misjoinder of defendants and causes of action, that no facts were set forth from which malice can be inferred, and that no special damages were alleged. The court sustained the general demurrer, and the plaintiff excepted.

Cobb, J.:

The petition really contains two counts—one for a libel, and the other for a violation of the plaintiff's right of privacy.... We will first deal with the general demurrer to the second count, which claimed damages on account of an alleged violation of the plaintiff's right of privacy. The question therefore to be determined is whether an individual has a right of privacy which he can enforce, and which the courts will protect against invasion. It is to be conceded that prior to 1890 every adjudicated case, both in this country and in England, which might be said to have involved a right of privacy, was not based upon the existence of such right, but was founded upon a supposed right of property, or a breach of trust or confidence, or the like, and that therefore a claim to a right of privacy, independent of a property or contractual right, or some right of a similar nature, had, up

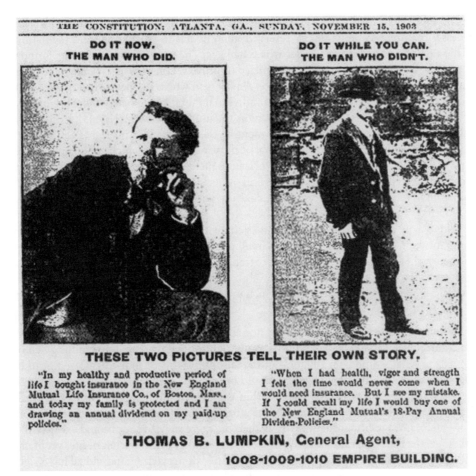

Figure 1-2. The advertisement in *Pavesich*

to that time, never been recognized in terms in any decision. The entire absence for a long period of time, even for centuries, of a precedent for an asserted right should have the effect to cause the courts to proceed with caution before recognizing the right, for fear that they may thereby invade the province of the lawmaking power; but such absence, even for all time, is not conclusive of the question as to the existence of the right. The novelty of the complaint is no objection, when an injury cognizable by law is shown to have been inflicted on the plaintiff. In such a case, "although there be no precedent, the common law will judge according to the law of nature and the public good." Where the case is new in principle, the courts have no authority to give a remedy, no matter how great the grievance; but where the case is only new in instance, and the sole question is upon the application of a recognized principle to a new case, "it will be just as competent to courts of justice to apply the principle to any case that may arise two centuries hence as it was two centuries ago." Broom's Legal Maxims (8th Ed.) 193. This results from the application of the maxim, "*Ubi jus ibi remedium*," which finds expression in our Code, where it is declared that "for every right there shall be a remedy, and every court having jurisdiction of the one may, if necessary, frame the other." Civ. Code 1895, § 4929.

The individual surrenders to society many rights and privileges which he would be free to exercise in a state of nature, in exchange for the benefits which he receives as a member of society. But he is not presumed to surrender all those rights, and the public has no more right, without his consent, to invade the domain of those rights which it is necessarily to be presumed he has reserved, than he has to violate the valid regulations of the organized government under which he lives. The right of privacy has its foundation in the instincts of nature. It is recognized intuitively, consciousness being the witness that can be called to establish its existence. Any person whose intellect is in a normal condition recognizes at once that as to each individual member of society there are matters private, and there are matters public so far as the individual is concerned. Each individual as instinctively resents any encroachment by the public upon his rights which are of a private nature as he does the withdrawal of those of his rights which are of a public nature. A right of privacy in matters purely private is therefore derived from natural law. This idea is embraced in the Roman's conception of justice, which "was not simply the external legality of acts, but the accord of external acts with the precepts of the law, prompted by internal impulse and free volition." McKeldey's Roman Law (Dropsie) § 123. It may be said to arise out of those laws sometimes characterized as "immutable," "because they are natural, and so just at all times and in all places that no authority can either change or abolish them." 1 Domat's Civil Law by Strahan (Cushing's Ed.) p. 49. It is one of those rights referred to by some law writers as "absolute" — such as would belong to their persons merely in a state of nature, and which every man is entitled to enjoy, whether out of society or in it." 1 [Blackstone] 123....

While neither Sir William Blackstone nor any of the other writers on the principles of the common law have referred in terms to the right of privacy, the illustrations given by them as to what would be a violation of the absolute rights of individuals are not to be taken as exhaustive, but the language should be allowed to include any instance of a violation of such rights which is clearly within the true meaning and intent of the words used to declare the principle. When the law guaranties to one the right to the enjoyment of his life, it gives to him something more than the mere right to breathe and exist. While, of course, the most flagrant violation of this right would be deprivation of life, yet life itself may be spared, and the enjoyment of life entirely destroyed. An individual has a right to enjoy life in any way that may be most agreeable and pleasant to him, according to his temperament and nature, provided that in such enjoyment he does not invade the rights of his neighbor, or violate public law or policy. The right of personal security is not fully accorded by allowing an individual to go through life in possession of all of his members, and his body unmarred; nor is his right to personal liberty fully accorded by merely allowing him to remain out of jail, or free from other physical restraints. The liberty which he derives from natural law, and which is recognized by municipal law, embraces far more than freedom from physical restraint. The term "liberty" is not to be so dwarfed, "but is deemed to embrace the right of a man to be free in the enjoyment of the faculties with which he has been endowed by his Creator, subject only to such restraints as are necessary for the common welfare. 'Liberty,' in its broad sense, as understood in this country, means the right not only of freedom from servitude, imprisonment, or restraint, but the right of one to use his faculties in all lawful ways, to live and work where he will, to earn his livelihood in any lawful calling, and to pursue any lawful trade or avocation." *See* Brannon on Fourteenth Amendment, 111. Liberty includes the right to live as one will, so long as that will does not interfere with the rights of another or of the public. One may desire to live a life of seclusion; another may desire to live a life of publicity; still another may wish to live a life of privacy as to certain matters, and of publicity as to others. One may wish to live a life of toil, where his work is of a nature that keeps him constantly before the public gaze, while another may wish to live a life of research and contemplation, only moving before the public at such times and under such circumstances as may be necessary to his actual existence. Each is entitled to a liberty of choice as to his manner of life, and neither an individual nor the public has a right to arbitrarily take away from him this liberty.... All will admit that the individual who desires to live a life of seclusion cannot be compelled, against his consent, to exhibit his person in any public place, unless such exhibition is demanded by the law of the land. He may be required to come from his place of seclusion to perform public duties—to serve as a juror and to testify as a witness, and the like; but, when the public duty is once performed, if he exercises his liberty to go again into seclusion, no one can deny him the right. One who desires to live a life of partial seclusion has a right to choose the times, places, and manner in which and at which he will submit himself to the public gaze. Subject to the limitation above referred to, the body of a person cannot be put on exhibition at any time or at any place without his consent. The right of one to exhibit himself to the public at all proper times, in all proper places, and in a proper manner is embraced within the right of personal liberty. The right to withdraw from the public gaze at such times as a person may see fit, when his presence in public is not demanded by any rule of law, is also embraced within the right of personal liberty. Publicity in one instance, and privacy in the other, are each guarantied. If personal liberty embraces the right of publicity, it no less embraces the correlative right of privacy, and this is no new idea in Georgia law. In *Wallace v.* [*Georgia C. & N.*] *Railway Company*, 94 Ga. 732, 22 S.E. 579 [(1894)], it was said: "Liberty of speech and of writing is secured by the Constitution, and incident thereto is the correlative liberty of silence, not less important nor less sacred." The right of privacy within certain limits is a right derived from natural law, recognized by the principles of municipal law, and guarantied to persons in this state both by the Constitutions of the United States and of the state of Georgia, in those provisions which declare that no person shall be deprived of liberty except by due process of law.

While, in reaching the conclusion just stated, we have been deprived of the benefit of the light that would be shed on the question by decided cases and utterances of law writers directly dealing with the matter, we have been aided by many side lights in the law. The "injuria" of the Roman law, sometimes translated "injury," and at other times "outrage," and which is generally understood at this time to convey the idea of legal wrong, was held to embrace many acts resulting in damage for which the law would give redress. It embraced all of those wrongs which were the result of a direct invasion of the rights of the person and the rights of property which are enumerated in all of the commentaries on the common law, and which are so familiar to every one at this time. But it included more. An outrage was committed not only by striking with the fists or with the club or lash, but also by shouting until a crowd gathered around one, and it was an outrage or legal wrong to merely follow an honest woman or young boy or girl; and it was declared in unequivocal terms that these illustrations were not exhaustive, but that an injury or legal wrong was committed "by numberless other acts." Sandar's Just. (Hammond's Ed.) 499; Poste's Inst. of Gaius (3d Ed.) 449. The punishment of one who had not committed any assault upon another, or impeded in any way his right of locomotion, but who merely attracted public attention to the other as he was passing along a public highway or standing upon his private grounds, evidences the fact that the ancient law recognized that a person had a legal right "to be let alone," so long as he was not interfering with the rights of other individuals or of the public. This idea has been carried into the common law, and appears from time to time in various places; a conspicuous instance being in the case of private nuisances resulting from noise which interferes with one's enjoyment of his home, and this, too, where the noise is the result of the carrying on of a lawful occupation. Even in such cases where the noise is unnecessary, or is made at such times that one would have a right to quiet, the courts have interfered by injunction in behalf of the person complaining. It is true that these cases are generally based upon the ground that the noise is an invasion of a property right, but there is really no injury to the property, and the gist of the wrong is that the individual is disturbed in his right to have quiet. Under the Roman law, "to enter a man's house against his will, even to serve a summons, was regarded as an invasion of his privacy." Hunter's Roman Law (3d Ed.) p. 149.... "Eavesdroppers, or such as listen under walls or windows or the eaves of a house to hearken after discourse, and thereupon to frame slanderous and mischievous tales," were a nuisance at common law, and indictable, and were required, in the discretion of the court, to find sureties for their good behavior. 4 [Blackstone] 168. The offense consisted in lingering about dwelling houses and other places where persons meet for private intercourse, and listening to what is said, and then tattling it abroad. 10 Am. & Eng. Enc. L. (2d Ed.) 440. A common scold was at common law indictable as a public nuisance to her neighborhood. 4 [Blackstone] 168. And the reason for the punishment of such a character was not the protection of any property right of her neighbors, but the fact that her conduct was a disturbance of their right to quiet and repose; the offense being complete even when the party indicted committed it upon her own premises. Instances might be multiplied where the common law has both tacitly and expressly recognized the right of an individual to repose and privacy. The right of the people to be secure in their persons, houses, papers, and effects, against unreasonable searches and seizures, which is so fully protected both in the Constitutions of the United States and of this state (Civ. Code 1895, §§ 6017, 5713), is not a right created by these instruments, but is an ancient right, which, on account of its gross violation at different times, was preserved from such attacks in the future by being made the subject of constitutional provisions. The right to search the papers or houses of another for the purpose of enforcing a claim of one individual against another in a civil proceeding, or in the maintenance of a mere private right, was never recognized at common law, but such search was confined entirely to cases of public prosecutions; and even in those cases the legality of the search was formerly doubted, and it has been said that it crept into the law by imperceptible practice. 25 Am. & Eng. Enc. L. (2d Ed.) 145. The refusal to allow such search as an aid to the assertion of a mere private right, and its allowance sparingly to aid in maintaining the rights of the public, is an implied recognition of the existence of a right of privacy, for the law on the subject of unreasonable searches cannot be based upon any other principle than the right of a person to be secure from invasion by the public into matters of a private nature, which can only be properly termed his right of privacy.

The right of privacy, however, like every other right that rests in the individual, may be waived by him, or by any one authorized by him.... This waiver may be either express or implied, but the existence of the waiver carries with it the right to an invasion of privacy only to such an extent as may be legitimately necessary and proper in dealing with the matter which has brought about the waiver. It may be waived for one purpose, and still asserted for another.... The most striking illustration of a waiver is where one either seeks or allows himself to be presented as a candidate for public office. He thereby waives any right to restrain or impede the public in any proper investigation into the conduct of his private life which may throw light upon his qualifications for the office, or the advisability of imposing upon him the public trust which the office carries. But even in this case the waiver does not extend into those matters and transactions of private life which are wholly foreign, and can throw no light whatever upon the question as to his competency for the office, or the propriety of bestowing it upon him.... So it is in reference to those belonging to the learned professions, who by their calling place themselves before the public, and thereby consent that their private lives may be scrutinized for the purpose of determining whether it is to the interest of those whose patronage they seek to place their interests in their hands. In short, any person who engages in any pursuit or occupation or calling which calls for the approval or patronage of the public submits his private life to examination by those to whom he addresses his call, to any extent that may be necessary to determine whether it is wise and proper and expedient to accord to him the approval or patronage which he seeks.

It may be said that to establish a liberty of privacy would involve in numerous cases the perplexing question to determine where this liberty ended, and the rights of others and of the public began. This affords no reason for not recognizing the liberty of privacy, and giving to the person aggrieved legal redress against the wrongdoer, in a case where it is clearly shown that a legal wrong has been done. It may be that there will arise many cases which lie near the border line which marks the right of privacy, on the one hand, and the right of another individual or of the public, on the other. But this is true in regard to numerous other rights which the law recognizes as resting in the individual. In regard to cases that may arise under the right of privacy, as in cases that arise under other rights where the line of demarcation is to be determined, the safeguard of the individual, on the one hand, and of the public, on the other, is the wisdom and integrity of the judiciary. Each person has a liberty of privacy, and every other person has, as against him, liberty in reference to other matters, and the line where these liberties impinge upon each other may in a given case be hard to define; but that such a case may arise can afford no more reason for denying to one his liberty of privacy than it would to deny to another his liberty, whatever it may be.... No greater difficulties will be encountered in such cases in determining the existence of the right than often will be encountered in determining the existence of other rights sought to be enforced by action.... With honest and fearless trial judges to pass in the first instance upon the question of law as to the existence of the right in each case, whose decisions are subject to review by the court of last resort, and with fair and impartial juries to pass upon the questions of fact involved, and assess the damages in the event of a recovery, whose verdict is, under our law, in all cases subject to supervision and scrutiny by the trial judge, ... there need be no more fear that the right of privacy will be the occasion of unjustifiable litigation, oppression, or wrong than that the existence of many other rights in the law would bring about such results.

The liberty of privacy exists, has been recognized by the law, and is entitled to continual recognition. But it must be kept within its proper limits, and in its exercise must be made to accord with the rights of those who have other liberties, as well as the rights of any person who may be properly interested in the matters which are claimed to be of purely private concern. Publicity in many cases is absolutely essential to the welfare of the public. Privacy in other matters is not only essential to the welfare of the individual, but also to the well-being of society. The law stamping the unbreakable seal of privacy upon communications between husband and wife, attorney and client, and similar provisions of the law, is a recognition not only of the right of privacy, but that, for the public good, some matters of private concern are not to be made public, even with the consent of those interested.

It therefore follows from what has been said that a violation of the right of privacy is a direct invasion of a legal right of the individual. It is a tort, and it is not necessary that special damages should have accrued from its violation in order to entitle the aggrieved party to recover. Civ. Code 1895, § 3807. In an action for an invasion of such right the damages to be recovered are those for which the law authorizes a recovery in torts of that character, and, if the law authorizes a recovery of damages for wounded feelings in other torts of a similar nature, such damages would be recoverable in an action for a violation of this right.

The stumbling block which many have encountered in the way of a recognition of the existence of a right of privacy has been that the recognition of such right would inevitably tend to curtail the liberty of speech and of the press. The right to speak and the right of privacy have been coexistent. Each is a natural right, each exists, and each must be recognized and enforced with due respect for the other.... The Constitution of the United States prohibits Congress from passing any law "abridging the freedom of speech or of the press." Civ. Code 1895, § 6014. The constitution of this state declares, "No law shall ever be passed to curtail or restrain the liberty of speech or of the press." Civ. Code 1895, § 5712. Judge Cooley says: "The constitutional liberty of speech and of the press, as we understand it, implies a right to freely utter and publish whatever the citizen may please, and to be protected against any responsibility for so doing, except so far as such publications, from their blasphemy, obscenity, or scandalous character, may be a public offense, or as by their falsehood and malice they may injuriously affect the standing, reputation, or pecuniary interests of individuals. Or, to state the same thing in somewhat different words, we understand liberty of speech and of the press to imply not only liberty to publish, but complete immunity from legal censure and punishment for the publication, so long as it is not harmful in its character, when tested by such standards as the law affords. For these standards we must look to the common-law rules which were in force when the constitutional guaranties were established, and in reference to which they have been adopted." Cooley Con. Lim. (5th Ed.) p. 521.... Mr. Justice Story defined the phrase to mean "that every man shall have a right to speak, write, and print his opinions upon any subject whatsoever, without any prior restraint, so, always, that he does not injure any other person in his rights, person, property, or reputation, and so, always, that he does not thereby disturb the public peace or attempt to subvert the government." Story, Const. § 1880....

The Constitution of this state declares what is meant by "liberty of speech" and "liberty of the press" in the following words: "Any person may speak, write and publish his sentiments on all subjects, being responsible for the abuse of that liberty." Civ. Code 1895, § 5712. The right preserved and guarantied against invasion by the Constitution is therefore the right to utter, to write, and to print one's sentiments, subject only to the limitation that in so doing he shall not be guilty of an abuse of this privilege, by invading the legal rights of others. The Constitution uses the word "sentiments," but it is used in the sense of thoughts, ideas, opinions. To make intelligent, forceful, and effective an expression of opinion, it may be necessary to refer to the life, conduct, and character of a person; and, so long as the truth is adhered to, the right of privacy of another cannot be said to have been invaded by one who speaks or writes or prints, provided the reference to such person, and the manner in which he is referred to, is reasonably and legitimately proper in an expression of opinion on the subject that is under investigation. It will therefore be seen that the right of privacy must in some particulars yield to the right of speech and of the press.... The truth may be spoken, written, or printed about all matters of a public nature, as well as matters of a private nature in which the public has a legitimate interest.... But there may arise cases where the speaking or printing of the truth might be considered an abuse of the liberty of speech and of the press, as in a case where matters of purely private concern, wholly foreign to a legitimate expression of opinion on the subject under discussion, are injected into the discussion for no other purpose and with no other motive than to annoy and harass the individual referred to. Such cases might be of rare occurrence, but, if such should arise, the party aggrieved may not be without a remedy. The right of privacy is unquestionably limited by the right to speak and print. It may be said that to give liberty of speech and of the press such wide scope as has been indicated would impose a very serious limitation upon the right of privacy, but, if it does, it is due to the fact that the law considers that the welfare of the public is better subserved by maintaining the liberty of speech and of the press than by allowing an individual to assert his right of privacy in such a way as to interfere with the free expression of one's sentiments, and the publication of every matter in which the public may be legitimately interested....

It seems that the first case in this country where the right of privacy was invoked as the foundation for an application to the courts for relief was the unreported case of *Manola v. Stevens*, which was an application for injunction to the Supreme Court of New York, filed on June 15, 1890. The complainant alleged that while she was playing in the Broadway Theatre, dressed as required by her role, she was, by means of a flash light, photographed surreptitiously and without her consent, from one of the boxes, by the defendant, and she prayed that an injunction issue to restrain the use of the photograph. An interlocutory injunction was granted *ex parte*. At the time set for a hearing there was no appearance for the defendant, and the injunction was made permanent. *See* 4 Harv. Law Rev. 195, note 7. The article in this magazine which refers to the case above mentioned appeared in 1890, and was written by Samuel D. Warren and Louis D. Brandeis. In it the authors ably and forcefully maintained the existence of a right of privacy, and the article attracted much attention at the time. It was conceded by the authors that there was no decided case in which the right of privacy was distinctly asserted and recognized, but it was asserted that there were many cases from which it would appear that this right really existed, although the judgment in each case was put upon other grounds when the plaintiff was granted the relief prayed.... Attention is called to the fact that in Prince Albert's Case, while the decision was put upon the ground above stated, Lord Cottenham declared that, with respect to the acts of the defendants, "privacy is the right invaded."

It must be conceded that the numerous cases decided before 1890 in which equity has interfered to restrain the publication of letters, writings, papers, etc., have all been based either upon the recognition of a right of property, or upon the fact that the publication would be a breach of contract, confidence, or trust. It is well settled that, if any contract or property right or trust relation has been violated, damages are recoverable. There are many cases which sustain such a doctrine. Cases involving the right of privacy that have arisen since 1890 will now be considered:

In *Mackenzie v. Mineral Springs Company* (1891) 18 N.Y. Supp. 240, an injunction was granted by the New York Supreme Court, Special Term, at the instance of a physician, to restrain the publication of an unauthorized recommendation of a medicinal preparation under his name, upon the grounds that such publication would be injurious to his professional reputation, and "an infringement of his right to the sole use of his own name," and prejudicial to public interest. While this case was not based upon the right of privacy, that right was impliedly recognized.

The first reported case in which the right of privacy was expressly recognized was the case of *Schuyler v. Curtis* (Sup. Ct. 1891) 15 N.Y. Supp. 787, where Justice O'Brien, of the Supreme Court of New York, granted an injunction to restrain the making and public exhibition of a statue of a deceased person, upon the ground that it was not shown that she was a public character. This judgment was affirmed by the Supreme Court, General Term, by Van Brunt and Barrett, JJ., in an opinion by the former, in which the rule was laid down that a person, whether a public character or not, has a right to enjoin the making and placing on exhibition of his statue, and, he being dead, a relative has this right. 19 N.Y. Supp. 264 [(Sup. Ct. 1892)]. When the case came before the Supreme Court, Special Term, in 1893, the judgment of the General Term was followed, and in an opinion by Ingraham, J., the rule was announced that a court of equity, at the instance of one

of the relatives of a deceased person, will enjoin the making and placing on public exhibition of a statue of the deceased by unauthorized persons, which the complaining relatives unite in alleging will cause them pain and distress, and will be considered by them
a disgrace; and this, too, whether or not the court be of the opinion that the proposed
representation should produce the alleged effect, and that such unauthorized act is not
within the provision of the state Constitution which secures to each person the right to
freely speak, write, and publish his sentiments on all subjects. 24 N.Y. Supp. 509. The
statue which it was proposed to exhibit was in no sense a caricature, and the exhibition
of the same would not have been a libel upon the deceased.

In 1893, in *Marks v. Jaffa*, 6 Misc. 290, 26 N.Y. Supp. 908, an injunction was granted
by the superior court of New York City, Special Term, to restrain the publication of a picture of the plaintiff in the defendant's newspaper, with an invitation to the readers of the
paper to vote on the question of the popularity of the plaintiff, as compared with another person, whose picture was also published in such newspaper. McAdam, J., in the
opinion said: "No newspaper or institution, no matter how worthy, has the right to use
the name or picture of any one for such a purpose without his consent." The decision was
apparently based upon the case of *Schuyler v. Curtis*, above referred to.

In 1893 an application was made to Judge Colt, of the United States Circuit Court for
the District of Massachusetts, by the widow and children of George H. Corliss, to enjoin
the publication and sale of a biographical sketch of Mr. Corliss, and from printing and
selling his picture in connection therewith. The bill did not allege that the publication contained any matter which was scandalous, libelous, or false, or that it affected any right of
property, but the relief was prayed upon the ground that the publication was an injury to
the feelings of the plaintiffs, and against their express prohibition. An injunction was refused as to the biography on the ground that Mr. Corliss was a public man, in the same sense
as authors or artists are public men; but an injunction was granted as to the publication
of the picture upon the ground that the publisher had obtained a copy of the photograph
upon certain conditions, and the publication would be a violation of those conditions.
Subsequently a motion was made to dissolve the injunction on the ground that the photograph from which the copies were made was not obtained in the manner above referred
to, but from a copy which was obtained in a lawful way; and the injunction was dissolved
upon the ground that neither a public character, nor his family after his death, has a right
to enjoin the publication of his portrait, when the publication would not be a violation of
a contract or a breach of trust or confidence. Judge Colt, in the opinion, uses this language:
"Independently of the question of contract, I believe the law to be that a private individual has a right to be protected in the representation of his portrait in any form, that this is
a property as well as a personal right, and that it belongs to the same class of rights which
forbids the reproduction of a private manuscript or painting, or the publication of private
letters, or of oral lectures delivered by a teacher to his class, or the revelation of the contents of a merchant's books by a clerk." *Corliss v. Walker*, 57 Fed. 434 [(C.C.D. Mass. 1893)];
Id., 64 Fed. 280 [(C.C.D. Mass. 1894)]. It is to be noted that the ruling in this case goes no
further than that a public character has so waived his right of privacy, if he ever had it, as
to authorize the publication of his life and his picture, not only without his consent, but
also without the consent of his family after his death, when there is nothing in the biography or the picture which will reflect discredit upon the subject....

In 1895 the case of *Schuyler v. Curtis* reached the Court of Appeals of New York, and
the judgment of the lower court was reversed. 147 N.Y. 436, 42 N.E. 22. It was held that
if any right of privacy, in so far as it includes the right to prevent the public from making pictures or statues commemorative of the worth and services of the subject, exists at

all, it does not survive after death, and cannot be enforced by the relatives of the deceased. The opinion was delivered by Judge Peckham, in the course of which he uses this language: "If the defendants had projected such a work in the lifetime of Mrs. Schuyler, it would perhaps have been a violation of her individual right of privacy, because it might be contended that she had never occupied such a position towards the public as would have authorized such action by any one so long as it was in opposition to her wishes." Judge Gray dissented, saying in his opinion: "I cannot see why the right of privacy is not a form of property, as much as is the right of complete immunity of one's person." This case settles nothing as to the existence of a right of privacy, but merely rules that, if it exists at all, it is a personal right, and dies with the person.

In *Atkinson v. Doherty*, 121 Mich. 372, 80 N.W. 285 [(1899)], ... the Supreme Court of Michigan held that the use of the name and likeness of a deceased person as a label for a brand of cigars cannot be restrained by injunction, so long as they do not constitute a libel. Many, if not all, the cases above referred to, in reference to the right of privacy, are mentioned and reviewed in this case. While this decision apparently lays down the broad proposition that the right of privacy does not exist to such an extent as to prohibit one from publishing the picture of another without his consent, in reality the only question necessary to have been decided was whether this right of privacy was personal, and died with the person; and therefore the decision, on its facts, is authoritative no further than the decision of the New York Court of Appeals in *Schuyler v. Curtis*. While the right of privacy is personal, and may die with the person, we do not desire to be understood as assenting to the proposition that the relatives of the deceased cannot, in a proper case, protect the memory of their kinsman, not only from defamation, but also from an invasion into the affairs of his private life after his death. This question is not now involved, but we do not wish anything said to be understood as committing us in any way to the doctrine that, against the consent of relatives, the private affairs of a deceased person may be published, and his picture or statue exhibited....

In *Roberson v. Rochester Folding Box Company* (1901) 64 App. Div. 30, 71 N.Y. Supp. 876, decided by the Appellate Division of the Supreme Court of New York, it appeared that lithographic likenesses of a young woman, bearing the words "Flour of the Family," were, without her consent, printed and used by a flour milling company to advertise its goods.... It was held that the declaration was not demurrable. It was also held that, if a right of property was necessary to entitle the plaintiff to maintain the action, the case might stand upon the right of property which every one has in his own body. This case came before the Court of Appeals of New York in 1902, and the judgment was reversed. 171 N.Y. 540, 64 N.E. 442. This is the first and only decision by a court of last resort involving the existence of a right of privacy.... While the ruling of the majority is limited in its effect to the unwarranted publication of the picture of another for advertising purposes, the reasoning of Judge Parker goes to the extent of denying the existence in the law of a right of privacy, "founded upon the claim that a man has a right to pass through this world without having his picture published, his business enterprises discussed, or his eccentricities commented upon, whether the comment be favorable or otherwise." The reasoning of the majority is, in substance, that there is no decided case either in England or in this country in which such a right is distinctly recognized; that every case that might be relied on to establish the right was placed expressly upon other grounds, not involving the application of this right in any sense; that the right is not referred to by the commentators and writers upon the common law or the principles of equity; that the existence of the right is not to be legitimately inferred from anything that is said by any of such writers, and that a recognition of the existence of the right would bring about a vast amount of litigation; and that in many instances where the right would be asserted it would be difficult, if not impossible, to determine the line of demarcation between the plaintiff's right of privacy and the well-established rights of others and of the public. For these reasons the conclusion is reached that the right does not exist, has never existed, and cannot be enforced as a legal right. We have no fault to find with what is said by the distinguished and learned judge who voiced the views of the majority as to the existence of decided cases, and agree with him in his analysis of the various cases which he reviews — that the judgment in each was based upon other grounds than the existence of a right of privacy. We also agree with him so far as he asserts that the writers upon the common law and the principles of equity do not in express terms refer to this right. But we are utterly at variance with him in his conclusion that the existence of this right cannot be legitimately inferred from what has been said by commentators upon the legal rights of individuals, and from expressions which have fallen from judges in their reasoning in cases where the exercise of the right was not directly involved.... With all due respect to Chief Judge Parker and his associates who concurred with him, we think the conclusion reached by them was the result of an unconscious yielding to the feeling of conservatism which naturally arises in the mind of a judge who faces a proposition which is novel. The valuable influence upon society and upon the welfare of the public of the conservatism of the lawyer, whether at the bar or upon the bench, cannot be overestimated; but this conservatism should not go to the extent of refusing to recognize a right which the instincts of nature prove to exist, and which nothing in judicial decision, legal history, or writings upon the law can be called to demonstrate its nonexistence as a legal right.

We think that what should have been a proper judgment in the *Roberson* case was that contended for by Judge Gray in his dissenting opinion.... [The court here quotes extensively from Judge Gray's dissent.]

The decision of the Court of Appeals of New York in the *Roberson* case gave rise to numerous articles in the different law magazines of high standing in the country — some by the editors and others by contributors. In some the conclusion of the majority of the court was approved, in others the views of the dissenting judges were commended, and in still others the case and similar cases were referred to as apparently establishing that the claim of the majority was correct, but regret was expressed that the necessity was such that the courts could not recognize the right asserted. An editorial in the American Law Review (volume 36, p. 636) said: "The decision under review shocks and wounds the ordinary sense of justice of mankind. We have heard it alluded to only in terms of regret."...

As we have already said, cases may arise where it is difficult to determine on which side of the line of demarcation which separates the right of privacy from the well-established rights of others they are to be found; but we have little difficulty in arriving at the conclusion that the present case is one in which it has been established that the right of privacy has been invaded, and invaded by one who cannot claim exemption under the constitutional guaranties of freedom of speech and of the press. The form and features of the plaintiff are his own. The defendant insurance company and its agent had no more authority to display them in public for the purpose of advertising the business in which they were engaged than they would have had to compel the plaintiff to place himself upon exhibition for this purpose. The latter procedure would have been unauthorized and unjustifiable, as every one will admit, and the former was equally an invasion of the rights of his person. Nothing appears from which it is to be inferred that the plaintiff has waived his right to determine himself where his picture should be displayed in favor of the advertising right of the defendants. The mere fact that he is an artist does not of itself establish a waiver of this right, so that his picture might be used for advertising purposes.

If he displayed in public his works as an artist, he would, of course, subject his works and his character as an artist, and possibly his character and conduct as a man, to such scrutiny and criticism as would be legitimate and proper to determine whether he was entitled to rank as an artist, and should be accorded recognition as such by the public. But it is by no means clear that even this would have authorized the publication of his picture. The constitutional right to speak and print does not necessarily carry with it the right to reproduce the form and features of man. The plaintiff was in no sense a public character, even if a different rule in regard to the publication of one's picture should be applied to such characters. It is not necessary in this case to hold—nor are we prepared to do so—that the mere fact that a man has become what is called a public character, either by aspiring to public office, or by holding public office, or by exercising a profession which places him before the public, or by engaging in a business which has necessarily a public nature, gives to every one the right to print and circulate his picture. To use the language of Hooker, J., in *Atkinson v. Doherty, supra*: "We are loath to believe that the man who makes himself useful to mankind surrenders any right to privacy thereby, or that, because he permits his picture to be published by one person and for one purpose, he is forever thereafter precluded from enjoying any of his rights." It may be that the aspirant for public office, or one in official position, impliedly consents that the public may gaze not only upon him, but upon his picture, but we are not prepared now to hold that even this is true. It would seem to us that even the President of the United States, in the lofty position which he occupies, has some rights in reference to matters of this kind which he does not forfeit by aspiring to or accepting the highest office within the gift of the people of the several states. While no person who has ever held this position, and probably no person who has ever held public office, has even objected or ever will object to the reproduction of his picture in reputable newspapers, magazines, and periodicals, still it cannot be that the mere fact that a man aspires to public office or holds public office subjects him to the humiliation and mortification of having his picture displayed in places where he would never go to be gazed upon, at times when and under circumstances where if he were personally present the sensibilities of his nature would be severely shocked. If one's picture may be used by another for advertising purposes, it may be reproduced and exhibited anywhere. If it may be used in a newspaper, it may be used on a poster or a placard. It may be posted upon the walls of private dwellings or upon the streets. It may ornament the bar of the saloon keeper or decorate the walls of a brothel. By becoming a member of society, neither man nor woman can be presumed to have consented to such uses of the impression of their faces and features upon paper or upon canvas. The conclusion reached by us seems to be so thoroughly in accord with natural justice, with the principles of the law of every civilized nation, and especially with the elastic principles of the common law, and so thoroughly in harmony with those principles as molded under the influence of American institutions, that it seems strange to us that not only four of the judges of one of the most distinguished and learned courts of the Union, but also lawyers of learning and ability, have found an insurmountable stumbling block in the path that leads to a recognition of the right which would give to persons like the plaintiff in this case and the young woman in the *Roberson* case redress for the legal wrong, or what is by some of the law writers called the outrage, perpetrated by the unauthorized use of their pictures for advertising purposes.

What we have ruled cannot be in any sense construed as an abridgment of the liberty of speech and of the press as guaranteed in the Constitution. Whether the reproduction of a likeness of another which is free from caricature can in any sense be declared to be an exercise of the right to publish one's sentiments, certain it is that one who merely for advertising purposes, and from mercenary motives, publishes the likeness of another without his consent, cannot be said, in so doing, to have exercised the right to publish his sentiments. The publication of a good likeness of another, accompanying a libelous article, would give a right of action. The publication of a caricature is generally, if not always, a libel. Whether the right to print a good likeness of another is an incident to a right to express one's sentiments in reference to a subject with which the person whose likeness is published is connected, is a question upon which we cannot, under the present record, make any authoritative decision; but it would seem that a holding that the publication of a likeness under such circumstances without the consent of the person whose likeness is published is allowable would be giving to the word "sentiment" a very extended meaning.... There is in the publication of one's picture for advertising purposes not the slightest semblance of an expression of an idea, a thought, or an opinion, within the meaning of the constitutional provision which guaranties to a person the right to publish his sentiments on any subject. Such conduct is not embraced within the liberty to print, but is a serious invasion of one's right of privacy, and may in many cases, according to the circumstances of the publication and the uses to which it is put, cause damages to flow which are irreparable in their nature. The knowledge that one's features and form are being used for such a purpose, and displayed in such places as such advertisements are often liable to be found, brings not only the person of an extremely sensitive nature, but even the individual of ordinary sensibility, to a realization that his liberty has been taken away from him; and, as long as the advertiser uses him for these purposes, he cannot be otherwise than conscious of the fact that he is for the time being under the control of another, that he is no longer free, and that he is in reality a slave, without hope of freedom, held to service by a merciless master; and if a man of true instincts, or even of ordinary sensibilities, no one can be more conscious of his enthrallment than he is.

So thoroughly satisfied are we that the law recognizes, within proper limits, as a legal right, the right of privacy, and that the publication of one's picture without his consent by another as an advertisement, for the mere purpose of increasing the profits and gains of the advertiser, is an invasion of this right, that we venture to predict that the day will come that the American bar will marvel that a contrary view was ever entertained by judges of eminence and ability....

[The court also held that the first count stated a cause of action for libel.]

Judgment reversed. All the Justices concur.

Edison v. Edison Polyform Mfg. Co.
73 N.J. Eq. 136, 67 A. 392 (1907)

[Thomas Edison, the world-famous inventor of the light bulb and the phonograph, "early in his career compounded a medicinal preparation intended to relieve neuralgic pains by external application." The defendant manufactured and sold a liquid compound containing all of the ingredients in Edison's formula except the active ingredient, morphine. The label on each bottle contained a picture of Edison and the following words: "Edison's Polyform. I certify that this preparation is compounded according to the formula devised and used by myself. Thos. A. Edison." Edison testified that he never authorized the use of his picture and that he never made or authorized the certificate.]

[The defendant] is, by its corporate name, by the certificate, and by the picture, holding out that Mr. Edison is connected with the enterprise and supervising its work. The question is whether Mr. Edison is without standing to complain because he is not a business competitor.... If a man's name be his own property, ... it is difficult to understand why the peculiar cast of one's features is not also one's property, and why its pecuniary value, if it has one, does not belong to its owner, rather than to the person seeking to make an unauthorized use of it.... It is certain that a man in public life may not claim the same immunity from publicity that a private citizen may.... [However, it] is difficult to imagine a case in which preventive relief would be more appropriate than the present. In a perfectly unauthorized way a certificate falsely purporting to be made by Mr. Edison, and also false in fact, because the preparation is not compounded with all the ingredients of the formula, is put by a company bearing Edison's name upon every bottle of Polyform which it sells. That there may be no mistake as to who is intended, the certificate is accompanied with a likeness. I think an injunction should be granted restraining the defendant company from holding out, either in the name of the company, or by certificate, or by pictorial representation, that Mr. Edison has any connection with or part in the complainant's business.... The abstract question whether a company can innocently use, as a part of its title, the name of a distinguished living character, is not before me for decision, and no opinion is expressed about it.

Notes and Questions

1. Is there any meaningful distinction between the facts in *Roberson* and those in *Pavesich*? If not, why do the two cases come out so differently? How does the Georgia court explain the difference? Does the Georgia court deal adequately with the line-drawing problem that concerned the majority in *Roberson*? Is the Georgia court improperly intruding upon the province of the legislature? Or is that simply inherent in common-law adjudication?

2. The Fourth Amendment to the U.S. Constitution recognizes one type of privacy; namely, "[t]he right of the people to be secure in their persons, houses, papers, and effects, against unreasonable searches and seizures." Does this Amendment support the recognition of a broad right of privacy? Why or why not?

3. The Due Process Clause of the Fourteenth Amendment to the U.S. Constitution provides that "No State shall ... deprive any person of life, liberty, or property, without due process of law." The Georgia Constitution contains a similar provision. If you have taken Constitutional Law, you will recall that the Due Process Clause is the foundation for the doctrine of "substantive due process," which protects certain intimate marital and family decisions against state interference, including decisions about child-rearing, contraception, and abortion. Given this background, does the Due Process Clause support the recognition of a broad right of privacy enforceable against private actors, even in the absence of state action? Why or why not?

4. Both Warren & Brandeis and the Georgia Supreme Court in *Pavesich* relied in part on "the unreported case of *Manola v. Stevens*," in which an *ex parte* injunction was granted by the Supreme Court of New York (a trial court) in 1890. For the story of singer and stage actress Marion Manola, and the role her case played in the development of the right of privacy, *see* Dorothy Glancy, *Privacy and the Other Miss M*, 10 N. Ill. U. L. Rev. 401 (1990).

5. The *Edison* case suggests a very different basis for prohibiting the use of one's name and likeness for commercial purposes: false endorsement. Unlike the plaintiffs in *Rober-*

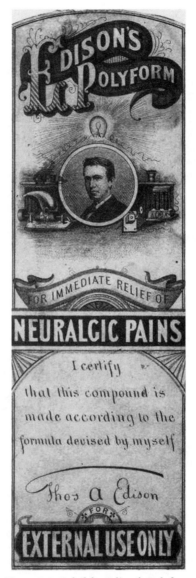

Figure 1-3. Label for Edison's Polyform

son and *Pavesich*, Thomas Edison was a well-known public figure who actively courted publicity in his role as a famous inventor. His endorsement of a product could be expected to increase sales. The gist of his complaint is not that he was embarrassed or humiliated by having his picture displayed in public, but that the public would be deceived, and his reputation might suffer, by a false statement that he endorsed the (presumably ineffective) medicinal preparation being sold by the defendants. However, lacking any well-developed cause of action for false statements other than libel, the New Jersey court relied instead on the newly-minted right of privacy to uphold the action.

Suppose the medicinal preparation *had* contained morphine, and was in fact made according to Edison's original formula. Should it be a violation of the right of privacy (or of the later-developed right of publicity) for the manufacturer to advertise that fact, so long as it did not imply that Edison was endorsing the particular manufacturer in question? Truth is an absolute defense to a libel action, but is it (or should it be) a defense to the rights of privacy or publicity? You may want to re-consider this question after you have read Chapters VII and VIII, below.

6. Following its recognition as a common-law right in *Pavesich*, the right of privacy was soon adopted in other states and developed into a broad-based right as envisioned by Warren & Brandeis. However, the right of privacy had some limitations as a vehicle for the protection of celebrity rights. First, the right of privacy was deemed to be a personal interest, rather than a property interest. This meant that the right of privacy did not survive the death of the celebrity, and it could not be assigned to, or enforced by, a mere licensee. Second, some courts held that a celebrity who placed himself or herself before the public, and actively courted publicity in his or her profession to earn a living, could not claim to be embarrassed and humiliated by the mere fact that his or her name or likeness was being used in a public manner. A prime example of this second limitation is the case that follows.

O'Brien v. Pabst Sales Co.
124 F.2d 167 (5th Cir. 1941)

[In 1938, Davey O'Brien, quarterback of the Texas Christian University football team, led TCU to an undefeated season and a victory in the Sugar Bowl, won the Heisman Trophy, and was named by sportswriter Grantland Rice to the Collier's All-American Football Team. In 1939, Pabst Blue Ribbon Beer published a calendar of college and pro football schedules that featured photos of several members of the All-American team, including a large photograph of O'Brien. O'Brien testified that he had not authorized the use of the photograph; that he was a member of the Allied Youth of America, which sought to discourage the use of alcohol by young people; "that he had had opportunities to sell his endorsement for beer and alcoholic beverages and had refused it; and that he was greatly embarrassed and humiliated when he saw the calendar and realized that his face and name was associated with publicity for the sale of beer." On cross-examination, O'Brien testified that he had posed for photographs for use in publicizing himself and the TCU football team; that TCU "had furnished numberless photographs to various people, periodicals and magazines" with his general approval and consent; and that the photo which was used on the calendar had previously been published in Collier's magazine.]

Claiming that this use of his photograph as part of defendant's advertising was an invasion of his right of privacy and that he had been damaged thereby, plaintiff brought this suit.... The first [defense] was that if the mere use of one's picture in truthful and respectable advertising would be an actionable invasion of privacy in the case of a private person, the use here was not, as to plaintiff, such an invasion, for as a result of his activities and prowess in football, his chosen field, and their nationwide and deliberate publicizing with his consent and in his interest, he was no longer, as to them, a private but a public person, and as to their additional publication he had no right of privacy....

The District Judge agreed with defendant that no case had been made out. He was of the opinion ... that considered from the standpoint merely of an invasion of plaintiff's right of privacy, no case was made out, because plaintiff was an outstanding national football figure and had completely publicized his name and his pictures. He was of the opinion too, that considered from the point of view that the calendar damaged him because it falsely, though only impliedly, represented that plaintiff was a user of or was commending the use of, Pabst beer, no case was made out because nothing in the calendar or football schedule could be reasonably so construed; every fact in it was truthfully stated and there was no representation or suggestion of any kind that O'Brien or any of the other football celebrities whose pictures it showed were beer drinkers or were recommending its drinking to others.... He directed a verdict for defendant.

Plaintiff is here urging that the judgment be reversed and the cause remanded for a new trial, first because as a matter of law plaintiff showed damage in that his name was used for the commercial purpose of advertising beer, and second, because there was an issue of fact as to whether the calendar reasonably conveyed to the public the false impression that plaintiff was a user of and was endorsing or recommending the use of beer. We cannot agree with appellant.... [Assuming] that an action for right of privacy would lie in Texas at the suit of a private person we think it clear that the action fails; because plaintiff is not such a person and the publicity he got was only that which he had been constantly seeking and receiving; ... and there were no statements or representations made in connection with it, which were or could be either false, erroneous or damaging to plaintiff.

[The dissenting judge said: "The decision of the majority leaves the appellant without remedy for any non-libellous use made of his picture by advertisers of beer, wine, whiskey, patent medicines, or other non-contraband goods, wares, and merchandise. It also places every other famous stage, screen, and athletic star in the same situation. If one is popular and permits publicity to be given to one's talent and accomplishment in any art or sport, commercial advertisers may seize upon such popularity to increase their sales of any lawful article without compensation of any kind for such commercial use of one's name and fame. This is contrary to usage and custom among advertisers in the marts of trade. They are undoubtedly in the habit of buying the right to use one's name or picture to create demand and good will for their merchandise.... It appears [from the facts alleged] that the appellee committed a tort in misappropriating a valuable property right of appellant."]

Notes and Questions

1. After graduating from TCU, Davey O'Brien played two seasons for the Philadelphia Eagles, during which he broke the NFL single-season record for passing yardage. He was an FBI agent for ten years, after which he entered the Texas oil business. He is remembered today as the namesake of the Davey O'Brien Award, which has been presented annually since 1981 to the outstanding quarterback in college football.

2. Much of the discussion contained in the above excerpt is dicta, since the district court also found that O'Brien had impliedly authorized the use of his picture by allowing TCU to distribute publicity photographs to anyone who asked for them. In agency law, the doctrine of apparent authority sometimes allows a person to be bound by the acts of another if the person created or does not dispel the impression that the other was acting as his or her agent. Should the doctrine be used to imply consent for the use of a name or likeness in advertising, or should the advertiser have to obtain more specific authorization?

3. Conversely, should the inclusion of photos of many different football players on a football calendar sponsored by a beer company be deemed to be an implied representation that the players depicted are sponsoring or endorsing that brand of beer? Should a court grant summary judgment on that issue, or should it leave the issue of implied endorsement to a jury? On this issue, you may wish to compare *O'Brien* with the opinion

of the Ontario Court of Appeal in *Krouse v. Chrysler Canada Ltd.*, which is reprinted in Chapter I.C., below.

4. The *O'Brien* case relies in part on outdated notions of what constitutes unfair competition. Had O'Brien agreed to endorse a particular brand of beer, the court would have enforced a contract requiring that he be paid for his endorsement, and it might have enjoined a competitor from using O'Brien's picture in its own advertisements. But since O'Brien refused to endorse any brand of beer at all, the majority held that he did not suffer any pecuniary loss by having his picture used in a calendar sponsored by a beer company without being paid.

5. The dissenting judge urged the majority to distinguish an action for invasion of privacy, a personal right, from an action for misappropriation of a property right by the use of one's name or likeness for commercial purposes. The next step in the development of the right of publicity came when a majority of a federal appellate panel endorsed such a distinction under New York law in the following case.

Haelan Laboratories, Inc. v. Topps Chewing Gum, Inc.
202 F.2d 866 (2d Cir. 1953)

Before SWAN, Chief Judge, and CLARK and FRANK, Circuit Judges.

FRANK, Circuit Judge:

After a trial without a jury, the trial judge dismissed the complaint on the merits. The plaintiff maintains that defendant invaded plaintiff's exclusive right to use the photographs of leading baseball-players. Probably because the trial judge ruled against plaintiff's legal contentions, some of the facts were not too clearly found.

1. So far as we can now tell, there were instances of the following kind:

(a). The plaintiff, engaged in selling chewing-gum, made a contract with a ball-player providing that plaintiff for a stated term should have the exclusive right to use the ball-player's photograph in connection with the sales of plaintiff's gum; the ball-player agreed not to grant any other gum manufacturer a similar right during such term; the contract gave plaintiff an option to extend the term for a designated period.

(b). Defendant, a rival chewing-gum manufacturer, knowing of plaintiff's contract, deliberately induced the ball-player to authorize defendant, by a contract with defendant, to use the player's photograph in connection with the sales of defendant's gum either during the original or extended term of plaintiff's contract, and defendant did so use the photograph.

Defendant argues that, even if such facts are proved, they show no actionable wrong, for this reason: The contract with plaintiff was no more than a release by the ball-player to plaintiff of the liability which, absent the release, plaintiff would have incurred in using the ball-player's photograph, because such a use, without his consent, would be an invasion of his right of privacy under Section 50 and Section 51 of the New York Civil Rights Law; this statutory right of privacy is personal, not assignable; therefore, plaintiff's contract vested in plaintiff no 'property' right or other legal interest which defendant's conduct invaded.

Both parties agree, and so do we, that, on the facts here, New York 'law' governs. And we shall assume, for the moment, that, under the New York decisions, defendant cor-

Figure 1-4. 1952 Topps Mickey Mantle Rookie Card

rectly asserts that any such contract between plaintiff and a ball-player, in so far as it merely authorized plaintiff to use the player's photograph, created nothing but a release of liability. On that basis, were there no more to the contract, plaintiff would have no actionable claim against defendant. But defendant's argument neglects the fact that, in the contract, the ball-player also promised not to give similar releases to others. If defendant, knowing of the contract, deliberately induced the ball-player to break that promise, defendant behaved tortiously.

Some of defendant's contracts were obtained by it through its agent, Players Enterprise, Inc; others were obtained by Russell Publishing Co., acting independently, and were then assigned by Russell to defendant. Since Players acted as defendant's agent, defendant is liable for any breach of plaintiff's contracts thus induced by Players. However, as Russell did not act as defendant's agent when Russell, having knowledge of plaintiff's contract with a player, by subsequently contracting with that player, induced a breach of plaintiff's contract, defendant is not liable for any breach so induced; nor did there arise such a liability against defendant for such an induced breach when defendant became the assignee of one of those Russell contracts.

2. The foregoing covers the situations where defendant, by itself or through its agent, induced breaches. But in those instances where Russell induced the breach, we have a different problem; and that problem also confronts us in instances—alleged in one paragraph of the complaint and to which the trial judge in his opinion also (although not altogether clearly) refers—where defendant, 'with knowledge of plaintiff's exclusive rights,' used a photograph of a ball-player without his consent during the term of his contract with plaintiff.

With regard to such situations, we must consider defendant's contention that none of plaintiff's contracts created more than a release of liability, because a man has no legal interest in the publication of his picture other than his right of privacy, *i.e.*, a personal and non-assignable right not to have his feelings hurt by such a publication.

A majority of this court rejects this contention. We think that, in addition to and independent of that right of privacy (which in New York derives from statute), a man has a right in the publicity value of his photograph, *i.e.*, the right to grant the exclusive privilege of publishing his picture, and that such a grant may validly be made 'in gross,' *i.e.*, without an accompanying transfer of a business or of anything else. Whether it be labelled a 'property' right is immaterial; for here, as often elsewhere, the tag 'property' simply symbolizes the fact that courts enforce a claim which has pecuniary worth.

This right might be called a 'right of publicity.' For it is common knowledge that many prominent persons (especially actors and ball-players), far from having their feelings bruised through public exposure of their likenesses, would feel sorely deprived if they no longer received money for authorizing advertisements, popularizing their countenances, displayed in newspapers, magazines, busses, trains and subways. This right of publicity would usually yield them no money unless it could be made the subject of an exclusive grant which barred any other advertiser from using their pictures.

We think the New York decisions recognize such a right. *See, e.g., Wood v. Lucy, Lady Duff Gordon*, 222 N.Y. 88, 118 N.E. 214 [(1917)]....

We think *Pekas Co., Inc. v. Leslie*, 52 N.Y.L.J. 1864, decided in 1915 by Justice Greenbaum sitting in the Supreme Court Term, is not controlling since—apart from a doubt as to whether an opinion of that court must be taken by us as an authoritative exposition of New York law—the opinion shows that the judge had his attention directed by plaintiff exclusively to Sections 50 and 51 of the New York statute, and, accordingly, held that the right of privacy was 'purely personal and not assignable' because 'rights for outraged feelings are no more assignable than would be a claim arising from a libelous utterance.'...

We said above that defendant was not liable for a breach of any of plaintiff's contracts induced by Russell, and did not become thus liable (for an induced breach) when there was assigned to defendant a contract between Russell and a ball-player, although Russell, in making that contract, knowingly induced a breach of a contract with plaintiff. But plaintiff, in its capacity as exclusive grantee of player's 'right of publicity,' has a valid claim against defendant if defendant used that player's photograph during the term of plaintiff's grant and with knowledge of it. It is no defense to such a claim that defendant is the assignee of a subsequent contract between that player and Russell, purporting to make a grant to Russell or its assignees. For the prior grant to plaintiff renders that subsequent grant invalid during the period of the grant (including an exercised option) to plaintiff, but not thereafter.[5]

3. We must remand to the trial court for a determination (on the basis of the present record and of further evidence introduced by either party) of these facts: (1) the date and contents of each of plaintiff's contracts, and whether plaintiff exercised its option to renew; (2) defendant's or Players' conduct with respect to each such contract.

Of course, if defendant made a contract with a ball-player which was not executed—or which did not authorize defendant to use the player's photograph—until the expira-

---

5. Since plaintiff asserts that, in all instances, defendant acted with knowledge of plaintiff's contracts, we need not consider whether and how far defendant would be liable to plaintiff, absent such knowledge, when, during the term of plaintiff's contract, defendant used a player's photograph without inducing a breach of that contract.

tion of the original or extended term of plaintiff's contract with that player, or which did not induce a breach of the agreement to renew, then defendant did no legal wrong to plaintiff. The same is true of instances where neither defendant nor Players induced a breach of plaintiff's contract, and defendant did not use the player's photograph until after the expiration of such original or extended or option term.

If, upon further exploration of the facts, the trial court, in the light of our opinion, concludes that defendant is liable, it will, of course, ascertain damages and decide what equitable relief is justified.

Reversed and remanded.

SWAN, Chief Judge (concurring in part):

I agree that the cause should be reversed and remanded, and I concur in so much of the opinion as deals with the defendant's liability for intentionally inducing a ball-player to breach a contract which gave plaintiff the exclusive privilege of using his picture.

Notes and Questions

1. What is the difference between the conception of the right of publicity, as set forth in *Haelan*, and the right of privacy, as set forth in *Pavesich*?

2. Note that in *Haelan*, the baseball player was not a party to the action. How does that affect the legal analysis? What other possible tort was available?

3. *Roberson* held that there was no common-law right of privacy in New York. Does the *Haelan* court satisfactorily answer the question of what to do about the precedent of *Roberson*?

4. One of the cases cited by the Second Circuit, *Wood v. Lucy, Lady Duff-Gordon*, may be familiar to you from your contracts class. In that case, the parties had entered into a contract under which Wood was to act as Lady Duff-Gordon's exclusive agent in endorsing fashion designs. He sued her for breach of contract, and was met with a defense of lack of consideration. Judge Cardozo's opinion for a unanimous court held that the consideration consisted of an implied promise of good faith in the contract which required Wood to use reasonable efforts in marketing Lady Duff-Gordon's endorsement. Does this case support the conclusion that there is an assignable "right of publicity" under New York law that is separate from the statutory right of privacy found in N.Y. Civil Rights Law sections 50 and 51?

5. Following *Haelan*, the newly-minted "right of publicity" received the endorsement of two influential commentators, which helped to encourage its adoption in other jurisdictions. The first of these was Melville B. Nimmer, who later became a professor at UCLA School of Law and authored a leading treatise on U.S. copyright law. In *The Right of Publicity*, 19 L. & Contemp. Probs. 203 (1954), Nimmer praised the Second Circuit's decision in *Haelan* and set forth his rationale for recognition of a separate right of publicity:

> The substance of the right of publicity must be largely determined by two considerations: first, the economic reality of pecuniary values inherent in publicity and, second, the inadequacy of traditional legal theories in protecting such publicity values. It is an unquestioned fact that the use of a prominent person's name, photograph or likeness (*i.e.*, his publicity values) in advertising a product or in

attracting an audience is of great pecuniary value. This is attested to by the now pervasive trade practice of paying well known personalities considerable sums for the right thus to use such publicity values. It is also unquestionably true that in most instances a person achieves publicity values of substantial pecuniary worth only after he has expended considerable time, effort, skill, and even money. It would seem to be a first principle of Anglo-American jurisprudence, an axiom of the most fundamental nature, that every person is entitled to the fruit of his labors unless there are important countervailing public policy considerations. Yet because of the inadequacy of traditional legal theories…, persons who have long and laboriously nurtured the fruit of publicity values may be deprived of them, unless judicial recognition is given to what is here referred to as the right of publicity—that is, the right of each person to control and profit from the publicity values which he has created or purchased.

The nature of the inadequacy of the traditional legal theories dictates in large measure the substance of the right of publicity. The right of publicity must be recognized as a property (not a personal) right, and as such capable of assignment and subsequent enforcement by the assignee. Furthermore, appropriation of publicity values should be actionable regardless of whether the defendant has used the publicity in a manner offensive to the sensibilities of the plaintiff.… Likewise, the measure of damages should be computed in terms of the value of the publicity appropriated by the defendant rather than, as in privacy, in terms of the injury sustained by the plaintiff. There must be no waiver of the right by reason of the plaintiff being a well known personality. Indeed, the right usually becomes important only when the plaintiff (or potential plaintiff) has achieved in some degree a celebrated status.

Id. at 215–16.

6. Six years later, William L. Prosser, Dean of the University of California at Berkeley School of Law and author of the treatise PROSSER ON TORTS, authored an influential article entitled simply *Privacy*, 48 Cal. L. Rev. 383 (1960), in which he contended:

The law of privacy comprises four distinct kinds of invasion of four different interests of the plaintiff, which are tied together by a common name, but otherwise have almost nothing in common except that each represents an interference with the right of the plaintiff … "to be let alone." Without any attempt to exact definition, the four torts may be described as follows:

1. Intrusion upon the plaintiff's seclusion or solitude, or into his private affairs.

2. Public disclosure of embarrassing private facts about the plaintiff.

3. Publicity which places the plaintiff in a false light in the public eye.

4. Appropriation, for the defendant's advantage, of the plaintiff's name or likeness.

It should be obvious at once that these four types of invasion may be subject, in some respects at least, to different rules; and that when what is said as to any one of them is carried over to another, it may not be at all applicable, and confusion may follow.

Id. at 389. Regarding the fourth category, Prosser said:

The interest protected is not so much a mental as a proprietary one, in the exclusive use of the plaintiff's name and likeness as an aspect of his identity. It

> seems quite pointless to dispute over whether such a right is to be classified as
> "property." If it is not, it is at least, once it is protected by law, a right of value
> upon which the plaintiff can capitalize by selling licenses. Its proprietary nature
> is clearly indicated by a decision of the Second Circuit that an exclusive license[e]
> has what has been called a "right of publicity" which entitles him to enjoin the
> use of the name or likeness by a third person. Although this decision has not yet
> been followed, it would seem clearly to be justified.

Id. at 406–07. Despite this endorsement of *Haelan*, however, Prosser recognized that
some of the limitations on the right of privacy should apply to the appropriation branch
as well:

> As to any one of the four, it is agreed that the plaintiff's right is a personal one,
> which does not extend to members of his family.... The right is not assignable;
> and while the cause of action may or may not survive his death, according to
> the survival rules of the particular state, there is no common law right of action
> for a publication concerning one who is already dead.

Id. at 408. It is difficult to square Prosser's conclusion that "[t]he right is not assignable"
with his express endorsement of the result in *Haelan*. As we will see, the subsequent history of the right of publicity has been colored heavily by the debate over whether it should
be recognized as a stand-alone right or as one branch of the right of privacy, together
with the implications of that choice for both assignability and recognition of post-mortem
rights of publicity.

7. Prosser's version of the four privacy torts (including commercial appropriation of
another's name or likeness) was incorporated into the Restatement (Second) of Torts
(1977), for which Prosser was the Reporter. The Second Restatement has since been superseded by the Restatement (Third) of Unfair Competition (1995), which provides
simply that "One who appropriates the commercial value of a person's identity by using
without consent the person's name, likeness, or other indicia of identity for purposes of
trade is subject to liability...." *Id.* § 46.

8. Note that *Haelan* was in federal court because of diversity of citizenship between the
parties. Accordingly, under the doctrine of *Erie Railroad Co. v. Tompkins*, 304 U.S. 64
(1938), the substantive law to be applied by the federal court was New York law, rather
than general federal common law. Another 30 years would pass before the New York
Court of Appeals (the highest court in the state of New York) took the opportunity to
rule on the validity of the "right of publicity" recognized by the federal court.

Stephano v. News Group Publications, Inc.

64 N.Y.2d 174, 474 N.E.2d 580, 485 N.Y.S.2d 220 (1984)

Wachtler, Judge:

The plaintiff, a professional model, claims that the defendant used his picture for trade
or advertising purposes without his consent, and thus violated his statutory right to privacy (Civil Rights Law, § 51), by publishing a picture of him modeling a "bomber jacket"
in a magazine article containing information regarding the approximate price of the jacket,
the name of the designer, and the names of three stores where the jacket might be purchased. Plaintiff also claims that the defendant's conduct violated a common-law right of
publicity....

Yes, Giorgio

From Giorgio Armani. Based on his now classic turn on the bomber jacket, this cotton-twill version with "fun fur" collar features the same cut at a far lower price—about $225. It'll be available in the stores next week. **—Henry Post**

BOMBER JACKET/*Barney's, Bergdorf Goodman, Bloomingdale's*

Figure 1-5. The "Best Bets" column in *Stephano*

In the summer of 1981 the plaintiff agreed to model for an article on men's fall fashions. The photographic session took place on August 11, 1981. The defendant used two of the photographs taken during that session to illustrate an article entitled "Classic Mixes", which appeared under the heading "Fall Fashions" in the September 7, 1981 issue of New York magazine. Another photograph taken during the session was used, a week earlier, in the August 31, 1981 issue of New York magazine, in a column entitled "Best Bets". That column, a regular feature in the magazine, contains information about new and unusual products and services available in the metropolitan area. One of the items included in the August 31 column was a bomber jacket modeled by the plaintiff. The text above the picture states: "Yes Giorgio—From Giorgio Armani. Based on his now classic turn on the bomber jacket, this cotton-twill version with 'fun fur' collar features the same cut at a far lower price—about $225. It'll be available in the stores next week.—Henry Post Bomber Jacket/Barney's, Bergdorf Goodman, Bloomingdale's."

It is the plaintiff's contention that he agreed to model for one article only—the September 7, 1981 article on Fall Fashions—and that the defendant violated his rights by publishing his photograph in the August 31 "Best Bets" column. The complaint alleges two causes of action. First the plaintiff claims that the defendant violated his civil rights by using his photograph for trade or advertising purposes without his consent. In his second cause of action the plaintiff claims that the defendant's conduct "invaded plaintiff's right of publicity". On each cause of action the plaintiff seeks $350,000 in compensatory damages and an equal amount in exemplary damages.

The defendant's answer asserts several affirmative defenses. The primary defense is that the photograph and article relating to it involve matters of legitimate public interest and concern and thus do not violate the plaintiff's rights under the Civil Rights Law (§§ 50, 51), or any common-law right of publicity. The defendant also urged that the second cause of action, for invasion of the plaintiff's right of publicity, does not set forth a claim "separate and distinct" from the first cause of action.…

[The trial court granted summary judgment to the defendant, concluding that the article reported a newsworthy event of fashion news, and was not published for trade or advertising purposes. The Appellate Division reversed, finding that factual questions were presented as to whether the defendant had used the plaintiff's picture for trade purposes and whether the article constituted an advertisement in disguise.] We now reverse.

Section 50 of the Civil Rights Law prohibits the use of "the name, portrait or picture of any living person" for advertising or trade purposes without the person's consent and declares a violation of the statute to be a misdemeanor. Section 51 of the statute provides civil remedies, including injunctive relief, compensatory damages and, if the defendant acted knowingly, exemplary damages.

The statutes have their origin in this court's 1902 decision in *Roberson v. Rochester Folding Box Co.*.… The Legislature responded the following year by amending the Civil Rights Law to establish a statutory "right to privacy."… Since the adoption of the statutes, this court has repeatedly held that the right of privacy is governed entirely by statute in this State.…

Section 51 of the Civil Rights Law has been applied in cases, such as the *Roberson* case, where the picture of a person who has apparently never sought publicity has been used without his or her consent for trade or advertising purposes. In such cases it has been noted that the statute serves "to protect the sentiments, thoughts and feelings of an individual" [citations omitted].

This history has led some courts to conclude that the statutory right to privacy is limited to the type of case which originally prompted its enactment and thus would not preclude the recognition in this State of a common-law "right of publicity" in cases where the defendant has exploited, without consent, and usually without payment, the name, picture, or portrait of an individual who has consciously sought to establish a publicity value for his personality (*see, e.g., Haelan Labs. v. Topps Chewing Gum*, 202 F.2d 866, 868 (2d Cir.1953) …). The statute, however, is not limited to situations where the defendant's conduct has caused distress to a person who wishes to lead a private life free of all commercial publicity.

By its terms the statute applies to any use of a person's picture or portrait for advertising or trade purposes whenever the defendant has not obtained the person's written consent to do so. It would therefore apply, and recently has been held to apply, in cases where the plaintiff generally seeks publicity, or uses his name, portrait, or picture, for commercial purposes but has not given written consent for a particular use. Thus where the written consent to use the plaintiff's name or picture for advertising or trade purposes has expired or the defendant has otherwise exceeded the limitations of the consent, the plaintiff may seek damages or other relief under the statute, even though he might properly sue for breach of contract. The right which the statute permits the plaintiff to vindicate in such a case may, perhaps, more accurately be described as a right of publicity. In this respect the statute parallels the common-law right of privacy which generally provides remedies for any commercialization of the individual's personality without his consent. Since the "right of publicity" is encompassed under the Civil Rights Law as an aspect of the right of privacy, which, as noted, is exclusively statutory in this State, the plaintiff cannot claim an independent common-law right of publicity.[2]

The only question then is whether the defendant used the plaintiff's picture for trade or advertising purposes within the meaning of the statute when it published his picture in the "Best Bets" column without his consent....

[The court held that the statute "should not be construed to apply to publications concerning newsworthy events or matters of public interest," and that the "newsworthiness exception applies not only to reports of political happenings and social trends, but also to news stories and articles of consumer interest including developments in the fashion world." The court also noted that the plaintiff did not bring an action for breach of contract.] Since the plaintiff chose to frame his complaint entirely in terms of rights covered by the Civil Rights Law, which we have concluded is not applicable in this case, the complaint should be dismissed.

Accordingly, the order of the Appellate Division should be reversed, the complaint dismissed and the certified question answered in the negative.

COOKE, C.J., and JASEN, JONES, MEYER, SIMONS and KAYE, JJ., concur.

Notes and Questions

1. The federal court in *Haelan* predicted that New York would recognize a common-law right of publicity. How was that right limited by *Stephano*? What is the significance of footnote 2 of the opinion? Should the states that recognized a common-law right of publicity after *Haelan* go back and reconsider that recognition after *Stephano*?

2. Note that the New York statute is limited to uses of another's name or likeness "for advertising purposes, or for the purposes of trade." The Court of Appeals interprets this phrase narrowly, holding that it does not apply to newsworthy items, including "articles of consumer interest." Does this holding leave Stephano without a remedy? Are there any other causes of action he could he have brought to protect his interest? For more on how New York has interpreted its "newsworthiness" exception, see Chapter VII, below.

3. New York is not the only state with a statute that governs rights of privacy and publicity. In 1971, California passed a similar statute. That statute was substantially revised in 1984 (the same year *Stephano* was decided) when California passed a companion statute for deceased personalities. The current versions of these statutes are contained in the Appendix to this casebook. As of this writing, 17 other states also have enacted right of publicity statutes. *See* J. Thomas McCarthy, THE RIGHTS OF PUBLICITY AND PRIVACY §6.8 (2d ed. 2008).

4. Even though Tony Stephano was a professional model, he was not a famous celebrity (unlike, say, the baseball players in *Haelan*). Is it helpful to have separate causes of action for celebrities (publicity) and non-celebrities (privacy), as *Haelan* and Nimmer suggest, or is it better to have a single cause of action available to all persons, as *Stephano* and Prossser believe?

"The distinction between the publicity and privacy actions ... relates primarily to the nature of the harm suffered by the plaintiff; similar substantive rules govern the determination

----

2. In view of the fact that the plaintiff is asserting his own right of publicity, we need not consider whether the statute would also control assignment, transfer or descent of publicity rights....

of liability." RESTATEMENT (THIRD) OF UNFAIR COMPETITION, § 46, cmt. a. Thus, in those jurisdictions that distinguish privacy and publicity, the right of privacy concerns "injury to personal feelings caused by an unauthorized use of the plaintiff's identity," whereas the right of publicity protects against "appropriation of the commercial value of the identity." *Id.* However, celebrities may sometimes suffer emotional injuries from misuse of their identities; and non-celebrities may well deserve to be paid for commercial use of their identities even if they have not suffered emotional harm. "Thus, an evaluation of the relative fame of the plaintiff is more properly relevant to the determination of the appropriate relief." *Id.*, § 46, cmt. d.

Today, while some states strictly maintain a distinction between the rights of publicity and privacy, *see, e.g., Curran v. Amazon.com, Inc.*, 86 U.S.P.Q.2d 1784 (S.D.W.V. 2008) (complaint stated a right of privacy claim, but plaintiff must plead he is a "public figure" to state a right of publicity claim); *People for the Ethical Treatment of Animals v. Berosini*, 111 Nev. 615, 636–39, 895 P.2d 1269, 1283–85 (1995) (common-law appropriation applies only to non-celebrities, while right of publicity tort involves celebrities and is purely statutory), most states allow anyone to recover for commercial appropriation (whether denominated privacy or publicity), so long as his or her identity has some commercial value. *See, e.g., Lauf v. Life Extension Foundation*, 547 F. Supp. 2d 771 (W.D. Mich. 2008). Many courts further hold that commercial value may be inferred from the very fact of use. *Id.* Consequently, as a practical matter, any distinction between celebrities and non-celebrities may be considered more a matter of form than a matter of substance.

B. Rationales for Recognizing Rights of Publicity

Look back at the *Haelan Laboratories* case. The court says that prominent persons "would feel sorely deprived if they no longer received money" for the use of their likenesses; but does the court explain *why* it thinks recognition of a right of publicity is a good idea? The excerpt that follows summarizes several possible rationales for rights of publicity, along with substantial criticisms of those rationales. (You will read the rest of the case in Chapter VIII.)

Cardtoons, L.C. v. Major League Baseball Players Association
95 F.3d 959 (10th Cir. 1996)

The justifications offered for the right of publicity fall into two categories, economic and noneconomic. The right is thought to further economic goals such as stimulating athletic and artistic achievement, promoting the efficient allocation of resources, and protecting consumers. In addition, the right of publicity is said to protect various noneconomic interests, such as safeguarding natural rights, securing the fruits of celebrity labors, preventing unjust enrichment, and averting emotional harm....

The principal economic argument made in support of the right of publicity is that it provides an incentive for creativity and achievement. Under this view, publicity rights induce people to expend the time, effort, and resources to develop the talents prerequisite to public recognition. While those talents provide immediate benefit to those with commercially valuable identities, the products of their enterprise—such as movies, songs, and sporting events—ultimately benefit society as a whole. Thus, it is argued, society has an interest in a right of publicity that is closely analogous to its interest in other intellectual property protections such as copyright and patent law....

This incentives argument is certainly a compelling justification for other forms of intellectual property. Copyright law, for example, protects the primary, if not only, source of a writer's income, and thus provides a significant incentive for creativity and achievement. The incentive effect of publicity rights, however, has been overstated. Most sports and entertainment celebrities with commercially valuable identities engage in activities that themselves generate a significant amount of income.... Thus, the analogy to the incentive effect of other intellectual property protections is strained because "[a]bolition of the right of publicity would leave entirely unimpaired a celebrity's ability to earn a living from the activities that have generated his commercially marketable fame." [Michael Madow, *Private Ownership of Public Image: Popular Culture and Publicity Rights*, 81 Cal. L. Rev. 127, 209 (1993)]....

Moreover, the additional inducement for achievement produced by publicity rights [is] often inconsequential because most celebrities with valuable commercial identities are already handsomely compensated.... [Thus,] "even without the right of publicity the rate of return to stardom in the entertainment and sports fields is probably high enough to bring forth a more than 'adequate' supply of creative effort and achievement." Madow, *supra*, at 210. In addition, even in the absence of publicity rights, celebrities would still be able to reap financial reward from authorized appearances and endorsements. The extra income generated by licensing one's identity does not provide a necessary inducement to enter and achieve in the realm of sports and entertainment. Thus, while publicity rights may provide some incentive for creativity and achievement, the magnitude and importance of that incentive has been exaggerated....

The second economic justification for the right of publicity is that it promotes the efficient allocation of resources, a version of the familiar tragedy of the commons argument used to prove the superiority of private property over common property. Without the artificial scarcity created by publicity rights, identities would be commercially exploited until the marginal value of each use is zero. [*Matthews v. Wozencraft*, 15 F.3d 432, 437–38 (5th Cir. 1994)]. "Creating artificial scarcity preserves the value to [the celebrity], to advertisers who contract for the use of his likeness, and in the end, to consumers, who receive information from the knowledge that he is being paid to endorse the product." *Id.* at 438. Giving people control of the commercial use of their identities, according to this analysis, maximizes the economic and informational value of those identities.

This efficiency argument is most persuasive in the context of advertising, where repeated use of a celebrity's likeness to sell products may eventually diminish its commercial value. The argument is not as persuasive, however, when applied to nonadvertising uses. It is not clear, for example, that the frequent appearance of a celebrity's likeness on t-shirts and coffee mugs will reduce its value; indeed, the value of the likeness may increase precisely because "everybody's got one." Madow, *supra*, at 222....

The final economic argument offered for rights of publicity is that they protect against consumer deception. The Lanham Act, however, already provides nationwide protection against false or misleading representations in connection with the sale of products....

There are also several noneconomic reasons advanced for the right of publicity. First, some believe that publicity rights stem from some notion of natural rights. McCarthy, for example, argues that a natural rights rationale, resting more upon "visceral impulses of 'fairness'" than upon reasoned argument, "seems quite sufficient to provide a firm support for the existence of a Right of Publicity." [J. Thomas McCarthy, THE RIGHTS OF PUBLICITY AND PRIVACY,] § 2.1[A] [(1996)]. McCarthy, however, offers little reason for this assertion, and blind appeals to first principles carry no weight in our ... analysis.

The second noneconomic justification is that publicity rights allow celebrities to enjoy the fruits of their labors. According to this argument, "[a] celebrity must be considered to have invested his years of practice and competition in a public personality which eventually may reach marketable status." [*Uhlaender v. Henrickson*, 316 F. Supp. 1277, 1282 (D. Minn. 1970).] People deserve the right to control and profit from the commercial value of their identities because, quite simply, they've earned it. Thus, in this view, the right of publicity is similar to the right of a commercial enterprise to profit from the goodwill it has built up in its name.

Celebrities, however, are often not fully responsible for their fame. Indeed, in the entertainment industry, a celebrity's fame may largely be the creation of the media or the audience. As one actor put it, "Only that audience out there makes a star. It's up to them. You can't do anything about it.... Stars would all be Louis B. Mayer's cousins if you could make 'em up." Jack Nicholson, *quoted in* Jib Fowles, *Starstruck: Celebrity Performers and the American Public* 84 (1992)....

The third, related justification for publicity rights is the prevention of unjust enrichment. In this view, whether the commercial value of an identity is the result of a celebrity's hard work, media creation, or just pure dumb luck, no social purpose is served by allowing others to freely appropriate it.... [In some cases, however, the defendant may have] added a significant creative component of its own to the celebrity identity and created an entirely new product....

A final justification offered for the right of publicity is that it prevents emotional injuries. For example, commercial misappropriation may greatly distress a celebrity who finds all commercial exploitation to be offensive. Even celebrities who crave public attention might find particular uses of their identities to be distressing. The right of publicity allows celebrities to avoid the emotional distress caused by unwanted commercial use of their identities. Publicity rights, however, are meant to protect against the loss of financial gain, not mental anguish. Laws preventing unfair competition, such as the Lanham Act, and laws prohibiting the intentional infliction of emotional distress adequately cover that ground. Moreover, fame is a double-edged sword—the law cannot allow those who enjoy the public limelight to so easily avoid the ridicule and criticism that sometimes accompany public prominence....

Notes and Questions

1. The first rationale offered by the court is that the right of publicity will serve as an incentive for people to engage in the types of activities that will bring them fame. Do you think that such activities are so beneficial to society that the law should seek to promote them? If so, do you think that the financial benefits offered by the right of publicity serve as a significant inducement to engage in such activities? Or do you think that a sufficient number of people would choose to engage in such activities even without the right of publicity? *See* Stacey L. Dogan & Mark A. Lemley, *What the Right of Publicity Can Learn from Trademark Law*, 58 Stan. L. Rev. 1161, 1186–1190 (2006); Michael Madow, *Private Ownership of Public Image: Popular Culture and Publicity Rights*, 81 Cal. L. Rev. 127, 206–15 (1993).

2. The second rationale offered by the court is economic efficiency. Essentially, the argument is that celebrity identities will be "over-exploited" if they are not actively managed by a rights holder, reducing the value of those identities to zero. The court acknowledges that this rationale carries significant weight in the context of advertising, but it questions it in the context of merchandising. Do you think that over-exploitation is a significant concern? What harm would be done to the *public* interest if a celebrity's image is commercially exploited by people other than those authorized by the celebrity? For a defense of this rationale, *see* Richard A. Posner, Economic Analysis of Law 45 (7th ed. 2007); and Mark F. Grady, *A Positive Economic Theory of the Right of Publicity*, 1 UCLA Ent. L. Rev. 97, 110–26 (1994). For criticisms of this rationale, *see* Madow, at 220–25; and Mark A. Lemley, *Ex Ante Versus Ex Post Justifications for Intellectual Property*, 71 U. Chi. L. Rev. 129, 141–48 (2004).

3. The third rationale offered by the court is avoiding consumer deception. Is the court correct that this interest can adequately be addressed by federal and state laws prohibiting false endorsement? Or is there a reason to believe that such laws are inadequate to address the issue? *See* Dogan & Lemley, at 1190–97 & 1208–13. You may wish to reconsider this question after you have studied the materials in Chapter 5.

4. The court also offers four non-economic justifications for the right of publicity. With regard to the first non-economic rationale, should a court recognize a "natural right" to prevent the use of one's name or likeness for a commercial purpose? What is the authority for doing so? Alternatively, should a court recognize a "natural right" for others to depict (or copy) the world around them, including the people in it? How should those competing rights be balanced?

5. Next, the court posits that celebrities may be entitled to the fruits of their labors. Is this a compelling or persuasive rationale? Are there other people in addition to "the media or the audience" that make a significant contribution to the value of a celebrity persona? *See* Dogan & Lemley at 1181; Madow, at 182–196. Is it relevant that in copyright law, the U.S. Supreme Court has rejected the "sweat of the brow" theory of protection, holding instead that "copyright rewards originality, not effort"? *See* Feist Publications, Inc. v. Rural Telephone Service Co., 499 U.S. 340 (1991).

6. Why should any "enrichment" earned by one who uses a celebrity's name or likeness for commercial purposes be considered "unjust"? Is "free riding" necessarily a bad thing? In our free-market economy, free competition is the default assumption; why should we depart from this assumption by granting exclusive rights to a celebrity? For criticisms of this rationale, *see* Dogan & Lemley, at 1182–83; Madow, at 196–205.

7. With regard to the final rationale, should the court so easily dismiss the emotional injuries of celebrities? Should a celebrity have an autonomy interest in how his or her name or likeness is used? If so, should the public have a countervailing interest in being able to depict a celebrity without being subject to the celebrity's control? How should those interests be balanced? Does the right of publicity offer something that the Lanham Act and tort law (such as intentional infliction of emotional distress) do not?

8. Keep these rationales in mind as you work through the materials in the rest of this book. For each case, try to identify which of these rationales are being served, whether the right of publicity is necessary or helpful to vindicating that interest, whether there are other interests that need to be taken into account, and whether some other body of law could adequately address the problems that are presented to the court.

C. Foundations of Rights of Publicity and Related Rights Outside the United States

The legal systems of United Kingdom and Canada share an important characteristic with the United States: a common-law tradition. That is, both countries have a legal system where a great deal of the law derives from court decisions in individual cases. By contrast, much of Europe (and many other countries as well) is steeped in a civil-law tradition, in which the primary source of law is statutes, and court decisions are not supposed to create law.

As in the United States, statutes have come to play an increasingly important role in the legal systems of both Canada and the U.K. In particular, the U.K's membership in the European Union has meant that European Union law plays an increasingly important role in the legal system of that country. However, although the European Union has implemented some fairly detailed statutory systems in the area of intellectual property, it has not enacted a legal regime relating to rights of publicity. (As we shall see in Chapter V, to some degree the European law of trademarks has begun to play a role in this area, but the foundations of the law in this area are still left to individual countries.) In addition, the European Convention on Human Rights, discussed in Chapter IX, also has begun to play a role in the area of the rights of individuals to control the use of their name, likeness, and persona.

Throughout this book, we will present cases and other materials from around the world to enable you to compare the form of protection available in the United States with that available in other countries. The materials in this section present some of the foundational cases in this area from the common-law jurisdictions of the United Kingdom, Canada, and Australia. In addition, there are textual materials that lay out the statutory schemes used in several civil law countries to protect celebrity rights. Interestingly enough, you will find that even in civil-law countries, case law plays a role in setting the parameters of these rights.

We have used the term "related rights" in the heading of this section because, as will be seen, countries outside of the United States do not necessarily grant rights to individuals on the same basis as U.S. courts. Rather, those rights are deemed a part of other branches of the law. As you read the following materials, consider in what ways the protection afforded by other countries is the same as, and different from, the protection afforded by United States courts.

Irvine v. Talksport, Ltd.

[2002] EWHC 367, [2002] 2 All E.R. 414, [2002] E.M.L.R. 32
(Eng. Ch. Div. 2002), *aff'd* [2003] EWCA Civ. 423,
[2003] E.M.L.R. 26 (Eng. Ct. App. 2003)

LADDIE, J.:

Introduction

1. This is the judgment in an action for passing off. It raises an important point of principle. The first claimant is Mr Edmund Irvine…. The defendant is Talksport Limited.

2. The evidence shows, as anyone interested in motor racing would know, that Mr Irvine, referred to generally as "Eddie Irvine", is a prominent driver on the Formula 1

("F1") racing circuit. He is one of a small group of British drivers who have achieved some success in recent years in that sport. 1999 has proved his most successful year to date. During that racing season, Mr Irvine was driving F1 cars made by Ferrari. By a narrow margin he missed being the F1 champion of the year, coming second.

3. Talksport Ltd. runs an eponymous radio station. It is now one of the largest commercial radio stations in the United Kingdom. Until the end of 1999, the station bore the name "Talk Radio".... In 1998 or early 1999, it was decided to refocus the area of interest away from news and general talk programmes towards sport.... Part of the implementation of that decision was the rebranding of the station by abandoning its existing name and adopting the name "Talksport".... In 1999 it obtained the rights to cover, inter alia, the F1 Grand Prix World Championship.

4. To support the change of direction and to generate interest among potential advertisers, the defendant embarked on a special promotional campaign. As part of that, it engaged the services of a marketing and communications agency called SMP Limited ("SMP") to produce a number of boxed packs to be sent to just under 1000 people who it was thought were likely to be responsible, directly or indirectly, for the placement of advertisements. Three such boxed sets were produced.... It is the second with which this action is concerned.

5. The second promotion consisted of a box bearing the image depicted at Annex 1 to this judgment. The car in the middle of the photograph is a F1 racing car. The two small photographs at opposite corners of the main image are of another famous F1 driver, Mr Michael Schumacher.... Inside the box is a pair of white shorts and a brochure or "flyer". The shorts bear on the back an imitation of the skid mark left on the road when a car accelerates too forcefully. On the front there are the words "Talk Radio 1053/1089 am". The brochure has four sides (*i.e.*, it is one piece of card folded down the middle).... Inside and on the back there is advertising copy extolling the virtues of Talk Radio including, in particular, as a vehicle for carrying sport-related advertisements. The reader is invited to contact a website: www.talksport.net. In the middle of pages 2 and 3 is a partial photograph of an F1 car. On the back page is a further photograph of another F1 car and a photograph of the winner's podium at the Monte Carlo F1 Grand Prix showing, amongst others, Michael Schumacher, Mikka Hakkinen and Eddie Irvine. All three are F1 drivers....

6. There was no dispute between the parties that the anonymous box and the shorts are likely to be discarded and the brochure retained, assuming that all three are not immediately thrown away by the recipient. It is the brochure which will stay on the recipient's desk or may be passed to others.

7. The photograph on the front of the brochure is of Eddie Irvine. There is no question of copyright infringement because the right to use this photograph was purchased from a sporting photograph agency. However the photograph as made available by the agency does not show Mr Irvine holding a radio. He is holding a mobile telephone. SMP took that image and manipulated it to cut out the mobile telephone and to replace it by an image of a portable radio to which the words "Talk Radio" had been added.

8. It is Mr Irvine's case that the distribution of the defendant's brochure bearing a manipulated picture of him is an actionable passing off....

9. Before considering the principles of law and the facts in this case, it will be useful to clear up one issue of terminology. Throughout the trial reference was made to sponsorship, endorsement and merchandising. The evidence sometimes referred to one, sometimes another and at times to all of these. As Ms Lane, who appeared for the claimants, explained, this case is concerned with endorsement. When someone endorses a product

or service he tells the relevant public that he approves of the product or service or is happy to be associated with it. In effect he adds his name as an encouragement to members of the relevant public to buy or use the service or product. Merchandising is rather different. It involves exploiting images, themes or articles which have become famous. To take a topical example, when the recent film, *Star Wars Episode 1* was about to be exhibited, a large number of toys, posters, garments and the like were put on sale, each of which bore an image of or reproduced a character or object in the film. The purpose of this was to make available a large number of products which could be bought by members of the public who found the film enjoyable and wanted a reminder of it. The manufacture and distribution of this type of spin-off product is referred to as merchandising. It is not a necessary feature of merchandising that members of the public will think the products are in any sense endorsed by the film makers or actors in the film. Merchandised products will include some where there is a perception of endorsement and some where there may not be, but in all cases the products are tied into and are a reminder of the film itself. An example of merchandising is the sale of memorabilia relating to the late Diana, Princess of Wales. A porcelain plate bearing her image could hardly be thought of as being endorsed by her, but the enhanced sales which may be achieved by virtue of the presence of the image is a form of merchandising.

The relevant law

10. As I have said, Ms Lane has argued that this is an endorsement case (or more strictly a false endorsement case) and falls squarely within modern application of the law of passing off. Mr Michael Hicks, who appears for the defendant, argues that even as an endorsement case, this fails to fall within the scope of passing off. At the forefront of his submission and encapsulating the various strands of his argument he relied on the following passage from the judgment of Simon Brown L.J. in *Elvis Presley Trade Marks* [1999] R.P.C. 567 at p. 597:

> "On analysis, as it seems to me, all the English cases upon which Enterprises seeks to rely (Mirage Studios not least) can be seen to have turned essentially upon the need to protect copyright or to prevent passing off (or libel). None creates the broad right for which in effect Mr Prescott contends here, a free standing general right to character exploitation enjoyable exclusively by the celebrity. As Robert Walker L.J. has explained, just such a right, a new 'character right' to fill a perceived gap between the law of copyright (there being no copyright in a name) and the law of passing off was considered and rejected by the Whitford Committee in 1977. Thirty years earlier, indeed, when it was contended for as a corollary of passing off law, it had been rejected in *McCulloch v. Lewis A. May* [1947] 2 All E.R. 845. I would assume to reject it. In addressing the critical issue of distinctiveness there should be no a priori assumption that only a celebrity or his successors may ever market (or licence the marketing of) his own character. Monopolies should not be so readily created."

11. At its heart, Mr Hicks' argument was that what Mr Irvine is trying to enforce here is just the sort of broad and novel right which Simon Brown L.J. rejected.

12. This dispute raises important questions as to the nature of the cause of action in passing off and whether, as Ms Lane asserted, that cause of action can prevent unauthorised endorsements assuming, of course, that what has happened here amounts to such an endorsement.

13. The sort of cases which come within the scope of a passing off action has not remained stationary over the years. This is for two reasons. First, passing off is closely con-

nected to and dependent upon what is happening in the market place. It is a judge made law which tries to ensure, in its own limited way, a degree of honesty and fairness in the way trade is conducted....

14. ... The law of passing off responds to changes in the nature of trade.

15. Second, the law itself has refined over the years....

16. ... The old cases provide us with the origin of the law. They do not illustrate more recent developments....

18. The need for goods-for-goods substitution as an essential ingredient in the tort was a feature in many nineteenth century cases and still can be discerned in some early decisions in the last century. Because the claimant had to show this substitution, it was inherent that the he also had to show that he was in business selling goods. Perhaps, to modern eyes, one of the most stark and surprising illustrations of this is to be seen in *Clark v. Freeman* (1848) 11 Beav. 112, an early case of false endorsement. The plaintiff, Sir James Clarke, was an eminent physician and Physician-in-Ordinary to Queen Victoria. The defendant sold certain pills under the name "Sir J. Clark's Consumption Pills". Before Lord Langdale M.R., the claim failed, a major reason being that the plaintiff did not carry on the business of selling pills so, it was held, he suffered no pecuniary injury by reason of the defendant's activities. It is interesting to note that Lord Langdale said that he could not conceive that anyone in the world would suppose that Sir James' professional name would be the least damaged by the defendant's "unscrupulous" use of it. Presumably that view made sense in an era when physicians were treated as the sort of gentlemen who would not soil their hands or their reputation by being involved "in trade".

19. *Clark v. Freeman* was followed, though without conspicuous enthusiasm, in *Williams v. Hodge & Co.* (1887) 4 T.L.R. 17, a case in which another eminent physician tried, but failed, to secure interlocutory relief against a manufacturer of surgical equipment who used his name to boost sales.

20. *Clark v. Freeman* was distinguished in another false endorsement case, *British Medical Association v. Marsh* (1931) 48 R.P.C. 565. Then as now, the plaintiff was the association for medical professionals. In 1874 it was registered as a company not for gain. It carried on no trade. Before the First World War it had published two books which contained the results of analyses which had been carried out on a large number of proprietary medicines. It disclosed which ones were ineffective and which were dangerous. The defendant, a pharmacist, had two retail shops. He sold medicines which were supposed to have been manufactured in accordance with the analyses in the plaintiff's books. He used the initials "BMA" as a trade mark for his medicines and made liberal reference to the British Medical Association. Maugham J. came to the conclusion that the initials would be recognised as referring to the plaintiff.

21. The defendant relied on the fact that the plaintiff was a non-trading company and had never manufactured or sold drugs or medical remedies and had never been associated with any firm or person who manufactured or sold such goods. The defendant said that it and its predecessors in title had been trading for seven years without complaint, so that the claim should fail as a result of delay and it argued that the plaintiff could not have suffered any damage and therefore was not entitled to relief. In holding that there was passing off, Maugham J. had to address the issue of damage. He held that no actual damage had been proved or had been suggested as having occurred. Notwithstanding this, he found damage by assuming loss of membership, based on an assumption that association with a pharmacist would damage the reputation of the Association. Thus it was damage to the reputation of the association which perfected the cause of action, the

loss of memberships was the consequence in money terms of that damage. To the best of my understanding, the correctness of *British Medical Association* has never been doubted. It is therefore not necessary to consider a number of other professional association cases which went the same way.

22. Counsel agreed that the most recent endorsement case in England is *McCulloch v. Lewis A. May (Produce Distributors Ltd)* (1947) 65 R.P.C. 58 in which the plaintiff was a famous presenter of children's radio programmes. He was known as "Uncle Mac". He had lost one leg and the use of one eye and had limited mobility. The defendant sold cereal food under the same name. It also used various advertising copy on the cartons in which its product was sold. They included "Uncle Mac loves children — and children love Uncle Mac!" and "You know the difficulties of travel these days, and will understand that Uncle Mac can't get about as freely as he would like to, but rest assured that all will come right in time and that he will always do his best to please his many friends." ...

24. [In that case,] Wynn-Parry J. [said] that, on the basis of the case law, including *British Medical Association*, the plaintiff needed to show the existence of a "common field of activity" in which it and the defendant were engaged. Finding against the plaintiff he said:

> "Upon the postulate that the plaintiff is not engaged in any degree in producing or marketing puffed wheat, how can the defendant, in using the fancy name used by the plaintiff, be said to be passing off the goods or the business of the plaintiff? I am utterly unable to see any element of passing off in this case." (p. 67)

25. With respect, it is difficult to agree with the suggestion that in *British Medical Association*, Maugham J. put forward the need to prove a common field of activity. If anything, that authority points decisively away from such a need.... It appears to me that Maugham J. accepted that there was no connection between the two businesses. The plaintiff was a non-trading association looking after the interests of the medical profession while the defendant was a retail pharmacist. The only connection between the parties was that the defendant's activities damaged the plaintiff's goodwill.

26. *McCulloch v. May* was considered and not followed by the High Court of New South Wales sitting in its appellate jurisdiction (Evatt C.J., Myers and Manning JJ.) in *Henderson v. Radio Corporation Pty. Ltd.* [1969] R.P.C. 218....

27. *Henderson* has been followed not only in Australia, but at least in Canada as well....

29. With respect, I agree [that *McCulloch* misstates the law]. The approach adopted ... in *Henderson* [is] to be preferred and seem to me to be consistent with a long line of English authority both before and since *McCulloch v. May*....

30. However, if the narrow approach in *McCulloch* is not right, so that identifying overlapping businesses is not a necessary ingredient in a passing off action, and nor is goods-for-goods or service-for-service substitution, what is the scope of the cause of action in its current form and does it cover false endorsement?

31. The law of passing off is not designed to protect a trader from fair competition. It is not even to protect him against others selling the same goods or copied goods. If the latter is possible at all it is only as a result of the application of the law of copyright, designs, patents or confidential information. Furthermore, passing off does not create or protect a monopoly in a name or get up.* ...

---

* "Get up" refers to what is known as "trade dress" in the United States. — *Eds.*

32. What is protected is goodwill. The nature of goodwill was described by the House of Lords in *Inland Revenue Commissioners v. Muller & Co.'s Margarine Ltd.* [1901] A.C. 217. The oft-quoted passage from the speech of Lord MacNaghton reads:

> "What is goodwill? It is a thing very easy to describe, very difficult to define. It is the benefit and advantage of the good name, reputation, and connection of a business. It is the attractive force which brings in custom."

33. However there is another passage in that speech which is just as important and throws light on rights held by the owner of goodwill:

> "It is very difficult, as it seems to me, to say that goodwill is not property. Goodwill is bought and sold every day. It may be acquired, I think, in any of the different ways in which property is usually acquired. When a man has got it he may keep it as his own. He may vindicate his exclusive right to it if necessary by process of law. He may dispose of it if he will—of course under the conditions attaching to property of that nature." (page 223)

34. Expressed in these terms, the purpose of a passing off action is to vindicate the claimant's exclusive right to goodwill and to protect it against damage. When a defendant sells his inferior goods in substitution for the claimant's, there is no difficulty in a court finding that there is passing off. The substitution damages the goodwill and therefore the value of it to the claimant. The passing off action is brought to protect the claimant's property. But goodwill will be protected even if there is no immediate damage in the above sense. For example, it has long been recognised that a defendant can not avoid a finding of passing off by showing that his goods or services are of as good or better quality than the claimant's. In such a case, although the defendant may not damage the goodwill as such, what he does is damage the value of the goodwill to the claimant because, instead of benefiting from exclusive rights to his property, the latter now finds that someone else is squatting on it. It is for the owner of goodwill to maintain, raise or lower the quality of his reputation or to decide who, if anyone, can use it alongside him. The ability to do that is compromised if another can use the reputation or goodwill without his permission and as he likes. Thus Fortnum & Mason is no more entitled to use the name F W Woolworth than F W Woolworth is entitled to use the name Fortnum & Mason....

38. In my view ... the law of passing off now is of greater width than as applied by Wynne-Parry J. in *McCulloch v. May*. If someone acquires a valuable reputation or goodwill, the law of passing off will protect it from unlicensed use by other parties. Such use will frequently be damaging in the direct sense that it will involve selling inferior goods or services under the guise that they are from the claimant. But the action is not restricted to protecting against that sort of damage. The law will vindicate the claimant's exclusive right to the reputation or goodwill. It will not allow others to so use goodwill as to reduce, blur or diminish its exclusivity. It follows that it is not necessary to show that the claimant and the defendant share a common field of activity or that sales of products or services will be diminished either substantially or directly, at least in the short term. Of course there is still a need to demonstrate a misrepresentation because it is that misrepresentation which enables the defendant to make use or take advantage of the claimant's reputation.

39. Not only has the law of passing off expanded over the years, but the commercial environment in which it operates is in a constant state of flux. Even without the evidence given at the trial in this action, the court can take judicial notice of the fact that it is common for famous people to exploit their names and images by way of endorsement. They do it not only in their own field of expertise but, depending on the extent of their fame or notoriety, wider afield also....

43. Manufacturers and retailers recognise the realities of the market place when they pay for well known personalities to endorse their goods. The law of passing off should do likewise. There appears to be no good reason why the law of passing off in its modern form and in modern trade circumstances should not apply to cases of false endorsement. Indeed, it seems to me that this is not a novel proposition in this country....

44. In my view nothing said above touches on the quite separate issues which may arise in character merchandising cases, a considerable number of which were cited to me during the trial. In those cases the defendant's activities do not imply any endorsement....

46. It follows from the views expressed above that there is nothing which prevents an action for passing off succeeding in a false endorsement case. However to succeed, the burden on the claimant includes a need to prove at least two, interrelated, facts. First that at the time of the acts complained of he had a significant reputation or goodwill. Second that the actions of the defendant gave rise to a false message which would be understood by a not insignificant section of his market that his goods have been endorsed, recommended or are approved of by the claimant....

[The judge then found that Mr. Irvine did have goodwill at the time.]

Did the actions of the defendant create a false message which would be understood by a not insignificant section of its market to mean that its radio programme or station had been endorsed, recommended or are approved of by Mr Irvine?

58. As pointed out already, this case is concerned with endorsement, not merchandising rights. For that reason, Miss Lane [counsel for Mr. Irvine] does not argue that her client can succeed simply by showing that his image was used for commercial purposes on the defendant's brochure. She accepts that she must go further and show that there was an implicit representation of endorsement or that members of the target audience would believe that to be the case....

73.... I have come to the conclusion that a not insignificant number of recipients of the brochure would have [assumed that the brochure constituted an endorsement]. I should add that Mr Hicks argued that the photograph was obviously doctored and this meant that it was less likely that anyone would believe that Mr Irvine had endorsed his client. Even if it were true that the photograph was obviously doctored, I do not see how that could make any significant difference to the impact the brochure would have on its recipients. Furthermore I am unable to accept that the doctoring was obvious. On the contrary, when I first saw the brochure it did not occur to me that the photograph was doctored. The replacement of the mobile telephone has been done so skillfully that, even now, it does not look like a doctored picture to me.

75. ... For reasons given above, Mr Irvine has a property right in his goodwill which he can protect from unlicensed appropriation consisting of a false claim or suggestion of endorsement of a third party's goods or business....

76. For the above reasons, I have come to the conclusion that Mr Irvine succeeds in this action.

77. By way of postscript I should refer to one other matter. At an early stage in the trial, I asked whether there was a Human Rights Act point in this case. I referred counsel to the provisions of Article 8 and those relating to the protection of property in Article 1 of the First Protocol ... Had I come to the conclusion that passing off had not developed sufficiently to cover false endorsements it would have been necessary to go on to consider whether this new strand of law was effective, to use the words of Sedley L.J. in *Douglas v. Hello! Ltd.* [2001] F.S.R. 40, to "give the final impetus" to reach that result.

As it is, for reasons set out above, I have come to the conclusion that the law of passing off secures to Mr Irvine the protection he seeks and no recourse needs to be had to the provisions of the Act.

Notes and Questions

1. The court decides this case on the basis of "passing off." Traditionally, "passing off" has meant the attempt by one merchant to make consumers believe that his or her goods are really those of another merchant. (For example, if I were to sell a homemade soda as Coca-Cola, I would be passing off my soda as that of another.) To what degree has the British court altered the traditional notion of passing off in this case? Is it a justifiable extension of that theory?

2. How is the passing off theory different from the basis of the claims made in the United States cases in the previous section? Would either Roberson or Pavesich have had a claim if their claims were brought under the British passing off theory?

3. Suppose a company puts Mr. Irvine's face on a commemorative plate and sells it at the racetrack where he races cars. Would the rationale of this case support a claim? Why or why not?

4. Note that *intent* to deceive the public is not a necessary element of the claim; even if there was no intent to deceive, if a significant portion of the public believed that Irvine was endorsing Talksport, that would be sufficient. However, the court did say that "what the defendant intended to achieve by the promotion can give some indication of what it was likely to achieve." Therefore, intent to deceive is not entirely irrelevant. (The same is essentially true in the United States.) In fact, in another part of the opinion (¶ 72—not included in the above edit) the judge stated that he was assuming that the intent was to create the impression of endorsement, in the absence of evidence from the marketing agency as to what its intent was. (The fact that the photograph was altered to make it appear that Irvine was listening to a radio with Talksport on also seemed to push the judge in the direction of finding that there was a false endorsement.)

5. Near the end of the opinion, Judge Laddie refers to a "property right" in Irvine's goodwill (representing his ability to license his name and likeness for endorsement purposes). That may presage the possibility of extensions of this case that would be broader than the rest of the case might suggest.

6. Judge Laddie's opinion discusses a number of the existing precedents in the area, most significantly *McCulloch v. May*. However, there is an interesting early British case that looks a great deal like *Midler v. Ford Motor Co.* (which you will encounter in Chapter II.A.). An actor (Alistair Sim) complained that a commercial used a simulation of his voice (by another actor), and asserted claims for both libel (he alleged that the commercial use reflected badly on his reputation) and passing off. Sims asked for an injunction against the use, but was refused. However, the refusal appears based more on technical grounds than substantive ones; the trial judge believed it would be an improper use of his discretion to grant an interlocutory injunction. However, that judge did state

> I am not at this stage going to rule upon the question whether, in any circumstances, an action of passing off would lie for the unauthorised use of a man's voice, be he actor or not an actor, *though it would seem to me to be a grave defect*

in the law if it were possible for a party, for the purpose of commercial gain, to make use of the voice of another party without his consent.

Sim v. H.J Heinz & Co., [1959] 1 All E.R. 547, [1959] R.P.C. 75 (Ct. App. 1959) (emphasis added). The trial judge's ruling was upheld on appeal. In that appeal, Lord Hodson called the passing off argument "novel," and went on to state the following:

> No doubt that [passing off] is an arguable case, but there are various questions to be determined in this action, which has not yet been tried, including the question whether this voice can in truth be regarded as a property and whether, in the circumstances of this case, there could be said to be anything in the nature of unfair trade competition in a common field, where in the one case you have an actor who uses his voice in the performance of his particular occupation and, on the other hand, another actor who, in some way or other, uses his voice to imitate a voice on television for advertising purposes.

Id. Having decided that the "common field" notion did not prevent passing off in *Irvine*, it is possible that a court would revisit this result (and, after all, the court did not actually reject the idea of a passing off claim in this context).

7. The British Court of Appeal upheld the finding of liability in *Irvine* and awarded damages of £25,000 — approximately $39,000 at the time (as opposed to the £2000 awarded by Judge Laddie). [2003] EWCA Civ 423 (Ct. App. 2003).

8. The last paragraph of the opinion refers to the British Human Rights Act of 1998, and Article 8 and Article 1 of the First Protocol of the European Convention on Human Rights. Although the court declined to rule on whether a claim could be founded on those provisions, we will discuss this possibility later, in Chapter IX.

Krouse v. Chrysler Canada, Ltd.

1 O.R. (2d) 225, 40 D.L.R. (3d) 15, 13 C.P.R. (2d) 28 (Ont. Ct. App. 1973)

ESTEY, J.A.:

1. The defendants appellants appeal from a judgment of the Honourable Mr. Justice Haines pronounced on the 1st day of November, 1971, whereby he awarded the plaintiff respondent damages in the sum of $1,000.00 and costs. The action arose out of the incorporation of a photograph depicting the respondent in an advertising piece produced by the appellants and which the respondent alleges was done without his authorization....

2. The appellant Chrysler, an automobile manufacturer, decided about 1969 to advertise some of its 1970 automobile models by means of a player identification device to be used by members of the television audience when viewing televised professional football games of the Canadian Football League (hereinafter referred to as "CFL") and the National Football League (hereinafter referred to as "NFL") in Eastern Canada. It may be significant that a competitor in the manufacture and sale of automobiles was a sponsor of CFL televised football games during the season in question.

3. The advertising device referred to at trial as the "Spotter" consists of a double sheet of cardboard between which have been inserted two rotating discs. On the one side of the discs, which may be viewed through windows cut into either side of the Spotter, are listed the players of the nine Canadian professional teams, and on the other side are listed the names of the players of the sixteen teams then playing in the NFL in the United States. By rotating the discs the television viewer can see the player line-ups of the two oppos-

ing teams (one for each team) and can thereby identify any of the players during the tele-cast by referring to the team line-ups in the two windows and locating the player's name opposite the number appearing on the back of his sweater. The information in the window also gives the player's position and indicates whether he plays on the offensive or defensive teams. This card was thus designed for the convenience of football enthusiasts in Eastern Canada in following a game during its broadcast by television.

4. In the centre of the CFL side of the Spotter there appears the photograph which gives rise to these proceedings. The photograph is flanked by four pictures of automobiles manufactured by the appellant Chrysler or its affiliates and appears below the two windows in which the team line-ups can be made to appear. This picture is approximately 5-3/4 inches by 6-1/4 inches and the Spotter is 16-1/2 inches by 11-1/4 inches. The size of each of the four automobile pictures is 5-3/4 inches by 2-1/2 inches. All appear to be printed in full colour. On the NFL side of the Spotter there is a photograph depicting three unidentifiable football players in uniform and above and below this photograph appear five photographs of Dodge and Chrysler automobiles manufactured and sold by the appellant Chrysler or its affiliates.

5. The Spotter was produced for the appellant Chrysler by the appellant Grant Advertising (of Canada) Limited and was sold by the appellant Chrysler to its Plymouth and Dodge dealers in Eastern Canada. The automobile dealers in turn distributed these Spotters to the public in and after the month of September, 1969.

6. The respondent Krouse has been a player on the football team of the Hamilton Tiger-Cats Football Club since the 1963 football season. In 1969, when the Spotter was distributed by the appellant Chrysler, Krouse was a regular member of the team playing the position of defensive back and wore on his uniform the number 14.

7. The learned trial Judge found that the evidence showed that "the Plaintiff is a good, competent, hardworking athlete ... it is clear that he is not a superstar". It is clear on the evidence that the respondent Krouse, who was once named as a member of the defensive All Star Team of the Eastern Division of the CFL, was one of the better native born players in the league and would at least in the Hamilton area be recognized as an important member of the Hamilton Football team.

8. Turning now to the photograph which has brought this all about, it is important to observe that by agreement of counsel no claim is made by the respondent against the appellants for defamation, infringement of copyright, breach of contract or breach of confidence. The photograph, which was acquired from the owner thereof by the appellant advertising agency, was taken in the 1967 season in Hamilton Civic Stadium to which the photographer was admitted by a Press Pass issued by the Hamilton Club at a time when Krouse wore, as he always has as a professional football player, No. 14.... The photograph shows a point in the action of the game when the defensive player No. 14 is blocking the ball carrier whose number cannot be discerned.... The artistic technique applied to the original photograph dramatically centres the reader's attention on the collision between the defensive player and the opposing ball carrier. The clearest and largest image in this colour picture is a rear view of the player wearing No. 14 who, with the ball carrier, shares the geometric and optical centre of the picture and the action depicted. While there is no serious attempt on the part of the appellants to deny that the picture represents the respondent Krouse and several other football players during the course of an actual football game, they say that the photograph only incidentally reproduces the respondent's image and was selected for the sole reason that it is an excellent illustration of the climactic action characteristic of a football game. In this way, it was no doubt in-

tended by the appellants to draw to the attention of the general public and particularly football enthusiasts the Spotter and its usefulness during the telecast of a game.

9.... In my view, the evidence is clear that neither of the appellants selected this photograph because it depicted the player Krouse, and that their respective staffs were not even aware of the identity of any of the players shown, although in the resolution of the issues arising this element is of receding importance.

10. In essence, the defence is that the picture was primarily inserted in the Spotter to depict typical football action and incidentally, perhaps, to illustrate the working of the Spotter's mechanism by which Krouse is identified as the member of the Hamilton defensive team wearing Sweater No. 14....

11. The substance of the respondent's claim is (a) his picture has been used to attract attention to the products of the appellant for its commercial advantage; and (b) the photograph is an implied endorsement by him of products of the appellant Chrysler; all without authorization by the respondent.

12. In order to succeed the respondent must establish that he has a right known to the law which was transgressed by the appellants; and that either such transgression is actionable per se, or that the respondent has in fact been damaged by such transgression.

13. In argument before us the respondent did not found his claim in the common law action of passing-off or, indeed, in any alleged right of privacy, but rather in the submission that as a professional athlete he has earning power not only in his role as a football player, but also in his ability to attach his endorsement to commercial products or undertakings or to participate otherwise in commercial advertising. It is this right, that is to say the right to realize upon this potential, that the respondent says has been injured by the conduct of the appellants....

15. In summary, it is clear in my view that (a) the action photograph included on the CFL side of the Spotter clearly shows a member of the Hamilton Tiger Cats football team and several players of another team; and (b) this photograph would be taken by the public as illustrating both the action of football in a dramatic manner and the usefulness of the Spotter to identify players quickly during a telecast of a game. I can find no reasonable basis for inferring or implying from the photograph that No. 14, whether he be Krouse or someone else, is thereby endorsing the products of the appellant Chrysler.

16. Bearing in mind the importance to the appellants of securing ready access to the large television football audience which had been revealed by their research, and the activity of one of their automotive competitors in sponsoring Canadian football telecasts, the efforts of the appellants to make the Spotter useful and attractive to the television viewer may take on added significance. That takes me to the broad and difficult issue as to whether our law recognizes a right in a personality from the world of professional sport to grant or withhold the right to use any part of his personality, including pictorial representation, in the promotion of the trade or business of another.

17. A member of a professional team by the very nature of his participation in a professional sport in a public stadium exposes himself to public view directly by people in the stadium and indirectly to the general public outside the stadium when the game is broadcast by television. Obviously the image of the respondent Krouse along with that of the other players would be telecast at those moments in which he participated in telecast games, in association with pictures of the products of the telecast sponsors. Equally inevitably, the respondent Krouse, as indeed the evidence showed here, would find his likeness printed in newspapers and sporting publications at least in the area in which he

performed as a football player. This exposure would be anticipated and encouraged by the team and by players such as the respondent, and the commercial success of the team owners who pay their salaries is dependent upon such public exposure. Indeed the object, value, and purpose of professional sport is to attract the public in the greatest numbers possible to the game, and in the final analysis the owners and, presumably, the players will reap rewards proportionate to the numbers thus attracted. It therefore follows that Krouse and the other participants by the clearest implication authorize and invite the communications media to photograph and write about their exploits. The photo in question was taken, as I have said, by a photographer who was issued a "press pass" by the respondent's employers for the purpose of photographing the game for possible use by the press.

18. Apart from promoting the success of the institution of professional football by directing the public's attention to its activities, the individual participants' notoriety and success rise and fall by the publicity given their individual exploits....

19. The question therefore arises as to what limitations, if any, the respondent can impose on the use of pictures taken of him during a football game. These events have been partially anticipated by a clause in the contract between the respondent and the Hamilton Tiger Cats Football Club [giving the club the exclusive right to pictures used for publicity for the club].

20. Counsel for the appellants in a thorough review of the authorities in this Country, the United Kingdom and the United States, which directly or by analogy have dealt with the issues herein arising, submitted:

(a) Heretofore such actions would be tried in libel, but none of the authorities would qualify the plaintiff in these circumstances;

(b) Actions for 'passing-off' similarly would not avail the plaintiff because there was no common field of endeavour between the plaintiff and the defendants, there being no evidence that the plaintiff was in the business of selling automobiles;

and therefore there is no cause of action known to our law vested in the respondent.

21. The respondent founded his claim on the existing principles of trespass and seeks to apply those principles to the relatively new field of commerce in which persons such as professional athletes enjoy large incomes from the possibilities of exploiting the publicity value of their notoriety and personality. Unfortunately, to date these claims have been confined to very isolated cases which can be explained on other grounds.

22. The essence of the facts and of the issue arising can be stated as follows: in producing the Spotter the appellants sought to appeal to followers of football by providing an attractive and handy device for the better enjoyment of a televised football game. The appellants have produced this device as a medium for the advertisement of their automobiles. To attract the attention of the public a photo of an interesting event in an actual football game has been included in the device. The photo shows players, including the respondent who alone can be identified by the number in the Spotter if the viewer recognizes his uniform colours as those of the Hamilton team. The simple question put to the court is: "Is this actionable by the respondent against the appellants?"

23. In the classification of claims such as those made herein by the respondent Krouse the courts have not been slow either to adapt or extend the ancient principles of law so as to apply them to new conditions prevailing in the community....

24. The respondent in this court and below sought to found his claim on several recognized principles to which courts in the past have resorted where one person with or without the motive of gain has in some way put to use another's name or, for want of a better word, another's personality. Sometimes the action has succeeded in contract, sometimes in tort, and sometimes on some vague theory of property law.

25. The appropriation of one's image by photography was first dealt with in the courts in England on the basis of an implied contract not to use the negative produced by the defendant for any commercial purpose without the authority of the person photographed [citing cases].

26. Sometimes the courts have sought to find the answer to a claim of appropriation of one's personality in the field of defamation. In *Tolley v. J.S. Fry and Sons Limited*, [1931] A.C. 333, the plaintiff, a prominent amateur golfer, recovered damages for the unauthorized use of his photograph in an advertisement by the defendant of its products which it was held would lead the public to believe that the plaintiff had been paid for this use of his image (when in fact he had not), with the result that his amateur standing, which was of considerable value to him, would be in jeopardy. The respondent Krouse is, of course, in a diametrically opposite position, namely, he is asserting the right to compensation for the use of his image by another for commercial purposes. While this case is of no assistance in the disposition of the issue herein arising, it does illustrate the extent to which customs of the community and commercial practices change so radically over a relatively short period of time, sometimes requiring modification in the application of recognized legal doctrines to meet these new circumstances.

27. At one time an attempt was made to establish a property right in a name so as to preclude its appropriation by another for his commercial advantage.

28. A more imaginative basis for this type of action has been explored in the United States where the courts of New York, for example, found a plaintiff in circumstances not unlike those affecting the respondent in the present proceedings had a right to enjoin the use of his photograph and name on the basis of a violation of his right to publicity: *Haelan Laboratories Inc. v. Topps Chewing Gum* (1953), 202 F.2d 866. Sometimes this type of claim was classified as a breach of privacy and more recently and accurately as breach of the right to publicity. Neither the courts of England or of this country have as yet recognized such a right.

29. The learned trial Judge has founded the claim of the respondent in the tort of passing-off. Traditionally the courts have restricted this doctrine to proceedings where the plaintiff and defendant are competing in a common trade or are each commercially associated in a common sector of the commercial world.... [The court discussed cases, including the British case *McCulloch v. May*. It also discussed the Australian case of *Henderson v. Radio Corp.*, which is reproduced below, as possible contrary authority.]

31. After a careful review of the evidence and with the greatest respect to the learned trial Judge, I have concluded that in this case the tort of passing-off would appear to have no application to the claim of the respondent because the buying public would not buy the products of the appellant on the assumption that they had been designed or manufactured by the respondent, nor would the public be understood to have accepted the Spotter as being something designed and produced by the respondent. Finally, the Spotter was not produced by the appellants to be passed off on the public in competition with a similar product marketed by the respondent.

32. The position of the respondent Krouse is different from the positions of the several plaintiffs who have in the past asserted the variety of claims that I have here attempted to

classify. Krouse, by reason of his profession as a professional athlete, has developed a notoriety which is a by-product of his athletic proficiency. It is doubtless true that his notoriety is smaller in degree and of lesser commercial significance than that of other professional athletes, including, perhaps, some of his own teammates. If he has a right known to the law, however, the difference in commercial value runs to damages and not to the presence or absence of a cause of action. Thus, I have approached the respondent's position on the basis that he is a well-known professional athlete, and while he may be a player of lesser public following than others, he is certainly prominent in the field of professional sport in the eyes of those following football in this province, and that he has the same rights, if any, as those enjoyed by the better known personalities in professional sport.

33. The appellants were not passing out the Spotter as a public service. In a calculated fashion they incurred the expense of producing the Spotter for the avowed purpose of improving the sales of their automobiles. In designing the Spotter to include the representation of an identifiable football player, in this case the respondent, they must be taken to have included the football action picture deliberately, either to attract the public to the Spotter as a ready identification device which could be tested on the spot with reference to No. 14, or to make the Spotter immediately attractive to the eyes of the potential automobile buyers, so as to lure thereby the recipient of the Spotter into a study of the products of the appellants in the hope of inducing him thereafter to purchase an automobile of the appellant Chrysler's manufacture. Perhaps the appellants had both objects in mind.

34. Such a use of the respondent's image certainly does not suggest an express endorsement by him of the represented products of the appellants as in the case of athletes who appear on television or in the newspaper advertisements driving automobiles and praising their qualities. Nor does it appear to be an endorsement by implication or inference of the automobiles of the appellants. Had the respondent been depicted standing by or sitting in an automobile such an inference might arise, but I do not believe that a reasonable inference of endorsement or approval by the respondent of the appellants' products can be drawn from the presence of the respondent in the photograph included on one side of the Spotter.

35. It therefore remains to be determined whether the use of the respondent's image by the appellants in this way is a wrongful appropriation, and therefore as urged by counsel a trespass against the respondent's right to realize, if he can, a commercial advantage from the notoriety which professional athletes in our community and in these times possess....

37. There is indeed some support in our law for the recognition of a remedy for the appropriation for commercial purposes of another's likeness, voice or personality. *Tolley v. J.S. Fry and Sons Limited*, supra, although based in the law of libel does in the end protect a public athletic figure from invasion of or aggression against his status as an athlete by commercial interests for their gain. Thus far the courts in this country and the United Kingdom have declined to found an award on any broad basis such as appropriation of personality or even an injury to the latent power of endorsement. Even in the United States such judgments, as have been granted, are largely based on statute.... There is, of course, no privacy legislation in Ontario....

38. I, therefore, conclude from the foregoing examination of the authorities in the several fields of tort related to the allegations made herein that the common law does contemplate a concept in the law of torts which may be broadly classified as an appropriation of one's personality. Assuming the existence of such a wrong in our law, it remains to be determined whether the respondent has established that the appellants have committed such a wrong and have thereby damaged the respondent....

40. On the evidence before us there was no attempt made to associate the respondent with the appellants' products, nor was there the vaguest suggestion that the respondent brought the Spotter into being or was in any way concerned in its production. No doubt the appellants' object was to obtain widespread acceptance of the Spotter as something useful to the sporting public and by using a football action shot in full colour which included a rear view image of the respondent, it was thought that the Spotter would be more readily recognized for what it was. No doubt, too, they cherished the hope that, by providing this convenience to the automobile buying public, the sale of its new products would be increased. The appellants in short have sought to gain a trade advantage by associating themselves with the popular game of football and not any particular team or participant. By publicizing the institution of football through the circulation of a ready index of participating teams and their players (both in the NFL and CFL), the appellants seek to attract the attention of football followers to their cars. By presenting such an index or guide in an attractive form, the appellants no doubt believed they would increase their chances of an effective distribution of their advertising piece in a selected section of the market, but it is the game of professional football that has been deliberately incorporated in this advertising device and not the personality of the respondent who is but one of many individual participants in the game.

41.... The Spotter appears to be just one more element in the promotion of the institution of professional football generally in a manner akin to the promotion of the game through the usual publicity organs.... In essence, the appellants' main purpose seems to be to utilize the promotion of the game of football generally to attract followers of that sport to the automobile showrooms of its affiliated dealers in the hope of selling the appellants' product.

42. The danger of extending the law of torts to cover every such exposure in public not expressly authorized is obvious. Progress in the law is not served by the recognition of a right which while helpful to some persons or classes of persons turns out to be unreasonable disruption to the community at large and to the conduct of its commerce. Much of this publicity will in reality be a mixed blessing involving the promotion of the game itself, but at the same time resulting in some minor or theoretical invasion of a player's individual potential for gainful exploitation. By way of illustration, a sports report on television might expose a motion or still picture of one or more well-known players immediately before or after the telecasting of a commercial message by an enterprise not associated with the telecasting of football games. The public in our community would not consider any players so represented on the screen as thereby endorsing the products advertised on the same program, nor would a viewer reasonably associate in any other way the players so depicted and the product mentioned in the program's commercial messages. Thus, it would be a gross exaggeration to say that the usefulness of the player's name or image in some form of commercial exploitation in the advertising world was thereby diminished. The use by the appellants of the respondent's image in this case is in no way parallel to the use of a hockey player's signature on a hockey stick, or of a photograph of a professional athlete driving an automobile of the advertisers. Aside from the laws of defamation the courts have not heretofore found it appropriate to bring acts of the kind complained of in the particular facts of this proceeding within the purview of the law of torts.

43. As I have indicated, there may well be circumstances in which the courts would be justified in holding a defendant liable in damages for appropriation of a plaintiff's personality, amounting to an invasion of his right to exploit his personality by the use of his image, voice or otherwise with damage to the plaintiff, but after a careful review of the

evidence in the present action, I have come to the conclusion that the respondent has not demonstrated any infringement by the appellants of any legal right of the respondent. I would, therefore, allow the appeal with costs, set aside the judgment in appeal, and direct that judgment issue in place thereof dismissing the action with costs.

SCHROEDER, J.:

44. I concur.

McGILLIVRAY, J:

45. I concur.

Notes and Questions

1. This case was decided almost thirty years before *Irvine*. As you can see from the opinion, Canadian courts consider British cases to be of precedential value in their courts. Do you think that this case would have been decided differently if *Irvine* had been decided already?

2. In *Irvine*, the court indicated that consumers might be deceived into believing that Irvine had endorsed the Talksport product. Why wasn't the same true in *Krouse*?

3. If Krouse had been a better known player (whose number would immediately identify him to football fans), would the result have been any different?

4. Even after rejecting a false endorsement claim, the court considered whether to grant a claim based on a theory that is similar to many U.S. cases, namely, a kind of personality-as-property claim. Why was the court unwilling to grant relief on that basis?

5. The court cites policy reasons for denying a broader claim of misappropriation of personality. In paragraph 42, the court states: "Progress in the law is not served by the recognition of a right which while helpful to some persons or classes of persons turns out to be unreasonable disruption to the community at large and to the conduct of its commerce. Much of this publicity will in reality be a mixed blessing involving the promotion of the game itself, but at the same time resulting in some minor or theoretical invasion of a player's individual potential for gainful exploitation." How is this different from the policy that animates the U.S. cases?

6. What change in the facts would have led the Canadian court to change the result?

7. Almost twenty-five years later, another Ontario court case indicated a broader rationale than was apparent in *Krouse*. A well-known hockey player (Tim Horton) had founded a chain of Tim Horton's Donut Shops. The shops, which were owned by a corporation, capitalized on Horton's fame as a hockey player. After Horton's death, a former shareowner in the corporation purchased the remaining shares from Horton's widow. At a later date, an affiliated entity, the Tim Horton Children's Foundation Inc., was formed and raised money for a summer camp for disadvantaged children in part by selling portraits and posters of Horton. At some point, Mrs. Horton and the owner of the corporation had a falling out; she then objected to one of the proposed portraits to be used to raise money for the charity. Although the court dismissed her claim for appropriation of personality, it did not view the claim as limited by the endorsement rationale of *Krouse*. Rather, the court recognized that a later case indicated that the tort (and the court did view it as a tort) viewed the primary issue as whether the use was primarily a commercial one, or whether it fell within a category of "public interest" uses. (The court cited U.S. cases for the existence of this supposedly exempt category.) The court then concluded:

It is inescapable and uncontradicted that the predominant purpose of the portrait is charitable and commemorative. It is neither exploitative, nor commercial. Its purpose and effect is to perpetuate in a dignified and creative fashion the memory of Tim Horton. Just as the author in *Gould* added his own creativity to the book on Gould's life, so here, has Mr. Danby [the artist who created the disputed portrait of Horton] sought to express through his artistic talent, a portrayal of a great Canadian sports figure. In my view, this is of as much public interest to the sports world as a book on Mr. Gould's life is to the music world. Any commercial purpose is incidental at best. Accordingly, the portrait falls into the protected category ... and there is no right of personality in Tim Horton which has been unlawfully appropriated.

Horton v. Tim Donut, Ltd., 24 O.T.C. 151 (Ont. Ct. Just. 1997).

8. As you read the next few chapters, you should consider whether U.S. courts would decide this case any differently. You should also consider whether some states might view this case differently than others.

Henderson v. Radio Corporation Pty. Ltd.

60 SR (NSW) 576, [1969] RPC 218
(New South Wales S.Ct. 1960)

EVATT, C.J. and MYERS, J.:

This is an appeal by the defendant in a passing off suit in which it was restrained by injunction from selling, distributing, or supplying copies of a gramophone record cover entitled "Strictly for Dancing" having upon it a representation of a photograph of the plaintiffs in the suit.

The respondents are husband and wife and are well-known professional ballroom dancers, particularly in professional dancing circles. They came to Australia from England in August 1957, and since that time have engaged in public performances, lectures and demonstrations. There is evidence that they are the best known dancers of their type here. They are known professionally as "The Hendersons"....

The record is one of music suitable for ballroom dancing and was described as strict tempo dance music. It was intended for the instruction of students in dancing and for use by dancing teachers, but might also be bought by the public.... The only question at the hearing and before us was whether there had been a passing off by the appellant which the respondents were entitled to have restrained.

The respondents [plaintiffs] have contended that the acts of the appellant were likely to lead to the belief that the business of the appellant was connected with the business of the respondents because, it was said, the picture of the respondents on the record cover would lead buyers of the record to believe that the respondents recommended the record as providing good music for ballroom dancing....

However, the facts relevant to this issue are not in dispute. The only question is the proper inference to be drawn from them, and in those circumstances we are entitled to form our own opinion....

Unaided by evidence, one might consider that the dancing figures merely indicate the type of music on the record and that it is not possible to come to the conclusion for which the respondents contend. But one is not unaided by evidence and, having regard to the fact that the record was primarily intended for professional dancing teachers, and to the uncontradicted evidence of four experts in that field, we are of opinion that the proper finding is that the class of persons for whom the record was primarily intended would probably believe that the picture of the respondents on the cover indicated their recommendation or approval of the record.

It still remains to be considered whether that finding establishes the necessary element of deception, namely, that the business of the appellant was connected with the business of the respondents. In our opinion it does.

The representation that the respondents recommended the record is an inducement to buy it. The recommendation can only be attributed to the respondents in their capacity of professional dancers, that is, a recommendation made in the course of their professional activities, and means that as professional dancers they have associated themselves with the appellant in promoting sales of the record, and that amounts to a connexion, in respect of the marketing of the record, between the business of the respondents and the business of the appellant....

It has been contended, however, that the court has no jurisdiction to grant an injunction unless there is what has been called a common field of activity and in this case, it is said, there is none. [Here the court cites *McCulloch v. May* from Great Britain] ...

We find it impossible to accept this view without some qualification. The remedy in passing off is necessarily only available where the parties are engaged in business, using that expression in its widest sense to include professions and callings. If they are, there does not seem to be any reason why it should also be necessary that there be an area, actual or potential, in which their activities conflict. If it were so, then, subject only to the law of defamation, any businessman might falsely represent that his goods were produced by another provided that other was not engaged, or not reasonably likely to be engaged, in producing similar goods. This does not seem to be a sound general principle....

In our view, once it is proved that A. is falsely representing his goods as the goods of B., or his business to be the same as or connected with the business of B., the wrong of passing off has been established and B. is entitled to relief.

While McCulloch's case is open to strong criticism, in actual fact the respondents here are in a real sense competing in the special area of providing gramophone records specially adapted to dancing and dancing teaching. Their activities are competitive in a broad sense. If so, McCulloch's case provides no obstacle to the plaintiffs' success in the suit.

[The judges stated that they would dismiss the defendant's appeal.]

MANNING, J.:

... [T]he problem as to the nature and extent of the right or interest which will be protected has, to an extent, been confused with another question, namely, whether as a matter of social justice, the protection should be extended beyond the limits which have come to be accepted. The question of what may be regarded as damage to support the action is really a part of the same problem and interwoven with it....

Such discussions seem to me to confuse the real problem. It is one thing to discuss what one feels the law should be, as a matter of social justice. It is an entirely different thing to consider what rights arise according to the common law.

I feel that there has been confusion, not only in relation to the desirability of protecting privacy of individuals as a proposed reform, but also in the application of the recognised rules to particular types of case during different eras, when commercial practices have differed widely....

For myself, I would have thought that where a man passes off another person's goods as his own, and induces prospective customers of the plaintiff to purchase them from him, the plaintiff suffers damage immediately the sale is made, inasmuch as his goodwill in his trade is thereby injured. The courts of equity have always been prepared to interfere in certain classes of case, without waiting for the actual occurrence which will precipitate the injury to the plaintiff, but the plaintiff has always been required to show a danger that, unless the defendant is restrained from continuing his conduct, imminent and substantial damage will be sustained by him....

The false representation of which a plaintiff can complain need not necessarily have been made to the plaintiff and may have been made either in relation to the plaintiff's goods, his services, his business, his goodwill or his reputation. Indeed I am of opinion that the categories in this regard may still be open and that the development of new or altered practices in business, in trade or in professions may in the future result in further classes becoming apparent. If in fact such a misrepresentation is made and as a result of such representation the plaintiff suffers damage the right of action arises....

There is implicit in the views I have expressed, the conclusion that *McCulloch v. Lewis A. May (Produce Distributors) Ltd.* (1947) 65 R.P.C. 58, was wrongly decided. The ratio of the decision in that case was that the plaintiff failed because the parties were not business rivals, having no common trading activities. I think it would be unsafe to adopt the view there expressed that what has been called a common field of activity must be established in every case to entitle the plaintiff to succeed. It is undoubtedly true to say that the existence of a common field of activity is a most cogent factor to be taken into account in considering whether the misrepresentation is calculated to deceive or likely to lead to deception and may also be a factor in considering the second question as to whether the plaintiff has suffered damage. But, in my view, it is going too far to say that the absence of this so-called common field of activity necessarily bars a plaintiff from relief.

It is not altogether easy to equate the position today with that which obtained twenty or thirty or more years ago. Commercial enterprise develops, competition becomes keen and those in whom the desire to succeed, at the expense of their competitors, is strongest, are forever seeking new and more attractive methods of presenting their goods to the public. In the early part of the century it doubtless would have been difficult if not impossible to envisage the development of advertising by radio. A quarter of a century ago only those with the greatest foresight could have envisaged the manner in which advertisers seek to catch the eye of a large proportion of the public by means to which we are (sadly so it seems to me) subjected if we tune in to a commercial television station....

The plaintiffs in this case had acquired a reputation which doubtless placed them in a position to earn a fee for any recommendation which they might be disposed to give to aid the sale of recorded dance music of the type in question.... I can see no distinction in any such cases provided, as has been established in this case, that the activity of the party concerned has resulted in their recommendation becoming a saleable commodity.

The result of the defendant's action was to give the defendant the benefit of the plaintiffs' recommendation and the value of such recommendation and to deprive the plaintiffs of the fee or remuneration they would have earned if they had been asked for their authority to do what was done. The publication of the cover amounted to an misrepresentation of the type which will give rise to the tort of passing off, as there was implied in the acts of the defendant an assertion that the plaintiffs had "sponsored" the record....

I am satisfied that the unauthorised use by the defendant of the commercially valuable reputation of the plaintiffs justifies the intervention of the court.

Notes and Questions

1. Part of what makes this case different from the previous two is the target audience of the record. How does that affect the outcome of this case?

2. Consider carefully this statement from the court's opinion: "The remedy in passing off is necessarily only available where the parties are engaged in business, using that expression in its widest sense to include professions and callings." How does this limit the passing off claim in a way that even the earlier U.S. cases did not?

Problem 1

Journalist Lori Wallerstein did an interview with the Beatles in 1966. The interview ran several hours and was recorded on tape. A number of photographs of the Beatles were taken at the same time. Ms. Wallerstein never published the interview. However, in 1975 she decided to allow Polydor Records, a British record company, to make a two-record album (the vinyl kind, not CDs) from the recordings. Also included with the album were several photographs of the Beatles. By the time the recording was released, one of the group had died, another had split up with the woman to whom he was married in 1966 (the photographs included one of her), and some of the things they said in the interview no longer represented their views. Two of the former Beatles, George Harrison and Ringo Starr (a/k/a Richard Starkey) filed suit seeking to enjoin the sale of the album on the grounds that it constitutes passing off. (You may assume that there is no copyright issue here.)

1. How would a British court rule?

2. How would a Canadian court rule?

3. How would an Australian court rule?

The countries of continental Europe (and many countries that were their former colonies in the Americas) have a different legal tradition than the U.S. — a civil law tradition. That is, they rely (at least in theory) on statutory provisions, rather than judicial decision making, as the source of their law. As you read these excerpts, you should try and determine how the civil law system appears to differ from the common law tradition. In addition, the European countries often have rather different views of the value of one's "image" than we do in the U.S. Hopefully you will see those philosophical differences in these article excerpts.

Eric H. Reiter, *Personality and Patrimony:*
Comparative Perspectives on the Right to One's Image
76 Tul. L. Rev. 673 (2002)

A. France

French law has grappled with the question of the right to one's image since early in the photographic era. In 1858, the actress Rachel was photographed on her deathbed, leading her heirs to seek an injunction preventing the sale and publication of the image. In that widely cited case, the court held

> que nul ne peut, sans le consentement formel de la famille, reproduire et livrer a la publicite les traits d'une personne sur son lit de mort, quelle qu'ait ete la celebrite de cette personne et … que le droit de s'opposer a cette reproduction est absolu [that no one can, without the formal consent of the family, reproduce and publish the features of a person on her deathbed, however famous the person was, and … that the right to oppose this reproduction is absolute].

Thus, rather than basing the decision on the regime of civil liability in article 1382 of the French Code civil, the court instead treated the issue as an absolute right, a kind of subjective right to one's image. Though this case dealt only with the right to one's image after death, subsequent cases extended this principle to living persons. In 1900, for example, the artist James Whistler was involved in an action for nondelivery of a commissioned painting. The court held that though Whistler was not obliged to hand over the painting (he had only to refund the plaintiff's deposit), he could neither sell nor exhibit it, because it contained the image of another person to which he did not have rights. Aside from being an interesting example of the right to one's image in a nonphotographic context, the case suggests analogies with moral rights (as in the droit d'auteur): though the subject contracted away an aspect of her right to her image in allowing Whistler to make the painting in the first place, she retained an intransmissible extrapatrimonial moral right to her image.

Since then, the right to one's image has generated considerable doctrinal interest in France, with its highly competitive media culture and its long experience with paparazzi. In this context, debate over the right to one's image has centered on whether it should be viewed simply as an aspect of the more general right to privacy or as an autonomous right. Some authors argue for a purely extrapatrimonial conception of personality rights, within which the right to one's image has no autonomous status outside the protection of privacy, reputation, and the like. According to this view, unauthorized use of one's image is a violation of one's right of privacy. Thus, any resultant commercial prejudice would be wholly within the realm of intellectual property and so would not, properly speaking, involve a personality right at all.

Certainly French courts, like those in Quebec, have sometimes treated the right to one's image as primarily a privacy concern, even when a commercial interest is involved. In an important 1975 case, for example, a French magazine published (without authorization) nude photos for which the actress Catherine Deneuve had earlier posed for publication in the United States in Playboy. Though there was a commercial aspect to the case (Playboy had sold the photos to the French magazine without Deneuve's consent), the decision was rendered on privacy grounds. Similarly, in 1982 the heirs of Maria Callas sued a radio station for broadcasting a tape that had been surreptitiously recorded during a vocal trial Callas made just before her death. Because the trial had been conducted in an empty theater, and hence was private, and because Callas was, at that time, unhappy with the state of her voice and had decided on that basis to stop performing, the court held that to broadcast the tape was "une intrusion fautive dans l'intimite de la vie artistique de Maria Callas et une atteinte grave a sa memoire [a wrongful intrusion into the intimacy of the artistic life of Maria Callas and a grave attack on her memory]." Properly speaking, this was not an image case (though the court did hold the voice to be the image sonore (sound image) of Maria Callas), but it does show the court basing its decision on the extrapatrimonial aspects of Maria Callas's talent, rather than on its undeniable commercial aspects. Weight was added to the privacy interpretation of personality rights in France when in 1970 a general right to privacy was inserted into the Code civil as article 9 ("Chacun a droit au respect de sa vie privee [Everyone has the right to the respect of his privacy] ..."), a right that the courts and doctrinal writers had already recognized. Though this article does not explicitly protect image, the long-standing doctrinal connection between privacy and image allows its use as a subjective-right supplement to the more usually used protection via civil liability under article 1382 of the Code civil.

Most doctrinal writers, however, argue (in various ways) that the right to one's image has a dual nature, both extrapatrimonial and patrimonial, touching both privacy and commercial issues. This view better mirrors the contemporary situation where images, as well as other attributes of the personality, have an undeniable pecuniary value, and it avoids the casuistry needed to argue this point away. Most, like Pierre Kayser, see the right as comprising an essential extrapatrimonial core based on privacy, with a patrimonial aspect that comes out in certain situations, but which is secondary to privacy because it cannot exist independently of it. This question of the ranking of personality rights is not without importance, because it brings up the issue of whether the patrimonial aspects of the right should receive the same absolute protection as other subjective rights of personality or whether they should be left to the general protection of civil liability. For this reason, Emmanuel Gaillard goes further than Kayser to argue for the existence of an independent patrimonial right to one's image in order to protect those cases where prejudice is commercial only. In a 1970 case, for example, Henri Charriere, author of Papillon, a memoir about his stay on Devil's Island, brought an action against the publisher of a book about his life. He claimed both violation of his right to privacy as well as unauthorized use of his image on the book's cover. While the court rejected his privacy argument because the image in question was taken in a public situation and the book's text made use of public documents only, it nonetheless granted him damages for the unauthorized use of his image.

Building on Gaillard's ideas, Acquarone has expressed the distinction more starkly as one between a droit a l'image and a droit sur l'image, the former treating one's image as an inherent part of the person, the latter as a commodity to be exploited. This conveniently expresses the difference between extrapatrimoniality and patrimoniality, or between privacy and publicity. An important theoretical consequence of conceptualizing the debate in this way is that the right to one's image is seen as fundamentally negative, protective, and passive, while the right over one's image is seen as positive, assertive, and active. In other words, the right to one's image, primarily the domain of the anonymous, prevents unwanted exploitation, while the right over one's image, exclusively the domain of the famous, allows the subject to exploit (or not to exploit) his or her own image for commercial ends. In a 1987 case, for example, the comedian Alain Delon sued a tabloid for publishing a story with a photograph of him after he had undergone surgery in a Cuban hospital.

His claim of "utilisation illegitime de son image et de sa vie privee a des fins commerciales et publicitaires [illegitimate use of his image and of his private life for commercial and advertising ends]" was rejected at trial, but the Cour de Cassation reversed, holding that in ruling only on moral damage the lower court did not sufficiently take into consideration the commercial prejudice suffered in the form of injury to Delon's career.

Most recently, Gregoire Loiseau has given strong articulation to a pragmatic view that is receiving increasing support: that a strictly or a predominantly extrapatrimonial conception of personality fails to accommodate current reality. Loiseau argues instead for the recognition of independent patrimonial personality rights, which would leave to extrapatrimonial rights the protection of intangible interests, while creating a recourse in cases of purely economic prejudice. In essence, as I will discuss more fully in Part IV below, Loiseau and others, like Gaillard and Acquarone, argue that the extrapatrimonial and patrimonial sides of personality rights are incompatible, and so should be protected each in specific and separate ways. A similar bifurcation is evident in France with the droit d'auteur, where many argue for a dualist conception, with the extrapatrimonial moral right of authorship separate from its patrimonial economic rights.

Rights of personality and rights of authorship share many features and are often compared in the literature. The shifting weight of doctrinal writing in France suggests that the right to one's image is moving in the direction of a dualist conception like the droit d'auteur, treating it less exclusively as a right of personality and more as a patrimonial right of exploitation.

Elisabeth Logeais & Jean-Baptiste Schroeder, *The French Right of Image: An Ambiguous Concept Protecting the Human Persona*
18 Loy. L.A. Ent. L.J. 511 (1998)

C. From the Acknowledgment of a Right to One's Image to a Right on One's Image

As discussed above, there is an abundance of French case law affirming the notion that everybody has an exclusive right in their own image. This right allows one to prohibit any unauthorized use or dissemination. There is also general consensus among most courts that the right of image is characterized as a personality right rather than as a property right, despite some courts' contrary statements. Additionally, various legal scholars and commentators have emphasized the ambiguous nature of the right of image by describing it as embodying two concepts.

On the one hand, the right to protect one's image from unwanted exposure embodies a privacy interest. This aspect flows from the general difficulty in placing a specific value on one's personal rights, while also recognizing the general consensus that one cannot alienate a personal attribute—the extrapatrimonial nature of the right. This concept has been called the right to the image, meaning that an individual has an exclusive right to his or her own image such that he or she can oppose its unauthorized use and dissemination. On the other hand, the right also embodies the desire to protect a marketable asset—the image of a popular person for which others are willing to offer compensation to use it. The relatively recent recognition of this patrimonial nature has been characterized as the right on the image (or the right to profit on the image)—the patrimonial nature.

It seems that French case law has followed suit, struggling with the replacement of the former concept with the latter. For example, a 1996 decision of the Paris Court of Appeal held that the right of image is a personality right that entitles the holder to oppose a dissemination and use of his or her image without prior consent; the violation of this right may cause moral and economic damage when the holder conferred commercial value to his or her image as a result of his or her notoriety.

Stephen R. Barnett, *"The Right to One's Own Image": Publicity and Privacy Rights in the United States and Spain*
47 Am. J. Comp. L. 555 (1999)

IV. "The Right to One's Own Image" in Spanish Law

Having outlined the American right of publicity and some of its current issues, I turn to the comparable Spanish law.

A. The Organic Law of May 5, 1982

The major relevant text of Spanish law is the Organic Law of May 5, 1982. This Law provides civil-law protection for the "fundamental right to honor, personal and family privacy, and one's own image" ("el derecho fundamental al honor, a la intimidad personal y familiar y a la propia imagen") that is guaranteed by Article 18 of the Spanish Constitution of 1978. Article 1 of the Organic Law states that this fundamental right is protected in civil law from any kind of illegitimate interference, as thereafter provided in the Organic Law. Article 7 of the Organic Law sets forth a list of acts that will be considered illegitimate interferences with the fundamental right. These include, in Article 7.5, "the taking, reproduction, or publication, by photography, film, or any other process, of a person's image captured in places or moments of his private life or outside of those settings...." Article 7.6 then lists as additional illegitimate conduct "the use of the name, voice, or picture of a person for purposes of advertising, business, or of a similar nature." Thus Article 7.6, with its requirement of a 'commercial' purpose, seems comparable to the American right of publicity; while Article 7.5, with its focus on 'private life,' seems analogous to the U.S. right of privacy.[56]

Article 8 then lists acts that will not be considered illegitimate interferences with the fundamental right. Article 8.1 protects, as a general rule, actions in which there is a "predominant and relevant historical, scientific, or cultural interest." In particular, Article 8.2(a) specifies that the right to one's own image does not prevent, among other things, "the taking, reproduction, or publication of one's image in any medium, when the subject is a public official or public figure and the image is captured in the course of a public act or in places open to the public."

When an illegitimate interference with the fundamental right has been established, the Organic Law provides, in Article 9.3, that harm will be presumed, and that compensation will include moral damages ("dano moral"). On the question of post mortem du-

---

56. The Spanish Supreme Court has recently elaborated:
> The right to one's own image is the right of every person that others not reproduce the essential characteristics of his appearance (figura) without his consent. Under this right, every act of taking, reproducing, or publishing by photography, film, or other process of a person's image captured in moments of his private life or outside of those settings is presumptively a violation of or attack on the fundamental right to one's image, as is the use of one's image for purposes of advertising, business, or of a similar nature....
> But the Organic Law itself imposes limits on the right to one's own image, arising from the conflict between that right and the right of information recognized in Article 20.1 of the Constitution....

Decision of 11 March 1999 (256/1999).

ration, the Organic Law provides that, in the absence of a will, the right to one's image can be enforced by family members alive at the time of the image-owner's death—thus apparently creating a post mortem term measured by the lives of those family members. In the absence of legatees or heirs, the right to one's image can be enforced by the Ministry of Justice for up to eighty years after death.

B. "One's Own Image" Versus the Right of Publicity

1. Commercial Purposes ("Fines Comerciales")

The Spanish right to "one's own image" appears to be distinctly broader than the American right of publicity in not being limited to uses that would be considered "commercial" in the United States. As we have seen, "commercial" in the United States generally bears not the broad meaning of a use for purposes of business or profit, but the narrow sense of a use in advertising or promotion. In Spain, the phrase "para fines publicitarios [o] comerciales" in Article 7.6 of the Organic Law carries a meaning broader than the American sense of "commercial" in two respects: one based on the word "comerciales," the other based on "publicitarios."

First, the term "comerciales" is not limited to advertising or promotion, but refers broadly to purposes of business or profit. As Professor Amat Llari writes, in addition to uses such as advertising or promotion, where the economic benefit is clear, that benefit can be produced "in a much more indirect manner, for example, when the image is used in words of information or entertainment; the authors of these works are not acting for philanthropic purposes, and although the benefit may not appear to take an economic form, at bottom it can also be valued." Accordingly, the use of someone's "image" in the news or entertainment pages of a magazine—a photo of a politician's wife, or supposed conversations between the plaintiff and her ex-husband, a famous bullfighter—has been held to be "para fines ... comerciales" under Article 7.6.[63]

In the United States, if the magazine used the "image" in its news or entertainment pages, and not in advertising, the use probably would not be considered "commercial," and hence probably would not violate the right of publicity. The plaintiff might still argue under U.S. law that the publication violated his or her right of privacy. But generally it would not, if the facts disclosed were true and arguably newsworthy, and at least if they

---

63. *See* Amat Llari, *supra* n. 26, at 16 n.42, citing the Decision of the Territorial Tribunal of Barcelona of 12 March 1987 in the Revista Juridica de Catalunya, 1987, Jurisprudencia civil, nos. 3 & 4, pp. 79–81, where the publication by the magazine Pronto of the picture of Dona Carmen, wife of the president of the Parliament of Cantabria, was found to be for a commercial purpose ("con fines comerciales") and hence to violate Article 7.6; see also *id.* at 112–14, citing STS 28 October 1988, where Dona Carmen Ordonez, ex-wife of the bullfighter Paquirri, succeeded in the Supreme Court in a suit against the magazine "Semana" for publishing her supposed conversations with him.

See also Igartua, supra n. 25, at 33–34, citing the Decision of 27 May 1986 of the Court of First Instance of Barcelona in *Carmen Gomez Ugarte v. Montserrat Padura, Montserrat Mayordomo y Publicaciones Eres, S.A.,* in which the magazine Pronto was held liable for using a picture of the plaintiff to illustrate an article; *see also id.* at 95, stating that "a clear case of appropriation for commercial purposes" was seen in the judgment of the First Instance No. 21 of Barcelona reported in El Pais for 29 January 1990, p.24, where the magazine Interviu published some photos "in which it was apparent that a well-known personality of Madrid high society was not wearing undergarments" ("en las que se apreciaba que una conocida personalidad de la alta sociedad madrilena no vestia ropa interior").

Thus, when Dr. Igartua states of the Spanish cases that "the large majority of cases in which the courts have found a violation of the right to one's image have involved a commercial appropriation of the image," it must be remembered that the scope of what is "commercial" is broader in Spain than in the United States.

were not so scandalous or disproportionate" to their news value as to overcome the First Amendment's protection.

2. Purposes of Advertising ("Fines Publicitarios")

Not only the concept of "fines … comerciales" under Article 7.6 of the Organic Law, but also the concept of "fines publicitarios" under that section, appears to go further in Spain than does its counterpart in the American right of publicity. "Publicitarios" seems to extend beyond the American concept of either "advertising" or "publicity." This was seen in a 1996 decision of the Spanish Supreme Court involving a booklet entitled "Respect for Seniors" ("Respeto a los mayores"), published by the City of Madrid as part of a public information campaign to promote respect for older people. In a suit brought by a child and adults whose photos, taken in a public place, appeared in the booklet without their consent, the court ruled that while the City's purpose in publishing the booklet was not "comercial"—since it did not involve business or hoped-for profit—it was nonetheless "publicitario." The court stated: "Article 7.6 covers purposes of advertising or publicity that are not commercial, that is to say, those in which there is no financial interest." The court did not explain what made the purpose one of advertising or publicity.

The court went on to deny the asserted defense of a "relevant cultural interest" under Article 8.1 of the Organic Law. Even admitting that the City's "Respect for Seniors" campaign embodied a certain "cultural" interest, it was not an interest sufficiently "relevant" to overcome the fundamental right of citizens to their own image, the court said. This was because the use of photos of identifiable people was not necessary in order for the City to fully realize its cultural interest. Under American law, the plaintiffs in the "Respect for Seniors" case would not have fared so well. . . .

3. "Images" Used in Advertising a Work in Which the Plaintiff Appears: The Zarzuela Case

In the United States, as we have seen, the right of publicity generally contains an exception for advertising that uses a person's name, likeness, or image to advertise a work or publication in which the person appears. It may be explained by saying that the advertising for the work functions as an extension of the work itself, and therefore falls on the "media" side of the media/advertising line.

Similar exceptions exist in Germany and France, and it has been suggested that the Spanish law is cut from the same cloth. But the Spanish Supreme Court, in one case in which it could have invoked such reasoning, did not. A light opera ("zarzuela") of 1934, "La Chulapona," was given a new production in 1988, and the revival was advertised with a poster of an actress, Dona Selica, as she appeared in the 1934 production. The actress having died, her daughter brought suit, claiming a violation of the right to one's own image through the utilization of her mother's picture for advertising and commercial purposes in violation of Article 7.6 of the Organic Law. The Supreme Court rejected her claim.

The court did not find that Dona Selica, by consenting to the use of her picture in the poster for "La Chulapona" in 1934, had consented to its use in the poster for the new production of 1988. Nor did the court take the approach of American, German, and French law, allowing use of a performer's image in advertising a work in which she appears (or possibly, as here, in an earlier version of which she had appeared). Rather, the Supreme Court reasoned that the new poster did not violate the actress's right to her own image because it was not made as much for the purpose of advertising under Article 7.6 of the Organic Law as for a cultural purpose ("interes … cultural") under Article 8.1. This cultural purpose was "to keep alive and promote the revival of a musical genre as typically Spanish as the zarzuela"—a purpose demonstrated, the court said, by the reduced prices at which the posters were sold.

Given the way the Supreme Court did decide the *Zarzuela* case, one may ask why the cultural interest in promoting the zarzuela prevailed there, while the City of Madrid's asserted cultural interest in promoting respect for its older citizens did not prevail in the "Respect for Seniors" case. Two answers seem possible. First, the court in the "Respect for Seniors" case argued that the use of photos of identifiable people was not essential to the fulfillment of the City's interest. By contrast, there would have been little point in using a photo of an actor or actress from the 1934 production of the zarzuela who would not have been identifiable. Second, the plaintiffs in "Respect for Seniors" were, as the court stressed, ordinary citizens, not public figures. In contrast, the actress in the *Zarzuela* case was a professional, who at least had been paid once for her performance back in 1934.

In general, while the results reached in the two jurisdictions in these cases are similar, the Spanish courts seem to take more of a "case by case" approach, heavily dependent on the facts of each case, than do the American tribunals. The approach of the American courts is more categorical, asking if the use is "commercial" in the sense of advertising, or if it is an advertisement for a work or publication in which the plaintiff appeared. Because the Spanish approach is more likely to depend on the facts of the case—for example, on whether the court finds the "cultural interest" that it discerned in the *Zarzuela* case but did not see in "Respect for Seniors"—the Spanish law here seems slightly less protective of the press, and more protective of interests in privacy or publicity rights, than is the American law.

Susanne Bergmann, *Publicity Rights in the United States and in Germany: A Comparative Analysis*
19 Loy. L.A. Ent. L.J. 479 (1999)

I. Introduction

... Germany does not recognize a right comparable to the U.S. right of publicity. However, celebrities may proceed against an unauthorized use of their identity, citing the commercial value at stake. Statutes provide for the protection of a person's identity, such as likeness or name. Beyond these statutory rights, it has been the task of the German courts to fill in the gaps and protect other aspects of a person's identity. On a case-by-case basis, the courts have developed a "general right of personality" (allgemeines Personlichkeitsrecht) which is an elaborate system of protection against defamation and unauthorized exploitation of a person's commercial value....

II. The Concept of the "General Right of Personality"

Part II reveals that the right of publicity in the U.S. has developed into a property right separate from the right of privacy. The American right of publicity affords an individual comprehensive protection against unauthorized exploitation of the commercial value of their identity. While an individual in Germany enjoys protection against unauthorized uses of their identity, no distinct right of publicity exists that is comparable to that in the U.S. In Germany, a person's commercial interests are protected by a much broader right, a general right of personality, that has been developed by statute and by the courts.

A. Development

Originally, the authors of the German Civil Code (BGB—Burgerliches Gesetzbuch) rejected the proposal of leading scholars to create a comprehensive right of personality. The legislature decided that only some specific interests should be protected. Specifically, a person's rights were protected under the general provision of the German law of torts and under the right of name. In 1907, the legislature created the "right to one's image" (Recht am eigenen Bild) in sections 22 and 23 of the Act of Artistic Creations (KUG— Kunsturhebergesetz). In isolated cases, the courts then extended the "right to one's image" to protect other aspects of an individual's personality where the defendant acted contra bonos mores (against good morals).[208]

In 1954, the Federal Supreme Court took the final step in developing an overall protection of personality by recognizing a "general right of personality." The Court stated that the "general right of personality" must be regarded as a constitutionally guaranteed fundamental right based on Articles 1 and 2 of the German Constitution of 1949 (GG— Grundgesetz). Furthermore, the court declared that this interest is protected under section 823 I BGB. At the time, the concept of the "general right of personality" was very vague. Today, it still acts as a blanket clause or catch-all for all misappropriation of identity claims, even though the multitude of decisions in this field have given this right more shape. Nevertheless, a general definition of the right has been difficult to develop and the Constitutional Court has never conclusively defined it. Therefore, when determining the scope of the right, courts must consider the particular circumstances of the individual and his personal values on a case-by-case basis.

In principle, all natural persons enjoy the "general right of personality," but it can also protect corporate entities and other organizations. Article 19 III GG states that fundamental rights shall also apply to domestic legal persons to the extent that such rights permit. In the *Carrera* case, the court granted protection to a limited partnership when the defendant depicted the partnership's name and racing car on toy racing car packages. The Federal Supreme Court recognized that the "general right of personality" is a fundamental right that should also protect legal entities. Thus, the right can protect the personality rights of legal persons within the limits of their intrinsic character and their legally assigned functions.

Today, the "general right of personality" is a bundle of rights that protect different aspects of an individual's personality from unauthorized public exposure. Moreover, it

---

208. Whereas the main part of the provisions of this law has been replaced in the copyright law reform by the Law on Copyright and Related Protected Rights of 9 September 1965 (UrhG—Urhebergesetz), these particular provisions expressly remain in force. See § 141 Nr. 5 UrhG.
    Section 22 KUG ("Right to one's image") states:
    Pictures or portraits may be distributed or displayed only with the consent of the person portrayed, i.e., the subject. In cases of doubt, consent is considered to have been given if the person portrayed has received a consideration for allowing himself to be portrayed. When the subject dies and for up to 10 years thereafter, the consent of the next of kin is required. Next of kin within the meaning of this law are the surviving spouse and children of the subject and, if neither the spouse nor the children are alive, the parents of the subject.
§ 22 KUG. Section 23 KUG describes the types of pictures that do not require consent:
    (1) The following may be distributed or publicly displayed without the required consent according to § 22:
        1. Pictures within the realm of contemporary history;
        2. Pictures in which the persons appear only incidentally in a landscape or other location;
        3. Pictures of meetings, receptions, processions and other gatherings in which the persons portrayed have participated;
        4. Pictures that have not been produced by order or request, but whose distribution or display would be in the higher interests of art.
    (2) Consent does not however extend to distribution and display in which the legitimate interests of the subject or the next of kin are infringed.
§ 23 KUG

guarantees the protection of human dignity and the right to freely develop one's personality. In addition, several aspects of the "general right of personality" are protected by special statutory provisions. These statutory rights are the "right to one's image" (sections 22 and 23 KUG) and the "right of name" (section 12 BGB). The "general right of personality" only applies when these provisions are not applicable.

Notes and Questions

1. France, Spain, and Germany are all civil law countries. Do the rationales used for protecting publicity rights in those countries have anything in common? Here is what one author had to say about the German right of personality:

> [T]he right of personality in Germany does not constitute an intellectual property right, but rather a personal right. It guarantees the protection of human dignity and the right to freely develop one's personality. Strongly based as it is on a Kantian theory of individual autonomy and freedom, the general personality right constitutes a personal right, integral to the self, which cannot be alienated. On the one hand, this underlying theory structures the scope of the right, providing an instructive example of how publicity rights based on autonomy theory in the United States might restrict the expansion the right of publicity has undergone since its inception as a separate intellectual property right, distinct from privacy. On the other hand, the issues German courts have encountered in confronting the restriction on alienability, for example, illustrate the necessity of a limited propertization of personality rights for modern commercial markets and thus affirms the desirability of a *sui generis* approach to publicity rights in general.

Ellen S. Bass, *A Right In Search of A Coherent Rationale—Conceptualizing Persona in a Comparative Context: The United States Right of Publicity and German Personality Rights*, 42 U.S.F. L. Rev. 799, 828–29 (2008).

2. How does the concept of a right of "personality" differ from the right as it exists in the United States? Is the personality right more limited or more expansive than the right of publicity?

3. How do you think the courts of France, Spain, and Germany would decide the three cases in this section (*Irvine, Krouse,* and *Henderson*)?

4. Revisit the Problem included earlier in this section. How would you expect the courts of France, Spain, and Germany to rule on that set of facts?

Chapter II

Issues of Identification

A. Domestic Law

In the cases we studied in the previous chapter, it was not disputed that the defendant had used a photograph or likeness of the plaintiff without permission. In this chapter, we consider to what extent the right of publicity extends beyond the name or likeness of the plaintiff to other indicia of his or her identity.

Motschenbacher v. R.J. Reynolds Tobacco Co.
498 F.2d 821 (9th Cir. 1974)

KOELSCH, Circuit Judge:

Lothar Motschenbacher appeals from the district court's order granting summary judgment in favor of defendants in his suit seeking injunctive relief and damages for the alleged misappropriation of his name, likeness, personality, and endorsement in nationally televised advertising for Winston cigarettes. The jurisdiction of the district court is founded on diversity of citizenship, 28 U.S.C. § 1332; appellate jurisdiction is predicated on 28 U.S.C. § 1291.

The 'facts' on which the district court rendered summary judgment are substantially as follows:[1] Plaintiff Motschenbacher is a professional driver of racing cars, internationally known and recognized in racing circles and by racing fans. He derives part of his income from manufacturers of commercial products who pay him for endorsing their products.

During the relevant time span, plaintiff has consistently 'individualized' his cars to set them apart from those of other drivers and to make them more readily identifiable as his own. Since 1966, each of his cars has displayed a distinctive narrow white pinstripe appearing on no other car. This decoration has adorned the leading edges of the cars' bodies, which have uniformly been solid red. In addition, the white background for his racing number '11' has always been oval, in contrast to the circular backgrounds of all other cars.

In 1970, defendants, R. J. Reynolds Tobacco Company and William Esty Company, produced and caused to be televised a commercial which utilized a 'stock' color photograph depicting several racing cars on a racetrack. Plaintiff's car appears in the foreground, and although plaintiff is the driver, his facial features are not visible.

In producing the commercial, defendants altered the photograph: they changed the numbers on all racing cars depicted, transforming plaintiff's number '11' into '71'; they

---

1. We of course express no opinion regarding what facts the evidence may ultimately establish; we simply accept the statements of plaintiff's affiants as true for the purposes of the motion.

Figure 2-1. Lothar Motschenbacher in his McLaren M8C Chevrolet
Image Courtesy Artemis Images/Raymond Golub Memorial Collection

'attached' a wing-like device known as a 'spoiler' to plaintiff's car; they added the word 'Winston,' the name of their product, to that spoiler and removed advertisements for other products from the spoilers of other cars. However, they made no other changes, and the white pinstriping, the oval medallion, and the red color of plaintiff's car were retained. They then made a motion picture from the altered photograph, adding a series of comic strip-type 'balloons' containing written messages of an advertising nature; one such balloon message, appearing to emanate from plaintiff, was: 'Did you know that Winston tastes good, like a cigarette should?' They also added a sound track consisting in part of voices coordinated with, and echoing, the written messages. The commercial was subsequently broadcast nationally on network television and in color.

Several of plaintiff's affiants who had seen the commercial on television had immediately recognized plaintiff's car and had inferred that it was sponsored by Winston cigarettes.

On these facts the district court, characterizing plaintiff's action as one 'for damages for invasion of privacy,' granted summary judgment for defendants, finding as a matter of law that

> '... the driver of car No. 71 in the commercial (which was plaintiff's car No. 11 prior to said change of number and design) is anonymous; that is, (a) the person who is driving said car is unrecognizable and unidentified, and (b) a reasonable inference could not be drawn that he is, or could reasonably be understood to be plaintiff, Lothar Motschenbacher, or any other driver or person.'...

Since the Winston commercial was broadcast on television throughout the United States, our initial inquiry in determining the correct legal standards to be applied on the motion for summary judgment is directed at the proper choice of law. In a diversity case, a federal court must follow the substantive law of the state in which it sits. *Erie Railroad Co. v. Tompkins*, 304 U.S. 64 (1938). This includes the conflict of laws rules of that state. *Klaxon Co. v. Stentor Electric Mfg. Co.*, 313 U.S. 487, 496, (1941)....

In this case, we believe that California courts ... would apply California local law.[4] By the same taken, noting the novelty of the factual situation presented and recognizing that the parties have each cited general case law in support of their respective positions, we think that California courts would not hesitate to consider relevant precedent from other jurisdictions in determining California local law.

In California, as in the vast majority of jurisdictions, the invasion of an individual's right of privacy is an actionable tort. In 1960 Dean Prosser, drawing on over 300 cases, observed that the tort is actually a complex of four separate and distinct torts, each of which is decided under an 'invasion of privacy' label. *See* Prosser, *Privacy*, 48 Calif. L. Rev. 383 (1960); Prosser, LAW OF TORTS 804 (4th ed. 1971). Prosser's four categories are: (1) intrusion upon the plaintiff's seclusion or solitude; (2) public disclosure of private facts; (3) placing the plaintiff in a false light in the public eye; and (4) appropriation, for defendant's advantage, of plaintiff's name or likeness. The case before us is of the fourth variety — commercial appropriation.

California courts have observed that 'the gist of the cause of action in a privacy case is not injury to the character or reputation, but a direct wrong of a personal character resulting in injury to the feelings without regard to any effect which the publication may have on the property, business, pecuniary interest, or the standing of the individual in the community.' *Fairfield v. American Photocopy Equip. Co.*, 138 Cal. App. 2d 82, 86, 291 P.2d 194, 197 (1955). But this observation is perhaps better applied to Prosser's first three categories than it is to the appropriation cases.

It is true that the injury suffered from an appropriation of the attributes of one's identity may be 'mental and subjective' — in the nature of humiliation, embarrassment, and outrage. However, where the identity appropriated has a commercial value,[10] the injury may be largely, or even wholly, of an economic or material nature.[11] Such is the nature of the injury alleged by plaintiff.

Some courts have protected this 'commercial' aspect of an individual's interest in his own identity under a privacy theory. [Citing cases.] Others have sought to protect it under the rubric of 'property' or a so-called 'right of publicity.' [Citing cases, including *Haelan*.]

Prosser synthesizes the approaches as follows:

'Although the element of protection of the plaintiff's personal feelings is obviously not to be ignored in such a case, the effect of the appropriation decisions is to recognize or create an exclusive right in the individual plaintiff to

---

4. First, it appears that California, the state of plaintiff's residency, has a greater interest in compensating its residents for injuries of the type here alleged than other jurisdictions may have in compensating foreigners so injured within their respective borders. Second, in cases of this type, the state of plaintiff's residency is normally the state of the greatest injury. Third, California, as the forum, has an interest in convenience and presumably can most easily ascertain its own law.... [Choice of law is discussed in detail in Chapter XII. — Eds.]

10. It would be wholly unrealistic to deny that a name, likeness, or other attribute of identity can have commercial value. As the court observed in *Uhlaender v. Henricksen*, 316 F. Supp. 1277 (D. Minn. 1970), at 1283: 'A name is commercially valuable as an endorsement of a product or for financial gain only because the public recognizes it and attributes good will and feats of skill or accomplishments of one sort or another to that personality.'...

11. Generally, the greater the fame or notoriety of the identity appropriated, the greater will be the extent of the economic injury suffered. However, it is quite possible that the appropriation of the identity of a celebrity may induce humiliation, embarrassment and mental distress, while the appropriation of the identity of a relatively unknown person may result in economic injury or may itself create economic value in what was previously valueless....

a species of trade name, his own, and a kind of trade mark in his likeness. It seems quite pointless to dispute over whether such a right is to be classified as 'property'; it is at least clearly proprietary in its nature. Once protected by the law, it is a right of value upon which the plaintiff can capitalize by selling licenses.'

LAW OF TORTS (4th ed. 1971), at 807.

So far as we can determine, California has no case in point; the state's appropriation cases uniformly appear to have involved only the 'injury to personal feelings' aspect of the tort. Nevertheless, from our review of the relevant authorities, we conclude that the California appellate courts would, in a case such as this one, afford legal protection to an individual's proprietary interest in his own identity. We need not decide whether they would do so under the rubric of 'privacy', 'property', or 'publicity'; we only determine that they would recognize such an interest and protect it.[16]

We turn now to the question of 'identifiability'. Clearly, if the district court correctly determined as a matter of law that plaintiff is not identifiable in the commercial, then in no sense has plaintiff's identity been misappropriated nor his interest violated.

Having viewed a film of the commercial, we agree with the district court that the 'likeness' of plaintiff is itself unrecognizable; however, the court's further conclusion of law to the effect that the driver is not identifiable as plaintiff is erroneous in that it wholly fails to attribute proper significance to the distinctive decorations appearing on the car. As pointed out earlier, these markings were not only peculiar to the plaintiff's cars but they caused some persons to think the car in question was plaintiff's and to infer that the person driving the car was the plaintiff.[17]

Defendant's reliance on *Branson v. Fawcett Publications, Inc.*, 124 F. Supp. 429 (E.D. Ill. 1954), is misplaced. In *Branson*, a part-time racing driver brought suit for invasion of privacy when a photograph of his overturned racing car was printed in a magazine without his consent. In ruling that 'the photograph * * * does not identify the plaintiff to the public or any member thereof,' 124 F. Supp. at 433, the court said:

> '[T]he automobile is pointed upward in the air and the picture shows primarily the bottom of the racer. The backdrop of the picture is not distinguishable. No likeness, face, image, form or silhouette of the plaintiff or of any person is shown. From all that appears from the picture itself, there is no one in the car. Moreover, no identifying marks or numbers on the car appear.... Plaintiff does not even assert that the car he was driving was the same color as that which appears in the colored reproduction.'

124 F. Supp. at 432.

---

16. Two recent instances of the expression of California public policy lend additional support to our conclusion. First, Article I, § 1, of the California Constitution was amended in November, 1972, to include 'pursuing and obtaining * * * privacy' as an alienable right. And second, the California legislature recently enacted Civ. Code § 3344, providing that anyone who knowingly uses another's name, photograph, or likeness for purposes of advertising or solicitation shall be liable for any damages sustained by the persons injured, in an amount no less than $300.... [T]he statute's concluding subsection states that 'the remedies provided for in this section are cumulative and shall be in addition to any others provided for by law.'

17. The addition of a 'Winston' spoiler to the plaintiffs car does not necessarily render the automobile impersonal, for plaintiff's cars have frequently used spoilers; it may be taken as contributing to the inference of sponsorship or endorsement. The alteration which may affect identifiability is the change in numbering, but this alteration does not preclude a finding of identifiability by the trier of fact.

But in this case, the car under consideration clearly has a driver and displays several uniquely distinguishing features.

The judgment is vacated and the cause is remanded for further proceedings.[18]

Carson v. Here's Johnny Portable Toilets, Inc.
698 F.2d 831 (6th Cir. 1983)

BAILEY BROWN, Senior Circuit Judge:

This case involves claims of unfair competition and invasion of the right of privacy and the right of publicity arising from appellee's adoption of a phrase generally associated with a popular entertainer.

Appellant, John W. Carson (Carson), is the host and star of "The Tonight Show," a well-known television program broadcast five nights a week by the National Broadcasting Company. Carson also appears as an entertainer in night clubs and theaters around the country. From the time he began hosting "The Tonight Show" in 1962, he has been introduced on the show each night with the phrase "Here's Johnny." This method of introduction was first used for Carson in 1957 when he hosted a daily television program for the American Broadcasting Company. The phrase "Here's Johnny" is generally associated with Carson by a substantial segment of the television viewing public. In 1967, Carson first authorized use of this phrase by an outside business venture, permitting it to be used by a chain of restaurants called "Here's Johnny Restaurants."

Appellant Johnny Carson Apparel, Inc. (Apparel), formed in 1970, manufactures and markets men's clothing to retail stores. Carson, the president of Apparel and owner of 20% of its stock, has licensed Apparel to use his name and picture, which appear on virtually all of Apparel's products and promotional material. Apparel has also used, with Carson's consent, the phrase "Here's Johnny" on labels for clothing and in advertising campaigns. In 1977, Apparel granted a license to Marcy Laboratories to use "Here's Johnny" as the name of a line of men's toiletries. The phrase "Here's Johnny" has never been registered by appellants as a trademark or service mark.

Appellee, Here's Johnny Portable Toilets, Inc., is a Michigan corporation engaged in the business of renting and selling "Here's Johnny" portable toilets. Appellee's founder was aware at the time he formed the corporation that "Here's Johnny" was the introductory slogan for Carson on "The Tonight Show." He indicated that he coupled the phrase with a second one, "The World's Foremost Commodian," to make "a good play on a phrase."

Shortly after appellee went into business in 1976, appellants brought this action alleging unfair competition, trademark infringement under federal and state law, and invasion of privacy and publicity rights. They sought damages and an injunction prohibiting appellee's further use of the phrase "Here's Johnny" as a corporate name or in connection with the sale or rental of its portable toilets.

After a bench trial, the district court issued a memorandum opinion and order, *Carson v. Here's Johnny Portable Toilets, Inc.*, 498 F. Supp. 71 (E.D. Mich. 1980), which served as its findings of fact and conclusions of law. The court ordered the dismissal of the appellants' complaint. On the unfair competition claim, the court concluded that the ap-

---

18. We have no occasion to discuss the measure of damages in the instant case, and our conclusion renders consideration of whether plaintiff has a cause of action under the California law of trade names or unfair competition unnecessary.

Figure 2-2. Johnny Carson in ad for Johnny Carson Apparel

pellants had failed to satisfy the "likelihood of confusion" test. On the right of privacy and right of publicity theories, the court held that these rights extend only to a "name or likeness," and "Here's Johnny" did not qualify.

I.

Appellants' first claim alleges unfair competition from appellee's business activities in violation of § 43(a) of the Lanham Act, 15 U.S.C. § 1125(a) (1976), and of Michigan com-

Figure 2-3. Logo for Here's Johnny Portable Toilets

mon law. The district court correctly noted that the test for equitable relief under both § 43(a) and Michigan common law is the "likelihood of confusion" standard....

[O]n the basis of [the district court's] findings, we agree with the district court that the appellants have failed to establish a likelihood of confusion. The general concept underlying the likelihood of confusion is that the public believe that "the mark's owner *sponsored or otherwise approved* the use of the trademark." *Warner Bros., Inc. v. Gay Toys, Inc.,* 658 F.2d 76, 79 (2d Cir. 1981) (emphasis added).... The facts as found by the district court do not implicate such likelihood of confusion, and we affirm the district court on this issue.

II.

The appellants also claim that the appellee's use of the phrase "Here's Johnny" violates the common law right of privacy and right of publicity.[1] The confusion in this area of the law requires a brief analysis of the relationship between these two rights.

In an influential article, Dean Prosser delineated four distinct types of the right of privacy: (1) intrusion upon one's seclusion or solitude, (2) public disclosure of embarrassing private facts, (3) publicity which places one in a false light, and (4) appropriation of one's name or likeness for the defendant's advantage. Prosser, *Privacy,* 48 Calif. L. Rev. 383, 389 (1960). This fourth type has become known as the "right of publicity." ...

Dean Prosser's analysis has been a source of some confusion in the law. His first three types of the right of privacy generally protect the right "to be let alone," while the right of publicity protects the celebrity's pecuniary interest in the commercial exploitation of his identity.... Thus, the right of privacy and the right of publicity protect fundamentally different interests and must be analyzed separately.

We do not believe that Carson's claim that his right of privacy has been invaded is supported by the law or the facts. Apparently, the gist of this claim is that Carson is embarrassed by and considers it odious to be associated with the appellee's product. Clearly, the association does not appeal to Carson's sense of humor. But the facts here presented do not, it appears to us, amount to an invasion of any of the interests protected by the right of privacy. In any event, our disposition of the claim of an invasion of the right of publicity makes it unnecessary for us to accept or reject the claim of an invasion of the right of privacy.

The right of publicity has developed to protect the commercial interest of celebrities in their identities. The theory of the right is that a celebrity's identity can be valuable in

---

1. Michigan law, which governs these claims, has not yet clearly addressed the right of publicity. But the general recognition of the right ... suggests to us that the Michigan courts would adopt the right. Michigan has recognized a right of privacy. *Beaumont v. Brown,* 401 Mich. 80, 257 N.W.2d 522 (1977).

the promotion of products, and the celebrity has an interest that may be protected from the unauthorized commercial exploitation of that identity. In *Memphis Development Foundation v. Factors Etc., Inc.*, 616 F.2d 956 (6th Cir.), *cert. denied*, 449 U.S. 953 (1980), we stated: "The famous have an exclusive legal right during life to control and profit from the commercial use of their name and personality." *Id.* at 957.

The district court dismissed appellants' claim based on the right of publicity because appellee does not use Carson's name or likeness. 498 F. Supp. at 77. It held that it "would not be prudent to allow recovery for a right of publicity claim which does not more specifically identify Johnny Carson." 498 F. Supp. at 78. We believe that, on the contrary, the district court's conception of the right of publicity is too narrow. The right of publicity, as we have stated, is that a celebrity has a protected pecuniary interest in the commercial exploitation of his identity. If the celebrity's identity is commercially exploited, there has been an invasion of his right whether or not his "name or likeness" is used. Carson's identity may be exploited even if his name, John W. Carson, or his picture is not used.

In *Motschenbacher v. R.J. Reynolds Tobacco Co.*, 498 F.2d 821 (9th Cir. 1974), the court held that the unauthorized use of a picture of a distinctive race car of a well known professional race car driver, whose name or likeness were not used, violated his right of publicity....

In *Ali v. Playgirl, Inc.*, 447 F. Supp. 723 (S.D.N.Y. 1978), Muhammad Ali, former heavyweight champion, sued Playgirl magazine under the New York "right of privacy" statute and also alleged a violation of his common law right of publicity. The magazine published a drawing of a nude, black male sitting on a stool in a corner of a boxing ring with hands taped and arms outstretched on the ropes. The district court concluded that Ali's right of publicity was invaded because the drawing sufficiently identified him in spite of the fact that the drawing was captioned "Mystery Man." The district court found that the identification of Ali was made certain because of an accompanying verse that identified the figure as "The Greatest." The district court took judicial notice of the fact that "Ali has regularly claimed that appellation for himself." *Id.* at 727.

In *Hirsch v. S.C. Johnson & Son, Inc.*, 90 Wis. 2d 379, 280 N.W.2d 129 (1979), the court held that use by defendant of the name "Crazylegs" on a shaving gel for women violated plaintiff's right of publicity. Plaintiff, Elroy Hirsch, a famous football player, had been known by this nickname. The court said:

> The fact that the name, "Crazylegs," used by Johnson, was a nickname rather than Hirsch's actual name does not preclude a cause of action. All that is required is that the name clearly identify the wronged person. In the instant case, it is not disputed at this juncture of the case that the nickname identified the plaintiff Hirsch. It is argued that there were others who were known by the same name. This, however, does not vitiate the existence of a cause of action. It may, however, if sufficient proof were adduced, affect the quantum of damages should the jury impose liability or it might preclude liability altogether. Prosser points out "that a stage or other fictitious name can be so identified with the plaintiff that he is entitled to protection against its use." 49 Cal. L. Rev., *supra* at 404. He writes that it would be absurd to say that Samuel L. Clemens would have a cause of action if that name had been used in advertising, but he would not have one for the use of "Mark Twain." If a fictitious name is used in a context which tends to indicate that the name is that of the plaintiff, the factual case for identity is strengthened. Prosser, *supra* at 403.

280 N.W.2d at 137.

In this case, Earl Braxton, president and owner of Here's Johnny Portable Toilets, Inc., admitted that he knew that the phrase "Here's Johnny" had been used for years to introduce Carson. Moreover, in the opening statement in the district court, appellee's counsel stated:

> Now, we've stipulated in this case that the public tends to associate the words "Johnny Carson", the words "Here's Johnny" with plaintiff, John Carson and, Mr. Braxton, in his deposition, admitted that he knew that and probably absent that identification, he would not have chosen it.

That the "Here's Johnny" name was selected by Braxton because of its identification with Carson was the clear inference from Braxton's testimony irrespective of such admission in the opening statement.

We therefore conclude that, applying the correct legal standards, appellants are entitled to judgment. The proof showed without question that appellee had appropriated Carson's identity in connection with its corporate name and its product.

Although this opinion holds only that Carson's right of publicity was invaded because appellee intentionally appropriated his identity for commercial exploitation, the dissent, relying on its interpretation of the authorities and relying on policy and constitutional arguments, would hold that there was no invasion here. We do not believe that the dissent can withstand fair analysis.

The dissent contends that the authorities hold that the right of publicity is invaded only if there has been an appropriation of the celebrity's "name, likeness, achievements, identifying characteristics or actual performances." After so conceding that the right is at least this broad, the dissent then attempts to show that the authorities upon which the majority opinion relies are explainable as involving an appropriation of one or more of these attributes. The dissent explains *Motschenbacher, supra,* where the advertisement used a photograph, slightly altered, of the plaintiff's racing car, as an "identifying characteristic" case. But the dissent fails to explain why the photograph any more identified Motschenbacher than the phrase "Here's Johnny" identifies appellant Carson. The dissent explains *Hirsch, supra,* by pointing out that there the use of the appellation "Crazylegs" by the defendant was in a "context" that suggested a reference to Hirsch and that therefore Hirsch was identified by such use. Here, the dissent states, there is no evidence of the use of "Here's Johnny" in such a suggestive "context." Putting aside the fact that appellee also used the phrase "The World's Foremost Commodian," we fail to see why "context" evidence is necessary where appellee's president admitted that it adopted the name "Here's Johnny" because it identified appellant Carson. We do not understand appellee to even contend that it did not successfully accomplish its intended purpose of appropriating his identity. The dissent explains *Ali, supra,* by pointing out that in that case the magazine used a drawing that "strongly suggests" it to be a representation of the famous fighter, but it is also true that the court put emphasis on the fact that the subject of the drawing was referred to as "The Greatest," which "further implied" that the individual was Ali. 447 F. Supp. at 726–27.

It should be obvious from the majority opinion and the dissent that a celebrity's identity may be appropriated in various ways. It is our view that, under the existing authorities, a celebrity's legal right of publicity is invaded whenever his identity is intentionally appropriated for commercial purposes. We simply disagree that the authorities limit the right of publicity as contended by the dissent. It is not fatal to appellant's claim that appellee did not use his "name." Indeed, there would have been no violation of his right of publicity even if appellee had used his name, such as "J. William Carson Portable Toilet" or the "John William Carson Portable Toilet" or the "J.W. Carson Portable Toilet." The reason is that, though literally using appellant's "name," the appellee would not have appropriated Carson's identity as a celebrity. Here there was an appropriation of Carson's identity without using his "name."

With respect to the dissent's general policy arguments, it seems to us that the policies there set out would more likely be vindicated by the majority view than by the dissent's view. Certainly appellant Carson's achievement has made him a celebrity which means that his identity has a pecuniary value which the right of publicity should vindicate. Vindication of the right will tend to encourage achievement in Carson's chosen field. Vindication of the right will also tend to prevent unjust enrichment by persons such as appellee who seek commercially to exploit the identity of celebrities without their consent.

The dissent also suggests that recognition of the right of publicity here would somehow run afoul of federal monopoly policies and first amendment proscriptions. If, as the dissent seems to concede, such policies and proscriptions are not violated by the vindication of the right of publicity where the celebrity's "name, likeness, achievements, identifying characteristics or actual performances" have been appropriated for commercial purposes, we cannot see why the policies and proscriptions would be violated where, as here, the celebrity's identity has admittedly been appropriated for commercial exploitation by the use of the phrase "Here's Johnny Portable Toilets."

The judgment of the district court is vacated and the case remanded for further proceedings consistent with this opinion.

CORNELIA G. KENNEDY, Circuit Judge, dissenting:

I respectfully dissent from that part of the majority's opinion which holds that appellee's use of the phrase "Here's Johnny" violates appellant Johnny Carson's common law right of publicity. While I agree that an individual's identity may be impermissibly exploited, I do not believe that the common law right of publicity may be extended beyond an individual's name, likeness, achievements, identifying characteristics or actual performances, to include phrases or other things which are merely associated with the individual, as is the phrase "Here's Johnny." The majority's extension of the right of publicity to include phrases or other things which are merely associated with the individual permits a popular entertainer or public figure, by associating himself or herself with a common phrase, to remove those words from the public domain.

The phrase "Here's Johnny" is merely associated with Johnny Carson, the host and star of "The Tonight Show" broadcast by the National Broadcasting Company. Since 1962, the opening format of "The Tonight Show," after the theme music is played, is to introduce Johnny Carson with the phrase "Here's Johnny." The words are spoken by an announcer, generally Ed McMahon, in a drawn out and distinctive manner. Immediately after the phrase "Here's Johnny" is spoken, Johnny Carson appears to begin the program. This method of introduction was first used by Johnny Carson in 1957 when he hosted a daily television show for the American Broadcasting Company. This case is not transformed into a "name" case simply because the diminutive form of John W. Carson's given name and the first name of his full stage name, Johnny Carson, appears in it. The first name is so common, in light of the millions of persons named John, Johnny or Jonathan that no doubt inhabit this world, that, alone, it is meaningless or ambiguous at best in identifying Johnny Carson, the celebrity. In addition, the phrase containing Johnny Carson's first stage name was certainly selected for its value as a double entendre. Appellee manufactures portable toilets. The value of the phrase to appellee's product is in the risque meaning of "john" as a toilet or bathroom. For this reason, too, this is not a "name" case.

Appellee has stipulated that the phrase "Here's Johnny" is associated with Johnny Carson and that absent this association, he would not have chosen to use it for his product and corporation, Here's Johnny Portable Toilets, Inc. I do not consider it relevant that appellee intentionally chose to incorporate into the name of his corporation and product a phrase that is merely associated with Johnny Carson. What is not protected by law is not taken from public use. Research reveals no case in which the right of publicity has been extended to phrases or other things which are merely associated with an individual and are not part of his name, likeness, achievements, identifying characteristics or actual performances. Both the policies behind the right of publicity and countervailing interests and considerations indicate that such an extension should not be made.

I. Policies Behind Right of Publicity

The three primary policy considerations behind the right of publicity are succinctly stated in Hoffman, *Limitations on the Right of Publicity,* 28 Bull. Copr. Soc'y, 111, 116–22 (1980). First, "the right of publicity vindicates the economic interests of celebrities, enabling those whose achievements have imbued their identities with pecuniary value to profit from their fame." *Id.* at 116. Second, the right of publicity fosters "the production of intellectual and creative works by providing the financial incentive for individuals to expend the time and resources necessary to produce them." [*Id.* at] 118. Third, "[t]he right of publicity serves both individual and societal interests by preventing what our legal tradition regards as wrongful conduct: unjust enrichment and deceptive trade practices." [*Id.*] ...

None of the above-mentioned policy arguments supports the extension of the right of publicity to phrases or other things which are merely associated with an individual. First, the majority is awarding Johnny Carson a windfall, rather than vindicating his economic interests, by protecting the phrase "Here's Johnny" which is merely associated with him. In *Zacchini* [*v. Scripps-Howard Broadcasting Co.,* 433 U.S. 562 (1977)], the Supreme Court stated that a mechanism to vindicate an individual's economic rights is indicated where the appropriated thing is "the product of ... [the individual's] own talents and energy, the end result of much time, effort and expense." *Zacchini, supra,* 433 U.S. at 575. There is nothing in the record to suggest that "Here's Johnny" has any nexus to Johnny Carson other than being the introduction to his personal appearances. The phrase is not part of an identity that he created. In its content "Here's Johnny" is a very simple and common introduction. The content of the phrase neither originated with Johnny Carson nor is it confined to the world of entertainment. The phrase is not said by Johnny Carson, but said of him. Its association with him is derived, in large part, by the context in which it is said—generally by Ed McMahon in a drawn out and distinctive voice[5] after the theme music to "The Tonight Show" is played, and immediately prior to Johnny Carson's own entrance. Appellee's use of the content "Here's Johnny," in light of its value as a double entendre, written on its product and corporate name, and therefore outside of the context in which it is associated with Johnny Carson, does little to rob Johnny Carson of something which is unique to him or a product of his own efforts.

The second policy goal of fostering the production of creative and intellectual works is not met by the majority's rule because in awarding publicity rights in a phrase neither

---

5. Ed McMahon arguably has a competing publicity interest in this same phrase because it is said by him in a distinctive and drawn out manner as his introduction to entertainers who appear on "The Tonight Show," including Johnny Carson.

created by him nor performed by him, economic reward and protection is divorced from personal incentive to produce on the part of the protected and benefited individual. Johnny Carson is simply reaping the rewards of the time, effort and work product of others.

Third, the majority's extension of the right of publicity to include the phrase "Here's Johnny" which is merely associated with Johnny Carson is not needed to provide alternatives to existing legal avenues for redressing wrongful conduct. The existence of a cause of action under section 43(a) of the Lanham Act, 15 U.S.C.A. § 1125(a) (1976) and Michigan common law does much to undercut the need for policing against unfair competition through an additional legal remedy such as the right of publicity. The majority has concluded, and I concur, that the District Court was warranted in finding that there was not a reasonable likelihood that members of the public would be confused by appellee's use of the "Here's Johnny" trademark on a product as dissimilar to those licensed by Johnny Carson as portable toilets. In this case, this eliminates the argument of wrongdoing. Moreover, the majority's extension of the right of publicity to phrases and other things merely associated with an individual is not conditioned upon wrongdoing and would apply with equal force in the case of an unknowing user. With respect to unjust enrichment, because a celebrity such as Johnny Carson is himself enriched by phrases and other things associated with him in which he has made no personal investment of time, money or effort, another user of such a phrase or thing may be enriched somewhat by such use, but this enrichment is not at Johnny Carson's expense. The policies behind the right of publicity are not furthered by the majority's holding in this case.

II. Countervailing Interests and Considerations

The right of publicity, whether tied to name, likeness, achievements, identifying characteristics or actual performances, etc. conflicts with the economic and expressive interests of others. Society's interests in free enterprise and free expression must be balanced against the interests of an individual seeking protection in the right of publicity where the right is being expanded beyond established limits. In addition, the right to publicity may be subject to federal preemption where it conflicts with the provisions of the Copyright Act of 1976.

A. Federal Policy: Monopolies

Protection under the right of publicity creates a common law monopoly that removes items, words and acts from the public domain.... In *Memphis Development* [*Foundation v. Factors Etc., Inc.,* 616 F.2d 956 (6th Cir. 1980)], this Court held that the right of publicity does not survive a celebrity's death under Tennessee law. In so holding, this Court recognized that commercial and competitive interests are potentially compromised by an expansive approach to the right of publicity. This Court was concerned that an extension of the right of publicity to the exclusive control of the celebrity's heirs might compromise the efficiency, productivity and fairness of our economic system without enlarging the stock or quality of the goods, services, artistic creativity, information, invention or entertainment available and detract from the equal distribution of economic opportunity available in a free market system. *Id.* 959–60. *Memphis Development* recognized that the grant of a right of publicity is tantamount to the grant of a monopoly, in that case, for the life of the celebrity. The majority's grant to Johnny Carson of a publicity right in the phrase "Here's Johnny" takes this phrase away from the public domain, giving him a common law monopoly for it, without extracting from Johnny Carson a personal contribution for the public's benefit.

Protection under the right of publicity confers a monopoly on the protected individual that is potentially broader, offers fewer protections and potentially competes with federal statutory monopolies. As an essential part of three federal monopoly rights, copyright, trademark and patents, notice to the public is required in the form of filing with the appropriate governmental office and use of an appropriate mark. This apprises members of the public of the nature and extent of what is being removed from the public domain and subject to claims of infringement. The right of publicity provides limited notice to the public of the extent of the monopoly right to be asserted, if one is to be asserted at all. As the right of privacy is expanded beyond protections of name, likeness and actual performances, which provide relatively objective notice to the public of the extent of an individual's rights, to more subjective attributes such as achievements and identifying characteristics, the public's ability to be on notice of a common law monopoly right, if one is even asserted by a given famous individual, is severely diminished. Protecting phrases and other things merely associated with an individual provides virtually no notice to the public at all of what is claimed to be protected. By ensuring the invocation of the adjudicative process whenever the commercial use of a phrase or other associated thing is considered to have been wrongfully appropriated, the public is left to act at their peril. The result is a chilling effect on commercial innovation and opportunity.

Also unlike the federal statutory monopolies, this common law monopoly right offers no protections against the monopoly existing for an indefinite time or even in perpetuity....

B. Federal Policy: Free Expression and Use of Intellectual Property

The first amendment protects the freedom of speech, including commercial speech. Strong federal policy permits the free use of intellectual property, words and ideas that are in general circulation and not protected by a valid copyright, patent or trademark.... Apart from the technical arguments regarding preemption, if federal law and policy does not protect phrases such as "Here's Johnny," which is certainly not an original combination of words, state law should not protect them either under a right of publicity for want of a sufficient interest justifying protection. In addition, because copyright does not restrain the use of a mere idea or concept but only protects particular tangible expressions of an idea or concept, it has been held not to run afoul of first amendment challenges. The protected tangible expressions are asserted to not run afoul of first amendment challenges because the notice requirements and limited duration of copyright protection balances the interest of individuals seeking protection under the copyright clause and the first amendment. Because the phrase "Here's Johnny" is more akin to an idea or concept of introducing an individual than an original protectable fixed expression of that idea and because the right of publicity in this instance is not complemented by saving notice or duration requirements, phrases such as "Here's Johnny" should not be entitled to protection under the right of publicity as a matter of policy and concern for the first amendment.

Apart from the possibility of outright federal preemption, public policy requires that the public's interest in free enterprise and free expression take precedence over any interest Johnny Carson may have in a phrase associated with his person.

III. Case Law

The common law right of publicity has been held to protect various aspects of an individual's identity from commercial exploitation: name, likeness, achievements, identifying characteristics, actual performances, and fictitious characters created by a performer.

Research reveals no case which has extended the right to publicity to phrases and other things which are merely associated with an individual.

The three cases cited by the majority in reaching their conclusion that the right of privacy should be extended to encompass phrases and other things merely associated with an individual and one other case merit further comment.... *Hirsch* simply stands for the principle accepted by the commentators, if not by the courts, that the right of publicity extends not only to an individual's name but to a nickname or stage name as well. *Hirsch* required that the name clearly identify the wronged person. *Hirsch, supra,* 280 N.W.2d at 137. *Hirsch* goes on to state that if a fictitious name is used, context may be sufficient to link the fictitious name with the complaining individual, and therefore give rise to protection under a right of publicity. In the *Hirsch* case, context supplied the missing link which is not present here. Hirsch, a/k/a "Crazylegs," was a famous football player and all around athlete.... He made a number of commercials and advertisements during his career and a movie was produced on his life.... The defendant in *Hirsch,* S.C. Johnson & Son, marketed a moisturizing shaving gel for women under the name of "Crazylegs." The context linking this product to Hirsch was Johnson's first promotion of its product at a running event for women, the use of a cheer in a television commercial similar to the "Crazylegs" cheer initiated at a college where Hirsch became athletic director, and the fact that the product was for women's legs. *Id.* 280 N.W.2d at 138. Based on this evidence of "context," the Wisconsin appellate court found a question of fact for the jury as to whether "Crazylegs" identified Hirsch. In this case, not only is the majority not dealing with a nickname or a stage name, but there is not a scintilla of evidence to support the context requirement of *Hirsch.* Appellee has only used the content of the "Here's Johnny" phrase on its product and its corporate name as transfigured by the double meaning of "John."

In *Ali,* Muhammad Ali sought protection under the right of publicity for the unauthorized use of his picture in Playgirl Magazine.... The essence of the case, and the unauthorized act from which Ali claims protection, is a drawing of a nude black man seated in the corner of a boxing ring with both hands taped and outstretched resting on the ropes on either side. The *Ali* court found that even a cursory inspection of the picture suggests that the facial characteristics of the man are those of Ali. The court stated: "The cheekbones, broad nose and wideset brown eyes, together with the distinctive smile and close cropped black hair are recognizable as the features of... [Ali]." *Ali supra,* at 726. Augmenting this likeness and reinforcing its identification with Ali was the context in which the likeness appeared—a boxing ring. The court found that identification of the individual depicted as Ali was further implied by the accompanying phrase "the Greatest." *Id.* at 727. Based on these facts, the court had no difficulty concluding that the drawing was Ali's portrait or picture. See *id.* 726. To the extent the majority uses the phrase "the Greatest" to support its position that the right of publicity encompasses phrases or other things which are merely associated with an individual, they misstate the law of *Ali.... Ali* is clearly a "likeness" case.... The result in that case is so dependent on the identifying features in the drawing and the boxing context in which the man is portrayed that the phrase "the Greatest" may not be severed from this whole and the legal propositions developed by the *Ali* court in response to the whole applied to the phrase alone. To be analogous, a likeness of Johnny Carson would be required in addition to the words "Here's Johnny" suggesting the context of "The Tonight Show"....

Motschenbacher, the third case cited by the majority, is an "identifying characteristics" case.... Identifying characteristics, such as Motschenbacher's racing car, are not synonymous with phrases or other things which are merely associated with an individual. In *Motschenbacher,* the Ninth Circuit determined that the car driver had "consistently 'individualized' his cars to set them apart from those of other drivers and to make them more readily identifiable as his own." ... Despite [the defendant's] alterations, the Ninth Circuit determined that car possessed identifying characteristics *peculiar* to Motschenbacher. *Id.* at 827.... The identifying characteristics, in the form of several decorations peculiar to his car, were the product of his personal time, energy, effort and expense and as such are inextricably interwoven with him as his individual work product, rather than being merely associated with him. Furthermore, the number and combination of the peculiar decorations on his cars results in a set of identifying characteristics, which although inanimate, are unique enough to resist duplication other than by intentional copying. This uniqueness provides notice to the public of what is claimed as part of his publicity right, as does an individual's name, likeness or actual performance, and narrowly limits the scope of his monopoly. In contrast to *Motschenbacher*, Johnny Carson's fame as a comedian and talk show host is severable from the phrase with which he is associated, "Here's Johnny." This phrase is not Johnny Carson's "thumbprint"; it is not his work product; it is not original; it is a common, simple combination of a direct object, a contracted verb and a common first name; divorced from context, it is two dimensional and ambiguous. It can hardly be said to be a symbol or synthesis, *i.e.,* a tangible "expression" of the "idea," of Johnny Carson the comedian and talk show host, as Motschenbacher's racing car was the tangible expression of the man....

Accordingly, neither policy nor case law supports the extension of the right of publicity to encompass phrases and other things merely associated with an individual as in this case. I would affirm the judgment of the District Court on this basis as well.

Midler v. Ford Motor Co.

849 F.2d 460 (9th Cir. 1988)

NOONAN, Circuit Judge:

This case centers on the protectibility of the voice of a celebrated chanteuse from commercial exploitation without her consent. Ford Motor Company and its advertising agency, Young & Rubicam, Inc., in 1985 advertised the Ford Lincoln Mercury with a series of nineteen 30 or 60 second television commercials in what the agency called "The Yuppie Campaign." The aim was to make an emotional connection with Yuppies, bringing back memories of when they were in college. Different popular songs of the seventies were sung on each commercial. The agency tried to get "the original people," that is, the singers who had popularized the songs, to sing them. Failing in that endeavor in ten cases the agency had the songs sung by "sound alikes." Bette Midler, the plaintiff and appellant here, was done by a sound alike.

Midler is a nationally known actress and singer. She won a Grammy as early as 1973 as the Best New Artist of that year. Records made by her since then have gone Platinum and Gold. She was nominated in 1979 for an Academy award for Best Female Actress in *The Rose,* in which she portrayed a pop singer. *Newsweek* in its June 30, 1986 issue described her as an "outrageously original singer/comedian." *Time* hailed her in its March 2, 1987 issue as "a legend" and "the most dynamic and poignant singer-actress of her time."

When Young & Rubicam was preparing the Yuppie Campaign it presented the commercial to its client by playing an edited version of Midler singing "Do You Want To Dance," taken from the 1973 Midler album, "The Divine Miss M." After the client accepted the idea and form of the commercial, the agency contacted Midler's manager, Jerry

Edelstein. The conversation went as follows: "Hello, I am Craig Hazen from Young and Rubicam. I am calling you to find out if Bette Midler would be interested in doing … ? Edelstein: "Is it a commercial?" "Yes." "We are not interested."

Undeterred, Young & Rubicam sought out Ula Hedwig whom it knew to have been one of "the Harlettes" a backup singer for Midler for ten years. Hedwig was told by Young & Rubicam that "they wanted someone who could sound like Bette Midler's recording of [Do You Want To Dance]." She was asked to make a "demo" tape of the song if she was interested. She made an *a capella* demo and got the job.

At the direction of Young & Rubicam, Hedwig then made a record for the commercial. The Midler record of "Do You Want To Dance" was first played to her. She was told to "sound as much as possible like the Bette Midler record," leaving out only a few "aahs" unsuitable for the commercial. Hedwig imitated Midler to the best of her ability.

After the commercial was aired Midler was told by "a number of people" that "sounded exactly" like her record of "Do You Want To Dance." Hedwig was told by "many personal friends" that they thought it was Midler singing the commercial. Ken Fritz, a personal manager in the entertainment business not associated with Midler, declares by affidavit that he heard the commercial on more than one occasion and thought Midler was doing the singing.

Neither the name nor the picture of Midler was used in the commercial; Young & Rubicam had a license from the copyright holder to use the song. At issue in this case is only the protection of Midler's voice. The district court described the defendants' conduct as that "of the average thief." They decided, "If we can't buy it, we'll take it." The court nonetheless believed there was no legal principle preventing imitation of Midler's voice and so gave summary judgment for the defendants. Midler appeals.

The First Amendment protects much of what the media do in the reproduction of likenesses or sounds.… The purpose of the media's use of a person's identity is central. If the purpose is "informative or cultural" the use is immune; "if it serves no such function but merely exploits the individual portrayed, immunity will not be granted." Felcher and Rubin, *Privacy, Publicity and the Portrayal of Real People by the Media*, 88 Yale L.J. 1577, 1596 (1979). Moreover, federal copyright law preempts much of the area. "Mere imitation of a recorded performance would not constitute a copyright infringement even where one performer deliberately sets out to simulate another's performance as exactly as possible." Notes of Committee on the Judiciary, 17 U.S.C.A. § 114(b). It is in the context of these First Amendment and federal copyright distinctions that we address the present appeal.

Nancy Sinatra once sued Goodyear Tire and Rubber Company on the basis of an advertising campaign by Young & Rubicam featuring "These Boots Are Made For Walkin'," a song closely identified with her; the female singers of the commercial were alleged to have imitated her voice and style and to have dressed and looked like her. The basis of Nancy Sinatra's complaint was unfair competition; she claimed that the song and the arrangement had acquired "a secondary meaning" which, under California law, was protectible. This court noted that the defendants "had paid a very substantial sum to the copyright proprietor to obtain the license for the use of the song and all of its arrangements." To give Sinatra damages for their use of the song would clash with federal copyright law. Summary judgment for the defendants was affirmed. *Sinatra v. Goodyear Tire & Rubber Co.*, 435 F.2d 711, 717–718 (9th Cir. 1970), *cert. denied*, 402 U.S. 906 (1971). If Midler were claiming a secondary meaning to "Do You Want To Dance" or seeking to prevent the defendants from using that song, she would fail like Sinatra. But that is not this case. Midler does not seek damages for Ford's use of "Do You Want To Dance," and thus her claim is not preempted by federal copyright law. Copyright protects "original works of authorship fixed in any tangible medium of expression." 17 U.S.C. § 102(a). A voice is not copyrightable. The sounds are not "fixed." What is put forward as protectible here is more personal than any work of authorship.

Bert Lahr once sued Adell Chemical Co. for selling Lestoil by means of a commercial in which an imitation of Lahr's voice accompanied a cartoon of a duck. Lahr alleged that his style of vocal delivery was distinctive in pitch, accent, inflection, and sounds. The First Circuit held that Lahr had stated a cause of action for unfair competition, that it could be found "that defendant's conduct saturated plaintiff's audience, curtailing his market." *Lahr v. Adell Chemical Co.,* 300 F.2d 256, 259 (1st Cir. 1962). That case is more like this one. But we do not find unfair competition here. One-minute commercials of the sort the defendants put on would not have saturated Midler's audience and curtailed her market. Midler did not do television commercials. The defendants were not in competition with her.

California Civil Code section 3344 is also of no aid to Midler. The statute affords damages to a person injured by another who uses the person's "name, voice, signature, photograph or likeness, in any manner." The defendants did not use Midler's name or anything else whose use is prohibited by the statute. The voice they used was Hedwig's, not hers. The term "likeness" refers to a visual image not a vocal imitation. The statute, however, does not preclude Midler from pursuing any cause of action she may have at common law; the statute itself implies that such common law causes of action do exist because it says its remedies are merely "cumulative." *Id.* § 3344(g).

The companion statute protecting the use of a deceased person's name, voice, signature, photograph or likeness states that the rights it recognizes are "property rights." *Id.* § 990(b). By analogy the common law rights are also property rights. Appropriation of such common law rights is a tort in California. *Motschenbacher v. R.J. Reynolds Tobacco Co.,* 498 F.2d 821 (9th Cir. 1974)....

Midler's case is different from Motschenbacher's. He and his car were physically used by the tobacco company's ad; he made part of his living out of giving commercial endorsements. But, as Judge Koelsch expressed it in *Motschenbacher,* California will recognize an injury from "an appropriation of the attributes of one's identity." *Id.* at 824. It was irrelevant that Motschenbacher could not be identified in the ad. The ad suggested that it was he. The ad did so by emphasizing signs or symbols associated with him. In the same way the defendants here used an imitation to convey the impression that Midler was singing for them.

Why did the defendants ask Midler to sing if her voice was not of value to them? Why did they studiously acquire the services of a sound-alike and instruct her to imitate Midler if Midler's voice was not of value to them? What they sought was an attribute of Midler's identity. Its value was what the market would have paid for Midler to have sung the commercial in person.

A voice is more distinctive and more personal than the automobile accouterments protected in *Motschenbacher.* A voice is as distinctive and personal as a face. The human voice is one of the most palpable ways identity is manifested. We are all aware that a friend is at once known by a few words on the phone. At a philosophical level it has been observed that with the sound of a voice, "the other stands before me." D. Ihde, *Listening and Voice* 77 (1976). A fortiori, these observations hold true of singing, especially singing by a singer of renown. The singer manifests herself in the song. To impersonate her voice is to pirate her identity. *See* W. Keeton, D. Dobbs, R. Keeton, D. Owen, *Prosser & Keeton on Torts* 852 (5th ed. 1984).

We need not and do not go so far as to hold that every imitation of a voice to advertise merchandise is actionable. We hold only that when a distinctive voice of a professional singer is widely known and is deliberately imitated in order to sell a product, the sellers have appropriated what is not theirs and have committed a tort in California. Midler has made a showing, sufficient to defeat summary judgment, that the defendants here for their own profit in selling their product did appropriate part of her identity.

REVERSED AND REMANDED FOR TRIAL.

White v. Samsung Electronics America, Inc.
971 F.2d 1395 (9th Cir. 1992)

GOODWIN, Senior Circuit Judge:

This case involves a promotional "fame and fortune" dispute. In running a particular advertisement without Vanna White's permission, defendants Samsung Electronics America, Inc. (Samsung) and David Deutsch Associates, Inc. (Deutsch) attempted to capitalize on White's fame to enhance their fortune. White sued, alleging infringement of various intellectual property rights, but the district court granted summary judgment in favor of the defendants. We affirm in part, reverse in part, and remand.

Plaintiff Vanna White is the hostess of "Wheel of Fortune," one of the most popular game shows in television history. An estimated forty million people watch the program daily. Capitalizing on the fame which her participation in the show has bestowed on her, White markets her identity to various advertisers.

The dispute in this case arose out of a series of advertisements prepared for Samsung by Deutsch. The series ran in at least half a dozen publications with widespread, and in some cases national, circulation. Each of the advertisements in the series followed the same theme. Each depicted a current item from popular culture and a Samsung electronic product. Each was set in the twenty-first century and conveyed the message that the Samsung product would still be in use by that time. By hypothesizing outrageous future outcomes for the cultural items, the ads created humorous effects. For example, one lampooned current popular notions of an unhealthy diet by depicting a raw steak with the caption: "Revealed to be health food. 2010 A.D." Another depicted irreverent "news"-show host Morton Downey Jr. in front of an American flag with the caption: "Presidential candidate. 2008 A.D."

The advertisement which prompted the current dispute was for Samsung video-cassette recorders (VCRs). The ad depicted a robot, dressed in a wig, gown, and jewelry which Deutsch consciously selected to resemble White's hair and dress. The robot was posed next to a game board which is instantly recognizable as the Wheel of Fortune game show set, in a stance for which White is famous. The caption of the ad read: "Longest-running game show. 2012 A.D." Defendants referred to the ad as the "Vanna White" ad. Unlike the other celebrities used in the campaign, White neither consented to the ads nor was she paid.

Following the circulation of the robot ad, White sued Samsung and Deutsch in federal district court under: (1) California Civil Code § 3344; (2) the California common law right of publicity; and (3) § 43(a) of the Lanham Act, 15 U.S.C. § 1125(a). The district court granted summary judgment against White on each of her claims. White now appeals.

I. *Section 3344*

White first argues that the district court erred in rejecting her claim under section 3344. Section 3344(a) provides, in pertinent part, that "[a]ny person who knowingly uses another's name, voice, signature, photograph, or likeness, in any manner, ... for purposes of advertising or selling, ... without such person's prior consent ... shall be liable for any damages sustained by the person or persons injured as a result thereof."

White argues that the Samsung advertisement used her "likeness" in contravention of section 3344. In *Midler v. Ford Motor Co.*, 849 F.2d 460 (9th Cir. 1988), this court rejected Bette Midler's section 3344 claim concerning a Ford television commercial in which a Midler "sound-alike" sang a song which Midler had made famous. In rejecting Midler's claim, this court noted that "[t]he defendants did not use Midler's name or anything else whose use is prohibited by the statute. The voice they used was [another person's], not hers. The term 'likeness' refers to a visual image not a vocal imitation." *Id.* at 463.

In this case, Samsung and Deutsch used a robot with mechanical features, and not, for example, a manikin molded to White's precise features. Without deciding for all purposes when a caricature or impressionistic resemblance might become a "likeness," we agree with the district court that the robot at issue here was not White's "likeness" within the meaning of section 3344. Accordingly, we affirm the court's dismissal of White's section 3344 claim.

II. *Right of Publicity*

White next argues that the district court erred in granting summary judgment to defendants on White's common law right of publicity claim. In *Eastwood v. Superior Court*, 149 Cal. App. 3d 409, 198 Cal. Rptr. 342 (1983), the California court of appeal stated that the common law right of publicity cause of action "may be pleaded by alleging (1) the defendant's use of the plaintiff's identity; (2) the appropriation of plaintiff's name or likeness to defendant's advantage, commercially or otherwise; (3) lack of consent; and (4) resulting injury." *Id.* at 417, 198 Cal. Rptr. 342 (citing Prosser, Law of Torts (4th ed. 1971) § 117, pp. 804–807). The district court dismissed White's claim for failure to satisfy *Eastwood's* second prong, reasoning that defendants had not appropriated White's "name or likeness" with their robot ad. We agree that the robot ad did not make use of White's name or likeness. However, the common law right of publicity is not so confined.

The *Eastwood* court did not hold that the right of publicity cause of action could be pleaded only by alleging an appropriation of name or likeness. *Eastwood* involved an unauthorized use of photographs of Clint Eastwood and of his name. Accordingly, the *Eastwood* court had no occasion to consider the extent beyond the use of name or likeness to which the right of publicity reaches. That court held only that the right of publicity cause of action "may be" pleaded by alleging, *inter alia,* appropriation of name or likeness, not that the action may be pleaded *only* in those terms.

The "name or likeness" formulation referred to in *Eastwood* originated not as an element of the right of publicity cause of action, but as a description of the types of cases in which the cause of action had been recognized. The source of this formulation is Prosser, *Privacy,* 48 Cal. L. Rev. 383, 401–07 (1960), one of the earliest and most enduring articulations of the common law right of publicity cause of action. In looking at the case law to that point, Prosser recognized that right of publicity cases involved one of two basic factual scenarios: name appropriation, and picture or other likeness appropriation. *Id.* at 401–02, nn.156–57.

Even though Prosser focused on appropriations of name or likeness in discussing the right of publicity, he noted that "[i]t is not impossible that there might be appropriation of the plaintiff's identity, as by impersonation, without the use of either his name or his likeness, and that this would be an invasion of his right of privacy." *Id.* at 401, n.155. At the time Prosser wrote, he noted however, that "[n]o such case appears to have arisen." *Id.*

Since Prosser's early formulation, the case law has borne out his insight that the right of publicity is not limited to the appropriation of name or likeness....

[The court's discussion of *Motschenbacher*, *Midler* and *Carson* is omitted.]

These cases teach not only that the common law right of publicity reaches means of appropriation other than name or likeness, but that the specific means of appropriation are relevant only for determining whether the defendant has in fact appropriated the plaintiff's identity. The right of publicity does not require that appropriations of identity be accomplished through particular means to be actionable. It is noteworthy that the *Midler* and *Carson* defendants not only avoided using the plaintiff's name or likeness, but they also avoided appropriating the celebrity's voice, signature, and photograph. The photograph in *Motschenbacher* did include the plaintiff, but because the plaintiff was not visible the driver could have been an actor or dummy and the analysis in the case would have been the same.

Although the defendants in these cases avoided the most obvious means of appropriating the plaintiffs' identities, each of their actions directly implicated the commercial interests which the right of publicity is designed to protect....

It is not important *how* the defendant has appropriated the plaintiff's identity, but *whether* the defendant has done so. *Motschenbacher, Midler,* and *Carson* teach the impossibility of treating the right of publicity as guarding only against a laundry list of specific means of appropriating identity. A rule which says that the right of publicity can be infringed only through the use of nine different methods of appropriating identity merely challenges the clever advertising strategist to come up with the tenth.

Indeed, if we treated the means of appropriation as dispositive in our analysis of the right of publicity, we would not only weaken the right but effectively eviscerate it. The right would fail to protect those plaintiffs most in need of its protection. Advertisers use celebrities to promote their products. The more popular the celebrity, the greater the number of people who recognize her, and the greater the visibility for the product. The identities of the most popular celebrities are not only the most attractive for advertisers, but also the easiest to evoke without resorting to obvious means such as name, likeness, or voice.

Consider a hypothetical advertisement which depicts a mechanical robot with male features, an African-American complexion, and a bald head. The robot is wearing black hightop Air Jordan basketball sneakers, and a red basketball uniform with black trim, baggy shorts, and the number 23 (though not revealing "Bulls" or "Jordan" lettering). The ad depicts the robot dunking a basketball one-handed, stiff-armed, legs extended like open scissors, and tongue hanging out. Now envision that this ad is run on television during professional basketball games. Considered individually, the robot's physical attributes, its dress, and its stance tell us little. Taken together, they lead to the only conclusion that any sports viewer who has registered a discernible pulse in the past five years would reach: the ad is about Michael Jordan.

Viewed separately, the individual aspects of the advertisement in the present case say little. Viewed together, they leave little doubt about the celebrity the ad is meant to depict. The female-shaped robot is wearing a long gown, blond wig, and large jewelry. Vanna White dresses exactly like this at times, but so do many other women. The robot is in the process of turning a block letter on a game-board. Vanna White dresses like this while turning letters on a game-board but perhaps similarly attired Scrabble-playing women do this as well. The robot is standing on what looks to be the Wheel of Fortune game show set. Vanna White dresses like this, turns letters, and does this on the Wheel of Fortune game show. She is the only one. Indeed, defendants themselves referred to their ad as the "Vanna White" ad. We are not surprised.

Television and other media create marketable celebrity identity value. Considerable energy and ingenuity are expended by those who have achieved celebrity value to exploit it for profit. The law protects the celebrity's sole right to exploit this value whether the celebrity has achieved her fame out of rare ability, dumb luck, or a combination thereof. We decline Samsung and Deutch's invitation to permit the evisceration of the common law right of publicity through means as facile as those in this case. Because White has alleged facts showing that Samsung and Deutsch had appropriated her identity, the district court erred by rejecting, on summary judgment, White's common law right of publicity claim.

III. *The Lanham Act*

... To prevail on her Lanham Act claim, White is required to show that in running the robot ad, Samsung and Deutsch created a likelihood of confusion over whether White was endorsing Samsung's VCRs....

Application of the [relevant] factors to this case indicates that the district court erred in rejecting White's Lanham Act claim at the summary judgment stage. In so concluding, we emphasize two facts, however. First, construing the motion papers in White's favor, as we must, we hold only that White has raised a genuine issue of material fact concerning a likelihood of confusion as to her endorsement. Whether White's Lanham Act claim should succeed is a matter for the jury. Second, we stress that we reach this conclusion in light of the peculiar facts of this case. In particular, we note that the robot ad identifies White and was part of a series of ads in which other celebrities participated and were paid for their endorsement of Samsung's products.

IV. *The Parody Defense*

[This portion of the court's opinion will be considered in connection with the discussion of parody in Chapter VIII, below.]

V. *Conclusion*

In remanding this case, we hold only that White has pleaded claims which can go to the jury for its decision.

AFFIRMED IN PART, REVERSED IN PART, and REMANDED.

ALARCON, Circuit Judge, concurring in part, dissenting in part:

Vanna White seeks recovery from Samsung based on three theories: the right to privacy, the right to publicity, and the Lanham Act. I concur in the majority's conclusions on the right to privacy. I respectfully dissent from its holdings on the right to publicity and the Lanham Act claims.

I.
RIGHT TO PRIVACY
(CAL. CIV. CODE § 3344(a))

I agree with the majority's conclusion that no reasonable jury could find that the robot was a "likeness" of Vanna White within the meaning of California Civil Code section 3344(a).

II.
RIGHT TO PUBLICITY

I must dissent from the majority's holding on Vanna White's right to publicity claim. The district court found that, since the commercial advertisement did not show a "likeness" of Vanna White, Samsung did not improperly use the plaintiff's identity. The majority asserts that the use of a likeness is not required under California common law. According to the majority, recovery is authorized if there is an appropriation of one's "identity." I cannot find any holding of a California court that supports this conclusion. Furthermore, the record does not support the majority's finding that Vanna White's "identity" was appropriated.

The district court relied on *Eastwood v. Superior Court,* 149 Cal. App. 3d 409, 198 Cal. Rptr. 342 (1983), in holding that there was no cause of action for infringement on the right to publicity because there had been no use of a likeness. In *Eastwood,* the California Court of Appeal described the elements of the tort of "commercial appropriation of the right of publicity" as "(1) the defendant's use of the plaintiff's identity; (2) *the appropriation of plaintiff's name or likeness* to defendant's advantage, ...; (3) lack of consent; and (4) resulting injury." *Id.* at 417, 198 Cal.Rptr. 342. (Emphasis added).

All of the California cases that my research has disclosed hold that a cause of action for appropriation of the right to publicity requires proof of the appropriation of a name or likeness. *See, e.g., Lugosi v. Universal Pictures,* 25 Cal. 3d 813, 603 P.2d 425, 160 Cal. Rptr. 323 (1979) ("The so-called right of publicity means in essence that the reaction of the public to name and likeness ... endows the name and likeness of the person involved with commercially exploitable opportunities.")....

Notwithstanding the fact that California case law clearly limits the test of the right to publicity to name and likeness, the majority concludes that "the common law right of publicity is not so confined." The majority relies on two factors to support its innovative extension of the California law. The first is that the *Eastwood* court's statement of the elements was permissive rather than exclusive. The second is that Dean Prosser, in describing the common law right to publicity, stated that it might be possible that the right extended beyond name or likeness. These are slender reeds to support a federal court's attempt to create new law for the state of California.

In reaching its surprising conclusion, the majority has ignored the fact that the California Court of Appeal in *Eastwood* specifically addressed the differences between the common law right to publicity and the statutory cause of action codified in California Civil Code section 3344. The court explained that "[t]he differences between the common law and the statutory actions are: (1) Section 3344, subdivision (a) requires *knowing* use whereas under case law, mistake and inadvertence are not a defense against commercial appropriation and (2) section 3344, subdivision (g) expressly provides that its remedies are cumulative and in addition to any provided by law." *Eastwood,* 149 Cal. App. 3d at n.6, 198 Cal. Rptr. 342 (emphasis in original). The court did not include appropriations of identity by means other than name or likeness among its list of differences between the statute and the common law.

The majority also relies on Dean Prosser's statement that "[i]t is not impossible that there might be an appropriation of the plaintiff's identity, as by impersonation, without the use of either his name or his likeness, and that this would be an invasion of his right of privacy." Prosser, *Privacy,* 48 Cal. L. Rev. 383, 401 n.155 (1960). As Dean Prosser noted, however, "[n]o such case appears to have arisen." *Id.*

The majority states that the case law has borne out Dean Prosser's insight that the right to publicity is not limited to name or likeness. As noted above, however, the courts of California have never found an infringement on the right to publicity without the use of the plaintiff's name or likeness.

The interest of the California Legislature as expressed in California Civil Code section 3344 appears to preclude the result reached by the majority. The original section 3344 protected only name or likeness. In 1984, ten years after our decision in *Motschenbacher v. R.J. Reynolds Tobacco Company*, 498 F.2d 821 (9th Cir. 1974) and 24 years after Prosser speculated about the future development of the law of the right of publicity, the California legislature amended the statute. California law now makes the use of someone's voice or signature, as well as name or likeness, actionable. Cal. Civ. Code sec. 2233(a) (Deering 1991 Supp.). Thus, California, after our decision in *Motschenbacher* specifically contemplated protection for interests other than name or likeness, but did not include a cause of action for appropriation of another person's identity. The ancient maxim, *inclusio unius est exclusio alterius,* would appear to bar the majority's innovative extension of the right of publicity. The clear implication from the fact that the California Legislature chose to add only voice and signature to the previously protected interests is that it wished to limit the cause of action to enumerated attributes.

The majority has focused on federal decisions in its novel extension of California Common Law. Those decisions do not provide support for the majority's decision.

In each of the federal cases relied upon by the majority, the advertisement affirmatively represented that the person depicted therein was the plaintiff. In this case, it is clear that a metal robot and not the plaintiff, Vanna White, is depicted in the commercial advertisement. The record does not show an appropriation of Vanna White's identity....

The common theme in these federal cases is that identifying characteristics unique to the plaintiffs were used in a context in which they were the only information as to the identity of the individual. The commercial advertisements in each case showed attributes of the plaintiff's identities which made it appear that the plaintiff was the person identified in the commercial. No effort was made to dispel the impression that the plaintiffs were the source of the personal attributes at issue. The commercials affirmatively represented that the plaintiffs were involved....

The case before this court is distinguishable from the factual showing made in *Motschenbacher, Midler,* and *Carson.* It is patently clear to anyone viewing the commercial advertisement that Vanna White was not being depicted. No reasonable juror could confuse a metal robot with Vanna White....

The majority appears to argue that because Samsung created a robot with the physical proportions of an attractive woman, posed it gracefully, dressed it in a blond wig, an evening gown, and jewelry, and placed it on a set that resembles the Wheel of Fortune layout, it thereby appropriated Vanna White's identity. But an attractive appearance, a graceful pose, blond hair, an evening gown, and jewelry are attributes shared by many women, especially in Southern California. These common attributes are particularly evident among game-show hostesses, models, actresses, singers, and other women in the entertainment field. They are not unique attributes of Vanna White's identity. Accordingly, I cannot join in the majority's conclusion that, even if viewed together, these attributes identify Vanna White and, therefore, raise a triable issue as to the appropriation of her identity.

The only characteristic in the commercial advertisement that is not common to many female performers or celebrities is the imitation of the "Wheel of Fortune" set. This set is the only thing which might possibly lead a viewer to think of Vanna White. The Wheel of Fortune set, however, is not an attribute of Vanna White's identity. It is an identifying characteristic of a television game show, a prop with which Vanna White interacts in her role as the current hostess. To say that Vanna White may bring an action when another blond female performer or robot appears on such a set as a hostess will, I am sure, be a surprise to the owners of the show. ...

The record shows that Samsung recognized the market value of Vanna White's identity. No doubt the advertisement would have been more effective if Vanna White had appeared in it. But the fact that Samsung recognized Vanna White's value as a celebrity does not necessarily mean that it appropriated her identity.... I quite agree that anyone seeing the commercial advertisement would be reminded of Vanna White. *Any* performance by another female celebrity as a game-show hostess, however, will also remind the viewer of Vanna White because Vanna White's celebrity is so closely associated with the role. But the fact that an actor or actress became famous for playing a particular role has, until now, never been sufficient to give the performer a proprietary interest in it. I cannot agree with the majority that the California courts, which have consistently taken a narrow view of the right to publicity, would extend law to these unique facts.

III.
THE LANHAM ACT

Vanna White's Lanham Act claim is easily resolved by applying the proper legal standard.... To succeed, Vanna White must prove actual deception of the consuming public. Vanna White offered no evidence that any portion of the consuming public was deceived. The district court was correct in granting summary judgment on Vanna White's Lanham Act claim.

IV.
SAMSUNG'S FIRST AMENDMENT DEFENSE

[This portion of the dissenting opinion will be considered in connection with the discussion of parody in Chapter VIII, below.]

V.
CONCLUSION

The protection of intellectual property presents the courts with the necessity of balancing competing interests. On the one hand, we wish to protect and reward the work and investment of those who create intellectual property. In so doing, however, we must prevent the creation of a monopoly that would inhibit the creative expressions of others. We have traditionally balanced those interests by allowing the copying of an idea, but protecting a unique expression of it. Samsung clearly used the idea of a glamorous female game show hostess. Just as clearly, it avoided appropriating Vanna White's expression of that role. Samsung did not use a likeness of her. The performer depicted in the commercial advertisement is unmistakably a lifeless robot. Vanna White has presented no evidence that any consumer confused the robot with her identity. Indeed, no reasonable consumer could confuse the robot with Vanna White or believe that, because the robot appeared in the advertisement, Vanna White endorsed Samsung's product.

I would affirm the district court's judgment in all respects.

Notes and Questions

1. The common issue in these four cases is whether and to what extent the right of publicity should be extended beyond a person's "name or likeness" to encompass other things that might identify that person in the public's mind; or more broadly, whether or not the use at issue takes unfair advantage of the person's identity or "persona." Before turning to that issue, however, there are a few procedural wrinkles that are worth considering briefly.

2. Note that all four of these cases were heard in federal court, either because of diversity of citizenship or because the right of publicity claims were supplemental to a federal claim under the Lanham Act. (We will examine the Lanham Act in Chapter V, below.) Under the *Erie* doctrine, the role of a federal court is to ascertain how the state's highest court would decide the issue. *See* Jack H. Friedenthal, Mary Kay Kane & Arthur Miller, Civil Procedure §4.6 at 235 (4th ed. 2005). Do you see any indication in these cases that the federal courts are attempting to predict how the state's highest court would rule, instead of just deciding what result they prefer?

3. At the time of *Haelan, Motschenbacher, Midler, Carson* and *White*, no procedure existed whereby a federal court could ask a state court to decide an unresolved question of state law. Today, however, 48 of the 50 states have adopted and implemented certification procedures that allow federal courts to certify unresolved questions of state law to the state's highest court for resolution. For example, Rule 7.305(B)(1) of the Michigan Rules of Court provides: "When a federal court ... considers a question that Michigan law may resolve and that is not controlled by Michigan Supreme Court precedent, the court may on its own motion or that of an interested party certify the question to the Michigan Supreme Court." Should a federal court considering an issue concerning the scope of a state's right of publicity utilize such a certification procedure? Why or why not? (We will see some examples of state courts deciding such certified questions in Chapters IV and VIII.) Do you think the widespread adoption of certification procedures will lead federal courts to defer to state courts more often? Is there any reason to believe that doing so would consistently lead to different outcomes?

4. As the court notes in *Motschenbacher*, if there is a question as to which state's law should be applied, then under the *Erie* doctrine the federal court must apply the choice of law rules of the state in which the district court is located. *Klaxon Co. v. Stentor Electric Mfg. Co.*, 313 U.S. 487 (1941). We will discuss choice of law rules in Chapter XII, below. For now, it is sufficient for you to note that the federal court predicts, using California's choice of law rules, that California state courts would apply California law to a case involving a plaintiff who resides permanently in California.

The other cases do not expressly discuss choice of law. The *Carson* court assumes that Michigan law applies to a case in which the defendant was doing business only in Michigan. By contrast, *Midler* and *White* assume, consistent with *Motschenbacher*, that California law applies because the plaintiffs were California residents. Should California law be applied to enjoin a national advertising campaign? Or should we be concerned that a state is regulating conduct occurring beyond its borders? See Chapter XIV for a full discussion of these issues.

5. Turning to the substantive issue in these cases, why should we extend the right of publicity beyond a person's name or likeness? Which of the purposes underlying the right

of publicity is being served by doing so? To the extent that the purpose is to protect the public from deception, can that interest be adequately served by a cause of action for false endorsement under the Lanham Act or common-law unfair competition? Why or why not?

6. The *Carson* case would appear to be a classic case of false endorsement, particularly since Carson used the phrase "Here's Johnny" as a trademark for apparel. Yet the court in *Carson* affirmed the district court's finding that there was no likelihood that the use of the phrase "Here's Johnny" on portable toilets would confuse the public into thinking that Johnny Carson had endorsed them. If the public is not confused, what justification is there for enjoining the defendant from using the phrase?

One possible justification is suggested by the trademark law doctrine of dilution by tarnishment. See Lanham Act § 43(c)(2)(C), 15 U.S.C. § 1125(c)(2)(C) (defining "dilution by tarnishment"). The notion is that even if the public is not confused, the trademark owner will be harmed by the association of the mark with less desirable goods or services. (The interplay of trademark law, including trademark dilution, and rights of publicity is discussed in Chapter V.)

7. Don't all of these cases reek a little of false endorsement? Suppose in *Midler*, the radio ad included a disclaimer that made it clear that the singer was *not* Bette Midler, and that Midler did not endorse Ford's cars. Would that have changed the outcome? Should it? Does the case deprive Ula Hedwig of her ability to earn a living as a celebrity impersonator? We consider the issues raised by celebrity impersonators more in Chapter III.

8. How far should the concept of "identity" be extended? In the 1980s, Bill Cosby was noted for wearing colorful sweaters on *The Bill Cosby Show*. Does that give Cosby the right to prohibit an advertiser from depicting a fatherly black man in a colorful sweater?

In *Carson*, the dissent suggests that we should limit the right of publicity to one's "name, likeness, achievements, identifying characteristics or actual performances." If one concedes that the right of publicity should extend beyond name and likeness, what justification is there for limiting the right to those five things? Assuming the right was so limited, could the phrase "Here's Johnny" be considered to be an "identifying characteristic" of Johnny Carson?

9. California Civil Code § 3344(a) forbids the use of a person's "name, voice, signature, photograph, or likeness" for commercial purposes. If none of those things is being used, should we extend the common-law right of publicity beyond them? Does doing so defeat the purpose of codifying the right of publicity? Note that the statute was not used in *Motschenbacher* because the events there occurred one year before the statute was enacted.

Civil Code § 3344(b) states that "photograph" means "any photograph or photographic reproduction ... such that the person is readily identifiable." Section 3344(b)(1) states that "A person shall be deemed to be readily identifiable from a photograph when one who views the photograph with the naked eye can reasonably determine that the person depicted in the photograph is the same person who is complaining of its unauthorized use." Had this section been in effect at the time of *Motschenbacher*, would it have applied to the case?

10. In *Newcombe v. Adolf Coors Co.*, 157 F.3d 686 (9th Cir. 1998), the Ninth Circuit held that the "readily identifiable" standard of § 3344(b) should be applied to a "likeness" as well as to a "photograph." The facts of the case were as follows: Don Newcombe was a star

pitcher for the Brooklyn Dodgers in the 1950s. In 1994, Coors published an advertisement for Killian's Irish Red beer which included a drawing of a baseball pitcher on the mound. The drawing was based on a photograph of Newcombe pitching in the 1949 World Series, although his uniform number was changed from "36" to "39" and the color of his cap was changed. The advertisement is depicted below. Should the advertisement be held to violate Newcombe's right of publicity? Is it relevant that Newcombe was a recovering alcoholic?

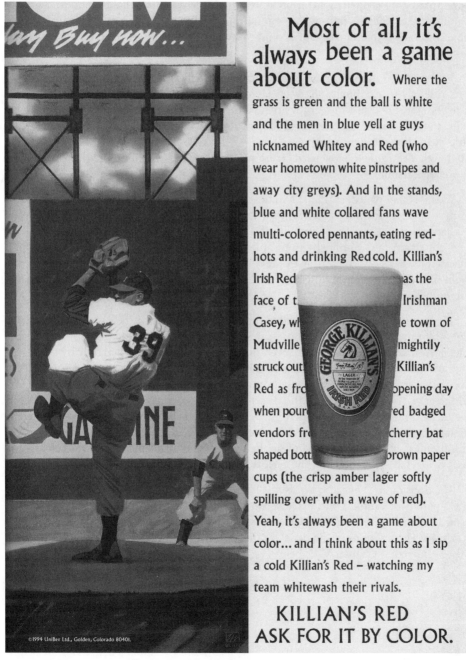

Figure 2-4. The advertisement in *Newcombe*

11. In *Carson*, is the dissent overreacting to the majority's holding? What actual harm might be caused by giving Johnny Carson the exclusive use of the phrase "Here's Johnny" for commercial purposes? How strong is the countervailing interest in allowing the defendant to use the phrase as a play on words to advertise his goods and services?

12. In 1980, Warner Brothers released a motion picture based on Stephen King's horror novel *The Shining*. In the movie, a woman is trapped in a bathroom when her husband, played by Jack Nicholson, breaks through the door with an axe and menacingly announces "Heeeeere's Johnny!" Assuming the producers of the motion picture did not obtain Johnny Carson's consent, should that use of the phrase violate Carson's right of publicity?

13. In 2005, Johnny Carson's sidekick, Ed McMahon, published his autobiography. The title of the autobiography was "Here's Johnny: My Memories of Johnny Carson, The Tonight Show, and 46 Years of Friendship." If McMahon did not obtain Carson's consent, should it violate Carson's right of publicity for McMahon to use the phrase for the title of his book? Why or why not? Would it make a difference if an author not affiliated with *The Tonight Show* used "Here's Johnny" as the title of an unauthorized biography of Carson?

14. In *Midler*, the defendants had licensed the music and lyrics to the song "Do You Want to Dance" from the copyright owner. The court suggests that if Midler had complained about the use of the song itself, the claim would have been preempted by federal copyright law. Similarly, preemption would be an issue if the defendants had licensed Midler's own recording of the song from the record label that owned the copyright in the sound recording. For a full discussion of the preemption issues, see Chapter X., below.

15. Is the decision in *White* simply the logical extension of the preceding cases? Or does it go significantly beyond those cases? In *Motschenbacher*, the plaintiff was the actual person depicted in the photo, even though he could be identified only by the markings on his race car and not by his facial features. In *Midler*, the use of a sound-alike apparently created confusion among the pubic as to whether Midler was the person singing in the advertisement. But isn't the dissent in *White* correct that no reasonable person would find that the robot depicted in the ad was actually Vanna White? Was the defendant trying to imply that Vanna White endorsed its VCRs? If not, is there some other justification for extending the right of publicity beyond actual depictions of the celebrity or uses which falsely suggest that the celebrity is endorsing the product?

The decision in *White* also involved a First Amendment defense that the advertisement was a parody of Vanna White, a defense that the majority rejected. The full court then denied a motion for rehearing *en banc*, which prompted a critical dissent from Judge Alex Kozinski. The opinions of the panel on the parody issue, and Judge Kozinski's response, are considered in Chapter VIII, below.

B. Comparative Law

Joseph v. Daniels
4 B.C.L.R. (2d) 239, 11 C.P.R. (3d) 544 (B.C. Sup. Ct. 1986)

WALLACE J.:

1. The plaintiff, an amateur body builder, sues the defendant for damages for wrongful misappropriation of personality arising from the alleged unauthorized use by the defendant of the plaintiff's portrait in posters and greeting cards.

Facts:

2. The plaintiff, Mr. Joseph, is an enthusiastic amateur body builder. He is a member of the Canadian Amateur Body Building Association and has competed successfully nationally and internationally in the middleweight category of the sport.

3. The defendant, Mr. Daniels, is a self-employed photographer, who creates photographs for advertising purposes. He was requested by Vancouver Magazine to create a picture publicizing a cat show. At a conference with the picture editor it was decided to picture a cat in a different way—a gray kitten against the background of a black body builder.

4. Mr. Daniels visited various gymnasiums inquiring if anyone knew a black body builder. He was referred to and met Mr. Joseph. I find that Mr. Daniels asked Mr. Joseph if he was interested in posing for a picture for Vancouver Magazine. He told him that the picture was to be basically a torso shot and he would be paid $50 for posing. I find Mr. Joseph agreed to this modelling fee. As he was concerned about his amateur status, he asked to be paid in cash. No mention was made of any other use to be made of the picture. The photographic session was held—a gray kitten was provided by the Association. Although the photograph was in colour, the following black and white … copy demonstrates the artistic creativity of the photographer and the role played by the plaintiff as a background for the picture of the kitten. [See Figure 2-5.]

5. After the photographic session Mr. Daniels, in accordance with his usual practice, asked Mr. Joseph to sign a release for unrestricted use of the photograph. Mr. Joseph refused to do so (presumably because of his concern about his amateur standing). I find Mr. Daniels paid Mr. Joseph $50 in cash and told him if he wished he could get copies of the finished photograph from Vancouver Magazine.

6. The photograph was published as a cover piece in Vancouver Magazine and, much to the surprise of Mr. Daniels who did not consider it an exceptional picture, it received considerable attention, both here and abroad. Vancouver Magazine entered it in a photographic competition and it won an award for graphic design. Several people proposed that they invest in producing posters of the picture. Mr. Daniels then decided to invest his own money by having posters, mini-posters and cards made of the picture. He realized at the time that he did not have a release from Mr. Joseph for unrestricted use of the photograph, and, although he was uncertain if it was necessary, he attempted to locate Mr. Joseph to obtain a release. However, he was not successful in locating Mr. Joseph and decided to proceed to produce the posters. Subsequently Mr. Joseph's girlfriend told him that she had seen one of the posters for sale at a local boutique. This action resulted.

Figure 2-5. Photo courtesy of Brent Daniels

7. The plaintiff claims damages for (a) breach of contract; (b) breach of the Privacy Act R.S.B.C. 1979, c. 336; and (c) wrongful misappropriation of personality; as well as pre-judgment interest and costs.

I. Wrongful Misappropriation of Personality

8. Counsel have referred me to two reported cases in which the emerging tort of wrongful appropriation of personality has been considered by Canadian courts. They advise me that as far as they have been able to ascertain they are the only Canadian cases dealing with the subject.

[The court here discusses the two cases, *Krouse v. Chrysler Canada*, (Chapter I.C.) and *Athans v. Canadian Adventure Camps Ltd.*, 17 O.R. (2d) 425 (Ont. 1977).]

12. Accepting, as I do, that the common law recognizes a claim in tort for the wrongful appropriation by another of one's personality, the question arises—has the defendant Daniels, in the circumstances of this case, committed such a wrong?

13. It is clear that the defendant made use of a photograph of the plaintiff's torso without having the plaintiff's consent or authority and he did so deliberately with a view to obtaining a monetary benefit. But in doing so, did he appropriate the plaintiff's personality?

14. From my review of the authorities I have concluded that it is the unauthorized use of a name or likeness of a person as a symbol of his identity that constitutes the essential element of the cause of action. The cause of action is proprietary in nature and the interest protected is that of the individual in the exclusive use of his own identity insofar as it is represented by his name, reputation, likeness or other value. For the defendant to be found liable he must be taking advantage of the name, reputation, likeness, or some other component of the plaintiff's individuality or personality which the viewer associates or identifies with the plaintiff.

15. By using the model's torso only, the defendant photographer deliberately designed his composition to avoid any reference to the identity of the person providing the background for the picture of the gray kitten. It is the juxtaposition of great strength with the fragility and helplessness of a wee kitten together with the colour contrast that gives the picture its artistic quality. None of these representations or values could be identified with the plaintiff by a viewer of the photograph. Therefore, the defendant has not used in his photographic composition any proprietary interest associated by the public with the plaintiff's individuality. The plaintiff has not established a necessary element of the claim for wrongful misappropriation of personality and his claim in this respect is dismissed.

II. Breach of Privacy Act

16. The relevant provisions of the Privacy Act, R.S.B.C. 1979, c. 336, are as follows:

Violation of privacy actionable

1. (1) It is a tort, actionable without proof of damage, for a person, wilfully and without a claim of right, to violate the privacy of another.

(2) The nature and degree of privacy to which a person is entitled in a situation or in relation to a matter is that which is reasonable in the circumstances, due regard being given to the lawful interests of others.

(3) In determining whether the act or conduct of a person is a violation of another's privacy, regard shall be given to the nature, incidence and occasion of the act or conduct and to any domestic or other relationship between the parties.

(4) Privacy may be violated by eavesdropping or surveillance, whether or not accomplished by trespass; but this subsection shall not be construed as restricting the generality of subsections (1) to (3).

Unauthorized use of name or portrait of another

3. (1) It is a tort, actionable without proof of damage, for a person to use the name or portrait of another for the purpose of advertising or promoting the sale of, or other trading in, property or services, unless that other, or a person entitled to consent on his behalf, consents to the use for that purpose.

(3) A person is not liable to another for the use, for the purposes stated in subsection (1), of his portrait in a picture of a group or gathering, unless the plaintiff is

(a) identified by name or description, or his presence is emphasized, whether by the composition of the picture or otherwise; or

(b) recognizable, and the defendant, by using the picture, intended to exploit the plaintiff's name or reputation.

(5) In this section "portrait" means a likeness, still or moving, and includes a likeness of another deliberately disguised to resemble the plaintiff, and a caricature.

17. A reading of the Privacy Act and in particular § 3, the reference to a "portrait of another" defined to be a "likeness of another" and the exemption of group pictures "unless the plaintiff is identified" or "his presence is emphasized" or "recognizable", clearly indicates the legislature's intention that an action is not maintainable under the Act unless the portrait is a recognizable likeness of the plaintiff. This requirement is not met in the present case: the photograph is not a "portrait" as defined by the Act since the photographer has intentionally avoided portraying an identified or recognizable likeness of the plaintiff. The plaintiff's claim under the Privacy Act is dismissed.

III. Breach of Contract

[The court held defendant had an obligation to pay plaintiff a modeling fee of $550.]

Holdke v. The Calgary Convention Centre Authority

2000 ABPC 80, 265 A.R. 381 (Alberta Prov. Ct. 2000)

JUDGE NORMAN R. HESS:

The Background

1. This [is] an action taken by the plaintiff claiming a misappropriation of his likeness by the defendant. No other cause of action is made out or alleged in the Civil Claim. The plaintiff claims damages equal to the loss of remuneration he could have earned had he been able to negotiate the use of his image. For the reasons which follow the plaintiff's action has failed.

The Facts

2. The plaintiff describes himself as a trick roper. He has been a trick roper since his retirement from his career employment in 1988. The plaintiff utilizes the persona of "Frank Holt" in conjunction with his appearances. At his performances the plaintiff performs his rope tricks for which he is paid a fee which he negotiates. When the plaintiff performs using his persona he is dressed in unique costuming which he has developed. The plaintiff testified he earns between $150.00 for a ten minute performance to $250.00 for an appearance at a convention. He has also appeared in ten to twelve movies, however, not utilizing his roping skills. I was not told what the plaintiff was paid for these appearances or if he used his persona of Frank Holt.

3. Since 1995 the defendant has staged *Canada's Cowboy Festival* ("the Festival")....

4. In 1997 the plaintiff attended the Festival as a patron. While in attendance and not dressed in the persona of Frank Holt, the plaintiff, for reasons which were not explained to me, put on a demonstration of his roping skills. The plaintiff's demonstration was observed by Gord Kelly, an on air personality with CFCN who was at the Festival with a cameraman for the purpose of gathering material for a television news item. Mr. Kelly asked the plaintiff if he would again demonstrate his skills. The cameraman then taped the demonstration. I am satisfied the plaintiff was aware his demonstration was being video taped and the purpose for which CFCN intended to use the tape. The plaintiff gave Mr. Kelly his business card. The plaintiff did not purport to place any restriction on the use of his image or performance.

5. CFCN compiled a two minute news report which aired the day or shortly after the plaintiff's performance was taped. The plaintiff was shown in two separate segments during the news report, once near the beginning and once at the end. The total of the depiction of the plaintiff's performance was less than ten seconds. The voice over for the first segment depicting the plaintiff identified him as Frank Holt, a trick roper and that he was "... a part of the informal entertainment ..." at the Festival....

7. In October, 1998 the plaintiff was contacted by Ms. Sloan via telephone. The plaintiff was asked if he was willing to appear at the 1999 Festival in exchange for promotional value. The plaintiff declined the opportunity and made it clear to Ms. Sloan that he was in the entertainment business and he did not work gratuitously.

8. In preparation for the 1999 Festival CFCN put together two television advertisements. The first was of fifteen seconds in duration and aired before Christmas of 1998.

The second was a thirty second advertisement and utilized some of the plaintiff's performance taped during his impromptu performance at the 1997 Festival. I have no evidence of the plaintiff appearing in the earlier, shorter advertisement. I also have no evidence that the producer of the advertisement was either aware of the identity of the plaintiff or was familiar with his persona....

10. The thirty second version of the advertisement depicts a collage of artists who were to appear at the 1999 Festival and a narration of the performers, activities and features to be presented. An excerpt of between two and three seconds in duration of the plaintiff's taped performance at the 1997 is included as part of the collage. No specific mention of the plaintiff is made in the narration. Unless a viewer was acquainted with the plaintiff or his persona, nothing in the advertisement would identify the plaintiff. The plaintiff first saw the advertisement on January 17, 1999 and subsequently video taped the advertisement on four more occasions. Ms. Sloan testified she thought the individual in question appearing in the advertisement was one of the performers at a previous Festival. As she had never met the plaintiff she had no idea he was the individual who was shown in the advertisement.

11. As I understand the plaintiff's complaint he says the unauthorized use of his image has caused him damage as he was not paid for the implied endorsement or promotion of the 1999 Festival. He says he has lost the opportunity to negotiate a fee and therefore an amount equal to the fee he could have negotiated for the use of his image and the persona of Frank Holt.

12. The plaintiff has not done any television advertisements and consequently could not assist me with what damages he might be entitled to receive for the lost opportunity to earn a fee or what value I might be able to assign to the use of his image, persona and performance. But as I have already said the plaintiff's persona was not used in the promotion of the 1999 Festival. The plaintiff did testify he had been in negotiations at one time for a television commercial with Canada Safeway, but I did not hear anything of the terms or the payment either offered to or expected by the plaintiff....

14. The plaintiff takes these proceedings claiming $7,500.00 (not coincidentally, I surmise, the monetary limit of the jurisdiction of this court) and as a result of "a misappropriation of the plaintiff's image, the plaintiff suffered a loss of remuneration that would have been paid had the defendant negotiated for the use of that image". No evidence was adduced by the plaintiff of any specified damages so I am left with what I take to be a claim for general damages for tort of misappropriation of an asset of the plaintiff's which has commercial value.

The Analysis

15. Each of the parties has submitted the decision of the Ontario Court of Appeal in the case of *Krouse v. Chrysler Canada Ltd. et al.* (1974), 40 D.L.R. (3rd) 15 [excerpted in Chapter I.C.] to be the leading case on the tort of misappropriation of something of commercial value. In *Krouse* the plaintiff was a professional football player and the defendant had published a spotter to assist television spectators with the identification of the participants. A depiction of the plaintiff taken in a game situation appeared in conjunction with photographs of four of the defendant's products was displayed on one side of the spotter. The plaintiff was easily identified by his uniform and number. The plaintiff had not consented to the use of his image.... Estey, J.A. found the mere use of Krouse's image did not suggest an express endorsement of Chrysler's products nor had any attempt been made to associate Krause with Chrysler's products nor was there an implication Krouse was in any way connected with the production of the spotter. At page 30 Estey, J.A. stated:

"… there may well be circumstances in which the Court would be justified in holding a defendant liable in damages for the appropriation of a plaintiff's personality, amounting to an invasion of his right to exploit his personality by the use of his image, voice, or otherwise with damage to the plaintiff …"

But the Court of Appeal determined on the evidence before the trial judge the plaintiff was not entitled to succeed. The Court found Chrysler was attempting to advertise its products in conjunction with the game of football, of which Krouse was a participant. It was not Krouse in particular, but rather the game of football in general, which Chrysler was seeking to associate with its products.

16. It seems to me that in order for the plaintiff to succeed there must be an attempt to in some way associate his persona with the Festival. In the present case there is no evidence of an attempt by the defendant to exploit the plaintiff or his persona for the benefit of either the defendant or the Festival.…

19. In *Krouse* there was no question as to his identity. The actual footage of the plaintiff used in the advertisement does not identify the plaintiff or his persona of Frank Holt by name, or otherwise. The plaintiff is not dressed in the manner of his alter ego. It seems to me the plaintiff's asset, which he alleges to have been misappropriated, is his skill as an entertainer coupled with the persona of Frank Holt. Otherwise the plaintiff would not have told me about his movie appearances which have nothing to do with his skills as a roper. But when the news footage was obtained the plaintiff did not trade upon the Frank Holt persona other than to identify himself to Mr. Kelly as Frank Holt. Neither the plaintiff's name or persona were used in the advertisement.

20. I have no evidence before me that the plaintiff or Frank Holt were so well known in the Calgary area that he or his persona would be recognizable in the advertisement. The plaintiff called two long standing friends to say they were aware of his value, skill and reputation as a western entertainer. But this evidence does not assist me assessing the public reputation and standing enjoyed by the plaintiff or Frank Holt. Likewise, I did not hear any evidence that someone viewing the news report in February, 1997 would, or would be likely to, recognize the plaintiff in January, 1999 from his earlier appearance during the newscast. In other words, in order for the plaintiff to succeed he must demonstrate the commercial value of the asset he owns and which has been misappropriated. This is an element in the tort of misappropriation. I am unable to find the plaintiff has established this element of his claim.…

22. For the foregoing reasons the plaintiff's claim is dismissed with costs.…

Notes and Questions

1. In both *Joseph* and *Holdke* there is no question that the defendant used the actual likeness of the plaintiff. Yet in both cases, the courts rejected right of publicity claims. (In *Joseph*, the court did award a small amount of damages on a breach of contract theory.) Was this because the uses were "noncommercial"? If that is not the reason, then we must ask some further questions.

2. In *Joseph*, the court considered two possible tort claims—one for violation of the right of personality and one for violation of a statutory right of privacy. Suppose that the plaintiff had a distinctive scar or tattoo on his body that was depicted in the photograph. Would that have changed the court's decision concerning the right of personality claim?

Would this change the court's observation that "[i]t is the juxtaposition of great strength with the fragility and helplessness of a wee kitten together with the colour contrast" that is the central theme of the photograph, rather than the plaintiff's identity?

3. As you can see, some of the provinces of Canada (including British Columbia), like some of the states of the United States, have laws protecting privacy interests that may overlap with rights of publicity. If the photograph had revealed the plaintiff's scar or tattoo, as hypothesized in Note 2, would that have changed the court's decision concerning the statutory right of privacy?

4. In *Holdke*, the advertisement in question clearly depicted Mr. Holdke, and clearly depicted him demonstrating his trick roping skills. Those skills (and Mr. Holdke's commercial use of those skills under the name of Frank Holt) were at the heart of the lawsuit. Why then did the court refuse any recovery? What were the missing elements of plaintiff's claim?

5. In *Athans v. Canadian Adventure Camps, Ltd.*, 17 O.R. (2d) 425 (Ont. High Ct. 1977), cited in *Joseph*, the defendant used a drawing of a water skier on a summer camp brochure. The drawing was a stylized version of a photograph of plaintiff, who had used it to promote his activities as a water skier. Although the drawing was not intended to be a recognizable depiction of plaintiff, and the court found that only "a relatively small number of very well-informed people would be likely to recognize the drawings as representations of [plaintiff]," that was sufficient to support a claim. Compare this holding to the one in *Newcombe*, discussed in the notes following *White* in Chapter II.A., above.

6. Would the *Carson* court in Chapter II.A. have granted relief to either of these plaintiffs? What about the *Motschenbacher* court? Conversely, would the courts in *Joseph* and *Holdke* have granted relief in *Carson*? In *White*?

7. Read the first three subsections of Cal. Civ. Code § 3344 in the Appendix. Would the defendant in either *Joseph* or *Holdke* have been liable under this statute?

———————

10th Cantanae Pty. Ltd. v. Shoshana Pty. Ltd.
79 A.L.R. 299 (Fed. Ct. Australia 1987)

WILCOX, PINCUS and GUMMOW JJ

WILCOX J.:

I have had the advantage of reading in draft form the reasons of Pincus J. I need not repeat the facts there set out. The essential complaint made by the respondents is that the appellants have, without their permission, exploited the name and identity of Ms Sue Smith, the second respondent. Ms Smith is a well-known television personality.

In the United States of America such a claim would fall within that aspect of the law of privacy which is called "appropriation". This was the first of the four separate torts, now treated as aspects of privacy law, to be recognised in that country as being actionable: see *Prosser and Keeton on Torts* 5th ed, 1984, pp. 851–4. It remains probably the most significant of those torts, although its inclusion amongst the interests protected under the rubric of "privacy" is somewhat ironic. Most American plaintiffs have not been concerned to maintain the privacy of their identity, but rather to safeguard their monopoly in the publicity value attaching to that identity.

Anglo-Australian law does not, of course, recognise privacy interests, as such, although the expansion of the protection given by the law of passing off which was effected in *Hen-*

derson v. Radio Corp Pty. Ltd. [1960] SR (NSW) 576 [excerpted in Chapter I.C.] goes some distance towards covering the appropriation cases. I see no reason to exclude the application of the law of passing off from a case such as the present, provided that the court were satisfied that the advertisement published by the appellants would be read as containing a representation that Ms Smith endorsed, or was otherwise associated with, the Blaupunkt video recorder....

Upon the assumption, once again, that the second respondent is the "Sue Smith" of the advertisement, I would not deny the respondents relief under §§ 52 and 53 of the Trade Practices Act 1974 (Cth)....

I see no reason to so limit the application of §§ 52 and 53 as to exclude "appropriation" cases from their ambit. Whilst there continues to be room for the view that consumers are sometimes influenced in their choices of goods and services because of a perceived association between those goods and services and a respected identity, it is salutory for the law to guard against their being misled as to the existence of such an association. Although the Trade Practices Act, unlike the American law of privacy, approaches the matter from the point of view of the consumer, rather than that of the person whose identity is appropriated, it is no disadvantage that the application to such cases of §§ 52 and 53 of that Act incidentally provides some protection against the unauthorised appropriation, for commercial purposes, of the reputations of other people.

However, there remains the critical question whether it can be said that the subject advertisement made any statement about the second respondent. I agree with what Pincus J has written on this topic. But, as it is a matter upon which I find myself in respectful disagreement with the view of the learned trial judge, I will elaborate.

Whether one approaches this case under the Trade Practices Act or under the law relating to passing off—indeed, even if it were considered as an "appropriation" case—the respondents must establish that a significant segment of the readers of the advertisement would be likely to associate Ms Smith with the "Sue Smith" of the advertisement. The relevant facts, as found by the trial judge, were that the second respondent was well known to television audiences, under the name "Sue Smith", but that she did not look like the lady pictured in the advertisement as being in control of the video recorder. The person pictured was clearly the person referred to in the advertisement as "Sue Smith". Although Ms Smith was well known to the public, the trial judge accepted evidence that she was in fact not known to those who compiled this advertisement and that the use by them of her name was merely coincidental. However, notwithstanding these findings and in the passage quoted by Pincus J, his Honour held that the respondents had established their case.

With respect to the trial judge, I cannot accept his process of reasoning. It seems to me to beg the critical question. The reasoning commences by assuming what is to be demonstrated: that there existed at the date of the advertisement a body of readers who would associate the second respondent with the "Sue Smith" of the advertisement. The argument recognises that the person depicted in the advertisements differs in appearance from the second respondent but, having made the first critical assumption, it copes with the difference in appearance by further assuming the existence of some readers, who knew the second respondent and who had already associated her in their minds with the Sue Smith of the Advertisement, but who were confused about, or forgetful of, her appearance. I cannot accept this latter assumption. Whatever may be the position regarding those who are well known by name and reputation but not by appearance, it is difficult to divorce the reputation of a television personality from his or her appearance. For the average viewer, the television personality exists only on the screen, or perhaps in magazine or newspaper articles, where photographs are commonly inserted. The effect of the assumption is to confer upon Ms Smith a monopoly of the use of the name "Sue Smith", at least in the absence of an explicit disavowal of any connection with her or of material identifying the "Sue Smith" of the advertisement as someone else, and thus implicitly excluding her. Although, as I have indicated, I would not be sorry to see §§ 52 and 53 of the Trade Practices Act, and the law of passing off, used in appropriate cases in such a manner as to protect well known people from the unathorised exploitation of their identities, it is another matter to confer upon them an exclusive right to use a particular name.

The critical question must always be whether the advertisement, having regard to all relevant aspects, is likely to result in members of the public being misled. In some cases that likelihood may be obvious. For example, in the case of an advertisement which unequivocally identifies a particular person, as by including a photograph or other information peculiar to that person. In other cases, the likelihood of readers being misled may arise out of the context in which the name is used. The example given by Stephen J in *Hornsby Building Information Centre Pty. Ltd. v. Sydney Building Information Centre Pty. Ltd.* (1978) 140 CLR 216 at 227, 18 ALR 639 of the unknown singer who shares the name of a famous prima donna comes to mind, the point being that the name is used in a context, an announcement of an opera, with which readers would readily associate the prima donna.

A third way in which the likelihood of deception may be demonstrated is by showing that the relevant name is so unusual that readers, or at least a significant proportion of them, would reason that there were unlikely to be two persons of that name and would make a connection accordingly. It is easy to apply this approach in the case of "concocted" names. It is much more difficult to do so in a case where the name is an ordinary descriptive name or uses a common first name and surname. The courts must assume that people would realise that Australia is likely to contain more than one John Brown or Alan Jones, so that the use of the name, without more, is not necessarily a reference, respectively, to the Minister for the Arts, Sport, the Environment, Tourism and Territories or to the racing car driver, although it may be taken as such if there is other identifying material or an appropriate context.

In the present case, there was nothing more than the bare name. The advertisement contained no information pointing unequivocally to Ms Smith. There was no relevant context. The two names "Sue" and "Smith" are common enough, whether considered separately or as a combination. The only additional material was a picture of the "Sue Smith" referred to in the advertisement. But, because it was a picture of a person dissimilar in appearance to the second respondent, it pointed the other way.

I would uphold the appeal upon the simple basis that the respondents failed to make out an essential ingredient of their case, namely that readers would be likely to read the advertisement as containing a reference to the second respondent.

I agree with the orders proposed by Pincus J.

PINCUS J.:

The appellants, who used the name "Sue Smith" in some advertisements in 1983, appeal against an award of damages made against them for so doing. The respondents are a lady called Sue Smith, who has appeared often on television, and her company.

The name was used in advertisements for Blaupunkt video recorders. The learned primary judge held that the advertisements were unlawful under the general law related to passing off, as well as under §§ 52, 53(c) and (d) of the Trade Practices Act 1974 (Cth).

To put the matter very generally, his Honour was of the view that the advertisements impermissibly suggested a connection between the second respondent and the video recorders.

Apart from these findings that the advertisements suggested a general association between the second respondent's name and the product, the learned primary judge made more specific findings. His Honour held that readers of a certain sort might well be led to believe that Sue Smith was endorsing the Blaupunkt video. He referred to "Sue Smith's apparent endorsement" of the brand of recorder and, most strongly, found that there was a representation "that the Blaupunkt video had the sponsorship and approval of Sue Smith which it did not have, and that the first-named respondent had her sponsorship and approval which it did not have: see § 53(c) and (d)".

The "first-named respondent" mentioned by the learned primary judge was the distributor of the videos, now one of the appellants.

Section 52, of course, proscribes engaging "in conduct that is misleading or deceptive or is likely to mislead or deceive". Section 53(c) and (d), with the introductory part of the section, is as follows: A corporation shall not, in trade or commerce, in connexion with the supply or possible supply of goods or services or in connexion with the promotion by any means of the supply or use of goods or services—

> ...

> (c) represent that goods or services have sponsorship, approval, performance characteristics, accessories, uses or benefits they do not have;

> (d) represent that the corporation has a sponsorship, approval or affiliation it does not have.

The advertisements the subject of these findings depicted a young woman in bed holding a cat and watching the screen of a television set, on which appeared a picture of another woman apparently grimacing or screaming. Written across each advertisement in large print appeared the words "Sue Smith just took total control of her video recorder". The smaller print of the advertisement had two versions, but each conveyed information along the same lines, namely that the Blaupunkt video recorder enabled the user, called "Sue" in the text, easily to control the functions of the recorder itself and the television to which it was attached.

"Sue" and "Smith" are of course both very common names, but the respondents' contention is based on the view that their use in combination, in circumstances of this sort, is proscribed both by the Trade Practices Act and by the general law, with the qualification that the illegality disappears if the respondents agree to the use.

That qualification, to my mind, points up an oddity of the result arrived at below. Although the award of damages is based on the view that it was untruthfully asserted, among other things, that the second respondent sponsored and approved the machine and its vendor, such an assertion might have had at best a tenuous claim to truth even if the second respondent had agreed to the use of the name and been paid for it. Her real complaint, in a commercial sense, is not the falsity of the advertisement, but that the name was used other than pursuant to an "endorsement" agreement involving a fee.

Passing off

It is desirable to say something of the applicable principles, before analysing the learned primary judge's findings further. His Honour, as appears from what is said above, accepted a wider view of the notion of passing off than that which had prevailed in this country before the decision in *Henderson v. Radio Corp Pty. Ltd.* [1960] SR (NSW) 576.

His Honour quoted ((1987) 79 ALR 279 at 288) and apparently accepted Mr Ricketson's statement that "any representation that the plaintiff is in some way associated with the defendant's business, whether by way of partnership, sponsorship or licensing, will suffice".

It should be noted that the apparent approval, in this passage, of the expansion of the tort of passing off does not go beyond instances in which people are led to believe that certain goods or services have a characteristic belonging to other goods or services; the question whether the law of passing off gives protection to the alleged proprietary right, "in gross", in the use of a well-known name, is left open. In the United States it appears there has been a ready acceptance of the idea that a well-known person (alive or dead) is entitled to the law's protection in the activity of selling others the right to use his name in association with goods or services, whether or not on the basis that the name properly belongs to any particular goods or services; protection is accorded to the bare name.

It appears to me a little artificial to assume that the ordinary reader is so gullible as to think, these days, that (for example) the application of the name of a well-known French clothing manufacturer to a great variety of goods necessarily implies anything about the "origin, selection or treatment of the goods" or, to quote further from Dixon J, that it implies anything other than that the owner of the same "must have sanctioned it".... It should not be too readily accepted that the mere mention of a name in an advertisement necessarily connotes that the goods advertised have any characteristic—for example, that they have been approved, or even examined, by the person named. In commercial parlance, it may be that a racing car driver "endorses" all the products referred to on his car and clothing, but he is not generally thought to be thereby expressing a view about them.

Putting this more shortly, passing off is not necessarily constituted by the mere authorized [sic] use of someone's name or picture or the name or picture of a well-known fictitious character, in an advertisement.

The findings of the primary judge

It was held below that the second respondent is very widely known in New South Wales and elsewhere in Australia as a prominent figure on national television.

An important question in the resolution of the issues arising on appeal is whether the women depicted in the advertisement look like the second respondent. A portfolio of a substantial number of photographs of the respondent, taken over a period of years, is available, and was available to the learned primary judge. His Honour said: Neither of the two females pictured appears actually to be the second applicant, though both are brunettes as is Sue Smith.

[I]f the finding that the advertisements were misleading is to be upheld, that must be done on the basis that the viewer depicted in the advertisement is the "Sue Smith" spoken of in the heading as just having taken control of her video recorder, who is in turn to be identified with the second respondent.

The point just made is of some importance in the determination of the appeal. Whereas the viewer shown in the advertisement plainly is not the second respondent, it is more difficult to be dogmatic as to the degree of resemblance between the face shown on the screen and the second respondent, because that face is distorted. It does not appear to me that there was anything misleading about use of the pictured viewer in the advertisement, as she looks quite unlike the second respondent. In my respectful opinion, this absence of resemblance substantially decreases the risk that anyone would be misled.

It cannot be enough, to sustain the award made against the appellants, merely to hold that it is conceivable that a person who had forgotten what the second respondent looks like might mistake the viewer depicted for her. If the judgment is to be upheld, that must be on the basis that the "Sue Smith" said in the heading to be in control of the recorder really might be thought to be the second respondent, although the person depicted as in control of the recorder does not resemble the second respondent.

Bases of liability

As to § 52(1), the appellants may have a slightly more difficult task, because under that provision it is enough to show that the advertisements are misleading or deceptive, or likely to mislead or deceive in any respect; the respondents are not confined to the particular sorts of representations mentioned in § 53. Nevertheless, it must be a rare case in which, an allegation of falsely representing that goods have the approval of a particular person being rejected, misleading conduct is found under § 52 on the basis that there is merely "some likely association" between the name and the goods. I incline to the view that the legislative intention is that allegations of this sort are to be tested under § 53. However that may be, it should not in my opinion be held that the use of the name "Sue Smith" was in the circumstances misleading or deceptive, or likely to mislead or deceive. Since the doctrine ... that it is necessary to show a misrepresentation has been accepted, it may be that the task of an applicant for a relief under § 52 of the Trade Practices Act has become harder than it would otherwise have been. If one asks if any misrepresentation relevant to the second respondent is made by these advertisements, the most which can be said in favour of the respondents is that some readers might suspect that, although the model described as "Sue Smith" is plainly not the second respondent, she permitted her name to be used in the advertisements. That is not enough, in my opinion, to uphold the view that the advertisements are made unlawful by § 52. For similar reasons, it appears to me that the allegation based on passing off must fail.

I would allow the appeal with costs and, in lieu of the order made below, dismiss the application with costs.

Gummow J.:

Introduction

This is an appeal from a decision of a judge of this court in which judgment was given in favour of the applicants (the present respondents) against each of the respondents (the present appellants) for $ 15,000. The liability of the appellants arose from activities which his Honour found constituted both passing off and contraventions of §§ 52 and 53(c) and (d) of the Trade Practices Act 1974 (the TP Act). The award of damages for contraventions of §§ 52 and 53 thus was based on § 82 of the TP Act; the liability for damages in respect of passing off arose from the general law as applied in the accrued jurisdiction of the court.

The advertisements appeared in the 10 May and 14 June 1983 issues of *The Bulletin*, in the May and June issues of *Video Age*, in the May issue of *Video and Communication* and in the issues of *Australian Business* of 5 May and 30 June.

In each case the advertisement was a prominent one, extending horizontally across two pages of the journal and taking up about half of each of those pages. Across the top of each advertisement in heavy bold print were the words: "Sue Smith just took total control of her video recorder."

Beneath the headline appeared the picture of a woman sitting up in bed nursing a cat and watching a television set equipped with a video recorder. Close to the hand of the viewer, on the bedspread, was a remote control device. On the television screen appeared a picture of the head and shoulders of a woman with an expression of some distress or agitation. Both women depicted in the advertisements were brunettes.

In any event, counsel for the appellants accepted that after the initial complaint in Sue Smith's letter of 30 May 1983, the advertisement of which she complained certainly was published in the issue of *Australian Business* for 30 June 1983 and *The Bulletin* on 14 June 1983 and possibly also in the issue of *Video Age* for June 1983. There was thus ample evidence to support his Honour's finding, which in any event was not challenged, that in the present case, on several occasions, the advertisement was published after notice and after no reply had been vouchsafed to the original complaint by Miss Smith. This is a finding of some importance to which I will return when considering the claim based on passing off.

It was also found and, indeed, it was not contested at the trial that the advertising agents, the third appellant and Mr James had devised the advertisement in ignorance of the second respondent, Sue Smith.

Since about 1970 Sue Smith has appeared as an interviewer and presenter for various news and current affairs programs, particularly on television, although, in 1978, she had broadcast a program over Radio 2UE, Sydney, between 9 am and 12 noon on weekdays. In January 1982 she had, as I have indicated, joined the Channel 10 Network. There she presented the weekend news, the program "Eyewitness News at 6" and, in addition, she had from time to time co-hosted the program "Good Morning Australia". She was also a member of the panel on the afternoon program "Beauty and the Beast". The programs "Good Morning Australia" and "Beauty and the Beast" were telecast over the Channel 10 Network throughout rural and metropolitan areas in New South Wales, Queensland, South Australia and Victoria.

Previously, she had been the first woman to compere* the well-known "Mike Walsh Show" which was telecast nationally throughout Australia and she was also the first woman to appear as "front person" for the leading public affairs program "A Current Affair". This also was telecast nationally. In 1977 she had won a Logie award for her performance as "front person" in "A Current Affair"; in 1978 she had won a Logie award as "Most Popular Female Personality"; and in 1983 she shared with Mr Ross Symonds the award of the Association for Better Hearing.

In consequence, like other television personalities, Sue Smith had become the subject of comment, news items and articles in the press. The evidence included more than 90 examples of such items in the period 1970–83. These items included the discussion of Sue Smith's personal life with photographs of her in various domestic settings. On at least one occasion, she was shown on a bed, if not in a bed, as in the advertisement with which this case is concerned. It is also apparent from these materials that Sue Smith is a brunette and that her hairstyle varied from time to time in the period before 1983.

His Honour found that in 1983 the name "Sue Smith" was extremely well known throughout Australia as the name of a popular television personality, particularly admired for the clarity of her presentation of information. His Honour said that he was assisted in understanding the evidence as to that last-mentioned attribute by his having heard and observed her in the witness box.

His Honour also found on the evidence, a finding not challenged, that persons in the position of Sue Smith were, "according to modern advertising practice, in significant demand for their endorsement of various products commonly sold by character merchandising", and that Miss Smith stood high in the category of persons suitable for this kind of work. The products sold by character merchandising, his Honour found,

---

* In Australia, "compere" refers to the announcer or host on a radio or television show. — *Eds.*

included television and video equipment. His Honour also found: "A feature of the technique of character merchandising ... is that the advertiser uses the public image of the personality concerned to develop in the minds of consumers an identification of the product with that personality. As a result, Sue Smith's endorsement of a particular product is likely in practice to preclude her obtaining a contract to endorse a competing product."

The impact of the advertisements

As I have indicated, the case for the respondents against the appellants was based both upon contraventions of §§ 52 and 53 of the TP Act and passing off. A central element in the consideration of each of these causes of action was the impact or likely impact of the advertisements upon the readers thereof. His Honour concluded that the advertisement would convey at a glance a good impression about the Blaupunkt video equipment and that that impression would be likely to be enhanced by an association of it with Sue Smith.

The striking feature in the advertisment, "the grab" as I have mentioned, was the headline "Sue Smith just took total control of her video recorder". Sue Smith and each of the women depicted in the advertisement were brunettes.

In his address before us, counsel for the appellants conceded that both the contraventions of § 52 and passing off would be made out if it could fairly be said of a substantial number of readers that they would take the advertisements as indicating that Sue Smith had endorsed the products in question. However, both at first instance and before us, much attention was devoted to what was said to be dissimilarities in appearance between Sue Smith and the two women shown in the advertisement. The dissimilarities were then relied upon for the conclusion that the reader would reason that the Sue Smith referred to in the headline was not the well-known Sue Smith of television fame but some other person of no fame or, indeed, "Everywoman".

His Honour dealt with the subject as follows: "The lady holding a cat appears younger than Sue Smith, but both the pictured ladies seem to me to bear some resemblance to her as might lead a casual reader of the advertisement, or a person not very familiar with Sue Smith's appearance but having a general recollection of it, to suppose that Sue Smith is pictured.... The performer pictured on the television screen could be Miss Smith, even to the eye of a more attentive reader with a fairly good recollection of her appearance, but if such a person read the small print as well as the caption with attention, he would see that the advertisement attributes the name Sue Smith to the other female pictured [*i.e.*, the woman holding the cat]."

I agree with this approach to the matter. In particular, it would be wrong, in my view, to place too much emphasis on the alleged dissimilarities in appearance in evaluating the likely overall effect of the advertisement upon readers. It is, as his Honour said, of the nature of glossy advertisements of this kind, that they create an impression and evoke a response which does not proceed from a discerning analysis. I also agree that the readers of the advertisement must include many who, by reason of the wide publicity given to Sue Smith's name in the press and on television, would immediately associate the heavy print of the headline of the advertisement with the well-known television personality even though, had it not been for the presence of the headline, they would not have recognised either photograph in the advertisement as that of Sue Smith.

No doubt there would have been a number of careful and attentive readers with the time and inclination to study with care the meaning of the message thrust before them in advertisements such as this. Those persons might well have decided that there was no endorsement by the famous Sue Smith because if there had been the picture would have been one of Sue Smith herself. But, in my view, it is important not to exaggerate the importance or numbers of such persons. Nor, in my view, should one place significance upon the circumstance that in its terms, the text of the advertisement does not state that Sue Smith approves or endorses the Blaupunkt equipment. That is the thrust of the advertisement and a reader who knew of Sue Smith's television fame might well ask why else has the advertiser featured her name so prominently in an advertisement for its television equipment?

Plainly, his Honour was correct in bearing in mind that one answers these questions not by close *ex post facto* analysis, but more by a perception of the usual manner in which ordinary people behave, bringing with them but an imperfect recollection of the appearance of Sue Smith in 1983 or her appearance at an earlier date.

As I have indicated, I agree with the conclusions reached by the learned trial judge. In any event, even if I had entertained doubts, they would have to have been sufficiently strong as to lead me to conclude that his Honour was wrong.

"Monopolisation"

The appellants stressed that the decision against them encouraged or tended to encourage "monopolies" in names that might be in use by appreciable numbers of the population. In my view, the use of the emotive term "monopoly" in a setting such as this is inapt. First, there is a well developed body of law dealing with the right of persons honestly to carry on business under their own names.

Secondly, passing off is concerned with the protection of a plaintiff's business or commercial interest, in a wide sense, but not with what might be thought of as an invasion of privacy by unathorised adoption of the name of a person with no celebrity or goodwill in that name: in the United States, the effect of federal and State legislation and the common law may be to establish the right of all citizens to privacy and against "misappropriation of personality" for commercial gain, but the interests of celebrities and private persons protected in this way differ: "Celebrities and private persons have two broad interests in the names and likenesses that the law should protect. The private person's primary interest rests on legal concern with the right to privacy. The celebrity's primary interest rests both on the law's traditional concern with protecting an individual's interest in the value of his services and on the desirability of preventing abuses of names and likenesses that can mislead consumers." Passing off as understood in Australia deals with the latter not the former category of interest.

Thirdly, the plaintiff's right to protection by the court cannot survive the life of his goodwill; it is a condition precedent to success that he can show the present subsistence of his reputation. There is thus no "monopoly" in the sense of rights conferred by statute for a certain term as with patents, copyright and registered designs.

Fourthly, if two or more persons of the same name have by their independent efforts achieved such celebrity as to endow each of them with the capability of earning money by endorsement of products, the law would deal with their rights *inter se* by the so-called doctrine of honest concurrent user; the result would be that whilst neither might enjoin the other, each might enjoin an interloper.

Passing off

On the footing that a reasonably significant number of persons reading the advertisements, being potential purchasers of the Blaupunkt equipment, would draw or be likely to draw from the advertisements the message that the media personality, Sue Smith, was giving her endorsement, I turn to consider the question whether the claim for passing off was made out. If so, then the further question arises as to the measure of damages for that passing off.

[T]he law as it has developed in the United States does not always provide very helpful or direct analogies in this area. This is in part because of the impact there of federal and State statutes upon the common law, differences in the common law between the States, and the blending of statute and common law in the reasoning in many decisions. It can be said that the law as to the "merchandising" of fictional characters such as "ET" and the "Bionic Man" fluctuates in emphasis, and in its doctrinal basis. Thus, doubts are expressed (particularly at the interlocutory level) as to "how prolonged a search would be required to identify a flesh and blood consumer who actually ... assumes that a coffee mug proclaiming 'I love ET' is necessarily connected with Universal City Studios Incorporated": Denicola, "Institutional Publicity Rights: An Analysis of the Merchandising of Famous Trade Symbols" (1985) 75 *Trade Mark Reporter* 41 at 47. However, the present is not a "merchandising" case in this sense. The United States decisions have tended to treat as a distinct subject the right of a celebrity to protection against false attribution of commercial endorsement.

In 1983, it could accurately be said of Sue Smith, to adapt the language of Cardozo J, that her favour would help a sale of the Blaupunkt television equipment: *cf Wood v. Lucy, Lady Duff-Gordon* (1917) 222 NY 88 at 90. To depict her as endorsing such products, without her consent, was a passing off.

It follows that, in my view, both the appeal and the cross-appeal fail.

ORDER:

(1) The appeal be allowed.

(2) The orders made by Burchett J be set aside and, in lieu thereof, it be ordered that the Application be dismissed with costs.

(3) The cross-appeal be dismissed.

(4) The respondents pay to the appellants their costs of the appeal.

———————

Notes and Questions

1. In Australia, as indicated in this decision and in the decisions excerpted in Chapter I.C., protection of rights of publicity is limited to a claim for "passing off." In this context, the claim could more accurately be described as one for false endorsement. Do the judges disagree fundamentally on matters of legal principle? If so, what is the nature of those disagreements? (Hint: look especially at Judge Gummow's discussion of monopolization and the discussions of the other judges of similar issues.)

2. What would be the smallest change in the facts that would have convinced Judge Gummow to concur in the result arrived at by the other two judges? Would an explicit disclaimer have satisfied him? Would something other than a disclaimer have been sufficient?

3. Suppose that the *White* or *Carson* cases (excerpted in Chapter II.A.) had been presented to these judges. What do you think would have been their reactions to those fact patterns? Conversely, suppose this fact pattern had been presented to the judges that decided those cases. What result do you think they would have come to?

4. If the issue is primarily one of fact—what would consumers think—do you believe that any of the methods used by the judges in this case is more appropriate than that used by the others?

5. Is it appropriate to consider the problem of other people's right to use the same name, or is the idea of "first come, first served" more appropriate in this situation?

Problem 2

Rod Laver is a very famous Australian tennis player (and the last male tennis player to win the Grand Slam in a single calendar year). Suppose that an Australian rugby player wanted to change his name from Rodd Lane to Rodd Layver. Do you think that the Australian courts would allow Rod Laver (the tennis player) to prevent Rodd Layver from endorsing products?

Susanne Bergmann, *Publicity Rights in the United States and in Germany: A Comparative Analysis*
19 Loy. L.A. Ent. L.J. 479 (1999)

B. Right to One's Image

The "right to one's image" grants individuals the exclusive right to decide to display and distribute their own likeness (Bildnis): "Only the person depicted is, as a holder of the right, entitled to decide whether, when and how he wishes to present himself to any third party or the public." The unauthorized public and private distribution of the likeness is prohibited....

1. Likeness

In Germany, the concept of likeness is broad. The medium of publication and its form are immaterial; it can be a photograph, photographic layout, drawing, painting, caricature, sculpture, or doll. However, determining whether the depicted person is recognizable is the decisive factor in determining if the use is actionable under section 22 KUG. It is sufficient that a person is recognizable by clothing, hair-style, or gestures. Therefore, a picture of a person's back or a silhouette can also be a likeness, even though the face of the person cannot be seen. For example, in the *Fußballtor* case, an advertisement for a television manufacturer depicted the back of a famous soccer goalkeeper. The Federal Supreme Court held that the goalkeeper was easily recognizable by his particular stature, posture, and haircut. It was not necessary that everyone recognized him, rather it was sufficient that a limited group of persons knew who was depicted. In another case, the Federal Supreme Court in *Nacktaufnahme* had to decide upon [these] facts[:] The picture in question showed the back of a nude woman which was recognized by her husband. [T]he Federal Supreme Court held that the person could be identified and, therefore, should be protected from unauthorized appropriation, even though facial features could not be seen.

Nevertheless, portraits of look-alikes or doubles do not fall within the scope of protection under section 22 KUG [a form of copyright protection discussed in Chapter I.C.]. Courts initially considered imitations to be likenesses. However, the current prevailing opinion grants protection on the basis of the "general right of personality."

Silvio Martuccelli, *The Right of Publicity under Italian Civil Law*
18 Loy. L.A. Ent. L.J. 543 (1998)

B. Use of Distinguishing Characteristics

The plaintiff must show that the defendant has used distinguishing characteristics of the celebrity, but not necessarily his or her physical attributes. In most cases, the misappropriation of another's persona is accomplished by actually using a statutorily protected element of one's identity, such as the person's real name, nickname, or professional name, or by a likeness embodied in a photograph, drawing, or videotape. However, the unauthorized use of other distinguishing characteristics of a person's identity can also infringe the right of publicity. Thus, the misappropriation of another's identity through the use or imitation of the person's performing persona, such as Charlie Chaplin's "Little Tramp" or Julius Marx's "Groucho," can violate the right of publicity if used for commercial purposes.

The use of other identifying characteristics or attributes can also violate the right of publicity if they are so closely identified with the person that their use enables the defendant to misappropriate the commercial value of the person's identity. Additionally, where the plaintiff's distinguishing characteristics are the only thing identifying the person in an advertisement, the plaintiff must show misappropriation of his or her persona. The Autovox advertisement, for example, used two distinguishing characteristics of Lucio Dalla*— his ever-present cap and glasses—clearly invoking his persona to sell Autovox products....

Accordingly, the means of appropriating the person's identity are irrelevant to the aims of protection. On the one hand, the right of publicity does not require that misappropriation of persona be accomplished through particular means to be actionable. On the other hand, the right of publicity is not infringed unless the defendant's use identifies the plaintiff.

Notes and Questions

1. The issue of rights of publicity in characters (such as the Little Tramp of Charlie Chaplin) and look-alikes is discussed in Chapter III.

2. How do you think that German courts would decide the "Sue Smith" case from Australia?

3. What is the justification for granting a cause of action if only one person recognizes the plaintiff's image? Does that correspond to the usual theories behind the right of publicity or the right of personality as discussed in Chapter I?

---

* Lucio Dalla is an Italian musician, singer and songwriter. (See www.luciodalla.it.)—*Eds.*

Chapter III

The Scope of Celebrity Rights

In Chapter II, we discussed the issue of identification—that is, under what circumstances is a celebrity sufficiently identifiable to justify a claim for a violation of his or her right of publicity. In this Chapter, we will look at a problem that ordinarily does not raise (but sometimes may intersect with) issues of identification—the extent to which celebrities have the right to control extensions of themselves, in the form of characters that they play, or impersonations of themselves by others.

A. Characters and Personas

Lugosi v. Universal Pictures
25 Cal. 3d 813, 160 Cal. Rptr. 323, 603 P.2d 425 (1979)

BY THE COURT:

We granted a hearing in this case in order to consider the important issues raised. After an independent study of these issues, we have concluded that the thoughtful opinion of Presiding Justice Roth for the Court of Appeal, Second Appellate District, in this case correctly treats the issues, and accordingly adopt it as our own. That opinion, with appropriate deletions and additions, is as follows:

In September 1930, Bela Lugosi and Universal Pictures Company, Inc. (Universal) concluded an agreement for the production of the film Dracula in which Lugosi contracted to and did play the title role....

[Plaintiffs are the heirs of Bela Lugosi.] The issue as framed by the trial judge is: "(Plaintiffs) seek to recover the profits made by (Universal) in its licensing of the use of the Count Dracula character to commercial firms and to enjoin (Universal) from making any additional grants, without (their) consent.... The action, therefore, raises the question of whether Bela Lugosi had granted to (Universal) in his contracts with (Universal) merchandising rights in his movie portrayal of Count Dracula, the nature of such rights, and whether any such rights, if retained by Bela Lugosi, descended to the (plaintiffs)...."

The trial court found in pertinent part that "the essence of the thing licensed" by Universal to each of its licensees was the "uniquely individual likeness and appearance of Bela Lugosi in the role of Count Dracula." The finding was based upon uncontradicted evidence that it was Lugosi's likeness that was used in the merchandising of Count Dracula notwithstanding the fact that other actors (Christopher Lee, Lon Chaney and John Carradine) appeared in the Dracula role in other Universal films.

The trial court concluded that: Lugosi during his lifetime had a protectable property or proprietary right in his facial characteristics and the individual manner of his likeness

119

Figure 3-1. Bela Lugosi as Dracula (1931)
Courtesy of Bela G. Lugosi. All Rights Reserved.

and appearance as Count Dracula; that said property or proprietary right was of such character and substance that it did not terminate with Lugosi's death but descended to his heirs; and that (they) acquired all right, title and interest in and to said property under the will of Lugosi.

(Plaintiffs) recovered a judgment for damages and an injunction. Universal appeals.

Bram Stoker's 1897 novel *Dracula* has always been in the public domain in the United States.[4] Universal's film *Dracula*, however, was copyrighted after the studio had purchased the motion picture rights from Florence Stoker, Stoker's heir, and from Hamilton Deane

---

4. Stoker failed to comply with the United States deposit requirements in effect in 1897. In England and other countries adhering to the Berne Convention the novel passed into the public domain in April 1962.

and John Balderston, the authors of the 1927 stage play *Dracula*. (Lugosi had played Count Dracula in the 1927 Deane-Balderston Broadway play.) The trial court found, notwithstanding Universal's copyright in the film, that the character of Count Dracula as described in Stoker's novel is in the public domain in the United States.

[The majority of the Court declined to decide whether Lugosi had a right of publicity that extended to the use of his likeness in the character of Count Dracula. Instead, for purposes of this case, the Court assumed that such a right existed. It then ruled against plaintiffs as follows.] We hold that the right to exploit name and likeness is personal to the artist and must be exercised, if at all, by him during his lifetime....

The judgment is reversed and the trial court is directed to enter a new judgment in favor of Universal....

MOSK, Justice, concurring:

With the majority of my colleagues I concur in the judgment, and in the opinion of [the Court of Appeal]. Because this is a matter of first impression in our court, I am impelled to add some observations.

Factually and legally this is a remarkable case. Factually: not unlike the horror films that brought him fame, Bela Lugosi rises from the grave 20 years after death to haunt his former employer. Legally: his vehicle is a strained adaptation of a common law cause of action heretofore unknown either in a statute or case law in California.

The plaintiffs, and my dissenting colleagues, erroneously define the fundamental issue, and consistently repeat their misconception. We are not troubled by the nature of Lugosi's right to control the commercial exploitation of *his* likeness. That right has long been established. The issue here is the right of Lugosi's successors to control the commercialization of a likeness of a dramatic character *i.e.*, Count Dracula, created by a novelist and portrayed for compensation by Lugosi in a film version produced by a motion picture company under license from the successor of the novelist. The error in discerning the problem pervades the trial court's conclusion. Inevitably one who asks the wrong question gets the wrong answer.

Bela Lugosi was a talented actor. But he was an actor, a practitioner of the thespian arts; he was not a playwright, an innovator, a creator or an entrepreneur. As an actor he memorized lines and portrayed roles written for him, albeit with consummate skill. In this instance the part he played was that of Count Dracula, a legendary character out of the novel originated by Bram Stoker, first published in England in 1897, and adapted for the screen by writers employed by Universal Pictures. Due to copyright omission, at all times involved herein the novel and its characters had been in the American public domain.

Merely playing a role under the foregoing circumstances creates no inheritable property right in an actor, absent a contract so providing. Indeed, as the record discloses, many other actors have portrayed the same role, notably Lon Chaney and John Carradine; the first movie was a European version released in 1922 with Max Schreck as the Count. Thus neither Lugosi during his lifetime nor his estate thereafter owned the exclusive right to exploit Count Dracula any more than Gregory Peck possesses or his heirs could possess common law exclusivity to General MacArthur, George C. Scott to General Patton, James Whitmore to Will Rogers and Harry Truman, or Charlton Heston to Moses.

I do not suggest that an actor can never retain a proprietary interest in a characterization. An original creation of a fictional figure played exclusively by its creator may well be protectible. Thus Groucho Marx just being Groucho Marx, with his moustache, cigar, slouch and leer, cannot be exploited by others. Red Skelton's variety of self-devised roles would appear to be protectible, as would the unique personal creations of Abbott and

Costello, Laurel and Hardy and others of that genre. Indeed the court in a case brought by the heirs of Stanley Laurel and Oliver Hardy (Price v. Hal Roach Studios (S.D.N.Y. 1975) 400 F. Supp. 836) observed ...: "we deal here with actors portraying themselves and developing their own characters...."

Here it is clear that Bela Lugosi did not portray himself and did not create Dracula, he merely acted out a popular role that had been garnished with the patina of age, as had innumerable other thespians over the decades. His performance gave him no more claim on Dracula than that of countless actors on Hamlet who have portrayed the Dane in a unique manner....

A salutary tendency today is to encourage the free dissemination of ideas — political, literary, artistic — even by commercial sources. If Bela Lugosi were alive today, he would be unable to claim an invasion of his right to privacy for Universal's exploitation not of Lugosi *qua* Lugosi but of products created in the image of Count Dracula, a role Lugosi played. On a right of privacy theory his successors concededly would be denied the substantial rewards they neither earned nor otherwise deserve two decades after Lugosi's death. To approve such a bonanza on a newly created cause of action, heretofore unknown in California, ill serves the principles of free expression and free enterprise.

I agree with the Court of Appeal that we must reverse the judgment.

BIRD, Chief Justice, dissenting:

...

I. THE FACTS

In 1960, four years after Lugosi's death, Universal began to enter into licensing agreements with various businesses for the use of the Count Dracula character in connection with certain commercial merchandising products. By 1966, when this action was filed, Universal had concluded approximately 50 such licensing agreements. The agreements authorized the use of the likeness of Count Dracula in connection with the sale of such products as plastic toy pencil sharpeners, plastic model figures, T-shirts and sweat shirts, card games, soap and detergent products, picture puzzles, candy dispensers, masks, kites, belts and belt buckles, and beverage stirring rods.

The licenses granted by Universal specifically authorized the use of Lugosi's likeness from his portrayal of Count Dracula in *Dracula*.... No agreement made reference to any other actor's portrayal of Count Dracula....

The trial court concluded that the essence of Lugosi's portrayal of Count Dracula was found in his "facial characteristics and in the uniquely individual manner of his likeness and appearance." The court further found that Universal had not granted its licensees the right to use a likeness of a Count Dracula character generally consistent with the character described in the novel *Dracula*. Rather, Universal had licensed the "uniquely individual likeness and appearance" of Lugosi in his portrayal of Count Dracula....

II. THE RIGHT OF PUBLICITY

...

B. THE SCOPE OF THE RIGHT OF PUBLICITY

The parameters of the right of publicity must now be considered. This case presents two questions: (1) whether the right extends to the likeness of an individual in his portrayal of the fictional character; and (2) whether the right dies with the individual or may be passed to one's heirs or beneficiaries.

Because the right protects against the unauthorized commercial use of an individual's identity, the right clearly applies to the person's name and likeness. However, such protection would appear to be insufficient because many people create public recognition not only in their "natural" appearance but in their portrayal of particular characters. Charlie Chaplin's Little Tramp, Carroll O'Connor's Archie Bunker and Flip Wilson's Judge and Geraldine exemplify such creations. Substantial publicity value exists in the likeness of each of these actors in their character roles. The professional and economic interests in controlling the commercial exploitation of their likenesses while portraying these characters are identical to their interests in controlling the use of their own "natural" likenesses. Indeed, to the extent one's professional endeavors have focused on the development of one or more particular character images, protection for one's likeness in the portrayal of those characters may well be considerably more important than protection for the individual's "natural" appearance. Hence, there appears to be no reason why the right of publicity should not extend to one's *own* likeness while portraying a particular fictional character.[26]

Lugosi's likeness in his portrayal of Count Dracula is clearly such a case. Many men have portrayed Count Dracula in motion pictures and on stage. However, the trial court found that Universal did not license the use of an undifferentiated Count Dracula character, but the distinctive and readily recognizable portrayal of Lugosi as the notorious Translyvanian count. Universal thereby sought to capitalize on the particular image of Lugosi in his portrayal of Count Dracula and the public recognition generated by his performance. Such use is illustrative of the very interests the right of publicity is intended to protect. Hence, Lugosi had a protectible property interest in controlling unauthorized commercial exploitation of *his* likeness in his portrayal of Count Dracula.

Recognizing Lugosi's legitimate interest in controlling the use of his portrayal of Count Dracula limits neither the author's exploitation of the novel *Dracula* nor Universal's use of its copyrighted motion picture. Lugosi only agreed to allow Universal to make limited use of his likeness in their 1930 contract. Further, Lugosi's right certainly does not prohibit others from portraying the character Count Dracula. Consequently, nothing established herein suggests that any of the individuals involved in contemporary cinematic or theatrical revivals of Count Dracula's nocturnal adventures have violated Lugosi's right of publicity. The only conduct prohibited is the unauthorized commercial use of *Lugosi's likeness* in his portrayal of Count Dracula. To the extent that Universal or another seeks such use, that right can be secured by contract....

[Chief Justice Bird's opinion then discussed a number of other issues, including the inheritability of the right of publicity, freedom of expression, and copyright preemption. These issues are discussed in Chapters IV, VIII and X, respectively. She concluded that "[t]he trial court properly found Lugosi had a right of publicity in his likeness in his portrayal of Count Dracula and that the right descended to plaintiffs as his beneficiaries."]

[Justices Tobriner and Manuel concurred in this opinion]

---

26. This protection extends only to the individual's likeness a representation or image of the person while portraying the particular character. Nothing herein is intended to extend protection to the idea for the character or to the character itself. Nothing in the right of publicity prohibits another person, for example, from developing and playing a sympathetic tramp character similar to the one portrayed by Chaplin.

McFarland v. Miller

14 F.3d 912 (3d Cir. 1994)

HUTCHINSON, Circuit Judge:

…

[W]e conclude that infringement of a person's right to exploit commercially his own name or the name of a character so associated with him that it identifies him in his own right is a cause of action that under New Jersey law survives the death of the person with whom the name has become identified.… [I]f McFarland's personal representatives can demonstrate on remand that the name Spanky McFarland identified George McFarland and not just the little urchin Spanky he portrayed in the movie and television series, Mc-Farland's right of publicity to exploit the name Spanky McFarland is superior to that of Miller and Anaconda. We will, therefore, remand this case to the district court in order to determine whether McFarland is inextricably linked to the name and image of Spanky McFarland.

Our reasons follow.

I.

In 1931, at the age of three, George McFarland joined "Our Gang" (later known as the "Little Rascals"), a theatrical group of mischievous children whose adventures were chronicled in a number of movie short films, known as serials, in the 1920s, 30s, and 40s. The "Gang" was a creation of the legendary Hollywood producer Hal Roach.

Initially, McFarland was hired to portray an unnamed small child in the group. Before his first appearance, a newspaper reporter dubbed McFarland "Spanky." The producer picked up on this nickname and the "Our Gang" series then used "Spanky" as the name of the character McFarland played. The nickname "Spanky" remained identified with Mc-Farland throughout his movie career.…

Sadly, George McFarland passed away during the pendency of this appeal at the age of sixty-four. At the time of his death, he was still receiving income from the licensing of his name "Spanky" and from various commercial ventures under the name "Spanky McFarland."

Miller is the principal shareholder and president of Anaconda. Anaconda leases a facility at 821 West Park Avenue in Ocean Township, New Jersey known as "Spanky Mc-Farland's" (the "Restaurant"). Anaconda also holds the liquor license for the establishment.

On July 31, 1989, the restaurant opened for business. In a deposition, Miller admitted he was solely responsible for choosing Spanky McFarland's as the name for his restaurant. He claimed he picked the name "McFarland" because it sounded Irish and "Spanky" was a nickname he once used for his son. He also admitted he was aware that the restaurant shared the name of an "Our Gang" character. In the restaurant, Miller has over 1,000 photos of movie characters including some of the "Little Rascals." The restaurant also displays two four-by-six-foot murals of "Our Gang." They include McFarland. Furthermore, the establishment's menu makes numerous references to the characters. McFarland never consented to the restaurant's use of his name or likeness.

On September 17, 1990, McFarland began this action for injunctive relief and damages.…

IV.

The district court held, in essence, that George McFarland had an extremely limited interest in exploitation of his childhood image or the name Spanky McFarland because Spanky was merely a character whom McFarland was employed to play. That holding naturally implied that the character belonged to some entity other than McFarland. That other party, the court concluded, was the Studio or its successors in interest. The court based that holding on its construction of the 1936 contract [between McFarland and Hal Roach Studio]. Specifically, it determined that the 1936 contract did not show that the parties believed McFarland's name was "Spanky," nor did it convey to McFarland any right to exploit either the name and image of the character Spanky, aside from using the name in personal appearances, or the right to prevent others from doing so. The law in this area has been likened to a "haystack in a hurricane." *See Ettore v. Philco Television Broadcasting Corp.*, 229 F.2d 481, 485 (3d Cir.), *cert. denied*, 351 U.S. 926 (1956). Still, we think the district court grasped the wrong bundle when it concluded that McFarland had no interest in the exploitation of the image or name Spanky McFarland.

The "right of publicity" "signif[ies] the right of an individual, especially a public figure or a celebrity, to control the commercial value and exploitation of his name and picture or likeness and to prevent others from unfairly appropriating this value for commercial benefit." [citation omitted] ...

The district court held, in effect, that an actor who portrays a character in such a manner that the character becomes inextricably intertwined with the individual, to such an extent that the individual comes to utilize the character's name as his own, has no proprietary interest in the exploitation of the name or image. We disagree. At its heart, the value of the right of publicity is associational. People link the person with the items the person endorses and, if that person is famous, that link has value. Celebrities' names and likenesses "are things of value. Defendant has made them so, for it has taken them for its own commercial benefit." *Canessa* [*v. J.I. Kislak, Inc.*, 235 A.2d 62,] 76 [(N.J. Super. 1967)].

Other courts have concluded that the value of the right of publicity lies in the association between celebrity and product....

[T]hese decisions recognize that without identification, the right of publicity is worthless. Here, we are presented with two subtly different questions: Was there an identification of George McFarland with the character Spanky and, if so, does a right of publicity follow and vest in the performer with whom the character has become identified?

The district court saw this case as one in which George McFarland had been an actor playing the role of Spanky in the course of an employment relationship with the Studio that produced "Our Gang." Where an actor plays a well-defined part which has not become inextricably identified with his own person, it has been suggested the actor receives no right of exploitation in his portrayal of the character. [citing Justice Mosk's opinion in *Lugosi*.]

In his concurrence in *Lugosi*, Justice Mosk recognized another distinct situation where the actor could obtain proprietary interests in a screen persona: "An original creation of a fictional figure played exclusively by its creator may well be protectible." *Id.* at 330, 603 P.2d at 432 (Mosk, J., concurring). We are inclined to agree, but we think the difference between the two situations Justice Mosk contrasts is not wholly dependent on originality as his concurrence suggests. While originality plays a role, a court should also consider the association with the real life actor. Where an actor's screen persona becomes so associated with him that it becomes inseparable from the actor's own public image, the actor obtains an interest in the image which gives him standing to prevent mere interlopers from using it without authority.[15] Thus, the actor who developed the image had the right to exploit it as superior to third parties which had nothing to do with the actor or the character identified with the actor....

In the current posture of this case, we do not have to decide whether Spanky McFarland was truly identical to George McFarland or whether Spanky was merely a character created by Hal Roach. Likewise, we do not have to determine whether McFarland had done a metamorphosis into Spanky McFarland over the years before or after the 1936 contract. The successor to the Studio is not before us. Therefore, we need not decide who would prevail in a contest between that entity and McFarland's estate. We hold only that there exists at least a triable issue of fact as to whether McFarland had become so inextricably identified with Spanky McFarland that McFarland's own identity would be invoked by the name Spanky. As the Wisconsin Supreme Court stated in *Hirsch v. S.C. Johnson & Son, Inc.,* 90 Wis. 2d 379, 280 N.W.2d 129, 137 (1979), "[a]ll that is required is that the name clearly identify the wronged person." *Id.* (holding that "Crazylegs Shaving Gel" infringes on the right of publicity of football great Elroy "Crazylegs" Hirsch). On the record now before us, there is evidence of identification between the name Spanky and the actor McFarland sufficient to show that he, and now his estate, have a right of publicity superior to that of the interloper, Miller, in exploiting the name and image of Spanky McFarland. Accordingly, summary judgment was inappropriate. While others may be able to claim that they were entirely responsible for the value of the name and image or, by assignment, own the right to exploit the publicity value of the name and image of Spanky McFarland, Miller has no such claim or defense. George McFarland has alleged facts sufficient to support a right superior to that of Miller or Anaconda to exploit the items that invoke his own image.

V.

In summary, we hold that in New Jersey, the right of publicity is a proprietary right based on the identity of a character or defining trait that becomes associated with a person when he gains notoriety or fame. The right to exploit the value of that notoriety or fame belongs to the individual with whom it is associated and a cause of action for its infringement that took place during the lifetime of the individual with whom the fame is associated descends to the personal representative of the holder in New Jersey. We conclude that by virtue of his on-screen portrayal of a cherubic boy in the "Our Gang" comedy series, McFarland developed an exploitable interest to which he may lay claim if he can persuade a fact finder that he has become identified with the name Spanky. There is no individual or entity presently before this court that has superior claim to the publicity value of the nickname Spanky. Accordingly, we will remand to the district court with instruction to vacate the summary judgment entered in favor of Miller and Anaconda and for further proceedings consistent with this opinion.

---

15. We think the case in which an actor becomes known for a single role such as Batman is different. *See* Carlos V. Lozano, *West Loses Lawsuit Over Batman TV Commercial,* L.A. Times, Jan. 18, 1990, at B3 (Actor Adam West failing in bid to stop retail chain from using a Batman in a commercial that West argued invoked his portrayal). West's association with the role of Batman or Johnny Weismuller's with the role of Tarzan is different than McFarland's identification with Spanky. West's identity did not merge into Batman and Weismuller did not become indistinguishable from Tarzan. McFarland, like Groucho Marx, may have become indistinguishable in the public's eye from his stage persona of Spanky.

Groucho Marx Prods. v. Day and Night Company, Inc.

523 F. Supp. 485 (S.D.N.Y. 1981), *rev'd*, 689 F.2d 317 (2d Cir. 1982)

CONNER, District Judge:

This action arises out of the production of the musical play, "A Day in Hollywood/A Night in the Ukraine" by defendants, Day and Night Company, Inc., Alexander Cohen and the Shubert Organization. (Plaintiffs' claims against the Shubert Organization have now been otherwise resolved.) Plaintiffs, Groucho Marx Productions, Inc. and Susan Marx, as Trustee under the will of Harpo Marx, claim, inter alia, that defendants have appropriated their rights of publicity in the names and likenesses of Groucho, Harpo and Chico Marx. In their amended complaint plaintiffs also allege causes of action under Section 43(a) of the Lanham Act, 15 U.S.C. §1125(a), for misappropriation of proprietary rights, for interference with contractual relations, and for infringement of common law copyright and unfair competition. In turn, defendants have asserted third-party claims against Richard K. Vosburgh and Frank Lazarus, authors of the play.

Presently before the Court are cross-motions for summary judgment. Plaintiffs seek summary judgment based on their right-of-publicity claim. Defendants and third-party defendants (hereinafter referred to as "defendants") have cross-moved for summary judgment on all of plaintiffs' causes of action....

Background

Plaintiffs assert that [their] rights [in the characters created by the Marx Brothers] have been infringed by the play, which originally opened in the New End Theatre in London, England on January 10, 1979. The play made several other stops before opening on Broadway on May 1, 1980. Plaintiffs take issue with the second half of the play which features performers simulating the unique appearance, style and mannerisms of the Marx Brothers....

In resolving the right of publicity claim several legal issues present themselves: (1) whether New York recognizes a common law right of publicity; (2) if so, whether such a right is descendible; and (3) whether the first amendment protection of entertainment limits the scope of the right of publicity as applied in this case.

[Here, the court decided that New York recognized a common law right of publicity separate and apart from its statutory right, and that this common law right is inheritable. When making this decision, the court did not have the benefit of the New York Court of Appeals decision in *Stephano*, set forth in Chapter I.]

C. First Amendment considerations

Defendants contend that the first amendment protects dramatic performances of literary works and therefore plaintiffs' claim of infringement of the right of publicity must fail. Unquestionably, first amendment interests must be considered in defining the scope of the right; the balance between the two has been analyzed in various cases. Although "entertainment ... enjoys First Amendment protection," *Zacchini, v. Scripps Howard Broadcasting Co.*, 433 U.S. [562,] 578 [(1977)], the purpose or function of such entertainment must be scrutinized in determining the scope of the right of publicity.

As a general rule, if the defendants' works are designed primarily to promote the dissemination of thoughts, ideas or information through news or fictionalization, the right of publicity gives way to protected expression. If, however, the defendants' use of the celebrity's name or likeness is largely for commercial purposes, such as the sale of merchandise, the right of publicity prevails.

Defendants contend that New York courts have indicated that great weight should be given to first amendment considerations in defining the right of publicity. They rely on *Frosch v. Grosset & Dunlap, Inc.*, [75 A.D.2d 768, 427 N.Y.S.2d 828 (1st Dept. 1980),] in which the First Department considered a claim by the estate of Marilyn Monroe that a fictional biography violated the estate's right of publicity.... [T]he court stated:

> "Plaintiff disputes the characterization of the book as a biography. We think it does not matter whether the book is properly described as a biography, a fictional biography, or any other kind of literary work. It is not for a court to pass on literary categories, or literary judgment. It is enough that the book is a literary work and not simply a disguised commercial advertisement for the sale of goods or services. The protection of the right of free expression is so important that we should not extend any right of publicity, if such exists, to give rise to a cause of action against the publication of a literary work about a deceased person." 427 N.Y.S.2d at 829.

Clearly, the situation at issue here is not analogous to that litigated in *Frosch*. The present case does not involve publication of a book discussing the lives or careers of the Marx Brothers; the play constitutes an unauthorized appropriation of the Marx Brothers' characters by imitation of their act.

Nevertheless, *Frosch* does make clear that literary works, including fictionalizations, are entitled to protection. By analogy to copyright law and the fair use doctrine, parody, burlesque, satire and critical review might be immune from the right of publicity because of their contribution as entertainment and as a form of literary criticism. In contrast to an imitator, who usurps a work for commercial gain without contributing substantially to the work, a commentator, parodist or satirist makes use of another's attributes in order to create a larger presentation.

Defendants contend that the play is a parody of the Marx Brothers' performance and cite reviews of the play terming it a "spoof," "compendium" and "parody." Defendants also rely on the affidavit of Richard Vosburgh, author of the play and a third-party defendant here, stating that his intention was to write a satiric comment on Hollywood movies using a parody of the Marx Brothers movies as one of the literary devices.

Applying the principles discussed above to the present case, I find as a matter of law that the defendants' production of the play is not protected expression. At the request of the parties, I reviewed the play in connection with an aborted motion for preliminary injunction. Although entertainment can merit first amendment protection, entertainment that merely imitates "even if skillfully and accurately carried out, does not really have its own creative component and does not have a significant value as pure entertainment." *Estate of Elvis Presley v. Russen*, 513 F. Supp. [1339,] 1359 [(D.N.J. 1981)].*

Although literary commentary may have been the intent of the playwright, any such intent was substantially overshadowed in the play itself by the wholesale appropriation of the Marx Brothers characters. Under the fair use doctrine in copyright law, a parodist is entitled to "conjure up" the original—a concept that allows the artist considerable leeway in building upon the original. Here, defendants have gone beyond merely building on the original to the point of duplicating as faithfully as possible the performances of the Marx Brothers, albeit in a new situation with original lines. The Marx Brothers themselves were a parody on life; the play does not present a parody on their parody but instead successfully reproduced the Marx Brothers' own style of humor. Although the

---

* [The *Presley* case is set forth in subsection B., below.—*Eds.*]

playwright may have intended to comment "about 1930's Hollywood, its techniques, its stars and its excesses," Vosburgh Affidavit at 5, the content of the relevant portion of the play attempts to accomplish that objective exactly as would the Marx Brothers themselves.

This conclusion finds support in two cases dealing with appropriations of performers' acts. In *Zacchini v. Scripps-Howard Broadcasting Co.*, 433 U.S. 562 (1977), the Supreme Court considered whether the first amendment immunized from suit a television news show that had broadcast a performer's human cannonball act without his authorization. In concluding that the first amendment did not protect the defendant when it had appropriated the performer's "entire act" the Court noted:

> "'[t]he rationale for [protecting the right of publicity] is the straightforward one of preventing unjust enrichment by the theft of good will. No social purpose is served by having the defendant get free some aspect of the plaintiff that would have market value and for which he would normally pay.'... Moreover, the broadcast of petitioner's entire performance, unlike the unauthorized use of another's name for purposes of trade or the incidental use of a name or picture by the press, goes to the heart of petitioner's ability to earn a living as an entertainer. Thus, in this case, Ohio has recognized what may be the strongest case for a 'right of publicity'—involving, not the appropriation of an entertainer's reputation to enhance the attractiveness of a commercial product, but the appropriation of the very activity by which the entertainer acquired his reputation in the first place." *Id.* at 576.

In *Estate of Elvis Presley v. Russen, supra*, the court gave careful consideration to whether the defendant's production of "The Big El Show" was protected expressive activity in a suit for infringement of the right of publicity. The show starred an individual who closely resembled Presley and who imitated the appearance, dress and performing style of the deceased artist. The court found that, despite an informational and entertainment element, the show was predominantly designed to exploit Presley's likeness without otherwise contributing anything of substantial value to society. Analyzing the informational value of the show the court noted that "in comparison to a biographical film or play of Elvis Presley or a production tracing the role of Elvis Presley in the development of rock 'n roll, the information about Presley which 'The Big El Show' provides is of limited value." [513 F. Supp.] at 1360.

In this case, like the *Presley* case, the defendants have not rebroadcast Marx Brothers acts but have reproduced their manner of performances by imitating their style and appearance. The play at issue is not biographical nor can it be viewed as an attempt to convey information about the Marx Brothers themselves or about the development of their characters.

For all the reasons stated, the Court finds that defendants' production of the play is not protected and has infringed the plaintiffs' rights of publicity in the Marx Brothers characters.

[On appeal, the Second Circuit reversed, on the grounds that the district court erroneously applied New York law, instead of California law, and that California law, as interpreted in *Lugosi*, did not allow the right of publicity to be inherited. (This issue is discussed in Chapter IV.) The Second Circuit did not reach the issue of whether the right of publicity should be interpreted to include characters created by the actor him or herself, nor did it discuss the First Amendment issues.]

Notes and Questions

1. The cases in this section all deal with variations on the same theme—to what extent does someone have a right of publicity in a role that they played and with which they

have become closely identified. This problem of "ownership" is further complicated by possible overlapping ownership claims by other people, in particular, those people who created the characters (and, where the character was first introduced in print, there are also the people who dramatized the character in a play or motion picture). There is the further question whether, even assuming we wish to grant ownership interests to the actor, a common law (or statutory) right of publicity is the best way to resolve the policy issues involved. (For example, it might be best to have a *sui generis* national law, or have it subsumed in copyright law, in order to maintain uniformity.)

2. Start with *Lugosi*. Do you understand why Justice Mosk thought it improper to grant Lugosi's heirs rights in his portrayal of Dracula? Do you understand the distinction he seems to draw between Dracula and characters such as Laurel and Hardy? Is that a useful distinction? And what is the nature of the disagreement between Justice Mosk and Chief Justice Bird?

3. Moving to *McFarland*, ask yourself whether this case is distinguishable from *Lugosi*. What would be the smallest change in the facts that might have altered the outcome in *McFarland*?

4. In what way is *Marx* different from both *Lugosi* and *McFarland*? Does this difference justify a different result?

5. *Marx* also raises some unique problems because the context of the challenged use is different. What is the difference? Should the court have given more weight to that different context? (We will return to this issue in the next subsection.)

6. In Chapter II, we discussed issues of identification, and found that aspects of a person's "persona" could be a sufficient identifying characteristic—it was not necessary that a person's actual name or picture be used in all cases. (This is, of course, a matter for state law—see the *Allen v. National Video* case, below.) Was there an issue of identification in any of these three cases? If so, which ones?

7. Suppose that in *Lugosi*, the Dracula figure had not looked anything like Bela Lugosi. Would that have made a difference in the way any of the justices viewed the case?

8. If the restaurant in *McFarland* had been called simply "Spanky's" and there had been no explicit connection made in the restaurant to "Our Gang" (no pictures, etc.), would the court have come to the same result? To what degree was it important that the restaurant sought to make the connection to the Spanky character in "Our Gang"?

9. Right of publicity cases concerning characters turn out to have a relatively old pedigree. In *Chaplin v. Amadour*, 93 Cal. App. 358, 269 P. 544 (1928), the actor Charlie Chaplin sued to enjoin the distribution of movies featuring a character named "Charlie Aplin," who was intended to be an imitation of the "Little Tramp" character made famous by Chaplin. (The stage name was chosen to be close to Chaplin's name.) Upholding a judgment for Chaplin, the Court of Appeal stated:

> The case of plaintiff does not depend on his right to the exclusive use of the role, garb, and mannerisms, etc.; it is based upon *fraud and deception*. The right of action in such a case arises from the *fraudulent purpose and conduct of appellant and injury caused to the plaintiff thereby, and the deception to the public,* and it exists independently of the law regulating trade-marks, or of the ownership of such trade-marks or trade-names by plaintiff. It is plaintiff's right to be protected against those who would injure him by fraudulent means—that is, by counterfeiting his role—or, in other words, plaintiff has the right to be protected against "unfair competition in business."

93 Cal. App. at 363, 269 P. at 546 (emphais in original). Thus, it appears that the court decided in favor of Chaplin not on a property rights basis, but on an unfair competition basis, with its attendant requirement of public confusion.

10. An interesting twist on the problem of ownership of characters was presented in *Wendt v. Host International, Inc.*, 125 F.3d 806 (9th Cir. 1997). Host created an airport bar with a theme modeled after the television show *Cheers*. *Cheers* was set in a bar in Boston that had various regular patrons with unique personalities. Host licensed the use of the Cheers setting and characters from the copyright owner, Paramount. Two of the unique bar patrons in the television show, "Norm" and "Cliff," were played by actors George Wendt and John Ratzenberger, whose portrayals of the characters arguably gave them a well-known identity. (Indeed, in general, the various roles in the television show were tied to the actors who played those roles, such as Ted Danson (Sam), Shelley Long (Diane), Rhea Perlman (Carla), and Kelsey Grammer (Frasier).) In its bar, Host used animatronic robots to simulate the characters of Cliff and Norm (although they called them by other names). Not surprisingly, the robots had some general resemblance to the actors who played the roles (George Wendt, for example, is rather heavy-set). Wendt and Ratzenberger sued, claiming that their California statutory and common-law rights of publicity had been violated. What result?

11. William Shatner and Leonard Nimoy gained considerable fame playing the characters of Captain James T. Kirk and Commander Spock in the original *Star Trek* television series and in several movies. In 2009, Paramount Pictures (owners of the rights to make movies based on Gene Roddenberry's creation) released a new Star Trek movie with new actors playing the roles of Kirk and Spock. Assume that the new actors do not look like the original actors.

a. Would Shatner and Nimoy be able to prevent Paramount from portraying Kirk and Spock with different actors?

b. Would the new actors be permitted to commercialize their roles as Kirk and Spock without the consent of Shatner and Nimoy (assuming that Paramount consented to this use)?

For one judge's take on this problem, *see Wendt v. Host International, Inc.*, 197 F.3d 1284 (9th Cir. 1999) (Kozinski, J., dissenting from denial of rehearing en banc). This opinion is reproduced in Chapter X, below.

12. Suppose, in *McFarland*, that George McFarland had played other roles for which he achieved substantial public recognition. Would that have affected the court's conclusion that the "Spanky" McFarland character had "merged into" George McFarland for right of publicity purposes? In Note 11 above, can it be said that William Shatner and Leonard Nimoy, both of whom played other television roles, have not "merged into" their most well-known roles? (Shatner played the title role, a police officer, in *T.J. Hooker* and lawyer Denny Crane on *Boston Legal*, among others; and Nimoy played a prominent role in the television series *Mission: Impossible*, though he was not a member of the original cast.)

13. Suppose a restaurant created a sandwich called a "Groucho." Could Groucho Marx (or his estate) sue to enjoin the sale of that item under his name? What if the sandwich featured a cigar-like pickle protruding from one side of the sandwich? What if all of the sandwiches on the menu are named after celebrities? Does that favor the plaintiff or the defendant? *Cf.* Celebrity Sandwich, at *www.celebritysandwich.com* (last visited July 15, 2009).

14. In *Frosch v. Grosset & Dunlap*, cited by the court in *Marx*, the estate of Marilyn Monroe claimed that an allegedly fictionalized biography of her violated her right of pub-

licity. The court, eschewing the specific characterization of the work as one necessarily of fiction, responded:

> we should not extend any right of publicity, if such exists, to give rise to a cause of action against the publication of a literary work about a deceased person.

427 N.Y.S.2d at 829. The *Marx* court distinguished *Frosch* on the apparent ground that the play involved in *Marx* was not *about* the Marx Brothers, but instead was an imitation of their creations. The play in question was, in part, intended to imagine how the Marx Brothers might have interpreted Anton Chekhov's play *The Bear*. (This fact is not mentioned in the court's opinion.) In copyright terms, the play arguably makes a "transformative" use of the characters, in that it uses them in a situation that was the creation of the playwright, not the Marx Brothers. When a use is denominated transformative, that normally counts in favor of the use being deemed a "fair use" that is permitted under copyright law.

Assuming that *Frosch* did involve a fictionalized biography of Marilyn Monroe, is that use distinguishable from the play in *Marx*, which is undoubtedly also a "literary work"? (You may wish to revisit this question after reading *Estate of Presley v. Russen* and *Joplin Enterprises v. Allen* in subsection B., below.) *See also* Hicks v. Casablanca Records, 464 F. Supp. 426 (S.D.N.Y. 1978), involving a book and movie that told a fictionalized version of an event in the life of mystery writer Agatha Christie; and Guglielmi v. Spelling-Goldberg Prods., 25 Cal. 3d 860, 160 Cal. Rptr. 352, 603 P.2d 454 (1979), involving a fictionalized television biography of silent-film star Rudolph Valentino. (*Guglielmi* is reproduced in Chapter VIII, below.)

B. Celebrity Impersonators

Estate of Presley v. Russen

513 F. Supp. 1339 (D.N.J. 1981)

Brotman, District Judge:

During his lifetime, Elvis Presley established himself as one of the legends in the entertainment business. On August 16, 1977, Elvis Presley died, but his legend and worldwide popularity have survived. As Presley's popularity has subsisted and even grown, so has the capacity for generating financial rewards and legal disputes. Although the present case is another in this line, it presents questions not previously addressed. As a general proposition, this case is concerned with the rights and limitations of one who promotes and presents a theatrical production designed to imitate or simulate a stage performance of Elvis Presley.

This action is currently before the court on a motion by plaintiff, the Estate of Elvis Presley, for a preliminary injunction ... It seeks a preliminary injunction restraining defendant, Rob Russen, d/b/a THE BIG EL SHOW (hereafter Russen), or anyone acting or purporting to act in his or its behalf or in collaboration with it from using the name and service mark THE BIG EL SHOW and design, the image or likeness or persona of Elvis Presley or any equivalent, the names Elvis, Elvis Presley, Elvis in Concert, The King, and TCB or any equivalent or similar names on any goods, in any promotional materials, in any advertising or in connection with the offering or rendering of any musical services....

FINDINGS OF FACT

Plaintiff

1. Plaintiff is the Estate of Elvis Presley (hereafter the Estate) located in Memphis, Tennessee, created by the Will of Elvis Presley and is, under the laws of the State of Tennessee, a legal entity with the power to sue and be sued.

2. The Estate came into being upon the death of Elvis Presley on August 16, 1977.

3. During his career, Elvis Presley established himself as one of the premier musical talents and entertainers in the United States, Europe and other areas of the world. He was the major force behind the American Rock and Roll movement, and his influence and popularity has continued to this day. During Presley's legendary career, his talents were showcased in many ways. He performed in concert, setting attendance records and selling out houses in Las Vegas and other cities in which his tour appeared. He starred in numerous motion pictures including one entitled *Viva Las Vegas,* which is also the name of the movie's title song which Presley sang. He made records which sold over one million copies and appeared on television programs and in television specials made from his tour programs.

4. The Elvis Presley tours were billed as "Elvis in Concert," and his nightclub performances were billed as the Elvis Presley Show, while Elvis Presley shows in Las Vegas were billed simply as "Elvis." Most of Elvis Presley's record albums used the name ELVIS on the cover as part of the title. One of his albums was entitled ELVIS IN CONCERT.

5. Elvis Presley adopted the initials TCB along with a lightning bolt design to identify entertainment services provided by him. This insignia appeared on letterheads, jackets for personnel associated with the show, a ring worn by Presley while performing, and tails of Presley's airplanes. Also, Presley's band was identified as the TCB band.

6. Elvis Presley's nickname was "THE KING."

7. Although Elvis Presley exhibited a range of talents and degrees of change in his personality and physical make-up during his professional career, he, in association with his personal manager, Thomas A. (Col.) Parker, developed a certain, characteristic performing style, particularly as to his live stage shows. His voice, delivery, mannerisms (such as his hips and legs gyrations), appearance and dress (especially a certain type of jumpsuit and a ring), and actions accompanying a performance (such as handing out scarves to the audience), all contributed to this Elvis Presley style of performance.

8. One particular image or picture of Presley became closely associated with and identifiable of the entertainment provided by Elvis Presley. This image (hereafter referred to as the "Elvis pose") consisted of a picture or representation of Elvis Presley dressed in one of his characteristic jumpsuits with a microphone in his hand and apparently singing.

9. Elvis Presley exploited his name, likeness, and various images during his lifetime through records, photographs, posters, merchandise, movies, and personal appearances.

10. As a result of Presley's own talent, as well as of the various promotional efforts undertaken on his behalf, the popularity of Elvis Presley and his entertainment services, as identified by certain trademark and service marks, reached worldwide proportions. Elvis Presley productions achieved a reputation for a certain level of quality and performance. Goodwill attached to Presley's performances and the merchandise bearing his name and picture....

25. Elvis Presley's popularity did not cease upon his death. His records and tapes are still sold in considerable dollar and unit amounts and Elvis Presley movies are still shown

in theaters and on television. Elvis Presley merchandise is still in demand and sold. Also, many people travel to Memphis, Tennessee to visit Presley's gravesite and to see Graceland Mansion, his former home. The extent of Presley's continued popularity and the value and goodwill associated with him and his performances on, for example, records, film, and tape, is evidenced by the over seven (7) million dollars in royalty and licensing payments which Presley's estate received in the first two years of its existence....

27. [T]he Estate ... has an interest in protecting the licensed rights not only for their value upon their reversion to it, but also to protect its continued royalties, which it receives from the licensees' sales of records, movies, merchandise and television performances of Elvis Presley. The Estate's licensees advertise and promote the marks identifying Presley's entertainment services and licensed merchandise to maintain their commercial value and goodwill.

28. The Estate has entered into a license agreement for the use of the logo TCB and the lightning bolt design to identify a band composed of the members of Elvis Presley's backup band. The Estate receives royalties.

29. The Estate, ... has entered into a movie contract with Warner Bros. Studio for a movie about Elvis Presley.

Defendant

31. Defendant, Rob Russen d/b/a THE BIG EL SHOW (hereafter Russen) is the producer of THE BIG EL SHOW.

32. THE BIG EL SHOW is a stage production patterned after an actual Elvis Presley stage show, albeit on a lesser scale, and featuring an individual who impersonates the late Elvis Presley by performing in the style of Presley. The performer wears the same style and design of clothing and jewelry as did Presley, hands out to the audience scarves as did Presley, sings songs made popular by Presley, wears his hair in the same style as Presley, and imitates the singing voice, distinctive poses, and body movements made famous by Presley.

33. Russen charges customers to view performances of THE BIG EL SHOW or alternatively charges fees to those in whose rooms or auditoriums THE BIG EL SHOW is performed who in turn charge customers to view THE BIG EL SHOW.

34. THE BIG EL SHOW production runs for approximately ninety minutes. The show opens with the theme from the movie "2001 — A Space Odyssey" which Elvis Presley also used to open his stage shows. The production centers on Larry Seth, "Big El," doing his Elvis Presley impersonation and features musicians called the TCB Band. The TCB Band was also the name of Elvis Presley's band; however THE BIG EL SHOW TCB Band does not consist of musicians from Presley's band.

35. From the inception of THE BIG EL SHOW, the star was Larry Seth. Seth, who is under a long-term contract with THE BIG EL SHOW, recently "retired" from the show; but he may return. THE BIG EL SHOW has continued its performances by using replacements for Seth.

36. THE BIG EL SHOW was first presented in 1975 and has been performed in the United States and Canada. For example, performances have been given in cities and towns in Connecticut, Maryland, New Jersey, Pennsylvania, and Nevada (one engagement at a Hotel-Casino in Las Vegas). In addition, Larry Seth as the star of THE BIG EL SHOW has appeared on television talk shows in Philadelphia and Las Vegas, and on the David Suskind Show, a nationally syndicated program.

37. Russen has advertised the production as THE BIG EL SHOW and displayed a photograph of the star, Larry Seth, or an artist's rendering of Seth dressed and posed as if in

performance. The advertisements make such statements as "Reflections on a Legend ... A Tribute to Elvis Presley," "Looks and Sounds LIKE THE KING," "12 piece Las Vegas show band."

38. Although the various pictures and artist's rendering associated with THE BIG EL SHOW are photographs of Larry Seth, or based on such photographs, a reasonable viewer upon seeing the pictures alone would likely believe the individual portrayed to be Elvis Presley. Even with a side-to-side comparison of photographs of Larry Seth as Big El and of certain photographs of Elvis Presley, it is difficult, although not impossible, to discern any difference.

39. On October 18, 1978, Russen applied to the United States Patent and Trademark Office to register the name THE BIG EL SHOW and the design feature, of that name, *i.e.*, an artist's rendition of Larry Seth as Big El, as a service mark. Plaintiff did prepare and timely file its Notice of Opposition in the United States Patent and Trademark Office to contest the defendant's right to register the mark. The proceeding before the Trademark Trial and Appeal Board has been stayed by the Board pending the results in the suit before this court.

40. Russen has produced or had produced for him records of THE BIG EL SHOW (including two albums and three 45 RPMs). Only a limited number of these records were pressed, and they were made for sales and promotional purposes. One record album, entitled "Viva Las Vegas", has on the cover of the jacket only the title and an artist's sketch which upon reasonable observation appears to be of Elvis Presley. It is only on the back of the jacket in a short blurb and in the credits that the name BIG EL SHOW appears. It is also indicated that the show stars Larry Seth as Big El and features the TCB Band. The other album is entitled BIG EL SHOW "In Concert" and also features an artist's drawing, ostensibly of Big El, but which looks like Elvis Presley, with microphone in hand, singing. Only one of the 45s has been presented to this court. THE BIG EL SHOW insignia appears on both sides. The artists are designated as Larry Seth and TCB Orchestra, on Side I, and Larry Seth and PCB [sic] Orchestra on Side II.

41. In addition to selling records at performances of THE BIG EL SHOW, Russen sold Big El pendants and a button with the picture of Larry Seth as Big El.

42. Russen began to produce THE BIG EL SHOW and to use his certain identifying marks, such as THE BIG EL SHOW logo, after Presley had become famous as one of the premier performers in the world and had used and established certain marks as strongly identifying his services and the merchandise licensed or sub-licensed by him.

43. Russen has never had any authorization from, license or contractual relation with Elvis Presley or with the Estate of Elvis Presley in connection with the production of THE BIG EL SHOW.

DISCUSSION AND CONCLUSIONS OF LAW

...

III. *Preliminary Injunction Standards*

  A. *Likelihood of Success on the Merits*

    1. *Right of Publicity*

The plaintiff has asserted that the defendant's production, THE BIG EL SHOW, infringes on the right of publicity which plaintiff inherited from Elvis Presley....

b. *Theatrical Imitations and The Right of Publicity*

Having found that New Jersey supports a common law right of publicity, we turn our attention to a resolution of whether this right of publicity provides protection against the defendant's promotion and presentation of THE BIG EL SHOW. In deciding this issue, the circumstances and nature of defendant's activity, as well as the scope of the right of publicity, are to be considered. In a recent law journal article, the authors conducted an extensive and thorough analysis of the cases and theories bearing on media portrayals, *i.e.,* the portrayal of a real person by a news or entertainment media production. Felcher & Rubin, *Privacy, Publicity, and the Portrayal of Real People by the Media,* [hereinafter "*Portrayal*"] 88 Yale L.J. 1577, 1596 (1979). They concluded that "[t]he primary social policy that determines the legal protection afforded to media portrayals is based on the First Amendment guarantee of free speech and press." *Id.* at 1596. Thus, the purpose of the portrayal in question must be examined to determine if it predominantly serves a social function valued by the protection of free speech. If the portrayal mainly serves the purpose of contributing information, which is not false or defamatory, to the public debate of political or social issues or of providing the free expression of creative talent which contributes to society's cultural enrichment, then the portrayal generally will be immune from liability. If, however, the portrayal functions primarily as a means of commercial exploitation, then such immunity will not be granted.

The idea that the scope of the right of publicity should be measured or balanced against societal interests in free expression has been recognized and discussed in the case law and by other legal commentators. In general, in determining whether a plaintiff's right of publicity can be invoked to prevent a defendant's activity, the courts have divided along the lines set out above. In cases finding the expression to be protected, the defendant's activity has consisted of the dissemination of such information as "thoughts, ideas, newsworthy events, … matters of public interest," and fictionalizations. The importance of protecting fictionalizations and related efforts as against rights of publicity was explained by Chief Justice Bird of the California Supreme Court:

> Contemporary events, symbols and people are regularly used in fictional works. Fiction writers may be able to more persuasively, more accurately express themselves by weaving into the tale persons or events familiar to their readers. The choice is theirs. No author should be forced into creating mythological worlds or characters wholly divorced from reality. The right of publicity derived from public prominence does not confer a shield to ward off caricature, parody and satire. Rather, prominence invites creative comment.[18]

Guglielmi, 25 Cal. 3d at 869, 160 Cal. Rptr. at 358, 603 P.2d at 460 (Bird, C.J., concurring).

On the other hand, most of those cases finding that the right of publicity, or its equivalence, prevails have involved the use of a famous name or likeness predominantly in connection with the sale of consumer merchandise or "solely 'for purposes of trade — *e.g.,* merely to attract attention.' [without being artistic, informational or newsworthy]

---

18. This idea of creative comment precluding a right of publicity claim can be analogized to the doctrine of fair use in the copyright law. Although the right of publicity is not the same as a right in a copyright, there are similarities, particularly where a personality's likeness or name is closely connected with a distinctive style of performance. In some respects this situation is similar to a copyright in a character.

The doctrine of fair use may provide guidance as to what types of uses of a name or likeness should be allowed. Fair use has been described as a "privilege in others than the owner of a copyright to use the copyright material in a reasonable manner without his consent, notwithstanding the monopoly granted to the owner…." Ball, COPYRIGHT AND LITERARY PROPERTY 260 (1944).

Grant v. Esquire, Inc., 367 F. Supp. 876, 881 (S.D.N.Y. 1973) [unauthorized use of photo of Cary Grant in fashion article]." *Ali v. Playgirl, Inc.,* 447 F. Supp. 723, 727, 728–29 (S.D.N.Y. 1978) (unauthorized drawing of nude man, recognizable as Muhammed Ali, seated in corner of boxing ring). In these cases, it seems clear that the name or likeness of the public figure is being used predominantly for commercial exploitation, and thus is subject to the right of publicity. As the court in *Palmer v. Schonhorn, supra,* noted, "While one who is a public figure or is presently newsworthy may be the proper subject of news or informative presentation, the privilege does *not extend to commercialization of his personality through a form of treatment distinct from the dissemination of news or information.*" *Id.* 96 N.J. Super. at 78, 232 A.2d 458 quoting *Gautier v. Pro-Football, Inc.,* 304 N.Y. 354, 359 (1952) (emphasis added by Palmer court).

In the present case, the defendant's expressive activity, THE BIG EL SHOW production, does not fall clearly on either side. Based on the current state of the record, the production can be described as a live theatrical presentation or concert designed to imitate a performance of the late Elvis Presley. The show stars an individual who closely resembles Presley and who imitates the appearance, dress, and characteristic performing style of Elvis Presley. The defendant has made no showing, nor attempted to show, that the production is intended to or acts as a parody, burlesque, satire, or criticism of Elvis Presley.[21] As a matter of fact, the show is billed as "A TRIBUTE TO ELVIS PRESLEY." In essence, we confront the question of whether the use of the likeness of a famous deceased entertainer in a performance mainly designed to imitate that famous entertainer's own past stage performances is to be considered primarily as a commercial appropriation by the imitator or show's producer of the famous entertainer's likeness or as a valuable contribution of information or culture. After careful consideration of the activity, we have decided that although THE BIG EL SHOW contains an informational and entertainment element, the show serves primarily to commercially exploit the likeness of Elvis Presley without contributing anything of substantial value to society. In making this decision, the court recognizes that certain factors distinguish this situation from the pure commercial use of a picture of Elvis Presley to advertise a product. In the first place, the defendant uses Presley's likeness in an entertainment form and, as a general proposition, "entertainment ... enjoys First Amendment protection." However, entertainment that is merely a copy or imitation, even if skillfully and accurately carried out, does not really have its own creative component and does not have a significant value as pure entertainment. As one authority has emphasized:

> The public interest in entertainment will support the sporadic, occasional and good-faith imitation of a famous person to achieve humor, to effect criticism or to season a particular episode, but it does not give a privilege to appropriate another's valuable attributes on a continuing basis as one's own without the consent of the other.

Netterville, *Copyright and Tort Aspects of Parody, Mimicry and Humorous Commentary*, 35 S. Cal. L. Rev. 225, 254 (1962).

---

21. Using an analogy to copyright law and the doctrine of fair use, *see* note 18, *supra,* a parody, burlesque, satire or critical review might be allowed because of their "historic importance and social value," *Berlin v. E.C. Publications, Inc.,* 329 F.2d 541, 544 (2nd Cir. 1964) and because of their contribution to society "both as entertainment and as a form of social and literary criticism." *Id.* at 545. Unlike a copier, a parodist or satirist adds his own new and creative touches to the original work, which, in this case, would be the likeness of Elvis Presley as he is performing. The original work basically becomes part of a new and different work which derives its popularity from the added creative elements. The original work, or the likeness of Elvis Presley, is being used in a different manner and for a different purpose.

In the second place, the production does provide information in that it illustrates a performance of a legendary figure in the entertainment industry. Because of Presley's immense contribution to rock 'n roll, examples of him performing can be considered of public interest. However, in comparison to a biographical film or play of Elvis Presley or a production tracing the role of Elvis Presley in the development of rock 'n roll, the information about Presley which THE BIG EL SHOW provides is of limited value.

This recognition that defendant's production has some value does not diminish our conclusion that the primary purpose of defendant's activity is to appropriate the commercial value of the likeness of Elvis Presley. Our decision receives support from two recent cases. In *Price v. Worldvision Enterprises, Inc.,* 455 F. Supp. 252 (S.D.N.Y. 1978), *aff'd without opinion,* 603 F.2d 214 (2nd Cir. 1979), the court found that the protection of the right of publicity could be invoked by the widows and beneficiaries, respectively, of Oliver Hardy and Stanley Laurel to enjoin the production or distribution of a television series entitled "Stan 'n Ollie," wherein two actors would portray the comedians Laurel and Hardy. Although the facts bearing on the content of the program are not entirely clear, it appears that the show was to be based on old Laurel and Hardy routines which the comedy team performed during the careers and was not a biographical portrayal of the lives of the two men. In this regard, the court can be deemed to have decided that an inherited "right of publicity" can be invoked to protect against the unauthorized use of the name or likeness of a famous entertainer, who is deceased, in connection with an imitation, for commercial benefit, of a performance of that famous entertainer.

In *Zacchini v. Scripps-Howard Broadcasting Co.,* 433 U.S. 562 (1977), the Supreme Court addressed a situation which implicated both a performer's right of publicity and the First Amendment. The Court held that the First Amendment did not prevent a state from deciding that a television news show's unauthorized broadcast of a film showing plaintiff's "entire act," a fifteen second human cannonball performance, infringed plaintiff's right of publicity.

In the present case, although the defendant has not shown a film of an Elvis Presley performance, he has engaged in a similar form of behavior by presenting a live performance starring an imitator of Elvis Presley. To some degree, the defendant has appropriated the "very activity [live stage show] by which [Presley initially] acquired his reputation ..." *id.* at 576, and from which the value in his name and likeness developed. The death of Presley diminishes the impact of certain of the court's reasons, especially the one providing for an economic incentive to produce future performances. However, through receiving royalties, the heirs of Presley are the beneficiaries of the "right of the individual to reap the reward of his endeavors." *Id.* at 573. Under the state's right of publicity, they are entitled to protect the commercial value of the name or likeness of Elvis Presley from activities such as defendant's which may diminish this value.

We thus find that the plaintiff has demonstrated a likelihood of success on the merits of its right of publicity claim with respect to the defendant's live stage production. In addition, we find this likelihood of success as to the defendant's unauthorized use of Elvis Presley's likeness on the cover or label of any records or on any pendants which are sold or distributed by the defendant....

B. *Irreparable Injury*

Having found that the plaintiff is likely to succeed on the merits as to certain claims, we must next examine the second requirement for a plaintiff seeking a preliminary injunction. The plaintiff must demonstrate that irreparable injury will result if an injunction is not granted *pendente lite.*

1. *Right of Publicity*

Although the plaintiff has shown a likelihood of success on the merits of its right of publicity claim, the plaintiff has not made a sufficient showing that irreparable injury will result if the defendant's production is not preliminarily enjoined. In making this decision, we note that we are treating a right of publicity claim different than a service mark infringement or unfair competition claim. Because the doctrine of the right of publicity emphasizes the protection of the commercial value of the celebrity's name or likeness, the plaintiff must demonstrate sufficiently that the defendant's use of the name and likeness of the celebrity has or is likely to result in an identifiable economic loss. In contrast, in the context of the service mark infringement, unfair competition, and §43(a) of the Lanham Act claims, we found that irreparable injury could result even in the absence of economic harm *per se*. One reason for this difference in approach stems from the public deception which is part of the latter three causes of action, but not part of the right of publicity claim. As a result of such public deception or confusion as to source, the plaintiff is being harmed. The plaintiff is being unfairly compelled to place the control of the good will attached to its entertainment services in the hands of the defendant.

In addition, and perhaps even more importantly, the close relationship in this case between the right of publicity and the societal considerations of free expression supports the position that the plaintiff in seeking relief for an infringement of its rights of publicity should demonstrate an identifiable economic harm. As we noted earlier, the defendant's activity when viewed simply as a skilled, good faith imitation of an Elvis Presley performance, *i.e.*, without the elements leading to a likelihood of confusion, is, in some measure, consistent with the goals of freedom of expression. Thus, before the harsh step of barring defendant's activity is undertaken, the plaintiff should have to make a showing of immediate, irreparable harm to the commercial value of the right of publicity and should not be able to rely on an intangible potentiality.

In light of these comments, we find that the plaintiff has not made a sufficient showing that the presentation of this particular production, THE BIG EL SHOW, has resulted in any loss of commercial benefits to the plaintiff or will result in an irreparable commercial harm in the near future. The plaintiff has not adequately demonstrated that the existence of defendant's activity has led to or is likely to lead to a diminished ability of the plaintiff to profit from the use of Elvis Presley's name or likeness. For example, there is insufficient evidence that plaintiff's (or its licensees') ability to enter into agreements licensing the use of Presley's name or likeness in connection with consumer products is seriously jeopardized by defendant's activity. As a matter of fact, it is even possible that defendant's production has stimulated the public's interest in buying Elvis Presley merchandise or in seeing films or hearing records embodying actual Elvis Presley performances. Thus, the defendant's show will not be preliminarily enjoined.

[The court found that other activities of the defendant should be enjoined, and issued a preliminary injunction against those activities.]

Joplin Enterprises v. Allen
795 F. Supp. 349 (W.D. Wash. 1992)

[This suit was brought to enjoin the production of *Janis*,] a two-act play about Janis Joplin, a renowned rock and blues singer who, sadly, died young in 1970. Act I fictionally portrays Ms. Joplin's experiences over the course of a day previous to an evening's concert performance.... Act I contains only one song.... Act II simulates an evening's concert performance by Ms. Joplin. [Plaintiff claims a violation of Joplin's right of publicity.]

... Acts I and II of *Janis* must be viewed together in the context of plaintiffs' right of publicity claims. Plaintiffs have attempted to pursue their claims against Act II of *Janis* as if Act I did not exist or could be analyzed separately. Yet they admit that "[a]s written and produced [*Janis*] occurs in two acts." They also admit that Act I is "a protected form of expression." ...

[The California statute, which contains an exemption for a "play, book [or] musical composition,"] clearly contemplates examining the use of a deceased personality's name, voice, etc., in terms of the total context in which it appears. Where a use is for the purpose of advertising goods or services, it is prohibited. Identical use in the context of a play is protected. To analyze Act II of *Janis* out of context would destroy the statutory exemption....

Allowing plaintiffs to assert a right of publicity only in a severable Act II would legitimate right of publicity claims based, for example, on a photograph in the back of a stage set, a comedian's imitation of a famous figure, or a celebrity's likeness on the cover of a biography. The right of publicity cannot rationally reach so far. Therefore, Act II of *Janis* occurs in the context of Act I and constitutes only a portion of the entire play. Under California law, plaintiffs cannot state a legally cognizable right of publicity claim in this case.

———————

Notes and Questions

1. You may wonder how, after *Presley*, there are so many Elvis impersonators in places like Las Vegas. The answer, at least for Las Vegas, is found in the Nevada statutes relating to rights of publicity. 52 Rev. Stat. Nev. § 597.790(2)(d) provides an exemption from liability for violating another's right of publicity if

> The use is an attempt to portray, imitate, simulate or impersonate a person in a play, book, magazine article, newspaper article, musical composition, film, or a radio, television or other audio or visual program, except where the use is directly connected with commercial sponsorship

2. Consider the following statutory provision, from the state of Washington:

> For purposes of RCW 63.60.050 [the Washington right of publicity statute], the use of a name, voice, signature, photograph, or likeness in connection with matters of cultural, historical, political, religious, educational, newsworthy, or public interest, including, without limitation, comment, criticism, satire, and parody relating thereto, shall not constitute a use for which consent is required under this chapter.

R.C.W. § 63.60.070. Would the Big El Show be exempt from liability under this statute?

3. Once the *Presley* court found a likelihood of success on the right of publicity claim, why did it not issue an injunction? If the right of publicity is truly a property right, why isn't it sufficient that defendant interfered with plaintiff's property?

4. Suppose that Russen started his show with a brief "dream" sequence or a séance calling up the image of Elvis Presley in concert, followed by the show. Would that suffice under *Joplin* to avoid a right of publicity claim under the California statute? If not, what would be the minimum Russen would have to do to comply with California law?

5. Suppose that Russen had written his own original songs and had them sung in the persona (and style) of Elvis Presley. Would that have changed the outcome of the case?

6. Does this case affect the ability of comedic celebrity impersonators to ply their trade? Can an impersonator like Rich Little or Frank Caliendo imitate a celebrity without violating the celebrity's right of publicity? Can an impersonator perform those imitations in advertisements for goods or services? On the latter issue, see *Allen v. National Video, Inc.*, below.

7. One entertainment phenomenon of relatively recent vintage is the "tribute band." As in *Russen*, such bands attempt to imitate faithfully a well-known band, especially one that either no longer gives concerts or that rarely does so. In some cases, courts have found against tribute bands on the grounds that they either interfere with the original artists' rights of publicity or that there is a likelihood of confusion about whether they are authorized. *See, e.g.*, Apple Corps Ltd. v. A.D.P.R., 843 F. Supp. 342 (M.D. Tenn. 1993); Apple Corps Ltd. v. Leber, 229 U.S.P.Q. 1015 (Cal. Super. 1986). *See generally* Krissi Geary, *Tribute Bands: Flattering Imitators or Flagrant Infringers*, 29 S. Ill U.L. Rev. 481 (2005). Is the fear that some people would be confused about either the identities of the members of the band, or the authorization of the original band for the tribute band, a realistic one?

Allen v. National Video, Inc.
610 F. Supp. 612 (S.D.N.Y. 1985)

MOTLEY, Chief Judge:

This case arises because plaintiff [Woody Allen], to paraphrase Groucho Marx, wouldn't belong to any video club that would have him as a member. More precisely, plaintiff sues over an advertisement for defendant National Video (National) in which defendant Boroff, allegedly masquerading as plaintiff, portrays a satisfied holder of National's movie rental V.I.P. Card. Plaintiff asserts that the advertisement appropriates his face and implies his endorsement, and that it therefore violates his statutory right to privacy, his right to publicity, and the federal Lanham Act's prohibition of misleading advertising....

Defendants, while conceding that Boroff looks remarkably like plaintiff, deny that the advertisement appropriates plaintiff's likeness or that it poses a likelihood of consumer confusion....

FACTS

... The present action arises from an advertisement, placed by National to promote its nationally franchised video rental chain, containing a photograph of defendant Boroff taken on September 2, 1983. The photograph portrays a customer in a National Video store, an individual in his forties, with a high forehead, tousled hair, and heavy black glasses. The customer's elbow is on the counter, and his face, bearing an expression at once quizzical and somewhat smug, is leaning on his hand. It is not disputed that, in general, the physical features and pose are characteristic of plaintiff.

The staging of the photograph also evokes associations with plaintiff. Sitting on the counter are videotape cassettes of "Annie Hall" and "Bananas," two of plaintiff's best known films, as well as "Casablanca" and "The Maltese Falcon." The latter two are Humphrey Bogart films of the 1940's associated with plaintiff primarily because of his play and film "Play It Again, Sam," in which the spirit of Bogart appears to the character played by Allen and

Figure 3-2. The National Video advertisement

offers him romantic advice. In addition, the title "Play It Again, Sam" is a famous, although inaccurate, quotation from "Casablanca."

The individual in the advertisement is holding up a National Video V.I.P. Card, which apparently entitles the bearer to favorable terms on movie rentals. The woman behind the counter is smiling at the customer and appears to be gasping in exaggerated excitement at the presence of a celebrity.

The photograph was used in an advertisement which appeared in the March 1984 issue of "Video Review," a magazine published in New York and distributed in the Southern District, and in the April 1984 issue of "Take One," an in-house publication which National distributes to its franchisees across the country. The headline on the advertisement reads "Become a V.I.P. at National Video. We'll Make You Feel Like a Star." The copy goes on to explain that holders of the V.I.P. card receive "hassle-free movie renting" and "special savings" and concludes that "you don't need a famous face to be treated to some pretty famous service."

The same photograph and headline were also used on countercards distributed to National's franchisees. Although the advertisement that ran in "Video Review" contained a disclaimer in small print reading "Celebrity double provided by Ron Smith's Celebrity Look-Alike's, Los Angeles, Calif.," no such disclaimer appeared in the other versions of the advertisement.

None of the defendants deny that the advertisements in question were designed, placed, and authorized by defendant National, that defendant Boroff was selected and posed as he was to capitalize on his resemblance to plaintiff and to attract the attention of movie watchers, that defendants Boroff and Smith were aware of this purpose in agreeing to supply Boroff's services, and that in fact Smith and Boroff have on other occasions offered the services of Boroff, a Los Angeles-based actor and director, as a look-alike for plaintiff. Moreover, defendants do not dispute that the photograph in question was used for commercial purposes, and that plaintiff did not give his consent to the use of the photograph....

DISCUSSION

Privacy and Publicity Claims

Plaintiff's right to privacy claim, upon which the parties have focused in this litigation, is based on sections 50 and 51 of the New York Civil Rights Law. These narrowly drawn provisions were enacted in the early years of the century when recognition of the novel right was controversial....

The right to privacy recognized by the Civil Rights law has been strictly construed, both because it is in derogation of New York common law and because of potential conflict with the First Amendment, particularly where public figures are involved. To make out a violation, a plaintiff must satisfy three distinct elements: 1) use of his or her name, portrait, or picture, 2) for commercial or trade purposes, 3) without written permission. Merely suggesting certain characteristics of the plaintiff, without literally using his or her name, portrait, or picture, is not actionable under the statute. Plaintiff here must therefore demonstrate, *inter alia,* that the advertisement in question appropriates his "portrait or picture." ...

Plaintiff argues that Boroff's physical resemblance to him, when viewed in conjunction with the undeniable attempt to evoke plaintiff's image through the selection of props and poses, makes the photograph in question a "portrait or picture" of plaintiff as a matter of law. Plaintiff notes that it is not necessary that all persons seeing the photograph actually identify him, only that he be *identifiable* from the photograph. Plaintiff contends that it is beyond cavil that some people will recognize him in this photograph. The cited cases, however, involved photographs which were not disputed to be of the plaintiffs; the only question was whether the pictures were too old or too obscure to be recognizable. They do not help us answer the more basic question of whether the photograph in the case at bar is, in fact, a "picture" or "portrait" of plaintiff.

More helpful are a line of cases holding that any recognizable likeness, not just an actual photograph, may qualify as a "portrait or picture." *See, e.g., Ali v. Playgirl, Inc.,* 447 F. Supp. 723, 726 (S.D.N.Y. 1978) ("clearly recognizable" drawing of plaintiff Muhammad Ali portrayed as boxer in ring, captioned "The Greatest," constitutes "portrait or picture")....

Therefore, if defendants had used, for example, a clearly recognizable painting or cartoon of plaintiff, it would certainly constitute a "portrait or picture" within the meaning of the statute. The case of a look-alike, however, is more problematic. A painting, drawing or manikin has no existence other than as a representation of something or someone; if the subject is recognizable, then the work is a "portrait." Defendant Boroff, however, is not a manikin. He is a person with a right to his own identity and his own face. Plaintiff's privacy claim therefore requires the court to answer the almost metaphysical question of when one person's face, presented in a certain context, becomes, as a matter of law, the face of another.

This question is not merely theoretical. The use in an advertisement of a drawing, which *has* no other purpose than to represent its subject, must give rise to a cause of action under the Civil Rights Law, because it raises the obvious implication that its subject has endorsed or is otherwise involved with the product being advertised. There is no question that this amounts to an appropriation of another's likeness for commercial advantage.

A living and breathing actor, however, has the right to exploit his or her own face for commercial gain. This right is itself protected by the Civil Rights Law. The privacy law does not prohibit one from evoking certain aspects of another's personality, but it does prohibit one from actually representing oneself as another person. The look-alike situation falls somewhere in between and therefore presents a difficult question.

The court is aware of only one case on point. In *Onassis v. Christian Dior N.Y. Inc.*, 122 Misc. 2d 603, 472 N.Y.S.2d 254 (Sup. Ct. 1983), plaintiff Jacqueline Kennedy Onassis won an injunction against an advertisement featuring a model who was made up to look like her. The advertisement was part of a series, which appeared for several weeks in major fashion and news magazines, featuring a trio of risque sophisticates known as "The Diors." The advertisements followed the developing relationship (and stunning Christian Dior wardrobes) of the imaginary *menage a trois*, including, in one week's installment, the marriage of two of the trio in a stylish, "legendary private affair." *Onassis*, 472 N.Y.S.2d at 257. Appearing among the guests at the soiree, which was portrayed in one large photograph, were several actual celebrities—actress Ruth Gordon, television personality Gene Shalit, and actress/model Shari Belafonte—and a Jacqueline Onassis double provided, as in this case, by Ron Smith's Celebrity Look-Alikes. *Id.*

The *Onassis* court found that the advertisement violated plaintiff's rights under section 51 of the Civil Rights Law. The court held that an exact duplication of plaintiff was not necessary to make out a cause of action under the statute, so long as the overall impression created clearly was that plaintiff had herself appeared in the advertisement. 472 N.Y.S.2d at 262.

> We are dealing here with actuality and appearance, where illusion often heightens reality and all is not quite what it seems. Is the illusionist to be free to step aside, having reaped the benefits of his creation, and be permitted to disclaim the very impression he sought to create? If we were to permit it, we would be sanctioning an obvious loophole to evade the statute. If a person is unwilling to give his or her endorsement to help sell a product, either at an offered price or any price, no matter—hire a double and the same effect is achieved.

472 N.Y.S.2d at 261.

The "illusion" created in *Onassis* was that plaintiff had actually appeared in the advertisement. Therefore, the court's holding was consistent with the long-standing requirement under section 51 that the commercial use complained of amount to a "portrait or picture" of an individual, not merely the suggestion of some aspect of a person's public persona. In other words, in the context of the advertisement, the look-alike's face was, as a matter of law, a portrait of Jacqueline Onassis. Important to the court's holding was the unusually realistic tone of the advertisement.

> The juxtaposition of the counterfeit figure just behind the real-life figures of a veteran actress, a TV personality, and a well-known model lends the whole ensemble an air of verisimilitude and accentuates the grievance, for it imparts an aura of authenticity to the trumped up tableau.

472 N.Y.S.2d at 262.

The question of whether a photograph presents a recognizable likeness of a person is ordinarily one for the jury. When, as in *Onassis*, the look-alike seems indistinguishable from the real person and the context of the advertisement clearly implies that he or she is the real celebrity, a court may hold as a matter of law that the look-alike's face is a "portrait or picture" of plaintiff. *Onassis* presented an unusual factual setting, in which the mixture of fantasy and reality suggested almost unavoidably the actual presence of the real-life celebrity. In order for the court to reach the same conclusion in the present case, it must conclude on the undisputed facts that the photograph in question similarly creates, as a matter of law, the illusion of Woody Allen's actual presence in the advertisement.

It is not disputed here that in this photograph defendant Boroff is meant to look like Woody Allen. The pose, expression, and props all support the suggestion. However, the question before the court is not whether some, or even most, people will be *reminded* of plaintiff when they see this advertisement. In order to find that the photograph contains plaintiff's "portrait or picture," the court would have to conclude that most persons who could identify an actual photograph of plaintiff would be likely to think that this was actually his picture. This standard is necessary since we deal not with the question of whether an undisputed picture of plaintiff is recognizable to some, but whether an undisputed picture of defendant Boroff should be regarded, as a matter of law, to *be* a portrait or picture of plaintiff.

The court notes several factors that might militate against summary adjudication of this question. First, there are several physical differences between plaintiff's face and that of defendant Boroff. Defendant's photo shows larger eyebrows, a wider face, and more uneven complexion than plaintiff's, and somewhat different glasses than plaintiff generally wears.

Moreover, the hair style and expression, while characteristic of the endearing "schlemiel" embodied by plaintiff in his earlier comic works, are out of step with plaintiff's post-"Annie Hall" appearance and the serious image and somber mien that he has projected in recent years. While this distinction would be of no moment if defendants had appropriated an actual photograph of plaintiff from 15 years ago such as those submitted by plaintiff for comparison, it is relevant to the question of whether the audience of movie watchers at whom this advertisement was aimed would conclude that plaintiff had actually appeared in the 1984 advertisement.

Finally, unlike in *Onassis,* where no other plausible interpretation was offered for the presence of the Jacqueline Onassis figure behind the real Ruth Gordon, *et al.,* here defendants argue for a view of the advertisement consistent with the presence of a look-alike who is not thought to be Woody Allen himself. The court has some doubts as to the ultimate persuasiveness of this interpretation. We are unable to conclude, however, that no reasonable jury could find that others would so interpret the advertisement, or at least recognize it to contain a look-alike, particularly in light of the distinctions noted above. Therefore, while the court finds that the advertisement at bar clearly makes *reference* to plaintiff, it hesitates to conclude that the photograph is, as a matter of law, plaintiff's portrait or picture.

[Because the plaintiff can obtain identical relief under the federal trademark statute, the Lanham Act,] the court finds it unnecessary to resolve plaintiff's privacy claim. Defendants' motion for summary judgment on the privacy claim therefore also need not be reached, except to the extent that similar counter-arguments are offered in the context of the Lanham Act discussion below.

[On the Lanham Act claim, the court reached the "inescapable conclusion that defendants' use of Boroff's photograph in their advertisement creates a likelihood of consumer confusion over plaintiff's endorsement or involvement," and issued an injunction.]*

---

* Lanham Act claims as a means of protecting rights of publicity are discussed below in Chapter V. — *Eds.*

Notes and Questions

1. This case required an interpretation of the New York right of privacy statute (New York, as you recall, does not have a separate right of publicity statute). Thus, the exact wording of the statute, rather than the general policy concerning rights of publicity, was in the forefront of the court's decision. This is not to say that New York is unique in this regard (although its statute may be more restrictive than many other states). Numerous states have statutory rights of publicity and courts must interpret the words of those statutes in order to determine whether the plaintiff has a cognizable claim. However, in some states the right of publicity is based on common law, which means that the court is not tied to any specific wording. (California has both statutory and common law rights.)

2. In the *Onassis* case cited by the *Allen* court, the New York court held that the use of a look-alike of Jacqueline Onassis constituted a violation of her right of publicity (or privacy, in New York terms). Yet the *Allen* court appeared reluctant to find a violation of the New York statute. Can you explain how the court distinguished this case from *Onassis*?

3. The advertiser in *Allen* had a small but readable disclaimer in the advertisement, stating that it had used a celebrity impersonator. Why didn't that change the outcome? What if Mr. Boroff had stated in a television advertisement "Although I'm not Woody Allen, he and I obviously have a lot in common. We both like movies, for example. And I am here to tell you that National Video is the best place to rent the movies that you like." Would that have been a violation of New York law?

4. If a celebrity can own the rights to her stage persona, and perhaps to characters with which she is closely identified, can she own rights to her "style" of doing things on stage? Analogous questions were raised in two New York cases. In *Miller v. Universal Pictures Co,* 11 A.D.2d 47, 201 N.Y.S.2d 632 (1st Dept. 1960), Universal, which owned the rights to the movie "The Glenn Miller Story," licensed an affiliate to sell recordings of the soundtrack. Universal had contracted with Miller's widow for various rights to make the movie, including the use of photographs of Miller and his family. The soundtrack did not use actual Glenn Miller band recordings—Universal hired a band to imitate the sound as precisely as possible. Although the contract between Universal and Miller's widow purported to include a license by the widow to Universal to use the Glenn Miller "sound," the court held that no such rights ever existed:

> Plaintiff never had, and certainly does not now have, any property interests in the Glenn Miller 'sound'. Indeed, in the absence of palming off or confusion, even while Glenn Miller was alive, others might have meticulously duplicated or imitated his renditions.

201 N.Y.S.2d at 634. (Even today, a sound recording copyright would not cover a recording made by another, even if the second recording was essentially identical to the original. *See* 17 U.S.C. § 114(b).)

In *Lombardo v. Doyle, Dane & Bernbach, Inc.,* 58 A.D.2d 620, 396 N.Y.S.2d 661 (2d Dept. 1977), band leader Guy Lombardo sued an advertising agency which used a New Year's Eve theme in an advertisement including a band playing music often associated with Lombardo's band and a bandleader who imitated Lombardo's conducting "style." (For more than forty years, Lombardo's band was broadcast nationally on New Year's

Eve — first on radio, later on television — and it became especially well-known for its rendition of "Auld Lang Syne.") The court rejected a claim brought under New York's statute:

> In the case at bar, plaintiff-respondent Guy Lombardo asks that the word "rep-utation" be equated to "name", and the words "mental image or likeness" to "pic-ture". As set forth above, the statute does not lend itself to such interpretation.... Accordingly, it is clear that the Civil Rights Law is to be strictly construed and is not to be applied so as to prohibit the portrayal of an individual's personality or style of performance.

396 N.Y.S.2d at 622. However, the court went on to allow a common-law claim for appropriation of personality (this was prior to the *Stephano* decision set out in Chapter 1):

> [T]here is no question but that a celebrity has a legitimate proprietary interest in his public personality. Guy Lombardo has invested 40 years in developing his public personality as Mr. New Year's Eve, an identity that has some marketable status. The combination of New Year's Eve, balloons, party hats, and "Auld Lang Syne" in this context might amount to an exploitation of that carefully and painstakingly built public personality. As such, it may be entitled to protec-tion....
>
> Moreover, if these allegations are proved, there would be an element of decep-tion of the public.... [T]he crux of the third cause of action herein is that the imitation is completely unfair, amounts to a deception of the public, and thus exploits the respondent's property right in his public personality.

Id. at 664–65. It is unclear from the court's discussion whether the common-law right thus described was essentially one of unfair competition, requiring some element of deception or confusion, or whether it was a right of property, granting Lombardo broad rights to prevent the use of New Year's Eve theme bands in advertising, even if it was clear that it was not his band that was being portrayed.

Problem 3

Robert Burck earns a living as a "street entertainer," who uses the persona of the "Naked Cowboy." He sings and plays the guitar while attired only in a cowboy hat, cowboy boots, and underwear. Mars, Inc., which makes M&Ms, decided to use the Naked Cowboy motif in an advertising campaign, but featuring an M&M dressed as the naked cowboy. Mars knew about Burck, and the fact that he used the Naked Cowboy persona, prior to launch-ing the advertising campaign. Mars never requested, or received permission from Burck to use the Naked Cowboy concept in its advertising. [See Figure 3.3.]

1. Would Burck have a claim under the New York right of privacy statute?

2. Would Burck have a claim under the California right of privacy statute?

3. Would Burck have a claim under the common law of California?

4. Would Burck have a claim under the common law of New Jersey?

Figure 3-3. The M&M and the Naked Cowboy

C. Comparative Law

In many common law countries, each of the judges issues his or her own opinion (sometimes merely concurring with that of another). They do not necessarily issue them in the expected order—*i.e.*, majority first. Therefore, one may have to read all of the opinions and count votes in order to determine who won the case.

Pacific Dunlop Ltd. v. Hogan

23 F.C.R. 553, 87 A.L.R. 14 (Fed. Ct. Australia 1989)

SHEPPARD, BEAUMONT and BURCHETT JJ.

SHEPPARD J.:

...

2. The case is concerned, as the orders suggest, with advertisements for shoes marketed by the appellant. The advertisements were intended to and did recall to the minds of persons seeing them a scene from the motion picture, "Crocodile Dundee" (now referred to as "Crocodile Dundee I") known as the "knife scene".

3. The film, "Crocodile Dundee I", is well known and has been the subject of much public discussion and comment. The star of the film is Mr. Hogan whose career is already well known to the great majority of Australians....

4. Mr. Hogan came under public notice in Australia when he played a prominent part in an extensive advertising campaign for cigarettes marketed under the name, "Winfield". The campaign was conducted from 1970 to 1979 when, so I believe, cigarette advertising was banned on television. As [the trial judge] has said, the campaign projected the char-

acter of Mr. Hogan as down-to-earth and irreverent and with something of the good-natured larrikin in him. Although the matter is not mentioned in this part of his Honour's judgment, Mr. Hogan was also well known for advertisements made for a well known brewer of beer and for a variety show, known as "The Paul Hogan Show", some excerpts from which are in evidence. In more recent times he has been featured in a large number of advertisements for the Australian Tourist Commission.... Unquestionably, all Mr. Hogan's advertising has been highly successful. It has given him a large public following in this country. The characters which he played in the variety show had a similar stamp about them to the character—Mr. Hogan himself is featured in the advertisements. In a broad sense they were extensions, or rather, exaggerations of Mr. Hogan's personality as revealed in the various advertising campaigns to which I have referred.

5. In the film Mr. Hogan stars as the principal character, Mick or Crocodile Dundee. This character, although fictitious, is another extension or exaggeration of Mr. Hogan's own personality, as projected in the various television advertisements to which I have referred. It is correct to say that the character undertakes many feats which, to use an expression used in the course of argument, are larger than life and highly improbable. Usually they are portrayed in a laconic, laid-back style and yet are all pervaded with a certain cockiness and insolence. All these characteristics are said to be dear to the hearts of many Australians and indeed to reveal the type of personality which Australians like to think they have, even if this involves a certain amount of self-deception....

7. [The trial judge's] description of the knife scene, which is critical for the case, is as follows:

> "Mick Dundee and Sue Charlton are walking arm in arm through the colonnade. They are approached by three young persons, one of whom asks the hero for a light. He replies 'Yeah sure kid. There you go', but the response is a demand for the hero's wallet. The heroine says in alarm 'Mick! give him your wallet'. Mick says in a relaxed fashion 'What for?' She replies 'He's got a knife'. Mick then laughs and responds 'That's not a knife', producing a formidable hunting knife with the words '*That's* a knife'. Mick uses the knife to slash the jacket of the mugger, then holds the knife to his face. The mugger and his accomplices then run off."

8. The television advertisement, which as I have said, was based on the knife scene, was described by his Honour as follows:

> "The television advertisement involves three persons, a couple set upon by a mugger. The advertisement depicts a scene at night in a dingy street with a couple advancing arm in arm, in light hearted mood. The female has fair hair, as does the Sue Charlton character in the film, but the clothing worn by the female character is quite different from that worn by Sue Charlton in the 'knife scene'. The clothes of the male character include a hat with a band displaying animal teeth and a vest worn over an open necked shirt with the sleeves rolled up above arm bands; he wears a necklet with several animal teeth affixed to it. The male character thus is dressed in clothing, the distinctive elements of which are similar to or identifiable as the clothing of the hero in the film. However, unlike Mr. Hogan, he is wearing jeans and 'Grosby Leatherz' shoes. The female character says 'He looked just like you Mick'. They are then confronted by a mugger wearing grotesque clothing and make-up, far more exaggerated than that of the mugger in the scene in the film. The mugger holds a knife and the female character says 'Mick give him your wallet. He's wearing leather shoes'. The male character then says in a confident tone 'You call those leather shoes? Now these are leather

shoes—Grosby leather, soft, comfortable, action packed leather'. The male character looks up and down and then kicks the knife out of the mugger's hand. The male character then takes further kicks at the mugger culminating in a running kick at the mugger in the crotch. The mugger then, in a very exaggerated manner, flies into the air and out of the frame of the film. As this happens, Mick says 'Made right here in Australia and only 40 bucks'. The male character delivers the parting message 'Grosby Leatherz—you'd be a mugger to pay any more for real leather'. There then appears superimposed on the film as the male and female character walk away a cartoon dog which then announces 'Grosby—they're great mate' and closes his remarks with 'woof!'. The cartoon dog was a device which had been used previously in advertising for Grosby products."

9. The advertisement on the posters shows a partially reclining figure wearing the same clothes as those worn in the television advertisement. The figure is wearing a pair of Grosby Leatherz. The face of the model is facing the camera and grinning. Beside the face appear in quotation marks the words in bold print, "You'd be a mugger to pay any more for real leather!" Above the shoes are the words in bold print, "Grosby Leatherz $40". The same actor appeared in the poster advertisement as in the television commercial and the same clothes were worn by him. The posters were shown at railway stations and on the sides of buses and trams....

11. A reading of the amended statement of claim shows that the respondents (the applicants at first instance) relied upon passing off and upon breach of §§ 52 and 53 (paras. (c) and (d)) of the Trade Practices Act. The essence of the respondents' case in relation to the cause of action for passing off was that the public were likely to be confused and led to believe that the appellant's footwear was marketed under franchise from the first or second respondent or both or marketed under licence or approval of those respondents whereby the appellant had passed off its footwear. In relation to the causes of action based on the Trade Practices Act the respondents' case was that the appellant falsely represented that it had the sponsorship or approval of or an affiliation with the first and or second respondents, falsely represented that the appellant's shoes had the sponsorship or approval of or an affiliation with the two respondents, and engaged in conduct which was misleading or deceptive or likely to mislead or deceive by making representations or otherwise leading or likely to lead members of the public to believe that the appellant or its goods had the endorsement of or was or were affiliated or associated with the first two respondents.

12. The learned primary Judge found the respondents' case in passing off established. He also found that the appellant's conduct constituted a breach of § 52 of the Trade Practices Act. He did not find any breach of § 53 of that Act....

30. The case made by the appellant is, in a sense, a simple one. Its advertisers say that they set out to gain the attention of television viewers and persons who saw the posters by reminding them of a well known scene in the film. Their intention was not to suggest that Mr. Hogan or the producers of the film had given permission for a spoof or send up of it to be made. Far less was it their intention to suggest that in some way Mr. Hogan endorsed or approved of Grosby shoes. What they endeavoured to do was to "grab" or "hook" the attention of television viewers and passers-by by reminding them of a funny incident in the film. They chose characters who did not look like Mr. Hogan (or Crocodile Dundee) or Miss Kozlowski who played the part of Sue Charlton in the film. The central feature of the action was not a knife or knives but shoes. The television advertisement was said to portray a scene which was exaggerated and "larger than life" in the sense that it built upon the already improbable sequence shown in the film and made the scene shown in

the advertisement even more unlikely. The actors playing the two parts were said to be caricatures of Crocodile Dundee and Sue Charlton and in no way to resemble them.

31. Because the character in the advertisement was not Mr. Hogan and viewers were not misled into thinking that it was he who was espousing the qualities of the shoes, the case brought against the appellant was a speculative one. It depended upon vague thoughts by members of the community concerning the legal rights film makers might have in ideas or characters and beliefs on the part of some people that in some general way permission was needed before use could be made of ideas or characters. To the extent that people had thought along these lines they had done so because they were under a misapprehension. They had thus deceived themselves and had not been misled by any conduct engaged in by the appellant. At bottom the advertisements had done no more than to cause people to become confused and to wonder what the situation was. This was not enough to warrant a finding of misleading and deceptive conduct nor of passing off. Certainly there was no basis for the view that Mr. Hogan had endorsed or approved of the product which was advertised.

32. The appellant tendered a series of excerpts from well known films—"Casablanca" and "Close Encounters of the Third Kind" are two examples—and then in juxtaposition with them on the reel what was said to be a spoof or send up of that scene. There were also a number of excerpts taken from "The Paul Hogan Show" in each of which Mr. Hogan was said to have sent up the advertisement for a well known product, for instance, Blue Omo washing powder and the Womens' Weekly Magazine. There was no evidence whether the owners of the copyright in any of these films or advertisements had consented to the spoof or send up. His Honour did not find the films of substantial assistance. The purpose of their tender was to attempt to show that what was done by the advertising agency in the present case was in accordance with well known practice in the industry and that persons seeing advertisements of this kind do not assume permission nor endorsement of products referred to in the spoofs. I share, with respect, his Honour's views about this evidence which I think is inconclusive and largely unhelpful.

33. In the course of the discussion which was had during the argument great emphasis was laid by counsel for the appellant on the submission that the advertisement was a spoof or send up of the scene in the film. Another word used was "parody". On reflection, I do not think that it helps greatly to come to a conclusion whether this is an accurate description of what was done. Some, including Mr. Jedlin, would think that to use the word "parody" in connection with the advertisement would be to dignify it with a characteristic it does not have; he along, perhaps, with others, might prefer to view it as a travesty, but, as I have indicated, I think the exercise tends to divert one from a proper consideration of the matter. It is a question of looking at the elements of each of the causes of action relied upon in determining whether they have been established by the evidence.

34. Two things need to be emphasized. Firstly, this is not a case of infringement of copyright. No infringement of copyright was alleged. Secondly, although the respondents contended at first instance that many people would believe that the principal character in the advertisement was Mr. Hogan, his Honour found to the contrary and there has been no challenge to that finding. In my opinion that was the only finding which was reasonably open. None of the seven lay witnesses thought the character was Mr. Hogan. I think it is clear that he was not. I say that not unmindful of the fact that people, in the ordinary course, do not see the film and the advertisement at the same time. The film leaves an impression and the advertisement recalls an aspect of it. Furthermore, the advertisement, like most advertisements, is shown without any warning of what viewers are about to see. It is flashed on the screen for 30 seconds or so at times when the attention

of viewers may be distracted so that they do not take it in fully. Nevertheless, Mr. Hogan was such a well known personality on television well before the film and the advertisement came into existence that his features, voice and manner were unmistakable. The actor who played the principal part in the advertisement could not possibly have been confused with him.

35. I propose first of all to deal with the question whether the appellant's conduct in broadcasting the television advertisement and displaying the posters constitutes passing off. The elements of that cause of action are:

> "(1) a misrepresentation (2) made by a trader in the course of trade, (3) to prospective customers of his or ultimate consumers of goods or services supplied by him, (4) which is calculated to injure the business or goodwill of another trader (in the sense that this is a reasonably foreseeable consequence) and (5) which causes actual damage to business or goodwill of the trader by whom the action is brought or (in a *quia timet* action) will probably do so."

So much was said by Lord Diplock in *Erven Warnink Besloten Vennootschap v. J. Townend & Sons (Hull) Limited* (1979) AC 731 at p 742....

36. The question whether there was a misrepresentation is at the heart of this case and I shall deal with it last. If there was, there is no doubt that it was made by the appellant as a trader in the course of trade (requirement (2)), to its prospective customers or ultimate consumers of goods supplied by it (requirement (3)). There are questions concerning the next two requirements, namely, whether any misrepresentation was calculated to injure the business or goodwill of the respondents and whether it caused actual damage to their business or goodwill or would probably do so.

37. I do not have great difficulty in resolving these questions favourably to the respondents in this appeal, particularly to Mr. Hogan himself. As I have indicated, he has for many years advertised products by himself appearing on television sponsoring or endorsing products. These products have been cigarettes, beer and Australia as a desirable tourist destination. It is clear, and the evidence establishes it, that he has been selective about the products he has chosen to advertise and that he has restricted his advertising activities to a small number of them. The appellant's advertising, if it amounted to a misrepresentation, would tend to damage the reputation which Mr. Hogan has because it would suggest that he was endorsing yet another product, although in a way different from the way in which his well known advertising campaigns had been conducted. Furthermore, the appellant's advertising would tend to reduce the impact of advertising in which Mr. Hogan himself might wish to engage by using parts of the film as a basis for it. What the appellant's advertising did, or at least had the potential to do, was to detract from Mr. Hogan's own opportunities of making money out of a film in which he himself had appeared and in which he or companies associated with him had copyright.

38. In the course of the argument it was submitted by counsel for the appellant that the character, Crocodile or Mick Dundee, was fictional and was certainly not Paul Hogan. On the other hand, the character in Mr. Hogan's advertising was not fictional, but was Mr. Hogan himself. I think this submission ignores the fact that Mr. Hogan, whether he is appearing personally to advertise a product or to portray fictional and exaggerated characters such as he did in the variety show which bears his name or in the film, is not really acting a part but is playing himself, notwithstanding that the character he plays may behave in an exaggerated and, at times, unbelievable fashion. The publicity for the film opens with the sentence, "Paul Hogan is Crocodile Dundee ..." I think this is unquestionably correct and was found to be so by the primary Judge.

39. I have found assistance in relation to the problems which Lord Diplock's elements (4) and (5) raise in the judgments of the High Court in *Radio Corporation Pty. Limited v. Disney* [1937] HCA 38; (1937) 57 CLR 448. The case concerned the application for the registration of trade marks for the names "Mickey Mouse" and "Minnie Mouse". The two characters had been invented by Mr. Disney and had acquired world-wide popularity in cinematograph pictures. The names and figures had been applied by traders under licence from Mr. Disney to many classes of goods other than films as an aid to selling them. The applicant for registration of the marks had no connection with or licence from Mr. Disney whose interests opposed the registration. The Court was concerned to construe and apply § 114 of the Trade Marks Act 1905 (see now § 28 of the Trade Marks Act 1955) which, so far as relevant, provided that no mark, the use of which would, by reason of its being likely to deceive or otherwise be deemed disentitled to protection in a court of justice, shall be used or registered as a trade mark or part of a trade mark. It is to be observed that the section used language not dissimilar from that used in § 52 of the Trade Practices Act. The case is relevant to the cause of action based on that section but I shall come to that matter a little later. In the course of his judgment Dixon J. (as he then was), ... said:

> "In the present case it is the same intangible advantage arising from public celebrity, widespread fame and interest, that the applicants seek. It is not a diversion of trade, custom or profit. Except for the refusal to pay licence fees, the continued use of the trade mark by the applicants will not affect any of the commercial operations of the opponents. It is clear, I think, that the opponents could on their part obtain no injunction for the protection of such an interest as that arising from the mere celebrity or reputation of Disney's productions. Further, in selling, so to speak, the advantage of that celebrity to traders as the opponents have done under their licensing system, they have done much to destroy the significance which they now seek to ascribe to it, namely, the significance of trade reputation based upon a mark. But these are matters which do not make it less right to keep off the register a mark improperly adopted by the applicants. If the circumstances are such that its adoption will give the applicants no right to protection by injunction or other remedy under the general law, then it should be kept off the register.... Further, the burden of establishing that the mark is free from this disqualification lies on the applicants.
>
> On the whole, I think there are present elements which leave them unable to discharge this burden. Those elements are, first, the belief which many people are not unlikely to hold that in some way or another Disney, or one of his companies has permitted, if not procured, the application of the name Mickey Mouse to the radio sets in connection with which it is used and, second, the unauthorized diversion to their own purposes on the part of the applicants of the celebrity and reputation obtained by the various activities of the opponents in relation to Mickey Mouse. The latter may give no cause of action but I think that, at any rate in conjunction with the former element, it would be enough to deprive the proposed mark of protection."

40. It is impossible, of course, to make comparisons between the impact that the Walt Disney characters must have had in Australia and other countries in the mid 1930s with the impact that Mr. Hogan has had in Australia and elsewhere in the 1970s and 80s. But the evidence establishes that that impact has been quite enormous. The considerations which apply in relation to him are precisely the same as those which Dixon J. found to apply in the case of the Disney characters.

41. The Disney case was not a passing off case but it seems to me that the considerations which are mentioned by Dixon J. provide assistance in the approach one should
make to the question whether the respondents have established elements (4) and (5)
stated by Lord Diplock in the *Warnink* case to be essential ingredients of the cause of
action.

42. Further assistance is to be found in the decision of the Full Court of the Supreme
Court of New South Wales in *Henderson v. Radio Corporation Pty. Limited*, (1960) 60 SR
NSW 576. The Hendersons, who were the plaintiffs, were well known professional ballroom dancers. The defendant made and distributed gramophone records. One of the
records was entitled, "Strictly for Dancing, Vol. I". The record was of music suitable for
ballroom dancing and was described as strict tempo dance music. It was intended for the
instruction of students in dancing and for use by dancing teachers, but might also be
bought by the public. The front cover featured as a background a ballroom scene in which
a dancing couple was a prominent feature. The couple was not identified in the print appearing on the cover but was recognized as the Hendersons by a number of witnesses
connected with professional ballroom dancing.

43. In the course of his judgment Manning J. said (pp 603–4):

> "The plaintiffs in this case had acquired a reputation which doubtless placed them
> on a position to earn a fee for any recommendation which they might be dis-
> posed to give to aid the sale of recorded dance music of the type in question.
> I have referred to those engaged in sporting activities because of the facts in
> *Tolley's Case* [1931] UKHL 1; (1931) AC 333, but the position of the plaintiffs
> is better compared with that of a well-known actress or model. I can see no
> distinction in any such cases provided (as has been established in this case) that
> the activity of the party concerned has resulted in their recommendation be-
> coming a saleable commodity. The result of the defendant's action was to give
> the defendant the benefit of the plaintiffs' recommendation and the value of
> such recommendation and to deprive the plaintiffs of the fee or remuneration
> they would have earned if they had been asked for their authority to do what
> was done. The publication of the cover amounted to a misrepresentation of
> the type which will give rise to the tort of passing-off, as there was implied in
> the acts of the defendant an assertion that the plaintiffs had 'sponsored' the
> record…." …

46. It follows in my opinion that, if there is here a misrepresentation, to use the language of Manning J. quoted earlier, the unauthorized use of Mr. Hogan's commercially
valuable reputation justifies the interference of the Court. I turn then to consider the critical question whether the televising of the advertisement and the display of the posters
amounted to a misrepresentation….

49. … Here I think the question is, "Would the portrayal of an advertisement evoca-
tive of the knife scene in the film lead a significant number of those seeing the broadcast
and the posters to think that Mr. Hogan had assented to the adaptation of the knife scene
from the film?"

50. The decisions in a number of cases show that questions such as this will sometimes be answered favourably and sometimes unfavourably to those claiming relief for
passing off. This is because of the wide variety of factual situations with which the courts
have had to grapple….

53. … As I have pointed out, this is not the case of a look alike, in other words, the
use of a character so similar in appearance to Mr. Hogan that a significant number of

people would think that it was he who was playing the principal part in the advertisement. It is a case rather of the adaptation (not in the copyright sense) of a scene from the film for the purpose of attracting viewers' attention. Having considered the whole of the circumstances, I do not think that one can say that more than this was involved.

54. That, however, does not end the inquiry. I have to place myself in the difficult position postulated by Lord Diplock in the *General Electric* case. I am entitled, indeed bound, to give effect to my own reactions and views. But, in doing so, I must be careful not to be too subjective about my approach and to endeavour to put aside any idiosyncratic notions that I may have. I ought to give substantial weight to the circumstances that viewers of the advertisements would see it under very different circumstances from those in which I saw it and I ought to have regard to the wide range of age groups, intellects and tastes of the numerous people who must have seen both the film and the advertisements.

55. Having performed this exercise as best I can, I have reached the conclusion that viewers of the advertisement could not reasonably conclude that Mr. Hogan had consented to or authorized the advertisement. In reaching this conclusion I have been much influenced by the very different advertising style used in the advertisements from the style used by Mr. Hogan himself. That style or stamp is, in a sense, an essential part of his case, because, as I have endeavoured to show, it is that which in effect is claimed to have been damaged as a result of the showing of the advertisements. I have been influenced also by the weakness, from the respondents' point of view, of the lay evidence. It crossed the mind of only two of the seven members of the public who were called that Mr. Hogan must, in some way, have approved of the advertisements. The three witnesses called in the appellant's case were firmly of the view that the showing of the advertisements did not imply consent. Two of the respondents' witnesses did not think about the matter until they were asked to do so by the solicitor who interviewed them. It seems to me that their reactions to his question reflected a vagueness and an uncertainty which militated against the evidence establishing that they were deceived or confused about the matter....

56. One can understand the indignation which the respondents and their own advertising agents must have felt when they saw one of the well-known scenes from this most successful film adapted in this way. But the question is whether what was done constituted a misrepresentation. There being no question of copyright, no right of property is involved. The only question is whether the use made of the advertisements caused a significant number of people to be misled or at least confused.

57. In reaching my conclusion, I have taken into account that I am differing from the primary Judge, who has had great experience in this area and who has given the matter very close and careful attention. That is a circumstance which has caused me to hesitate. But this Court is in as good a position to assess the evidence as was his Honour and if, upon proper reflection, it reaches the conclusion that a different view is warranted, it should give effect to its own views. For my part, I have reached that conclusion and I would propose that that be the view which the Court should adopt. It follows, in my opinion, that the respondents' claim based on passing off should have failed....

60. In the result I would allow the appeal, set aside the orders of the learned primary Judge and, in lieu thereof, order that the application be dismissed.

BEAUMONT, J.:

[The judge recounted the facts stated above in Judge Sheppard's opinion.]

12. There was evidence, accepted by the Judge, of a widespread practice of "character merchandising" in which persons holding copyright or other rights in fictional characters grant licences for reward to others to manufacture or deal in products in association with a representation of those characters. His Honour inferred from this evidence that the purchasing public would be aware, in a general way, of this practice. There was also evidence of the widespread use, for reward, of the services of sportsmen, entertainers and other figures in the public eye to promote a wide range of products and services. There was evidence that not every celebrity used in advertising campaigns appeared simply as himself or herself. He or she might appear as the "persona" of himself or herself.

13. Evidence was called by both sides from members of the public as an indication of the likely responses by consumers to the advertisements in question. Some did, but most did not, think that permission to display the advertising would have been sought from the first respondent or from the producers of the film.

14. The Judge made the following findings: (1) A very large number of television viewers in the target audience would be aware, first, of the character Mick Dundee as played by the first respondent in the film "Crocodile Dundee" and, secondly, of the incident comprising the knife scene of the film. (2) The first respondent was well regarded by those persons as an individual in the public eye who represented "archetypal Australian attitudes and values". (3) Many of those television viewers would recall fairly closely the dialogue in the knife scene: "He's got a knife." "That's not a knife. *That's* a knife." (4) These persons would have "pleasant memories" of the film and the knife scene in particular. (5) Many of those television viewers would be aware "in a general way" of business practices whereby licences for reward were given for marketing of products in association with representations of well known fictional characters and whereby persons in the public eye agreed to associate themselves with the marketing of products. (6) The television advertisement was devised with the desire (which his Honour found would have been achieved as regards many television viewers in the target audience) of "grabbing" or "hooking" the attention of viewers by having them draw an "immediate association" with the "knife scene" and the first respondent; that attention would be (and was) retained throughout the advertisement. (7) A substantial number of those viewers would believe that the male actor was a "send-up" of the Mick Dundee character played by the first respondent, and the advertisement was intended to achieve this result. (8) The objective of the advertisement was that a substantial number of viewers take away a favourable impression of "Crocodile Dundee" and the first respondent in connection with "Grosby Leatherz", rather than that they go away to analyse differences between the real thing and the character in the advertisement dressed up like "Crocodile Dundee"; and that intention was realised.

15. The Judge held that a substantial number of viewers in the target audience would, as a matter of real, not remote, likelihood have responded to the advertisement "on the footing that in accordance with general or normal practice", permission would have been sought for the advertisement from the first respondent, the film makers or both, and that they had "some association of a commercial nature with" the production of the advertisement, or, more generally, with "Grosby Leatherz" shoes. His Honour made similar findings with respect to the posters.

16. The Judge held that both passing-off and misleading conduct contrary to § 52 had been made out....

21. [In *Tolley v. J.S. Fry & Sons Ltd.*], the defendants published as an advertisement for their chocolate a caricature of the plaintiff in the act of playing golf. The plaintiff was a

well-known amateur golfer. It was held, in a libel action, that it was open to the jury to infer that the cartoon had been published with the plaintiff's approval. Viscount Hailsham was "not satisfied that it would not be open to a jury, acting on their own knowledge as ordinary citizens, to assume that no reputable firm would have the effrontery and bad taste to take the name and reputation of a well known man for an advertisement commending their goods without first obtaining his consent" (at p 339). Viscount Dunedin found that the cartoon of the plaintiff,

> "innocent itself as a caricature, is so to speak imbedded in the advertisement. It is held out as part of an advertisement, so that its presence there gives rise to speculation as to how it got there, or in other words provokes in the minds of the public an inference as to how and why the plaintiff's picture, caricatured as it was, became associated with a commercial advertisement. The inference that is suggested (by the plaintiff) is that his consent was given either gratuitously or for a consideration to its appearance" (at p 342).

Viscount Dunedin concluded (at p 343) that the first proposition to be considered was as follows:

> "(1) Would the caricature associated with the advertisement admit of a reasonable inference that the plaintiff had assented to be so depicted? That depends on the view taken of the picture, of its surroundings, and of its use."

22. Lord Buckmaster said (at p 344) that all the circumstances of the issue of the publication must be considered. The first is that "the picture is not a mere caricature, it is an advertisement; and ... the question of whether a well known and respectable trader would be assumed to have the effrontery to use a man's portrait and his reputation to advertise goods without his assent is exactly the class of question on which the opinion of a juror might well be invoked." Lord Tomlin said (at p 350) that, "regarded *in vacuo*", a drawing in the nature of a caricature of the plaintiff was innocent; but, having regard to the circumstances or "environment" surrounding its publication, including the fact that it was published by the defendants as part of an advertisement used for promoting the sale of their goods, "reasonable minds" might infer that the plaintiff had assented to the publication.

23. In *Henderson's Case*, the trial Judge, Sugerman J., referred to the observation made by Dixon J. in *Radio Corporation Pty. Ltd. v. Disney* ... that an injunction could not be obtained "for the protection of such an interest as that arising from the mere celebrity or reputation of Disney's Productions". In Disney's Case, the appellant unsuccessfully sought to register the words "Mickey Mouse" and "Minnie Mouse" as trade marks in respect of radio sets. Dixon J. said (at p 457) that the use of these words would not produce an impression that related primarily to the origin, selection or treatment of the goods. Rather "(t)he reason for using the names is to attract the attention of members of a public that has found pleasure and amusement in the grotesque forms and absurd antics of Disney's creatures, and at the same time to give to the goods a name or means of description at once familiar and pleasing or interesting to the possible buyer. No doubt this means that the trader makes use of elements which belong to the reputation and fame of Disney's creations and it may be that in some vague way the buyer supposes that Disney must have sanctioned it."

24. Dixon J. later (at p 459) referred to "the belief which many people are not unlikely to hold that in some way or another Disney, or one of his companies has permitted, if not procured, the application of the name Mickey Mouse to the radio sets in connection with which it is used".

25. It appears that Dixon J. was of the opinion that no cause of action arose in pass-ing-off. However, he was of the view that, in the language of § 114 of the Trade Marks Act 1905, the use by the applicants of a mark consisting in the words would, by reason of its being "likely to deceive or otherwise, be disentitled to protection in a court of jus-tice"....

27. Questions of "character merchandising" were considered in three earlier cases in this Court.

28. In *Newton-John v. Scholl-Plough (Australia) Ltd.* (1985) 11 FCR 233, a well-known entertainer alleged a breach of § 52 and passing-off in respect of pictorial advertisements for cosmetics. Burchett J. dismissed the claim because "the casual reader would get the im-pression that indeed the advertiser had made use of Olivia Newton-John's reputation to the extent of gaining attention, but not to the extent of making any suggestion of an as-sociation" (at p 235).

29. In *Shoshana Pty. Ltd. v. 10th Cantanae Pty. Ltd.* (1987) 18 FCR 285, an advertise-ment using the name of a well known television personality, Sue Smith, was held by [the trial judge] to amount to a passing-off and a breach of § 52 since "deception (was) struck by the advertisement out of a correct public understanding that television personalities use the images conveyed by their well known and admired names for commercial gain by endorsing products" (at p 292). On appeal, [the court found no deception]. [The appel-late opinion is reprinted in Chapter II.] ...

30. In *Hogan v. Koala Dundee Pty. Ltd.* (1988) 20 FCR 314, Mr. Hogan and other "in-terests associated with the 'Crocodile Dundee' films" ... complained that the respondents, who sold Australian souvenirs bearing similarities to, and strongly reminiscent of, the central character in the film, had breached § 52. Relief was also sought in passing-off. Pincus J. enjoined the respondents.... His Honour was of the view that "the inventor of a sufficiently famous fictional character having certain visual or other traits may prevent others using his character to sell their goods." (p 323). In upholding the common law claim in passing-off, he said (at p 327):

> "Here, Mr Chesterman QC argued that the koala image was akin to a parody of the image of Paul Hogan in the film and he relied upon certain United States parody cases.... He contended that people would be likely to think that, if the respondents were using 'Crocodile Dundee' images in the shop by licence, Paul Hogan's face would not have been replaced by that of a koala, nor would all men-tion of Paul Hogan's name have been omitted. I agree. In my opinion, however, there is nevertheless a clear representation of association with the film's images. Mr. Chesterman pointed out that each of the elements complained of is by it-self common enough. For example, koalas are, as are bush hats and, perhaps less so, hats with teeth in the band and so forth, but the combination of images is something else again."

31. The question for the Judge to decide in the present case was whether a significant section would be misled into believing, contrary to the fact, that a commercial arrange-ment had been concluded between the first respondent and the appellant under which the first respondent agreed to the advertising. If such a misrepresentation were established to the satisfaction of the Judge, a case of both passing-off and conduct contrary to § 52 would be made out.

34. The nature of the issue, involving as it did matters of impression, is one in which particular respect and weight should be given to the decision of the trial Judge unless some error in his judgment has been demonstrated....

35. In my opinion, no such error has been demonstrated.

36. On behalf of the appellant, it was strongly submitted that, although the attention of consumers may have been "grabbed" by reference to the film "Crocodile Dundee", consumers were induced to buy by reason of the subsequent "sales pitch", which, it was said, was a different thing. In my view, the distinction sought to be drawn is unlikely to be made by viewers. The thrust of the advertising is to identify the image of "Crocodile Dundee" with the product to be sold. That image and the appellant's product are not portrayed as separate. On the contrary, the image is put forward as endorsing the product. The message conveyed is that Dundee is recommending the shoes.

37. It is true that the Dundee figure in the advertising does not appear to be the first respondent. But it does not follow that the image of "Crocodile Dundee" is not projected as sponsoring the product. Viewers are given the impression that a variant of the Dundee figure is endorsing the shoes. The question for the Judge was whether this impression would be seen as connected with the first respondent in a commercial context.

38. It was further argued on behalf of the appellant that the effect of his Honour's decision would be to proscribe the use of parody in advertising or, indeed generally. But the essential question is whether the appellant has conveyed the message that the first respondent has agreed to an advertisement for the appellant's goods in which an image identified with the respondents is seen to endorse the goods. As in *Tolley v. Fry*, there is a real distinction to be drawn between a "mere" caricature on the one hand and a caricature "embedded" in an advertisement on the other. The former is innocent because viewers would receive the impression that the person caricatured would not have agreed. The latter carries with it a different impression, favourable to the subject of the caricature, in which he or she is perceived as endorsing the object of the advertising. The distinction between the "mere" caricature and one "embedded" in the advertising is of critical significance. If it were appropriate to divide the advertisement into two discrete parts, one part devoted to a parody of the Dundee figure and the other a sales promotion, it may be that no relevant misrepresentation could be made out. But such a division of the advertising is not possible. The Dundee figure, albeit a variant of the original image, is seen as sponsoring the appellant's shoes. The advertising is not a "mere" caricature.

39. The appellant also argued that there could be no relevant misrepresentation here unless there was a belief that there was a universal practice that permission would be sought in the present circumstances, whereas the Judge found that this was the "general or normal" practice. In my opinion, the point is without substance. His Honour was entitled to take a by and large approach in this area, considering the matter, as he was, from the standpoint of viewers of the advertisement who would not reasonably be expected to draw such fine distinctions. The appellant sought to use this submission as a platform for a further argument that there was no misrepresentation here and that the difficulty was no more than an "erroneous assumption" as to the legal relationship between the appellant and the first respondent. But the case does not depend upon any erroneous assumption. Either the advertisements do, or they do not, carry with them a message or suggestion of the first respondent's agreement with their tenor. If they do, there is a misrepresentation. If they do not, there can be no cause of action.

40. Reliance was also placed by the appellant upon the absence of evidence that the misrepresentation caused damage to consumers. It was further contended by the appellant that there could be no passing-off here in the absence of evidence of any causal nexus between the misrepresentation alleged and any damage claimed to have been suffered by the first respondent.

41. In my opinion, neither of the appellant's arguments should be accepted....

43. I would dismiss the appeal.

BURCHETT, J.:

1. The facts of this case are set out in the judgment of Beaumont J., and I shall not repeat them. To the extent that the question is whether a significant section of the viewing public would infer a consent of some kind by Mr Hogan to the showing of the appellant's advertisement, I agree with the reasons Beaumont J. has given for not disturbing the findings of the trial Judge.

2. But, to my mind, the matter may be approached more directly and more realistically by asking whether the advertisement conveys a false message of endorsement of the shoes themselves, which were its subject, by Mr Hogan. Whether the advertisement does convey any identifiable and relevant message is, of course, a question of fact. I do not think the truly legal questions in the case are controversial. However, the ultimate conclusion whether the advertisement was likely to mislead should not depend upon precisely that analysis which would be sufficient for an advertisement appearing only in print, as in *Tolley v. J.S. Fry and Sons, Limited* [1931] UKHL 1; (1931) AC 333, or for the kind of representation constituted by the display of a trademark, as in *Radio Corporation Proprietary Limited v. Disney* [1937] HCA 38; (1937) 57 CLR 448. The advertisement here in question uses the still relatively new technology of television, and the even newer techniques of the exploitation of personality, projected by that medium, in order to promote products. In considering whether such a television advertisement involves conduct likely to mislead, within the meaning of §52, or deception liable to attract the principle of passing off, it is necessary to bear in mind the nature of the advertising, and of the unique appeal advertising of that kind makes to those to whom it is directed.

3. Character merchandising through television advertisements should not be seen as setting off a logical train of thought in the minds of television viewers. Its appeal is nothing like the insistence of a logical argument on behalf of a product, which may persuade, but also may repel. An association of some desirable character with the product proceeds more subtly to foster favourable inclination towards it, a good feeling about it, an emotional attachment to it. No logic tells the consumer that boots are better because Crocodile Dundee wears them for a few seconds on the screen (cf. the remarks of Lord Brightman in *In re American Greetings Corporation's Application* (1984) 1 WLR 189 at 197); but the boots are better in his eyes, worn by his idol. The enhancement of the boots is not different in kind from the effect produced when an alpine pass makes a grander impact on the tourist whose mind's eye captures a vision of Hannibal urging elephants and men to scale it.

4. To ask whether the consumer reasons that Mr Hogan authorised the advertisement is therefore to ask a question which is a mere side issue, and far from the full impact of the advertisement. The consumer is moved by a desire to wear something belonging in some sense to Crocodile Dundee (who is perceived as a persona, almost an avatar, of Mr Hogan). The arousal of that feeling by Mr Hogan himself could not be regarded as misleading, for then the value he promises the product will have is not in its leather, but in its association with himself. When, however, an advertisement he did not authorise makes the same suggestion, it is misleading; for the product sold by that advertisement really lacks the one feature the advertisement attributes to it.

5. The whole importance of character merchandising is the creation of an association of the product with the character; not the making of precise representations. Precision

would only weaken an impression which is unrelated to logic, and would in general be logically indefensible. Yet the impression must be powerful to be effective. The only medium likely to convey the vague message of character merchandising, while giving it the force and immediacy of an exciting visual impact, is television. That is why the technique has grown in importance with the rise of the television industry. Its implications have hardly yet been explored in the courts. Their exploration involves the application of established principles in an unfamiliar setting, where a pervasive feature is not so much the making of statements that may mislead the mind directly, as suggestions that may inveigle the emotions into false responses.

6. The suggestion in the present case, as his Honour found the facts, was of an endorsement of the appellant's shoes by Mr Hogan's almost universally appreciated Crocodile Dundee personality, and through that of an association between Mr Hogan and the product so endorsed. The television audience would accordingly hold the shoes in higher regard. On the evidence, some evocation of Crocodile Dundee was admittedly both intended and achieved; I do not see any basis for disturbing Gummow J.'s view of its true effect. That view owed much to the special nature and circumstances of Mr Hogan's portrayal of a character really indistinguishable from his own public image. It is, too, consistent with the concession made by the advertisement's author, as noted by his Honour, "that the intention of the advertisement was that viewers should get an impression of 'Crocodile Dundee' in connection with Grosby shoes". I reject the appellant's attempt to avoid, by miscalling its advertisement a parody, the consequences of representing Crocodile Dundee (actually addressed in the advertisement by his name Mick) as endorsing its shoes. The essence of Mr Hogan's performance is parody, which can hardly itself be parodied, at least by what would be more accurately described as a parasitic copy—parasitic because its vitality is drawn entirely from the audience's memory of the original. As well might an attempt to imitate "H.M.S. Pinafore" be called a parody of Gilbert and Sullivan!

7. I also reject the argument that the figure in the advertisement is differentiated from Mick Dundee by virtue of his companion's statement: "He looked just like you Mick." I regard as fanciful the suggestion that more than a tiny minority of viewers would infer from this an otherwise unmentioned visit to a picture theatre showing "Crocodile Dundee", and that the word "he" referred to Mick Dundee. Such an advertisement is not analysed like a crossword puzzle. It comes as a caller upon a family relaxing in the evening, from whom it asks an uncritical welcome. There is little chance that the words in question, which are not emphasized, would even be noticed by many viewers. What the thirty seconds caller would leave behind would be a satisfying feeling that it would be good to have these "Crocodile Dundee" shoes, associated with Mr Hogan. That is just the sort of message character merchandising ordinarily aims to implant....

11. ... I do not think the appellant's conduct derived its misleading character from any pre-existing misconception on the part of members of the public. It was submitted, for the appellant, that only persons who already had a misconception of the extent of the legal protection available to the creator of an artistic work, such as a film, would be misled. As I have seen the matter, this argument cannot be sustained. On the alternative approach discussed in the judgment of Beaumont J., with which I have also expressed agreement, I do not think a person who inferred Mr Hogan's consent had been given to the advertisement would do so by reason of a misunderstanding of the law. The ordinary viewer would well appreciate that the niceties of the law of intellectual property were quite outside his own area of precise knowledge, and would base his conclusion, not on any assumption about the law, but on his correct perception of what normally happens in commercial and advertising practice. However, an acceptance of the proposition that

deception here grows out of error and confusion on the part of some consumers would not necessarily be fatal to the respondents' case. [The trial judge] found that the intention of the appellant's agents was to create the deceptive impression. Generally, intention is irrelevant to § 52, except in the evidentiary sense that a court may more readily infer deception was achieved where it is shown to have been intended. But if intentional advantage is taken by a corporation of a misconception harboured by some consumers, I think at least it can be said it will not be open to the corporation to rely on the misconception, or on some confusion about it, in order to negative the quality of its own conduct as a breach of § 52. Here, the appellant intended to stimulate in the minds of consumers, including those who had the relevant preconceptions, an impression that there was an association between Grosby Shoes and Mr Hogan in the guise of Mick Dundee.

12. For these reasons, the appeal should be dismissed with costs.

Notes and Questions

1. Compare this case to the U.S. cases in sections A. and B. above. Which U.S. case most closely resembles *Hogan* on its facts? Is the outcome of *Hogan* consistent with the U.S. case? Is the analysis used the same?

2. Suppose there had been a clear disclaimer in the advertisement (or at the end of the advertisement), stating that neither Paul Hogan nor anyone associated with his movies had anything to do with the advertisement, and that Paul Hogan did not endorse the product. Would that have changed the outcome of the case?

3. How do you think the Australian court would have decided the *Lugosi* and *McFarland* cases in the previous section?

4. How do you think the Australian court would have decided the *Presley* case? What about the Naked Cowboy problem?

5. As you can see from the opinions, in an earlier case the Australian courts had ruled in favor of Hogan and against someone trying to merchandise his face and Crocodile Dundee character outside of the context of an advertisement. Do you think that the same result would have been reached in either Britain or Canada?

6. How do you think the courts of Germany would react to the facts of this case?

Chapter IV

Post-Mortem Rights of Publicity

A. Domestic Law

How long should the right of publicity last? Should it die with the person, or should it descend to the person's heirs and assigns and be enforceable after the person's death? If the right is inheritable, how long should it last after death? Other intellectual property rights that may be inherited are nonetheless subject to durational limits; patents last for only 20 years, while the duration of most copyrights in the U.S. is 70 years after the death of the author. The cases in this chapter explore these issues.

————

Memphis Development Foundation v. Factors Etc., Inc.
616 F.2d 956 (6th Cir. 1980)

Before WEICK and MERRITT, Circuit Judges, and CECIL, Senior Circuit Judge.

MERRITT, Circuit Judge:

This appeal raises the interesting question: Who is the heir of fame? The famous have an exclusive legal right during life to control and profit from the commercial use of their name and personality. We are called upon in this diversity case to determine whether, under Tennessee law, the exclusive right to publicity survives a celebrity's death. We hold that the right is not inheritable. After death the opportunity for gain shifts to the public domain, where it is equally open to all.

I.

Elvis Presley died in Memphis on August 16, 1977. To honor him, the Memphis Development Foundation, a Tennessee non-profit corporation, laid plans to erect a large bronze statue of Presley in downtown Memphis. The Foundation solicited public contributions to pay for the sculpture. Donors of $25 or more received an eight-inch pewter replica of the proposed statue from the Foundation.

The District Court held that the heirs and assigns of Presley retained his exclusive right of publicity after his death. It held that the exclusive right to exploit Elvis Presley's name and likeness currently belongs to Factors Etc., Inc., the assignee of Elvis Presley's right of publicity. The District Court thus enjoined further distribution of the replicas by the Foundation.

Prior to his death, Presley had conveyed the exclusive right to exploit the commercial value of his name and likeness to Boxcar Enterprises in exchange for royalties. Colonel Tom Parker, Presley's manager, was the majority shareholder of Boxcar. Parker owned 56% of the shares; Presley and Tom Dishkin, President of Boxcar, each owned 22%. Two days after Presley's death, Boxcar sold a license to use its rights to Factors for $150,000. Presley's father agreed to the sale on behalf of Elvis' estate.

The Foundation instituted this action seeking a declaratory judgment that Factors' license does not preclude distribution by the Foundation of the pewter replicas and that the Foundation has the right to erect the Presley statue.

Factors in turn by counterclaim seeks damages and an injunction against further distribution of the replicas by the Foundation. Factors claims that the Foundation is selling the statuettes for $25 apiece, and thus appropriating Factors' exclusive right to reap commercial value from the name and likeness of Elvis Presley.

The District Court issued an injunction against the Foundation. The injunction allows the Foundation to build the Presley memorial but prohibits it from manufacturing, selling or distributing any statuette bearing the image or likeness of Elvis Presley, or utilizing commercially in any manner or form the name, image, photograph or likeness of Elvis Presley.

II.

At common law, there is a right of action for the appropriation or unauthorized commercial use of the name or likeness of another. An individual is entitled to control the commercial use of these personal attributes during life. But the common law has not heretofore widely recognized this right to control commercial publicity as a property right which may be inherited. *See* W. Prosser, Handbook of The Law of Torts § 117, at 804, 815 (4th ed. 1971).

Recently, a few cases have characterized the right of publicity as property which may be passed on to heirs or assigns. In addition, a recent law journal article advocates recognition of such a right after death where a person has exploited his fame during life by assigning it to an agent or otherwise entering into a contract for its use. The theory is that the law should recognize that "the possibility of providing for one's heirs may have a motivational effect during one's life." Assignment during life is the touchstone because "if no contract has been created, the identification of ... harm is ... difficult" and evidently "such concerns were not a substantial motivation." The article thus distinguishes between "the unrealized potential ability of a person to profit from his attributes," an interest insufficient to establish an inheritable right, and the conscious exploitation of the right during life, the continuation of which after death fulfills "the social policy of encouraging individual creativity." Felcher & Rubin, *Privacy, Publicity, and the Portrayal of Real People by the Media*, 88 Yale L.J. 1577, 1618–19 (1979).

Tennessee courts have not addressed this issue directly or indirectly, and we have no way to assess their predisposition. Since the case is one of first impression, we are left to review the question in the light of practical and policy considerations, the treatment of other similar rights in our legal system, the relative weight of the conflicting interests of the parties, and certain moral presuppositions concerning death, privacy, inheritability and economic opportunity. These considerations lead us to conclude that the right of publicity should not be given the status of a devisable right, even where as here a person exploits the right by contract during life.

III.

Recognition of a post-mortem right of publicity would vindicate two possible interests: the encouragement of effort and creativity, and the hopes and expectations of the decedent and those with whom he contracts that they are creating a valuable capital asset.

Figure 4-1. The Elvis Presley memorial statue in Memphis
Photograph courtesy of Michelle Doscher.

Although fame and stardom may be ends in themselves, they are normally by-products
of one's activities and personal attributes, as well as luck and promotion. The basic motivations are the desire to achieve success or excellence in a chosen field, the desire to contribute to the happiness or improvement of one's fellows and the desire to receive the
psychic and financial rewards of achievement. As John Rawls has written, such needs
come from the deep psychological fact that the individuals want the respect and good
will of other persons and enjoy the exercise of their realized capacities (their innate or
trained abilities), and this enjoyment increases the more the capacity is realized, or the
greater its complexity. (Footnote omitted.) According to Rawls:

> (Such) activities are more enjoyable because they satisfy the desire for variety
> and novelty of experience, and leave room for feats of ingenuity and invention.
> They also evoke the pleasures of anticipation and surprise, and often the over-

all form of the activity, its structural development, is fascinating and beautiful. A Theory of Justice 426–27 (1971).

Fame is an incident of the strong motivations that Rawls describes. The desire to exploit fame for the commercial advantage of one's heirs is by contrast a weak principle of motivation. It seems apparent that making the right of publicity inheritable would not significantly inspire the creative endeavors of individuals in our society.

IV.

On the other hand, there are strong reasons for declining to recognize the inheritability of the right. A whole set of practical problems of judicial line-drawing would arise should the courts recognize such an inheritable right. How long would the property interest last? In perpetuity? For a term of years? Is the right of publicity taxable? At what point does the right collide with the right of free expression guaranteed by the first amendment? Does the right apply to elected officials and military heroes whose fame was gained on the public payroll, as well as to movie stars, singers and athletes? Does the right cover posters or engraved likenesses of, for example, Farah Fawcett Majors or Mahatma Gandhi, kitchen utensils ("Revere Ware"), insurance ("John Hancock"), electric utilities ("Edison"), a football stadium ("RFK"), a pastry ("Napoleon"), or the innumerable urban subdivisions and apartment complexes named after famous people? Our legal system normally does not pass on to heirs other similar personal attributes even though the attributes may be shared during life by others or have some commercial value. Titles, offices and reputation are not inheritable. Neither are trust or distrust and friendship or enmity descendible. An employment contract during life does not create the right for heirs to take over the job. Fame falls in the same category as reputation; it is an attribute from which others may benefit but may not own.

The law of defamation, designed to protect against the destruction of reputation including the loss of earning capacity associated with it, provides an analogy. There is no right of action for defamation after death. The two interests that support the inheritability of the right of publicity, namely, the effort and creativity and the hopes and expectations of the decedent, would also support an action for libel or slander for destruction of name and reputation after death. Neither of these reasons, however, is sufficient to overcome the common law policy terminating the action for defamation upon death.

Fame often is fortuitous and fleeting. It always depends on the participation of the public in the creation of an image. It usually depends on the communication of information about the famous person by the media. The intangible and shifting nature of fame and celebrity status, the presence of widespread public and press participation in its creation, the unusual psychic rewards and income that often flow from it during life and the fact that it may be created by bad as well as good conduct combine to create serious reservations about making fame the permanent right of a few individuals to the exclusion of the general public. Heretofore, the law has always thought that leaving a good name to one's children is sufficient reward in itself for the individual, whether famous or not. Commercialization of this virtue after death in the hands of heirs is contrary to our legal tradition and somehow seems contrary to the moral presuppositions of our culture.

There is no indication that changing the traditional common law rule against allowing heirs the exclusive control of the commercial use of their ancestor's name will increase the efficiency or productivity of our economic system. It does not seem reasonable to expect that such a change would enlarge the stock or quality of the goods, services, artistic creativity, information, invention or entertainment available. Nor will it enhance the fairness of our political and economic system. It seems fairer and more efficient for the commercial, aesthetic, and political use of the name, memory and image of the famous to be open to all rather than to be monopolized by a few. An equal distribution of the opportunity to use the name of the dead seems preferable. The memory, name and pictures of famous individuals should be regarded as a common asset to be shared, an economic opportunity available in the free market system.

These same considerations also apply to the Presley assigns' more narrow argument based on the fact that Presley entered into contracts during his life for the commercial use of his image. It is true that the assignment of the right of publicity during life shows that Presley was aware of the value of the asset and intended to use it. The assignment also suggests that he intended to convert a mere opportunity or potential for profit into a tangible possession and consciously worked to create the asset with, perhaps, the hope of devising it.

The question is whether the specific identification and use of the opportunity during life is sufficient to convert it into an inheritable property right after death. We do not think that whatever minimal benefit to society may result from the added motivation and extra creativity supposedly encouraged by allowing a person to pass on his fame for the commercial use of his heirs or assigns outweighs the considerations discussed above.

Accordingly, the judgment of the District Court is reversed and the case is remanded for further proceedings consistent with the principles announced above.

State ex rel. Elvis Presley Int'l Memorial Foundation v. Crowell
733 S.W.2d 89 (Tenn. App. 1987)

What remains to be decided by the courts in Tennessee is whether a celebrity's right of publicity is descendible at death under Tennessee law. The only reported opinion holding that Tennessee law does not recognize a *postmortem* right of publicity is *Memphis Development Foundation v. Factors, Etc., Inc.*, 616 F.2d 956 (6th Cir. 1980). We have carefully reviewed this opinion and have determined that it is based upon an incorrect construction of Tennessee law and is inconsistent with the better reasoned decisions in this field....

We have also concluded that recognizing that the right of publicity is descendible promotes several important policies that are deeply ingrained in Tennessee's jurisprudence. First, it is consistent with our recognition that an individual's right of testamentary distribution is an essential right. If a celebrity's right of publicity is treated as an intangible property right in life, it is no less a property right at death.

Second, it recognizes one of the basic principles of Anglo-American jurisprudence that "one may not reap where another has sown nor gather where another has strewn." [citations] This unjust enrichment principle argues against granting a windfall to an advertiser who has no colorable claim to a celebrity's interest in the right of publicity.

Third, recognizing that the right of publicity is descendible is consistent with a celebrity's expectation that he is creating a valuable capital asset that will benefit his heirs and assigns after his death.... While a celebrity's expectation that his heirs will benefit from his right of publicity might not, by itself, provide a basis to recognize that the right of publicity is descendible, it does recognize the effort and financial commitment celebrities make in their careers. This investment deserves no less recognition and protection than investments celebrities might make in the stock market or in other tangible assets.

Fourth, concluding that the right of publicity is descendible recognizes the value of the contract rights of persons who have acquired the right to use a celebrity's name and likeness. The value of this interest stems from its duration and its exclusivity. If a celebrity's name and likeness were to enter the public domain at death, the value of any existing contract made while the celebrity was alive would be greatly diminished.

Fifth, recognizing that the right of publicity can be descendible will further the public's interest in being free from deception with regard to the sponsorship, approval or certification of goods and services. Falsely claiming that a living celebrity endorses a product or service violates [Tennessee law]. It should likewise be discouraged after a celebrity has died....

[We] conclude that Elvis Presley's right of publicity survived his death and remains enforceable by his estate and those holding licenses from the estate.

Lugosi v. Universal Pictures
25 Cal. 3d 813, 160 Cal. Rptr. 323, 603 P.3d 425 (1979)

By the Court:

[Plaintiffs, the heirs of Bela Lugosi, sued Universal to recover the profits made by Universal from its licensing of the "uniquely individual likeness and appearance of Bela Lugosi in the role of Count Dracula." A more detailed recounting of the facts is reprinted in the excerpt in Chapter III.]

The trial court concluded that: Lugosi during his lifetime had a protectable property or proprietary right in his facial characteristics and the individual manner of his likeness and appearance as Count Dracula; that said property or proprietary right was of such character and substance that it did not terminate with Lugosi's death but descended to his heirs; and that (they) acquired all right, title and interest in and to said property under the will of Lugosi....

Before discussing the applicable law, it should be noted:

There is no allegation in the complaint, no evidence in the record, and no finding of the court that Lugosi in his lifetime alone or with others used his name and/or likeness as Dracula or otherwise in connection with any business, product or service so as to impress a secondary meaning on such business, product or service.

However, Lugosi could have created during his lifetime through the commercial exploitation of his name, face and/or likeness in connection with the operation of any kind of business or the sale of any kind of product or service a general acceptance and good will for such business, product or service among the public, the effect of which would have been to impress such business, product or service with a secondary meaning, protectable under the law of unfair competition....

The trial court found, and the parties have extensively briefed and argued, that the interest in question is one of "property" as that term is defined in Civil Code section 654. We agree, however, with Dean Prosser who considers a dispute over this question "pointless." (Prosser, *Privacy* (1960) 48 Cal.L.Rev. 383, 406.) "*Once protected by the law,* (the right of a person to the use of his name and likeness) ... is a right of value upon which plaintiff can capitalize by selling licenses." (Italics added; Prosser, Law of Torts (4th ed. 1971) p. 807.)

In brief, Lugosi in his lifetime had a right to create in his name and/or likeness "... a right of value," which could have been transmuted into things of value or Lugosi could, if he elected not to exercise such right, protect it from invasion by others by a suit for injunction and/or damages. However, insofar as the record shows, Lugosi had no occasion in his lifetime to sue or restrain anyone because of a purported invasion of his right to commercially exploit his name and likeness.

Such "... a right of value" to create a business, product or service of value is embraced in the law of privacy and is protectable during one's lifetime but it does not survive the death of Lugosi. "The law of privacy comprises four distinct kinds of invasion of four different interests of the plaintiff ... [including] 4. Appropriation, for the defendant's advantage, of the plaintiff's name or likeness." (Prosser, *Privacy*, *supra*, 48 Cal.L.Rev. 383, 389.)[6]

Assuming *arguendo* that Lugosi, in his lifetime, based upon publicity he received and/or because of the nature of his talent in exploiting his name and likeness in association with the Dracula character, had established a business under the name of Lugosi Horror Pictures and sold licenses to have "Lugosi as Dracula"[7] imprinted on shirts, and in so doing built a large public acceptance and/or good will for such business, product or service, there is little doubt that Lugosi would have created during his lifetime a business or a property wholly apart from the rights he had granted to Universal to exploit his name and likeness in the characterization of the lead role of Count Dracula in the picture *Dracula*.

However, even on the above assumption, whether Lugosi's heirs would have succeeded to such property depends entirely on how it was managed before Lugosi died. Lugosi may have sold the property and spent the consideration before he died, or sold it for installment payments and/or royalties due after his death, in which latter event such payments and/or royalties would, of course, be a part of his estate.

"There has ... been a good deal of consistency in the rules that have been applied to the four disparate torts under the common name. As to any of the four, it is agreed that the plaintiff's right is a personal one, which does not extend to members of his family, unless, as is obviously possible, their own privacy is invaded along with his. The right is not assignable, and while the cause of action may or may not survive after his death, according to the survival rules of the particular state, *there is no common law right of action for a publication concerning one who is already dead*." (Italics added, fns. omitted, Prosser, Law of Torts, *supra*, pp. 814–815.)

(Although, as we discuss hereafter, the right to exploit one's name or likeness may be assignable,) a number of decisions support the italicized conclusion.

In *Maritote v. Desilu Productions, Inc.* (7th Cir. 1965) 345 F.2d 418, the administratrix of the estate of Al Capone brought an action for unjust enrichment arising out of the defendant's alleged appropriation of the name, likeness and personality of Al Capone. The widow and son of Al Capone brought an action for invasion of their privacy, based on the same appropriation. The plaintiffs argued that the property rights of Al Capone, his name, likeness and personality, did not fall into the public domain upon his death, but passed to his heirs. Defendants argued that the action for unjust enrichment was in essence an action for the invasion of the right of privacy of Al Capone, which could not survive his death. The court agreed with the defendants, holding that the relief sought by the plain-

---

6. Item 4 of Dean Prosser's classification of invasions of privacy has been complemented legislatively by Civil Code section 3344, adopted in 1971.... (Significantly, section 3344 does not purport to create a descendible right enforceable by the heirs of the person whose identity was appropriated.)

7. For the purpose of the illustration, we assume (plaintiffs') position that Universal would have had no conflicting rights. As stated *infra* we do not decide this question.

tiffs was essentially that of a claimed invasion of a right of privacy, and judgment was entered for the defendants....

In *Schumann v. Loew's Inc.* (N.Y. Sup. Ct. 1954) 135 N.Y.S.2d 361 [reprinted in Chapter XII], some of the great-grandchildren of composer Robert Schumann brought suit against the defendant for misappropriation of a property right once belonging to the famous composer in the latter's name.... In denying recovery to plaintiffs, the court stated: "None of them (cases cited by the plaintiffs) supports plaintiff's contention that a motion picture depicting the life of one who died almost one hundred years earlier is an infringement upon the deceased's property right in his name which descended to his heirs or next of kin." [*Id.* at 369.]

In *James v. Screen Gems, Inc.* (1959) 174 Cal. App. 2d 650, 344 P.2d 799, the widow of Jesse James, Jr., brought suit against a film producer of a television show portraying the life of her husband. Both the first and second causes of action alleged that there had been "exploitation of plaintiff's deceased husband's personality and name for commercial purposes." (174 Cal. App. 2d at p. 651, 344 P.2d 799, 800.) The court treated both causes of action as personal to the deceased so that even if there was an invasion of the right of privacy it was not a right that survived death.

When the right invaded was more strictly the privilege "to be let alone," the courts in this state have refused to extend to the heirs of the (potential) plaintiff the right to recover for the invasion of that right: "It is well settled that the right of privacy is purely a personal one; it cannot be asserted by anyone other than the person whose privacy has been invaded, that is, plaintiff must plead and prove that *his* privacy has been invaded.... Further, the right does not survive but dies with the person." (*Hendrickson v. California Newspapers, Inc.* (1975) 48 Cal. App. 3d 59, 62, 121 Cal. Rptr. 429, 431.)

There is good reason for the rule. The very decision to exploit name and likeness is a personal one. It is not at all unlikely that Lugosi and others in his position did not during their respective lifetimes exercise their undoubted right to capitalize upon their personalities, and transfer the value thereof into some commercial venture, for reasons of taste or judgment or because the enterprise to be organized might be too demanding or simply because they did not want to be bothered.

It seems to us rather novel to urge that because one's immediate ancestor did not exploit the flood of publicity and/or other evidence of public acceptance he received in his lifetime for commercial purposes, *the opportunity* to have done so is property which descends to his heirs. Yet (plaintiffs') claim boils down to this: now that Bela Lugosi is dead, they are the only ones who should have the opportunity to exploit their ancestor's personality.

If the opportunities of a person to exploit a name or likeness in one's lifetime is inheritable property, may it be assumed that if the first heirs thereof, like their immediate ancestor, do not exploit similar opportunities the right to do so is automatically transferred to succeeding heirs? (May the remote descendants of historic public figures obtain damages for the unauthorized commercial use of the name of likeness of their distinguished ancestors? If not, where is the line to be drawn, and who should draw it? Assuming that some durational limitation would be appropriate, it has been suggested that the adoption of such a limitation would be "beyond the scope of judicial authority," and that "legislative action will be required...." (Note (1978) 29 Hastings L.J. 751, 774.) Certainly the Legislature by appropriate amendment to Civil Code section 3344 might recognize a right of action on behalf of the family or immediate heirs of persons such as Lugosi. For the reasons stated above, however, we decline to adopt judicially any such rule.

Thus, under present law,) upon Lugosi's death anyone, related or unrelated to Lugosi, with the imagination, the enterprise, the energy and the cash could, in (his or her) own name or in a fictitious name, or a trade name coupled with that of Lugosi, have impressed a name so selected with a secondary meaning and realized a profit or loss by so doing depending upon the value of the idea, its acceptance by the public and the management of the enterprise undertaken. After Lugosi's death, his name was in the public domain. Anyone, including (plaintiffs), or either of them, or Universal, could use it for a legitimate commercial purpose.

We are not prepared to say, however, that (plaintiffs) or any person other than Universal could have attempted to build a business with a secondary meaning, which business exploited the name Lugosi, and coupled Lugosi's name with that of Dracula. That question is not before us.

The learned trial judge, in holding that the name and likeness are "property" which can pass to the heirs, relied on a line of cases which purport to recognize such a "property right" as opposed to the right of privacy founded in tort (*e.g., Haelan Laboratories v. Topps Chewing Gum* (2d Cir. 1953) 202 F.2d 866; *Uhlaender v. Henricksen* (D. Minn. 1970) 316 F. Supp. 1277; *Cepeda v. Swift and Co.* (8th Cir. 1969) 415 F.2d 1205.)

The question which these cases pose is this: if the right to exploit name and likeness can be assigned because it is a "property" right, is there any reason why the same right cannot pass to the heirs?

Assignment of the right to exploit name and likeness by the "owner" thereof is synonymous with its exercise. In all of the above cases *the owner* of the right did assign it in his lifetime and, too, Lugosi did precisely this in his lifetime when he assigned his name and likeness to Universal for exploitation in connection with the picture *Dracula*. Assertion by the heirs of the right to exploit their predecessor's name and likeness to commercial situations he left unexploited simply is *not* the exercise of that right by *the person* entitled to it.[8] Thus, whether or not the right sounds in tort or property, and we think with Dean Prosser that a debate over this issue is pointless, what is at stake is the question whether this right is or ought to be personal.

The so-called right of publicity means in essence that the reaction of the public to name and likeness, which may be fortuitous or which may be managed or planned, endows the name and likeness of the person involved with commercially exploitable opportunities. The protection of name and likeness from unwarranted intrusion or exploitation is the heart of the law of privacy.

If rights to the exploitation of artistic or intellectual property never exercised during the lifetime of their creators were to survive their death, neither society's interest in the free dissemination of ideas nor the artist's rights to the fruits of his own labor would be served. Authority, as noted, supports the strong policy considerations which underlie the conclusion that the right is personal.

We hold that the right to exploit name and likeness is personal to the artist and must be exercised, if at all, by him during his lifetime. (End of Court of Appeal opinion.)

---

8. We have analyzed *Price v. Hal Roach Studios, Inc.* (S.D.N.Y. 1975) 400 F. Supp. 836, which relies in part on the trial court's opinion. (Roach found "no logical reason to terminate this right (of publicity) upon death of the person protected." [*Id.* at 844.] To the contrary, as we have explained, a rule of non-descendibility is justified by the personal nature of the right, coupled with the difficulty in judicially selecting an appropriate durational limitation were it held descendible to one's heirs. (*See also Factors Etc., Inc. v. Pro Arts, Inc.* (2d Cir. 1978) 579 F.2d 215, 220–222.))

The judgment is reversed and the trial court is directed to enter a new judgment in favor of Universal for its costs. Plaintiffs' cross-appeal is dismissed as moot. Universal shall recover its costs of appeal.

MOSK, Justice, concurring:

… Finally, I must comment briefly on the problems my dissenting colleagues face when they attempt to determine the temporal limitations of their version of the right of publicity. May the descendants of George Washington sue the Secretary of the Treasury for placing his likeness on the dollar bill? May the descendants of Abraham Lincoln obtain damages for the commercial exploitation of his name and likeness by the Lincoln National Life Insurance Company or the Lincoln division of the Ford Motor Company? May the descendants of James and Dolly Madison recover for the commercialization of Dolly Madison confections?

Although conceding it is inherently a policy decision, and without statutory guidance or case authority, the dissent by mere *ipse dixit* selects the copyright period, *i.e.*, the author's life plus 50 years.

I suggest that if the copyright statute can be adapted to an artistic or literary creation where there is no actual recorded American copyright, then all rights to exploitation of Dracula would have been vested not in Lugosi and his heirs but in the author, Bram Stoker. Parenthetically, Stoker retained copyright protection abroad, and his book did not fall into the public domain in England and in countries adhering to the Berne Convention until April of 1962. This was, of course, long after Lugosi's performances for Universal. While Universal protected itself by contracting in 1930 with Florence Stoker, Bram Stoker's successor, and with the playwrights who adapted the Broadway theatrical version of *Dracula*, if Lugosi had attempted to exploit Dracula in 1948, 1931, or 1936, he would have been liable in damages to the Stoker estate. The heirs should have no greater rights now than Lugosi would have had in his lifetime.…

BIRD, Chief Justice, dissenting:

I respectfully dissent.

Although Bela Lugosi died more than 20 years ago, his name still evokes the vivid image of Count Dracula, a role he played on stage and in motion pictures. So impressed in the public's memory, the image of Lugosi as Dracula was profitably marketed by defendant Universal Pictures, which had employed Lugosi to portray Count Dracula in the motion picture *Dracula*. Specifically, Universal Pictures concluded licensing agreements which authorized the use of Lugosi's likeness in his portrayal of Count Dracula in connection with the sale of numerous commercial merchandising products.

Plaintiffs, beneficiaries under Bela Lugosi's will, commenced this action for damages and an injunction against further licensing of Lugosi's likeness on the ground that such use was unauthorized and infringed on their interest in controlling the commercial use of Lugosi's likeness. This case thus presents the novel question in California of the nature and scope of an individual's interest in controlling the commercial exploitation of his or her likeness. I conclude that Universal Picture's licensing of Lugosi's image was unauthorized and infringed on Lugosi's proprietary interest in his likeness. Since that interest is inheritable, the trial court correctly held that plaintiffs are entitled to damages and injunctive relief.

I. THE FACTS

… In 1960, four years after Lugosi's death, Universal began to enter into licensing agreements with various businesses for the use of the Count Dracula character in connection with certain commercial merchandising products. By 1966, when this action was filed, Universal had concluded approximately 50 such licensing agreements. The agreements authorized the use of the likeness of Count Dracula in connection with the sale of such products as plastic toy pencil sharpeners, plastic model figures, T-shirts and sweat shirts, card games, soap and detergent products, picture puzzles, candy dispensers, masks, kites, belts and belt buckles, and beverage stirring rods....

Plaintiffs, Lugosi's surviving son and widow, learned of the commercial use of Lugosi's likeness in his portrayal of Count Dracula in April 1963. They filed suit in August 1963 seeking damages and injunctive relief on the ground that licensing his likeness was unauthorized and infringed on a valuable property right, the commercial value of Lugosi's likeness. Universal moved to dismiss the complaint on the ground that Lugosi's estate was the proper plaintiff. Plaintiffs were subsequently granted a voluntary dismissal without prejudice so that Lugosi's estate could be reopened to determine the distribution of property not considered in the earlier decree of distribution. In 1966, after plaintiffs had been awarded all causes of action belonging to the estate, the present action was filed....

II. THE RIGHT OF PUBLICITY

The fundamental issue in this case is the nature of Lugosi's right to control the commercial exploitation of his likeness. The trial court found Universal's licensing agreements constituted a tortious interference with Lugosi's proprietary or property interest in the commercial use of his likeness, an interest which had descended to plaintiffs. Universal asserts that Lugosi's interest is protected only under the rubric of the right of privacy. Since that right is personal and ceased with Lugosi's death, plaintiffs cannot recover damages based on Universal's conduct.[8] Accordingly, the critical question is whether an individual's interest in the commercial use of his likeness is protected solely as an aspect of the right of privacy or whether additional or alternative protection exists.

A. PRIVACY OR PUBLICITY

... The appropriation of an individual's likeness for another's commercial advantage often intrudes on interests distinctly different than those protected by the right of privacy. Plaintiffs in this case have not objected to the manner in which Universal used Lugosi's likeness nor claimed any mental distress from such use. Rather, plaintiffs have asserted that Universal reaped an economic windfall from Lugosi's enterprise to which they are rightfully entitled.

Today, it is commonplace for individuals to promote or advertise commercial services and products or, as in the present case, even have their identities infused in the products. Individuals prominent in athletics, business, entertainment and the arts, for example, are frequently involved in such enterprises. When a product's promoter determines that the commercial use of a particular person will be advantageous, the promoter is often willing to pay handsomely for the privilege. As a result, the sale of one's persona in connection with the promotion of commercial products has unquestionably become big business.

Such commercial use of an individual's identity is intended to increase the value or sales of the product by fusing the celebrity's identity with the product and thereby siphoning some of the publicity value or good will in the celebrity's persona into the prod-

---

8. It is not disputed that the right of privacy is a personal right, which is not assignable and ceases with an individual's death. Thus, if the use of Lugosi's likeness in the sale of commercial products violated only Lugosi's right of privacy, such use after Lugosi's death would not entitle plaintiffs to any relief.

uct. This use is premised, in part, on public recognition and association with that person's name or likeness, or an ability to create such recognition. The commercial value of a particular person's identity thus primarily depends on that person's public visibility and the characteristics for which he or she is known.

Often considerable money, time and energy are needed to develop one's prominence in a particular field. Years of labor may be required before one's skill, reputation, notoriety or virtues are sufficiently developed to permit an economic return through some medium of commercial promotion. For some, the investment may eventually create considerable commercial value in one's identity.

In this context, the marketable product of that labor is the ability of a person's name or likeness to attract the attention and evoke a desired response in a particular consumer audience. That response is a kind of good will or recognition value generated by that person. While this product is concededly intangible, it is not illusory.

An unauthorized commercial appropriation of one's identity converts the potential economic value in that identity to another's advantage. The user is enriched, reaping one of the benefits of the celebrity's investment in himself. The loss may well exceed the mere denial of compensation for the use of the individual's identity. The unauthorized use disrupts the individual's effort to control his public image, and may substantially alter that image. The individual may be precluded from future promotions in that as well as other fields. Further, while a judicious involvement in commercial promotions may have been perceived as an important ingredient in one's career, uncontrolled exposure may be dysfunctional. As a result, the development of his initial vocation his profession may be arrested. Finally, if one's identity is exploited without permission to promote products similar to those which the individual has already endorsed, the unauthorized use resembles unfair competition. While the product which first used the celebrity paid for the privilege of trading on his publicity value, the second product has secured a costless endorsement. The simultaneous presence in the market of these competing products may cause the latter to be mistaken for the former and will probably diminish the value of the endorsement.

Accordingly, the gravamen of the harm flowing from an unauthorized commercial use of a prominent individual's likeness in most cases is the loss of potential financial gain, not mental anguish.[11] The fundamental objection is not that the commercial use is offensive, but that the individual has not been compensated. Indeed, the representation of the person will most likely be flattering, since it is in the user's interest to project a positive image. The harm to feelings, if any, is usually minimal.

The individual's interest thus threatened by most unauthorized commercial uses is significantly different than the personal interests protected under the right of privacy. Recognition of this difference has prompted independent judicial protection for this economic interest. The individual's interest in the commercial value of his identity has been regarded as proprietary in nature and sometimes denominated a common law "right of

---

11. This is not to suggest that commercial misappropriations of one's likeness may not inflict noneconomic injuries. Commercial misappropriations may injure a person's feelings in several ways. First, the person may find any commercial exploitation undesirable and offensive. Second, while certain commercial uses may be acceptable or even desirable, a particular use may be distressing. (*See, e. g., O'Brien v. Pabst Sales Co.* (5th Cir. 1942) 124 F.2d 167, 170.) Third, other individuals, unaware that the use is unauthorized, may disparage one who would sell their identity for that purpose, thereby inducing embarrassment, anger or mental distress. Further, any unauthorized use infringes on one's effort to control the public projection of one's identity, including the desire for solitude and anonymity.

publicity." This right has won increasing judicial recognition, as well as endorsements by legal commentators. . . .

Underlying these decisions is a recognition that each person has a "right to enjoy the fruits of his own industry," the right to decide how and when the commercial value in his identity will be exploited. When one makes an unauthorized use of another's identity for his own commercial advantage, he is unjustly enriched, having usurped both profit and control of that individual's public image. . . .

Universal argues that judicial recognition of an independent right of publicity is unnecessary in light of the adequate protection afforded under the common law right of privacy. However, the interest at stake in most commercial appropriation cases is ill-suited to protection under the umbrella of the right of privacy. . . . [I]f information about a person is already in the public domain, there can be no claim for an invasion of privacy; to that extent, the right of privacy has been waived. Yet it is publicity which frequently creates value in the individual's identity. To deny a claim for damages for commercial misappropriation because the claimant is prominent is to deny the right to the very individuals to whom the right is most valuable. [Also,] if treated as an aspect of privacy, the use of one's identity for commercial purposes may not be assigned because privacy is a personal, nonassignable right. Such a limitation precludes transferring this economic interest, thereby substantially diminishing its value. . . .

The reasons for affording independent protection for the economic value in one's identity are substantial and compelling, as attested by the increasing number of jurisdictions which have done so. I am similarly persuaded that an individual's right of publicity is entitled to the law's protection.

B. THE SCOPE OF THE RIGHT OF PUBLICITY

The parameters of the right of publicity must now be considered. This case presents two questions: (1) whether the right extends to the likeness of an individual in his portrayal of the fictional character; and (2) whether the right dies with the individual or may be passed to one's heirs or beneficiaries. . . . [Chief Justice Bird's discussion of the first issue is excerpted in Chapter III.]

The right of publicity protects the intangible proprietary interest in the commercial value in one's identity. Like other intangible property rights, its value often cannot be reaped if the individual may not transfer all or part of that interest to another for development. Indeed, an exclusive grant of publicity rights may be required before an attempt to use or promote that person's likeness will be undertaken. Since it is clear that the right of publicity is hardly viable unless assignable, I agree with the numerous authorities that have recognized the right is capable of assignment.

It is equally clear that the right may be passed to one's heirs or beneficiaries upon the individual's death. In considering the question of the right's descendibility, it must be remembered that what is at issue is the *proprietary* interest in the value of one's name and likeness in commercial enterprises, not a personal right like the right of privacy. No policy has been suggested which persuades me that the right of publicity ". . . should not descend at death like any other intangible property right." (*Factors Etc., Inc. v. Creative Card Co.* [(S.D.N.Y. 1977)] 444 F. Supp. [279,] 284.) Further, as with copyright protection, granting protection after death provides an increased incentive for the investment of resources in one's profession, which may augment the value of one's right of publicity. If the right is descendible, the individual is able to transfer the benefits of his labor to his immediate successors and is assured that control over the exercise of the right can be vested is a suitable beneficiary. "There is no reason why, upon a celebrity's death, advertisers should receive a windfall in the form of freedom to use with impunity the name or likeness of the deceased celebrity who may have worked his or her entire life to attain celebrity status. The financial benefits of that labor should go to the celebrity's heirs...." (Note, 42 Brooklyn L.Rev. [527,] 547 [(1976)].)

However, encouraging the investment of resources in activities and careers from which publicity values arise and providing protection for the resulting proprietary interest does not necessitate perpetual protection for the right of publicity. Assurance that one's immediate family and successors will be entitled to the residual value of one's right of publicity after death is a sufficient incentive. Further, recognition of the right of publicity is premised in part on an individual's interest in controlling the manner in which he or she is commercially exploited, so that such use furthers rather than undermines his or her professional activities. With death, the *individual's* need to control the commercial uses of his identity as an adjunct to his career ceases. Providing legal protection long after death basically serves to protect the continuing exploitation of the right, a protection which may already be available under the theory of unfair competition. Finally, with the passage of time, an individual's identity is woven into the fabric of history, as a heroic or obscure character of the past. In that sense, the events and measure of his life are in the public domain and are questionably placed in the control of a particular descendant.

The fixing of the precise date for the termination of the right of publicity is inherently a policy decision, once that the Legislature may be best able to determine. However, in the absence of legislative action, a limit must be prescribed. In fashioning common law rights and remedies in the past, this court has often considered federal and state statutory schemes for guidance. Since the right of publicity recognizes an interest in intangible property similar in many respects to creations protected by copyright law, that body of law is instructive.

The Copyright Act of 1976 (17 U.S.C. § 101 *et seq.*) provides that a copyright in new works shall be recognized during the author's life and for 50 years thereafter. That period represents a reasonable evaluation of the period necessary to effect the policies underlying the right of publicity. Therefore, I would hold that the right of publicity should be recognized during the subject's life and for 50 years thereafter.[31]

The final question presented is whether an individual must exercise the right of publicity during his or her lifetime as a condition of its inheritability. The weight of authority holds that an individual need *not* exercise one's right of publicity "to protect it from use by others or to preserve any potential right of one's heirs." (*Price v. Hal Roach Studios, Inc., supra*, 400 F. Supp. at p. 846.) A person may not have commercially exploited his name or likeness during his lifetime due to the absence of the appropriate medium or an early death. Perhaps the individual chose not to exercise the right to retain its full value as a legacy for his heirs. Since those choices do not conflict with the rationale for recognizing the right, the failure to exercise the right should not affect its inheritability.

Further, there is no reasonable method for ascertaining in a particular case if the right has been sufficiently exploited to warrant passing the right to the decedent's beneficiaries. There are no practical standards for measuring which uses and what period of use

---

31. Universal asserts that the recognition of any right after death will deluge the courts with trivial and specious complaints concerning the use of the names of long-dead notables, *e.g.*, Henry VIII. This argument is unpersuasive. The statutes of limitations, the absolute limitation on the duration of the right, and the difficulties of proving ownership of that right, not mere descendency, will provide ample barriers to stale claims.

are required to create a protectible right. Absent clear rules, the right of publicity might be lost by the unwary. Hence, requiring the exercise of the right of publicity during the person's lifetime as a condition for inheritability is not only inconsistent with the rationale underlying the right but imposes an ill-defined prerequisite on its preservation.

In summary, I would hold that a prominent person's interest in the economic value of commercial uses of his or her name and likeness is protected under the common law. This interest is denominated a right of publicity and is assignable. The right is descendible and is accorded legal protection during the individual's lifetime and for a period of 50 years thereafter. Having found Universal licensed Lugosi's likeness in his distinctive portrayal of Count Dracula, the trial court properly held such use infringed on Lugosi's right of publicity. Since plaintiffs inherited that right upon Lugosi's death, they are entitled to relief for Universal's tortious conduct....

C. COPYRIGHT, PREEMPTION AND FREEDOM OF EXPRESSION

... Finally, I am sensitive to the fact that enforcement of the right of publicity may conflict with freedom of expression in some cases. However, such a conflict is not presented in this case. Plaintiffs challenged Universal's licensing of Lugosi's likeness in his portrayal of Count Dracula in connection with the sale of such objects as plastic toy pencil sharpeners, soap products, target games, candy dispensers and beverage stirring rods. Such conduct hardly implicates the First Amendment. This unauthorized exploitation of plaintiffs' proprietary interest in these commercial merchandising products is no more insulated from suit by the constitutional guarantees of freedom of expression than Universal's refusal to pay Lugosi for his services in portraying Count Dracula in Dracula would be....

V. CONCLUSION

Judicial recognition and protection of the proprietary interest in one's name and likeness is not an unjustified foray by the judiciary into the legislative domain but a recognition of the common law's sensitivity to the evolution of societal needs and its ability to adapt to new conditions. The trial court properly found Lugosi had a right of publicity in his likeness in his portrayal of Count Dracula and that the right descended to plaintiffs as his beneficiaries....

TOBRINER and MANUEL, JJ., concur.

Martin Luther King Center for Social Change, Inc. v. American Heritage Products, Inc.
250 Ga. 135, 296 S.E.2d 697 (1982)

HILL, Presiding Justice:

These are certified questions regarding the "right of publicity". The certification comes from the United States Court of Appeals for the Eleventh Circuit. The facts upon which the questions arise are as follows:

The plaintiffs are the Martin Luther King, Jr. Center for Social Change (the Center), Coretta Scott King, as administratrix of Dr. King's estate, and Motown Record Corporation, the assignee of the rights to several of Dr. King's copyrighted speeches. Defendant James F. Bolen is the sole proprietor of a business known as B & S Sales, which manu-

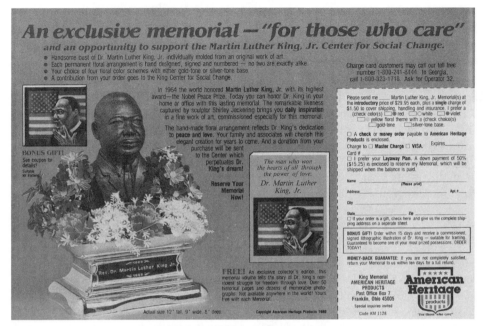

Figure 4-2. The American Heritage advertisement

factures and sells various plastic products as funeral accessories. Defendant James E. Bolen, the son of James F. Bolen, developed the concept of marketing a plastic bust of Dr. Martin Luther King, Jr., and formed a company, B & S Enterprises, to sell the busts, which would be manufactured by B & S Sales. B & S Enterprises was later incorporated under the name of American Heritage Products, Inc.

Although Bolen sought the endorsement and participation of the Martin Luther King, Jr. Center for Social Change, Inc., in the marketing of the bust, the Center refused Bolen's offer. Bolen pursued the idea, nevertheless, hiring an artist to prepare a mold and an agent to handle the promotion of the product. Defendant took out two half-page advertisements in the November and December 1980 issues of Ebony magazine, which purported to offer the bust as "an exclusive memorial" and "an opportunity to support the Martin Luther King, Jr., Center for Social Change." The advertisement stated that "a contribution from your order goes to the King Center for Social Change." Out of the $29.95 purchase price, defendant Bolen testified he set aside 3% or $.90, as a contribution to the Center. The advertisement also offered "free" with the purchase of the bust a booklet about the life of Dr. King entitled "A Tribute to Dr. Martin Luther King, Jr."

In addition to the two advertisements in Ebony, defendant published a brochure or pamphlet which was inserted in 80,000 copies of newspapers across the country. The brochure reiterated what was stated in the magazine advertisements, and also contained photographs of Dr. King and excerpts from his copyrighted speeches. The brochure promised that each "memorial" (bust) is accompanied by a Certificate of Appreciation "testifying that a contribution has been made to the Martin Luther King, Jr., Center for Social Change."

Defendant James E. Bolen testified that he created a trust fund for that portion of the earnings which was to be contributed to the Center. The trust fund agreement, however, was never executed, and James E. Bolen testified that this was due to the plaintiffs' attorneys' request to cease and desist from all activities in issue. Testimony in the district court disclosed that money had been tendered to the Center, but was not accepted by its governing board. Also, the district court found that, as of the date of the preliminary injunction, the defendants had sold approximately 200 busts and had outstanding orders for 23 more.

On November 21, 1980, and December 19, 1980, the plaintiffs demanded that the Bolens cease and desist from further advertisements and sales of the bust, and on December 31, 1980, the plaintiffs filed a complaint in the United States District Court for the Northern District of Georgia. The district court held a hearing on the plaintiffs' motion for a preliminary injunction and the defendants' motion to dismiss the complaint. The motion to dismiss was denied and the motion for a preliminary injunction was granted in part and denied in part. The motion for an injunction sought (1) an end to the use of the Center's name in advertising and marketing the busts, (2) restraint of any further copyright infringement and (3) an end to the manufacture and sale of the plastic busts. The defendants agreed to discontinue the use of the Center's name in further promotion. Therefore, the court granted this part of the injunction. The district court found that the defendants had infringed the King copyrights and enjoined all further use of the copyrighted material.

In ruling on the third request for injunction, the court confronted the plaintiffs' claim that the manufacture and sale of the busts violated Dr. King's right of publicity which had passed to his heirs upon Dr. King's death. The defendants contended that no such right existed, and hence, an injunction should not issue. The district court concluded that it was not necessary to determine whether the "right of publicity" was devisable in Georgia because Dr. King did not commercially exploit this right during his lifetime. As found by the district court, the evidence of exploitation by Dr. King came from his sister's affidavit which stated that he had received "thousands of dollars in the form of honorariums from the use of his name, likeness, literary compositions, and speeches." The district court further found that "Dr. King apparently sold his copyrights in several speeches to Motown Records Corporation." *Martin Luther King, Jr. Center for Social Change, Inc. v. American Heritage Products, Inc.*, 508 F. Supp. 854 (N.D. Ga. 1981).

On plaintiffs' appeal of the partial denial of the preliminary injunction, the Eleventh Circuit Court of Appeals has certified the following questions:

(1) Is the "right of publicity" recognized in Georgia as a right distinct from the right of privacy?

(2) If the answer to question (1) is affirmative, does the "right to publicity" survive the death of its owner? Specifically, is the right inheritable and devisable?

(3) If the answer to question (2) is also affirmative, must the owner have commercially exploited the right before it can survive his death?

(4) Assuming the affirmative answers to questions (1), (2) and (3), what is the guideline to be followed in defining commercial exploitation and what are the evidentiary prerequisites to a showing of commercial exploitation?

… As is known to all, from 1955 until he was assassinated on April 4, 1968, Dr. King, a Baptist minister by profession, was the foremost leader of the civil rights movement in the United States. He was awarded the Nobel Prize for Peace in 1964. Although not a public official, Dr. King was a public figure, and we deal in this opinion with public figures who are neither public officials nor entertainers. Within this framework, we turn to the questions posed.

1. Is the "right of publicity" recognized in Georgia as a right distinct from the right of privacy?

Georgia has long recognized the right of privacy. Following denial of the existence of the right of privacy in a controversial decision by the New York Court of Appeals in *Roberson v. Rochester Folding-Box Co.*, 171 N.Y. 538, 64 N.E. 442 (1902), the Georgia Supreme Court became the first such court to recognize the right of privacy in *Pavesich v. New England Life Ins. Co.*, 122 Ga. 190, 50 S.E. 68 (1905)....

[A]lthough recognizing the right of privacy, the *Pavesich* court left open the question facing us involving the likeness of a public figure....

[In] *Cabaniss v. Hipsley*, 114 Ga. App. 367, 151 S.E.2d 496 (1966) ... the court held that the plaintiff, an exotic dancer, could recover from the owner of the Atlanta Playboy Club for the unauthorized use of the dancer's misnamed photograph in an entertainment magazine advertising the Playboy Club. Although plaintiff had had her picture taken to promote her performances, she was not performing at the Playboy Club.... Although Ms. Hipsley was an entertainer (i.e., a public figure), the court found she was entitled to recover from the Playboy Club (but not from the magazine which published the Club's ad) for the unauthorized use of her photograph....

In *McQueen v. Wilson*, 117 Ga. App. 488, 161 S.E.2d 63, *reversed on other grounds*, 224 Ga. 420, 162 S.E.2d 313 (1968), the Court of Appeals upheld the right of an actress, Butterfly McQueen, who appeared as "Prissie" in the movie *Gone With the Wind*, to recover for the unauthorized use of her photograph....

Thus, the courts in Georgia have recognized the rights of private citizens, as well as entertainers, not to have their names and photographs used for the financial gain of the user without their consent, where such use is not authorized as an exercise of freedom of the press. We know of no reason why a public figure prominent in religion and civil rights should be entitled to less protection than an exotic dancer or a movie actress. Therefore, we hold that the appropriation of another's name and likeness, whether such likeness be a photograph or sculpture, without consent and for the financial gain of the appropriator is a tort in Georgia, whether the person whose name and likeness is used is a private citizen, entertainer, or as here a public figure who is not a public official.

In *Pavesich*, this right not to have another appropriate one's photograph was denominated the right of privacy; in *Cabaniss v. Hipsley*, it was the right of publicity. Mr. Pavesich was not a public figure; Ms. Hipsley was. We conclude that while private citizens have the right of privacy, public figures have a similar right of publicity, and that the measure of damages to a public figure for violation of his or her right of publicity is the value of the appropriation to the user. As thus understood the first certified question is answered in the affirmative.

2. Does the "right of publicity" survive the death of its owner (i.e., is the right inheritable and devisable)?

Although the *Pavesich* court expressly did not decide this question, the tenor of that opinion is that the right to privacy at least should be protectable after death. *Pavesich*, *supra*, 122 Ga. at 210, 50 S.E. at 76.

The right of publicity is assignable during the life of the celebrity, for without this characteristic, full commercial exploitation of one's name and likeness is practically impossible. That is, without assignability the right of publicity could hardly be called a "right". Recognizing its assignability, most commentators have urged that the right of publicity must also be inheritable.

The courts that have considered the problem are not as unanimous....

In *Factors Etc., Inc. v. Pro Arts, Inc.*, 579 F.2d 215 (2d Cir. 1978), Elvis Presley had assigned his right of publicity to Boxcar Enterprises, which assigned that right to Factors after Presley's death. Defendant Pro Arts published a poster of Presley entitled "In Memory". In affirming the grant of injunction against Pro Arts, the Second Circuit Court of Appeals said (579 F.2d at 221): "The identification of this exclusive right belonging to Boxcar as a transferable property right compels the conclusion that the right survives Presley's death. The death of Presley, who was merely the beneficiary of an income interest in Boxcar's exclusive right, should not in itself extinguish Boxcar's property right. Instead, the income interest, continually produced from Boxcar's exclusive right of commercial exploitation, should inure to Presley's estate at death like any other intangible property right. To hold that the right did not survive Presley's death, would be to grant competitors of Factors, such as Pro Arts, a windfall in the form of profits from the use of Presley's name and likeness. At the same time, the exclusive right purchased by Factors and the financial benefits accruing to the celebrity's heirs would be rendered virtually worthless."

In *Lugosi v. Universal Pictures*, 25 Cal. 3d 813, 160 Cal. Rptr. 323, 603 P.2d 425 (1979), the Supreme Court of California, in a 4 to 3 decision, declared that the right of publicity expires upon the death of the celebrity and is not descendible....

In *Memphis Development Foundation v. Factors Etc., Inc.*, 616 F.2d 956 (6th Cir. 1980), Factors, which had won its case against Pro Arts in New York, lost against the Memphis Development Foundation under the Court of Appeals for the Sixth Circuit's interpretation of Tennessee law.... The Sixth Circuit reversed the grant of an injunction favoring Factors, holding that a celebrity's right of publicity was not inheritable even where that right had been exploited during the celebrity's life.[4] The court reasoned that although recognition of the right of publicity during life serves to encourage effort and inspire creative endeavors, making the right inheritable would not. The court also was concerned with unanswered legal questions which recognizing inheritability would create. We note, however, that the court was dealing with a non-profit foundation attempting to promote Presley's adopted home-place, the City of Memphis. The court was not dealing, as we do here, with a profit making endeavor....

For the reasons which follow we hold that the right of publicity survives the death of its owner and is inheritable and devisable. Recognition of the right of publicity rewards and thereby encourages effort and creativity. If the right of publicity dies with the celebrity, the economic value of the right of publicity during life would be diminished because the celebrity's untimely death would seriously impair, if not destroy, the value of the right of continued commercial use. Conversely, those who would profit from the fame of a celebrity after his or her death for their own benefit and without authorization have failed to establish their claim that they should be the beneficiaries of the celebrity's death. Finally, the trend since the early common law has been to recognize survivability, notwithstanding the legal problems which may thereby arise. We therefore answer question 2 in the affirmative.

3. Must the owner of the right of publicity have commercially exploited that right before it can survive?

Exploitation is understood to mean commercial use by the celebrity other than the activity which made him or her famous, *e.g.*, an *inter vivos* transfer of the right to the use of one's name and likeness.

---

4. The Second Circuit has now accepted the Sixth Circuit's interpretation of Tennessee law. *Factors Etc., Inc. v. Pro Arts, Inc.*, 652 F.2d 278 (2d Cir. 1981). [This decision is reprinted in Chapter XII.—*Eds.*]

The requirement that the right of publicity be exploited by the celebrity during his or her lifetime in order to render the right inheritable arises from the case involving Agatha Christie, *Hicks v. Casablanca Records*, [464 F. Supp. 426 (S.D.N.Y. 1978)] at 429. The Hicks court cited three authorities, *Factors Etc., Inc. v. Pro Arts, Inc.*, supra, 579 F.2d at 222 (n. 11); *Guglielmi v. Spelling-Goldberg Prods.*, 73 Cal. App. 3d 436, 140 Cal. Rptr. 775 (1977); and "see also" *Price v. Hal Roach Studios, Inc.*, [400 F. Supp. 836 (S.D.N.Y. 1975)]. However, footnote 11 in *Factors v. Pro Arts, supra*, shows that the issue was not decided there. The *Guglielmi* case, brought by an heir of Rudolph Valentino, involved the movie "Legend of Valentino: A Romantic Fiction," and the California Court of Appeals decision in that case was affirmed on the ground of nondescendibility. *Guglielmi v. Spelling-Goldberg Productions*, [25 Cal. 3d 860, 160 Cal. Rptr. 352, 603 P.2d 454 (1979)]. And in *Price v. Hal Roach Studios, Inc., supra*, the court said: "There cannot, therefore, be any necessity to exercise the right of publicity during one's life in order to protect it from use by others or to preserve any potential right of one's heirs." 400 F. Supp. at 846. Moreover, the Hicks court held that the fictional account of Agatha Christie's 11-day disappearance was protected by the first amendment. Thus, the finding that exploitation during life was necessary to inheritability was actually unnecessary to that decision.

Nevertheless, the *Hicks* dicta has been relied upon. *See Groucho Marx Productions, Inc. v. Day & Night Co.*, 523 F. Supp. 485, 490 (S.D.N.Y. 1981).[5] However, in this case, involving the Marx brothers, it was found that, although Leo and Adolpho Marx ("Chico" and "Harpo") had not made *inter vivos* or specific testamentary dispositions of their rights, they had earned their livelihoods by exploiting the unique characters they created and thus had exploited their rights to publicity so as to make such rights descendible. Thus, even in the Southern District of New York where the requirement arose, exploitation beyond the "activity which made him or her famous" is not now required.

The cases which have considered this issue, see above, involved entertainers. The net result of following them would be to say that celebrities and public figures have the right of publicity during their lifetimes (as others have the right of privacy), but only those who contract for bubble gum cards, posters and tee shirts have a descendible right of publicity upon their deaths. That we should single out for protection after death those entertainers and athletes who exploit their personae during life, and deny protection after death to those who enjoy public acclamation but did not exploit themselves during life, puts a premium on exploitation. Having found that there are valid reasons for recognizing the right of publicity during life, we find no reason to protect after death only those who took commercial advantage of their fame.

Perhaps this case more than others brings the point into focus. A well known minister may avoid exploiting his prominence during life because to do otherwise would impair his ministry. Should his election not to take commercial advantage of his position during life *ipso facto* result in permitting others to exploit his name and likeness after his death? In our view, a person who avoids exploitation during life is entitled to have his image protected against exploitation after death just as much if not more than a person who exploited his image during life.

Without doubt, Dr. King could have exploited his name and likeness during his lifetime. That this opportunity was not appealing to him does not mean that others have the right to use his name and likeness in ways he himself chose not to do. Nor does it

---

5. On appeal of this case, the Second Circuit reversed, finding the law of California applicable, where, as noted above, the right of publicity is not inheritable. *Groucho Marx Productions, Inc. v. Day & Night Co.*, 689 F.2d 317 (2d Cir. 1982).

strip his family and estate of the right to control, preserve and extend his status and memory and to prevent unauthorized exploitation thereof by others. Here, they seek to prevent the exploitation of his likeness in a manner they consider unflattering and unfitting. We cannot deny them this right merely because Dr. King chose not to exploit or commercialize himself during his lifetime.

Question 3 is answered in the negative, and therefore we need not answer question 4.

All the Justices concur, except WELTNER, J., who concurs specially.

WELTNER, Justice, concurring specially:

I concur specially because, although this matter is one of certified questions, I believe that the complaint states a claim upon which relief can be granted. I disagree most decidedly with the substantive portion of the majority opinion, for reason that it generates more unsettling questions than it resolves....

[I]n proclaiming this new "right of publicity," we have created an open-ended and ill-defined force which jeopardizes a right of unquestioned authenticity—free speech....

But the majority says that the fabrication and commercial distribution of a likeness of Dr. King is not "speech," thereby removing the inquiry from the ambit of First Amendment or Free Speech inquiries.

To this conclusion I most vigorously dissent. When our Constitution declares that anyone may "speak, write and publish his sentiments, on all subjects" it does not confine that freedom exclusively to verbal expression. Human intercourse is such that ofttimes the most powerful of expressions involve no words at all, *e.g.*, Jesus before Pilate; Thoreau in the Concord jail; King on the bridge at Selma.

Do not the statutes of the Confederate soldiers which inhabit so many of our courthouse squares express the sentiments of those who raised them?

Are not the busts of former chief justices, stationed within the rotunda of this very courthouse, expressions of sentiments of gratitude and approval?

Is not the portrait of Dr. King which hangs in our Capitol an expression of sentiment? Manifestly so.

If, then, a two-dimensional likeness in oil and canvas is an expression of sentiment, how can it be said that a three-dimensional likeness in plastic is *not*?

But, says the majority, our new right to publicity is violated only in cases involving financial gain.

Did the sculptors of our Confederate soldiers, and of our chief justices, labor without gain? Was Dr. King's portraitist unpaid for his work?

If "financial gain" is to be the watershed of violation *vel non* of this new-found right, it cannot withstand scrutiny. It is rare, indeed, that any expression of sentiment beyond casual conversation is not somehow connected, directly or indirectly, to "financial gain." For example, a school child wins a $25 prize for the best essay on Dr. King's life. Is this "financial gain?" Must the child then account for the winnings?

The essay, because of its worth, is reprinted in a commercial publication. Must the publisher account?

The publication is sold on the newsstand. Must the vendor account?

The majority will say "free speech." Very well. The same child wins a $25 prize in the school art fair. His creation—a bust of Dr. King.

Must he account?

The local newspaper prints a photograph of the child and of his creation. Must it account?

The school commissions replicas of the bust to raise money for its library. Must it account?

UNICEF reproduces the bust on its Christmas cards. Must it account?

Finally, a purely commercial venture undertakes to market replicas of the bust under circumstances similar to those of this case. Must it account?

Obviously, the answers to the above questions will vary, and properly so, because the circumstances posited are vastly different. The dividing line, however, cannot be fixed upon the presence or absence of "financial gain." Rather, it must be grounded in the community's judgment of what is unconscionable.

Were it otherwise, this "right of publicity," fully extended, would eliminate scholarly research, historical analysis, and public comment, because food and shelter, and the financial gain it takes to provide them, are still essentials of human existence.

Were it otherwise, no newspaper might identify any person or any incident of his life without accounting to him for violation of his "right to publicity."

Were it otherwise, no author might refer to any event in history wherein his reference is identifiable to any individual (or his heirs!) without accounting for his royalties....

The doctrine of unjust enrichment ... can be applied to just such a matter as that before us. Were we to do so, we could avoid entering the quagmire of combining considerations of "right of privacy," "right of publicity," and considerations of *inter vivos* exploitation. We would also retain our constitutional right of free speech uncluttered and uncompromised by these new impediments of indeterminate application.

And we could sanction relief *in this case*—where relief is plainly appropriate.

———————

Notes and Questions

1. In *Memphis Development Foundation*, what reasons does the court give for refusing to recognize the descendibility of the right of publicity? Do you find these reasons persuasive? In particular, are you persuaded by the court's view that allowing the right to descend "would not significantly inspire the creative endeavors of individuals in our society"?

2. The court in *Memphis Development* might have been influenced by its view of the merits of the claim. Do you think the Foundation should be required to get the permission of the Presley estate to erect a statue in memory of Elvis Presley? If not, why does it matter that they are financing the statue by selling miniature replicas of the statue? Is there a meaningful difference between a large public statue and the smaller versions from a policy standpoint?

3. In the *Crowell* case, the Tennessee Court of Appeals takes a very different view of the question. What five reasons does the court give for recognizing the inheritability of the right of publicity? Do you find these reasons persuasive? Do the various justifications have the same weight for advertising uses, merchandising uses, and other uses?

4. Under the *Erie* doctrine, the Tennessee court's interpretation of Tennessee law is binding on federal courts. (Technically, a federal court is supposed to predict how the state's highest court would rule; but in the absence of conflicting authority, the U.S. Supreme Court has directed the federal courts to follow a decision of a state's intermediate appellate court.)

In any case, the Tennessee legislature rendered the question moot by enacting a statute recognizing a post-mortem right of publicity. *See* Tenn. Code Ann. §47-25-1101 et seq. Similarly, five years after the *Lugosi* decision, the California legislature enacted a post-mortem right of publicity. (The California statute, which became effective January 1, 1985, was originally codified at Cal. Civ. Code §990. The statute was later amended and renumbered; it is now codified at Cal. Civ. Code §3344.1.) The current version of the California statute is included in the Appendix.

Currently, fourteen states have enacted post-mortem right of publicity laws, and five states recognize post-mortem rights under their common law. Of the five states in which courts have held that there is no post-mortem right under common law, three have now recognized post-mortem rights by statute (California, Ohio and Tennessee). Only two states (New York and Wisconsin) continue to hold that there is no post-mortem right, because the statutes in those states limit the right to "any living person." *See generally* 2 J. Thomas McCarthy, The Rights of Publicity and Privacy §9.18 (2d ed. 2008).

5. Among the states that have recognized a descendible right of publicity by common law is New Jersey. *See Estate of Presley v. Russen*, 513 F. Supp. 1339, 1355 (D.N.J. 1981) (excerpted in Chapter III). A closely related issue is whether a cause of action that accrued during the celebrity's lifetime survives his or her death. The latter issue was decided in favor of the plaintiff under New Jersey law in *McFarland v. Miller*, 14 F.3d 912, 917–18 (3rd Cir. 1994) (also excerpted in Chapter III). Although similar, the two issues need not be resolved identically. A court could hold that a celebrity has no cause of action for conduct occurring after his or her death, while still allowing his or her estate to sue for conduct occurring before death.

6. The *Lugosi* decision adds an additional consideration to the question of descendibility. The opinion draws an analogy to trademark and unfair competition law, and suggests that a property right could have been created if Lugosi's name or likeness had been commercially exploited during his lifetime. Presumably, however, such a right would be appurtenant to the business and would be owned as an asset by the business rather than by Lugosi's heirs.

The *King* court, on the other hand, rejects the notion that the right must have been exploited during the person's lifetime in order to be descendible. Do you think the right of publicity should be so limited? Why or why not?

7. The *King* court was probably influenced by its view of the merits of the case. The advertisement being run by American Heritage Products is positively dripping with a false implication of endorsement. Could the courts have granted relief in the *King* case without recognizing a descendible right of publicity? The concurring judge certainly seems to think so. Do you agree with the concurrence's concern about the effect of the decision on free speech? If so, what is the appropriate way to address the problem? For more on freedom of expression, see Chapters VII and VIII, below.

8. One of the reasons given by the *Lugosi* majority (and emphasized in Justice Mosk's concurring opinion) for refusing to recognize a post-mortem right is the difficulty of determining how long the right should last after death. A specific term of years is inherently a legislative act rather than a judicial one. On what basis does the dissent in *Lugosi* suggest that the court borrow the federal copyright term of life-plus-50 years? Isn't Justice Mosk correct that this would be judicial lawmaking?

9. A legislature, of course, can choose an arbitrary term of years without difficulty. How long should the right of publicity last after a celebrity's death? The various states have enacted terms ranging from 20 years (Virginia) to 100 years (Indiana and Oklahoma). Tennessee has a unique provision: the right lasts for at least ten years after death,

but "[c]ommercial exploitation of the property right" maintains the right indefinitely, until the right is abandoned by non-use for two consecutive years. *See* Tenn. Code. Ann. § 47-25-1104. Thus, the Elvis Presley estate has a right of publicity of potentially indefinite duration.

The most common term of years (in effect in four states) is 50 years after the celebrity's death. These states were undoubtedly influenced by the life-plus-50-years term of the 1976 Copyright Act (which was itself borrowed from the Berne Convention for the Protection of Literary and Artistic Works). In 1998, however, Congress extended the basic term of copyright to life of the author plus 70 years. As a result, California amended its statute to increase its term from life-plus-50-years to life-plus-70 years. Should other states follow suit? Why or why not?

10. The vast majority of decisions concerning choice of law have concerned the issue of whether to recognize a post-mortem right of publicity. (See Chapter XII.) The situation was particularly tangled in the early 1980s. As a result of the *Lugosi* and *Memphis Development* decisions, California and Tennessee did not recognize a post-mortem common-law right; while federal courts in New York held that New York law *would* recognize a post-mortem common-law right. As a result, the estates of dead celebrities tried to get courts to adopt New York law, while defendants tried to avoid New York law. *See, e.g., Groucho Marx Prods. v. Day and Night Company, Inc.*, 523 F. Supp. 485 (S.D.N.Y. 1981) (excerpted in Chapter III) (applying New York law), *rev'd*, 689 F.2d 317 (2d Cir. 1982) (applying California law and dismissing the action). But in 1984, the situation reversed: both California and Tennessee passed statutes recognizing a post-mortem right of publicity, and the New York Court of Appeals (in the *Stephano* decision reprinted in Chapter I) held that New York did *not* recognize a common-law right of publicity of any kind. Because the New York statute is limited to living persons, and thus does not apply after death, suddenly the strategic positions of celebrity estates and defendants reversed as well.

11. The following case implicates the choice of law issue. In 1962, Marilyn Monroe died in her home in California. At the time of her death, however, Monroe also owned an apartment in New York City, where she resided when she wasn't filming a movie. As a result, there was a legal question whether Monroe was domiciled in New York or California at the time of her death. The following case does not directly answer the question. Instead, the court assumes that a post-mortem right of publicity exists in Marilyn Monroe's name and likeness, and asks instead: who is entitled to assert that right?

Shaw Family Archives, Ltd. v. CMG Worldwide, Inc.

486 F. Supp. 2d 309 (S.D.N.Y. 2007)

McMahon, District Judge:

On March 23, 2005, Plaintiffs Marilyn Monroe, LLC ("MMLLC") and CMG Worldwide, Inc. ("CMG") filed a complaint against the Shaw Family Archives and Bradford Licensing Associates ("the SFA parties"), in the United States District Court for the Southern District of Indiana…. In its Second Amended Complaint pursuant to the Indiana action, MMLLC alleges, among other things, that SFA and Bradford have violated Marilyn Monroe's right of publicity by using her name, image and likeness for commercial purposes without consent in violation of Indiana's right of publicity Act, 32 Ind. Code, Art. 36, Chap. 1, §§ 1–20, and that MMLLC has suffered damages as a result of that alleged violation of Ms. Monroe's right of publicity….

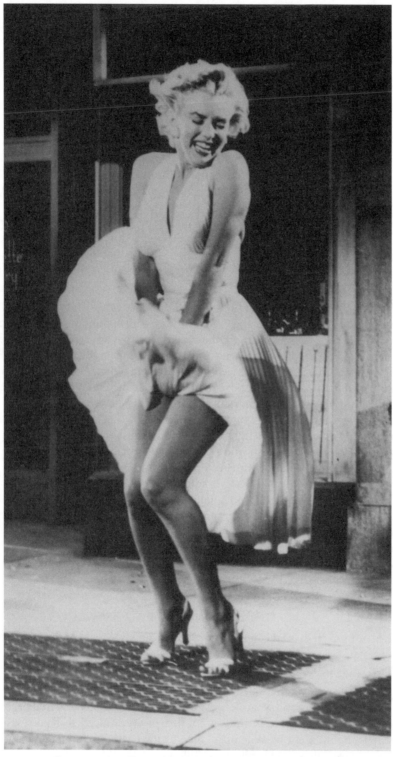

Figure 4-3. Marilyn Monroe on the set of *The Seven Year Itch*
© 1954 Sam Shaw, Inc., Photo by Sam Shaw.
Courtesy of the Shaw Family Archives, Ltd.

On April 19, 2005, apparently prior to being served in the Indiana action, SFA and others brought suit in this court against MMLLC and CMG (the "New York Action") seeking a declaratory judgment on whether there is any postmortem right of privacy or publicity in the name, likeness, and image of Marilyn Monroe.... [The Indiana action was transferred to the Southern District of New York and consolidated with this action. The court previously decided that because the transfer was discretionary rather than mandatory, Indiana's choice of law principles would apply to the consolidated action.]

On October 25, 2006, MMLLC moved for summary judgment on the right of publicity claims set forth in Count II of its Second Amended Complaint, asserting that MMLLC is the holder of a 100% interest in Ms. Monroe's postmortem publicity rights under Indiana law, that Indiana's postmortem publicity statute applies to its right of publicity claims regardless of Marilyn Monroe's state of domicile at the time of her death, and that the SFA parties violated MMLLC rights under the statute by using Marilyn Monroe's name, photograph, image, and likeness on T-shirts that were marketed and sold in the State of Indiana and by maintaining a website that gives customers the ability to purchase licenses for the use of Ms. Monroe's picture, image, and likeness on commercial products.

On November 30, 2006, SFA and Bradford filed a cross-motion for summary judgment on Count II against MMLLC and CMG and served an opposition brief in which they argued, *inter alia,* that the Indiana right of publicity Act does not create any independent postmortem publicity rights but rather provides a mechanism for vindicating preexisting publicity rights when infringements occur in the state of Indiana; that Marilyn Monroe's right of publicity could not survive her because she died domiciled in New York, a state that does not recognize postmortem publicity rights; and that, regardless of where Ms. Monroe was domiciled at the time of her death, MMLLC cannot show an ownership interest in Marilyn Monroe's right of publicity because she lacked the testamentary capacity to devise by will a right she did not own under the law of any state in which she could have been domiciled at the time of her death in 1962. In support of their cross-motion for summary judgment SFA and Bradford further argued that MMLLC should be judicially and collaterally estopped from arguing that Ms. Monroe died a California domiciliary by virtue of four decades of various proceedings in which representatives of the Monroe Estate purportedly maintained, and judicial tribunals purportedly determined that Ms. Monroe died a New York domiciliary....

For the reasons stated below, Count II of MMLLC's Second Amended Complaint is dismissed.

Factual Background

Marilyn Monroe, perhaps the most famous American sex symbol of the twentieth century, died testate on August 5, 1962. Her will, which did not expressly bequeath a right of publicity, contained the following residuary clause:

> SIXTH: All the rest, residue and remainder of my estate, both real and personal of whatsoever nature and whatsoever situate, of which I shall die seized or possessed or to which I shall be in any way entitled, or over which I shall possess any power of appointment by Will at the time of my death, including any lapsed legacies, I give, devise and bequeath as follows:
>
> (a) To MAY REIS the sum of $40,000 or 25% of the total remainder of my estate, whichever shall be the lesser.

(b) To Dr. Marianne Kris 25% of the balance thereof, to be used by her as set forth in Article Fifth (d) of this my Last Will and Testament.

(c) To Lee Strasberg the entire remaining balance.

The will also named Aaron Frosch, Ms. Monroe's New York-based attorney, as the executor. It was subject to primary probate in New York County Surrogate's Court.

In 1968, six years after probate of the Monroe Estate had commenced, Lee Strasberg married Anna Strasberg. Lee Strasberg died in 1982, leaving his wife Anna Strasberg as the sole beneficiary under his will. Upon the death of Mr. Frosch in 1989, the New York Surrogate's Court appointed Anna Strasberg as Administratrix of the Monroe Estate. The Monroe Estate remained open until June 19, 2001, on which date the Surrogate's Court authorized the Administratrix to close the estate and transfer the residuary assets to MMLLC, a Delaware company formed by Ms. Strasberg to hold and manage the intellectual property assets of the residuary beneficiaries of Marilyn Monroe's will.

SFA is a limited liability company organized under New York law with its primary place of business in New York. Its principals are the three children of the late photographer Sam Shaw. Among the photographs owned by SFA and comprising the Shaw Collection is a series of photographs of Marilyn Monroe, including many "canonical" Marilyn images. The copyrights to the Marilyn photographs are purportedly owned by Sam Shaw's daughters, Edith Marcus and Meta Stevens.

This dispute arises out of (1) the alleged sale of a T-shirt at a Target retail store in Indianapolis, Indiana on September 6, 2006, which bore a picture of Marilyn Monroe and the inscription of the "Shaw Family Archives" on the inside neck label and tag, and (2) the alleged maintenance of a website by SFA and Bradford through which customers could purchase licenses for the use of Ms. Monroe's picture, image and likeness on various commercial products. MMLLC asserts that it is the successor-in-interest to the postmortem right of publicity that was devised through the residuary clause of Ms. Monroe's will, and that the commercial use of Ms. Monroe's picture, image, and likeness by SFA and Bradford without MMLLC's consent violates its rights under Indiana's 1994 right of publicity Act. This statute, passed over three decades after Ms. Monroe's death, by a state with which she had (as far as the court is aware) absolutely no contact during her life, creates a descendible and freely transferable right of publicity that survives for 100 years after a personality's death. The statute purports to apply to an act or event that occurs within Indiana, regardless of a personality's domicile, residence, or citizenship. *See* Ind. Code §§ 32–36-1-1 to -20.

Standard of Review

Under Federal Rule of Civil Procedure 56(c), a court will grant summary judgment if the evidence offered shows that there is no genuine issue as to any material fact and that the moving party is entitled to judgment as a matter of law. *See Celotex Corp. v. Catrett,* 477 U.S. 317 (1986)....

Discussion

In their cross-motion for summary judgment, the SFA parties argue, *inter alia,* that even if a postmortem right of publicity in Marilyn Monroe's name, likeness and persona exists, MMLLC and CMG cannot demonstrate that they are the owners of that right because only property actually owned by a testator at the time of her death can be devised by will. Since neither New York nor California (the only possible domiciles of Ms. Monroe at the time of her death) — nor for that matter, Indiana — recognized descendible postmortem publicity rights at the time of Ms. Monroe's death in 1962, she could not transfer any such rights through her will, and MMLLC cannot be a successor-in-interest to them. Moreover, the SFA parties contend, neither the California nor the Indiana right of publicity statutes allow for the transfer of the publicity rights they recognize through the wills of personalities who were already deceased at the time of their enactment. The court agrees.

1. *Ms. Monroe did not have the testamentary capacity to devise property rights she did not own at the time of her death.*

MMLLC argues that its ownership interest in Ms. Monroe's postmortem right of publicity—assuming *arguendo* that such a right exists—stems from Ms. Monroe's valid devise of this right to Lee Strasberg through the residuary clause in her will. The court concludes—regardless of Ms. Monroe's domicile at the time of her death, and regardless of any rights purportedly conferred after her death by the Indiana right of publicity Act or by Cal. Civil Code § 3344.1—Ms. Monroe could not devise by will a property right she did not own at the time of her death in 1962.

Descendible postmortem publicity rights were not recognized, in New York, California, or Indiana at the time of Ms. Monroe's death in 1962. To this day, New York law does not recognize any common law right of publicity and limits its statutory publicity rights to living persons. *See e.g. Pirone v. MacMillan, Inc.,* 894 F.2d 579, 586 (2d Cir. 1990) (citing *Stephano v. News Group Pub.,* 64 N.Y.2d 174, 183, 485 N.Y.S.2d 220, 474 N.E.2d 580 (1984)). California recognized descendible publicity rights when it passed its postmortem right of publicity statute in 1984, 22 years after Ms. Monroe's death. *See* Cal. Civil Code 3344.1 (formerly Cal. Civil Code § 990). Prior to that time, a common law right of publicity existed, but it was not freely transferable or descendible. *See Guglielmi v. Spelling-Goldberg Productions,* 25 Cal.3d 860, 861, 160 Cal. Rptr. 352, 603 P.2d 454 (1979); *Gionfriddo v. Major League Baseball,* 94 Cal. App. 4th 400, 408–09, 114 Cal. Rptr. 2d 307 (2001). Indiana first recognized a descendible, postmortem right of publicity in 1994, when it passed the Indiana right of publicity Act. *See* Ind. Code §§ 32–36-1-1–20; *Phillips v. Scalf,* 778 N.E.2d 480, 483 (Ind. App. 2002). Prior to that time, rights of publicity were inalienable in Indiana, since they could only be vindicated through a personal tort action for invasion of privacy. *See Continental Optical Co. v. Reed,* 119 Ind. App. 643, 86 N.E.2d 306, 309 (1949); *see also Time Inc. v. Sand Creek Partners, L.P.,* 825 F. Supp. 210, 212 (S.D. Ind. 1993); Ind. Code § 34-9-3-1.

Thus, at the time of her death in 1962 Ms. Monroe did not have any postmortem right of publicity under the law of any relevant state. As a result, any publicity rights she enjoyed during her lifetime were extinguished at her death by operation of law.

Nevertheless, MMLLC argues that her will should be construed as devising postmortem publicity rights that were later conferred on Ms. Monroe by statute. Such a construction is untenable.

Indiana follows the majority rule that the law of the domicile of the testator at his or her death applies to all questions of a will's construction. *White v. United States,* 511 F. Supp. 570 (S.D. Ind. 1981). There are disputed issues of fact concerning whether Ms. Monroe was domiciled in New York or California at the time of her death. (There is absolutely no doubt that she was *not* domiciled in Indiana.) However, it is not necessary to resolve the question of domicile because neither New York nor California—the only two states in which Ms. Monroe could conceivably have been domiciled—permitted a testator to dispose by will of property she does not own at the time of her death.

It is well-settled that, under New York law, "A disposition by the testator of all his property passes all of the property he was entitled to dispose of *at the time of his death.*" N.Y. Est. Powers & Trusts Law § 3-3.1 (formerly N.Y. Decedent Est. Law § 14) (emphasis added). The corollary principle recognized by the courts is that property not owned by the testator at the time of his death is not subject to disposition by will. *In re Van Winkle's Will,* 86 N.Y.S.2d 597, 600 (N.Y. Sur. Ct. 1949). *See also In re Estate of Gernon,* 35 Misc.2d 12, 226 N.Y.S.2d 940 (1962) ("In the absence of a contrary intent the will must be interpreted as applying to all property owned by [the testator] *at the date of his death*") (emphasis added.)

MMLLC—which clearly derived any interest in Monroe's postmortem right of publicity through her will (via the legatees)—tries to distinguish *Gernon* by arguing that a testator's "contrary intent" can overcome the prohibition on passing property not owned by the testator at the time of his death. The argument is unpersuasive. The "contrary intent" contemplated by *Gernon* and the cases cited therein is an intent to devise only the property owned by the testator at the time of the will's execution rather than at the time of death. The legislative history of EPTL § 3-3.1 makes clear that it was enacted to codify the rule that a will is deemed pass all of the property the testator owns at the time of his death, rather than only the property owned at the time when the will was executed. Thus, when the *Gernon* court and others refer to "after-acquired" property, the term signifies property acquired after the execution of the will and before the testator's death—not property acquired after the testator's death. Nothing in EPTL § 3-3.1 or *Gernon* stands for the proposition that any intent on the part of the testator can overcome his testamentary incapacity to devise property he does not own at the time of his death.

California law does not differ from New York's. Section 21105 of the California Probate Code provides that, with inapplicable exceptions, "A will passes all property *the testator owns at death,* including property acquired after execution of the will." (emphasis added). In *In re Buzza's Estate,* the court held that a testator/wife could not devise an inter vivos trust that terminated by operation of law when her husband predeceased her. 194 Cal. App. 2d 598, 601, 15 Cal. Rptr. 518 (1961) The *Buzza* court explained the probate rule as follows:

> It is settled law that a will is construed as applying to and disposing of the estate in its condition at the time of death. A testator may dispose only of such property as is subject to his testamentary power, and the testator is presumed to know the law. In interpreting a will, a court should view the will in a manner which will reveal the intent of the testator as disclosed by the language in the will and, if possible, effectuate the intent. This does not mean, however, that a testator may validly dispose of non-existent property.

Id. (citations omitted). *See also* ... 80 Am.Jur.2d Wills 1168 ("A person cannot make a postmortem distribution of property which he or she did not own, at the time of his or her death, or in which such a person had no legal or equitable right. Thus, property acquired by a testator's estate after his or her death may not pass under the residuary clause of the will."); 96 C.J.S. Wills 1088 (same).

MMLLC cites various provisions of the EPTL and the California Probate Code and asks this court to draw the inference that property not owned by Ms. Monroe at the time of her death can nonetheless pass through the residuary clause in her will. However, those provisions do not speak to the precise question presented—whether Ms. Monroe had the testamentary capacity to devise a right she did not own at the time of her death. Faced with the unequivocal language of the provisions and cases that are precisely on point, the court is unpersuaded by MMLLC's endeavor to reason from attenuated analogies.

Nor does §2-602 of the Uniform Probate Code, which states that a will may pass "property acquired by the estate after the testator's death," have anything to do with the present case, because neither New York nor California is among the 18 states that have adopted the Uniform Probate Code in whole or even in part. This court has not found, nor has MMLLC cited, any provision in either the New York or the California probate laws that codifies §2-602....

Even if, as MMLLC implies, there has been some recent shift away from the unequivocal rule that only property owned by the testator at the time of death can be passed by will (as evidenced by §2-602 of the Uniform Probate Code), it does not help MMLLC's cause. "Testamentary disposition ... is controlled by the law in effect *as of the date of death.*" *Dep't of Health Services v. Fontes,* 169 Cal. App. 3d 301, 305, 215 Cal. Rptr. 14 (1985) (emphasis added); *In re Smith's Estate,* 182 Misc. 711, 48 N.Y.S.2d 631 (N.Y. Sur. 1944). There is no question—based on the case law recited above—that at the time of Ms. Monroe's death in 1962, neither New York nor California permitted a testator to dispose by will of property she did not own at the time of her death. Any argument that the residuary clause of Ms. Monroe's will could devise a postmortem right of publicity is thus doubly doomed because the law in effect at the time of Ms. Monroe's death did not recognize descendible postmortem publicity rights and did not allow for distribution under a will of property not owned by the testator at the time of her death.

2. *Ms. Monroe did not "intend" to devise any rights she may have acquired under the Indiana or California right of publicity statute through the residuary clause of her will.*

MMLLC argues that Marilyn Monroe intended to bequeath a postmortem right of publicity to her testamentary legatees. The argument is unpersuasive....

First, the language Ms. Monroe used does not reveal any actual intent to devise property she did not own at the time of her death, much less an intent to devise a postmortem right of publicity whose existence Ms. Monroe could not have contemplated.... Because there is no comma separating the phrases "of which I shall die seized or possessed" and "to which I shall be in any way entitled," they are part of a single term or clause and must be construed together.... [Thus,] Ms. Monroe explicitly recognizes that her powers of testamentary disposition are limited to property she owns at the time of her death....

Second, a testator is presumed, as a matter of law, to know that he cannot dispose of property over which he has no testamentary power, including property he does not own at the time of his death....

Even if the language Ms. Monroe employed clearly demonstrated her intent to devise property she had no capacity to devise, the effect would be to render the disposition invalid, because she had no legal right to dispose of property that did not exist at the time of her death. In *In re Van Winkle's Will,* the New York Surrogate's Court stated the rule unequivocally: "Under no circumstances, in the absence of a valid power, can any amount of testamentary intent produce the effect of subjecting property not owned by a testator at the date of his death to any disposition whatever." 86 N.Y.S.2d at 600; *see also In re Buzza's Estate,* 194 Cal. App. 2d at 601, 15 Cal. Rptr. 518.

Finally, MMLLC's argument that refusing to allow property that did not exist at the time of Ms. Monroe's death to pass through the residuary clause of her will improperly favors intestacy without any countervailing considerations borders on the absurd. The countervailing consideration that MMLLC refuses to recognize is Ms. Monroe's legal incapacity to devise what she did not own. *See In re Braman's Estate,* 435 Pa. at 578, 258 A.2d 492 (Principle that residuary clause should be construed broadly to avoid intestacy does not apply "until it has been demonstrated that the testator at the time of death actually had an interest, recognized in law or in equity, as opposed to an expectancy in the property; absent such an interest, postmortem disposition of the property cannot be exercised.").

3. Neither the California nor the Indiana postmortem right of publicity statutes allows for testamentary disposition of the rights it recognizes by celebrities already deceased at the time of its enactment.

Finally, MMLLC's case is doomed because both the California and Indiana postmortem right of publicity statutes recognize that an individual cannot pass by will a statutory property right that she did not possess at the time of her death. California's Civ. Code § 3344.1(b)-(d) provides that, if no transfer of a personality's postmortem right of publicity has occurred before the personality's death, either "by contract or by means of a trust or testamentary documents," then the rights vest in certain statutorily specified heirs. Since a testamentary transfer has no effect until the testator's death, such a transfer could not be effectuated "before death" for purposes of the California statute. Thus, any rights bestowed by § 3344.1 on a personality already deceased at the time of its enactment could not be transferred by will (which is how the purported property right came to MMLLC from the Administratrix at the time the Monroe Estate wound up). It would vest instead in the persons provided for by statute.

The Indiana statute likewise provides that if a personality has not transferred her right of publicity by "contract," "license," "gift," "trust," or "testamentary document," the right will "vest" in those individuals entitled to her property through the "[o]peration of the laws of intestate succession applicable to the state administering the estate and property of the intestate deceased personality, regardless of whether the state recognizes the property rights set forth under this chapter." *See* Ind. Code §§ 32–36-1-16 to -18. Ms. Monroe's legatees under her will are not her statutory heirs for intestacy purposes.

Thus, even if a postmortem right of publicity in Marilyn Monroe's persona could have been created after her death, neither of the statutes that arguably bestowed that right allows for it to be transferred through the will of a "personality" who, like Ms. Monroe, was already deceased at the time of the statute's enactment. To the extent that other courts … [have] assumed without explicitly deciding that California's right of publicity statute allows for the disposition of the rights it recognizes through wills of personalities already deceased at the time of its enactment, and that such disposition is permissible under the applicable probate principles, this court respectfully disagrees.

Having determined that any postmortem right of publicity in Marilyn Monroe could not have passed to MMLLC's predecessors-in-interest through the residuary clause in her will, the court need not consider the SFA parties' alternative arguments.

Conclusion

MMLLC's motion for summary judgment on Count II of its Second Amended Complaint is denied, and SFA's cross-motion for summary judgment on the same Count is granted.

Notes and Questions

1. In order for CMG and MMLLC to obtain an injunction and damages, it was necessary for them to show first that Marilyn Monroe owned a post-mortem right of pub-

licity. CMG and MMLLC argued that Monroe possessed such a right under the law of either Indiana (the state in which CMG is located and in which the alleged infringement occurred) or California (the state in which Marilyn Monroe died). The declaratory judgment plaintiffs in *Shaw Family Archives* contended that Monroe did *not* possess a post-mortem right, because even though she died in California, she was domiciled in New York at the time of her death, and New York law did not and does not recognize a post-mortem right of publicity.

The resolution of this issue depends on the applicable choice-of-law principles. In this case, Indiana's choice-of-law principles provided that the applicable law was the law of the state in which Monroe was domiciled at the time of her death. As noted above, however, there was a genuine issue of material fact as to whether Monroe was domiciled in New York of California at the time of her death. Thus, summary judgment on that basis was inappropriate. (For more on the choice of law issue, see Chapter XI, below.)

2. In order to avoid a trial, the plaintiffs in *Shaw Family Archives* made a different argument. They argued that even assuming that Marilyn Monroe was entitled to a post-mortem right of publicity (under either California or Indiana law), CMG and MMLLC were not the owners of that right, because that right did not exist at the time that Marilyn Monroe died, and therefore it could not have been transferred by will to her testamentary beneficiaries. Because CMG and MMLLC claimed ownership of the right by transfer from her testamentary beneficiaries, a ruling that the rights could not be transferred by will would deprive them of standing to pursue their infringement claims.

The California statute, originally enacted in 1984 (and effective January 1, 1985), provided that:

> The rights recognized by this section are property rights, freely transferable, in whole or in part, by contract or by means of trust or testamentary documents, whether the transfer occurs before the death of the deceased personality, by the deceased personality or his or her transferee, or, after the death of the deceased personality, by the person or persons in whom the rights vest under this section or the transferees of that person or persons.

Former Cal. Civ. Code 990(b). The district court construed this section to mean that a will executed by a person during his or her lifetime was sufficient to transfer the right of publicity, but only if the right existed at the time of the person's death. If the right did not exist at the time of the person's death, or if no will was executed during his or her lifetime, then the right vested instead in the person's statutory beneficiaries, under the law of intestate succession.

3. Assuming Marilyn Monroe had a post-mortem right, and that her will was ineffective to transfer that right, who were Marilyn Monroe's statutory beneficiaries? Under the California statute, the right passes to the deceased person's surviving spouse and children (or to the children of any dead child), if any. Cal. Civ. Code § 3344.1(d)(1)-(2). "If there is no surviving spouse, and no surviving children or grandchildren, then the entire interest in those rights belong to the surviving parent or parents of the deceased personality." Cal. Civ. Code § 3344.1(d)(3). Finally, "[i]f any deceased personality does not transfer his or her rights under this section by contract, or by means of a trust or testamentary document, and there are no surviving persons as described in subdivision (d), then the rights ... shall terminate." Cal. Civ. Code § 3344.1(e).

Although Marilyn Monroe was married three times (including famously to New York Yankees' Hall-of-Fame center-fielder Joe DiMaggio and playwright Arthur Miller), she was divorced at the time of her death and did not have any children. Accordingly, under the California statute, any post-mortem right of publicity would have passed to her mother, Gladys Baker (who died in 1984), and her father, Edward Mortensen (who died in 1981). Since both of her parents had died by the time California's post-mortem right came into effect on January 1, 1985, under *Shaw Family Archives*, Monroe's right of publicity would have terminated upon her death.

4. Two weeks after the ruling in *Shaw Family Archives*, a federal district court in California reached the same conclusion, holding that Marilyn Monroe "could not have devised a statutory right that was created only decades after her death." *See Milton H. Greene Archives, Inc. v. CMG Worldwide, Inc.*, 568 F. Supp. 2d 1152 (C.D. Cal. 2008) (paraphrasing the court's previous order). The twin rulings set off a flurry of lobbying activity in California and New York. In New York, MMLLC unsuccessfully attempted to get the New York legislature to enact a post-mortem right of publicity. In California, however, MMLLC met with greater success. Senate Bill 771, enacted on October 10, 2007, amended California Civil Code subsection (b) to read in part as follows:

> The rights recognized under this section are property rights, freely transferable or descendible, in whole or in part, by contract or by means of any trust or any other testamentary instrument, executed before or after January 1, 1985. The rights recognized under this section shall be deemed to have existed at the time of death of any deceased personality who died prior to January 1, 1985, and ... shall vest in the persons entitled to these property rights under the testamentary instrument of the deceased personality effective as of the date of his or her death. In the absence of an express transfer in a testamentary instrument of the deceased personality's rights..., a provision in the testamentary instrument that provides for the disposition of the residue of the deceased personality's assets shall be effective to transfer the rights recognized under this section in accordance with the terms of that provision.

SB 771 also added subsection (p) to California Civil Code section 3344.1, stating: "The rights recognized by this section are expressly made retroactive, including to those deceased personalities who died before January 1, 1985." Finally, SB 771 expressly provided: "It is the intent of the Legislature to abrogate the summary judgment orders entered in *The Milton H. Greene Archives, Inc. v. CMG Worldwide, Inc.*, United States District Court, Central District of California, Case No. CV 05-2200 MMM (MCx), filed May 14, 2007, and in *Shaw Family Archives Ltd. v. CMG Worldwide, Inc.*, United States District Court, Southern District of New York, Case No. 05 Civ. 3939 (CM), dated May 2, 2007."

5. On January 7, 2008, in the *Milton H. Greene Archives* case, Judge Margaret M. Morrow held that under the amended statute, CMG and MMLLC did have standing to pursue a claim for violation of Monroe's statutory post-mortem right of publicity. The court declined to grant summary judgment, however, because discovery regarding the issue of Monroe's domicile was still ongoing.

Seven months later, however, Judge Morrow ruled that CMG and MMLLC were judicially estopped from asserting that Monroe was a California domiciliary at the time of her death. The court noted that Monroe's estate had previously taken the position that Monroe was domiciled in New York at the time of her death, in order to avoid California inheritance taxes; that the estate submitted several sworn declarations to that effect; that CMG and MMLLC were in privity with Monroe's estate; and that having benefited from those representations, they would obtain an unfair advantage if they were now permitted to try to establish otherwise. *See Milton H. Greene Archives, Inc. v. CMG Worldwide, Inc.*, 568 F. Supp. 2d 1152 (C.D. Cal. 2008).

Relying on Judge Morrow's order, the district court in New York subsequently held that CMG and MMLLC were collaterally estopped from relitigating the issue of Monroe's domicile. *See Shaw Family Archives Ltd. v. CMG Worldwide, Inc.*, 2008 WL 4127830 (S.D.N.Y. 2008). Unless these cases are overturned on appeal, the net result is that Marilyn Monroe's estate has no enforceable post-mortem right of publicity.

6. From a policy point of view, should a newly-enacted right of publicity statute be held to be retroactive to celebrities who were deceased before it was enacted? Why or why not? If the person dies without having transferred the right, and without expressly mentioning the right in her will, should the right be owned by the deceased person's surviving spouse and children or next of kin, or by her testamentary beneficiaries?

In Marilyn Monroe's case, neither option is particularly attractive. As noted above, Monroe had no surviving spouse or children. Monroe's parents were separated at the time of her birth, and her father played no role in her life. Her mother placed her in foster care until she was seven years old. She then lived with her mother for a few months, until her mother had a breakdown and was committed to a mental hospital. After that, she was declared a ward of the state and was returned to foster care until she married at the age of 16.

Monroe's will left the residue of her estate to three people: May Reis, her personal secretary; Marianne Kris, her psychoanalyst; and Lee Strasberg, her acting coach and mentor. Monroe was close to Strasberg and his second wife Paula. But Paula Strasberg died in 1966, and Lee Strasberg later remarried. Thus, from the time of Lee Strasberg's death until the rulings in these two cases, Monroe's estate and right of publicity were controlled by Anna Strasberg, a woman who was not related to and who never knew or met Monroe.

7. The possibility that the right of publicity could be devised to or inherited by more than one person raises some interesting questions regarding joint ownership. Can one joint owner authorize a use that the other joint owners do not approve of? In the copyright context, the answer is generally "yes": any one of the joint owners may authorize a non-exclusive use, but agreement of all of the joint owners is required to assign an exclusive right. If a use is authorized by any of the joint owners, then the licensee is not liable for infringement, but each co-owner must share any profits earned with the others.

Does this resolution make sense for the right of publicity? Suppose a celebrity is survived by two children who do not get along. Could each child authorize the use of the celebrity's name and likeness for a different brand of cars? Is there a legal basis for treating the right of publicity different from other types of intangible property?

8. Assuming that the rulings in *Shaw Family Archives* and *Milton H. Greene Archives* are upheld on appeal, what will become of the millions of dollars that CMG and MMLLC received from licensing Monroe's right of publicity up to 2008? If a licensee who paid royalties sues to get those royalties back, presumably the statute of limitations will be deemed to have run from the time the license fee was paid, rather than from the time of the *Shaw* and *Greene* decision, since any licensee could have challenged CMG's right to collect royalties at any time. For those royalties that were paid within the limitations period, will a court hold that the licensee is entitled to a refund? Or did the licensee receive a valuable benefit from the license, saving the millions of dollars in legal fees it would have cost to contest ownership of those rights?

9. Although the construction of California Civil Code section 3344.1 in *Shaw Family Archives* has been overturned by amendment, the reasoning of that case remains relevant in any other case in which a post-mortem right of publicity was enacted after the death of the celebrity at issue.

B. Comparative Law

The following materials include an excerpt from a law review article discussing how the issue of descendibility has been addressed in France, and two cases, one from Canada and one from Germany. As you read these materials, consider how the approaches to descendibility in these cases differ from each other and from the approaches taken in the United States.

Elisabeth Logeais & Jean-Baptiste Schroeder, *The French Right of Image: An Ambiguous Concept Protecting the Human Persona*
18 Loy. L.A. Ent. L.J. 511 (1998)

* * *

V. A Transferable and Descendible Asset

A. Transferability

As already explained, the French right of image prohibits any unauthorized use of a person's image that fails to respect his privacy. Consent is the prerequisite for the use of a person's image. Thus, anybody may give their consent for free or bargain for compensation in exchange for it. This compensation may take the form of a flat fee or a royalty payment based on the scope of the authorized use. The Paris Court of Appeal stated that the general principle as: "Prior consent must be explicit with respect to its term and scope; therefore, consent given by a model to reproduce her photographs 'for commercial exploitation' can only be deemed given for a reasonable term (usually two years for a model) and predictable customary uses...."

Various court decisions have acknowledged the exclusive right of any person to commercially exploit his or her image. Two professions, modeling and the performing arts, have contributed to the recognition by case law of the patrimonial aspect of the right of image. However, recently passed legislation concerning these two professions have failed to expressly acknowledge their right of image as an economic asset worthy of protection. Articles L 763-1 and L 763-2 of the French Labor Code (Law No. 90-603 of July 12, 1990) defining the payment terms and conditions for the sale or exploitation of the services provided by a model, do not make any reference to their right of image as an individual right. Similarly, Law No. 85-660 of July 3, 1985, establishing the neighboring rights of performing artists by granting them protection for their name, quality, and performance, does not consider their right of image in itself, but rather through its embodiment in the protected performance. The silence in the law reflects the ambiguous nature of the right of image, which has yet to be expressly incorporated into statutory law as was the right of privacy under Article 9 of the French Civil Code.

The cautious legislative approach has not prevented French courts from protecting the goodwill attached to the image of these professionals. As stated by one decision,

[I]n the artistic field, fame stems from talent, work and lengthy, painstaking efforts along one's career, ... a capital ... the person enjoying it is the only one to decide how and when to exploit it.... Everybody is entitled to oppose any impairment of his or her persona, any prejudice to the representation which he or she may legitimately expect that people or the public will have of him or her.

This view appears to reflect the new concept of "brand image" or reputation rights attached to a person.

Furthermore, the fact that consent may be contractually granted has allowed for the development of image licensing and marketing (for instance, character merchandising, sports licensing, endorsement, sponsorship, etc.). General rules of contract law apply to agreements consenting to the use of a person's image. In this respect, contracts that are against public policy and morality standards are null and void. Also, because the right of image is and remains a personality right, a general and perpetual waiver or transfer would probably be successfully challenged in courts, especially considering the existence of a right to oblivion....

B. Descendibility

The descendibility of the right of image depends directly on the characterization of the right as based either on privacy or on its economic value, that is, whether it is extra-patrimonial or patrimonial in nature. This has been a long debated issue in the courts. After initially denying the descendibility of the right of image, the courts appear to finally be moving toward recognizing descendibility.

1. The Right of Image as a Personality Right Cannot Be Transmitted to Heirs

In accordance with the majority of case law, the personality rights are not descendible to heirs.[140] The majority view is illustrated by a decision involving the heirs of the popular French singer Claude Francois.[141] Mr. P, the tutor of Francois' two minor children, assigned by contract to the Bonnet company the exclusive rights to reproduce, use, and sell, affixed to mirrors, four photographs of the deceased singer. A second contract extended the scope of the license to all forms of the singer's image in connection with mirrors. Upset by the fact that other competitors were exploiting the image of the singer as well, the Bonnet company sued its competitors for copyright infringement and unfair competition. After having denied copyright protection to the photographs, the Court dismissed the plaintiff's claims, holding that the right of image is a personality right terminating upon the death of the person. As such, the tutor of the heirs could not have validly granted exclusive rights to the Bonnet Company.

On the other hand, the court stated that heirs have a right to object to the use of their father's image that would be offending to his memory, but they cannot assign this right to a third party. Therefore, the Bonnet company could not invoke such a right. The result of the court's holding here is that one cannot commercially exploit the image of a deceased singer without the prior consent of his or her heirs.

Even if the rationale for denying descendibility was initially because the right of image belongs only to living persons, it has nevertheless always been admitted that heirs may claim

---

140. Cass. civ. 1e ch., Oct. 10, 1995, JCP 1997, II, 22765, note Ravanas. In this recent case, the widow of the last Emperor of China sued the French publishing company Robert Laffont, [and] the High Court held that the widow could not claim unlawful invasion of the private life of her deceased husband.

141. CA Paris, 4e ch., June 7, 1983, Gaz. Pal. 1984, 2, 258, note Pochon & Lamoureux [Société Bonnet v. Société Cashart United Diffusion Moderne].

their own personality rights. Courts have acknowledged the right of families to prohibit the taking and the using of images of a relative in his or her death bed, in order to preserve the memory of one's deceased parent.

For example, on January 25, 1996, Paris Match published photographs of the former President of France, Francois Mitterand, on his death bed.[152] These photographs were taken in his home and without the knowledge of his family. The Paris Court of Appeal strongly reaffirmed that "[t]he right of privacy only belongs to living persons and can not be passed onto heirs." Although there is no post-mortem private life, it has been held that the unauthorized photographing of a person's remains amounts to an invasion of the family's private life, as well as to an impairment of the peaceful rest of the deceased ("paix des morts"). This action, the court indicated, violated the general principles of human dignity.

2. The Evolution of Case Law Toward Recognition of Descendibility

The first decision clearly recognizing the descendibility of the right of image was rendered in 1988 in a case involving the widow of the famous French actor Raimu and an advertising company that had used a caricature of her late husband to promote the advertiser's real estate.[156] The court characterized the widow's claims as ones for invasion of privacy and damage to the image, fame, and memory of her deceased husband. It disallowed the damage to dignity claim but awarded her damages to compensate for her lost share of the profits made from the advertising use of her husband's image. The court stated:

> The right to one's image has a moral and patrimonial character; the patrimonial right which allows the contracting of the commercial exploitation of the image for monetary compensation, is not purely personal and passes on to heirs. For a great actor to achieve celebrity, far from allowing the free use of his image for commercial purposes, makes it more necessary on the contrary to obtain his consent which he may deny for dignity reasons or grant subject to payment. In the present case, the use of an actor's image for advertising purpose is not offensive; yet it was subject to his heirs' authorization for she could have derived profit from such use according to the law of demand on the advertising market.

The decision is significant for three reasons. First, it affirms the dual nature of the right of image. Second, it establishes the general principle of descendibility of the patrimonial aspect of the right of image (without relying on corresponding statutory provisions concerning performing artists introduced by the Law of July 3, 1985). Finally, it concludes that heirs may object to impairment of the image of the deceased ascendant, whether such impairment is of a moral character (harm to the memory of the deceased) or of an economic character (loss of profits and eventual depreciation of the notoriety of the deceased's image).

A 1996 decision confirmed the descendibility of the right of image in a case involving the widow of the Famous French comedic actor "Coluche," and the publisher of a book discussing his life.[160] The book contained several photographs of the deceased actor that

---

152. CA Paris, 11e ch., July 2, 1997, D. 1997, 596. The editor of Paris Match was sued before the criminal courts on the basis of articles L 226-1 and 226-2 of the French Criminal Code and ordered to pay a fine of 200,000 [francs], and the plaintiffs were awarded 1 [franc] in damages.

156. T.G.I. Aix en Provence, Nov. 24, 1988, JCP éd. G. 1989, II, 21329, note J. Henderycksen [Mme Brun v. SA Expobat], aff'd sub nom, CA Aix en Provence, 2e ch., May 21, 1991, R.J.D.A. 8-9/91, 756 [SARL Propulsion v. Brun].

160. CA Paris, Sep. 10, 1996, R.D.P.I., no. 68, 63 [Les Editions Sand & M. Pascuito v. M. Kantor, Mme Colucci]. Coluche: The Book of Souvenir was released in 1993, several years after the actor's accidental death.

had already been published, including some taken in a private context (e.g., family pictures with his parents, children, and his divorced wife) and at the funeral.

The Court of Appeal upheld the lower judgment and found that the publication of the book unlawfully invaded his privacy and prejudiced the image of the widow and children as well as the image of the deceased actor. Concerning the right of image, the Court made the following clear statement:

> The right of image is a personality right which entitles anyone to oppose the dissemination and use of his or her image without prior consent.... [T]he violation of this right may cause to its holder moral damage and, as the case may be, economic damage whenever the holder conferred a commercial value to his or her image due to his or her activities or notoriety.

The court went on to say:

> Whereas heirs may seek relief for the moral harm caused by such violation only if the selection and display of the image is likely to impair the perception that the public may have of the deceased artist, they are entitled to full compensation of the economic damage stemming from said violation.

In this case, the court found that the heirs of Coluche could not claim a moral harm resulting from the publication of the contentious book of the images of Coluche and his mother, both deceased. However, the court stated that the heirs were entitled to recover for the economic damage resulting from the unauthorized use of Coluche's image, but not for the unauthorized use of the image of his deceased mother. Apparently, the court found that Coluche's mother did not appear to have acquired any commercial value in her image during her lifetime.

A very recent case illustrates the express descendibility provisions concerning the neighboring rights of performing artists. Article L 212-2 of the French C.P.I. provides that the right of the performing artist to have his or her name, quality and performance respected passes on to his or her heirs to ensure protection of the performance and memory of the deceased artist. In this case, the copyright owner of the famous French film noir *Les Tontons Flingueurs* starring Bernard Blier, authorized the use of movie excerpts for an advertising campaign promoting the French bank Banc National de Paris.[168] The advertising posters showed edited excerpts of the image and postures of Blier with new fabricated partners in the place of the original fellow actors and displayed them in an overall decolorized ambiance.

The son and daughter of the deceased actor unsuccessfully petitioned the court to enjoin the campaign, complaining, *inter alia*, of a mutilation of the artist's performance. The court made a strict yet correct interpretation of Article L 212-2 C.P.I., stating:

> The descendibility of the right of respect of the performance and memory of the artist is based on the principle of a continuation of the defunct. Therefore, an heir may not exercise such right in his personal interest in an attempt to protect the image which he wants people to have of himself; he may only exercise this right in the sole interest of the deceased artist.

The court's rationale parallels the traditional reasoning with respect to descendibility of the moral and patrimonial rights of a deceased author with respect to his or her work of authorship. The court found that advertisements using the movie excerpts did not

---

168. See T.G.I. Paris, 1e ch., Apr. 23, 1997 [Bertand Blier et Brigitte Blier v. BNP, EURO RSCG France, Gaumont et Annette Blier], cited in Gazette du Palais, Nov. 22, 1997, at 2.

harm the memory of the deceased artist, especially since he had performed in commercials while still alive. The court further held that the performance of the actor was not impaired by the editing of the scenes nor depreciated by the association of his name with the advertising of the bank.

It is interesting to note, however, that the court seemed to rely only on the provisions of Article L 212-2 of the C.P.I. and did not refer to the right of image every person enjoys, regardless of his social and professional status. The potential market value of images, as well as the uncertainty about the exact scope for post-mortem enforcement of their right of image, is highlighted by the current advertising campaign run by Apple Computer displaying images of deceased personalities such as Pablo Picasso, Albert Einstein, La Callas, and Indira Gandhi.

———————

Gould Estate v. Stoddart Publishing Co.
30 O.R. (3d) 520 (Ont. Ct. J. 1996)
aff'd on other grounds, 39 O.R. (3d) 545 (Ont. Ct. App. 1998)

LEDERMAN, J.:

Background

1. In 1956, Glenn Gould ("Gould"), then a young concert pianist, was interviewed by Jock Carroll ("Carroll") for an article in Weekend Magazine. They talked on a variety of occasions and in numerous venues, including Carroll accompanying Gould on a vacation to the Bahamas. During this time, Carroll took approximately 400 photographs of Gould and copious notes, including some tape-recordings, of their conversations. Certain of these photographs and comments of Gould were used in the magazine article. Nearly forty years later, in 1995, Carroll published through Stoddart Publishing Co. Limited a book entitled "Glenn Gould: Some Portraits of the Artist as a Young Man." Gould had died in 1982 and Gould's Estate did not authorize its publication or receive royalties from the book.

2. The book makes use of over 70 of the original 400 photographs and draws very extensively on the conversations that Carroll recorded back in 1956. The text of the book is largely comprised of extracts from these conversations. It is undisputed that Carroll is the owner of the copyright in the photographs. Gould's Estate, however, in these two actions, seeks damages claiming (i) that use of the photographs amounts to the tort of appropriation of personality, the cause of action for which may be asserted by the Estate; and (ii) that copyright in the oral conversations recorded by Carroll rests with Gould (now his Estate) and as such the conversations may not be used without the permission of the Estate.

The Photograph Action

. . .

4. In 1956, [Gould's agent] invited Carroll to take pictures of, and do a story on, Gould.... The photos and interview took place one year after Gould's major U.S. concert debut, less than one year after his first U.S. record release and the same year as a major North American concert tour. Given the number of photographs taken, Carroll was of the view that Gould would have been delighted if Carroll used them in subsequent publications so as to create further publicity for him. At no time during his life, did Gould or anyone on his behalf ever take the position that he had the right to restrict or control the use

of these photographs. On this basis, the defendants say that Carroll was free to use the photographs in any manner he saw fit.

5. On the other hand, the Gould Estate argued that it was well known that Gould was an intensely private individual who guarded his privacy. He took great care with the management of his personal image and reputation, and was scrupulously careful about the quality of materials which were released under his name, or projects in which he participated. He has been referred to as "Canada's own Greta Garbo"....

6. If Gould has a proprietary right to his personality, then the onus is on the defendants to show that Carroll had permission to appropriate that right by publishing the photographs of Gould. The onus should not be on the holder of the right to prove that he had placed restrictions on the exploitation of his own property.

7. The first question should then be: Did Gould in fact have any proprietary rights in his image, likeness or personality which have been appropriated by the publication of the photographs in the book?

i) The Tort of Appropriation of Personality

8. In Ontario, the common law tort of misappropriation of personality was first articulated by Estey J.A. in the Court of Appeal in *Krouse v. Chrysler Canada Ltd. et al.* (1973), 40 D.L.R. (3d) 15. While no formal definition of the tort was offered, he stated at pp. 30-1:

> ... there may well be circumstances in which the Courts would be justified in holding a defendant liable in damages for appropriation of a plaintiff's personality, amounting to an invasion of his right to exploit his personality by the use of his image, voice, or otherwise with damage to the plaintiff....

[The court then cites and quotes two other cases, *Athans v. Canadian Adventure Camps Ltd.*, 17 O.R. (2d) 425 (Ont. High Ct. J. 1977), and *Joseph v. Daniels* (1986), 11 C.P.R. (3d) 544 (B.C. Sup. Ct. 1986)]

11. The same type of tort, usually under the name "right of publicity", is also well-recognized in the United States....

12. The Gould Estate submits that the book in question is a compilation of photographs of Gould and the act of selling the book constitutes commercial exploitation. Accordingly, it argues that this amounts to unlawful appropriation of Gould's personality.

13. The few Canadian cases dealing with this tort have generally involved situations in which the name or image of an individual enjoying some celebrity status has been used in the advertising or promotion of the defendant's business or products....

14. Generally then, there has been an implication that the celebrity is endorsing the activity of the defendant. This contextual factor seems to have been an important underlying consideration in the courts' reasoning. In *Krouse, supra*, for example, Estey J.A. pointed out, at p. 29:

> ... Here the photograph was not used in such a way as to associate the respondent with the commercial enterprise or production of the Spotter [the name of a product] a fact which is not without legal significance.

Similarly, in *Athans*, Henry J. was concerned with whether the material in question had "the effect of establishing any connection in the minds of the relevant public between Mr. Athans and the [summer] camp" (p. 436). It should be pointed out that in *Athans, supra*, damages were ultimately awarded despite the judge's finding that people viewing the material in question would not conclude that the plaintiff was actually endorsing the defendant's waterskiing school. Instead, the plaintiff recovered on the basis that:

… the commercial use of his representational image by the defendants without his consent constituted an invasion and *pro tanto* an impairment of his exclusive right to market his personality and this, in my opinion, constitutes an aspect of the tort of appropriation of personality. [p. 437]

While at first glance this decision may seem to support the present defendants' broad interpretation of commercialization, the decision is consistent with the endorsement context. *Athans* was a situation where an identifiable "representational image" was utilized by a waterskiing school in the school's promotional brochure. Therefore, on the basis of these Canadian authorities it would seem open to the court to conclude, on a contextual basis, that the tort of appropriation of personality is restricted to endorsement-type situations.

15. More broadly, it also seems clear that in articulating this tort the court must be mindful of the public interest…. While not explicitly offering any principles that ought to guide the development of this tort, the [*Krouse*] Court at p. 30 did warn:

> The danger of extending the law of torts to cover every such exposure in public not expressly authorized is obvious.

16. The U.S. courts have similarly recognized the necessity of limits on the right of personality. These limits are usually discussed in terms of First Amendment considerations: "the scope of the right of publicity should be measured or balanced against societal interests in free expression" ([*Estate of*] *Presley* [*v. Russen*], *supra*, p. 1356)…. Accordingly, the right of publicity has not been successfully invoked in cases where the activity in question consists of thoughts, ideas, newsworthy events or matters of public interest. In this regard, it is important to note that:

> the scope of the subject matter which falls within the protected area of the 'newsworthy' or of 'public interest' extends far beyond the dissemination of news in the sense of current events and includes all types of factual, educational and historical data, or even entertainment and amusement. (*Current Audio Inc. v. RCA Corp.*, 337 N.Y.S. 2d 949 (Sup. Ct. 1972) at 954–56).

17. Conversely, the right of publicity has been upheld in situations where famous names or likeness are used "predominately in connection with the sale of consumer merchandise or solely for purposes of trade—e.g. merely to attract attention" (*Presley*, p. 1358)….

18. While Canada does not have a constitutional provision akin to the First Amendment which is applicable to the private law, no principled argument has been advanced to suggest that freedom of expression considerations should not animate Canadian courts in identifying the public interest and placing limits on the tort of appropriation of personality. Indeed, freedom of expression would seem to be a compelling and reasonably coherent basis for defining the "obvious" need for limits noted by Estey J.A. in *Krouse*, *supra*.

19. In the end then, and perhaps at the risk of oversimplifying, it seems that the courts have drawn a "sales vs. subject" distinction. Sales constitute commercial exploitation and invoke the tort of appropriation of personality. The identity of the celebrity is merely being used in some fashion. The activity cannot be said to be about the celebrity. This is in contrast to situations in which the celebrity is the actual subject of the work or enterprise, with biographies perhaps being the clearest example. These activities would not be within the ambit of the tort. To take a more concrete example, in endorsement situations, posters and board games, the essence of the activity is not the celebrity. It is the use of some attributes of the celebrity for another purpose. Biographies, other books, plays, and satirical skits are by their nature different. The subject of the activity is the celebrity and the work is an attempt to provide some insights about that celebrity.

20. Adapted to the present case, the book in question contains 26 pages of text by Carroll together with photographs depicting Gould in posed and spontaneous moments at the beginning of his concert career. I agree with the comment on the overleaf:

> They capture the passion and brilliance of Gould as pianist, the solitude of Gould as artist and the boyish nature of Gould as a young man.

Although it is primarily through Gould's own images and words, this book provides insight to anyone interested in Gould, the man and his music. The author added his own creativity in recounting his time spent with Gould and in making decisions about which photographs and text to use and how they should be arranged to provide this glimpse into Gould's solitary life. There is a public interest in knowing more about one of Canada's musical geniuses. Because of this public interest, the book therefore falls into the protected category and there cannot be said to be any right of personality in Gould which has been unlawfully appropriated by the defendants.

ii) Survivability, of the Right of Publicity

21. Although not necessary to the decision in view of the above finding, the issue had arisen as to whether the tort of appropriation of personality survives the death of the individual and I am impelled to make some comments about this. Of those U.S. jurisdictions which have considered the matter, the substantial majority recognize that the right of publicity is devisable and descendible. It also seems clear that the modern trend is toward this recognition....

22. The defendants place some reliance on the fact that in the three provincial Privacy Acts which provide for a cause of action for the appropriation of personality (Newfoundland, Saskatchewan and British Columbia), the right of action is extinguished by the death of the individual whose rights are alleged to have been violated. However, this factor is not persuasive in the case at bar. In creating a statutory right of action, the legislature may obviously impose statutory restrictions on that cause of action. Here though, the case is grounded in a common law cause of action. As such it is not constrained by the restrictions which apply to the statutory right of action.

23. A more theoretical approach to distinguishing the Privacy Acts can be found in U.S. law. There, several cases have recognized a distinction between the right of privacy and the right of publicity. The former is considered a personal tort and is designed to protect an individual's interest in dignity and peace of mind. The right of publicity, on the other hand, protects the commercial value of a person's celebrity status. As such, it is a form of intangible property, akin to copyright or patent, that is descendible. Given that the Canadian statutory rights of action are found in Privacy Acts, it would certainly seem that, following the U.S. reasoning, whatever statutory restrictions there may be on the rights of action for privacy violations and unauthorized use of personality, they should not be applied to the common law tort of appropriation of personality.

24. The right of publicity, being a form of intangible property under Ontario law akin to copyright, should descend to the celebrity's heirs. Reputation and fame can be a capital asset that one nurtures and may choose to exploit and it may have a value much greater than any tangible property. There is no reason why such an asset should not be devisable to heirs....

As a final comment on this topic, the U.S. cases on both sides of the right of publicity debate have expressed concern over whether there should be a durational limit on the right of publicity after it is inherited (see *Presley, supra,* 1355 fn. 10, and *Lugosi v. Universal Pictures, Cal.,* 603 P. 2d 425 (Sup. Ct. 1979) at p. 430). For the present purposes though, suffice it to say that Gould passed away in 1982, and it seems reasonable to conclude that whatever the durational limit, if any, it is unlikely to be less than 14 years. The protection granted by other intangible property rights such as patents and copyrights is longer. So, too, any durational limit on Gould's right of publicity would not yet have expired.

The Words Action

26. The issue in this action is whether Gould, and now his Estate, has copyright in the oral conversations which occurred between himself and Carroll and form the essence of the text in the book in question.

[The court found no right of action under Canada's Copyright Act.]

Disposition

33. There is no basis in law for the plaintiffs' actions. Accordingly, there will be summary judgment dismissing both actions....

———————

Marlene Dietrich

Case No. 1 ZR 49/97 (Dec. 1, 1999), BGHZ 143, 214
Bundesgerichtshof (Federal Supreme Court) (Germany)

Translated by Raymond Youngs
Copyright 2001 by Professor Basil Markesinis

Facts:

The claimant is the only child and sole heir of the actress Marlene Dietrich, who died on the 6th May 1992. She is also the executrix of her mother's estate.

The first defendant ("the defendant") produced a musical on the life of Marlene Dietrich in 1993. It had its première at the beginning of April 1993 in Berlin and was performed to start with until the end of May 1993 under the title "Tell me where the flowers are" and then until the end of June 1993 under the title "Marlene". There were no further performances of the musical, which was not very successful. The defendant was the sole manager of the Lighthouse Musical Production Company Ltd. ("Lighthouse Musical"), which no longer exists. He is the owner of trade mark no. 2022193 "Marlene" which, following an application in June 1992, was registered in the same year for, amongst other things, the development, production and performance of literary and/or musical entertainments for stage and film. The claimant has already withdrawn at first instance an application to extinguish this trade mark.

Lighthouse Musical granted to FIAT Automobil AG — in accordance with a confirmatory letter by the defendant of the 23rd June 1993 — rights to the production and marketing of two hundred models of the special Lancia type Y 10 "Marlene" and allowed it in particular to use the signature "Marlene", a picture of Marlene Dietrich from the year 1930 and the registered trade mark "Marlene". In return, FIAT advertised for the musical in accordance with the agreement when displaying the vehicle. It offered the Lancia special model "Marlene" with considerable advertising expenditure and sold a hundred of the vehicles.

In the programme for the performance of the Musical "Tell me where the flowers are," a doublesided advertisement for the Ellen Betrix enterprise was printed, advertising cosmetics under the heading "the Marlene Look" and using a drawing of Marlene Dietrich.

In return for this, the enterprise made available all the make-up materials for the performance of the musical to a value of 2,000 to 3,000 DM.

Lighthouse Musical also arranged for numerous so-called promotion articles (telephone cards, mugs, T-shirts, watches and badges) and postcards to be produced, which were provided with a picture of Marlene Dietrich and—with the exception of the badges—with the original title of the musical "Tell me where the flowers are". These objects were offered for sale in June 1993 at a stand in front of the theatre.

The claimant is claiming from the defendant injunctive relief, a declaration of his duty to compensate for harm and provision of information in respect of the use of the picture, name and signature of Marlene Dietrich, on the basis of her own rights and her legal status as executrix for the estate of her mother. She considers that the claims she is making arise from infringement of the posthumous personality rights of her mother. She has also based the claims she is making on the rights of the American law enterprises Marlene Inc and M Dietrich Inc which have been transferred to her.

The claimant in the end applied—insofar as it is still of importance for the decision on the appeal in law—

1. for the defendant to be ordered under threat of punitive measures (Ordnungsmitteln) to refrain from:

a) using the name Marlene for the purpose of the advertising and/or labeling of goods by way of business and/or letting the name be used in connection with the person, life and work of Marlene Dietrich;

b) producing, and/or offering and/or disseminating objects of a commercial kind by way of business which are provided with pictures of Marlene Dietrich and/or letting them be produced and/or offered and/or disseminated;

c) producing, and/or offering and/or disseminating objects of a commercial kind by way of business which are provided with a handwritten signature of Marlene Dietrich by her first name and/or letting them be produced and/or offered and/or disseminated;

if these actions at a) to c) do not in each case occur within the framework of an artistic analysis of Marlene Dietrich or the interests of the general public in information about Marlene Dietrich as an absolute person of contemporary history;

[or] alternatively:

for the defendant to be ordered to refrain, in order to avoid punitive measures (Ordnungsmitteln) being taken, from

a) allowing third parties to use pictures of Marlene Dietrich and/or to use pictures of Marlene Dietrich together with her handwritten signature and/or the name "Marlene" for the labelling of goods or commercial services and in advertising for goods or commercial services;

b) disseminating written material which contains advertisements by enterprises in which goods and commercial services are advertised by use of the name "Marlene" and a pictorial representation of Marlene Dietrich;

c) offering goods for sale, letting them be offered, disseminating them or letting them be disseminated, on which there is a picture of Marlene Dietrich, if the goods contain no additional verbal or symbolic information about the person, life or impact of Marlene Dietrich;

2. for a declaration that the defendant must compensate her for all harm which she has suffered so far from the actions from which he is to refrain and which she will in future suffer or that the defendant must hand over the enrichment he has obtained;

3. further that the defendant be ordered to give information to her about the extent of the actions causing harm which correspond to the requirements of the injunctions …

The defendant has defended the claim. He is of the opinion that any possible invasion of the general right of personality of Marlene Dietrich by advertising measures for the musical is covered by artistic freedom. Besides this, an infringement of posthumous personality rights could not be the basis of any claims to compensation for harm, because these rights only protected non-material interests.

The Landgericht granted the application for injunctive relief in the form of the main application, and rejected the claim in other respects. In response to the appeal against this decision lodged by both sides, the Kammergericht—rejecting the appeal in other respects—allowed the application for injunctive relief in the form of the alternative application with limitations (reference omitted), and ordered the defendant, under threat of punitive measures (Ordnungsmitteln), to refrain from:

a) Allowing third parties to use pictures of Marlene Dietrich and/or to use pictures of Marlene Dietrich together with her written signature and/or the name "Marlene" for labeling goods or commercial services or in advertising goods or commercial services, if this occurs as in the agreement between Lighthouse Musical and FIAT Automobil AG in accordance with the defendant's letter of the 23rd June 1993;

b) Disseminating written material which contains advertisements of enterprises in which goods or commercial services are advertised using the name "Marlene" and a pictorial representation of Marlene Dietrich, if this occurs as with the advertising of cosmetics by the "Ellen Betrix" enterprise in the programme for the performance of the musical "Tell me where the flowers are".

c) Offering goods for sale, or letting them to be offered, disseminating them or letting them be disseminated, on which there is a picture of Marlene Dietrich, if the goods contain no additional verbal or symbolic information about the person, life or impact of Marlene Dietrich or advertise for works of art which concern Marlene Dietrich.

The Senate has accepted for decision the claimant's appeal in law against this decision only insofar as the claimant is not suing on the basis of a transferred right. Within the scope of this acceptance, the claimant is pursuing the applications ultimately lodged by her. The defendant applies for the appeal in law to be rejected.

Reasons:

The appeal in law is unsuccessful insofar as it objects to the appeal court only allowing the claim for injunctive relief in the limited form of the alternative application. It is however successful insofar as it is directed against rejection of the claim for a declaration and information.

Within this scope the appeal in law leads to quashing of the judgment on appeal and to an order being made against the defendant.

[The Court first held that the injunction was properly "limited to the actual form of the infringement in each case." It then turned to the second issue.]

II. The application for a declaration and the giving of information:

The objection by the appeal in law to the rejection by the appeal court of the applications for a declaration and the giving of information is successful. The appeal court was admittedly correct here in proceeding on the basis that a claim to enrichment against the defendant does not fall to be considered, because the person obliged to compensate for the enrichment would not have been the defendant personally but Lighthouse Musical. However, the appeal court's assumption that the claimant has no right to compensation for harm from any legal standpoint proves to be legally incorrect. Contrary to this view, the claimant can demand from the defendant compensation for harm under § 823(1) of the BGB. The general personality right protected by § 823(1) of the BGB and its special forms of manifestation, like the right to one's own picture and the right to one's name, do not only serve the protection of non-material personality interests, but also ones which are of financial value (see 1.). The corresponding components—protecting the interests which are of financial value—of Marlene Dietrich's right of personality passed on her death to the claimant (see 2.). The defendant infringed these rights unlawfully and culpably, and therefore has to pay compensation for harm and give information to the claimant (see 3.). Under these circumstances, no decision is needed on whether such a claim could also arise under § 1 of the UWG (see 4.).

1. The general right of personality has been recognised in the case law of the Bundesgerichtshof since 1954 as a basic right constitutionally guaranteed by Arts 1 and 2 of the Basic Law and at the same time as an "other right" protected in civil law under § 823(1) of the BGB (constant case law since BGHZ 13, 334, 338—*Readers' Letters*). It guarantees as against all the world the protection of human dignity and the right to free development of the personality. Special forms of manifestation of the general right of personality are the right to one's own picture (§§ 22 ff. of the KUG) and the right to one's name (§ 12 of the BGB). They guarantee protection of the personality for the sphere regulated by them (reference omitted).

The general right of personality and its special forms of manifestation primarily serve the protection of non-material interests, in particular the protection of the claim of the personality to worth and respect. This protection is realised by the fact that on an infringement of these rights, besides defensive claims, claims to compensation for harm come into consideration which aim at compensating not only material but also—when it is a question of a serious intrusion and the harm cannot be satisfactorily compensated in another way—non-material harm. This compensation is admittedly not based on a claim to compensation for pain and suffering under § 847 of the BGB, but on a legal remedy which originates directly from the protective mandate in Arts 1 and 2 para 1 of the Basic Law (see BVerfGE 34, 269, 282 and 292 = GRUR 1974, 44, 46, 48 and 50—*Soraya*). The granting of monetary compensation in cases of this kind rests on the concept that without such a claim, violations of the dignity and honour of human beings frequently remain without sanction, with the consequence that legal protection of the personality would atrophy (references omitted).

But besides this, the general right of personality and its special forms also protect those interests of the person which are of financial value. A considerable economic value can attach to the image, name and other features of the personality, like for example the voice. This value is generally based on the person's fame and reputation in the public eye—mostly as a result of special achievements in, for example, the areas of sport or the arts. A well-known personality can exploit this popularity and the image connected with it economically by allowing third parties to use his picture or his name and also other features of his personality which facilitate recognition in advertising for goods or services in return for money. Frequently therefore fewer non-material than commercial interests of the person affected are harmed by an unauthorised use of the features of his personality for the purpose for instance of advertising, because he will feel himself harmed less in his honour and his reputation than he will see himself as disadvantaged financially (references omitted).

The Bundesgerichtshof has always included the commercial interests in the personality within the protection guaranteed by the personality rights. The personality rights should accordingly protect the right of free decision, belonging only to the person entitled, on the question of whether and under what conditions his picture or his name—and the same applies for other characteristic features of the personality—is used for the business interests of third parties (references omitted). In relation to economic interests in the personality, the Bundesgerichtshof has recognised that the right of personality also shows elements which are of financial value (BGHZ 50, 133, 137—*Mephisto*). It has accordingly described the right to one's own picture as a exclusive right of financial value and generally regarded claims for compensation as possible on violation of the right of personality (references omitted).

2. The elements of financial value in the right of Marlene Dietrich to her own picture and name have passed to the claimant as sole heir. This is because, regardless of their transferability between living persons, these elements are—in contrast to the highly personal elements which protect non-material interests—inheritable.

a) Insofar as the rights of personality protect non-material interests, they are indissolubly bound to the person of the holder of them and, as highly personal rights, are not renounceable and are inalienable, and are therefore not transferable and not inheritable (see BGHZ 50, 133, 137—*Mephisto*; other references omitted). No-one can relinquish his right to his own picture, his right to his name or another personality right completely and conclusively. This would contradict the guarantee of human dignity (Art 1 of the Basic Law) and of the right to self-determination (Art 2 of the Basic Law; other references omitted).

b) The question of whether the elements of the right of personality which are of financial value and which protect commercial interests in the personality are transferable and inheritable has not yet been expressly decided by the Bundesgerichtshof. But in some decisions it has already been intimated that the principle of non-transferability and non-inheritability does not necessarily apply for all elements of the personality right. Thus it has stated in the *Mephisto* decision "that the right of personality—apart from its elements which are of financial value—is, as a highly personal right, not transferable and not inheritable" (BGHZ 50, 133, 137). In the "*NENA*" decision, it left open whether the transfer of the right to one's own picture is ruled out because of its legal character as a general personality right (reference omitted). A considerable part of the academic literature argues for transferability and inheritability of the property law powers which are connected with the rights of personality (references omitted). Others consider these powers to be simply non-transferable because of their personality right character (references omitted).

c) A number of considerations argue for the elements of the right of personality which are of financial value not being indissolubly bound to the person of the holder of the right in the same manner as the part of the right of personality which protects non-material interests. There is also the special need for protection which can only be taken into account by regarding the elements of the personality right which are of financial value as inheritable. Whether this part of the right of personality can be transferred between living persons or whether rights to the use of it can be granted does not, however, need to be decided in the present case.

aa) First the examples of other rights show that the character of a right can change in the estimation of the legal order.

Thus the Reichsgericht has regarded the right to the name of a firm as still being the right to a name and therefore as a right of personality (references omitted). The Bundesgerichtshof has not maintained this case law. It has classified the material right to a firm's name as a property right, and based this on the fact that the name in this area has largely become separated from a particular person and becomes associated with an object—an enterprise or an association of persons. Considerable property law interests would thereby come into play which could outweigh the non-material interests in the name and completely displace them (reference omitted). Even the firm which contains the name of a person can therefore—together with the trading enterprise (see §§ 22 and 23 of the Commercial Code)—in principle be transferred and inherited without limitations.

Trade mark law was likewise categorised by the Reichsgericht as still being a personality right (references omitted). The trade mark has since become completely detached from its relationship to a business and the personality of an entrepreneur. It can be acquired without a business (§ 7 of the Trade Marks Act) and it can be transferred and inherited (§ 27(1) of the Trade Marks Act). Even a mark which consists of a person's name or picture is today a non-material property right capable of being freely dealt with.

bb) The picture, name and other characterising features of the personality have always been capable—as a reflection of the defensive rights granted by the legal order against an unauthorised use—of being exploited commercially and in particular of being used for advertising purposes (reference omitted). Protection of interests of financial value was also always connected with this, but it did not necessarily have to be regarded as an independent element of the right of personality. However in past decades technical, economic and business conditions have changed (reference omitted). Features of the personality can with improved technical opportunities be recorded in sound and vision, and copied and disseminated. They have become economically exploitable to an extent not previously known, because of the continuing development of the mass media. So-called image transfer has a large role to play in advertising. It involves diverting the positive associations, which consumers connect with a well known personality, to the product to be advertised. In this respect well-known personalities contribute to creation of value to a considerable extent. The possibility of marketing the personality of, for instance, well-known figures in sport or the arts has—without passing judgment on this occurrence—become an important factor in product development which can no longer be imagined as not existing.

cc) Recognition of the inheritability of the elements of the right of personality which are of financial value is required to guarantee protection from commercial exploitation of a name, a picture and other features of the personality of a deceased person by those who are not entitled to do so. An effective posthumous protection of the elements of the right of personality which are of financial value is only guaranteed if the heir can step into the role of the holder of the right of personality and can, in defending the presumed interests of the deceased, proceed in the same way as that person could have done against an unauthorised exploitation.

It is true that, according to constant case law, the continuing image of the personality is also protected after death against serious distortions (BGHZ 50, 133, 136 ff.—*Mephisto*; other references omitted). Likewise at any rate the right to one's own picture (§ 22 sentence 3 of the KUG) and possibly also the right to a name (reference omitted) continue to have an effect beyond death. But, on a posthumous violation of these rights, only defensive claims are granted to the person entitled to exercise them, and not claims to compensation for harm, because a deceased person could not suffer harm which is compensable by a money payment (references omitted). In these cases it is only a question of the infringement of non-material interests, for the protection of which the highly personal claim to respect continues to have an effect. This admittedly is not transferable and not inheritable, but it can be exercised after death for defensive purposes by a person authorised to do so (BGHZ 50, 133, 137 f.—*Mephisto*). The defensive claims granted are of little use, however, if the violation of the right—as is frequently the case—has already ended, before the person entitled to the claim obtains knowledge of it. Besides this, it seems unfair to surrender the financial value created by the achievements of the deceased and embodied in his picture, his name or his other personality features after his death to the clutches of just any third party, instead of giving this financial value to his heirs or relations or other persons who were close to him when he was alive (references omitted).

Doubts are certainly raised in part in the academic literature about promoting the increasing commercialisation of the personality. It is said that this is a possible unsatisfactory development in society, against which the legal order must take a stand, because the creation of a marketable non-material property right is in the end result directed against the individual and makes his personality available for third parties (references omitted). These doubts should certainly not be simply dismissed, but in the end they do not prevail. For one thing, the protection of the personality is strengthened rather than weakened by the recognition of an independent inheritable element of the right of personality which has financial value, and on the violation of which the person entitled can acquire his own defensive rights and rights to compensation for harm. This applies not least in cases in which the name, picture or other personality features of a deceased person are used by a third party for commercial purposes contrary to the wishes of the heir and/or relatives and contrary to the presumed wishes of the deceased holder of the right of personality. This is because the right of personality in this situation will not be effectively protected with the help of defensive claims alone, as sanctions are only available in the case of repetition. A claim to enrichment can also fail in these cases, if—as here—the violator himself has not been enriched. Besides this, a claim for enrichment (reference omitted) also assumes a corresponding legal assignment of assets (reference omitted).

For another thing, it has to be borne in mind that the legal order in relation to marketing of legally protected positions does not form a rigid system to which reality would have to orientate itself. Instead, besides the indisputable task of setting predetermined boundaries by value judgments, the law also has an assisting function in that it must also offer a regulatory framework for new forms of marketing which are in the interest of the marketer as well as of the person who might permit such marketing of his personality. It is true that the legal order must confront the demands which arise from the growing commercialisation of the right of personality where legal or ethical principles of higher rank demand this (references omitted). But an ineffective protection of the right of personality, limited to defensive powers, does not constitute a remedy against undesired exploitation of the personality. The interest which exists in not harming the image of a deceased person by unrestricted commercial exploitation of features of his personality can best be served by the heir being able to resist unauthorised exploitation, as holder of the elements of the right of personality which are of financial value. In this connection he has in principle at his disposal the same claims as the living holder of the right of personality—despite the differences which can arise after the death in respect of the scope of the content of the right (see BGHZ 50, 133, 140 f.—*Mephisto*).

Finally, it should be pointed out that the powers of the heir derive from the holder of the right of personality and cannot be used in a manner contrary to his presumed wishes. The power of the heir to exploit the elements of the right of personality which are of financial value by taking action against an unauthorised use of the picture or name of a deceased person is therefore not linked to an unlimited positive right of use which could be exploited even against the express or presumed interests of the deceased holder of the personality right. The heir is only allowed to use the opportunities for marketing which exist or continue after the death on taking the deceased's will into account. In the present case, which concerns compensation for an unauthorised use, it is beyond doubt that the measures taken by the claimant are in the interest of her deceased mother.

d) Whilst the defensive claims which protect the deceased's non-material interests are to be made by the relatives (§ 22 sentences 3 and 4 of the KUG) or by a person entitled to exploit them appointed for this purpose (see BGHZ 50, 133, 139 f. — *Mephisto*), only the heirs are to be considered as holders of the powers which are of financial value (reference omitted) and they are not necessarily identical with the persons just mentioned. It is not however an argument against the inheritability of the elements of the right of personality which are of financial value that different persons can become entitled to the non-material and the financial interests.

If the elements of the right of personality which are of financial value are inherited, they still remain, for the preservation of the non-material interests of the holder of the right, inseparably linked with the inalienable highly personal elements of the right of personality. This is because commercial exploitation frequently also affects the powers which belong to the relatives (§ 22 sentence 2 of the KUG) and other persons entitled to exploit them. In this respect the position is no different from that applying in copyright law. Here the powers in copyright personality law which are likewise aimed at protecting non-material interests (§§ 11 ff. of the Copyright Act) are frequently not in the same hands as the rights of use (references omitted). This means that uses which also interfere with powers in copyright personality law need not only the consent of the person entitled to the use but also of the owner of the copyright personality right. The situation is no different if, for example, the picture of the deceased is to be used for commercial purposes. Here the consent of the heirs as well as of the owner of the elements of the right of personality which are of financial value and also of the relatives is necessary (§ 22 sentence 3 of the KUG). Likewise the non-material interests of the deceased protected by the general right of personality can be affected by a commercial use of features of the personality, with the result that the person with the right of exploitation could take action against such a use in spite of agreement by the heirs. In the present case, such rights are however in one person's hands, because the claimant is the sole heir, as well as the only relative of Marlene Dietrich (see § 22 sentence 4 of the KUG).

e) Nor can the objection of lack of legal certainty be successfully raised against the inheritability of the elements of the right of personality which are of financial value. The possibility of commercial exploitation of the features of the personality has developed — as explained above (under II.2. c) aa)) — from the protection under the personality right of non-material interests. Therefore it seems reasonable to assume that the protection of commercial interests cannot extend in time beyond the protection of non-material interests in the personality. The ten-year period of § 22 sentence 2 of the KUG offers a clue in this respect. But it can remain open whether longer protection of the commercial interests should be considered if and insofar as longer protection of non-material interests arises exceptionally from the general right of personality (see BGHZ 50, 133, 140 f. — *Mephisto*). This because in the present case it is a question of the use of the name and picture of Marlene Dietrich in the period shortly after her death.

3. The defendant has unlawfully and culpably violated the elements of financial value of the right of Marlene Dietrich to her own picture and name which have passed to the claimant and he is therefore obliged to provide compensation for harm as well as to supply information.

Contrary to the view of the reply to the appeal in law, the application which has been made for a declaration that there is a duty to provide compensation does not require a special intensity of interference on violation of the right. It is true that, for violations of non-material interests, claims for monetary compensation only come into consideration in the lifetime of the holder of the right of personality (see above under II.1.) and only in relation to serious encroachments. But this does not apply on a violation of material interests of the kind under discussion here. A person who culpably violates the elements of the right of personality which are of financial value is liable for the harm which occurs, just as for a violation of other exclusive rights which are of financial value, regardless of how serious the interference was.

a) The right of Marlene Dietrich to her own picture (§ 22 of the KUG) has—as the appeal court has correctly accepted—been violated by her picture having been used without the necessary consent for the special model Lancia Y 10 "Marlene", for the cosmetics advertisement by the Ellen Betrix enterprise and for promotion articles.

aa) The photographs and drawings used are pictures in the sense of § 22 sentence 1 of the KUG. A picture in the sense of this provision is a portrayal of a person which reproduces their outward appearance in a manner recognisable to a third party (references omitted). It does not matter in this connection how the picture has been produced, so the protection of pictures does not only include photographs but also other forms of portrayal as for example drawings (reference omitted).

bb) These pictures have been disseminated without the consent of the claimant as the owner of the elements of the right of personality which are of financial value and—which admittedly does not matter as the basis of an obligation to provide compensation for harm—as the person entitled under § 22 sentence 3 of the KUG.

cc) The consent of the claimant was also not dispensable. It is true that pictures from the realm of contemporary history may be disseminated under § 23(1) no. 1 of the KUG without the consent necessary under § 22 of the KUG. Marlene Dietrich was—and the reply to the appeal in law also does not question this—a so-called absolute person of contemporary history (references omitted). But a person who by publication is not fulfilling any interest of the general public in information which is worthy of protection, but is only using the picture of another for advertisement purposes to satisfy his business interest cannot refer to the exception provision of § 23(1) no. 1 of the KUG (references omitted). That is the position here. The use of the picture was not to give information about the life or work of Marlene Dietrich, but exclusively to advertise cars, cosmetics and promotion articles.

The defendant can also not successfully claim that these were advertising measures for the musical which are covered by artistic freedom. Admittedly advertising for a work of art falls within the protection of Art 5 paragraph 3 sentence 1 of the Basic Law. This is because artistic freedom does not only protect the actual artistic activity, the "work area" ("Werkbereich") of the artistic work, but also the "effect area" ("Wirkbereich") in which access to the work of art is provided to the public. Advertisement for the work of art is also included in this (references omitted). But the picture and name of Marlene Dietrich were not used to advertise for the musical, but exclusively to promote the sales of the products provided with it. According to the findings of the appeal court, which are free of legal error, there is no connection which is recognisable for third parties between these products and the musical. No reference is made to the musical on these products; even the words "Tell me where the flowers are" on the telephone cards, the wrist watches and the mugs were not only the former title of the musical, but also the title of a song which contributed in a special way to Marlene Dietrich's fame. No different assessment is required just because for instance the FIAT and Ellen Betrix enterprises have each provided consideration for the use of the picture and name of Marlene Dietrich, which was to benefit the musical. This does not change the fact that the picture of Marlene Dietrich was not directly used as a means to draw the public's attention to the musical.

b) The right to determine whether one's own name may be used for advertising purposes, to which the claimant is entitled as heir of Marlene Dietrich, has further been infringed by the mention of the name "Marlene" in the advertising (references omitted). This power likewise constitutes an inheritable element of the right of personality which is of financial value insofar as it protects commercial interests of the bearer of the name. It is not a question here of violation of the powers under the law on names (§ 12 of the BGB), which can possibly come into consideration even with a use which is not related to the name if the impression would arise in the ordinary affairs of life that the bearer of the name has granted to the user a right to appropriate use of the name (references omitted).

The appeal court has correctly assumed that the use to which objection has been made of the signature "Marlene" is to be seen as an unauthorised utilisation of the name of Marlene Dietrich. It is true that first names on their own are mostly not understood as a reference to a certain person. This may be different in the case of Marlene Dietrich in view of her outstanding fame and the comparatively strong identification power of her first name (reference omitted). But this can be left open here because in the actual form of the violation which the appeal court has alone made the subject of the judgment, the first name has not been used on its own, but has on each occasion been used with a picture of Marlene Dietrich.

c) The defendant must assume liability for the violation of the elements of the right of personality of Marlene Dietrich which are of financial value.

d) The defendant must therefore compensate the claimant for the harm to her which has already arisen and will yet arise in the future through violations of the right of personality. The claimant can calculate the harm which has arisen for her either actually or by analogy with a licence, or demand the violator's profits (reference omitted). In order to be able to choose the form of calculation of harm which is most favourable for her and in order to calculate the harm, the claimant has a claim to the supply of the information for which she has applied.

4. Under the given circumstances it does not need to be clarified whether the claimant is also entitled to claims under § 1 of the UWG. Competition law would anyway offer no possibility of resolving the present case without recourse to the right of personality. Even if a competition relationship existed between the parties, classification of the marketing opportunities is not to be founded on competition law but only on the right of personality. . . .

————

Notes and Questions

1. Can you articulate what the difference is in France between the majority view and the more recent view (according to the authors)? How would the Marlene Dietrich case be decided under French law?

2. In the French judicial system, the Tribunal de Grande Instance (T.G.I.), is a trial court. The Cour d'Appel (CA), or Court of Appeal, is the intermediate appellate court; and the Cour de Cassation (Cass.), is the court of last resort (the French equivalent of the U.S. Supreme Court). The C.P.I. is the Code de la propriété intellectuelle, or Intellectual Property Code. Art. 212-2 of the C.P.I., cited in the excerpt, states: "A performer shall have the right to respect for his name, his capacity, and his performance. This inalienable and imprescriptible right shall attach to his person. It may be transmitted to his heirs in order to protect his performance and his memory after his death." ("Imprescriptible" means that the right is not subject to any statute of limitations.)

3. In the *Gould* case, was the ruling on the descendibility of the right to prevent misappropriation of personality necessary to the decision? If not, why did the judge feel "impelled to make some comments about this"? How much weight should those "comments" be given in subsequent cases?

4. The court in *Gould* declines to decide how long the right of publicity should last after death, remarking only that if there is to be a limit, "it is unlikely to be less than 14 years." What is the basis for this conclusion? Is the analogy to patent (which carries a 20-year term) and copyright (life-plus-50 years in Canada) a persuasive one?

5. In the *Gould* case, where does the court draw the line between appropriations that are permitted and those that are forbidden? How does that line compare with that drawn in the United States? This issue will be considered further in Chapters VII and VIII, below.

6. The decision in the *Gould* case was appealed from the Ontario Court of Justice (a trial court) to the Ontario Court of Appeal. Although the decision was affirmed, the Court of Appeal decided the case on very different grounds:

> The principal focus of the motions judge was on the second basis of the claim, misappropriation of personality.... I agree with the motions judge's ultimate disposition and accordingly would dismiss the appeal, but my view of the issues differs from his in that I would decide the case on the basis of conventional principles relating to copyright. In my opinion, it is not necessary to decide the issues in this case on the basis of the relatively new development in tort of appropriation of personality when this case so clearly sounds in intellectual property. Put shortly, the motions judge addressed Gould's right to preserve his privacy and exploit commercially his own fame, whereas I would address the proprietary rights Carroll had in the photographs and other material created by Carroll in 1956 and again in 1995.

This approach raises the question whether the right of publicity is preempted by copyright law, which specifies that the owner of the copyright in a photograph is the photographer, rather than the subject. If a third party purchases the right to reproduce a photograph from the copyright owner, should the subject have standing to complain? Does it matter to what use the photograph will be put? These issues will be addressed from a U.S. perspective in Chapter X, below.

7. In the German Judicial System, the Landgericht (LG) is a trial court; and the Oberlandesgericht (OLG), or Regional Court, is an intermediate appellate court. (The Kammergericht is the OLG for the State of Berlin; it retains a different name for purely historical reasons.) The Bundesgerichtshof (BGH), or Supreme Court of Justice, is the highest court for ordinary civil matters. (There is a different court of last resort for Constitutional matters: the Bundesverfassungsgericht (BVG), or Constitutional Court of Justice.) Decisions of the BGH are published in BGHZ; the standard citation format is BGHZ (volume), (page number of the decision), (page number of the reference). The BGH was formerly known as the Reichsgericht.

The Basic Law is the German Constitution. The BGB (Bürgerliches Gesetzbuch) is the Civil Code. The KUG (Kunsturhebergesetz) is the Act on the Protection of Copyright in Works of Art and Photographs. (The copyright act for all other works is the Urheberrechtsgesetz, or UrhG). The UWG (Gesetz gegen den unlauteren Wettbewerb) is the Unfair Competition Act.

8. In the *Marlene Dietrich* case, the claimant sought a declaration that the defendants owed her damages for violating her mother's right of personality. The difficulty was the BGH had previously held (in the *Mephisto* case) that the right of personality recognized under the Basic Law did not descend. The *Mephisto* case allowed for the possibility of an injunction after the death of the celebrity, but not damages. How does the BGH avoid this holding in the *Marelene Dietrich* case?

9. In a subsequent case, the BGH addressed the duration of post-mortem rights of personality. Noting that under section 22 of the KUG, the right of a person to consent to the public use of his or her image may be exercised by his or her heirs until 10 years after his or her death, the BGH held that the same term should apply to other types of violations of the right of personality. In re Kinski-Klaus.de, Case No. 1 ZR 277/08 (Oct. 5, 2006), BGHZ 169, 193. Do you find it odd that the duration of a *constitutional* right is limited by a term of years contained in a *statute*? Does this holding shed new light on the *Gould* court's view that the term, if any, "is unlikely to be less than 14 years"?

Chapter V

Alternative Means of Protection: Celebrities as Trademarks

A. Domestic Law

1. Introduction

Rights of publicity in the United States are primarily a creation of state law. Therefore, it may surprise you to learn that federal trademark law provides an alternative mechanism for protecting rights of publicity. On further reflection, however, it should not be that surprising to see trademark law injected into the protection of rights of publicity. By now, we are all familiar with the efforts of many celebrities to make themselves into a "brand." Celebrities serve as spokespersons for companies, and, more importantly, they seek to project a particular image that becomes the public "brand" image of the celebrity. Although the classical right of publicity as explained in Chapters I to IV can be of help in creating and protecting this "brand" image, trademark law is another (and perhaps more logical) strand of law for this purpose.

Trademark law protects words, symbols, and devices used by companies to identify and distinguish the source of their goods and services from those of other companies. Coca-Cola, the Nike swoosh, and the distinctive colors on a box of Kodak film (in addition to the Kodak name) are all examples of such source identifiers. Although trademark, like rights of publicity, can trace its roots to state common law (and, to some degree, state statutory law), today trademark owners normally use a federal statute to obtain protection. (They also may use state trademark law, but in most circumstances the standard for infringement will be the same.) The federal statute is the Lanham Act (named for its most prominent sponsor) and it is codified at 15 U.S.C. §§ 1051 *et seq*.

Three separate provisions of the Lanham Act contain provisions relevant to rights of publicity. In order to understand these provisions, a small amount of background is in order.

First, in order to claim true *trademark* infringement one must have a trademark. The Lanham Act contains the following definition:

> The term "trademark" includes any word, name, symbol, or device, or any combination thereof—
>
> (1) used by a person, or
>
> (2) which a person has a bona fide intention to use in commerce and applies to register on the principal register established by this Act,

to identify and distinguish his or her goods, including a unique product, from those manufactured or sold by others and to indicate the source of the goods, even if that source is unknown.

15 U.S.C. § 1127. Thus, if Tiger Woods creates a "Tiger Woods" line of clothing, the name "Tiger Woods" could be an actual trademark, because the "Tiger Woods" name on the clothing labels denotes a unique source of the goods, even though the source may not be known. As you can see from the definition, a trademark need not be a word or name. It can be almost anything—a picture, a signature, a sound—that denotes a unique source of goods or services. However, in order to act as a true trademark, the celebrity's name or image must be a source identifier; that is, it must denote the source of some goods or services. It is not enough that the name or image is recognized by the public, or that the celebrity is an endorser of the product.

Many of the provisions of the Lanham Act are related to the process of, and rights granted by, registration of trademarks with the Patent and Trademark Office ("PTO"). It is not necessary to register a trademark in order to assert trademark protection under the common law (and unregistered trademarks can even claim protection under a provision of the Lanham Act discussed below). However, if a trademark satisfies the statutory criteria, it is entitled to be registered. In fact, in some cases, celebrities have registered their names or likenesses as trademarks with the PTO. In addition to various administrative criteria (filing an application and the internal examination process of the PTO), the statutory criteria for registration include affirmative criteria (that is, attributes a trademark must possess to be capable of registration), and negative criteria (attributes that would prevent registration).

Two provisions encompassing negative criteria relate, both directly and indirectly, to rights of publicity. In essence, they permit people to prevent registration of trademarks that incorporate their names, likenesses, or other indicia without their consent. We will discuss those provisions in the next section of this Chapter. Upon registration, a trademark acquires certain advantages in any infringement litigation against a second user. Therefore, if a celebrity can register her name, likeness, or other indicia as a trademark, he or she will be able to avail herself of those advantages in a subsequent litigation. We will discuss infringement issues in subsection A.3. of this Chapter.

Although the greatest part of the Lanham Act deals with the process of registration and its resulting advantages, the Lanham Act also contains a provision granting protection to unregistered marks. This provision, which is Section 43(a) of the Lanham Act,* is written in broad language, and grants a cause of action under circumstances where one might not expect a trademark law to apply.

Section 43(a) provides in part as follows:

(a) Civil action

(1) Any person who, on or in connection with any goods or services, or any container for goods, uses in commerce any word, term, name, symbol, or device, or any combination thereof, or any false designation of origin, false or misleading description of fact, or false or misleading representation of fact, which—

---

* The various sections of the Lanham Act are commonly referred to by the number assigned in the original legislation, rather than by their section number in the United States Code. (Section 1 of the Lanham Act is codified at 15 U.S.C. § 1051; Section 2 is codified at 15 U.S.C. § 1052, and so on.) Section 43(a) is codified at 15 U.S.C. § 1125(a).

(A) is likely to cause confusion, or to cause mistake, or to deceive as to the affiliation, connection, or association of such person with another person, or
as to the origin, sponsorship, or approval of his or her goods, services, or
commercial activities by another person ...

shall be liable in a civil action by any person who believes that he or she is likely
to be damaged by such act.

This language grants a federal cause of action to owners of trademarks that are not
registered, if someone's unauthorized use of a trademark is likely to cause confusion about
the source or affiliation of goods or services. Thus, to the extent that celebrities have created a true trademark with their names or likenesses, Section 43(a) also allows them to
protect that trademark, regardless of whether it is registered. More critical to our discussion, § 43(a) also provides a basis for a claim of "false or misleading representation of
fact" that causes confusion. This language has given rise to a claim for what is known as
"false endorsement" — when a celebrity's name, image, or persona is used in an advertisement without permission, courts may find that the use would cause consumers to assume, improperly, that the celebrity endorsed the goods or services in question. (You
may recall that such a claim was discussed in the *Pabst* case in Chapter I.A., and the *Irvine*
case from Great Britain in Chapter I.C., and it is a frequent basis for claims in other common law countries.)

Thus, the key to a claim under § 43(a) is a likelihood of confusion. If the public is confused about whether the celebrity is endorsing a product, then there may be a claim. This
is not quite the same as trademark infringement, because the second use is not a use as
another's trademark; instead, the wrong is in the implicit (or explicit) misrepresentation
that the celebrity endorses the product. In addition, if someone else uses the celebrity's
name, likeness, etc., as a source identifier (*i.e.*, as a brand name or logo) for a product without the celebrity's authorization, that may also cause confusion — the public may believe
that the product originated with (or at least is in some way connected with) the celebrity.
That, too, would be subject to a claim under § 43(a), but as a more traditional claim for
infringement of an unregistered trademark.

Equally important, § 43(a) may apply even when the use in question would not satisfy
the strictures of state law. As seen in Chapter III, in *Allen v. National Video*, the court
questioned whether an advertisement featuring a celebrity impersonator was a "portrait"
under New York law. However the court stated that § 43(a) "is broader than the standard
under [the New York statute]," and went on to consider a claim under § 43(a). As a result,
many right of publicity cases include a claim under § 43(a) of the Lanham Act. (Such
claims also provide a basis for subject-matter jurisdiction in federal court. *See* Chapter XII,
below.) *Allen*'s discussion of § 43(a) is excerpted in subsection A.3., below.

Before discussing trademark infringement and false endorsement claims under § 43(a),
we shall take a look at the effect of rights of publicity on the ability of a trademark owner
to obtain a federal registration of that trademark.

———————

2. Registration Issues

As noted in the Introduction to this Chapter, two provisions of the Lanham Act that limit
a trademark applicant's ability to obtain a federal registration are directly related to the issue
of rights of publicity. Those provisions are Sections 2(a) and 2(c), and they read as follows:

No trademark by which the goods of the applicant may be distinguished from the goods of others shall be refused registration on the principal register on account of its nature unless it—

(a) Consists of or comprises immoral, deceptive, or scandalous matter; *or matter which* may disparage or *falsely suggest a connection with persons, living or dead*, institutions, beliefs, or national symbols, or bring them into contempt, or disrepute; or a geographical indication which, when used on or in connection with wines or spirits, identifies a place other than the origin of the goods and is first used on or in connection with wines or spirits by the applicant on or after one year after the date on which the WTO Agreement ... enters into force with respect to the United States....

(c) Consists of or comprises a *name, portrait, or signature identifying a particular living individual* except by his written consent, or the name, signature, or portrait of a deceased President of the United States during the life of his widow, if any, except by the written consent of the widow.

15 U.S.C. § 1052 (emphasis added). In order for this section even to be an issue, of course, the applicant must apply to register a "trademark" as that term is defined in the statute (the statutory definition is set out in the Introduction to this Chapter).

The issue of rights of publicity is not a common problem with registration, perhaps because the statute is relatively clear on this point. However, these sections are not entirely without ambiguity, as the next case illustrates. This decision was rendered by the Trademark Trial and Appeal Board, or TTAB, which is a quasi-judicial body within the PTO that hears appeals from decisions of trademark examiners who refuse registration, as well as contested proceedings such as an opposition to a registration brought by someone who believes that he or she may be harmed by the registration of the mark in question.

In re Debbie Sauer

27 U.S.P.Q.2d 1073 (TTAB 1993),
aff'd mem. 26 F.3d 140 (Fed. Cir. 1994)

[Note: Bo Jackson, referred to in the opinion, played professional football for the Oakland Raiders and professional baseball for the Kansas City Royals.]

On August 30, 1989 Debbie Sauer applied to register the mark shown below on the Principal Register for "an oblong shaped ball made of white leather with red stitching at the seams."

... Registration has been finally refused under Sections 2(a) and 2(c) of the Lanham Act....

The refusal under Section 2(a) of the Act is based on the contention that the mark falsely suggests a connection with Bo Jackson, a well-known professional athlete. The refusal under Section 2(c) is based on the contention that the mark consists of the name identifying Mr. Jackson, and thus cannot be registered by applicant without Mr. Jackson's written consent to registration.

Based on the materials of record in this application, we conclude that prospective purchasers of applicant's balls would mistakenly view the mark in its entirety as suggesting

Figure 5-1. The proposed "Bo Ball" trademark

a connection with Bo Jackson. This makes the mark unregistrable under Section 2(a) of the Act. Such purchasers of these products would also recognize the name "Bo," as it appears in the mark on these goods, as Mr. Jackson's name. In the absence of a written consent from him, this runs afoul of Section 2(c) of the Act....

[T]he test for determining the propriety of a refusal to register based on Section 2(a) has four parts. The mark must be shown to be the same as or a close approximation of the person's previously used name or identity. It must be established that the mark (or part of it) would be recognized as such. It must be shown that the person in question is not connected with the goods or services of the applicant, and finally, the person's name or identity must be of sufficient fame that when it is used as part or all of the mark on applicant's goods, a connection with that person is likely to be made by someone considering purchasing the goods....

The evidence submitted by the Examining Attorney establishes that Bo Jackson is a famous athlete who has played both professional football and baseball. Included in these materials are Bo Jackson baseball cards; Bo Jackson football cards; advertisements for Bo Jackson figurines and toys; a copy of a tag from a Bo Jackson model baseball glove; a copy of a Cheerios cereal box referring to Bo Jackson; and copies of magazines with articles about and cover references to Bo Jackson. These materials show that Bo Jackson is well known and has been a highly regarded collegiate and professional athlete in both baseball and football. The aforementioned evidence establishes that "Bo" is widely recognized and used as Bo Jackson's nickname, which he has had since childhood. He is frequently referred to by "Bo" alone, without any reference at all to his surname.

Applicant argues that "Bo" is also the given name of several other widely recognized celebrities, such as Bo Diaz, Bo Belinsky, Bo Bo Osborne and Bo Schembechler,* and that therefore "Bo" would not necessarily be understood to refer to Bo Jackson. While these other people named "Bo" have been in the public eye to varying degrees, the record does not show that any of them is famous to nearly the same degree as Bo Jackson is, or that any of them is famous as both a baseball and football star like Bo Jackson is. Further, there is no evidentiary support for the proposition that any of the other people named by applicant has ever commercially exploited his or her nickname in connection with the sale of products as Bo Jackson has.

The mark uses Bo Jackson's famous nickname in combination with the generic term "Ball" and the design of a ball which appears to be a combination of a baseball and a football (oblong like a football, but with exposed stitching like a baseball). Applicant's press release confirms this dual nature of the ball. The evidence also confirms the dual nature of Bo Jackson's notoriety as both a baseball player and a football player. The use of his name "Bo" as part of a mark which suggests both kinds of balls on goods like these plainly would be recognized by prospective purchasers of such goods as a reference to Bo Jackson.

As to the third part of the test, the record does not reflect any connection between applicant and Bo Jackson, nor has applicant claimed that any such connection exists. The record is clear that Bo Jackson has achieved great fame and notoriety, so that when his nickname is used as part of the "Bo Ball" and design mark on applicant's goods, purchasers will likely make a connection between him and applicant's products. In that all four parts of the test for refusal under Section 2(a) are met, the refusal is affirmed.

The refusal based on Section 2(c) of the Act is also well taken. That section prohibits registration of a mark which "consists of or comprises a name ... identifying a particular living individual except by his written consent ..." The section operates to bar the registration of marks containing not only full names, but also surnames, shortened names, nicknames, etc., so long as the name in question does, in fact, "identify" a particular living individual.... A name is deemed to "identify" a particular living individual, for purposes of Section 2(c), only if the "individual bearing the name in question will be associated with the mark as used on the goods, either because that person is so well known that the public would reasonably assume the connection, or because the individual is publicly connected with the business in which the mark is used." See *Martin v. Carter Hawley Hale Stores, Inc.*, 206 USPQ 931 (TTAB 1979).

In the case at hand this test is met. The record establishes that Bo Jackson is widely known by his nickname, and that when his nickname is used without his surname in connection with the goods of applicant, an association between him and the goods or with applicant's business would be assumed by purchasers of such products. His fame as both a baseball player and a football player, and the fact that he has commercially endorsed other products support this conclusion. He has not given applicant his written consent to use and register his name.

Decision: The refusal under Section 2(c) is therefore affirmed as well as the refusal under Section 2(a).

---

* Bo Diaz, Bo Belinsky, and Bo Bo Osborne were all major league baseball players, although Bo Belinsky was probably the only one to gain any significant notoriety (Bo Diaz was probably the most skilled player of the three). Bo Schembechler was the long-time football coach at the University of Michigan. — *Eds.*

Notes and Questions

1. Does "identity" for purposes of §§ 2(a) and (c) mean the same as it does under the common law of rights of publicity (recall the *Carson* case here)? Does it incorporate any privacy aspects?

2. The court states that, under § 2(a), the person must be sufficiently famous such that a connection will be presumed. How can one reasonably derive that requirement from the statutory language? Is the requirement of "fame" under this section any different from the common law?

3. Is the requirement of fame any different under § 2(c) than under § 2(a)?

4. Suppose the person was famous at one point but now is forgotten. Should that alter the analysis under § 2(a) or § 2(c)?

5. Suppose the "Bo Ball" design had been a tennis ball, or a soccer ball. Would that have changed the Board's opinion?

6. As an illustration of just how broadly famous nicknames can preempt potential registrations, in 1996 (shortly after Tiger Woods turned professional to much fanfare), an applicant sought to register LITTLE TIGER as a trademark for "golf equipment for children, namely, golf bags and golf clubs, excluding golf balls." The TTAB upheld the examining attorney's refusal to register under both § 2(a) and § 2(c). In re The Junior Golf Co., 2000 TTAB LEXIS 602 (TTAB 2000) (non-precedential). In this case, the applicant only sought to register the word mark. Suppose the applicant had added a picture of a tiger? *See id.*, n.3.

7. Any number of famous sports figures have registered, or allowed others to register, their names as marks. For example, basketball star LeBron James allowed Nike to register the mark LEBRON for footwear and apparel. Reg. No. 3370246 (Jan. 15, 2008). James himself previously had filed an application to register LEBRON JAMES for clothing, but the application was abandoned in 2003. Serial No. 78193435. On March 5, 2008, an Ohio company filed an application to register LEBRONASTY for hats, jackets and shirts. Problem?

8. Joe DiMaggio, the Hall-of-Fame center fielder for the New York Yankees, was nicknamed "The Yankee Clipper." Suppose a person (without any authorization from DiMaggio's estate) applies to register the mark "Yankee Clipper" for shoes. Would that be prohibited by § 2(a)? If DiMaggio were still alive, could he oppose it on the basis of § 2(c)? Could his estate oppose it under § 2(c)? What if the application was for model sailing ships?

9. Under § 2(c) it is not necessary that the person be generally famous; it is sufficient, for example, if the person is well known in the particular field of endeavor encompassed by the goods on which the trademark is to be used. Ross v. Analytical Technology, Inc., 51 U.S.P.Q.2d 1269 (TTAB 1999).

10. The TTAB has ruled that it is not necessary for the opposer to introduce consumer surveys or other similar evidence in order to prove a false association claim under § 2(a). Association Pour la Defense et la Promotion de L'oeuvre de Marc Chagall Dite Comite Marc Chagall v. Bondarchuk, 82 U.S.P.Q.2d 1838 (TTAB 2007).

11. Under § 2(a), how should we deal with people who are still well known, but who died many years ago? Does this mean that one cannot register "Charlemagne" as a trademark? *See* Lucien Picard Watch Corp. v. Since 1868 Crescent Corp., 314 F. Supp. 329 (S.D.N.Y. 1970) (use of "DaVinci" as a trademark on jewelry). *Cf.* In re Sloppy Joe's International, Inc., 43 U.S.P.Q.2d 135 (TTAB 1997) (upholding refusal to register a mark containing a portrait of Ernest Hemingway to be used in connection with a bar).

12. You should understand that the inability to register a trademark under the Lanham Act does not necessarily preclude the existence of trademark rights under common law. In other words, a mark that is not registrable under either Section 2(a) or 2(c) might still be protected under state law (or perhaps under §43(a) of the Lanham Act). However, a mark deemed deceptive probably would not receive common-law protection, since likelihood of confusion is a cornerstone of state trademark law and unfair competition law in general.

In re MC MC S.r.l.

88 U.S.P.Q.2d 1378 (TTAB 2008)

MC MC S.r.l., an Italian corporation, filed an application to register the mark MARIA CALLAS on the Principal Register for [a variety of] goods [consisting largely of jewelry items]. The application contains a statement that the mark does not identify a living individual [Maria Callas having died in 1977].

The trademark examining attorney refused registration under Section 2(a) of the Trademark Act, 15 U.S.C. § 1052(a), on the ground that applicant's mark falsely suggests a connection with, as stated in her brief, "Maria Callas, the famous, deceased opera singer, her heirs and/or her estate."

Applicant appealed....

Trademark Act Section 2(a) states, in relevant part, that "[n]o trademark by which the goods of the applicant may be distinguished from the goods of others shall be refused registration on the principal register on account of its nature unless it—(a) consists of or comprises ... matter which may disparage or falsely suggest a connection with persons living or dead, institutions, beliefs, or national symbols, or bring them into contempt or disrepute."

For over twenty years ... the Board has utilized a four-part test to determine whether a false suggestion of a connection under Trademark Act Section 2(a) has been established. As applied in *ex parte* proceedings, the test is articulated as follows:

> 1) that the marks are the same as, or a close approximation of, the name or identity previously used by the other person; 2) that the marks would be recognized as such, in that they point uniquely and unmistakably to that person; 3) that the person named by the marks is not connected with the activities performed by applicant under the marks; and 4) that the prior user's name or identity is of sufficient fame or reputation that a connection with such person would be presumed when applicant's marks are used on applicant's goods.

In re Wielinski, 49 U.S.P.Q.2d 1754, 1757 (TTAB 1998).... The examining attorney argues that:

> (1) the name in the proposed mark, MARIA CALLAS, is the same as the name of the famous, deceased opera singer Maria Callas, (2) the proposed mark would be recognized as being the same as that of the singer Maria Callas, (3) no one associated with the deceased singer Maria Callas, her heirs and/or her estate is connected with the goods sold by applicant, and (4) the fame and reputation of the singer Maria Callas is such that consumers of applicant's goods will presume a connection between her and the applicant's goods.

Brief, (unnumbered) p. 4.

The examining attorney attached evidence to her Office Actions to support these assertions.

Applicant, on the other hand, argues that its mark does not falsely suggest a connection with the singer Maria Callas because there is no estate vested with rights to control use of her name or persona. Brief, p. 3. Specifically, applicant so contends "because the cumulative evidence of record establishes that the rights of privacy and publicity in the name 'Maria Callas' have extinguished with the death of the opera singer in 1977 and her legal heirs thereafter." *Id.*, p. 4. That being so, applicant argues that the test for false suggestion of a connection "has limited applicability in an *ex parte* proceeding where the existence of a cognizable right of privacy and publicity in the name 'Maria Callas' is in question." Brief, p. 9....

In response to applicant's arguments that there is no successor-in-interest to the rights once held by Ms. Callas in her name and/or persona, the examining attorney argues that the evidence she has submitted indicates there is an estate of Maria Callas "which appears to authorize releases and re-releases of Maria Callas' intellectual property, including her music." Brief, (unnumbered) p. 9. She also argues that "there is evidence of a Greek law firm that claims to represent clients in the entertainment industry, including the estate of Maria Callas." *Id.*, (unnumbered) p. 10. The examining attorney points out that "the requirements for establishing a Section 2(a) claim do not mandate that the Office prove beyond any doubt that there currently exists heirs and/or an estate of Maria Callas to protect her rights." *Id.*, (unnumbered) p. 15.

[However, in *In re Wielinski*,] the Board stated:

> A natural person's right to the use of a designation which points uniquely to his or her persona may not be protected under Section 2(a) after his or her death unless heirs or other successors are entitled to assert that right....

In this case, ... we must find whether or not there is someone (this may be a natural person, estate, or juristic entity) with rights in the name "Maria Callas."[5] ...

Based on the evidence of record, we have doubt as to whether there is any successor in interest entitled to assert rights, as contemplated under Section 2(a), to the Maria Callas name or persona. In other words, it is unclear whether the rights that Ms. Callas once possessed in her name or persona devolved to anyone. The record is replete with contradictory information on this point.... Ultimately, after evaluating all of the evidence, significant doubt remains as to whether there is a successor in interest to Maria Callas' rights in her name or persona.

The burden is on the examining attorney (representing the Trademark Office) to establish that applicant's mark falsely suggests a connection with the name or persona. Where contradictions in the evidence raise significant doubt as to whether the examin-

---

5. Again, for sake of clarity, the "rights" to which the Board references in this decision are those contemplated by Section 2(a). Our primary reviewing court and the Board have determined that Section 2(a) emanates from a desire to protect "one's right of privacy, or the related right of publicity." *University of Notre Dame du Lac*, 703 F.2d 1372, 217 USPQ at 509; *see also Buffett v. Chi-Chi's, Inc.*, 226 U.S.P.Q. 428, 429 (TTAB 1985) ("that portion of Section 2(a) respecting the 'false suggestion of a connection' evolved out of, and embraced, the then nascent concepts of the rights of privacy and publicity," referencing the findings of the Federal Circuit in *University of Notre Dame du Lac*). Moreover, there is no overriding public interest to protect. "The rights protected under the § 2(a) false suggestion provision are not designed primarily to protect the public, but to protect persons and institutions from exploitation of their persona." *Bridgestone/Firestone Research, Inc. v. Automobile Club De L'Quest De La France*, 245 F.3d 1359 (Fed. Cir. 2001).

ing attorney has established the elements of false suggestion of a connection, such doubt should be resolved in applicant's favor. Resolving in applicant's favor significant doubts about whether there exists a successor to the rights in a name or persona removes the possibility that we might be denying registration to an applicant based on non-existent rights.... In this regard, we further note that a Section 2(a) claim is not time barred under Section 14 of the Trademark Act;* thus, any person or entity alleging rights in the name or persona will have recourse.

In view of the significant doubt remaining as to whether anyone currently possesses rights in the name "Maria Callas," and resolving such doubt in applicant's favor, we find that the examining attorney has not met her burden in establishing the false suggestion of a connection refusal under Section 2(a).

Decision: The refusal to register under Trademark Act § 2(a) is reversed.

_____

Notes and Questions

1. Review the four elements set forth in the *Wielinski* case for use in analyzing a § 2(a) case, and then look at the examining attorney's argument with respect to the four elements as applied to the mark MARIA CALLAS. Which one of those elements was the focal point of the TTAB's decision regarding the MARIA CALLAS application? Does § 2(a) expressly require that the person be alive, or that there be an entity capable of vindicating the person's right of publicity?

2. Footnote 5, which discusses the TTAB's view of the policy behind § 2(a), presents a possible reason for the TTAB's decision. Can you identify the policy that seems to guide the decision here? Do you think that the TTAB's reasoning is supported by the statutory language? Does the fact that § 2(c), which does not require confusion or deception, protects only living individuals support or contradict the TTAB's conclusion here?

3. As indicated in the opinion, this was an *ex parte* proceeding, meaning that there was no one opposing the application as yet (except, of course, for the examining attorney at the PTO). (The *Debbie Sauer* case also was an *ex parte* proceeding.) Why should that make a difference? Is the main significance the "rule of doubt" that the PTO uses when dealing with an *ex parte* situation? Is that rule of doubt appropriate?

_____

3. Infringement Issues: Registered and Unregistered Marks

The infringement issues in these cases rely largely on Section 43(a) of the Lanham Act, discussed in the Introduction to this Chapter. If one has a federal registration, then protection from infringement is granted under Section 32 of the Lanham Act. But, whether the trademark is registered or not, the standard for judging whether there has been infringement is the same. As you read the cases, ask yourself to what extent a trademark in-

_____

* Section 14(3) permits someone to initiate a proceeding to cancel a registration "*At any time,* if ... registration was obtained ... contrary to ... subsection (a), (b) or (c) of section 1052 [i.e., § 2(a), (b), or (c) of the Lanham Act]" (emphasis added). — *Eds.*

fringement action (which requires a showing of likelihood of confusion) differs from a claim of false endorsement (which also requires a showing of likelihood of confusion); or, if you decide that they are really the same, is that appropriate?

ETW Corp. v. Jireh Publishing, Inc.
332 F.3d 915 (6th Cir. 2003)

GRAHAM, District Judge (sitting by designation):

[Golfer Tiger Woods sued artist Rick Rush for various alleged violations, including trademark infringement and violation of Woods' right of publicity. Rush had created a lithograph "entitled *The Masters of Augusta*, which commemorates Woods's victory at the Masters Tournament in Augusta, Georgia, in 1997.... In the foreground of Rush's painting are three views of Woods in different poses. In the center, he is completing the swing of a golf club, and on each side he is crouching, lining up and/or observing the progress of a putt. To the left of Woods is his caddy, Mike "Fluff" Cowan, and to his right is his final round partner's caddy. Behind these figures is the Augusta National Clubhouse. In a blue background behind the clubhouse are likenesses of famous golfers of the past looking down on Woods. These include Arnold Palmer, Sam Snead, Ben Hogan, Walter Hagen, Bobby Jones, and Jack Nicklaus. Behind them is the Masters leader board." The court's opinion as to Woods' right of publicity and related claims is reproduced in Chapter VIII.A. below. This excerpt deals only with the trademark claims.]

II. *Trademark Claims Based on the Unauthorized Use of the Registered Trademark "Tiger Woods"*

… ETW claims that Jireh infringed the registered mark "Tiger Woods" by including these words in marketing materials which accompanied the prints of Rush's painting. The words "Tiger Woods" do not appear on the face of the prints, nor are they included in the title of the painting. The words "Tiger Woods" do appear under the flap of the envelopes which contain the prints, and Woods is mentioned twice in the narrative which accompanies the prints.

The Lanham Act provides a defense to an infringement claim where the use of the mark "is a use, otherwise than as a mark, … which is descriptive of and used fairly and in good faith only to describe the goods … of such party[.]" In evaluating a defendant's fair use defense, a court must consider whether defendant has used the mark: (1) in its descriptive sense; and (2) in good faith.

A celebrity's name may be used in the title of an artistic work so long as there is some artistic relevance. *See Rogers v. Grimaldi*, 875 F.2d 994, 997 (2d Cir. 1989).… The use of Woods's name on the back of the envelope containing the print and in the narrative description of the print are purely descriptive and there is nothing to indicate that they were used other than in good faith. The prints, the envelopes which contain them, and the narrative materials which accompany them clearly identify Rush as the source of the print. Woods is mentioned only to describe the content of the print.

The district court properly granted summary judgment on ETW's claim for violation of its registered mark, "Tiger Woods," on the grounds that the claim was barred by the fair use defense as a matter of law.[4]

---

4. The dissent misunderstands the basis for our holding that defendant's use of the registered mark "Tiger Woods" is not infringing. We find only that defendant's use of the mark was a fair use under established trademark law. This finding is not linked in any way with our separate finding that

III. *Trademark Claims Under 15 U.S.C. § 1125(a) Based on the Unauthorized Use of the Likeness of Tiger Woods*

... ETW has registered Woods's name as a trademark, but it has not registered any image or likeness of Woods. Nevertheless, ETW claims to have trademark rights in Woods's image and likeness....

The essence of a trademark is a designation in the form of a distinguishing name, symbol or device which is used to identify a person's goods and distinguish them from the goods of another. Not every word, name, symbol or device qualifies as a protectable mark; rather, it must be proven that it performs the job of identification, *i.e.,* to identify one source and to distinguish it from other sources. If it does not do this, then it is not protectable as a trademark.

"[A] trademark, unlike a copyright or patent, is not a 'right in gross' that enables a holder to enjoin all reproductions." *Boston Athletic Ass'n v. Sullivan,* 867 F.2d 22, 35 (1st Cir. 1989) (citing *Univ. of Notre Dame du Lac v. J.C. Gourmet Food Imports Co.,* 703 F.2d 1372, 1374 (Fed. Cir. 1983)).

Here, ETW claims protection under the Lanham Act for any and all images of Tiger Woods.[5] This is an untenable claim. ETW asks us, in effect, to constitute Woods himself as a walking, talking trademark. Images and likenesses of Woods are not protectable as a trademark because they do not perform the trademark function of designation. They do not distinguish and identify the source of goods. They cannot function as a trademark because there are undoubtedly thousands of images and likenesses of Woods taken by countless photographers, and drawn, sketched, or painted by numerous artists, which have been published in many forms of media, and sold and distributed throughout the world. No reasonable person could believe that merely because these photographs or paintings contain Woods's likeness or image, they all originated with Woods.

We hold that, as a general rule, a person's image or likeness cannot function as a trademark. Our conclusion is supported by the decisions of other courts which have addressed this issue. In *Pirone v. MacMillan, Inc.,* 894 F.2d 579 (2d Cir.1990), the Second Circuit rejected a trademark claim asserted by the daughters of baseball legend Babe Ruth. The plaintiffs objected to the use of Ruth's likeness in three photographs which appeared in a calendar published by the defendant. The court rejected their claim, holding that "a

---

defendant's use of Woods's image was not an infringement of plaintiff's claimed unregistered trademark in all images and likenesses of Woods. The dissent's discussion of plaintiff's evidence of consumer confusion in connection with plaintiff's claim of violation of the registered trademark "Tiger Woods" is inapposite because the survey subjects were shown only the Rush print, which does not contain the words "Tiger Woods."

5. The dissent states that we have incorrectly characterized plaintiff's claim, and that the plaintiff is not seeking to protect any and all images of Woods, but only the image which appears in Rush's print, and that there is "at the very least ... a question of fact ... as to whether Woods has used this image as a trademark...." We stand by our characterization of plaintiff's claim. Plaintiff's first amended complaint does not allege that Woods has used any specific image or likeness as a trademark. There is no evidence in the record that Woods has consistently used any specific image or likeness as a trademark. As the district court correctly pointed out, all of the images of Woods which were submitted by the plaintiff in the course of the summary judgment proceedings are different. The image of Woods in the Nike poster referred to in the dissent is readily distinguishable from the central image in the Rush print. It features, among other things, a different facial expression, a different position of the hands, and a different position of the golf club. Finally, we note that there is not just one but three very different images of Woods in the Rush print: one standing and swinging a club, and two crouching— one with hands on the ball and club, and the other with hands over eyes. Plaintiff claims that all three violated its unregistered trademark in Woods's likeness and image.

photograph of a human being, unlike a portrait of a fanciful cartoon character, is not inherently 'distinctive' in the trademark sense of tending to indicate origin." *Id.* at 583. The
court noted that Ruth "was one of the most photographed men of his generation, a larger
than life hero to millions and an historical figure[.]" *Id.* The Second Circuit Court concluded that a consumer could not reasonably believe that Ruth sponsored the calendar:

> [A]n ordinarily prudent purchaser would have no difficulty discerning that these
> photos are merely the subject matter of the calendar and do not in any way in-
> dicate sponsorship. No reasonable jury could find a likelihood of confusion.

Id. at 585. The court observed that "[u]nder some circumstances, a photograph of a person may be a valid trademark—if, for example, a particular photograph was consistently
used on specific goods." *Id.* at 583. The court rejected plaintiffs' assertion of trademark
rights in every photograph of Ruth....

Here, ETW does not claim that a particular photograph of Woods has been consistently used on specific goods. Instead, ETW's claim is identical to that of the plaintiffs in
Pirone, a sweeping claim to trademark rights in every photograph and image of Woods.
Woods, like Ruth, is one of the most photographed sports figures of his generation, but
this alone does not suffice to create a trademark claim. The district court properly granted
summary judgment on ETW's claim of trademark rights in all images and likenesses of
Tiger Woods....

CLAY, Circuit Judge, dissenting.

[Judge Clay's dissent as to the non-trademark claims is presented in Chapter VIII with
the court's opinion on those claims.]

I. Trademark Claims Based Defendant's Unauthorized Use of the Unregistered Mark— § 43(a) of the Lanham Act, 15 U.S.C. § 1125(a)

At the outset, it should be noted that the majority's characterization of this claim as
the "Unauthorized Use of the Likeness of Tiger Woods" is misleading. Such a characterization bolsters the majority's unfounded position that Plaintiff is seeking protection
under the Lanham Act for any and all images of Tiger Woods, but, indeed, such is not the
case. Plaintiff's amended complaint squarely sets forth Defendant's conduct to which
Plaintiff takes issue—Defendant's portrayal of Woods in his famous golf swing at the
Masters Tournament in Augusta as set forth in Rush's print. Plaintiff provided evidence
that there was a "high incidence" of consumer confusion as to Woods being the origin or
sponsor of *The Masters of Augusta* print by Rick Rush, thus demonstrating, at the very least,
that a question of fact remains for trial as to whether Woods used this image as a trademark and whether Defendant's print infringed upon the mark.

The majority's contention as set forth in footnote 5 of its opinion, that "Plaintiff's first
amended complaint does not allege that Woods has used any specific image or likeness
as a trademark," misses the point. That is, Plaintiff's complaint expressly takes issue with
Defendant's unauthorized sale of Rush's print depicting Woods, and Plaintiff has proffered
evidence to show that consumers are confused as to Woods being the sponsor or origin
of the print, thereby establishing, particularly for purposes of summary judgment, that
the image of Woods in Rush's print has been used as a trademark. The majority's repeated
disagreement with this point ... flies in the face of several propositions of law....

The majority ignores this body of well established jurisprudence by holding that "as a
general rule, a person's image or likeness cannot function as a trademark." Indeed, if a plaintiff alleging infringement in the unregistered mark of his image or likeness in the product of another brings forth evidence of consumer confusion, then the image or likeness

of the plaintiff may very well be functioning "as a trademark" for purposes of § 1125(a), and a question of fact may be created as to whether the defendant's unauthorized use of the mark infringed on the plaintiff's rights....

Simply stated, contrary to the majority's contention, the jurisprudence clearly indicates that a person's image or likeness *can* function as a trademark as long as there is evidence demonstrating that the likeness or image was used as a trademark; which is to say, the image can function as a trademark as long as there is evidence of consumer confusion as to the source of the merchandise upon which the image appears....

With that said, it is difficult to conceive how the majority arrives at its conclusion that Plaintiff "does not claim that a particular photograph of Woods has been consistently used on specific goods" but instead makes "a sweeping claim to trademark rights in every photograph and image of Woods." As indicated in the outset of this discussion, Plaintiff's complaint specifically takes issue with the image of Woods as depicted in Rush's *Masters of Augusta* print and, moreover, Plaintiff has come forward with strong evidence of consumer confusion to support its claim that this image of Woods has been used as a trademark for purposes of supporting its § 43(a) claim. The majority's failure to acknowledge the significance of this evidence constitutes a fatal flaw in its analysis because it is settled that "if the defendant's unauthorized use creates a false suggestion of endorsement or a likelihood of confusion as to source or sponsorship, liability may also be imposed for ... trademark or trade name infringement." Restatement (Third) of Unfair Competition § 46 cmt. b, 537 (1995); *see also Bird*, 289 F.3d at 877 (noting that "the key question in cases where a plaintiff alleges trademark infringement and unfair competition is whether the defendant's actions create a likelihood of confusion as to the origin of the parties' goods or services").

Finally, as explained in the next section, even by adopting the Second Circuit's balancing approach when considering a Lanham Act claim involving an artistic expression,* Plaintiff's likelihood of confusion evidence should, and indeed must, be considered in deciding Plaintiff's claim for infringement of the unregistered mark....

Notes and Questions

1. The majority refers in its opinion to a registered trademark in the name "Tiger Woods." Under United States law, it is possible to register a name (whether well-known or not) as a trademark, provided it meets certain criteria. Primarily, the name must act as a *trademark*, not merely a name—that is, it must act as an indicator of the source of some goods or services. Thus, if Tiger Woods created a line of "Tiger Woods" golf wear, the name Tiger Woods would be acting as a trademark. (Many clothing designers, such as Anne Klein, and Ralph Lauren use their names in this manner.)

2. Assuming Tiger Woods has a validly registered trademark in the words "Tiger Woods," the artist's use of Woods' image does not constitute a use that infringes Tiger Woods's

---

* In *Rogers v. Grimaldi*, 875 F.2d 994 (2d Cir. 1989), former dancer Ginger Rogers sued to enjoin production of a movie entitled "Ginger and Fred" about an Italian dancing couple. The Second Circuit stated that when one challenges the title of a movie, one must balance the interest of the celebrity against the First Amendment interest in allowing the use of the title, and that the use of the title should be allowed unless there was no connection between the title and the underlying expressive work. The issue of celebrity names and images and the First Amendment in the context of expressive works is analyzed in Chapter VIII. —*Eds.*

trademark because he used an *image*, not the trademark, and he used it *as an image*, not as a trademark. Now, suppose that the artist had written "Tiger Woods and the Ghosts of the Masters" across the top of the lithograph. Would that have constituted trademark infringement?

3. The court also found that the use of Woods' image did not infringe any *unregistered* trademark rights that Woods has in his image. Can you explain why? Does it have to be a particular image that is used as a trademark, or will any image do? The dissenting judge believed that there was at least a factual issue in this regard. Do you agree? The same court dealt with a somewhat similar issue in a conventional trademark suit in Rock and Roll Hall of Fame and Museum, Inc. v. Gentile Productions, 134 F.3d 749 (6th Cir. 1998).

4. Suppose that someone wishes to use a short clip from a movie starring a celebrity as part of another movie that neither features the celebrity in a starring role, nor is about the celebrity. Assuming that the second movie producer obtains proper authorization from the copyright owner of the clip, can the celebrity claim that the clip is a trademark and thus subject to §43(a)? See Comedy III Productions, Inc. v. New Line Cinema, 200 F.3d 593 (9th Cir. 2000).

5. *Trademark dilution and rights of publicity.* As the cases indicate, trademark infringement normally requires the trademark owner to show that the unauthorized use leads to a "likelihood of confusion" between the unauthorized use and the authorized one. In a right of publicity context, the confusion is usually about whether the celebrity endorsed, or authorized the use of his or her name (or likeness, or persona) by the unauthorized user. However, there is another form of trademark protection available, known as trademark dilution. Unlike ordinary infringement, dilution does not require any showing of likelihood of confusion. Instead, dilution requires a showing either that the unauthorized use will "impair the distinctiveness" (lessen the source-identifying power) of the trademark (often called "blurring"), or that the unauthorized use will "harm the reputation of" the trademark (often called "tarnishment"). See Lanham Act §43(c)(2)(B), (C), 15 U.S.C. §1125(c)(2)(B), (C) (defining "dilution by blurring" and "dilution by tarnishment"). Protection from dilution is also provided by the laws of a majority of the states. *See, e.g.*, Cal. Bus. & Prof. Code §14247 (West Supp. 2008); N.Y. Gen. Bus. L. §360-*l* (McKinney Supp. 2008); 765 Ill. Comp. Stat. Ann. §§1036/5, 1036/65 (West 2001). A complete list of state laws can be found in David S. Welkowitz, Trademark Dilution: Federal, State, and International Law (BNA Books 2002 & 2008 Supp.).

The use of dilution in the rights of publicity context is somewhat problematic. First, the celebrity must have an actual trademark—a point discussed in the case and the Notes above. Second, it appears that, at least under federal law, the unauthorized use must be a use *as a trademark*, that is, more than simply a merchandising use, but rather as a source identifier for some goods or services. Third, under federal law the mark must be "famous" among the "general consuming public" to be protected. See Lanham Act §43(c)(2)(A). However, assuming that these requirements are met, dilution potentially grants broad protection to such a trademark, possibly akin to the protection granted under the common law and/or statutory law of many states. The tarnishment branch of dilution, which would protect the celebrity from unappealing uses of his or her likeness—as long as the celebrity has actual trademark rights in the name or likeness—also has very broad potential. However, federal law, and the law of most states, contain exceptions that significantly circumscribe the tarnishment claim, particularly with respect to parodies and what are termed "noncommercial" uses. Lanham Act §43(c)(3)(A)-(C).

Problem 4

Hazel Blue is a writer whose self-professed area of expertise is human sexuality. She has written numerous columns on the subject for various publications and as a blogger on the Internet. She also has written erotica and pornography, which have been published in print form. Ada Martin is an actress who has appeared in dozens of adult films. She uses the name "Hazel Blue" as a stage name. When she adopted that stage name, she was unaware of the author (for whom that is an actual given name). Hazel Blue, the author, has now become aware of the actress and wishes to prevent Ms. Martin from using the Hazel Blue stage name. The author claims that she has trademark rights in the name that precede its adoption as Ms. Martin's stage name.

Assuming that Ms. Blue (the author) began writing columns and books prior to Ms. Martin's adoption of the stage name, would she be granted trademark rights in the name? If so, should Ms. Martin's use of the Hazel Blue stage name be enjoined?

Allen v. National Video, Inc.
610 F. Supp. 612 (S.D.N.Y. 1985)

[The facts of this case, and the court's analysis of the state law right of publicity claim, are set out in Chapter III. The excerpt that follows deals only with the Lanham Act claim.]

Plaintiff seeks summary judgment on his claim under section 43(a) of the federal Lanham Act ("the Act"), which prohibits false descriptions of products or their origins. The Act is more than a mere codification of common law trademark infringement. Its purpose is "the protection of consumers and competitors from a wide variety of misrepresentations of products and services in commerce." ...

The Act has therefore been held to apply to situations that would not qualify formally as trademark infringement, but that involve unfair competitive practices resulting in actual or potential deception. To make out a cause of action under the Act, plaintiff must establish three elements: 1) involvement of goods or services, 2) effect on interstate commerce, and 3) a false designation of origin or false description of the goods or services.

Application of the act is limited, however, to potential deception which threatens economic interests analogous to those protected by trademark law. One such interest is that of the public to be free from harmful deception. Another interest, which provides plaintiff here with standing, is that of the "trademark" holder in the value of his distinctive mark. As the Supreme Court, per Justice Frankfurter, has said:

> The protection of trade-marks is the law's recognition of the psychological value of symbols. If it is true that we live by symbols, it is no less true that we purchase goods by them. A trade-mark is a merchandising shortcut which induces a purchaser to select what he wants, or what he has been led to believe he wants. The owner of the mark exploits this human propensity by making every effort to impregnate the atmosphere of the market with the drawing power of a congenial symbol. *Whatever the means employed, the aim is the same*—to convey through the mark, in the minds of the potential customer, the desirability of the commodity upon which it appears. Once this is attained, the trademark owner has some-

thing of value. If another poaches upon the commercial magnetism of the symbol he has created, the owner can obtain legal redress.

Mishawaka Rubber & Woolen Mfg. Co. v. S.S. Kresge Co., 316 U.S. 203, 205 (1942) (emphasis added).

A celebrity has a similar commercial investment in the "drawing power" of his or her name and face in endorsing products and in marketing a career. The celebrity's investment depends upon the good will of the public, and infringement of the celebrity's rights also implicates the public's interest in being free from deception when it relies on a public figure's endorsement in an advertisement. The underlying purposes of the Lanham Act therefore appear to be implicated in cases of misrepresentations regarding the endorsement of goods and services....

The Act's prohibitions, in fact, have been held to apply to misleading statements that a product or service has been endorsed by a public figure. [discussing cases]

[These cases] suggest that the unauthorized use of a person's name or photograph in a manner that creates the false impression that the party has endorsed a product or service in interstate commerce violates the Lanham Act. Application of this standard to the case at bar, however, is complicated by defendants' use of a look-alike for plaintiff, rather than plaintiff's actual photograph ... or pseudonym.... Unlike the state law privacy claim discussed in the foregoing section [*see* Chapter III], the plaintiff's Lanham Act theory does not require the court to find that defendant Boroff's photograph is, as a matter of law, plaintiff's "portrait or picture." The court must nevertheless decide whether defendant's advertisement creates the likelihood of consumer confusion over whether plaintiff endorsed or was otherwise involved with National Video's goods and services.[6]

This inquiry requires the court to consider whether the look-alike employed is sufficiently *similar* to plaintiff to create such a likelihood—an inquiry much like that made in cases involving similar, but not identical, trademarks. The court therefore finds it helpful, in applying the likelihood of confusion standard to the facts of this case, to refer to traditional trademark analysis.

[T]he Second Circuit [has] suggested six factors for a court to consider in deciding the issue of likelihood of confusion: 1) the strength of plaintiff's marks and name; 2) the similarity of plaintiff's and defendant's marks; 3) the proximity of plaintiff's and defendant's products; 4) evidence of actual confusion as to source or sponsorship; 5) sophistication of the defendant's audience; and 6) defendant's good or bad faith. These factors provide a helpful structure for the court's application of the Lanham Act to the facts of this case.

[The court found the first two factors to clearly favor plaintiff. As to the third, it stated that plaintiff's movie-making and defendant's video rental were at least related businesses. There was no evidence of actual confusion, but the court found that even sophisticated customers might be fooled. As to the factor of bad faith, the court stated that] [d]efendants may not have intended to imply that plaintiff actually endorsed their product, but they happily risked creating that impression in an attempt to gain commercial advantage

---

6. The court rejects defendants' argument that the perception that plaintiff appeared in National's advertisement does not give rise to an inference that he endorses their product. It is disingenuous to suggest that consumers would assume no more than that plaintiff had been hired as an actor. When a public figure of Woody Allen's stature appears in an advertisement, his mere presence is inescapably to be interpreted as an endorsement. Moreover, defendant's pose in National's advertisement—smiling at the camera while holding up the V.I.P. card—is the classic stance of the product spokesperson.

through reference to plaintiff's public image. The failure of defendant National to include any disclaimer on all but one of the uses of the photograph also supports a finding of, at best, dubious motives.

A review of all these factors leads the court to the inescapable conclusion that defendants' use of Boroff's photograph in their advertisement creates a likelihood of consumer confusion over plaintiff's endorsement or involvement. In reaching this conclusion, the court notes several distinctions between plaintiff's Lanham Act and privacy claims which make this case more appropriate for resolution under the Lanham Act.

First and most important, the likelihood of confusion standard applied herein is broader than the strict "portrait or picture" standard under the [New York] Civil Rights Law. Evocation of plaintiff's general persona is not enough to make out a violation of section 51 [of the Civil Rights Law], but it may create a likelihood of confusion under the Lanham Act.... Similarly, even if the public does not believe that plaintiff actually appeared in the photograph, it may be led to believe by the intentional reference to plaintiff that he is somehow involved in or approves of their product. This broader standard is justified since the Lanham Act seeks to protect not just plaintiff's property interest in his face, but the public's interest in avoiding deception.

Second, the likelihood of confusion standard is easier to satisfy on the facts of this case. Enough people may realize that the figure in the photograph is defendant Boroff to negate the conclusion that it amounts to a "portrait or picture" of plaintiff as a matter of law. All that is necessary to recover under the Act, however, is that a *likelihood* of confusion exist. While defendants, as noted above, have urged an interpretation of the advertisement which might defeat a finding of "portrait or picture," the court finds that no such explanation can remove the likelihood of confusion on the part of "any appreciable number of ordinarily prudent" consumers.

Third, although the question of identifiability under the Civil Rights Law is generally one of fact for the jury, the likelihood of confusion standard may be applied by the court. While confusing similarity is technically a question of fact, it has sometimes been regarded as "one for the court to decide through its own analysis, comparison, and judgment."

In seeking to forestall summary judgment, defendants Smith and Boroff maintain that the disclaimer which they insisted be included in the advertisement would have avoided consumer confusion. The court disagrees. Even with regard to the one version of the advertisement in which the requisite disclaimer was included, there exists a likelihood of consumer confusion. The disclaimer, in tiny print at the bottom of the page, is unlikely to be noticed by most readers as they are leafing through the magazine. Moreover, the disclaimer says only that a celebrity double is being used, which does not in and of itself necessarily dispel the impression that plaintiff is somehow involved with National's products or services. To be effective, a disclaimer would have to be bolder and make clear that plaintiff in no way endorses National, its products, or its services....

Plaintiff seeks an injunction preventing defendants from presenting defendant Boroff as plaintiff in advertising. Defendant Boroff argues that any such injunction would interfere impermissibly with his ability to earn a living and his First Amendment rights....

[T]he court hesitates sweepingly to enjoin defendant Boroff from ever appearing as a look-alike for plaintiff, since that could interfere with his ability to make money and express himself in settings where there is no likelihood of consumer confusion.

What plaintiff legitimately seeks to prevent is not simply defendant Boroff dressing up as plaintiff, but defendant *passing himself off* as plaintiff or an authorized surrogate. Therefore, defendant must be enjoined from appearing in advertising that creates the likelihood that a reasonable person might believe that he was really plaintiff or that plaintiff had approved of his appearance. Defendant may satisfy the injunction by ceasing his work as a Woody Allen look-alike, but he may also satisfy it by simply refusing to collaborate with those advertisers, such as National Video in this case, who recklessly skirt the edges of misrepresentation. Defendant may sell his services as a look-alike in any setting where the overall context makes it completely clear that he *is* a look-alike and that plaintiff has nothing to do with the project—whether that is accomplished through a bold and unequivocal disclaimer, the staging of the photograph, or the accompanying advertising copy.

Notes and Questions

1. Is the court's assumption that, *as a matter of law*, the public is likely to believe that Woody Allen endorses National Video factually supportable? If the public would understand that the ad features a look-alike and not Woody Allen, is it supportable? Is the court's statement that the "public *may* be led to believe by the intentional reference to plaintiff that he is somehow involved" the same as a *likelihood* of confusion?

2. What sort of disclaimer would be sufficient to avoid liability? Would "Celebrity Impersonator: No endorsement intended" at the bottom of the advertisement be sufficient?

3. If some sort of disclaimer would avoid liability, what is the difference between the Lanham Act right and the right of publicity under state law?

4. Note here that, unlike the Tiger Woods situation, there was no trademark claim. But the false endorsement claim was said by the court to be within the language of §43(a). Do you agree? (Note that the language of §43(a) has been changed since *Allen* was decided.)

5. Section 43(a) has been invoked in a variety of situations, even outside of advertisements (the context of the *Allen* case). In *Wendt v. Host International, Inc.*, 125 F.3d 806 (9th Cir. 1997) (excerpted in Chapter X), the court found that the use of animatronic figures resembling the characters of "Norm" and "Cliff" in the television series "Cheers" in an airport bar setting could trigger a false endorsement claim. However, in *Carson v. Here's Johnny Portable Toilets, Inc.*, 698 F.2d 831 (6th Cir. 1983) (reprinted in Chapter II), the court upheld a finding that defendant's use of "Here's Johnny" as the name of its portable toilets did not cause a likelihood of confusion as to possible sponsorship or association with Johnny Carson, despite finding that the use violated Carson's common-law right of publicity.

6. *Standing to bring claims under §43(a).* Claims brought under §43(a) are often characterized as federal unfair competition claims. However, putting false endorsement claims in that category may engender some doctrinal problems. "Unfair competition" implies that the two parties to the lawsuit are, in some manner, in competition with each other. Neither Tiger Woods nor Woody Allen was in competition with the respective defendants (an artist and a video store, respectively). There is case law indicating that a non-competitor lacks standing to bring a claim under §43(a). *E.g., Halicki v. United Artists Communications, Inc.*, 812 F.2d 1213 (9th Cir. 1987). (You may recall that this problem arose in Britain, in the *Irvine v. Talksport* case (Chapter I.C.), where the defendant argued that the two sides were not engaged in any analogous businesses. Perhaps the denomination

"passing off," rather than "unfair competition" made it easier for the court to reject the defendant's argument.) However, federal courts have not applied that requirement to false endorsement claims. In *Waits v. Frito-Lay, Inc.*, 973 F.2d 1093 (9th Cir. 1992), singer Tom Waits sued Frito-Lay over the latter's use of a sound-alike to imitate Waits' voice in a commercial. His suit included a claim for false endorsement under § 43(a). Defendant claimed Waits lacked standing to bring such a claim because he was not in competition with Frito-Lay. The Ninth Circuit distinguished its *Halicki* opinion, saying that *Halicki*'s competitive standing requirement applied when the claim was a false advertising claim about the qualities of a particular product, but that Waits' claim was about "false association," which was more like a trademark infringement claim. In the latter situation, competition was not a necessary element of a claim under § 43(a). 973 F.2d at 1108–10.

Although § 43(a) claims may not require any competition between the parties, such a requirement may exist for unfair competition claims brought under state law. *E.g.*, *Sinatra v. Goodyear Tire & Rubber Co.*, 435 F.2d 711, 714 (9th Cir. 1970).

7. *"Likelihood of confusion."* As you can see from the cases, the standard for both trademark infringement and false endorsement is whether there is a likelihood of confusion caused by the unauthorized use of the celebrity's name, likeness, or persona. The determination of likelihood of confusion is often a rather lengthy, fact-laden process. Each federal Circuit has promulgated a (remarkably similar) set of factors to guide trial courts in their analysis of likelihood of confusion. These factors include the "strength" of the mark (which might also be the fame of the celebrity in a false endorsement case), the similarity of the marks, the similarity of the goods sold by the two parties, any evidence (including survey evidence) of actual confusion, and the intent of the unauthorized user. Some of these factors are difficult to apply in a false endorsement situation. Nevertheless, in right of publicity cases brought under the Lanham Act, courts typically will use several of these factors. In this casebook, our intent is simply to make you aware of the existence of this multifactor analysis; the details of how these tests are applied are best discussed in a course in Trademark Law.

B. Comparative Law

Elvis Presley Enterprises, Inc. v. Sid Shaw Elvisly Yours
[1999] R.P.C. 567 (Eng. Ct. App. 1999)

LORD JUSTICE ROBERT WALKER:

I

The litigation

This is an appeal from an order of Laddie J made on 18 March 1997 in a trade mark case. On 26 January 1989 Elvis Presley Enterprises Inc (Enterprises [or EPEI]) of Memphis, Tennessee made three applications to register trade marks under the Trade Marks Act 1938 (the 1938 Act). The numbers of the applications and the marks applied for were as follows:

　　1371624 signature 'Elvis A. Presley'

　　1371627 ELVIS

　　1371637 ELVIS PRESLEY

The first of these has been referred to as the signature mark. All three applications were for the same specification of goods, that is

> "Toilet preparations, perfumes, eau de cologne; preparations for the hair and teeth; soaps, bath and shower preparations; deodorants, antiperspirants and cosmetics; all included in Class 3."

The applications survived their initial examination in the Patent Office and were advertised in the official journal on different dates between March and May 1991. On 27 December 1991 notices of opposition to all three applications were put in by Mr Sid Shaw, who trades as 'Elvisly Yours' and is registered proprietor of that trade mark for a wide range of goods.... The notices stated six grounds of opposition, including lack of distinctiveness and conflict with Mr Shaw's own mark.

Mr Shaw's opposition led to a hearing before the Registrar, in the person of Mr M.J.Tuck as hearing officer. In a written decision dated 31 January 1996 Mr Tuck found that the grounds of opposition were not made out, and did not think it appropriate to exercise the Registrar's discretion to refuse registration. Mr Shaw appealed to the High Court, where Laddie J allowed his appeal, and Enterprises in turn appeals to this court.

II

The legislation

... The 1938 Act has in principle been repealed [and replaced by the Trade Marks Act of 1994, which made various changes in the law], but that is subject to the very important exception that under the transitional provisions in Schedule 3 to the 1994 Act, the 1938 Act continues to apply to pending applications for registration. So Enterprises' applications have to be determined under the 1938 Act but if they result in registration the marks will then be subject to the provisions of the 1994 Act....

Section 68(1) of the 1938 Act contains some definitions which provide the best starting-point:

> "mark" includes a device, brand, heading, label, ticket, name, signature, word, letter, numeral, or any combination thereof

> "trade mark" means [with an irrelevant exception] a mark used or proposed to be used in relation to goods for the purpose of indicating, or so as to indicate, a connection in the course of trade between the goods and some person having the right either as proprietor or as registered user of that mark, whether with or without any indication of the identity of that person ...

[The court then quotes several other statutory provisions. The essence of these provisions is that a trademark must be distinctive and that an application to register a trademark cannot be granted if the trademark in question is "so near as to be likely to deceive or cause confusion" with another, pre-existing trademark.]

III

The facts and factual issues

Most of the material facts are not in dispute.... Elvis Presley was born in Tupelo, Mississippi in 1935 and died in Memphis, Tennessee in 1977. He gained great fame and riches as a rock and roll singer and starred in many films. His fame has endured since his death and there are still devoted fans of his in many parts of the world. His house in Memphis, called Graceland, is still a place of pilgrimage for his fans, and there they can buy a wide range of souvenirs.

Enterprises is based at Memphis and it runs Graceland. It carries on merchandising activities previously carried on by or on behalf of Elvis Presley. Mr Shaw does not dispute that Enterprises should be regarded as the successor to Elvis Presley's merchandising business....

Mr Sid Shaw has had a varied career.... For the last 20 years of his career his activities have centred on Elvis Presley. He trades through a company named Elvisly Yours Limited but Mr Shaw personally is the registered proprietor of the trade mark ELVISLY YOURS which (in a cursive script with an elaborate E and Y) is registered for a wide specification of goods..., but limited (as the applications by Enterprises are not limited) to goods relating to Elvis Presley. Mr Shaw's application for his trade mark was made on 17 November 1987. Mr Shaw's company makes wholesale and retail supplies of a range of goods, all somehow related to Elvis Presley, to customers in this country and overseas. It also publishes a magazine, Elvisly Yours, for Elvis Presley fans. The company did at one time supply goods for sale at Graceland itself, but Mr Shaw and Enterprises no longer enjoy an amicable relationship. There has been litigation between them in the United States resulting in an injunction against Mr Shaw and his company.

... I am satisfied that Mr Shaw and his company have traded under the Elvisly Yours mark on a significant scale since 1980 at latest, and in toiletries (including soap, on which Mr Prescott concentrated) since 1986.

No evidence of deception or of actual confusion was adduced by either side. So far as the evidence goes, there is no reason not to accept the Judge's observation

> "that although Mr Shaw has sold millions of pounds worth of memorabilia bearing the name of Elvis or Elvis Presley over the last 18 or so years, it has not been suggested that anyone has ever thought they emanated from Enterprises".

On the contrary, occasional references in the Elvisly Yours magazine to disputes between Mr Shaw and Enterprises suggest that Elvis Presley fans in this country who read the magazine would be well aware of the true state of affairs.

The Court gave leave to Enterprises to adduce further evidence as to the names of well-known persons or fictional characters which have been registered as trade marks in recent years. But the court has not derived any real assistance from that evidence in deciding the issues on this appeal....

I must also refer to a difference in terminology which was indicative of a difference of principle between the parties. Both sides put in evidence of the type of goods which have been sold, or are currently sold, by Enterprises and Mr Shaw's company respectively. Mr Soden exhibited a publication called 'Elvis Collectibles' which is described as "an identification and value guide to hundreds of pieces of memorabilia for the most promoted celebrity of them all." He also exhibited pictures of some of the goods sold through an outlet (now closed) which Enterprises had in England. Mr Shaw has exhibited several copies of the magazine 'Elvisly Yours' which contain numerous advertisements for his company's goods.

The 'Elvisly Yours' products cover what is, in terms of specifications for trade mark purposes, quite a wide range: magazines, calendars, framed and unframed pictures, mugs, T-shirts, soap, cheap jewellery, pennants, rosettes, and so on. Some of these items are described in the magazines as 'memorabilia' or 'collectibles'. Goods of the same type appear in Mr Soden's exhibits and he says of them,

> "These products are, in some instances, souvenirs or memorabilia of Elvis Presley, and in other instances, commercial consumer items."

Mr Soden then referred (in terms which I have already quoted) to trade marks. He sought to identify the trade marks with commercial consumer items, and particularly with items such as soap or cologne which diminish and disappear with use.

The Judge seems to have been disinclined to accept any sharp distinction between 'memorabilia' and commercial consumer goods. The judgment refers to "the wide range of products sold as Elvis Presley memorabilia" and contains several other references to memorabilia, mementoes and souvenirs. I think the Judge was right not to accept any sharp distinction. The consumer is a label which economists use to distinguish the eventual end-purchaser from the producer, but it is not essential that consumer goods should be useful, or that they should have a predictably short life. I think the Judge was right to conclude that all these products, including the soap and the cologne, were being marketed primarily on the strength of their bearing the name or image of Elvis Presley. The Judge did not go so far as to say that the real product was Elvis Presley himself, but that thought seems to have been not far below the surface of the Judge's reasoning on distinctiveness.

IV

Distinctiveness

In relation to all three applications the Judge allowed the appeals on grounds related to distinctiveness or capability of distinguishing.... In his judgment the Judge said,

> "The distinctiveness addressed by the Act is not a quality of the mark which exists in a vacuum. It is a particular type of distinctiveness, namely the ability to distinguish the proprietor's goods from the same or similar goods marketed by someone else. The more a proposed mark alludes to the character, quality or non-origin attributes of the goods on which it is used or proposed to be used, the lower its inherent distinctiveness."

[T]he authorities show that one of the most common reasons for failure on the ground of lack of distinctiveness is if a mark is descriptive of the goods on which it is to be used....

Descriptiveness of the goods in question is not the only way in which a proposed trade mark may fail in terms of distinctiveness. It may fail simply because it is too commonplace, such as a surname (with or without an added first name) of fairly frequent occurrence....

The two main obstacles to distinctiveness—being too descriptive and being too commonplace—come together in the very well-known statement in the speech of Lord Parker in *Registrar of Trade Marks v. W & G Du Cros* [1913] AC 624, 634–5

> "In my opinion, in order to determine whether a mark is distinctive it must be considered quite apart from the effects of registration. The question, therefore, is whether the mark itself, if used as a trade mark, is likely to become actually distinctive of the goods of the person so using it. The applicant for registration in effect says, "I intend to use this mark as a trade mark, *i.e.*, for the purpose of distinguishing my goods from the goods of other persons," and the Registrar or the Court has to determine before the mark be admitted to registration whether it is of such a kind that the applicant, quite apart from the effects of registration, is likely or unlikely to attain the object he has in view. The applicant's chance of success in this respect must, I think, largely depend upon whether other traders are likely, in the ordinary course of their business and without any improper motive, to desire to use the same mark, or some mark nearly resembling it, upon or in connection with their own goods. It is apparent from the history of trade

marks in this country that both the Legislature and the Courts have always shewn a natural disinclination to allow any person to obtain by registration under the Trade Marks Acts a monopoly in what others may legitimately desire to use."

V

Character merchandising

Both sides referred in their written and oral submissions to character merchandising. We were referred to several recent cases (both in this country and in Australia) and to articles in academic publications and in the trade press. Character merchandising has been big business for at least 30 years. As long ago as 1977 the Whitford Committee considered, but did not regard as feasible, the introduction of a new 'character right' which would fill a perceived gap between the law of copyright and that of passing off.

The traditional attitude of the English court to claims of that sort appears clearly from the judgment of Wynn-Parry J in *McCulloch v. May* [1947] 2 AER 845, 851, the case in which 'Uncle Mac' of BBC's Children's Hour sued the distributors of 'Uncle Mac's Puffed Wheat,'

> "On the postulate that the plaintiff is not engaged in any degree in producing or marketing puffed wheat, how can the defendant, in using the fancy name used by the plaintiff, be said to be passing off the goods or the business of the plaintiff? I am utterly unable to see any element of passing off in this case. If it were anything, it were libel, as to which I say nothing. Passing off, in my judgment, it certainly is not. If I were to accede to the plaintiff's claim I should, as I see it, not merely be extending quite unjustifiably the scope of the action of passing off, but I should be establishing an entirely new remedy, and that I am quite unprepared to do."

[The court then cited and quoted extensively from several subsequent cases, indicating that, although some of the judges expressed disquiet about the result, they agreed that there was no general right in Britain to protect oneself against unauthorized character merchandising, except for a passing off action or violation of some intellectual property right, such as copyright.]

However this appeal is not an appropriate occasion on which to attempt to define precisely how far the law of passing off has developed in response to the growth of character merchandising, still less to express views as to how much further it should develop or in what direction. This appeal is concerned solely with trade mark law and although I have (out of deference to the interesting submissions made to us) gone through some of the principal authorities concerned with character merchandising which were cited to us, they are relevant to the appeal only so far as they affect either (i) distinctiveness and distinguishing under §§9 and 10 of the 1938 Act or (ii) deceptiveness or confusion under §§11 and 12.

I did not find it easy to see exactly how the character merchandising cases were said to fit into counsel's arguments on §§9–12, and I may have overlooked some of the refinements of the arguments. But Mr Prescott [counsel for Enterprises] relied on the cases principally in order (i) to suggest that the *Tarzan* decision must be restricted to its special facts (a fictitious character whose name had once been an invented word) and is no longer (if it ever was) of wide significance; and (ii) to suggest that the Judge misapplied Lord Parker's test in *W & G du Cros*, because other traders could not legitimately wish to use the names Elvis and Elvis Presley. Therefore, Mr Prescott said, the Judge was wrong to conclude that the ELVIS and ELVIS PRESLEY marks have very little inherent distinctiveness.

In his written and oral submissions Mr Prescott enlarged on these basic points. He argued that the law has now evolved to the stage where there is a general rule that a trader may not make unauthorised use of the name of a celebrity in order to sell his own goods. He expressed the rule primarily in terms of a living celebrity, but argued that the death of Elvis Presley does not matter in view of his abiding fame and Enterprises' unchallenged status as his successor. Mr Prescott allowed some exceptions to the rule (comparable, although he did not put it like that, to the doctrine of 'fair dealing' in the law of copyright infringement) such as the publication (without copyright infringement) of portrait photographs or biographical material. He mentioned the Abba case as an example falling within the exceptions. But (in the words of Mr Prescott's written submissions)

> "those instances—the 'product' is really text or other information *about* the celebrity—are remote from the present case. We are concerned with consumable commercial items like soap, toothpaste and perfume, the general case."

In the general case, Mr Prescott submitted, to use the name of a living celebrity for the purpose of selling a consumable commercial item implies authority, and therefore endorsement, by that person. He said that as a matter of everyday experience, reputable traders do not use the name of a living person in connection with their merchandise without obtaining authority. That had been a matter of judicial notice for 70 years, he said, with a reference to *Tolley v. Fry*. (But, as I have already noted, it was an essential part of Mr Tolley's case that he was an amateur in days when the distinction between amateur and professional sportsmen was still very important. That brings out one of many paradoxical features of this case, that some celebrities wish to prevent 'appropriation of personality' as a means of defending their privacy; others wish to prevent unauthorised appropriation so as to secure a monopoly of commercial exploitation of their names, images and fame….)

Mr Prescott also relied on an assertion of the same general rule in his submissions on §§ 11 and 12. Enterprises was, he said, the undisputed successor to the rights which Elvis Presley had: how could there be any deception or confusion in Enterprises using for its trading purposes names which are so readily recognised as referring to the world-famous singer whose rights now belong to Enterprises?

Mr Meade [counsel for Shaw] challenged almost all these submissions. He described it as a bold contention that in any case of use of a well-known name (whether the name was that of an individual celebrity, living or dead, or a fictional character) there was a universal or general public assumption that use of the name must have been franchised. (In some cases there will be a further twist as to whether the celebrity is real or fictional, or a mixture of the two: Kojak was played by one well-known actor but James Bond by at least three; Mr Paul Hogan was well-known for commercials on Australian television before he played Crocodile Dundee. But it is unnecessary to pursue that here.) Mr Meade said that any such assumption must be proved by evidence appropriate to the particular case, and could not be established by citation of what had been said in other cases on different facts….

Mr Meade submitted that the Judge was right to conclude that the ELVIS and ELVIS PRESLEY marks have very little inherent distinctiveness, especially when applied to goods which are sold as memorabilia of Elvis Presley, or when applied to goods as decoration. He described Elvis Presley as having become an important part of popular culture whose name and image other traders might legitimately wish to make use of. To the paradox which Mr Prescott put in the forefront of his submissions—

> "Can it be the law that the more famous a man becomes, the harder it will be for him to register his name as a trade mark in respect of goods in which he intends to trade?"

—Mr Meade would give an affirmative answer, subject to the important qualification that the answer applied to goods sold (in the Judge's words) as "memorabilia and mementoes" of Elvis Presley and in circumstances where the average purchaser "is buying a likeness, not a product from a particular source."

As to Mr Prescott's submissions on §§ 11 and 12, Mr Meade said that Enterprises could not (any more than the defendant in the Kojak passing-off case could) rely on a title derived from the owners of other intellectual property rights which were not being infringed. Enterprises had, Mr Meade said, failed to educate the British public that Elvis and Elvis Presley were being used by Enterprises and its licensees in a trade mark sense.

VI

The judgment of Laddie J

The views of the Registrar (in the person of the hearing officer) are entitled to respect. But so also are the views of Laddie J, a judge of great experience (at the bar and on the bench) in intellectual property matters. I intend no disrespect to the hearing officer if I concentrate on the judgment immediately under appeal....

[Judge Laddie] concluded that none of the marks merited registration because all were lacking in sufficient inherent distinctiveness to succeed without evidence of factual distinctiveness (which, as Mr Prescott concedes, was not there). The Judge did not discuss §§ 11 and 12 in relation to the ELVIS and ELVIS PRESLEY marks beyond the brief comment that he would have difficulty seeing how Mr Shaw's extensive use of his registered mark could fail to give rise to an objection. He did consider §§ 11 and 12 in relation to the signature mark and concluded that its similarity to Mr Shaw's mark would be likely to give rise to deception or confusion and so constituted a further obstacle to registration.

In my judgment the Judge was right to conclude that the ELVIS mark has very little inherent distinctiveness. That conclusion was reached by a number of intermediate steps, one of which was the Judge's finding that members of the public purchase Elvis Presley merchandise not because it comes from a particular source, but because it carries the name or image of Elvis Presley. Indeed the Judge came close to finding (although he did not in terms find) that for goods of the sort advertised by Elvisly Yours (or by Enterprises in the United States) the commemoration of the late Elvis Presley *is* the product, and the article on which his name or image appears (whether a poster, a pennant, a mug or a piece of soap) is little more than a vehicle. I consider that the Judge was right to treat all these goods as memorabilia or mementoes, and not to treat some as being in a different class of consumable commercial goods. (On any view, of course, these categories cut across the statutory classes of goods.) Given that conclusion, and given that the *Tarzan* decision was binding on him (as it is on this court) the Judge's final conclusion as to very low inherent distinctiveness followed almost inevitably, and factual distinctiveness is no longer asserted.

I feel more doubt about the Judge's clear but not fully reasoned view that the ELVIS mark would also have failed under §§ 11 and 12. The hearing officer said that Mr Shaw's Elvisly Yours mark

> "is in my view a clever invention a sort of mock valediction. I have no evidence before me as to how the public would view these marks, but my own reaction to them is that the opponents' mark draws special attention to itself and this would serve to reduce any possibility of confusion."

I am inclined to agree with that view, and it derives some support from the point (made by Mr Meade himself, for another purpose) that there is no positive evidence of any actual confusion during the period of 20 years when both sides have been trading. However as I think the Judge was right about distinctiveness it is not necessary to express a final view on the alternative ground of objection.

The Judge then dealt with the ELVIS PRESLEY mark quite briefly.... The most relevant point is in paragraph 8-74,

> "[The 1938 Act] faced the Registry and the courts with the need to define registrability for new and newish marks. Here a sort of rule of thumb is available: to ask whether the mark is one a rival trader would want to use in referring to his goods [with a reference to *Always* [1986] RPC 93] and if so, whether it has gone too far towards distinctiveness for an honest rival to do so?"

The ELVIS PRESLEY mark differed from the ELVIS mark by the addition of a not particularly common surname. Had it been almost any other surname (except Costello) it would have made the mark more distinctive in the trade mark sense. But in this case it simply confirmed the descriptive character of the mark.

In those circumstances I think the Judge was bound to come to the same conclusion about the ELVIS PRESLEY mark....

Finally the Judge considered the signature mark (without, as I have noted, reaching any conclusion as to its authenticity). He set out and discussed the structure of §9(1) of the 1938 Act and said,

> "Although the Registry and the court must start from the premise that signatures are *prima facie* distinctive, they are not inevitably so.... Someone ... may adopt a signature which consists of his surname spelt out in precise capitals or in a perfect script which is indistinguishable from, say, Times Roman font. Such writings, though signatures, would be indistinguishable from the printed form of the name and, it seems to me, would not be distinctive."

... [T]he example given by the judge is a very extreme case—so extreme that the court might simply decline to treat the mark as a signature at all. The "Elvis A. Presley" mark is miles away from that and I consider that the Judge was wrong, [in light of an earlier case], to conclude that the signature mark was not distinctive under §9(1)(b).

However I agree with the Judge's alternative ground of decision under §§11 and 12. Mr Shaw's registered Elvisly Yours mark is in a cursive script with a Greek E which (while more regular and more florid) bears at least some resemblance to the Greek E at the beginning of the Elvis A Presley signature. The test ... is whether, if the two rival marks are used in a fair and normal manner, the court is satisfied that there is no reasonable likelihood of deception or confusion being caused to a substantial number of members of the public. For this purpose the public is to be regarded as ordinary persons, neither specially careful nor specially careless, who would be in the market as possible purchaser of the goods in question. The burden of proof is on the applicant for the later registration.

The hearing officer considered all three marks together in relation to [deceptiveness], and concluded that there was no valid objection to any of them as regards deception or confusion. I have already indicated that I am inclined to agree with this view in relation to the word marks ELVIS and ELVIS PRESLEY. But the signature mark appears to me to call for separate consideration, because its impact is more visual and it and Mr Shaw's mark share a cursive script. It is very much a matter of impression, on which lengthy reasons are inappropriate. I prefer the Judge's view on this point.

I would therefore dismiss the appeal in respect of all three applications.

LORD JUSTICE MORRITT:

... The circumstances relevant to this appeal have been fully described by Robert Walker LJ. I gratefully adopt his account of them. The issues for our determination fall into two broad categories, namely distinctiveness and the likelihood of confusion. Such issues arise in respect of three marks which, though similar to each other, are not the same. It is therefore necessary to give separate consideration to each mark in respect of each issue....

[I]t is an essential feature of a trade mark that it should indicate a connection in the course of trade between the goods in respect of which it is registered and the person having the right to use the mark. A trade mark must indicate the source of the goods not their type or quality.

A mark, in order to indicate the source of goods, must be distinctive....

The Signature Mark

I consider first the Signature Mark....

For my part I do not accept that the authenticity of the signature has been established on the balance of probability.... In those circumstances I would dismiss the appeal in respect of the Signature Mark.

If, contrary to my view, the signature mark is authentic then the issue of distinctiveness arises. Prima facie an authentic signature is distinctive of the individual who signed. But it does not, I think, follow that the signature is on that account distinctive of the goods as denoting the necessary connection between the goods and the proprietor of the mark. In my view, there is no distinction to be drawn in this respect between the signature mark and the marks ELVIS or ELVIS PRESLEY.

ELVIS

... In my view it is necessary ... to keep in mind that part of the definition of trade mark which requires that the mark is capable of indicating the connection in the course of trade between the goods and EPEI.

... It is true that the goods in respect of which registration is sought, for instance soap, are consumer items. To market those goods under the mark ELVIS would obviously seek to turn to account the name and memory of Elvis Presley; but it would seek to do so as descriptive of a popular hero not as distinctive of the connection between the soap and EPEI as the proprietor of the mark. The soap would be sold as Elvis soap. The character of the soap would be Elvis soap. To my mind it is clear that the mark could not [be considered a source identifier] for it would be a direct reference to the character of the soap.

... [As a] consequence, as apparently accepted by counsel for EPEI, [it] must be that ... the appeal should be dismissed with regard to this mark also.

ELVIS PRESLEY

... The issue is whether this mark is "capable ... of distinguishing the goods with which the proprietor of the trade mark is or may be connected in the course of trade from goods in the case of which no such no such connection subsists ...". In deciding that issue one must have regard to both inherent and factual capability to distinguish. Some degree of both inherent and factual capability must be shown.

For EPEI it was submitted that, subject to the effect of the fame of Elvis Presley, the answer was in the affirmative. In a sustained criticism of the judge's conclusion counsel for EPEI submitted that the fame of Elvis Presley in fact confirmed the conclusion because of the effect of what has now come to be known as "character merchandising". That activity is one in which a notable public figure lends his name to a particular product or range of products so as, apparently, to endorse that product. The consequence relied on is that the consumer comes to regard goods bearing that name as having the approbation of or licence from his or her "idol". EPEI relied on a number of reported cases so as to suggest that over the last 20 years the court has come to conclude, without the need for affirmative evidence on the point, that such endorsement does distinguish the goods he or she endorses from those he or she does not. Robert Walker LJ has considered those cases in detail and it is unnecessary for me to repeat the exercise.

I do not accept that submission. First, the judge concluded that there was no evidence of use by EPEI of ELVIS PRESLEY in the United Kingdom. There is no appeal from that conclusion. Second, Mr Shaw has sold in the United Kingdom quantities of his products by reference to Elvis, which, the public would generally appreciate, was a reference to Elvis Presley. For example his brand of soap was called Elvis Soap because it was impregnated with an "image [of Elvis which] remains right to the end". It is not suggested that Mr Shaw has ever claimed any connection with EPEI. Third, the fame of Elvis Presley was as a singer. He was not a producer of soap. There is no reason why he or any organisation of his should be concerned with toiletries so as to give rise to some perceived connection between his name and the product. In these circumstances I do not accept without evidence to that effect that the mark ELVIS PRESLEY would connote to anyone a connection between EPEI and Elvis soap so as to distinguish their soap from that of Mr Shaw's soap.

Counsel for EPEI forcefully contended that such a conclusion would leave the door wide open to unscrupulous traders seeking to cash in on the reputations of others. This is true if, but only if, the mark has become so much a part of the language as to be descriptive of the goods rather than distinctive of their source. But in that event I can see no objection to any trader being entitled to use the description. In the field of memorabilia, which I consider includes consumer items bearing the name or likeness of a famous figure, it must be for that person to ensure by whatever means may be open to him or her that the public associate his or her name with the source of the goods. In the absence of evidence of such association in my view the court should be very slow to infer it.

For all these reasons I consider that the judge was right to reject each of the three marks on the ground of lack of distinctiveness. In those circumstances the question of confusion does not arise. But in view of the full argument we heard and the possibility that this case may go further I should deal, briefly, with the question of confusion.

Likelihood of confusion

... The [first] question ... is whether if the signature mark or the marks ELVIS or ELVIS PRESLEY were registered their respective use would be likely to cause deception or confusion. In approaching this question I have to assume that such marks are distinctive in a trade mark sense. But in that event I do not understand how the use of such marks could fail to cause confusion given, for example, Mr Shaw's trade in Elvis soap....

[To determine confusion,] it is necessary to compare mark for mark, that is to say ELVISLY YOURS with the signature mark and with ELVIS and ELVIS PRESLEY. It is also necessary to consider notional fair use by each protagonist. Although the goods in respect of which ELVISLY YOURS is registered are limited to those "relating to the late Elvis Presley" that more limited class of goods is included in the wider class for which EPEI seeks registration. Thus all four marks relate to the same goods.

Do the marks for which EPEI seeks registration so resemble ELVISLY YOURS as to be likely to deceive or cause confusion? Again if it is to be assumed that the marks for which EPEI contends are distinctive in a trade mark sense the answer is in the affirmative....

Conclusion

For all these reasons I would dismiss this appeal.

LORD JUSTICE SIMON BROWN:

I agree with Lord Justice Robert Walker's judgment on all points (and also with Lord Justice Morritt's judgment save only insofar as he would find in the respondent's favour on the issue of the authenticity of the signature) and wish to add a few thoughts of my own only because of the obvious importance and interest of the case. My Lords' judgments so comprehensively set out the relevant facts, law and argument that my own can be very short. It is directed only to the proposed marks 'Elvis' and 'Elvis Presley', not to the signature and only to the issue of distinctiveness.

... It cannot be right, [Mr. Prescott, counsel for Enterprises] submits, that the more famous the celebrity, the more difficult it becomes to register his name as a trade mark. Rather, he argues, the general public will nowadays assume that the commercial exploitation of his name has the endorsement (i.e. the licence and approval) of the celebrity himself (or, after his death, of those lawfully succeeding to his rights). That is true equally of real people as of invented characters....

If objection be taken that registration would confer upon the appellants "a monopoly in what other traders may legitimately desire to use" ... Mr Prescott's answer is that any desire in other traders to exploit the name Elvis Presley is not legitimate but illegitimate: it would be intrinsically wrong for other traders to benefit from the prestige given to the name by the celebrity himself. It is one thing to exclude from registration geographical names (like "Glastonbury" and "Yorkshire"), simple initials (like "W & G"), descriptive words (like "Electrix"), laudatory words (like "Perfection"), and commonplace descriptive indicia (like "pale green" for pharmaceutical tablets or "Joy" for perfumes); quite another to forbid the registration of a celebrity's own name lest others may wish themselves to benefit from its acquired significance and attraction.

There are thus two central strands to the appellant's argument: one that the public's awareness of merchandising practices means that they will always assume that products of famous personalities or fictitious characters come from a particular "genuine" source, namely the person himself or his estate or someone granted the relevant rights (and in the case of fictitious characters the creator or his successors); the other that it would be wrong to deny registration of a celebrity's name by reference to Lord Parker's test in the *W & G* case—that the rights should "largely depend on whether other traders are likely, in the ordinary course of their business and without any improper motive, to desire to use the same mark ... in connection with their own goods"—because, although other traders doubtless want to use Elvis Presley's name(s) to market their own goods, their motive for doing so would be improper: it would be to exploit a commercial value in the name that properly belongs only to the character and his successors.

This, it will readily be perceived, is a very wide argument indeed. It applies virtually irrespective of the nature of the products to be marketed (exceptions being made only for non-consumable souvenirs and biographical material), irrespective of when registration is applied for (unless only it is sought for truly historical characters), irrespective of whether it is sought by the personality himself or by his legal successors, and irrespective of what if any trading in the relevant products has previously been effected either by whoever seeks registration or by competing traders. If, of course, it is sound, then it will greatly enhance the role played by trade mark registration in the promotion and protection of character merchandising. But its difficulty is that both its limbs depend ultimately upon the general proposition that character merchandising is already established and accepted in the public mind as properly the exclusive preserve of the character himself, and that, to my mind, represents an altogether too simplistic view of the effect of the many authorities in this field and discounts utterly the well-established principle that all these cases ultimately must turn upon their own facts.

Pre-eminent amongst the facts here are, first, that there is no connection whatsoever between the class of products in question (toiletries) and the things for which Elvis Presley was and remains famous ...; second, that such marketing of this class of products as has taken place in the UK since Elvis Presley's death has been effected not by Enterprises but rather by the respondent himself (who, moreover, so far from claiming any endorsement for his products from Enterprises has on the contrary made plain his differences with them); and third, that the Elvis Presley legend is such as would inevitably attract a wide demand for memorabilia, little of which (at any rate (a) in the United Kingdom, and (b) following his death) would the general public suppose to be officially licensed and approved.

On analysis, as it seems to me, all the English cases upon which Enterprises seeks to rely can be seen to have turned essentially upon the need to protect copyright or to prevent passing off (or libel). None creates the broad right for which in effect Mr Prescott contends here, a free standing general right to character exploitation enjoyable exclusively by the celebrity. As Robert Walker LJ has explained, just such a right, a new "character right" to fill a perceived gap between the law of copyright (there being no copyright in a name) and the law of passing off was considered and rejected by the Whitford Committee in 1977. Thirty years earlier, indeed, when it was contended for as a corollary of passing off law, it had been rejected in *McCulloch v. May* [1947] 2 AER 845. I would continue to reject it. In addressing the critical issue of distinctiveness there should be no *a priori* assumption that only a celebrity or his successors may ever market (or licence the marketing of) his own character. Monopolies should not be so readily created.

Notes and Questions

1. Why did the British court say that the various Elvis marks were not "distinctive"? Was it because they identify more than one person?

2. Notice that the second ground for rejecting the application — that there would be confusion between the Elvis marks used by Enterprises and the prior Elvisly Yours mark used by Shaw — was much easier to demonstrate. Mr. Shaw already had established a source connection between his goods and the "Elvis" mark. However, in reality, the type of confusion that might have resulted is what is called in the United States "reverse confusion." This occurs when the first (or "senior") user is relatively small and the second (or "junior") user is relatively large, and the public assumes that it is the senior user who is the interloper, not the junior user. The court did not comment on that possibility.

3. Suppose that Mr. Shaw had not used the Elvisly Yours mark in Britain. Would that have eliminated all of the barriers to registering the three Elvis marks?

4. Unlike the situation under the Lanham Act in the United States, there is no specific provision in the British law that protects living or deceased celebrities from having their names registered by others as trademarks without their permission. An opposition to such a registration must rely on traditional grounds, such as confusion or lack of distinctiveness. However, Section 3(6) of the current British trademark statute states: "A trade mark shall not be registered if or to the extent that the application is made in bad faith." The history of this section indicates that when Parliament considered the statute, it had before it an interpretation of this section that specifically referred to the unauthorized registration of a celebrity's name or picture as an example of bad faith. Thus, it may be that a celebrity could prevent another from registering his or her name as a trademark on that basis. On the other hand, there appear to be limits to this ground. In *In the Matter of Application No 2117532 By Corsair Toiletries Ltd. To Register The Mark Jane Austen*, (U.K. Trade Marks Registry 1999), the Hearing Officer (albeit in dicta) rejected an opposition to the registration of JANE AUSTEN as a mark based on Section 3(6). The officer expressed some doubt about whether the provision even applied to deceased celebrities. But, more to the point, the officer indicated that the provision may not have a very broad reach even if it applies to deceased celebrities:

> Specifically it is said that the applicants should have been aware of the Jane Austen nomenclature and works; that registration and use will prejudice and damage the literary and educational heritage of Jane Austen; and that there is no connection between the application in suit and the literary works of Jane Austen and the Memorial Trust. It is said on the applicants' behalf that the choice of mark was intended to "conjure up old fashioned fragrances and images of bonneted ladies". There is no suggestion that the applicants were aware of or should have been aware of the Memorial Trust. It is true that the application appears to have been filed at about the time that particular interest was being generated by television and film dramatisation of the novels. That might suggest commercial opportunism but not in my view bad faith.

> Mr Cuddigan [counsel for the Memorial Trust] suggested that it was inappropriate for the name of a historical literary figure to be registered as a trade mark. I cannot see that any general presumption of this kind exists though as I have already indicated such names may be open to objection for other reasons depending on the particular circumstance of the case. It follows also that I cannot accept that there will be any damage to Jane Austen's literary heritage. Trade in the goods at issue under the mark would in my view have no discernible effect on Jane Austen's standing as an author.

However, following the rationale of the *Elvis Presley* case, the Hearing Officer found the JANE AUSTEN mark to be lacking in distinctiveness and therefore incapable of registration on that basis.

5. Although the British statute contains no specific references to celebrities, the manual used by trademark examiners in Britain does contain some specific guidelines in these areas. Four of those guidelines are as follows:

21.2 Mere Image Carriers

The name of a famous person or group is likely to be perceived as merely descriptive of the subject matter of posters, photographs, transfers and figurines. Names of famous persons or groups are therefore unlikely to be accepted by consumers as trade marks for these goods because they will usually be seen as mere descriptions of the subject matter of the product. Objections will arise under Section 3(1)(b) & (c) of the Act.

21.3 Badges of Allegiance

The name of a famous person or group may serve to identify the trade source of badges of allegiance (including T-shirts, mugs, scarves etc) even if the possibility of other traders producing unofficial merchandise cannot be ruled out. Consequently, such marks will normally be accepted for such goods unless there is a particular reason to believe that the mark in question cannot fulfil the function of a trade mark, for example, the names of some members of the Royal Family may be incapable of performing a trade mark function for such goods because of the widespread historical trade in Royal souvenirs.

21.4 Names of Deceased Famous Individuals or Defunct Groups

In these circumstances the name is more likely to be seen by consumers as merely an historical reference to the subject matter of the goods or services, rather than to the trade source of the goods. However, each such case must be judged on its own facts taking account of the length of time that has passed since the person concerned died, or the group became defunct, and the relationship (if any) between the goods/services in the application and those associated with the dead person or defunct group. A Team Leader will be involved in each case.

21.5 Pictures of Famous Persons (living and deceased) and Groups

Pictures of famous persons/groups present similar issues to famous names. However, depending upon the goods, they may be more likely (compared to a name) to be taken as mere decoration and therefore to lack a trade mark character. Each case will be judged on its own merits and a Hearing Officer will be involved in each case.

6. *The European Union: Community Trade Marks.* In addition to the trademark laws of individual countries, the European Union has its own separate trademark system, called the Community Trade Mark (or CTM). A CTM is valid throughout the entire European Union, whereas trademarks registered in individual countries must rely on the law of that country for protection. To obtain a CTM one must register it with the EU's Office for the Harmonization of the Internal Market (OHIM) in Alicante, Spain.

The CTM is governed by Council Regulation (EC) No. 207/2009 (superseding Council Regulation (EC) No. 40/94). The provisions relating to what marks are and are not eligible for registration are found primarily in Articles 4, 7 and 8. Among the provisions are the following:

Article 4 Signs of which a Community trade mark may consist

A Community trade mark may consist of any signs capable of being represented graphically, particularly words, including personal names, designs, letters, numerals, the shape of goods or of their packaging, provided that such signs are capable of distinguishing the goods or services of one undertaking from those of other undertakings.

Article 7 Absolute grounds for refusal

1. The following shall not be registered:

   (a) signs which do not conform to the requirements of Article 4;

   (b) trade marks which are devoid of any distinctive character; ...

Suppose that a famous tennis player, such as Roger Federer, wants to register a picture of himself (not his name) as a CTM. (Although Federer is Swiss and Switzerland is not a member of the European Union, that does not bar him from registering a mark as a CTM. *See* CTM Regulation, Article 5.) Would the provisions of Articles 4 and/or 7 pose an obstacle to registration?

7. Another provision of the CTM Regulation (and also a feature of the trademark laws of virtually every member country of the European Union) provides that the following acts will constitute an infringement:

Article 9 Rights conferred by a Community trade mark

1. A Community trade mark shall confer on the proprietor exclusive rights therein. The proprietor shall be entitled to prevent all third parties not having his consent from using in the course of trade: ...

(c) any sign which is identical with or similar to the Community trade mark in relation to goods or services which are not similar to those for which the Community trade mark is registered, where the latter has a reputation in the Community and where use of that sign without due cause takes unfair advantage of, or is detrimental to, the distinctive character or the repute of the Community trade mark.

Suppose Roger Federer were to succeed in his application to register a picture of himself as a Community Trade Mark, which is valid throughout the European Union.

a. If Professor Ochoa were to create and sell t-shirts in Germany with the same picture on it as Federer registered, would that constitute trademark infringement under these regulations? Is there any additional information you would need to answer the question?

b. If Professor Welkowitz were to create and sell t-shirts in Ireland with a *different* picture of Federer (say, one that he took himself at a tennis tournament), would that constitute infringement under these regulations? If Federer had registered the picture mark in Australia and Prof. Welkowitz sold his t-shirts there, would it constitute infringement? (See also Note 8 below.)

8. The trademark law of the Benelux countries (Belgium, the Netherlands, and Luxembourg, which have a unified trademark law) contains a provision similar to CTM Article 9(c), but also one which is potentially broader:

Article 13

A.1. Without prejudice to the possible application of ordinary civil law in matters of civil liability, the proprietor of a mark may, by virtue of his exclusive right, prohibit: ...

(c) any use in the course of trade, without due cause, made of a mark that has a reputation in the Benelux territory, or of a similar sign, for goods that are not similar to those for which the mark is registered, where use of such sign takes unfair advantage of or is detrimental to the distinctive character or the repute of the mark;

(d) any use in the course of trade, without due cause, of a mark or a similar sign in any way other than to distinguish goods where use of such sign takes unfair advantage of or is detrimental to the distinctive character or the repute of the mark.

Article 13.A.1.(c) is almost identical to CTM Article 9(c) (in fact, it is derived from the EU's Trademark Harmonization Directive, which directed the member countries to harmonize their laws, and which contained the same language). However, Article 13.A.1.(d) appears designed to grant protection beyond those other provisions. It dispenses with the "mark that has a reputation" language and, perhaps more important, specifically applies to uses of the mark in a manner other than as a trademark (in other words, the offending use need not be a use that is a source identifying use). If either of the t-shirts discussed in Note 7 (a) or (b) above were sold in the Benelux countries, would Federer have a claim under Article 13 (assuming he registered under Benelux law)?

9. The CTM Regulation contains a separate provision, somewhat analogous to Section 2 of the Lanham Act, that permits the invalidation of a CTM consisting of a personal name where a prior law of the relevant member state (or the European Community) granted protection of the personal name. CTM Reg., Article 52(2). In *Fiorucci v. OHIM*, Case T-165/06 (C.F.I. 2009), the Court of First Instance held that the fashion designer Emilio Fiorucci could invoke Italian law, which prevented registration of a "well known" personal name without the consent of the person, to invalidate an application for a trademark for EMILIO FIORUCCI.

10. Even when a celebrity successfully obtains a trademark in his or her name, that does not guarantee broad protection. The estate of Pablo Picasso has licensed the Picasso name and signature for use on automobiles. When Daimler Chrysler (as it was then known) applied for a Community Trade Mark for the word PICARO, for use on motor vehicles, the Picasso heirs opposed. Unlike the *Presley* case in Britain, however, the focus in the European Trade Mark Office (known as OHIM) was not distinctiveness, but likelihood of confusion between the two marks. OHIM rejected the Picasso estate's opposition to the PICARO mark, finding no likelihood of confusion. This decision was upheld by the European Court of Justice. Ruiz-Picasso v. OHIM, Case No. C-361/04 (E.C.J. 2004). In another Picasso-related case, the British Trade Marks Registry rejected the Picasso family's opposition to the registration of the mark PQASSO (which the mark owner claimed would be pronounced PKWASSO and which stands for Practical Quality Assurance Systems for Small Organisations). The Hearing Officer found that the application was not a bad faith attempt to capitalize on the fame of the Picasso name (such bad faith being a ground for rejection under the current British trademark statute), nor was the mark lacking in distinctiveness. In re Farley's Application, [2002] E.T.M.R. 30 (U.K. Trade Marks Registry 2001).

11. In Japan, the owner of Albert Einstein's rights of publicity (which, by bequest, happens to be the Hebrew University of Jerusalem) successfully opposed the registration of the name "Einstein" in a stylized script, on the grounds that the registration would be contrary to "public order and morality" (which is a recognized basis under Japanese law for refusing or rescinding a registration). Reported in John A. Tessensohn & Shusaku Yamamoto, *Japan: Trade Marks—Registration of Famous Persons' Names*, [2001] E.I.P.R. N136 (decision dated December 12, 2000).

12. Musidor BV v. Tansing, [1994] FCA 1242; (1994) 123 ALR 593 (Fed. Ct. Australia 1994), is a case that resembles the Tiger Woods case in the previous section. This was a claim of trademark infringement regarding the sale of a CD containing a bootleg performance of the Rolling Stones. The infringement claim was based on the CD label, which had a picture of the group and the Rolling Stones name on it. The majority upheld the trial judge, who ruled that the use was not a trademark use. There was a lengthy dissent, arguing to the contrary. What, precisely, do you think the judges meant when they said it was not a "trademark use"? The dissent cited a number of U.S. cases, which were distinguished by the majority on the grounds that Australian law was not as broad as U.S. law. How do you think that a U.S. court would rule on this matter?

13. Elvis Presley apparently fared no better in Australia than in Britain. The opposition of Elvis Presley Enterprises to the mark "ElvisFINANCE" was rejected by a hearing examiner in the Australian trademark office. Elvis Presley Enterprises, Inc. v. Jelcic, [2008] ATMO 103 (Reg. of Trade Marks 2008).

———————

Problem 5

The picture below depicts a scene from the championship game of the 2006 World Cup, in which a French soccer player (or footballer if you are not from the U.S.), Zinedine Zidane, head-butted an Italian player (and was thrown out of the game). At the time, the incident was televised around the world and was the subject of a great deal of commentary.

Figure 5-2. The Zidane Head-Butt

An enterprising person decided to turn the incident into a unique commercial opportunity. He applied to register the following as a trademark:*

———————

* In fact, such an application was made in China. —Eds.

Figure 5-3. The proposed Head-Butt "trademark"

If the application was made under the Community Trade Mark regulations of Europe, would it be granted? (If you believe it is relevant, you may assume that Zidane did not authorize the use and that he would bring an opposition to the mark if necessary.) Would your answer be the same if British law applied?

Chapter VI

Internet Domain Names and Rights of Publicity

A. Introduction

The Internet has brought some new and unique challenges to the study of rights of publicity. As is the case with other areas of intellectual property law, the ability to make identical copies of electronic files, coupled with the ability to transfer that information to a virtually unlimited number of people in an instant, creates the possibility of large-scale infringement of the rights of the owners of a valuable persona. In addition, the advent of the World Wide Web, where one accesses information by navigating to a web site, has created a new wrinkle for the law of celebrity rights. In most instances, one navigates the Internet by the use of *addresses* (technically, internet protocol addresses, or IP addresses); these are numbers that represent "places" or web pages on the Internet. However, using numbers to navigate would be difficult for most people. Therefore, the numerical addresses have been made to correspond with *domain names*—words with appropriate prefixes and suffixes that allow for easier navigation to the desired place on the internet. The most common prefix is "www" which stands for World Wide Web. Common suffixes are .com, .edu., .org, .gov, etc., which designate different types of organizations. Thus, .com (or "dot com") normally designates a business or commercial enterprise, .edu designates an educational institution (such as a college or university), .org a non-profit organization (such as a public radio station or network—npr.org is the domain name address used by National Public Radio, for example), and .gov refers to a governmental organization. These suffixes are referred to as top-level domains, or TLDs. Domain names are leased through *registrars*, who have been designated by a non-profit organization (the Internet Corporation for Assigned Names and Numbers, or ICANN) as the proper entities for making domain names available. Anyone can acquire a domain name, provided it has not already been assigned to someone else, by signing up with a properly accredited registrar for the desired TLD.

The use of domain names makes it relatively easy for businesses and other organizations to create useful web sites that potential customers can remember. One can, for example, register a domain name in the form of www.yourbusinessname.com and communicate that to the public. It has become common for companies to use their trademarks as domain names (e.g., cocacola.com). Indeed, there is no reason why someone cannot register a personal name as a domain name as well—something like myname.com. Since anyone can register a domain name that has not yet been assigned, it is also possible to register someone else's name or trademark as your domain name. In the early days of the Internet, this was a common practice, and the registrants often attempted to get the owner of the trademark (or the person whose name had been registered) to pay the registrant for turning over the domain name. This practice, often called cybersquatting,

255

became very widespread and led to protests by people and businesses who felt that this constituted a misuse of the system.

One solution was to use existing statutes to deal with the problem. But ordinary trademark law proved to be an imperfect vehicle for dealing with the problem of cybersquatting. Dissatisfaction with existing law led to specific statutory solutions aimed at domain name issues, including the Anti-Cybersquatting Consumer Protection Act (ACPA), which added § 43(d) to the Lanham Act. The ACPA is discussed in Section C., below.

But specific statutory protections are not the only means by which individuals can prevent the unauthorized registration of their names as domain names. In the next section, we will discuss a process by which individuals may force the transfer of such domain names to themselves without a court procedure.

B. Arbitration under the UDRP

The problem of cybersquatting and cyberpiracy on the Internet obviously crosses the boundaries of any single country. Thus, even to the extent that countries enact statutes to protect individuals and trademark owners from such situations, their courts may face a difficult problem when the parties attempt to enforce the judgments. In an effort to assist people with these situations, and to offer a non-judicial means of resolving domain name disputes, ICANN developed the Uniform Domain Name Dispute Resolution Policy, commonly referred to as the UDRP. ICANN requires all accredited domain name registrars to adhere to the UDRP. See http://www.icann.org/en/udrp/ (last visited June 30, 2009). The UDRP mandates what ICANN calls an "administrative proceeding"—essentially an arbitration proceeding—to resolve domain name disputes. ICANN has authorized various providers to conduct these proceedings, but by far the most widely-used provider is the World Intellectual Property Organization (WIPO). Since 1999, WIPO has resolved an average of over 1,500 disputes per year.

The UDRP sets forth rules of both substance and procedure for the conduct of these dispute resolution proceedings. Perhaps most pertinent to our discussion is Paragraph 4 of the UDRP, which provides as follows:

4. **Mandatory Administrative Proceeding.**

This Paragraph sets forth the type of disputes for which you are required to submit to a mandatory administrative proceeding. These proceedings will be conducted before one of the administrative-dispute-resolution service providers listed at www.icann.org/udrp/approved-providers.htm (each, a "Provider").

a. Applicable Disputes. You are required to submit to a mandatory administrative proceeding in the event that a third party (a "complainant") asserts to the applicable Provider, in compliance with the Rules of Procedure, that

(i) your domain name is identical or confusingly similar to a trademark or service mark in which the complainant has rights; and

(ii) you have no rights or legitimate interests in respect of the domain name; and

(iii) your domain name has been registered and is being used in bad faith.

In the administrative proceeding, the complainant must prove that each of these three elements are present.

b. Evidence of Registration and Use in Bad Faith. For the purposes of Paragraph 4(a)(iii), the following circumstances, in particular but without limitation, if found by the Panel to be present, shall be evidence of the registration and use of a domain name in bad faith:

(i) circumstances indicating that you have registered or you have acquired the domain name primarily for the purpose of selling, renting, or otherwise transferring the domain name registration to the complainant who is the owner of the trademark or service mark or to a competitor of that complainant, for valuable consideration in excess of your documented out-of-pocket costs directly related to the domain name; or

(ii) you have registered the domain name in order to prevent the owner of the trademark or service mark from reflecting the mark in a corresponding domain name, provided that you have engaged in a pattern of such conduct; or

(iii) you have registered the domain name primarily for the purpose of disrupting the business of a competitor; or

(iv) by using the domain name, you have intentionally attempted to attract, for commercial gain, Internet users to your web site or other on-line location, by creating a likelihood of confusion with the complainant's mark as to the source, sponsorship, affiliation, or endorsement of your web site or location or of a product or service on your web site or location.

c. How to Demonstrate Your Rights to and Legitimate Interests in the Domain Name in Responding to a Complaint. When you receive a complaint, you should refer to Paragraph 5 of the Rules of Procedure in determining how your response should be prepared. Any of the following circumstances, in particular but without limitation, if found by the Panel to be proved based on its evaluation of all evidence presented, shall demonstrate your rights or legitimate interests to the domain name for purposes of Paragraph 4(a)(ii):

(i) before any notice to you of the dispute, your use of, or demonstrable preparations to use, the domain name or a name corresponding to the domain name in connection with a bona fide offering of goods or services; or

(ii) you (as an individual, business, or other organization) have been commonly known by the domain name, even if you have acquired no trademark or service mark rights; or

(iii) you are making a legitimate noncommercial or fair use of the domain name, without intent for commercial gain to misleadingly divert consumers or to tarnish the trademark or service mark at issue.

As you can see, not every domain name dispute is cognizable under the UDRP. Essentially, only those involving a "bad faith" registration, as defined in Paragraph 4, are subject to this procedure. In so doing, the UDRP tracks the ACPA, discussed in the Introduction and below in Section C.

The arbitration decisions are publicly available and many contain a fairly detailed explanation of their decisions. The opinions in this section are illustrative of some of the key issues involved when the dispute concerns the unauthorized use of a person's name as part of (or as the entire) domain name.

Julia Fiona Roberts v. Russell Boyd

Case No. D2000-0210
(WIPO Arbitration and Mediation Center May 29, 2000)

1. The Parties

Claimant is Julia Fiona Roberts a United States citizen....

Respondent is Russell Boyd a United States citizen....

2. The Domain Name and Registrar

The domain name at issue is <juliaroberts.com> ...

4. Factual Background

The Complainant, Julia Fiona Roberts, is a famous motion picture actress.... The Complainant is widely featured in celebrity publications, movie reviews, and entertainment publications and television shows, and she has earned two Academy Award nominations. Her latest film, Erin Brockovich (released nationwide on March 16, 2000), is currently ranked #1 at the box office.

Respondent registered the subject domain name on November 9, 1998. As of March 24, 2000, the website www.juliaroberts.com featured a photograph of a woman named "Sari Locker". The Respondent has placed the domain name up for auction on the commercial auction website, "eBay" ...

The Respondent has also registered over fifty (50) other domain names, including names incorporating other movie stars names within <madeleinestowe.com> and <alpacino.com> and a famous Russian gymnast's name within <elenaprodunova.com>. Respondent lists his email address as mickjagger@home.com. Respondent was offered US$2,550 in the eBay auction for the domain name registration.

5. Parties' Contentions

A. Complainant contends that the domain name <juliaroberts.com> is identical to and confusingly similar with the name "Julia Roberts" and the common law trademark rights which she asserts in her name pursuant to the Policy paragraph 4(a)(I).

Complainant contends that Respondent has no rights or legitimate interest in the domain name <juliaroberts.com> pursuant to the Policy paragraph 4(a)(ii).

Complainant contends that Respondent registered and is using the domain name <juliaroberts.com> in bad faith in violation of the Policy paragraph 4(a)(iii).

B. Respondent does not contest that the domain name <juliaroberts.com> is identical with and confusingly similar to Complainant's name. Respondent does contest whether Complainant has common law trademark rights in her name. Respondent admits that he selected the domain name <juliaroberts.com> because of the well known actress.

Respondent contends that he has rights and legitimate interest in <juliaroberts.com> because of his registration and use of the domain name.

Respondent contends that his registration and use of <juliaroberts.com> is in good faith.

6. Discussion and Findings

Identity or Confusing Similarity

The initial consideration of the Panel was whether Complainant had sufficiently alleged the existence of common law trademark rights in her Complaint. On page 5 of her

Complaint, Complainant alleges that "The Respondent's use of www.juliaroberts.com infringes upon the name and trademark of Complainant and clearly causes a likelihood of confusion as defined by Section 2(d) of the United States Lanham Act, Section 2(d), 15 U.S.C. Section 1052(d)." From this allegation, the Panel understood that Complainant asserted common law trademark rights in her name. The Panel further decided that registration of her name as a registered trademark or service mark was not necessary and that the name "Julia Roberts" has sufficient secondary association with Complainant that common law trademark rights do exist under United States trademark law.

A recent decision citing English law found that common law trademark rights exist in an author's name. The Policy does not require that the Complainant should have rights in a registered trademark or service mark. It is sufficient that the Complainant should satisfy the Administrative Panel that she has rights in common law trademark or sufficient rights to ground an action for passing off.

Having decided that Complainant has common law trademark rights in her name, the next consideration was whether the domain name <juliaroberts.com> was identical to or confusingly similar with Complainant's name. The second level domain name in <juliaroberts.com> is identical to the Complainant's name. Therefore, the Panel finds that the requirement of the Policy paragraph 4(a)(i) is satisfied.

Rights or Legitimate Interest

Respondent has no relationship with or permission from Complainant for the use of her name or mark. The domain name was registered with the Registrar on November 9, 1998. At this time Complainant has already been featured in a number of motion pictures and had acquired common law trademark rights in her name. Respondent admits at page 13 of his Response that "I registered JuliaRoberts.com because, after seeing several of her movies, I had a sincere interest in the actor …"

In the conclusion of the Response on page 16, the Respondent elaborates that "If Julia Roberts had picked up a phone and said, 'Hi Russ, can we talk about the domain name juliaroberts.com?' she would own it by now." Then Respondent concludes "But as I mentioned at the beginning of this response, I still think Julia is nifty crazy wacko cool."

The original content posted on the website www.juliaroberts.com had little if anything to do with Julia Roberts. It was not until this dispute arose that her likeness was posted.

In addition, Respondent admits that he has registered other domain names including other well-known movie and sports stars and having placed the disputed domain name <juliaroberts.com> for auction on eBay.

The Complainant has established a prima facie case that the Respondent has no rights or legitimate interest in the domain name and the Respondent has not provided any evidence to rebut this. It is clear from the submissions and evidence provided to this Administrative Panel that Respondent has failed to show (a) use of the domain name in connection with the offering of any goods or services, (b) common knowledge that he is known by the domain name, (c) legitimate noncommercial or fair use of the domain name, or (d) any other basis upon which he can assert rights or a legitimate interest.

Therefore, the Panel finds that Respondent has no rights or legitimate interest in the domain name <juliaroberts.com> and that the requirement of the Policy paragraph 4(a)(ii) is satisfied.

Bad Faith

Paragraph 4 of the Policy provides that evidence of bad faith registration and use includes circumstances showing:

(ii) you have registered the domain name in order to prevent the owner of the trademark or service mark from reflecting the mark in a corresponding domain name, provided that you have engaged in a pattern of such conduct.

The Respondent admits that he has registered other domain names including several famous movie and sports stars. Such actions necessarily prevent Complainant from using the disputed domain name and demonstrate a pattern of such conduct.

Therefore, the Panel finds that Respondent has registered and used the domain name <juliaroberts.com> in bad faith and that the requirement of the Policy paragraph 4(a)(iii) is satisfied.

In addition, the Respondent has placed the domain name up for auction on the commercial website eBay. When considered in conjunction with the pattern of registrations described above, the Panel finds that such action constitutes additional evidence of bad faith.

7. Decision

The Panel concludes (a) that the domain name <juliaroberts.com> is identical to Complainant's common law trademark in her name "Julia Roberts," (b) that Respondent has no rights or legitimate interest in the domain name and (c) that Respondent registered and used the domain name in bad faith. Therefore, pursuant to paragraphs 4(i) of the Policy and 15 of the Rules, the Panel orders that the domain name <juliaroberts.com> be transferred to Complainant Julia Fiona Roberts.

Israel Harold Asper v. Communication X Inc.

Case No. D2001-0540
(WIPO Arbitration and Mediation Center June 11, 2001)

1. The Parties

1.1 The Complainant is Israel Harold Asper, the Executive Chairman of the Board of CanWest Global Communications Corp. (CanWest)....

1.2 The Respondent is, according to the BulkRegister.com Whois database, Peter Zahoruk, President and Director, Communication X Inc., an Ontario corporation with its head office at 3077 New Street, Burlington, Ontario, L7N 1M6, Canada.

2. The Domain Names and Registrar

2.1 The Domain Names are: <izzyasper.com>, <izzyasper.net>, and <izzyasper.org>.

2.2 The Domain Names were registered with BulkRegister.com, Inc.,.... on August 4, 2000....

4. Factual Background

4.1 The Complainant, Israel Harold Asper, is a businessman who has typically been known by his nickname "Izzy". It is asserted on his behalf in the Complaint that "Izzy Asper has achieved widespread public recognition throughout Canada and internationally as the founder of CanWest Global Communications Corp. (CanWest), an international and diversified media company. He has also been known as an accomplished lawyer, politician and philanthropist. Despite his achievements as a lawyer, author and politician, Izzy Asper is most famous as a broadcaster." This Panel accepts this as a fact. While diversified, his business achievements have been primarily in the news media. He is the founder, majority controlling shareholder, and Executive Chairman of the Board, of a national Canadian broadcasting network (Global Television), a new media business (CanWest Interactive), and has a significant international broadcasting presence in New Zealand, Australia, and Ireland. CanWest is also Canada's largest daily newspaper publisher with 14 major metropolitan newspapers, over 120 community newspapers and a fifty-percent interest in one of Canada's national newspapers, the *National Post*. His name is closely associated with the broadcasting business in Canada and internationally. In 1995, he was inducted as an Officer of the Order of Canada, and awarded the North American Broadcasters Association International Achievement Award in 1999. He also has received the International Distinguished Entrepreneur award.

4.2 "Izzy" Asper's career in the above-noted endeavours, and his notoriety therein, have endeared [sic] for a period of time well in excess of twenty-five years.

4.3 The Complainant does not hold a registered trademark in his name, but lays claim to rights in a common law trademark sufficient to ground an action for passing off.

4.4 On August 4, 2000, the Respondent registered the following Domain Names, which are the subject of this proceeding:

<izzyasper.com>
<izzyasper.net>
<izzyasper.org>

Collectively the Domain Names.

4.5 On or about August 5, 2000, CanWest received an e-mail from the attorney on behalf of the Respondent.

"Please contact me so we can discuss my ownership of the domain names of

<IzzyAsper.com>
<IzzyAsper.org>
<IzzyAsper.net>
<LeonardAsper.com>
<LeonardAsper.org>
<LeonardAsper.net>

Peter Zahoruk
(905) 333-9740"

4.6 The Complaint in this matter was filed in April 2001.

5. Parties' Contentions

A. Complainant

5.1 Complainant contends that the Domain Names

<izzyasper.com>
<izzyasper.net>
<izzyasper.org>

are virtually identical to a common law mark to which the Complainant has rights and that the Respondent's use of the Domain Names in question infringes on Complainant's rights by confusing the public as to the origins of the

<izzyasper.com>
<izzyasper.net>
<izzyasper.org>

pursuant to the Policy, paragraph 4(a)(i).

5.2 Complainant contends that Respondent has no rights or legitimate interests in the Domain Names

    <izzyasper.com>
    <izzyasper.net>
    <izzyasper.org>

pursuant to the Policy, paragraph 4(a)(ii).

5.3 Complainant contends that Respondent registered and used the Domain Names

    <izzyasper.com>
    <izzyasper.net>
    <izzyasper.org>

in bad faith in violation of the Policy, paragraph 4(a)(iii).

B. Respondent

5.4 Although the Respondent has submitted a Response in accordance with the Uniform Domain Name Dispute Resolution Policy, this does not address, specifically, the entitlement of the Complainant to assert a common law mark to which he has rights under the Policy. Nevertheless, this must be proved to the satisfaction of the Panel.

5.5 The Respondent claims to hold a legitimate interest in the acquisition of the disputed Domain Names.

5.6 The Respondent denies any bad faith in regard to his application for and his use of the Domain Names

    <izzyasper.com>
    <izzyasper.net>
    <izzyasper.org>

...

6. Discussion and Findings

6.1 The Complaint was submitted on the basis of the provisions of a Registration Agreement in effect between the Respondent and Network Solutions which incorporates by reference, the Uniform Domain Name Dispute Resolution Policy (the "Policy") in effect at the time of the dispute. The Policy requires that domain name registrants such as Respondent agree in writing to submit to a mandatory administrative proceeding regarding third-party allegations or abuse of domain name registration (Policy, paragraph 49(a)). No registration is approved in the absence of such a written submission.

6.2 Such administrative proceedings are conducted by ICANN-approved dispute resolution service providers such as WIPO. The Policy provides an administrative means for resolving disputes concerning allegations of abuse of domain name registration, subject to referral of the dispute to a court of competent jurisdiction for independent resolution (Policy, paragraph 4(a)).

6.3 The Policy, and the Rules for Uniform Domain Name Dispute Resolution Policy (the "Rules"), establish procedures intended to assure that respondents are given adequate notice of proceedings commenced against them, and a reasonable opportunity to respond (See e.g. paragraph 2(a), Rules).

Applicable Law

6.4 The Complainant has cited, in support of its case, a Canadian judicial decision, a Canadian text, and a number of decisions of Administrative Panels pursuant to the Policy and the Rules of ICANN. The Respondent has not referred to any specific legal authority, national or international.

6.5 Paragraph 15(a) of the Rules instructs this Panelist as to the principles to be used in rendering a decision: "A Panel shall decide a complaint on the basis of the statements and documents submitted and in accordance with the Policy, these Rules and any rules and principles of law that it deems applicable."

6.6 Where the Complainant and Respondent are domiciled in the same country, previous Panels have held that this country's laws may be used "to the extent that it would assist the Panel in determining whether the Complainant has met its burden as established by paragraph(4)(a) of the Policy."

6.7 While the Panel agrees that in this matter references to Canadian law are applicable as both the Complainant and the Respondent are situated in Canada, it must also be borne in mind that there are essential differences between trademarks and domain names, and between the bases for proving causes of action available in various courts as contrasted with what is necessary to enable this Panel to reach its determinations under the Policy and Rules. This is also the case in regard to the remedies available through domestic courts and those obtainable under the Policy. With trademarks, there can be more than one registrant of the same mark and its effect may be limited by the category of goods to which it relates, and the geographic boundaries of its territorial protection. There are no such limitations with domain names. Due to the latter's technological limitations and borderless use, only one entity can be registered in each gTLD name throughout the world. Thus, there is justification for different legal principles to apply to the Uniform Domain Name Dispute Resolution Policy, its Rules, and the interpretation given these by Administrative Panels operating thereunder. It is these Rules with which all applicants for the registration of domain names agree to be bound. In any event, no one is precluded from seeking any remedies available from national courts.

6.8 The Complainant has the burden of proof in all material issues. The Role of the Panel is to make findings of fact based on the evidence presented, provided the matters at issue are within the scope of the Policy. The appropriate standard for fact-finding is the civil standard of a preponderance of the evidence. Under the preponderance of the evidence standard a fact is proved for the purpose of reaching a decision when it appears more likely than not to be true based on the evidence.

6.9 This case arises in the midst of an active dialogue concerning the issue of the extent to which a person is given a right to use the ICANN Policy and the WIPO Rules to obtain a transfer of a Domain Name or its cancellation. In the Interim Report of the Second WIPO Internet Domain Name Process relating to the Recognition of Rights and the Use of Names in the Internet Domain Name System issued on April 12, 2001, the subject is dealt with at length. This document bears review by anyone involved in Domain Name disputes concerning a claim to protection for a personal name, which has not been registered as a trademark. It addresses the right to protect one's own identity, often referred to as a "personality right, which "focuses on an individual's right to control *the commercial use* of his or her identity." [Emphasis added] This right, it is said, "serves to prohibit the unauthorized *commercial use* of a person's name, likeness or other personal characteristics closely associated with him or her." [Emphasis added]

6.10 The Final Report of the WIPO Internet Domain Name Process, April 30, 1999, addressed this issue in the context of The Scope of the Administrative Procedure, commencing at paragraph 163. It put the matter as follows:

164. The views of commentators on the desirable scope of the administrative procedure were divided. Certain commentators favored the broad approach of opening the procedure to any intellectual property dispute with respect to a domain name registration. In general, they favored the development of a body of administrative law that would, through the procedure, provide an effective international enforcement mechanism for intellectual property rights as an alternative to expensive and time-consuming multijurisdictional litigation.

165. The preponderance of views, however, was in favor of restricting the scope of the procedure, at least initially, in order to deal first with the most offensive forms of predatory practices and to establish the procedure on a sound footing. Two limitations on the scope of the procedure were, as indicated above, favored by these commentators.

166. The first limitation would confine the availability of the procedure to cases of deliberate, bad faith abusive registrations....

167. The second limitation would define abusive registration by reference only to trademarks and service marks. Thus, registrations that violate trade names, geographical indications or personality rights would not be considered to fall within the definition of abusive registration for the purposes of the administrative procedure. Those in favor of this form of limitation pointed out that the violation of trademarks (and service marks) was the most common form of abuse and that the law with respect to trade names, geographical indications and personality rights is less evenly harmonized throughout the world, although international norms do exist requiring the protection of trade names and geographical indications.

168. We are persuaded by the wisdom of proceeding firmly but cautiously and of tackling, at the first stage, problems which all agree require a solution....

6.11 It was as a result of the above that it was concluded that the Policy should be worded as they are now found therein as paragraph 4(a).

6.12 The Interim Report of the Second WIPO Internet Domain Name Process further noted that there were four important aspects, including certain commonalties and differences with respect to the protection afforded under trademark law and under the law of personality rights, which may be relevant to the discussion of protection of personal names in the DNS. These included:

(iii) Infringement of both a trademark or personality right occurs through unauthorized use by a third party. However, under trademark law the right is infringed only if a third party's use of the mark is likely to cause a likelihood of confusion among consumers as to the source of goods or services. The personality right, on the other hand, does not require the demonstration of any confusion; instead, it is infringed when the public can identify the person in question from the third party's unauthorized commercial use.

(iv) Both are concerned with a commercial exploitation by a third party that infringes upon the right. However, under trademark law, the mark itself for which protection is sought must be *used in commerce* as a precondition to relief, whereas the personality right may protect a person who does not commercially exploit his or her own identity, but nevertheless desires to prevent others from doing so.

6.13 Since the introduction of the Policy numerous Panels have been faced with deciding whether the use of an identical or confusingly similar name to that of a well-known person offends the Policy. These cases fall into a number of categories.

6.14 The first category involves entertainers, both living and deceased, in respect of whom there has been near unanimous success. [The arbitrator cited numerous cases.] There were two Complaints from entertainers, which were denied.[5] One was the case of *Bruce Springsteen v. Jeff Burgar and Bruce Springsteen Club* WIPO Case No. D2000-1532.

6.15 Authors have also sought to protect their personal names, and were successful in [several cases].

6.16 Professional athletes have sought protection in a number of cases [citing cases]

6.17 There have been few cases involving claims by or on behalf of business people [citing cases]

6.18 Yet another category is "royalty", with a case involving Princess Diana—*CMG Worldwide, Inc. v. Naughtya Page* (NAF FA0009000095641).

6.19 Finally, there has been one case of a politician, namely Anne McLellan, the Minister of Justice and Attorney General of Canada, eResolution case no. AF0303.

In order to obtain the relief requested under the Policy, Complainant must prove in the administrative proceeding that each of the three elements of paragraph 4(a) are present:

(i) The domain name registered by Respondent is identical or confusingly similar to a trademark or service mark in which Complainant has rights.

6.20 There are numerous decisions in which Panels have recognized the right of a Complainant to claim a common law mark where there is no registered trademark. In other cases the Complainant will have registered his or her name as a trademark, in which event that name will be protected within that geographic area whose law recognizes the trademark in question, and the protection for that trademark will be limited to the categories of products designated in the certificate of registration. The case involving *Madonna* is an example in the cases referred to above in paragraphs 6.14–6.17. In the *Bruce Springsteen* case, the Complainant had registered the Domain Name <brucespringsteen.net>, which was used as the host site for an official Bruce Springsteen web site. The Respondent registered the Domain Name <brucespringsteen.com>.

6.21 In the Daniel Marino case, the Panel ... found that the name "Dan Marino" had acquired sufficient secondary meaning within the American sports, entertainment and public service communities to constitute a valid common law trademark. The Panel in the case involving Steven Rattner emphasized the importance of understanding that the protection at common law must be determined on a case-by-case basis, depending greatly on the factual basis of each individual case. "At common law, as the primary task is to determine if there is confusion in the mind of the consumer, the notoriety of a particular mark is gauged relative to a number of factors, including the territory within which the mark is used, the products for which it is being used, etc." The *Cho Yong Pil* Panel found it necessary to review the evidence with a mind to determining whether the name 'Cho Yong Pil' "functions as the Complainant's mark". In *Monty and Pat Roberts, Inc. v. J. Bartell,* the Panel determined that "[i]f Complainant can establish that 'Monty Roberts' is a famous mark, then it may be able to protect that mark against dilution, even if an infringer is not involved in the same or competing channel of trade."[6]

---

5. There was another case of a performer not being entitled to the transfer of his stage name. This was *Gordon Sumner a/k/a Sting v. Michael Urvan*, WIPO Case No. D2000-0596. This case turned primarily on the fact that the name "Sting" was not a personal name and was too generic to obtain its protection.

6. However, as the Panel in this case footnotes the Lanham Act as authority for this proposition, its relevance to our case may be questionable as Canada has no comparable legislation recognizing the

6.22 In the cases mentioned in paragraphs 6.14–6.17 above where the Complainant was successful he or she either used the personal name in question as a marketable commodity, allowing his or her name or image to be used for a fee, to promote someone else's goods or services, or for direct commercial purposes in the marketing of his or her own goods and services. In some of these, including *Monty and Pat Roberts*, there were multipurposes. The pure business cases are more problematic. An obvious difference between them and the above situations is that it is less likely that a business person will use his or her name to market their own goods or services, and very unlikely that they will do so to market someone else's. Take, by way of examples, Henry Luce, Kenneth Thomson, Conrad Black and Rupert Murdoch. Are their publications marketed as a product connected to the person in question? Not likely. It is also not likely that someone would pay a fee to use these names in the promotion of a good or service with which they have no connection. Yet, each of these gentlemen is or was a famous businessman with a very high profile in the publishing business and held in high regard by many. This doesn't mean that a businessperson's name is not entitled to protection as a Domain Name. As demonstrated in the Supreme Court of Canada decision in *Hurlbut Co. Ltd. v. Hulburt Shoe* [1925] 2 D.L.R. 121 a person may be able to use his personal name to prevent its improper use if he or she can show that if "all persons whom in any way it concerns" has come to know that a particular article associated with his or her name means that he or she is responsible for its source. Under this circumstance, the personal name takes on a secondary meaning. Probably, when the T. Eaton Co. was owned by Timothy Eaton and Macy's owned by someone of that name, their names could have been protected on this basis. There is no evidence in the Complaint that the name of the Complainant has formed a part of the name of any of his companies.

6.23 It is the view of this Panel that it would be helpful in these personal name cases if the Complaint, when dealing with the criteria in 4(a)(i) identified what the nature of the commercial connection would be in the Complainant's use of the Domain Name in issue. In many cases, this will be so obvious as not to need any further embellishment. It would only be in such cases, as here, where this is not apparent that such evidence would be needed. In this case, the Complainant has not shown on a preponderance of the evidence that he uses his personal name for the purpose of the merchandising or other commercial promotion of goods or services, or that he intended to do so.

6.24 In this case, there is no evidence that the Complainant has ever used his personal name for the purpose of merchandising or other commercial promotion of goods or services, or that he intended to do so. There is evidence that as a result of a very large donation by Izzy Asper to the University of Manitoba, its business school was renamed the Asper School of Business in May 2000. Also, his name appears in connection with other charitable endeavours including the Asper Foundation and the Asper Jewish Community Campus. But it is not argued on his behalf that there was any commercial consideration given to his name being included in the name of any of these bodies. It would not therefore be appropriate for this Panel to draw any such conclusions.

6.25 The cases involving claims by or on behalf of business people, shown in paragraph 6.17 above, do not demonstrate a pattern. The *Monty and Pat Roberts* cases clearly show a commercial attachment to the use of their names. Similarly, in the case of *Steven Rattner*, he provided investment banking and corporate advisory services under his own name and therefore would have an obvious interest in protecting that name for com-

---

effect of dilution. [In fact, Canada does have a statute relating to trademark dilution, which is a form of trademark infringement that does not require confusion.—*Eds.*]

mercial uses. There is no evidence on the record in this case that Izzy Asper has ever used his name as part of a corporate name. In *Harrod's Limited v. Robert Boyd, supra,* it should be noted that the Complainant was not the person whose name was in question, but Harrod's Limited, the well-known British department store on whose Board Dodi al-Fayed served, thus the Panel in that case concluded that "The commercial impression is that domain name is associated with goods and services sponsored by or affiliated with the late Dodi Fayed or his estate". This distinguishes that case from the one before this Panel. Further, the case was one of the very early ones decided without benefit of the subsequent material available to this Panel which reserves the right to disagree with the reasoning in an appropriate subsequent matter.

6.26 There are two dominant concerns inducing the protection of marks. The first is the protection of consumers who associate the name with goods and services of a known source and quality. The second is to preserve the value of goodwill built up over time by the owner of the mark. In the case of those (primarily entertainers and professional athletes) who sell their goodwill to others in the marketing of goods and services not directly associated with the holder, the first rationale, above, is likely to be dominant. This is much less likely to be the case with other personal name marks, particularly those, which have not obtained a secondary meaning. It is the view of this Panel that the name of the Complainant falls within the latter category.

6.27 As for the cases involving royalty and a politician, their factors are sufficiently distant from those applicable in this case as not to be considered here. This is particularly the case given the current active dialogue on the subject of personal names referred to in paragraph 6.9 above.

6.28 In *Ahmanson Land Company v. Save Open Space and Electronic Imaging Systems,* WIPO Case No. D2000-0858 and *Ahmanson Land Company v. Vince Curtis,* WIPO Case No. D2000-0859, the Panels found that trade names or marks that have, through usage, become distinctive of the users' goods or services in commerce may be protectable as they have acquired a "secondary meaning". In the former case, it said: "A mark comprising a personal name has acquired secondary meaning if a substantial segment of the public understand the designation, when used in connection with services or a business, not as a personal name, but as referring to a particular source or organization." This Panel does not find this to be the case with the personal name of the Complainant. In Canada, the ownership of interests in newspapers change as frequently as that of major league sports coaches. The first *Ahmanson* Panel further held that personal names used as marks are treated as strong marks upon a showing of secondary meaning and a mark comprising a personal name will acquire secondary meaning if a substantial segment of the public understands the designation, when used in connection with services or a business, not as a personal name, but as referring to a particular source or organization. No such secondary meaning has been proved in the name "Izzy Asper".

6.29 While, therefore, this Panel has no doubt that the Complainant, known as Izzy Asper, has a deservedly famous name and that this attribute may provide him with a remedy in a national court for an alleged improper use of his name, the present Policy and Rules which bind this Panel do not permit a finding that he has rights in a trademark or service mark of such a nature as to successfully challenge a Domain Name which is identical or confusingly similar.

(ii) Respondent has no rights or legitimate interests in respect of the domain name.

6.30 The Policy in paragraph 4(c)(iii) indicates that a Respondent may demonstrate its rights to and legitimate interest in the Domain Name in responding to a Complaint if the Panel finds it to be proved, based on its evaluation of all evidence presented, that the Respondent is "making a legitimate non commercial or fair use of the Domain Name, without intent for commercial gain to misleadingly divert consumers or to tarnish the trademark or service mark at issue."

6.31 The Panel in the *Jules I. Kendall* case focused closely upon the necessity of showing a commercial relationship when it held that it was material that the Respondent did not register the Domain Name to disrupt the business of a competitor in that there was no indication that the Respondent had intentionally attempted to attract Internet users to its site for commercial gain, based on confusion with the name of the Complainant.

6.32 In the *Monty Roberts* case, the Respondent lost its fair use argument as its web site was used for commercial activity in that it directed users to sites where merchandise could be purchased, including some which competed with that marketed by the Complainant.

6.33 In the *Jeanette Winterson* case, the Respondent failed to succeed in demonstrating any legitimate right he may have had to use the name for a site promoting the Complainant's works and as a "fan club" by virtue of the fact that he offered the name in question for sale.

6.34 In the case concerning the *Jimi Hendrix* name the site was used to advertise vanity e-mail addresses incorporating the <Jimihendrix.com> Domain Name.

6.35 The question of "fair use" has come up in a number of cases. Recently, it has been the subject of an award in *Ahmanson Land Company v. Vince Curtis, supra*. In that case the Panel found a fair use where the purpose of Respondent's web sites were shown to have served as non-commercial platforms to criticize the commercial activities of Complainant. The Panel said "[d]eterminations regarding legitimate non-commercial and fair use under the Policy require a balancing of trademark holder and other public interests." This Panel agrees with this statement.

6.36 The Respondent says that his possession of the three Domain Names involving the Complainant is integral for it to maintain both the artistic merit and the purely satirical nature of a web site created by him entitled **Who Wants To Be A Canadian Media Baron**. The site, he says, "was designed in response to the both the popularity of the program WHO WANT TO BE A MILLIONAIRE *[sic]*, and the public outcry over Canadian media mergers and acquisitions, particularly those of the complainants." The site was operated as a game with people answering a question "Who Wants to Be A Canadian Media Baron" with the options including the Complainant in this case. This site is not now available, says the Respondent, due to the fact that the Domain registrar required that it be disabled, although a screen shot of one of the frames from the multimedia project is annexed to the Response. A copy of the communications from the registrar to this effect is not provided.

6.37 Previous Panel decisions have held that it is not appropriate to use the name of the entity whom one wishes to criticize on the basis of "fair use" to divert Internet traffic to the site.

6.38 While the onus is on the Complainant to prove each of the three elements of the Policy, once he makes a *prima facie* showing that a Respondent lacks rights in the Domain Name, the burden of proof shifts to the Respondent to come forward with demonstrable evidence proving a legitimate interest in the Domain Name. This is consistent with the Policy in paragraph 4(c)(iii), which speaks in terms of the Respondent demonstrating his rights or legitimate interests to the Domain Name for legitimate non-commercial or fair use purposes. The Policy in the opinion of this Panel, strikes the correct relationship between the overall onus of proof in regard to an issue in a case as contrasted with the proof of a fact material to that issue. In regard to the latter, the onus is always on a person who asserts a proposition of fact, which is not self-evident. See *Robins v. Na-*

tional Trust Co.Ltd. et al. [1927] 2 D.L.R. 98, [1927] A.C. 515 (P.C.). Thus, while the effect of the assertion, as above, made by the Respondent may have amounted to fair use, its credibility is significantly negated by reason of the elements of bad faith as addressed below in connection with paragraph 4(a)(iii) of the Policy.

6.39 This Panel finds that the Respondent has no rights or legitimate interests in respect of the Domain Name(s).

<izzyasper.com>
<izzyasper.net>
<izzyasper.org>

(iii) The domain name has been registered and is being used in bad faith.

6.40 Complainant must establish not only bad faith registration, but also bad faith use.

6.41 The term "use in bad faith" in paragraph 4(a)(iii) does not refer to "use in commerce" in the trademark sense of the word, but refers in the broad sense to a pattern of conduct respecting the registered Domain Name in dispute, while passive holding of the Domain Name, without use in commerce, may support a holding of use in bad faith.

6.42 While this Panel is prepared to accept that the e-mail from the Respondent to the corporate office of the Complainant one-day after the Respondent registered its Domain Name is not necessarily evidence of an offer to sell the domain in question, it is evidence of bad faith. The e-mail stated:

"Please contact me so we can discuss my ownership of the domain names of

<IzzyAsper.com>
<IzzyAsper.org>
<IzzyAsper.net>
<LeonardAsper.com>
<LeonardAsper.org>
<LeonardAsper.net>

Peter Zahoruk
(905) 333-9740"

This is, in the opinion of this Panel, inconsistent with the alleged plan of fair use by the Respondent of the Domain Name(s) as recited above in paragraph 6.36. In addition, the e-mail header indicated the e-mail was from "Izzy Asper" and the e-mail address used to send the e-mail was <izzyasper@hotmail.com>. This was followed by a notification by the Respondent that he was forwarding his original e-mail and the response from Complainant's office to several newsrooms throughout Canada. On balance, and in the absence of any explanation by the Respondent to the allegation in the Complaint that there could be no bona fide reason for this e-mail, the Panel accepts the allegation.

6.43 There is also evidence that the Respondent has engaged in a pattern of such conduct by registering other Domain Names which are identical or confusingly similar to the names of famous persons such as the name of a former Canadian Prime Minister, a celebrated businessman and publisher, an American wrestler, and of the son of the Complainant who was being groomed to eventually succeed his father in the family businesses.

6.44 This Panel finds that the Domain Names <izzyasper.com>, <izzyasper.net>, and <izzyasper.org> have been registered and are being used in bad faith.

7. Decision

7.1 The only remedy sought by the Complainant, as set out in paragraph 51 of the Complaint is that this Administrative Panel issue a decision that the contested Domain

Names be transferred to the Complainant. As the Rules in paragraph 3(b)(x) require that the Complaint specify, in accordance with the Policy, the remedies sought, and as the Complainant has not asked for a cancellation of the registrations in question, only the former remedy will be addressed.

7.2 The Panel finds and decides:

(i) the Domain Name is not identical or confusingly similar to a trademark in which Complainant has rights;

(ii) Complainant has established that Respondent has no rights or legitimate interests in respect of the Domain Names;

(iii) Complainant has established that the Domain Name has been registered and is being used in bad faith.

7.3 The request that the Administrative Panel appointed in this administrative proceeding issue a decision that the contested Domain Names <izzyasper.com>, <izzyasper.net>, and <izzyasper.org> be transferred to the Complainant is denied.

Notes and Questions

1. In both cases, the complaining party had to overcome the same barrier under the UDRP. Can you identify that barrier? Can you explain why Julia Roberts was able to overcome that barrier, but not Mr. Asper? Does the difficulty have anything to do with the relative renown of the two people? What does that tell you about the ability of celebrities to use the UDRP to protect against unauthorized registration of their names as domain names?

2. Why do you suppose that limitation (the one that ultimately kept Mr. Asper from winning) was built into the UDRP?

3. How does the policy behind the UDRP (cited in the WIPO Report, quoted in the *Asper* case) compare to the policies underlying the protection of rights of publicity that you have seen in Chapters I–V?

4. As can be seen from these two cases, UDRP proceedings may involve parties from different countries, and certainly from countries other than the United States. What body of law is relevant when deciding the rights of celebrities in their names? Is state law relevant? Is a state right of publicity law like that of California, or the common law (such as that in California) relevant?

5. In the *Asper* case, the panel found bad faith, but still did not find in favor of Mr. Asper. Would a sliding scale of trademark use vs. bad faith be a superior method of dealing with the problem? Should personal names be dealt with differently under the UDRP, or would that simply cause other problems?

Friends of Kathleen Kennedy Townsend v. B. G. Birt
Case No. D2002-0451 (WIPO 2002)

[Kathleen Kennedy Townsend, daughter of the late Sen. Robert Kennedy and the then-Lieutenant Governor of Maryland, brought a WIPO complaint against the registrant of several domain names consisting of variations of her name. That complaint was rejected on the grounds that she was not using her name as a trademark, but the panel suggested that a fundraising committee for Townsend might have standing to complain. Such a committee brought the present action. The panel treated the present action as a refiling of the previous action.]

[In a prior case a panel stated:]

"... some general principles about the determination of this issue [entertaining a Refiled Complaint] can and should be stated.... First, the burden of establishing that the Refiled Complaint should be entertained under the Uniform Policy rests on the refiling complainant. Secondly, that burden is high...." ...

In this case, whether or not Friends [a fundraising organization for Townsend] has any rights under the alleged mark is open to serious doubt. The alleged license [between Townsend and Friends] is not before the panel. Nothing about its terms and conditions, or when it was entered into, is known. Nothing is known about Friends's actual use, if any, of the alleged mark. Nothing is known about any control the owner of the mark has, may have, or may have exercised, over any use or proposed use by Friends of the mark.

The panel in the prior proceeding did not adjudicate that Friends was in fact and in law a proper complainant with respect to the alleged mark. The prior panel simply stated a general proposition, *viz.*: it is the legal fundraising entity, not the individual political figure, who would be an appropriate complainant—assuming the fundraising entity did indeed have rights under a mark.

Here, Friends has not discharged its high burden of demonstrating its rights under the mark. Accordingly, Friends has no standing here.

[The panel then considered what, if any, trademark rights Friends might have:]

Friends relies on a common law mark. As we read the current complaint, Friends urges only that it *will* use the mark "Kathleen Kennedy Townsend". Those averments appeared in the January 15, 2002, complaint, as well as the May 8, 2002, complaint here. No contemporaneous document supporting such averments accompanies the complaint. No document showing actual use of the alleged mark is in the record—even in the intervening four months since the filing of the first complaint.

If Ms. Townsend had filed an intent-to-use application to register her name as a mark in the U. S. Patent and Trademark Office, she would have had to meet the requirements of 15 U.S.C. § 1051(b). This record does not reflect the verified showing that she would have had to make under 15 U.S.C. Nor does the record reflect either factual support or legal authorization for a finding that Ms. Townsend has any common law trademark or service mark rights in her name based on her, or Friends', alleged intent to use the mark.

Even if Ms. Townsend had properly granted to Friends rights under a common law mark, this record falls far short of establishing what that mark is, when those common law rights arose, or whether they remain extant. Accordingly, Friends has failed to satisfy its burden of proof with respect to Paragraph 4.a. of the Policy....

[T]he majority of the panel orders that the complaint be dismissed with prejudice....

[There was a dissent filed by one of the three panelists:]

In the prior ruling referred to as *Townsend I*, the panel noted that the fundraising entity, not the politician, has standing to assert rights under the Policy. Now that the fundraising entity has asserted a claim, the majority of the panelists rejects the claim as not being significantly different from the arguments previously made by the politician herself.

I would find that the Complainant has shown sufficient rights in the trademark. I would, thereafter, consider the claims of this Complainant and engage in the analyses of confusing similarity between the mark and the domain name, rights or legitimate interest of the Respondent and the existence or lack of good faith by Respondent in the registration and use of the domain name.

Notes and Questions

1. Is Kathleen Kennedy Townsend's fame more akin to that of Julia Roberts or to Izzy Asper?

2. Was the Friends of Kathleen Kennedy Townsend organization acting without her authorization?

3. Which country's trademark law would apply to this proceeding?

4. In light of this ruling how, if at all, can a political figure use the UDRP to protect herself from this sort of problem?

5. Suppose that a person named Paul McCartney, no relation to the former Beatle, has owned a clothing store in Christchurch, New Zealand, called Paul McCartney Haberdashers since 1975 (the Beatles became famous in the 1960s). Mr. McCartney has registered the domain name paulmccartney.com, which he uses to advertise his clothing store. If Sir Paul McCartney (the former Beatle) brought a complaint under the UDRP, whose law would apply to the key element of the claim? Could Sir Paul successfully challenge the New Zealander under the UDRP?

C. The Anti-Cybersquatting Consumer Protection Act

The UDRP was an attempt to solve the cybersquatting problem without invoking the court processes of individual countries. However, this did not stop countries from enacting their own solutions to the problem. In the United States, the Anticybersquatting Consumer Protection Act of 1999 (the ACPA) gave a right of action against those who registered domain names with a "bad faith intent to profit" from the registration. *See* Lanham Act § 43(d), 15 U.S.C. § 1125(d). For the most part, the right of action was given to *trademark* owners, to protect them against diversion of trade from the unauthorized use of web sites whose domain names were identical or confusingly similar to a trademark. As we have seen in Chapter V and in Section B., above, and as will be discussed below, this can create obstacles for individuals who want to prevent their names from being registered without authorization.

1. Provisions Specific to the Protection of Individuals

One part of the ACPA specifically targeted the registration of personal names by people other than the person represented by the domain name. 15 U.S.C. § 8131* provides in part:

---

* This section was originally codified at 15 U.S.C. § 1129.

§ 8131. Cyberpiracy protections for individuals

(1) **In general**

(A) Civil liability

Any person who registers a domain name that consists of the name of another living person, or a name substantially and confusingly similar thereto, without that person's consent, with the specific intent to profit from such name by selling the domain name for financial gain to that person or any third party, shall be liable in a civil action by such person....

(2) **Remedies**

In any civil action brought under paragraph (1), a court may award injunctive relief, including the forfeiture or cancellation of the domain name or the transfer of the domain name to the plaintiff. The court may also, in its discretion, award costs and attorneys fees to the prevailing party.

As you can see, this provision is rather limited in scope. It only applies to *living* individuals, and it only prohibits registrations made "with the specific intent to profit ... by selling the domain name." In many ways, this section is an analog to Section 2(c) of the Lanham Act, which prohibits the registration of the name of a living person as a trademark. (See Chapter V.A.2.)

Some celebrities have invoked the somewhat broader provisions of § 43(d); those situations will be discussed below.

Some states have enacted analogous statutes, which outlaw the unauthorized registration of someone else's name as a domain name under more generalized circumstances. *See, e.g.,* Cal. Bus. & Prof. Code § 17525 (protects living persons and "deceased personalit[ies]" and requires only a generalized "bad faith intent"); Cal. Elec. Code § 18320 (outlawing domain names that seek to "to deny a person access to a political Web site, deny a person the opportunity to register a domain name for a political Web site, or cause a person reasonably to believe that a political Web site has been posted by a person other than the person who posted the Web site, and would cause a reasonable person, after reading the Web site, to believe the site actually represents the views of the proponent or opponent of a ballot measure"); Haw. Rev. Stat. § 481B-22(b) (protects against bad faith registration of name of a living person); La. Stat. Ann. RS § 300.12 (protection limited to living persons, including their nicknames or aliases, and to intent to profit by reselling the domain name to that person or another).

In view of the limitations of the UDRP, would Mr. Izzy Asper have had better luck if Canada had a statute similar to 15 U.S.C. § 8131?

---

2. General Provisions of the ACPA

Section 8131 and analogous state laws would seem to be the simpler and more direct statutory mode of protection. However, those statutes have some limits. In some states, the statute has not been interpreted to grant a private right of action (reserving the right to a state official). As we have seen in Chapter V, personal names can act as trademarks and in such cases celebrities may use trademark law as a means of protection. In the main portion of the ACPA, which became Section 43(d) of the Lanham Act (15 U.S.C. § 1125(d)), Congress recognized this possibility. Section 43(d)(1)(A) provides, in part:

> A person shall be liable in a civil action by the owner of a mark, including a personal name which is protected as a mark under this section, if, without regard to the goods or services of the parties, that person—

> (i) has a bad faith intent to profit from that mark, *including a personal name which is protected as a mark under this section* ...

15 U.S.C. § 1125 (d)(1)(A) (emphasis added). Under this section, plaintiff must show more than that the domain name is plaintiff's personal name; the name must also act as a trademark. *See, e.g.,* Dawson v. Brandsberg, 2006 WL 2915234 (W.D. Va. 2006). That plaintiff's name is well known is not relevant. If the name acts as a mark, then it is protected from cyberpiracy under § 43(d)(1)(A). As seen from the statute, the mere unauthorized registration of another's name, even if it acts as a mark, is not sufficient to trigger liability under the statute. The registration must be made with "a bad faith intent to profit from [the] mark." The statute sets out nine factors to assist courts in making that determination. It also contains an exemption for situations where the defendant had a reasonable belief that he or she had a right to use the domain name.

One of the advantages of using Section 43(d) is that one can also avail oneself of the remedies contained in Section 35(a) (15 U.S.C. § 1117(a)), which allows damages for violations of all portions of Section 43, including 43(d). An even greater advantage is Section 35(d), which provides statutory damages for violations of Section 43(d):

> (d) **Statutory damages for violation of section 1125(d)(1)**

> In a case involving a violation of section 1125(d)(1) of this title, the plaintiff may elect, at any time before final judgment is rendered by the trial court, to recover, instead of actual damages and profits, an award of statutory damages in the amount of not less than $1,000 and not more than $100,000 per domain name, as the court considers just.

Section 8131(2) does not allow any damage remedies, although it does permit the recovery of attorneys fees "in [the] discretion [of the court]." Section 35(a) also allows recovery of attorneys fees, but only in an "exceptional case."

Finally, the student should be aware that the UDRP and the ACPA do not necessarily work in harmony. United States courts are not obligated to recognize the results of UDRP proceedings as preclusive of ACPA suits. *See* Storey v. Cello Holdings, L.L.C., 347 F.3d 370, 382 (2d Cir. 2003); Sallen v. Corinthians Licenciamentos Ltda., 273 F.3d 14, 27–30 (1st Cir. 2001).

Chapter VII

Newsworthiness as an Exception to Rights of Publicity

A. News Reporting and the First Amendment

The preceding chapters have demonstrated that the right of publicity (whether or not one considers the additional modes of protection under trademark law) is a very broad right to control the use of one's persona. Obviously, such a broad right in a communicative vehicle—and the persona of a celebrity certainly can be considered communicative (think of Paris Hilton, Bill Cosby, and Clint Eastwood and imagine the different images they convey)—runs the risk of butting up against the First Amendment's protection of freedom of expression. In the Chapters that follow, we will see how different courts, including foreign courts, attempt to reconcile the protection of rights of publicity with free expression in many different ways. One of the most obvious situations in which these two ideas may collide is in the reporting of news about a celebrity. Where is the line between the legitimate needs of news reporting and "commercial exploitation"? The cases in this Chapter address this problem.

We begin with the only United States Supreme Court decision to address rights of publicity. In addition to discussing the First Amendment issue, the Court offers its rationale for the right of publicity, which you should compare to the discussion in Chapter I.B. In some ways, this case is factually quite different from the usual right of publicity case; as you read the case, think about how the unique facts of the case shape the opinion and whether these facts might make it difficult to apply the Court's reasoning in other situations.

Zacchini v. Scripps-Howard Broadcasting Co.
433 U.S. 562 (1977)

Mr. Justice WHITE delivered the opinion of the Court.

Petitioner, Hugo Zacchini, is an entertainer. He performs a 'human cannonball' act in which he is shot from a cannon into a net some 200 feet away. Each performance occupies some 15 seconds. In August and September 1972, petitioner was engaged to perform his act on a regular basis at the Geauga County Fair in Burton, Ohio. He performed in a fenced area, surrounded by grandstands, at the fair grounds. Members of the public attending the fair were not charged a separate admission fee to observe his act.

On August 30, a freelance reporter for Scripps-Howard Broadcasting Co., the operator of a television broadcasting station and respondent in this case, attended the fair. He carried a small movie camera. Petitioner noticed the reporter and asked him not to film

275

Figure 7-1. An Advertisement for Hugo Zacchini, The Human Cannonball

the performance. The reporter did not do so on that day; but on the instructions of the producer of respondent's daily newscast, he returned the following day and videotaped the entire act. This film clip[,] approximately 15 seconds in length, was shown on the 11 o'clock news program that night, together with favorable commentary.[1]

Petitioner then brought this action for damages, alleging that he is "engaged in the entertainment business," that the act he performs is one "invented by his father and ... performed only by his family for the last fifty years," that respondent "showed and commercialized the film of his act without his consent," and that such conduct was an "unlawful appropriation of plaintiff's professional property." Respondent answered and moved for summary judgment, which was granted by the trial court.

The Court of Appeals of Ohio reversed. The majority held that petitioner's complaint stated a cause of action for conversion and for infringement of a common-law copyright, and one judge concurred in the judgment on the ground that the complaint stated a cause of action for appropriation of petitioner's "right of publicity" in the film of his act. All three judges agreed that the First Amendment did not privilege the press to show the entire performance on a news program without compensating petitioner for any financial injury he could prove at trial.

Like the concurring judge in the Court of Appeals, the Supreme Court of Ohio rested petitioner's cause of action under state law on his "right to the publicity value of his per-

---

1. The script of the commentary accompanying the film clip read as follows:
   "This ... now ... is the story of a true spectator sport ... the sport of human cannon-balling ... in fact, the great Zacchini is about the only human cannonball around, these days ... just happens that, where he is, is the Great Geauga County Fair, in Burton ... and believe me, although it's not a long act, it's a thriller ... and you really need to see it in person ... to appreciate it...."

formance." 47 Ohio St.2d 224, 351 N.E.2d 454, 455 (1976). The opinion syllabus, to which we are to look for the rule of law used to decide the case, declared first that one may not use for his own benefit the name or likeness of another, whether or not the use or benefit is a commercial one, and second that respondent would be liable for the appropriation over petitioner's objection and in the absence of license or privilege, of petitioner's right to the publicity value of his performance. *Ibid.* The court nevertheless gave judgment for respondent because, in the words of the syllabus:

> "A TV station has a privilege to report in its newscasts matters of legitimate public interest which would otherwise be protected by an individual's right of publicity, unless the actual intent of the TV station was to appropriate the benefit of the publicity for some non-privileged private use, or unless the actual intent was to injure the individual." *Ibid.*

We granted certiorari to consider an issue unresolved by this Court: whether the First and Fourteenth Amendments immunized respondent from damages for its alleged infringement of petitioner's state law "right of publicity." Insofar as the Ohio Supreme Court held that the First and Fourteenth Amendments of the United States Constitution required judgment for respondent, we reverse the judgment of that court....

II

The Ohio Supreme Court held that respondent is constitutionally privileged to include in its newscasts matters of public interest that would otherwise be protected by the right of publicity, absent an intent to injure or to appropriate for some nonprivileged purpose. If under this standard respondent had merely reported that petitioner was performing at the fair and described or commented on his act, with or without showing his picture on television, we would have a very different case. But petitioner is not contending that his appearance at the fair and his performance could not be reported by the press as newsworthy items. His complaint is that respondent filmed his entire act and displayed that film on television for the public to see and enjoy. This, he claimed, was an appropriation of his professional property. The Ohio Supreme Court agreed that petitioner had "a right of publicity" that gave him "personal control over commercial display and exploitation of his personality and the exercise of his talents." This right of "exclusive control over the publicity given to his performances" was said to be such a "valuable part of the benefit which may be attained by his talents and efforts" that it was entitled to legal protection. It was also observed, or at least expressly assumed, that petitioner had not abandoned his rights by performing under the circumstances present at the Geauga County Fair Grounds.

The Ohio Supreme Court nevertheless held that the challenged invasion was privileged, saying that the press "must be accorded broad latitude in its choice of how much it presents of each story or incident, and of the emphasis to be given to such presentation. No fixed standard which would bar the press from reporting or depicting either an entire occurrence or an entire discrete part of a public performance can be formulated which would not unduly restrict the 'breathing room' in reporting which freedom of the press requires." 47 Ohio St.2d, at 235, 351 N.E.2d, at 461. Under this view, respondent was thus constitutionally free to film and display petitioner's entire act.[5]

---

5. The court's explication was as follows:
"The proper standard must necessarily be whether the matters reported were of public interest, and if so, the press will be liable for appropriation of a performer's right of publicity only if its actual intent was not to report the performance, but, rather, to appropriate the performance for some other private use, or if the actual intent was to injure the performer.

The Ohio Supreme Court relied heavily on *Time, Inc. v. Hill*, 385 U.S. 374 (1967), but that case does not mandate a media privilege to televise a performer's entire act without his consent. Involved in *Time, Inc. v. Hill* was a claim under the New York "Right of Privacy" statute that Life Magazine, in the course of reviewing a new play, had connected the play with a long-past incident involving petitioner and his family and had falsely described their experience and conduct at that time. The complaint sought damages for humiliation and suffering flowing from these nondefamatory falsehoods that allegedly invaded Hill's privacy. The Court held, however, that the opening of a new play linked to an actual incident was a matter of public interest and that Hill could not recover without showing that the Life report was knowingly false or was published with reckless disregard for the truth—the same rigorous standard that had been applied in *New York Times Co. v. Sullivan*, 376 U.S. 254 (1964).

Time, Inc. v. Hill, which was hotly contested and decided by a divided Court, involved an entirely different tort from the "right of publicity" recognized by the Ohio Supreme Court.... The Court was aware that it was adjudicating a "false light" privacy case involving a matter of public interest, not a case involving "intrusion," "appropriation" of a name or likeness for the purposes of trade, or "private details" about a non-newsworthy person or event. It is also abundantly clear that *Time, Inc. v. Hill* did not involve a performer, a person with a name having commercial value, or any claim to a "right of publicity." This discrete kind of "appropriation" case was plainly identified in the literature cited by the Court and had been adjudicated in the reported cases.

The differences between these two torts are important. First, the State's interests in providing a cause of action in each instance are different. "The interest protected" in permitting recovery for placing the plaintiff in a false light "is clearly that of reputation, with the same overtones of mental distress as in defamation." Prosser, [*Privacy*], 48 Calif. L. Rev. [383,] 400 [(1960)]. By contrast, the State's interest in permitting a "right of publicity" is in protecting the proprietary interest of the individual in his act in part to encourage such entertainment. As we later note, the State's interest is closely analogous to the goals of patent and copyright law, focusing on the right of the individual to reap the reward of his endeavors and having little to do with protecting feelings or reputation. Second, the two torts differ in the degree to which they intrude on dissemination of information to the public. In "false light" cases the only way to protect the interests involved is to attempt to minimize publication of the damaging matter, while in "right of publicity" cases the only question is who gets to do the publishing. An entertainer such as petitioner usually has no objection to the widespread publication of his act as long as he gets the commercial benefit of such publication. Indeed, in the present case petitioner did not seek to enjoin the broadcast of his act; he simply sought compensation for the broadcast in the form of damages.

Nor does it appear that our later cases ... require or furnish substantial support for the Ohio court's privilege ruling. These cases, like *New York Times*, emphasize the protection extended to the press by the First Amendment in defamation cases, particularly when suit is brought by a public official or a public figure. None of them involve an alleged appropriation by the press of a right of publicity existing under state law.

Moreover, [those cases] all involved the reporting of events; in none of them was there an attempt to broadcast or publish an entire act for which the performer ordinarily gets

---

It might also be the case that the press would be liable if it recklessly disregarded contract rights existing between the plaintiff and a third person to present the performance to the public, but that question is not presented here" 47 Ohio St. 2d, at 235, 351 N.E.2d, at 461.

paid. It is evident, and there is no claim here to the contrary, that petitioner's state-law right of publicity would not serve to prevent respondent from reporting the newsworthy facts about petitioner's act. Wherever the line in particular situations is to be drawn between media reports that are protected and those that are not, we are quite sure that the First and Fourteenth Amendments do not immunize the media when they broadcast a performer's entire act without his consent. The Constitution no more prevents a State from requiring respondent to compensate petitioner for broadcasting his act on television than it would privilege respondent to film and broadcast a copyrighted dramatic work without liability to the copyright owner, or to film and broadcast a prize fight, or a baseball game, where the promoters or the participants had other plans for publicizing the event. There are ample reasons for reaching this conclusion.

The broadcast of a film of petitioner's entire act poses a substantial threat to the economic value of that performance. As the Ohio court recognized, this act is the product of petitioner's own talents and energy, the end result of much time, effort, and expense. Much of its economic value lies in the "right of exclusive control over the publicity given to his performance"; if the public can see the act free on television, it will be less willing to pay to see it at the fair.[12] The effect of a public broadcast of the performance is similar to preventing petitioner from charging an admission fee. "The rationale for (protecting the right of publicity) is the straightforward one of preventing unjust enrichment by the theft of good will. No social purpose is served by having the defendant get free some aspect of the plaintiff that would have market value and for which he would normally pay." Kalven, *Privacy in Tort Law—Were Warren and Brandeis Wrong?*, 31 Law & Contemp. Prob. 326, 331 (1966). Moreover, the broadcast of petitioner's entire performance, unlike the unauthorized use of another's name for purposes of trade or the incidental use of a name or picture by the press, goes to the heart of petitioner's ability to earn a living as an entertainer. Thus, in this case, Ohio has recognized what may be the strongest case for a "right of publicity" involving, not the appropriation of an entertainer's reputation to enhance the attractiveness of a commercial product, but the appropriation of the very activity by which the entertainer acquired his reputation in the first place.

Of course, Ohio's decision to protect petitioner's right of publicity here rests on more than a desire to compensate the performer for the time and effort invested in his act; the protection provides an economic incentive for him to make the investment required to produce a performance of interest to the public. This same consideration underlies the patent and copyright laws long enforced by this Court....

These laws ... were "intended definitely to grant valuable, enforceable rights" in order to afford greater encouragement to the production of works to benefit the public. The Constitution does not prevent Ohio from making a similar choice here in deciding to protect the entertainer's incentive in order to encourage the production of this type of work.

There is no doubt that entertainment, as well as news, enjoys First Amendment protection. It is also true that entertainment itself can be important news. But it is important to note that neither the public nor respondent will be deprived of the benefit of petitioner's performance as long as his commercial stake in his act is appropriately recognized. Petitioner does not seek to enjoin the broadcast of his performance; he simply

---

12. It is possible, of course, that respondent's news broadcast increased the value of petitioner's performance by stimulating the public's interest in seeing the act live. In these circumstances, petitioner would not be able to prove damages and thus would not recover. But petitioner has alleged that the broadcast injured him to the extent of $25,000, and we think the State should be allowed to authorize compensation of this injury if proved.

wants to be paid for it. Respondent knew that petitioner objected to televising his act, but nevertheless displayed the entire film.

We conclude that although the State of Ohio may as a matter of its own law privilege the press in the circumstances of this case, the First and Fourteenth Amendments do not require it to do so.

Reversed.

Mr. Justice POWELL, with whom Mr. Justice BRENNAN and Mr. Justice MARSHALL join, dissenting.

Disclaiming any attempt to do more than decide the narrow case before us, the Court reverses the decision of the Supreme Court of Ohio based on repeated incantation of a single formula: "a performer's entire act." ...

I doubt that this formula provides a standard clear enough even for resolution of this case.[1] In any event, I am not persuaded that the Court's opinion is appropriately sensitive to the First Amendment values at stake, and I therefore dissent.

Although the Court would draw no distinction, I do not view respondent's action as comparable to unauthorized commercial broadcasts of sporting events, theatrical performances, and the like where the broadcaster keeps the profits. There is no suggestion here that respondent made any such use of the film. Instead, it simply reported on what petitioner concedes to be a newsworthy event, in a way hardly surprising for a television station—by means of film coverage. The report was part of an ordinary daily news program, consuming a total of 15 seconds. It is a routine example of the press' fulfilling the informing function so vital to our system.

The Court's holding that the station's ordinary news report may give rise to substantial liability[2] has disturbing implications, for the decision could lead to a degree of media self-censorship. Hereafter, whenever a television news editor is unsure whether certain film footage received from a camera crew might be held to portray an "entire act,"[3] he may decline coverage—even of clearly newsworthy events—or confine the broadcast to watered-down verbal reporting, perhaps with an occasional still picture. The public is

---

1. Although the record is not explicit, it is unlikely that the "act" commenced abruptly with the explosion that launched petitioner on his way, ending with the landing in the net a few seconds later. One may assume that the actual firing was preceded by some fanfare, possibly stretching over several minutes, to heighten the audience's anticipation: introduction of the performer, description of the uniqueness and danger, last-minute checking of the apparatus, and entry into the cannon, all accompanied by suitably ominous commentary from the master of ceremonies. If this is found to be the case on remand, then respondent could not be said to have appropriated the "entire act" in its 15-second newsclip and the Court's opinion then would afford no guidance for resolution of the case. Moreover, in future cases involving different performances, similar difficulties in determining just what constitutes the "entire act" are inevitable.

2. At some points the Court seems to acknowledge that the reason for recognizing a cause of action asserting a "right of publicity" is to prevent unjust enrichment.... But the remainder of the opinion inconsistently accepts a measure of damages based not on the defendant's enhanced profits but on harm to the plaintiff regardless of any gain to the defendant. Indeed, in this case there is no suggestion that respondent television station gained financially by showing petitioner's flight (although it no doubt received its normal advertising revenue for the news program revenue it would have received no matter which news items appeared). Nevertheless, in the unlikely event that petitioner can prove that his income was somehow reduced as a result of the broadcast, respondent will apparently have to compensate him for the difference.

3. Such doubts are especially likely to arise when the editor receives film footage of an event at a local fair, a circus, a sports competition of limited duration (e. g., the winning effort in a ski-jump competition), or a dramatic production made up of short skits, to offer only a few examples.

then the loser. This is hardly the kind of news reportage that the First Amendment is meant to foster.

In my view the First Amendment commands a different analytical starting point from the one selected by the Court. Rather than begin with a quantitative analysis of the performer's behavior — is this or is this not his entire act? — we should direct initial attention to the actions of the news media: what use did the station make of the film footage? When a film is used, as here, for a routine portion of a regular news program, I would hold that the First Amendment protects the station from a "right of publicity" or "appropriation" suit, absent a strong showing by the plaintiff that the news broadcast was a subterfuge or cover for private or commercial exploitation.[4]

... [H]aving made the matter public — having chosen, in essence, to make it newsworthy — [Zacchini] cannot, consistent with the First Amendment, complain of routine news reportage.

Since the film clip here was undeniably treated as news and since there is no claim that the use was subterfuge, respondent's actions were constitutionally privileged. I would affirm.

[Justice Stevens' dissenting opinion, on procedural grounds, is omitted.]

————————

Notes and Questions

1. Who has the better argument, in your view, the majority or the dissent?

2. The Court analogizes the role of the right of publicity to that of copyright and patent: providing an incentive to create a performance. Is that an accurate characterization of the cases that you have read up to this point? In what ways is Zacchini's situation similar to those of other plaintiffs? In what ways is it different?

3. If "the opening of a new play linked to an actual incident was a matter of public interest," isn't a human cannonball act that is part of a local carnival a matter of public interest? If so, why doesn't *Time, Inc. v. Hill* require a different result?

4. What problem does the Supreme Court posit will occur if Zacchini does not have a right of action against the station in this case?

5. Does the dissent adequately respond to the problem the Court identifies? What problem does the dissent have with the majority's analysis of the problem?

6. Is the dissent correct that the majority opinion is severely limited by its characterization of what was protected? Test your understanding with a few examples:

    a. Suppose that the news broadcast had shown a still photograph of Mr. Zacchini landing in a net triumphantly after being shot out of the cannon (accompanied by a verbal description of the act). Would that have led to a different outcome? Why?

    b. Would your answer to the previous question be different if the broadcast showed a video clip of Mr. Zacchini landing in the net (without showing him being

————————

4. This case requires no detailed specification of the standards for identifying a subterfuge, since there is no claim here that respondent's news use was anything but bona fide. I would point out, however, that selling time during a news broadcast to advertisers in the customary fashion does not make for "commercial exploitation" in the sense intended here.

shot out of the cannon)? What if the broadcast showed a still photograph of Mr. Zacchini in the cannon and then a video of him landing in the net?

c. Suppose the television station subsequently used a still photograph of Mr. Zacchini landing in the net on its promotional commercials for the news broadcast as an example of the type of news viewers might see. Would that be a violation of Mr. Zacchini's right of publicity?

7. Suppose that, instead of seeking damages, Zacchini sought to enjoin any broadcast of his act by the television station. Would the result have been the same? Assuming he wins, what sort of damages could he claim? How would he prove the existence and amount of damages?

8. If, on remand from the Supreme Court, the Ohio Supreme Court decided that, notwithstanding the U.S. Supreme Court's decision, it wanted to limit the right of publicity by disallowing claims in cases like this, would it be permitted to do so?

9. As noted in Chapter I, a number of states have statutes granting rights of publicity. Many of those statutes contain provisions that exempt uses in news broadcasts. California's statute is illustrative:

> For purposes of this section, a use of a name, voice, signature, photograph, or likeness in connection with any news, public affairs, or sports broadcast or account, or any political campaign, shall not constitute a use for which consent is required....

Cal. Civ. Code § 3344(d). How would this provision affect the result in *Zacchini*?

10. Although we will reserve discussion of other countries' approaches to newsworthiness and free expression until Chapter IX, it is appropriate to note in conjunction with *Zacchini* that there are several international treaties that protect the right of a performer to control the fixation of his or her performances. *See* International Convention for the Protection of Performers, Producers of Phonograms, and Broadcasting Organizations, Arts. 4, 7 (1961) (Rome Convention); Agreement on Trade-Related Aspects of Intellectual Property Rights, Art. 14(1) (1994) (TRIPS Agreement); WIPO Performances and Phonograms Treaty, Arts. 5–10 (1996) (WPPT). The United States is not a party to the Rome Convention, but it is a party to the TRIPS Agreement and the WPPT.

B. Defamation, Newsworthiness, and Rights of Publicity

1. Introduction: Constitutional Limits on Defamation and Privacy

In *Zacchini*, it was clear that plaintiff's remedial interest in the lawsuit was financial. Zacchini, a performer, believed that the broadcast of his "entire act" diminished the financial value of his performance. However, in many right of publicity cases, the plaintiff's interest is far more complicated. A celebrity often will believe that the unauthorized commercial exploitation of her name, picture, or persona is in some way insulting. In those cases, the plaintiff's remedial interest is more than financial; it is a matter of personal honor.

Tort law typically provides a remedy for injuries to one's personal honor through the torts of defamation and false-light invasion of privacy. If a person is defamed (verbally or in writing), or if he or she is portrayed in a manner that is false, then a cause of action exists to remedy the insult. However, when the object of the alleged defamation or false light portrayal is a celebrity, then the First Amendment places certain restrictions on the state's ability to make the harm actionable.

As you may have studied in your Torts class, in the landmark case of *New York Times v. Sullivan*, 376 U.S. 254 (1964), the Supreme Court held that a public official may recover for defamation only upon a showing that the defendant acted with "actual malice." That is, the public official must show that the defendant made a false statement that he or she knew was false, or that the defendant acted with reckless disregard of the truth or falsity of the statement. Moreover, the plaintiff must prove actual malice by "clear and convincing" evidence, a higher standard than the usual "preponderance of the evidence" (more likely than not) standard in a civil case. The purpose of the *New York Times* test was to make sure that news media were not so fearful of incurring liability for false reports that they hesitated to report on stories of public interest.

The Court has extended the *New York Times* test beyond public officials to "public figures." *See Curtis Publishing Co., Inc. v. Butts*, 388 U.S. 130 (1967) (opinions of Warren, C.J., and Brennan, J.). It further extended *New York Times* to claims of "false-light privacy" violations in *Time, Inc. v. Hill*, 385 U.S. 374 (1967) (cited in the *Zacchini* case above). (In a claim of "false-light privacy," the plaintiff claims that a publication placed him or her in a "false light" in the public eye, even though the allegedly false facts are not necessarily defamatory. Not all states recognize a cause of action for "false-light" privacy.)

One final case that is worthy of mention is *Hustler Magazine v. Falwell*, 485 U.S. 46 (1988). In that case, Rev. Jerry Falwell was insulted by the portrayal of him in a parody advertisement contained in Hustler Magazine. (The Hustler parody was a take-off on a series of advertisements by Campari about the "first time" for celebrities—the first time that they drank Campari liqueur. Falwell's "first time" was portrayed as "a drunken incestuous rendezvous with his mother in an outhouse.") He brought a claim for intentional infliction of emotional distress and claimed that that cause of action was not governed by the *New York Times* test. The Court disagreed and held that a plaintiff could not circumvent the *New York Times* test merely by relabeling the cause of action.

As a consequence of this series of cases, many claims of violations of rights of publicity—particularly, but not exclusively, those where the alleged wrong is an "intrusive" one—may resemble the type of claims at issue in *New York Times* and *Time v. Hill*. This is especially true of claims made against media defendants, where the premise of the *New York Times* test applies most directly. As the next series of cases demonstrates, courts are sensitive to the constitutional dimensions in the obvious cases. However, as you may have noted in other chapters, courts are not always willing to view right of publicity actions as disguised substitutes for defamation claims, particularly where the defendant is not a traditional news media organization. *See generally* David S. Welkowitz and Tyler T. Ochoa, *The Terminator As Eraser: How Arnold Schwarzenegger Used The Right Of Publicity To Terminate Non-Defamatory Political Speech*, 45 Santa Clara L. Rev. 651 (2005).

2. Case Law: Newsworthiness

Eastwood v. Superior Court

149 Cal. App. 3d 409, 198 Cal. Rptr. 342 (1983)

THOMPSON, Associate Justice:

In this proceeding in mandate, we inquire into the propriety of the respondent court's ruling sustaining without leave to amend the general demurrer of the real party in interest, National Enquirer, Inc. (Enquirer), to the second cause of action of the complaint of petitioner, Clint Eastwood (Eastwood), for commercial appropriation of the right of publicity. We consider whether the unauthorized use of a celebrity's name, photograph, or likeness on the cover of a publication and in related telecast advertisements, in connection with a published nondefamatory article, which is false but presented as true, constitutes an actionable infringement of that person's right of publicity under both the common law and Civil Code section 3344, subdivision (a). We have determined that such use constitutes commercial exploitation and is not privileged or protected by constitutional considerations or expressly exempted as a news account under Civil Code section 3344, subdivision (d). Accordingly, we have concluded that the respondent court improperly sustained the general demurrer to the second cause of action without leave to amend.

Facts and Proceedings Below

The facts before this court as set forth in the petition of Eastwood and the return of the Enquirer are not in substantial dispute.

Eastwood, a well-known motion picture actor, filed a complaint containing two causes of action against the Enquirer. The gist of the first cause of action is for false light invasion of privacy. The second cause of action is for invasion of privacy through the commercial appropriation of name, photograph and likeness under both the common law and Civil Code section 3344.

The following pertinent facts emerge from the allegations of the first cause of action. The Enquirer publishes a weekly newspaper known as the "National Enquirer" which enjoys wide circulation and is read by a great number of people. In its April 13, 1982 edition of the National Enquirer, the Enquirer published a 600-word article about Eastwood's romantic involvement with two other celebrities, singer Tanya Tucker and actress Sondra Locke. On the cover of this edition appeared the pictures of Eastwood and Tucker above the caption "Clint Eastwood in Love Triangle with Tanya Tucker."[2]

The article is headlined "Clint Eastwood in Love Triangle" and appears on page 48 of this edition. Eastwood alleges the article is false and in this regard alleges:

"(a) The offending article falsely states that Eastwood 'loves' Tucker and that Tucker means a lot to him.

"(b) The offending article falsely states that Eastwood was, in late February, 1982, swept off his feet and immediately smitten by Tucker; that Tucker makes his head spin; that Tucker used her charms to get what she wanted from Eastwood; and that Eastwood now daydreams about their supposedly enchanted evenings together.

"(c) The offending article falsely states that Eastwood and Tucker, in late February, 1982, shared 10 fun-filled romantic evenings together; were constantly, during

---

2. Copies of the cover of this publication and the subject article are attached in the appendix to this opinion.

that period, in each other's arms; publicly 'cuddled' and publicly gazed romantically at one another; and publicly kissed and hugged.

"(d) The offending article falsely states that Eastwood is locked in a romantic triangle involving Tucker and Sondra Locke ('Locke'); is torn between Locke and Tucker; can't decide between Locke and Tucker; is involved in a romantic tug-of-war involving Locke and Tucker; that Locke and Tucker are dueling over him; that Tucker is battling Locke for his affections; and that when he is with Locke, Tucker is constantly on his mind.

"(e) The offending article falsely states that, in or about late February of 1982, there were serious problems in Eastwood's relationship with Locke; that he and Locke at that time had a huge argument over marriage; that he and Locke had a nasty fight; and that Locke stormed out of his presence.

"(f) The offending article falsely states that after his supposed romantic interlude with Tucker, Locke camped at his doorstep and, while on hands and knees, begged Eastwood to 'keep her', vowing that she wouldn't pressure him into marriage; but that Eastwood acted oblivious to her pleas."

Eastwood further asserts that Enquirer "published the offending article maliciously, willfully and wrongfully, with the intent to injure and disgrace Eastwood, either knowing that the statements therein contained were false or with reckless disregard of ... their ... falsity." Enquirer used Eastwood's name and photograph without his consent or permission. As a consequence thereof, Eastwood alleges that he has suffered mental anguish and emotional distress and seeks both compensatory and punitive damages.

The second cause of action of the complaint incorporates all the allegations of the first cause of action concerning the status of Enquirer and the falsity of the article. It does not, however, incorporate the allegation that the article was published with knowledge or in reckless disregard of its falsity.

Additionally, Eastwood alleges that the Enquirer made a telecast advertisement in which it featured Eastwood's name and photograph and mentioned prominently the subject article. Moreover, Eastwood alleges that the telecast advertisements as well as the cover of the April 13 publication were calculated to promote the sales of the Enquirer. Eastwood asserts that the unauthorized use of his name and photograph has damaged him in his right to control the commercial exploitation of his name, photograph and likeness, in addition to injuring his feelings and privacy. Eastwood seeks damages under both the common law and Civil Code section 3344.

Enquirer did not challenge the legal sufficiency of the first cause of action for invasion of privacy by placing Eastwood in a false light in the public eye.

Enquirer demurred to the second cause of action for invasion of privacy through appropriation of name, photograph and likeness on the basis it failed to state a cause of action on two grounds: (1) Eastwood's name and photograph were not used to imply an endorsement of the Enquirer; and (2) Eastwood's name and photograph were used in connection with a news account.

The respondent court sustained the general demurrers of Enquirer without leave to amend, and this petition followed....

Issues

This petition poses two basic issues: (1) Has Eastwood stated a cause of action for commercial appropriation of the right of publicity under either the common law or Civil

Code section 3344? (2) Is the conduct of the Enquirer privileged so as not to constitute an infringement of Eastwood's right of publicity?

Discussion

... Eastwood has framed his complaint against Enquirer on the third and fourth branches of the right of privacy. His first cause of action, which is not at issue here, rests on the theory that the subject publication placed him in a false light in the public eye. The focus of this tort is the falsity of the published article. His second cause of action, which is at issue here, rests on alternative theories. One is the common law action of commercial appropriation. The other is the statutory remedy provided in Civil Code section 3344, subdivision (a), for the knowing use, without consent, of another's name, photograph or likeness for the purposes of advertising or solicitation of purchases.

A common law cause of action for appropriation of name or likeness may be pleaded by alleging (1) the defendant's use of the plaintiff's identity; (2) the appropriation of plaintiff's name or likeness to defendant's advantage, commercially or otherwise; (3) lack of consent; and (4) resulting injury.

In addition, to plead the statutory remedy provided in Civil Code section 3344, there must also be an allegation of a knowing use of the plaintiff's name, photograph or likeness for purposes of advertising or solicitation of purchases. Furthermore, recent judicial construction of section 3344 has imposed an additional requirement. A "direct" connection must be alleged between the use and the commercial purpose....

Here, Eastwood has alleged that the Enquirer employed his name, photograph and likeness on the front page of the subject publication and in related telecast advertisements, without his prior consent, for the purpose of promoting the sales of the Enquirer. Therefore, Eastwood states an actionable claim in his second cause of action under either the common law or section 3344, or both, if two conditions are satisfied: (1) Enquirer's use of Eastwood's name, photograph and likeness constitutes an appropriation for commercial purposes, and (2) Enquirer's conduct constitutes an impermissible infringement of Eastwood's right of publicity.

I

Eastwood Has Stated Facts Showing An Appropriation of His Right of Publicity for Commercial Purposes

Enquirer argues ... that the failure of Eastwood to allege the appearance of an "endorsement" of the Enquirer is fatal to stating a cause of action for commercial appropriation.

California law has not imposed any requirement that the unauthorized use or publication of a person's name or picture be suggestive of an endorsement or association with the injured person....

Moreover, the appearance of an "endorsement" is not the *sine qua non* of a claim for commercial appropriation. Thus, in *Stilson v. Reader's Digest Assn., Inc.* (1972) 28 Cal. App. 3d 270, 104 Cal. Rptr. 581, the allegedly wrongful use involved a magazine's inclusion of individuals' names in letters soliciting participation in a sweepstake designed to promote subscription. The letters stated that the recipient and other named individuals had been chosen to receive "lucky numbers." No statement or implication that these individuals had consented to promote the magazine was made or implied. Assessing the legal significance of this promotional endeavor, the court stated that "[t]he unauthorized use of one's name for commercial exploitation is actionable." (*Id.*, at p. 273.) ...

Turning to whether the Enquirer has commercially exploited Eastwood's name, photograph or likeness, we note that one of the primary purposes of advertising is to motivate a decision to purchase a particular product or service.

The first step toward selling a product or service is to attract the consumers' attention. Because of a celebrity's audience appeal, people respond almost automatically to a celebrity's name or picture. Here, the Enquirer used Eastwood's personality and fame on the cover of the subject publication and in related telecast advertisements. To the extent their use attracted the readers' attention, the Enquirer gained a commercial advantage. Furthermore, the Enquirer used Eastwood's personality in the context of an alleged news account, entitled "Clint Eastwood in Love Triangle with Tanya Tucker" to generate maximum curiosity and the necessary motivation to purchase the newspaper.

Moreover, the use of Eastwood's personality in the context of a news account, allegedly false but presented as true, provided the Enquirer with a ready-made "scoop" — a commercial advantage over its competitors which it would otherwise not have.

Absent a constitutional or statutory proscription, we find that Eastwood can show that such use is a subterfuge or cover-up for commercial exploitation.

We therefore conclude that Eastwood has sufficiently alleged that the Enquirer has commercially exploited his name, photograph, and likeness under both the common law and section 3344, subdivision (a).

II

Enquirer's Conduct May Constitute An Infringement of Eastwood's Right of Publicity

Enquirer argues that Eastwood's second cause of action fails to state an actionable claim under California law because the use of his name and photograph in the telecast advertisements, the cover page, and the story is expressly exempted from liability as a news account under the provisions of Civil Code section 3344, subdivision (d).

Civil Code section 3344, subdivision (d) provides inter alia that "[f]or purposes of this section, a use of a name, photograph or likeness in connection with any news ... shall not constitute a use for purposes of advertising or solicitation."

While the issue raised by the Enquirer's argument solely involves the statutory remedy of Civil Code section 3344, subdivision (a), its resolution will necessarily determine Eastwood's ability to maintain a cause of action for commercial appropriation under the common law. The reason is that implicit in this issue are major constitutional questions which we must confront and determine. Publication of matters in the public interest, which rests on the right of the public to know, and the freedom of the press to tell it, cannot ordinarily be actionable. [citing cases]

In *Carlisle v. Fawcett Publications, Inc.* [201 Cal. App. 2d 733, 20 Cal. Rptr. 405 (1962)], the court defined "matters in the public interest" as follows: "The privilege of printing an account of happenings and of enlightening the public as to matters of interest is not restricted to current events; magazines and books, radio and television may legitimately inform and entertain the public with the reproduction of past events, travelogues and biographies." (*Id.*, 201 Cal. App. 2d at p. 746.)

Hence we are called upon to determine the boundaries of Eastwood's ability to control the commercial exploitation of his personality in the publication field. This determination will necessitate a weighing of the private interest of the right of publicity against matters of public interest calling for constitutional protection, and a consideration of the character of these competing interests.

Freedom of the press is constitutionally guaranteed, and the publication of daily news is an acceptable and necessary function in the life of the community. The scope of the privilege extends to almost all reporting of recent events even though it involves the publication of a purely private person's name or likeness.

Moreover, "there is a public interest which attaches to people who, by their accomplishments, mode of living, professional standing or calling, create a legitimate and widespread attention to their activities. Certainly, the accomplishments and way of life of those who have achieved a marked reputation or notoriety by appearing before the public such as actors ... may legitimately be mentioned and discussed in print...." (*Carlisle v. Fawcett Publications, Inc., supra,* 201 Cal. App. 2d at p. 746.) Thus, a celebrity has relinquished "'a part of his right of privacy to the extent that the public has a legitimate interest in his doings, affairs or character.'" (*Id.,* at p. 747.)

Yet absolute protection of the press in the case at bench requires a total sacrifice of the competing interest of Eastwood in controlling the commercial exploitation of his personality. Often considerable money, time and energy are needed to develop the ability in a person's name or likeness to attract attention and evoke a desired response in a particular consumer market. Thus, a proper accommodation between these competing concerns must be defined, since "the rights guaranteed by the First Amendment do not require total abrogation of the right to privacy", and in the case at bench, the right of publicity.

Ordinarily, only two branches of the law of privacy, namely, public disclosure and false light, create tension with the First Amendment, because of their intrusion on the dissemination of information to the public. Normally, in a commercial appropriation case involving the right of publicity, the only question is who gets to do the publishing, since the celebrity is primarily concerned with whether he gets the commercial benefit of such publication.

All fiction is false in the literal sense that it is imagined rather than actual. However, works of fiction are constitutionally protected in the same manner as topical new stories.

Therefore, since Eastwood asserts that the alleged news account is entirely false, and is a cover-up or subterfuge for commercial appropriation of his name and likeness, we must consider First Amendment limitations.

We have no doubt that the subject of the Enquirer article — the purported romantic involvements of Eastwood with other celebrities — is a matter of public concern, which would generally preclude the imposition of liability. However, Eastwood argues that the article, and thereby the related advertisements, are not entitled to either constitutional protection or exemption from liability as a news account because the article is a calculated falsehood.

Since *New York Times v. Sullivan* (1964) 376 U.S. 254, 279–280, it is clear that the First Amendment generally precludes the imposition of liability upon a publisher for its expressive activities, except upon a finding of fault. Thus, our analysis must determine whether Eastwood has alleged the kinds of fault and the appropriate standard that may constitutionally warrant liability in this case.

In actions where the fault involves defamatory statements, the cases have focused on the status of plaintiff to determine the standard of fault necessary to impose liability on a media defendant. For example, in the case of a public official or public figure, the Supreme Court established the rule that a plaintiff may not recover except upon showing that the defendant published defamatory statements with *actual malice* (hereafter "scienter"), i.e., either with knowledge of their falsity or with reckless disregard for the truth. However, in defamation actions brought by private individuals, the Supreme Court has allowed any appropriate standard of fault less than scienter to be used, short of liability without fault. Thus, a private-party plaintiff may sue for negligent publication of defamatory falsehoods.

Similarly, in privacy actions involving deliberate fictionalization presented as truth, the cases have focused on the materials published to determine the standard of fault required to impose liability on a publisher. For example, where the materials published, although assertedly private and nondefamatory, are matters of public interest, the target of the publication must prove knowing or reckless falsehood.

Moreover, the standard of scienter, whether in a defamation or privacy case, reflects the Supreme Court's recognition that while a calculated falsehood has no constitutional value, such statements are inevitable in the continuing debate on public issues and thus, the fruitful exercise of the freedoms of speech and press requires "breathing space" for speech that matters.

Accordingly, we conclude whether the focus is on the status of Eastwood, or upon the materials published in the Enquirer article, scienter of the alleged calculated falsehood is the proper standard of fault to impose liability on the Enquirer, contrary to the position of Eastwood, that calculated falsehood alone is enough.

Enquirer contends, however, that it is the manifest character of the article which is determinative as to whether it is news under section 3344, subdivision (d). Enquirer argues that the statute, by its terms, refers only to generic categories; it does not distinguish between news accounts that are true or false. Thus, whether an article is a news account does not turn on the truth or falsity of its content. We disagree.

The spacious interest in an unfettered press is not without limitation. This privilege is subject to the qualification that it shall not be so exercised as to abuse the rights of individuals. Hence, in defamation cases, the concern is with defamatory lies masquerading as truth. Similarly, in privacy cases, the concern is with nondefamatory lies masquerading as truth. Accordingly, we do not believe that the Legislature intended to provide an exemption from liability for a knowing or reckless falsehood under the canopy of "news." We therefore hold that Civil Code section 3344, subdivision (d), as it pertains to news, does not provide an exemption for a knowing or reckless falsehood.

Moreover, wherever the line in a particular situation is to be drawn between news accounts that are protected and those that are not, we are quite sure that the First Amendment does not immunize Enquirer when the entire article is allegedly false.

Finally, Enquirer contends that falsity is the predicate, not for commercial appropriation, but for false light claims. We disagree.

As noted earlier, all fiction is literally false, but enjoys constitutional protection.

However, the deliberate fictionalization of Eastwood's personality constitutes commercial exploitation, and becomes actionable when it is presented to the reader as if true with the requisite scienter.[10]

---

10. Although the issue is unsettled under California common law, we see no constitutional barrier to imposing damages under section 3344, subdivision (a) measured not only by the harm done to the plaintiff but additionally by the benefit enjoyed by defendant.

Here, Eastwood failed to incorporate from his first cause of action that the article was published with knowledge or in reckless disregard of its falsity. Accordingly, we find that such failure renders the second cause of action insufficient to make the Enquirer's expressive conduct actionable under the common law or Civil Code section 3344, subdivision (a).

Manifestly, such defect is capable of being cured by amendment. Thus, where it appears that the trial court has made a ruling which deprives a party of the opportunity to plead his cause of action or defense, relief by mandamus may be appropriate to prevent a needless and expensive trial and reversal.

Let a peremptory writ of mandamus issue requiring the respondent court to set aside its order sustaining the demurrer to Eastwood's second cause of action without leave to amend, and to grant Eastwood leave to amend his second cause of action.

SCHAUER, P.J., and JOHNSON, J., concur.

APPENDIX

EXHIBIT A

Figure 7-2. Exhibit A in *Eastwood I*

EXHIBIT B

Figure 7-3. Exhibit B in *Eastwood I*

Notes and Questions

1. At the time of the *Eastwood* decision, the California statute was limited to unauthorized uses for commercial advertising or solicitation. Since that time, the statute has been amended to include other unauthorized uses: uses on "products," which includes merchandising uses (such as commemorative plates, t-shirts, etc.). Some of the cases involving the amended statute are discussed in Chapter II.

2. Why is false endorsement not an element of a Section 3344 claim? Do you agree with the court's interpretation of the statute?

3. Did the court say that Clint Eastwood's complaint failed to allege a critical element of Section 3344? Did he fail to allege a critical element of a common-law right of publicity claim? If so, what element(s) did he fail to allege?

4. In Part II, the court discusses the issue of newsworthiness. Examine closely the parameters of this doctrine. Clearly, it is intended to give "breathing space" to the press under the First Amendment. The question is how much space to give. In what sense is a story about Clint Eastwood's love life "newsworthy" (even assuming that it is true)? What does that tell you about the scope of what is considered "news"?

5. Is the court's invocation of *New York Times* appropriate in this case? Does it matter that Eastwood claims that the newspaper sought to capitalize on his celebrity by putting a headline about the alleged interview on the cover of the tabloid?

6. Eastwood claims that the alleged interview is a fabrication. Does the court's decision mean that fiction is not protected by the First Amendment? If not, what is the significance of the possible fabrication of an interview to the outcome of the case?

7. The court ultimately sent the case back to the trial court. What do you expect happened next?

Clint Eastwood and the National Enquirer's "relationship" did not end with this incident. Years later, another dispute again landed them in court together (only this time in federal court). Although they involve separate incidents, we will refer to these cases as *Eastwood I* (the above case) and *Eastwood II* (the case below). The gist of *Eastwood II* is the proper standard to be applied to cases where the alleged violation of rights of publicity constitutes matter that is newsworthy. *Eastwood I* sketched out the requirements; *Eastwood II* fills in many of the details of the standard.

Eastwood v. National Enquirer, Inc.
123 F.3d 1249 (9th Cir. 1997)

KOZINSKI, Circuit Judge:

Did defendant falsely represent that plaintiff had given it an interview? Or did it avoid learning that the purported interview was a fabrication? And was the jury right in finding "actual malice"?

Enquiring judges want to know.

* * *

On December 21, 1993, the front page of the *National Enquirer* touted an "Exclusive Interview" with Clint Eastwood. *See* Figure 1. Under the headline "Clint Eastwood at 63: Being a new dad has made my day," the "interview" featured "quotes" from Eastwood about his relationship with actress Frances Fisher ("I propose marriage to her from time to time and sometimes she says yes and sometimes she says no."), their new baby ("Frances and I ... take turns getting up [in the middle of the night].") and his career ("For me to be ... wiping out tons of people, that's over. I think I'll leave that for the newer guys on the scene."). The by-line of Don Gentile, an *Enquirer* assistant editor, and the inclusion of such phrases as "[Eastwood] said with a chuckle" suggested that the writer and the movie star had conversed. *See* Figure 2.

In fact, Eastwood never spoke to the *Enquirer*; the interview, he claims, is a fabrication. In a suit in Federal District Court, Eastwood alleged that the article misrepresented its origin, association and/or endorsement in violation of section 43(a) of the Lanham Act, 15 U.S.C. § 1125(a), and invaded his privacy and misappropriated his name, likeness and personality under Cal. Civ. Code § 3344 and California common law. The gist of the complaint is that Eastwood's reputation was damaged by the suggestion that he would grant an interview to a sensationalist tabloid.

After a seven-day trial and four days of deliberation, the jury returned a unanimous verdict for Eastwood; it awarded him $150,000. Pursuant to the Lanham Act and California law, Judge Davies awarded Eastwood $653,156 in attorney's fees but denied $185,163 in costs, including expert witness fees. The *Enquirer* appeals the verdict and the fee award....

I.

Under the rule first announced in *New York Times v. Sullivan*, 376 U.S. 254, 279–80 (1964), a public figure can recover damages from a news organization, for harms perpetrated by its reporting, only by proving "actual malice." This phrase does not mean

> ill will or "malice" in the ordinary sense of the term.... Actual malice, instead, requires ... that the statements were made with a reckless disregard for the truth. And although the concept of "reckless disregard" "cannot be fully encompassed in one infallible definition," we have made clear that the defendant must have made [the decision to publish] with a "high degree of awareness of ... probable falsity," or must have "entertained serious doubts as to the truth of his publication."

Harte-Hanks Communications v. Connaughton, 491 U.S. 657, 666–67 (1989) (citations and footnote omitted) (quoting *St. Amant v. Thompson*, 390 U.S. 727, 730 (1968)). Thus Eastwood was entitled to prevail if the *Enquirer* knowingly made a false statement that hurt his reputation.

Alternatively, he could prevail if the *Enquirer* had "obvious reasons to doubt the veracity" of its reporting, *St. Amant*, 390 U.S. at 732, but engaged in "purposeful avoidance of the truth." *Harte-Hanks*, 491 U.S. at 692.... Mere negligence would not be enough. "Even an extreme departure from accepted professional standards of journalism will not suffice to establish actual malice; nor will any other departure from reasonably prudent conduct, including the failure to investigate before publishing." *Newton v. National Broadcasting Co.*, 930 F.2d 662, 669 (9th Cir. 1990); *see also St. Amant*, 390 U.S. at 733 ("Failure to investigate does not in itself establish bad faith.").

The jury here was properly instructed.[3] Nonetheless, we must satisfy ourselves that "actual malice" was proven. This is because "'[j]udges, as expositors of the Constitution,' have a duty to 'independently decide whether the evidence in the record is sufficient to

---

3. The jury was told: ...
> To prove actual malice, the plaintiff must prove by clear and convincing evidence that the defendant published the interview with knowledge that it was fabricated or with reckless disregard for whether it was genuine or not.
> A reckless disregard for the truth requires more than a departure from reasonably prudent conduct. Reckless disregard is not shown by sloppy journalism, carelessness, or gross negligence. Even an extreme departure from accepted professional standards of journalism will not suffice to prove actual malice.
> Rather, to prove actual malice the plaintiff must provide clear and convincing proof that the defendant in fact entertained serious doubts as to whether the interview was genuine, or actually had a high degree of awareness of probable falsity. This is a subjective test focusing on defendant's state of mind at the time of publication....

[overcome] the constitutional ... [bar to the entry of any judgment] ... not supported by clear and convincing proof of "actual malice."'" *Harte-Hanks,* 491 U.S. at 686 (quoting *Bose Corp. v. Consumers Union,* 466 U.S. 485, 511 (1984))....

In conducting our review, it is not enough for us to determine that a reasonable jury could have found for the plaintiff—a kind of sufficiency-of-the-evidence test, permitting us to affirm even though we would have reached a different conclusion. Rather, "First Amendment questions of 'constitutional fact' compel [us to conduct a] *de novo* review." *Bose,* 466 U.S. at 508 n.27. We ourselves must be convinced that the defendant acted with malice....

The purpose of our review is to satisfy ourselves that plaintiff proved malice by clear and convincing evidence, which we have described as a "heavy burden," far in excess of the preponderance sufficient for most civil litigation....

Nonetheless, even a properly instructed juror may have difficulty gauging whether a proposition was proven by clear and convincing evidence, or merely by a preponderance.... The task is somewhat easier for judges.... Thus it falls to us to decide if the heightened standard was met. If the jury could only have found "actual malice" by a preponderance, we must reverse.

II.

As we have yet to see a defendant who admits to entertaining serious subjective doubt about the authenticity of an article it published, we must be guided by circumstantial evidence. By examining the editors' actions we try to understand their motives.

A. Eastwood first asserts that the interview never took place at all—it was a fabrication. The *Enquirer's* "exclusive interview" first appeared in *Today,* a British tabloid. *Enquirer* article editor Steve Plamann phoned *Today,* only to learn that a freelance writer, Cameron Docherty, was the source of the interview and had retained the rights. Plamann phoned Docherty, who "confirmed" that he had interviewed Eastwood. Plamann did not ask when and where the interview took place, nor did Docherty volunteer this information. Docherty told Plamann he had taped the interview but had erased the tapes.

Plamann again phoned *Today*; he testified that an assistant features editor, Sharon, told him that Docherty had done "good work" and that "there never had been any complaints about" his stories. However, Plamann never obtained Sharon's last name, nor did he ask if she had ever worked with Docherty. Next, Plamann called Jerry Pam, a Hollywood press agent who once represented Eastwood, purportedly to ask about Docherty's credentials. Pam was moving that day and Plamann did not reach him. A secretary who answered the phone said—quite ambiguously—"We know Docherty."

In the meantime, Plamann had his staff see what the *Enquirer's* competitors had been saying about Eastwood—a process known to tabloid editors as a "playcheck." The playcheck revealed that the *Star* (a tabloid under the same ownership as the *Enquirer*) had recently run an article by Cameron Docherty containing identical quotes from Eastwood. Plamann phoned Docherty, who claimed he had interviewed Eastwood again after the *Star* interview appeared and had combined new and old material for the *Today* piece.[6]

---

6. The existence of the *Star* interview decreased the value of the *Enquirer's* "exclusive" yet increased Plamann's confidence that Docherty was on the level; Eastwood had—to the best of Plamann's knowledge—not complained to the *Star.*

Finally, the story was referred to the *Enquirer*'s outside counsel, David Kendall, for pre-publication review. Kendall performed no new investigation. In giving the *Enquirer* approval to run the piece he considered mainly that similar reporting had been published elsewhere without complaint, and that the article "was a very sympathetic account of his becoming a father at the age of 63." It is fair to say that what Kendall did was satisfy himself that the *Enquirer* would probably not get sued, largely because, in his view, nothing in the article cast Eastwood in an especially negative light.

As the *Enquirer* views these facts, it had little reason to doubt Docherty's story: *Today* "is a reputable daily newspaper, reporting on national affairs, matters of local interest, financial developments, sports, and entertainment news," Plamann— "who earned a journalism degree from the University of Wisconsin,"—found that the interview "rang true" because it was consistent with other published articles about Eastwood; and Kendall has sufficient tabloid experience to have reliably concluded that the interview was on the level.

Eastwood takes a very different view, arguing that the *Enquirer* had plenty of reason to suspect that the Docherty interview was fake: First, he contends, *Today* is not a reputable paper but a "sensationalist tabloid much like the *Enquirer*." Second, Docherty provided no corroborating details of the interview, and—suspiciously for someone peddling an interview with a litigious mega-star—claimed he'd erased the tapes. In addition, the *Enquirer*'s editors must have known that Eastwood never gave interviews without retaining some control over the time and place of publication—a policy which would have precluded speaking to a freelancer like Docherty.[9] Finally, Eastwood points out that at least one assertion in the Docherty interview, that Eastwood "never work[ed] out," directly contradicted a celebrity fitness story that the *Enquirer* had run just a few weeks before, and which Plamann was almost certainly aware of.

For all these reasons, Eastwood argues, Plamann must have had serious subjective doubts about the interview, which his conversations with Docherty could not have assuaged. But the *Enquirer* claims that it made a legitimate effort to satisfy itself the interview was real before making the final decision to publish. Plamann, after all, called *Today* and Pam not knowing what he would hear. Thus, according to the *Enquirer*, it did not engage in "purposeful avoidance."

In Eastwood's view, Plamann's calls were intended to create the appearance of investigation, without running the risk of uncovering anything. In calling *Today*, Eastwood contends, Plamann accepted a cursory answer from the first person he spoke to; he did the same in his call to Jerry Pam. That he then exaggerated what he was told in both cases suggests that the calls were designed to cover his mass circulation publication.

Eastwood makes much of the *Enquirer*'s failure to call him or any of his representatives to ask whether the interview took place. But even without phoning Eastwood or one of his reps, there is plenty more the *Enquirer* could have done: It could have refused to buy the interview if Docherty could not produce tapes—or a photo or a witness—placing him with Eastwood. It could have asked Docherty more about where and when the interview occurred, and who arranged it. From the answers to these questions, it might well have figured out Docherty was lying. Indeed, given the *Enquirer* 's desire to make the interview seem up close and personal by inserting scene-setting language, it's hard to imagine a diligent editor not asking Docherty to describe exactly Where and When (two of

---

9. Docherty's later assertion that he had interviewed Eastwood twice is, to Eastwood's lawyers, preposterous. In their view, one Docherty-Eastwood interview stretches credulity; two Docherty-Eastwood interviews would tip off a corpse.

the five "W's" of journalism) the meeting had happened. That the editor here didn't, supports Eastwood's argument that the *Enquirer* was taking a see-no-evil, hear-no-evil tack. And, of course, Plamann could have asked to speak to someone at *Today* besides the surnameless Sharon, and made more of an effort to locate the out-of-the-office, but not-out-of-the-country, Jerry Pam.

We therefore believe that a preponderance of the evidence supports the jury's verdict; that is to say, the *Enquirer* more likely than not did what Eastwood says it did. But a preponderance is not enough. A number of facts—that similar material had been published in two other publications, which apparently were satisfied that Docherty was on the level; that two people who knew Docherty slightly suggested his work was okay; that most of the material in the interview was consistent with what Plamann knew about Clint Eastwood—support the view that the *Enquirer*'s editors could have believed the interview was genuine. Therefore, we cannot say that Eastwood established, by clear and convincing evidence, that the *Enquirer* published the interview knowing it was false.

B. Eastwood presented an alternate theory under which he could show malice even if the *Enquirer* editors believed the interview was genuine. Eastwood contended at trial that the defendant misdesignated the interview by labeling it "Exclusive," and by signalling, through text and graphics, that he had willingly talked to the *Enquirer*. Because it is undisputed that Eastwood did not consent to be interviewed by the *Enquirer*, Eastwood could succeed on this theory even if he had, in fact, been interviewed by Cameron Docherty.[14]

Did the *Enquirer* editors mislabel the interview as having been given to *them* by Clint Eastwood? The interview is marked "Exclusive" in three places—on the cover, near the top of page 5 (in bold, underlined, uppercase type, lest anyone overlook it), and in the article itself ("In an exclusive interview, the superstar gave a rare glimpse of his private life."). The *Enquirer* explains that—among magazine editors—"exclusive" means only "no one else is publishing this article in our market." Moreover, it argues, *Cher v. Forum Int'l*, 692 F.2d 634 (9th Cir. 1982), requires us to accept the labeling of an interview originally intended for another outlet as "exclusive." But even if *Cher* applies—which is doubtful[16]—there is more here than the word "exclusive." The *Enquirer* gave the by-line (or, more properly, the tag-line) to Don Gentile, who is identified in the same issue as an assistant editor at the *Enquirer*. It inserted scene-setting phrases. It quoted Eastwood in the "simple past" tense; using "Eastwood has said" instead of "Eastwood said" would have informed readers that the statement was not directed to the article's purported author. (For that matter, using "Eastwood told freelance writer Cameron Docherty" would have eliminated any ambiguity whatever.) And it labeled a baby picture "Exclusive Photo"—hinting at access to Eastwood. *See* Figure 2.

We are not suggesting that any one of these things is dispositive (or, conversely, that the *Enquirer* would have solved the problem with a single alteration). Rather, we look to the totality of the *Enquirer*'s presentation of the interview and find that the editors falsely suggested to the ordinary reader of their publication—as well as those who merely glance

---

14. The *Enquirer* does not dispute that, as a matter of state law, an individual can be defamed by the suggestion that he granted an interview to a publication when he in fact did not consent to be interviewed by that publication.

16. *Cher* pertains only to quotations not previously published. *See* 692 F.2d at 638 ("*Star* was entitled to inform its readers that the issue contained an article about Cher, that the article was based on an interview with Cher herself, and that the article had not previously appeared elsewhere."). The *Enquirer* knew the Eastwood interview had previously appeared elsewhere. Thus, its use of "Exclusive" does not fall under the *Cher* umbrella.

at the headlines while waiting at the supermarket checkout counter—that Eastwood had willingly chatted with someone from the *Enquirer*.

Of course, under *New York Times v. Sullivan*, it is not dispositive that most, even all, of the *Enquirer's* readers believed Eastwood had granted an interview to the *Enquirer*; there is no actual malice where journalists unknowingly mislead the public. *Bose*, 466 U.S. at 513 (warning that absent the subjective test, "any individual using a malapropism might be liable ... even though he did not realize his folly at the time"). To affirm, we must find the editors knew or should have known that their statements would be misleading.

In this case, there was testimony that the *Enquirer* uses a kind of code, applying the label "*Enquirer* Interview" where an interview is given to the *Enquirer* directly, and "Exclusive Interview" where it is not. Assuming the truth of this testimony, we do not believe the absence of the phrase "*Enquirer* Interview" would inform the average reader (or the average browser) that the subject had not spoken to the *Enquirer*, or that the editors could have believed their code sufficient for that purpose. Rather, we find, from the totality of their choices, that the editors intended to convey the impression—known by them to be false—that Eastwood wilfully submitted to an interview by the *Enquirer*. This intentional conduct satisfies the "actual malice" standard, permitting a verdict for Eastwood.

III.

[The court upheld the jury's award of $150,000.]

Affirmed.

FIGURE 1

Figure 7-4. Figure 1 in *Eastwood II*

FIGURE 2

Figure 7-5. Figure 2 in *Eastwood II*

Notes and Questions

1. It is important to remember that the causes of action involved here are a right of publicity claim under California law and a false endorsement claim under the Lanham

Act. (The latter theory is discussed in Chapter V.) The court begins its discussion by asserting that in order to recover on these claims, Eastwood must satisfy the standard set forth by the Supreme Court in *New York Times v. Sullivan*, which was a defamation case. Neither of the causes of action alleged are (at least directly) defamation claims. Why, then, is the actual malice standard of *New York Times* the appropriate standard to use in this case?

2. The *New York Times* standard has two important facets: (1) a plaintiff who is a public figure must show that the defendant *knew* that the statement was false, or *recklessly* (not merely negligently) disregarded the truth or falsity of the statement; and (2) this showing must be made by "clear and convincing" evidence, which is a much higher standard of proof than the conventional standard for civil cases, which is a "preponderance of the evidence," *i.e.*, that it is more likely than not that the plaintiff's version is true. In addition, unlike a normal case, where the appellate court would be very deferential to the jury's verdict, the appellate court is not supposed to give that deference under the *New York Times* standard, but is instead obliged to review the jury's verdict *de novo*.

a. Why is the appellate court not supposed to give the usual deference to a jury's verdict in this case? What important policy functions does requiring *de novo* review serve? Do you think that the court carried out its mandate here?

b. The court says that Eastwood had proven that the Enquirer knew the interview was false by a preponderance of the evidence, but not by clear and convincing evidence. What was it that prevented the court from finding clear and convincing evidence?

c. If the court could not uphold the jury's finding that the Enquirer knew the interview was false, on what theory did it uphold the jury's verdict? How does the court determine that the evidence on this point was "clear and convincing"?

d. Did the court's decision to uphold the jury verdict allow Eastwood to recover for activity that the court already ruled was constitutionally protected? Or is that not an accurate characterization of the court's actions?

3. The use of a standard originally intended for defamation cases suggests that this case is more like a defamation case in tort than a "property rights" case. Do you think that is an accurate statement? Are there instances where a right of publicity plaintiff could seek damages for injury to his or her reputation without having to satisfy the *New York Times* standard? Should we permit celebrities (or even non-celebrities) to recover for damage to their reputation without satisfying the *New York Times* standard? See David S. Welkowitz and Tyler T. Ochoa, *The Terminator as Eraser: How Arnold Schwarzenegger Used The Right of Publicity to Terminate Non-Defamatory Political Speech*, 45 Santa Clara L. Rev. 651 (2005).

4. In *Zacchini*, the Supreme Court held that the First Amendment did not bar Ohio from allowing a claim for violation of rights of publicity when a television news report showed Zacchini's "entire act." Are *Eastwood I* and *Eastwood II* consistent with *Zacchini*? Would the Supreme Court agree that the *New York Times* standard (which is a First Amendment standard) is the proper standard to apply?

5. Suppose the Supreme Court would not require the application of *New York Times* to these cases. Could California impose that standard even if it is not required by the First Amendment?

Messenger v. Gruner + Jahr Printing and Publishing
94 N.Y.2d 436, 727 N.E.2d 549, 706 N.Y.S.2d 52 (2000)

PER CURIAM.

Plaintiff, a 14-year-old aspiring Florida model, posed for a series of photographs in New York to appear in Young and Modern (YM), a magazine for teenage girls published by defendant Gruner + Jahr Printing. Plaintiff consented to the photo shoot, but YM did not obtain written consent from her parent or legal guardian. YM used the photos to illustrate the "Love Crisis" column in its June/July 1995 issue.

The column began with a letter to Sally Lee, YM's editor-in-chief, from a 14-year-old girl identified only as "Mortified." Mortified writes that she got drunk at a party and then had sex with her 18-year-old boyfriend and two of his friends. Lee responds that Mortified should avoid similar situations in the future, and advises her to be tested for pregnancy and sexually transmitted diseases. Above the column, in bold type, is a pull-out quotation stating, "I got trashed and had sex with three guys." Three full-color photographs of plaintiff illustrate the column—one, for example, shows her hiding her face, with three young men gloating in the background. The captions are keyed to Lee's advice: "Wake up and face the facts: You made a pretty big mistake;" "Don't try to hide—just ditch him and his buds;" and "Afraid you're pregnant? See a doctor."

Plaintiff brought this diversity action in the United States District Court for the Southern District of New York, alleging, among other things, that YM violated sections 50 and 51 of the New York Civil Rights Law by using her photographs for trade purposes without obtaining the requisite consent. Defendants moved for summary judgment, arguing that they could not be held liable under the Civil Rights Law because the photographs had been used to illustrate a newsworthy column, the pictures had a real relationship to the article and the column was not an advertisement in disguise. Plaintiff conceded these facts but argued that the "newsworthiness" exception did not apply because the column and pictures together created the false impression that plaintiff was the author of the letter. The District Court denied summary judgment, holding that the newsworthiness exception does not apply where the juxtaposition of a photograph to an article creates a substantially fictionalized implication.[1] The court dismissed plaintiff's additional claims for defamation, intentional infliction of emotional distress, negligent infliction of emotional distress and negligence. Following trial on the Civil Rights Law claim, the jury awarded plaintiff $100,000 in compensatory damages.

Defendants appealed to the United States Court of Appeals for the Second Circuit, arguing that the newsworthiness exception barred recovery under the Civil Rights Law. The Second Circuit observed that New York had, in older cases, recognized a "fictionalization limitation" on the newsworthiness exception. The court noted, however, that our more recent cases have held that, where a photograph illustrates an article on a matter of public interest, the newsworthiness exception bars recovery unless there is no real relationship between the photograph and the article, or the article is an advertisement in disguise (*see, e.g.*, *Finger v. Omni Publs. Intl.*, 77 N.Y.2d 138, 141–42 [(1990)]). Uncertain whether

---

1. Plaintiff also sought to introduce evidence that the article itself was substantially fictionalized in that the letter had in fact been invented by YM's editorial staff. The District Court, however, barred plaintiff from exploring this subject at trial, holding that the only inquiry relevant to plaintiff's Civil Rights Law § 51 claim was whether the juxtaposition of the photographs to the article—not the article itself—was substantially fictionalized. The fictionalization alleged was that the use of the photograph in conjunction with the article conveyed the false impression that plaintiff was the author of Mortified's letter and had the experiences described in it.

Figure 7-6. The "Love Crisis" column in *Messenger*

Finger "signaled the end of the fictionalization limitation," the Second Circuit *sua sponte* certified to us the following two questions, which we accepted for review (93 N.Y.2d 948):

"1. May a plaintiff recover under New York Civil Rights Law §§ 50 and 51 where the defendant used the plaintiff's likeness in a substantially fictionalized way without the plaintiff's consent, even if the defendant's use of the image was in conjunction with a newsworthy column?"

"2. If so, are there any additional limitations on such a cause of action that might preclude the instant case?"

We answer the first question in the negative, and therefore need not reach the second.

Analysis

New York does not recognize a common-law right of privacy. In response to *Roberson* [*v Rochester Folding Box Co.*], the Legislature enacted Civil Rights Law §§ 50 and 51, which provide a limited statutory right of privacy....

This Court has consistently restated several basic principles concerning the statutory right of privacy. First, recognizing the Legislature's pointed objective in enacting sections 50 and 51, we have underscored that the statute is to be narrowly construed and "strictly limited to nonconsensual commercial appropriations of the name, portrait or picture of a living person". Second, we have made clear that these sections do not apply to reports of newsworthy events or matters of public interest. This is because a newsworthy article is not deemed produced for the purposes of advertising or trade. Additionally, these principles reflect "constitutional values in the area of free speech" (*Howell v. New York Post Co., supra,* 81 N.Y.2d [115 (1993)], at 123).

Third, this Court has held that "newsworthiness" is to be broadly construed. Newsworthiness includes not only descriptions of actual events but also articles concerning political happenings, social trends or any subject of public interest. Significantly, the fact that a publication may have used a person's name or likeness "solely or primarily to increase the circulation" of a newsworthy article — and thus to increase profits — does not mean that the name or likeness has been used for trade purposes within the meaning of the statute. Indeed, "most publications seek to increase their circulation and also their profits". Whether an item is newsworthy depends solely on "the content of the article" — not the publisher's "motive to increase circulation".

Applying these principles, courts have held that a wide variety of articles on matters of public interest — including those not readily recognized as "hard news" — are newsworthy (*see, e.g., Stephano v. News Group Publs., supra,* 64 N.Y.2d [174 (1984)], at 179–86 [picture of plaintiff wearing leather bomber jacket in column about "new and unusual products and services"]; *Abdelrazig v. Essence Communications,* 225 A.D.2d 498 [picture of plaintiff in "African garb" concerned "newsworthy fashion trends in the Black community"], *leave denied,* 88 N.Y.2d 810 [(1996)]; *Creel v. Crown Publs.,* 115 A.D.2d 414 [(1995)] [picture of plaintiffs illustrating guide to nude beaches]; *Lopez v. Triangle Communications,* 70 A.D.2d 359, 360 [(1979)] ["make-over" pictures in Seventeen magazine]; *Rand v. Hearst Corp.,* 31 A.D.2d 406, 407–11 [(1969)] [quotation on book cover comparing author to plaintiff], *affd* 26 N.Y.2d 806 [(1990)]; *Stern v. Delphi Internet Servs. Corp.,* 165 Misc. 2d 21, 22–27 [(1995)] [lewd photograph of plaintiff used in connection with promotion for internet news service]; *Welch v. Group W. Prods.,* 138 Misc. 2d 856 [(1987)] [use of television commercial in connection with Clio awards]; *Namath v. Sports Illustrated,* 80 Misc. 2d 531, 533–535 [photographs of plaintiff in promotional material], *affd* 48 A.D.2d 487 [(1975)], *affd* 39 N.Y.2d 897 [(1976)]; *Ann–Margret v. High Socy. Mag.,* 498 F. Supp. 401, 405 [(S.D.N.Y. 1980)] [partially nude photograph of plaintiff]).

Consistent with the statutory — and constitutional — value of uninhibited discussion of newsworthy topics, we have time and again held that, where a plaintiff's picture is used to illustrate an article on a matter of public interest, there can be no liability under sections 50 and 51 unless the picture has no real relationship to the article or the article is an advertisement in disguise. That has been so even where a plaintiff's photograph, when juxtaposed with an article, could reasonably have been viewed as falsifying or fictionalizing plaintiff's relation to the article.

In the recent case of *Finger* [*v. Omni Publications Int'l, Inc.*, 77 N.Y. 2d 138 (1990)], for example, defendant used a photograph of plaintiffs Joseph and Ida Finger and their six children to illustrate an article on caffeine-aided *in vitro* fertilization. Plaintiffs sought damages for defendant's use of their photograph, arguing that none of their children were conceived through *in vitro* fertilization, and that they did not participate in the caffeine-aided fertility project. While this Court was made well aware of the false impression potentially created by defendant's use of the photograph, we nevertheless upheld dismissal of plaintiffs' Civil Rights Law claim, repeating once again that the article was newsworthy, that there was a real relationship between the photograph and the article, and that the article was not an advertisement in disguise....

[I]n *Murray*, plaintiff's photograph, taken while attending a St. Patrick's Day Parade in green regalia, appeared on the cover of the defendant's magazine. "Directly above that photograph" was the caption, "The Last of the Irish Immigrants" (*Murray v. New York Mag. Co.*, *supra*, 27 N.Y.2d [406 (1971)], at 408). The article discussed "contemporary attitudes of Irish-Americans in New York City" (*id.*, at 409). Although the *Murray* plaintiff was "not of Irish extraction" (*id.*, at 408), we ruled that defendant was entitled to summary judgment, because the article was newsworthy and not advertising in disguise, and because a genuine relationship existed between the photograph and the article (*id.*, at 408–10).

Thus, it is clear that a Civil Rights Law §§ 50 and 51 claim does not lie where a plaintiff's photograph is used to illustrate a newsworthy article. There are two limitations: first, there must be a real relationship between the article and the photograph, and second, the article cannot be an advertisement in disguise. Of course, a Civil Rights Law claim may lie if a plaintiff's picture is used purely for trade purposes, and not in connection with a newsworthy article (*see, Brinkley v. Casablancas*, 80 A.D.2d 428 [(1981)] [Civil Rights Law action lies for defendants' distribution of pin-up posters without plaintiff's consent]).

Applying these settled principles, we answer the first certified question in the negative. Plaintiff concedes that the "Love Crisis" column was newsworthy, since it is informative and educational regarding teenage sex, alcohol abuse and pregnancy—plainly matters of public concern. Further, she concedes that the photographs bore a real relationship to the article, and there is no allegation that the article was an advertisement in disguise. Given these facts, *Finger*, *Arrington* and *Murray* dictate that plaintiff may not recover under the Civil Rights Law, regardless of any false implication that might be reasonably drawn from the use of her photographs to illustrate the article.[2]

Notwithstanding these precedents, plaintiff contends that an action lies under the Civil Rights Law where a photograph, juxtaposed with an article, creates a "substantially fictionalized" implication....

We see no inherent tension between the *Finger-Arrington-Murray* line and the *Binns-Spahn* line. *Finger*, *Arrington* and *Murray*, which are directly on point, state the rule applicable here. All three cases involved the unauthorized, and allegedly false and damaging, use of plaintiffs' photographs to illustrate newsworthy articles. Because the photographs

---

2. We have not been asked to, and do not, pass on the question whether a reasonable reader could conclude that plaintiff was the person identified as "Mortified," given that the pictures were obviously contrived and she was not identified as the author of the letter.

illustrated newsworthy articles, because there was a real relationship between the photographs and the articles, and because the articles were not advertisements in disguise, we concluded that none of those plaintiffs stated a Civil Rights Law claim. Nor does plaintiff here.

By contrast, *Binns* and *Spahn* concerned a strikingly different scenario from the one before us. In those cases, defendants invented biographies of plaintiffs' lives. The courts concluded that the substantially fictional works at issue were nothing more than attempts to trade on the persona of Warren Spahn or John Binns. Thus, under *Binns* and *Spahn*, an article may be so infected with fiction, dramatization or embellishment that it cannot be said to fulfill the purpose of the newsworthiness exception. Here, by contrast, the "Love Crisis" column was concededly newsworthy. Thus, this case is controlled by *Finger*—not by *Binns* or *Spahn*.

The dissent argues that *Binns* and *Spahn* permit a plaintiff to recover if the plaintiff's name or likeness is used in a substantially fictionalized way—including where, as here, the use of a plaintiff's picture in juxtaposition to a newsworthy article creates a false implication. This, however, conflicts with our holdings in *Finger*, *Arrington* and *Murray* that the use of a photograph to illustrate a newsworthy article does not state a claim under the Civil Rights Law—regardless of any false impression created by the use of the photograph—so long as the article is not an advertisement and there is a real relationship between the photograph and the article.[3] ...

Also contrary to the dissent, our result would be the same whether plaintiff were Jamie Messenger or a famous person, like Shirley Temple. The test is not whether plaintiff is a public or private figure. Rather, the analysis centers on whether the photograph bears a real relationship to a newsworthy article and is not an advertisement in disguise. Where those requirements are met, there is no cause of action under the Civil Rights Law.

Notably, if the newsworthiness exception is forfeited solely because the juxtaposition of a plaintiff's photograph to a newsworthy article creates a false impression about the plaintiff, liability under Civil Rights Law § 51 becomes indistinguishable from the common-law tort of false light invasion of privacy.

Accordingly, the first certified question should be answered in the negative, and we need not address the second.

BELLACOSA, J. (Dissenting):

I respectfully disagree and would answer the first question in the affirmative. Under the analysis of the *Per Curiam* opinion, no matter what *the published photographs* of plaintiff depict or connote, if *the words of the column* project an abstractly newsworthy subject matter, then the judicially created newsworthiness exemption forecloses the remedy of Civil Rights Law §§ 50 and 51. This latest extension marginalizes the statutory authorization that was enacted expressly to supply potential redress for aggrandizing uses of a person's "portrait or picture."

We all agree that the courts have properly created a newsworthiness exception to liability pursuant to the Civil Rights statute. The courts have, however, also harnessed a

---

3. As is evident from its opening, the dissent misinterprets our decision. We do not hold that the newsworthiness exception forecloses liability under the Civil Rights Law whenever "*the words of the column* project an abstractly newsworthy subject matter".... Rather, we hold only that there is no Civil Rights Law action for a photograph illustrating a newsworthy article if there is a real relationship between the photograph and the article, and the article is not an advertisement in disguise. Our holding follows settled law and neither marginalizes nor immobilizes the statutory remedy.

runaway newsworthiness exemption with exceptions. Part of the puzzle here is whether there are two exceptions—advertisement in disguise and no "real relationship"—or three—also a distinctive "material and substantial falsification" prong....

If the "fictionalization exception" remains part of New York law, as I contend, then despite the newsworthiness of part of the published column—which might otherwise operate to block this plaintiff's invocation of the remedial statute against defendants—Messenger's victory before a Federal jury could be sustainable. If, on the other hand, the "fictionalization exception" is rendered a "dead letter"—and newsworthiness reigns—then Messenger's Federal lawsuit is equally comatose....

II.

This Court enunciated a fictionalization exception to newsworthiness immunity, ... when it found that a substantially fictionalized biography constituted an unauthorized exploitation of the plaintiff's personality "for purposes of trade" (*see, Spahn v. Julian Messner, Inc.,* 18 N.Y.2d 324 [(1966)], *adhered to on reargument,* 21 N.Y.2d 124 [(1967)]). The Court recognized that even a public figure's "personality" may be "fictionalized," and as such, the baseball star's story was found to have exploited his persona for commercial value.

On reargument of *Spahn* in light of the United States Supreme Court's *Time, Inc. v. Hill* (385 U.S. 374 [(1967)]) decision, this Court stood by its initial decision with respect to the fictionalized account of the professional athlete's life. The Court, of course, also necessarily imbued the authoritative interpretation of New York substantive law with the requisite constitutional speech protections:

> "[B]efore recovery by a public figure may be had for an unauthorized presentation of his life, it must be shown, *in addition to the other requirements of the statute, that the presentation is infected with material and substantial falsification* and that the work was published with knowledge of such falsification or with a reckless disregard for the truth" (*Spahn v. Julian Messner, Inc.,* 21 N.Y.2d 124, 127 [(1967)] [emphasis added]).

The Court found that the use of "invented dialogue" to supply "a dramatic portrayal attractive to the juvenile reader" in a manner "customary" for the type of book involved did not entitle the defendants to publish such "knowing fictionalization," which was "destructive of an individual's right ... to be free of the commercial exploitation of his name and personality" (*Spahn v. Julian Messner, Inc.,* 21 N.Y.2d, *supra,* at 127–129). Thus, if there was any doubt after *Gautier* that the courts should make a fictionalization/falsification examination in a "purposes of trade" inquiry, *Spahn II* provided enduring insights. The quoted language offers significant relevance, not the ephemeral distinguishments proffered by the majority....

If a Shirley Temple-like set of photos were used with this identical column, that would more than likely be actionable, as trading on the persona of a famous individual. The 14-year-old plaintiff adolescent, a private person who cannot even legally give consent to the use of her photos, should have no less a remedy for someone trading on her persona and aspirations, the particular protection tendered by the statute. This contrast dramatizes the irony of a real tension, as I see it, between the extant precedential lines and a growing atrophy of the Civil Rights statute.

III.

... In any event, the substantive law question of this case was simply not the dispositive or necessarily implicated thrust in *Finger*. Thus, the instant case is also demonstrably distinguishable from *Finger* on its facts and import. In *Finger*, "[n]either the article nor the caption mentioned plaintiffs' names or *indicated in any fashion* that the adult plaintiffs used caffeine or that the children were produced through *in vitro* fertilization" (*Finger v. Omni Publs. Intl., supra*, at 140 [emphasis added]).

Here, the caption juxtaposed next to and across a large picture of Jamie Messenger, looking "hung over," states, "*I* got trashed and had sex with three guys ... Even worse, *I* heard them laughing about it the next day" (emphasis added). The smaller caption *within* the photograph with Messenger reads, "*You* made a pretty big mistake" (emphasis added). Another caption within another picture of Messenger looking distraught reads, "Afraid *you're* pregnant?" (emphasis added). These captions, "pull quotes" and photographs leap off the page with the real relationship to the published material—which is not contested—but also with the substantial falsification of the photographs in the *kind, manner* and *degree* to which they were exploited. In *Finger*, there was *no* indication in any fashion that the plaintiffs in the associated picture had experienced what was described in the content of the article. In this case, that very linkage is soldered together and dramatized. In my opinion, that is what takes this case over tolerable lines and limits.

Here, a Federal court jury found that reasonable readers would think Messenger was unquestionably the subject and signatory of an ersatz letter. Despite the abstracted public-interest newsworthy quality of the editor's answer to the letter, the falsified connection— "*I* got trashed"—personalizes the matter in a devastating fashion. Even though the column enjoys the academic quality of a newsworthy subject matter, its presentation publicly paraded plaintiff as the epitomized subject for sensationalized impact. That should not be immune from the statute's reach.

I am unable to discern support in this Court's developed line of analysis—until today— for the conclusion that this substantially fictionalized portrayal of Messenger's likeness is beyond the statute's ken just because something about it is newsworthy in a general way. That, as I understand it—or misinterpret it, as the majority characterizes my view—is the bottom line of the majority's negative answer transmitted to the Second Circuit. For me, New York law supports a more nuanced and generous approach to the applicability of this now largely immobilized statute that is functionally and realistically foreclosed by today's ruling.

In sum, the practical and theoretical consequence of the negative answer justifies a too-facile escape valve from the operation of the statute, one that is also unilaterally within the control of the alleged wrongdoer. The paradigm for editors is a "newsworthy" homily to lovesick adolescents or any other audience; they then just have to use a journalistic conceit of tying the advice to a purported letter to the editor, with an inescapable first person identification of the letter as originating with any adolescent in the photo array. When an aggrieved person like Messenger reaches for the statutory lifeline, the newsworthiness notion dissipates it into a dry mirage. That is not fair or right.

Strong New York jurisprudence and protection of constitutional speech guarantees— that I too support—are urged as overarching policy reasons for courts to be very circumspect with respect to claims under the Civil Rights statutes. That should not be a preemptive justification for courts to neutralize, in functional applications, a remedial statute that this Court nudged into existence. In the endeavor to live up to this Court's and New York's robust tradition of free speech and free press protections, statutory rights and reputations of individuals can also be proportionately safeguarded and legitimately redressed.

Chief Judge KAYE and Judges SMITH, LEVINE, CIPARICK, WESLEY and ROSENBLATT concur in PER CURIAM opinion; Judge BELLACOSA dissents and votes to answer certified question No. 1 in the affirmative in a separate opinion.

Notes and Questions

1. *Messenger* grants broad protection under the "newsworthiness" label. Is the protection it grants lesser than, equal to, or greater than that given by *Eastwood I* and *Eastwod II*? Or, perhaps, is it simply different, yet consistent?

2. Is the result in *Messenger* required by the First Amendment? Notice that, unlike the *Eastwood* cases, *Messenger* does not rely on federal constitutional law. Therefore, even if its protection exceeds the requirements of the First Amendment, the Supreme Court would not have any reason to rule on its validity (unless the scope of its protection violated some other constitutional norm).

3. Suppose the caption had *explicitly* (and deliberately) falsely identified Ms. Messenger as the girl who wrote the letter (for example, suppose the letter was signed "Jill" and the caption for the photograph read "Here is Jill, regretting her decision"). Do you think that the court would have decided the case the same way?

4. Does Jaime Messenger have any recourse under federal law (e.g., the Lanham Act, discussed in Chapter 5)? The court indicates that the decision would not be different even if the photograph had been one of a celebrity. Suppose the photograph had been one of an under-age celebrity (such as Miley Cyrus). Would the celebrity have a claim under federal law?

5. If the cover of the magazine featured the caption and photograph (without the letter, but with a reference to the inside page), would that have been actionable? Would it then matter if the photograph was of a celebrity? If the magazine had taken out advertisements for this issue showing the caption and the photograph, would that have been actionable under New York law? If so, how do we distinguish actionable from nonactionable situations under the newsworthiness exception?

6. Is a fictionalization exception (such as the one represented by the *Spahn* and *Binns* cases) a good idea? How do we distinguish "substantial" fictionalizations from other ones? Does fictionalization make the book or movie any more "commercial" than a documentary? If the book is expressly fictional — that is, the cover makes it clear that this is a work of fiction, not fact, is it actionable under New York law? Under California law? For more on "docudramas" (fictionalized or dramatized motion pictures based on real events), *see* Chapter VIII.C.

7. Suppose a tennis player consents to pose for pictures for a magazine in New York. Some of the pictures are later republished in a foreign magazine, along with an article about the tennis player. Does this violate New York law? *See* Myskina v. Conde Nast Publications, Inc., 386 F. Supp. 2d 409 (S.D.N.Y. 2005) (finding this to be within the newsworthiness exception).

8. Suppose that after a celebrity is murdered, an adult magazine prints an article on her life and career, and includes nude photos of her that were taken some 20 years earlier. Is there a "real relationship" between the photos and the article under New York law? In the actual case, decided under Georgia law, the Eleventh Circuit held that "[t]he fact of Benoit's nudity was not in and of itself newsworthy," commenting that "[t]he photos were not incidental to the article. Rather, the article was incidental to the photos." Toffoloni v. LFP Publishing Goup, LLC, 572 F.3d 1201 (11th Cir. 2009).

C. Other Uses of Newsworthy Information

C.B.C. Distribution and Marketing, Inc. v.
Major League Baseball Advanced Media, L.P.
505 F.3d 818 (8th Cir. 2007)

ARNOLD, Circuit Judge:

C.B.C. Distribution and Marketing, Inc., brought this action for a declaratory judgment against Major League Baseball Advanced Media, L.P., to establish its right to use, without license, the names of and information about major league baseball players in connection with its fantasy baseball products. Advanced Media counterclaimed, maintaining that CBC's fantasy baseball products violated rights of publicity belonging to major league baseball players and that the players, through their association, had licensed those rights to Advanced Media, the interactive media and Internet company of major league baseball. The Major League Baseball Players Association intervened in the suit, joining in Advanced Media's claims and further asserting a breach of contract claim against CBC. The district court granted summary judgment to CBC, see C.B.C. Distrib. and Mktg., Inc. v. Major League Baseball Advanced Media, L.P., 443 F. Supp. 2d 1077 (E.D. Mo. 2006), and Advanced Media and the Players Association appealed. We affirm.

I.

CBC sells fantasy sports products via its Internet website, e-mail, mail, and the telephone. Its fantasy baseball products incorporate the names along with performance and biographical data of actual major league baseball players. Before the commencement of the major league baseball season each spring, participants form their fantasy baseball teams by "drafting" players from various major league baseball teams. Participants compete against other fantasy baseball "owners" who have also drafted their own teams. A participant's success, and his or her team's success, depends on the actual performance of the fantasy team's players on their respective actual teams during the course of the major league baseball season. Participants in CBC's fantasy baseball games pay fees to play and additional fees to trade players during the course of the season.

From 1995 through the end of 2004, CBC licensed its use of the names of and information about major league players from the Players Association pursuant to license agreements that it entered into with the association in 1995 and 2002. The 2002 agreement, which superseded in its entirety the 1995 agreement, licensed to CBC "the names, nicknames, likenesses, signatures, pictures, playing records, and/or biographical data of each player" (the "Rights") to be used in association with CBC's fantasy baseball products.

In 2005, after the 2002 agreement expired, the Players Association licensed to Advanced Media, with some exceptions, the exclusive right to use baseball players' names and performance information "for exploitation via all interactive media." Advanced Media began providing fantasy baseball games on its website, MLB.com, the official website of major league baseball. It offered CBC, in exchange for a commission, a license to promote the MLB.com fantasy baseball games on CBC's website but did not offer CBC a license to continue to offer its own fantasy baseball products. This conduct by Advanced Media prompted CBC to file the present suit, alleging that it had "a reasonable apprehension that it will be sued by Advanced Media if it continues to operate its fantasy baseball games."

The district court granted summary judgment to CBC. It held that CBC was not infringing any state-law rights of publicity that belonged to major league baseball players. *C.B.C.*, 443 F. Supp. 2d at 1106–07.The court reasoned that CBC's fantasy baseball products did not use the names of major league baseball players as symbols of their identities and with an intent to obtain a commercial advantage, as required to establish an infringement of a publicity right under Missouri law (which all parties concede applies here). *Id.* at 1085–89. The district court further held that even if CBC were infringing the players' rights of publicity, the first amendment preempted those rights. *Id.* at 1091–1100....

II.

A.

An action based on the rights of publicity is a state-law claim. In Missouri, "the elements of a rights of publicity action include: (1) That defendant used plaintiff's name as a symbol of his identity (2) without consent (3) and with the intent to obtain a commercial advantage." *Doe v. TCI Cablevision*, 110 S.W.3d 363, 369 (Mo. 2003). The parties all agree that CBC's continued use of the players' names and playing information after the expiration of the 2002 agreement was without consent. The district court concluded, however, that the evidence was insufficient to make out the other two elements of the claim, and we address each of these in turn.

With respect to the symbol-of-identity element, ... we entertain no doubt that the players' names that CBC used are understood by it and its fantasy baseball subscribers as referring to actual major league baseball players. CBC itself admits that: In responding to the appellants' argument that "this element is met by the mere confirmation that the name used, in fact, refers to the famous person asserting the violation," CBC stated in its brief that "if this is all the element requires, CBC agrees that it is met." We think that by reasoning that "identity," rather than "mere use of a name," "is a critical element of the rights of publicity," the district court did not understand that when a name alone is sufficient to establish identity, the defendant's use of that name satisfies the plaintiff's burden to show that a name was used as a symbol of identity.

It is true that with respect to the "commercial advantage" element of a cause of action for violating publicity rights, CBC's use does not fit neatly into the more traditional categories of commercial advantage, namely, using individuals' names for advertising and merchandising purposes in a way that states or intimates that the individuals are endorsing a product. *Cf.* RESTATEMENT (THIRD) OF UNFAIR COMPETITION § 47 cmt. a, b. But the Restatement ... also says that a name is used for commercial advantage when it is used "in connection with services rendered by the user" and that the plaintiff need not show that "prospective purchasers are likely to believe" that he or she endorsed the product or service. RESTATEMENT (THIRD) OF UNFAIR COMPETITION § 47 & cmt. a. We note, moreover, that in Missouri, "the commercial advantage element of the rights of publicity focuses on the defendant's intent or purpose to obtain a commercial benefit from use of the plaintiff's identity." *Doe*, 110 S.W.3d at 370–71. Because we think that it is clear that CBC uses baseball players' identities in its fantasy baseball products for purposes of profit, we believe that their identities are being used for commercial advantage and that the players therefore offered sufficient evidence to make out a cause of action for violation of their rights of publicity under Missouri law.

B.

CBC argues that the first amendment nonetheless trumps the right-of-publicity action that Missouri law provides. Though this dispute is between private parties, the state action necessary for first amendment protections exists because the right-of-publicity claim exists only insofar as the courts enforce state-created obligations that were "never explicitly assumed" by CBC. *See Cohen v. Cowles Media Co.,* 501 U.S. 663, 668 (1991).

The Supreme Court has directed that state law rights of publicity must be balanced against first amendment considerations, *see Zacchini v. Scripps-Howard Broad.,* 433 U.S. 562 (1977), and here we conclude that the former must give way to the latter. First, the information used in CBC's fantasy baseball games is all readily available in the public domain, and it would be strange law that a person would not have a first amendment right to use information that is available to everyone. It is true that CBC's use of the information is meant to provide entertainment, but "[s]peech that entertains, like speech that informs, is protected by the First Amendment because '[t]he line between the informing and the entertaining is too elusive for the protection of that basic right.'" *Cardtoons, L.C. v. Major League Baseball Players Ass'n,* 95 F.3d 959, 969 (10th Cir. 1996) (quoting *Winters v. New York,* 333 U.S. 507, 510 (1948)); *see also Zacchini,* 433 U.S. at 578. We also find no merit in the argument that CBC's use of players' names and information in its fantasy baseball games is not speech at all. We have held that "the pictures, graphic design, concept art, sounds, music, stories, and narrative present in video games" is speech entitled to first amendment protection. *See Interactive Digital Software Ass'n v. St. Louis County, Mo.,* 329 F.3d 954, 957 (8th Cir. 2003). Similarly, here CBC uses the "names, nicknames, likenesses, signatures, pictures, playing records, and/or biographical data of each player" in an interactive form in connection with its fantasy baseball products. This use is no less expressive than the use that was at issue in *Interactive Digital.*

Courts have also recognized the public value of information about the game of baseball and its players, referring to baseball as "the national pastime." *Cardtoons,* 95 F.3d at 972. A California court, in a case where Major League Baseball was itself defending its use of players' names, likenesses, and information against the players' asserted rights of publicity, observed, "Major league baseball is followed by millions of people across this country on a daily basis … The public has an enduring fascination in the records set by former players and in memorable moments from previous games … The records and statistics remain of interest to the public because they provide context that allows fans to better appreciate (or deprecate) today's performances." *Gionfriddo v. Major League Baseball,* 94 Cal. App. 4th 400, 411, 114 Cal. Rptr. 2d 307 (2001). The Court in *Gionfriddo* concluded that the "recitation and discussion of factual data concerning the athletic performance of [players on Major League Baseball's website] command a substantial public interest, and, therefore, is a form of expression due substantial constitutional protection." *Id.* We find these views persuasive.

In addition, the facts in this case barely, if at all, implicate the interests that states typically intend to vindicate by providing rights of publicity to individuals. Economic interests that states seek to promote include the right of an individual to reap the rewards of his or her endeavors and an individual's right to earn a living. Other motives for creating a publicity right are the desire to provide incentives to encourage a person's productive activities and to protect consumers from misleading advertising. *See Zacchini,* 433 U.S. at 573, 576; *Cardtoons,* 95 F.3d at 973. But major league baseball players are rewarded, and handsomely, too, for their participation in games and can earn additional large sums from endorsements and sponsorship arrangements. Nor is there any danger here that consumers will be misled, because the fantasy baseball games depend on the inclusion of all players and thus cannot create a false impression that some particular player with "star power" is endorsing CBC's products.

Then there are so-called non-monetary interests that publicity rights are sometimes thought to advance. These include protecting natural rights, rewarding celebrity labors, and avoiding emotional harm. *See Cardtoons,* 95 F.3d at 973. We do not see that any of these interests are especially relevant here, where baseball players are rewarded separately for their labors, and where any emotional harm would most likely be caused by a player's actual performance, in which case media coverage would cause the same harm. We also note that some courts have indicated that the right of publicity is intended to promote only economic interests and that noneconomic interests are more directly served by so-called rights of privacy. For instance, although the court in *Cardtoons,* 95 F.3d at 975–76, conducted a separate discussion of noneconomic interests when weighing the countervailing rights, it ultimately concluded that the non-economic justifications for the rights of publicity were unpersuasive as compared with the interest in freedom of expression. "Publicity rights ... are meant to protect against the loss of financial gain, not mental anguish." *Id.* at 976. We see merit in this approach.

Because we hold that CBC's first amendment rights in offering its fantasy baseball products supersede the players' rights of publicity, we need not reach CBC's alternative argument that federal copyright law preempts the players' state law rights of publicity.

III.

[Here, the court held that CBC was not estopped from challenging the validity of Players Associations's rights of publicity by a provision in the contract under which "CBC undertook not to 'dispute or attack the title or any rights of Players' Association in and to the Rights and/or the Trademarks or the validity of the license granted,' either during or after the expiration of the agreement." This issue is discussed briefly in the Notes below.]

IV.

For the foregoing reasons, the district court's grant of summary judgment to CBC is affirmed.

COLLOTON, Circuit Judge, dissenting:

I agree with the court's discussion of the rights of publicity in Missouri and the application of the First Amendment in this context. I would resolve the contractual issues differently, however, and I therefore respectfully dissent.

[Judge Colloton's dissent on the contractual issues is omitted.]

Notes and Questions

1. As a prelude to the First Amendment issue, note how broad the Missouri common-law right of publicity is. In most cases, the defendant is using the "selling power" of the celebrity's "identity" to make money, either in an advertisement for goods and services or by selling celebrity merchandise. Here, the defendant is using the names and statistics of the players to offer fantasy baseball services. Does this conduct rely on the "selling power" of the players' "identities"? The court holds that it doesn't matter; under Missouri law, simply making money from the use is enough.

2. The main issue in the case, of course, is whether the use of the players' names and statistics is protected by the First Amendment. Do you think the defendant's conduct should be protected? Is the defendant contributing to the marketplace of ideas? Is the de-

fendant engaging in individual self-expression? If not, what is the rationale for protecting the defendant's use of the information?

3. Is the defendant reporting news when it uses the players' names and statistics for fantasy baseball? Can one comfortably draw a line between news reporting and commercial exploitation of the players' identities and statistics?

4. The players' names and statistics are undoubtedly "newsworthy" when they are reported in newspapers and magazines (and on the Internet) during the season. How long does that information remain "newsworthy"? In *Gionfriddo* (discussed in *C.B.C.*), baseball players who played before 1947 (when the standard major league contract was changed to expressly assign to the clubs the rights to film and photograph players) challenged Major League Baseball's use of their names, photos, statistics and performances in game programs, websites and video clips. The court held that the use was protected by the First Amendment:

> Major league baseball is followed by millions of people across this country on a daily basis. Likewise, baseball fans have an abiding interest in the history of the game. The public has an enduring fascination in the records set by former players and in memorable moments from previous games. Statistics are kept on every aspect of the game imaginable. Those statistics and the records set throughout baseball's history are the standards by which the public measures the performance of today's players. The records and statistics remain of interest to the public because they provide context that allows fans to better appreciate (or deprecate) today's performances. Thus, the history of professional baseball is integral to the full understanding and enjoyment of the current game and its players.

94 Cal. App. 4th at 411, 114 Cal. Rptr. 2d at 315. The court noted that "the public interest is not limited to current events; the public is also entitled to be entertained and informed about our history." *Id.* at 411, 114 Cal. Rptr. at 314.

5. Ultimately, the *C.B.C.* case is about whether there should be only one authorized provider of "fantasy" baseball, or whether there should be competition in providing such services. What are the policy arguments for and against these positions? Should your argument be affected by the fact that Major League Baseball famously enjoys a judicially-created exemption from federal antitrust law, while other sports do not?

6. In a follow-on case that demonstrates the advantages of forum shopping, CBS won a summary judgment that it does not have to pay the National Football League or its players royalties for the use of their names and statistics in offering fantasy football services. *See* CBS Interactive, Inc. v. National Football League Players Ass'n, ___ F.R.D. ___, 2009 WL 1151982 (D. Minn. 2009). The District of Minnesota, of course, lies within the Eighth Circuit, and the Players were unsuccessful in trying to get the suit heard in the Southern District of Florida instead. Sports leagues, however, are continuing to litigate the issue, likely hoping for a circuit split that might encourage the U.S. Supreme Court to take the case. (The Court denied *certiorari* in the *C.B.C.* case.)

7. In a portion of the opinion omitted above, the court discussed whether CBC should be estopped from challenging the validity of the Players Association's rights of publicity by a contractual provision, under which "CBC undertook not to 'dispute or attack the title or any rights of Players' Association in and to the Rights and/or the Trademarks or the validity of the license granted,' either during or after the expiration of the agreement." Do you think such a clause should be enforceable? What are the argument for and against enforcing such a clause?

The district court invalidated the clause on the authority of *Lear v. Adkins*, 395 U.S. 653 (1969), in which the Supreme Court held that a patent licensee could not be estopped from challenging the validity of the patent. The majority noted that *Lear* has been applied to other areas of intellectual property law, including trademark and copyright, but that "[t]he district court's application of the *Lear* principles to a state law right-of-publicity action, however, was unique so far as we can determine." The majority declined to reach the issue, holding instead that the clause was unenforceable because the Players Association had breached a warranty of title by stating in its contract that it "'is the sole and exclusive holder of all right, title and interest' in and to the names and playing statistics of virtually all major league baseball players." The court held this statement was untrue, *because* the Players could not prevent others from using the information under the First Amendment. What do you think of that argument?

The dissent criticized the majority on this point, stating that "CBC surely can 'agree,' as a matter of good business judgment, to bargain away any uncertain First Amendment rights that it may have in exchange for the certainty of what it considers to be an advantageous contractual arrangement." The dissent was also of the view that *Lear* should be limited to situations in which state law might interfere with federal policy under the Supremacy Clause.

8. Even uses that might otherwise be seen as merchandising can sometimes qualify for newsworthiness protection. In *Montana v. San Jose Mercury News, Inc.*, 34 Cal. App. 4th 790, 60 Cal. Rptr. 2d 639 (1995), the San Jose Mercury News ran a "Souvenir Section" in its Sunday newspaper following the San Francisco 49ers' victory in the 1990 Super Bowl. This section included "an artist's rendition of [Joe] Montana [the 49ers' quarterback] on the front page." That picture was made into a poster; most were given away, but about 30% of them were sold to the public for $5 each. Montana sued, claiming a violation of California statutory and common law. The California Court of Appeal affirmed summary judgment for the newspaper:

> In summary, the First Amendment protects the posters complained about here for two distinct reasons: first, because the posters themselves report newsworthy items of public interest, and second, because a newspaper has a constitutional right to promote itself by reproducing its originally protected articles or photographs.

Do you agree? Can this holding be reconciled with *Eastwood I* and *Messenger* (even though the latter, admittedly, is from a different state)? When you read the materials concerning the newsworthiness exception in other countries (in Chapter IX), consider whether the poster in *Montana*, or, for that matter, the material in any of the cases in this Chapter, would be protected under the laws of other countries.

Chapter VIII

Celebrity Rights and Freedom of Expression in the United States

In Chapter VII we discussed one set of limits on rights of publicity, in cases in which the use of use of the celebrity's name, image, or likeness is considered newsworthy. The newsworthiness doctrine, which derives from both state law and the First Amendment, focuses on freedom of the press as a limitation on rights of publicity. In this Chapter, we explore a larger panoply of limitations on rights of publicity deriving more generally from the idea of free expression (*i.e.*, not limited to uses in traditional news media). The cases in this Chapter include uses in various expressive contexts, such as works of art, parodies, and entertainment.

A. Works of Art

The two cases that follow raise a fundamental question regarding the conflict between celebrity rights and freedom of expression: should an artist have to obtain the consent of a celebrity in order to sell copies of works of art depicting that celebrity? The two courts reach different conclusions on this fundamental question. As you read the materials, consider whether it is possible to harmonize the two holdings, or whether two courts simply feel differently about the relative importance of the two rights involved.

Comedy III Prods. Inc. v. Gary Saderup, Inc.
25 Cal. 4th 387, 106 Cal. Rptr. 2d 126, 21 P.3d 797 (2001)

Mosk, J.:

A California statute grants the *right of publicity* to specified successors in interest of deceased celebrities, prohibiting any other person from using a celebrity's name, voice, signature, photograph, or likeness for commercial purposes without the consent of such successors. (Former Civ. Code, § 990.)[1] The United States Constitution prohibits the states

---

1. After we granted review, the Legislature renumbered the statute as section 3344.1 of the Civil Code. (Stats.1999, ch. 998, § 1; *id.*, ch. 1000, § 9.5.) At the same time, it amended the wording of the

from abridging, among other fundamental rights, freedom of speech. (U.S. Const., 1st and 14th Amends.) In the case at bar we resolve a conflict between these two provisions. The Court of Appeal concluded that the lithographs and silkscreened T-shirts in question here received no First Amendment protection simply because they were reproductions rather than original works of art. As will appear, this was error: reproductions are equally entitled to First Amendment protection. We formulate instead what is essentially a balancing test between the First Amendment and the right of publicity based on whether the work in question adds significant creative elements so as to be transformed into something more than a mere celebrity likeness or imitation. Applying this test to the present case, we conclude that there are no such creative elements here and that the right of publicity prevails. On this basis, we will affirm the judgment of the Court of Appeal.

I. The Statute

In this state the right of publicity is both a statutory and a common law right. The statutory right originated in Civil Code section 3344 (hereafter section 3344), enacted in 1971, authorizing recovery of damages by any living person whose name, photograph, or likeness has been used for commercial purposes without his or her consent. Eight years later, in *Lugosi v. Universal Pictures* (1979) 25 Cal. 3d 813, 160 Cal. Rptr. 323, 603 P.2d 425 (*Lugosi*), we also recognized a common law right of publicity, which the statute was said to complement (*id.* at p. 818 and fn. 6). But because the common law right was derived from the law of privacy, we held in *Lugosi* that the cause of action did not survive the death of the person whose identity was exploited and was not descendible to his or her heirs or assignees.

In 1984 the Legislature enacted an additional measure on the subject, creating a second statutory right of publicity that *was* descendible to the heirs and assignees of deceased persons. (Stats. 1984, ch. 1704, §1, p. 6169.) The statute was evidently modeled on section 3344: many of the key provisions of the two statutory schemes were identical. The 1984 measure is the statute in issue in the case at bar. At the time of trial and while the appeal was pending before the Court of Appeal, the statute was numbered section 990 of the Civil Code....

The statute provides a number of exemptions from the requirement of consent to use. Thus a use "in connection with any news, public affairs, or sports broadcast or account, or any political campaign" does not require consent. (§990, subd. (j).) Use in a "commercial medium" does not require consent solely because the material is commercially sponsored or contains paid advertising; "Rather it shall be a question of fact whether or not the use ... was so directly connected with" the sponsorship or advertising that it requires consent. (*Id.*, subd. (k).) Finally, subdivision (n) provides that "[a] play, book, magazine, newspaper, musical composition, film, radio or television program" (*id.*, subd. (n)(1)), work of "political or newsworthy value" (*id.*, subd. (n)(2)), "[s]ingle and original works of fine art" (*id.*, subd. (n)(3)), or "[a]n advertisement or commercial announcement" for the above works (*id.*, subd. (n)(4)) are all exempt from the provisions of the statute.

II. Facts

Plaintiff Comedy III Productions, Inc. (hereafter Comedy III), brought this action against defendants Gary Saderup and Gary Saderup, Inc. (hereafter collectively Saderup),

---

statute in several respects. Because we interpret the former statute, we will refer to it throughout, in the present tense, as section 990.

seeking damages and injunctive relief for violation of section 990 and related business torts. The parties waived the right to jury trial and the right to put on evidence, and submitted the case for decision on the following stipulated facts:

Comedy III is the registered owner of all rights to the former comedy act known as The Three Stooges, who are deceased personalities within the meaning of the statute.

Saderup is an artist with over 25 years' experience in making charcoal drawings of celebrities. These drawings are used to create lithographic and silkscreen masters, which in turn are used to produce multiple reproductions in the form, respectively, of lithographic prints and silkscreened images on T-shirts. Saderup creates the original drawings and is actively involved in the ensuing lithographic and silkscreening processes.

Without securing Comedy III's consent, Saderup sold lithographs and T-shirts bearing a likeness of The Three Stooges reproduced from a charcoal drawing he had made. These lithographs and T-shirts did not constitute an advertisement, endorsement, or sponsorship of any product.

Saderup's profits from the sale of unlicensed lithographs and T-shirts bearing a likeness of The Three Stooges was $75,000 and Comedy III's reasonable attorney fees were $150,000.

On these stipulated facts the court found for Comedy III and entered judgment against Saderup awarding damages of $75,000 and attorney fees of $150,000 plus costs. The court also issued a permanent injunction restraining Saderup from violating the statute by use of any likeness of The Three Stooges in lithographs, T-shirts, "or any other medium by which [Saderup's] art work may be sold or marketed." The injunction further prohibited Saderup from "Creating, producing, reproducing, copying, distributing, selling or exhibiting any lithographs, prints, posters, t-shirts, buttons, or other goods, products or merchandise of any kind, bearing the photograph, image, face, symbols, trademarks, likeness, name, voice or signature of The Three Stooges or any of the individual members of The Three Stooges." The sole exception to this broad prohibition was Saderup's original charcoal drawing from which the reproductions at issue were made.

Saderup appealed. The Court of Appeal modified the judgment by striking the injunction. The court reasoned that Comedy III had not proved a likelihood of continued violation of the statute, and that the wording of the injunction was overbroad because it exceeded the terms of the statute and because it "could extend to matters and conduct protected by the First Amendment...."

The Court of Appeal affirmed the judgment as thus modified, however, upholding the award of damages, attorney fees, and costs. In so doing, it rejected Saderup's contentions that his conduct (1) did not violate the terms of the statute, and (2) in any event was protected by the constitutional guaranty of freedom of speech.

We granted review to address these two issues.

III. Discussion

A. The Statutory Issue

Saderup contends the statute applies only to uses of a deceased personality's name, voice, photograph, etc., for the purpose of advertising, selling, or soliciting the purchase of, products or services. He then stresses the stipulated fact (and subsequent finding) that the lithographs and T-shirts at issue in this case did not constitute an advertisement, endorsement, or sponsorship of any product. He concludes the statute therefore does not apply in the case at bar. As will appear, the major premise of his argument—his construction of the statute—is unpersuasive.

As noted above, the statute makes liable any person who, without consent, uses a deceased personality's name, voice, photograph, etc., "in any manner, *on or in products, merchandise, or goods, or* for purposes of advertising or selling, or soliciting purchases of, products, merchandise, goods, or services...." (§ 990, subd.(a), italics added.) Saderup's construction reads the emphasized phrase out of the statute. Yet the Legislature deliberately inserted it, as the following sequence of events demonstrates. When first enacted in 1971, section 3344—the companion statute applying to living personalities—contained no such phrase: the statute simply made liable any person who uses another's identity "in any manner, for purposes of advertising products, merchandise, goods or services, or for purposes of solicitation of" such purchases. (Stats. 1971, ch. 1595, § 1, p. 3426.) The Legislature inserted the phrase, "on or in products, merchandise, or goods, or," when it amended section 3344 in 1984. (Stats. 1984, ch. 1704, § 2, p. 6172.) And in the very same legislation, the Legislature adopted section 990 and inserted the identical phrase in that statute as well. (Stats. 1984, ch. 1704, § 1, p. 6169.)

We therefore give effect to the plain meaning of the statute: it makes liable any person who, without consent, uses a deceased personality's name, voice, photograph, etc., either (1) "on or in" a product, *or* (2) in "advertising or selling" a product. The two uses are not synonymous: in the apt example given by the Court of Appeal, there is an obvious difference between "placing a celebrity's name on a 'special edition' of a vehicle, and using that name in a commercial to endorse or tout the same or another vehicle."

Applying this construction of the statute to the facts at hand, we agree with the Court of Appeal that Saderup sold more than just the incorporeal likeness of The Three Stooges. Saderup's lithographic prints of The Three Stooges are themselves tangible personal property, consisting of paper and ink, made as products to be sold and displayed on walls like similar graphic art. Saderup's T-shirts are likewise tangible personal property, consisting of fabric and ink, made as products to be sold and worn on the body like similar garments. By producing and selling such lithographs and T-shirts, Saderup thus used the likeness of The Three Stooges "on ... products, merchandise, or goods" within the meaning of the statute....

B. The Constitutional Issue

Saderup next contends that enforcement of the judgment against him violates his right of free speech and expression under the First Amendment. He raises a difficult issue, which we address below.

The right of publicity is often invoked in the context of commercial speech when the appropriation of a celebrity likeness creates a false and misleading impression that the celebrity is endorsing a product. Because the First Amendment does not protect false and misleading commercial speech, and because even nonmisleading commercial speech is generally subject to somewhat lesser First Amendment protection, the right of publicity may often trump the right of advertisers to make use of celebrity figures.

But the present case does not concern commercial speech. As the trial court found, Saderup's portraits of The Three Stooges are expressive works and not an advertisement for or endorsement of a product. Although his work was done for financial gain, "[t]he First Amendment is not limited to those who publish without charge.... [An expressive activity] does not lose its constitutional protection because it is undertaken for profit." (*Gugliemi v. Spelling-Goldberg Productions* (1979) 25 Cal. 3d 860, 868, 160 Cal. Rptr. 352, 603 P.2d 454 (conc. opn. of Bird, C.J.).)[7]

---

7. Chief Justice Bird's concurring opinion in *Gugliemi* was signed by Justices Tobriner and Manuel. The principles enunciated in her concurrence were also endorsed by Justice Newman, who nonetheless did not join the opinion because he shared the view of the majority that the common law right of publicity was not descendible (the case predated the passage of section 990). Therefore, Chief Jus-

The tension between the right of publicity and the First Amendment is highlighted by recalling the two distinct, commonly acknowledged purposes of the latter. First, "'to preserve an uninhibited marketplace of ideas' and to repel efforts to limit the '"uninhibited, robust and wide-open" debate on public issues.'" (*Guglielmi, supra,* 25 Cal. 3d at p. 866.) Second, to foster a "fundamental respect for individual development and self-realization. The right to self-expression is inherent in any political system which respects individual dignity. Each speaker must be free of government restraint regardless of the nature or manner of the views expressed unless there is a compelling reason to the contrary." (*Ibid.*)

The right of publicity has a potential for frustrating the fulfillment of both these purposes. Because celebrities take on public meaning, the appropriation of their likenesses may have important uses in uninhibited debate on public issues, particularly debates about culture and values. And because celebrities take on personal meanings to many individuals in the society, the creative appropriation of celebrity images can be an important avenue of individual expression. As one commentator has stated: "Entertainment and sports celebrities are the leading players in our Public Drama. We tell tales, both tall and cautionary, about them. We monitor their comings and goings, their missteps and heartbreaks. We copy their mannerisms, their styles, their modes of conversation and of consumption. Whether or not celebrities are 'the chief agents of moral change in the United States,' they certainly are widely used—far more than are institutionally anchored elites—to symbolize individual aspirations, group identities, and cultural values. Their images are thus important expressive and communicative resources: the peculiar, yet familiar idiom in which we conduct a fair portion of our cultural business and everyday conversation." (Madow, *Private Ownership of Public Image: Popular Culture and Publicity Rights* (1993) 81 Cal. L. Rev. 125, 128.)

As Madow further points out, the very importance of celebrities in society means that the right of publicity has the potential of censoring significant expression by suppressing alternative versions of celebrity images that are iconoclastic, irreverent, or otherwise attempt to redefine the celebrity's meaning. A majority of this court recognized as much in *Guglielmi:* "The right of publicity derived from public prominence does not confer a shield to ward off caricature, parody and satire. Rather, prominence invites creative comment." (*Guglielmi, supra,* 25 Cal. 3d at p. 869.)

For similar reasons, speech about public figures is accorded heightened First Amendment protection in defamation law. As the United States Supreme Court held in *Gertz v. Robert Welch, Inc.* (1974) 418 U.S. 323, public figures may prevail in a libel action only if they prove that the defendant's defamatory statements were made with actual malice, *i.e.,* actual knowledge of falsehood or reckless disregard for the truth, whereas private figures need prove only negligence. The rationale for such differential treatment is, first, that the public figure has greater access to the media and therefore greater opportunity to rebut defamatory statements, and second, that those who have become public figures have done so voluntarily and therefore "invite attention and comment." Giving broad scope to the right of publicity has the potential of allowing a celebrity to accomplish through the vigorous exercise of that right the censorship of unflattering commentary that cannot be constitutionally accomplished through defamation actions.

Nor do Saderup's creations lose their constitutional protections because they are for purposes of entertaining rather than informing. As Chief Justice Bird stated in *Guglielmi,* invoking the dual purpose of the First Amendment: "Our courts have often observed that

---

tice Bird's views in *Guglielmi* commanded the support of the majority of the court. Hereafter, all references to *Guglielmi* in this opinion will be to the Chief Justice's opinion.

entertainment is entitled to the same constitutional protection as the exposition of ideas. That conclusion rests on two propositions. First, '[t]he line between informing and entertaining is too elusive for the protection of the basic right. Everyone is familiar with instances of propaganda through fiction. What is one man's amusement, teaches another doctrine.'" (*Guglielmi, supra,* 25 Cal. 3d at p. 867.) "Second, entertainment, as a mode of self-expression, is entitled to constitutional protection irrespective of its contribution to the marketplace of ideas. 'For expression is an integral part of the development of ideas, of mental exploration and of the affirmation of self. The power to realize his potentiality as a human being begins at this point and must extend at least this far if the whole nature of man is not to be thwarted.'" (*Ibid.*)

Nor does the fact that expression takes a form of nonverbal, visual representation remove it from the ambit of First Amendment protection. In *Bery v. City of New York* (2d Cir. 1996) 97 F.3d 689, the court overturned an ordinance requiring visual artists— painters, printers, photographers, sculptors, etc.—to obtain licenses to sell their work in public places, but exempted the vendors of books, newspapers or other written matter. As the court stated: "Both the [district] court and the City demonstrate an unduly restricted view of the First Amendment and of visual art itself. Such myopic vision not only overlooks case law central to First Amendment jurisprudence but fundamentally misperceives the essence of visual communication and artistic expression. Visual art is as wide ranging in its depiction of ideas, concepts and emotions as any book, treatise, pamphlet or other writing, and is similarly entitled to full First Amendment protection.... One cannot look at Winslow Homer's paintings on the Civil War without seeing, in his depictions of the boredom and hardship of the individual soldier, expressions of anti-war sentiments, the idea that war is not heroic." (*Id.* at p. 695.)

Moreover, the United States Supreme Court has made it clear that a work of art is protected by the First Amendment even if it conveys no discernable message: "[A] narrow, succinctly articulable message is not a condition of constitutional protection, which if confined to expressions conveying a 'particularized message,' [citation], would never reach the unquestionably shielded painting of Jackson Pollock, music of Arnold Schoenberg, or Jabberwocky verse of Lewis Carroll." (*Hurley v. Irish-American Gay, Lesbian and Bisexual Group of Boston, Inc.* (1995) 515 U.S. 557, 569.)

Nor does the fact that Saderup's art appears in large part on a less conventional avenue of communications, T-shirts, result in reduced First Amendment protection. As Judge Posner stated in the case of a defendant who sold T-shirts advocating the legalization of marijuana, "its T-shirts ... are to [the seller] what the *New York Times* is to the Sulzbergers and the Ochs—the vehicle of her ideas and opinions." (*Ayres v. City of Chicago* (7th Cir. 1997) 125 F.3d 1010, 1017; *see also Cohen v. California* (1971) 403 U.S. 15 [jacket with words "Fuck the Draft" on the back is protected speech].) First Amendment doctrine does not disfavor nontraditional media of expression.

But having recognized the high degree of First Amendment protection for noncommercial speech about celebrities, we need not conclude that all expression that trenches on the right of publicity receives such protection. The right of publicity, like copyright, protects a form of intellectual property that society deems to have some social utility. "Often considerable money, time and energy are needed to develop one's prominence in a particular field. Years of labor may be required before one's skill, reputation, notoriety or virtues are sufficiently developed to permit an economic return through some medium of commercial promotion. [Citations.] For some, the investment may eventually create considerable commercial value in one's identity." (*Lugosi, supra,* 25 Cal. 3d at pp. 834–835 (dis. opn. of Bird, C. J.).)

The present case exemplifies this kind of creative labor. Moe and Jerome (Curly) Howard and Larry Fein fashioned personae collectively known as The Three Stooges, first in vaudeville and later in movie shorts, over a period extending from the 1920's to the 1940's. The three comic characters they created and whose names they shared—Larry, Moe, and Curly—possess a kind of mythic status in our culture. Their journey from ordinary vaudeville performers to the heights (or depths) of slapstick comic celebrity was long and arduous. Their brand of physical humor—the nimble, comically stylized violence, the "nyuk-nyuks" and "whoop-whoop-whoops," eye-pokes, slaps and head conks—created a distinct comedic trademark. Through their talent and labor, they joined the relatively small group of actors who constructed identifiable, recurrent comic personalities that they brought to the many parts they were scripted to play. "Groucho Marx just being Groucho Marx, with his moustache, cigar, slouch and leer, cannot be exploited by others. Red Skelton's variety of self-devised roles would appear to be protectible, as would the unique personal creations of Abbott and Costello, Laurel and Hardy and others of that genre.... '[W]e deal here with actors portraying themselves and developing their own characters.'" (*Lugosi, supra,* 25 Cal. 3d at pp. 825–26 (conc. opn. of Mosk, J.).)

In sum, society may recognize, as the Legislature has done here, that a celebrity's heirs and assigns have a legitimate protectible interest in exploiting the value to be obtained from merchandising the celebrity's image, whether that interest be conceived as a kind of natural property right or as an incentive for encouraging creative work. Although critics have questioned whether the right of publicity truly serves any social purpose, there is no question that the Legislature has a rational basis for permitting celebrities and their heirs to control the commercial exploitation of the celebrity's likeness.

Although surprisingly few courts have considered in any depth the means of reconciling the right of publicity and the First Amendment, we follow those that have in concluding that depictions of celebrities amounting to little more than the appropriation of the celebrity's economic value are not protected expression under the First Amendment. We begin with *Zacchini v. Scripps-Howard Broadcasting Co.* (1977) 433 U.S. 562, 576 (*Zacchini*), the only United States Supreme Court case to directly address the right of publicity....

To be sure, *Zacchini* was not an ordinary right of publicity case: the defendant television station had appropriated the plaintiff's entire act, a species of common law copyright violation. Nonetheless, two principles enunciated in *Zacchini* apply to this case: (1) state law may validly safeguard forms of intellectual property not covered under federal copyright and patent law as a means of protecting the fruits of a performing artist's labor; and (2) the state's interest in preventing the outright misappropriation of such intellectual property by others is not automatically trumped by the interest in free expression or dissemination of information; rather, as in the case of defamation, the state law interest and the interest in free expression must be balanced, according to the relative importance of the interests at stake.

Guglielmi adopted a similar balancing approach. The purported heir of Rudolph Valentino filed suit against the makers of a fictional film based on the latter's life. *Guglielmi* concluded that the First Amendment protection of entertainment superseded any right of publicity.... *Guglielmi* proposed a balancing test to distinguish protected from unprotected appropriation of celebrity likenesses: "an action for infringement of the right of publicity can be maintained only if the proprietary interests at issue clearly outweigh the value of free expression in this context." (*Guglielmi, supra,* 25 Cal. 3d at p. 871.)

[The court also discussed *Estate of Presley v. Russen*, 513 F. Supp. 1339 (D.N.J. 1981) and *Groucho Marx Productions, Inc. v. Day & Night Co.*, 523 F. Supp. 485 (S.D.N.Y. 1981), *reversed on other grounds*, 689 F.2d 317 (2d Cir. 1982). Both of these cases are excerpted in Chapter III, above.]

It is admittedly not a simple matter to develop a test that will unerringly distinguish between forms of artistic expression protected by the First Amendment and those that must give way to the right of publicity. Certainly, any such test must incorporate the principle that the right of publicity cannot, consistent with the First Amendment, be a right to control the celebrity's image by censoring disagreeable portrayals. Once the celebrity thrusts himself or herself forward into the limelight, the First Amendment dictates that the right to comment on, parody, lampoon, and make other expressive uses of the celebrity image must be given broad scope. The necessary implication of this observation is that the right of publicity is essentially an economic right. What the right of publicity holder possesses is not a right of censorship, but a right to prevent others from misappropriating the economic value generated by the celebrity's fame through the merchandising of the "name, voice, signature, photograph, or likeness" of the celebrity. (§ 990.)

Beyond this precept, how may courts distinguish between protected and unprotected expression? Some commentators have proposed importing the fair use defense from copyright law (17 U.S.C. § 107), which has the advantage of employing an established doctrine developed from a related area of the law. Others disagree, pointing to the murkiness of the fair use doctrine and arguing that the idea/expression dichotomy, rather than fair use, is the principal means of reconciling copyright protection and First Amendment rights.

We conclude that a wholesale importation of the fair use doctrine into right of publicity law would not be advisable. At least two of the factors employed in the fair use test, "the nature of the copyrighted work" and "the amount and substantiality of the portion used" (17 U.S.C. § 107(2), (3)), seem particularly designed to be applied to the partial copying of works of authorship "fixed in [a] tangible medium of expression" (17 U.S.C. § 102); it is difficult to understand why these factors would be especially useful for determining whether the depiction of a celebrity likeness is protected by the First Amendment.

Nonetheless, the first fair use factor—"the purpose and character of the use" (17 U.S.C. § 107(1))—does seem particularly pertinent to the task of reconciling the rights of free expression and publicity. As the Supreme Court has stated, the central purpose of the inquiry into this fair use factor "is to see, in Justice Story's words, whether the new work merely 'supersede[s] the objects' of the original creation [citations], or instead adds something new, with a further purpose or different character, altering the first with new expression, meaning, or message; it asks, in other words, whether and to what extent the new work is 'transformative.' [Citation.] Although such transformative use is not absolutely necessary for a finding of fair use, [citation] the goal of copyright, to promote science and the arts, is generally furthered by the creation of transformative works." (*Campbell v. Acuff-Rose Music, Inc.* (1994) 510 U.S. 569, 579.)

This inquiry into whether a work is "transformative" appears to us to be necessarily at the heart of any judicial attempt to square the right of publicity with the First Amendment. As the above quotation suggests, both the First Amendment and copyright law have a common goal of encouragement of free expression and creativity, the former by protecting such expression from government interference, the latter by protecting the creative fruits of intellectual and artistic labor. The right of publicity, at least theoretically, shares this goal with copyright law. When artistic expression takes the form of a literal depiction or imitation of a celebrity for commercial gain,[9] directly trespassing on the right of publicity without adding significant expression beyond that trespass, the state law interest in protecting the fruits of artistic labor outweighs the expressive interests of the imitative artist.

On the other hand, when a work contains significant transformative elements, it is not only especially worthy of First Amendment protection, but it is also less likely to interfere with the economic interest protected by the right of publicity. As has been observed, works of parody or other distortions of the celebrity figure are not, from the celebrity fan's viewpoint, good substitutes for conventional depictions of the celebrity and therefore do not generally threaten markets for celebrity memorabilia that the right of publicity is designed to protect. (*See Cardtoons, L.C. v. Major League Baseball Players Association* (10th Cir. 1996) 95 F.3d 959, 974 (*Cardtoons*).) Accordingly, First Amendment protection of such works outweighs whatever interest the state may have in enforcing the right of publicity. The right-of-publicity holder continues to enforce the right to monopolize the production of conventional, more or less fungible, images of the celebrity.[10] ...

Another way of stating the inquiry is whether the celebrity likeness is one of the "raw materials" from which an original work is synthesized, or whether the depiction or imitation of the celebrity is the very sum and substance of the work in question. We ask, in other words, whether a product containing a celebrity's likeness is so transformed that it has become primarily the defendant's own expression rather than the celebrity's likeness. And when we use the word "expression," we mean expression of something other than the likeness of the celebrity.

We further emphasize that in determining whether the work is transformative, courts are not to be concerned with the quality of the artistic contribution—vulgar forms of expression fully qualify for First Amendment protection. (*See, e.g., Hustler Magazine v. Falwell* [(1988)] 485 U.S. 46; *see also Campbell v. Acuff-Rose Music, Inc., supra,* 510 U.S. at p. 582.) On the other hand, a literal depiction of a celebrity, even if accomplished with great skill, may still be subject to a right of publicity challenge. The inquiry is in a sense

---

9. Inquiry into the "purpose and character" of the work in copyright law also includes "whether such use is of a commercial nature or is for nonprofit educational purposes." (17 U.S.C. §107(1).) It could be argued that reproduction of a celebrity likeness for noncommercial use—e.g., T-shirts of a recently deceased rock musician produced by a fan as a not-for-profit tribute—is a form of personal expression and therefore more worthy of First Amendment protection. This is an issue, however, that we need not decide in this case. It is undisputed that Saderup sold his reproductions for financial gain.

10. There is a fourth factor in the fair use test not yet mentioned, "the effect of the use upon the potential market for or value of the copyrighted work" (17 U.S.C. §107(4)), that bears directly on this question. We do not believe, however, that consideration of this factor would usefully supplement the test articulated here. If it is determined that a work is worthy of First Amendment protection because added creative elements significantly transform the celebrity depiction, then independent inquiry into whether or not that work is cutting into the market for the celebrity's images—something that might be particularly difficult to ascertain in the right of publicity context—appears to be irrelevant. Moreover, this "potential market" test has been criticized for circularity: it could be argued that if a defendant has capitalized in any way on a celebrity's image, he or she has found a potential market and therefore could be liable for such work. The "transformative" test elaborated in this opinion will, we conclude, protect the right-of-publicity holder's core interest in monopolizing the merchandising of celebrity images without unnecessarily impinging on the artists' right of free expression.

more quantitative than qualitative, asking whether the literal and imitative or the creative elements predominate in the work.[11]

Furthermore, in determining whether a work is sufficiently transformative, courts may find useful a subsidiary inquiry, particularly in close cases: does the marketability and economic value of the challenged work derive primarily from the fame of the celebrity depicted? If this question is answered in the negative, then there would generally be no actionable right of publicity. When the value of the work comes principally from some source other than the fame of the celebrity—from the creativity, skill, and reputation of the artist—it may be presumed that sufficient transformative elements are present to warrant First Amendment protection. If the question is answered in the affirmative, however, it does not necessarily follow that the work is without First Amendment protection—it may still be a transformative work.

In sum, when an artist is faced with a right of publicity challenge to his or her work, he or she may raise as affirmative defense that the work is protected by the First Amendment inasmuch as it contains significant transformative elements or that the value of the work does not derive primarily from the celebrity's fame.

Turning to the present case, we note that the trial court, in ruling against Saderup, stated that "the commercial enterprise conducted by [Saderup] involves the sale of lithographs and T-shirts which are not original single works of art, and which are not protected by the First Amendment; the enterprise conducted by [Saderup] was a commercial enterprise designed to generate profits solely from the use of the likeness of The Three Stooges which is the right of publicity ... protected by section 990." Although not entirely clear, the trial court seemed to be holding that *reproductions* of celebrity images are categorically outside First Amendment protection. The Court of Appeal was more explicit in adopting this rationale: "Simply put, although the First Amendment protects speech that is sold [citation], reproductions of an image, made to be sold for profit do not per se constitute speech." But this position has no basis in logic or authority. No one would claim that a published book, because it is one of many copies, receives less First Amendment protection than the original manuscript. It is true that the statute at issue here makes a distinction between a single and original work of fine art and a reproduction. (§ 990, subd. (n)(3).) Because the statute evidently aims at preventing the illicit merchandising of celebrity images, and because single original works of fine art are not forms of merchandising, the state has little if any interest in preventing the exhibition and sale of such works, and the First Amendment rights of the artist should therefore prevail. But the inverse—that a reproduction receives no First Amendment protection—is patently false: a reproduction of a celebrity image that, as explained above, contains significant creative elements is entitled to as much First Amendment protection as an original work of art. The trial court and the Court of Appeal therefore erred in this respect.

---

11. Saderup also cites *ETW Corp. v. Jireh Publishing, Inc.* (N.D. Ohio 2000) 99 F. Supp. 2d 829, 835–836, in which the court held that a painting consisting of a montage of likenesses of the well-known professional golfer Eldridge "Tiger" Woods, reproduced in 5,000 prints, was a work of art and therefore protected under the First Amendment. We disagree with the *ETW Corp.* court if its holding is taken to mean that any work of art, however much it trespasses on the right of publicity and however much it lacks additional creative elements, is categorically shielded from liability by the First Amendment. Whether the work in question in that case would be judged to be exempt from California's right of publicity, either under the First Amendment test articulated in this opinion or under the statutory exception for material of newsworthy value, is, of course, beyond the scope of this opinion.

Rather, the inquiry is into whether Saderup's work is sufficiently transformative. Correctly anticipating this inquiry, he argues that all portraiture involves creative decisions, that therefore no portrait portrays a mere literal likeness, and that accordingly all portraiture, including reproductions, is protected by the First Amendment. We reject any such categorical position. Without denying that all portraiture involves the making of artistic choices, we find it equally undeniable, under the test formulated above, that when an artist's skill and talent is manifestly subordinated to the overall goal of creating a conventional portrait of a celebrity so as to commercially exploit his or her fame, then the artist's right of free expression is outweighed by the right of publicity....

On the other hand, we do not hold that all reproductions of celebrity portraits are unprotected by the First Amendment. The silkscreens of Andy Warhol, for example, have as their subjects the images of such celebrities as Marilyn Monroe, Elizabeth Taylor, and Elvis Presley. Through distortion and the careful manipulation of context, Warhol was able to convey a message that went beyond the commercial exploitation of celebrity images and became a form of ironic social comment on the dehumanization of celebrity itself. Such expression may well be entitled to First Amendment protection. Although the distinction between protected and unprotected expression will sometimes be subtle, it is no more so than other distinctions triers of fact are called on to make in First Amendment jurisprudence.

Turning to Saderup's work, we can discern no significant transformative or creative contribution. His undeniable skill is manifestly subordinated to the overall goal of creating literal, conventional depictions of The Three Stooges so as to exploit their fame. Indeed, were we to decide that Saderup's depictions were protected by the First Amendment, we cannot perceive how the right of publicity would remain a viable right other than in cases of falsified celebrity endorsements.

Moreover, the marketability and economic value of Saderup's work derives primarily from the fame of the celebrities depicted. While that fact alone does not necessarily mean the work receives no First Amendment protection, we can perceive no transformative elements in Saderup's works that would require such protection.

Saderup argues that it would be incongruous and unjust to protect parodies and other distortions of celebrity figures but not wholesome, reverential portraits of such celebrities. The test we articulate today, however, does not express a value judgment or preference for one type of depiction over another. Rather, it reflects a recognition that the Legislature has granted to the heirs and assigns of celebrities the property right to exploit the celebrities' images, and that certain forms of expressive activity protected by the First Amendment fall outside the boundaries of that right. Stated another way, we are concerned not with whether conventional celebrity images should be produced but with who produces them and, more pertinently, who appropriates the value from their production. Thus, under section 990, if Saderup wishes to continue to depict The Three Stooges as he has done, he may do so only with the consent of the right-of-publicity holder.

IV. Disposition

The judgment of the Court of Appeal is affirmed.

GEORGE, C.J., KENNARD, J., BAXTER, J., WERDEGAR, J., CHIN, J., BROWN, J., concur.

APPENDIX

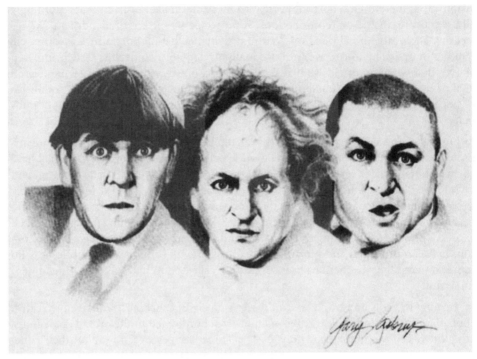

Figure 8-1. Saderup's portrait of The Three Stooges

ETW Corp. v. Jireh Publishing, Inc.

332 F.3d 915 (6th Cir. 2003)

GRAHAM, District Judge (sitting by designation):

Plaintiff-Appellant ETW Corporation ("ETW") is the licensing agent of Eldrick "Tiger" Woods ("Woods"), one of the world's most famous professional golfers. Woods, chairman of the board of ETW, has assigned to it the exclusive right to exploit his name, image, likeness, and signature, and all other publicity rights. ETW owns a United States trademark registration for the mark "TIGER WOODS" (Registration No. 2,194,381) for use in connection with "art prints, calendars, mounted photographs, notebooks, pencils, pens, posters, trading cards, and unmounted photographs."

Defendant-Appellee Jireh Publishing, Inc. ("Jireh") of Tuscaloosa, Alabama, is the publisher of artwork created by Rick Rush ("Rush"). Rush, who refers to himself as "America's sports artist," has created paintings of famous figures in sports and famous sports events. A few examples include Michael Jordan, Mark McGuire, Coach Paul "Bear" Bryant, the Pebble Beach Golf Tournament, and the America's Cup Yacht Race. Jireh has produced and successfully marketed limited edition art prints made from Rush's paintings.

In 1998, Rush created a painting entitled *The Masters of Augusta,* which commemorates Woods's victory at the Masters Tournament in Augusta, Georgia, in 1997. At that event, Woods became the youngest player ever to win the Masters Tournament, while setting a 72-hole record for the tournament and a record 12-stroke margin of victory. In the foreground of Rush's painting are three views of Woods in different poses. In the center, he is completing the swing of a golf club, and on each side he is crouching, lining up and/or observing the progress of a putt. To the left of Woods is his caddy, Mike "Fluff" Cowan, and to his right is his final round partner's caddy. Behind these figures is the Augusta National Clubhouse. In a blue background behind the clubhouse are likenesses of famous golfers of the past looking down on Woods. These include Arnold Palmer, Sam Snead, Ben Hogan, Walter Hagen, Bobby Jones, and Jack Nicklaus. Behind them is the Masters leader board.

The limited edition prints distributed by Jireh consist of an image of Rush's painting which includes Rush's signature at the bottom right hand corner. Beneath the image of the painting, in block letters, is its title, "The Masters Of Augusta." Beneath the title, in block letters of equal height, is the artist's name, "Rick Rush," and beneath the artist's name, in smaller upper and lower case letters, is the legend "Painting America Through Sports."

As sold by Jireh, the limited edition prints are enclosed in a white envelope, accompanied with literature which includes a large photograph of Rush, a description of his art, and a narrative description of the subject painting. On the front of the envelope, Rush's name appears in block letters inside a rectangle, which includes the legend "Painting America Through Sports." Along the bottom is a large reproduction of Rush's signature two inches high and ten inches long. On the back of the envelope, under the flap, are the words "Masters of Augusta" in letters that are three-eights of an inch high, and "Tiger Woods" in letters that are one-fourth of an inch high. Woods's name also appears in the narrative description of the painting where he is mentioned twice in twenty-eight lines of text. The text also includes references to the six other famous golfers depicted in the background of the painting as well as the two caddies.[1] Jireh published and marketed two hundred and fifty 22½" x 30" serigraphs and five thousand 9" x 11" lithographs of *The Masters of Augusta* at an issuing price of $700 for the serigraphs and $100 for the lithographs.

ETW filed suit against Jireh on June 26, 1998, in the United States District Court for the Northern District of Ohio, alleging trademark infringement in violation of the Lan-

---

1. The narrative reads as follows: **The Masters of Augusta** Undeniably, the essence of golf is Augusta National, The Masters. And, as sure as Spring itself, when the azaleas' plethora of color burst upon this uniquely manicured playground of golf's greatest, an almost heavenly awe overtakes the crowd. Because there is something about Augusta—a golden thread of nostalgia that weaves its way through the entire spectacle. Something will happen here that has happened for decades. Greatness will emerge. A Tiger Woods will unleash an incomparable swing and bury his opponents in his wake.

Amid the memorable hanging baskets of the Augusta National Clubhouse, Ben Hogan's Bridge, the 13th rock wall, and the dazzling floral logo that greets each guest, a star is born, and he's for real. And attesting from the Leader Board are the men who have formed a golfer's "field of dreams."

Men like Arnold Palmer with his omnipresent "Arnie's Army" roaring its approval; there's flamboyant Slammin' Sammy Snead or the irrepressible Ben Hogan; of course, you'll find Walter Hagen, who played his first Masters in 1934. And who can forget Bobby Jones, a truly great one, who always played as an amateur here, never as a professional. Last there's the Golden Bear, Jack Nicklaus, standing tall with six Masters to his credit, a man whose golfing prowess sets him apart from mere mortals.

But the center of their gaze is 1997 winner Tiger Woods, here flanked by his caddie, "Fluff", and final round player partner's (Constantino Rocca) caddie on right, displaying that awesome swing that sends a golf ball straighter and truer than should be humanly possible. Only his uncanny putting ability serves to complete his dominating performance that lifts him alongside the Masters of Augusta.

In this unique work of art, America's Sports Artist, Rick Rush has blended the charm and boastful beauty of nature with the magnificence of a gilded golfing history and unabashed power and confidence of youth to deliver a masterpiece: "The Masters of Augusta."

Figure 8-2. *The Masters of Augusta* by Rick Rush

ham Act, 15 U.S.C. § 1114; dilution of the mark under the Lanham Act, 15 U.S.C. § 1125(c); unfair competition and false advertising under the Lanham Act, 15 U.S.C. § 1125(a); unfair competition and deceptive trade practices under Ohio Revised Code § 4165.01; unfair competition and trademark infringement under Ohio common law; and violation of Woods's right of publicity under Ohio common law. Jireh counterclaimed, seeking a declaratory judgment that Rush's art prints are protected by the First Amendment and do not violate the Lanham Act. Both parties moved for summary judgment.

The district court granted Jireh's motion for summary judgment and dismissed the case. *See ETW Corp. v. Jireh Pub., Inc.*, 99 F. Supp. 2d 829 (N.D. Ohio 2000). ETW timely perfected an appeal to this court....

[The portions of the court's opinion (and the dissent) relating to the trademark claims are set forth in Chapter V.]

IV. *Lanham Act Unfair Competition and False Endorsement Claims, Ohio Right to Privacy Claims, and the First Amendment Defense*

A. *Introduction*

ETW's claims under § 43(a) of the Lanham Act, 15 U.S.C. § 1125(a), include claims of unfair competition and false advertising in the nature of false endorsement. ETW has also asserted a claim for infringement of the right of publicity under Ohio law. The elements of a Lanham Act false endorsement claim are similar to the elements of a right of publicity claim under Ohio law.... Therefore, cases which address both these types of claims should be instructive in determining whether Jireh is entitled to summary judgment on those claims.

In addition, Jireh has raised the First Amendment as a defense to all of ETW's claims, arguing that Rush's use of Woods's image in his painting is protected expression. Cases involving Lanham Act false endorsement claims and state law claims of the right of publicity have considered the impact of the First Amendment on those types of claims. We will begin with a discussion of the scope of First Amendment rights in the context of works of art, and will then proceed to examine how First Amendment rights have been balanced against intellectual property rights in cases involving the Lanham Act and state law rights of publicity. Finally, we will apply the relevant legal principles to the facts of this case.

B. *First Amendment Defense*

The protection of the First Amendment is not limited to written or spoken words, but includes other mediums of expression, including music, pictures, films, photographs, paintings, drawings, engravings, prints, and sculptures. *See Hurley v. Irish-American Gay, Lesbian and Bisexual Group of Boston,* 515 U.S. 557, 569 (1995) ("[T]he Constitution looks beyond written or spoken words as mediums of expression.").... *Kaplan v. California,* 413 U.S. 115, 119–120 (1973) ("[P]ictures, films, paintings, drawings, and engravings ... have First Amendment protection[.]"); *Bery v. City of New York,* 97 F.3d 689, 695 (2nd Cir. 1996) ("[V]isual art is as wide ranging in its depiction of ideas, concepts and emotions as any book, treatise, pamphlet or other writing, and is similarly entitled to full First Amendment protection.").

Speech is protected even though it is carried in a form that is sold for profit. *See Time, Inc. v. Hill,* 385 U.S. 374, 397 (1967) (" 'That books, newspapers, and magazines are published and sold for profit does not prevent them from being a form of expression whose liberty is safeguarded by the First Amendment.' "); *New York Times Co. v. Sullivan,* 376 U.S. 254 (1964) (solicitation to pay or contribute money). The fact that expressive materials are sold does not diminish the degree of protection to which they are entitled under the First Amendment. *City of Lakewood v. Plain Dealer Publ'g Co.,* 486 U.S. 750, 756 n.5 (1988).

Publishers disseminating the work of others who create expressive materials also come wholly within the protective shield of the First Amendment. *See, e.g., Sullivan,* 376 U.S. at 286–88 (finding New York Times fully protected by the First Amendment for publishing a paid editorial advertisement).[8]

Even pure commercial speech is entitled to significant First Amendment protection. [Citations] Commercial speech is "speech which does 'no more than propose a commercial transaction [.]'" *Virginia State Bd. of Pharmacy* [*v. Virginia Citizens Consumer Council, Inc.*], 425 U.S. [748,] 762 [(1976)]; *see also Central Hudson Gas and Electric Corp.* [*v. Pub. Serv. Comm'n of New York*], 447 U.S. [557,] 566 [(1980)] (articulating a four part test to bring commercial speech within the protection of the First Amendment).

Rush's prints are not commercial speech. They do not propose a commercial transaction. Accordingly, they are entitled to the full protection of the First Amendment. Thus, we are called upon to decide whether Woods's intellectual property rights must yield to Rush's First Amendment rights.

C. *Lanham Act False Endorsement Claim*

The district court did not specifically discuss ETW's false endorsement claim in granting summary judgment to Jireh. The gist of the false endorsement claim is that the presence of Woods's image in Jireh's print implies that he has endorsed Jireh's product. Courts

---

8. ETW's argument that only the original work and not its copies are protected would lead to absurd results. For example, the original manuscript of an unauthorized biography would be protected, but not the published copies. The original script of a play or a movie would be protected, but not live performances or films produced from it.

have recognized false endorsement claims under § 43(a) of the Lanham Act where a celebrity's image or persona is used in association with a product so as to imply that the celebrity endorses the product.

False endorsement occurs when a celebrity's identity is connected with a product or service in such a way that consumers are likely to be misled about the celebrity's sponsorship or approval of the product or service. *See, e.g., Wendt v. Host Int'l, Inc.,* 125 F.3d 806 (9th Cir. 1997) (animatronic robotic figures resembling actors in *Cheers* television program used to advertise chain of airport bars modeled on Cheers set); *Abdul-Jabbar v. General Motors Corp.,* 85 F.3d 407 (9th Cir. 1996) (athlete's name and accomplishments used in television advertisement for Oldsmobile automobiles); *Waits v. Frito-Lay, Inc.,* 978 F.2d 1093 (9th Cir. 1992) (imitation of singer's unique voice used in radio commercial advertising Dorito Chips); *White v. Samsung Electronics America, Inc.,* 971 F.2d 1395 (9th Cir. 1992) (female robot bearing resemblance to television celebrity, Vanna White, turning letters in what appeared to be the "Wheel of Fortune" game show set in television commercial advertising electronics products); *Allen v. National Video, Inc.,* 610 F. Supp. 612 (S.D.N.Y. 1985) (photograph of Woody Allen look-alike in national advertising campaign for video club).

In the ordinary false endorsement claim, the controlling issue is likelihood of confusion. This court has formulated an eight-factor test to determine the likelihood of confusion.... However, for the reasons discussed below, we conclude that where the defendant has articulated a colorable claim that the use of a celebrity's identity is protected by the First Amendment, the likelihood of confusion test is not appropriate because it fails to adequately consider the interests protected by the First Amendment.

In *Rogers v. Grimaldi,* 875 F.2d 994 (2nd Cir. 1989), Ginger Rogers, the surviving member of one of the most famous duos in show business history, brought suit against the producers and distributors of a movie entitled *Ginger and Fred.* The film was not about Ginger Rogers and Fred Astaire, but about two fictional Italian cabaret performers who imitated Rogers and Astaire and became known in Italy as "Ginger and Fred." Rogers asserted claims under § 43(a) of the Lanham Act. The Second Circuit began its analysis by noting that "[m]ovies, plays, books, and songs are all indisputably works of artistic expression and deserve protection." *Id.* at 997. The court concluded that "[b]ecause overextension of Lanham Act restrictions in the area of titles might intrude on First Amendment values, we must construe the Act narrowly to avoid such a conflict." *Id.* at 998.

The Second Circuit court rejected Rogers' argument that First Amendment concerns are implicated only where the author has no alternative means of expression. Her argument was based on *Lloyd Corp. v. Tanner,* 407 U.S. 551, 566–67 (1972), where the Supreme Court held that respondents had no First Amendment right to distribute handbills in the interior mall area of petitioner's privately-owned shopping center, noting that respondents had adequate alternative means of communication. Noting that this test had been applied by several courts in the trademark context, the *Rogers* court rejected the "no alternative means" test because it "does not sufficiently accommodate the public's interest in free expression[.]" 875 F.2d at 999. The court concluded:

> We believe that in general the Act should be construed to apply to artistic works only where the public interest in avoiding consumer confusion outweighs the public interest in free expression. In the context of allegedly misleading titles using a celebrity's name, that balance will normally not support application of the Act unless the title has no artistic relevance to the underlying work whatsoever, or, if it has some artistic relevance, unless the title explicitly misleads as to the source or the content of the work.

Id.

Although Rogers produced some evidence of consumer confusion, the court found:

> The survey evidence, even if its validity is assumed, indicates at most that some members of the public would draw the incorrect inference that Rogers had some involvement with the film. But that risk of misunderstanding, not engendered by any overt claim in the title, is so outweighed by the interests in artistic expression as to preclude application of the Lanham Act.

Id. at 1001. The Second Circuit affirmed the district court's decision granting summary judgment to the defendants.

In *Cliffs Notes, Inc. v. Bantam Doubleday Dell Pub. Group, Inc.,* 886 F.2d 490, 495 (2nd Cir. 1989), the Second Circuit held that the *Rogers* test is not limited to literary titles but is generally applicable to Lanham Act claims against works of artistic expression. Like Rogers, ETW argues that the district court should have considered whether alternative means existed for Jireh to express itself without violating Woods's intellectual property rights. We agree with the Second Circuit's conclusion that the "no alternative means" test does not sufficiently accommodate the public's interest in free expression.

In *Mattel, Inc. v. MCA Records, Inc.,* 296 F.3d 894 (9th Cir. 2002), the Ninth Circuit adopted and applied the *Rogers* test where the plaintiff asserted Lanham Act claims against the producer of a song entitled "Barbie Girl" which evoked the image of plaintiff's famous doll.... Thus, both the Second Circuit and the Ninth Circuit have held that in Lanham Act false endorsement cases involving artistic expression, the likelihood of confusion test does not give sufficient weight to the public interest in free expression. Both courts rejected the "no alternative means" test. They held instead that the Lanham Act should be applied to artistic works only where the public interest in avoiding confusion outweighs the public interest in free expression. They agreed that the public interest in free expression should prevail if the use of the celebrity's image has artistic relevance, unless it is used in such a way that it explicitly misleads as to the source of the work.[11]

In *Parks v. LaFace Records,* 329 F.3d 437 (6th Cir. 2003), we joined the Second and Ninth Circuits in holding that the likelihood of confusion and "alternative means" tests do not give sufficient weight to the public interest in freedom of expression. In *Parks,* we adopted the *Rogers* test as the law of the Sixth Circuit....

D. *Right of Publicity Claim*

ETW claims that Jireh's publication and marketing of prints of Rush's painting violates Woods's right of publicity. The right of publicity is an intellectual property right of recent origin which has been defined as the inherent right of every human being to control the commercial use of his or her identity. *See* McCARTHY ON PUBLICITY AND PRIVACY, § 1:3. The right of publicity is a creature of state law and its violation gives rise to a cause of action for the commercial tort of unfair competition. *Id.*

---

11. We disagree with the dissent's suggestion that the rule of *Rogers* and *Mattel* is limited to titles of artistic works. We believe that the principles identified in these decisions are generally applicable to all cases involving literary or artistic works where the defendant has articulated a colorable claim that the use of a celebrity's identity is protected by the First Amendment.

The dissent contends that we have overlooked the comment in *Mattel* that the result in *Rogers* may have been different if, for example, "a pair of dancing shoes had been labeled Ginger and Fred, [because] a dancer might have suspected that Rogers was associated with the shoes (or at least one of them), just as Michael Jordan has endorsed Nike sneakers that claim to make you fly through the air." *Mattel,* 296 F.3d at 901. We fail to see the relevance of this distinction, because Woods's image in Rush's print is not used to identify a product.

The Ohio Supreme Court[14] recognized the right of publicity in 1976 in *Zacchini v. Scripps-Howard Broadcasting Co.,* 47 Ohio St. 2d 224, 351 N.E.2d 454 (1976). [The U.S. Supreme Court's decision on appeal from the Ohio Supreme Court is included in Chapter VII.] …

When the Ohio Supreme Court recognized the right of publicity, it relied heavily on the Restatement (Second) Of Torts, §652. *See Zacchini,* 47 Ohio St. 2d at 230, 351 N.E.2d 454.…

The Restatement originally treated the right of publicity as a branch of the right of privacy and included it in a chapter entitled "Invasion of Privacy." In 1995, the American Law Institute transferred its exposition of the right of publicity to the Restatement (Third) Of Unfair Competition, Chapter 4, §46 … [which] defines the right of publicity as follows:

> Appropriation of the Commercial Value of a Person's Identity: The Right of Publicity
>
> One who appropriates the commercial value of a person's identity by using without consent the person's name, likeness, or other indicia of identity for purposes of trade is subject to liability for the relief appropriate under the rules stated in §§ 48 and 49.

Id.

In §46, Comment c, *Rationale for Protection,* the authors of the Restatement suggest that courts may justifiably be reluctant to adopt a broad construction of the right.

> The rationales underlying recognition of a right of publicity are generally less compelling than those that justify rights in trademarks or trade secrets. The commercial value of a person's identity often results from success in endeavors such as entertainment or sports that offer their own substantial rewards. Any additional incentive attributable to the right of publicity may have only marginal significance. In other cases the commercial value acquired by a person's identity is largely fortuitous or otherwise unrelated to any investment made by the individual, thus diminishing the weight of the property and unjust enrichment rationales for protection. In addition, the public interest in avoiding false suggestions of endorsement or sponsorship can be pursued through the cause of action for deceptive marketing. Thus, courts may be properly reluctant to adopt a broad construction of the publicity right. See §47.

In §47, Comment c, the authors of the Restatement note, "The right of publicity as recognized by statute and common law is fundamentally constrained by the public and constitutional interest in freedom of expression." In the same comment, the authors state that "[t]he use of a person's identity primarily for the purpose of communicating information or expressing ideas is not generally actionable as a violation of the person's right of publicity." Various examples are given, including the use of the person's name or likeness in news reporting in newspapers and magazines. The Restatement recognizes that this limitation on the right is not confined to news reporting but extends to use in "entertainment and other creative works, including both fiction and non-fiction." *Id.* The authors list examples of protected uses of a celebrity's identity, likeness or image, including

---

14. ETW is a Florida corporation with its principal place of business in Cleveland, Ohio. Both parties have argued this case on the premise that Ohio law applies to ETW's right of publicity claim. Thus, the court will apply Ohio law.…

unauthorized print or broadcast biographies and novels, plays or motion pictures. *Id.* According to the Restatement, such uses are not protected, however, if the name or likeness is used solely to attract attention to a work that is not related to the identified person, and the privilege may be lost if the work contains substantial falsifications. *Id.*

We believe the courts of Ohio would follow the principles of the Restatement in defining the limits of the right of publicity....

There is an inherent tension between the right of publicity and the right of freedom of expression under the First Amendment. This tension becomes particularly acute when the person seeking to enforce the right is a famous actor, athlete, politician, or otherwise famous person whose exploits, activities, accomplishments, and personal life are subject to constant scrutiny and comment in the public media....

In a series of recent cases, other [courts] have been called upon to establish the boundaries between the right of publicity and the First Amendment. [The court quotes extensively from the opinions in *Rogers, White, Cardtoons, Hoffman,* and *Saderup.* The free speech portions of *White, Cardtoons* and *Hoffman* are excerpted later in this Chapter.] ...

We conclude that in deciding whether the sale of Rush's prints violate Woods's right of publicity, we will look to the Ohio case law and the RESTATEMENT (THIRD) OF UNFAIR COMPETITION. In deciding where the line should be drawn between Woods's intellectual property rights and the First Amendment, we find ourselves in agreement with the dissenting judges in *White,* the Tenth Circuit's decision in *Cardtoons* [*L.C. v. Major League Baseball Players Assoc.,* 95 F.3d 959 (10th Cir. 1996)], and the Ninth Circuit's decision in *Hoffman* [*v. Capital Cities/ABC, Inc.,* 255 F.3d 1180 (9th Cir. 2001)], and we will follow them in determining whether Rush's work is protected by the First Amendment. Finally, we believe that the transformative elements test adopted by the Supreme Court of California in *Comedy III Productions,* [*Inc. v. Gary Saderup, Inc.,* 25 Cal. 4th 387, 106 Cal. Rptr. 2d 126, 21 P.3d 797 (2001)] will assist us in determining where the proper balance lies between the First Amendment and Woods's intellectual property rights. We turn now to a further examination of Rush's work and its subject.

E. *Application of the Law to the Evidence in this Case*

The evidence in the record reveals that Rush's work consists of much more than a mere literal likeness of Woods. It is a panorama of Woods's victory at the 1997 Masters Tournament, with all of the trappings of that tournament in full view, including the Augusta clubhouse, the leader board, images of Woods's caddy, and his final round partner's caddy. These elements in themselves are sufficient to bring Rush's work within the protection of the First Amendment. The Masters Tournament is probably the world's most famous golf tournament and Woods's victory in the 1997 tournament was a historic event in the world of sports. A piece of art that portrays a historic sporting event communicates and celebrates the value our culture attaches to such events. It would be ironic indeed if the presence of the image of the victorious athlete would deny the work First Amendment protection. Furthermore, Rush's work includes not only images of Woods and the two caddies, but also carefully crafted likenesses of six past winners of the Masters Tournament: Arnold Palmer, Sam Snead, Ben Hogan, Walter Hagen, Bobby Jones, and Jack Nicklaus, a veritable pantheon of golf's greats. Rush's work conveys the message that Woods himself will someday join that revered group.

Turning first to ETW's Lanham Act false endorsement claim, we agree with the courts that hold that the Lanham Act should be applied to artistic works only where the public interest in avoiding confusion outweighs the public interest in free expression. The *Rogers* test is helpful in striking that balance in the instant case. We find that the presence of

Woods's image in Rush's painting *The Masters of Augusta* does have artistic relevance to the underlying work and that it does not explicitly mislead as to the source of the work. We believe that the principles followed in *Cardtoons, Hoffman* and *Comedy III* are also relevant in determining whether the Lanham Act applies to Rush's work, and we find that it does not.

We find, like the court in *Rogers,* that plaintiff's survey evidence, even if its validity is assumed, indicates at most that some members of the public would draw the incorrect inference that Woods had some connection with Rush's print.[19] The risk of misunderstanding, not engendered by any explicit indication on the face of the print, is so outweighed by the interest in artistic expression as to preclude application of the Act. We disagree with the dissent's suggestion that a jury must decide where the balance should be struck and where the boundaries should be drawn between the rights conferred by the Lanham Act and the protections of the First Amendment.

In regard to the Ohio law right of publicity claim, we conclude that Ohio would construe its right of publicity as suggested in the RESTATEMENT (THIRD) OF UNFAIR COMPETITION, Chapter 4, Section 47, Comment d, which articulates a rule analogous to the rule of fair use in copyright law. Under this rule, the substantiality and market effect of the use of the celebrity's image is analyzed in light of the informational and creative content of the defendant's use. Applying this rule, we conclude that Rush's work has substantial informational and creative content which outweighs any adverse effect on ETW's market and that Rush's work does not violate Woods's right of publicity.

We further find that Rush's work is expression which is entitled to the full protection of the First Amendment and not the more limited protection afforded to commercial speech. When we balance the magnitude of the speech restriction against the interest in protecting Woods's intellectual property right, we encounter precisely the same considerations weighed by the Tenth Circuit in *Cardtoons.* These include consideration of the fact that through their pervasive presence in the media, sports and entertainment celebrities have come to symbolize certain ideas and values in our society and have become a valuable means of expression in our culture. As the Tenth Circuit observed "[c]elebrities ... are an important element of the shared communicative resources of our cultural domain." *Cardtoons,* 95 F.3d at 972.

In balancing these interests against Woods's right of publicity, we note that Woods, like most sports and entertainment celebrities with commercially valuable identities, engages in an activity, professional golf, that in itself generates a significant amount of income which is unrelated to his right of publicity. Even in the absence of his right of publicity, he would still be able to reap substantial financial rewards from authorized appearances and endorsements. It is not at all clear that the appearance of Woods's likeness in artwork prints which display one of his major achievements will reduce the commercial value of his likeness.

While the right of publicity allows celebrities like Woods to enjoy the fruits of their labors, here Rush has added a significant creative component of his own to Woods's iden-

---

19. Respondents in the survey were handed a copy of Rush's print and were asked the question: "Do you believe that Tiger Woods has an affiliation or connection with this print or that he has given his approval or has sponsored it?" Sixty-two percent answered "Yes"; eleven percent said "No"; and twenty-seven percent said "Don't Know." The terms "affiliated with" and "connected with" were not defined. Some respondents may have thought that Woods's mere presence in the print was itself an affiliation or connection. No control questions were asked to clarify this. Furthermore, the respondents were not given the packaging in which Jireh distributed the prints which prominently features Rush and contains no suggestion that Woods sponsored or approved the print.

tity. Permitting Woods's right of publicity to trump Rush's right of freedom of expression would extinguish Rush's right to profit from his creative enterprise.

After balancing the societal and personal interests embodied in the First Amendment against Woods's property rights, we conclude that the effect of limiting Woods's right of publicity in this case is negligible and significantly outweighed by society's interest in freedom of artistic expression.

Finally, applying the transformative effects test adopted by the Supreme Court of California in *Comedy III*, we find that Rush's work does contain significant transformative elements which make it especially worthy of First Amendment protection and also less likely to interfere with the economic interest protected by Woods' right of publicity. Unlike the unadorned, nearly photographic reproduction of the faces of The Three Stooges in *Comedy III*, Rush's work does not capitalize solely on a literal depiction of Woods. Rather, Rush's work consists of a collage of images in addition to Woods's image which are combined to describe, in artistic form, a historic event in sports history and to convey a message about the significance of Woods's achievement in that event. Because Rush's work has substantial transformative elements, it is entitled to the full protection of the First Amendment. In this case, we find that Woods's right of publicity must yield to the First Amendment.

V. *Conclusion*

In accordance with the foregoing, the judgment of the District Court granting summary judgment to Jireh Publishing is affirmed.

CLAY, Circuit Judge, dissenting:

Genuine issues of material fact remain for trial as to the [trademark, unfair competition and false endorsement] claims brought by Plaintiff ...; therefore, I would reverse the district court's judgment and remand the case for trial as to these claims. No genuine issue of material fact remains for trial that Defendant ... violated Plaintiff's right of publicity under Ohio common law; therefore, I would reverse the district court's judgment on Plaintiff's right of publicity claim and remand with instructions that the district court enter summary judgment in favor of Plaintiff. For these reasons, I respectfully dissent from the majority opinion, and shall address Plaintiff's claims in an order somewhat different than that utilized by the majority....

II. Lanham Act Unfair Competition & False Endorsement Claims — § 1125(a)

Regarding Plaintiff's claim for false endorsement, the majority concludes that "where the defendant has articulated a colorable claim that the use of a celebrity's identity is protected by the First Amendment, the likelihood of confusion test is not appropriate because it fails to adequately consider the interests protected by the First Amendment." In support of this conclusion, the majority relies upon the Second Circuit's decision in *Rogers v. Grimaldi*, 875 F.2d 994 (2d Cir. 1989) and *Mattel, Inc. v. MCA Records, Inc.*, 296 F.3d 894 (9th Cir. 2002), and ultimately holds that under these cases, the Lanham Act is not applicable to Plaintiff's claim, thus obviating the need to address Plaintiff's evidence of consumer confusion. The majority misapplies the test set forth and applied in these cases, and thus reaches an erroneous result.

This dissent focuses on the majority's misapplication of the *Rogers* balancing test and resulting erroneous conclusion; however, this dissent should not be interpreted as endorsing the application of the *Rogers* test to the facts of this case. Rather, the point made by the dissent is that even under the *Rogers* standard, questions of fact remain precluding summary judgment....

... [I]n applying the *Rogers* balancing test to facts if this case, the majority fails to consider Plaintiff's survey evidence of consumer confusion.... Instead, without any meaningful consideration whatsoever of Plaintiff's survey evidence, or for that matter any meaningful explanation of why Rush's print has artistic relevance for purposes of conducting a balancing of interests of any significance, the majority simply concludes that "the presence of Woods' image in Rush's painting *The Masters of Augusta* does have artistic relevance to the underlying work and that it does not explicitly mislead as to the source of the work." ...

The majority's contention that this case is like *Rogers* because the survey evidence merely indicates that some members of the public would draw the incorrect inference that Woods had some connection with Rush's print fails to account for the differences in the type of survey evidence in this case as opposed to that in *Rogers*. In *Rogers* the survey evidence indicated that only about 14% of the consumers polled indicated that Ginger Rogers was "involved in any way with making the film[;]" however, in this case, 62% of the consumers polled indicated that they believed that Woods had an "affiliation" or "connection" with Rush's print, or "approved" or "sponsored" the print. *See* 875 F.2d at 1001 n.8.... The majority's misleading and wholesale use of language from *Rogers* cannot serve to compel the outcome it argues for where the evidence and the facts involved differ so significantly.

In response to this dissent, the majority added what appears as footnote 11 of its opinion stating, among other things, that it fails to see the significance of the comment made in *Mattel* that the result in *Rogers* may have been different if a pair of dancing shoes had been labeled Ginger and Fred, inasmuch as "Woods's image in Rush's print is not used to identify a product." The "product" in this case *is* Rush's print, and Rush prominently depicts Woods holding his swing at the Masters Tournament in the print, entitled *The Masters of Augusta*, such that the evidence indicates that consumers believe that Woods sponsored or approved of the print....

Even under the *Rogers* standard, it is necessary for this case to be remanded on the issue of Plaintiff's false endorsement claim since questions of fact remain as to the degree of consumer confusion associated with Rush's print and Woods' endorsement thereof ... This is not to say that the ultimate outcome here would necessarily be a favorable one for Plaintiff; however, a jury should be able to make that decision after hearing all of the evidence presented by Plaintiff, as opposed to the majority's truncated and abbreviated approach which fails to engage in any meaningful consideration of pertinent and relevant evidence of consumer confusion, and fails to engage in any significant balancing of the interests....

V. Ohio Common Law Right of Publicity Claim

The majority makes a somewhat disjointed holding regarding Plaintiff's right of publicity claim. It first concludes that, under the rule of the Restatement, "Rush's work has substantial informational and creative content which outweighs any adverse effect on ETW's [Plaintiff's] market and that Rush's work does not violate Woods's right of publicity." Then, the majority appears to engage in a separate analysis or balancing of the interests under the law of various circuits when it takes into account the degree of First Amendment protection that should be afforded Rush's print against Woods' "intellectual property right" in order to conclude that "[p]ermitting Woods' right of publicity to trump Rush's right of freedom of expression would extinguish Rush's right to profit from his creative enterprise." Finally, engaging in yet a separate analysis under the "transformative effects test" pronounced by the California Supreme Court, the majority concludes that "[b]ecause Rush's work has substantial transformative elements, it is entitled to the full protection of the First Amendment. In this case, we find that Woods's right of publicity must yield to the First Amendment." Thus, it appears that the majority engages in three separate analyses, and arrives at three separate holdings, although all of which reach the same result.

The majority's analysis not only fails in its disjointed approach but in its outcome as well. The approach best suited for addressing Plaintiff's right of publicity claim in this case is that taken by the California Supreme Court in *Comedy III Productions v. Gary Saderup, Inc.*, 25 Cal. 4th 387, 106 Cal. Rptr. 2d 126, 21 P.3d 797 (2001). This is so because the Court in *Comedy III* took account of a celebrity's right of publicity and the principles of the right in general, as balanced against competing First Amendment concerns, in arriving at a test for purposes of adjudicating a case that is nearly on all fours with the matter at hand. This approach takes into account all of the competing interests while allowing for a single well-determined outcome that provides guidance and adds to the jurisprudence as a whole. Before applying the *Comedy III* approach to the facts of this case, it is useful to review the background of the birth of the right of publicity, the considerations embodied in the right, and the competing First Amendment interests in freedom of expression.

A. Background of the Right of Publicity

… Despite the various commentary and scholarship assessing the virtues and drawbacks to the right of publicity when compared to First Amendment principles, the fact remains that the right of publicity is an accepted right and striking the balance between an individual's right of publicity against the speaker's First Amendment right is not an easy one. Bearing in mind the principles justifying the two rights, it is clear why Woods' right of publicity does not bow to Defendant's First Amendment rights in this case.

B. Woods' Right of Publicity Claim in this Case

… "The right of publicity has often been invoked in the context of commercial speech when the appropriation of a celebrity likeness creates a false and misleading impression that the celebrity is endorsing a product." *See Comedy III Prods., Inc. v. Saderup, Inc.*, 25 Cal. 4th 387, 106 Cal. Rptr. 2d 126, 21 P.3d 797, 802 (2001)…. In this case, to the extent that the district court was correct in characterizing Defendant's prints as expressive works and not as commercial products, even though Defendant was selling the prints for financial gain, the issue becomes what degree of First Amendment protection should be afforded to Defendant's expressive work.

In answering this question, one must look beyond *Zacchini*…. With that in mind, guidance is provided by the California Supreme Court because it has addressed the specific issue in a case nearly on all fours with that presented here; namely, *Comedy III Productions v. Gary Saderup, Inc.*, 25 Cal. 4th 387, 106 Cal. Rptr. 2d 126, 21 P.3d 797 (2001)…. [The dissent's discussion of *Saderup* is omitted.]

In the instant case, where we are faced with an expressive work and the question of whether that work is protected under the First Amendment, the reasoning and transformative test set forth in *Comedy III* are in line with the Supreme Court's reasoning in *Zacchini* as well as in harmony with the goals of both the right to publicity and the First Amendment. Applying the test here, it is difficult to discern any appreciable transformative or creative contribution in Defendant's prints so as to entitle them to First Amendment protection. "A literal depiction of a celebrity, even if accomplished with great skill, may still be subject to a right of publicity challenge. The inquiry is in a sense more quantitative than qualitative, asking whether the literal and imitative or the creative elements predominate in the work." *Comedy III*, 106 Cal. Rptr. 2d 126, 21 P.3d at 809 (footnote omitted).

Indeed, the rendition done by Rush is nearly identical to that in the poster distributed by Nike. Although the faces and partial body images of other famous golfers appear in blue sketch blending in the background of Rush's print, the clear focus of the work is Woods in full body image wearing his red shirt and holding his famous swing in the pose which is nearly identical to that depicted in the Nike poster. Rush's print does not depict Woods in the same vein as the other golfers, such that the focus of the print is not the Masters Tournament or the other golfers who have won the prestigious green jacket award, but that of Woods holding his famous golf swing while at that tournament. Thus, although it is apparent that Rush is an adequately skilled artist, after viewing the prints in question it is also apparent that Rush's ability in this regard is "subordinated to the overall goal of creating literal, conventional depictions of [Tiger Woods] so as to exploit his ... fame [such that Rush's] right of free expression is outweighed by [Woods'] right of publicity." *See id.* at 811.

Accordingly, contrary to the majority's conclusion otherwise, it is clear that the prints gain their commercial value by exploiting the fame and celebrity status that Woods has worked to achieve. Under such facts, the right of publicity is not outweighed by the right of free expression. *See Comedy III,* 106 Cal. Rptr. 2d 126, 21 P.3d at 811 (noting that the marketability and economic value of the defendant's work was derived primarily from the fame of the three celebrities that it depicted and was therefore not protected by the First Amendment).

I therefore respectfully dissent from the majority opinion affirming summary judgment to Defendant as to all of Plaintiff's claims.

———————

Notes and Questions

1. The first step in analyzing the First Amendment issue is to determine whether the First Amendment applies. Are works of art depicting celebrities "speech" within the meaning of the First Amendment? The *Saderup* court considers and rejects six reasons why the t-shirts and lithographs at issue might not be given full First Amendment protection. What are they? (Hint: one is found at the outset of the Constitutional analysis; four are considered in consecutive paragraphs shortly thereafter; and the sixth is found near the end of the opinion, when the court explains an error made by the lower courts.)

The *Saderup* court also explains that the First Amendment serves two purposes that might be frustrated by full enforcement of the right of publicity. What are they?

2. Having held that the t-shirts and lithographs are entitled to full First Amendment protection, the *Saderup* opinion then briefly discusses the purposes of the right of publicity and concludes that "the Legislature has a *rational basis* for permitting celebrities and their heirs to control the commercial exploitation of the celebrity's likeness" (emphasis added).

If you have taken Constitutional Law, you will recall that "rational basis" review is typically applied to economic legislation, such as laws regulating wages and workplace conditions. But when government-enforced restrictions on free speech are involved, courts typically impose some type of heightened review. "Content-based" restrictions are subject to strict scrutiny: to be valid, the speech restriction must be "necessary to serve a compelling state interest," and must be "narrowly drawn to achieve that end." *Perry Education Ass'n v. Perry Local Educators' Ass'n,* 460 U.S. 37, 45 (1983). By contrast, "content-neutral" restrictions, including "time, place, and manner" restrictions, are subject to intermediate scrutiny: to be valid, the speech restriction must "promote[] a substantial government interest" unrelated to the suppression of free expression, and may not "burden substantially more speech than is necessary to further the government's legitimate interests." *Ward v. Rock Against Racism*, 491 U.S. 781, 799–800 (1989). (As we will see in the next section, intermediate scrutiny is also used in commercial speech cases.)

Which of these categories best describes the right of publicity? Is the right of publicity "content-based," because it forbids the use of images of celebrities without their consent? Or is "content-neutral," because the purpose of the law is unrelated to the suppression of expression? In either case, given the direct impact that the right of publicity has on free speech, it is hard to justify applying a "rational basis" standard of review applicable to mere economic regulation.

3. Now consider the standard that the *Saderup* court announces to "distinguish between forms of artistic expression protected by the First Amendment and those that must give way to the right of publicity." What forms of artistic expression fall into the former category? What forms of artistic expression fall into the latter category? And what is the "subsidiary inquiry" that courts "may find useful..., particularly in close cases"?

4. Is the *Saderup* court consistent in its treatment of the "commercial" nature of the work? On the one hand, the court reminds us that "[a]lthough [Saderup's] work was done for financial gain, ... [it] does not lose its constitutional protection because it is undertaken for profit." On the other hand, the court states that "[w]hen artistic expression takes the form of a literal depiction or imitation of a celebrity *for commercial gain*, ... the state law interest ... outweighs the expressive interests of the imitative artist" (emphasis added). If speech does not lose its constitutional protection because it is undertaken for profit, why should "commercial gain" be considered in deciding when that constitutional protection may be disregarded by the legislature?

5. Similarly, is the *Saderup* court consistent in its treatment of whether the lithographs must contain some sort of "message"? The court notes that "[an] articulable message is not a condition of constitutional protection"; but the "transformative use" standard that it applies expressly inquires whether the work "adds something new, ... altering the first with new expression, meaning, or message." That standard comes from U.S. Supreme Court's opinion in *Campbell*, a copyright case. Arguably, however, the Constitutional basis for copyright (in Art. I, §8, cl. 8) gives copyright a stronger government interest to balance against the First Amendment than that of the right of publicity, a state law which is subordinate to the First Amendment under the Supremacy Clause.

6. The First Amendment analysis in the *ETW* case likewise begins by considering and rejecting four reasons why the lithographs of Tiger Woods might not be given full First Amendment protection. What are they?

One of the four reasons is the possibility that "commercial speech" may be given less First Amendment protection that non-commercial speech. Perhaps somewhat counterintuitively, on this point, both courts agree that although the works of art at issue were being sold for profit, they are *not* "commercial speech." As the *ETW* case reminds us, "commercial speech" has a very limited definition in First Amendment jurisprudence: it refers to "speech that does no more than propose a commercial transaction," *i.e.*, advertising. Hence, the fact that the works are being sold for money does not render them less entitled to full First Amendment protection.

7. The *ETW* court also considers and rejects a balancing test that would deny First Amendment protection if the defendant had "adequate alternative means of communication." The case that articulates this standard, *Lloyd Corp. v. Tanner*, 407 U.S. 551 (1972),

used this standard to balance freedom of speech against an ownership interest in *real* property. Is this an appropriate balancing test to use when balancing freedom of speech against an ownership interest in intangible *intellectual* property? Why or why not?

8. Instead, the *ETW* court prefers the balancing test announced by the Second Circuit in *Rogers v. Grimaldi*, and adopted by the Sixth Circuit in *Parks*. As the *ETW* court notes, the *Rogers* test was developed for balancing the right of publicity against freedom of speech in the context of *titles* of artistic works. The test asks, in part, whether the title has "artistic relevance" to the content of the artistic work. Both the Second and Ninth Circuit have also applied this test to the use of trademarks in the artistic work itself. Does the *Rogers* test make sense when applied to the use of celebrity images in an artistic work? How would a court determine whether the celebrity image has "artistic relevance" to the work?

9. The dissent in *ETW* argues that the evidence of confusion is so great that a jury should decide whether there is a violation. How does the majority respond to this argument? What ought to be the role of confusion in the analysis? Should *any* level of confusion (even if not the intended result of the defendant) be sufficient to outweigh First Amendment concerns?

10. *Parks v. LaFace Records*, 329 F.3d 437 (6th Cir. 2003) (cited in *ETW*), involved a right of publicity claim by civil rights icon Rosa Parks against the performers, producers and distributors of a rap song titled "Rosa Parks." The Sixth Circuit described the plaintiff as follows:

> Rosa Parks is an historical figure who first gained prominence as a symbol of the civil rights movement in the United States during the 1950's and 1960's. In 1955, while riding in the front of a segregated bus in Montgomery, Alabama, she refused to yield her seat to a white passenger and move to the back of the bus as blacks were required to do by the then-existing laws requiring segregation of the races.... Her single act of defiance has garnered her numerous public accolades and awards, and she has used that celebrity status to promote various civil and human rights causes as well as television programs and books inspired by her life story.

The defendants' rap song included the following lyrics in the chorus, or "hook," which was repeated several times during the song:

> Ah ha, hush that fuss
>
> Everybody move to the back of the bus
>
> Do you wanna bump and slump with us
>
> We the type of people make the club get crunk

How would you apply the *Rogers* standard to these facts? Does the title have "artistic relevance" to the song? Does it "explicitly mislead" consumers as to whether the work was endorsed or approved by Rosa Parks?

11. The *ETW* court also holds that the lithograph of Tiger Woods would be protected under the *Saderup* standard. Do you agree? If so, what facts distinguish the lithograph of Tiger Woods from the lithographs and t-shirts involved in *Saderup*? Under the *Saderup* standard, how would an artist know in advance of publication whether he or she needed to seek permission before marketing copies of his or her work?

12. In the interests of full disclosure, it should be noted that the authors of this casebook both signed an *amicus* brief in support of the defendant in *ETW*, *see* Tyler T. Ochoa, *Introduction: Tiger Woods and the First Amendment*, 22 Whittier L. Rev. 381 (2000); Diane

Leenheer Zimmerman, Amicus Curiae *Brief of Seventy-Three Law Professors in Support of Jireh Publishing, Inc.*, 22 Whittier L. Rev. 391 (2000); and that Prof. Welkowitz authored an amicus brief in support of the defendant in *Saderup*, which Prof. Ochoa also signed.

13. In *Bleistein v. Donaldson Lithographing Co.*, 188 U.S. 239 (1903), Justice Holmes issued a warning against asking judges to make artistic determinations, in holding that a circus poster was entitled to copyright protection:

> It would be a dangerous undertaking for persons trained only in the law to constitute themselves final judges of the worth of pictorial illustrations, outside of the narrowest and most obvious limits. At the one extreme, some works of genius would be sure to miss appreciation. Their very novelty would make them repulsive until the public had learned the new language in which their author spoke.... At the other end, copyright would be denied to pictures which appealed to a public less educated than the judge....

Id. at 251–52. This famous passage has become known as the "aesthetic non-discrimination" principle. Doesn't the *Rogers* standard run afoul of the "aesthetic non-discrimination principle" by inviting judges to determine the "artistic relevance" of a celebrity image? Doesn't the *Saderup* standard likewise invite judges to make artistic judgments? Are such artistic judgments unavoidable? Or can you articulate a First Amendment standard that would not require judges to make such artistic determinations?

B. Parody and Satire

White v. Samsung Electronics America, Inc.
971 F.2d 1395 (9th Cir. 1992)

GOODWIN, Senior Circuit Judge:

[The facts are set forth in detail in Chapter II; they are only briefly recounted here.]

... The dispute in this case arose out of a series of advertisements prepared for Samsung [Electronics America, Inc.] by [David] Deutsch [Associates, Inc., Samsung's advertising agency]....

The advertisement which prompted the current dispute was for Samsung video-cassette recorders (VCRs). The ad depicted a robot, dressed in a wig, gown, and jewelry which Deutsch consciously selected to resemble White's hair and dress. The robot was posed next to a game board which is instantly recognizable as the Wheel of Fortune game show set, in a stance for which White is famous. The caption of the ad read: "Longest-running game show. 2012 A.D." Defendants referred to the ad as the "Vanna White" ad. Unlike the other celebrities used in the campaign, White neither consented to the ads nor was she paid.

Following the circulation of the robot ad, White sued Samsung and Deutsch in federal district court under: (1) California Civil Code § 3344; (2) the California common law right of publicity; and (3) § 43(a) of the Lanham Act, 15 U.S.C. § 1125(a). The district court granted summary judgment against White on each of her claims. White now appeals....

[Parts I–III of the opinion, holding that White had not stated a claim under § 3344, but that she had stated claims under California common law and the Lanham Act, are reproduced in Chapter II. In this Chapter, only the parody defense will be discussed.]

IV. *The Parody Defense*

In defense, defendants cite a number of cases for the proposition that their robot ad constituted protected speech. The only cases they cite which are even remotely relevant to this case are *Hustler Magazine v. Falwell*, 485 U.S. 46 (1988) and *L.L. Bean, Inc. v. Drake Publishers, Inc.*, 811 F.2d 26 (1st Cir. 1987). Those cases involved parodies of advertisements run for the purpose of poking fun at Jerry Falwell and L.L. Bean, respectively. This case involves a true advertisement run for the purpose of selling Samsung VCRs. The ad's spoof of Vanna White and Wheel of Fortune is subservient and only tangentially related to the ad's primary message: "buy Samsung VCRs." Defendants' parody arguments are better addressed to non-commercial parodies.[3] The difference between a "parody" and a "knock-off" is the difference between fun and profit.

V. *Conclusion*

In remanding this case, we hold only that White has pleaded claims which can go to the jury for its decision.

AFFIRMED IN PART, REVERSED IN PART, and REMANDED.

ALARCON, Circuit Judge, concurring in part, dissenting in part:

    … I concur in the majority's conclusions on the right to privacy. I respectfully dissent from its holdings on the right to publicity and the Lanham Act claims …

[Parts II and III of Judge Alarcon's dissent, discussing the common law and Lanham Act claims, are reproduced in Chapter II.]

IV.

SAMSUNG'S FIRST AMENDMENT DEFENSE

The majority gives Samsung's First Amendment defense short shrift because "[t]his case involves a true advertisement run for the purpose of selling Samsung VCRs." Majority opinion at p. 1401. I respectfully disagree with the majority's analysis of this issue as well.

The majority's attempt to distinguish this case from *Hustler Magazine v. Falwell*, 485 U.S. 46 (1988), and *L.L. Bean, Inc. v. Drake Publishers, Inc.*, 811 F.2d 26 (1st Cir. 1987), is unpersuasive. The majority notes that the parodies in those cases were made for the purpose of poking fun at the Reverend Jerry Falwell and L.L. Bean. But the majority fails to consider that the defendants in those cases were making fun of the Reverend Jerry Falwell and L.L. Bean for the purely commercial purpose of selling soft-core pornographic magazines.

Generally, a parody does not constitute an infringement on the original work if it takes no more than is necessary to "conjure up" the original. *Walt Disney Prods. v. Air Pirates*,

---

3. In warning of a first amendment chill to expressive conduct, the dissent reads this decision too broadly. This case concerns only the market which exists in our society for the exploitation of celebrity to sell products, and an attempt to take a free ride on a celebrity's celebrity value…. [E]ven if some forms of expressive activity, such as parody, do rely on identity evocation, the first amendment hurdle will bar most right of publicity actions against those activities. In the case of commercial advertising, however, the first amendment hurdle is not so high. *Central Hudson Gas & Electric Corp. v. Public Service Comm'n of New York*, 447 U.S. 557, 566 (1980). Realizing this, Samsung attempts to elevate its ad above the status of garden-variety commercial speech by pointing to the ad's parody of Vanna White. Samsung's argument is unavailing. Unless the first amendment bars all right of publicity actions—and it does not, *see Zacchini v. Scripps-Howard Broadcasting Co.*, 433 U.S. 562 (1977)—then it does not bar this case.

581 F.2d 751, 756 (9th Cir. 1978). The majority has failed to consider these factors properly in deciding that Vanna White may bring an action for damages solely because the popularity of the fame show, Wheel of Fortune.

The effect of the majority's holding on expressive conduct is difficult to estimate. The majority's position seems to allow any famous person or entity to bring suit based on any commercial advertisement that depicts a character or role performed by the plaintiff. Under the majority's view of the law, Gene Autry could have brought an action for damages against all other singing cowboys. Clint Eastwood would be able to sue anyone who plays a tall, soft-spoken cowboy, unless, of course, Jimmy Stewart had not previously enjoined Clint Eastwood. Johnny Weismuller would have been able to sue each actor who played the role of Tarzan. Sylvester Stallone could sue actors who play blue-collar boxers. Chuck Norris could sue all karate experts who display their skills in motion pictures. Arnold Schwarzenegger could sue body builders who are compensated for appearing in public....

V.

CONCLUSION

The protection of intellectual property presents the courts with the necessity of balancing competing interests. On the one hand, we wish to protect and reward the work and investment of those who create intellectual property. In so doing, however, we must prevent the creation of a monopoly that would inhibit the creative expressions of others. We have traditionally balanced those interests by allowing the copying of an idea, but protecting a unique expression of it. Samsung clearly used the idea of a glamorous female game show hostess. Just as clearly, it avoided appropriating Vanna White's expression of that role. Samsung did not use a likeness of her. The performer depicted in the commercial advertisement is unmistakably a lifeless robot. Vanna White has presented no evidence that any consumer confused the robot with her identity. Indeed, no reasonable consumer could confuse the robot with Vanna White or believe that, because the robot appeared in the advertisement, Vanna White endorsed Samsung's product.

I would affirm the district court's judgment in all respects.

White v. Samsung Electronics America, Inc.
989 F.2d 1512 (9th Cir. 1993)

Kozinksi, Circuit Judge, with whom Circuit Judges O'Scannlain and Kleinfeld join, dissenting from the order rejecting the suggestion for rehearing *en banc*:

I

Saddam Hussein wants to keep advertisers from using his picture in unflattering contexts.[1] Clint Eastwood doesn't want tabloids to write about him.[2] Rudolf Valentino's heirs

---

1. *See* Eben Shapiro, *Rising Caution on Using Celebrity Images*, N.Y. Times, Nov. 4, 1992, at D20 (Iraqi diplomat objects on right of publicity grounds to ad containing Hussein's picture and caption "History has shown what happens when one source controls all the information").

2. *Eastwood v. Superior Court*, 149 Cal. App. 3d 409, 198 Cal. Rptr. 342 (1983).

want to control his film biography.[3] The Girl Scouts don't want their image soiled by association with certain activities.[4] George Lucas wants to keep Strategic Defense Initiative fans from calling it "Star Wars."[5] Pepsico doesn't want singers to use the word "Pepsi" in their songs.[6] Guy Lombardo wants an exclusive property right to ads that show big bands playing on New Year's Eve.[7] Uri Geller thinks he should be paid for ads showing psychics bending metal through telekinesis.[8] Paul Prudhomme, that household name, thinks the same about ads featuring corpulent bearded chefs.[9] And scads of copyright holders see purple when their creations are made fun of.[10]

---

3. *Guglielmi v. Spelling-Goldberg Prods.*, 25 Cal. 3d 860, 160 Cal. Rptr. 352, 603 P.2d 454 (1979) (Rudolph Valentino); *see also Maheu v. CBS, Inc.*, 201 Cal. App. 3d 662, 668, 247 Cal. Rptr. 304 (1988) (aide to Howard Hughes). *Cf.* Frank Gannon, *Vanna Karenina*, in *Vanna Karenina and Other Reflections* (1988) (A humorous short story with a tragic ending. "She thought of the first day she had met VR__SKY. How foolish she had been. How could she love a man who wouldn't even tell her all the letters in his name?").

4. *Girl Scouts v. Personality Posters Mfg.*, 304 F. Supp. 1228 (S.D.N.Y. 1969) (poster of a pregnant girl in a Girl Scout uniform with the caption "Be Prepared").

5. *Lucasfilm Ltd. v. High Frontier*, 622 F. Supp. 931 (D.D.C. 1985).

6. Pepsico Inc. claimed the lyrics and packaging of grunge rocker Tad Doyle's "Jack Pepsi" song were "offensive to [it] and [...] likely to offend [its] customers," in part because they "associate [Pepsico] and its Pepsi marks with intoxication and drunk driving." Deborah Russell, *Doyle Leaves Pepsi Thirsty for Compensation*, Billboard, June 15, 1991, at 43. Conversely, the Hell's Angels recently sued Marvel Comics to keep it from publishing a comic book called "Hell's Angel," starring a character of the same name. Marvel settled by paying $35,000 to charity and promising never to use the name "Hell's Angel" again in connection with any of its publications. *Marvel, Hell's Angels Settle Trademark Suit*, L.A. Daily J., Feb. 2, 1993, §II, at 1.

Trademarks are often reflected in the mirror of our popular culture. *See* Truman Capote, *Breakfast at Tiffany's* (1958); Kurt Vonnegut, Jr., *Breakfast of Champions* (1973); Tom Wolfe, *The Electric Kool-Aid Acid Test* (1968) (which, incidentally, includes a chapter on the Hell's Angels); Larry Niven, *Man of Steel, Woman of Kleenex*, in *All the Myriad Ways* (1971); *Looking for Mr. Goodbar* (1977); *The Coca-Cola Kid* (1985) (using Coca-Cola as a metaphor for American commercialism); *The Kentucky Fried Movie* (1977); *Harley Davidson and the Marlboro Man* (1991); *The Wonder Years* (ABC 1988-present) ("Wonder Years" was a slogan of Wonder Bread); Tim Rice & Andrew Lloyd Webber, *Joseph and the Amazing Technicolor Dream Coat* (musical). *Hear* Janis Joplin, *Mercedes Benz*, on *Pearl* (CBS 1971); Paul Simon, *Kodachrome*, on *There Goes Rhymin' Simon* (Warner 1973); Leonard Cohen, *Chelsea Hotel*, on *The Best of Leonard Cohen* (CBS 1975); Bruce Springsteen, *Cadillac Ranch*, on *The River* (CBS 1980); Prince, *Little Red Corvette*, on *1999* (Warner 1982); dada, *Dizz Knee Land*, on *Puzzle* (IRS 1992) ("I just robbed a grocery store—I'm going to Disneyland/I just flipped off President George—I'm going to Disneyland"); Monty Python, *Spam*, on *The Final Rip Off* (Virgin 1988); Roy Clark, *Thank God and Greyhound [You're Gone]*, on *Roy Clark's Greatest Hits Volume I* (MCA 1979); Mel Tillis, *Coca-Cola Cowboy*, on *The Very Best of* (MCA 1981) ("You're just a Coca-Cola cowboy/You've got an Eastwood smile and Robert Redford hair ..."). *Dance to* Talking Heads, *Popular Favorites 1976–92: Sand in the Vaseline* (Sire 1992); Talking Heads, *Popsicle*, on *id*. *Admire* Andy Warhol, *Campbell's Soup Can*. *Cf.* REO Speedwagon, 38 Special, and Jello Biafra of the Dead Kennedys.

The creators of some of these works might have gotten permission from the trademark owners, though it's unlikely Kool-Aid relished being connected with LSD, Hershey with homicidal maniacs, Disney with armed robbers, or Coca-Cola with cultural imperialism. Certainly no free society can *demand* that artists get such permission.

7. *Lombardo v. Doyle, Dane & Bernbach, Inc.*, 58 A.D.2d 620, 396 N.Y.S.2d 661 (1977).

8. *Geller v. Fallon McElligott*, No. 90-Civ-2839 (S.D.N.Y. July 22, 1991) (involving a Timex ad).

9. *Prudhomme v. Procter & Gamble Co.*, 800 F. Supp. 390 (E.D. La. 1992).

10. *E.g.*, *Acuff-Rose Music, Inc. v. Campbell*, 972 F.2d 1429 (6th Cir. 1992); *Cliffs Notes v. Bantam Doubleday Dell Publishing Group, Inc.*, 886 F.2d 490 (2d Cir. 1989); *Fisher v. Dees*, 794 F.2d 432 (9th Cir. 1986); *MCA, Inc. v. Wilson*, 677 F.2d 180 (2d Cir. 1981); *Elsmere Music, Inc. v. NBC*, 623 F.2d 252 (2d Cir. 1980); *Walt Disney Prods. v. The Air Pirates*, 581 F.2d 751 (9th Cir. 1978); *Berlin v. E.C. Publications, Inc.*, 329 F.2d 541 (2d Cir. 1964); *Lowenfels v. Nathan*, 2 F. Supp. 73 (S.D.N.Y. 1932).

Something very dangerous is going on here. Private property, including intellectual property, is essential to our way of life. It provides an incentive for investment and innovation; it stimulates the flourishing of our culture; it protects the moral entitlements of people to the fruits of their labors. But reducing too much to private property can be bad medicine. Private land, for instance, is far more useful if separated from other private land by public streets, roads and highways. Public parks, utility rights-of-way and sewers reduce the amount of land in private hands, but vastly enhance the value of the property that remains.

So too it is with intellectual property. Overprotecting intellectual property is as harmful as underprotecting it. Creativity is impossible without a rich public domain. Nothing today, likely nothing since we tamed fire, is genuinely new: Culture, like science and technology, grows by accretion, each new creator building on the works of those who came before. Overprotection stifles the very creative forces it's supposed to nurture.

The panel's opinion is a classic case of overprotection. Concerned about what it sees as a wrong done to Vanna White, the panel majority erects a property right of remarkable and dangerous breadth: Under the majority's opinion, it's now a tort for advertisers to *remind* the public of a celebrity. Not to use a celebrity's name, voice, signature or likeness; not to imply the celebrity endorses a product; but simply to evoke the celebrity's image in the public's mind. This Orwellian notion withdraws far more from the public domain than prudence and common sense allow. It conflicts with the Copyright Act and the Copyright Clause. It raises serious First Amendment problems. It's bad law, and it deserves a long, hard second look.

II

The ad that spawned this litigation starred a robot dressed in a wig, gown and jewelry reminiscent of Vanna White's hair and dress; the robot was posed next to a Wheel-of-Fortune-like game board. *See* Appendix. The caption read "Longest-running game show. 2012 A.D." The gag here, I take it, was that Samsung would still be around when White had been replaced by a robot.

Perhaps failing to see the humor, White sued, alleging Samsung infringed her right of publicity by "appropriating" her "identity." Under California law, White has the exclusive right to use her name, likeness, signature and voice for commercial purposes. But Samsung didn't use her name, voice or signature, and it certainly didn't use her likeness. The ad just wouldn't have been funny had it depicted White or someone who resembled her — the whole joke was that the game show host(ess) was a robot, not a real person. No one seeing the ad could have thought this was supposed to be White in 2012.

The district judge quite reasonably held that, because Samsung didn't use White's name, likeness, voice or signature, it didn't violate her right of publicity. Not so, says the panel majority: The California right of publicity can't possibly be limited to name and likeness. If it were, the majority reasons, a "clever advertising strategist" could avoid using White's name or likeness but nevertheless remind people of her with impunity, "effectively eviscerat[ing]" her rights. To prevent this "evisceration," the panel majority holds that the right of publicity must extend beyond name and likeness, to any "appropriation" of White's "identity" — anything that "evoke[s]" her personality.

III

But what does "evisceration" mean in intellectual property law? Intellectual property rights aren't like some constitutional rights, absolute guarantees protected against all kinds of interference, subtle as well as blatant. They cast no penumbras, emit no emanations: The very point of intellectual property laws is that they protect only against certain specific kinds of appropriation. I can't publish unauthorized copies of, say, *Presumed Innocent*; I can't make a movie out of it. But I'm perfectly free to write a book about an idealistic young prosecutor on trial for a crime he didn't commit.[14] So what if I got the idea from *Presumed Innocent*? So what if it reminds readers of the original? Have I "eviscerated" Scott Turow's intellectual property rights? Certainly not. All creators draw in part on the work of those who came before, referring to it, building on it, poking fun at it; we call this creativity, not piracy.

The majority isn't, in fact, preventing the "evisceration" of Vanna White's existing rights; it's creating a new and much broader property right, a right unknown in California law.[16] It's replacing the existing balance between the interests of the celebrity and those of the public by a different balance, one substantially more favorable to the celebrity. Instead of having an exclusive right in her name, likeness, signature or voice, every famous person now has an exclusive right to *anything that reminds the viewer of her*. After all, that's all Samsung did: It used an inanimate object to remind people of White, to "evoke [her identity]." 971 F.2d at 1399.[17]

Consider how sweeping this new right is. What is it about the ad that makes people think of White? It's not the robot's wig, clothes or jewelry; there must be ten million blond women (many of them quasi-famous) who wear dresses and jewelry like White's. It's that the robot is posed near the "Wheel of Fortune" game board. Remove the game board from the ad, and no one would think of Vanna White. *See* Appendix. But once you include the game board, anybody standing beside it — a brunette woman, a man wearing women's clothes, a monkey in a wig and gown — would evoke White's image, precisely the way the robot did. It's the "Wheel of Fortune" set, not the robot's face or dress or jewelry that evokes White's image. The panel is giving White an exclusive right not in what she looks like or who she is, but in what she does for a living.[18]

This is entirely the wrong place to strike the balance. Intellectual property rights aren't free: They're imposed at the expense of future creators and of the public at large. Where would we be if Charles Lindbergh had an exclusive right in the concept of a

---

14. It would be called "Burden of Going Forward with the Evidence," and the hero would ultimately be saved by his lawyer's adept use of Fed. R. Evid. 301.

16. In fact, in the one California case raising the issue, the three state Supreme Court Justices who discussed this theory expressed serious doubts about it. *Guglielmi v. Spelling-Goldberg Prods.*, 25 Cal. 3d 860, 864 n.5, 160 Cal. Rptr. 352, 355 n.5, 603 P.2d 454, 457 n.5 (1979) (Bird, C.J., concurring) (expressing skepticism about finding a property right to a celebrity's "personality" because it is "difficult to discern any easily applied definition for this amorphous term").

17. Some viewers might have inferred White was endorsing the product, but that's a different story. The right of publicity isn't aimed at or limited to false endorsements, that's what the Lanham Act is for. Note also that the majority's rule applies even to advertisements that unintentionally remind people of someone. California law is crystal clear that the common-law right of publicity may be violated even by unintentional appropriations.

18. Once the right of publicity is extended beyond specific physical characteristics, this will become a recurring problem: Outside name, likeness and voice, the things that most reliably remind the public of celebrities are the actions or roles they're famous for. A commercial with an astronaut setting foot on the moon would evoke the image of Neil Armstrong. Any masked man on horseback would remind people (over a certain age) of Clayton Moore. And any number of songs — "My Way," "Yellow Submarine," "Like a Virgin," "Beat It," "Michael, Row the Boat Ashore," to name only a few — instantly evoke an image of the person or group who made them famous, regardless of who is singing.

heroic solo aviator? If Arthur Conan Doyle had gotten a copyright in the idea of the detective story, or Albert Einstein had patented the theory of relativity? If every author and celebrity had been given the right to keep people from mocking them or their work? Surely this would have made the world poorer, not richer, culturally as well as economically.

This is why intellectual property law is full of careful balances between what's set aside for the owner and what's left in the public domain for the rest of us: The relatively short life of patents; the longer, but finite, life of copyrights; copyright's idea-expression dichotomy; the fair use doctrine; the prohibition on copyrighting facts; the compulsory license of television broadcasts and musical compositions; federal preemption of overbroad state intellectual property laws; the nominative use doctrine in trademark law; the right to make soundalike recordings [under copyright law]. All of these diminish an intellectual property owner's rights. All let the public use something created by someone else. But all are necessary to maintain a free environment in which creative genius can flourish.

The intellectual property right created by the panel here has none of these essential limitations: No fair use exception; no right to parody; no idea-expression dichotomy. It impoverishes the public domain, to the detriment of future creators and the public at large. Instead of well-defined, limited characteristics such as name, likeness or voice, advertisers will now have to cope with vague claims of "appropriation of identity," claims often made by people with a wholly exaggerated sense of their own fame and significance. Future Vanna Whites might not get the chance to create their personae, because their employers may fear some celebrity will claim the persona is too similar to her own.[21] The public will be robbed of parodies of celebrities, and our culture will be deprived of the valuable safety valve that parody and mockery create.

Moreover, consider the moral dimension, about which the panel majority seems to have gotten so exercised. Saying Samsung "appropriated" something of White's begs the question: *Should* White have the exclusive right to something as broad and amorphous as her "identity"? Samsung's ad didn't simply copy White's schtick—like all parody, it created something new. True, Samsung did it to make money, but White does whatever she does to make money, too; the majority talks of "the difference between fun and profit," 971 F.2d at 1401, but in the entertainment industry fun *is* profit. Why is Vanna White's right to exclusive for-profit use of her persona—a persona that might not even be her own creation, but that of a writer, director or producer—superior to Samsung's right to profit by creating its own inventions? Why should she have such absolute rights to control the conduct of others, unlimited by the idea-expression dichotomy or by the fair use doctrine?

... [I]t may seem unfair that much of the fruit of a creator's labor may be used by others without compensation. But this is not some unforeseen byproduct of our intellectual

---

21. If Christian Slater, star of "Heathers," "Pump up the Volume," "Kuffs," and "Untamed Heart"—and alleged Jack Nicholson clone—appears in a commercial, can Nicholson sue? Of 54 stories on LEXIS that talk about Christian Slater, 26 talk about Slater's alleged similarities to Nicholson. Apparently it's his nasal wisecracks and killer smiles, St. Petersburg Times, Jan. 10, 1992, at 13, his eyebrows, Ottawa Citizen, Jan. 10, 1992, at E2, his sneers, Boston Globe, July 26, 1991, at 37, his menacing presence, USA Today, June 26, 1991, at 1D, and his sing-song voice, Gannett News Service, Aug. 27, 1990 (or, some say, his insinuating drawl, L.A. Times, Aug. 22, 1990, at F5). That's a whole lot more than White and the robot had in common.

property system; it is the system's very essence. Intellectual property law assures authors the right to their original expression, but encourages others to build freely on the ideas that underlie it. This result is neither unfair nor unfortunate: It is the means by which intellectual property law advances the progress of science and art. We give authors certain exclusive rights, but in exchange we get a richer public domain. The majority ignores this wise teaching, and all of us are the poorer for it.[23] ...

[Parts IV and V of Judge Kozinski's opinion, discussing possible preemption of the right of publicity by the Copyright Act, are omitted. Preemption is discussed in Chapter X.]

VI

Finally, I can't see how giving White the power to keep others from evoking her image in the public's mind can be squared with the First Amendment. Where does White get this right to control our thoughts? The majority's creation goes way beyond the protection given a trademark or a copyrighted work, or a person's name or likeness. All those things control one particular way of expressing an idea, one way of referring to an object or a person. But not allowing *any* means of reminding people of someone? That's a speech restriction unparalleled in First Amendment law.[28]

What's more, I doubt even a name-and-likeness-only right of publicity can stand without a parody exception. The First Amendment isn't just about religion or politics—it's also about protecting the free development of our national culture. Parody, humor, irreverence are all vital components of the marketplace of ideas. The last thing we need, the last thing the First Amendment will tolerate, is a law that lets public figures keep people from mocking them, or from "evok[ing]" their images in the mind of the public.

The majority dismisses the First Amendment issue out of hand because Samsung's ad was commercial speech. So what? Commercial speech may be less protected by the First Amendment than noncommercial speech, but less protected means protected nonetheless. *Central Hudson Gas & Elec. Corp. v. Public Serv. Comm'n*, 447 U.S. 557 (1980). And there are very good reasons for this. Commercial speech has a profound effect on our culture and our attitudes. Neutral-seeming ads influence people's social and political attitudes, and themselves arouse political controversy. "Where's the Beef?" turned from an advertising catchphrase into the only really memorable thing about the 1984 presidential campaign. Four years later, Michael Dukakis called George Bush "the Joe Isuzu of American politics."

In our pop culture, where salesmanship must be entertaining and entertainment must sell, the line between the commercial and noncommercial has not merely blurred; it has

---

23. The majority opinion has already earned some well-deserved criticisms on this score. Stephen R. Barnett, *In Hollywood's Wheel of Fortune, Free Speech Loses a Turn*, Wall St. J., Sept. 28, 1992, at A14; Stephen R. Barnett, *Wheel of Misfortune for Advertisers: Ninth Circuit Misreads the Law to Protect Vanna White's Image*, L.A. Daily J., Oct. 5, 1992, at 6; Felix H. Kent, *California Court Expands Celebrities' Rights*, N.Y.L.J., Oct. 30, 1992, at 3 ("To speak of the 'evisceration' of such a questionable common law right in a case that has probably gone the farthest of any case in any court in the United States of America is more than difficult to comprehend")....

28. Just compare the majority's holding to the intellectual property laws upheld by the Supreme Court. The Copyright Act is constitutional precisely because of the fair-use doctrine and the idea-expression dichotomy, two features conspicuously absent from the majority's doctrine. The right of publicity at issue in *Zacchini v. Scripps-Howard Broadcasting Co.*, 433 U.S. 562, 576 (1977) was only the right to "broadcast of petitioner's entire performance," not "the unauthorized use of another's name for purposes of trade." Even the statute upheld in *San Francisco Arts & Athletics, Inc. v. United States Olympic Comm.*, 483 U.S. 522, 530 (1987), which gave the USOC sweeping rights in the word "Olympic," didn't purport to protect all expression that reminded people of the Olympics.

disappeared. Is the Samsung parody any different from a parody on Saturday Night Live or in Spy Magazine? Both are equally profit-motivated. Both use a celebrity's identity to sell things—one to sell VCRs, the other to sell advertising. Both mock their subjects. Both try to make people laugh. Both add something, perhaps something worthwhile and memorable, perhaps not, to our culture. Both are things that the people being portrayed might dearly want to suppress.

Commercial speech is a significant, valuable part of our national discourse. The Supreme Court has recognized as much, and has insisted that lower courts carefully scrutinize commercial speech restrictions, but the panel totally fails to do this. The panel majority doesn't even purport to apply the *Central Hudson* test, which the Supreme Court devised specifically for determining whether a commercial speech restriction is valid. The majority doesn't ask, as *Central Hudson* requires, whether the speech restriction is justified by a substantial state interest. It doesn't ask whether the restriction directly advances the interest. It doesn't ask whether the restriction is narrowly tailored to the interest. These are all things the Supreme Court told us—in no uncertain terms—we must consider; the majority opinion doesn't even mention them.

Maybe applying the test would have convinced the majority to change its mind; maybe going through the factors would have shown that its rule was too broad, or the reasons for protecting White's "identity" too tenuous. Maybe not. But we shouldn't thumb our nose at the Supreme Court by just refusing to apply its test.

VII

For better or worse, we *are* the Court of Appeals for the Hollywood Circuit. Millions of people toil in the shadow of the law we make, and much of their livelihood is made possible by the existence of intellectual property rights. But much of their livelihood— and much of the vibrancy of our culture—also depends on the existence of other intangible rights: The right to draw ideas from a rich and varied public domain, and the right to mock, for profit as well as fun, the cultural icons of our time.

In the name of avoiding the "evisceration" of a celebrity's rights in her image, the majority diminishes the rights of copyright holders and the public at large. In the name of fostering creativity, the majority suppresses it. Vanna White and those like her have been given something they never had before, and they've been given it at our expense. I cannot agree.

APPENDIX

[See Figures 8-3 and 8-4.]

Notes and Questions

1. In Chapter III, we discussed another "robotic" case, *Wendt v. Host International, Inc.*, 125 F.3d 806 (9th Cir. 1997) (animatronic robots in an airport bar violated the rights of publicity of the actors who portrayed those characters in the television show "Cheers"). Judge Kozinski also wanted the full circuit to hear that case, but, as here, the request was denied. 197 F.3d 1284 (9th Cir. 1999) (Kozinski, J., dissenting from denial of rehearing *en banc*). Judge Kozinski's opinion in *Wendt* is reprinted in Chapter X.

2. Some of the problems raised by Judge Kozinski—that celebrities may be able to preclude others from playing roles identified with them—are analogous to the problems

Figure 8-3. Vanna White

discussed in Chapter III regarding publicity rights in characters. You may wish to review those cases in connection with your study of the cases in this section. This does, however, bring up a larger question: To what extent is Judge Kozinski's dissent related to the parodic nature of the advertisement, and to what extent is he making a larger argument about the proper scope of protection for celebrities?

3. In his dissent in *White*, Judge Kozinski writes the following:

> In our pop culture, where salesmanship must be entertaining and entertainment must sell, the line between the commercial and noncommercial has not merely blurred; it has disappeared. Is the Samsung parody any different from a parody on Saturday Night Live or in Spy Magazine? Both are equally profit-motivated. Both use a celebrity's identity to sell things—one to sell VCRs, the other to sell advertising.

Do you agree? Or is there something different about an advertisement that makes it more susceptible to liability using rights of publicity?

Figure 8-4. Ms. C3PO?

4. Judge Kozinski makes a distinction between Samsung's use of a robot in its advertisement and the use of an actual "likeness" of Vanna White. Can you explain why this would have made a difference (assuming that Samsung used the same caption: "Longest running game show 2012 A.D.")? Is there something different about using a device that "evokes" a famous personality as opposed to using that person's name or likeness?

5. Compare this case to *Pacific Dunlop Ltd. v. Hogan*, the Australian case in Chapter III (about a parody of the Crocodile Dundee character used in a shoe commercial). How do you think that the panel majority, Judge Alarcon, and Judge Kozinski would view that case?

6. In addition to a right of publicity claim under California common law, White asserted a claim for false endorsement under §43(a) of the Lanham Act (and the court allowed that claim to go forward). As we saw in Chapter V, a claim of false endorsement requires the plaintiff to show that consumers would be likely to be confused about whether

the celebrity had endorsed (or was otherwise connected with) the product in question. No such confusion is required for a right of publicity claim. Does the existence of the Lanham Act claim change the analysis? Does it make a difference that at least one of the celebrities portrayed in the Samsung advertisements (Morton Downey, Jr.) consented to the use of his "image" (and apparently was paid for his consent)? *Should* that make a difference?

7. Judge Kozinski's opinion only makes passing reference to the Lanham Act. Do you think he believes that White has a valid Lanham Act claim on these facts?

8. Recall from our discussion of *ETW* earlier in this chapter that several courts (including the Ninth Circuit) have adopted the Second Circuit's analysis in *Rogers v. Grimaldi* for determining whether a use of the celebrity's name or image is protected by the First Amendment against a Lanham Act claim. Does the *Rogers* test have any relevance here?

9. If a humor magazine (such as Mad Magazine) had run a fake advertisement for electronic consumer goods featuring the identical robotic caricature of Vanna White (in the same Wheel of Fortune setting, with the same caption), do you think that the panel majority would have allowed her to proceed with her claim? If not, how is that situation different from the one presented in the actual case? Alternatively, suppose that the publishers of Mad Magazine sold a series of posters, each intended as a parody of a celebrity. One of the posters contained the robot in front of the Wheel of Fortune set that was at issue in *White*. Would that have been actionable under the panel majority's reasoning?

10. Judge Kozinski takes the panel majority to task for, among other things, not applying the Supreme Court's commercial speech test to the situation in *White*. As he relates in his opinion, the test requires a showing of a substantial governmental interest favoring the restriction, and a showing that the restriction directly advances that interest. If the majority had applied that test to the Vanna White advertisement, would that have changed its result?

Cardtoons, L.C. v. Major League Baseball Players Association
95 F.3d 959 (10th Cir. 1996)

Tacha, Circuit Judge:

Cardtoons, L.C., ("Cardtoons") brought this action to obtain a declaratory judgment that its parody trading cards featuring active major league baseball players do not infringe on the publicity rights of members of the Major League Baseball Players Association ("MLBPA"). The district court held that the trading cards constitute expression protected by the First Amendment and therefore read a parody exception into Oklahoma's statutory right of publicity. MLBPA appeals, arguing that (1) the district court lacked jurisdiction to issue a declaratory judgment and (2) Cardtoons does not have a First Amendment right to market its trading cards. We exercise jurisdiction pursuant to 28 U.S.C. § 1291. Because Cardtoons' First Amendment right to free expression outweighs MLBPA's proprietary right of publicity, we affirm.

I. Background

Cardtoons formed in late 1992 to produce parody trading cards featuring caricatures of major league baseball players. Cardtoons contracted with a political cartoonist, a sports artist, and a sports author and journalist, who designed a set of 130 cards. The majority of the cards, 71, have caricatures of active major league baseball players on the front and humorous commentary about their careers on the back. The balance of the set is comprised of 20 "Big Bang Bucks" cards (cartoon drawings of currency with caricatures of the most highly paid players on the front, yearly salary statistics on the back), 10 "Spectra" cards (caricatures of active players on the front, nothing on the back), 10 retired player cards (caricatures of retired players on the front, humorous commentary about their careers on the back), 11 "Politics in Baseball" cards (cartoons featuring caricatures of political and sports figures on the front, humorous text on the back), 7 standing cards (caricatures of team logos on the front, humorous text on the back), and 1 checklist card. Except for the Spectra cards, the back of each card bears the Cardtoons logo and the following statement: "Cardtoons baseball is a parody and is NOT licensed by Major League Baseball Properties or Major League Baseball Players Association."

A person reasonably familiar with baseball can readily identify the players lampooned on the parody trading cards. The cards use similar names, recognizable caricatures, distinctive team colors, and commentary about individual players. For example, the card parodying San Francisco Giants' outfielder Barry Bonds calls him "Treasury Bonds," and features a recognizable caricature of Bonds, complete with earring, tipping a bat boy for a 24 carat gold "Fort Knoxville Slugger." The back of the card has a team logo (the "Gents"), and the following text:

Redemption qualities and why Treasury Bonds is the league's most valuable player:

1. Having Bonds on your team is like having money in the bank.

2. He plays so hard he gives 110 percent, compounded daily.

3. He turned down the chance to play other sports because he has a high interest rate in baseball.

4. He deposits the ball in the bleachers.

5. He is into male bonding.

6. He is a money player.

7. He has a 24-karat Gold Glove.

8. He always cashes in on the payoff pitch.

NOTICE: Bonds is not tax-free in all states but is double exempt. [See Figures 8-5 and 8-6.]

At the end of the 1992 season, Barry Bonds was a two-time winner of the National League's Most Valuable Player award, a three-time winner of a Gold Glove award, and had just signed a six-year contract for $43.75 million, making him the highest-paid player in baseball. No one the least bit familiar with the game of baseball would mistake Cardtoons' "Treasury Bonds" for anyone other than the Giants' Barry Bonds. Other caricatures, such as "Ken Spiffy, Jr." of the "Mari-Nerds" (Ken Griffey, Jr., of the Seattle Mariners), are equally identifiable.

The trading cards ridicule the players using a variety of themes. A number of the cards, including the "Treasury Bonds" card and all of the Big Bang Bucks cards, humorously criticize players for their substantial salaries. (The irony of MLBPA's counterclaim for profits from the cards is not lost on this panel.) Other trading cards mock the players' narcissism, as exemplified by the card featuring "Egotisticky Henderson" of the "Pathetics," parodying Ricky Henderson, then of the Oakland Athletics. The card features a caricature of Henderson raising his finger in a "number one" sign while patting himself on the back, with the following text:

Egotisticky Henderson, accepting the "Me-Me Award" from himself at the annual "Egotisticky Henderson Fan Club" banquet, sponsored by Egotisticky Henderson:

"I would just like to thank myself for all I have done. (Pause for cheers.) I am the greatest of all time. (Raise arms triumphantly.) I love myself. (Pause for more cheers.)

Figure 8-5. Front of "Treasury Bonds" card

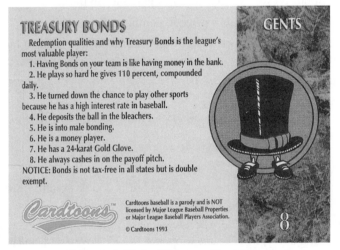

Figure 8-6. Back of "Treasury Bonds" card

I am honored to know me. (Pause for louder cheers.) I wish there were two of me so I could spend more time with myself. (Wipe tears from eyes.) I couldn't have done it without me. (Remove cap and hold it aloft.) It's friends like me that keep me going. (Wave to crowd and acknowledge standing ovation.)

The remainder of the cards poke fun at things such as the players' names ("Chili Dog Davis" who "plays the game with relish," a parody of designated hitter Chili Davis), physical characteristics ("Cloud Johnson," a parody of six-foot-ten-inch pitcher Randy Johnson), and onfield behavior (a backflipping "Ozzie Myth," a parody of shortstop Ozzie Smith).

The format of the parody trading cards is similar to that of traditional baseball cards. The cards, printed on cardboard stock measuring 2 1/2 by 3 1/2 inches, have images of players on the front and player information on the back. Like traditional cards, the parody cards use a variety of special effects, including foil embossing, stamping, spectra etching, and U-V coating. Cardtoons also takes advantage of a number of trading card industry techniques to enhance the value of its cards, such as limiting production, serially numbering cases of the cards, and randomly inserting subsets and "chase cards" (special trading cards) into the sets.

After designing its trading cards, Cardtoons contracted with a printer (Champs Marketing, Inc.) and distributor (TCM Associates) and implemented a marketing plan. As part of that plan, Cardtoons placed an advertisement in the May 14, 1993, issue of Sports Collectors Digest. That advertisement tipped off MLBPA, the defendant in this action, and prompted its attorney to write cease and desist letters to both Cardtoons and Champs.

MLBPA is the exclusive collective bargaining agent for all active major league baseball players, and operates a group licensing program in which it acts as the assignee of the individual publicity rights of all active players. Since 1966, MLBPA has entered into group licensing arrangements for a variety of products, such as candy bars, cookies, cereals, and, most importantly, baseball trading cards, which generate over seventy percent of its licensing revenue. MLBPA receives royalties from these sales and distributes the money to individual players.

After receiving the cease and desist letter from MLBPA, Champs advised Cardtoons that it would not print the parody cards until a court of competent jurisdiction had determined that the cards did not violate MLBPA's rights. Cardtoons then filed this suit seeking a declaratory judgment that its cards do not violate the publicity or other property rights of MLBPA or its members. MLBPA moved to dismiss for lack of subject matter jurisdiction, and counterclaimed for a declaratory judgment, injunction, and damages for violation of its members' rights of publicity under Oklahoma law.

The district court ... held that a fair use analysis requires recognition of a parody exception to the Oklahoma publicity rights statute, and issued a declaratory judgment in favor of Cardtoons. This appeal followed....

III. The Merits

Cardtoons asks for a declaration that it can distribute its parody trading cards without the consent of MLBPA. There are three steps to our analysis of this issue. First, we determine whether the cards infringe upon MLBPA's property rights as established by either the Lanham Act or Oklahoma's right of publicity statute. If so, we then ascertain whether the cards are protected by the First Amendment. Finally, if both parties have cognizable rights at stake, we proceed to a final determination of the relative importance of those rights in the context of this case.

A. MLBPA's Property Rights

1. The Lanham Act

We begin by determining whether the cards violate MLBPA's property rights under the Lanham Act.

The hallmark of a Lanham Act suit is proof of the likelihood of confusion....

The district court found that Cardtoons' parody cards created no likelihood of confusion. We agree that no one would mistake MLBPA and its members as anything other than the targets of the parody cards. Most of the cards have a Cardtoons logo and a statement that they are not licensed by MLBPA. In addition, as with all successful parodies, the effect of the cards is to amuse rather than confuse.... Cardtoons' success depends upon the humorous association of its parody cards with traditional, licensed baseball cards, not upon public confusion as to the source of the cards. The district court's decision that the parody cards do not create a likelihood of confusion is not clearly erroneous, and thus the cards do not infringe upon MLBPA's property rights under the Lanham Act.

2. The Right of Publicity

... Publicity rights ... are a form of property protection that allows people to profit from the full commercial value of their identities.

Oklahoma first recognized the right of publicity as early as 1965, but expanded the right in a 1985 statute that is virtually identical to California's right of publicity statute, Cal. Civ. Code §§ 990 and 3344. ... Thus, a civil suit for infringement of MLBPA's publicity right under [Okla. Stat. tit. 12,] § 1449(A) requires proof of three elements: (1) knowing use of player names or likenesses (2) on products, merchandise, or goods (3) without MLBPA's prior consent. If MLBPA proves these three elements, then the burden shifts to Cardtoons to raise a valid defense.

There is little question that Cardtoons knowingly uses the names and likenesses of major league baseball players [without their consent].... Cardtoons' parody cards, then, do infringe upon MLBPA's publicity right as defined in § 1449(A).

The Oklahoma publicity statute contains two exceptions designed to accommodate the First Amendment. The first, a "news" exception, exempts use of a person's identity in connection with any news, public affairs, or sports broadcast or account, or any political campaign, from the dictates of the statute. Okla. Stat. tit. 12, § 1449(D). The second exception, roughly analogous to the First Amendment concept of "incidental use," exempts use in a commercial medium that is not directly connected with commercial sponsorship or paid advertising. Okla. Stat. tit. 12, § 1449(F). The news and incidental use exceptions, however, provide no haven for Cardtoons. Cardtoons' commercial venture is not in connection with any news account. Moreover, the company's use of player likenesses is directly connected with a proposed commercial endeavor; indeed, the players were specifically selected for their wide market appeal. Thus, notwithstanding any First Amendment defense, Cardtoons' use of player likenesses on its cards violates the Oklahoma statute and infringes upon the property rights of MLBPA.

B. Cardtoons' First Amendment Right

Because the parody trading cards infringe upon MLBPA's property rights, we must consider whether Cardtoons has a countervailing First Amendment right to publish the cards. The First Amendment only protects speech from regulation by the government. Although this is a civil action between private parties, it involves application of a state statute that Cardtoons claims imposes restrictions on its right of free expression. Application of that statute thus satisfies the state action requirement of Cardtoons' First Amendment claim.

Cardtoons' parody trading cards receive full protection under the First Amendment. The cards provide social commentary on public figures, major league baseball players, who are involved in a significant commercial enterprise, major league baseball. While not core political speech (the cards do not, for example, adopt a position on the Ken Griffey, Jr., for President campaign), this type of commentary on an important social institution constitutes protected expression.

The cards are no less protected because they provide humorous rather than serious commentary. Speech that entertains, like speech that informs, is protected by the First Amendment because "[t]he line between the informing and the entertaining is too elusive for the protection of that basic right." *Winters v. New York,* 333 U.S. 507, 510 (1948). Moreover, Cardtoons makes use of artistic and literary devices with distinguished traditions. Parody, for example, is a humorous form of social commentary that dates to Greek antiquity, and has since made regular appearances in English literature. In addition, cartoons and caricatures, such as those in the trading cards, have played a prominent role in public and political debate throughout our nation's history. Thus, the trading cards' commentary on these public figures and the major commercial enterprise in which they work receives no less protection because the cards are amusing.

MLBPA contends that Cardtoons' speech receives less protection because it fails to use a traditional medium of expression. The protections afforded by the First Amendment, however, have never been limited to newspapers and books. Thus, even if the trading cards are not a traditional medium of expression, they nonetheless contain protected speech.

Moreover, even if less common mediums of expression were to receive less First Amendment protection (perhaps out of concern for whether they contain any expression at all), trading cards do not fall into that category. Baseball cards have been an important means of informing the public about baseball players for over a century. In addition, non-sports trading cards have also been an important medium for disseminating information. Some recent examples feature topics such as saints, Norman Rockwell paintings, presidential candidates, the rise and fall of the Soviet Union, local police officers, and Rodney King. All of these trading cards, regardless of their topic, convey information about their subject and therefore constitute an important means of expression that deserves First Amendment protection.

MLBPA also maintains that the parody trading cards are commercial merchandise rather than protected speech. However, we see no principled distinction between speech and merchandise that informs our First Amendment analysis. The fact that expressive materials are sold neither renders the speech unprotected, nor alters the level of protection under the First Amendment. Cardtoons need not give away its trading cards in order to bring them within the ambit of the First Amendment.

MLBPA further argues that the parody cards are commercial speech and should therefore receive less protection under the First Amendment. The Supreme Court has defined commercial speech as "expression related solely to the economic interests of the speaker and its audience." *Central Hudson Gas & Elec. Corp. v. Public Serv. Comm'n,* 447 U.S. 557, 561 (1980). Speech that does no more than propose a commercial transaction, for example, is commercial speech. Thus, commercial speech is best understood as speech that merely advertises a product or service for business purposes. As such, commercial speech may receive something less than the strict review afforded other types of speech.

Cardtoons' trading cards, however, are not commercial speech—they do not merely advertise another unrelated product. Although the cards are sold in the marketplace, they are not transformed into commercial speech merely because they are sold for profit. Contrary to MLBPA's argument, therefore, the cards are unlike the parody in the only other circuit court decision addressing the constitutional tensions inherent in a celebrity parody, *White v. Samsung Electronics America, Inc.,* 971 F.2d 1395 (9th Cir.), *cert. denied,* 508 U.S. 951 (1992). We disagree with the result in that case for reasons discussed in the two dissents that it engendered. Moreover, our case is distinguished by the fact that the speech involved is not commercial, but rather speech subject to full First Amendment protection. *White,* therefore, is inapposite, and we must directly confront the central problem in this case: whether Cardtoons' First Amendment right trumps MLBPA's property right.

C. Balancing Free Speech Rights with Property Rights

In resolving the tension between the First Amendment and publicity rights in this case, we find little guidance in cases involving parodies of other forms of intellectual property.

Trademark and copyright, for example, have built-in mechanisms that serve to avoid First Amendment concerns of this kind. As discussed above, proof of trademark infringement under the Lanham Act requires proof of a likelihood of confusion, but, in the case of a good trademark parody, there is little likelihood of confusion, since the humor lies in the difference between the original and the parody. ... Oklahoma's right of publicity statute, however, does not provide a similar accommodation for parody, and we must therefore confront the First Amendment issue directly.

MLBPA urges us to adopt the framework established in *Lloyd Corp. v. Tanner*, 407 U.S. 551 (1972), in order to reconcile the free speech and property rights at stake in this case. The issue in *Lloyd* was whether a private shopping center could prevent the distribution of handbills on its premises. The Court focused on the availability of "adequate alternative avenues of communication." *Id.* at 567. The Court held that the First Amendment did not require the shopping center to allow distribution of the handbills because the public side-walks and streets surrounding the center provided an adequate alternative avenue of communication. *Id.* at 567–68. This type of analysis, usually applied to time, place, and manner restrictions, has also been applied in several cases where intellectual property rights have conflicted with the right to free expression. *E.g., Mutual of Omaha Ins. Co. v. Novak*, 836 F.2d 397, 402–03 (8th Cir. 1987) (holding that "Mutant of Omaha," a parody of Mutual of Omaha's logo, constitutes trademark infringement), *cert. denied*, 488 U.S. 933 (1988).

MLBPA argues that application of the *Lloyd* analysis requires protection of its propri-etary right of publicity. First, MLBPA maintains that there are many ways that Cardtoons could parody the institution of baseball that would not require use of player names and likenesses. Cardtoons could, for example, use generic images of baseball players to poke fun at the game. Second, MLBPA contends that Cardtoons could use recognizable play-ers in a format other than trading cards, such as a newspaper or magazine, without in-fringing on its right of publicity. MLBPA argues that these alternative means of communication are adequate and, therefore, that we may uphold its property rights with-out seriously infringing upon Cardtoons' right to free expression.

We find, however, that in the context of intellectual property, *Lloyd's* "no adequate alter-native avenues" test does not sufficiently accommodate the public's interest in free expression. *See Rogers v. Grimaldi*, 975 F.2d 994, 999 (2d Cir. 1989); *Mutual of Omaha Ins. Co.*, 836 F.2d at 405–06 (Heaney, J., dissenting). Intellectual property, unlike real estate, includes the words, images, and sounds that we use to communicate, and "we cannot indulge in the facile assumption that one can forbid particular words without also running a substantial risk of suppressing ideas in the process," *Cohen [v. California]*, 403 U.S. [15,] 26 [(1971)]; *see San Francisco Arts & Athletics [v. United States Olympic Committee]*, 483 U.S. [522 (1987)] at 569–70 (Brennan, J., dissenting). Restrictions on the words or images that may be used by a speaker, therefore, are quite different than restrictions on the time, place, or manner of speech.

In this case, Cardtoons' expression requires use of player identities because, in addi-tion to parodying the institution of baseball, the cards also lampoon individual players. Further, Cardtoons' use of the trading card format is an essential component of the par-ody because baseball cards have traditionally been used to celebrate baseball players and their accomplishments. Cardtoons expresses ideas through the use of major league base-ball player identities, and MLBPA's attempts to enjoin the parody thus goes to the con-tent of the speech, not merely to its time, place, or manner. For that reason, the *Lloyd* test is inapplicable in this case.

This case instead requires us to directly balance the magnitude of the speech restric-tion against the asserted governmental interest in protecting the intellectual property right. We thus begin our analysis by examining the importance of Cardtoons' right to free expression and the consequences of limiting that right. We then weigh those consequences against the effect of infringing on MLBPA's right of publicity.

1. The Effect of Infringing Upon Cardtoons' Right to Free Speech

Cardtoons' interest in publishing its parody trading cards implicates some of the core concerns of the First Amendment. "Parodies and caricatures," noted Aldous Huxley, "are the most penetrating of criticisms." A parodist can, with deft and wit, readily expose the foolish and absurd in society. Parody is also a valuable form of self-expression that allows artists to shed light on earlier works and, at the same time, create new ones. Thus, parody, both as social criticism and a means of self-expression, is a vital commodity in the marketplace of ideas.

Parodies of celebrities are an especially valuable means of expression because of the role celebrities play in modern society. As one commentator explained, celebrities are "common points of reference for millions of individuals who may never interact with one another, but who share, by virtue of their participation in a mediated culture, a common experience and a collective memory." John B. Thompson, *Ideology and Modern Culture: Critical Social Theory in the Era of Mass Communication* 163 (1990). Through their pervasive presence in the media, sports and entertainment celebrities come to symbolize certain ideas and values. ...

Because celebrities are an important part of our public vocabulary, a parody of a celebrity does not merely lampoon the celebrity, but exposes the weakness of the idea or value that the celebrity symbolizes in society. Cardtoons' trading cards, for example, comment on the state of major league baseball by turning images of our sports heroes into modern-day personifications of avarice. In order to effectively criticize society, parodists need access to images that mean something to people, and thus celebrity parodies are a valuable communicative resource. Restricting the use of celebrity identities restricts the communication of ideas.

Without First Amendment protection, Cardtoons' trading cards and their irreverent commentary on the national pastime cannot be freely distributed to the public. Instead, as required by Oklahoma law, the production and distribution of the cards would be subject to MLBPA's consent. The problem with this scheme, as the Supreme Court noted in the context of copyright parody, is that "the unlikelihood that creators of imaginative works will license critical reviews or lampoons of their own productions removes such uses from the very notion of a potential licensing market." *Campbell* [*v. Acuff-Rose Music, Inc.*], 510 U.S. [569, 592 (1994)]. The potential for suppression is even greater in the context of publicity rights because the product involved is the celebrity's own persona. Indeed, the director of licensing for MLBPA testified that MLBPA would never license a parody which poked fun at the players. Thus, elevating the right of publicity above the right to free expression would likely prevent distribution of the parody trading cards. This would not only allow MLBPA to censor criticism of its members, but would also have a chilling effect upon future celebrity parodies. ...

2. The Effect of Infringing Upon MLBPA's Right of Publicity

We now turn to an evaluation of society's interest in protecting MLBPA's publicity right. The justifications offered for the right of publicity fall into two categories, economic and noneconomic. The right is thought to further economic goals such as stimulating athletic and artistic achievement, promoting the efficient allocation of resources, and protecting consumers. In addition, the right of publicity is said to protect various noneconomic interests, such as safeguarding natural rights, securing the fruits of celebrity labors, preventing unjust enrichment, and averting emotional harm. We examine the applicability of each of these justifications to the facts of this case.

The principal economic argument made in support of the right of publicity is that it provides an incentive for creativity and achievement. Under this view, publicity rights induce people to expend the time, effort, and resources to develop the talents prerequisite to public recognition. While those talents provide immediate benefit to those with commercially valuable identities, the products of their enterprise—such as movies, songs, and sporting events—ultimately benefit society as a whole. Thus, it is argued, society has an interest in a right of publicity that is closely analogous to its interest in other intellectual property protections such as copyright and patent law. *Zacchini*, 433 U.S. at 576.

This incentives argument is certainly a compelling justification for other forms of intellectual property. Copyright law, for example, protects the primary, if not only, source of a writer's income, and thus provides a significant incentive for creativity and achievement. The incentive effect of publicity rights, however, has been overstated. Most sports and entertainment celebrities with commercially valuable identities engage in activities that themselves generate a significant amount of income; the commercial value of their identities is merely a by-product of their performance values. Although no one pays to watch Cormac McCarthy write a novel, many people pay a lot of money to watch Demi Moore "act" and Michael Jordan play basketball. Thus, the analogy to the incentive effect of other intellectual property protections is strained because "[a]bolition of the right of publicity would leave entirely unimpaired a celebrity's ability to earn a living from the activities that have generated his commercially marketable fame." [Michael] Madow, [*Private Ownership of Public Image: Popular Culture and Publicity Rights*, 81 Cal. L. Rev. 127,] 209 [(1993)].

This distinction between the value of a person's identity and the value of his performance explains why *Zacchini*, the Supreme Court's sole case involving a right of publicity claim, is a red herring. Hugo Zacchini, a performer in a human cannonball act, brought an action against a television station to recover damages he suffered when the station videotaped and broadcast his entire performance. The Supreme Court held that the First Amendment did not give the station the right to broadcast Zacchini's entire act in contravention of his state protected right of publicity. Zacchini, however, complained of the appropriation of the economic value of his *performance,* not the economic value of his *identity.* The Court's incentive rationale is obviously more compelling in a right of performance case than in a more typical right of publicity case involving the appropriation of a celebrity's identity.

Moreover, the additional inducement for achievement produced by publicity rights are often inconsequential because most celebrities with valuable commercial identities are already handsomely compensated. Actor Jim Carrey, for example, received twenty million dollars for starring in the movie *The Cable Guy,* and major league baseball players' salaries currently average over one million dollars per year. Such figures suggest that "even without the right of publicity the rate of return to stardom in the entertainment and sports fields is probably high enough to bring forth a more than 'adequate' supply of creative effort and achievement." Madow, *supra,* at 210. In addition, even in the absence of publicity rights, celebrities would still be able to reap financial reward from authorized appearances and endorsements. The extra income generated by licensing one's identity does not provide a necessary inducement to enter and achieve in the realm of sports and entertainment. Thus, while publicity rights may provide some incentive for creativity and achievement, the magnitude and importance of that incentive has been exaggerated.

The argument that publicity rights provide valuable incentives is even less compelling in the context of celebrity parodies. Since celebrities will seldom give permission for their identities to be parodied, granting them control over the parodic use of their identities would not directly provide them with any additional income. It would, instead, only allow them to shield themselves from ridicule and criticism. The only economic incentive gained by having control over the use of one's identity in parody is control over the potential effect the parody would have on the market for nonparodic use of one's identity. MLBPA claims, for example, that publication of the parody cards will decrease demand for traditional baseball cards because Cardtoons and other makers of parody trading cards would compete with manufacturers of licensed cards in the same limited trading card market. Parody, however, rarely acts as a market substitute for the original, and there is no evidence in this record that convinces us otherwise. Even if there is some substitutive effect, and card collectors with limited resources decide to buy parody cards instead of traditional, licensed cards, the small amount of additional income generated by suppressing parody cards will have little, if any, effect on the incentive to become a major league baseball player.

The incentives argument would be even more tenuous, indeed perverse, if good-humored celebrities were to license use of their identities for parody. The right of publicity would then provide an incentive to engage in the socially undesirable behavior that might give rise to a reason to parody. Although part of any parody's market appeal depends upon the prominence of the celebrity, the critical element of the parody's value hinges on the accuracy of the caricature or criticism. Society does not have a significant interest in allowing a celebrity to protect the type of reputation that gives rise to parody.

We recognize that publicity rights do provide some incentive to achieve in the fields of sports and entertainment. However, the inducements generated by publicity rights are not nearly as important as those created by copyright and patent law, and the small incentive effect of publicity rights is reduced or eliminated in the context of celebrity parodies. In sum, it is unlikely that little leaguers will stop dreaming of the big leagues or major leaguers will start "dogging it" to first base if MLBPA is denied the right to control the use of its members' identities in parody.

The second economic justification for the right of publicity is that it promotes the efficient allocation of resources, a version of the familiar tragedy of the commons argument used to prove the superiority of private property over common property. Without the artificial scarcity created by publicity rights, identities would be commercially exploited until the marginal value of each use is zero. [*Matthews v. Wozencraft*, 15 F.3d 432, 437–38 (5th Cir. 1994)]. "Creating artificial scarcity preserves the value to [the celebrity], to advertisers who contract for the use of his likeness, and in the end, to consumers, who receive information from the knowledge that he is being paid to endorse the product." *Id.* at 438. Giving people control of the commercial use of their identities, according to this analysis, maximizes the economic and informational value of those identities.

This efficiency argument is most persuasive in the context of advertising, where repeated use of a celebrity's likeness to sell products may eventually diminish its commercial value. The argument is not as persuasive, however, when applied to nonadvertising uses. It is not clear, for example, that the frequent appearance of a celebrity's likeness on t-shirts and coffee mugs will reduce its value; indeed, the value of the likeness may increase precisely because "everybody's got one." Madow, *supra*, at 222. Further, celebrities with control over the parodic use of their identities would not use the power to "ration the use of their names in order to maximize their value over time," *Matthews*, 15 F.3d at 438 n.2. They would instead use that power to suppress criticism, and thus permanently remove a valuable source of information about their identity from the marketplace.

The final economic argument offered for rights of publicity is that they protect against consumer deception. The Lanham Act, however, already provides nationwide protection against false or misleading representations in connection with the sale of products. Moreover, as discussed above, the use of celebrity names or likenesses in parodies in general, and in Cardtoons' trading cards in particular, are not likely to confuse or deceive consumers. Thus, this final economic justification has little merit.

There are also several noneconomic reasons advanced for the right of publicity. First, some believe that publicity rights stem from some notion of natural rights. McCarthy, for example, argues that a natural rights rationale, resting more upon "visceral impulses of 'fairness'" than upon reasoned argument, "seems quite sufficient to provide a firm support for the existence of a Right of Publicity." [1 J. Thomas] McCarthy, [THE RIGHTS OF PUBLICITY AND PRIVACY] § 2.1[A] [(1996)]. McCarthy, however, offers little reason for this assertion, and blind appeals to first principles carry no weight in our balancing analysis.

The second noneconomic justification is that publicity rights allow celebrities to enjoy the fruits of their labors. According to this argument, "[a] celebrity must be considered to have invested his years of practice and competition in a public personality which eventually may reach marketable status." *Uhlaender [v. Henricksen]*, 316 F. Supp. [1277,] 1282 [(D. Minn. 1970)]. People deserve the right to control and profit from the commercial value of their identities because, quite simply, they've earned it. Thus, in this view, the right of publicity is similar to the right of a commercial enterprise to profit from the goodwill it has built up in its name.

Celebrities, however, are often not fully responsible for their fame. Indeed, in the entertainment industry, a celebrity's fame may largely be the creation of the media or the audience. As one actor put it, "Only that audience out there makes a star. It's up to them. You can't do anything about it.... Stars would all be Louis B. Mayer's cousins if you could make 'em up." Jack Nicholson, *quoted in* Jib Fowles, *Starstruck: Celebrity Performers and the American Public* 84 (1992). Professional athletes may be more responsible for their celebrity status, however, because athletic success is fairly straightforwardly the result of an athlete's natural talent and dedication. Thus, baseball players may deserve to profit from the commercial value of their identities more than movie stars. Once again, however, the force of this justification is diminished in the case of parody, because there is little right to enjoy the fruits of socially undesirable behavior.

The third, related justification for publicity rights is the prevention of unjust enrichment. In this view, whether the commercial value of an identity is the result of a celebrity's hard work, media creation, or just pure dumb luck, no social purpose is served by allowing others to freely appropriate it. Cardtoons, however, is not merely hitching its wagon to a star. As in all celebrity parodies, Cardtoons added a significant creative component of its own to the celebrity identity and created an entirely new product. Indeed, allowing MLBPA to control or profit from the parody trading cards would actually sanction the theft of Cardtoons' creative enterprise.

A final justification offered for the right of publicity is that it prevents emotional injuries. For example, commercial misappropriation may greatly distress a celebrity who finds all commercial exploitation to be offensive. Even celebrities who crave public attention might find particular uses of their identities to be distressing. The right of publicity allows celebrities to avoid the emotional distress caused by unwanted commercial use of their identities. Publicity rights, however, are meant to protect against the loss of financial gain, not mental anguish. Laws preventing unfair competition, such as the Lanham Act, and laws prohibiting the intentional infliction of emotional distress adequately cover that ground. Moreover, fame is a double-edged sword—the law cannot allow those who enjoy the public limelight to so easily avoid the ridicule and criticism that sometimes accompany public prominence.

Thus, the noneconomic justifications for the right of publicity are no more compelling than the economic arguments. Those justifications further break down in the context of parody, where the right to profit from one's persona is reduced to the power to suppress criticism. In sum, the effect of limiting MLBPA's right of publicity in this case is negligible.

IV. Conclusion

One of the primary goals of intellectual property law is to maximize creative expression. The law attempts to achieve this goal by striking a proper balance between the right of a creator to the fruits of his labor and the right of future creators to free expression. Underprotection of intellectual property reduces the incentive to create; overprotection creates a monopoly over the raw material of creative expression. The application of the Oklahoma publicity rights statute to Cardtoons' trading cards presents a classic case of overprotection. Little is to be gained, and much lost, by protecting MLBPA's right to control the use of its members' identities in parody trading cards. The justifications for the right of publicity are not nearly as compelling as those offered for other forms of intellectual property, and are particularly unpersuasive in the case of celebrity parodies. The cards, on the other hand, are an important form of entertainment and social commentary that deserve First Amendment protection. Accordingly, we AFFIRM.

Notes and Questions

1. In this case, the right of publicity was a function of state law (Oklahoma, in this situation). The statute provided certain defenses designed to protect free speech; however, the court found them inapplicable. Therefore, it had to decide whether the First Amendment trumped plaintiffs' rights under the statute. Since this was a suit between private parties, the court had to determine whether there was the requisite "state action" for the application of the First Amendment. What was the state action involved in this case?

2. Both *Cardtoons* and *White* involved caricatures (one literal, one robotic) of well known individuals. Yet the courts came to opposite results regarding the First Amendment protection for the expression in question. Can the two cases be reconciled? If so, what are the major features distinguishing the two cases?

3. How much should context matter? In both cases, the object of the parody was clearly the individual. However, in one, the "commercial" context was said to outweigh the free speech values. Are there any circumstances in which "commercial" speech can also contain sufficient expressive content so as to outweigh the right of publicity involved? Or does the very nature of "commercial" speech mean it cannot carry that burden? *Cf. Louis Vuitton Malletier S.A. v. Haute Diggity Dog, LLC,* 507 F.3d 252 (4th Cir. 2007) (finding no likelihood of dilution of Louis Vuitton trademarks by "Chewy Vuiton" dog toys, despite the commercial nature of the use of plaintiff's trademarks).

4. The *Cardtoons* court cites various possible reasons to uphold rights of publicity, but rejects them all on the facts of this case. Do you agree that none of those possible justifications outweighs the free speech interests here? The court gives especially short shrift to non-economic justifications, such as the "visceral" one noted by Professor McCarthy in his treatise. In copyright, the concept of "moral rights" gives authors a certain level of control over the use of their creations by others, even trumping the rights

of the copyright owner (in the event that the author has transferred the copyright to someone). *See* Berne Convention For The Protection Of Literary And Artistic Works, Art. 6*bis*(1):

> Independently of the author's economic rights, and even after the transfer of the said rights, the author shall have the right to claim authorship of the work and to object to any distortion, mutilation or other modification of, or other derogatory action in relation to, the said work, which would be prejudicial to his honor or reputation.

Is this what Professor McCarthy had in mind? Should similar rights be granted to celebrities? What problems might this create? You should also know that, although the United States is a signatory to the Berne Convention, its implementation of Article 6*bis* is not as broad as the language seems to intend. *See* 17 U.S.C. § 106A (the Visual Artists Rights Act).

5. If MLBPA could show (by a survey, for example) that many people think that even a parody baseball card requires the consent of the player, would that have changed the result in this case? (Recall that the court rejected a Lanham Act claim.)

6. In the realm of copyright, parody is considered a "transformative" use, which often leads to a conclusion that the fair use defense of 17 U.S.C. § 107 will apply. *See Campbell v. Acuff-Rose Music, Inc.*, 510 U.S. 569, 579–83 (1994). However, some courts have distinguished between parody, which spoofs the work in question, and satire, which makes a larger point without specifically targeting the work for criticism. *See Dr. Seuss Enterprises, L.P. v. Penguin Books USA, Inc.*, 109 F.3d 1394, 1400–01 (9th Cir. 1997); *see also* Tyler T. Ochoa, *Dr. Seuss, The Juice and Fair Use: How the Grinch Silenced a Parody*, 45 J. Copyr. Soc'y USA 546 (1998) (criticizing the distinction). Do you think that the distinction between parody and satire is relevant to the issue of the proper scope of rights of publicity? Some state right of publicity laws specifically exempt both parody and satire. *E.g.*, RCW § 63.60.070(1). The *Winter* case below also contains a brief discussion of this issue.

7. Suppose someone had written a fictional novel about baseball, in which the writer included various well-known players as characters. If the players (and/or MLBPA) sued, would the *Cardtoons* precedent prevent plaintiffs from recovering?

8. Suppose that Marvel Comics decided to come out with a special comic book issue, in which one of its superheroes (say, Spiderman) defeats an evil superhuman baseball player, transformed into a superpowered villain by nasty chemicals. The villain is loosely (and identifiably) based on Boston Red Sox pitcher Jonathan Papelbon. Would *Cardtoons* preclude recovery? You may wish to return to this question after considering the next two cases.

Winter v. DC Comics

30 Cal. 4th 881, 69 P.3d 473, 134 Cal. Rptr. 2d 634 (2003)

CHIN, J.:

... In this case, we apply the same balancing test [as in *Comedy III Productions v. Gary Sadrup, Inc.*] to comic books containing characters that evoke musician brothers Johnny and Edgar Winter. We conclude that, in contrast to a drawing of the Three Stooges, the comic books do contain significant creative elements that transform them into something more than mere celebrity likenesses. Accordingly, the comic books are entitled to First Amendment protection.

I. FACTS AND PROCEDURAL HISTORY

In the 1990's, DC Comics published a five-volume comic miniseries featuring "Jonah Hex," a fictional comic book "anti-hero." The series contains an outlandish plot, involving giant worm-like creatures, singing cowboys, and the "Wilde West Ranch and Music and Culture Emporium," named for and patterned after the life of Oscar Wilde. The third volume ends with a reference to two new characters, the "Autumn brothers," and the teaser, "Next: The Autumns of Our Discontent." The cover of volume 4 depicts the Autumn brother characters, with pale faces and long white hair. (See append., *post;* the Autumn brothers are the two lower figures.) One brother wears a stovepipe hat and red sunglasses, and holds a rifle. The second has red eyes and holds a pistol. This volume is entitled *Autumns of Our Discontent* and features brothers Johnny and Edgar Autumn, depicted as villainous half-worm, half-human offspring born from the rape of their mother by a supernatural worm creature that had escaped from a hole in the ground. At the end of volume 5, Jonah Hex and his companions shoot and kill the Autumn brothers in an underground gun battle.

Plaintiffs, Johnny and Edgar Winter, well-known performing and recording musicians originally from Texas, sued DC Comics and others alleging several causes of action including, as relevant here, appropriation of their names and likenesses under Civil Code section 3344. They alleged that the defendants selected the names Johnny and Edgar Autumn to signal readers the Winter brothers were being portrayed; that the Autumn brothers were drawn with long white hair and albino features similar to plaintiffs'; that the Johnny Autumn character was depicted as wearing a tall black top hat similar to the one Johnny Winter often wore; and that the title of volume 4, *Autumns of Our Discontent,* refers to the famous Shakespearian phrase, "the winter of our discontent." They also alleged that the comics falsely portrayed them as "vile, depraved, stupid, cowardly, subhuman individuals who engage in wanton acts of violence, murder and bestiality for pleasure and who should be killed."

Defendants moved for summary judgment, partly relying on the First Amendment. The trial court granted summary judgment on all causes of action and entered judgment in defendants' favor. The Court of Appeal originally affirmed the judgment.... [W]e remanded the matter for the Court of Appeal to reconsider its decision in light of *Comedy III.* This time, the Court of Appeal affirmed the summary adjudication of all causes of action other than the one for misappropriation of likeness. On the misappropriation cause of action, the court concluded that triable issues of fact exist whether or not the comic books are entitled to protection under the test in *Comedy III.* It reversed the judgment and remanded for further proceedings on that cause of action.

We granted the defendants' petition for review to determine whether the comic books are protected under the *Comedy III* transformative test.

II. DISCUSSION

... Application of the [*Saderup*] test to this case is not difficult. We have reviewed the comic books and attach a copy of a representative page. We can readily ascertain that they are not just conventional depictions of plaintiffs but contain significant expressive content other than plaintiffs' mere likenesses. Although the fictional characters Johnny and Edgar Autumn are less-than-subtle evocations of Johnny and Edgar Winter, the books do not depict plaintiffs literally. Instead, plaintiffs are merely part of the raw materials from which the comic books were synthesized. To the extent the drawings of the Autumn brothers resemble plaintiffs at all, they are distorted for purposes of lampoon, parody, or caricature. And the Autumn brothers are but cartoon characters—half-human and half-worm—in a larger story, which is itself quite expressive. The characters and their portrayals do not greatly threaten plaintiffs' right of publicity. Plaintiffs' fans who want to purchase pictures of them would find the drawings of the Autumn brothers unsatisfactory as a substitute for conventional depictions. The comic books are similar to the trading cards caricaturing and parodying prominent baseball players that have received First Amendment protection. [citing *Cardtoons*]

Citing *Dr. Seuss Enterprises L.P. v. Penguin Books* (9th Cir. 1997) 109 F.3d 1394, plaintiffs argue, and the Court of Appeal agreed, that the comic books do not technically qualify as parody of plaintiffs (although the Court of Appeal found they may qualify as parody of Jonah Hex). That case, however, involved alleged copyright and trademark infringement, allegations not involved here. *Comedy III* did not adopt copyright law wholesale. The distinction between parody and other forms of literary expression is irrelevant to the *Comedy III* transformative test. It does not matter what precise literary category the work falls into. What matters is whether the work is transformative, not whether it is parody or satire or caricature or serious social commentary or any other specific form of expression.

Plaintiffs also argue, and the Court of Appeal found, that the record contains evidence that defendants were trading on plaintiffs' likenesses and reputations to generate interest in the comic book series and increase sales. This, too, is irrelevant to whether the comic books are constitutionally protected. The question is whether a work is transformative, not how it is marketed. If the work is sufficiently transformative to receive legal protection, "it is of no moment that the advertisement may have increased the profitability of the [work]." *Guglielmi v. Spelling-Goldberg Productions* [(1979) 25 Cal. 3d 860] at p. 873, 160 Cal. Rptr. 352, 603 P.2d 454 (conc. opn. of Bird, C.J.).) If the challenged work is transformative, the way it is advertised cannot somehow make it nontransformative.[3]

Accordingly, we conclude that the Court of Appeal erred in finding the existence of triable issues of fact. "[B]ecause unnecessarily protracted litigation would have a chilling effect upon the exercise of First Amendment rights, speedy resolution of cases involving free speech is desirable." [Citation omitted.] As in *Comedy III, supra*, courts can often resolve the question as a matter of law simply by viewing the work in question and, if necessary, comparing it to an actual likeness of the person or persons portrayed. Because of these circumstances, an action presenting this issue is often properly resolved on summary judgment or, if the complaint includes the work in question, even demurrer. This is one of those cases.

III. CONCLUSION

The artist in *Comedy III* essentially sold, and devoted fans bought, pictures of the Three Stooges, not transformed expressive works by the artist. Here, by contrast, defendants essentially sold, and the buyers purchased, DC Comics depicting fanciful, creative characters, not pictures of the Winter brothers. This makes all the difference. The comic books here are entitled to First Amendment protection.

Accordingly, we reverse the judgment of the Court of Appeal and remand the matter for further proceedings consistent with our opinion.

---

3. Plaintiffs also claim that the way the comic books were advertised is itself actionable, for example, by falsely implying plaintiffs endorsed the product. This question is beyond the scope of our grant of review and the Court of Appeal's opinion, which focused on whether the comic books were constitutionally protected. We leave it to the Court of Appeal on remand to decide whether plaintiffs have preserved a cause of action based solely on the advertising and, if so, whether that cause of action is susceptible to summary adjudication.

APPENDIX

Figure 8-7. Volume 4 of *Jonah Hex*

Doe v. TCI Cablevision

110 S.W.3d 363 (Mo. 2003)

Stephen N. Limbaugh, Jr., Judge:

Appellant Anthony Twist, also known as Tony Twist, is a former professional hockey player in the National Hockey League. After learning of the existence of a comic book, titled *Spawn,* that contained a villainous character sharing his name, Twist brought misappropriation of name and defamation claims against respondents, the creators, publishers and marketers of *Spawn* and related promotional products. Respondents defended on First Amendment grounds. The circuit court dismissed the defamation count, but allowed the misappropriation of name count to go to trial, which resulted in a jury verdict in favor of Twist in the amount of $24,500,000. The circuit court, however, granted respondents' motion for judgment notwithstanding the verdict and, in the alternative, ordered a new trial in the event that its judgment notwithstanding the verdict was overturned on appeal. A request for injunctive relief was also denied. After appeal to the Court of Appeals, Eastern District, this Court granted transfer.

I.

Tony Twist began his NHL career in 1988 playing for the St. Louis Blues, later to be transferred to the Quebec Nordiques, only to return to St. Louis where he finished his career in 1999, due to injuries suffered in a motorcycle accident. During his hockey career, Twist became the League's preeminent "enforcer," a player whose chief responsibility was to protect goal scorers from physical assaults by opponents. In that role, Twist was notorious for his violent tactics on the ice. Describing Twist, a *Sports Illustrated* writer said: "It takes a special talent to stand on skates and beat someone senseless, and no one does it better than the St. Louis Blues left winger." Austin Murphy, *Fighting For A Living: St. Louis Blues Enforcer Tony Twist, Whose Pugilistic Talents Appear To Run In The Family, Doesn't Pull Any Punches On The Job,* Sports Illustrated, Mar. 16, 1998, at 42. The article goes on to quote Twist as saying, "I want to hurt them. I want to end the fight as soon as possible and I want the guy to remember it." *Id.*

Despite his well-deserved reputation as a tough-guy "enforcer," or perhaps because of that reputation, Twist was immensely popular with the hometown fans. He endorsed products, appeared on radio and television, hosted the "Tony Twist" television talk show for two years, and became actively involved with several children's charities. It is undisputed that Twist engaged in these activities to foster a positive image of himself in the community and to prepare for a career after hockey as a sports commentator and product endorser.

Respondent Todd McFarlane, an avowed hockey fan and president of Todd McFarlane Productions, Inc. (TMP), created *Spawn* in 1992. TMP employs the writers, artists and creative staff responsible for production of the comic book. *Spawn* is marketed and distributed monthly by Image Comics, Inc., which was formed by McFarlane and others.

Spawn is "a dark and surreal fantasy" centered on a character named Al Simmons, a CIA assassin who was killed by the Mafia and descended to hell upon death. Simmons, having made a deal with the devil, was transformed into the creature Spawn and returned to earth to commit various violent and sexual acts on the devil's behalf. In 1993, a fictional character named "Anthony 'Tony Twist' Twistelli" was added to the *Spawn* storyline. The fictional "Tony Twist" is a Mafia don whose list of evil deeds includes multiple murders, abduction of children and sex with prostitutes. The fictional and real Tony Twist bear no physical resemblance to each other and, aside from the common nickname, are similar only in that each can be characterized as having an "enforcer" or tough-guy persona.

Figure 8-8. "Tony Twist" from *Spawn*

Each issue of the *Spawn* comic book contains a section entitled "Spawning Ground" in which fan letters are published and McFarlane responds to fan questions. In the September 1994 issue, McFarlane admitted that some of the *Spawn* characters were named after professional hockey players, including the "Tony Twist" character: "Antonio Twistelli, a/k/a Tony Twist, is actually the name of a hockey player of the Quebec Nordiques." And, again, in the November 1994 issue, McFarlane stated that the name of the fictional character was based on Twist, a real hockey player, and further promised the readers that they "will continue to see current and past hockey players' names in my books."

In April 1996, *Wizard,* a trade magazine for the comic book industry, interviewed McFarlane. In the published article, "Spawning Ground: A Look at the Real Life People Spawn Characters Are Based Upon," McFarlane is quoted as saying that he uses the names of real-life people to create the identities of the characters. Brief biographies and drawings of the *Spawn* characters follow the McFarlane interview. The paragraph devoted to the "Tony Twist" character contained a drawing of the character accompanied by the following description:

First Appearance: Spawn # 6

Real-Life Persona: Tony Twist.

Relation: NHL St. Louis Blues right winger.

The Mafia don that has made life exceedingly rough for Al Simmons and his loved ones, in addition to putting out an ill-advised contract on the Violator, is named for former Quebec Nordiques hockey player Tony Twist, now a renowned enforcer (*i.e.* "Goon") for the St. Louis Blues of the National Hockey League.

Below the character description was a photo of a Tony Twist hockey trading card, in which Twist was pictured in his St. Louis Blues hockey jersey.

In 1997, Twist became aware of the existence of *Spawn* and of the comic book's use of his name for that of the villainous character. On one occasion, several young hockey fans approached Twist's mother with Spawn trading cards depicting the Mafia character "Tony Twist." Subsequently, at an autograph session Twist was asked to sign a copy of the *Wizard* article in which McFarlane was interviewed and Twist's hockey trading card was pictured.

In October 1997, Twist filed suit against McFarlane and various companies associated with the *Spawn* comic book (collectively "respondents"), seeking an injunction and damages for, *inter alia,* misappropriation of name and defamation, the latter claim being later dismissed. McFarlane and the other defendants filed motions for summary judgment asserting First Amendment protection from a prosecution of the misappropriation of name claim, but the motions were overruled.

At trial, McFarlane denied that the comic book character was "about" the real-life Tony Twist despite the fact that the names were the same. McFarlane also denied that he or the other defendants had attained any benefit by using Twist's name. Twist, however, presented evidence that McFarlane and the other defendants had indeed benefited by using his name. For example, Twist introduced evidence suggesting that in marketing Spawn products, McFarlane directly targeted hockey fans — Twist's primary fan base — by producing and licensing Spawn logo hockey pucks, hockey jerseys and toy zambonis. On cross-examination, McFarlane admitted that on one occasion defendants sponsored "Spawn Night" at a minor league hockey game, where McFarlane personally appeared and distributed Spawn products, including products containing the "Tony Twist" character. Another "Spawn Night" was planned to take place at a subsequent NHL game, but the event never occurred. On the issue of damages, Twist, through purported expert testimony, offered a formula for determining the fair market value that McFarlane and the other defendants should have paid Twist to use his name. In addition, Twist introduced evidence that his association with the *Spawn* character resulted in a diminution in the commercial value of his name as an endorser of products. To that end, Sean Philips, a former executive of a sports nutrition company, testified that his company withdrew a $100,000 offer to Twist to serve as the company's product endorser after Philips learned that Twist's name was associated with the evil Mafia don in the *Spawn* comic book.

As noted, at the conclusion of the trial, the jury returned a verdict in favor of Twist and against the defendants jointly in the amount of $24,500,000. On motions for a judgment notwithstanding the verdict or in the alternative a new trial, the circuit court overturned the verdict finding that Twist had failed to make a submissible case on the misappropriation of name count. The court further held that in the event the judgment notwithstanding the verdict was reversed on appeal, the motion for new trial was granted for evidentiary and instructional errors. Finally, the circuit court denied Twist's request for injunctive relief.

II.

... In this case, Twist seeks to recover the amount of the fair market value that respondents should have paid to use his name in connection with Spawn products and for damage done to the commercial value — in effect the endorsement value — of his name....

To summarize, ... the elements of a right of publicity action include: (1) That defendant used plaintiff's name as a symbol of his identity (2) without consent (3) and with the intent to obtain a commercial advantage.

In this case, the circuit court's entry of JNOV was based on a finding that Twist failed to make a submissible case on the commercial advantage element. In addition, and though the court implicitly held otherwise, respondents claim that the grant of JNOV was also justified because Twist failed to prove that his name was used as [a] "symbol of his identity." ...

A.

Respondents' initial contention that Twist did not prove that his name was used as a "symbol of his identity" is spurious. To establish that a defendant used a plaintiff's name as a symbol of his identity, "the name used by the defendant must be understood by the audience as referring to the plaintiff." RESTATEMENT (THIRD) OF UNFAIR COMPETITION sec. 46 cmt. d....

Here, all parties agree that the "Tony Twist" character is not "about" him, in that the character does not physically resemble Twist nor does the *Spawn* story line attempt to track Twist's real life. Instead, Twist maintains that the sharing of the same (and most unusual) name and the common persona of a tough-guy "enforcer" create an unmistakable correlation between Twist the hockey player and Twist the Mafia don that, when coupled with Twist's fame as a NHL star, conclusively establishes that respondents used his name and identity. This Court agrees. Indeed, respondent McFarlane appears to have conceded the point by informing his readers in separate issues of *Spawn* and in the *Wizard* article that the hockey player Tony Twist was the basis for the comic book character's name.

Arguably, without these concessions, some *Spawn* readers may not have made the connection between Twist and his fictional counterpart. However, other evidence at trial clearly demonstrated that, at some point, *Spawn's* readers did in fact make the connection, for both Twist and his mother were approached by young hockey fans under the belief that appellant was somehow affiliated with the *Spawn* character. On this record, respondents cannot seriously maintain that a good many purchasers of *Spawn* did not readily understand that respondents' use of the name referred to appellant. Accordingly, this Court holds that Twist presented sufficient evidence to prove that his name was used as a symbol of his identity.

B.

As noted, the grant of JNOV was based on the commercial advantage element of the cause of action. Specifically, the court held that the record was devoid of credible evidence that respondents intended (1) "to injure Twist's marketability," (2) "to capitalize on the market recognition of the name," or (3) "derived any pecuniary benefit whatsoever from the use of that name."

At the outset, two of the premises for the circuit court's rationale are incorrect: Twist was under no obligation to prove that respondents intended to injure Twist's marketability or that respondents actually derived a pecuniary benefit from the use of his name. As explained, the commercial advantage element of the right of publicity focuses on the defendant's intent or purpose to obtain a commercial benefit from use of the plaintiff's identity. But in meeting the commercial advantage element, it is irrelevant whether defendant intended to injure the plaintiff, or actually succeeded in obtaining a commercial advantage from using plaintiff's name. That said, it still was incumbent upon Twist to prove that respondents used his name intending to obtain a commercial advantage.

Twist contends, and this Court again agrees, that the evidence admitted at trial was sufficient to establish respondents' intent to gain a commercial advantage by using Twist's name to attract consumer attention to *Spawn* comic books and related products.... At a minimum, respondents' statements and actions reveal their intent to create the impression that Twist was somehow associated with the *Spawn* comic book, and this alone is sufficient to establish the commercial advantage element in a right of publicity action....

But this is not all. At trial, Twist introduced evidence that respondents marketed their products directly to hockey fans. For example, respondents produced and distributed Spawn hockey jerseys and pucks and sponsored a "Spawn Night" at a minor league hockey game where other Spawn products were distributed, including products featuring the character "Tony Twist." Additionally, Twist points to McFarlane's statement in the November 1994 issue of *Spawn,* in which he promised readers that "they will continue to see current and past hockey players' names in [his] books." This statement, Twist correctly contends, amounts to an inducement to *Spawn* readers, especially those who are also hockey fans, to continue to purchase the comic book in order to see the name Tony Twist and other hockey players. This is evidence from which the jury could infer that respondents used his name to obtain a commercial advantage....

... Therefore, this Court holds that Twist presented sufficient evidence to establish that respondents used his name for a commercial advantage.

III.

Having determined that Twist made a submissible case at trial, we next address whether the right of publicity claim is nevertheless prohibited by the First Amendment.... Of course, not all speech is protected under the First Amendment, and in cases like this, courts often will weigh the state's interest in protecting a plaintiff's right to the commercial value of his or her name and identity against the defendant's right to free speech.

Zacchini v. Scripps-Howard Broadcasting Co., 433 U.S. 562 (1977), is the first and only right of publicity case decided by the Supreme Court.... Because the *Zacchini* Court limited its holding to the particular facts of the case — the appropriation of plaintiff's "entire act" — it does not control the case at hand. Nonetheless, there are larger lessons that are certainly applicable.

First, the Court acknowledged, as had many lower courts previously, that the right of publicity is not always trumped by the right of free speech....

Second, the Court distinguished claims for right of publicity or name appropriat[ion] from claims for defamation like those adjudicated in *New York Times v. Sullivan*, 376 U.S. 254 (1964) and *Hustler Magazine v. Falwell*, 485 U.S. 46 (1988).... Because property interests are involved in the former categories but not the latter, *Zacchini*, 433 U.S. at 573, the Court refused to apply the *New York Times v. Sullivan* "actual malice" standard.... As the Court later made clear in *Hustler, Zacchini* stands for the proposition that "the 'actual malice' standard does not apply to the tort of appropriation of a right of publicity...." 485 U.S. at 52.

Right to publicity cases, both before and after *Zacchini*, focus instead on the threshold legal question of whether the use of a person's name and identity is "expressive," in which case it is fully protected, or "commercial," in which case it is generally not protected. For instance, the use of a person's identity in news, entertainment, and creative works for the purpose of communicating information or expressive ideas about that person is protected "expressive" speech. [Citing cases, including *Cardtoons*.] On the other hand, the use of a person's identity for purely commercial purposes, like advertising goods or services or the use of a person's name or likeness on merchandise, is rarely protected. [Citing cases, including *White* and *Midler*.]

Several approaches have been offered to distinguish between expressive speech and commercial speech. The Restatement, for example, employs a "relatedness" test that protects the use of another person's name or identity in a work that is "related to" that person. The catalogue of "related" uses includes "the use of a person's name or likeness in news reporting, whether in newspapers, magazines, or broadcast news ... use in entertainment and other creative works, including both fiction and nonfiction ... use as part of an article published in a fan magazine or in a feature story broadcast on an entertainment program ... dissemination of an unauthorized print or broadcast biography, [and use] of another's identity in a novel, play, or motion picture...." RESTATEMENT (THIRD) OF UNFAIR COMPETITION sec. 47 cmt. c at 549. The proviso to that list, however, is that "if the name or likeness is used solely to attract attention to a work that is *not related* to the identified person, the user may be subject to liability for a use of the other's identity in advertising...." *Id.* (Emphasis added.)

California courts use a different approach, called the "transformative test," that was most recently invoked in *Winter v. D.C. Comics*, 30 Cal. 4th 881, 134 Cal. Rptr. 2d 634, 69 P.3d 473 (2003), a case with a remarkably similar fact situation [to this case]....

The weakness of the Restatement's "relatedness" test and California's "transformative" test is that they give too little consideration to the fact that many uses of a person's name and identity have both expressive and commercial components. These tests operate to preclude a cause of action whenever the use of the name and identity is in any way expressive, regardless of its commercial exploitation. Under the relatedness test, use of a person's name and identity is actionable only when the use is solely commercial and is otherwise unrelated to that person. Under the transformative test, the transformation or fictionalized characterization of a person's celebrity status is not actionable even if its sole purpose is the commercial use of that person's name and identity. Though these tests purport to balance the prospective interests involved, there is no balancing at all — once the use is determined to be expressive, it is protected. At least one commentator, however, has advocated the use of a more balanced balancing test — a sort of predominant use test — that better addresses the cases where speech is both expressive and commercial:

> If a product is being sold that predominantly exploits the commercial value of an individual's identity, that product should be held to violate the right of publicity and not be protected by the First Amendment, even if there is some "expressive" content in it that might qualify as "speech" in other circumstances. If, on the other hand, the predominant purpose of the product is to make an expressive comment on or about a celebrity, the expressive values could be given greater weight.

[Mark S.] Lee, [*Agents of Chaos: Judicial Confusion in Defining the Right of Publicity-Free Speech Interface,* 23 Loy. L.A. Ent. L. Rev. 471,] 500 [(2003)].

The relative merit of these several tests can be seen when applied to the unusual circumstances of the case at hand. As discussed, Twist made a submissible case that respondents' use of his name and identity was for a commercial advantage. Nonetheless, there is still an expressive component in the use of his name and identity as a metaphorical reference to tough-guy "enforcers." And yet, respondents agree (perhaps to avoid a defamation claim) that the use was not a parody or other expressive comment or a fictionalized account of the real Twist. As such, the metaphorical reference to Twist, though a literary device, has very little literary value compared to its commercial value. On the record here, the use and identity of Twist's name has become predominantly a ploy to sell comic books and related products rather than an artistic or literary expression, and under these circumstances, free speech must give way to the right of publicity.

VI.

[The court ultimately remanded for a new trial, agreeing with the appellate court that the trial court had given the jury an improper instruction. It also agreed that the injunction sought was overly broad.]

All concur.

Notes and Questions

1. In both of these cases, the plaintiffs questioned whether the material involved was technically a "parody" of the plaintiff. Do you think that either or both should qualify as a parody? Should that label matter in the analysis? If so, in what way is the characterization of "parody" important to the analysis?

2. As the *Doe* court indicates, *Winter* and *Doe* involve very similar facts. In both cases, an author created a comic-book character based on an actual person, and, in both cases, the comic-book character was an unsavory one, clearly insulting the plaintiffs in these cases. However, the courts come to very different results. *Winter* uses the test of *Comedy III Productions v. Saderup*, which was discussed earlier in this Chapter. Do you think that the court properly applied the *Saderup* test in *Winter*? Should it matter that the *Saderup* lithograph and t-shirts portrayed a far more benign view of the Three Stooges than the comic book in *Winter* did of the Winter brothers?

3. The transformative test of *Saderup* produced, in the view of the California Supreme Court, a simple case in *Winter*. Should the court have modified the test in view of the possibly different interests involved here? In *Saderup*, the court noted that rights of publicity have much in common with copyright, which includes a transformative test as part of the fair use analysis. Is this case similarly imbued with copyright overtones?

4. How is the Restatement test different from the *Saderup* test? Would the Restatement test have produced a different result in *Winter*?

5. *Doe* rejects both the *Saderup* test and the Restatement test. What test does the *Doe* court settle on? In what way is this test more favorable to the plaintiffs than the rejected tests? Do you think that the test appropriately accounts for all of the interests—including society's interest in free speech? Does the court tell you how one determines whether the commercial interest is the "predominate" interest? How would the *Doe* court's test apply to the play "A Day in Hollywood/A Night in the Ukraine," set out in the *Groucho Marx Prods.* case in Chapter III? How would it apply to a fictional account of an historical figure in a novel? Does it matter that the medium of expression in *Doe* was a comic book?

6. Is the true gravamen of the *Doe* and *Winter* complaints a violation of right of publicity, or is it really a defamation claim in disguise? The complaints in both cases in fact included defamation counts. (The lower courts in *Winter* rejected the defamation count.

That decision was not appealed.) Assuming that the plaintiffs in the two cases would be considered "public figures," they would have faced serious obstacles to recovery on their defamation counts. As noted in Chapter VII, the Constitution precludes recovery absent a showing of "actual malice," by clear and convincing evidence. Should plaintiffs be permitted to use rights of publicity as a means of avoiding these constitutional restrictions on recovery? See David S. Welkowitz & Tyler T. Ochoa, *The Terminator as Eraser: How Arnold Schwarzenegger Used The Right Of Publicity To Terminate Non-Defamatory Political Speech*, 45 Santa Clara L. Rev. 651, 652–62 (2005).

7. The Missouri Supreme Court states that the plaintiff sought the "endorsement value" of his identity. Although it held that there was a submissible case, it also sent the case back for retrial due to an improper jury instruction. On remand, the new trial resulted in a verdict of $15 million for the plaintiff (who was not one of the best known hockey players in the NHL), which was affirmed on appeal. *See Doe v. McFarlane*, 207 S.W.3d 52 (Mo. App. 2006).

Parody, Satire, and Political Speech

How should the parody and satire cases be applied to right of publicity cases brought by politicians and other public officials? Certainly political speech is considered "core" protected speech under the First Amendment, and politicians are aware that they would look bad in the eyes of their constituents if they attempted to suppress criticism of themselves. Perhaps for that reason, politicians are very circumspect about suing, and there are very few reported right of publicity cases involving politicians on the books. However, occasionally there are situations in which the use is sufficiently "commercial" that a right of publicity suit is threatened or filed.

The most prominent example occurred in 1997, when New York Magazine entered into a contract with the New York Metropolitan Transit Authority (MTA) to run an advertisement on city buses using the slogan "Possibly the only good thing in New York Rudy hasn't taken credit for." One week after the ads first appeared, the office of then-Mayor Rudy Giuliani "called the MTA and asked that the Advertisement be removed, objecting to the use of the Mayor's name to promote a commercial product, claiming this violated" New York's statutory right of privacy. *See New York Magazine v. Metro. Transp. Auth.*, 136 F.3d 123, 125–26 (2d Cir. 1998). New York Magazine sued, seeking an injunction requiring the MTA to restore the ads. Recognizing that "protecting the right to express skeptical attitudes toward the government ranks among the First Amendment's most important functions," *id.* at 131, the Second Circuit ruled that the MTA's action was an impermissible prior restraint, *id.* at 131–32, and it affirmed a preliminary injunction against the MTA without reaching the merits of the Mayor's right of publicity claim.

In a footnote in the Vanna White case (omitted in the excerpt above), Judge Kozinski described another right of publicity case involving a public official:

> The majority's failure to recognize a parody exception to the right of publicity would apply equally to parodies of politicians as of actresses. Consider the case of Wok Fast, a Los Angeles Chinese food delivery service, which put up a billboard with a picture of then-L.A. Police Chief Daryl Gates and the text "When you can't leave the office. Or won't." (This was an allusion to Chief Gates's refusal to retire despite pressure from Mayor Tom Bradley [in the aftermath of the riots that followed the acquittal of four police officers for the beating of Rodney King].)

Gates forced the restaurant to take the billboard down by threatening a right of publicity lawsuit. Leslie Berger, *He Did Leave the Office—And Now Sign Will Go, Too*, L.A. Times, July 31, 1992, at B2.

White v. Samsung Electronics America, Inc., 989 F.2d 1512, 1519 n.29 (9th Cir. 1993) (Kozinski, J., dissenting from denial of reh'g en banc).

In both of these cases, there was a mixture of political speech and commercial speech. How should these "hybrid" cases be handled? Is it plausible in either case that the public might mistakenly believe that the politician had endorsed the product or service in question? Should it matter? Unlike § 43(a) of the Lanham Act, state right of publicity laws do not require a showing of false endorsement; and as we saw in *White*, implied criticism of the celebrity was not enough to persuade a majority of the court that the use was protected by the First Amendment. Does *White* run the risk of throwing out the political-speech baby with the commercial-speech bathwater? (A similar issue is raised in the *Hoffman* case, excerpted below.) The following problem, based on actual case, squarely presents the issue.

———————

Problem 6

Arnold Schwarzenegger was a famed body-builder who became a star in action movies such as *Terminator* (1984), *Kindergarten Cop* (1990), and *True Lies* (1994). In 2003, he won a special election and became Governor of California. In 2004, Ohio Discount Merchandise, Inc. (ODM) released a series of bobblehead dolls of several politicians and political candidates, including Schwarzenegger. The Schwarzenegger bobblehead doll depicts the Governor in a gray business suit, white shirt and red tie, standing on a red circular base inscribed with his name, holding an assault rifle and wearing an ammunition belt over his shoulder, as shown in Figure 8-9.

The corporation to whom Schwarzenegger assigned his right of publicity sued, claiming that the bobblehead dolls are merchandise that violate the Governor's right of publicity. ODM claims that the dolls are political speech that is protected by the First Amendment. What arguments can you make for and against the positions of the two parties?

For commentary on the actual case (which settled), *see Symposium: The Schwarzenegger Bobblehead Case*, 45 Santa Clara L. Rev. 547 (2005).

———————

C. Other Free Expression Issues

1. Works of Fiction

Guglielmi v. Spelling-Goldberg Prods.
25 Cal. 3d 860, 160 Cal. Rptr. 352, 603 P.2d 454 (1979)

BY THE COURT:

Appellant allegedly is the nephew of the actor Rudolph Valentino, who died in 1926. According to the complaint herein, in 1975, respondents exhibited on television a "fic-

Figure 8-9. The Schwarzenegger bobblehead doll (Photo by Eric B. Johnson)

tionalized version" of Valentino's life, depicting the actor's name, likeness and personality without obtaining the prior consent of either Valentino or appellant. In the present action, appellant seeks damages and injunctive relief on the theory that respondents have misappropriated Valentino's "right of publicity," and that appellant as Valentino's legal heir is the present owner of that right. Respondents' demurrer to the complaint was sustained and, upon appellant's refusal to amend, the complaint was ordered dismissed. This appeal followed.

In *Lugosi v. Universal Pictures*, 25 Cal. 3d 813, 160 Cal. Rptr. 323, 603 P.2d 425, we hold that the right of publicity protects against the unauthorized use of one's name, likeness or personality, but that the right is not descendible and expires upon the death of the person so protected. *Lugosi* controls the disposition of the present case and makes it unnecessary to discuss any further issues raised by the parties.

The judgment is affirmed.

BIRD, Chief Justice, concurring:

This court must decide whether the use of a deceased celebrity's name and likeness in a fictional film exhibited on television constitutes an actionable infringement of that person's right of publicity. It is clear that appellant's action cannot be maintained. Therefore, the trial court properly dismissed his complaint.

I

In his complaint, appellant alleges that Rudolpho Guglielmi, also known as Rudolph Valentino, was his paternal uncle. Valentino was a world-renowned silent motion picture actor who created substantial commercial value in his identity through his motion picture performances. Appellant contends that Valentino had a protectible proprietary interest in the commercial uses of his name, likeness and personality. Appellant alleges that he inherited this right of publicity, under Valentino's will following Valentino's death in 1926.

On November 23, 1975, respondents exhibited on the [ABC] television network … a film entitled *Legend of Valentino: A Romantic Fiction*. Appellant alleges that "(s)aid film purports to represent a portion of the life of Rudolph Valentino and employs the name, likeness and personality of Rudolph Valentino." However, appellant asserts that while the principal character is identified as Valentino, the film is "a work of fiction about the life and loves of an Italian actor who became Hollywood's first romantic screen star and who died at the height of his fame." Hence, the film is a "fictionalized version of Rudolph Valentino's life." Appellant alleges that respondents knew that the film did not truthfully portray Valentino's life, and that the film was made without Valentino's or appellant's consent. Appellant contends that respondents also used Valentino's name, likeness and personality in advertising the film "to solicit and to sell commercial sponsorship exhibited in conjunction with the exhibition of said film and to solicit viewers for the exhibition of said film."

Appellant argues that by incorporating Valentino's identity in the film and related advertisements, respondents "were able to derive greater income from their film by attracting more viewers and sponsors than they would have …" if Valentino's name had not been used. This unauthorized use in a "work of fiction" which respondents knew was not an accurate portrayal of Valentino's life allegedly constituted a misappropriation of Valentino's right of publicity. For this allegedly tortious conduct, appellant seeks damages and injunctive relief.

Respondents demurred to appellant's complaint, asserting that it failed to state facts sufficient to constitute a cause of action. The trial court sustained the demurrer with leave to amend. However, the court offered to sustain the demurrer without leave to amend and dismiss the complaint if appellant wished to challenge the court's ruling. Appellant elected to stand on the unamended complaint and his complaint was dismissed. This appeal followed.

II

… The gravamen of appellant's complaint is that respondents used Valentino's name, likeness and personality in a fictionalized film which did not accurately portray his life.

Figure 8-10. Rudolph Valentino in *The Sheik* (1921)

They thereby infringed on appellant's inherited interest in Valentino's right of publicity. Appellant seeks recovery of the amounts respondents were unjustly enriched by the unauthorized use of Valentino's right of publicity and damages for diminishing its value. No claim was made that respondents' fictional work defamed or invaded the privacy of either Valentino or appellant.[4] Therefore, appellant's complaint states a cause of action if two conditions are satisfied: (1) Rudolph Valentino had a right of publicity in the commercial uses of his name, likeness and personality, a right which could be transferred to his heirs, and (2) respondents' conduct constituted an impermissible infringement on that right.

In light of my conclusions [in dissent] in *Lugosi...*, I believe that plaintiff's complaint satisfies the first condition....

It must therefore be determined whether respondents' conduct constituted an infringement of Valentino's right of publicity. In resolving that question, the context and

---

4. There was no allegation that Appellant's name or likeness was used in respondents' film. Appellant recognizes that any injury to Valentino's personal rights, such as his right to privacy, would not be actionable after his death.

nature of the use is of pre-eminent concern. Valentino's name and likeness were allegedly used in a work of fiction broadcast on television. Appellant characterized respondents' film as "a work of fiction about the life and loves of an Italian actor who became Hollywood's first romantic screen star and who died at the height of his fame." Valentino was identified as that character.[6]

Film is a "significant medium for the communication of ideas." (*Joseph Burstyn, Inc. v. Wilson* (1952) 343 U.S. 495, 501.) Whether exhibited in theaters or on television, a film is a medium which is protected by the constitutional guarantees of free expression....

Appellant contends that the Valentino film is not entitled to the cloak of constitutional protection because respondents incorporated Valentino's name and likeness in: (1) a work of fiction, (2) for financial gain, (3) knowing that such film falsely portrayed Valentino's life. The critical issue is whether the presence of these factors, individually or collectively, sufficiently outweighs any protection this expression would otherwise enjoy under the United States and California Constitutions.

In emphasizing the fictional nature of the film, appellant's argument reveals a fundamental misconception of the nature of the constitutional guarantees of free expression....

The First Amendment and article I, section 2 of the California Constitution serve "to preserve an uninhibited marketplace of ideas" and to repel efforts to limit the "'uninhibited, robust and wide-open' debate on public issues." (*Red Lion Broadcasting Co. v. FCC* [(1969) 395 U.S. 367,] 390; *Gertz v. Welch* (1974) 418 U.S. 323, 340.) These rights are essential in a democratic system of government. Free speech is also guaranteed because of our fundamental respect for individual development and self-realization. The right to self-expression is inherent in any political system which respects individual dignity. Each speaker must be free of government restraint regardless of the nature or manner of the views expressed unless there is a compelling reason to the contrary....

Our courts have often observed that entertainment is entitled to the same constitutional protection as the exposition of ideas. That conclusion rests on two propositions. First, "(t)he line between the informing and the entertaining is too elusive for the protection of the basic right. Everyone is familiar with instances of propaganda through fiction. What is one man's amusement, teaches another doctrine." (*Winters v. New York* (1948) 333 U.S. 507, 510.) Second, entertainment, as a mode of self-expression, is entitled to constitutional protection irrespective of its contribution to the marketplace of ideas. "For expression is an integral part of the development of ideas, of mental exploration and of the affirmation of self. The power to realize his potentiality as a human being begins at this point and must extend at least this far if the whole nature of man is not to be thwarted...." (Emerson, [*Toward a General Theory of the First Amendment,*] 72 Yale L.J. [877,] 879 [(1963)].)

It is clear that works of fiction are constitutionally protected in the same manner as political treatises and topical news stories. Using fiction as a vehicle, commentaries on our values, habits, customs, laws, prejudices, justice, heritage and future are frequently expressed. What may be difficult to communicate or understand when factually reported may be

---

6. Such statements establish that this is not a case in which the use is wholly unrelated to the individual. A different result may follow if, for example, respondents had published *Rudolph Valentino's Cookbook* and neither the recipes nor the menus described in the book were in any fashion related to Rudolph Valentino. While Valentino's name was allegedly used to advertise this particular film, this is not a case in which a celebrity's name is used to promote or endorse a collateral commercial product or is otherwise associated with a product or service in an advertisement.

poignant and powerful if offered in satire, science fiction or parable. Indeed, Dickens and Dostoevski may well have written more trenchant and comprehensive commentaries on their times than any factual recitation could ever yield. Such authors are no less entitled to express their views than the town crier with the daily news or the philosopher with his discourse on the nature of justice. Even the author who creates distracting tales for amusement is entitled to constitutional protection.

Thus, no distinction may be drawn in this context between fictional and factual accounts of Valentino's life. Respondents' election of the former as the mode for their views does not diminish the constitutional protection afforded speech. If respondents are to be held liable for their expression, a more persuasive basis must be established.

Next, appellant contends that Valentino's name and likeness were used because they increased the value or marketability of the film. It is argued that such motivation diminishes the constitutional protection otherwise mandated. This contention appears to encompass three distinct bases of liability. First, the film was produced and broadcast for profit. Second, respondents could have expressed themselves without using Valentino's name and likeness. To permit such unauthorized use allows them to benefit unjustifiably from Valentino's prominence. Third, the use of Valentino's name and likeness in a *fictional* account poses a unique threat to the value of Valentino's right of publicity.

The first argument can be readily dismissed. The First Amendment is not limited to those who publish without charge. Whether the activity involves newspaper publication or motion picture production, it does not lose its constitutional protection because it is undertaken for profit. (*Time, Inc. v. Hill* (1967) 385 U.S. 374, 397.) The fact that respondents sought to profit from the production and exhibition of a film utilizing Valentino's name and likeness is not constitutionally significant.

The second prong of appellant's argument is more subtle. In essence, it is that the use of Valentino's name and likeness in the film was unnecessary, that Valentino's identity was incorporated in the film solely to increase the film's value. If this analysis were used to determine whether an expression is entitled to constitutional protection, grave harm would result. Courts would be required not merely to determine whether there is some minimal relationship between the expression and the celebrity (see fn. 6, *ante*), but to compel the author to justify the use of the celebrity's identity. Only upon satisfying a court of the necessity of weaving the celebrity's identity into a particular publication would the shadow of liability and censorship fade. Such a course would inevitably chill the exercise of free speech—limiting not only the manner and form of expression but the interchange of ideas as well.

Contemporary events, symbols and people are regularly used in fictional works. Fiction writers may be able to more persuasively, more accurately express themselves by weaving into the tale persons or events familiar to their readers. The choice is theirs. No author should be forced into creating mythological worlds or characters wholly divorced from reality. The right of publicity derived from public prominence does not confer a shield to ward off caricature, parody and satire. Rather, prominence invites creative comment. Surely, the range of free expression would be meaningfully reduced if prominent persons in the present and recent past were forbidden topics for the imaginations of authors of fiction.

The facts of the present case are strikingly illustrative. Valentino was a Hollywood star. His life and career are part of the cultural history of an era. As the title of respondents' film suggests, Valentino became a "legend," a symbol of the romantic screen idol and lover. His lingering persona is an apt topic for poetry or song, biography or fiction.[13] Whether respondents' work constitutes a serious appraisal of Valentino's stature or mere fantasy is a judgment left to the reader or viewer, not the courts.

The third strand in appellant's argument is that the incorporation of a prominent person's identity in a fictional work poses a threat to the value of his right of publicity not found in truthful accounts. Yet truthful accounts, no less than fictional ones, may trade upon the publicity value in Valentino's identity and thereby diminish its value. The author of an unauthorized truthful publication may be inspired by, and seek to profit from, the public's interest in Valentino's career or legend. The truthful account may sate the public's desire for "contact" with Valentino, making any other plan for exploitation or revelation a profitless venture. Conversely, the false report, no less than the truthful, may stimulate interest and infuse great value in the previously insignificant publicity value in a celebrity's identity. A fictional account is as likely to laud as to denigrate. It may either augment or diminish the value of a celebrity's right of publicity. Therefore, any assertion that fictional accounts pose a unique threat to the right of publicity not found in truthful reports is simply not justified.[15]

Finally, appellant claims that the film is not entitled to constitutional protection because respondents acted with "knowledge or reckless disregard of the falsity" of their broadcast concerning Valentino. However, appellant's effort to import the "actual malice" standard of liability in defamation actions of *New York Times Co. v. Sullivan* (1964) 376 U.S. 254 is misguided.

That standard reflects the Supreme Court's recognition that while defamatory false statements of fact have no constitutional value, such statements are inevitable in the continuing debate on public issues. Accordingly, to provide adequate protection to "speech that matters," the court held that even false statements of fact concerning public figures and officials are not actionable unless they are published with knowledge of their falsity or reckless disregard for the truth.

No such constitutional dichotomy exists in this area between truthful and fictional accounts. They have equal constitutional stature and each is as likely to fulfill the objectives underlying the constitutional guarantees of free expression. Moreover, in defamation cases, the concern is with defamatory lies masquerading as truth. In contrast, the author who denotes his work as fiction proclaims his literary license and indifference to "the facts." There is no pretense. All fiction, by definition, eschews an obligation to be faithful to historical truth. Every fiction writer knows his creation is in some sense "false." That is the nature of the art. Therefore, where fiction is the medium—as alleged by appellant in this case and as evident in the film's title, *A Romantic Fiction*—it is meaningless to charge that the author "knew" his work was false.

Clearly, appellant's basis for distinguishing respondents' film from other expressive works, whether factual or fictional, is unpersuasive. Appellant has not established any analytic framework which logically differentiates respondents' film from other expressions. Hence, an action for infringement of the right of publicity can be maintained only if the proprietary interests at issue clearly outweigh the value of free expression in this context.

---

13. *Amicus curiae* informs the court that, in addition to the film at issue, at least five biographies and three motion pictures concerning Valentino have been produced.

15. False or fictional accounts may pose a unique danger to the subject's reputation. However, appellant has expressly disavowed any intention of pursuing a claim that respondents' film defamed Valentino.

While few courts have addressed the question of the parameters of the right of publicity in the context of expressive activities, their response has been consistent. Whether the publication involved was factual and biographical or fictional, the right of publicity has not been held to outweigh the value of free expression. Any other conclusion would allow reports and commentaries on the thoughts and conduct of public and prominent persons to be subject to censorship under the guise of preventing the dissipation of the publicity value of a person's identity. Moreover, the creation of historical novels and other works inspired by actual events and people would be off limits to the fictional author. An important avenue of self-expression would be blocked and the marketplace of ideas would be diminished....

A cause of action for the appropriation of Valentino's right of publicity through the use of his name and likeness in respondents' film may not be maintained. The trial court properly sustained the demurrer and dismissed the complaint.

A similar result is compelled for the use of Valentino's name and likeness in advertisements for the film. That use was merely an adjunct to the exhibition of the film. It was not alleged that the advertisements promoted anything but the film. Having established that any interest in financial gain in producing the film did not affect the constitutional stature of respondents' undertaking, it is of no moment that the advertisement may have increased the profitability of the film. It would be illogical to allow respondents to exhibit the film but effectively preclude any advance discussion or promotion of their lawful enterprise. Since the use of Valentino's name and likeness in the film was not an actionable infringement of Valentino's right of publicity, the use of his identity in advertisements for the film is similarly not actionable....

In contrast, the facts underlying *Lugosi v. Universal Pictures, supra,* are substantially different than those in the present case. Lugosi involved the use of Bela Lugosi's likeness in connection with the sale of such commercial products "as plastic toy pencil sharpeners, soap products, target games, candy dispensers and beverage stirring rods." These objects, unlike motion pictures, are not vehicles through which ideas and opinions are regularly disseminated.[21] This case involves the use of a celebrity's identity in a constitutionally protected medium of expression, a work of fiction on film. Lugosi simply did not address the viability of a cause of action for appropriation of the right of publicity under these circumstances.

Finally, *Zacchini v. Scripps-Howard Broadcasting Co.,* 433 U.S. 562 [(1977)], does not require that appellant be accorded protection. In *Zacchini,* respondent filmed petitioner's "entire act" in a human cannonball performance and broadcast his performance on television. Under state law, petitioner had the "right to the publicity value of his performance," the right to control its commercial display and exploitation. The Supreme Court found that the broadcast went "to the heart of petitioner's ability to earn a living as an entertainer" and posed a "substantial threat to the economic value of (petitioner's) performance." (*Id.,* at pp. 575–576.) In light of the nature of this interest, the court held that a suit for damages based on respondent's broadcast of petitioner's "entire act" was not precluded by the First Amendment.[22]

---

21. This is not to suggest that the incorporation of a prominent person's name or likeness in a commercial product could never be considered an expression entitled to constitutional protection. (*See* Smith & Sobel, *The Mickey Mouse Watch Goes to Washington: Would the Law Stop the Clock?* (1972) 62 Trademark Rep. 334....)

22. The court noted that permitting petitioner to maintain an action would not diminish the dissemination of information, as petitioner only sought compensation for the broadcast. In this case, appellant asked the trial court to enjoin exhibition of respondents' film.

In the present case, respondents did not surreptitiously film a performance by Valentino and incorporate that film in a motion picture. They did not appropriate "an entire act for which the performer ordinarily gets paid," thereby undercutting his ability to earn a living. Rather, respondents produced a fictional film about the legend of Valentino. Respondents' conduct was thus much more akin to commenting upon or reporting the facts of Zacchini's performance, which the Supreme Court regarded as entirely permissible....

TOBRINER and MANUEL, JJ., concur.

NEWMAN, Justice, concurring:

I concur in the Court's opinion. Further, I concur in the discussion in the Chief Justice's opinion that sets forth principles for determining whether an action based on the invasion of an individual's right of publicity may be maintained in the face of a claim that the challenged use is an exercise of freedom of expression. While the Chief Justice applies those principles under the facts of this case to a suit by the heir of a prominent person, it seems clear that the principles similarly would apply to a suit brought by that person.

Tyne v. Time Warner Entertainment Co.
901 So.2d 802 (Fla. 2005)

[In 1991, the fishing vessel *Andrea Gail* was caught in a "massively powerful" storm and was lost at sea. The story of the *Andrea Gail* was told in a 1997 book by Sebastian Junger called *The Perfect Storm*. In 2000, Warner Brothers released a motion picture based on Junger's book, starring George Clooney as Captain Billy Tyne.] Unlike the book, the Picture presented a concededly dramatized account of both the storm and the crew of the *Andrea Gail*.... Warner Bros. took additional liberties with the land-based interpersonal relationships between the crewmembers and their families.

While the Picture did not hold itself out as factually accurate, it did indicate at the beginning of the film that "THIS FILM IS BASED ON A TRUE STORY." A disclaimer inserted during the closing credits [stated]: "This film is based on actual historical events contained in 'The Perfect Storm' by Sebastian Junger. Dialogue and certain events and characters in the film were created for the purpose of fictionalization." ...

[Shortly after the movie was released, the children of two of the fishermen sued Warner Brothers, alleging that the false depiction of their fathers in the movie violated Florida's right of publicity statute, Fla. Stat. §540.08. That statute prohibits the use of a person's likeness "for purposes of trade or for any commercial or advertising purpose." The U.S. Court of Appeals for the Eleventh Circuit certified the interpretation of that section to the Florida Supreme Court.]

In *Loft* [v. *Fuller*, 408 So.2d 619 (Fla. App. 1981)], Dorothy Loft and her two children brought an action for ... violation of section 540.08 for the alleged unauthorized publication of the name and likeness of the Lofts' deceased husband and father, Robert Loft. Robert Loft had been the captain of an Eastern Airlines flight that crashed while en route from New York to Miami in 1972. The crash was followed by reports of the appearance of apparitions of the flight's crew members, including Robert Loft, on subsequent flights.... [These events were recounted in the book and movie, *The Ghost of Flight 401*.] The Fourth District held as follows:

In our view, section 540.08, by prohibiting the use of one's name or likeness for trade, commercial or advertising purposes, is designed to prevent the unauthorized use of a name *to directly promote the product or service of the publisher.* Thus, the publication is harmful not simply because it is included in a publication that is sold for a profit, but rather because of the way it associates the individual's name or his personality with something else. Such is not the case here.

While we agree that at least one of the purposes of the author and publisher in releasing the publication in question was to make money through sales of copies of the book and that such a publication is commercial in that sense, this in no way distinguishes this book from almost all other books, magazines or newspapers and simply does not amount to the kind of commercial exploitation prohibited by the statute. We simply do not believe that the term "commercial," as employed by Section 540.08, was meant to be construed to bar the use of people's names in such a sweeping fashion. We also believe that acceptance of appellants' view of the statute would result in substantial confrontation between this statute and the first amendment to the United States Constitution guaranteeing freedom of the press and of speech....

Loft, 408 So.2d at 622–23 (emphasis added) (citations omitted).

We approve the Fourth District's logical construction of section 540.08 in *Loft.* This construction has been applied to cases construing the statute for more than thirty years, and the statute has remained unchanged by the Legislature for this period.... [We] hold that the term "commercial purpose" as used in section 540.08(1) does not apply to publications, including motion pictures, which do not directly promote a product or service.

Notes and Questions

1. A majority of the court in *Guglielmi* dismissed the suit on the ground that California common-law did not recognize a post-mortem right of publicity. Nonetheless, Chief Justice Bird's concurring opinion in *Guglielmi* was influential, because it was endorsed by a different majority comprising four of the seven justices (Justice Newman concurring in both opinions).

Five years after *Guglielmi,* of course, the California legislature enacted a statutory post-mortem right of publicity (Civil Code § 990, now codified as amended at Civil Code § 3344.1). That statute codifies and expands the ruling in *Guglielmi* in subsection (a)(2):

> "For purposes of this subdivision, a play, book, magazine, newspaper, musical composition, audiovisual work, radio or television program, ... or an advertisement or commercial announcement for any of these works, shall not be considered a product, article of merchandise, good, or service if it is fictional or nonfictional entertainment, or a dramatic, literary, or musical work."

For living persons, however, *Guglielmi* continues to be a leading authority protecting the depiction of real people in movies, whether in dramatized "docudramas" or in more heavily fictionalized works. *See, e.g., Taylor v. National Broadcasting Co.,* 22 Media L. Rep. 2433 (Cal. Super. Ct. 1994) (dismissing action by Elizabeth Taylor to enjoin NBC's broadcast of a mini-series about her life); *see also* RESTATEMENT (THIRD) OF UNFAIR COMPETITION § 47 (1995) ("use 'for purposes of trade' does not ordinarily include the use of a person's identity in … entertainment, works of fiction or nonfiction, or in advertising that is incidental to such uses.").

2. Chief Justice Bird's opinion in *Guglielmi* concludes that Rudolph Valentino's heir cannot recover for a fictionalized version of his uncle's life. But why? Compare the facts of this case to those in *Saderup*. Isn't the Valentino movie as much of a commercial exploitation as the t-shirts and lithographs in *Saderup*? If so, then the only distinction between them is that the California Supreme Court believes that the First Amendment values the speech in *Guglielmi* more than the speech in *Saderup*. Why should that be the case?

Chief Justice Bird identifies two purposes underlying the First Amendment: "to preserve an uninhibited marketplace of ideas," and to respect "individual self-expression." Which of these purposes is served by the fictional life of Valentino? Which of these purposes is served by the Three Stooges t-shirts and lithographs? Is it fair to say that the former purpose receives greater First Amendment protection than the latter? If so, what should we make of the assertion in *Saderup* than an "articulable message is not a condition of constitutional protection"?

3. The line subsequently drawn by the *Saderup* court is whether the defendant's work is "transformative," that is, whether the defendant added enough of his own self-expression to the work to avoid being "a literal depiction or imitation of a celebrity for commercial gain." Clearly a fictional version of Valentino's life meets that standard. Does that mean that any narrative account of a celebrity will receive greater protection than a work of visual art? Why do the courts value self-expression in works of visual art less than self-expression in a book or movie? Whatever the reason, there can be no doubt that, as a practical matter, traditional media get more respect when the First Amendment implications of their works are assessed.

4. As we saw in Chapter VII, false news accounts of public figures are protected by the First Amendment *unless* they were made with knowledge or reckless disregard of their falsity (the *New York Times* standard of "actual malice"). The plaintiff in *Guglielmi* alleged that the Valentino film was made and broadcast "with knowledge or reckless disregard of its falsity." Why wasn't that allegation enough to survive a demurrer?

Chief Justice Bird draws a distinction between "defamatory lies masquerading as truth" and fiction, which "eschews an obligation to be faithful to historical truth." Even if one agrees with that distinction, it may be a difficult line to draw in practice. Should one consider a tabloid newspaper that regularly features articles on alien visitation to be "news" or "fiction"? What about the dramatized movie in *Tyne*? Is the label "This Film is Based on a True Story" enough to signal to audiences that some parts of the movie have been entirely invented by the film makers?

5. The court in *Tyne* takes a different approach, interpreting the Florida statute narrowly to avoid tackling the constitutional question directly. Under the Florida court's interpretation, which limits the statute to "publications … which directly promote a product or service," is it clear that movies simply are not actionable, no matter how heavily they are fictionalized? Would *Tyne* have been decided differently if the movie had been labeled "This is a True Story"?

6. The opinions in *Guglielmi* and *Tyne* are consistent with two earlier cases upholding the right to publish allegedly fictionalized biographies under New York Law. In *Frosch v. Grosset & Dunlap, Inc.*, 75 A.D.2d 768, 427 N.Y.S.2d 828 (1980), involving a biography of Marilyn Monroe by Norman Mailer, the court stated: "We think it does not matter whether the book is properly described as a biography, a fictional biography, or any other kind of literary work.… It is enough that the book is a literary work and not simply a disguised commercial advertisement for the sale of goods and services."

Likewise, in *Hicks v. Casablanca Records*, 464 F. Supp. 426 (S.D.N.Y. 1978), the court allowed the defendants to publish and release an admittedly fictional book and movie that speculated about the truth behind the mysterious eleven-day disappearance of famed mystery writer Agatha Christie in 1922. In so holding, the court distinguished a previous New York case, *Spahn v. Julian Messner, Inc.*, 18 N.Y.2d 324, 274 N.Y.S.2d 877, 221 N.E.2d 543 (1966), which held that a deliberately fictionalized biography of pitcher Warren Spahn was *not* protected by the First Amendment. The court in *Hicks* explained:

> It is clear ... that the presence or absence of deliberate falsifications or an attempt by defendant to present the disputed events as true determines whether the scales in this balancing process shall tip in favor of or against protection of the speech at issue. Since [here] there were no deliberate falsifications alleged by plaintiffs, and the reader ... by the presence of the word "novel" would know that the work is fictitious, this Court finds that the first amendment protection usually accorded novels and movies outweighs whatever publicity rights plaintiffs may possess....

464 F. Supp. at 433. Both *Frosch* and *Hicks* can now be considered *dicta*, as it now clear that New York provides no protection at all to the estates or heirs of deceased celebrities.

7. Finally, note an important subsidiary holding in *Guglielmi*: once the court has decided that a film about a celebrity is not actionable, the use of the celebrity's likeness to advertise the film also will not be actionable, because "it would be illogical to allow respondents to exhibit the film but effectively preclude any advance discussion or promotion of their lawful enterprise." *See also* Restatement (Third) of Unfair Competition, §47 and comment a.

---

2. News vs. Advertising: Noncommercial vs. Commercial Speech

Hoffman v. Capital Cities/ABC, Inc.
255 F.3d 1180 (9th Cir. 2001)

Boochever, Circuit Judge:

In 1982, actor Dustin Hoffman starred in the movie "Tootsie," playing a male actor who dresses as a woman to get a part on a television soap opera. One memorable still photograph from the movie showed Hoffman in character in a red long-sleeved sequined evening dress and high heels, posing in front of an American flag. The still carried the text, "What do you get when you cross a hopelessly straight, starving actor with a dynamite red sequined dress? You get America's hottest new actress." [See Figure 8-11.]

In March 1997, Los Angeles Magazine ("LAM") published the "Fabulous Hollywood Issue!" An article from this issue entitled "Grand Illusions" used computer technology to alter famous film stills to make it appear that the actors were wearing Spring 1997 fashions. The sixteen familiar scenes included movies and actors such as "North by Northwest" (Cary Grant), "Saturday Night Fever" (John Travolta), "Rear Window" (Grace Kelly and Jimmy Stewart), "Gone with the Wind" (Vivian Leigh and Hattie McDaniel), "Jailhouse Rock" (Elvis Presley), "The Seven Year Itch" (Marilyn Monroe), "Thelma and Louise" (Susan Sarandon and Geena Davis), and even "The Creature

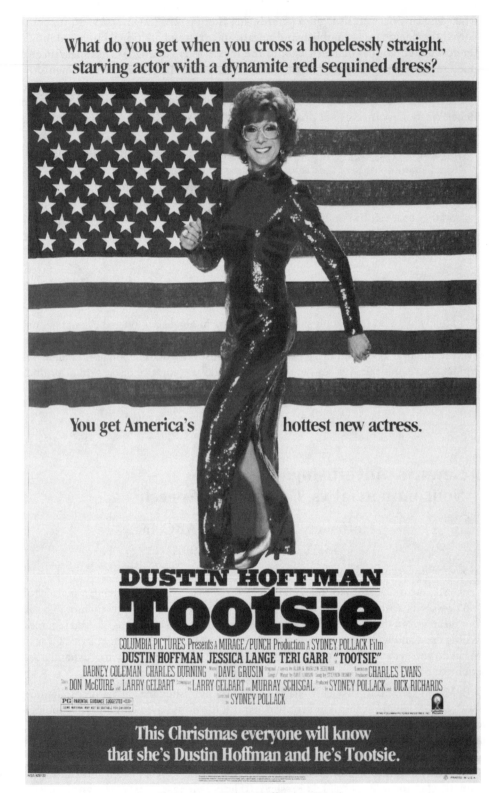

Figure 8-11. Dustin Hoffman as *Tootsie*

from the Black Lagoon" (with the Creature in Nike shoes). The final shot was the "Toot-sie" still. The American flag and Hoffman's head remained as they appeared in the orig-inal, but Hoffman's body and his long-sleeved red sequined dress were replaced by the body of a male model in the same pose, wearing a spaghetti-strapped, cream-colored, silk evening dress and high-heeled sandals. LAM omitted the original caption. The text on the page identified the still as from the movie "Tootsie," and read, "Dustin Hoffman isn't a drag in a butter-colored silk gown by Richard Tyler and Ralph Lauren heels."

LAM did not ask Hoffman for permission to publish the altered photograph. Nor did LAM secure permission from Columbia Pictures, the copyright holder. In April 1997, Hoffman filed a complaint in California state court against LAM's parent company, Cap-ital Cities/ABC, Inc. (now ABC, Inc. or "ABC"). The complaint alleged that LAM's pub-lication of the altered photograph misappropriated Hoffman's name and likeness in violation of (1) the California common law right of publicity; (2) the California statu-tory right of publicity, Civil Code § 3344; (3) the California unfair competition statute, Business and Professions Code § 17200; and (4) the federal Lanham Act, 15 U.S.C. § 1125(a).

ABC removed the case to federal court. Hoffman added LAM as a defendant. After a bench trial, the district court found for Hoffman and against LAM on all of Hoffman's claims, rejecting LAM's defense that its use of the photograph was protected by the First Amendment.... *Hoffman v. Capital Cities/ABC, Inc.*, 33 F. Supp. 2d 867 (C.D. Cal. 1999).... It also held that ABC was not liable for any of LAM's actions.... [The court awarded Hoffman $1.5 million in compensatory damages, $1.5 million in punitive damages, and $270,000 in attorney fees. LAM appealed.]

ANALYSIS

California recognizes, in its common law and its statutes, "the right of a person whose identity has commercial value—most often a celebrity—to control the commercial use of that identity." *Waits v. Frito-Lay, Inc.*, 978 F.2d 1093, 1098 (9th Cir. 1992) (as amended). Hoffman claims that LAM violated his state right of publicity by appropriating his name and likeness. He also claims that LAM violated his rights under the federal Lanham Act.

LAM replies that its challenged use of the "Tootsie" photo is protected under the First Amendment. We evaluate this defense aware of "the careful balance that courts have grad-ually constructed between the right of publicity and the First Amendment and federal in-tellectual property laws." *Landham v. Lewis Galoob Toys, Inc.*, 227 F.3d 619, 626 (6th Cir. 2000).

LAM argues that the "Grand Illusions" article and the altered "Tootsie" photograph con-tained therein are an expression of editorial opinion, entitled to protection under the First Amendment. Hoffman, a public figure, must therefore show that LAM, a media defendant, acted with "actual malice," that is, with knowledge that the photograph was false, or with reck-less disregard for its falsity. *See New York Times Co. v. Sullivan*, 376 U.S. 254, 279–80 (1964). Because Hoffman did not produce clear and convincing evidence that LAM acted with ac-tual malice, LAM contends that all Hoffman's claims are barred by the First Amendment.

The district court rejected this argument. First, it concluded that the magazine article was commercial speech not entitled to constitutional protection: "[t]he First Amendment does not protect the exploitative commercial use of Mr. Hoffman's name and likeness." *Hoffman*, 33 F. Supp. 2d at 874. Second, the court found that LAM acted with actual mal-ice, and "the First Amendment does not protect knowingly false speech." Id. at 875.[2]

---

2. In *Comedy III Prods., Inc. v. Gary Saderup, Inc.*, 25 Cal. 4th 387, 106 Cal. Rptr. 2d 126, 21 P.3d 797 (Cal. 2001), the California Supreme Court held that there was no First Amendment defense to a California right of publicity claim when "artistic expression takes the form of a literal depiction or im-

Commercial speech

The district court concluded that LAM's alteration of the "Tootsie" photograph was an "exploitative commercial" use not entitled to First Amendment protection. We disagree.

"Commercial speech" has special meaning in the First Amendment context. Although the boundary between commercial and noncommercial speech has yet to be clearly delineated, the "core notion of commercial speech" is that it "does no more than propose a commercial transaction." *Bolger v. Youngs Drug Prods. Corp.*, 463 U.S. 60, 66 (1983) (quotations omitted). Such speech is entitled to a measure of First Amendment protection. *See, e.g., Greater New Orleans Broad. Ass'n, Inc. v. United States*, 527 U.S. 173, 183 (1999) (setting out four-part test to evaluate constitutionality of governmental regulation of "speech that is commercial in nature"). Commercial messages, however, do not receive the same level of constitutional protection as other types of protected expression. *See 44 Liquormart, Inc. v. Rhode Island*, 517 U.S. 484, 498 (1996). False or misleading commercial speech is not protected. *See Florida Bar v. Went For It, Inc.*, 515 U.S. 618, 623–24 (1995). When speech is properly classified as commercial, a public figure plaintiff does not have to show that the speaker acted with actual malice. *See Procter & Gamble Co. v. Amway Corp.*, 242 F.3d 539, 556 (5th Cir. 2001).

In many right of publicity cases, the question of actual malice does not arise, because the challenged use of the celebrity's identity occurs in an advertisement that "does no more that propose a commercial transaction" and is clearly commercial speech. [Citing *Newcombe, Abdul-Jabbar, Waits, White*, and *Midler*.] In all these cases, the defendant used an aspect of the celebrity's identity entirely and directly for the purpose of selling a product. Such uses do not implicate the First Amendment's protection of expressions of editorial opinion. *Cf. White*, 971 F.2d at 1401 (advertisement in which "spoof" is entirely subservient to primary message to "buy" identified product not protected by First Amendment).

Hoffman points out that the body double in the "Tootsie" photograph was identified as wearing Ralph Lauren shoes and that there was a Ralph Lauren advertisement (which does not feature shoes) elsewhere in the magazine. (Insofar as the record shows, Richard Tyler, the designer of the gown, had never advertised in LAM.) Hoffman also points to the "Shopper's Guide" in the back of the magazine, which provided stores and prices for the shoes and gown.

These facts are not enough to make the "Tootsie" photograph pure commercial speech. If the altered photograph had appeared in a Ralph Lauren advertisement, then we would be facing a case much like those cited above. But LAM did not use Hoffman's image in a traditional advertisement printed merely for the purpose of selling a particular product. Insofar as the record shows, LAM did not receive any consideration from the designers for featuring their clothing in the fashion article containing the altered movie stills. Nor did the article simply advance a commercial message. "Grand Illusions" appears as a feature article on the cover of the magazine and in the table of contents. It is a complement to and a part of the issue's focus on Hollywood past and present. Viewed in context, the

---

itation of a celebrity for commercial gain." *Id.* at 808. An artist who added "significant transformative elements" could still invoke First Amendment protection. *Id.* Even if we were to consider LAM an "artist" and the altered "Tootsie" photograph "artistic expression" subject to the Comedy III decision, there is no question that LAM's publication of the "Tootsie" photograph contained "significant transformative elements." Hoffman's body was eliminated and a new, differently clothed body was substituted in its place. In fact, the entire theory of Hoffman's case rests on his allegation that the photograph is not a "true" or "literal" depiction of him, but a false portrayal. Regardless of the scope of *Comedy III*, it is clear to us that it does not strip LAM of First Amendment protection.

DUSTIN HOFFMAN
ISN'T A DRAG IN A
BUTTER-COLORED
SILK GOWN BY
RICHARD TYLER
AND RALPH
LAUREN HEELS.

Figure 8-12. The altered photo in *Los Angeles Magazine*

article as a whole is a combination of fashion photography, humor, and visual and verbal editorial comment on classic films and famous actors. Any commercial aspects are "inextricably entwined" with expressive elements, and so they cannot be separated out "from the fully protected whole." *Gaudiya Vaishnava Soc'y v. City & County of San Francisco*, 952 F.2d 1059, 1064 (9th Cir. 1991) (as amended). "[T]here are commonsense differences between speech that does no more than propose a commercial transaction and other varieties," *Va. State Bd. of Pharmacy v. Va. Citizens Consumer Council, Inc.*, 425 U.S. 748, 771 n.24 (1976) (quotations and citation omitted), and common sense tells us this is not a simple advertisement.

The district court also concluded that the article was not protected speech because it was created to "attract attention." 33 F. Supp. 2d at 874. A printed article meant to draw attention to the for-profit magazine in which it appears, however, does not fall outside of the protection of the First Amendment because it may help to sell copies. While there was testimony that the Hollywood issue and the use of celebrities was intended in part to "rev up" the magazine's profile, that does not make the fashion article a purely "commercial" form of expression.

We conclude that LAM's publication of the altered "Tootsie" photograph was not commercial speech.

Actual malice

The district court went on to state that even if LAM could raise a First Amendment defense, LAM acted with actual malice, and "the First Amendment does not protect knowingly false speech," 33 F. Supp. 2d at 875 (citing *New York Times Co. v. Sullivan*, 376 U.S. 254 (1964)). The court found that the magazine altered Hoffman's image, and then published that image knowing it was false and intending that the readers believe the falsehood:

> [LAM] knew that Mr. Hoffman had never worn the designer clothes he was depicted as wearing, and that what they were showing was not even his body. Moreover, [LAM] admitted that it intended to create the false impression in the minds of the public "that they were seeing Mr. Hoffman's body."

Id.

We have concluded that LAM is entitled to the full First Amendment protection accorded noncommercial speech. Because a public figure such as Hoffman can recover damages for noncommercial speech from a media organization such as LAM only by proving "actual malice," we now must determine whether the district court was correct in concluding that LAM acted with "reckless disregard for the truth" or a "high degree of awareness of probable falsity."

We review the district court's finding of actual malice de novo. *Eastwood v. Nat'l Enquirer, Inc.*, 123 F.3d 1249, 1252 (9th Cir. 1997). We give to "credibility determinations the special deference to which they are entitled," and then "determine whether the believed evidence establishes actual malice." *Id.* We must "satisfy ourselves that plaintiff proved malice by clear and convincing evidence, which we have described as a heavy burden, far in excess of the preponderance sufficient for most civil litigation." *Id.*

We must first identify the purported false statement of fact in issue. Hoffman alleged, and the district court found, that the altered "Tootsie" photograph and the accompanying text were "false" because they created the impression that Hoffman himself posed for the altered photograph (that is, that Hoffman was wearing the Richard Tyler dress and the Ralph Lauren shoes which replaced the red sequined dress and the shoes Hoffman wore in the original photograph). To show actual malice, Hoffman must demonstrate by clear and convincing evidence that LAM intended to create the false impression in the minds of its readers that when they saw the altered "Tootsie" photograph they were seeing Hoffman's body. It is not enough to show that LAM unknowingly misled readers into thinking Hoffman had actually posed for the altered photograph. Mere negligence is not enough to demonstrate actual malice. *Dodds v. American Broad. Co.*, 145 F.3d

1053, 1063 (9th Cir. 1998) (citing *Masson v. New Yorker Magazine, Inc.*, 501 U.S. 496, 510 (1991)). "[S]ubjective or actual intent is required and ... 'there is no actual malice where journalists unknowingly mislead the public.'" *Id.* at 1064 (quoting *Eastwood*, 123 F.3d at 1256). The evidence must clearly and convincingly demonstrate that LAM knew (or purposefully avoided knowing) that the photograph would mislead its readers into thinking that the body in the altered photograph was Hoffman's. *See Eastwood*, 123 F.3d at 1256.

The altered photograph retains Hoffman's head and the American flag background from the "Tootsie" still, but grafts onto it a body dressed in different clothing. The body is similar in appearance to Hoffman's in the original. On the page directly facing the altered "Tootsie" photograph the magazine printed small copies of all sixteen original, unaltered stills, including the original "Tootsie" photograph. By providing a point of comparison to the original, this next page made it clear that LAM had altered the film still. This direct comparison does not, however, alert the reader that Hoffman did not participate in the alteration.

We must go beyond the altered photograph itself and examine the "totality of [LAM's] presentation," to determine whether it "would inform the average reader (or the average browser)" that the altered "Tootsie" photograph was not a photograph of Hoffman's body. The article is featured on the magazine cover as "The Ultimate Fashion Show Starring Grace Kelly, Marilyn Monroe and Darth Vader." The table of contents describes the "Grand Illusions" article: "By using state-of-the-art digital magic, we clothed some of cinema's most enduring icons in fashions by the hottest designers." The accompanying full-page photo is of Humphrey Bogart and Ingrid Bergman as they appeared in "Casablanca," wearing current designer clothing, with a caption stating, "Digital composite by ZZYZX."

A few pages later, the "editor's note" describes the article:

> The movie stills in our refashioned fashion spectacular, "Grand Illusions" (page 104) *have* appeared before—in fact, they're some of the most famous images in Hollywood history. But you've never seen them quite like this. Cary Grant, for example, is still ducking that pesky plane in *North by Northwest*, but now he is doing it as a runway model, wearing a suit from Moschino's spring collection. We know purists will be upset, but who could resist the opportunity to produce a 1997 fashion show with mannequins who have such classic looks?

The Contributors page states: "'With computers,' says Elisabeth Cotter of ZZYZX, 'you can transform anything—even the past.' She proved it by using the latest in computer software to give old movie stars makeovers for 'Grand Illusions.'"

The "Grand Illusions" article itself states on the title page, "With the help of digital magic and today's hottest designers, we present the ultimate Hollywood fashion show—starring Cary Grant, Marilyn Monroe, Rita Hayworth and the Creature from the Black Lagoon. Photographs by Alberto Tolot. Digital Composites by ZZYZX." Each photograph that follows identifies the actor whose "body" is clothed in designer clothing with a reference to the featured film. Representative captions read "Cary Grant is dashing in...." (as he runs from the cropduster in "North by Northwest"), "Harold Lloyd looks timely in...." (as he hangs from the clock in "Safety Last"), "Marilyn Monroe cools off in...." (as she stands on the grate in "The Seven Year Itch"), "Jimmy Stewart likes to watch in...." (as he looks at Grace Kelly in "Rear Window"), "Susan Sarandon takes on mankind in...." (as she aims a gun in "Thelma and Louise"), and "Judy Garland hits the bricks in...." (as she runs through a field in "The Wizard of Oz" with the Cowardly Lion, the Tin Man, and the Scarecrow, "who is stuffed into" a designer suit printed with bricks).

Finally, the "Tootsie" photograph appears, with its caption "Dustin Hoffman isn't a drag in a butter-colored silk gown by Richard Tyler and Ralph Lauren heels," immediately followed by the page showing all the original stills. The only remaining reference to the article is the "shopping guide," which, almost twenty pages later, provides prices and the names of stores carrying some of the clothing featured in the photographs.

We do not believe that the totality of LAM's presentation of the article and the "Tootsie" photograph provides clear and convincing evidence that the editors intended to suggest falsely to the ordinary reader that he or she was seeing Hoffman's body in the altered "Tootsie" photograph. All but one of the references to the article in the magazine make it clear that digital techniques were used to substitute current fashions for the clothes worn in the original stills. Although nowhere does the magazine state that models' bodies were digitally substituted for the actors' bodies, this would be abundantly clear given that the vast majority of the featured actors were deceased. While LAM never explicitly told its readers that the living actors did not pose for the altered photographs in the article, there is certainly no clear and convincing evidence in the magazine itself that LAM intended to suggest the opposite—that it convinced Hoffman (or, for that matter, John Travolta, Elizabeth Taylor, Susan Sarandon, and Geena Davis) to recreate poses from their past roles for this fashion article.

The district court stated that LAM "admitted that it intended to create the false impression in the minds of the public 'that they were seeing Mr. Hoffman's body.'" This is a quotation from a portion of the style editor's testimony, in which she explained that she wanted the male model whose body would appear in the altered "Tootsie" photograph to have Hoffman's body type. She later explained, however, that she did not intend to convey to readers that Hoffman had participated in some way in the article's preparation, and never thought that readers would believe Hoffman posed for the photograph in the new dress.

We defer to the district court when it makes a credibility determination. *See Eastwood*, 123 F.3d at 1252. In this case, the district court made no express credibility finding, as it did not state that it believed this one statement and disbelieved the remainder of the editor's testimony. But even if the district court had determined that only this quoted portion of her testimony were worthy of belief, it does not constitute clear and convincing evidence that LAM intended to *mislead* its readers. This single statement, whose meaning is ambiguous in the context of other testimony, the text of the article, and the entire magazine, is not sufficient to strip the magazine of its First Amendment protection.

We conclude that LAM is entitled to the full First Amendment protection awarded noncommercial speech. We also conclude that Hoffman did not show by clear and convincing evidence, which is "far in excess of the preponderance sufficient for most civil litigation," *Eastwood*, 123 F.3d at 1252, that LAM acted with actual malice in publishing the altered "Tootsie" photograph. Because there is no clear and convincing evidence of actual malice, we must reverse the district court's judgment in Hoffman's favor and the court's award of attorney fees to Hoffman, and direct that judgment be entered for LAM.

REVERSED.

———

Stephano v. News Group Publications, Inc.
64 N.Y.2d 174, 474 N.E.2d 580, 485 N.Y.S.2d 220 (1984)

[New York magazine printed a photograph of the plaintiff wearing a "bomber jacket" designed by Giorgio Armani in its weekly "Best Bets column." The caption listed the price of the jacket and three stores where it could be purchased. (See photo in Chapter I.)]

The plaintiff's affidavit ... stated: "While it may be that a party whose service or product is included in 'Best Bets' does not pay a direct advertising fee to be included, the benefits to the magazine are obtained in an indirect manner. Stores, designers, and retailers featured there have all advertised in New York magazine at other times and places, and giving them this 'breakout' feature in the 'Best Bets' column acts as barter for such advertising at another time and place." The plaintiff further stated that the designer and the stores mentioned ... had previously advertised in New York magazine and observed that "the publicity benefits in the column to the designer and retail outlets mentioned are evident from a fair reading of the column." ...

It is settled that a "'picture illustrating an article on a matter of public interest is not considered used for the purposes of trade or advertising within the prohibition of the statute * * * unless it has no real relationship to the article * * * or unless the article is an advertisement in disguise'" [citations omitted].... The plaintiff's primary contention is that his picture was used for advertising purposes within the meaning of the statute. Although the article was not presented to the public as an advertisement, and was published in a column generally devoted to newsworthy items, the plaintiff claims that it is in fact an advertisement in disguise. In addition, although the defendant has submitted affidavits that the article was published solely as a matter of public interest, without any consideration for advertising concerns, and that the magazine received no payment for including the item in its "Best Bets" column, the plaintiff nevertheless contends that he has presented sufficient facts to require a trial on the issue....

The circumstances on which [the plaintiff] bases his claim are (1) the fact that the news column contains information normally included in an advertisement identifying the designer of the jacket, the approximate price, and three places where the jacket may be purchased, and (2) the fact that some or all of those stores mentioned in the article had previously advertised products in the magazine. Those circumstances are not enough to raise a jury question as to whether the article was published for advertising purposes.

The plaintiff does not dispute the fact that the information provided in the article is of legitimate reader interest. Indeed, similar information is frequently provided in reviews or news announcements of books, movies, shows or other new products including fashions. Nor does the plaintiff contend that it is uncommon for commercial publishers to print legitimate news items or reviews concerning products by persons or firms who have previously advertised in the publisher's newspaper or magazine. In short, the plaintiff has not presented any facts which would set this particular article apart from the numerous other legitimate news items concerning new products. He offers only his speculative belief that in this case the information on the jacket was included in the defendant's column for advertising purposes or perhaps, more vaguely, to promote additional advertising. That, in our view, is insufficient to defeat the defendant's motion for summary judgment.

———

Notes and Questions

1. *Hoffman* raises the question of what types of uses will be considered an advertisement for a product or service. The Los Angeles Magazine article demonstrated how digital technology could be used to place new clothing on the bodies of famous actors or actresses in iconic photos from their movies; but the captions specified the brand-name

designers of the clothing depicted, and a "Shopper's Guide" in the back of magazine listed the prices and stores where those items could be purchased. Isn't that an implicit invitation or advertisement to buy the item in question?

Taking the Supreme Court's definition seriously (commercial speech is speech that "does no more than propose a commercial transaction"), the Ninth Circuit limits commercial speech to "a traditional advertisement printed *merely* for the purpose of selling a particular product" (emphasis added). It holds that the photo at issue was not "commercial speech," because the magazine "did not receive any consideration from the designers for featuring their clothing in the fashion article," and because "any commercial aspects are 'inextricably intertwined' with expressive elements." Do you agree that the definition of "commercial speech" should be narrowly limited to avoid constitutional problems? Should the court have ruled differently if it had deemed the photograph to constitute an advertisement?

2. Compare *Hoffman* to the false endorsement cases we have studied, including *Allen v. National Video* and *White v. Samsung*. Should the court have applied the multi-factor test for likelihood of confusion instead of the *New York Times* standard for defamatory speech? Does the likelihood of confusion test only apply in cases of commercial speech? If the court did apply a likelihood of confusion standard, should it have found a triable issue of fact? Why or why not?

3. Alternatively, having found that the *Los Angeles Magazine* article was artistic expression rather than commercial speech, should the court have applied the *Rogers* standard instead of the *New York Times* standard? If the court had applied the *Rogers* standard, would you say that Hoffman's likeness had "artistic relevance" to the article? Was the use explicitly misleading?

4. *Hoffman* is consistent with the New York Court of Appeals' ruling in *Stephano*. The question presented there was whether the trier of fact could reasonably conclude that the article was "an advertisement in disguise" where the stores listed all had previously advertised in the magazine. The plaintiff alleged the existence of an implicit *quid pro quo* arrangement, in which advertisers who received free publicity in the editorial pages of the magazine would be more likely to purchase advertisements in later issues of the magazine. Is that theory so far-fetched that it should not be submitted to the trier of fact? If such an arrangement in fact existed, what additional evidence could the plaintiff submit to demonstrate its existence?

5. Compare *Hoffman* and *Stephano* to *Facenda v. NFL Films, Inc.*, 542 F.3d 1007 (3d Cir. 2008). The plaintiff was the estate of John Facenda, a longtime narrator for NFL Films, whose deep baritone voice was described in the opinion as "distinctive, recognizable, legendary, and ... known by many football fans as the Voice of God" (internal quotations omitted). Facenda had licensed to NFL Films "the unequivocal rights to use the audio and visual film sequences recorded of me, or any part of them ... in perpetuity and by whatever media or manner NFL Films sees fit ... provided, however, such use does not constitute an endorsement of any product or service."

Two decades after Facenda's death, NFL Films produced "The Making of Madden NFL '06," a 22-minute "documentary" extolling the "Madden NFL '06" video game and comparing it favorably to real NFL games. The film was shown eight times in the three days preceding the release of the video game in stores. The program contained three sentences spoken by Facenda, totalling 13 seconds. The Third Circuit rejected application of the *Rogers* test and held that the program was commercial speech, likening it to a "late-night, half-hour long 'infomercial.'" Accordingly, it affirmed summary judgment in favor of Facenda under Pennsylvania's post-mortem right of publicity statute. However, the court held there was a genuine issue of material fact as to whether the public would be confused as to whether Facenda endorsed "Madden '06", and it remanded the Lanham Act §43(a) claim for trial.

Are the court's two holdings consistent? Doesn't the contract waive any right of publicity claim unless the use "constitute[s] an endorsement"? If so, and if there is a triable issue of fact as to whether the use of Facenda's voice would be perceived as an endorsement, isn't there also a triable issue as to whether Facenda's right of publicity claim was waived? Or does the contract distinguish between an actual endorsement and the perception of one? Shouldn't an actual endorsement be harder to prove than whether there was a likelihood of confusion about whether an endorsement exists?

Problem 7

John Riggins is a former professional football player who played for the New York Jets and Washington Redskins, and was inducted into the Hall of Fame. After his divorce, his ex-wife, a real-estate agent, decided to sell the house they had once owned jointly. She held a "broker's open" to generate interest in the home among other real-estate agents, and made up the following flyer to advertise the event:

BROKERS OPEN
June 16 — 11 AM to 1 PM
COME SEE ...
John Riggins'
Former Home,

$849,500
Register to win an autographed football

Menu
Honey Baked Ham
Famous Rice Ring
Homemade Chocolate Cake and
Lemon Squares etc.

Directions: From 66, Rt. 123 North to a left on Hunter Hill Rd.
Go 3.2 miles to a left onto Wickens. Take the first left onto
Vickers Drive. Go to the Col-de-Sac and it's the second driveway.

10611 Vickers Dr.

Mary Lou Riggins
Home: 938-4199
Office: 938-5800

Riggins sued his wife's employer, Town & Country Properties, Inc., for violating his right of publicity. Using the cases above, what arguments can you make for and against his claim? For the actual outcome, *see* Town & Country Properties, Inc. v. Riggins, 249 Va. 387, 457 S.E.2d 356 (1995).

Chapter IX

Celebrity Rights and Freedom of Expression Outside the United States

A. Introduction

As we have seen in Chapters VII and VIII, in the United States the First Amendment provides protection both for the press (which may be sued for publishing pictures, etc., of celebrities) and for others, such as artists, who may make use of celebrity images or "personas" as part of their own expressions. The case law relating to the clashes between rights of publicity and freedom of expression in the United States is fairly robust.

Although other countries do not have quite the same tradition (or constitutional mandates) as the U.S., they do typically have some form of protection for the press and for free expression. Sometimes that protection may be contained in a constitution; other times it is in statutory provisions. (Britain, which has no written constitution, has a combination of traditional common law rules and statutory provisions.) The differences in the legal protections for rights of publicity and free expression in other countries make it difficult to present precise analogies for all of the situations in which First Amendment values inform the law of rights of publicity in the U.S. Therefore, the next section contains material from various countries concerning the interplay of rights of publicity (or rights of privacy, which may be the closest available analogue in the case law) and free expression. Although most of the cases deal with what we would call newsworthiness, you should compare these materials to the various U.S. situations that are contained in Chapter VIII as well. In other words, you should use these materials to attempt to develop answers to the variety of problems that may be raised concerning the rights of publicity on the one hand, and the rights of free expression on the other.

B. The European Convention on Human Rights

In the aftermath of World War II, European nations were determined to prevent a repeat of the human rights abuses of the previous generation. The result was the Convention for the Protection of Human Rights and Fundamental Freedoms (the "European Convention on Human Rights"), a treaty under which signatories agree to provide specific protections against human rights abuses. To date, the number of signatories to the Convention has grown to forty-seven, including all 27 countries of the European Union, and twenty other countries. The Convention permits parties who claim to have been injured by violations committed by member countries to sue the countries in the European Court of Human Rights, located in Strasbourg, France.

But what, you may ask, does this have to do with rights of publicity (or even free speech)? Quite a bit, as it turns out. The Convention contains two provisions that are particularly relevant to these issues. One protects the right to privacy (recall the origins of the U.S. right of publicity from Chapter I); another protects freedom of speech and the press. In the next case, the European Court of Human Rights was called upon to reconcile those two provisions in a situation involving a rather well-known European personality. The court's decision provides insight into the European approach to the protection of celebrities as well as freedom of expression.

––––––

Von Hannover v. Germany
[2005] 40 E.H.R.R. 1 (Eur. Ct. H. R. 2004)

[Princess Caroline of Monaco, who lives in Paris, brought this action in the European Court of Human Rights, claiming that the German courts, which refused to give her complete relief, improperly denied her rights provided by the European Convention on Human Rights (particularly Article 8, which provides protection for one's privacy). Her original complaint concerned several series of photographs of her that were taken in France but published in German publications (because of stricter French laws regarding publication of such photos). The photos in question included some with her children, others with one or more friends, all in technically "public" places, though some in locations, such as restaurants, where she may have had an expectation of privacy from photographers. Lower German courts refused any relief against publication in Germany, on the grounds, essentially, that she is a public figure and does not have an expectation of privacy. The German Federal Court of Justice (Bundesgerichtshof) granted limited relief relating to the photographs in a restaurant, because it was a "secluded place" where she would have an expectation of privacy. She appealed that judgment to the Federal Constitutional Court of Germany (the Bundesverfassungsgericht), "submitting that there had been an infringement of her right to the protection of her personality rights."]

25. In a landmark judgment of 15 December 1999, delivered after a hearing, the Constitutional Court allowed the applicant's appeal in part on the ground that the three photos that had appeared in the 32nd and 34th editions of *Bunte* magazine, dated 5 August 1993 and 19 August 1993, featuring the applicant with her children had infringed her right to the protection of her personality rights guaranteed by sections 2(1) and 1(1) of the [German] Basic Law, reinforced by her right to family protection under section 6 of the Basic Law. It referred the case to the Federal Court of Justice on that point. However, the Constitutional Court dismissed the applicant's appeal regarding the other photos.

The relevant extract of the judgment reads as follows:

"The appeal is well-founded in part.

...

II.

The decisions being appealed do not fully satisfy the requirements of section 2(1) read in conjunction with section 1(1) of the Basic Law.

The provisions of sections 22 and 23 of the KUG (*Kunsturhebergesetz*—Copyright Act) on which the civil courts based their decisions in the present case are, however, compatible with the Basic Law.

Under section 2(1) of the Basic Law general personality rights are guaranteed only within the framework of the constitutional order. The provisions concerning the publication of photographical representations of persons listed in sections 22 and 23 of the KUG are part of that constitutional order. They derive from an incident which at the time caused a scandal (photos of Bismarck on his deathbed ...) and from the ensuing politico-legal debate sparked by this incident..., and aim to strike a fair balance between respect for personality rights and the community's interest in being informed....

Under section 22, first sentence, of the KUG, pictures can only be disseminated or exposed to the public eye with the express approval of the person represented. Pictures relating to contemporary society are excluded from that rule under section 23(1) of the KUG.... Under 23(2) of the KUG, however, that exception does not apply where the dissemination interferes with a legitimate interest of the person represented. The protection by degrees under these rules ensures that they take account of both the need to protect the person being represented and the community's desire to be informed and the interest of the media which satisfy that desire. That much has already been established by the Federal Constitutional Court....

...

(b) In the instant case regard must be had, in interpreting and applying sections 22 and 23 of the KUG, not only to general personality rights, but also to the freedom of the press guaranteed by section 5(1), second sentence, of the Basic Law in so far as the provisions in question also affect those freedoms.

...

The fact that the press fulfils the function of forming public opinion does not exclude entertainment from the functional guarantee under the Basic Law. The formation of opinions and entertainment are not opposites. Entertainment also plays a role in the formation of opinions. It can sometimes even stimulate or influence the formation of opinions more than purely factual information. Moreover, there is a growing tendency in the media to do away with the distinction between information and entertainment both as regards press coverage generally and individual contributions, and to disseminate information in the form of entertainment or mix it with entertainment ("infotainment"). Consequently, many readers obtain information they consider to be important or interesting from entertaining coverage....

Nor can mere entertainment be denied any role in the formation of opinions. That would amount to unilaterally presuming that entertainment merely satisfies a desire for amusement, relaxation, escapism or diversion. Entertainment can also convey images of reality and propose subjects for debate that spark a process of discussion and assimilation relating to philosophies of life, values and behaviour models. In that respect it fulfils important social functions.... When measured against the aim of protecting press freedom, entertainment in the press is neither negligible nor entirely worthless and therefore falls within the scope of application of fundamental rights....

The same is true of information about people. Personalization is an important journalistic means of attracting attention. Very often it is this which first arouses interest in a problem and stimulates a desire for factual information. Similarly, interest in a particular event or situation is usually stimulated by personalised accounts. Additionally, celebrities embody certain moral values and lifestyles. Many people base their choice of lifestyle on their example. They become points of crystallisation for adoption or rejection and act as examples or counter-examples. This is what explains the public interest in the various ups and downs occurring in their lives.

As regards politicians this public interest has always been deemed to be legitimate from the point of view of transparency and democratic control. Nor can it in principle be disputed that it exists in respect of other public figures. To that extent it is the function of the press to show people in situations that are not limited to specific functions or events and this also falls within the sphere of protection of press freedom. It is only when a balancing exercise has to be done between competing personality rights that an issue arises as to whether matters of essential interest for the public are at issue and treated seriously and objectively or whether private matters, designed merely to satisfy the public's curiosity, are being disseminated....

(c) The decision of the Federal Court of Justice largely stands up to an examination of its compatibility with the constitutional rules.

(aa) ... Under section 23(1) no. 1 of the KUG the publication of pictures portraying an aspect of contemporary society are exempted from the obligation to obtain the consent of the person concerned within the meaning of section 22 of the KUG. Judging from the drafting history to the Act ... and from the meaning and purpose of the words used, the provision in question takes into consideration the community's interest in being informed and the freedom of the press. Accordingly, the interpretation of this element (*Tatbestandsmerkmal*) must take account of the interests of the public. Pictures of people who are of no significance in contemporary society should not be made freely accessible to the public: they require the prior consent of the person concerned. The other element that is affected by fundamental rights, that of a "legitimate interest" for the purposes of section 23(2) of the KUG, concerns only—and this must be stressed at the outset—figures of contemporary society and cannot therefore take sufficient account of the interests of the freedom of the press if these have previously been neglected when the circle of the persons concerned was defined.

It is in keeping with the importance and scope of the freedom of the press, and not unreasonably restrictive of the protection of personality rights, that the concept of contemporary society referred to in section 23(1) no. 1 of the KUG should not only cover, in accordance with a definition given by the courts, events of historical or political significance, but be defined on the basis of the public interest in being informed.... The kernel of press freedom and the free formation of opinions requires the press to have sufficient margin of manoeuvre to allow it to decide, in accordance with its publishing criteria, what the public interest demands and the process of forming opinion to establish what amounts to a matter of public interest. As has been stated, entertaining coverage is no exception to these principles.

Nor should the Federal Court of Justice be criticised for including in the "domain of contemporary society", within the meaning of section 23(1) no. 1 of the KUG, pictures of people who have not only aroused public interest at a certain point on the occasion of a particular historical event but who, on account of their status and importance, attract the public's attention in general and not just on the odd occasion. Account should also be taken in this regard of the fact that, compared to the situation at the time the Copyright Act was passed, increased importance is given today to illustrated information. The concept of a "figure of contemporary society *par excellence*" (*absolute Person der Zeitgeschichte*), often employed in this respect in the case-law and legal theory, does not conclusively derive from statute or the Constitution. If, as was done by the Court of Appeal and the Federal Court of Justice, it is interpreted as a shortened expression designating people whose image is deemed by the public to be worthy of respect out of consideration for the people concerned, it is irreproachable from the point of view of constitutional law at least as long as a balancing exercise is carried out, in the light of the circumstances of the case, between the public's interest in being informed and the legitimate interests of the person concerned.

General personality rights do not require publications that are not subject to prior consent to be limited to pictures of figures of contemporary society in the exercise of their function in society. Very often the public interest aroused by such figures does not relate exclusively to the exercise of their function in the strict sense. It can, on the contrary, by virtue of the particular function and its impact, extend to information about the way in which these figures behave generally—that is, also outside their function—in public. The public has a legitimate interest in being allowed to judge whether the personal behaviour of the individuals in question, who are often regarded as idols or role models, convincingly tallies with their behaviour on their official engagements.

If, on the other hand, the right to publish pictures of people considered to be figures of contemporary society were to be limited to their official functions, insufficient account would be taken of the public interest properly aroused by such figures and this would, moreover, favour a selective presentation that would deprive the public of certain necessary judgmental possibilities in respect of figures of socio-political life, having regard to the function of role model of such figures and the influence they exert. The press is not, however, allowed to use any picture of figures of contemporary society. On the contrary, section 23(2) of the KUG gives the courts adequate opportunity to apply the protective provisions of section 2(1) read in conjunction with section 1(1) of the Basic Law....

(bb) In theory the criteria established by the Federal Court of Justice for interpreting the concept of "legitimate interest" used in section 23(2) of the KUG are irreproachable from the point of view of constitutional law.

According to the decision being appealed, the privacy meriting protection that must also be afforded to "figures of contemporary society *par excellence*" presupposes that they have retired to a secluded place with the objectively perceptible aim of being alone and in which, confident of being alone, they behave differently from how they would behave in public. The Federal Court of Justice accepted that there had been a breach of sections 22 and 23 of the KUG where this type of picture was taken secretly or by catching the person unawares....

Lastly, there is nothing unconstitutional, when balancing the public interest in being informed against the protection of private life, in attaching importance to the method used to obtain the information in question.... It is doubtful, however, that the mere fact of photographing the person secretly or catching them unawares can be deemed to infringe their privacy outside the home. Having regard to the function attributed to that privacy under constitutional law and to the fact that it is usually impossible to determine from a photo whether the person has been photographed secretly or caught unawares, the existence of unlawful interference with that privacy cannot in any case be made out merely because the photo was taken in those conditions. As, however, the Federal Court of Justice has already established in respect of the photographs in question that the appellant was not in a secluded place, the doubts expressed above have no bearing on the review of its decision.

(cc) However, the constitutional requirements have not been satisfied in so far as the decisions of which the appellant complains did not take account of the fact that the right to protection of personality rights of a person in the appellant's situation is strengthened by section 6 of the Basic Law regarding that person's intimate relations with their children.

(dd) ... The three photos of the applicant with her children require a fresh examination ... in the light of the constitutional rules set out above.... The decision must therefore be set aside in that respect and remitted to the Federal Court of Justice for a fresh decision....

3. *The third set of proceedings*

[Princess Caroline reapplied to the German courts for relief regarding photographs taken of her at a beach club, which apparently were taken at some distance from a neighboring building. The German courts reaffirmed their earlier rulings and held that the beach club was a public place, even if a restricted one.]

II. RELEVANT DOMESTIC AND EUROPEAN LAW

A. The Basic Law

39. The relevant provisions of the Basic Law [of Germany] are worded as follows:

Article 1 § 1

"The dignity of human beings is inviolable. All public authorities have a duty to respect and protect it."

Article 2 § 1

"Everyone shall have the right to the free development of their personality provided that they do not interfere with the rights of others or violate the constitutional order or moral law (*Sittengesetz*)."

Article 5 §§ 1 and 2

"(1) Everyone shall have the right freely to express and disseminate his or her opinions in speech, writing and pictures and freely to obtain information from generally accessible sources. Freedom of the press and freedom of reporting on the radio and in films shall be guaranteed. There shall be no censorship.

(2) These rights shall be subject to the limitations laid down by the provisions of the general laws and by statutory provisions aimed at protecting young people and to the obligation to respect personal honour (*Recht der persönlichen Ehre*)."

Article 6 §§ 1 and 2

"(1) Marriage and the family enjoy the special protection of the State.

(2) The care and upbringing of children is the natural right of parents and a duty primarily incumbent on them. The State community shall oversee the performance of that duty."

B. The Copyright (Arts Domain) Act

40. Section 22(1) of the Copyright (Arts Domain) Act provides that images can only be disseminated with the express approval of the person concerned.

41. Section 23(1) no. 1 of that Act provides for exceptions to that rule, particularly where the images portray an aspect of contemporary society (*Bildnisse aus dem Bereich der Zeitgeschichte*) on condition that publication does not interfere with a legitimate interest (*berechtigtes Interesse*) of the person concerned (section 23(2)).

C. Resolution 1165 (1998) of the Parliamentary Assembly of the Council of Europe on the right to privacy

42. [T]his resolution, adopted by the Parliamentary Assembly on 26 June 1998, is worded as follows:

> "1. The Assembly recalls the current affairs debate it held on the right to privacy during its September 1997 session, a few weeks after the accident which cost the Princess of Wales her life.
>
> 2. On that occasion, some people called for the protection of privacy, and in particular that of public figures, to be reinforced at the European level by means of a convention, while others believed that privacy was sufficiently protected by national legislation and the European Convention on Human Rights, and that freedom of expression should not be jeopardised.
>
> 3. In order to explore the matter further, the Committee on Legal Affairs and Human Rights organised a hearing in Paris on 16 December 1997 with the participation of public figures or their representatives and the media.
>
> 4. The right to privacy, guaranteed by Article 8 of the European Convention on Human Rights, has already been defined by the Assembly in the declaration on mass communication media and human rights, contained within Resolution 428 (1970), as "the right to live one's own life with a minimum of interference".
>
> 5. In view of the new communication technologies which make it possible to store and use personal data, the right to control one's own data should be added to this definition.
>
> 6. The Assembly is aware that personal privacy is often invaded, even in countries with specific legislation to protect it, as people's private lives have become a highly lucrative commodity for certain sectors of the media. The victims are essentially public figures, since details of their private lives serve as a stimulus to sales. At the same time, public figures must recognise that the special position they occupy in society—in many cases by choice—automatically entails increased pressure on their privacy.
>
> 7. Public figures are persons holding public office and/or using public resources and, more broadly speaking, all those who play a role in public life, whether in politics, the economy, the arts, the social sphere, sport or in any other domain.
>
> 8. It is often in the name of a one-sided interpretation of the right to freedom of expression, which is guaranteed in Article 10 of the European Convention on Human Rights, that the media invade people's privacy, claiming that their readers are entitled to know everything about public figures.

9. Certain facts relating to the private lives of public figures, particularly politicians, may indeed be of interest to citizens, and it may therefore be legitimate for readers, who are also voters, to be informed of those facts.

10. It is therefore necessary to find a way of balancing the exercise of two fundamental rights, both of which are guaranteed by the European Convention on Human Rights: the right to respect for one's private life and the right to freedom of expression.

11. The Assembly reaffirms the importance of every person's right to privacy, and of the right to freedom of expression, as fundamental to a democratic society. These rights are neither absolute nor in any hierarchical order, since they are of equal value.

12. However, the Assembly points out that the right to privacy afforded by Article 8 of the European Convention on Human Rights should not only protect an individual against interference by public authorities, but also against interference by private persons or institutions, including the mass media.

13. The Assembly believes that, since all member states have now ratified the European Convention on Human Rights, and since many systems of national legislation comprise provisions guaranteeing this protection, there is no need to propose that a new convention guaranteeing the right to privacy should be adopted.

14. The Assembly calls upon the governments of the member states to pass legislation, if no such legislation yet exists, guaranteeing the right to privacy containing the following guidelines, or if such legislation already exists, to supplement it with these guidelines:

(i) the possibility of taking an action under civil law should be guaranteed, to enable a victim to claim possible damages for invasion of privacy;

(ii) editors and journalists should be rendered liable for invasions of privacy by their publications, as they are for libel;

(iii) when editors have published information that proves to be false, they should be required to publish equally prominent corrections at the request of those concerned;

(iv) economic penalties should be envisaged for publishing groups which systematically invade people's privacy;

(v) following or chasing persons to photograph, film or record them, in such a manner that they are prevented from enjoying the normal peace and quiet they expect in their private lives or even such that they are caused actual physical harm, should be prohibited;

(vi) a civil action (private lawsuit) by the victim should be allowed against a photographer or a person directly involved, where paparazzi have trespassed or used "visual or auditory enhancement devices" to capture recordings that they otherwise could not have captured without trespassing;

(vii) provision should be made for anyone who knows that information or images relating to his or her private life are about to be disseminated to initiate emergency judicial proceedings, such as summary applications for an interim order or an injunction postponing the dissemination of the information, subject to an assessment by the court as to the merits of the claim of an invasion of privacy;

(viii) the media should be encouraged to create their own guidelines for publication and to set up an institute with which an individual can lodge complaints of invasion of privacy and demand that a rectification be published....

THE LAW

I. ALLEGED VIOLATION OF ARTICLE 8 OF THE CONVENTION

43. The applicant submitted that the German court decisions had infringed her right to respect for her private and family life guaranteed by Article 8 of the Convention, which is worded as follows:

"1. Everyone has the right to respect for his private and family life, his home and his correspondence.

2. There shall be no interference by a public authority with the exercise of this right except such as is in accordance with the law and is necessary in a democratic society in the interests of national security, public safety or the economic well-being of the country, for the prevention of disorder or crime, for the protection of health or morals, or for the protection of the rights and freedoms of others."

A. Submissions of the parties and interveners

1. The applicant

44. The applicant stated that she had spent more than ten years in unsuccessful litigation in the German courts trying to establish her right to the protection of her private life. She alleged that as soon as she left her house she was constantly hounded by paparazzi who followed her every daily movement, be it crossing the road, fetching her children from school, doing her shopping, out walking, engaging in sport or going on holiday. In her submission, the protection afforded to the private life of a public figure like herself was minimal under German law because the concept of a "secluded place" as defined by the Federal Court of Justice and the Federal Constitutional Court was much too narrow in that respect. Furthermore, in order to benefit from that protection the onus was on her to establish every time that she had been in a secluded place.... She affirmed that in France her prior agreement was necessary for the publication of any photos not showing her at an official event. Such photos were regularly taken in France and then sold and published in Germany....

2. The Government

45. The Government submitted that German law, while taking account of the fundamental role of the freedom of the press in a democratic society, contained sufficient safeguards to prevent any abuse and ensure the effective protection of the private life of even public figures. In their submission, the German courts had in the instant case struck a fair balance between the applicant's rights to respect for her private life guaranteed by Article 8 and the freedom of the press guaranteed by Article 10, having regard to the margin of appreciation available to the State in this area. The protection of the private life of a figure of contemporary society *par excellence* did not require the publication of photos without his or her authorisation to be limited to showing the person in question engaged in their official duties. The public had a legitimate interest in knowing how the person behaved generally in public.... Furthermore, the concept of a secluded place was only one factor, albeit an important one, of which the domestic courts took account when balancing the protection of private life against the freedom of the press. Accordingly, while private life was less well protected where a public figure was photographed in a public place other factors could also be taken into consideration, such as the nature of the photos, for example, which should not shock the public....

3. The interveners

46. The Association of Editors of German Magazines submitted that German law, which was half way between French law and United Kingdom law, struck a fair balance between the right to protection of private life and the freedom of the press....

47. ... Since the death of her mother in 1982 the applicant had officially been First Lady of the reigning family in Monaco and was as such an example for the public (*Vorbildfunktion*). Moreover, the Grimaldi family had always sought to attract media attention and was therefore itself responsible for the public interest in it. The applicant could not therefore, especially if account were taken of her official functions, be regarded as a victim of the press....

B. The Court's assessment

...

2. As regards the applicability of Article 8

50. The Court reiterates that the concept of private life extends to aspects relating to personal identity, such as a person's name, or a person's picture.

Furthermore, private life, in the Court's view, includes a person's physical and psychological integrity; the guarantee afforded by Article 8 of the Convention is primarily intended to ensure the development, without outside interference, of the personality of each individual in his relations with other human beings. There is therefore a zone of interaction of a person with others, even in a public context, which may fall within the scope of "private life"....

53. In the present case there is no doubt that the publication by various German magazines of photos of the applicant in her daily life either on her own or with other people falls within the scope of her private life.

3. Compliance with Article 8

a. The domestic courts' position

54. The ... Federal Constitutional Court ... balanc[ed] the requirements of the freedom of the press against those of the protection of private life, that is, the public interest in being informed against the legitimate interests of the applicant.... The court attached decisive weight to the freedom of the press, even the entertainment press, and to the public interest in knowing how the applicant behaved outside her representative functions....

b. General principles governing the protection of private life and the freedom of expression

56. In the present case the applicant did not complain of an action by the State, but rather of the lack of adequate State protection of her private life and her image.

57. The Court reiterates that although the object of Article 8 is essentially that of protecting the individual against arbitrary interference by the public authorities, it does not merely compel the State to abstain from such interference: in addition to this primarily negative undertaking, there may be positive obligations inherent in an effective respect for private or family life. These obligations may involve the adoption of measures designed to secure respect for private life even in the sphere of the relations of individuals between themselves. That also applies to the protection of a person's picture against abuse by others.

The boundary between the State's positive and negative obligations under this provision does not lend itself to precise definition. The applicable principles are, nonetheless, similar. In both contexts regard must be had to the fair balance that has to be struck between the competing interests of the individual and of the community as a whole; and in both contexts the State enjoys a certain margin of appreciation.

58. That protection of private life has to be balanced against the freedom of expression guaranteed by Article 10 of the Convention. In that context the Court reiterates that the freedom of expression constitutes one of the essential foundations of a democratic society. Subject to paragraph 2 of Article 10, it is applicable not only to "information" or "ideas" that are favourably received or regarded as inoffensive or as a matter of indifference, but also to those that offend, shock or disturb. Such are the demands of that pluralism, tolerance and broadmindedness without which there is no "democratic society".

In that connection the press plays an essential role in a democratic society. Although it must not overstep certain bounds, in particular in respect of the reputation and rights of others, its duty is nevertheless to impart—in a manner consistent with its obligations and responsibilities—information and ideas on all matters of public interest. Journalistic freedom also covers possible recourse to a degree of exaggeration, or even provocation.

59. Although freedom of expression also extends to the publication of photos, this is an area in which the protection of the rights and reputation of others takes on particular importance. The present case does not concern the dissemination of "ideas", but of images containing very personal or even intimate "information" about an individual. Furthermore, photos appearing in the tabloid press are often taken in a climate of continual harassment which induces in the person concerned a very strong sense of intrusion into their private life or even of persecution.

60. In the cases in which the Court has had to balance the protection of private life against the freedom of expression it has always stressed the contribution made by photos or articles in the press to a debate of general interest.... [I]n a recent case concerning the publication by President Mitterand's former private doctor of a book containing revelations about the President's state of health, the Court held that "the more time passed the more the public interest in President Mitterand's two seven-year presidential terms prevailed over the requirements of the protection of his rights with regard to medical confidentiality" and held that there had been a breach of Article 10.

c. Application of these general principles by the Court

61. The Court points out at the outset that in the present case the photos of the applicant in the various German magazines show her in scenes from her daily life, thus engaged in activities of a purely private nature such as practising sport, out walking, leaving a restaurant or on holiday. The photos, in which the applicant appears sometimes alone and sometimes in company, illustrate a series of articles with such anodyne titles as "Pure happiness", "Caroline ... a woman returning to life", "Out and about with Princess Caroline in Paris" and "The kiss. Or: they are not hiding anymore."

62. The Court also notes that the applicant, as a member of the Prince of Monaco's family, represents the ruling family at certain cultural or charitable events. However, she does not exercise any function within or on behalf of the State of Monaco or one of its institutions.

63. The Court considers that a fundamental distinction needs to be made between reporting facts—even controversial ones—capable of contributing to a debate in a democratic society relating to politicians in the exercise of their functions, for example, and reporting details of the private life of an individual who, moreover, as in this case, does not exercise official functions. While in the former case the press exercises its vital role of

"watchdog" in a democracy by contributing to "impart[ing] information and ideas on matters of public interest it does not do so in the latter case.

64. Similarly, although the public has a right to be informed, which is an essential right in a democratic society that, in certain special circumstances, can even extend to aspects of the private life of public figures, particularly where politicians are concerned..., this is not the case here. The situation here does not come within the sphere of any political or public debate because the published photos and accompanying commentaries relate exclusively to details of the applicant's private life.

65. As in other similar cases it has examined, the Court considers that the publication of the photos and articles in question, of which the sole purpose was to satisfy the curiosity of a particular readership regarding the details of the applicant's private life, cannot be deemed to contribute to any debate of general interest to society despite the applicant being known to the public.

66. In these conditions freedom of expression calls for a narrower interpretation.

67. In that connection the Court also takes account of the resolution of the Parliamentary Assembly of the Council of Europe on the right to privacy, which stresses the "one-sided interpretation of the right to freedom of expression" by certain media which attempt to justify an infringement of the rights protected by Article 8 of the Convention by claiming that "their readers are entitled to know everything about public figures".

68. The Court finds another point to be of importance: even though, strictly speaking, the present application concerns only the publication of the photos and articles by various German magazines, the context in which these photos were taken—without the applicant's knowledge or consent—and the harassment endured by many public figures in their daily lives cannot be fully disregarded.

In the present case this point is illustrated in particularly striking fashion by the photos taken of the applicant at the Monte Carlo Beach Club tripping over an obstacle and falling down. It appears that these photos were taken secretly at a distance of several hundred metres, probably from a neighbouring house, whereas journalists and photographers' access to the club was strictly regulated.

69. The Court reiterates the fundamental importance of protecting private life from the point of view of the development of every human being's personality. That protection—as stated above—extends beyond the private family circle and also includes a social dimension. The Court considers that anyone, even if they are known to the general public, must be able to enjoy a "legitimate expectation" of protection of and respect for their private life.

70. Furthermore, increased vigilance in protecting private life is necessary to contend with new communication technologies which make it possible to store and reproduce personal data. This also applies to the systematic taking of specific photos and their dissemination to a broad section of the public.

71. Lastly, the Court reiterates that the Convention is intended to guarantee not rights that are theoretical or illusory but rights that are practical and effective.

72. The Court has difficulty in agreeing with the domestic courts' interpretation of section 23(1) of the Copyright (Arts Domain) Act, which consists in describing a person as such as a figure of contemporary society *par excellence*. Since that definition affords the person very limited protection of their private life or the right to control the use of their image, it could conceivably be appropriate for politicians exercising official func-

tions. However, it cannot be justified for a "private" individual, such as the applicant, in whom the interest of the general public and the press is based solely on her membership of a reigning family whereas she herself does not exercise any official functions.

In any event the Court considers that, in these conditions, the Act has to be interpreted narrowly to ensure that the State complies with its positive obligation under the Convention to protect private life and the right to control the use of one's image.

73. Lastly, the distinction drawn between figures of contemporary society "*par excellence*" and "relatively" public figures has to be clear and obvious so that, in a state governed by the rule of law, the individual has precise indications as to the behaviour he or she should adopt. Above all, they need to know exactly when and where they are in a protected sphere or, on the contrary, in a sphere in which they must expect interference from others, especially the tabloid press.

74. The Court therefore considers that the criteria on which the domestic courts based their decisions were not sufficient to protect the applicant's private life effectively. As a figure of contemporary society "*par excellence*" she cannot — in the name of freedom of the press and the public interest — rely on protection of her private life unless she is in a secluded place out of the public eye and, moreover, succeeds in proving it (which can be difficult). Where that is not the case, she has to accept that she might be photographed at almost any time, systematically, and that the photos are then very widely disseminated even if, as was the case here, the photos and accompanying articles relate exclusively to details of her private life.

75. In the Court's view, the criterion of spatial isolation, although apposite in theory, is in reality too vague and difficult for the person concerned to determine in advance. In the present case merely classifying the applicant as a figure of contemporary society "*par excellence*" does not suffice to justify such an intrusion into her private life.

d. Conclusion

76. As the Court has stated above, it considers that the decisive factor in balancing the protection of private life against freedom of expression should lie in the contribution that the published photos and articles make to a debate of general interest. It is clear in the instant case that they made no such contribution since the applicant exercises no official function and the photos and articles related exclusively to details of her private life.

77. Furthermore, the Court considers that the public does not have a legitimate interest in knowing where the applicant is and how she behaves generally in her private life even if she appears in places that cannot always be described as secluded and despite the fact that she is well known to the public.

Even if such a public interest exists, as does a commercial interest of the magazines in publishing these photos and these articles, in the instant case those interests must, in the Court's view, yield to the applicant's right to the effective protection of her private life.

78. Lastly, in the Court's opinion the criteria established by the domestic courts were not sufficient to ensure the effective protection of the applicant's private life and she should, in the circumstances of the case, have had a "legitimate expectation" of protection of her private life.

79. Having regard to all the foregoing factors, and despite the margin of appreciation afforded to the State in this area, the Court considers that the German courts did not strike a fair balance between the competing interests.

80. There has therefore been a breach of Article 8 of the Convention....

CONCURRING OPINION OF JUDGE CABRAL BARRETO
(Translation)

I am of the opinion that there has been a violation of Article 8 of the Convention, but am unable to follow the entire reasoning of the majority.

1. ... In my view, ... the applicant is a public figure and the public does have a right to be informed about her life.

The solution therefore needs to be found in the fair balance that has to be struck between the applicant's right to her private life and the public's right to be informed.

2. The applicant is a public figure, even if she does not perform any function within or on behalf of the State of Monaco or one of its institutions.

"Public figures are persons holding public office and/or using public resources and, more broadly speaking, all those who play a role in public life, whether in politics, the economy, the arts, the social sphere, sport or in any other domain"—paragraph 7 of Resolution 1165 (1998) of the Parliamentary Assembly of the Council of Europe on the right to privacy.

It is well known that the applicant has for years played a role in European public life, even if she does not perform any official functions in her own country.

To measure the degree of public interest in her, it is sufficient to look at the amount of media coverage devoted to her public or private life.

Very recently the press drew attention to the fact that, on her arrival at the ceremony of the marriage of Crown Prince Felipe of Spain, the applicant was one of the people from Europe's and the world's high society to be the most widely greeted by the public.

The applicant is, in my view, a public figure and information about her life contributes to a debate of general interest.

The general interest does not have to be limited to political debate. As pointed out by the Parliamentary Assembly "certain facts relating to the private lives of public figures, particularly politicians, may indeed be of interest to citizens ..."

If that is true of politicians it is also true for all other public figures in whom the public takes an interest.

It is therefore necessary to strike a balance between two fundamental rights: the right of public figures to respect for their private life and everyone's right to freedom of expression, which embraces the right of the public to be informed.

I agree with the majority that the private life of a public figure does not stop at their front door.

However, it has to be acknowledged that, in view of their fame, a public figure's life outside their home, and particularly in public places, is inevitably subject to certain constraints.

Fame and public interest inevitably give rise to a difference in treatment of the private life of an ordinary person and that of a public figure.

As the Federal Constitutional Court pointed out, "the public has a legitimate interest in being allowed to judge whether the personal behaviour of the individuals in question, who are often regarded as idols or role models, convincingly tallies with their behaviour on their official engagements".

Admittedly, determining the limit of a public figure's private life is no easy task.

Furthermore, a strict criterion might lead to solutions that do not correspond to the "nature of things".

It is clear that if the person is in an isolated spot everything that happens there must be covered by the protection of private life.

It appears to me, however, that the criterion of spatial isolation used by the German courts is very restrictive.

In my view, whenever a public figure has a "legitimate expectation" of being safe from the media his or her right to private life prevails over the right to freedom of expression or the right to be informed.

It will never be easy to define in concrete terms the situations that correspond to this "legitimate expectation" and a case-by-case approach is therefore justified.

This casuistic approach may also give rise to differences of opinion.

The majority attach importance, for example, to the fact that the photos at the Monte Carlo Beach Club had been taken secretly.

I do not dispute the need to take account of the fact that the photos were taken from a distance, particularly if the person was somewhere they could legitimately believe did not expose them to public view.

However, the beach club swimming pool was an open place frequented by the general public and, moreover, visible from the neighbouring buildings.

Is it possible in such a place to entertain a reasonable expectation of not being exposed to public view or to the media?

I do not think so.

I believe that this same criterion is valid for photos showing the applicant in other situations in her daily life in which she cannot expect her private life to be protected.

I have in mind the photos of her doing her shopping.

However, other photos—for example those of the applicant on horseback or playing tennis—were taken in places and circumstances that would call for the opposite approach.

It is thus in the knowledge of the limits to the exercise (I refer in this connection to Judge Zupančič's opinion) that I have found a violation of Article 8 of the Convention.

CONCURRING OPINION OF JUDGE ZUPANČIČ

I adhere to the hesitations raised by my colleague, Judge Cabral Barreto. And while I find the distinctions between the different levels of permitted exposure, as defined by the German legal system, too *Begriffsjurisprudenz*-like, I nevertheless believe that the balancing test between the public's right to know on the one hand and the affected person's right to privacy on the other hand must be adequately performed. He who willingly steps upon the public stage cannot claim to be a private person entitled to anonymity. Royalty, actors, academics, politicians etc. perform whatever they perform publicly. They may not seek publicity, yet, by definition, their image is to some extent public property.

Here I intend to concentrate not so much on the public's right to know—this applies first and foremost to the issue of the freedom of the press and the constitutional doctrine concerning it—but rather on the simple fact that it is impossible to separate by an iron curtain private life from public performance....

It is time[, however,] that the pendulum swung back to a different kind of balance between what is private and secluded and what is public and unshielded.

The question here is how to ascertain and assess this balance. I agree with the outcome of this case. However, I would suggest a different determinative test ... which speaks of a "reasonable expectation of privacy"....

Notes and Questions

1. Although all European Union members are signatories to the European Human Rights Convention, the number of adhering countries goes far beyond just the EU. Forty-seven countries are members of the Council of Europe, which administers the Convention (ironically, the latest addition was Monaco). Thus, the potential effect of this decision is much greater, in some respects, than a decision of the European Court of Justice (which has jurisdiction over European Union law). The Court of Human Rights is empowered to issue judgments for money—its judgments are not merely advisory opinions on the interpretation of the Convention. Like any treaty, enforcement of the Convention's provisions, including judgments of the Court, can be problematic. However, European Union countries tend to respect its judgments (in the *von Hannover* case, there was a subsequent monetary settlement).

2. Did the German court ignore Articles 8 and 10 in the ruling reversed by the Court of Human Rights? If so, why? If not, in what way did the German court and the Court of Human Rights interpret the Convention provisions differently?

3. Why wasn't it sufficient that Princess Caroline was a famous public figure? (Recall that under U.S. law, public figures have less protection against certain intrusions into their privacy.)

4. If Princess Caroline had been the actual head of state of Monaco, would that have changed the outcome?

5. The Court engages in what it describes as a balancing of different interests. What factors are relevant to this balancing test?

6. Under some circumstances, the Court of Human Rights gives what it calls a "margin of appreciation" (a form of deference) to the findings of the courts of member states of the Convention. Did the Court of Human Rights give any deference to the analysis of the German court? What level of deference would be appropriate in this kind of case? Would it be reasonable to give different countries different levels of deference?

7. How do the analyses of the concurring judges differ from that of the majority? Were they in favor of greater protection for Princess Caroline or greater protection of the press? Did either fundamentally disagree with the balancing test of the majority?

C. The United Kingdom

Timothy Pinto, *The Influence of the European Convention on Human Rights on Intellectual Property Rights*[*]
24 E.I.P.R. 209 (2002)

The best evidence of the influence of the European Convention on Human Rights ("ECHR") on intellectual property rights is to be found in English law. This is because the ECHR was only incorporated into English law, via the Human Rights Act 1998 ("HRA"), on October 2, 2000. There is a discernable dividing line between English intellectual property cases before and after the HRA came into force. This article will focus on the influence of the ECHR on the English law of intellectual property rights....

The European Convention on Human Rights

The Second World War and the Nuremberg trials left Western Europe in a state of shock. As a result, the Council of Europe ("the Council") was founded in 1949 to guard against the rise of new dictatorships, another European war and the spread of communism. It recognised that dictatorships did not arrive overnight but arose gradually; the first steps usually being the suppression of individual rights, for example restricting the freedom of the press.

The Council hoped to lay down a mechanism so that if a Contracting State started down the slope towards totalitarianism, other States could react and prevent the slide. This mechanism would uphold the rule of law and principles of democracy. It became enshrined in the ECHR which was first signed in 1950 and came into force in 1953.

Convention rights which influence intellectual property

The following Convention rights have already affected or are likely to affect intellectual property rights:

(1) Article 10—freedom of expression;

(2) Article 8—right to respect for private and family life, home and correspondence; and

(3) Article 1 of the First Protocol ("Article 1FP")—right to property.

This list is not exhaustive. The ingenuity of lawyers, litigants and judges, exceptional cases, the development of the jurisprudence of the European Court of Human Rights ("E Ct HR") and changes in intellectual property rights can bring other Convention rights into play....

Principles of interpretation of the ECHR

The interpretation of the Convention rights is governed by principles deriving from the jurisprudence of the E Ct HR. The E Ct HR recognises that Contracting States have a certain margin of appreciation (*i.e.* discretion) in assessing an interference with a Convention right. There are circumstances when national courts are in a better position than an international court to judge whether or not it is appropriate to restrict a Convention right. Nevertheless, the margin is subject to supervision by the E Ct HR. National courts

---

[*] Courtesy of Timothy Pinto, Taylor Wessing LLP, London, U.K.

have a wide margin where a measure is taken to protect morality and in the areas of unfair competition and advertising.

Another principle of interpretation is that of proportionality. Any measure restricting a Convention right must be "proportionate to the legitimate aim pursued". This means that the measure must be justified, not more than necessary to achieve its objective and not be arbitrary, unfair or based on irrational considerations.

Article 10 — freedom of expression

The right to freedom of expression potentially impacts on all intellectual property rights. This is because an intellectual property right enables its owner to control to an extent the use of the information or idea protected. Such control is in conflict with the principle of freedom of expression. The text of Article 10 is as follows:

> 1. Everyone has the right to freedom of expression. This right shall include freedom to hold opinions and to receive and impart information and ideas without interference by public authority and regardless of frontiers. This Article shall not prevent States from requiring the licensing of broadcasting, television or cinema enterprises.

> 2. The exercise of these freedoms, since it carries with it duties and responsibilities, may be subject to such formalities, conditions, restrictions or penalties as are prescribed by law and are necessary in a democratic society, in the interests of national security, territorial integrity or public safety, for the prevention of disorder or crime, for the protection of health or morals, for the protection of the reputation or rights of others, for preventing the disclosure of information received in confidence, or for maintaining the authority and impartiality of the judiciary.

Nature of the right under Article 10

The E Ct HR has held that freedom of expression constitutes one of the essential foundations of a democratic society and for the development of every man. Freedom of the press is particularly important as it enables everyone to participate in the free political debate which is at the very core of the concept of a democratic society. Journalistic freedom even admits a degree of exaggeration or provocation. Article 10 protects journalists' rights to divulge information of general interest provided they act in good faith and on an accurate factual basis and provide reliable and precise information in accordance with the ethics of journalism. Almost every copyright and confidentiality case discussed below involves journalists fighting for their freedom of expression.

Scope of Article 10(1)

The "expression" to which Article 10(1) refers is very wide in scope. It is applicable not only to "information" and "ideas" that are favourably received or regarded as inoffensive or as a matter of indifference, but also to those that offend, shock or disturb the state or any sector of the population. Furthermore, Article 10(1) does not apply solely to certain types of information, ideas or forms of expression. As well as political speech, it includes freedom of information of a commercial nature, advertising and freedom of artistic expression. Article 10 applies to natural and legal persons, including profit-making companies.

Interference

If the expression comes within Article 10(1) then the court will examine whether or not there has been an interference with it. As Lester and Pannick explain, "[t]he protection from interference is not limited to prior censorship and includes the prohibitions by way of post-expression sanctions. ... Other types of restraints on expression have included forfeiture of property, the denial of a licence and libel damages and an injunction".

An example of interference is the interim injunctions imposed against various newspapers preventing them from publishing material about Peter Wright's employment in the British security service which he described in his book *Spycatcher*.

If there has been an interference with the right to freedom of expression, it is for the interferer to prove that it came within the requirements of Article 10(2). If these are not met, there has been a violation of Article 10.

Restrictions on Freedom of expression—Article 10(2)

There are three requirements which must be satisfied in order to prove that there has not been a violation of freedom of expression, namely:

(1) the interference must be prescribed by law;

(2) it must pursue one or more of the legitimate aims set out in Article 10(2); and

(3) It must be necessary in a democratic society to achieve one or more of the legitimate aims.

These exceptions to the right to freedom of expression must be narrowly interpreted and the necessity for any restriction must be convincingly established.

Prescribed by law

Any restriction on the right to freedom of expression must have some basis in domestic law, whether statute or common law. However, there must not only be a basis in domestic law, but also the law in question must be of sufficient quality. It must therefore fulfil two criteria, namely:

(a) the law must be adequately accessible; and

(b) it must be formulated with sufficient precision to enable the citizen to regulate his conduct: he must be able—if need be with appropriate advice—to foresee, to a degree that is reasonable in the circumstances, the consequences which a given action may entail.

Nonetheless, the E Ct HR recognises that frequently laws are framed in a manner that is not absolutely precise. It has held that section 1 of the German Unfair Competition Act 1909 which prohibits "acts contrary to honest practices" was sufficiently precise as it dealt with a sphere in which the situation is constantly changing in accordance with developments in the market and in the field of communication. Similarly, states have been accorded a wide margin of appreciation in formulating laws governing advertising. ...

The permitted aims

The legitimate aims for restricting freedom of expression, which are most pertinent to intellectual property rights, are the protection of the rights of others (i.e. the intellectual property rights of others) and the prevention of the disclosure of information received in confidence.

Nevertheless, any of the aims may be involved in an intellectual property context. For example, in *The Observer and The Guardian v. United Kingdom*, the British Government cited as the aims of restricting the freedom of expression of the claimants (by obtaining interim injunctions for breach of confidence), the maintenance of the authority of the judiciary and the interests of national security.

Necessary in a democratic society

The E Ct HR has held that the word "necessary" in Article 10(2) "is not synonymous with 'indispensible', neither has it the flexibility of such expressions as 'admissible', 'ordinary', 'useful', 'reasonable' or 'desirable'." The national court must assess "whether the interference complained of corresponded to a 'pressing social need', whether it was 'proportionate to the legitimate aim pursued', [and] whether the reasons given by the national authorities are 'relevant and sufficient'".

Article 8 — Right to respect for private and family life, home and correspondence

There is no independent cause of action for breach of privacy in English law. Intellectual property (especially confidentiality and copyright) is used to protect privacy. Article 8 states that:

1. Everyone has the right to respect for his private and family life, his home and correspondence.

2. There shall be no interference by a public authority with the exercise of this right except such as is in accordance with the law and is necessary in a democratic society in the interests of national security, public safety or the economic well-being of the country, for the protection of health or morals, or for the protection of the rights and freedoms of others.

Nature of the right under Article 8

Although the object of Article 8 is essentially that of protecting the individual against arbitrary interference by public authorities, states have an obligation to provide individuals as between themselves with protection of the rights specified in Article 8(1). The provisions of Article 8(2) are interpreted in the same way as those in Article 10(2).

Scope of Article 8

Article 8 only applies to human beings. As Lester and Pannick point out, Article 8 "protects more than privacy simpliciter. It covers a broad range of personal interests: family life, home and correspondence." They go on to state that "Article 8 encompasses, more broadly, the right to be oneself, to live as oneself and to keep oneself."

The E Ct HR has held that the concept of private life "covers the physical and moral integrity of the person including his or her sexual life", and comprises "to a certain degree the right to establish and develop relationships with other human beings".

The concepts of family life, home and correspondence have also been broadly interpreted. The concept of home includes business premises. "Correspondence" includes telephone calls made from business premises as well as from home....

Article 1FP: Right to property

Most intellectual property rights are property rights. Article 1FP states that:

Every natural or legal person is entitled to the peaceful enjoyment of his possessions. No one shall be deprived of his possessions except in the public interest and subject to the conditions provided for by law and by the general principles of international law.

The proceeding provision shall not, however, in any way impair the right of a state to enforce such laws as it deems necessary to control the use of property in accordance with the general interest or to secure the payment of taxes or other contributions or penalties.

Scope of Article 1FP

The right to property applies to a wide variety of property including patents and, it is submitted, copyright, trade marks and designs. Confidential information is not traditionally classified as property because of the requirement for an obligation of confidence between the confider and confidant. Nevertheless, Article 1FP may cover commercial information, such as know-how, as this is often treated as property. For example, know-how is often the subject of licensing. In contrast, personal information or activities, e.g. sunbathing in one's garden (where the publication of photographs could be protected by confidentiality), are unlikely to come within Article 1FP as they are not possessions which a state can control.

Restriction of the right to property

Any interference with a person's Convention right to property must be justified by being prescribed by law, in the public interest and proportional to the aim to be achieved. States are given a wide margin of appreciation in deciding whether such interference is in the public interest.

The Human Rights Act 1998

Compatibility and public authorities

Section 3(1) of the HRA states that "[i]n so far as it is possible to do so, primary legislation and subordinate legislation must be read and given effect in a way which is compatible with the Convention rights". Section 6(1) of the HRA states that "[i]t is unlawful for a public authority to act in a way which is incompatible with a Convention right". "[P]ublic authority includes—(a) a court or tribunal, and (b) any person certain of whose functions are functions of a public nature ... ".

Thus, a United Kingdom court must consider the Convention rights in order to ensure it is acting compatibly with them. In doing so, it must take Strasbourg jurisprudence into account. The Trade Marks Registry, Patent Office and Copyright Tribunal are almost certainly public authorities for the purposes of the HRA.

Section 12

Section 12 of the HRA is specifically designed to safeguard legitimate journalistic activity while protecting individuals from unjustified interference in their private lives. It applies if a court is considering whether to grant any relief which, if granted, might affect the exercise of freedom of expression.

Section 12(3)

Section 12(3) states that the court must not grant an interim injunction restraining publication unless it is "satisfied that the applicant is likely to establish that publication should not be allowed."

This indicates the great importance which parliament gives to freedom of expression. On first sight, the use of the word "likely" changes the *American Cyanamid* test to determine whether to grant an interim injunction, namely, if there is a serious question to be tried, the court must weigh the balance of convenience (without considering the merits). In *Douglas v. Hello!*, Keene L.J. considered that section 12(3) "does not seek to give priority to one Convention right over another ... [and] requires the court to look at the merits of the case and not merely to apply the *American Cyanamid* test".

In *Imutran Ltd. v. Uncaged Campaign Ltd.*, Morritt V.-C. held that "[t]heoretically and as a matter of language likelihood is slightly higher in the scale of probability than a real prospect of success. But the difference is so small that I cannot believe that there will be many (if any) cases which would have succeeded under the *American Cyanamid* test but will now fail because of the terms of section 12(3)".

Section 12(4)

Section 12(4) states that the "court must have particular regard to the importance of the Convention right to freedom of expression". Where the proceedings relate to journalistic, literary or artistic material the court must have particular regard to "(a) the extent to which— (i) the material has, or is about to, become available to the public; or (ii) it is, or would be, in the public interest for the material to be published; (b) any relevant privacy code".

The privacy code to which the courts have so far had regard is clause 3 of the Code of Practice of the Press Complaints Commission.

In *Ashdown v. Telegraph Group Ltd.* the Vice Chancellor considered that the phrase "must have particular regard to" in section 12(4) does not mean that freedom of expression and the other factors should be given extra weight but that it "points to the need for the court to consider the matters to which the subsection refers specifically and separately from other relevant considerations"....

Privacy

Arguably the most important recent development in the law of confidentiality has been due to the influence of Article 8.

There has traditionally been no right to privacy in English law. This was illustrated in the 1990 case of *Kaye v. Robertson*. The claimant had undergone brain surgery in hospital. Whilst recovering, a reporter and a photographer from the Sunday Sport newspaper, ignoring signs that visitors contact a member of hospital staff, entered his hospital room and interviewed him. The newspaper intended to publish the interview. Fortunately, the court moulded the action of malicious falsehood to fit the facts and granted the injunction. Glidewell L.J. stated "[i]t is well-known that in English law there is no right to privacy, and accordingly no right of action of a person's privacy. The facts of the present case are a graphic illustration of the desirability of Parliament considering whether and in what circumstances statutory provision can be made to protect the privacy of individuals."

Four years later, in the case of *Hellewell v. Chief Constable of Derbyshire*, Laws J. stated obiter that "[i]f someone with a telephoto lens were to take from a distance and with no authority a picture of another engaged in some private act, his subsequent disclosure of the photograph would, in my judgment, as surely amount to a breach of confidence as if he had found or stolen a letter or diary in which the act was recounted and proceeded to publish it. In such a case, the law would protect what might reasonably be called a right of privacy, although the name accorded to the cause of action would be breach of confidence." The judge was making the point that, notwithstanding *Kaye v. Robertson*, breach of confidence was flexible enough to protect the fundamental right of a person's privacy.

Shortly after the judgment in *Hellewell*, the News of the World published an article entitled "Di's sister-in-law in booze and bulimia clinic". This detailed some of the personal problems of Countess Spencer and included a photograph taken with a telephoto lens while she walked in the grounds of a private clinic. Earl Spencer complained to the Press Complaints Commission which concluded there was a clear breach of its code vis-a-vis his wife.

Instead of suing the newspapers, the Earl and Countess applied to the European Commission on Human Rights ("E Com HR") complaining that English law failed to provide adequate respect for their privacy and so violated Article 8. The E Com HR decided in 1998 that the applicants had not exhausted their domestic remedies and dismissed the application. It held that the common law remedy of breach of confidence was available to them and, if necessary, had the ability to develop.

The dicta of Laws J. and the ruling of the *Spencer* case did not amount to a right of privacy. However, the tide of opinion was about to turn.

On January 8, 2001, 50 years after the United Kingdom ratified the ECHR, Sedley L.J. in *Douglas v. Hello! Ltd.* stated: "we have reached a point at which it can be said with confidence that the law recognises and will appropriately protect a right of personal privacy." This was the watershed which the above case law had been building up to. The judge gave two reasons for his comment. First, that equity and the common law had to respond to an increasingly invasive social environment. Secondly, that such recognition was required by the HRA and in particular Article 8. He went on to say that since *Kaye v. Robertson* had been decided, "the legal landscape has altered" and that the right of privacy was grounded in the equitable doctrine of breach of confidence.

The main reason why breach of confidence was not previously able to provide adequate protection of privacy was because a claimant had to prove the three elements in *Coco v. Clark*, the second element of which is that the information must have been imparted in circumstances importing an obligation of confidence. Invasions of privacy are often done by those with no relationship with the victim, for instance by a journalist with a telephoto lens. With no relationship between confider and confidant, the obligation of confidence is not established and a claimant would not have succeeded in a confidentiality action.

On this issue Sedley L.J. said: "what a concept of privacy does, however, is accord recognition to the fact that the law has to protect not only those people whose trust has been abused but also those who simply find themselves subjected to an unwanted intrusion into their personal lives. The law no longer needs to construct an artificial relationship of confidentiality between intruder and victim: it can recognise privacy itself as a legal principle drawn from the fundamental value of personal autonomy."

The facts of the case were that Michael Douglas and Catherine Zeta-Jones had given OK! magazine exclusive rights to publish photographs of and an article about their wedding. There were tight security and confidentiality arrangements to ensure that neither guests nor those employed at the wedding could take photographs of the occasion. Hello! magazine managed to acquire some unauthorised photographs and was about to publish them.

The Court of Appeal discharged the interim injunctions partly because Mr and Mrs Douglas had sold most of their privacy to OK! and partly because, had they been wrongly granted, it would have been very difficult to quantify the damage suffered by Hello!. The claimants had entered into a contract for their mutual profit: the couple would be paid by OK! for the exclusive rights and OK! would be able to sell more copies of its magazine as a result of the wedding feature. Furthermore, the Douglas' wedding did not remain private for long, as they were quite happy for it to be widely publicised by OK!. The case of *Douglas v. Hello!* was in reality a commercial breach of confidence case and privacy was only used by the claimants to bolster their position.

The case of *Beckham v. MGN* fell more squarely as an invasion of privacy. In that case Eady J. upheld an interim injunction in favour of David and Victoria Beckham to prevent publication in the Sunday People of photographs of their matrimonial home. Relying on clause 3 of the Press Complaints Code, the HRA and *Douglas v. Hello!*, the judge ruled that it was appropriate to "grant an injunction to protect the claimants from unwarranted intrusions into their privacy, and with regard to material which the law recognises as being confidential".

In *Douglas v. Hello!* the claimants had set out to make a profit from the wedding but Hello! scooped the exclusive deal. In contrast, *Beckham v. MGN* did not have that commercial backdrop and the photographs were taken inside the Beckhams' home, not at a celebrity wedding in the Plaza Hotel.

Although Mr and Mrs Beckham were themselves considering selling the rights to allow publication of certain photographs of their house, they were particularly concerned that the unauthorised photographs might reveal and thereby jeopardise some of the security measures taken to protect them and their home. Eady J. reversed the decision of the duty judge that the claimants give a cross-undertaking not to publish photographs of their house, holding that this would have prejudiced their basic rights of privacy and freedom of contract.

Eady J. confirmed the development of the law of confidence in protecting privacy in *B v. H Bauer Publishing Ltd.* when he explained that "[o]ne of the inhibiting factors about this area of law, hitherto, has been that it was traditionally necessary to establish a duty of confidence — most frequently associated with a prior relationship of some kind. It is becoming easier now, however, to establish that an obligation of confidence can arise (in equity) without the parties having been in any such prior relationship ... ".

The law of confidential information now protects citizens against invasions of their Convention right to privacy.

Trade marks

The Trade Marks Act 1994 and passing off

It is possible that trade mark owners will start citing their right to property under the Convention. Similarly, although the law of passing off aims to achieve a balance between protecting the goodwill attached to marks and legitimate competition, owners of goodwill may argue that their Convention rights to property must be respected. The other side of the coin is that a person accused of infringing a registered trade mark or passing off could present their right of freedom of expression as a defence.

In the author's view, assuming that a trade mark fell within Article 10(1), it is unlikely that freedom of expression will significantly influence trade mark rights. This is because the Trade Marks Act 1994 ("TMA") and passing off already take into account a person's right to use their own name or use a mark descriptively or otherwise than to indicate source. Similarly, the author does not consider that Article 1FP will influence registered trade mark or passing-off rights which already recognise a trade mark owner's right of property.

Other Convention rights might crop up in trade mark cases. English trade mark law does not easily protect personality rights. Thus, where a person's name or likeness is registered as a trade mark, that person might object to certain use of that trade mark citing their right to privacy under Article 8. Article 14, which prohibits discrimination, could be employed to supplement the ground of refusal to register a trade mark which is contrary to public policy under section 3(3)(a) of the TMA.

The following case applies the principles of the Human Rights Act discussed in the preceding article and the *Von Hannover* case. As you read this case you should understand

(a) that the House of Lords was the highest judicial body in the U.K.,[*] and (b) the Lords often issue their opinions seriatim, without regard to how they voted. Therefore, you must read each opinion carefully and count votes in order to determine who wins the case.

———————

Campbell v. MGN Limited
[2004] U.K.H.L. 22, [2004] 2 A.C. 457,
[2004] 2 All ER 995, [2004] E.M.L.R. 15
(H.L. 2004)

THE LORD NICHOLLS OF BIRKENHEAD:

My Lords,

1. Naomi Campbell is a celebrated fashion model. Hers is a household name, nationally and internationally. Her face is instantly recognisable. Whatever she does and wherever she goes is news.

2. On 1 February 2001 the 'Mirror' newspaper carried as its first story on its front page a prominent article headed 'Naomi: I am a drug addict'. The article was supported on one side by a picture of Miss Campbell as a glamorous model, on the other side by a slightly indistinct picture of a smiling, relaxed Miss Campbell, dressed in baseball cap and jeans, over the caption 'Therapy: Naomi outside meeting'....

4. The article made mention of Miss Campbell's efforts to rehabilitate herself, and that one of her friends said she was still fragile but 'getting healthy'. The article gave a general description of Narcotics Anonymous therapy, and referred to some of Miss Campbell's recent publicised activities....

5. In the middle of the double page spread, between several innocuous pictures of Miss Campbell, was a dominating picture over the caption 'Hugs: Naomi, dressed in jeans and baseball hat, arrives for a lunchtime group meeting this week'. The picture showed her in the street on the doorstep of a building as the central figure in a small group. She was being embraced by two people whose faces had been pixelated. Standing on the pavement was a board advertising a named cafe. The article did not name the venue of the meeting, but anyone who knew the district well would be able to identify the place shown in the photograph.

6. The general tone of the articles was sympathetic and supportive with, perhaps, the barest undertone of smugness that Miss Campbell had been caught out by the 'Mirror'. The source of the newspaper's information was either an associate of Miss Campbell or a fellow addict attending meetings of Narcotics Anonymous. The photographs of her attending a meeting were taken by a free lance photographer specifically employed by the newspaper to do the job. He took the photographs covertly, while concealed some distance away inside a parked car....

The proceedings and the further articles

8. On the same day as the articles were published Miss Campbell commenced proceedings against MGN Ltd., the publisher of the 'Mirror'. The newspaper's response was to publish further articles, this time highly critical of Miss Campbell....

———————

[*] As of October 1, 2009, the judicial functions of the House of Lords were transferred to the newly-created Supreme Court of the United Kingdom. —Eds.

10. In the proceedings Miss Campbell claimed damages for breach of confidence and compensation under the Data Protection Act 1998. The article of 7 February formed the main basis of a claim for aggravated damages. Morland J. upheld Miss Campbell's claim. He made her a modest award of £2,500 plus £1,000 aggravated damages in respect of both claims. The newspaper appealed. The Court of Appeal, comprising Lord Phillips of Worth Matravers MR, Chadwick and Keene LJJ, allowed the appeal and discharged the judge's order: Miss Campbell has now appealed to your Lordships' House.

Breach of confidence: misuse of private information

11. In this country, unlike the United States of America, there is no over-arching, all-embracing cause of action for 'invasion of privacy': see *Wainwright v. Home Office* [2003] 3 WLR 1137. But protection of various aspects of privacy is a fast developing area of the law, here and in some other common law jurisdictions.... In this country development of the law has been spurred by enactment of the Human Rights Act 1998.

12. The present case concerns one aspect of invasion of privacy: wrongful disclosure of private information. The case involves the familiar competition between freedom of expression and respect for an individual's privacy. Both are vitally important rights. Neither has precedence over the other. The importance of freedom of expression has been stressed often and eloquently, the importance of privacy less so. But it, too, lies at the heart of liberty in a modern state. A proper degree of privacy is essential for the well-being and development of an individual. And restraints imposed on government to pry into the lives of the citizen go to the essence of a democratic state.

13. The common law or, more precisely, courts of equity have long afforded protection to the wrongful use of private information by means of the cause of action which became known as breach of confidence....

14.... The continuing use of the phrase 'duty of confidence' and the description of the information as 'confidential' is not altogether comfortable. Information about an individual's private life would not, in ordinary usage, be called 'confidential'. The more natural description today is that such information is private. The essence of the tort is better encapsulated now as misuse of private information.

15.... The extent to which the common law as developed thus far in this country protects other forms of invasion of privacy is not a matter arising in the present case. It does not arise because, although pleaded more widely, Miss Campbell's common law claim was throughout presented in court exclusively on the basis of breach of confidence, that is, the wrongful publication by the 'Mirror' of private information.

16. The European Convention on Human Rights, and the Strasbourg jurisprudence, have undoubtedly had a significant influence in this area of the common law for some years. The provisions of article 8, concerning respect for private and family life, and article 10, concerning freedom of expression, and the interaction of these two articles, have prompted the courts of this country to identify more clearly the different factors involved in cases where one or other of these two interests is present. Where both are present the courts are increasingly explicit in evaluating the competing considerations involved. When identifying and evaluating these factors the courts, including your Lordships' House, have tested the common law against the values encapsulated in these two articles. The development of the common law has been in harmony with these articles of the Convention.

17. The time has come to recognise that the values enshrined in articles 8 and 10 are now part of the cause of action for breach of confidence.... Further, it should now be recognised that for this purpose these values are of general application. The values em-

bodied in articles 8 and 10 are as much applicable in disputes between individuals or between an individual and a non-governmental body such as a newspaper as they are in disputes between individuals and a public authority.

18. In reaching this conclusion it is not necessary to pursue the controversial question whether the European Convention itself has this wider effect. Nor is it necessary to decide whether the duty imposed on courts by section 6 of the Human Rights Act 1998 extends to questions of substantive law as distinct from questions of practice and procedure. It is sufficient to recognise that the values underlying articles 8 and 10 are not confined to disputes between individuals and public authorities. This approach has been adopted by the courts in several recent decisions, reported and unreported, where individuals have complained of press intrusion....

19. In applying this approach, and giving effect to the values protected by article 8, courts will often be aided by adopting the structure of article 8 in the same way as they now habitually apply the Strasbourg court's approach to article 10 when resolving questions concerning freedom of expression. Articles 8 and 10 call for a more explicit analysis of competing considerations than the three traditional requirements of the cause of action for breach of confidence identified in *Coco v. A N Clark (Engineers) Ltd.* [1969] RPC 41.

20. I should take this a little further on one point. Article 8(1) recognises the need to respect private and family life. Article 8(2) recognises there are occasions when intrusion into private and family life may be justified. One of these is where the intrusion is necessary for the protection of the rights and freedoms of others. Article 10(1) recognises the importance of freedom of expression. But article 10(2), like article 8(2), recognises there are occasions when protection of the rights of others may make it necessary for freedom of expression to give way. When both these articles are engaged a difficult question of proportionality may arise. This question is distinct from the initial question of whether the published information engaged article 8 at all by being within the sphere of the complainant's private or family life

21. Accordingly, in deciding what was the ambit of an individual's 'private life' in particular circumstances courts need to be on guard against using as a touchstone a test which brings into account considerations which should more properly be considered at the later stage of proportionality. Essentially the touchstone of private life is whether in respect of the disclosed facts the person in question had a reasonable expectation of privacy....

The present case

23. I turn to the present case and consider first whether the information whose disclosure is in dispute was private. Mr Caldecott QC placed the information published by the newspaper into five categories: (1) the fact of Miss Campbell's drug addiction; (2) the fact that she was receiving treatment; (3) the fact that she was receiving treatment at Narcotics Anonymous; (4) the details of the treatment—how long she had been attending meetings, how often she went, how she was treated within the sessions themselves, the extent of her commitment, and the nature of her entrance on the specific occasion; and (5) the visual portrayal of her leaving a specific meeting with other addicts.

24. It was common ground between the parties that in the ordinary course the information in all five categories would attract the protection of article 8. But Mr Caldecott recognised that, as he put it, Miss Campbell's 'public lies' precluded her from claiming protection for categories (1) and (2).... As the Court of Appeal noted, where a public figure chooses to present a false image and make untrue pronouncements about his or her life, the press will normally be entitled to put the record straight. Thus the area of dispute at the trial concerned the other three categories of information.

25. Of these three categories I shall consider first the information in categories (3) and (4), concerning Miss Campbell's attendance at Narcotics Anonymous meetings.... [T]he relevant question can be framed along the following lines: Miss Campbell having put her addiction and treatment into the public domain, did the further information relating to her attendance at Narcotics Anonymous meetings retain its character of private information sufficiently to engage the protection afforded by article 8?

26. I doubt whether it did. Treatment by attendance at Narcotics Anonymous meetings is a form of therapy for drug addiction which is well known, widely used and much respected.... Given the extent of the information, otherwise of a highly private character, which admittedly could properly be disclosed, the additional information was of such an unremarkable and consequential nature that to divide the one from the other would be to apply altogether too fine a toothcomb. Human rights are concerned with substance, not with such fine distinctions.

27. For the same reason I doubt whether the brief details of how long Miss Campbell had been undergoing treatment, and how often she attended meetings, stand differently....

28. But I would not wish to found my conclusion solely on this point. I prefer to proceed to the next stage and consider how the tension between privacy and freedom of expression should be resolved in this case, on the assumption that the information regarding Miss Campbell's attendance at Narcotics Anonymous meetings retained its private character. At this stage I consider Miss Campbell's claim must fail. I can state my reason very shortly. On the one hand, publication of this information in the unusual circumstances of this case represents, at most, an intrusion into Miss Campbell's private life to a comparatively minor degree. On the other hand, non-publication of this information would have robbed a legitimate and sympathetic newspaper story of attendant detail which added colour and conviction. This information was published in order to demonstrate Miss Campbell's commitment to tackling her drug problem. The balance ought not to be held at a point which would preclude, in this case, a degree of journalistic latitude in respect of information published for this purpose.

29. It is at this point I respectfully consider Morland J. fell into error. Having held that the details of Miss Campbell's attendance at Narcotics Anonymous had the necessary quality of confidentiality, the judge seems to have put nothing into the scales under article 10 when striking the balance between articles 8 and 10. This was a misdirection. The need to be free to disseminate information regarding Miss Campbell's drug addiction is of a lower order than the need for freedom to disseminate information on some other subjects such as political information. The degree of latitude reasonably to be accorded to journalists is correspondingly reduced, but it is not excluded altogether.

30. There remains category (5): the photographs taken covertly of Miss Campbell in the road outside the building she was attending for a meeting of Narcotics Anonymous.... Miss Campbell, expressly, makes no complaint about the taking of the photographs. She does not assert that the taking of the photographs was itself an invasion of privacy which attracts a legal remedy. The complaint regarding the photographs is of precisely the same character as the nature of the complaints regarding the text of the articles: the information conveyed by the photographs was private information. Thus the fact that the photographs were taken surreptitiously adds nothing to the only complaint being made.

31. In general photographs of people contain more information than textual description. That is why they are more vivid. That is why they are worth a thousand words. But the pictorial information in the photographs illustrating the offending article of 1 February 2001 added nothing of an essentially private nature....

32. For these reasons and those given by my noble and learned friend Lord Hoffmann, I agree with the Court of Appeal that Miss Campbell's claim fails. It is not necessary for me to pursue the claim based on the Data Protection Act 1998. The parties were agreed that this claim stands or falls with the outcome of the main claim.

34. That Miss Campbell should suffer real distress under all these heads is wholly understandable. But in respect of none of these causes of distress does she have reason for complaint against the newspaper for misuse of private information....

LORD HOFFMAN:

My Lords,

36. The House is divided as to the outcome of this appeal, but the difference of opinion relates to a very narrow point which arises on the unusual facts of this case. The facts are unusual because the plaintiff is a public figure who had made very public false statements about a matter in respect of which even a public figure would ordinarily be entitled to privacy, namely her use of drugs. It was these falsehoods which, as was conceded, made it justifiable, for a newspaper to report the fact that she was addicted. The division of opinion is whether in doing so the newspaper went too far in publishing associated facts about her private life. But the importance of this case lies in the statements of general principle on the way in which the law should strike a balance between the right to privacy and the right to freedom of expression, on which the House is unanimous. The principles are expressed in varying language but speaking for myself I can see no significant differences.

37. Naomi Campbell is a famous fashion model who lives by publicity. What she has to sell is herself: her personal appearance and her personality. She employs public relations agents to present her personal life to the media in the best possible light just as she employs professionals to advise her on dress and make-up. That is no criticism of her. It is a trade like any other. But it does mean that her relationship with the media is different from that of people who expose less of their private life to the public.

38. The image which she has sought to project of herself to the international media is that of a black woman who started with few advantages in life and has by her own efforts attained international success in a glamorous profession. There is much truth in this claim. Unfortunately she has also given wide publicity, in interviews with journalists and on television, to a claim which was false, namely that (unlike many of her colleagues in the fashion business) she had not succumbed to the temptation to take drugs.

39. In January 2001 the Mirror obtained information that Ms Campbell had acknowledged her drug dependency by going regularly to meetings of Narcotics Anonymous ("NA") for help in ridding herself of the addiction. It was told that she would be going to a meeting at an address in the King's Road. The informant was either a member of Ms Campbell's numerous entourage or another participant in the meetings. The Mirror sent a photographer to sit unobtrusively in a car. As she left the meeting, he took a couple of pictures of her on the pavement....

42. On the same day as the article appeared, Ms Campbell issued proceedings for damages for "breach of confidence and/or unlawful invasion of privacy". The narrowness of the dispute between the parties emerged at the trial when Mr Caldecott QC conceded that because of the publicity which Ms Campbell had given to her claim that she had "never had a drug problem" the Mirror was entitled to publish that she was an addict and also, in fairness to her, that she was now attempting to deal with it. The matters which were alleged to be in breach of confidence or an unlawful invasion of privacy were, first,

the fact that she was attending meetings at NA, secondly, the published details of her attendance and what happened at the meetings and thirdly, the photographs taken in the street without her knowledge or consent.

43. In order to set both the concession and the residual claim in their context and to identify the point of law at issue, I must say something about the cause of action on which Ms Campbell relies. This House decided in *Wainwright v. Home Office* [2003] 3 WLR 1137 that there is no general tort of invasion of privacy. But the right to privacy is in a general sense one of the values, and sometimes the most important value, which underlies a number of more specific causes of action, both at common law and under various statutes. One of these is the equitable action for breach of confidence, which has long been recognised as capable of being used to protect privacy....

44. But although the action for breach of confidence could be used to protect privacy in the sense of preserving the confidentiality of personal information, it was not founded on the notion that such information was in itself entitled to protection....

46. In recent years, however, there have been two developments of the law of confidence, typical of the capacity of the common law to adapt itself to the needs of contemporary life. One has been an acknowledgement of the artificiality of distinguishing between confidential information obtained through the violation of a confidential relationship and similar information obtained in some other way. The second has been the acceptance, under the influence of human rights instruments such as article 8 of the European Convention, of the privacy of personal information as something worthy of protection in its own right....

49. ... Until the Human Rights Act 1998 came into force, there was no equivalent in English domestic law of article 8 the European Convention or the equivalent articles in other international human rights instruments which guarantee rights of privacy. So the courts of the United Kingdom did not have to decide what such guarantees meant. Even now that the equivalent of article 8 has been enacted as part of English law, it is not directly concerned with the protection of privacy against private persons or corporations. It is, by virtue of section 6 of the 1998 Act, a guarantee of privacy only against public authorities. Although the Convention, as an international instrument, may impose upon the United Kingdom an obligation to take some steps (whether by statute or otherwise) to protect rights of privacy against invasion by private individuals, it does not follow that such an obligation would have any counterpart in domestic law.

50. What human rights law has done is to identify private information as something worth protecting as an aspect of human autonomy and dignity. And this recognition has raised inescapably the question of why it should be worth protecting against the state but not against a private person. There may of course be justifications for the publication of private information by private persons which would not be available to the state—I have particularly in mind the position of the media, to which I shall return in a moment—but I can see no logical ground for saying that a person should have less protection against a private individual than he would have against the state for the publication of personal information for which there is no justification. Nor, it appears, have any of the other judges who have considered the matter.

51.... As Sedley LJ observed in a perceptive passage in his judgment in *Douglas v. Hello! Ltd.* [2001] QB 967, 1001, the new approach takes a different view of the underlying value which the law protects. Instead of the cause of action being based upon the duty of good faith applicable to confidential personal information and trade secrets alike, it focuses upon the protection of human autonomy and dignity—the right to control the dissemination of information about one's private life and the right to the esteem and respect of other people.

52. These changes have implications for the future development of the law. They must influence the approach of the courts to the kind of information which is regarded as entitled to protection, the extent and form of publication which attracts a remedy and the circumstances in which publication can be justified.

53. In this case, however, it is unnecessary to consider these implications because the cause of action fits squarely within both the old and the new law....

54. What is said to make this case different is, first, that Ms Campbell is a public figure who has sought publicity about various aspects of her private life and secondly, that the aspects of her private life which she has publicised include her use of drugs, in respect of which she has made a false claim. The Mirror claims that on these grounds it was entitled in the public interest to publish the information and photographs and that its right to do so is protected by article 10 of the European Convention.

55. I shall first consider the relationship between the freedom of the press and the common law right of the individual to protect personal information. Both reflect important civilised values, but, as often happens, neither can be given effect in full measure without restricting the other. How are they to be reconciled in a particular case? There is in my view no question of automatic priority. Nor is there a presumption in favour of one rather than the other. The question is rather the extent to which it is necessary to qualify the one right in order to protect the underlying value which is protected by the other. And the extent of the qualification must be proportionate to the need.

56. If one takes this approach, there is often no real conflict. Take the example I have just given of the ordinary citizen whose attendance at NA is publicised in his local newspaper. The violation of the citizen's autonomy, dignity and self-esteem is plain and obvious. Do the civil and political values which underlie press freedom make it necessary to deny the citizen the right to protect such personal information? Not at all. While there is no contrary public interest recognised and protected by the law, the press is free to publish anything it likes. Subject to the law of defamation, it does not matter how trivial, spiteful or offensive the publication may be. But when press freedom comes into conflict with another interest protected by the law, the question is whether there is a sufficient public interest in that particular publication to justify curtailment of the conflicting right. In the example I have given, there is no public interest whatever in publishing to the world the fact that the citizen has a drug dependency. The freedom to make such a statement weighs little in the balance against the privacy of personal information.

57. One must therefore proceed to consider the grounds why the Mirror say there was a public interest in its publication of information about Ms Campbell which it would not have been justified in publishing about someone else. First, there is the fact that she is a public figure who has had a long and symbiotic relationship with the media. In my opinion, that would not in itself justify publication. A person may attract or even seek publicity about some aspects of his or her life without creating any public interest in the publication of personal information about other matters. I think that the history of Ms Campbell's relationship with the media does have some relevance to this case, to which I shall return in due course, but that would not without more justify publication of confidential personal information.

58. The reason why Mr Caldecott concedes that the Mirror was entitled to publish the fact of her drug dependency and the fact that she was seeking treatment is that she had specifically given publicity to the very question of whether she took drugs and had falsely

said that she did not. I accept that this creates a sufficient public interest in the correction of the impression she had previously given.

59. The question is then whether the Mirror should have confined itself to these bare facts or whether it was entitled to reveal more of the circumstantial detail and print the photographs. If one applies the test of necessity or proportionality which I have suggested, this is a matter on which different people may have different views....

61. That brings me to what seems to be the only point of principle which arises in this case. Where the main substance of the story is conceded to have been justified, should the newspaper be held liable whenever the judge considers that it was not necessary to have published some of the personal information? Or should the newspaper be allowed some margin of choice in the way it chooses to present the story?

62. In my opinion, it would be inconsistent with the approach which has been taken by the courts in a number of recent landmark cases for a newspaper to be held strictly liable for exceeding what a judge considers to have been necessary. The practical exigencies of journalism demand that some latitude must be given. Editorial decisions have to be made quickly and with less information than is available to a court which afterwards reviews the matter at leisure. And if any margin is to be allowed, it seems to me strange to hold the Mirror liable in damages for a decision which three experienced judges in the Court of Appeal have held to be perfectly justified.

63. Ms Campbell now concedes the truth of the essentials of the Mirror's story but the editor said in evidence that he thought at the time, in view of her previous falsehoods, that it was necessary to include some detail and photographs by way of verification. It is unreasonable to expect that in matters of judgment any more than accuracy of reporting, newspapers will always get it absolutely right. To require them to do so would tend to inhibit the publication of facts which should in the public interest be made known....

64. A similar point, in relation to the protection of private information, was made by the European Court of Human Rights in *Fressoz and Roire v. France* (2001) 31 EHRR 28. 'Le Canard enchaine' published the salary of M. Calvet, the chairman of Peugeot (which was publicly available information), and also, by way of confirmation, photographs of the relevant part of his tax assessment, which was confidential and could not lawfully be published. The Strasbourg court said that the conviction of the journalists for publishing the assessment infringed their right of free speech under article 10....

65. In my opinion the Court of Appeal was right in the present case to say [2003] QB 633, 662, para 64:

> "Provided that publication of particular confidential information is justifiable in the public interest, the journalist must be given reasonable latitude as to the manner in which that information is conveyed to the public or his article 10 right to freedom of expression will be unnecessarily inhibited." ...

69. The [trial] judge ... said:

> "In my judgment clearly the publication of information about details of her therapy in regularly attending meetings of [NA] was to Miss Naomi Campbell's detriment. It was, viewed objectively, likely to affect adversely her attendance and participation in therapy meetings."

70. The judge did not analyse the details which were said to be likely to have this effect or explain why they should have this effect when the bare revelation that she was a drug addict seeking therapy would not....

72. That leaves the question of the photographs. In my opinion a photograph is in principle information no different from any other information. It may be a more vivid form of information than the written word ("a picture is worth a thousand words"). That has to be taken into account in deciding whether its publication infringes the right to privacy of personal information. The publication of a photograph cannot necessarily be justified by saying that one would be entitled to publish a verbal description of the scene. But the principles by which one decides whether or not the publication of a photograph is an unjustified invasion of the privacy of personal information are in my opinion the same as those which I have already discussed.

73. In the present case, the pictures were taken without Ms Campbell's consent. That in my opinion is not enough to amount to a wrongful invasion of privacy. The famous and even the not so famous who go out in public must accept that they may be photographed without their consent, just as they may be observed by others without their consent....

74. But the fact that we cannot avoid being photographed does not mean that anyone who takes or obtains such photographs can publish them to the world at large. In the recent case of *Peck v. United Kingdom* (2003) 36 EHRR 41, Mr Peck was filmed on a public street in an embarrassing moment by a CCTV camera. Subsequently, the film was broadcast several times on the television. The Strasbourg court said (at p. 739) that this was an invasion of his privacy contrary to article 8:

> "the relevant moment was viewed to an extent which far exceeded any exposure to a passer-by or to security observation and to a degree surpassing that which the applicant could possibly have foreseen when he walked in Brentwood on August 20, 1995."

75. In my opinion, therefore, the widespread publication of a photograph of someone which reveals him to be in a situation of humiliation or severe embarrassment, even if taken in a public place, may be an infringement of the privacy of his personal information. Likewise, the publication of a photograph taken by intrusion into a private place (for example, by a long distance lens) may in itself by such an infringement, even if there is nothing embarrassing about the picture itself: *Hellewell v. Chief Constable of Derbyshire* [1985] 1 WLR 804, 807. As Lord Mustill said in *R v. Broadcasting Standards Commission, Ex p BBC* [2001] QB 885, 900, "An infringement of privacy is an affront to the personality, which is damaged both by the violation and by the demonstration that the personal space is not inviolate."

76. In the present case, however, there was nothing embarrassing about the picture, which showed Ms Campbell neatly dressed and smiling among a number of other people.

77. No doubt it would have been possible for the Mirror to have published the article without pictures. But that would in my opinion again be to ignore the realities of this kind of journalism as much as to expect precision of judgment about the amount of circumstantial detail to be included in the text. We value the freedom of the press but the press is a commercial enterprise and can flourish only by selling newspapers. From a journalistic point of view, photographs are an essential part of the story. The picture carried the message, more strongly than anything in the text alone, that the Mirror's story was true. So the decision to publish the pictures was in my opinion within the margin of editorial judgment and something for which appropriate latitude should be allowed.

78. I would therefore dismiss the appeal.

LORD HOPE OF CRAIGHEAD:

My Lords,

79. The facts of this case have been described by my noble and learned friend, Lord Nichols of Birkenhead, and I gratefully adopt his account of them. But I should like to say a few more words about the general background before I explain why I have reached the conclusion that this appeal must be allowed....

The background ...

82. The question in this case is whether the publicity which the respondents gave to Miss Campbell's drug addiction and to the therapy which she was receiving for it in an article which was published in "The Mirror" newspaper on 1 February 2001 is actionable on the ground of breach of confidence. Miss Campbell cannot complain about the fact that publicitly was given in this article to the fact that she was a drug addict. This was a matter of legitimate public comment, as she had not only lied about her addiction but had sought to benefit from this by comparing herself with others in the fashion business who were addicted. As the Court of Appeal observed, where a public figure chooses to make untrue pronouncements about his or her private life, the press will normally be entitled to put the record straight.

83. Miss Campbell's case is that information about the treatment she was receiving for the addiction falls to be treated differently. This is because it was not the subject of any falsehood that was in need of correction and because it was information which any reasonable person who came into possession of it would realise was obtained in confidence....

84. The respondents' answer is based on the proposition that the information that was published about her treatment was peripheral and not sufficiently significant to amount to a breach of the duty of confidence that was owed to her. They also maintain that the right balance was struck between Miss Campbell's right to respect for her private life under article 8(1) of the European Convention for the Protection of Human Rights and Fundamental Freedoms and the right to freedom of expression that is enshrined in article 10(1) of the Convention....

86. The language has changed following the coming into operation of the Human Rights Act 1998 and the incorporation into domestic law of article 8 and article 10 of the Convention. We now talk about the right to respect for private life and the countervailing right to freedom of expression. The jurisprudence of the European Court offers important guidance as to how these competing rights ought to be approached and analysed. I doubt whether the result is that the centre of gravity, as my noble and learned friend Lord Hoffmann says, has shifted. It seems to me that the balancing exercise to which that guidance is directed is essentially the same exercise, although it is plainly now more carefully focussed and more penetrating....

[Lord Hope discussed whether the information was confidential.]

95. I think that the judge was right to regard the details of Miss Campbell's attendance at Narcotics Anonymous as private information which imported a duty of confidence.... The private nature of these meetings encourages addicts to attend them in the belief that they can do so anonymously.... I would hold that these details are obviously private....

99. The approach which the Court of Appeal took to this issue seems to me, with great respect, to be quite unreal.... They were also in error, in my opinion, when they were asking themselves whether the disclosure would have offended the reasonable man of ordinary susceptibilities. The mind that they examined was the mind of the reader. This is

wrong. It greatly reduces the level of protection that is afforded to the right of privacy. The mind that has to be examined is that, not of the reader in general, but of the person who is affected by the publicity. The question is what a reasonable person of ordinary sensibilities would feel if she was placed in the same position as the claimant and faced with the same publicity....

The competing rights of free speech and privacy

103. Morland J. did not give any detailed reasons in para 70 of his judgment for his conclusion that, striking the balance between articles 8 and 10 and having full regard to section 12(4) of the Human Rights Act 1998, Miss Campbell was entitled to the remedy of damages. But he did recognise in para 98 that neither article 10 nor article 8 had pre-eminence, the one over the other. Court of Appeal's approach to the respondents' entitlement to publish what they described as the peripheral details was based on their view that the provision of these details as background to support the story that Miss Campbell was a drug addict was a legitimate part of the journalistic package which was designed to demonstrate that she had been deceiving the public when she said that she did not take drugs: [2003] QB 633, 662, para 62. In para 64 they said that its publication was justified in order to give a factual account that had the detail necessary to carry credibility. But they do not appear to have attempted to balance the competing Convention rights against each other. No doubt this was because they had already concluded that these details were peripheral and that their publication was not, in its context, sufficiently significant to amount to a breach of duty of confidence: para 58.

104. In my opinion the Court of Appeal's approach is open to the criticism that, because they wrongly held that these details were not entitled to protection under the law of confidence, they failed to carry out the required balancing exercise.

105. The context for this exercise is provided by articles 8 and 10 of the Convention. The rights guaranteed by these articles are qualified rights. Article 8(1) protects the right to respect for private life, but recognition is given in article 8(2) to the protection of the rights and freedoms of others. Article 10(1) protects the right to freedom of expression, but article 10(2) recognises the need to protect the rights and freedoms of others. The effect of these provisions is that the right to privacy which lies at the heart of an action for breach of confidence has to be balanced against the right of the media to impart information to the public. And the right of the media to impart information to the public has to be balanced in its turn against the respect that must be given to private life.

106. There is nothing new about this, as the need for this kind of balancing exercise was already part of English law. But account must now be taken of the guidance which has been given by the European Court on the application of these articles....

107. I accept, of course, that the importance which the Court of Appeal attached to the journalistic package finds support in the authorities....

108. The freedom of the press to exercise its own judgment in the presentation of journalistic material was emphasised in a further passage in *Jersild* [*v Denmark* (1994) 19 EHRR 1] where the court said, at p 26, para 31:

> "At the same time, the methods of objective and balanced reporting may vary considerably, depending among other things on the media in question. It is not for this court, nor for the national courts for that matter, to substitute their own views for those of the press as to what technique of reporting should be adopted

by journalists. In this context the court recalls that article 10 protects not only the substance of the ideas and information expressed, but also the form in which they are conveyed." ...

109. There was no need for the court in Jersild's case to examine the question how the article 10 right which was relied on was to be balanced against a competing right under article 8 of the Convention....

110. The need for a balancing exercise to be carried out is also inherent in the provisions of article 10 itself, as the court explained in *Bladet Tromsø and Stensaas v. Norway* (2000) 29 EHRR 125. In that case a newspaper and its editor complained that their right to freedom of expression had been breached when they were found liable in defamation proceedings for statements in articles which they had published about the methods used by seal hunters in the hunting of harp seals. At p 167, para 59 the court said:

> "Although the press must not overstep certain bounds, in particular in respect of the reputation and rights of others and the need to prevent the disclosure of confidential information, its duty is nevertheless to impart—in a manner consistent with its obligations and responsibilities—information and ideas on all matters of public interest."

The court dealt with the question of balance at p169, para 65:

> "Article 10 of the Convention does not, however, guarantee a wholly unrestricted freedom of expression even with respect to press coverage of matters of serious public concern. Under the terms of paragraph 2 of the Article the exercise of this freedom carries with it 'duties and responsibilities' which also apply to the press. These 'duties and responsibilities' are liable to assume significance when, as in the present case, there is question of attacking the reputation of private individuals and examining the 'rights of others'. As pointed out by the government, the seal hunters' right to protection of their honour and reputation is itself internationally recognised under Article 17 of the International Covenant on Civil and Political Rights. Also of relevance for the balancing of competing interests which the Court must carry out is the fact that under article 6(2) of the Convention the seal hunters had a right to be presumed innocent of any criminal offence until proved guilty. By reason of the duties and responsibilities' inherent in the exercise of the freedom of expression, the safeguard afforded by article 10 to journalists in relation to reporting on issues of general interest is subject to the proviso that they are acting in good faith to provide accurate and reliable information in accordance with the ethics of journalism."

111. Section 12(4) of the Human Rights Act 1998 provides:

> "The court must have particular regard to the importance of the Convention right to freedom of expression and, where the proceedings relate to material which the respondent claims, or which appears to the court, to be journalistic, literary or artistic material (or to conduct connected with such material), to—
>
> (a) the extent to which—
>
> (i) the material has, or is about to, become available to the public; or
>
> (ii) it is, or would be, in the pubic interest for the material to be published; or
>
> (b) any relevant privacy code."

But, as Sedley LJ said in *Douglas v. Hello! Ltd.* [2001] QB 967, 1003, para 133, you cannot have particular regard to article 10 without having equally particular regard at the very least to article 8: *see also In re S (A Child) (Identifications: Restrictions on Publication)* [2003] 3 WLR 1425, 1450, para 52 where Hale LJ said that section 12(4) does not give either article pre-eminence over the other. These observations seem to me to be entirely consistent with the jurisprudence of the European Court....

Striking the balance

112. There is no doubt that the presentation of the material that it was legitimate to convey to the public in this case without breaching the duty of confidence was a matter for the journalists. The choice of language used to convey information and ideas, and decisions as to whether or not to accompany the printed word by the use of photographs, are pre-eminently editorial matters with which the court will not interfere. The respondents are also entitled to claim that they should be accorded a reasonable margin of appreciation in taking decisions as to what details needed to be included in the article to give it credibility. This is an essential part of the journalistic exercise.

113. But decisions about the publication of material that is private to the individual raise issues that are not simply about presentation and editing. Any interference with the public interest in disclosure has to be balanced against the interference with the right of the individual to respect for their private life. The decisions that are then taken are open to review by the court. The tests which the court must apply are the familiar ones. They are whether publication of the material pursues a legitimate aim and whether the benefits that will be achieved by its publication are proportionate to the harm that may be done by the interference with the right to privacy. The jurisprudence of the European Court of Human Rights explains how these principles are to be understood and applied in the context of the facts of each case. Any restriction of the right to freedom of expression must be subjected to very close scrutiny. But so too must any restriction of the right to respect for private life. Neither article 8 nor article 10 has any pre-eminence over the other in the conduct of this exercise. As Resolution 1165 of the Parliamentary Assembly of the Council of Europe (1998), para 11, pointed out, they are neither absolute not in any hierarchical order, since they are of equal value in a democratic society.

The article 10 right

114. In the present case it is convenient to begin by looking at the matter from the standpoint of the respondents' assertion of the article 10 right and the court's duty as a public authority under section 6(1) of the Human Rights Act 1998, which section 12(4) reinforces, not to act in a way which is incompatible with that Convention right.

115. The first question is whether the objective of the restriction on the article 10 right—the protection of Miss Campbell's right under article 8 to respect for her private life—is sufficiently important to justify limiting the fundamental right to freedom of expression which the press assert on behalf of the public. It follows from my conclusion that the details of Miss Campbell's treatment were private that I would answer this question in the affirmative. The second question is whether the means chosen to limit the article 10 right are rational, fair and not arbitrary and impair the right as minimally as is reasonably possible. It is not enough to assert that it would be reasonable to exclude these details from the article. A close examination of the factual justification for the restriction on the freedom of expression is needed if the fundamental right enshrined in article 10 is to remain practical and effective. The restrictions which the court imposes on the article 10 right must be rational, fair and not arbitrary, and they must impair the right no more than is necessary.

116. In my opinion the factors that need to be weighed are, on the one hand, the duty to impart information and ideas of public interest which the public has a right to receive, and the need for the court to leave it to journalists to decide what material needs to be reproduced to ensure credibility; and, on the other hand, the degree of privacy to which Miss Campbell was entitled under the law of confidence as to the details of her therapy....

117. But it should also be recognised that the right of the public to receive information about the details of her treatment was of a much lower order than the undoubted right to know that she was misleading the public when she said that she did not take drugs.... Clayton and Tomlinson, THE LAW OF HUMAN RIGHTS (2000), para 15.162, point out that the court has distinguished three kinds of expression: political expression, artistic expression and commercial expression, and that it consistently attaches great importance to political expression and applies rather less rigorous principles to expression which is artistic and commercial. According to the court's well-established case law, freedom of expression constitutes one of the essential foundations of a democratic society and one of the basic conditions for its progress and the self-fulfilment of each individual. But there were no political or democratic values at stake here, nor has any pressing social need been identified.

The article 8 right

119. Looking at the matter from Miss Campbell's point of view and the protection of her article 8 Convention right, publication of details of the treatment which she was undertaking to cure her addiction ... had the potential to cause harm to her, for the reasons which I have already given. So I would attach a good deal of weight to this factor.

120. As for the other side of the balance, a person's right to privacy may be limited by the public's interest in knowing about certain traits of her personality and certain aspects of her private life. But it is not enough to deprive Miss Campbell of her right to privacy that she is a celebrity and that her private life is newsworthy. A margin of appreciation must, of course, be given to the journalist. Weight must be given to this. But to treat these details merely as background was to undervalue the importance that was to be attached to the need, if Miss Campbell was to be protected, to keep these details private. And it is hard to see that there was any compelling need for the public to know the name of the organisation that she was attending for the therapy, or for the other details of it to be set out. The presentation of the article indicates that this was not fully appreciated when the decision was taken to publish these details. The decision to publish the photographs suggests that greater weight was being given to the wish to publish a story that would attract interest rather than to the wish to maintain its credibility.

121. Had it not been for the publication of the photographs, and looking to the text only, I would have been inclined to regard the balance between these rights as about even. Such is the effect of the margin of appreciation that must, in a doubtful case, be given to the journalist. In that situation the proper conclusion to draw would have been that it had not been shown that the restriction on the article 10 right for which Miss Campbell argues was justified on grounds of proportionality. But the text cannot be separated from the photographs.... The reasonable person of ordinary sensibilities would also regard publication of the covertly taken photographs, and the fact that they were linked with the text in this way, as adding greatly overall to the intrusion which the article as a whole made into her private life.

122. The photographs were taken of Miss Campbell while she was in a public place, as she was in the street outside the premises where she had been receiving therapy. The taking of photographs in a public street must be taken to be one of the ordinary incidents of living in a free community. The real issue is whether publicising the content of the photographs would be offensive. A person who just happens to be in the street

when the photograph was taken and appears in it only incidentally cannot as a general rule object to the publication of the photograph.... But the situation is different if the public nature of the place where a photograph is taken was simply used as background for one or more persons who constitute the true subject of the photograph. The question then arises, balancing the rights at issue, where the public's right to information can justify dissemination of a photograph taken without authorisation. The European Court has recognised that a person who walks down a public street will inevitably be visible to any member of the public who is also present and, in the same way, to a security guard viewing the scene through closed circuit television. But, as the court pointed out in the same paragraph, private life considerations may arise once any systematic or permanent record comes into existence of such material from the public domain....

123.... [T]hese were not just pictures of a street scene where she happened to be when the photographs were taken. They were taken deliberately, in secret and with a view to their publication in conjunction with the article. The zoom lens was directed at the doorway of the place where the meeting had been taking place. The faces of others in the doorway were pixilated so as not to reveal their identity. Hers was not, the photographs were published and her privacy was invaded....

Conclusion

125. Despite the weight that must be given to the right to freedom of expression that the press needs if it is to play its role effectively, I would hold that there was here an infringement of Miss Campbell's right to privacy that cannot be justified. In my opinion publication of the third, fourth and fifth elements in the article (see para 88) was an invasion of that right for which she is entitled to damages. I would allow the appeal and restore the orders that were made by the trial judge.

THE BARONESS HALE OF RICHMOND:

My Lords,

126. This case raises some big questions. How is the balance to be struck between everyone's right to respect for their private and family life under Article 8 of the European Convention on Human Rights and everyone's right to freedom of expression, including the freedom to receive and impart information and ideas under Article 10? How do those rights come into play in a dispute between two private persons? But the parties are largely agreed about the answers to these. They disagree about where that balance is to be struck in the individual case. In particular, how far is a newspaper able to go in publishing what would otherwise be confidential information about a celebrity in order to set the record straight? And does it matter that the article was illustrated by a covertly taken photograph?

The facts

[Baroness Hale's recitation of the facts is omitted.]

The basic principles

132. Neither party to this appeal has challenged the basic principles which have emerged from the Court of Appeal in the wake of the Human Rights Act 1998. The 1998 Act does not create any new cause of action between private persons. But if there is a relevant cause of action applicable, the court as a public authority must act compatibly with both parties' Convention rights. In a case such as this, the relevant vehicle will usually be the action for breach of confidence....

133. The action for breach of confidence is not the only relevant cause of action. But the courts will not invent a new cause of action to cover types of activity which were not

previously covered.... But where existing remedies are available, the court not only can but must balance the competing Convention rights of the parties.

134. This begs the question of how far the Convention balancing exercise is premissed on the scope of the existing cause of action.... Inside its scope is what has been termed 'the protection of the individual's informational autonomy' by prohibiting the publication of confidential information. How does the scope of the action for breach of confidence accommodate the Article 8 rights of individuals? ... The position we have reached is that the exercise of balancing article 8 and article 10 may begin when the person publishing the information knows or ought to know that there is a reasonable expectation that the information in question will be kept confidential....

137. It should be emphasised that the 'reasonable expectation of privacy' is a threshold test which brings the balancing exercise into play. It is not the end of the story. Once the information is identified as 'private' in this way, the court must balance the claimant's interest in keeping the information private against the countervailing interest of the recipient in publishing it. Very often, it can be expected that the countervailing rights of the recipient will prevail.

138. The parties agree that neither right takes precedence over the other. This is consistent with Resolution 1165 (1998) of the Parliamentary Assembly of the Council of Europe, para 11:

> "The Assembly reaffirms the importance of everyone's right to privacy, and of the right to freedom of expression, as fundamental to a democratic society. These rights are neither absolute nor in any hierarchical order, since they are of equal value."

139. Each right has the same structure. Article 8(1) states that "everyone has the right to respect for his private and family life, his home and his correspondence". Article 10(1) states that "Everyone has the right to freedom of expression. This right shall include freedom to hold opinions and to receive and impart information and ideas without interference by public authorities and regardless of frontiers...." Unlike the article 8 right, however, it is accepted in article 10(2) that the exercise of this right 'carries with it duties and responsibilities.' Both rights are qualified. They may respectively be interfered with or restricted provided that three conditions are fulfilled:

> (a) The interference or restriction must be 'in accordance with the law'; it must have a basis in national law which conforms to the Convention standards of legality.

> (b) It must pursue one of the legitimate aims set out in each article. Article 8(2) provides for "the protection of the rights and freedoms of others". Article 10(2) provides for "the protection of the reputation or rights of others" and for "preventing the disclosure of information received in confidence". The rights referred to may either be rights protected under the national law or, as in this case, other Convention rights.

> (c) Above all, the interference or restriction must be "necessary in a democratic society"; it must meet a "pressing social need" and be no greater than is proportionate to the legitimate aim pursued; the reasons given for it must be both "relevant" and "sufficient" for this purpose.

140. The application of the proportionality test is more straightforward when only one Convention right is in play: the question then is whether the private right claimed offers sufficient justification for the degree of interference with the fundamental right. It is

much less straightforward when two Convention rights are in play, and the proportionality of interfering with one has to be balanced against the proportionality of restricting the other. As each is a fundamental right, there is evidently a "pressing social need" to protect it. The Convention jurisprudence offers us little help with this.... In the national court, the problem of balancing two rights of equal importance arises most acutely in the context of disputes between private persons.

141. Both parties accepted the basic approach of the Court of Appeal in *In re S* [2003] 3 WLR 1425, 1451–1452, at paras 54 to 60. This involves looking first at the comparative importance of the actual rights being claimed in the individual case; then at the justifications for interfering with or restricting each of those rights; and applying the proportionality test to each. The parties in this case differed about whether the trial judge or the Court of Appeal had done this, the appellant arguing that the Court of Appeal had assumed primacy for the Article 10 right while the respondent argued that the trial judge had assumed primacy for the Article 8 right.

Striking the balance

...

143. ... Put crudely, [this case is about] a prima donna celebrity against a celebrity-exploiting tabloid newspaper. Each in their time has profited from the other. Both are assumed to be grown-ups who know the score. On the one hand is the interest of a woman who wants to give up her dependence on illegal and harmful drugs and wants the peace and space in which to pursue the help which she finds useful. On the other hand is a newspaper which wants to keep its readers informed of the activities of celebrity figures, and to expose their weaknesses, lies, evasions and hypocrisies. This sort of story, especially if it has photographs attached, is just the sort of thing that fills, sells and enhances the reputation of the newspaper which gets it first. One reason why press freedom is so important is that we need newspapers to sell in order to ensure that we still have newspapers at all. It may be said that newspapers should be allowed considerable latitude in their intrusions into private grief so that they can maintain circulation and the rest of us can then continue to enjoy the variety of newspapers and other mass media which are available in this country. It may also be said that newspaper editors often have to make their decisions at great speed and in difficult circumstances, so that to expect too minute an analysis of the position is in itself a restriction on their freedom of expression.

144. Examined more closely, however, this case is far from trivial. What is the nature of the private life, respect for which is in issue here? The information revealed by the article was information relating to Miss Campbell's health, both physical and mental. Drug abuse can be seriously damaging to physical health; indeed it is sometimes life-threatening....

145. It has always been accepted that information about a person's health and treatment for ill-health is both private and confidential....

146. The Court of Appeal in this case held that the information revealed here was not in the same category as clinical medical records. That may be so, in the sense that it was not the notes made by a doctor when consulted by a patient. But the information was of exactly the same kind as that which would be recorded by a doctor on those notes: the presenting problem was addiction to illegal drugs, the diagnosis was no doubt the same, and the prescription was therapy....

147. I start, therefore, from the fact—indeed, it is common ground—that all of the information about Miss Campbell's addiction and attendance at NA which was revealed

in the Daily Mirror article was both private and confidential.... It had also been received from an insider in breach of confidence.... [T]he starting point must be that it was all private and its publication required specific justification.

148. What was the nature of the freedom of expression which was being asserted on the other side? There are undoubtedly different types of speech, just as there are different types of private information, some of which are more deserving of protection in a democratic society than others. Top of the list is political speech. The free exchange of information and ideas on matters relevant to the organisation of the economic, social and political life of the country is crucial to any democracy. Without this, it can scarcely be called a democracy at all. This includes revealing information about public figures, especially those in elective office, which would otherwise be private but is relevant to their participation in public life. Intellectual and educational speech and expression are also important in a democracy, not least because they enable the development of individuals' potential to play a full part in society and in our democratic life. Artistic speech and expression is important for similar reasons, in fostering both individual originality and creativity and the free-thinking and dynamic society we so much value. No doubt there are other kinds of speech and expression for which similar claims can be made.

149. But it is difficult to make such claims on behalf of the publication with which we are concerned here. The political and social life of the community, and the intellectual, artistic or personal development of individuals, are not obviously assisted by pouring over the intimate details of a fashion model's private life. However, there is one way in which the article could be said to be educational. The editor had considered running a highly critical piece, adding the new information to the not inconsiderable list of Miss Campbell's faults and follies detailed in the article, emphasising the lies and hypocrisy it revealed. Instead he chose to run a sympathetic piece, still listing her faults and follies, but setting them in the context of her now-revealed addiction and her even more important efforts to overcome it. Newspaper and magazines often carry such pieces and they may well have a beneficial educational effect.

150. The crucial difference here is that such pieces are normally run with the co-operation of those involved. Private people are not identified without their consent. It is taken for granted that this is otherwise confidential information. The editor did offer Miss Campbell the opportunity of being involved with the story but this was refused. Her evidence suggests that she was concerned for the other people in the group. What entitled him to reveal this private information about her without her consent?

151. The answer which she herself accepts is that she had presented herself to the public as someone who was not involved in drugs.... The press must be free to expose the truth and put the record straight.

152. That consideration justified the publication of the fact that, contrary to her previous statements, Miss Campbell had been involved with illegal drugs. It also justified publication of the fact that she was trying to do something about it by seeking treatment. It was not necessary for those purposes to publish any further information, especially if this might jeopardise the continued success of that treatment....

154. Publishing the photographs contributed both to the revelation and to the harm that it might do. By themselves, they are not objectionable. Unlike France and Quebec, in this country we do not recognise a right to one's own image. We have not so far held that the mere fact of covert photography is sufficient to make the information contained in the photograph confidential. The activity photographed must be private....

155. But here the accompanying text made it plain that these photographs were different. They showed her coming either to or from the NA meeting. They showed her in the company of others, some of whom were undoubtedly part of the group. They showed the place where the meeting was taking place, which will have been entirely recognisable to anyone who knew the locality....

156. There was no need to do this. The editor accepted that even without the photographs, it would have been a front page story. He had his basic information and he had his quotes. There is no shortage of photographs with which to illustrate and brighten up a story about Naomi Campbell....

157. The weight to be attached to these various considerations is a matter of fact and degree. Not every statement about a person's health will carry the badge of confidentiality or risk doing harm to that person's physical or moral integrity. The privacy interest in the fact that a public figure has a cold or a broken leg is unlikely to be strong enough to justify restricting the press's freedom to report it. What harm could it possibly do? Sometimes there will be other justifications for publishing, especially where the information is relevant to the capacity of a public figure to do the job. But that is not this case and in this case there was, as the judge found, a risk that publication would do harm. The risk of harm is what matters at this stage, rather than the proof that actual harm has occurred....

158. The trial judge was well placed to assess these matters....

160. I would therefore allow this appeal and restore the order of the judge.

Lord Carswell:

My Lords,

161. I have had the advantage of reading in draft the opinions of my noble and learned friends, Lord Hope of Craighead and Baroness Hale of Richmond, and I agree with them that the appeal should be allowed....

165. I am unable to agree with the distinction drawn by the Court of Appeal and for the reasons given by Lord Hope and Lady Hale I consider that the information was private. It seems to me that the publication of the details of the appellant's course of treatment at NA and of the photographs taken surreptitiously in the street of her emerging from a meeting went significantly beyond the publication of the fact that she was receiving therapy or that she was engaged in a course of therapy with NA. ... This in my view went beyond disclosure which was, in the words of the Court of Appeal, "peripheral to" the publication of the information that the appellant was a drug addict who was receiving treatment and was capable of constituting breach of confidence....

166. It follows that it is not necessary in this case to ask ... whether disclosure of the information would be highly offensive to a reasonable person of ordinary sensibilities. It is sufficiently established by the nature of the material that it was private information which attracted the duty of observing the confidence in which it was imparted to the respondents....

167. One must then move to the balancing exercise, which involves consideration of articles 8 and 10 of the European Convention on Human Rights.... The carrying out of the balancing is at the centre of this case and forms the point at which the two currents of opinion divide. I agree with the analysis contained in paragraphs 105 to 113 of Lord Hope's opinion in the present appeal and am gratefully content to adopt it. I also agree with him that in order to justify limiting the article 10 right to freedom of expression the restrictions imposed must be rational, fair and not arbitrary, and they must impair the right no more than necessary....

169. In my opinion it is a delicately balanced decision, and the answer to the questions which one must ask is by no means self-evident. My own conclusion is the same as that reached by Lord Hope and Lady Hale....

171. I would accordingly hold that the publication of the third, fourth and fifth elements in the article constituted an infringement of the appellant's right to privacy that cannot be justified and that she is entitled to a remedy. I would allow the appeal and restore the judge's order.

Notes and Questions

1. Let's start with a comparative question: How do you think this case would come out if it were brought in the United States? Would Naomi Campbell's right to privacy trump the interests of the press, or would the rights of the press win out?

2. Make sure you understand the basic facts here. Were any of the photographs at issue falsified in any way? Were any of them in what might be regarded as non-public settings? How do the settings of these pictures compare with those in *Von Hannover*?

3. Obviously, the Lords did not all agree on the proper outcome of this case. (Did you remember to count the votes?) The question is on what points they disagreed. Start with the fundamental applicable legal principles. On what principles did the Lords actually agree? Look at paragraph 36, where Lord Hoffman says that "the difference of opinion relates to a very narrow point which arises on the unusual facts of this case." Is he correct? If so, then there should be a substantial amount of agreement here.

4. Does either Lord Nicholls or Lord Hoffman dispute the applicability of the Human Rights Act of 1998? Does either dispute that both Article 8 and Article 10 of the European Human Rights Convention need to be considered in the analysis?

5. If the issue is the proper balance among competing rights, then what principles do the two sides use to strike the balance and how did those principles differ in this case?

6. The Lords referred to the cause of action as one for "breach of confidence." Was there any confidential information involved here? Did a third party betray a confidence bestowed by Ms. Campbell?

7. Notice the distinction drawn between the law in the U.K. and the law in the United States as stated in paragraph 11 of Lord Nicholls' opinion. Can you articulate the significant differences between the right in the U.S. and that in the U.K?

8. Suppose Ms. Campbell had been walking down the street with a friend, and her picture was taken by a news photographer (without her knowledge), and subsequently published on the front page of a tabloid newspaper. Would she have had any claim against the newspaper?

9. Suppose an enterprising manufacturer had obtained (legitimately) a photograph of Ms. Campbell and put it on a commemorative plate that it sold to the public. Would this case have any relevance to that situation?

10. How do you think the House of Lords would have decided the *Eastwood* cases in Chapter VII?

11. *Douglas v. Hello! Ltd.*, [2005] EWCA Civ 595 (Ct. App. 2005), was a suit for breach of confidence by Michael Douglas and Catherine Zeta-Jones over the unauthorized publication of photographs of their wedding. The couple's wedding was not public, but they had granted exclusive rights to take and publish photographs to OK! Magazine. As to the applicability of the European Convention of Human Rights, the Court of Appeal stated:

> We conclude that, in so far as private information is concerned, we are required to adopt, as the vehicle for performing such duty as falls on the courts in relation to Convention rights, the cause of action formerly described as breach of confidence. As to the nature of that duty, it seems to us that sections 2, 3, 6 and 12 of the Human Rights Act all point in the same direction. The court should, insofar as it can, develop the action for breach of confidence in such a manner as will give effect to both Article 8 and Article 10 rights. In considering the nature of those rights, account should be taken of the Strasbourg jurisprudence. In particular, when considering what information should be protected as private pursuant to Article 8, it is right to have regard to the decisions of the ECtHR. We cannot pretend that we find it satisfactory to be required to shoe-horn within the cause of action of breach of confidence claims for publication of unauthorised photographs of a private occasion.

Hello! did not argue that the photographs were inherently subject to free press guarantees under Article 10. Rather, the magazine argued that, by agreeing to allow OK! to publish photographs, the Douglases had, in essence, placed their wedding in the public domain. However, the court rejected that argument:

> Once intimate personal information about a celebrity's private life has been widely published it may serve no useful purpose to prohibit further publication. The same will not necessarily be true of photographs. Insofar as a photograph does more than convey information and intrudes on privacy by enabling the viewer to focus on intimate personal detail, there will be a fresh intrusion of privacy when each additional viewer sees the photograph and even when one who has seen a previous publication of the photograph, is confronted by a fresh publication of it.

The court then considered whether the law protected the couple's *commercial* interest in their wedding and concluded that they did have a right of action.

12. The *Douglas* case also involved the question of whether OK! Magazine could recover damages from Hello!, as the assignee of an exclusive license to publish from Douglas and Zeta-Jones. The trial judge had awarded damages to OK!, but the Court of Appeals held that the cause of action for breach of confidence was personal, and that OK! could not recover. On appeal to the House of Lords, however, the Lords held 3–2 that OK! magazine could recover as well, and reinstated the trial judge's award. *Douglas v. Hello! Ltd.* [2007] UKHL 21. (The appeal did not involve the award to Douglas and Zeta-Jones, which Hello! did not appeal.)

D. Canada and Australia

Aubry v. Éditions Vice-Versa Inc.

1 S.C.R. 591, 157 D.L.R. (4th) 577, 78 C.P.R. (3d) 288
(S.Ct. Canada 1998)

[Note: In the original, the dissent of the Chief Justice appears first. That order has been changed to make the case more readable.]

English version of the judgment of L'HEUREUX-DUBE, GONTHIER, CORY, IACOBUCCI and BASTARACHE JJ. delivered by

L'HEUREUX-DUBE and BASTARACHE JJ.

38. This appeal concerns the scope of the right to one's image as an element of the more general right to privacy. It also involves a balancing of the right to privacy and freedom of expression....

I. Facts

40. The respondent, Pascale Claude Aubry, brought an action in civil responsibility against the appellants, Gilbert Duclos and Les Éditions Vice-Versa Inc., for taking and publishing a photograph showing the respondent sitting on a step in front of a building on Ste-Catherine Street in Montreal. Both sides accept that the photograph was taken in a public place and published without the respondent's consent. According to the evidence, it was the appellant Gilbert Duclos who took the respondent's photograph. The photograph was published by the appellant Les Éditions Vice-Versa inc. in the June issue of Vice-Versa, a magazine dedicated to the arts, and 722 copies of the issue in question were sold. The photograph was drawn to the respondent's attention by a friend who had purchased a copy of the magazine. The respondent, who was 17 at the time, brought this action for damages in the amount of $10,000, half as compensatory damages and the other half as exemplary damages.

II. Judicial History

A. Court of Québec

41. At trial, Judge Bourret of the Court of Québec allowed the respondent's action in part. Recognizing that the unauthorized publication of the photograph constituted a fault to which both the magazine's publisher and the photographer who handed over the photograph to the magazine had contributed, he ordered them to pay $2,000 jointly and severally. However, the judgment is somewhat ambiguous regarding the nature of the damage this amount was intended to compensate. Judge Bourret wrote in this connection (at p. 423):

> "[TRANSLATION] In the court's view, to learn through teasing by friends her own age that her picture had been published in a prestigious, large-circulation magazine without her even knowing that her picture had been taken by a third party and without her having ever authorized its publication, merits compensation of at least $ 2,000 for the humiliation suffered as a result of the invasion of her privacy and injury to her reputation."

42. This passage suggests that the $ 2,000 would cover both the damages resulting from the injury to her reputation and the loss of privacy resulting from the publication of the photograph.

43. However, since the photograph was not defamatory in nature either in itself or by association with the accompanying text in the magazine, Judge Bourret denied any com-

pensation on this ground. He also refused to award exemplary damages, as there was no evidence of malice on the part of the defendants.

B. Court of Appeal

44. The majority of the Court of Appeal affirmed Judge Bourret's decision. LeBel J.A. and Biron J. (*ad hoc*) both found that the fault lay not in the taking of the photograph but in its publication. According to LeBel J.A., writing for the majority, since the respondent was in a public place when the photograph was taken, that act alone could not be considered an invasion of her privacy. However, the unauthorized publication of the photograph constituted an infringement of her anonymity, which is an essential element of the right to privacy.

45. LeBel J.A. recognized that the unauthorized publication of a photograph could be justified on the basis of the public's legitimate interest in information. In his view, however, Québec law recognizes no such exception for artistic activity. Even in the absence of bad faith, the dissemination of the photograph was, therefore, wrongful.

46. While the judges of the majority recognized that there was only limited evidence of moral prejudice, they refused to alter Judge Bourret's decision.... [T]hey noted that an appellate court must show deference to findings of fact drawn from the evidence by the trial judge.

47. Baudouin J.A.'s dissent focussed essentially on the question of damages. In his view, damages cannot be found to have been sustained solely because the photograph was wrongfully disseminated. Nor can the absence of evidence of damages be concealed under the head "nominal damages". This was particularly important, in his view, where the right to privacy is claimed as against freedom of information or artistic freedom. In this case, Baudouin J.A. refused to consider the respondent's sole statement that [translation] "people laughed at me" as sufficient evidence. In his view, therefore, the issue was not one of credibility warranting an appellate court's deference but rather one of lack of evidence.

III. Relevant Statutory Provisions

48. Charter of Human Rights and Freedoms, R.S.Q., c. C-12:

> "3. Every person is the possessor of the fundamental freedoms, including freedom of conscience, freedom of religion, freedom of opinion, freedom of expression, freedom of peaceful assembly and freedom of association.
>
> 4. Every person has a right to the safeguard of his dignity, honour and reputation.
>
> 5. Every person has a right to respect for his private life.
>
> 9.1. In exercising his fundamental freedoms and rights, a person shall maintain a proper regard for democratic values, public order and the general well-being of the citizens of Québec.
>
> In this respect, the scope of the freedoms and rights, and limits to their exercise, may be fixed by law.
>
> 49. Any unlawful interference with any right or freedom recognized by this Charter entitles the victim to obtain the cessation of such interference and compensation for the moral or material prejudice resulting therefrom.
>
> In case of unlawful and intentional interference, the tribunal may, in addition, condemn the person guilty of it to exemplary damages."

IV. Analysis

49. The case at bar raises a problem of civil law and it is in light of that law that it must be resolved. The infringement of a right guaranteed by the Charter of Human Rights and

Freedoms (hereinafter the "Québec Charter") gives rise, under § 49 para. 1, to an action for moral and material prejudice. Such an action is subject to the civil law principles of recovery. As a result, the traditional elements of liability, namely fault, damage and causal connection, must be established.

50. It should be mentioned at the outset that our analysis will be limited to the sole issue before this Court, namely publication of a photograph taken without permission.

51. There is a debate in French law, and a corresponding uncertainty in Québec law, as to whether the right to one's image is a separate right of personality or an element of the right to privacy. In our view, the right to one's image, which has an extrapatrimonial and a patrimonial aspect, is an element of the right to privacy under § 5 of the Québec Charter. This is consistent with the liberal interpretation given to the concept of privacy in the recent decision *Godbout v. Longueuil (City)*, [1997] 3 S.C.R. 844, and in past judgments of this Court.

52. … It should be noted, finally, that art. 36 of the new Civil Code of Québec, S.Q. 1991, c. 64, although not applicable here, confirms this interpretation since it recognizes that the use of a person's name, image, likeness or voice for a purpose other than the legitimate information of the public is an invasion of privacy.

53. Since the right to one's image is included in the right to respect for one's private life, it is axiomatic that every person possesses a protected right to his or her image. This right arises when the subject is recognizable. There is, thus, an infringement of the person's right to his or her image, and therefore fault, as soon as the image is published without consent and enables the person to be identified.

54. The right to respect for one's private life should not be confused with the right to one's honour and reputation under § 4 of the Québec Charter even though, in certain cases, wrongful publication of an image may in itself result in an injury to one's honour and reputation. Since every person is entitled to protection of his or her privacy, and since the person's image is protected accordingly, it is possible for the rights inherent in the protection of privacy to be infringed even though the published image is in no way reprehensible and has in no way injured the person's reputation. In the case at bar, the judges at trial and on appeal found that the photograph was in no way reprehensible and did not injure the respondent's honour or reputation. The Court of Appeal also found that the manner in which the photograph was juxtaposed with the text did not make it possible to associate the two elements and that, at any rate, the text was serious and not open to ridicule.

55. The right to respect for one's private life comes into conflict here with another right protected by the Québec Charter, in § 3, namely the right to freedom of expression. LeBel J.A. and Biron J. stated that Québec law does not yet consider artistic expression to be a separate right. It is our view that freedom of expression includes freedom of artistic expression. It is, therefore, unnecessary to create a special category to take freedom of artistic expression into account. Artistic expression does not require a special category to be effective. Nor is there any justification for giving it a status superior to that of general freedom of expression. An artist can assert his or her right to freedom of expression under the same conditions as any other person. There is, thus, no need to distinguish freedom of artistic expression from journalistic reporting, as we have been asked to do.

56. The right to respect for one's private life, like freedom of expression, must be interpreted in accordance with the provisions of § 9.1 of the Québec Charter. For this purpose, it is necessary to balance these two rights.

57. The public's right to information, supported by freedom of expression, places limits on the right to respect for one's private life in certain circumstances. This is because the expectation of privacy is reduced in certain cases. A person's right to respect for his or her private life may even be limited by the public's interest in knowing about certain traits of his or her personality. In short, the public's interest in being informed is a concept that can be applied to determine whether impugned conduct oversteps the bounds of what is permitted.

58. The public interest so defined is thus conclusive in certain cases. The balancing of the rights in question depends both on the nature of the information and on the situation of those concerned. This is a question that depends on the context. Thus, it is generally recognized that certain aspects of the private life of a person who is engaged in a public activity or has acquired a certain notoriety can become matters of public interest. This is true, in particular, of artists and politicians, but also, more generally, of all those whose professional success depends on public opinion. There are also cases where a previously unknown individual is called on to play a high-profile role in a matter within the public domain, such as an important trial, a major economic activity having an impact on the use of public funds, or an activity involving public safety. It is also recognized that a photographer is exempt from liability, as are those who publish the photograph, when an individual's own action, albeit unwitting, accidentally places him or her in the photograph in an incidental manner. The person is then in the limelight in a sense. One need only think of a photograph of a crowd at a sporting event or a demonstration.

59. Another situation where the public interest prevails is one where a person appears in an incidental manner in a photograph of a public place. An image taken in a public place can then be regarded as an anonymous element of the scenery, even if it is technically possible to identify individuals in the photograph. In such a case, since the unforeseen observer's attention will normally be directed elsewhere, the person "snapped without warning" cannot complain. The same is true of a person in a group photographed in a public place. Such a person cannot object to the publication of the photograph if he or she is not its principal subject. On the other hand, the public nature of the place where a photograph was taken is irrelevant if the place was simply used as background for one or more persons who constitute the true subject of the photograph.

60. In the context of freedom of expression, which is at the heart of the public's interest in being informed, the person's express or tacit consent to the publication of his or her image must, therefore, be taken into account....

61. LeBel J.A. and Biron J. analysed this question on the basis of the notion of "socially useful information" (p. 2149). In their view, freedom of expression and the public's right to information will prevail where the expression at issue concerns information that is "socially useful". This notion seems to have been borrowed from American law, which draws a distinction between useful information, in the sense of the public's right to be informed, and information whose sole purpose is commercial. *See Estate of Presley v. Russen*, 513 F.Supp. 1339 (D.N.J. 1981), and *Current Audio Inc. v. RCA Corp.*, 337 N.Y.S.2d 949 (Sup. Ct. 1972). Only the first category is protected in the United States. In the United States, freedom of expression and public information prevail over the right to privacy except where the information's sole purpose is commercial. We agree with the intervener that this notion of "socially useful" refers only to the fact that the information in question has an economic, political, artistic, cultural, sporting or other value. A photograph of a single person can be "socially useful" because it serves to illustrate a theme. That does not make its publication acceptable, however, if it infringes the right to privacy. We do not consider it appropriate to adopt the notion of "socially useful" for the pur-

poses of legal analysis. The distinction based on commercial purpose is inconsistent with §9.1 of the Québec Charter. Only one question arises, namely the balancing of the rights at issue. It must, therefore, be decided whether the public's right to information can justify dissemination of a photograph taken without authorization.

62. In the case at bar, the appellants are liable *a priori*, since the photograph was published when the respondent was identifiable. In our view, the artistic expression of the photograph, which was alleged to have served to illustrate contemporary urban life, cannot justify the infringement of the right to privacy it entails. It has not been shown that the public's interest in seeing this photograph is predominant. The argument that the public has an interest in seeing any work of art cannot be accepted, especially because an artist's right to publish his or her work, no more than other forms of freedom of expression, is not absolute. The wording of §9.1 of the Québec Charter should be borne in mind here, together with the fact that this Court has stated on a number of occasions that freedom of expression must be defined in light of the other values concerned.

63. An artist's right to publish his or her work cannot include the right to infringe, without any justification, a fundamental right of the subject whose image appears in the work. While the artist's right must be taken into consideration, so must the rights of the photograph's subject. If it is accepted that publishing the artist's work is an exercise of freedom of expression, the respondent's right not to consent must also be taken into consideration. That is what this Court held in the context of the Canadian Bill of Rights in *R. v. CKOY Ltd.*, [1979] 1 S.C.R. 2, at pp. 14–15, where the Court denied a radio station the right to broadcast an interview without the consent of the person interviewed.

64. When the values at issue in a case must be balanced, it is important to bear in mind that our law is characterized by recognition of interrelated rights whose purpose is to strengthen the democratic ideal. Individual freedom is at the heart of that ideal. Dickson J. (as he then was) stated the following in this regard in *R. v. Big M Drug Mart Ltd.*, [1985] 1 S.C.R. 295, at pp. 336–37:

> "Freedom can primarily be characterized by the absence of coercion or constraint. If a person is compelled by the state or the will of another to a course of action or inaction which he would not otherwise have chosen, he is not acting of his own volition and he cannot be said to be truly free. One of the major purposes of the Charter is to protect, within reason, from compulsion or restraint. Coercion includes not only ... blatant forms of compulsion ... [but also] includes indirect forms of control which determine or limit alternative courses of conduct available to others."

65. None of the exceptions mentioned earlier based on the public's right to information is applicable here. Accordingly, there appears to be no justification for giving precedence to the appellants other than their submission that it would be very difficult in practice for a photographer to obtain the consent of all those he or she photographs in public places before publishing their photographs. To accept such an exception would, in fact, amount to accepting that the photographer's right is unlimited, provided that the photograph is taken in a public place, thereby extending the photographer's freedom at the expense of that of others. We reject this point of view. In the case at bar, the respondent's right to protection of her image is more important than the appellants' right to publish the photograph of the respondent without first obtaining her permission.

V. Damages

66. The appellants argued that there was no causal connection between the publication of the photograph and the damages. In our view, no particular problem arises here

since the damages are the logical, direct and immediate consequence of the fault. A teenager's sensitivity and the possibility of being teased by her friends are eminently foreseeable.

67. Nonetheless, it was necessary for the respondent to establish that she had suffered prejudice. Such prejudice may be extrapatrimonial and/or patrimonial.

68. Where extrapatrimonial damages are concerned, we agree with Baudouin J.A. that the infringement of a right guaranteed by the Québec Charter is in itself insufficient to establish that damage has been sustained. Nor is an award of symbolic damages justified when the courts wish to punish the infringement of a right that will, in most cases, result in minimal injury. This would be contrary to the principles of civil responsibility.

69. The damages must, therefore, be proven....

70. In the case at bar, the evidence of moral damages is limited. The moral prejudice is described in a few lines. Nonetheless, it is possible for a trial judge in a case such as this to assess the victim's conduct and, going beyond his or her words, to detect a violation of dignity....

71. Although the evidence is limited, we agree with LeBel J.A. and Biron J. that, having been accepted by the trial judge, it could serve as a basis for the damages awarded....

73. It is clear, however, that the trial judge erred with respect to the extent of the dissemination of the magazine. He also erred in stating that the damages would compensate in part for the humiliation suffered by the respondent as a result of the injury to her reputation, whereas no injury to her honour and reputation had been proven. However, these errors in the assessment do not call into question the existence of moral damages resulting from the infringement of the respondent's right to respect for her private life. Accordingly, they do not warrant this Court's intervention to reduce a compensatory award that is still within reasonable limits.

74. With respect to the patrimonial aspect of the invasion of privacy, we are of the view that the commercial or promotional exploitation of an image, whether of a well-known person or a private individual, can cause the victim material prejudice. The compensation must, then, be calculated on the basis of the loss actually sustained and the lost profit (art. 1073 C.C.L.C.). In this regard, the respondent is correct in stating that the magazine does not cease to be "commercial" merely because it has an artistic content. In the case at bar, the photograph was used for commercial purposes, in particular to sell the magazine. The trial judge stated that the amount of $2,000 was compensation for moral damages only. Neither the trial judge nor the judges of the Court of Appeal discussed the patrimonial aspect of the damages. The respondent was, however, entitled to claim an amount in exchange for the use of her image. The respondent argued that there was commercial exploitation and adduced evidence in support of her claim for damages in respect thereof. The testimony of Gilbert Duclos disclosed that he usually has to pay between $30 and $40 an hour for the services of a model, generally for a period of two to four hours. Thus, the respondent would ordinarily have been entitled to a sum of money. In the present case, this was the only evidence available to this Court for calculating these damages. In other circumstances, where the evidence so permits, it is not impossible to compensate for patrimonial damages through profit-sharing based on the principles of profit lost and loss sustained. Since no cross-appeal was brought with respect to the amount of the damages, we will not vary the amount awarded by the trial judge.

75. The appeal is dismissed with costs....

LAMER, C.J. (dissenting):

1. I have had the opportunity to read the joint reasons of Justices L'Heureux-Dube and Bastarache and, while I generally agree with them, I cannot fully subscribe to their analytical approach or their conclusion. I wish to make certain comments concerning the nature of the right to one's image and how I believe rights should be incorporated into an analysis of civil liability. Furthermore, I would allow this appeal because there is no evidence of damage.

I. Civil Liability and Rights

2. To a great extent, the oral arguments of the parties in this Court concerned the scope of the right to one's image and the limits imposed on it by the freedom of expression of a photographer and that of a publishing company. To this effect, the intervener Canadian Broadcasting Corporation relied on this Court's freedom of expression jurisprudence to challenge the scope of a person's right to his or her image. The important role played by freedom of expression in our society was raised. While these submissions are most relevant to the resolution of the case, I think it is important to clarify first how rights influence our analysis of civil liability. This approach makes clear to us how to reconcile the conflicting values at issue.

3. I would stress that the concept of fault is central to the resolution of this case. Before the Québec legislature enacted a charter of human rights and freedoms, it was the law of civil liability, with all its flexibility, that protected privacy and the individual's interest in his or her image in Québec private law. I read with interest the reasons of the judges of the Court of Appeal on this topic. In enacting its Charter of Human Rights and Freedoms, the legislature thus consolidated the advances of civil liability in the protection of human rights....

5. My intention here is to place the analytical approach that characterizes the dispute in this case as being primarily a conflict between the rights of the respondent and those of the appellants in its proper theoretical context. Accordingly, even though she relies on a certain right to her image, the plaintiff respondent must prove that a fault committed by the appellants caused her prejudice.

6. I also wish to point out that the parties referred us to a number of public law cases. I do not doubt that the law of civil liability is informed by the constitutional or "quasi-constitutional" rights protected by the Charters. I am certain that a reasonable person respects everyone's right to privacy, right to his or her image and freedom of expression in accordance with the Charters. However, I believe that it is important to emphasize the comprehensive and contextual nature of civil fault. We should be reluctant to view fault as amounting to a violation of rights alone. In my view, such an approach is riddled with obstacles....

9. It would therefore be wrong to define the scope of the right to privacy between citizens solely on the basis of the decisions relating to [rights against the state]. Although I agree with the functional definitions of privacy adopted by this Court, it seems to me that the right to privacy can have a different scope in private law.

10. The analysis under the Canadian Charter can also be distinguished from civil liability analysis in another way. In Charter matters, this Court has developed a two-stage approach: the plaintiff must first show that a right or freedom has been infringed before the defendant attempts to demonstrate that the limit on the protected rights and freedoms is reasonable. For example, freedom of expression enjoys very broad protection in Canada. Any peaceful activity that conveys or attempts to convey meaning is protected by freedom of expression. According to this definition, even defamatory remarks are protected

by freedom of expression. Therefore, the person who maintains the validity of a limit on such expression has the burden of proving that the limit is reasonable. Where the Canadian Charter is concerned, the burden of justification is always on the state.

11. In contrast, the rules of civil liability are different. First, mere infringement of a right or freedom does not in my view necessarily constitute fault. For example, firefighters who interrupt a political meeting to evacuate a burning building do not commit a fault. Only unjustifiable infringements of freedom of expression, as this freedom is defined in public law, constitute fault.

12. Second, I do not think that a civil liability analysis allows the burden of proof to be shifted between the parties in the same manner as is permitted in Charter law. Section 9.1 of the Charter of Human Rights and Freedoms is relevant here. It reads as follows:

> "9.1. In exercising his fundamental freedoms and rights, a person shall maintain a proper regard for democratic values, public order and the general well-being of the citizens of Québec.
>
> In this respect, the scope of the freedoms and rights, and limits to their exercise, may be fixed by law."

15. ... I believe that we must give the first paragraph of §9.1 an interpretative significance and adapt the law of civil liability, as needed, to make it consistent with the rights guaranteed by the Québec Charter....

17. In short, the real issue is whether the appellants committed a fault. This approach recognizes the flexible and contextual nature of the concept of fault, and its capacity to reconcile the rights relied upon in this case. A reasonable person respects the rights and freedoms of everyone and carries out his or her obligations while bearing his or her own rights in mind.

18. This approach is also consistent with the wording of §9.1 of the Québec Charter. The parliamentary proceedings that resulted in the adoption of §9.1 show that the legislature's intention was for the first paragraph of §9.1 to place limits on private relations rather than on the law itself. The statement made by the Québec Minister of Justice when the provision was adopted in 1982 can also be noted, with appropriate caution:

> "[TRANSLATION] The purpose of §9.1 is to temper the absolute nature of the freedoms and rights set out in §§1 to 9 both from the perspective of the limits imposed on the holders of those rights and freedoms in respect of other citizens, which is the case for the first paragraph, and from that of the limits the legislature may place on the community as a whole, a principle formed in the second paragraph."

(Journal des debats: Commissions parlementaires, 3rd sess., 32nd Leg., December 16, 1982, at p. B-11609.)

19. This case cannot be resolved merely by relying upon the respondent's right to her image or the appellants' freedom of expression; the rights concerned must also be balanced. Since freedom of expression is fairly well known, I shall now discuss the right to one's image.

II. Right to One's Image

20. The Québec courts have applied the principles of civil liability to allow compensation for the prejudice resulting from the use of a person's image without his or her consent. According to the authors, these judicial interventions have created a right to one's image at issue in the present case. The reasons of the Court of Appeal include a detailed

account of the evolution of Québec and French jurisprudence and doctrine, and that account is entirely satisfactory. However, I wish to add the following comments.

21. I would hesitate to conclude that the right to one's image has no existence independent of the right to privacy. It is common knowledge that this Court has defined the right to privacy very broadly (albeit in the public law context).... I believe that the right to privacy can be analysed in similar terms in private law. Furthermore, this right certainly includes a person's right to his or her image. Nevertheless, I do not rule out the possibility that a person's commercial interest in his or her image does not derive uniquely from his or her right to privacy. As a result, it may be advisable to preserve the integrity of the concept of privacy.

22. I also agree with my colleagues that the right to one's image is primarily a personality right, an interest of an extrapatrimonial nature. I do not consider it necessary to go further and determine whether there is also a right to one's image of a patrimonial nature.... I would note simply that it is not contrary to public order for individuals, whether famous or not, to profit from consenting to the use of their image.

23. In the case at bar, I am of the view that the dissemination of the respondent's image constituted a violation of her privacy and of her right to her image. In the abstract, to appropriate another person's image without his or her consent to include it in a publication constitutes a fault. I am of the view that a reasonable person would have been more diligent and would at least have tried to obtain the respondent's consent to the publication of her photograph. The appellants did not do everything necessary to avoid infringing the respondent's rights....

24. I do not doubt that freedom of expression provides the appellants with powerful arguments to the effect that they acted reasonably. However, as § 9.1 of the Québec Charter provides, rights and freedoms must be exercised in relation to each other, with proper regard for public order, democratic values and general well-being. Thus, the rights of the appellants and the respondent must be harmonized in the facts of the case. The concept of the public interest is intended to play this role in matters involving the right to one's image as in the case of the right to one's honour and reputation. This rule should now be examined.

III. Public Interest

25. The respondent's right to privacy must be interpreted in a manner consistent with the appellants' freedom of expression and the public's right to information, which is guaranteed by § 44 of the Québec Charter. As the Court of Appeal recently stated in *The Gazette (Division Southam Inc.) v. Valiquette*, [1997] R.J.Q. 30 (C.A.), at p. 36:

> "[TRANSLATION] The right to privacy, on the other hand, is not absolute. It is subject to a series of limits, and its application requires a balancing with other fundamental rights, including the public's right to information. A violation of the right to privacy thus cannot be characterized as illicit or wrongful if there is a reasonable justification or a legitimate purpose, or if it can be concluded that the person consented to the invasion of his or her privacy."

26. It is inevitable that the concept of public interest is imprecise. In her work on defamation, Nicole Vallieres writes of the public interest in this context: [TRANSLATION] "this abstract concept is difficult to delimit, and as far as we know, no definition of the public interest has been applied to the press by the Québec courts": *La presse et la diffamation* (1985), at p. 90. In my view, the content of the concept of public interest depends on the nature of the information conveyed by the image and on the situation of the

parties involved. On the other hand, it must be balanced against the reasonable expectation of privacy of the person whose image is reproduced and, generally, against the severity of the infringement of the parties' rights.

27. With respect, I believe that LeBel J.A. of the Court of Appeal erred in limiting the notion of public interest to the right to receive [TRANSLATION] "socially useful" information ([1996] R.J.Q. 2137, at p. 2149). This concept appears to me to be too narrow. Be that as it may, it is my view that in the case at bar the public interest does not justify the appellants' fault. The appellant Duclos could easily have obtained the respondent's consent, but did not do so. It is possible for the public interest to justify the dissemination of the image of a person who is in a crowd or is at the scene of an important event in a purely incidental manner. However, I will express no opinion on this subject, and I do not think it appropriate to specify, in the context of the present case, the circumstances in which the public interest prevails over a person's right to his or her image. It is sufficient to state that the appellants committed a fault. Since causality is not at issue here, it is now necessary to consider damage and the proof thereof.

IV. Damage

28. The Québec law of civil liability requires proof of prejudice resulting from the fault. This is an essential element of civil liability. On this question of damage, I agree with Baudouin J.A. that the plaintiff respondent has not proven that she suffered prejudice....

31. I believe that if the respondent had stated, "I felt humiliated when I saw the photograph published in *Vice-Versa* magazine," there would have been sufficient evidence of damage in this case, provided that Judge Bourret believed her....

32. However, in my view the statement "people laughed at me" does not *in itself* constitute sufficient evidence of damage, since it does not provide any information about how the respondent Aubry felt. The fact that the trial judge accepted this evidence, without giving any reasons or explanation, suggests to me that he erred in presuming damage solely because the respondent's classmates laughed at her. On re-reading the Court of Québec's judgment, I cannot convince myself that Judge Bourret considered this essential element of civil liability.

33. The respondent nonetheless suggests that her prejudice consists of the fact that she has become well-known, thereby losing her anonymity. With respect, there is no evidence on the record tending to show that the respondent is now a "well-known figure"....

35. According to one French author, damage in the case of an infringement of the right to one's image [TRANSLATION] "may consist simply in the annoyance felt by a person at becoming a 'celebrity'". With respect, this statement cannot mean that the infringement of a personality right on its own results in civil liability in Québec in the absence of evidence of prejudice, contrary to what seems to be possible in France.

36. For these reasons, I do not rule out the possibility that the dissemination of a person's image without consent might result in damage for which he or she can be compensated....

V. Disposition

37. I am of the view that the evidence is insufficient to conclude that the wrongful dissemination of the photograph of the respondent Aubry caused her moral prejudice. For this reason, I would allow the appeal, set aside the judgments below and dismiss the action, with costs.

Major J. (dissenting):

82. I agree with the result reached by the Chief Justice and would allow the appeal for the reasons of Baudouin J.A. that there was no evidence of damage.

———————

Notes and Questions

1. Make sure you understand the facts: where was the plaintiff when the picture was taken? Was this a private place?

2. Given these facts, why did the plaintiff's right of privacy trump any rights of free expression of the photographer? Can you identify the factors used by the court to decide whether privacy or free expression should win?

3. If the photographer had taken the picture and hung it up on a wall in his house, would plaintiff have been able to sue (assuming she found out)? Suppose only one copy had been made and hung in a museum?

4. Suppose that a newspaper reporter doing a story about the city of Montreal had taken the picture and it had been published in the newspaper. Would that have changed the result?

5. The court indicates that U.S. cases give greater protection to the press and free expression over privacy rights than do Canadian cases. Do you agree? How do you think a U.S. court would have decided this case?

6. Compare the *Aubry* case to the previous two cases. Do you think that either of the other two courts (in *von Hannover* and *Campbell*) would have decided this case the same way as the Canadian court? Would this court have decided those cases any differently than the Court of Human Rights or the House of Lords did?

7. *Parody and satire.* The Canadian courts have not yet had an opportunity to address the issue of parody and satire in the context of rights of privacy or publicity. However, there are some cases concerning trademark and copyright that may shed some light on how the Canadian courts would deal with the issue, and how they might react to the *von Hannover* and *Campbell* cases.

8. In *Source Perrier (Societe Anonyme) v. Fira-Less Marketing Co. Ltd.,* 1983 A.C.W.S.J. 474679; 18 A.C.W.S. (2d) 365 (Fed. Ct. Tr. Div. 1983), the defendant manufactured bottled water in a bottle whose shape, color, and labels strongly resembled those used by Perrier. However, the defendant's bottles were labeled "Pierre Eh!", a spoof of the name of the former Canadian Prime Minister, Pierre Trudeau. Trudeau did not sue, but Perrier did, claiming that the spoof infringed its trademark rights. Defendant cited various U.S. cases in support of its position that its parody was protected expression. However, the Canadian court held for Perrier. The judge stated:

> In my view, the most liberal interpretation of "freedom of expression" does not embrace the freedom to depreciate the goodwill of registered trade marks, nor does it afford a licence to impair the business integrity of the owner of the marks merely to accommodate the creation of a spoof. It must be borne in mind that this application for an injunction does not originate from the targets of the parody — those in the political trade are expected to be blessed with a broad sense of humour — but from the owner of the trade marks.

Id. at ¶ 20. Why should it matter that it was the trademark owner who sued, rather than the politician? Does this aside suggest the court would have ruled differently if Trudeau had sued?

9. In *Cie Générale des Établissements Michelin-Michelin & Cie v. C.A.W.-Canada*, 71 C.P.R. (3d) 348 (Fed. Ct. Tr. Div. 1996), the tire-maker Michelin sued the union that represents its workers for trademark and copyright infringement in leaflets distributed by the union during an organizing campaign. The leaflets contained the Michelin trademark and a parody depicting Michelin's "Bibendum" (the Michelin Man) stepping on union workers. The court found no trademark infringement, but it did find copyright infringement. The court rejected defendant's claim that parody was equivalent to "criticism"—a defense under Canadian copyright law. The court then turned to the union's claim that its rights of free speech were violated:

> I recognize ... how free expression is "fundamental because in a free, pluralistic and democratic society we prize a diversity of ideas and opinions for their inherent value both to the community and the individual." ... [However, one] cannot give free rein to unions to use the property of another merely because they are in the midst of an organizing campaign. Freedom of expression is not an absolute value....

> Copyright is an intangible property right.... But just because the right is intangible, it should not be any less worthy of protection as a full property right.... No infringer could credibly allege that freedom of expression gives him or her the right to subvert the content or message of the painting by physically drawing a moustache on [a] painting. However, what if the infringer asserted the right to copy or substantially reproduce the painting with a moustache? Our instincts might not be so certain about the scope of the infringer's freedom of expression because our perceptions are coloured by the intangible nature of the copyholder's right. We should guard against our instincts in this instance since they might lead us to undervalue the nature of the Plaintiff's copyright and overestimate the breadth of the Defendants' freedom of expression.... The Defendants cannot logically assert a right to use the Plaintiff's private property within the scope of their freedom of expression, because then the Plaintiff would have a reciprocal duty to give the Defendants access to this property....

> The Plaintiff argues that the Defendants' use of its property in fact subverts the third value—the diversity of ideas by enhancing self-fulfillment—of expression. Copyright promotes the third value by protecting and providing an incentive for authors to create works of expression because their works will be protected under the aegis of the Copyright Act from unauthorized reproduction. I have no reason to doubt that the Plaintiff is intent on protecting its interest in its copyright against all unauthorized users....

> I hold that a person using the private property of another like a copyright, must demonstrate that his or her use of the property is compatible with the function of the property before the Court can deem the use a protected form of expression under the Charter. In the present case, subjecting the Plaintiff's "Bibendum" to ridicule as the object of parody is not compatible with the function of the copyright. A "Bibendum" about to stomp hapless workers into submission does not present the original author's intent of a favourable corporate image or provide an incentive for compensating artists for the integrity of their vision.

Do you agree with the judge's analogy between a copyright and tangible personal property such as a painting? Why or why not? Does the doctrine of "fair use" in the U.S. (or "fair dealing" in British and Canadian law) improperly impose upon defendants an obligation to give the public "access" to their property? Are there any parodies that would pass the judge's standard of being "compatible with the function of the copyright"? Would you expect Canadian courts to treat rights of privacy or publicity with greater or less deference than a copyright or trademark? Why?

The following case deals with privacy interests, rather than publicity interests, and does not involve a celebrity, or even a natural person. However, the principles it enunciates appear applicable to cases that are more akin to rights of publicity. There are several opinions in this case, so be sure you read them all and count votes!

Australian Broadcasting Corp. v. Lenah Game Meat Pty. Ltd.

[2001] H.C.A. 63, 185 A.L.R. 1 (High Ct. Australia 2001)

Gleeson CJ, Gaudron, Gummow, Kirby, Hayne and Callinan JJ

Gleeson CJ:

1. This appeal concerns an application for an interlocutory injunction, pending the hearing of an action brought by the respondent against the appellant and another party, to restrain the broadcasting of a film of the respondent's operations at a "brush tail possum processing facility". The film was made surreptitiously and unlawfully, and was given to the appellant with the evident purpose that the appellant would broadcast it. . . .

The facts

23. The respondent is a processor and supplier of game meat. It sells possum meat for export. Tasmanian brushtail possums are killed and processed at licensed abattoirs. The respondent's business is conducted according to law, and with the benefit of all necessary licences. The methods by which the possums are killed, although lawful, are objected to by some people, including people associated with Animal Liberation Ltd., on the ground that they are cruel.

24. A person or persons unknown broke and entered the respondent's premises and installed hidden cameras. The possum-killing operations were filmed, without the knowledge or consent of the respondent. The film was supplied to Animal Liberation Ltd., which, in turn, supplied the film, or part of it, to the appellant, with the intention that the appellant would broadcast it. [It is also apparent that the broadcaster knew it had been obtained unlawfully.] . . .

25. It is not suggested that the operations that were filmed were secret, or that requirements of confidentiality were imposed upon people who might see the operations. . . . There is no evidence that, at least before the events giving rise to this case, any special precautions were taken by the respondent to avoid its operations being seen by people outside its organisation. But, like many other lawful animal slaughtering activities, the respondent's activities, if displayed to the public, would cause distress to some viewers. It is claimed that loss of business would result. . . .

The respondent's claim of right

28. . . . There is no claim by the respondent to copyright, or any other form of intellectual property, in relation to the film, or what is depicted on the film. No trade secrets are at risk.

29. The film is the means by which the trespassers recorded, and intended to communicate to others, what goes on in the slaughtering process. Because it is an effective method of doing so, it is clearly relevant to any harm which the respondent is likely to suffer. But does it have additional relevance? If the trespassers had simply entered the premises themselves, secretly observed what was happening, and later described on television what they had seen, what difference would that have made to the respondent's case, except on the question of damage? ... One possible answer to those questions is that the film itself is a visual image, and a sound recording, in a potent form, which the respondent did not wish to be available for public display. The images and sounds recorded on a film may themselves constitute information; and the circumstances in which the film was made, the nature of the activities recorded, a person's concern that they not be seen by the general public, and an inference that trespassers and broadcasters or publishers knew of that concern, could make the image and the sounds confidential.

30. The respondent contends that the conduct of the appellant in publishing a film known to have been taken as the result of a trespass would on that account alone be unconscionable, and should be restrained.... [I]t is argued [that] all information obtained as the result of trespass ought to be treated in the same way as confidential information.

31. The Attorney-General of the Commonwealth, intervening, made the following submissions:

1. A court of equity has jurisdiction to grant an injunction to restrain the use of information where the information has been obtained by a trespasser, or by some other illegal, tortious, surreptitious or otherwise improper means and use of the information would be unconscionable.

2. The jurisdiction extends to ordering an injunction against any person to whom the information has been conveyed, whether or not that person is implicated in the trespass or other illegal, tortious, surreptitious or otherwise improper conduct.

3. In determining whether the use of the information would be unconscionable, the court should take account of all the circumstances of the case, including the competing public interests in preserving the rule of law, protecting private property and in otherwise protecting the relevant information, and the public interest in freedom of speech.

4. In all cases, the fact that the information was improperly obtained should weigh heavily against allowing the information to be used.

5. The onus of showing that the publication is in the public interest should rest on the person seeking to publish the improperly obtained information....

34. ... In *Hellewell v. Chief Constable of Derbyshire*, [4 All E.R. 473, 476 (Q.B. 1995) (Eng.)], Laws J. said:

If someone with a telephoto lens were to take from a distance and with no authority a picture of another engaged in some private act, his subsequent disclosure of the photograph would, in my judgment, as surely amount to a breach of confidence as if he had found or stolen a letter or diary in which the act was recounted and proceeded to publish it. In such a case, the law would protect what might reasonably be called a right of privacy, although the name accorded to the cause of action would be breach of confidence. It is, of course, elementary that, in all such cases, a defence based on the public interest would be available.

35. I agree with that proposition, although, to adapt it to the Australian context, it is necessary to add a qualification concerning the constitutional freedom of political communication earlier mentioned. The present is at least as strong a case for a plaintiff as photography from a distance with a telephoto lens. But it is the reference to "some private act" that is central to the present problem. The activities filmed were carried out on private property. They were not shown, or alleged, to be private in any other sense....

37. In *Douglas v. Hello! Ltd.*, [discussed in the Notes above,] there was some difference of opinion between members of the English Court of Appeal as to whether a celebrity wedding to which 250 guests were invited, and at which photography was closely controlled, was private. However, images of the wedding were treated as confidential information.

38. An argument for the respondent invoked privacy in a somewhat different context. The respondent invited this court to depart from old authority; declare that Australian law now recognises a tort of invasion of privacy; hold that it is available to be relied upon by corporations as well as individuals; and conclude that this is the missing cause of action for which everyone in the case has so far been searching....

41. But the lack of precision of the concept of privacy is a reason for caution in declaring a new tort of the kind for which the respondent contends. Another reason is the tension that exists between interests in privacy and interests in free speech. I say "interests", because talk of "rights" may be question-begging, especially in a legal system which has no counterpart to the First Amendment to the United States Constitution or to the Human Rights Act 1998 of the United Kingdom. The categories that have been developed in the United States for the purpose of giving greater specificity to the kinds of interest protected by a "right to privacy" illustrate the problem. The first of those categories, which includes intrusion upon private affairs or concerns, requires that the intrusion be highly offensive to a reasonable person. Part of the price we pay for living in an organised society is that we are exposed to observation in a variety of ways by other people....

48. In *Bartnicki v. Vopper*, [532 U.S. 514, 529–30 (2001),] Stevens J., speaking for the majority of the Supreme Court of the United States, said:

> The normal method of deterring unlawful conduct is to impose appropriate punishment on the person who engages in it. If the sanctions that presently attach to a violation of [the statute] do not provide sufficient deterrence, perhaps those sanctions should be more severe. But it would be quite remarkable to hold that speech by a law-abiding possessor of information can be suppressed in order to deter conduct by a non-law-abiding third party.

49. That statement, it is true, was made in a context influenced by the First Amendment to the United States Constitution....

51. There is judicial support for the proposition that the trespassers, if caught in time, could have been restrained from publishing the film....

55. For reasons already given, I regard the law of breach of confidence as providing a remedy, in a case such as the present, if the nature of the information obtained by the trespasser is such as to permit the information to be regarded as confidential. But, if that condition is not fulfilled, then the circumstance that the information was tortiously obtained in the first place is not sufficient to make it unconscientious of a person into whose hands that information later comes to use it or publish it. The consequences of such a proposition are too large.

Conclusion

56. Underwood J [the trial judge] was correct to dismiss the respondent's application on the first ground of his decision. It is unnecessary to consider the other ground.

57. I would allow the appeal. I agree with the orders proposed by Gummow and Hayne JJ.

GAUDRON J.:

58. I agree with the judgment of Gummow and Hayne JJ and with the orders they propose....

GUMMOW and HAYNE JJ.:

63. The appellant, the Australian Broadcasting Corporation (the ABC), seeks from this court an order discharging an interlocutory injunction granted by the Full Court of the Supreme Court of Tasmania on 2 November 1999. The injunction restrains, until further order, the ABC, its servants and agents "from distributing, publishing, copying or broadcasting a video tape or video tapes filmed by a trespasser or trespassers showing [Lenah's] brush tail possum processing facility at 315 George Town Road Rocherlea in Tasmania." The Full Court allowed an appeal by the present respondent, Lenah Game Meats Pty. Ltd. (Lenah) against an order made on 3 May 1999 by a judge of the Supreme Court (Underwood J) dismissing Lenah's application for interlocutory relief.... [B]efore the hearing of the appeal, the ABC had televised segments of the videotape in question....

No equity to injunctive relief

105. The ABC's submission on this branch of the case should be accepted. The conferral upon the Supreme Court by statute of the power to grant interlocutory injunctions in cases in which it appears to the court to be just or convenient to do so is not at large. Here, the statute did not confer on the court power to make an order on the application of Lenah other than in protection of some legal or equitable right of Lenah which the court might enforce by final judgment. It becomes necessary then to consider the submission by Lenah that, in any event, there is such a right which is the subject of the tort dealing with invasions of privacy....

116. Nothing in *Douglas* [*v. Hello!*] suggests that the right to privacy ... is enjoyed other than by natural persons. Further, the necessarily tentative consideration of the topic in that case assumes rather than explains what "privacy" comprehends and what would amount to a tortious invasion of it. The difficulties in obtaining in this field something approaching definition rather than abstracted generalisation have been recognized for some time....

118. It is in the United States that, in many jurisdictions, the subject has received much judicial attention and it was to that learning that Lenah invited us to have closest regard. However, what the law is said to be may diverge from its practical operation, as seen at first hand. Some caution in this regard may be prudent in considering the position in the United States. There, the application of state and federal laws, protective of the privacy of the individual, in some circumstances may violate the First Amendment. This is because in those cases "privacy concerns give way when balanced against the interest in publishing matters of public importance". [*Bartnicki v. Vopper*, 532 U.S. 514, 534 (2001).] ...

119. It recently has been said by an academic commentator:

> But privacy is not the only cherished American value. We also cherish information, and candour, and freedom of speech. We expect to be free to discover and

discuss the secrets of our neighbours, celebrities, and public officials. We expect government to conduct its business publicly, even if that infringes the privacy of those caught up in the matter. Most of all, we expect the media to uncover the truth and report it—not merely the truth about government and public affairs, but the truth about people.

The law protects these expectations too—and when they collide with expectations of privacy, privacy almost always loses. Privacy law in the United States delivers far less than it promises, because it resolves virtually all these conflicts in favour of information, candour, and free speech. The sweeping language of privacy law serves largely to mask the fact that the law provides almost no protection against privacy-invading disclosures. (As we shall see later, the law is more successful in protecting against commercial exploitation, although for reasons that have more to do with commerce than privacy.)

With that warning in mind, it is convenient to turn to consider the position in the United States, which has been treated as the fount of privacy jurisprudence.... [The judges canvassed the precedents, but ultimately found no right of privacy existed for a corporation, as opposed to an individual.]

Conclusions

139. The appeal should be allowed....

Kirby J.:

... 200. *Conclusion: no invalid law*: There is nothing in the general language of the Tasmanian legislation, conferring on the Supreme Court the power to grant interlocutory injunctions, that is inconsistent with the representative democracy created by, or implied in, the Constitution.

201. Nor, in my view, is the provision of relief by way of interlocutory injunction to restrain the use of information obtained illegally by a trespasser, where such use would be unconscionable, incompatible with the principle in *Lange*. That principle does not establish a rule expelling all legal restraints. Neither in what this court said in *Lange*, nor in what it did there or in *Levy v. Victoria*, is there any support for such an extreme position. It is not one appropriate to the text of, or implications derived from, the Constitution. It is not one compatible with the protection of other values (such as individual reputation) upheld during the entire operation of the Constitution to date. It would not be compatible with the recognition, in statements of fundamental human rights, of values which sometimes compete with free expression (including defence of reputation and privacy). It would be incompatible with the approach taken in other representative democracies similar to our own.

202. Only in the United States is the rule in favour of free speech as stringent as the appellant appeared to urge. But that rule, which is particularly wide with reference to discussion about public figures, is itself based on an interpretation of an express prohibition in the constitution of that country. It is an express prohibition that has no counterpart in the Australian Constitution. Analogous principles have been rejected by this court and by courts in the United Kingdom, Canada and South Africa, and by legal bodies....

211. *The weighing of competing interests*: This result establishes an approach to the exercise of the power, enjoyed by a judge or the court, in a way more conformable with past practice and less rigid than the appellant urged. The public interest in free speech would not always "trump" individual interests. Instead, this approach would require that proper attention be given to the value of free speech, which is necessary for the operation of the

polity established by the Constitution, but in a context where other values are also respected. Such other values would include the rights of individuals to protection of the law against arbitrary or unlawful attacks on their reputation and privacy, to the extent that the law upholds those values....

220. *Conclusion: discretion miscarried*: It follows that I consider that the Full Court erred in the exercise of its discretion in failing to give proper weight to the constitutional consideration favouring discussion in the appellant's television program of animal welfare as a legitimate matter of governmental and political concern. This was a matter of federal concern in the present case because the product involved was wholly exported and the appellant is the national broadcaster, established by federal law with national functions. It follows that the orders which the Full Court made must be vacated.

221. When the constitutional consideration favouring free discussion of governmental and political issues of animal welfare in this context is given due weight, a proper exercise of the discretion obliges that the interlocutory injunction be refused. The *power* to grant an injunction existed. But the *exercise* of that power miscarried. Such exercise should have upheld free speech. The respondent would then be left to the recovery of damages for any cause of action it could prove against the appellant.

222. I agree in the orders proposed by Gummow and Hayne JJ.

CALLINAN J.:

...

224. ... [In a previous case, a] freelance photographer commissioned by a newspaper, initially lawfully present at the scene of a photography session for the production of a cover for a new album of a record for the pop group Oasis, surreptitiously took photographs of the tableau vivant devised for that purpose by the group leader, at a time when, as the photographer well knew, further photography was embargoed. The High Court of Justice granted an interlocutory injunction to restrain the newspaper from any further publication of the photographs on the grounds that there was a sufficiently arguable case that the taking of the photographs and their publication were a breach of confidence.

225. Despite [this and other] decisions, the appellant here contends that it should be free to telecast video footage provided to it for nothing and surreptitiously made on private property during the course of the commission of an offence of trespass, probably following the even more serious offence of breaking and entering, the general nature of which the appellant knows, in circumstances in which such a telecast is likely to do great, indeed incurable financial harm to the occupier of the premises, and is to the financial advantage of the appellant. The large question in this appeal is whether that contention is right....

297. ... The film was brought into existence, and the appellant acquired it, in circumstances in which it cannot in good conscience use it without the permission of the respondent. If the facts remain at the trial as they appear to be now, the appellant should then be obliged to deliver the film to the respondent. There is therefore an underlying remedy sufficient to support an interlocutory injunction....

303. The conclusion ... recognises the reality of the value of images. If they have value, the right to control the making of them plainly also has value. If there is no right to control the making of them, that is, for example, if they can be made in, or from a public place or places upon which their maker may go, then on the current state of the law, the maker will not be able to be restrained from using them. But if the position, as here, be otherwise, then an occupier should not be denied rights in respect of them because their

maker has been able, surreptitiously, to violate the occupier's rights. It may also be that the law should and may come to recognise that the creator of a spectacle has a property right in respect of it but it is unnecessary to decide whether that is so in this case....

331. Australian courts need to be wary about applying any decisions of the courts of the United States in which any asserted right to publication is involved, as the question on the merits will usually be bound up with an assertion of constitutional rights under the First Amendment.

332. The recognition of a tort of invasion of privacy as part of the common law of Australia does not involve acceptance of all, or indeed any of the jurisprudence of the United States which is complicated by the First Amendment. There is good reason for not importing into this country all of the North American law particularly because of the substantial differences in our political and constitutional history. Any principles for an Australian tort of privacy would need to be worked out on a case by case basis in a distinctly Australian context....

334. Ultimately the questions involved are ones of proportion and balance. The value of free speech and publication in the public interest must be properly assessed, but so too must be the value of privacy. The appropriate balance would need to be struck in each case. This is not an unfamiliar exercise for all courts in all constitutional democracies....

352. I am unconvinced as to the need for the continued operation of the doctrine of judicial restraint with respect to interlocutory injunctions adopted by judges—it is entirely a judge-made doctrine. In any event, it can have no operation in a case of this kind. There is no reason here why the respondent should not have its injunction continued....

Notes and Questions

1. Unlike the previous cases in this Chapter, the plaintiff in this case was a corporation. Should a corporation have rights of privacy? What policy considerations either favor or disfavor conferring such a right? Assuming that corporations should have rights of privacy, should they also have rights of publicity? What would be the implications of granting such rights?

2. Hopefully you deduced that the court ruled in favor of the broadcaster, though not unanimously. How was the analysis used by the judges analogous to the analysis used in *von Hannover* and *Campbell*? In what ways was it different?

3. If this court had to decide the *Campbell* case, how do you think it would have come out? Would your answer be the same for the *von Hannover* case? Why or why not?

4. The various judges are careful to say that Australian law is not (and, for some, should not be) the same as U.S. law regarding free speech. In what way do they seem to think Australian law differs from that of the U.S.? Do you agree with their understanding of U.S. law?

5. In what way is Judge Callinan's analysis different from that of his colleagues? Do you think that he would decide either *von Hannover* or *Campbell* differently than his colleagues?

6. Consider some of the cases discussed in Chapter VIII. Those cases involve rights of publicity, rather than defamation. Would that make a difference to this court? How do you think that this court would have decided the *Comedy III* case? What about *Winter*?

7. How do you think this court would have decided the *Eastwood* cases in Chapter VII?

8. The court indicates that there must be some action on the part of defendant that is tortious before an injunction can issue. Even then, the court must balance the rights of free speech against whatever violation has occurred. Suppose that Lenah decides it would be satisfied with monetary damages. Would this court grant damages on these facts? If so, how is that reconcilable with the refusal to uphold the injunction?

E. Free Speech in Other Countries

Elisabeth Logeais & Jean-Baptiste Schroeder, *The French Right of Image: An Ambiguous Concept Protecting the Human Persona*
18 Loy. L.A. Ent. L.J. 511 (1998)

B. Freedom of Speech and the Right to Provide News Information

Article 10 of the European Convention on Human Rights establishes and promotes the freedom of speech and information. The French Law on the Liberty of the Press, the backbone of the legal regulation of the press in France, also provides for such freedom. Therefore, reproduction and publication of one's image in a newsworthy context is the second exception to enforcement of the right of image.

1. *"Information" is a Broadly Construed Term*

A person who participates in an event likely to trigger the legitimate public interest falls into the realm of "public information" and thus he or she loses the full protection of his or her image, provided that the right of privacy is respected. This exception was clearly illustrated by the Paris Court in a matter concerning the publication of photographs taken of the 1995 bomb attacks in the St. Michel subway station....

2. *The Use of a Person's Image Must Be for Genuinely Informational Purposes*

Consistent with the purpose of the information exception, the photograph must be taken "in circumstances directly linked to the events at stake or their factual consequences." Based on this requirement, courts have prohibited the publication of old photographs in which the traumatizing impact for the victims was not outweighed by their informative value. Commercial use of an image also precludes claiming the exemption of newsworthiness. However, the concept of commercial speech was acknowledged by the Strasbourg Court. The court held that advertising was protected under Article 10 of the European Convention for Human Rights, which did not distinguish between profit and non-profit advertising messages.

3. *Freedom of Speech and the Right of Information May Be Undermined by the Right to Human Dignity*

The French courts allowed the publication of photographs showing the dismembered corpse of a Dutch student killed by a fellow Japanese student. French legislation amending the Law of September 30, 1986, which allowed this publication and regulates audio-visual communication, now expressly provides for the respect of human dignity. Based on this provision, the Conseil Superieur de l'Audiovisuel ("CSA"), the French administrative authority in charge of supervising proper enforcement of the law, admonished television channels that had broadcast the mortal agony of a French soldier shot in former Yugoslavia.

The right of dignity also arose in an interesting case involving a controversial advertising campaign run by the clothing company Benetton. The campaign consisted of three advertising posters reproduced in the media, each showing a naked torso, buttock, and groin area tattooed with the words "HIV-positive." The French Court of Appeal affirmed the right of dignity, holding that any business is ordinarily free to promote its activities by commenting on any social or contemporary issues, including very serious ones, even if the message does not relate to the company's products or services. In this specific case, however, the court condemned Benetton's exercise of commercial speech on the ground that it violated the dignity rights of AIDS patients. The court found that the advertising posters, absent captions providing an explanation of the message or the nature of the purported debate, degraded the dignity of AIDS patients and would likely spur detrimental social rejection of these individuals.

C. The Parody Exception

French Case law acknowledges that prior consent for the use of a person's image is not required when the use is for parody purposes. Parody is a humorous form of social commentary and literary criticism that dates back to Greek antiquity. The French Courts have reasoned by analogy to the parody exception expressly provided by French copyright law (droit d'auteur) defining a parody of copyrighted work as a non-infringing use.

Parody is a method of exercising one's freedom of speech and is essential in a democratic society. By definition, parody is not an objective depiction of reality and truth. To qualify as an exception to the right of image, the parodistic use must have a humorous, non-offensive, and informative purpose.

Furthermore, while a parody of a person has been long recognized as acceptable, the parody exception does not apply to the mocking of a person associated with the trademark. In a recent case, the French High Court held that repeated mockery of the manager of the French car company Peugeot was detrimental to the Peugeot trademark and the parody exception was not available as a defense.

Stephen R. Barnett, *"The Right to One's Own Image": Publicity and Privacy Rights in the United States and Spain*
47 Am. J. Comp. L. 555 (1999)

III. Some Current Issues in Right-of-Publicity Law in the United States

Against that background, I will now describe some of the current issues in the right-of-publicity law of the United States.

C. Possible Free Speech Defenses to the Right of Publicity

In one case, Kareem Abdul-Jabbar, the former basketball player, brought suit over an Oldsmobile television commercial, broadcast during the NCAA Mens' College Basketball Tournament that included a basketball "trivia quiz." The quiz asked, "Who holds the record for being voted the most times the most outstanding player in this tournament?" It answered: "Lew Alcindor"—Abdul-Jabbar's name before he converted to Islam. Abdul-Jabbar thus claimed that his name (or former name) had been used in an advertisement without his permission, violating his right of publicity. General Motors claimed "fair use" and free speech, arguing that the name was used as a true fact of news and history and was only "incidental" to the selling of Oldsmobiles. The Ninth Circuit ruled for Abdul-

Jabbar, apparently holding that a celebrity's name may not be used in an advertisement, however "incidentally," without his permission.

Meanwhile, a case from New York City presented the issue beautifully. New York Magazine ran ads, for itself, on New York City buses. The ads featured the magazine's logo with the text: "Possibly the only good thing in New York that Rudy hasn't taken credit for." Mayor Rudolph Giuliani of New York ordered the ads taken down, claiming that their use of his name violated his right of publicity. The magazine sued to keep the ads up, and won a preliminary injunction in the district court. The court relied on the First Amendment and on two exceptions to the right of publicity under New York law, for "incidental" use and for "public interest and newsworthiness." ...

3. May There Be a Free Speech Defense for the Use of One's Image in Advertising?

We may ask finally what is the Spanish law on the question presented in the United States by the cases of Kareem Abdul-Jabbar and Mayor Giuliani: May there be a free-speech defense for the use of a celebrity's name, likeness, or image, without his or her consent, in what is plainly an advertisement?

The answer in Spain may seem to be no. The Spanish Supreme Court, in a case involving trading cards of soccer players, has declared that the exceptions for public officials, public figures, and public information provided by Article 8.2 of the Organic Law "never" apply to uses in advertising:

> The public nature of the person whose image is reproduced without his or her consent can legitimate the taking, reproduction, or publication of that image only for purposes of information alone, and never when the image is being exploited for purposes of advertising. In support of this position, the court stated that the right to one's own image can give way only to a right of the same rank, like the public's right of information, and not to "the mere financial interest of a third person." Commentators on the Spanish law have expressed similar views.

a. The *Gades* Case

While the court's statement in the soccer-cards case was apparently "dictum," a decision of the Spanish Supreme Court that seems to follow that position involved facts resembling the *Abdul-Jabbar* case. The suit was brought by Antonio Gades, the famous dance director. As the facts are recounted by Dr. Igartua:

> An [advertising] campaign for a well-known whisky presented photos of various well-known artists, accompanied in each case by a small resume containing some facts of the artist's professional and personal life and also some of his or her preferences, which in respect of beverages included, of course, the whisky in question. One of these ads, featuring the actress Laura del Sol, listed as its first professional credit: "Most recent work completed: Carmen, together with Antonio Gades, a film nominated for the Academy Award in 1984."

> Señor Gades sued, claiming that his name had been used for purposes of advertising without his consent. He asked damages of 20 million pesetas (about $130,000). The Court of First Instance awarded him one million pesetas (about $7,000); the Court of Second Instance reduced this to 100,000 pesetas (about $700); and the Supreme Court let that stand. The Supreme Court noted that the "illegal text" contained nothing that was damaging to Gades or that related to his private life; that this text was very small in relation to the poster as a whole; that it contained facts which might have been disclosed in other publications

having no commercial purpose; and that it in no way transgressed the limits of free speech. The court took the view that some damages nonetheless had to be awarded to Gades for the "unlawful use of his artistic name," especially given the presumption of harm established by Article 9.3 of the Organic Law. The court concluded that the 100,000 pesetas awarded by the Second Instance was enough.

The *Gades* case thus appears to hold, like the *Abdul-Jabbar* case in the United States, that any unauthorized use of a celebrity's name in an advertisement, even as a true fact of history or biography and in a way "incidental" to the commercial message of the ad, violates the right to one's own image....

The Spanish law, however, may not be as absolute as the *Gades* case suggests. Dr. Igartua writes of the case: "I do not believe ... that this decision closes off totally the possibility of using incidentally in an advertisement the name of a well-known person." That possibility, one would think, should not be closed off totally. In the *Gades* case, the name of Antonio Gades was used as a recent, biographical fact in the life of the actress, Laura del Sol; her most recent work, together with Antonio Gades on the movie, Carmen, which was nominated for an Academy Award, was part of Laura's curriculum vitae. Since she was entitled to use her name, together with the biographical facts of her life, in endorsing the whisky, it does not seem right that she should be obliged to delete certain of those biographical facts because they involve other people. Those facts are parts of her life, and are merely incidental to the ad's message in favor of the whisky.

One wonders how the Spanish courts would have ruled if the ad had not been for a whisky, but for a film or play in which Laura was appearing. If an ad or poster for such a film or play similarly presented a few facts of Laura's professional biography, such as the fact that her last movie had been "Carmen, together with Antonio Gades," would such a use entitle Gades to collect damages? Dr. Igartua observes, "It is necessary to judge on the facts of each case how important is the reference to the celebrity in the context of the ad." In comparison with the whisky ad, the use of the name Antonio Gades in the hypothetical ad for the film or play would be more relevant to what was being sold, and hence more justified as a matter of public information. By the same token, however, it would be less "incidental" than in the whisky ad, which also could be considered to make it more offensive to Gades (especially if he did not drink alcoholic beverages, or perhaps 'was a recovering alcoholic').

The language of the Spanish Supreme Court in the soccer cards case may seem to compel liability, even in the case of the hypothetical ad for the film or play in which Laura appears. The court said that the interest in public information protected by Article 8.2 applies "only for purposes of information alone, and never when the image is being exploited for purposes of advertising." The court may have overlooked the fact, however, that in some cases both purposes—public information and advertising—may be present. The communication of facts of Laura's professional career may contribute to public information, even if those facts are communicated in the context of an advertisement. This may not be what the court called "the mere financial interest of a third person," but the public's interest in information as well.

An ad hoc, fact-dependent approach to these cases, as suggested by Dr. Igartua, may seem inconsistent with the principles of freedom of speech that ordinarily oppose basing judicial judgments on speech content. Such an ad hoc approach, however, seems indicated by the American law as well. If one rejects a per se rule of liability for any unconsented use of a name or likeness in an ad, as may be the holding of the *Abdul-Jabbar* case, one is forced to make ad hoc judgments—to decide, for example, that the comment about Mayor Giuliani in the *New York Magazine* case was political satire, "incidental" to the commercial purpose of the ad, and therefore should be permitted. The American law is uncertain, with *Abdul-Jabbar* on the one hand but *New York Magazine* and *Cardtoons* [discussed in Chapter VIII], on the other. The Spanish law has the *Gades* case on the one hand but, apparently, no Supreme Court case on the other.

   b. The *New York Magazine* Case in Spain

When one asks how the *New York Magazine* case would be decided in Spain, however, another provision of Spanish law also may come into play. The federal district court in New York found that the use of the name "Rudy" in the ad for New York magazine was protected by two defenses in New York law: (1) "incidental" use, conveying the "nature and content" of the magazine being advertised, and (2) material of "public interest," as the court found was true of the political satire in the ad. The ad was "a hybrid of commercial speech and political satire," and it "could not mock the Mayor's eagerness to take credit for all the City's successes without mentioning him," the court said.

While the Giuliani case might be regarded as involving an "incidental" use, that apparently would not be enough to protect the magazine in Spain, given the *Gades* decision and the remarks of the Supreme Court in the soccer-cards case. But perhaps there is another defense in Spain, based on the satirical nature of the ad. Article 8.2 (b) of the Organic Law provides a defense for "the use of a caricature of a person who is a public official or public figure, consistently with social convention." There appears to be little authority and little agreement in Spanish law, in either the jurisprudence or the commentary, on the scope of this "caricature" defense. The meaning of the Spanish word "caricatura," however, is not limited to pictorial representations, but includes literary and other forms—any "graphic or literary representation that exaggerates certain features with a comic or satirical intent." The New York Magazine ad thus could be said to involve a "caricature" of Mayor Giuliani, exaggerating what the judge called his "alleged penchant for taking credit for all of New York's achievements." ...

The exception for "la caricature" in Article 8.2 (b) of the Organic Law thus might be interpreted to include various forms of parody and satire aimed at celebrities. The result might be to provide the Spanish law of "one's own image" with a defense based on "safeguarding the liberty of expression," a defense protecting satire and parody in the name of "caricature," even in an advertisement.

Edward J. Eberle, *Human Dignity, Privacy, and Personality in German And American Constitutional Law*
1997 Utah L. Rev. 963

2. *Lebach*: Right to Personal Honor and Control Over Presentation of One's Self in Society

   [T]he Constitutional Court, in the *Lebach* decision, concluded that the privacy interests recognized in *Soraya* outweighed any public speech interest in publicizing an individual's role in a crime for which he had already paid the penalty. In *Lebach*, a convicted robber was able to halt a planned television broadcast of a documentary film depicting, accurately, his and others' participation in a notorious armed robbery of an army munitions depot which resulted in the death of four soldiers. The Court grounded its decision in the felon's personality right in being let alone, free from publicity, so that he could concentrate on his reentry into society. This concern took precedence over even highly ranked expression freedoms, just as personality interests had trumped expression in *Soraya*....

From here, it is not much of a step to the general right of informational self-determination. Personality rights "also encompass( ) the right to one's own likeness and utterances, especially the right to decide what to do with pictures of oneself. In principle, everyone has the right to determine for himself whether and to what extent others may make a public account of either certain incidents from his life or his entire life story."

Of course, these rights ran directly counter to the broadcasters' expression rights, guaranteed in Article 5. Expression rights are highly valued in Germany, as in America, and are themselves reflections of human dignity. Thus, the Court was faced with resolving the conflict between the two fundamental values.

In such cases, the Court strives to achieve concordance (Konkordanz) between the values, attempting to interpret both in a manner such that the essence of each can be preserved and, hopefully, optimized. This requires a careful assessment and application of differing values, which seems to work better in theory than in practice. It is not always possible to achieve such harmony in the hard realities of a case. It was not possible in *Lebach*.

The Court chose personality rights over expression rights. Ordinarily, the public has a significant interest in learning a crime. However, there is an important difference between a crime that is ongoing and one that is past.... Thus, the only public interest was in publicizing an event that had already occurred....

Lebach thus illustrates how the assertion of dignitarian rights can operate to limit other fundamental rights, even especially highly valued ones like expression freedoms. This limiting influence that personality rights may have on other rights is mainly foreign to American law. *Lebach* further illustrates the communitarian bent of German law. The Court's concern for reintegrating the felon into society took precedence over individual and social interests in expression. It is hard to find a more dramatic contrast with American law; it is a contrast which illustrates the strength of dignity and personality in German law and society. Certainly one does not ordinarily find such solicitude for individual welfare in American law. On its face, *Lebach* is also a remarkable act of judicial activism: The Court inferred rights from the textual enumeration of personality rights to eclipse textually secure expression rights.

Deborah Fisch Nigri & Silvia Regina Dain Gandelman, *The Right of Publicity in the Brazilian Legal System*
18 Loy. L.A. Ent. L.J. 469 (1998)

V. Defense Based on the Public's Right to Know

Freedom of information is granted by the Brazilian Constitution among its "Fundamental Rights and Guarantees." Accordingly, when analyzing a celebrity's right to privacy, it is necessary to balance the public interest's right to know with the celebrity's interest in privacy. Public figures, in theory, renounce their right to privacy and the right to be let alone in specific situations. Nevertheless, a limitation must be imposed on the public's right to know.

In order to constitute a public interest, the information must be more than mere public curiosity. Antonio Chaves argues that "the true harassment suffered by famous people through photographers, professionals or not, push them to their limit of exasperation that sometimes they appeal to the use of violence, as a persuasive form, or as a dissuasive form in defense of their disturbed tranquillity." The determination of what is or is not the subject of public concern normally requires a careful appreciation of the collective interest. Curiosity regarding a public figure or an artist is not sufficient to justify public interest and will be considered simple curiosity.

Notes and Questions

1. As you can see from the first three excerpts, continental Europe places a great deal of emphasis on dignity interests. All three countries—France, Spain, and Germany— seem willing to sacrifice some free expression in favor of protecting the dignity of individuals. Is this emphasis on dignity consistent with the approach in *von Hannover*?

2. Does French law, as described in the first excerpt above, conform to the European Court of Human Rights decision in *von Hannover v. Germany*?

3. How would the *White* and *Cardtoons* cases in Chapter VIII be decided under French law?

4. In what way is Spanish law the same as French law? In what way are they different? Do you think that the *Gades* case would be decided the same way under French law?

5. How do you think that Spain and Germany would decide the various cases in Chapter VIII? In particular, consider the works of art and the parody cases. Do you think any of those cases would be decided the way the U.S. courts decided them?

6. How do you think a U.S. court would decide the *Gades* and *Lebach* cases? In what way is the dignitarian German interest and Spanish right of image the same as and different from the U.S. right of publicity?

7. As you think about the German law, remember that *von Hannover* originated in Germany. Although the Court of Human Rights disagreed with the German approach in that particular case, the general approach of the German courts may be used in other situations that do not raise the same privacy problems.

8. Outside of the U.S., the laws of the various countries (including Brazil) seem to emphasize community over individualism. That may be the greatest conceptual difference between U.S. free speech concepts and similar concepts in other countries. Do you see how this difference leads to different results in the case law?

Chapter X

Preemption

Under the 1909 Copyright Act, the United States had a dual system of copyright protection. Before a work was published, it was protected by state law (common-law copyright). After a work was published, state common-law protection ended, and one of two things happened. If the work was published with proper copyright notice, it received a federal statutory copyright of limited duration. If the work was published without proper notice, it immediately and irrevocably entered the public domain.

One of the goals of the 1976 Copyright Act was to unify all of copyright into a single federal law. Works would be protected by federal copyright from the moment they were "fixed in a tangible medium of expression" regardless of publication, and state law would be eliminated for fixed works. (Unfixed works would, in theory, still be protected by state law. This was considered necessary because the Copyright Clause only permits Congress to grant exclusive rights to "Authors" for their "Writings," a term which has been interpreted to require a "physical rendering" of the author's creativity. *See Goldstein v. California*, 412 U.S. 546, 561 (1973).)

Congress also wanted to clarify the scope of federal preemption. The Supremacy Clause of the U.S. Constitution states: "This Constitution, and the Laws of the United States which shall be made in Pursuance thereof…, shall be the supreme Law of the Land; and the Judges in every State shall be bound thereby, any Thing in the Constitution or Laws of any State to the Contrary notwithstanding." U.S. Const., Art. VI, para. 2. In the 1960s and 1970s, a series of cases in the U.S. Supreme Court had interpreted the Supremacy Clause and applied it to alleged conflicts between state intellectual property laws and the federal patent and copyright acts. These cases left the law of preemption in a somewhat confused state.

Accordingly, section 301 of the 1976 Act was intended by Congress "to preempt and abolish any rights under the common law or statutes of a State that are equivalent to copyright and that extend to works coming within the scope of the Federal copyright law." H.R. Rep. No. 94-1476, at 130 (1976). (The text of the statute is quoted in the opinions below.) Congress also stated that "section 301 is intended to be stated in the clearest and most unequivocal language possible, so as to foreclose any conceivable misinterpretation … and to avoid the development of any vague borderline areas between State and Federal Protection." *Id.* Unfortunately, section 301 failed miserably in that goal. As the following cases demonstrate, the law of preemption remains in a confused state, particularly as applied to state rights of publicity.

What follows are two pairs of cases, from the Seventh and Ninth Circuits respectively. In each pair, one case holds that a state right of publicity is preempted, and the other case holds that the right is not preempted. As you read these materials, see if you can explain the divergent outcomes in a way that makes coherent sense of the statutory language and the policy behind it.

Baltimore Orioles, Inc. v.
Major League Baseball Players Association
805 F.2d 663 (7th Cir. 1986)

Before COFFEY and FLAUM, Circuit Judges, and ESCHBACH, Senior Circuit Judge.

ESCHBACH, Senior Circuit Judge:

The primary issue involved in this appeal is whether major league baseball clubs own exclusive rights to the televised performances of major league baseball players during major league baseball games. For the reasons stated below, we will affirm in part, vacate in part, and remand for further proceedings.

I

This appeal arises out of a long-standing dispute between the Major League Baseball Clubs ("Clubs") and the Major League Baseball Players Association ("Players") regarding the ownership of the broadcast rights to the Players' performances during major league baseball games. After decades of negotiation concerning the allocation of revenues from telecasts of the games, the Players in May of 1982 sent letters to the Clubs, and to television and cable companies with which the Clubs had contracted, asserting that the telecasts were being made without the Players' consent and that they misappropriated the Players' property rights in their performances. The mailing of these letters led the parties to move their dispute from the bargaining table to the courtroom.

On June 14, 1982, the Clubs filed an action in the United States District Court for the Northern District of Illinois, in which they sought a declaratory judgment that the Clubs possessed an exclusive right to broadcast the games and owned exclusive rights to the telecasts. Each count sought essentially the same relief, but was premised upon a different theory: Count I was based upon copyright law, in particular the "works made for hire" doctrine of 17 U.S.C. § 201(b); Count II rested upon state master-servant law; Count III was predicated upon the collective bargaining agreement between the Clubs and the Players, including the Uniform Player's Contract; and Count IV was based upon the parties' customs and dealings.

On July 1, 1982, three major league players brought an action against the Clubs in the United States District Court for the Southern District of New York. The three players sought a declaration that the game telecasts misappropriated their property rights in their names, pictures, and performances, and also asked for damages and injunctive relief. The *Rogers* complaint asserted six claims for relief, based upon the Players' alleged property rights in their names, pictures, and performances, the doctrine of unjust enrichment, and sections 50 and 51 of the New York Civil Rights Statute, N.Y. Civ. Rights Law §§ 50–51. After the district court in Chicago denied a motion to transfer the *Baltimore Orioles* action to New York, the parties stipulated to a transfer of the *Rogers* suit from New York to Chicago, and to consolidation of the two cases.

The parties moved for summary judgment on Counts I and II of the *Baltimore Orioles* complaint, which concerned the Clubs' copyright and master-servant claims. On May 23, 1985, the district court granted the Clubs summary judgment on these two counts. *See Baltimore Orioles, Inc. v. Major League Baseball Players Association*, Copyright L. Dec. (CCH) ¶ 25,822 (N.D. Ill. 1985). On June 14, 1985, the Players filed a notice of appeal from the grant of summary judgment for the Clubs in the *Baltimore Orioles* action.

II

...

B. *Copyright Claim*

The Clubs sought a declaratory judgment "that the telecasts of Major League Baseball games constitute copyrighted 'works made for hire' in which defendant and Major League Baseball players have no rights whatsoever." [Complaint] The district court found that the Clubs, not the Players, owned a copyright in the telecasts as works made for hire and that the Clubs' copyright in the telecasts preempted the Players' rights of publicity in their performances. Accordingly, it granted summary judgment and entered final judgment for the Clubs on this claim. The Players argue that the district court erred in holding that a baseball player's live performance, as embodied in a copyrighted telecast of the game, constitutes a work made for hire so as to extinguish the player's right of publicity in his performance.

1. *Works Made for Hire Under 17 U.S.C. § 201(b)*

Our analysis begins by ascertaining whether the Clubs own a copyright in the telecasts of major league baseball games. In general, copyright in a work "vests initially in the author or authors of the work," 17 U.S.C. § 201(a); however, "[i]n the case of a work made for hire, the employer or other person for whom the work was prepared is considered the author ... and, unless the parties have expressly agreed otherwise in a written instrument signed by them, owns all of the rights comprised in the copyright." 17 U.S.C. § 201(b). A work made for hire is defined in pertinent part as "a work prepared by an employee within the scope of his or her employment." 17 U.S.C. § 101. Thus, an employer owns a copyright in a work if (1) the work satisfies the generally applicable requirements for copyrightability set forth in 17 U.S.C. § 102(a), (2) the work was prepared by an employee, (3) the work was prepared within the scope of the employee's employment, and (4) the parties have not expressly agreed otherwise in a signed, written instrument.

a. *Copyrightability of the telecasts*

The district court concluded that the telecasts were copyrightable works. We agree. Section 102 sets forth three conditions for copyrightability: first, a work must be fixed in tangible form; second, the work must be an original work of authorship; and third, it must come within the subject matter of copyright. *See* 17 U.S.C. § 102(a). Although there may have been some question at one time as to whether simultaneously recorded live broadcasts were copyrightable, this is no longer the case. Section 101 expressly provides that "[a] work consisting of sounds, images, or both, that are being transmitted, is 'fixed' ... if a fixation of the work is being made simultaneously with its transmission." Since the telecasts of the games are videotaped at the same time that they are broadcast, the telecasts are fixed in tangible form.

Moreover, the telecasts are original works of authorship. The requirement of originality actually subsumes two separate conditions, *i.e.,* the work must possess an independent origin and a minimal amount of creativity. It is obvious that the telecasts are independent creations, rather than reproductions of earlier works.

As for the telecasts' creativity, courts long have recognized that photographing a person or filming an event involves creative labor. For example, one court held that the Zapruder film of the Kennedy assassination was copyrightable because it embodied

> many elements of creativity. Among other things, Zapruder selected the kind of camera (movies, not snapshots), the kind of film (color), the kind of lens (tele-

photo), the area in which the pictures were to be taken, the time they were to be taken, and (after testing several sites) the spot on which the camera would be operated.

Time Inc. v. Bernard Geis Associates, 293 F. Supp. 130, 143 (S.D.N.Y. 1968). The many decisions that must be made during the broadcast of a baseball game concerning camera angles, types of shots, the use of instant replays and split screens, and shot selection similarly supply the creativity required for the copyrightability of the telecasts. *See* House Report at 52, *reprinted in* 1976 U.S. Code Cong. & Ad. News at 5665 ("When a football game is being covered by four television cameras, with a director guiding the activities of the four cameramen and choosing which of their electronic images are sent to the public and in which order, there is little doubt that what the cameramen and the director are doing constitutes 'authorship.'").[7]

Furthermore, the telecasts are audiovisual works, which under § 102 come within the subject matter of copyright. The telecasts are, therefore, copyrightable works.

b. *Employer-employee relationship*

With regard to the relationship between the Clubs and the Players, the district court found, and the Players do not dispute, that the Players are employees of their respective Clubs. We add only that this finding is consistent with the broad construction given to the term "employee" by courts applying the "work made for hire" doctrine.

c. *Scope of employment*

The district court further found that the scope of the Players' employment encompassed the performance of major league baseball before "live and remote audiences." *See Baltimore Orioles,* 1985 Copyright L. Dec. at 19,731....

[T]he Players do not identify any evidence that would create a genuine issue of material fact as to the scope of the Players' employment. In contrast to the Players' perfunctory claim that playing baseball for television audiences is not within the scope of their employment, the Clubs brought forth detailed evidence in support of their motion for summary judgment that the scope of the Players' employment encompassed performances before broadcast audiences.[10] ...

d. *Written agreements*

Because the Players are employees and their performances before broadcast audiences are within the scope of their employment, the telecasts of major league baseball games, which consist of the Players' performances, are works made for hire within the meaning of § 201(b). Thus, in the absence of an agreement to the contrary, the Clubs are presumed to own all of the rights encompassed in the telecasts of the games. The district court

---

7. The Players argue that their performances are not copyrightable works because they lack sufficient artistic merit. We disagree. Only a modicum of creativity is required for a work to be copyrightable.... A recording of a performance generally includes creative contributions by both the director and other individuals responsible for recording the performance and by the performers whose performance is captured.... Moreover, even if the Players' performances were not sufficiently creative, the Players agree that the cameramen and director contribute creative labor to the telecasts. The work that is the subject of copyright is not merely the Players' *performances,* but rather the *telecast* of the Players' performances. The creative contribution of the cameramen and director alone suffices for the telecasts to be copyrightable.

10. For example, the Clubs adduced evidence that the Players are acutely aware of the fact that major league baseball games are televised, and that the Players understand that television revenues have a bearing on the level of the salaries that they receive.

found that there was no written agreement that the Clubs would not own the copyright to the telecasts, and, therefore, that the copyright was owned by the Clubs....

Under § 201(b), an agreement altering the statutory presumption that the employer owns the copyright in a work made for hire must be express. This is to say, the parties' agreement must appear on the face of the signed written instrument. Section 201(b) thus bars the use of parol evidence to imply a provision not found within the four corners of the parties' agreement....

We thus conclude that there are no genuine issues of material fact as to the ownership of the copyright in the telecasts, and that the parties did not expressly agree to rebut the statutory presumption that the employer owns the copyright in a work made for hire. We, therefore, hold that the Clubs own the copyright in telecasts of major league baseball games.[18]

2. Preemption under 17 U.S.C. § 301(a)

Although the Clubs own the copyright to the telecasts of major league baseball games, the Players claim that broadcasts of these games made without their express consent violate their rights to publicity in their performances. For the reasons stated below, we hold that the Clubs' copyright in the telecasts of major league baseball games preempts the Players' rights of publicity in their game-time performances.

Section 301(a) of Title 17 provides that

> all legal or equitable rights that are equivalent to any of the exclusive rights within the general scope of copyright as specified by section 106 in works of authorship that are fixed in a tangible medium of expression and come within the subject matter of copyright as specified by sections 102 and 103, whether created before or after that date and whether published or unpublished, are governed exclusively by this title. Thereafter, no person is entitled to any such right or equivalent right in any such work under the common law or statutes of any State.

17 U.S.C. § 301(a). This provision sets forth two conditions that both must be satisfied for preemption of a right under state law: First, the work in which the right is asserted must be fixed in tangible form and come within the subject matter of copyright as specified in § 102. Second, the right must be equivalent to any of the rights specified in § 106.

a. Section 102 test

The works in which the Players claim rights are the telecasts of major league baseball games. As established above, the telecasts are fixed in tangible form because they are recorded simultaneously with their transmission and are audiovisual works which come within the subject matter of copyright. The first condition for preemption is, therefore, satisfied.

The Players argue, however, that the works in which they claim rights are their performances, rather than the telecasts of the games in which they play, and that performances *per se* are not fixed in tangible form. They contend that, since the works in which they assert rights are not fixed in tangible form, their rights of publicity in their performances are not subject to preemption. We disagree. Under § 101, "[a] work is 'fixed' in a

---

18. We have not been called upon to decide whether the copyrights in the telecasts of the various games are owned separately by individual clubs or jointly by some combination of clubs. We also have not been asked to determine whether the copyrights in the telecasts are owned exclusively by the Clubs or jointly by the Clubs and the television stations or networks that record and broadcast the games. We express no opinion on these issues.

tangible medium of expression when its embodiment in a copy…, by or under the authority of the author, is sufficiently permanent and stable to permit it to be perceived, reproduced, or otherwise communicated for a period of more than transitory duration." The Players' performances are embodied in a copy, *viz*, the videotape of the telecast, from which the performances can be perceived, reproduced, and otherwise communicated indefinitely. Hence, their performances are fixed in tangible form, and any property rights in the performances that are equivalent to any of the rights encompassed in a copyright are preempted.

It is, of course, true that unrecorded performances *per se* are not fixed in tangible form. Among the many such works not fixed in tangible form are "choreography that has never been filmed or notated, an extemporaneous speech, 'original works of authorship' communicated solely through conversations or live broadcasts, and a dramatic sketch or musical composition improvised or developed from memory and without being recorded or written down." House Report at 131, *reprinted in* 1976 U.S. Code Cong. & Ad. News at 5747. Because such works are not fixed in tangible form, rights in such works are not subject to preemption under § 301(a). Indeed, § 301(b), which represents the obverse of § 301(a), expressly allows the states to confer common law copyright protection upon such works, and protection has been afforded to unfixed works by some states. *See, e.g.*, Cal. Civil Code § 980 (West 1982 & 1986 Supp.) (protecting "any original work of authorship that is not fixed in any tangible medium of expression"). Nonetheless, once a performance is reduced to tangible form, there is no distinction between the performance and the recording of the performance for the purpose of preemption under § 301(a). Thus, if a baseball game were not broadcast or were telecast without being recorded, the Players' performances similarly would not be fixed in tangible form and their rights of publicity would not be subject to preemption. *See* NIMMER [ON COPYRIGHT], § 1.08[C] (using the example of a live broadcast of a baseball game). By virtue of being videotaped, however, the Players' performances are fixed in tangible form, and any rights of publicity in their performances that are equivalent to the rights contained in the copyright of the telecast are preempted.[22]

The Players also contend that to be a "work[ ] of authorship that … [is] fixed in a tangible medium of expression" within the scope of § 301(a), a work must be copyrightable.

---

22. An example illustrates this point. Take the case of *Zacchini v. Scripps-Howard Broadcasting Co.*, 433 U.S. 562 (1977), in which Hugo Zacchini sued a television station for violating his right of publicity by broadcasting the entirety of his human cannonball act. *Zacchini* was decided before § 301(a) became effective, but let us suppose that the same case arises again today. Assuming that Zacchini did not videotape or otherwise record his performance, his human cannonball act would not be fixed in tangible form and could not be copyrighted. Nonetheless, because the work in which he asserts rights would not be fixed in a tangible medium of expression, his right of publicity in his performance would not be subject to preemption. Thus, if a television station were to broadcast his act, he still could sue successfully for violation of his right of publicity in his performance. Merely that the television station might videotape its telecast would not grant the station a copyright in the broadcast of Zacchini's performance or preempt Zacchini's right of publicity. To be "fixed" in tangible form, a work must be recorded "by or under the authority of the author," here Zacchini. *See* 17 U.S.C. § 101 (definition of "fixed"). Because Zacchini did not consent to the telecast, the broadcast could not be "fixed" for the purpose of copyrightability and Zacchini's right of publicity would not be subject to preemption. Assume, however, that Zacchini, after the fashion of championship prize fights, transmitted his live act over closed-circuit television and simultaneously recorded it for later broadcast over a cable television network, and that the satellite signal for the closed-circuit show was intercepted and rebroadcast by a television station. Zacchini sues the station for violation of his copyright and his right to publicity. He would prevail on the copyright infringement claim only. Nevertheless, because his act was videotaped, the work in which he asserts rights would be fixed in tangible form and thus copyrightable. Assuming *arguendo* that a right of publicity is equivalent to one of the rights encompassed in a copyright—a subject that we soon shall take up—his right of publicity in his perfor-

They assert that the works in which they claim rights, namely their performances, are not copyrightable because they lack sufficient creativity. They consequently conclude that because the works in which they claim rights are not works within the meaning of § 301(a), their rights of publicity are not subject to preemption. There is a short answer to this argument. Congress contemplated that "[a]s long as a work fits within one of the general subject matter categories of section 102 and 103, ... [section 301(a)] prevents the States from protecting it even if it fails to achieve Federal copyright because it is too minimal or lacking in originality to qualify." House Report at 131, *reprinted in* 1976 U.S. Code Cong. & Ad. News at 5747.[23] Hence, § 301(a) preempts all equivalent state-law rights claimed in any work within the subject matter of copyright whether or not the work embodies any creativity. Regardless of the creativity of the Players' performances, the works in which they assert rights are copyrightable works which come within the scope of § 301(a) because of the creative contributions of the individuals responsible for recording the Players' performances. Therefore, the Players' rights of publicity in their performances are preempted if they are equivalent to any of the bundle of rights encompassed in a copyright.[24]

b. Section 106 test

A right under state law is "equivalent" to one of the rights within the general scope of copyright if it is violated by the exercise of any of the rights set forth in § 106. That section grants the owner of a copyright the exclusive rights to reproduce (whether in original or derivative form), distribute, perform, and display the copyrighted work. *See* 17 U.S.C. § 106; *see also* NIMMER, § 1.01[B][1]. Thus, a right is equivalent to one of the rights comprised by a copyright if it "is infringed by the mere act of reproduction, performance, distribution or display." *Id.*

In particular, the right to "perform" an audiovisual work means the right "to show its images in any sequence or to make the sounds accompanying it audible." 17 U.S.C. § 101 (definition of "perform"). Thus, the right to perform an audiovisual work encompasses the right to broadcast it. Hence, a right in a work that is conferred by state law is equivalent to the right to perform a telecast of that work if the state-law right is infringed merely by broadcasting the work.

In this case, the Players claim a right of publicity in their performances. As a number of courts have held, a right of publicity in a performance is violated by a televised broadcast of the performance. *See Ettore v. Philco Television Broadcasting Corp.*, 229 F.2d 481 (3d Cir.), *cert. denied*, 351 U.S. 926 (1956) (broadcast of boxing match); *Lombardo v. Doyle, Dane & Bernbach, Inc.*, 58 A.D.2d 620, 396 N.Y.S.2d 661 (1977) (broadcast of commercial depicting bandleader's performance); *Zacchini v. Scripps-Howard Broadcasting Co.*, 54 Ohio St. 2d 286, 376 N.E.2d 582 (1978), *on remand from* 433 U.S. 562 (1977) (broadcast

---

mance would be preempted. *See* Shipley, *Publicity Never Dies; It Just Fades Away: The Right of Publicity and Federal Preemption*, 66 Cornell L. Rev. 673, 710–11 (1981).

23. The reason that § 301(a) preempts rights claimed in works that lack sufficient creativity to be copyrightable is to prevent the states from granting protection to works which Congress has concluded should be in the public domain.

24. The Players' rights of publicity in their performances are preempted only if they would be violated by the exercise of the Clubs' copyright in the telecasts. A player's right of publicity in his name or likeness would not be preempted if a company, without the consent of the player, used the player's name to advertise its product, *cf. Cepeda v. Swift & Co.*, 415 F.2d 1205, 1206 (8th Cir. 1969), placed the player's photograph on a baseball trading card, *cf. Fleer Corp. v. Topps Chewing Gum, Inc.*, 658 F.2d 139, 148–49 (3d Cir. 1981), *cert. denied*, 455 U.S. 1019 (1982); *Haelan Laboratories, Inc. v. Topps Chewing Gum, Inc.*, 202 F.2d 866, 868 (2d Cir.), *cert. denied*, 346 U.S. 816 (1953), or marketed a game based upon the player's career statistics, *cf. Uhlaender v. Henricksen*, 316 F. Supp. 1277, 1282 (D. Minn. 1970).

of human cannonball act). Indeed, from the start of this litigation, the Players consistently have maintained that their rights of publicity permit them to control telecasts of their performances, and that televised broadcasts of their performances made without their consent violate their rights of publicity in their performances. Because the exercise of the Clubs' right to broadcast telecasts of the games infringes the Players' rights of publicity in their performances, the Players' rights of publicity are equivalent to at least one of the rights encompassed by copyright, *viz.*, the right to perform an audiovisual work. Since the works in which the Players claim rights are fixed in tangible form and come within the subject matter of copyright, the Players' rights of publicity in their performances are preempted.

The Players argue that their rights of publicity in their performances are not equivalent to the rights contained in a copyright because rights of publicity and copyrights serve different interests.[26] In their view, the purpose of federal copyright law is to secure a benefit to the public, but the purpose of state statutory or common law concerning rights of publicity is to protect individual pecuniary interests. We disagree.

The purpose of federal copyright protection is to benefit the public by encouraging works in which it is interested. To induce individuals to undertake the personal sacrifices necessary to create such works, federal copyright law extends to the authors of such works a limited monopoly to reap the rewards of their endeavors. Contrary to the Players' contention, the interest underlying the recognition of the right of publicity also is the promotion of performances that appeal to the public.... Because the right of publicity does not differ in kind from copyright, the Players' rights of publicity in their performances cannot escape preemption.

In this litigation, the Players have attempted to obtain *ex post* what they did not negotiate *ex ante*. That is to say, they seek a judicial declaration that they possess a right—the right to control the telecasts of major league baseball games—that they could not procure in bargaining with the Clubs. The Players' aim is to share in the increasingly lucrative revenues derived from the sale of television rights for over-the-air broadcasts by local stations and national networks and for distribution by subscription and pay cable services. Contrary to the Players' contention, the effect of this decision is not to grant the Clubs perpetual rights to the Players' performances. The Players remain free to attain

---

26. The Players cite to four opinions to support their assertion that § 301(a) does not preempt the right of publicity. Each opinion is premised upon an erroneous analysis of preemption. [Three cases] assert without discussion that the right of publicity is not preempted because the work that it protects— a public figure's persona—cannot be fixed in a tangible medium of expression. We disagree. Because a performance is fixed in tangible form when it is recorded, a right of publicity in a performance that has been reduced to tangible form is subject to preemption.

[Another] court stated without extended discussion or citation to authority that the right of publicity is not preempted because it requires additional elements other than the reproduction, performance, distribution or display of a copyrighted work. We disagree.... [A] right is equivalent to a copyright if (1) it is infringed by the mere act of reproduction, performance, distribution, or display, or (2) it requires additional elements to make out a cause of action, but the additional elements do not differ in kind from those necessary for copyright infringement. *Cf. Crow v. Wainwright,* 720 F.2d 1224, 1226 (11th Cir. 1983) (publication with scienter not qualitatively different), *cert. denied,* 469 U.S. 819 (1984); *Mayer v. Josiah Wedgewood & Sons, Ltd.,* 601 F. Supp. 1523, 1535 (S.D.N.Y. 1985) (reproduction with intent, knowledge, or commercial immorality not different in kind) (discussing cases).... Because the right of publicity does not require a qualitatively different additional element, it is equivalent to a copyright and is preempted to the extent that it is claimed in a tangible work within the subject matter of copyright.

their objective by bargaining with the Clubs for a contractual declaration that the Players own a joint or an exclusive interest in the copyright of the telecasts.[29]

C. *Master-Servant Claim*

The Clubs sought a judgment "declaring (a) that the plaintiffs, as employers who create the product, Major League Baseball games, own all rights in and to Major League Baseball games, including the right to telecast them, and (b) that the Major League Baseball players, by virtue of their employment, have no rights in and to the product."[30] The district court found that the Clubs, as employers, retain all rights in their employees' work product. It thus granted summary judgment and entered final judgment for the Clubs on this claim. On appeal, the Players argue that the district court erred in holding that their status as employees extinguished their rights of publicity in their performances....

The threshold issue that we must decide is what law governs the Clubs' master-servant claims. The parties offer no assistance. Instead of considering the choice-of-law question, they rely upon "traditional principles of master-servant common law." Notwithstanding the parties' assumptions to the contrary, master-servant common law exists only with reference to the laws of particular states. As Justice Brandeis once stated, "[t]here is no federal general common law." *Erie Railroad Co. v. Tompkins*, 304 U.S. 64, 78 (1938). For a federal court to base its decision on "established principles of master-servant common law" that are independent of the law of any state would contravene *Erie* by creating a federal common law of master-servant relationships.

In general, a federal district court sitting in diversity, and this court on appeal, must follow the choice-of-law rules of the state in which the district court sits. *See Klaxon Co. v. Stentor Electric Manufacturing Co.*, 313 U.S. 487, 496–97 (1941). Although diversity of citizenship is not present in this case, federal courts, reasoning by analogy from diversity cases, have applied *Klaxon* to determine what law governs pendent state claims. We agree that the choice-of-law rule for pendent state claims should be that of the forum....

It would be understating matters to say that the conflicts question in this case is complex. The 26 Clubs are located in 14 states and in Canada. The Major League Baseball Players Association is an unincorporated association of individuals from most, if not all, the states and many foreign countries. The Players' contracts were negotiated and executed in various states and call for performance at stadiums across the country. The Players' rights of publicity might be violated wherever their performances are broadcast without their consent.

Because we cannot ascertain on the basis of the record before us the state or states whose law governs the Clubs' master-servant claim, we will vacate the district court's opinion and judgment with respect to Count II of the *Baltimore Orioles* complaint and remand this matter for further proceedings. On remand, the district court should determine the appropriate choice-of-law rule under Illinois conflicts law and should make the factual findings necessary to identify the state or states whose law controls....

---

29. The Players also are at liberty to attempt to negotiate a contractual limitation excluding performances before broadcast audiences from their scope of employment.

30. The Clubs' copyright and master-servant claims are distinct. With respect to the first claim, the Clubs contend that their copyright in the simultaneously recorded telecasts of major league baseball games preempts the Players' rights of publicity in their performances. This claim, however, is limited to games that are fixed in tangible form. With respect to the second claim, the Clubs assert that, as employers, they own the right to broadcast the Players' performances, regardless of whether the game is reduced to tangible form. This claim extends to games that are not broadcast or that are televised without being videotaped.

III

For the reasons stated above, the district court's judgment is AFFIRMED with respect to the Clubs' copyright claim and is VACATED with respect to the Clubs' master-servant claim and REMANDED for further proceedings consistent with this opinion and law.

Toney v. L'Oreal USA, Inc.
406 F.3d 905 (7th Cir. 2005)

KANNE, Circuit Judge:

June Toney's photograph was used to advertise a hair product marketed by Johnson Products Company. Toney consented to the use of her photograph for a limited time, but when a successor company later used the photograph without her permission, Toney filed suit alleging that her right of publicity had been violated. The district court dismissed her claim after finding that it was preempted by federal copyright law. Toney appeals, and we reverse.

I. Background

In November 1995, June Toney, a model who has appeared in print advertisements, commercials, and runway shows, authorized Johnson Products Company to use her likeness on the packaging of a hair-relaxer product called "Ultra Sheen Supreme" from November 1995 until November 2000. In addition, Toney authorized the use of her likeness in national magazine advertisements for the relaxer from November 1995 until November 1996. Additional uses (e.g., promotion of other products and/or for extended time periods) were contemplated by the agreement, but, as specifically stated in the agreement, the particular terms for any such uses were to be negotiated separately.

In August 2000, L'Oreal USA, Inc., acquired the Ultra Sheen Supreme line of products from Carson Products, which had previously acquired that same product line from Johnson. Subsequently, in December 2000, the Wella Corporation purchased and assumed control of the line and brand from L'Oreal.

In her complaint filed in state court, Toney asserted that L'Oreal, Wella Corporation, and Wella Personal Care of North America, Inc., (collectively, "defendants") used her likeness in connection with the packaging and promotion of the Ultra Sheen Supreme relaxer product beyond the authorized time period. Specifically, she claimed that the defendants thereby violated (1) her right to publicity in her likeness as protected under the Illinois Right of Publicity Act, 765 Ill. Comp. Stat. 1075/1-60 ("IRPA"), and (2) the Lanham Trademark Act of 1946, 15 U.S.C. § 1125(a).

The case was properly removed to federal district court on the basis of federal question jurisdiction. Following the defendants' motion to dismiss under Rule 12(b)(6) of the Federal Rules of Civil Procedure, the district court found that the IRPA-based claim met the conditions set out in § 301 of the Copyright Act ("Act"), 17 U.S.C. § 301, and was therefore preempted. Toney later voluntarily dismissed her Lanham Act claim with prejudice and the case was closed. She now appeals the district court's preemption determination. For the reasons stated herein, we reverse.

II. Analysis

The question we must address is whether Toney's claim, brought under the IRPA, is preempted by the Copyright Act. We review this legal question and the district court's decision to grant the defendants' motion to dismiss *de novo*....

The IRPA grants an individual the "right to control and to choose whether and how to use an individual's identity for commercial purposes." 765 Ill. Comp. Stat. 1075/10. Moreover, the IRPA provides that "[a] person may not use an individual's identity for commercial purposes during the individual's lifetime without having obtained previous written consent from the appropriate person...." 765 Ill. Comp. Stat. 1075/30. However, these state law rights are only valid if they do not interfere with federal copyright protections....

A. Toney's Claim Has Not Been Waived

Before interpreting the statutes at issue, we will dispose of the defendants' waiver argument. The defendants argue that Toney has waived any claim that the IRPA protects her "identity," as compared to her likeness fixed in photographic form. They point out that the word "identity" does not appear in her complaint and that "a plaintiff cannot amend [her] complaint by a brief that [she] files in the ... court of appeals." *Harrell v. United States,* 13 F.3d 232, 236 (7th Cir. 1993); *see also Bell v. Duperrault,* 367 F.3d 703, 709 n.1 (7th Cir. 2004) (citing *Williams v. REP Corp.,* 302 F.3d 660, 666 (7th Cir. 2002) ("A party waives any argument that it does not raise before the district court....") (quotation omitted)). In addition to finding problems with the complaint, the defendants point to the fact that in Toney's response to the defendants' motion to dismiss before the district court, she expressly stated that her claim "is narrowly directed to the use of her likeness, captured in photograph or otherwise."

Although Toney's complaint could have been more clear, we find that the minimal requirements for notice pleading have been met here. Under Federal Rule of Civil Procedure 8(a)(2), a pleading must contain a "short and plain statement of the claim showing that the pleader is entitled to relief," as well as a jurisdictional statement and a demand for relief. *Id.* Toney was required only to provide the defendants with "fair notice of what the plaintiff's claim is and the grounds upon which it rests." *Leatherman v. Tarrant County Narcotics Intelligence & Coordination Unit,* 507 U.S. 163, 168 (1993) (quotation omitted). Toney's complaint alleges unauthorized commercial use of her likeness by the defendants under the IRPA. The complaint does not explain the legal theory that Toney relies upon, but it was not required to do so. We find that Toney provided the defendants with adequate notice of her claim. The identity claim was not waived.

B. Toney's Claim Survives Preemption

The IRPA states that a person's "identity" is protected by the statute. Identity is defined to mean "any attribute of an individual that serves to identify that individual to an ordinary, reasonable viewer or listener, including but not limited to (i) name, (ii) signature, (iii) photograph, (iv) image, (v) likeness, or (vi) voice." 765 Ill. Comp. Stat. 1075/5. In short, the IRPA protects a person's right to publicity. The subject matter of such a claim "is *not* a particular picture or photograph of plaintiff. Rather, what is protected by the right of publicity is the very identity or persona of the plaintiff as a human being." J. Thomas McCarthy, 2 RIGHTS OF PUBLICITY & PRIVACY § 11:52 (2d ed. 2004) (emphasis in original) (internal citations and quotations omitted). A photograph "is merely one copyrightable 'expression' of the underlying 'work,' which is the plaintiff as a human being. There is only one underlying 'persona' of a person protected by the right of publicity." *Id.* In contrast, "[t]here may be dozens or hundreds of photographs which fix certain moments in that person's life. Copyright in each of these photographs might be separately owned by dozens or hundreds of photographers." *Id.* A persona, defined in this way, "can hardly be said to constitute a 'writing' of an 'author' within the meaning of the copyright clause of the Constitution." *Downing v. Abercrombie & Fitch,* 265 F.3d 994, 1003–04 (9th

Cir. 2001) (quotation omitted); *see also Landham v. Lewis Galoob Toys, Inc.*, 227 F.3d 619, 623 (6th Cir. 2000); *Brown v. Ames*, 201 F.3d 654, 658 (5th Cir. 2000).

Having reviewed the rights protected by the IRPA, we must now determine whether Toney's claim has been preempted by federal law. Section 301 of the Copyright Act delineates two conditions which, if met, require the preemption of a state-law claim in favor of the rights and remedies available under federal law. Section 301(a) states:

> On and after January 1, 1978, all legal or equitable rights that are equivalent to any of the exclusive rights within the general scope of copyright as specified by section 106 in works of authorship that are fixed in a tangible medium of expression and come within the subject matter of copyright as specified by section[ ] 102 ... are governed exclusively by this title. Thereafter, no person is entitled to any such right or equivalent right in any such work under the common law or statutes of any State.

17 U.S.C. § 301(a). We will take the questions in reverse order, first determining whether the work at issue is fixed in a tangible form and whether it comes within the subject matter of copyright as specified in § 102. Second, we consider whether the right is equivalent to the general copyright protections which are set out in § 106.

Section 102 of the Act defines the subject matter of copyright as "original works of authorship fixed in any tangible medium of expression," including "pictorial" works. 17 U.S.C. § 102(a). The Act's definitional section explains that a work is "fixed" in a tangible medium of expression "when its embodiment in a copy ... is sufficiently permanent or stable to permit it to be perceived, reproduced, or otherwise communicated for a period of more than transitory duration." 17 U.S.C. § 101.

The second aspect of the test requires a showing that the right to be enforced is "equivalent" to any of the rights set forth in § 106. The notes and commentary accompanying § 106 make it clear that copyright holders have five exclusive and fundamental rights: reproduction, adaptation, publication, performance, and display. 17 U.S.C. § 106. A copyright is violated or infringed when, without permission, someone other than the copyright holder exercises one of these fundamental rights. Put differently, to avoid preemption, a state law must regulate conduct that is qualitatively distinguishable from that governed by federal copyright law—i.e., conduct other than reproduction, adaptation, publication, performance, and display. *See, e.g., Trandes Corp. v. Guy F. Atkinson Co.*, 996 F.2d 655, 659–60 (4th Cir. 1993); 1 Melville B. Nimmer & David Nimmer, NIMMER ON COPYRIGHT § 1.01[B] [1] (1999).

Applying the facts of this case to the requirements for preemption, we find that Toney's identity is not fixed in a tangible medium of expression. There is no "work of authorship" at issue in Toney's right of publicity claim. A person's likeness—her persona—is not authored and it is not fixed. The fact that an image of the person might be fixed in a copyrightable photograph does not change this. From this we must also find that the rights protected by the IRPA are not "equivalent" to any of the exclusive rights within the general scope of copyright that are set forth in § 106. Copyright laws do not reach identity claims such as Toney's. Identity, as we have described it, is an amorphous concept that is not protected by copyright law; thus, the state law protecting it is not preempted.

We also note that the purpose of the IRPA is to allow a person to control the commercial value of his or her identity. Unlike copyright law, "commercial purpose" is an element required by the IRPA. The phrase is defined to mean "the public use or holding out of an individual's identity (i) on or in connection with the offering for sale or sale of a product, merchandise, goods, or services; (ii) for purposes of advertising or promoting products, merchandise, goods, or services; or (iii) for the purpose of fundraising." 765 Ill. Comp. Stat. 1075/5. Clearly the defendants used Toney's likeness without her consent for their commercial advantage. The fact that the photograph itself could be copyrighted, and that defendants owned the copyright to the photograph that was used, is irrelevant to the IRPA claim. The basis of a right of publicity claim concerns the message—whether the plaintiff endorses, or appears to endorse the product in question. One can imagine many scenarios where the use of a photograph without consent, in apparent endorsement of any number of products, could cause great harm to the person photographed. The fact that Toney consented to the use of her photograph originally does not change this analysis. The defendants did not have her consent to continue to use the photograph, and therefore, they stripped Toney of her right to control the commercial value of her identity.

C. Conflicting Precedent

Our decision in *Baltimore Orioles v. Major League Baseball Players Ass'n*, 805 F.2d 663 (7th Cir. 1986), has been widely criticized by our sister circuits and by several commentators. Many interpret the case as holding that the right of publicity as protected by state law is preempted by § 301 in all instances. We take this opportunity to clarify our holding. The case simply does not stand for the proposition that the right of publicity as protected by state law is preempted in all instances by federal copyright law; it does not sweep that broadly.

Baltimore Orioles holds that state laws that intrude on the domain of copyright are preempted even if the particular expression is neither copyrighted nor copyrightable. Such a result is essential in order to preserve the extent of the public domain established by copyright law. Therefore, states may not create rights in material that was published more than 75 years ago, even though that material is not subject to federal copyright. Also, states may not create copyright-like protections in materials that are not original enough for federal protection, such as a telephone book with listings in alphabetical order. *See Feist Publ'ns, Inc. v. Rural Tel. Serv. Co.*, 499 U.S. 340 (1991). *Baltimore Orioles* itself makes clear that "[a] player's right of publicity in his name or likeness would not be preempted if a company, without the consent of the player, used the player's name to advertise its product." 805 F.2d at 666 n.24. Therefore, the bottom line is that Toney's claim under the Illinois right of publicity statute is not preempted by federal copyright law.

III. Conclusion

For the reasons stated above, the dismissal of Toney's right of publicity claim is VACATED; this case is REMANDED for further proceedings in the district court.

Laws v. Sony Music Entertainment, Inc.

448 F.3d 1134 (9th Cir. 2006)

BYBEE, Circuit Judge:

Plaintiff Debra Laws ("Laws") brought suit against defendant Sony Music Entertainment, Inc. ("Sony") for misappropriating her voice and name in the song "All I Have" by Jennifer Lopez and L.L. Cool J. The district court found that Sony had obtained a license to use a sample of Laws's recording of "Very Special" and held that Laws's claims for violation of her common law right to privacy and her statutory right of publicity were preempted by the Copyright Act. We agree with the district court that the Copyright Act preempts Laws's claims, and we affirm.

I. FACTS AND PROCEEDINGS

In 1979, professional vocalist and recording artist Debra Laws and Spirit Productions ("Spirit") entered into a recording agreement with Elektra/Asylum Records ("Elektra") to produce master recordings of Laws's vocal performances for Elektra. The agreement gave Elektra the "sole and exclusive right to copyright such master recordings" and "the exclusive worldwide right in perpetuity ... to lease, license, convey or otherwise use or dispose of such master recordings." Elektra also secured the right "to use and to permit others to use your name, the Artist's name ... likeness, other identification, and biographical material concerning the Artist ... in connection with such master recordings." Notwithstanding these provisions, Elektra agreed that "we shall not, without your prior written consent, utilize or authorize others to utilize the Masters in any so-called 'audio-visual' or 'sight and sound' devices intended primarily for home use," and "we or our licensees shall not, without your prior written consent, sell records embodying the Masters hereunder for use as premiums or in connection with the sale, advertising or promotion of any other product or service." In 1981, Laws recorded the song "Very Special," which was released on Laws's album on the Elektra label. Elektra copyrighted the song that same year.

In November 2002, Elektra's agent, Warner Special Products, Inc., entered into an agreement with Sony Music Entertainment, Inc. ("Sony") to grant Sony a non-exclusive license to use a sample of Debra Laws's recording of "Very Special" in the song "All I Have," performed by recording artists Jennifer Lopez and L.L. Cool J. The agreement required Sony to include a credit stating, "Featuring samples from the Debra Laws recording Very Special" in any reproduction. Warner, Elektra's agent, did not seek permission from Laws or Spirit before it released the disc and video, and neither Laws nor Spirit was compensated.

Sony subsequently released a Jennifer Lopez compact disc and music video incorporating brief samples of "Very Special" into her recording of "All I Have." The sampled portions include a segment approximately ten seconds in length at the beginning of "All I Have," and shorter segments repeated in the background throughout the song. Sony included the required credit in the booklet accompanying the compact disc. The song and Lopez's album, "This is Me ... Then," became a huge commercial success, netting over forty million dollars. At one time "All I Have" was the number one song in the United States.

In February 2003, Laws brought an action in the Superior Court of California alleging multiple claims. The two claims relevant to this appeal were: (1) a common law claim for invasion of privacy for the misappropriation of Laws's name and voice and (2) a claim for misappropriation of Laws's name and voice for a commercial purpose under California Civil Code § 3344. The complaint sought injunctive and monetary relief.

Sony removed the case to the U.S. District Court for the Central District of California and sought to join Elektra as a necessary party. The court denied the motion. Sony filed a summary judgment motion, which the district court granted, ruling that both of Laws's misappropriation claims were preempted by the Copyright Act. Laws filed a timely appeal.

II. STANDARD OF REVIEW

A grant of summary judgment is reviewed de novo ... We must view the evidence in the light most favorable to Laws and determine whether there is any genuine issue of material fact and whether the district court properly applied the relevant substantive law....

III. ANALYSIS

The Copyright Clause of the U.S. Constitution provides that "Congress shall have the Power ... To promote the Progress of Science and useful Arts, by securing for limited Times to Authors and Inventors the exclusive Right to their respective Writings and Discoveries...." U.S. Const. art. I, §8, cl. 8. Pursuant to this authority, Congress enacted the Copyright Act to define and protect the rights of copyright holders. Under the Act, "the owner of copyright ... has the exclusive rights to do and to authorize" others to display, perform, reproduce or distribute copies of the work, and to prepare derivative works. 17 U.S.C. §106. The copyright is the right to control the work, including the decision to make the work available to or withhold it from the public.

Sections 301(a) and (b) of Title 17 describe when the Act preempts legal and equitable rights granted by state common law or statute. Section (a) states:

On and after January 1, 1978, all legal and equitable rights that are equivalent to any of the exclusive rights within the general scope of copyright as specified by section 106 in works of authorship that are fixed in a tangible medium of expression and come within the subject matter of copyright as specified by sections 102 and 103 ... are governed exclusively by this title. Thereafter, no person is entitled to any such right or equivalent right in any such work under the common law or statutes of any State.

Id. §301(a). Section (b) states:

Nothing in this title annuls or limits any rights or remedies under the common law or statutes of any State with respect to ... subject matter that does not come within the subject matter of copyright as specified by sections 102 and 103, including works of authorship not fixed in any tangible medium of expression....

Id. §301(b). Congress explained what the statute made obvious: "[t]he intention of section 301 is to preempt and abolish any rights under the common law or statutes of a State that are equivalent to copyright and that extend to works [coming] within the scope of the Federal copyright law." H.R. Rep. No. 94-1476, at 130 (1976); *see also Maljack Prods. v. GoodTimes Home Video Corp.,* 81 F.3d 881, 888 (9th Cir. 1996).

We have adopted a two-part test to determine whether a state law claim is preempted by the Act. We must first determine whether the "subject matter" of the state law claim falls within the subject matter of copyright as described in 17 U.S.C. §§102 and 103. Second, assuming that it does, we must determine whether the rights asserted under state law are equivalent to the rights contained in 17 U.S.C. §106, which articulates the exclusive rights of copyright holders. *See Downing v. Abercrombie & Fitch,* 265 F.3d 994, 1003 (9th Cir. 2001).

Laws alleges two causes of action. First, she asserts a claim for protection of her voice, name and likeness under California's common law right of privacy. To sustain this action, Laws must prove: "(1) the defendant's use of the plaintiff's identity; (2) the appropriation of plaintiff's name or likeness to defendant's advantage, commercially or otherwise; (3) lack of consent; and (4) resulting injury." *Eastwood v. Superior Court,* 149 Cal. App. 3d 409, 198 Cal. Rptr. 342, 347 (1983); *see also Downing,* 265 F.3d at 1001. Second, Laws asserts a statutory misappropriation or "right of publicity" claim under California Civil Code §3344(a), which provides that:

Any person who knowingly uses another's name, voice, signature, photograph, or likeness, in any manner, on or in products, merchandise, or goods, or for purposes of advertising or selling, or soliciting purchases of, products, merchandise, goods or services, without such person's prior consent ... shall be liable for any damages sustained by the person or persons injured as a result thereof.

We have observed that "[t]he remedies provided for under California Civil Code § 3344 complement the common law cause of action; they do not replace or codify the common law." *Downing*, 265 F.3d at 1001. Nevertheless, for purposes of our preemption analysis, section 3344 includes the elements of the common law cause of action. *See id.* ("Under section 3344, a plaintiff must prove all the elements of the common law cause of action" plus "knowing use" and "a direct connection between the alleged use and the commercial purpose."). For convenience's sake, we will refer to Laws's claims as "right of publicity" claims.

Sony does not argue that common law privacy actions and statutory claims under section 3344 are preempted generally by section 301; rather, it argues that they are preempted as applied to the facts of this case. We thus turn to (1) whether the subject matter of Laws's right of publicity claims comes within the subject matter of copyright, and (2) whether the rights Laws asserts under California law are equivalent to those created under the Copyright Act.

A. The "Subject Matter" of Copyright

We first consider whether the subject matter of Laws's misappropriation claim is within the subject matter of the Copyright Act. We conclude that it is. Sections 102 and 103 of the Act identify the works of authorship that constitute the "subject matter" of copyright. Section 102 of the Act extends copyright protection to "original works of authorship fixed in any tangible medium of expression ... from which they can be ... reproduced, ... either directly or with the aid of a machine or device." 17 U.S.C. § 102(a). That section defines a "work of authorship" to include "sound recordings." *Id.* § 102(a)(7). "A work is fixed in a tangible medium of expression when its embodiment in a copy or phonorecord, by or under the authority of the author, is sufficiently permanent or stable to permit it to be perceived, reproduced, or otherwise communicated for a period of more than transitory duration." *Id.* § 101. Laws's master recordings held by Elektra are plainly within these definitions.

Laws nevertheless contends that the subject matter of a copyright claim and a right of publicity claim are substantively different. She argues that a copyright claim protects ownership rights to a work of art, while a right of publicity claim concerns the right to protect one's persona and likeness. Sony, by contrast, contends that the subject matter of a right of publicity in one's voice is not different from a copyright claim when the voice is embodied within a copyrighted sound recording. Sony argues that once a voice becomes part of a sound recording in a fixed tangible medium it comes within the subject matter of copyright law.

Our jurisprudence provides strong guidance to the resolution of this question. In *Sinatra v. Goodyear Tire & Rubber Co.*, 435 F.2d 711 (9th Cir. 1970), Nancy Sinatra filed suit against Goodyear Tire on the basis of an advertising campaign that featured "These Boots Are Made for Walkin'," a song that Sinatra made famous. Goodyear Tire had obtained a license from the copyright proprietor for the use of music, lyrics, and arrangement of the composition. Goodyear Tire subsequently used the music and lyrics in its ads, which were sung by unknown vocalists. She alleged the song had taken on a "secondary meaning" that was uniquely injurious to her. We rejected her claim:

> [A]ppellant's complaint is not that her sound is uniquely personal; it is that the sound in connection with the music, lyrics and arrangement, which made her

the subject of popular identification, ought to be protected. But as to these latter copyrightable items she had no rights. Presumably, she was required to obtain permission of the copyright owner to sing "Boots", and to make an arrangement of the song to suit her own tastes and talents. Had she desired to exclude all others from use of the song so that her "secondary meaning" with the song could not be imitated she could have purchased those rights from the copyright proprietor. One wonders whether her voice ... would have been identifiable if another song had been presented, and not "her song," which unfortunately for her was owned by others and licensed to the defendants.

Id. at 716. Although *Sinatra* was decided prior to passage of the modern-day preemption provision in section 301, we nonetheless ruled that the Copyright Act impliedly preempted Sinatra's state law claim. *Id.* at 717–18. We later confirmed this holding in *Midler v. Ford Motor Co.,* 849 F.2d 460, 462 (9th Cir. 1988), when we observed that "[t]o give Sinatra damages for [defendants'] use of the song would clash with federal copyright law."

In *Midler,* recording and performing artist Bette Midler filed suit against an advertising agency and its client when a professional "sound alike" was used to imitate Midler's voice from her hit song "Do You Want to Dance." The agency did not acquire a license to use Midler's recording; instead, it had obtained a license from the song's copyright holder and then attempted to get Midler to do the commercial. When Midler's agent advised the agency that she was not interested, the agency hired someone who had been a backup singer for Midler and could imitate her voice and style. Indeed, the singer was instructed to sound as much like Bette Midler as possible. We held that Midler's common law misappropriation claim was not preempted by copyright law because the "thing" misappropriated, her voice, was not copyrightable in that instance. We explained:

> Midler does not seek damages for [the defendant's] use of "Do You Want To Dance," and thus her claim is not preempted by federal copyright law. Copyright protects "original works of authorship fixed in any tangible medium of expression." A voice is not copyrightable. The sounds are not "fixed." What is put forward as protectible here is more personal than any work of authorship.

Id. at 462. What Midler sought was relief from an unauthorized vocal imitation for advertising purposes, and that was not the subject of copyright.

We subsequently applied *Midler* in *Waits v. Frito-Lay, Inc.,* 978 F.2d 1093 (9th Cir. 1992). The voice of Tom Waits, a professional singer, songwriter, and actor, was imitated and then broadcast in a commercial for Frito-Lay. Waits filed a right of publicity claim under California law. We held that the claim was not preempted by copyright law because it was "for infringement of voice, not for infringement of a copyrightable subject such as sound recording or musical composition." *Id.* at 1100. Thus, the issues in *Waits* were "whether the defendants had deliberately imitated Waits' voice rather than simply his style and whether Waits' voice was sufficiently distinctive and widely known to give him a protectible right in its use. These elements are 'different in kind' from those in a copyright infringement case challenging the unauthorized use of a song or recording." *Id.*

In this case, Laws's voice misappropriation claim is plainly different from the claims in *Midler* and *Waits* and falls within the subject matter of copyright. In contrast to *Midler* and *Waits,* where the licensing party obtained only a license to the song and then imitated the artist's voice, here Sony obtained a license to use Laws's recording itself. Sony was not imitating "Very Special" as Laws might have sung it. Rather, it used a portion of "Very Special" as sung by Debra Laws....

Laws does not dispute Sony's contention that the recording of "Very Special" was a copyrighted sound recording fixed in a tangible medium of expression. Laws's right of publicity claim is based exclusively on what she claims is an unauthorized duplication of her vocal performance of the song "Very Special." Although California law recognizes an assertable interest in the publicity associated with one's voice, we think it is clear that federal copyright law preempts a claim alleging misappropriation of one's voice when the entirety of the allegedly misappropriated vocal performance is contained within a copyrighted medium. Our conclusion is consistent with our holdings in *Midler* and *Waits*, where we concluded that the voice misappropriation claim was not preempted, because the alleged misappropriation was the imitation of the plaintiffs' voices. Neither of those imitations was contained in a copyrighted vocal performance. Moreover, the fact that the vocal performance was copyrighted demonstrates that what is put forth here as protectible is *not* "more personal than any work of authorship." *Midler*, 849 F.2d at 462.

Laws points to two cases for support. Both cases, however, involve photographs used in advertising, and are distinguishable from this case. In *Downing*, we held that a claim based on the right of publicity was not preempted by the Copyright Act. In *Downing*, retailer Abercrombie & Fitch was developing a surfing theme for its subscription catalog. Abercrombie published a photo of the plaintiffs, who were participants in a surf championship in Hawaii in 1965. Abercrombie ran the photo, which it had purchased from the photographer (who held the copyright), and it identified the plaintiffs by name. Abercrombie went well beyond mere republication of the photograph. Without obtaining plaintiffs' consent to use their names and images, it also offered t-shirts exactly like those worn by the plaintiffs in the photo. We noted that the photograph itself was within the subject matter protected by the Copyright Act. But Abercrombie had not merely published the photograph. Rather, it published the photo in connection with a broad surf-themed advertising campaign, identified the plaintiffs-surfers by name, and offered for sale the same t-shirts worn by the plaintiffs in the photo. By doing so, it had suggested that the surfers had endorsed Abercrombie's t-shirts. Accordingly, we concluded that "it is not the publication of the photograph itself, as a creative work of authorship, that is the basis for [plaintiffs'] claims, but rather, it is the use of the [plaintiffs'] likenesses and their names pictured in the published photograph." 265 F.3d at 1003. We thus concluded that the claim was not within the subject matter of copyright because "[a] person's name or likeness is not a work of authorship within the meaning of 17 U.S.C. § 102." *Downing*, 265 F.3d at 1004.

Laws also relies on a second case, *Toney v. L'Oreal USA, Inc.*, 406 F.3d 905 (7th Cir. 2005), in which the Seventh Circuit held that a claim under the Illinois Right of Publicity Act was not preempted by the Copyright Act. Toney was a model who had posed for photographs used to promote hair-care products on packaging and in national advertisements. Defendants owned the copyright for the photograph of Toney that was used, and had a right to use it from November 1995 to November 2000; any other use would be negotiated separately. In apparent violation of their understanding, defendants continued to use the photographs in their advertising beyond 2000. Toney alleged that this use violated her right of publicity under Illinois law. The Seventh Circuit concluded that

> Toney's identity is not fixed in a tangible medium of expression. There is no "work of authorship" at issue in Toney's right of publicity claim. A person's likeness — her persona — is not authored and it is not fixed. The fact that an image of the person might be fixed in a copyrightable photograph does not change this.... The fact that the photograph itself could be copyrighted, and that defendants owned the copyright to the photograph that was used, is irrelevant to

the [right of publicity] claim.... The defendants did not have her consent to
continue to use the photograph....

Id. at 910. The fact that the photograph was copyrighted could not negate the fact that
Toney had reserved artistic control over her image for any period beyond the contractual
time frame. The Seventh Circuit concluded that Toney's claim was not preempted.[4]

In contrast, Jennifer Lopez's song "All I Have" incorporated samples of Deborah Laws's
"Very Special" and gave her the attribution negotiated by Elektra and Sony. Sony did not
use Laws's image, name, or the voice recording in any promotional materials. Her state
tort action challenges control of the artistic work itself and could hardly be more closely
related to the subject matter of the Copyright Act.

We find more to the point, and quite persuasive, the California Court of Appeal's decision in *Fleet v. CBS, Inc.,* 50 Cal. App. 4th 1911, 58 Cal. Rptr. 2d 645 (1996). There, defendant CBS owned the exclusive rights to distribute a motion picture in which plaintiffs
performed. A third party who financed the operation of the movie refused to pay plaintiffs their previously agreed-to salaries. Plaintiffs brought suit against CBS alleging, *inter
alia,* that by airing the motion picture using their names, pictures, and likenesses without
their consent, CBS had violated their statutory right of publicity. The Court of Appeal
held that the Copyright Act preempted the action. As the court observed, "it was not merely
[plaintiffs'] likenesses which were captured on film—it was their dramatic performances
which are ... copyrightable." *Id.* at 651. "[O]nce [plaintiffs'] performances were put on
film, they became 'dramatic work[s]' 'fixed in[a] tangible medium of expression....' At
that point, the performances came within the scope or subject matter of copyright law
protection," and the claims were preempted. *Id.* at 650; *see also Downing,* 265 F.3d at 1005
n. 4 ("In *Fleet,* the plaintiffs were actors in a copyrighted film. The claims of the plaintiffs
were based on their dramatic performance in a film CBS sought to distribute.... This is
clearly distinguishable from this case where the Appellants' claim is based on the use of
their names and likenesses, which are not copyrightable."). In effect, the plaintiffs' right of
publicity claim was a question of control over the distribution, display or performance of
a movie CBS owned. Since CBS's use of plaintiffs' likenesses did not extend beyond the
use of the copyrighted material it held, there was no right of publicity at issue, aside from
the actors' performances. Had the court held otherwise, each actor could claim that any
showing of the film violated his right to control his image and persona.

Laws makes much of the fact that she possessed a right of first refusal in all future uses
of "Very Special" under the original production agreement with Elektra. She contends
that this right expressly gives her control over the use of her name and voice in connection with any use of "Very Special." She also contends that "[i]f the copyright holder itself, Elektra/Asylum, was not ceded such rights, then as a matter of law its licensee does
not possess those rights." In effect, Laws contends that her contractual reservation gives
her an interest in the copyright and, concomitantly, renders Elektra's copyright partially
subject to her control.

We express no view as to the effect of Laws's reservation in the production agreement
and no view as to any remedies that Laws may have against Elektra. Whether or not the
two parties contracted around the actual use of a copyright does not affect our preemption analysis. To the extent that Laws has enforceable, contractual rights regarding the

---

4. ... The facts of this case would be analogous to *Toney* if Laws had brought her right of publicity claim against Elektra, which holds the copyright to the song and may have agreed to licensing limitations. We express no views on the correctness of *Toney* or its application to any claims against
Elektra.

use of Elektra's copyright, her remedy may lie in a breach of contract claim against Elektra for licensing "Very Special" without her authorization.[5]

In sum, we hold that Laws's cause of action is within the subject matter of copyright.

B. *Equivalent Rights*

We must next determine whether the rights she asserts under California law are equivalent to the rights protected under the Copyright Act. We conclude that they are. In *Del Madera Properties v. Rhodes & Gardner*, 820 F.2d 973 (9th Cir. 1987), we outlined the test for determining whether state rights were "equivalent" to those under the Copyright Act:

> To satisfy the "equivalent rights" part of the preemption test ... the ... alleged misappropriation ... must be equivalent to rights within the general scope of copyright as specified by section 106 of the Copyright Act. Section 106 provides a copyright owner with the exclusive rights of reproduction, preparation of derivative works, distribution, and display. To survive preemption, the state cause of action must protect rights which are qualitatively different from the copyright rights. The state claim must have an extra element which changes the nature of the action.

Id. at 977 (quotations and citations omitted). In *Del Madera Properties,* the plaintiff alleged that the defendants had allegedly misappropriated a copyrighted land map to plan a new development. Plaintiff advanced an unfair competition claim and argued that it was qualitatively different from copyright because the unfair competition claim required the breach of a fiduciary duty, an element not required under copyright. We squarely rejected Del Madera's argument:

> This argument ... does not add any "extra element" which changes the nature of the action. The argument is constructed upon the premise that the documents and information ... belonged to Del Madera and were misappropriated by the defendants. Del Madera's ownership of this material, and the alleged misappropriation by the defendants, are part and parcel of the copyright claim.

Id.; see also Harper & Row, Publishers, Inc. v. Nation Enters., 501 F. Supp. 848, 853–54 (S.D.N.Y. 1980) ("[T]he contract claim is redundant because the additional elements ... do not afford plaintiff rights that are different in kind from those protected by the copyright laws."), *rev'd on other grounds*, 471 U.S. 539 (1985).

Laws contends that her right of publicity claim under California Civil Code § 3344 requires proof of a use for a "commercial purpose," which is not an element of a copyright infringement claim. She concedes that a right which is the "equivalent to copyright" is one that is infringed by the mere act of reproduction; however, she argues that her claim is not based on Sony's mere act of reproduction, but "is for the use of ... Laws'[s] voice, the combination of her voice with another artist, and the commercial exploitation of her voice and name in a different product without her consent."

Sony argues that Laws's claims are based exclusively on the reproduction of "Very Special" in "All I Have." It asserts that the rights protected under Laws's voice misappropriation claim are not qualitatively different from the rights protected under copyright law because the sole basis for her voice misappropriation claim is the unauthorized reproduction of her copyrighted vocal performance.

---

5. Counsel represented to this Court during oral argument that it had in fact filed a breach of contract claim in state court.

The essence of Laws's claim is, simply, that she objects to having a sample of "Very Special" used in the Jennifer Lopez-L.L. Cool J recording. But Laws gave up the right to reproduce her voice—at least insofar as it is incorporated in a recording of "Very Special"—when she contracted with Elektra in 1981 and acknowledged that Elektra held the "sole and exclusive right to copyright such master recordings," including the right "to lease, license, convey or otherwise use or dispose of such master recordings." At that point, Laws could have either retained the copyright, or reserved contractual rights in Elektra's use of the recording. Indeed, Laws claims that the latter is precisely what she did. But if Elektra licensed "Very Special" to Sony in violation of its contract with Laws, her remedy sounds in contract against Elektra, not in tort against Sony.

The mere presence of an additional element ("commercial use") in section 3344 is not enough to qualitatively distinguish Laws's right of publicity claim from a claim in copyright. The extra element must transform the nature of the action. Although the elements of Laws's state law claims may not be identical to the elements in a copyright action, the underlying nature of Laws's state law claims is part and parcel of a copyright claim. *See Fleet,* 58 Cal. Rptr. 2d at 649. Under the Act, a copyright owner has the exclusive right "to reproduce the copyrighted work." 17 U.S.C. § 106(1). Laws's claims are based on the premise that Sony reproduced a sample of "Very Special" for commercial purposes without her permission. But Sony obtained a limited license from the copyright holder to use the copyrighted work for the Lopez album. The additional element of "commercial purpose" does not change the underlying nature of the action....

IV. CONCLUSION

Both copyright and the right of publicity are means of protecting an individual's investment in his or her artistic labors. As the Court said of copyright:

> The economic philosophy behind the clause empowering Congress to grant patents and copyrights is the conviction that encouragement of individual effort by personal gain is the best way to advance public welfare through the talents of authors and inventors in "Science and useful Arts." Sacrificial days devoted to such creative activities deserve rewards commensurate with the services rendered.

Mazer v. Stein, 347 U.S. 201, 219 (1954). Similarly, the Supreme Court has said that the

> right of publicity ... rests on more than a desire to compensate the performer for the time and effort invested in his act; the protection provides an economic incentive for him to make the investment required to produce a performance of interest to the public.

Zacchini v. Scripps-Howard Broad. Co., 433 U.S. 562, 576 (1977). On the one hand, we recognize that the holder of a copyright does not have "a license to trample on other people's rights." *See* J. Thomas McCarthy, THE RIGHTS OF PUBLICITY AND PRIVACY § 11:60, at 788 (2d ed. 2005). On the other hand, however, the right of publicity is not a license to limit the copyright holder's rights merely because one disagrees with decisions to license the copyright. We sense that, left to creative legal arguments, the developing right of publicity could easily supplant the copyright scheme. This, Congress has expressly precluded in § 301. Were we to conclude that Laws's voice misappropriation claim was not preempted by the Copyright Act, then virtually every use of a copyrighted sound recording would infringe upon the original performer's right of publicity. We foresaw this distinct possibility in *Sinatra:*

> An added clash with the copyright laws is the potential restriction which recognition of performers' "secondary meanings" places upon the potential market of the copyright proprietor. If a proposed licensee must pay each artist who has played or sung the composition and who might therefore claim unfair competition-performer's protection, the licensee may well be discouraged to the point of complete loss of interest.

Sinatra, 435 F.2d at 718. It is hard to imagine how a copyright would remain meaningful if its licensees were potentially subject to suit from any performer anytime the copyrighted material was used.

To be clear, we recognize that not every right of publicity claim is preempted by the Copyright Act. Our holding does not extinguish common law or statutory rights of privacy, publicity, and trade secrets, as well as the general law of defamation and fraud (or any other similar causes of action), so long as those causes of action do not concern the subject matter of copyright and contain qualitatively different elements than those contained in a copyright infringement suit. Elektra copyrighted Laws's performance of "Very Special" and licensed its use to Sony. If Laws wished to retain control of her performance, she should (and may) have either retained the copyright or contracted with the copyright holder, Elektra, to give her control over its licensing. In any event, her remedy, if any, lies in an action against Elektra, not Sony.

We therefore agree with the district court's conclusion that Laws's right of publicity claims are preempted by the Copyright Act. The judgment is AFFIRMED.

———————

Wendt v. Host Int'l, Inc.

35 U.S.P.Q.2d (BNA) 1315 (9th Cir. 1995)

Before: FERGUSON, BEEZER and NOONAN, Circuit Judges.

MEMORANDUM*

Plaintiffs George Wendt and John Ratzenberger appeal the district court's grant of summary judgment in favor of defendant Host International, Inc. ("Host") and applicant in intervention Paramount Pictures Corporation ("Paramount"), as well as the district court's orders awarding Host and Paramount their attorney fees. This case involves claims arising from the alleged appropriation of plaintiffs' identities in the design of animatronic figures placed in bars operated by defendant Host. We have jurisdiction, 28 U.S.C. § 1291, and we reverse....

II

At the outset, we wish to make it clear that this is not a preemption case. Plaintiffs' causes of action are not preempted by federal copyright law. *Midler v. Ford Motor Co.,* 849 F.2d 460, 462–63 (9th Cir. 1988) ("What is put forward as protectable here is more personal than any work of authorship.... A voice is *as distinctive as a face.*") (emphasis added).

———————

* This disposition is not appropriate for publication and may not be cited to or used by the courts of this circuit except as provided by Ninth Circuit Rule 36-3.

More broadly, plaintiffs' claims are not preempted by the federal copyright statute so long as they "contain elements, such as the invasion of personal rights ... that are different in kind from copyright infringement." *Waits v. Frito Lay, Inc.*, 978 F.2d 1093, 1100 (9th Cir. 1992) (quoting H.R. Rep. No. 1476, 94th Cong., 2d Sess. 132, *reprinted in* 1976 U.S.C.C.A.N. 5659, 5748), *cert. denied*, 113 S.Ct. 1047 (1993).

In *Waits*, we held that the unauthorized commercial use of one's identity is an invasion of "a personal property right," different in kind from copyright infringement. 978 F.2d at 1100. This is true because the torts at issue require the proof of additional elements beyond those essential to show copyright infringement. *See id.* For example, both section 3334 and the common law right of publicity tort require proof that the defendant's use of the plaintiff's "likeness" or "identity" was commercial (*i.e.* connected with selling or promoting a product), whereas copyright infringement occurs with any unauthorized copying of the protected material. *See* 17 U.S.C. §§ 106, 501; *Brown Bag Software v. Symantec Corp.*, 960 F.2d 1465, 1472 (9th Cir.), *cert. denied*, 113 S.Ct. 198 (1992).

Plaintiffs' state law causes of action are not preempted by the operation of federal copyright statutes....

[The merits of the memorandum opinion are summarized in the published opinion that follows.]

Wendt v. Host Int'l, Inc.
125 F.3d 806 (9th Cir. 1997)

Before: FLETCHER and TROTT, Circuit Judges, and JENKINS,* District Judge.

FLETCHER, Circuit Judge:

Actors George Wendt and John Ratzenberger appeal the district court's grant of summary judgment in favor of Host International, Inc. ("Host") and applicant in intervention Paramount Pictures Corporation ("Paramount"), dismissing their action for violations of the Lanham Act, 15 U.S.C. § 1125(a), and California's statutory and common law right of publicity. We reverse.

I. OVERVIEW

Wendt and Ratzenberger argue that the district court erred in dismissing their action because they have raised issues of material fact as to whether Host violated their trademark and publicity rights by creating animatronic robotic figures (the "robots") based upon their likenesses without their permission and placing these robots in airport bars modeled upon the set from the television show *Cheers*. They also appeal the district court's orders excluding appellants' survey evidence, barring presentation of expert testimony, and awarding Host and Paramount attorney's fees. We have jurisdiction, 28 U.S.C. § 1291, and we reverse and remand for trial.

---

* Honorable Bruce S. Jenkins, Senior United States District Judge for the District of Utah, sitting by designation.

Figure 10-1. "Hank" and "Bob"

II. PROCEDURAL HISTORY

In *Wendt v. Host*, 1995 WL 115571 (9th Cir. 1995) ("*Wendt I*"), we reversed the first grant of summary judgment in this action and remanded. We held that appellants' state law causes of action were not preempted by federal copyright law and that disputed issues of material fact precluded summary judgment because the district court's comparison of photographs of appellants Wendt and Ratzenberger with photographs of the animatronic figures was not sufficient to resolve their claims under Cal. Civ.Code § 3344:

> The question here is whether the three dimensional animatronic figures are sufficiently similar to plaintiffs to constitute their likenesses. Based on the limited record before us, it cannot be said as a matter of law that the figures are so dissimilar from plaintiffs that no reasonable trier of fact could find them to be 'likenesses.' That question must be determined by a comparison of the actual, three-dimensional entities.

1995 WL 115571 at *2. We concluded that this comparison must be decided without reference to the context in which the image appears. *Id.* We found that there were disputed issues of material fact concerning the appellants' common law right of publicity claims because the similarity between appellants' physical characteristics and those of the robots is disputed. *Id.* at *3. Finally, we held that the appellants' claims for unfair competition under § 43(a) of the Lanham Act, 15 U.S.C. § 1125(a), require the application of a "well settled eight factor test" to determine whether Host's conduct has created a likelihood of confusion as to whether appellants were endorsing Host's product. *Id.*

Upon remand, the district court granted summary judgment for a second time after an in-court inspection of the robots. It held that it could not "find, by viewing both the robotics and the live persons of Mr. Wendt and Mr. Ratzenberger, that there is any similarity at all ... except that one of the robots, like one of the plaintiffs, is heavier than the other ... The facial features are totally different." The district court then awarded attorney's fees to Host and Paramount pursuant to Cal. Civ.Code § 3344.

Appellants argue that despite the district court's comparison of the animatronic figures and the appellants, dismissal was inappropriate because material issues of fact remain as to the degree to which the animatronic figures appropriate the appellants' likenesses. Appellants claim that the district court erred in determining that the robots were not likenesses of the appellants because the "likeness" need not be identical or photographic. Further, they argue that the likeness determination is an issue for the jury to decide in this case. We agree.

III. ANALYSIS

We review a grant of summary judgment de novo.... Our review is governed by the 'law of the case' doctrine, which prevents courts from "reconsidering an issue previously decided by the same court, or a higher court in the identical case." *Securities Investor Protection Corp. v. Vigman,* 74 F.3d 932, 937 (9th Cir. 1996).

A. The Statutory Right of Publicity

California Civil Code § 3344 provides in relevant part:

> [a]ny person who knowingly uses another's name, voice, signature, photograph, or likeness, in any manner, ... for purposes of advertising or selling, ... without such person's prior consent ... shall be liable for any damages sustained by the person or persons injured as a result thereof.

In *White,* 971 F.2d at 1397, we ruled that a robot with mechanical features was not a "likeness" under § 3344. However, we specifically held open the possibility that a manikin molded to Vanna White's precise features, or one that was a caricature or bore an impressionistic resemblance to White might become a likeness for statutory purposes. *Id.* The degree to which these robots resemble, caricature, or bear an impressionistic resemblance to appellants is therefore clearly material to a claim of violation of Cal. Civ. Code § 3344. Summary judgment would have been appropriate upon remand only if *no* genuine issues of material fact concerning that degree of resemblance were raised by appellants. Fed. R. Civ. P. 56.

Despite the district court's assertions that no reasonable jury could find that the robots are "similar in any manner whatsoever to Plaintiffs," we respectfully disagree. Without making any judgment about the ultimate similarity of the figures to the appellants, we conclude from our own inspection of the robots that material facts exist that might cause a reasonable jury to find them sufficiently "like" the appellants to violate Cal. Civ. Code § 3344.

We reject appellees' assertion that *Fleet v. CBS,* 50 Cal. App. 4th 1911, 58 Cal. Rptr. 2d 645 (1996) is new controlling authority that requires us to revisit the determination on first appeal that appellants' § 3344 claims are not preempted by federal copyright law. *Wendt I,* 1995 WL 115571, at * 1. *Fleet* is not controlling new authority on the preemption issue. It holds that an actor may not bring an action for misappropriation under Cal. Civ. Code § 3344 when the *only* claimed exploitation occurred through the distribution of the actor's performance in a copyrighted movie. *Id.* at 651 ("Appellants may choose to call their claims misappropriation of right to publicity, but if all they are seeking is to prevent a party from exhibiting a copyrighted work they are making a claim equivalent to an exclusive right within the general scope of copyright.") (internal quotations omitted).

Appellants here are not seeking to prevent Paramount from exhibiting its copyrighted work in the *Cheers* series. As we stated in *Wendt I,* their "claims are not preempted by the federal copyright statute so long as they 'contain elements, such as the invasion of personal rights ... that are different in kind from copyright infringement.'" *Wendt I,* 1995 WL 115571 at * 1 (quoting *Waits v. Frito-Lay, Inc.,* 978 F.2d 1093, 1100 (9th Cir. 1992)) (citing H.R. Rep. No. 1476, 94th Cong., 2d Sess. 132 (1976)). The *Fleet* court acknowledged that it simply found a fact-specific exception to the general rule that "as a general proposition section 3344 is intended to protect rights which cannot be copyrighted." *Fleet,* 58 Cal. Rptr. 2d at 649.

Appellants' claims are not preempted by federal copyright law. Issues of material fact exist concerning the degree to which the robots are like the appellants. We reverse the grant of summary judgment on the claim under Cal. Civ. Code § 3344.

B. Common-Law Right of Publicity

California recognizes a common law right of privacy that includes protection against appropriation for the defendant's advantage of the plaintiff's name or likeness....

We have held that this common-law right of publicity protects more than the knowing use of a plaintiff's name or likeness for commercial purposes that is protected by Cal. Civ. Code § 3344. It also protects against appropriations of the plaintiff's identity by other means....

Appellees argue that the figures appropriate only the identities of the characters Norm and Cliff, to which Paramount owns the copyrights, and not the identities of Wendt and Ratzenberger, who merely portrayed those characters on television and retain no licensing rights to them. They argue that appellants may not claim an appropriation of identity by relying upon indicia, such as the *Cheers* Bar set, that are the property of, or licensee of, a copyright owner.

Appellants freely concede that they retain no rights to the characters Norm and Cliff; they argue that the figures, named "Bob" and "Hank," are not related to Paramount's copyright of the creative elements of the characters Norm and Cliff. They argue that it is the physical likeness to Wendt and Ratzenberger, not Paramount's characters, that has commercial value to Host.

While it is true that appellants' fame arose in large part through their participation in *Cheers,* an actor or actress does not lose the right to control the commercial exploitation of his or her likeness by portraying a fictional character.

Appellants have raised genuine issues of material fact concerning the degree to which the figures look like them. Because they have done so, appellants have also raised triable issues of fact as to whether or not appellees sought to appropriate their likenesses for their own advantage and whether they succeeded in doing so. The ultimate issue for the jury to decide is whether the defendants are commercially exploiting the likeness of the figures to Wendt and Ratzenberger intending to engender profits to their enterprises. We therefore reverse the grant of summary judgment on the common law right of publicity claim.

C. Unfair Competition

Section 43(a) of the Lanham Act (15 U.S.C. § 1125(a)) prohibits, *inter alia,* the use of any symbol or device which is likely to deceive consumers as to the association, sponsorship, or approval of goods or services by another person. The appellants' claim is for false endorsement—that by using an imitation of their unique physical characteristics, Host misrepresented their association with and endorsement of the *Cheers* bars concept.

In *Wendt I* we held that appellants would have a claim if "Host's conduct had created a likelihood of confusion as to whether plaintiffs were endorsing Host's product." 1995 WL 115571 at *3. In order to determine whether or not such confusion is likely to occur, we referred to a "well settled eight factor test" to be applied to celebrity endorsement cases....

On remand, however, the district court simply compared the robots with the appellants in the courtroom and awarded judgment because there was "no similarity at all." The district court erred in failing independently to analyze any of the other relevant factors to determine whether or not there was a likelihood of confusion *to consumers* as to whether appellants sponsored, approved of, or were otherwise associated with the *Cheers* bars....

A reasonable jury could conclude that most of the factors weigh in appellants' favor and that Host's alleged conduct creates at least the likelihood of consumer confusion. Whether appellants' Lanham Act claim should succeed, of course, is a matter for the jury. Accordingly, we reverse the dismissal of the unfair competition claim and remand....

Wendt v. Host Int'l, Inc.
197 F.3d 1284 (9th Cir. 1999)

KOZINSKI, Circuit Judge, with whom Judges KLEINFELD and TASHIMA join, dissenting from the order rejecting the suggestion for rehearing *en banc*:

Robots again. In *White v. Samsung Elecs. Am., Inc.*, 971 F.2d 1395, 1399 (9th Cir. 1992), we held that the right of publicity extends not just to the name, likeness, voice and signature of a famous person, but to anything at all that evokes that person's identity. The plaintiff there was Vanna White, Wheel of Fortune letter-turner extraordinaire; the offending robot stood next to a letter board, decked out in a blonde wig, Vanna-style gown and garish jewelry. Dissenting from our failure to take the case en banc, I argued that our broad application of the right of publicity put state law on a collision course with the federal rights of the copyright holder. *See* 989 F.2d 1512, 1517–18 (9th Cir. 1993).

The conflict in *White* was hypothetical, since the defendant (Samsung) did not have a license from the Wheel of Fortune copyright holder. Here it is concrete: The panel holds that *licensed* animatronic figures based on the copyrighted *Cheers* characters Norm and Cliff infringe on the rights of the actors who portrayed them. As I predicted, *White*'s voracious logic swallows up rights conferred by Congress under the Copyright Act.

I

Though a bit dated now, *Cheers* remains near and dear to the hearts of many TV viewers. Set in a friendly neighborhood bar in Boston, the show revolved around a familiar scene. Sam, the owner and bartender, entertained the boys with tales of his glory days pitching for the Red Sox. Coach piped in with sincere, obtuse advice. Diane and Frasier chattered self-importantly about Lord Byron. Carla terrorized patrons with acerbic comments. And there were Norm and Cliff, the two characters at issue here. Norm, a fat, endearing, oft-unemployed[1] accountant, parked himself at the corner of the bar, where he was joined by Cliff, a dweebish[2] mailman and something of a know-it-all windbag.[3] After eleven years on the air, the gang at *Cheers* became like family to many fans, ensuring many more years in syndication. *See* Gebe Martinez, *"Cheers" Fans Cry in Their Beers as Sitcom Ends Long Run*, L.A. Times, May 21, 1993, at B1.

---

1. Sam: "Hey, what's happening, Norm?"
Norm: "Well, it's a dog-eat-dog world, and I'm wearing Milk Bone underwear."
2. "There's no rule against postal workers not dating women. It just works out that way."
3. "It's a little known fact that the tan became popular in what is known as the Bronze Age."

Defendant Host International decided to tap into this keg of goodwill. After securing a license from Paramount, the copyright holder, Host opened a line of *Cheers* airport bars. To help get patrons into a *Cheers* mood, Host populated the bars with animatronic figures[4] resembling Norm and Cliff: One is fat; the other is dressed as a mailman.[5]

Plaintiffs George Wendt and John Ratzenberger, the only actors who ever portrayed Norm and Cliff, sued Host for unfair competition and violation of their right of publicity. Paramount intervened, claiming that its copyright preempted any claim Wendt and Ratzenberger might have under state law. The district court granted summary judgment for the defendants because it found that the robots didn't look like the plaintiffs: "[T]here is [no] similarity at all ... except that one of the robots, like one of the plaintiffs, is heavier than the other.... The facial features are totally different." 125 F.3d at 809. Relying on *White,* the panel here reverses but offers little explanation beyond the curt assertion that "material facts exist that might cause a reasonable jury to find [the robots] sufficiently 'like' [Wendt and Ratzenberger] to violate" their right of publicity. *Id.* at 810.

II

This case, unlike *White,* pits actor against copyright holder. The parties are fighting over the same bundle of intellectual property rights—the right to make dramatic representations of the characters Norm and Cliff. Host and Paramount assert their right under the Copyright Act to present the *Cheers* characters in airport bars; Wendt and Ratzenberger assert their right under California law to control the exploitation of their likenesses. But to millions of viewers, Wendt and Ratzenberger *are* Norm and Cliff; it's impossible to exploit the latter without also evoking thoughts about the former.

So who wins? The Copyright Act makes it simple, at least insofar as the plaintiffs interfere with Paramount's right to exploit the *Cheers* characters. Section 301 of the Copyright Act preempts any state law "legal or equitable rights that are equivalent to any of the exclusive rights within the general scope of copyright[.]" 17 U.S.C. § 301(a). The copyright to *Cheers* carries with it the right to make derivative works based on its characters. *See generally Warner Bros., Inc. v. American Broadcasting Cos.,* 720 F.2d 231, 235 (2d Cir. 1983) (Superman copyright belongs to Warner Brothers). The presentation of the robots in the *Cheers* bars is a derivative work, just like a TV clip, promotion, photograph, poster, sequel or dramatic rendering of an episode. Thus, under federal law, Host has the unconditional right to present robots that resemble Norm and Cliff.

Instead, the panel allows the plaintiffs to pick up where Vanna left off: Copyright or no copyright, anyone who wants to use a figure, statue, robot, drawing or poster that reminds the public of Wendt and Ratzenberger must first obtain (and pay for) their consent. This cannot be squared with the right of the copyright holder to recreate Norm and Cliff however it sees fit. At the very least, Paramount must be able to reproduce the characteristics that bring Norm and Cliff to mind.

The problem lies with the sweeping standard we adopted in *White.* The right of publicity, as defined by the state courts, is limited to using a celebrity's name, voice, face or signature. A copyright holder can generally avoid using any of these tangible elements in exploiting its copyright. *White* exploded the right of publicity to include anything that brings the celebrity to mind. *See White,* 971 F.2d at 1399. It's inevitable that so broad and

---

4. As best the record discloses, these are life-size stuffed dolls that move somewhat and play prerecorded quips.

5. In a half-hearted attempt to avoid litigation, Host changed the robots' names to "Hank" and "Bob."

ill-defined a property right will trench on the rights of the copyright holder. According to the panel, Paramount and Host may not use Norm and Cliff in a way that reminds people of the actors who played them and whose identity is therefore fused in the public mind. This is a daunting burden. Can Warner Brothers exploit Rhett Butler without also reminding people of Clark Gable? Can Paramount cast Shelley Long in *The Brady Bunch Movie* without creating a triable issue of fact as to whether it is treading on Florence Henderson's right of publicity? How about Dracula and Bela Lugosi? Ripley and Sigourney Weaver? Kramer and Michael Richards?

When portraying a character who was portrayed by an actor, it is impossible to recreate the character without evoking the image of the actor in the minds of viewers. Suppose the *Seinfeld* minions create a spin-off called *Kramer*. One of the *Seinfeld* characters was Newman, a fat mailman. Suppose Wayne Knight—the actor who played Newman—won't do *Kramer*. So *Kramer* brings in someone else to play Newman, a corpulent actor who (when dressed as a mailman) reminds people of Wayne Knight. What happens when Knight sues? Under *White* and the panel decision here, Knight can go to trial on a claim that the new Newman evokes his (Knight's) identity, even though Castle Rock owns the rights to make derivative works based on *Seinfeld*. It would be no defense that everyone knows the new actor is not Wayne Knight; no one, after all, thinks the robots here or in *White* were, in fact, Wendt, Ratzenberger or White. So long as the casting director comes up with a new Newman who *reminds* the public of the old Newman (i.e. Knight), Knight has a right-of-publicity claim that will at least survive summary judgment. Under the unbounded right of publicity announced in *White*, copyright holders will seldom be able to avoid trial when sued for infringement of the right to publicity. Remember Vanna: Even though the robot looked nothing like her, a jury awarded her $400,000. *See* Vanna White Wins Suit, Wall St. J., Jan. 24, 1994, at B2.[6]

III

The panel's refusal to recognize copyright preemption puts us in conflict with the Seventh Circuit in *Baltimore Orioles, Inc. v. Major League Baseball Players Ass'n*, 805 F.2d 663 (7th Cir. 1986). *Baltimore Orioles* held that the baseball clubs—not the players—own the rights to baseball telecasts under copyright law, and the players can't use their state law right of publicity to veto the telecast of their performance. This was so even though the telecast (obviously) used the players' identities and likenesses.

… The same reasoning applies here: The plaintiffs' right to control the use of their likeness is preempted by Paramount's right to exploit the Norm and Cliff characters however it sees fit. If Wendt and Ratzenberger wanted to control how the *Cheers* characters were portrayed after they left the show, they should have negotiated for it beforehand.

IV

Coming home to roost is yet another problem I warned about in *White*—that a broad reading of the state right of publicity runs afoul of the dormant Copyright Clause, which preempts state intellectual property laws to the extent they "prejudice the interests of other States." *Goldstein v. California*, 412 U.S. 546, 558 (1973). Just as a state

---

6. To avoid going to trial in such a situation, producers will have to cast new actors who look and sound very different from the old ones. A *Seinfeld* spin-off thus ends up in a bizarre world where a skinny Newman sits down to coffee with a svelte George, a stocky Kramer, a fat Jerry and a lanky blonde Elaine. Not only is goodwill associated with the old show lost, the artistic freedom of the screenwriters and producers is severely cramped.

law regulating the length of trucks is invalid under the dormant Commerce Clause if it poses an undue burden on interstate commerce, so California's right of publicity law is invalid if it substantially interferes with federal copyright law, even absent preemptive legislation.

A copyright licensee must be able to exercise rights which are inherently federal in nature without worrying that 50 separate states will burden those rights. This is most obviously true when state law restricts the display of derivative works outside the borders of its state. Yet that is exactly what the panel approves here: Plaintiffs are using California law to stop Host from displaying a copyrighted work in Kansas City and Cleveland. Why California should set the national standard for what is a permissible use of a licensed derivative work is beyond me. Rather than construe the right of publicity narrowly to avoid this constitutional conundrum, the panel compounds *White*'s errors by enforcing California's right of publicity way beyond California's borders.

V

The First Amendment concerns raised by *White* are even more pressing here. *White* was an advertisement and therefore subject to the less demanding commercial speech standard of *Central Hudson Gas & Elec. Corp. v. Public Serv. Comm.*, 447 U.S. 557, 561–63 (1980). Here, the portrayal of the *Cheers* characters is core protected speech: Using Norm and Cliff dummies in a *Cheers*-themed bar is a dramatic presentation.[8] It's like a play. *Cheers* may not have the social impact of *Hair*, but it's a literary work nonetheless, worthy of the highest First Amendment protection from intrusive state laws like California's right-of-publicity statute. *See Cardtoons, L.C. v. Major League Baseball Players Ass'n*, 95 F.3d 959, 970–72 (10th Cir. 1996). Host did not plaster Wendt's face on a billboard with a Budweiser logo. It cashed in on the *Cheers* goodwill by creatively putting its familiar mise-en-scene to work. The robots are a new derivation of a copyrighted work, not unlike a TV series based on a movie or a Broadway play based on a novel. The novelty of using animatronic figures based on TV characters ought to prick up our ears to First Amendment concerns. Instead we again let the right of publicity snuff out creativity.

VI

As I noted in *White*, "No California statute, no California court has actually tried to reach this far. It is ironic that it is we who plant this kudzu in the fertile soil of our federal system." 989 F.2d at 1519. We pass up yet another opportunity to root out this weed. Instead, we feed it Miracle-Gro. I dissent.

––––––––––

Notes and Questions

1. As the cases note, section 301 contains two requirements that must be met for a state law to be preempted. First, the subject matter of the state-law claim must fall within the subject matter of copyright as described in sections 102 and 103. Second, the rights asserted under state law must be "equivalent" to any of the exclusive the rights contained in section 106.

––––––––––

8. No doubt the decision to put animatronic Norm and Cliff figures in the bars was profit-driven. But that doesn't mean *Central Hudson* applies: The Supreme Court limits the outhouse of commercial speech to pure advertising—speech that does no more than propose a commercial transaction. *Virginia State Bd. of Pharmacy v. Virginia Citizens Consumer Council, Inc.*, 425 U.S. 748, 762 (1976).

2. Section 102(a) of the 1976 Copyright Act grants copyright protection to "original works of authorship fixed in any tangible medium of expression," and lists eight categories of works (including pictorial, graphic and sculptural works; audiovisual works; and sound recordings). Section 103 specifies that the subject matter of copyright includes compilations (selections and arrangements of preexisting material) and derivative works (works based on one or more preexisting works), so long as they are made lawfully. Both sections are subject to the idea/expression dichotomy, which is codified in § 102(b). Thus, copyright protection extends only to the original expression of authors, and not to the ideas contained within their works.

As noted in *Baltimore Orioles*, Congress intended the scope of preemption to be broader than the scope of copyright protection. "As long as a work fits within one of the general subject matter categories of sections 102 and 103, the bill prevents the States from protecting it even if it fails to achieve Federal statutory copyright because it is too minimal or lacking in originality to qualify, or because it has fallen into the public domain." H.R. Rep. No. 94-1476, at 131 (1976).

3. Nonetheless, these cases disagree sharply on how to interpret the subject-matter requirement of § 301. *Baltimore Orioles* finds that the telecasts of baseball players' performances are fixed in a tangible medium, and *Laws* finds that a sound recording of Laws' voice was fixed in a tangible medium, leaving the claims in those cases potentially subject to preemption. But *Toney* and the panel decisions in *Wendt* hold that a person's "identity" or "likeness" is not fixed, and therefore the right of publicity claim cannot be preempted.

Can these decisions be reconciled? Both *Baltimore Orioles* and *Laws* involve performances that were fixed on videotape and audiotape, respectively. But Wendt's and Ratzenberger's performances as Norm and Cliff were also fixed on videotape; and the claim in *Toney* involved the use of a particular photograph of the plaintiff, which had been fixed with her consent. In both *Laws* and *Toney*, the plaintiff bargained for a contract that limited the use of the copyrighted work; but in *Laws* the court says that the plaintiff's only recourse is to sue for breach of contract; while in *Toney*, the court allows suit for violating the right of publicity.

It may be interesting to note that the panel in *Toney* originally held unanimously that the photograph was fixed and that the claim *was* preempted. 384 F.3d 486 (7th Cir. 1986). The firestorm of criticism that followed the decision prompted the panel the grant the petition for rehearing and to reverse its prior decision. Was the problem with the original decision the holding that the photograph was fixed, or that the rights were equivalent, or both?

4. Moving to the second requirement, section 106 grants the copyright owner five exclusive rights. How should a court decide if the state-law claim is "equivalent" to one of these rights? Two principal approaches have emerged. Some courts ask whether the state right is violated by the mere act of reproducing, adapting, publicly distributing, publicly performing or publicly displaying the copyrighted work. If so, the state-law claim is equivalent. Other courts ask whether the state-law claim requires "extra elements" that are not required for a copyright infringement claim. However, as noted in *Baltimore Orioles*, the "extra elements" must be ones that make the action qualitatively different from an infringement action. Elements such as scienter, knowledge, intent, or "commercial immorality" generally do not suffice to save the state-law claim.

Once again, these cases are irrevocably split on how to apply these tests to a right of publicity claim. *Baltimore Orioles* takes a "mere act of reproducing" approach, as does

Fleet (a California case relied on in *Laws* and distinguished in *Wendt*). *Laws* applies an extra element test, but finds that the element of "commercial use" is "*not* enough to qualitatively distinguish Law's right of publicity claim from a claim in copyright" (emphasis added). *Toney*, however, finds that the element of "commercial purpose" *is* enough to distinguish the right of publicity claim from a copyright infringement. The *Wendt* panel opinions assert (without analysis) that the right of publicity claims are not preempted because they contain "elements, such as the invasion of personal rights ... that are different in kind from copyright infringement." Exactly what is it that makes the right of publicity claim in *Wendt* different from a claim of unauthorized preparation of an adaptation or derivative work?

5. It makes a lot more sense to hold that a state-law claim is not preempted when the gravamen of the claim is false endorsement. The implication of endorsement arises from the use of the plaintiff's "identity" in *any* form, not just in the particular (fixed) form used; and the extra element of likelihood of confusion surely makes the claim different in kind from an infringement claim. But as we have seen, the right of publicity does not require proof of false endorsement or likelihood of confusion. When the court in *Toney* states that "[t]he basis of a right of publicity claim concerns the message—whether the plaintiff endorses, or appears to endorse the product in question," that is simply an incorrect statement of Illinois law.

Like *Toney*, *Wendt* can also be viewed as a "false endorsement" case. Although Judge Kozinski views the robots as simply a derivative work of *Cheers* (a type of "performance art"), the panel seems to think that the "identity" of Wendt and Ratzenberger are being used to advertise the restaurant services at issue. If that is the rationale, the decision makes more sense: surely Wendt and Ratzenberger have a right not to have their likenesses used to sell products or services without their consent. But again, nothing in the California right of publicity statute or common law requires a showing of false endorsement in order to prevail.

Assuming that state-law false endorsement claims should not be preempted, what is the best way to achieve that goal? Reasoning that the claim involves "identity" rather than a fixed work seems far too broad, eliminating from preemption claims that conflict with federal copyright law; but can we in good faith distinguish right of publicity claims involving false endorsement from those that do not, when the cause of action does not require proof of falsity or confusion in order to prevail? Perhaps the problem is with the "tests" developed by the courts, which seem inadequate to the task. Certainly the results of the cases are more easily reconciled than their rationales.

It is worth noting that Wendt and Ratzenberger also included a claim for "false endorsement" under §43(a) of the Lanham Act. Because the Lanham Act is a federal law, it cannot be preempted by the Copyright Act or by the Supremacy Clause. *See* 17 U.S.C. §301(d) ("Nothing in this title annuls or limits any rights or remedies under any other Federal statute."). This is consistent with the notion that state-law claims based on false endorsement also should not be preempted.

6. As Judge Kozinski notes, his dissent in *Wendt* was not his first encounter with the problem of copyright preemption. In his dissent in *White v. Samsung Electronics America, Inc.* (reprinted in Chapter VIII), he expressed the problem as follows:

> By refusing to recognize a parody exception to the right of publicity, the panel directly contradicts the federal Copyright Act. Samsung didn't merely parody Vanna White. It parodied Vanna White appearing in "Wheel of Fortune," a copyrighted television show, and parodies of copyrighted works are governed by federal copyright law....

It's impossible to parody a movie or a TV show without at the same time "evok[ing]" the "identit[ies]" of the actors.[26] You can't have a mock *Star Wars* without a mock Luke Skywalker, Han Solo and Princess Leia, which in turn means a mock Mark Hamill, Harrison Ford and Carrie Fisher. You can't have a mock *Batman* commercial without a mock Batman, which means someone emulating the mannerisms of Adam West or Michael Keaton. *See* Carlos V. Lozano, *West Loses Lawsuit over Batman TV Commercial,* L.A. Times, Jan. 18, 1990, at B3 (describing Adam West's right of publicity lawsuit over a commercial produced under license from DC Comics, owner of the Batman copyright). The public's right to make a fair use parody and the copyright owner's right to license a derivative work are useless if the parodist is held hostage by every actor whose "identity" he might need to "appropriate."

Our court is in a unique position here. State courts are unlikely to be particularly sensitive to federal preemption, which, after all, is a matter of first concern to the federal courts. The Supreme Court is unlikely to consider the issue because the right of publicity seems so much a matter of state law. That leaves us. It's our responsibility to keep the right of publicity from taking away federally granted rights, either from the public at large or from a copyright owner. We must make sure state law doesn't give the Vanna Whites and Adam Wests of the world a veto over fair use parodies of the shows in which they appear, or over copyright holders' exclusive right to license derivative works of those shows. In a case where the copyright owner isn't even a party—where no one has the interests of copyright owners at heart—the majority creates a rule that greatly diminishes the rights of copyright holders in this circuit.

989 F.2d at 1518–19.

7. Judge Kozinski's dissent in *Wendt* also highlights another substantial difficulty. On what basis is California law being used to enjoin the use of Norm and Cliff robots in Missouri and Ohio? Not only does this raise an issue of choice of law (unaddressed in the panel opinion), but it also raises a Constitutional issue, which Judge Kozinski characterizes as the Dormant Copyright Clause (by analogy to the Dormant Commerce Clause). As Kozinski stated in his dissent in *White*:

The broader and more ill-defined one state's right of publicity, the more it interferes with the legitimate interests of other states. A limited right that applies to unauthorized use of name and likeness probably does not run afoul of the Copyright Clause, but the majority's protection of "identity" is quite another story. Under the majority's approach, any time anybody in the United States— even somebody who lives in a state with a very narrow right of publicity—creates an ad, he takes the risk that it might remind some segment of the public of somebody, perhaps somebody with only a local reputation, somebody the advertiser has never heard of. So you made a commercial in Florida and one of the characters reminds Reno residents of their favorite local TV anchor (a California domiciliary)? Pay up.

This is an intolerable result, as it gives each state far too much control over artists in other states. . . .

---

26. 17 U.S.C. § 301(b)(1) limits the Copyright Act's preemptive sweep to subject matter "fixed in any tangible medium of expression," but White's identity—her look as the hostess of Wheel of Fortune—is definitely fixed: It consists entirely of her appearances in a fixed, copyrighted TV show. *See Baltimore Orioles v. Major League Baseball Players Ass'n,* 805 F.2d 663, 675 & n.22 (7th Cir. 1986).

989 F.2d at 1519. For an analysis of the problem in a different context, *see* David S. Welkowitz, *Preemption, Extraterritoriality, and the Problem of State Antidilution Laws*, 67 Tulane L. Rev. 1 (1992). The extraterritorial effect of rights of publicity is explored in Chapter XIV.

8. When an existing sound recording is used in a new work, two copyrights are implicated. The first is the copyright in the *musical work* (the notes and lyrics), which is initially owned by the composer and lyricist; and the second is the copyright in the *sound recording* (the particular recorded performance), which is typically owned by the record label (as assignee of the performer and sound engineers). Unlike the copyright in the musical work, the copyright in a sound recording is expressly limited as follows:

> The exclusive rights of the owner of copyright in a sound recording ... do not extend to the making or duplication of another sound recording that consists entirely of an independent fixation of other sounds, even though such sounds imitate or simulate those in the copyrighted sound recording.

17 U.S.C. § 114(b) (emphasis added). In other words, anyone can make a *sound-alike* recording without violating the copyright of the existing sound recording, as long as the person obtains a license to use the underlying musical work.

Now reconsider *Midler v. Ford Motor Co.*, which we encountered in Chapter II. There, Ford did exactly what section 114(b) says is permitted: it obtained a license to use the song "Do You Want to Dance," and it hired a singer to imitate the voice of Bette Midler to make a new recording. Should this claim be preempted by federal copyright law? How is this case different from *Laws*?

9. For an academic analysis of the preemption problem, and a proposed solution, *see* Jennifer E. Rothman, *Copyright Preemption and the Right of Publicity*, 36 U.C. Davis L. Rev. 199 (2002).

Chapter XI

Other Defenses to Rights of Publicity

A. Consent

The essence of the right of publicity is that one should not exploit the identity of another without that person's consent. This case raises the issue of whether and how consent is properly obtained.

Miller v. Glenn Miller Prods.
454 F.3d 975 (9th Cir. 2006)

PER CURIAM.

Steven and Jonnie Miller, adopted children of Helen Miller, wife of the world-renowned bandleader Glenn Miller, and their exclusive licensing agent CMG Worldwide Inc. (collectively "Appellants") appeal from the district court's order granting defendant Glenn Miller Productions, Inc. ("GMP") summary judgment and dismissing their complaint on the basis of laches. *See Miller v. Glenn Miller Prods.*, 318 F. Supp. 2d 923 (C.D. Cal. 2004). GMP cross-appeals the district court's determination that it is engaged in unauthorized sublicensing. In his well-reasoned opinion, District Judge A. Howard Matz ruled that a licensee of trademark and related publicity rights may not sublicense those rights to third parties without express permission from the original licensor. We agree with this extension of the well-established "sublicensing rule" from copyright and patent law to the licensing of trademark and related publicity rights such as occurred here, and with the district court's reasons for extending the rule. The district court also correctly ruled, however, that Appellants are barred by the doctrine of laches from taking legal action now, based on undisputed evidence establishing that they should have known of GMP's allegedly infringing activities well beyond the statutory period for bringing suit. Accordingly, we affirm and adopt the district court's thorough opinion [with certain exceptions not relevant here].... We also reprint the incorporated portions as an appendix to this opinion....

APPENDIX

MATZ, District Judge:

This matter is before the Court on Plaintiffs' Motion for Summary Adjudication and Defendant's Motion for Summary Judgment.

Figure 11-1. Glenn Miller

FACTUAL BACKGROUND

The principal facts of this case are either undisputed or not genuinely disputed. Glenn Miller was a popular musician and band leader who formed the Glenn Miller Orchestra in 1938. During the 1930s and 1940s, Glenn Miller recorded and released sound recordings using his name and the name "Glenn Miller Orchestra." On December 15, 1944, Glenn Miller was aboard an armed services airplane that crashed in the English Channel. One year later, he was pronounced dead. Glenn Miller's last will and testament did not contain an express provision bequeathing his publicity rights, trademarks or other intellectual property rights. His widow, Helen Miller, inherited the residue of his will, which would include whatever intellectual property rights he had.

On either April 20, 1956 or April 23, 1956, David Mackay, Sr. (Glenn Miller's close friend and lawyer during his lifetime) incorporated Glenn Miller Productions, Inc. ("GMP").... At the first Board of Director's meeting, David Mackay, Sr. was elected President of GMP and he remained president until his death in 1980. Helen Miller was elected Vice-President of GMP and she served in that role until her death in 1966....

Sometime between April 25, 1956 and June 6, 1956 (in any case, shortly after GMP was incorporated), Helen Miller executed a written license agreement (the "1956 license agreement") in favor of GMP. The agreement consisted of one paragraph which read, in its entirety:

> For and in consideration of the sum of ONE AND NO 100THS ($1.00) DOL-
> LAR and other good and valuable consideration, the undersigned, individually

and as Executrix of the estate of Glenn Miller deceased, hereby grants to Glenn Miller Productions, Inc. the right and license to use the name and likeness of Glenn Miller and the library of music belonging to the Estate of Glenn Miller and/or the undersigned in connection with the business activities of Glenn Miller Productions, Inc.

Notwithstanding the amount of consideration (*i.e.*, $1.00) specified in the 1956 license agreement, the minutes of a June 6, 1956 GMP Board meeting state that the Board agreed to pay Helen Miller $13,000 per year in return for permission to use Glenn Miller's name, likeness and library of music (the same rights conveyed by the 1956 license agreement).

Sometime after the 1956 license agreement was executed, GMP began operating an orchestra called the Glenn Miller Orchestra and engaging in a variety of promotional activities.... [I]n 1961, GMP authorized ... a production company to produce a television show on CBS titled "Glenn Miller Time" featuring the Glenn Miller Orchestra.... [T]he production company received the rights to "use the Glenn Miller name, picture, likeness, music and arrangements in connection with the television show, and usual accompanying promotion and publicity." There is no evidence in the record that Helen Miller objected to this licensing of Glenn Miller's name, likeness and publicity rights....

In 1965, GMP obtained a federal trademark registration for the "Glenn Miller Orchestra" mark, which it renewed in 1985. Helen Miller died on June 2, 1966.... Upon Helen Miller's death, David Mackay, Jr. (the son of David Mackay, Sr.) was appointed vice president of GMP (Helen Miller's former position).

Like her deceased husband's will, Helen Miller's will did not contain an express provision which bequeathed any of Glenn Miller's publicity rights, trademarks or other intellectual property rights that she may have inherited. Her two adopted children, Steven Miller and Jonnie Soper Miller, would have inherited any such rights only through the residue of Helen Miller's will.

In the late 1970s, Steven and Jonnie Miller filed three separate lawsuits against David Mackay, Sr.... based in part on a dispute over the ownership of GMP. On April 23, 1980, the parties entered into an oral stipulation ("the settlement agreement").... As part of the settlement agreement, the parties agreed as follows:

> Petitioners [Jonnie and Steven Miller] ratify and confirm the agreement dated April 25, 1956, made by Helen Miller granting *inter alia* Glenn Miller Productions, Inc. 'The right and license to use the name and likeness of Glenn Miller and/or [Helen Miller]' and petitioners agree not to directly or indirectly organize and/or operate or cause to be organized and/or operate a band or orchestra using the name of Glenn Miller or any facsimile thereof. Respondent [presumably, David Mackay, Sr. or GMP] agrees to pay the petitioners the sum of $50,000.00 ($25,000.00 to each petitioner) in consideration of Glenn Miller Productions, Inc., past and continued use in perpetuity of the name, likeness and library of music of Glenn Miller.

... On May 12, 1980, David Mackay, Sr. died. Upon his death, David Mackay, Jr. became the president of GMP.

Since at least the 1980s, an ensemble calling itself the Glenn Miller Orchestra has performed at many events and festivals.... Since 1981, GMP has operated one regular Glenn Miller Orchestra band, as well as "special units" of the Glenn Miller Orchestra which supplement the regular Glenn Miller Orchestra band during times of high demand. These "special units" are comprised of different band leaders and musicians hired and supervised by GMP, and they work on a performance-by-performance basis....

Also since 1988, GMP has sub-licensed to third parties the right to operate orchestras called the Glenn Miller Orchestra. These sub-licensees have operated Glenn Miller Orchestras in the United States, Canada, Germany and the United Kingdom. Currently, GMP has two sub-licensees: Schmidt & Salden GmbH & Co., which operates in Germany, and Ray McVay, who operates in the United Kingdom. Both sub-license agreements set forth detailed "performance standards" which provide, for example, that the orchestra shall consist of at least 16 musicians plus a leader and one male and one female vocalist, that the sub-licensee's bandstands must be similar to that used by the Glenn Miller Orchestra operated by GMP, that the orchestra shall consist of a particular number of various types of instruments, and that the orchestra "shall at all times behave and be groomed in accordance with the highest standards of the Glenn Miller Orchestra." The sub-license agreements also provide that a failure to conform to those standards constitutes a default. Finally, the sub-license agreements provide that they are not assignable or transferable. Counsel for GMP represented at the hearing on these motions that David Mackay, Jr. assures that the sub-licensees are complying with the terms of the sub-license agreements by observing their performances and monitoring their bookings.

Beginning in 1983, GMP also has been selling merchandise, including cassette tapes, videotapes, CDs, DVDs, t-shirts and polo shirts bearing the "Glenn Miller Orchestra" mark or the "GMO" logo. This merchandise is sold primarily at GMO performances.... Since September of 1998, merchandise has also been available on GMP's website.... Counsel for GMP represented at the hearing that GMP's annual worldwide revenue is approximately $2 million dollars.

During the 1980s and 1990s, counsel for Steven and Jonnie Miller sent at least eight cease and desist letters to third parties who were not authorized to use or otherwise exploit Glenn Miller's name or likeness, but who were, nevertheless, apparently doing so.... However, the Millers never sent any cease and desist letters to GMP. Indeed, before they filed this lawsuit, the Millers had never communicated with GMP regarding any qualitative aspect of GMP's business activities, such as its operation of the Glenn Miller Orchestra, its sublicensing to third parties of the right to operate a Glenn Miller Orchestra, or its sale of merchandise bearing the "Glenn Miller Orchestra" mark.

In 1994, the Millers hired the Roger Richman Agency, for a period of two years, to be their exclusive licensing agent for use of the Glenn Miller name "in connection with all video recording and tapes; look-alikes; sound-alikes; advertising; commercials; theater and other dramatic uses; animation; newspaper; book and magazine syndication; endorsements; promotions; premiums; sale of merchandise and/or use in all services." However, excluded from the grant of rights to the Roger Richman Agency were rights previously granted by GMP to certain third parties, including "Orchestras of Glenn Miller Productions, Inc., a New York Corporation." In 1996, the Millers hired Plaintiff CMG Worldwide, Inc. ("CMG") to be their exclusive licensing agent, subject to the same exclusion for the pre-existing rights of "Orchestras of Glenn Miller Productions, Inc., a New York Corporation." ...

Steven Miller claims that he first learned in 2000 or 2001 that there was more than one functioning Glenn Miller Orchestra, although he does not specify how he learned. Steven Miller also claims that he did not learn until April 2003 (after filing this lawsuit) that GMP has entered into sub-license agreements with third parties to use Glenn Miller's name and likeness in the United States and in foreign counties. The record does not indicate when Steven Miller learned that GMP has been selling merchandise bearing the Glenn Miller Orchestra mark.

On June 22, 2003, Steven Miller, Jonnie Miller, and CMG Worldwide, Inc. (collectively "Plaintiffs") filed this action against GMP, asserting eleven claims for relief [including]: (1) breach of written contract [and] (3) infringement of statutory right of publicity..., all based on GMP's sale of merchandise bearing Glenn Miller's name, likeness and identity, and GMP's sub-licensing to third parties of the right to operate orchestras named the Glenn Miller Orchestra.

Plaintiffs currently move for summary adjudication of one narrow issue in this case. They seek a ruling from the Court that GMP may not sub-license any intellectual property rights conveyed to it pursuant to the 1956 license agreement without express permission from the licensors (now the Millers), and therefore that GMP's admitted sub-licensing constitutes a material breach of the 1956 license agreement. Defendant has filed a cross-motion for summary judgment, contending that the 1956 license agreement and 1980 settlement agreement give GMP the right to sell merchandise and to operate and sub-license multiple bands, and in any case, that all of Plaintiffs' claims are barred by the doctrine of laches. Although the Court ultimately finds that Plaintiffs' claims are barred by ... laches, the Court will proceed to examine the other issues raised by the parties because the Court anticipates an appeal from the laches ruling and believes that if the Court is found to be in error, on remand it would be in the parties' best interest to have their respective rights and obligations previously clarified. Indeed, such clarification may assist the parties in settling their surprisingly bitter and very costly dispute.

ANALYSIS

* * *

B. *Plaintiffs' Motion for Summary Adjudication: May GMP Sub-License Intellectual Property Rights Without Plaintiffs' Permission?*

It is well established in patent and copyright law that a patent or copyright licensee may not sub-license his licensed intellectual property rights without express permission from the licensor. *See Gardner v. Nike, Inc.,* 279 F.3d 774 (9th Cir. 2002); *Everex Systems v. Cadtrak Corp.,* 89 F.3d 673, 679 (9th Cir. 1996). (The Court will henceforth refer to this rule as "the sub-licensing rule.") Although the Ninth Circuit has not addressed whether the sub-licensing rule applies to trademark licenses, the courts that have addressed the issue have uniformly held it does, and thus that a trademark licensee may not sub-license a mark without express permission from the licensor. *See Tap Publications, Inc. v. Chinese Yellow Pages (New York), Inc.,* 925 F. Supp. 212, 218 (S.D.N.Y. 1996); *In re Travelot Co.,* 286 B.R. 447, 455 (Bankr. S.D. Ga.2002); J. Thomas McCarthy, *McCarthy on Trademarks and Unfair Competition,* § 18:43 (4th ed.) (hereinafter "*McCarthy*"). The reasoning behind the courts' extension of the sub-licensing rule to the trademark context is that, "[s]ince the licensor-trademark owner has the duty to control the quality of goods sold under its mark, it must have the right to pass upon the abilities of new potential licensees." *McCarthy, supra,* § 25:33.

In Plaintiffs' motion for summary adjudication, Plaintiffs ask the Court to apply the sub-licensing rule to trademark licenses. Plaintiffs also ask the Court to extend the sub-licensing rule to licenses of publicity rights. Finally, Plaintiffs seek a ruling that because the 1956 license agreement did not grant GMP express permission to sub-license, GMP does not have the right to sub-license any intellectual property rights it obtained under the 1956 license agreement.

1. *Defendant's Threshold Arguments That the 1956 Agreement Did Not Convey a License.*

Defendant argues, first, that as a matter of contract law, the 1956 agreement between Helen Miller and GMP did not convey a license. Defendant also argues that even if the parties did intend the agreement to convey a license, at the time, there were no existing trademark rights that could be licensed.

a. *The Only Reasonable Interpretation of the 1956 Agreement is That it Conveys to GMP Both a Trademark License and a License of Glenn Miller's Publicity Rights.*

… The 1956 license agreement conveyed to GMP "the right and license to use the name and likeness of Glenn Miller … in connection with the business activities of [GMP]." The license agreement does not explicitly convey to GMP either the right to license any existing Glenn Miller trademark or Glenn Miller's publicity rights, or both. However, the terms "name" and/or "likeness" are found in both the Lanham Act definition of a trademark and in the definitions of California's statutory and common law rights to publicity.…

It is undisputed that Helen Miller executed the 1956 license agreement shortly after incorporating GMP.… GMP's Certificate of Incorporation provided that GMP was authorized to "manufacture, purchase, sell and generally to trade and deal in and with goods, wares, products and merchandise of every kind, nature and description" as well as to "organize, own, operate, manage, direct and control, directly or through others, one or more orchestras or musical organizations." It is hard to imagine that GMP would be able to sell and trade merchandise and operate orchestras bearing the Glenn Miller mark without exploiting Glenn Miller's identity or likeness for promotional purposes. Likewise, it is hard to imagine that GMP could exploit Glenn Miller's publicity rights without using a trademark containing the Glenn Miller name. Therefore, the Court finds that 1956 agreement is susceptible to only one reasonable interpretation—that it conveys both a trademark license and a license of Glenn Miller's publicity rights.

b. *The Court Rejects GMP's Arguments That, as a Matter of Law, the 1956 Agreement Could Not Have Conveyed a Trademark License.*

GMP next argues that regardless of how the terms are construed, as a matter of law, the 1956 agreement could not have conveyed a trademark license to GMP because neither Plaintiffs nor their predecessors owned a "Glenn Miller" trademark in 1956. Therefore, GMP argues, the 1956 agreement must have conveyed only a license of Glenn Miller's publicity rights. This argument is unpersuasive.

An individual may acquire trademark protection in a personal name in one of two ways. First, an individual may obtain a federal trademark registration from the Patent and Trademark Office. It is undisputed that neither Plaintiffs nor their predecessors have, at any time, obtained a federal registration for the mark "Glenn Miller." Second, an individual may prove that through usage, a personal name has acquired a secondary meaning. "Secondary meaning is the consumer's association of the mark with a particular source or sponsor." *See E. & J. Gallo Winery v. Gallo Cattle Co.*, 967 F.2d 1280, 1291 (9th Cir. 1992).…

Plaintiffs present evidence of pre-1956 advertising and use of the Glenn Miller name in connection with the sale of goods and services, such as radio shows, advertisements for agents, record labels, cigarettes, transcription services, concerts, record compilations, musical instruments, commemorative clothing, photographs and specialty items. This evidence is sufficient to permit a reasonable jury to conclude that by 1956, consumers associated the name "Glenn Miller" with a particular source or quality of product, and thus that the Glenn Miller name had acquired a secondary meaning. Therefore, the Court rejects GMP's argument that the 1956 agreement could not have conveyed a trademark license because in 1956 Helen Miller had no trademark to convey.…

Having found, first, that the only reasonable interpretation of the language of the 1956 agreement is that it conveyed both a trademark license and a license of Glenn Miller's publicity rights, and second, that a jury could reasonably find that Helen Miller owned a trademark that she could license, the Court now will turn to the merits of Plaintiffs' summary adjudication motion.

2. *The Policy Reasons For the Sub-Licensing Rule in the Patent and Copyright Contexts Support Extending the Rule to the Trademark Context.*

Acting on its own, GMP has sub-licensed to third parties the rights it acquired in the 1956 agreement. Could it do so, lawfully? In *Harris v. Emus Records Corp.*, 734 F.2d 1329 (9th Cir. 1984), the Ninth Circuit addressed for the first time whether under the 1909 Copyright Act, a copyright licensee could transfer his license to a third party without permission from the original licensor. The Ninth Circuit held that a copyright licensee could not do so. *Id.* at 1334. In support of its ruling, the Ninth Circuit discussed several policy issues, including that a copyright licensor's retained rights in the copyright would be jeopardized if the licensee could sub-license without notifying or receiving permission from him. *Id.* The Ninth Circuit reasoned: "By licensing rather than assigning his interest in the copyright, the owner reserves certain rights, including that of collecting royalties. His ability to monitor use would be jeopardized by allowing sublicensing without notice." *Id.* Eighteen years later, in *Gardner v. Nike, Inc.*, 279 F.3d 774, 781 (9th Cir. 2002), the Ninth Circuit held that the same rule applied to the 1976 Copyright Act, for the same reason. In addition to agreeing with the *Harris* court's concern about the ability of a copyright licensor to monitor use, the Ninth Circuit also recognized that in the absence of such a requirement, disputes between a licensor and a licensee regarding whether a sub-licensee was acting within the scope of the original license would trigger litigation (an undesirable result). *Id.*

The policy rationales cited by the Ninth Circuit in *Harris* and *Gardner* apply with equal force to the sub-licensing of trademarks.... [A] trademark owner has an affirmative duty to supervise and control the licensee's use of its mark, in order to protect the public's expectation that all products sold under a particular mark derive from a common source and are of like quality. *See McCarthy, supra,* §§ 18:42, 18:48. Licensors who fail to meet this obligation may lose their right to enforce the trademark license. *Id.* § 18:48. Common sense suggests that if a trademark licensee could unilaterally sub-license a mark without notifying or obtaining consent from the licensor, then a trademark licensor would lose his ability to police his mark, thereby becoming estopped from enforcing his ownership rights vis-a-vis the licensee. Such a result is illogical, undesirable, and at odds with the nature of intellectual property rights. Moreover, if a trademark licensor could not control the capacity of a licensee to sub-license its mark, then disputes about the suitability of a potential sub-licensee or about whether a sub-licensee is acting within the scope of the original license would trigger litigation. As the Ninth Circuit recognized in *Gardner,* this result is also undesirable.

The Court acknowledges that ... there are "fundamental differences" between patent and copyright law on the one hand, and trademark law on the other hand. For example, while the basic policies underlying copyright and patent protection are to encourage creative authorship and invention, the purposes of trademark protection are to protect the public's expectation regarding the source and quality of goods. However, despite these differences, copyright and trademark licensors share a common retained interest in the ownership of their intellectual property—an interest that would be severely diminished if a licensee were allowed to sub-license without the licensor's express permission. For these reasons, the Court finds that the policies underlying the sub-licensing rule in patent and copyright law apply with equal force to trademark law. Accordingly, a trademark licensee such as GMP may not sub-license without express permission from the original licensor.

3. *The Same Policies Also Support an Extension of the Sub-licensing Rule to Licenses of Publicity Rights.*

Plaintiffs also argue that the sub-licensing rule should apply to licenses of an individual's publicity rights. Plaintiffs cite no authority for this proposition, but merely rely on the same policy arguments and rationales discussed above.

Although trademarks and publicity rights share many common features, they are also dissimilar in several ways. For example, while trademark laws protect the trademark owner by fortifying the public's expectation regarding the source and quality of goods and services, the right of publicity protects an individual's "persona" from commercial exploitation by others. However, the distinction most relevant for the purposes of this motion is that a licensor of an individual's publicity rights, unlike a trademark licensor, lacks an affirmative statutory or common law duty to police its license and to ensure that the licensee is maintaining sufficient quality controls. Therefore, one of the two policy rationales supporting the extension of the sub-licensing rule to trademark licenses—that unfettered sub-licensing will prevent the licensor from satisfying his obligation to supervise the licensee—does not apply to licenses of publicity rights.

Nevertheless, a licensor of publicity rights may, in many instances—indeed, in probably *all* instances and respects—have a powerful incentive to supervise the licensee's use of those rights. The facts of this case are instructive. If GMP were permitted to sub-license Glenn Miller's publicity rights without notifying or obtaining permission from the owner of those rights ... it could sub-license Glenn Miller's publicity rights to a third party who used his name or photograph or likeness to promote fascism or pornography. Such use presumably would horrify Glenn Miller if he were alive; it also would adversely affect the image of Glenn Miller that Plaintiffs (successors to their mother, the original licensor) may wish to preserve. However, absent a sub-licensing rule, Plaintiffs would have no ability to prevent GMP from sullying their father's name (and, in fact, would have no right to even know that GMP was doing so). In addition, any disputes about whether GMP could sub-license Glenn Miller's right of publicity to a particular third party, or whether a third party sub-licensee was acting beyond the scope of the original license, would trigger litigation. These are undesirable results.

Moreover, in practice, many licenses convey both trademark rights and publicity rights. In such cases, "the special rules of trademark licensing must be followed in order to preserve the trademark significance of the licensed identity or persona." *McCarthy, supra*, §28:14. Again, the facts of this case help illustrate this principle. If, without Plaintiffs' knowledge or permission, GMP could sub-license the Glenn Miller mark to third parties who use the mark to sell products or causes at odds with what Glenn Miller stood for, the public's image of Glenn Miller's persona surely would become tainted in a manner that Plaintiffs did not intend. Conversely, if GMP could sub-license Glenn Miller's publicity rights to third parties who use his name or photograph or likeness to sell a wide variety of products whose quality is not controlled, then the Glenn Miller mark may become diluted. For these reasons, at least in cases such as this one in which a license conveys both trademark and publicity rights, the sub-licensing rule should be extended to cover publicity rights.

For these reasons, if a jury were to find that at the time Helen Miller executed the 1956 license agreement, she actually had a trademark in Glenn Miller's name to convey, then because the 1956 license agreement does not expressly grant GMP unilateral authority to sub-license the mark, GMP may not do so. In addition, because the 1956 license agreement does not grant GMP express permission to unilaterally sub-license Glenn Miller's publicity rights, GMP may not do so....

C. *Defendant's Motion for Summary Judgment.*

GMP has filed a cross-motion for summary judgment, contending that: (1) the 1956 license agreement and 1980 settlement agreement grant GMP the right to sell merchandise bearing the Glenn Miller Orchestra mark; (2) the same two agreements grant GMP the right to operate and sub-license multiple bands; (3) because GMP has the right to sell merchandise and to operate and sub-license multiple bands, all of Plaintiffs' eleven claims for relief necessarily fail; and (4) all of Plaintiffs' claims are barred by the doctrine of laches. Although the Court rejects GMP's first three contentions, it agrees that Plaintiffs' claims are barred by laches....

1. *GMP Lacks the Unilateral Right to Sub-License Multiple Ensembles Using the Name "The Glenn Miller Orchestra."*

GMP argues that the only reasonable interpretation of the 1956 license agreement and the 1980 settlement agreement is that they permit GMP to sub-license to an unlimited number of third parties the right to operate orchestras named the Glenn Miller Orchestra. However, because the Court has already ruled that a trademark and publicity rights licensee (such as GMP) may not sub-license those rights without the express permission of the licensor, and because it is undisputed that the two agreements do not expressly authorize GMP to sub-license, as a matter of law, GMP lacks the unilateral authority to sub-license its right to operate a band named the Glenn Miller Orchestra.

2. *There Are Fact Issues Concerning Any Right of GMP to Directly Operate "Special Units" of the Glenn Miller Orchestra and to Sell Merchandise.*

GMP also argues that the only reasonable interpretation of the 1956 license agreement and the 1980 settlement agreement shows that Helen Miller and Plaintiffs actually granted to GMP the right to itself operate more than one ensemble named the Glenn Miller Orchestra, such as ensembles referred to as "special units,"[9] and to sell merchandise bearing the Glenn Miller Orchestra mark, including cassette tapes, videotapes, CDs, DVDs, t-shirts and polo shirts. GMP relies on the following undisputed evidence in support of its interpretation:

1. GMP's Certificate of Incorporation provides that GMP is authorized to "organize, operate, manage, direct, and control, directly or through others, one or more orchestras or musical organizations," and to "manufacture, purchase, sell and generally to trade and deal in and with goods, wares, products and merchandise of every kind, nature and description"....

4. At GMP's first Board of Directors meeting on April 25, 1956, David Mackay, Sr. (the then-chairman) stated: "The main business of the corporation would be to own and operate a traveling orchestra." ...

7. GMP has operated "special units" of the Glenn Miller Orchestra since 1981 and Plaintiffs never objected.

8. GMP has openly sold merchandise bearing the Glenn Miller Orchestra mark at concerts since 1983 (six of which Steven Miller attended), and has sold merchandise on its website since September 1998. However, Plaintiffs never objected.

In contrast to the foregoing facts, which definitely do constitute powerful evidence favoring GMP, the record also shows that for at least 25 years after the execution of the

---

9. Since the operation of "special units" does not constitute sub-licensing, the sub-licensing rule does not bar GMP from itself operating more than one Glenn Miller Orchestra absent express permission from the Millers.

1956 license agreement (and during the entirety of Helen Miller and David Mackay, Sr.'s respective lifetimes), GMP did not operate more than one Glenn Miller Orchestra or sell merchandise bearing the Glenn Miller Orchestra mark. This lengthy history, which is consistent with the language of item 4, above ("... a traveling orchestra"), would at least permit a jury to infer that Helen Miller's intent in executing the 1956 license agreement, and the intent of GMP and the Millers when they entered into the 1980 settlement agreement, was to have only one orchestra. Accordingly, the Court DENIES summary adjudication of this issue....

[The district court nonetheless granted summary judgment in favor of the defendants on the ground of laches, holding that the plaintiffs were aware of the challenged uses, that their "delay in filing suit was unreasonable," and that "GMP has been substantially prejudiced by the delay." This portion of the opinion is discussed in subsection D, below.]

CONCLUSION

For the foregoing reasons, the Court concludes that as a matter of contract law, in the 1956 agreement Helen Miller conveyed both a trademark license and a license to the right of publicity. It concludes that as a matter of trademark law, Helen Miller was in a position to convey a trademark license and that a jury could reasonably find facts establishing that she did. And it concludes that the sub-licensing rule applies to both such conveyances—*i.e.,* trademark and rights of publicity. However, despite having found that Plaintiffs have legal claims that the law could recognize, the Court nevertheless GRANTS IN WHOLE Defendant's motion for summary judgment and dismisses the complaint because under the doctrines of laches, Plaintiffs waited too long to assert those claims....

IT IS SO ORDERED.

Notes and Questions

1. Although the Ninth Circuit characterizes the sublicensing rule as "well established," it is worth noting that the Ninth Circuit's application of the sublicensing rule to copyrights under the 1976 Copyright Act has been the subject of serious criticism, and at least two district courts have disagreed with its conclusion in the copyright context. *See Traicoff v. Digital Media, Inc.,* 439 F. Supp. 2d 872 (S.D. Ind. 2006); *In re Golden Books Family Entertainment, Inc.,* 269 B.R. 311 (Bankr. D. Del. 2001). Thus, it is worth asking whether a prohibition on sublicensing the right of publicity without express consent makes sense as an independent matter.

2. Of course, the parties to a licensing agreement can expressly provide by contract either to allow or to disallow sublicensing by the licensee. What is disputed in the *Miller* case is what the default rule should be when the license agreement is silent: should sub-licenses be allowed unless expressly forbidden, or should sub-licenses be prohibited unless expressly permitted? In answering this question, ask yourself which of the parties to a licensing agreement typically is in a better position to protect itself through private bargaining? Should we construe an ambiguous license agreement against the drafter, rather than having a single default rule?

3. The other issue in the case is whether the license agreement permits GMP to operate more than one orchestra and to sell merchandise with the "Glenn Miller Orchestra" mark. The court holds that there is a genuine issue of material fact in this regard. Note that if a contract is ambiguous, parol evidence may be admitted as an aid to interpreting

the agreement. Here, the district court holds that there is a genuine issue of material fact regarding the interpretation of the agreement, which would require a trial to resolve. Only the court's ruling on laches allows it to resolve the case on summary judgment.

4. Note that although the 1956 license agreement was silent on the issue of duration, the 1980 settlement agreement specified that the license was "in perpetuity." If the agreement is silent, how long should a right of publicity license last? In some cases, courts have allowed the termination of a gratuitous license at any time, although sometimes they will hold that equitable principles of estoppel, laches or acquiescence allow continued use. Absent the 1980 settlement, would it have been fair in the *Miller* case to allow the 1956 license to be terminated? Does the recital of valuable consideration (or the receipt of actual consideration) change your answer?

B. First-Sale Doctrine

Allison v. Vintage Sports Plaques
136 F.3d 1443 (11th Cir. 1998)

Before TJOFLAT and HULL, Circuit Judges, and KRAVITCH, Senior Circuit Judge.

KRAVITCH, Senior Circuit Judge:

The issue presented in this case is whether the "first-sale doctrine," a well-established limitation on intellectual property rights, applies to the common-law right of publicity. We hold that it does. Accordingly, we affirm the district court, which granted summary judgment to the defendant.

I.

Elisa Allison ("Allison") is the widow of Clifford Allison, a well-known race-car driver who had a licensing agreement with Maxx Race Cards ("MAXX") whereby Maxx would manufacture and market trading cards bearing his likeness in exchange for a royalty of 18% of sales receipts, which is now paid to his estate. Orel Hershisher ("Hershisher") is a well-known professional baseball player who has a licensing agreement with the Major League Baseball Players Association ("MLBPA") that grants MLBPA the right to use and license his name and image for commercial purposes in exchange for a *pro rata* share of all revenues derived therefrom. MLBPA has licensed Hershisher's name and image to various trading card companies, which have manufactured and marketed cards bearing his image.

Vintage Sports Plaques ("Vintage") purchases trading cards from licensed card manufacturers and distributors and, without altering the cards in any way, frames them by mounting individual cards between a transparent acrylic sheet and a wood board. Vintage then labels each plaque with an identification plate bearing the name of the player or team represented. In addition to the mounted trading card, some of the plaques feature a clock with a sports motif. Vintage markets each plaque as a "Limited Edition" and an "Authentic Collectible." Vintage is not a party to any licensing agreement that grants it the right to use the appellants' names or likenesses for commercial purposes and has never paid a royalty or commission to the appellants for its use of their names or images. Appellants presumably have received, however, pursuant to their respective licensing agreements, royalties from the card manufacturers and distributors for the *initial* sale of the cards to Vintage.

Allison filed suit against Vintage in Alabama state court alleging infringement of licensure rights, violation of the right of publicity, and conspiracy, and Vintage removed the action to the United States District Court for the Northern District of Alabama on the basis of diversity of citizenship. Allison then filed an amended complaint seeking to join Hershisher as a plaintiff and to certify a plaintiff class. The amended complaint alleged violation of the right of publicity and conspiracy and included a prayer for injunctive and declaratory relief. Vintage moved for summary judgment, and the district court, concluding that "it would be provident to consider [the motion] to determine if a legally cognizable claim is stated in the amended complaint ... [b]efore considering the issue of class certification," granted the motion. The district court first decided that although appellants established a *prima facie* case of violation of the right of publicity, the first-sale doctrine operates as a defense in such actions. The district court then concluded that because "[t]his is more appropriately classified as a case of an entrepreneur repackaging or displaying the trading cards in a more attractive way to consumers," rather than a case of an opportunist "using Plaintiffs' names and likenesses to sell frames and clocks," Vintage was entitled to summary judgment on the right of publicity claim.

II.A.

As a preliminary matter, we note that as a court sitting in diversity we are bound to apply state substantive law. *See Erie R.R. Co. v. Tompkins*, 304 U.S. 64 (1938). In reaching its conclusions, the district court purported to apply Alabama law, and we do the same.[6] The district court cited only one Alabama case, *Birmingham Broadcasting Co. v. Bell*, 259 Ala. 656, 68 So.2d 314 (1953), for the proposition that Alabama has recognized a cause of action for violation of the right of publicity. In *Bell*, the court held that the only cause of action available to a well-known radio announcer against a broadcaster who had used the announcer's name without his permission was for "violation of his privacy." *Id.* at 319. Noting that the earlier case of *Smith v. Doss*, 251 Ala. 250, 37 So.2d 118 (1948), impliedly had recognized a cause of action for violation of the right of privacy, the court held that the "privacy of a public personage may not be lawfully invaded by the use of his name or picture for commercial purposes without his consent, not incidental to an occurrence of legitimate news value." *Bell*, 68 So.2d at 319. Although it does not appear that Alabama courts ever have recognized a right denominated as "publicity," we conclude that the Alabama right of privacy contains an analogous right....

Alabama has not denominated the interest protected by its commercial appropriation invasion of privacy tort as the right of publicity. We read Alabama's commercial appropriation privacy right, however, to represent the same interests and address the same harms as does the right of publicity as customarily defined. Indeed, the elements of Al-

---

6. The district court did not address choice of law in its Order, but rather seemed to assume that Alabama law applied. A district court must apply the choice-of-law rules of the state in which it sits. *See Klaxon Co. v. Stentor Elec. Mfg. Co.*, 313 U.S. 487 (1941). Alabama uses a vested rights approach in determining the applicable law in tort actions, an approach that ordinarily results in application of the law of the state where the injury occurred. Because Alabama courts have not addressed choice-of-law issues in cases similar to the one before us, it is difficult to determine what choice-of-law principles an Alabama state court would apply in this case. For example, it is not clear whether the locus of the injury would be the location of the plaintiff or instead the situs of the allegedly tortious conduct. To complicate matters, the right of publicity has been treated in some jurisdictions as a property right, and some courts accordingly have used choice-of-law rules applicable to personal property. Because Allison resides in Alabama, treatment of right of publicity claims as property actions likely would result in application of Alabama substantive law. Although there are certain ambiguities, we nevertheless conclude that an Alabama court would apply Alabama law to resolve this case.

abama's commercial appropriation invasion of privacy tort, which bases liability on commercial, rather than psychological interests, do not differ significantly from those of the tort of violation of the right of publicity. As a technical matter, then, we construe appellants' claim as one sounding in commercial appropriation, rather than in publicity, although we conclude that the distinction is largely semantic.[7]

Although the Alabama Supreme Court has addressed the tort of commercial appropriation only twice and thus has provided us with little guidance in determining the contours of the cause of action, we read Alabama law to permit a cause of action for invasion of privacy when the defendant appropriates without consent the "plaintiff's name or likeness to advertise the defendant's business or product, or for some other similar commercial purpose." *Kyser-Smith* [*v. Upscale Communications, Inc.*], 873 F. Supp. [1519 (M.D. Ala. 1995)] at 1525. The plaintiff must demonstrate that there is a "unique quality or value in [his] likeness [ ]" that, if appropriated, would result in "commercial profit" to the defendant. *Schifano* [*v. Greene County Greyhound Park, Inc.*], 624 So.2d [178 (Ala. 1993)] at 181.

B.

The district court concluded that the first-sale doctrine precludes appellants from holding Vintage liable in tort. The first-sale doctrine provides that once the holder of an intellectual property right "consents to the sale of particular copies ... of his work, he may not thereafter exercise the distribution right with respect to such copies...." M. Nimmer and D. Nimmer, *Nimmer on Copyright* § 8.12[B][1] (1997). Any other rule would extend the monopoly created by the intellectual property right so far as to permit control by the right-holder over the disposition of lawfully obtained tangible personal property. Therefore, "the policy favoring [an intellectual property right monopoly] ... gives way to the policy opposing restraints of trade and restraints on alienation." *Id.* at § 8.12[A]. The first-sale doctrine limits the three principal forms of intellectual property rights: (1) copyright, *see* 17 U.S.C. § 109(a); (2) patent, *see Intel Corp. v. ULSI Sys. Tech., Inc.*, 995 F.2d 1566, 1568 (Fed. Cir. 1993); and (3) trademark, *see NEC Electronics v. CAL Circuit ABCO*, 810 F.2d 1506, 1509 (9th Cir. 1987).

Appellants argue that we should not apply the first-sale doctrine to common-law actions to enforce the right of publicity. There is virtually no case law in any state addressing the application of the first-sale doctrine to the right of publicity, perhaps because the applicability of the doctrine is taken for granted.[8] The cases cited by appellants do not show that the doctrine is inapplicable to publicity actions, but rather address instances either of unauthorized use of likenesses that *never* have been licensed for use, or of use by a licensee that exceeds the scope of the license.

Appellants argue that the right of publicity differs from other forms of intellectual property because the former protects "identity," whereas the latter protect "a particular photograph or product." The first-sale doctrine should not apply, they reason, because a celebrity's identity continues to travel with the tangible property in which it is embodied after the first sale. We find two significant problems with appellants' argument. First, the distinction that appellants draw between what is protected by the right of publicity and what is protected by other forms of intellectual property rights, such as copyright, is not sound. Copyright law, for example, does not exist merely to protect the tangible items,

---

7. Because we conclude that there is no significant difference between Alabama's commercial appropriation privacy tort and the right of publicity, we use the terms interchangeably during the remainder of the opinion.

8. We note that some states that statutorily have recognized a right of publicity have codified the first-sale doctrine. *See, e.g.*, Fla.Stat.Ann. § 540.08(3)(b).

such as books and paintings, in which the underlying expressive material is embodied; rather, it protects as well the author's or artist's *particular* expression that is included in the tangible item.

Second, and more important in our view, accepting appellants' argument would have profoundly negative effects on numerous industries and would grant a monopoly to celebrities over their identities that would upset the delicate "balance between the interests of the celebrity and those of the public." *White v. Samsung Electronics Amer., Inc.*, 989 F.2d 1512, 1515 (9th Cir. 1993) (Kozinski, J., dissenting from the order rejecting the suggestion for rehearing en banc). Indeed, a decision by this court not to apply the first-sale doctrine to right of publicity actions would render tortious the resale of sports trading cards and memorabilia and thus would have a profound effect on the market for trading cards, which now supports a multi-billion dollar industry. Such a holding presumably also would prevent, for example, framing a magazine advertisement that bears the image of a celebrity and reselling it as a collector's item, reselling an empty cereal box that bears a celebrity's endorsement, or even reselling a used poster promoting a professional sports team. Refusing to apply the first-sale doctrine to the right of publicity also presumably would prevent a child from selling to his friend a baseball card that he had purchased, a consequence that undoubtedly would be contrary to the policies supporting that right.

A holding that the first-sale doctrine does limit the right of publicity, on the other hand, would not eliminate completely a celebrity's control over the use of her name or image; the right of publicity protects against unauthorized use of an image, and a celebrity would continue to enjoy the right to license the use of her image *in the first instance*—and thus enjoy the power to determine when, or if, her image will be distributed. Appellants in this case, for example, have received sizable royalties from the use of their images on the trading cards at issue, images that could not have been used in the first place without permission. Because application of the first-sale doctrine to limit the right of publicity under Alabama law will maintain the appropriate balance between the rights of celebrities in their identities and the rights of the public to enjoy those identities, we conclude that the Alabama Supreme Court would apply the first-sale doctrine in this case and that the district court properly so applied it.

C.

Having concluded that the first-sale doctrine applies to limit the right of publicity under Alabama law, we turn to the question of whether the district court correctly granted summary judgment in favor of Vintage. Appellants cannot prevail under a commercial appropriation cause of action if Vintage merely resells the trading cards that bear appellants' likenesses because the resale of licensed images falls under the protective scope of the first-sale doctrine.

The district court correctly observed:

> Vintage would probably violate the right of publicity if [it] attached a trading card to a baseball glove and sold it as "an official Orel Hershisher glove" or if [it] affixed a Clifford Allison card onto a model car and sold it as "an official Clifford Allison car." Thus, this court must decide if the Vintage Clocks and plaques are more like reselling the trading cards or more like using Plaintiffs' names and likenesses to sell frames and clocks, similar to selling an Allison car or a Hershisher glove.

Because the district court concluded that "Vintage is selling the trading cards after presenting them in, what some consumers deem to be, a more attractive display," and because the first-sale doctrine permits such resale, the court granted summary judgment on the right of publicity claim. Appellants contend that the issue of whether Vintage's plaques are "more like reselling the trading cards or more like using Plaintiffs' names and likenesses to sell frames and clocks" involves questions of material fact that should not have been resolved at the summary judgment stage.

The issue before us, then, is whether the district court properly resolved as a matter of law that Vintage's plaques merely are the cards themselves repackaged, rather than products separate and distinct from the trading cards they incorporate. If they are the latter, as appellants contend that they are, then arguably Vintage is selling a product by "commercially exploiting the likeness[es of appellants] intending to engender profits to their enterprise," *Wendt v. Host Int'l, Inc.,* 125 F.3d 806, 811 (9th Cir. 1997), a practice against which the right of publicity seems clearly to protect....

We conclude that the district court properly determined that, as a matter of law, Vintage merely resells cards that it lawfully obtains. We think it unlikely that anyone would purchase one of Vintage's plaques for any reason other than to obtain a display of the mounted cards themselves. Although we recognize that the plaques that include a clock pose a closer case, we conclude that it is unlikely that anyone would purchase one of the clock plaques simply to obtain a means of telling time, believing the clock to be, for example, a "Hershisher Clock" or an "Allison Clock."[15] Because reselling a product that was lawfully obtained does not give rise to a cause of action for violation of the right of publicity, we hold that the district court correctly entered summary judgment in favor of Vintage on the right of publicity claim.[16]

III.

The judgment of the district court in favor of appellee is AFFIRMED.

Notes and Questions

1. As the court notes, the first-sale doctrine (also known as the doctrine of exhaustion) is well-established in other areas of intellectual property law. The doctrine holds that the purchaser of a lawfully made item is entitled to re-sell or otherwise dispose of the possession of that item without the consent of the intellectual property owner. The doctrine thus vindicates the strong policy against restraints on the alienation of property.

Note that the doctrine applies only to goods that have been made and distributed with the consent of the right owner. It is clear, however, that despite the name "first-sale doctrine," the doctrine applies even when ownership has been obtained by gift, rather than by sale. *See, e.g., UMG Recordings, Inc. v. Augusto,* 558 F. Supp. 2d 1055 (C.D. Cal. 2008) (promotional CDs).

---

15. Appellants make much of the fact that Vintage markets its plaques as "Limited Edition[s]" and "Authentic Collectible[s]." In our view, however, these designations in no way change the fundamental nature of the plaques.

16. Appellants also argue that Vintage violated their right of publicity merely by using the appellants' names on the plaques. Although appellants are correct that unauthorized use of a celebrity's *name,* in contrast to a celebrity's image, to promote a product ordinarily constitutes a violation of the right of publicity, it does not violate the right of publicity to use the celebrity's name to identify the likeness if the *image* is lawfully used. Appellants' argument about the use of their names thus rises and falls with their arguments about the applicability of the first-sale doctrine and the nature of the product that Vintage sells. Because we conclude that the first-sale doctrine applies and that Vintage's displays merely repackage the trading cards, Vintage's use of appellants' names to label the displays does not violate their common-law right of publicity.

2. A related question is the extent to which the first-sale doctrine can be modified by contract. In the original first-sale doctrine case in copyright law, *Bobbs-Merrill Co. v. Straus*, 210 U.S. 339 (1908), the U.S. Supreme Court held that a department store that had purchased lawfully made copies of a book at wholesale could resell those copies at 89 cents per copy, notwithstanding a notice printed in the book that read "The price of this book at retail is $1 net. No dealer is licensed to sell it at a less price, and a sale at a less price will be treated as an infringement of the copyright." Notwithstanding this decision, software manufacturers have sometimes been successful in persuading a court that copies of their software were "licensed" rather than "sold," and that restrictions on resale contained in an "End-User License Agreement" (or EULA) are therefore valid. *Compare, e.g., Adobe Systems, Inc. v. Stargate Software, Inc.*, 216 F. Supp. 2d 1051 (N.D. Cal. 2002) *and Adobe Systems, Inc. v. One Stop Micro, Inc.*, 84 F. Supp. 2d 1086 (C.D. Cal. 2001) (license) *with Vernor v. Autodesk, Inc.*, 555 F. Supp. 2d 1164 (W.D. Wash. 2008) *and Softman Prods. Co. v. Adobe Systems, Inc.*, 171 F. Supp. 2d 1075 (C.D. Cal. 2001) (sale). In your opinion, when should a transfer of possession be considered a sale rather than a license?

3. The doctrine of exhaustion also has an international dimension. The issue is whether authorized merchandise sold in one country can be imported into and resold in another country without the permission of the rights owner. On this question, countries have very different rules. Some countries follow a rule of international exhaustion, so that authorized merchandise sold anywhere in the world can be resold there. The European Union follows a rule of regional exhaustion, so that authorized merchandise sold within the E.U. can be resold in any E.U. country, but authorized merchandise from outside the E.U. can be prohibited. *See, e.g., Silhouette Int'l Schmied GmbH v. Hartlauer Handelsgesellschaft mbH*, Case No. C-355/96 (E.C.J. 1998) (trademark). In the U.S., exhaustion applies if the good was manufactured in the U.S., even if it was first sold overseas. *See Quality King Distributors, Inc. v. L'anza Research Int'l, Inc.*, 523 U.S. 135 (1998); *Jazz Photo Corp. v. Int'l Trade Comm'n*, 254 F.3d 1094 (Fed. Cir. 2001).

4. On the merits of the case, do you agree with the court's conclusion that mounting a baseball card on a plaque (with or without a clock) is merely a resale and not the creation of a new product? In the copyright context, courts have split over whether mounting an authorized copy of a work of art on a ceramic tile and reselling it was the preparation of a "derivative work" that was infringing, or whether it was protected by the first-sale doctrine. *Compare Mirage Editions, Inc. v. Albuquerque A.R.T. Co.*, 856 F.2d 1341 (9th Cir. 1988) (infringing) *with Lee v. A.R.T. Co.*, 125 F.3d 580 (7th Cir. 1997) (not infringing). Does this debate shed any light on the court's decision in *Allison*?

C. Abandonment and Fair Use

Abdul-Jabbar v. General Motors Co.
85 F.3d 407 (9th Cir. 1996)

T.G. NELSON, Circuit Judge:

Former basketball star Kareem Abdul-Jabbar appeals the district court's summary judgment in favor of General Motors Corporation ("GMC") and its advertising agency, Leo Burnett Co., in his action alleging violations of the Lanham Act, 15 U.S.C. §1125(a), and

California's statutory and common law right of publicity. Abdul-Jabbar argues that GMC violated his trademark and publicity rights by using his former name, Lew Alcindor, without his consent, in a television commercial aired during the 1993 NCAA men's basketball tournament. The district court based its judgment on all causes of action largely on its findings that Abdul-Jabbar had abandoned the name "Lew Alcindor," and that GMC's use of the name could not be construed as an endorsement of its product by Abdul-Jabbar.... [W]e reverse and remand for trial.

FACTS AND PROCEDURAL HISTORY

This dispute concerns a GMC television commercial aired during the 1993 NCAA men's basketball tournament. The record includes a videotape of the spot, which plays as follows: A disembodied voice asks, "How 'bout some trivia?" This question is followed by the appearance of a screen bearing the printed words, "You're Talking to the Champ." The voice then asks, "Who holds the record for being voted the most outstanding player of this tournament?" In the screen appear the printed words, "Lew Alcindor, UCLA, '67, '68, '69." Next, the voice asks, "Has any car made the 'Consumer Digest's Best Buy' list more than once? [and responds:] The Oldsmobile Eighty-Eight has." A seven-second film clip of the automobile, with its price, follows. During the clip, the voice says, "In fact, it's made that list three years in a row. And now you can get this Eighty-Eight special edition for just $18,995." At the end of the clip, a message appears in print on the screen: "A Definite First Round Pick," accompanied by the voice saying, "it's your money." A final printed message appears: "Demand Better, 88 by Oldsmobile."

The following facts are undisputed. Kareem Abdul-Jabbar was named Ferdinand Lewis ("Lew") Alcindor at birth, and played basketball under that name throughout his college career and into his early years in the National Basketball Association ("NBA"). While in college, he converted to Islam and began to use the Muslim name "Kareem Abdul-Jabbar" among friends. Several years later, in 1971, he opted to record the name "Kareem Abdul-Jabbar" under an Illinois name recordation statute, and thereafter played basketball and endorsed products under that name.[1] He has not used the name "Lew Alcindor" for commercial purposes in over ten years.

GMC did not obtain Abdul-Jabbar's consent, nor did it pay him, to use his former name in the commercial described above. When Abdul-Jabbar complained to GMC about the commercial, the company promptly withdrew the ad. The ad aired about five or six times in March 1993 prior to its withdrawal. The parties dispute whether Abdul-Jabbar abandoned the name Lew Alcindor and whether the ad could be construed as an endorsement by Abdul-Jabbar of the 88 Oldsmobile.

Abdul-Jabbar brought suit in federal district court in May 1993, alleging claims under the Lanham Act and California's statutory and common law rights of publicity. The district court held a hearing on March 14, 1994. During the hearing, ... the district court announced its "tentative finding that plaintiff has abandoned the name Lew Alcindor, and has abandoned the right to protect that name, and the right to assert any other rights that flow from his having had that name at one time in the past." This finding

---

1. The record judgment read that "said petitioner's name be, and the same is hereby changed from FERDINAND LEWIS ALCINDOR to KAREEM ABDUL-JABBAR by which said last-mentioned name shall be hereafter known and called." Illinois' name recordation laws, like California's, are permissive. *See Reinken v. Reinken,* 351 Ill. 409, 184 N.E. 639, 640 (1933); *In re Ritchie,* 159 Cal. App. 3d 1070, 206 Cal. Rptr. 239, 240 (1984).

forms the basis for the district court's decision to grant summary judgment in favor of GMC on both the Lanham Act and the state law causes of action.[2] Abdul-Jabbar timely appealed.

ANALYSIS

I

The Lanham Act

"[A]n express purpose of the Lanham Act is to protect commercial parties against unfair competition." *Waits v. Frito-Lay, Inc.,* 978 F.2d 1093, 1108 (9th Cir. 1992). In *Waits,* we held as a matter of first impression that false endorsement claims are properly cognizable under section 43(a), 15 U.S.C. § 1125(a), of the Lanham Act. *Id.* at 1107. "Section 43(a) [as amended in 1988] ... expressly prohibits, *inter alia,* the use of any symbol or device which is likely to deceive consumers as to the association, sponsorship, or approval of goods or services by another person." *Id.* Accordingly, we held actionable:

> [a] false endorsement claim based on the unauthorized use of a celebrity's identity ... [which] alleges the misuse of a trademark, i.e., a symbol or device such as a visual likeness, vocal imitation, or other uniquely distinguishing characteristic, which is likely to confuse consumers as to the plaintiff's sponsorship or approval of the product.

Id. at 1110. Abdul-Jabbar contends that GMC's unauthorized use of his birth name, Lew Alcindor, was likely to confuse consumers as to his endorsement of the Olds 88, and thus violates the Lanham Act.

GMC offers two defenses in response to this claim: 1) Abdul-Jabbar lost his rights to the name Lew Alcindor when he "abandoned" it; and 2) GMC's use of the name Lew Alcindor was a nominative fair use which is not subject to the protection of the Lanham Act. The district court held both defenses applicable.

a) *Abandonment under the Lanham Act*

While the district court found that there was no dispute as to GMC's failure to seek or obtain Abdul-Jabbar's consent to use his former name in its commercial, and that "on its face, the Lanham Act applies," it held that GMC was entitled to summary judgment on the basis of its finding that Abdul-Jabbar had abandoned his former name through nonuse under the Lanham Act. Title 15 U.S.C. § 1127 (1992) provides in pertinent part:

> A mark shall be deemed to be "abandoned" when either of the following occurs:
>
> (1) When its use has been discontinued with intent not to resume such use. Intent not to resume may be inferred from circumstances. Nonuse for two consecutive years shall be prima facie evidence of abandonment.* "Use" of a mark means the bona fide use of that mark made in the ordinary course of trade, and not merely to reserve a right in a mark.
>
> (2) When any course of conduct of the owner, including acts of omission as well as commission, causes the mark to become ... generic....

---

2. The district court did not distinguish between defendants GMC and Burnett, but assumed for purposes of the summary judgment motion that "if one is liable, both are liable; if one is entitled to the grant of the motion, both are entitled to it."

* Under current law, the period is three years of consecutive non-use, rather than two. — *Eds.*

Once created, a prima facie case of abandonment may be rebutted by showing valid reasons for nonuse or lack of intent to abandon the mark. *Star-Kist Foods, Inc. v. P.J. Rhodes & Co.*, 769 F.2d 1393, 1396 (9th Cir. 1985). Because Abdul-Jabbar acknowledged that he had not used the name Lew Alcindor in over ten years, and because the district court found that plaintiff's proffered religious reasons for nonuse were not applicable,[5] the court held that Abdul-Jabbar had in effect abandoned the name.

Trademark law withdraws its protection from a mark that has become generic and deems it available for general use. Given that

> the primary cost of recognizing property rights in trademarks is the removal of words from (or perhaps non-entrance into) our language, ... the holder of a trademark will be denied protection if it is (or becomes) generic, i.e., if it does not relate exclusively to the trademark owner's product.

New Kids on the Block v. News America Pub., Inc., 971 F.2d 302, 306 (9th Cir. 1992). Similarly, the law ceases to protect the owner of an abandoned mark. Rather than countenancing the "removal" or retirement of the abandoned mark from commercial speech, trademark law allows it to be used by another. Accordingly, courts have held that an unused mark may not be held in abeyance by its original owner....

While the Lanham Act has been applied to cases alleging appropriation of a celebrity's identity, the abandonment defense has never to our knowledge been applied to a person's name or identity. We decline to stretch the federal law of trademark to encompass such a defense. One's birth name is an integral part of one's identity; it is not bestowed for commercial purposes, nor is it "kept alive" through commercial use. A proper name thus cannot be deemed "abandoned" throughout its possessor's life, despite his failure to use it, or continue to use it, commercially.

In other words, an individual's given name, unlike a trademark, has a life and a significance quite apart from the commercial realm. Use or nonuse of the name for commercial purposes does not dispel that significance. An individual's decision to use a name other than the birth name—whether the decision rests on religious, marital, or other personal considerations—does not therefore imply intent to set aside the birth name, or the identity associated with that name.

While the issue of whether GMC's use of the name Lew Alcindor constituted an endorsement of its product is far from clear, we hold that GMC cannot rely on abandonment as a defense to Abdul-Jabbar's Lanham Act claim.

b) *Lanham Act "fair use" doctrine*

The district court cited the "fair use" defense, 15 U.S.C. § 1115(b)(4), as an alternative ground for dismissal of plaintiff's Lanham Act claim. We discussed this defense in *New Kids*, where we held that the use by two newspapers of the "New Kids" name to conduct phone-in polls measuring the group's popularity was a nominative or non-trademark "fair use" of the name not subject to protection under the Lanham Act. 971 F.2d at 306–09.

---

5. We need not decide whether Abdul-Jabbar's proffered reasons for non-use of his birth name would serve to rebut a prima facie case of abandonment. Abdul-Jabbar argues that the district court's abandonment ruling substantially burdens his First Amendment right to free exercise of religion. The gist of this argument is that by holding that one loses rights to his given name on adopting a new name for religious purposes, the court puts pressure on a religious believer to "modify his behavior and violate his beliefs." *See Frazee v. Illinois Dep't of Employment Sec.*, 489 U.S. 829, 832 (1989). Because we hold GMC failed to establish a prima facie case of abandonment under the Lanham Act, we do not reach or resolve this argument.

"[T]rademark law recognizes a defense where the mark is used only 'to describe the goods or services of [a] party, or their geographic origin.'" *Id.* at 306 (quoting 15 U.S.C. § 1115(b)(4)). We cited the example of a Volkswagen repair shop which used the name "Volkswagen" in the sign advertising its business. *Volkswagenwerk Aktiengesellschaft v. Church,* 411 F.2d 350, 352 (9th Cir. 1969). There, we had recognized that it "'would be difficult, if not impossible, ... to avoid altogether the use of the word "Volkswagen" or its abbreviation "VW" ... [to] signify appellant's cars.'... Therefore, his use of the Volkswagen trademark was not an infringing use." *Id.* at 307 (quoting *Volkswagenwerk Aktiengesellschaft v. Church,* 411 F.2d 350, 352 (9th Cir. 1969)).

We explained that "[c]ases like these are best understood as involving a non-trademark use of a mark—a use to which the infringement laws simply do not apply." *Id.*

> [W]e may generalize a class of cases where the use of the trademark does not attempt to capitalize on consumer confusion or to appropriate the cachet of one product for a different one. Such *nominative use* of a mark—where the only word reasonably available to describe a particular thing is pressed into service— lies outside the strictures of trademark law: Because it does not implicate the source-identification function that is the purpose of the trademark, it does not constitute unfair competition; such use is fair because it does not imply sponsorship or endorsement by the trademark holder.

Id. at 307–08.

New Kids was not the classic fair use case because the New Kids trademark was being used not to describe the defendant's own product (newspapers), but to describe the plaintiff's product (rock band). *Id.* at 308. However, we held that in such cases, a commercial user is nevertheless entitled to the nominative fair use defense if it meets three requirements:

> First, the product or service in question must be one not readily identifiable without use of the trademark; second, only so much of the mark or marks may be used as is reasonably necessary to identify the product or service; and third, the user must do nothing that would, in conjunction with the mark, suggest sponsorship or endorsement by the trademark holder.

Id. (footnotes omitted). Because 1) the New Kids rock band could not be referenced without using its name; and 2) the newspapers used the name only to the extent necessary to identify them; and 3) nothing in the newspaper announcements implied sponsorship or endorsement by the New Kids, we held that the papers were entitled to the nominative fair use defense. *Id.* at 308–10.

The district court here found that GMC met the three *New Kids* requirements as a matter of law. We conclude, however, that there was a genuine issue of fact as to the third requirement, implied endorsement or sponsorship. Like the newspapers in *New Kids,* General Motors could not refer to plaintiff without using his name, and it used no more than was necessary to refer to him. Also, analogously to the newspapers in *New Kids* asking their readers which New Kid was the best, sexiest, etc., the defendant was selling something, newspapers or cars, different from the product the plaintiff was selling, and their products could not be confused.

The distinction between this case and *New Kids* is that use of celebrity endorsements in television commercials is so well established by commercial custom that a jury might find an implied endorsement in General Motors' use of the celebrity's name in a commercial, which would not inhere in a newspaper poll. Newspapers and magazines commonly use celebrities' names and photographs without making endorsement contracts, so the public does not infer an endorsement agreement from the use. Many people may assume that when a celebrity's name is used in a television commercial, the celebrity endorses the product advertised. Likelihood of confusion as to endorsement is therefore a question for the jury. *White v. Samsung Elec. Am., Inc.,* 971 F.2d 1395, 1400–01 (9th Cir. 1992) (holding that use of a robot dressed and posed like Vanna White next to a "Wheel of Fortune" set raised sufficient question of fact as to endorsement under the Lanham Act to preclude summary judgment), *cert. denied,* 508 U.S. 951 (1993).

Had GMC limited itself to the "trivia" portion of its ad, GMC could likely defend the reference to Lew Alcindor as a nominative fair use. But by using Alcindor's record to make a claim for its car—like the basketball star, the Olds 88 won an "award" three years in a row, and like the star, the car is a "champ" and a "first round pick"—GMC has arguably attempted to "appropriate the cachet of one product for another," if not also to "capitalize on consumer confusion." *New Kids* at 308. We therefore hold that there is a question of fact as to whether GMC is entitled to a fair use defense.

c) *Abdul-Jabbar's Lanham Act claim*

In considering celebrities' claims of violation under the Lanham Act, we have considered the following factors to determine whether a plaintiff has raised a genuine issue of material fact as to likelihood of confusion over endorsement: "(1) strength of the plaintiff's mark; (2) relatedness of the goods; (3) similarity of the marks; (4) evidence of actual confusion; (5) marketing channels used; (6) likely degree of purchaser care; (7) defendant's intent in selecting the mark." *White,* 971 F.2d at 1400.

The parties dispute the applicability of the factors. GMC concedes that the fifth factor, marketing channels, favors Abdul-Jabbar, but contests the rest. Because a jury could reasonably conclude that most of the factors weigh in plaintiff's favor, we hold that the question of whether Abdul-Jabbar's Lanham Act claim should succeed is a question for the jury.

II

State law claims: Common Law and Statutory Rights of Privacy

"California has long recognized a common law right of privacy … [which includes protection against] appropriation, for the defendant's advantage, of the plaintiff's name or likeness." *Eastwood v. Superior Court for Los Angeles County,* 149 Cal. App. 3d 409, 198 Cal. Rptr. 342, 346 (1983) (citations omitted). The right to be protected against such appropriations is also referred to as the "right of publicity." *Id.,* 198 Cal.Rptr. at 347.…

As set out in *Eastwood,* a common law cause of action for appropriation of name or likeness may be pleaded by alleging "(1) the defendant's use of plaintiff's identity; (2) the appropriation of plaintiff's name or likeness to defendant's advantage, commercially or otherwise; (3) lack of consent; and (4) resulting injury." 198 Cal. Rptr. at 347.…

California's common law cause of action is complemented legislatively by Civil Code section 3344. As the *Eastwood* court explained, the statute is best understood as "complementing," rather than enacting, the common law cause of action, because the two are not identical. 198 Cal. Rptr. at 346.…

In addition to the common law elements, the statute requires two further allegations: 1) knowing use; and 2) a "direct connection … between the use and the commercial purpose." 198 Cal. Rptr. at 347 (quotations omitted). Furthermore, unlike the common law cause of action, section 3344 is apparently limited to commercial appropriations. As the

Eastwood court pointed out, however, "California law has not imposed any requirement that the unauthorized use or publication of a person's name or picture be suggestive of an endorsement or association with the injured person." *Id.* at 347. This caveat apparently applies to both the common law and statutory causes of action. *See id.* at 348 ("the appearance of an 'endorsement' is not the *sine qua non* of a claim for commercial appropriation.").

We have construed the statute's protection of "name, voice, signature, photograph, or likeness" more narrowly than the common law's protection of "identity." *See, e.g., White,* 971 F.2d at 1397 (holding plaintiff stated a cause of action under common law but not under section 3344 where likeness in question was robot impersonating celebrity); *Midler v. Ford Motor Co.,* 849 F.2d 460, 463 (9th Cir.1988) (holding common law but not statutory cause of action applicable to appropriation of singer's voice by voice-impersonator).

The district court ruled that GMC was entitled to summary judgment on both the statutory and common law causes of action. The court reasoned that section 3344 did not apply because: 1) Abdul-Jabbar had abandoned his former name; and 2) GMC did not "use" plaintiff's name because Abdul-Jabbar "did not [at the time of the ad] and does not have the name used." While the court found that GMC knowingly used the name Lew Alcindor for commercial purposes without obtaining plaintiff's consent, it concluded that GMC had not used *plaintiff's* name because he no longer bore that name.

The district court found that Abdul-Jabbar abandoned the name Lew Alcindor when he legally recorded his present name in 1971. The court acknowledged that "[w]e have no case law in California that abandonment is a defense [to § 3344], but as I would construe the law, it surely must be." The court further found, "regardless of abandonment," that because Abdul-Jabbar no longer uses the name Lew Alcindor, "there has been no use of plaintiff's name." Extrapolating from our holdings in *White* and *Midler* that, under section 3344, "use must be of actual voice or actual likeness," the court concluded that "the actual name must be used in a name case, and ... our case does not involve the use of plaintiff's actual name."

The court dismissed the common law cause of action on similar grounds. The court referred to and distinguished *Carson v. Here's Johnny Portable Toilets, Inc.,* 698 F.2d 831 (6th Cir. 1983) (holding distributor's use of the phrase "Here's Johnny" actionable under Michigan common law, *see id.* at 837) and *Ali v. Playgirl, Inc.,* 447 F. Supp. 723, 728 (S.D.N.Y. 1978) (holding magazine's publication of drawing of nude black man labelled "the greatest" entitled plaintiff to preliminary injunctive relief for violations of New York statutory and common law right of publicity), on the grounds that "[o]ne cannot say that Lew Alcindor equals Kareem Abdul-Jabbar in anywhere near the same sense that 'Here's Johnny' equals Johnny Carson ... or the way 'the greatest' equalled Muhammed Ali, when [those cases were] tried." The court described the "essence" of the holdings in *Carson* and *Ali* to be "that the sobriquet or nickname must be in the most common present use so that it clearly identifies the person seeking recovery" and opined without reviewing any of the California cases that "[*Carson* and *Ali*] might well come out the same under California common [law]."

We have frequently held that California's common law right of publicity protects celebrities from appropriations of their *identity* not strictly definable as "name or picture." [The court cites *Motschenbacher, Midler* & *White* (all reprinted in Chapter II)] ...

Neither the cases cited by the district court, nor the cases listed above stand for the proposition that the reference must be "in common, present use" under the statute or under California common law. Rather, they stand for the proposition that "identity" is a more flexible proposition and thus more permissive than the statutory "laundry list" of particular means of appropriation. *White*, 971 F.2d at 1398; *see also Carson*, 698 F.2d at 835 ("All that is required [under Michigan's common law right of publicity] is that the name clearly identify the wronged person.").

The district court's "common, present use" analysis appears to be a variation on its abandonment theme (*e.g.*, Abdul-Jabbar can only sue for use of his present name, because he has abandoned his former name). Abdul-Jabbar argues that abandonment cannot be a defense to appropriation because the right of publicity protects not only a celebrity's "sole right to exploit" his identity, *White*, 971 F.2d at 1399, but also his decision not to use his name or identity for commercial purposes. *See, e.g., Waits*, 978 F.2d 1093 (applying right of publicity protection to singer with moral and aesthetic objections to advertising). We agree.

Abdul-Jabbar cites *Price v. Hal Roach Studios, Inc.*, 400 F. Supp. 836, 846 (S.D.N.Y. 1975), wherein the court dismissed as "nonsensical" defendants' argument that Laurel and Hardy's failure to use their caricatures and imitations between 1940 and 1954 constituted abandonment: "It cannot be possible for Laurel and Hardy to lose rights in their own names and likenesses through 'non-use.'" *Id.* at 846 (citing New York statutory law protecting persons from commercial exploitation by others and case) and *see id.* at n.15 (citing *Grant v. Esquire*, 367 F. Supp. 876, 880 (S.D.N.Y. 1973), for the proposition that nonuse of commercial value of name and likeness does not preclude against violation by others). We find this argument persuasive.

We hold that Abdul-Jabbar has alleged sufficient facts to state a claim under both California common law and section 3344. The statute's reference to "name or likeness" is not limited to present or current use. To the extent GMC's use of the plaintiff's birth name attracted television viewers' attention, GMC gained a commercial advantage. *See East-wood*, 198 Cal. Rptr. at 349 ("The first step toward selling a product or service is to attract the consumers' attention."). Whether or not Lew Alcindor "equals" Kareem Abdul-Jabbar in the sense that "'Here's Johnny' equal [led] Johnny Carson," or "'the greatest' equal[led] Muhammed Ali"—or the glamorously dressed robot equalled Vanna White—is a question for the jury. *See Waits*, 978 F.2d at 1102 (observing that a celebrity's renown is relative and "adequately reflected in the amount of damages recoverable").

As to injury, ... Abdul-Jabbar alleges, and submits evidence to show, that he was injured economically because the ad will make it difficult for him to endorse other automobiles, and emotionally because people may be led to believe he has abandoned his current name and assume he has renounced his religion. These allegations suffice to support his action....

GMC makes a final argument that its use of the name Lew Alcindor was "incidental" and therefore not actionable, citing *Namath v. Sports Illustrated*, 80 Misc.2d 531, 363 N.Y.S.2d 276 (1975), for the proposition that "newsworthy" items are privileged under right of publicity laws. The district court correctly rejected this line of reasoning as irrelevant. The *Namath* court held that Sports Illustrated was entitled under the First Amendment to use its own news stories to promote sales of its magazine. 363 N.Y.S.2d at 279–80.

A recent California case, *Montana v. San Jose Mercury News, Inc.*, 34 Cal. App. 4th 790, 40 Cal. Rptr. 2d 639 (1995), reaches a similar conclusion. The California Court of Appeal denied football star Joe Montana's claim that a newspaper's use of his image, taken from its Super Bowl cover story and sold in poster form, violated his section 3344 and common law right of publicity, holding that: 1) the posters represented newsworthy events, and 2) a newspaper has a constitutional right to promote itself by reproducing its news stories. *Id.* at 641–42. As the court noted, section 3344(d) provides that no prior consent is required for use of a "name, voice, signature, photograph, or likeness in connection with any news, public affairs, or sports broadcast or account, or any political campaign." Cal.Civ.Code § 3344; *Montana,* 40 Cal. Rptr. 2d at 640.

While Lew Alcindor's basketball record may be said to be "newsworthy," its use is not automatically privileged. GMC used the information in the context of an automobile advertisement, not in a news or sports account. Hence GMC is not protected by section 3344(d).

For the reasons set out above, we reverse the judgment of the district court and remand for trial on the claims alleging violation of the California common law right of publicity and section 3344, as well as the claims alleging violation of the Lanham Act.

REVERSED and REMANDED

Notes and Questions

1. The argument that the right of publicity is abandoned by non-use has more than a little in common with the idea, introduced in Chapter 4, that one's identity must be commercially exploited in order to be protected post-mortem. As we saw in Chapter 4, although the latter argument was endorsed in dicta in the *Lugosi* decision, it largely has not been successful. Is there any reason to distinguish between the two situations? Is relinquishing a name entirely different from failing to commercially exploit it?

2. In trademark law, a personal name must be used in connection with goods and services in order to be protected as a mark. A personal name must also have acquired "secondary meaning," that is, it must be perceived by the public to signify the source or origin of goods and services rather than merely be descriptive, in order to protected as a mark. Should these trademark law doctrines be adopted by analogy for the right of publicity? Why or why not?

3. Kareem Abdul-Jabbar was already famous under the name Lew Alcindor before he adopted his Muslim name. Similarly, Cassius Clay was already famous as a boxer before he adopted his Muslim name, Muhammad Ali. In both cases, arguably there was a significant amount of residual goodwill accumulated by the former name. But it is common for singers and movie stars to adopt stage names at the outset of their careers, before they become famous. In such a case, should the issue of abandonment be treated any differently? Should the estate of actor John Wayne be able to prevent commercial use of the name Marion Morrison? Should singer Elton John be able to prevent commercial use of the name Reginald Dwight?

4. General Motors also argued that the use of the name "Lew Alcindor" as the answer to a trivia question was newsworthy, even though it occurred in the context of an advertisement. This is a good time to review the material in Chapter VII on newsworthiness. On remand, what arguments could you make that this use should be permitted? Should it matter whether or not the public perceives the advertisement as an endorsement of Oldsmobile cars?

5. Note that federal trademark law contains two related but distinct "fair use" doctrines: descriptive use and nominative fair use. Descriptive fair use is codified in section 33(b)(4) of the Lanham Act. It provides a defense when:

> [T]he use of the name, term, or device charged to be an infringement is a use, otherwise than as a mark ... of a term or device which is descriptive of and used fairly in good faith only to describe the goods and services of such party ...

17 U.S.C. § 1115(b)(4). Descriptive fair use would apply, for example, in a case covered by the first-sale doctrine: because it is lawful to re-sell genuine celebrity merchandise, it is lawful to use the celebrity's name to describe what the merchandise is. We have seen a similar principle at work in some of the First Amendment cases we studied in Chapters VII and VIII: because it is lawful to publish a news article or release a movie about a celebrity, it is also lawful to use the celebrity's name in describing what the article or movie is about.

6. "Nominative" fair use is the use of a trademark to describe the trademark owner or its goods and services. As Judge Kozinski pointed out in the *New Kids on the Block* case (cited in *Abdul-Jabbar*):

> With many well-known trademarks, such as Jell-O, Scotch tape and Kleenex, there are equally informative non-trademark words describing the products (gelatin, cellophane tape and facial tissue). But sometimes there is no descriptive substitute, and a problem ... is presented when many goods and services are effectively identifiable only by their trademarks. For example, one might refer to "the two-time world champions" or "the professional basketball team from Chicago," but it's far simpler (and more likely to be understood) to refer to the Chicago Bulls. In such cases, use of the trademark does not imply sponsorship or endorsement of the product because the mark is used only to describe the thing, rather than to identify its source.

971 F.2d at 306. To deal with such cases, Judge Kozinski invented the "nominative" fair use doctrine, which has three elements, as discussed in *Abdul-Jabbar*.

The district court in *Abdul-Jabbar* held that nominative fair use applied as matter of law. On what basis did the Ninth Circuit reverse and remand the Lanham Act claim for trial? Which of the three elements of "nominative fair use" was potentially problematic? If you were a juror, would you find that "nominative fair use" applies here?

7. The Ninth Circuit discussed abandonment twice: first for the Lanham Act claim, and again for the right of publicity claim. But the court only discussed "nominative fair use" in conjunction with the Lanham Act claim. Does "nominative fair use" apply to right of publicity claims? Should it? In which of the cases that we have studied might nominative fair use change the outcome if it did apply?

8. Note that copyright law also contains a "fair use" doctrine, but that the copyright version is completely distinct from the trademark "fair use" doctrines. As codified in the 1976 Copyright Act, the copyright version states:

> [T]he fair use of a copyrighted work, ... for purposes such as criticism, comment, news reporting, teaching..., scholarship, or research, is not an infringement of copyright. In determining whether the use made of a work in any particular case is a fair use the factors to be considered shall include—
>
> (1) the purpose and character of the use, including whether such use is of a commercial nature or is for nonprofit educational purposes;
>
> (2) the nature of the copyrighted work;
>
> (3) the amount and substantiality of the portion used in relation to the copyrighted work as a whole; and
>
> (4) the effect of the use upon the potential market for or value of the copyrighted work.

17 U.S.C. § 107. Do you think the "fair use" doctrine, or something like it, should apply to rights of publicity? Why or why not? Do factors two and three make much sense in the

context of rights of publicity? Recall that in *Comedy III Prods. v. Saderup* (reprinted in Chapter VIII), the California Supreme Court thought that only the first factor, which under case law includes consideration of whether the use is "transformative," should be applied.

As we have seen, the absence of a "fair use" doctrine (or something like it) in rights of publicity cases forces many such cases to be decided under the First Amendment, as a matter of Constitutional law, rather than as a matter of statute or common law.

9. In 1995, Sharmon Shah, a running back at UCLA, was given the name "Karim Abdul-Jabbar," which means "most generous servant of the Creator," in a Muslim naming ceremony. In 1996, Karim was drafted by the Miami Dolphins and became an NFL star, which led to increased sales of Dolphins jerseys bearing his new name. In 1997, Karim was sued by Kareem Abdul-Jabbar, the basketball player, for trademark infringement and violation of his right of publicity.

Although both men adopted or were given the name for religious reasons, Kareem alleged that Karim wore the number "33", both at UCLA and in Miami, in order to exploit the similarity of their names. (Karim contended that he picked the number "33" because of Dallas Cowboys running back Tony Dorsett, and that he had used it long before he was given a Muslim name.) Kareem also alleged that he had contacted Karim in 1995, before any commercial exploitation had occurred, and suggested that Karim adopt another name.

How would you analyze the issues in this case? In real life, the lawsuit was settled in April 1998, with the younger Karim agreeing to use only the name "Abdul" on his jerseys and merchandise, rather than the full name "Abdul-Jabbar."

D. Statutes of Limitations and Laches

Christoff v. Nestlé USA, Inc.
47 Cal. 4th 468, 97 Cal. Rptr. 3d 798, 213 P.3d 132 (2009)

Moreno, J.:

In 1986, professional model Russell Christoff was paid $250 to pose for a photograph to be used in Canada on a label for bricks of coffee. Sixteen years later, Christoff saw his face on a jar of Taster's Choice instant coffee in the United States and discovered that his image had been used without his consent on millions of labels sold internationally for the preceding five years. Christoff filed the present action for appropriation of his likeness six years after Nestlé USA, Inc. (Nestlé), began using his image on the Taster's Choice label but less than a year after his discovery.

The trial court applied a two-year statute of limitations and instructed the jury to determine under the discovery rule whether Christoff knew or should have known earlier that Nestlé had used his image. The jury found that Christoff did not know, and should not reasonably have suspected prior to seeing the jar, that his image was being used without his consent and awarded him more than $15 million in damages.

The Court of Appeal reversed, holding that under the single-publication rule, because Christoff had not filed his lawsuit within two years after Nestlé first "published" the label, his cause of action is barred by the statute of limitations unless, on remand, the trier of fact finds that Nestlé had hindered Christoff's discovery of the use of his photograph, or that the label had been "republished." We granted review.

We agree with the Court of Appeal that the judgment must be reversed because the trial court erroneously ruled that the single-publication rule does not apply to claims for appropriation of likeness. But we do not agree with the Court of Appeal that this means that Christoff's action necessarily is barred by the statute of limitations unless he can show on remand that Nestlé had hindered his discovery of the use of his photograph, or that the label had been "republished." The Court of Appeal's ruling presupposes that Nestlé's various uses of Christoff's likeness, including its production of the product label for a five-year period, necessarily constituted a "single publication" within the meaning of the single-publication rule. Because the parties were prevented by the trial court's erroneous legal ruling from developing a record concerning whether the single-publication rule applied, we remand the matter for further proceedings.

FACTS

In 1986, Russell Christoff, an actor and professional model, posed gazing at a cup of coffee, as if he enjoyed the aroma. The photo shoot was arranged by Nestlé Canada.[2] Christoff was paid $250 for a two-hour photo shoot and received a contract providing that if Nestlé Canada used the picture on a label it was designing for a brick of Taster's Choice coffee, Christoff would be paid $2,000 plus an agency commission. The price for any other use of Christoff's image would require further negotiations. Without informing Christoff, or paying him according to the terms of the contract, Nestlé Canada used Christoff's image on the coffee brick.

Eleven years later, in 1997, Nestlé decided to redesign its label for Taster's Choice instant coffee, which, for three decades, had prominently featured a "taster," that is a person peering into a cup of coffee. The high resolution artwork of the original "taster" used to produce the existing label had been lost. Nestlé searched without success for other high resolution artwork of the original "taster," but found instead the photograph of Christoff that Nestlé Canada had used on the coffee brick, which satisfied the requirements.

Nestlé decided to use Christoff's image because he looked "distinguished" and resembled the original "taster." Christoff's photograph was "youthened" to make him appear younger and more similar to the original "taster." Nestlé believed that it had authority to use Christoff's image because it had been widely used in Canada. Nestlé never investigated the scope of the consent and never asked Christoff if he consented to the use of his image. Christoff's image was used in the redesigned Taster's Choice label beginning in 1998. The redesigned label was used on several different Taster's Choice jars, including regular coffee, decaffeinated, and various flavors. Labels bearing Christoff's image also were produced in different languages and placed on jars of coffee to be sold internationally. For the label used in Mexico, Christoff's image was altered to add sideburns and darken his complexion. Images of jars of coffee bearing Christoff's image appeared in Nestlé's multiple advertising campaigns for Taster's Choice, including transit ads, coupons in newspapers, magazine advertisements, and Internet advertisements.

In 2002, a person standing in line with Christoff at a hardware store remarked that he "look[ed] like the guy on my coffee jar." A month or so later, on June 4, 2002, Christoff

---

2. Nestlé Canada is a corporation affiliated with but separate from respondent and is not a party to this appeal.

saw a jar of Taster's Choice instant coffee on a store shelf and, for the first time, recognized his photograph on the label. He purchased the jar of coffee and called his agent.

In 2003, Nestlé again redesigned its label using another model, James Vaccaro, as the "taster." Vaccaro was paid $150,000 for the use of his image for 10 years. The new label started circulating in May 2003, but jars of Taster's Choice with Christoff's image were still in Nestlé's inventory and could have been shipped to retailers.

PROCEDURAL BACKGROUND

In 2003, Christoff sued Nestlé, alleging causes of action for unauthorized commercial use of another's likeness in violation of Civil Code section 3344, common law appropriation of likeness, quantum meruit (initially labeled "quasi-contract"), and unjust enrichment. The trial court denied Nestlé's motion for summary judgment based on the statute of limitations, ruling that the Uniform Single Publication Act as codified in Civil Code section 3425.3 (hereafter section 3425.3), which states that "[n]o person shall have more than one cause of action for damages for libel or slander or invasion of privacy or any other tort founded upon any single publication or exhibition or utterance, such as any one issue of a newspaper or book or magazine,"[5] did not apply to Christoff's claims because they were not "based on defamation." The trial court reasoned that the single-publication rule "was developed in the common law to avoid the problems that mass publication of books and newspapers created for the tort of defamation." The court explained that Christoff's "claim is not defamation-like because he is not alleging that he suffered damages from offensive communications," but rather his "claim arises from the alleged unauthorized use of his likeness, which is protected by his right of publicity." Christoff "does not claim that this use was offensive, but instead seeks compensation for the defendant's use of his likeness in advertising."

The court applied a two-year statute of limitations under Code of Civil Procedure section 339 and instructed the jury that because Christoff filed his complaint on February 7, 2003, he could "claim damages that took place at any time on or after February 7, 2001." The court further instructed the jury that "the rule of delayed discovery" would apply and Christoff could "also seek damages that took place from the time Nestlé USA first used his image" if Christoff proved that "prior to his discovery of the facts he did not previously suspect, or should have suspected, that his photograph was on the Taster's Choice label." The trial court denied Nestlé's motion for summary adjudication, in which it asserted that there was no evidence it knowingly used Christoff's photograph without his consent....

The jury concluded as follows: (1) Nestlé knowingly used Christoff's photograph or likeness on the Taster's Choice labels for commercial purposes without Christoff's consent; (2) prior to 2002, Christoff did not know and should not have known or reasonably suspected that his photograph was being used for commercial purposes; (3) Christoff suffered $330,000 in actual damages; (4) the profits attributable to the use of Christoff's photograph or likeness were $15,305,850.... Nestlé appealed from the judgment and the order awarding costs and attorney fees.

The Court of Appeal reversed the judgment and remanded the case for a new trial, ruling that the single-publication rule codified in section 3425.3 applied to the tort of ap-

---

5. Section 3425.3 states: "No person shall have more than one cause of action for damages for libel or slander or invasion of privacy or any other tort founded upon any single publication or exhibition or utterance, such as any one issue of a newspaper or book or magazine or any one presentation to an audience or any one broadcast over radio or television or any one exhibition of a motion picture. Recovery in any action shall include all damages for any such tort suffered by the plaintiff in all jurisdictions."

propriation of likeness. The court applied our decision in *Shively v. Bozanich* (2003) 31 Cal. 4th 1230, 1245 (hereafter *Shively*), which held that the defamation cause of action in that case accrued upon the "first general distribution of the publication to the public," and reasoned that whether the discovery rule delayed the accrual of the cause of action depended upon whether Nestlé hindered Christoff's discovery of the use of his photograph. The court directed that, in a retrial, the trier of fact must consider whether Nestlé hindered Christoff's discovery of the use of his photograph and "whether any republications occurred within the two-year limitations period."[7]

DISCUSSION

The Court of Appeal ruled that the single-publication rule as codified in section 3425.3 applied to Christoff's cause of action for unauthorized commercial use of his likeness and, thus, the statute of limitations was triggered when Nestlé first "published" the label and expired two years later unless accrual of Christoff's action was delayed by the delayed discovery rule or the statute of limitations began anew because Nestlé "republished" the label. We agree that, in general, the single-publication rule as codified in section 3425.3 applies to causes of action for unauthorized commercial use of likeness, but in order to determine when the statute of limitations was triggered for Christoff's action, we must decide whether Nestlé's unauthorized use of Christoff's image, including its production of the label, constituted a "single publication" within the meaning of the single-publication rule. As explained below, the record on appeal is insufficient to permit this court to answer this question.

The Court of Appeal was correct that the single-publication rule as codified in section 3425.3 applies, in general, to a cause of action for unauthorized commercial use of likeness. The language of section 3425.3 is quite broad and applies by its terms to any action "for libel or slander or invasion of privacy *or any other tort* founded upon any single publication or exhibition or utterance, such as any one issue of a newspaper or book or magazine or any one presentation to an audience or any one broadcast over radio or television or any one exhibition of a motion picture." (Italics added.) "When the Legislature inserted the clause '*or any other tort*' it is presumed to have meant exactly what it said." (*Strick v. Superior Court* (1983) 143 Cal. App. 3d 916, 924.) The rule announced in section 3425.3 is "'not aimed at the particular tort alleged, but rather at the manner in which the tort is executed.'" (*Ibid.*) ... We agree with the Court of Appeal, therefore, that the trial court erred in ruling that section 3425.3 did not apply to Christoff's claims because they were not "based on defamation."

The Court of Appeal then turned to our decision in *Shively*, which held that a cause of action that is governed by the single-publication rule accrues "from the date of the '"first general distribution of the publication to the public."' (*Shively, supra*, 31 Cal. 4th at p. 1245.)" Christoff argues, *inter alia*, that the single-publication rule does not apply to Nestlé's printing of its product label because it is not "a single 'publication,' a one-time occurrence," such as a newspaper, book, magazine, or television broadcast. Nestlé counters that "the rule was intended to apply to multiple printings of the same publication." The question is more subtle than either of these positions would suggest.

In order to apply the single-publication rule, a court first must identify what constitutes a "single integrated publication" (*Belli v. Roberts Brothers Furs* (1966) 240 Cal. App.

---

7. The Court of Appeal further ruled that the two-year statute of limitations set forth in Code of Civil Procedure section 339 applied, that Nestlé knowingly used Christoff's likeness within the meaning of Civil Code section 3344, [and] that the award of more than $15 million for profits attributable to the use of Christoff's photograph was not supported by substantial evidence....

2d 284, 289) within the meaning of the rule, such as the printing and distribution of a particular issue of a newspaper, magazine, or book. Whether the printing of a product label over a five-year period constitutes a single integrated publication within the meaning of the single-publication rule is an issue of first impression in this state. In addition to producing the product label, Nestlé also used Christoff's likeness in other forms, including transit ads, coupons in newspapers, magazine advertisements, and Internet advertisements. This raises questions whether each of these activities constituted a "single integrated publication," whether the entire advertising campaign should be considered a "single integrated publication," or whether Nestlé's first use of Christoff's image triggered the running of the statute of limitations for all subsequent uses in whatever form. These are important questions, and there is little authority to turn to for guidance.

The single-publication rule was created to address the problem that arose with the advent of mass communication from the general rule in defamation cases that "each time the defamatory statement is communicated to a third person … the statement is said to have been 'published,'" giving rise to a separate cause of action. (*Shively, supra,* 31 Cal. 4th at p. 1242.) "[T]he principle that each communication of a defamatory remark to a new audience constitutes a separate 'publication,' giving rise to a separate cause of action, led to the conclusion that each sale or delivery of a copy of a newspaper or book containing a defamation also constitutes a separate publication of the defamation to a new audience, giving rise to a separate cause of action for defamation. [Citations.] This conclusion had the potential to subject the publishers of books and newspapers to lawsuits stating hundreds, thousands, or even millions of causes of action for a single issue of a periodical or edition of a book." (*Id.* at pp. 1243–1244.) "As one commentator stated: '… Regardless of whether it was an appropriate rule in 1849 it is horrendous today when magazine readers and radio and TV audiences may total many millions.' [Citation.]" (*Hebrew Academy of San Francisco v. Goldman* (2007) 42 Cal. 4th 883, 891, fn. 2.)

The common law rule that each "publication" of a defamatory statement created a new cause of action "also had the potential to disturb the repose that the statute of limitations ordinarily would afford, because a new publication of the defamation could occur if a copy of the newspaper or book were preserved for many years and then came into the hands of a new reader.… The statute of limitations could be tolled indefinitely, perhaps forever, under this approach." (*Shively, supra,* 31 Cal. 4th 1230, 1244.) We cited as an example "a 19th-century English case that concluded a plaintiff could bring an action seeking redress for libel against a publisher based upon an allegedly defamatory remark contained in a newspaper issued 17 years prior to the plaintiff's discovery of the defamation, on the theory that the sale to the plaintiff of the long-forgotten copy of the newspaper constituted a new publication, starting anew the running of the period of limitations. [Citation.]" (*Ibid.*) We observed "courts recognized that the advent of books and newspapers that were circulated among a mass readership threatened unending and potentially ruinous liability as well as overwhelming (and endless) litigation, as long as courts adhered to the rule that each sale of a copy of a newspaper or a book, regardless how long after original publication, constituted a new and separate publication." (*Ibid.*)

To correct these problems, "courts fashioned what became known as the single-publication rule, holding that, for any single edition of a newspaper or book, there was but a single potential action for a defamatory statement contained in the newspaper or book, no matter how many copies of the newspaper or the book were distributed. [Citations.]" (*Shively, supra,* 31 Cal. 4th at p. 1245.) The common law single-publication rule was codified in 1955 when California adopted the Uniform Single Publication Act by enacting section 3425.3.… The prefatory note to the uniform act states that under the single-publication rule "any single integrated publication, such as one edition of a newspaper or magazine, or one broadcast, is treated as a unit, giving rise to only one cause of action." (U. Single Pub. Act (2005) 14 U. Laws Ann. 469.)[8]

The decision in *Gregoire v. G.P. Putnams Sons* (N.Y. 1948) 81 N.E.2d 45, upon which we relied in *Shively*, recognized that the purpose of the single-publication rule was to give meaning to the statute of limitations as "a statute of repose — designed 'to spare the courts from litigation of stale claims, and the citizen from being put to his defense after memories have faded, witnesses have died or disappeared, and evidence has been lost.' [Citation.]" (*Id.* at p. 48.) The plaintiff in *Gregoire* filed a suit for defamation nearly five years after the book *Total Espionage* first was published. Although approximately 6,000 copies of the book had been sold in each of the first two years of its distribution, only 60 copies had been sold from stock in the year prior to the filing of the action. The plaintiff argued that these relatively few sales from stock caused the book to be "republished," triggering a new limitations period. The court observed that accepting the plaintiffs view would mean that "although a book containing libelous material may have been the product of but one edition or printing fifty years ago, if, by sale from stock or by display, the publisher continues to make unsold copies of the single publication available to the public today, such conduct would amount to a republication of any libel the book contains and thereby would become actionable. Under such a rule the Statute of Limitation would never expire so long as a copy of such book remained in stock and is made by the publisher the subject of a sale or inspection by the public." (*Id.* at pp. 48–49.)

The court in *Gregoire* thus held that the publisher was entitled to repose following the initial process of printing and releasing the book to the public and that subsequent sales from the stock so produced would not begin the statute of limitations anew. The court stated "that the publication of a libelous book, involving styling, printing, binding and those other acts which enable a publisher on a given date to release to the public thousands of copies of a single printing or impression, affords the one libeled a legal basis for only one cause of action which arises when the finished product is released by the publisher for sale in accord with trade practice." [*Id.* at 49.]

The first California case to apply the single-publication rule, *Belli v. Roberts Brothers Furs, supra,* 240 Cal. App. 2d 284, held that the February 14, 1962, issue of the San Francisco Chronicle newspaper, which was composed of six editions that were issued over a two-day period was "a single, integrated publication." (*Id.* at p. 289.) The court concluded that "the Legislature intended to abrogate the right to bring a separate action based upon defamatory matter appearing in several editions of a newspaper or magazine, where, as here, all of the editions comprise a single issue of a particular date." (*Id.* at p. 289.)

The Court of Appeal therefore concluded that "[t]he various editions of the Chronicle for February 14, 1962, comprise a single integrated publication, namely the issue of the newspaper for that date. As we have seen, the allegedly defamatory matter appeared in the first edition and was repeated without change in each and every edition that followed. It has generally been held that, in the case of a single, integrated publication, the cause of action based upon objectionable matter appearing in the publication accrues upon the first general distribution of the publication to the public. [Citation.]" (*Belli v. Roberts Brothers Furs, supra,* 240 Cal. App. 2d at p. 289.) ...

---

8. The Uniform Single Publication Act has been adopted in six other states — Arizona, Idaho, Illinois, New Mexico, North Dakota, and Pennsylvania — and the "great majority" of the remaining states follow the single-publication rule by judicial decision. (*Keeton v. Hustler Magazine, Inc.* (1984) 465 U.S. 770, 777, fn. 8.)

The single-publication rule is intended to prevent a "single integrated publication" from resulting in numerous causes of action because the publication is received by a mass audience. (*Rinaldi v. Viking Penguin, Inc.* (N.Y. 1981) 420 N.E.2d 377, 381 ["neither the time nor the circumstance in which a copy of a book or other publication finds its way to a particular consumer is, in and of itself, to militate against the operation of the unitary, integrated publication concept"].) As the Court of Appeal recognized in *Miller v. Collectors Universe, Inc.* (2008) 159 Cal. App. 4th 988, 998: "The original purpose of the single-publication rule is apparent, both from its history and from the language of the California statute implementing it. The rule was originally directed at *mass* communications, such as communications in newspapers, books, magazines, radio and television broadcasts, and speeches to an audience. Where the offending language is read or heard by a large audience, the rule limits the plaintiff to a single cause of action for each mass communication. A separate cause of action for each member of the public audience is disallowed."

The rule does not address the issue of repeated publications of the same libelous material over a substantial period of time. (See *Kanarek v. Bugliosi* (1980) 108 Cal. App. 3d 327, 332 ["the Uniform Single Publication Act ... was not designed to give unending immunity for repeated publications of libelous matter].) This distinction is clearly made in the Restatement Second of Torts, which adopts the single-publication rule that "[a]ny one edition of a book or newspaper, or any one radio or television broadcast, exhibition of a motion picture or similar aggregate communication is a single publication." (Rest. 2d Torts, 577A, p. 208.) The comments explain: "An exceptional rule, sometimes called the single publication rule, is applied in cases where the same communication is heard at the same time by two or more persons. In order to avoid multiplicity of actions and undue harassment of the defendant by repeated suits by new individuals, as well as excessive damages that might have been recovered in numerous separate suits, the communication to the entire group is treated as one publication, giving rise to only one cause of action. (*Id.,* cmt. b, p. 209.) The single publication rule applies also to the issue of any one edition of a newspaper, magazine or book; to any one broadcast over radio or television; to any one exhibition of a motion picture; to any one theatrical performance or other presentation to an audience; and to any similar aggregate communication that reaches a large number of persons at the same time...." (*Id.,* cmt. c, p. 209.)

It is not clear whether the production of a product label over a period of years is a "single integrated publication" that triggers the running of the statute of limitations when the first such label is distributed to the public. Publishing an issue of a newspaper or magazine or an edition of a book is a discrete publishing event. A publisher that prints and distributes an issue of a magazine or an edition of a book is entitled to repose from the threat that a copy of that magazine or book will surface years later and trigger a lawsuit. But as we stated earlier, there is little case law or academic commentary discussing whether a manufacturer that produces a product label for a period of years is entitled to the same repose, especially while that product label is still being produced....

We decline to resolve this important issue without the benefit of a sufficient factual record that reveals the manner in which the labels were produced and distributed, including when production of the labels began and ceased. The parties did not have a reason or an opportunity to present such evidence in light of the trial court's erroneous ruling that the single-publication rule did not apply to claims for misappropriation of likeness. The parties will have that opportunity on remand to the superior court. If on remand it is established that all or some portion of the production of the label constituted a single integrated publication, then the superior court should further consider whether the statute of limitation began anew because the label was "republished" within the meaning of the single-publication rule.

Whether producing the product labels was a "single integrated publication" is not the only issue that the trial court will face on remand. Evidence was introduced at trial that Christoff's image also was used without his consent in various forms of advertising, including transit ads, coupons in newspapers, magazine advertisements, and Internet advertisements. Nestlé may be able to show that the production of some or all of these items were single integrated publications and that the statute of limitations was triggered as to that item when it first was distributed to the public.

The Court of Appeal further held that the trial court erred in instructing the jury to apply the delayed discovery rule if it found that "prior to his discovery of the facts [Christoff] did not previously suspect, or should have suspected, that his photograph was on the Taster's Choice label." We agree. "[C]ourts uniformly have *rejected* the application of the discovery rule to libels published in books, magazines, and newspapers, pointing out that application of the discovery rule would undermine the protection provided by the single-publication rule." (*Shively, supra,* 31 Cal. 4th at p. 1250.) The same logic applies to a product label such as the one in the present case that is "not published in an inherently secretive manner" (*Hebrew Academy of San Francisco v. Goldman, supra,* 42 Cal. 4th 883, 894), but is distributed widely to the public.

DISPOSITION

The judgment of the Court of Appeal is reversed to the extent that it holds that, for purposes of the statute of limitations, Christoff's cause of action necessarily accrued when Nestlé first "published" the label under the rule we announced in *Shively v. Bozanich, supra,* 31 Cal. 4th 1230. In all other respects, the judgment of the Court of Appeal is affirmed and the matter is remanded to the Court of Appeal for further proceedings consistent with our opinion.

George, C.J., Kennard, Baxter, Werdegar, Chin, and Corrigan, JJ., concur.

Werdegar, J., Concurring:

I concur fully in the majority opinion. In particular, I agree that without a better factual record we cannot determine how California's single publication rule (Civ. Code, § 3425.3 (hereafter section 3425.3)) should apply here and hence whether, or to what extent, plaintiff's action is barred by the statute of limitations. Nonetheless, I believe some general principles relevant to that question may be discerned from the language of section 3425.3.

Leaving aside any Taster's Choice labels on which plaintiff's image was significantly altered, and further disregarding advertisements that employed photographs of a label,[2] the broadest question posed here is whether *all* distribution of labels employing the original misappropriated image, whenever they occurred, should be deemed to constitute a single publication for purposes of section 3425.3. Phrased more generally, should a series of temporally distinct publications be treated as a single publication because each consisted of substantially the same text or images?

On this question, California courts have not spoken, and courts from other jurisdictions have reached diverse results. Some have held that multiple broadcasts, distributions or displays of identical material constitute a single publication for purposes of the statute

---

2. That both these categories constituted separate publications from the original labels themselves seems clear, as they differed in contents from the original labels and were apparently aimed at different audiences. (See *Rinaldi v. Viking Penguin, Inc.* (N.Y. Sup. Ct. 1979) 422 N.Y.S.2d 552, 556; *Kanarek v. Bugliosi* (1980) 108 Cal. App. 3d 327, 332–333.)

of limitations, and not a series of republications. (See, e.g., *Blair v. Nevada Landing Partnership* (Ill. App. 2006) 859 N.E.2d 1188, 1193–1194 [use of the plaintiff's image in various advertisements within a casino and on the casino's Web site over a nine-year period treated as a single publication]; *Auscape Intern. v. National Geographic Soc.* (S.D.N.Y. 2006) 461 F. Supp. 2d 174, 185–187 [the defendant, which each year distributed a digital compilation of past magazine issues, including in each year's compilation all the prior years' contents, did not thereby republish the prior years' issues]; *Zoll v. Jordache Enterprises, Inc.* (S.D.N.Y. 2002) 2002 WL 31873461, pp. *9–*11 [rebroadcast of 1978 television commercial in 2000 was not a republication of the original 1978 broadcast].)

Other courts have looked on each broadcast or display as a separate publication, or republication, each of which, if it violates the plaintiff's rights, begins a new limitations period. (*See, e.g., Wells v. Talk Radio Network-FM, Inc.* (N.D. Ill. 2008) 2008 WL 4888992, pp. *1–*3 [each unauthorized use of the plaintiff's voice in radio advertisements broadcast repeatedly for two years was a rebroadcast triggering a new statute of limitations period]; *Lehman v. Discovery Communications, Inc.* (E.D.N.Y. 2004) 332 F. Supp. 2d 534, 535–536 [where the defendant broadcast a program 17 times over more than two years, each broadcast was a republication of the allegedly defamatory material]; *Baucom v. Haverty* (Fla. App. 2001) 805 So.2d 959, 960–961 [where, over several years, the defendant repeatedly used the plaintiff's name and image in marketing presentations to potential clients, each such presentation was a new publication].)

In my view, the latter approach is more consistent with our statutory language. As illustrative of a single publication, section 3425.3 refers to "any one issue of a newspaper or book or magazine or any one presentation to an audience or any one broadcast over radio or television or any one exhibition of a motion picture." The statute thus dictates we treat as a separate publication any reissue, rebroadcast or reexhibition, even though the publication's contents or the manner of its distribution or display has not been changed. Section 3425.3's reference to "any one broadcast," for example, appears to preclude a result like that in *Zoll v. Jordache Enterprises, Inc., supra,* where two broadcasts of the same advertisement, separated by 22 years, were deemed to be a single publication.

Granted, determining what is a single "issue" of printed material presents special difficulties. When large numbers of a book are printed and distributed at one time, the later distribution of smaller numbers from stock is considered part of the original publication. (*Gregoire v. G.P. Putnam's Sons* (N.Y. 1948) 81 N.E.2d 45, 46, 49.) The same rule has been applied to additional printings of a single book edition, at least within a short time of its original publication. (See *Fleury v. Harper & Row, Publishers, Inc.* (9th Cir. 1983) 698 F.2d 1022, 1028 [where a book was published in November 1978, "continued printing of the book into 1979" was part of the same publication].) Would the same rule apply if there were no initial mass printing, but individual copies or small batches of copies were printed and sent out to readers on demand? Arguably it should, for each instance of access to text on the Internet is not considered a separate publication (*Firth v. State* (N.Y. Ct. Cl. 2000) 706 N.Y.S.2d 835, 841–843), nor presumably would be each download of text in digital form to an electronic reader or audio device; the use of printed paper as a distribution medium should not lead to a different result.

A useful distinction lies in earlier cases' criterion of a republication decision that is "conscious [and] independent" (*Barres v. Holt, Rinehart & Winston, Inc.* (N.J. Super. 1974) 330 A.2d 38, 46, *aff'd* (N.J. 1977) 378 A.2d 1148) or "conscious and deliberate" (*Rinaldi v. Viking Penguin, Inc.* (N.Y. 1981) 420 N.E.2d 377, 382). Where the publisher has set up a more or less automated system for printing and distributing an item or for downloading it in digital form and does not make a separate publishing decision as to each copy or small batch of copies, to call each such distribution a new "issue" of the material would defeat the purposes of the single publication rule. Conversely, where a publication has been out of print or unavailable in digital form for some time and the publisher makes a conscious decision to reissue it or again make it available for download, no reason appears in the text or purposes of section 3425.3 why the publisher should not be separately responsible for any tort committed in republishing.

For these reasons, I doubt defendant's entire five-year course of printing and distributing labels may be deemed a single publication simply because the labels were not substantially altered during that time. The trial court should consider as well whether the production and distribution of labels was predetermined by a single initial decision or whether defendant (that is, the officers or managing agents of defendant corporation) made at any relevant time a conscious, deliberate choice to continue, renew or expand the use of labels bearing plaintiff's misappropriated image. If any such decisions occurred during the period defined by the statute of limitations, plaintiff should be able to recover damages caused by publication pursuant to those decisions.

Notes and Questions

1. As the court notes, the single publication rule has been applied to right of publicity actions in New York, and in other states as well. *See* J. Thomas McCarthy, THE RIGHTS OF PUBLICITY AND PRIVACY § 11:40 (2d ed. 2008). However, "it can be argued that the policy of the single publication rule should not apply in right of publicity cases to the infringing use of identity on a label on a consumer product which is sold in stores over a long period of time." *Id.* at 748. Prof. McCarthy also notes that in copyright and trademark cases, damages typically are allowed to be recovered for all infringements that occurred within the limitations period. Should a right of publicity suit based on continuous sales of merchandise be subject to the single publication rule, or should it follow the rule in copyright and trademark cases?

2. The *Christoff* court also notes that there is considerable disagreement over what constitutes a "republication" under the Single Publication Rule. Previous cases have held that hardback and paperback editions of a book are separate "publications," and that theatrical and DVD releases of a movie are separate "publications." Given these decisions, would it make sense to hold that coffee labels, transit ads, newspaper coupons, magazine ads and Internet ads were only a single "publication"? Would such a holding be consistent with the language of the California statute? Does Justice Werdegar's approach help in making this determination?

3. A corollary to the Single Publication Rule is that the cause of action accrues, for purposes of the statute of limitations, when the material is first released to the public. This can create a trap for the unwary, because it is common for magazines to be published earlier than the dates that appear on their covers. Thus, in the *Belli* case (cited in *Christoff*) the court dismissed an action filed on February 14, 1963, based on an alleged libel published in the February 14, 1962 edition of the *San Francisco Chronicle*, as untimely, because the *Chronicle* had distributed and sold copies of the February 14 newspaper the evening before. If there is a lesson here, it is: don't wait until the last possible day to file a lawsuit.

4. Next, the court rejects the application of the discovery rule, noting that it would defeat the purposes of the single publication rule. Under *Shively*, the discovery rule does

not apply unless the document was "hidden from view," as in a personnel file, such that the plaintiff "lacked a meaningful ability to discover the use of his likeness." Thus, a plaintiff is deemed to have constructive knowledge of a nationwide publication of a magazine, even if he or she never saw or read that particular edition of the magazine. Similarly, if on remand it is determined that a single publication occurred more than two years before Christoff filed suit, an action based on that publication will be barred.

5. The choice of a particular statute of limitations is often difficult. For example, is an action based on the common-law right of publicity an action "for injury ... to one caused by the wrongful act or neglect of another" (former Cal. Civ. Proc. Code § 340(3), one year) or an action "upon a contract, obligation or liability not founded upon an instrument of writing" (Cal. Civ. Proc. Code § 339(1), two years)? The Court of Appeal in *Christoff* chose the latter, noting that it has been held to apply to "torts protecting property rights." The California Supreme Court did not review this portion of the lower court's opinion (see footnote 7); and because California amended its statutes in 2002 to increase the statute of limitations for personal injury to two years (Cal. Civ. Proc. Code § 335.1), the choice between these two no longer matters in California. Arguably, however, the statutory rights of publicity in California (including the post-mortem right of publicity) are actions "upon a liability created by statute" (Cal. Civ. Proc. 338(a)), which would make the statute of limitations three years instead of two.

6. Even where the statute of limitations does not apply because of an ongoing infringement, relief may be barred by the equitable doctrine of laches. Laches is an equitable defense based on unreasonable delay in bringing an action that results in unfair prejudice to the opposing party. For example, in the *Miller* case, discussed in subsection A. above, the district court held that the two plaintiffs reasonably should have known for at least five years (and possibly more than twenty) that GMP was sublicensing other orchestras and selling merchandise using Glenn Miller's name and likeness. (Steven Miller had attended concerts at which merchandise was sold, and received financial statements showing income from "Licensing."). Unfair prejudice was shown because GMP had "invested a significant amount of time and money in developing its merchandising program," and because GMP would "suffer a tremendous loss of goodwill among its existing licensees and clients" (and possibly be liable for breach of contract) if it was forced to discontinue its licensing. *Miller v. Glenn Miller Prods.*, 454 F.3d 975, 997–1000 (9th Cir. 2006).

Chapter XII

Jurisdiction and Choice of Law

A. Jurisdiction in the United States

1. Subject-Matter Jurisdiction

Because rights of publicity are based on state common law and state statutes, one might think that litigation concerning rights of publicity would ordinarily occur in state courts. As we have seen, however, rights of publicity cases are frequently litigated in federal court. Rights of publicity cases can end up in federal court in one of several ways. First, there may be diversity of citizenship between the parties, and an amount in controversy exceeding the jurisdictional threshold (currently $75,000). *See* 28 U.S.C. § 1332. Second, state right of publicity claims are often joined with federal Lanham Act claims, thereby coming into federal court under the supplemental jurisdiction statute. *See* 28 U.S.C. § 1367. (Jurisdiction over Lanham Act claims can be founded on 28 U.S.C. § 1331 or 28 U.S.C. § 1338.) Third, even if a right of publicity claim in one of the previous two categories is filed initially in state court, the defendant in such a case can ordinarily remove the case to federal court. *See* 28 U.S.C. § 1441.

---

2. Personal Jurisdiction

For a case to be heard in either state or federal court, the court must also have jurisdiction over the parties to the dispute. The plaintiff voluntarily subjects itself to the court's jurisdiction by the act of filing a lawsuit; but the court must analyze whether the defendant is subject to the court's jurisdiction. As you learned in first-year Civil Procedure, in order for a state court to have personal jurisdiction over the defendant, there must be a statute authorizing the court to exercise jurisdiction over the defendant, and the exercise of jurisdiction must be consistent with the Due Process Clause of the Fourteenth Amendment to the U.S. Constitution. Under Federal Rule of Civil Procedure 4(k)(1)(A), those same limits generally apply in federal court as well.[1]

---

1. Rule 4(k)(1)(A) provides that service of process establishes personal jurisdiction over a defendant "who is subject to the jurisdiction of a court of general jurisdiction in the state where the district court is located." There are a few limited exceptions to this general rule, but those exceptions do not apply in a typical right of publicity case.

Under the Due Process Clause, if an individual defendant resides permanently in the state, or a corporate defendant is incorporated in or has its principal place of business in the state, then the court has general jurisdiction over that defendant (*i.e.*, the court has jurisdiction over the defendant for any kind of claim, no matter where the events occurred). However, if the defendant resides or has its principal place of business out of state, then the court must analyze whether the defendant has "minimum contacts" with the forum state, "such that the maintenance of the suit does not offend traditional notions of fair play and substantial justice." *International Shoe Co. v. Washington*, 326 U.S. 310, 316 (1945). In such a case, the court would have "specific jurisdiction" over the defendant (*i.e.*, the court has jurisdiction over the defendant only with respect to claims arising out of the jurisdictional contacts).

The case that follows analyzes whether the *International Shoe* standard was met in an international dispute involving the use of a Texas resident's image in an advertisement that was displayed only in Australia.

Chang v. Virgin Mobile USA, LLC

2009 WL 111570, 2009 U.S. Dist. LEXIS 3051 (N.D. Tex. 2009)

SIDNEY A. FITZWATER, Chief Judge:

Defendant's motion to dismiss presents questions concerning the court's constitutional power to exercise personal jurisdiction over an Australian defendant arising from its use in Australia of a photograph downloaded from a public photo-sharing website. Concluding that plaintiffs have failed to make the required prima facie showing of personal jurisdiction, the court grants defendant's motion and dismisses this action without prejudice.

I

Plaintiffs Susan Chang ("Chang"), as next friend of Alison Chang ("Alison"), a minor, and Justin Ho-Wee Wong ("Wong") sued defendant Virgin Mobile Pty. Ltd. ("Virgin Australia"), an Australian-based company, in Texas state court on claims for invasion of privacy, libel, breach of contract, and copyright infringement[2] based on Virgin Australia's use of an image of Alison ("the photograph") in its "Are You With Us or What" advertising campaign (the "Campaign"). The case was removed to this court based on diversity jurisdiction, and Virgin Australia now moves to dismiss for lack of personal jurisdiction....

Virgin Australia is an Australian company with its principal place of business in Sydney, New South Wales, Australia. Virgin Australia provides a range of mobile phone products and services, including prepaid and postpaid mobile phones. Its geographical area of operation is limited to the area of domestic Australia covered by the Optus telecommunications network.

In 2007 Virgin Australia launched the Campaign in select Australian cities, such as Sydney and Adelaide. The Campaign featured a collection of over 100 photographs downloaded at no cost to Virgin Australia from Yahoo!'s ("Yahoo's") public photo-sharing website, Flickr. Alison's photograph was taken by her church counselor, Wong, a resident of

---

2. Plaintiffs also originally sued Virgin Mobile USA, LLC ("Virgin USA"), alleging the same claims alleged against Virgin Australia, and Creative Commons Corporation, alleging negligence in the creation of the licenses that governed the photographs placed on Flickr. Plaintiffs later voluntarily dismissed the actions against these defendants, and only Virgin Australia remains as a defendant.

Fort Worth, Texas, who then published the photograph on Flickr under a Creative Commons Attribution 2.0 license agreement that provides for the most unrestricted use available to any worldwide user (including commercial use and no monetary payment). Virgin Australia used the photograph in an advertisement encouraging viewers to "DUMP YOUR PEN FRIEND" and advertising "FREE VIRGIN TO VIRGIN TEXTING." The advertisement was placed on bus shelter ad shells in major metropolitan areas in Australia. Virgin Australia never distributed the advertisement incorporating Alison's image in the United States, including Texas, and it never posted the photograph on its website or on any other website.

Figure 12-1. Photo by Brenton Cleeland.
http://flickr.com/sesh00

Several weeks after Wong uploaded the photograph onto Flickr, Alison received an email from one of her friends with a picture of her on a billboard affixed to a bus shelter in Adelaide, Australia. A member of the Flickr online blogger community then posted the picture of the billboard to the World Wide Web. The advertisement eventually garnered the interest of news stations, legal commentators, and website bloggers.

Virgin Australia moves to dismiss, contending that it lacks minimum contacts with the state of Texas....

II

A

... The Due Process Clause permits a court to exercise personal jurisdiction over a nonresident defendant if

> (1) that defendant has purposefully availed himself of the benefits and protections of the forum state by establishing "minimum contacts" with the forum state; and (2) the exercise of jurisdiction over that defendant does not offend "traditional notions of fair play and substantial justice." To comport with due process, the defendant's conduct in connection with the forum state must be such that he "should reasonably anticipate being haled into court" in the forum state.

Latshaw v. Johnston, 167 F.3d 208, 211 (5th Cir. 1999) (footnotes omitted).... Specific jurisdiction is appropriate when a nonresident corporation "has purposefully directed its activities at the forum state and the litigation results from alleged injuries that "arise out of or relate to" those activities." [*Alpine View Co. v. Atlas Copco AB*, 205 F.3d 208, 215 (5th Cir. 2000)] (*quoting Burger King Corp. v. Rudzewicz*, 471 U.S. 462, 472 (1985))....

III

... Plaintiffs essentially argue that Virgin Australia is amenable to personal jurisdiction in Texas based on three contacts with the state: (1) Virgin Australia's accessing a Flickr server located in Texas; (2) Virgin Australia's contract with a Texas resident; and (3) the intrastate effects of Virgin Australia's use of Alison's photograph in the Campaign.

A

Plaintiffs maintain that Virgin Australia had contact with a Flickr server located in Texas, and they argue that this constitutes sufficient minimum contact to satisfy due process. Assuming *arguendo* that contact with a computer server fortuitously located in the state of Texas can establish personal jurisdiction here, plaintiffs have failed to make a *prima facie* showing that the server in this case was in fact located in Texas.... Consequently, ... this contact is insufficient to establish personal jurisdiction.

B

Alternatively, even if the court assumes that plaintiffs made the *prima facie* showing of contact with a Texas server, they cannot rely on the fortuitous location of Flickr's servers to establish personal jurisdiction over Virgin Australia.

... [P]laintiffs contend that, by virtue of the fact that Virgin Australia (through its vendors) deliberately directed its activity toward Flickr.com (*i.e.*, by visiting the website and downloading the photograph from Flickr.com), Virgin Australia can be haled into any forum where Flickr.com's servers are located. The cases plaintiffs cite, however, are readily distinguishable, either because they arise in the context of spam-email or because the harm alleged in the complaint was directed toward the plaintiff's server. *See Travel Jungle* [*v. Am. Airlines, Inc.*], 212 S.W.3d [841 (Tex. App. 2006)] at 850 (defendant allegedly sent electronic spiders to plaintiff's website, accessing the site 2,972 times in one day and using valuable computer capacity); *Verizon Online Servs., Inc. v. Ralsky*, 203 F. Supp. 2d 601, 604 (E.D. Va. 2002) (defendant allegedly bombarded plaintiff's servers with spam, overwhelming the servers and causing delays in processing legitimate emails).... Therefore, even if plaintiffs had made a prima facie showing that Virgin Australia made contact with a Flickr server located in Texas, such contact would be insufficient to establish minimum contacts.

C

Assuming *arguendo* that Virgin Australia contracted with Wong (a Texas resident) to use Alison's photograph under the terms of the license agreement and then breached the contract, this conduct does not establish specific personal jurisdiction over Virgin Australia. "[M]erely contracting with a resident of the forum state does not establish minimum contacts." *Moncrief Oil Int'l Inc. v. Oao Gazprom*, 481 F.3d 309, 311 (5th Cir. 2007) (citing cases). Furthermore, "a plaintiff's unilateral activities in Texas do not constitute minimum contacts [in a breach of contract case] where the defendant did not perform any of its obligations in Texas, the contract did not require performance in Texas, and the contract is centered outside of Texas." *Id.* at 312.

Here, the license agreement did not require Virgin Australia to perform any of its obligations in Texas; on the contrary, the license permitted Alison's photograph to be used anywhere in the world. Furthermore, plaintiffs have failed to show that Virgin Australia performed any of its obligations in Texas. It used the photograph solely in Australia, the one place that, according to Virgin Australia's evidence, it is authorized to sell its products and services. Finally, because Virgin Australia only used the photograph in Australia, the contract that permits the use of the photograph is centered in Australia, not Texas. Consequently, the unilateral activity of Wong—*i.e.*, taking the photograph and publishing it in Texas on Flickr under the Creative Commons Attribution 2.0 license agreement—does not satisfy the requirement of contact between Virgin Australia and the state of Texas....

Virgin Australia's vendor searched through hundreds of millions of Flickr photographs publicly available on the Internet and fortuitously selected Alison's photograph. Neither the nationality or residence of the photographed individual nor the location where the photograph was taken are clear from the image itself, and even if Virgin Australia should have known, based on Wong's Flickr profile, that Wong was a Texas resident, Wong's Texas location was irrelevant to the contract. The mere fortuity that a party to a contract happens to be a Texas resident, coupled with that party's unilateral performance in the forum state, is not enough to confer jurisdiction. Thus the facts of plaintiffs' breach of contract claim will not support a finding of specific personal jurisdiction over Virgin Australia.

D

Plaintiffs invoke the effects test articulated by the Supreme Court in *Calder v. Jones*, 465 U.S. 783 (1984), contending that, with respect to plaintiffs' intentional tort claims,[17] personal jurisdiction is established by the intrastate effects of Virgin Australia's conduct. "In *Calder*, the Supreme Court held that when an alleged tort-feasor's intentional actions are expressly aimed at the forum state, and the tort-feasor knows that the brunt of the injury will be felt by a particular resident in the forum, the tort-feasor must reasonably anticipate being haled into court there to answer for its tortious actions." *Southmark Corp. v. Life Investors, Inc.*, 851 F.2d 763, 772 (5th Cir. 1988) (citing *Calder*, 465 U.S. at 789–790). This holds true even if the tortfeasor's conduct occurred in a state other than the forum state. *See id.*

In *Noonan v. Winston Co.*, 135 F.3d 85 (1st Cir. 1998), the *Calder* effects test was applied to a substantially analogous case. Noonan, a Massachusetts resident, brought an action alleging misappropriation, defamation, invasion of privacy, and related claims against French advertising agency Lintas:Paris, French cigarette manufacturer RJR France, and

---

17. Plaintiffs allege intentional tort claims of invasion of privacy, libel, and copyright infringement.

others based on the unauthorized use of his photograph[18] in a cigarette advertising campaign in France. The advertisement pictured Noonan in his Boston Police uniform on horseback at Faneuil Hall in Boston. Without the knowledge of Lintas:Paris, several hundred copies of various French magazines containing the advertisement were distributed to, and sold from, retail magazine outlets in the Boston area. Noonan became aware of the advertisement when several of his acquaintances, some of whom had seen the advertisement in France and some of whom had seen it in Boston, told Noonan about it. After some people denounced him for supporting the cigarette industry, Noonan filed suit.

Holding that the exercise of personal jurisdiction over Lintas:Paris and RJR France would offend due process, the First Circuit reasoned that while Noonan had satisfied the injurious-effects part of the *Calder* test, Lintas:Paris and RJR France had not acted with "sufficient intent to make them reasonably anticipate being haled into court [in Massachusetts]." *Id.* at 90 (internal quotation marks omitted).

> Like [the plaintiff in *Calder*], [Noonan] felt a tortious effect in the forum state where [he] lived and worked. Moreover, the content of the picture—a Boston Police Officer in uniform, sitting on a saddle blanket decorated with the Boston Police insignia, in front of a distinctive Boston landmark—indicated where any injury would be felt.

> For the first part of *Calder'*s framework to be satisfied, however, the defendants must have acted toward the forum state with sufficient intent to make them "reasonably anticipate being haled into court there." In *Calder,* the court found that the defendants' intentional conduct was "*calculated* to cause injury to respondent in California." There is no analogous intentional behavior here....

> The defendants did not direct their actions toward Massachusetts. That the advertisement contains French text and a French phone number suggests Lintas:Paris created it for a French audience. This interpretation is corroborated, without contradiction, by a Lintas:Paris representative who stated that "[t]he advertisement was aimed solely at the French consumer market." Furthermore, Lintas:Paris "was not aware that some copies of the magazines bearing the advertisement" would reach Massachusetts.

Id. at 90–91 (citations omitted; emphasis and brackets in original).

Here, as in *Noonan,* plaintiffs have satisfied the injurious-effects part of the *Calder* test but have failed to make a prima facie showing of intent. Although Alison felt a tortious effect in Texas after the advertisement incorporating her picture garnered the interest of news stations, legal commentators, and website bloggers, Virgin Australia did not direct its actions toward Texas. Like the defendants in *Noonan,* who aimed their advertisement solely at the French consumer market and did not intentionally target Massachusetts, Virgin Australia aimed the Campaign solely at Australia and did not intentionally target Texas.

If anything, the lack of intentional behavior aimed at the forum state is even more pronounced here than in *Noonan.* The advertisement in *Noonan* was placed in publications with international circulations, and although the defendants in *Noonan* claimed

---

18. The offending photograph was taken without Noonan's permission by an employee of the English book packaging house Colour Library Books ("CLB"). The photograph remained in CLB's files until CLB published it in *An American Moment.* Two years later, CLB sold the photograph to Lintas:Paris with no restrictions on its use and without advising Lintas:Paris that Noonan had not granted a release. Linta:Paris then used the photograph in the advertising campaign for client RJ France. *Noonan,* 135 F.3d 87.

ignorance of the distribution, 305 copies of various French magazines containing the advertisement were distributed to retailers in the Boston area. Here, by contrast, Alison's photograph was only used on billboards at bus stations in Australian cities, and Alison only learned about the use of her image in Virgin Australia's Campaign after a third party saw the billboard at a bus station in Adelaide, Australia, took a picture of it, and then posted it on the Internet. The nondescript content of Alison's photograph, moreover, unlike the picture in *Noonan*, did not clearly indicate where any injury would be felt.

Alison's Texas injury—i.e., her distress at seeing her image used in an allegedly disparaging way—is insufficient to support personal jurisdiction in the state of Texas over Virgin Australia.... "To find otherwise would inappropriately credit random, isolated, or fortuitous contacts and negate the reason for the purposeful availment requirement." *Noonan*, 135 F.3d at 92.

E

Because none of the three contacts on which plaintiffs rely establishes sufficient minimum contacts between Virgin Australia and the state of Texas, the court cannot constitutionally exercise personal jurisdiction over Virgin Australia....

Notes and Questions

1. This case, and the *Noonan* case cited within it, both hearken back to *Roberson* and *Pavesich* from Chapter I, in which an advertiser used a picture of the plaintiff without authorization. However, here the problem is that the advertisement was not published or displayed in Texas, but only in Australia, creating a problem of personal jurisdiction over the defendant. Suppose that the defendant had been located in Michigan, and only ran the advertisement in Michigan (with perhaps some spillover into neighboring Illinois and Indiana). If plaintiff had sued in Texas, do you think that the court would have come to the same result?

2. Suppose that the Virgin advertisement had been uploaded by someone to YouTube, where it could be seen by anyone in the world. Would that have made any difference in the outcome? What if Virgin employees had done the uploading?

3. The jurisdiction issue masks a larger problem, namely choice of law. Traditionally, intellectual property on an international scale has been guided by a principle of territoriality: generally speaking, one must rely on the courts and law of the country where infringement occurs to vindicate one's rights. Suppose that Virgin Australia was not a separate corporate entity, but was simply a division of Virgin Atlantic which, let us assume, would be subject to general jurisdiction in Texas. In that case, the next question would be: whose law should the Texas court apply? Should Texas law apply, or is Australian law the more reasonable choice? That issue will be addressed in the second part of this Chapter.

A related problem concerns enforcement of judgments. If Australia law applies, is a U.S. court empowered to interpret and enforce Australian law? If Texas law applies, can and should a U.S. court enforce an order to do something in another country? As to those questions, see Chapter XIV (Extraterritoriality).

4. If Australian law had been applied, what result do you think would have been reached? Some commentators have asserted that the plaintiff would not have had a rem-

edy. Do you agree? In the *Noonan* case, cited in *Chang*, if French law had been applied, what result do you think would have been reached?

5. Suppose Ms. Chang had posted some pictures of herself on a personal web site she had created, and that Virgin Australia copied one of those pictures for use in its Australian advertising campaign. Would that have been sufficient to subject Virgin to jurisdiction in Texas? Would it have been sufficient to allow the application of Texas law?

B. Choice of Law in the United States

1. The *Erie* Doctrine

Except where federal law provides otherwise, the Rules of Decision Act specifies that "[t]he laws of the several states … shall be regarded as rules of decision in civil actions in the courts of the United States, in cases where they apply." 28 U.S.C. § 1652. In the landmark case of *Erie Railroad Co. v. Tompkins*, 304 U.S. 64 (1938), the U.S. Supreme Court held that the phrase "the laws of the several states" included a State's decisional law as well as its statutes (and implied that its decision was compelled by the U.S. Constitution). Thus, in cases in which jurisdiction is based on diversity of citizenship or supplemental jurisdiction, rather than on a federal question, *Erie* requires that state substantive law be applied to resolve the dispute. Thus, a federal court sitting in diversity would apply state right of publicity statutes and common law rules.

In *Erie* itself, the parties and the Court agreed that the state law to be applied was the law of Pennsylvania, where the accident had occurred (even though the suit was heard in New York). Three years later, the Court made express the basis of that decision. In *Klaxon Co. v. Stentor Elec. Mfg. Co.*, 313 U.S. 487 (1941), the Court held that a federal court must apply the conflict of law rules of the state in which the district court is located.

The law to be applied when a diversity case is transferred from one federal court to another depends on the reason for the transfer. If jurisdiction and venue were proper, and the case was transferred for discretionary reasons under 28 U.S.C. § 1404, then "the transferee court will apply the law that would have been applied in the transferor court under the conflicts-of-laws rules of the state from which the action was transferred." 15 Charles Alan Wright, Arthur R. Miller & Edward H. Cooper, FEDERAL PRACTICE & PROCEDURE § 3846 (2009). However, "if venue was improper or personal jurisdiction was lacking over the defendant in the transferor court, the transferee court will apply the law that would have been applied if the action had been commenced in the transferee court." *Id.*

2. Choice of Law Principles

In the absence of a governing statute, American states typically take one of two general approaches to choice of law issues. The traditional approach utilizes black-letter rules derived from common-law cases. Under this approach, for example, a court might say that in a tort case, the law to be applied is the law of the state in which the wrong occurred (*lex loci delicti*); but in a case involving real or personal property, the law to be applied is the law of the state in which the property is located. *See* RESTATEMENT OF CONFLICT OF

Laws § 378 (1934) (tort); *id.*, § 211 (property). The more modern approach is a multi-factor analysis that attempts to identify the law of the state that has "the most significant relationship to the occurrence and to the parties." *See, e.g.,* RESTATEMENT (SECOND) OF CONFLICT OF LAWS § 145 (1971); *see also id.*, § 222 (most significant relationship to the property). Factors to be considered include the substantive policies of the forum state and of other interested states and the justified expectations of the parties. *Id.* § 6. The court then weighs and balances these factors in determining which state's law to apply.* Under the principle of *dépeçage*, a court might decide to apply different laws to different issues in the case.

The following cases attempt to apply these approaches to multistate and multinational disputes involving rights of publicity. In international intellectual property, the priniciple of territoriality—that each country may regulate acts of infringement that take place in that country, but not those taking place outside the country—is a strong, though not absolute, principle. As you read these materials, consider whether it makes sense to apply the law of a single state (or nation) to these disputes, or whether it would be more appropriate to allow different states or nations to enforce their own policies.

Schumann v. Loew's Inc.
135 N.Y.S.2d 361 (Sup. Ct. 1954)

HECHT, Justice:

This is a motion to dismiss the second amended complaint for alleged failure to state a good cause of action....

The four plaintiffs allege that they are great grandchildren of Robert Schumann, the celebrated composer, who died in 1856; that Schumann became insane and died suffering from 'said mental disease'; that a sister of his also suffered from the same malady; that defendant in recent years produced and exhibited a motion picture entitled 'Song of Love', which depicted Schumann's life, including the mental illness which overtook him and from which he suffered until his death; that the picture also brought to the public's attention the fact that Schumann's sister was similarly afflicted.

Plaintiff's allege that the distribution of the motion picture was without their consent; that its tendency is 'to instill suspicion in the minds of the public that plaintiffs are or may be subjected to such possible mental illness', and that plaintiffs have, as a result, suffered in the esteem of others.

Plaintiffs claim that the distribution of the motion picture constituted (1) an unlawful invasion of their right of privacy, and of the right to privacy of Robert Schumann; (2) an injury to the property rights of themselves and Schumann, and (3) a libel upon the memory of Schumann. They also maintain that defendant has been 'unjustly enriched' by the profits it has made from the exhibition of the motion picture and that they, as heirs and kinsmen of Robert Schumann, are entitled to recover from defendant the gross proceeds derived from the exhibition of the picture.

---

* This is a vast oversimplification. A recent treatise identifies no fewer than seven different approaches taken by American states in determining conflict of law issues in tort cases. *See* Eugene F. Scoles, Peter Hay, Patrick J. Borchers & Symeon C. Symeonides, CONFLICT OF LAWS §§ 2.20–2.25 (4th ed. 2004).

Figure 12-2. Robert Schumann (1810–1856)
Portrait by Carl Jaeger.

The pleading contains 61 causes of action; one for each state of the United States and the District of Columbia; and the rest for Alaska; Hawaii; Canada; Mexico; all the countries of Central America; all the countries of South America; the West Indies; the British Isles; all the countries of Europe; Japan; all the countries of Asia; all the countries of Africa; and Australia. In short, plaintiffs claim that the exhibition of the motion picture violated their rights and those of Robert Schumann under the laws of every country in the world and they seek redress therefor in this court in the form of damages and injunctive relief.

Taking up first the plaintiffs' claim that there was an unlawful violation of their right of privacy as well as of Robert Schumann's right of privacy, we find that the New York Court of Appeals, in the leading and controlling case on the subject in this state, has held that there is no right of privacy at common law. *Roberson v. Rochester Folding Box Co.*, 171 N.Y. 538, 64 N.E. 442 [(1902)]. The only right of privacy in New York State is a statutory one. The statute, sections 50 and 51, Civil Rights Law, by its express terms, applies only where the name, portrait or picture used for advertising or trade purposes is that of a 'living person'. As Robert Schumann and his sister were no longer alive at the time the picture was produced and exhibited, it is clear that no recovery may be had either under the common law or the statutory law of this state, on the theory of a violation of the right of privacy.

In the sixth cause of action recovery is sought under the law of Connecticut. The complaint expressly admits that no case as to the existence or non-existence of a right of privacy has ever been rendered by the courts of Connecticut and that no statute conferring such a right has ever been enacted in Connecticut. In the absence of a showing that the common law of a sister state is different from our own, 'we must presume that the common law (of the sister state) is the same as the common law of New York'. *Southworth v. Morgan*, 205 N.Y. 293, 295, 98 N.E. 490, 491 [(1912)]. It follows that no cause of action for violation of a right of privacy under Connecticut law is made out by the complaint. It is important to note, in addition, that even if a right of privacy were recognized by the courts of Connecticut, it would not follow that the plaintiffs, great grandchildren of the person whose privacy was invaded, would possess a good cause of action, for even in those states where a right of privacy is recognized the right 'is a personal right and cannot, as a general rule, be asserted by any one other than him whose privacy is invaded'. 138 A.L.R. 51.

The allegations of the causes of action under the laws of Delaware (7th), Idaho (11th), Illinois (12th), Iowa (14th), Maine (18th), Maryland (19th), Minnesota (22nd), Nebraska (26th), New Mexico (29th), North Dakota (33rd), South Dakota (40th), Tennessee (41st), Vermont (44th), West Virginia (47th), Wyoming (49th), Hawaii (51st) are similar to those relating to the law of Connecticut and are insufficient for the reasons on the basis of which the conclusion has been reached that no cause of action based upon a right of privacy has been made under the Connecticut law.

The causes of action based upon the law as to a right of privacy prevailing in Canada, Mexico, Central America, South America, the West Indies, Europe, Japan, Asia, Africa and Australia, are also insufficient. As to common law countries, the courts of this state will assume, in the absence of a contrary showing, that their common law is the same as that of this state, which recognizes no right of privacy. As to other than common law countries, no assumption will be indulged in that their law is the same as ours, *Sonnesen v. Panama Transport Co.*, 298 N.Y. 262, 267, 82 N.E.2d 569, 570 [(1948)], and the foreign law must be proved. No allegations are made, in the causes of action dealt with in this paragraph, that the laws of the respective countries referred to (either common law countries or others) recognize a right of privacy. The causes of action above referred to all proceed on the express theory that because plaintiffs and defendant are residents of the United States the common law should be applied to the causes of action based upon the laws of said countries. Since there is no claim made in any of the causes of action referred to in this paragraph that the laws of the foreign countries recognize a right of privacy, and since plaintiffs claim our common law is applicable, the courts of this state must apply the common law of this state as formulated by our Court of Appeals in *Roberson v. Rochester Folding Box Co.*, *supra*, under which no right of privacy exists.

The causes of action based upon an alleged right of privacy under the laws of Alabama (1st), Arizona (2nd), Arkansas (3rd), California (4th), Colorado (5th), the District of Columbia (8th), Florida (9th), Georgia (10th), Indiana (13th), Kansas (15th), Kentucky (16th), Louisiana (17th), Massachusetts (20th), Michigan (21st), Missouri (23rd), Mississippi (24th), Montana (25th), New Jersey (28th), Nevada (31st), North Carolina (32nd), Ohio (34th), Oklahoma (35th), Oregon (36th), Pennsylvania (37th), Rhode Island (38th), South Carolina (39th), Texas (42nd), Washington (46th), Wisconsin (48th), Alaska (50th), and the British Isles (57th), differ from the causes of action previously considered in that they cite decisions of courts of the respective jurisdictions involved which, plaintiffs claim, recognize the existence of a right of privacy (except as to Wisconsin, where the complaint admits that 'the court has not definitely indicated its tendency toward the recognition of a right for the invasion or violation of the right of privacy.')

Examination of the cases cited discloses that almost all of them related to the right by a living person to enforce his own right to privacy....

The cause of action under the laws of Utah (43rd) is based upon a statute of that state which confers a right of action upon 'the heirs or personal representatives of any deceased person, whose name, portrait or picture is used within this state for advertising purposes or for purposes of trade, without the written consent first obtained as provided in the next preceding section'. U.C.A.1953, §76-4-9. However, in *Donahue v. Warner Brothers Pictures Distributing Corporation*, 2 Utah 2d 256, 272 P.2d 177, 184 [(1954)], the Supreme Court of Utah held that the statute was intended only to prohibit the use of names, portraits or pictures in connection with the advertising or promotion of the sale of collateral items, and therefore affirmed the judgment of the trial court that 'semifictional portrayal of Jack Donahue in 'Look for the Silver Lining' was not for 'purposes of trade' within the meaning of the prohibition contained in' the Utah statute. In view of this decision, the present plaintiffs, on the basis of the allegations of their complaint, possess no cause of action under Utah law.

The cause of action under the law of Virginia (45th) refers to a Virginia statute prohibiting the use of a dead person's name, portrait or picture, 'without * * * the written consent * * * of his surviving consort, or if none, his next of kin'. Code 1950 Va. §8-650. The first sentence of the Virginia statute makes it a crime to use the name, portrait or picture 'of any person resident in the State' for advertising or trade purposes. Although the following sentences of the statute do not use the quoted language, it is open to serious question whether the legislature intended those sentences to apply where the name, portrait or picture used was that of a non-resident of Virginia. However that may be, the allegations of the complaint do not establish that the plaintiffs are the next of kin of Robert Schumann within the meaning of the Virginia statute. The complaint is consistent with the possibility that both under the laws of the country where Robert Schumann was domiciled at his death and under the laws of Virginia, the plaintiffs, some of the great grandchildren of the deceased, are not included among his 'next of kin'. Plaintiffs claim to be grandchildren of one of Robert Schumann's seven children. Nothing is said in the complaint about Robert Schumann's six other children. Some of them, or their children, could conceivably be alive and, in that event, it is possible that plaintiffs, as great grandchildren, would not be next of kin under the laws of the country of Robert Schumann's domicile or under the laws of Virginia. In the circumstances, the allegations of the 45th cause of action fail to make out a good cause of action in plaintiffs under the law of Virginia.

For the reasons indicated, each and every cause of action in the complaint is insufficient to entitle plaintiffs to recover upon the theory of a violation of a right to privacy.

Nor are plaintiffs' rights any better on the theory that the defendant libeled them. The allegations of the complaint affirmatively admit that Robert Schumann and his sister were insane as depicted in defendant's motion picture.... [N]o cause of action in libel is made out where the complaint shows that the article complained of was true....

Plaintiffs also claim that the defendant has misappropriated the name of Robert Schumann, which was a property right belonging to him, and that they may enforce that right as descendants of Robert Schumann.... None of [the authorities cited] supports plaintiffs' contention that a motion picture depicting the life of one who died almost one hundred years earlier is an infringement upon the deceased's property right in his name which descended to his heirs or next of kin. Furthermore, even if it were assumed that Robert Schumann did possess a property right in his name which could be transferred to others and enforced by the latter against those using his name after his death, the complaint fails to allege sufficient facts to establish that plaintiffs are the persons who presently own the right. For aught that appears in the pleading, Robert Schumann may have died testate and his will may have disposed of his property, including his property right in his name, in such manner that the present plaintiffs would possess no valid claim to that right. Even if Robert Schumann died intestate as to the property right in his name, the complaint fails to show that plaintiffs inherited that right under the laws of the country where Robert Schumann was domiciled at the time of his death. All that the complaint establishes is that plaintiffs are some of the great grandchildren of Robert Schumann....

For the reason indicated, this motion in so far as it seeks to dismiss the second amended complaint for insufficiency is granted, with $10 costs, with leave to serve a further amended complaint within twenty days from the service of a copy of this order with notice of entry.

Factors Etc., Inc. v. Pro Arts, Inc.
652 F.2d 278 (2d Cir. 1981)

NEWMAN, Circuit Judge:

The merits of this appeal concern the interesting state law question whether a person has a protected interest in publicizing his name and likeness after his death, or, as the matter has been put, is there a descendible right of publicity? Despite the fascination of this question, what divides the members of this panel and forms the basis for the majority's disposition of this appeal is the more esoteric question, apparently of first impression, concerning the deference a federal court exercising diversity jurisdiction should give to a ruling by a court of appeals deciding the law of a state within its circuit. Believing that conclusive deference should be given, except in certain situations not applicable here, we reverse the judgment of this case.

FACTS

The facts are set forth in this Court's first encounter with this litigation, *Factors Etc., Inc. v. Pro Arts, Inc.*, 579 F.2d 215 (2d Cir. 1978), *cert. denied*, 440 U.S. 908 (1979) (*Factors I*), and need be recounted only briefly here. During his life, Elvis Presley, the well-known popular singer, formed a Tennessee corporation, Boxcar Enterprises, Inc., and assigned it exclusive ownership of all rights to use for commercial purposes his name and likeness. On August 18, 1977, two days after Presley's death, Boxcar granted to plaintiff-appellee Factors Etc., Inc., a Delaware corporation, an exclusive license for 18 months, renewable at the licensee's option for up to four years, to use Presley's name and likeness in connection with the manufacture and sale of any kind of merchandise. The licensee agreed to pay a royalty of 5% of sales, subject to a minimum royalty for the first 18 months of $150,000, and also subject to certain minimum royalties on specified items, for example $.08 for each poster.

On August 19, 1977, defendant-appellant Pro Arts, Inc., an Ohio corporation, published a poster displaying a photograph of Presley and the dates 1935–1977. Pro Arts had purchased the copyright in the photograph from the newspaper photographer who had taken it. Pro Arts marketed the poster through various retailers, including co-defendant-appellant Stop and Shop Companies, Inc., which sold the poster through its Bradlee Stores Division in the Southern District of New York. After communication between Boxcar, Factors, and Pro Arts, Factors brought this suit in the Southern District of New York and obtained a preliminary injunction restraining defendants from manufacturing, selling, or distributing the Presley poster and from making any commercial use of Presley's

Figure 12-3. "In Memory" of Elvis Presley

name or likeness. *Factors Etc., Inc. v. Pro Arts, Inc.*, 444 F. Supp. 288 (S.D.N.Y. 1977). We affirmed that injunction in *Factors I.*

Contemporaneously with the initiation of this suit, Factors found itself in litigation on another front. The Memphis Development Foundation, an organization formed in Memphis, Tennessee, to construct a bronze statue of Presley in downtown Memphis, sued Factors in the District Court for the Western District of Tennessee to prevent Factors from interfering with the Foundation's efforts to raise funds by selling eight-inch pewter replicas of the proposed Presley statue priced at $25. Factors counterclaimed for an injunction to restrain the Foundation's distribution of the statuettes and secured a preliminary injunction, *Memphis Development Foundation v. Factors, Etc., Inc.*, 441 F. Supp. 1323 (W.D. Tenn. 1977), *aff'd without opinion*, 578 F.2d 1381 (6th Cir. 1978). On motion for summary judgment in the Tennessee litigation, Factors obtained a permanent injunction in the District Court. However, the Sixth Circuit reversed, holding that Presley's right of publicity did not survive his death. *Memphis Development Foundation v. Factors Etc., Inc.*, 616 F.2d 956 (6th Cir.), *cert. denied*, 449 U.S. 953 (1980).

Thereafter Factors moved for summary judgment in the New York litigation. Appellants (hereafter collectively "Pro Arts") brought to the District Court's attention the Sixth Circuit's reversal in *Memphis Development*, contending that *Memphis Development* collaterally estopped Factors from asserting that it possessed any exclusive publicity rights to the name and likeness of Presley after his death. Implicitly rejecting this contention, the District Court granted Factors' motion and issued a permanent injunction, from which this appeal has been taken. 496 F. Supp. 1090 (S.D.N.Y. 1980).

DISCUSSION

The District Court, exercising its diversity jurisdiction, was obliged to apply the substantive law of the state to which the forum state, New York, would have turned had the suit been filed in state court. *Klaxon Co. v. Stentor Electric Manufacturing Co.*, 313 U.S. 487 (1941). Curiously, the choice of law issue had received no attention from the parties in this litigation prior to the Sixth Circuit's reversal in *Memphis Development*. Perhaps assuming that the law governing this infringement action was the law of the place of the wrong, as appellees now explicitly contend on this appeal, the parties did not refer to choice of law rules on the prior appeal, and this Court, without discussion, simply observed that the issue of the duration of the right of publicity is "one of state law, more specifically the law of the State of New York," 579 F.2d at 220. That choice of law ruling, made in the course of affirming the preliminary injunction, does not preclude our reexamination of the point on this appeal from a final adjudication of the case, especially now that the parties have put the choice of law issue in dispute.

Factors not only contends that New York law is applicable as the law of the place of the wrong, but also asserts that even if a "significant contacts" test were applied, the significant contacts of this dispute, *i.e.*, those that "relate to the purpose of the particular law in conflict," [citation omitted], are with New York. Factors points not only to the sale of the infringing poster, which occurred in New York, but also to the fact that New York, as a center of communications and the locale where the publicity value of many personas has developed, has an interest in ensuring against misappropriation of a celebrity's right of publicity. Against this rather sparse showing, Pro Arts points out that Tennessee is where Presley was domiciled, Boxcar was incorporated, and the agreement between Boxcar and Factors was made. Moreover, the latter agreement specifically provides that it is to be construed in accordance with Tennessee law. We think it likely that these facts would persuade a New York court to look to the law of Tennessee. But even if a New York court would apply New York law in considering some elements of Factors' claim, such as the occurrence of an infringement, we feel certain that Tennessee law would be referred to in deciding whether Boxcar had a right of publicity in Presley's name and likeness, after his death, that was capable of being contracted for by Factors. *Cf.* RESTATEMENT (SECOND) OF CONFLICT OF LAWS (1971) § 147, Comment (i), noting that tort conflicts rules apply to issue of conversion of property, but property conflicts rules apply to whether plaintiff has title to property allegedly converted.

All members of the panel agree that we should turn to Tennessee law to determine what rights the Boxcar-Factors contract conveyed to Factors. We find, as the Sixth Circuit concluded in *Memphis Development*, that Tennessee statutory and decisional law affords no answer to the question. We are thus brought to the issue that divides the panel: whether deference should be accorded to the decision in *Memphis Development*.

Somewhat to our surprise, there has been hardly a mention in the appellate reports of the appropriate deference a court of appeals should give to a decision made by the court of appeals of another circuit on the law of a state within that other circuit. It has frequently been observed that a court of appeals should give considerable weight to state law rulings made by district judges, within the circuit, who possess familiarity with the law of the state in which their district is located. *See* 1A MOORE'S FEDERAL PRACTICE ¶ 0.309(2), at 3125 n.28 (collecting cases). The Supreme Court has expressed similar views concerning state law interpretations by a panel of circuit judges whose circuit includes the relevant state. *MacGregor v. State Mutual Life Assurance Co.*, 315 U.S. 280 (1942). But no case appears to have turned on whether one court of appeals should defer to another circuit as to the law of a state within that circuit.

In deciding *Memphis Development*, the Sixth Circuit was expounding Tennessee's version of the common law. It makes no difference that the Court was unable to find any Tennessee decisional law to guide its resolution of the issue before it, leaving it, as Judge Merritt candidly acknowledged, with "no way to assess" the predisposition of the Tennessee courts. 616 F.2d at 958. The Sixth Circuit may have lacked any sure basis for predicting what the Tennessee courts would do and therefore felt obliged to make its decision "in the light of practical and policy considerations, the treatment of other similar rights in our legal system, the relative weight of the conflicting interests of the parties, and certain moral presuppositions concerning death, privacy, inheritability and economic opportunity." *Ibid.* But this recourse to such general considerations did not alter the function that the Sixth Circuit was performing. In adjudicating a state-created right in the exercise of its diversity jurisdiction the Court was "for that purpose, in effect, only another court of the State." *Guaranty Trust Co. v. York*, 326 U.S. 99, 108 (1945). It had no power "to declare substantive rules of common law," *Erie Railroad Co. v. Tompkins*, 304 U.S. 64, 78 (1938); it could only declare the law of Tennessee....

Of course reasonable minds may differ as to the preferable course that the common law of Tennessee ought to follow on the merits of Factors' claim. The writer would probably uphold a descendible right of publicity, were he serving on the Tennessee Supreme Court, and perhaps if he served on the Sixth Circuit when *Memphis Development* was decided. But the issue for this Court is not which view of the merits is wiser policy; it is whether, and under what circumstances, a ruling by a court of appeals, interpreting the common law of a state within its circuit, should be regarded as authoritative by the other federal courts of the nation. The answer is illuminated by consideration of the functioning of diversity jurisdiction.

One distinct shortcoming of diversity jurisdiction is the interruption of the orderly development and authoritative exposition of state law occasioned by sporadic federal court adjudications. Except in those few jurisdictions permitting a federal court to certify an unsettled question of state law to the state's highest court, a federal court's decision on state law cannot be corrected, for the benefit of the litigants in the particular case, by the state's authoritative tribunal. As long as diversity jurisdiction exists, this price must be paid. However, the opportunities for federal court departure from the normal paths of state law development should be held to a minimum, for the benefit of both the orderly development of state law and fairness to those subject to state law requirements. Both values are served by recognizing, within the federal system, the authoritativeness of decisions on the law of a particular state rendered by the court of appeals for the circuit in which the state is located. Orderly development is enhanced because the state legislature will know that the decision of the pertinent court of appeals will determine legal rights, unless superseded by a later state supreme court decision. This knowledge will focus state legislative efforts on the appropriateness of a statutory change. Fairness to the public is promoted by making clear that there is a single, authoritative answer to the particular state law issue, instead of leaving the matter subject to the varying interpretations of the courts of appeals for the several circuits.[6] If this Court were to disregard the Sixth

---

6. Even if uniformity is achieved throughout the federal courts, the possibility remains that the courts of various states, obliged to consider Tennessee law because of their conflicts rules, might reach different predictions of Tennessee law. We think it more likely that state courts would share our in-

Circuit's view and declare that Tennessee law recognizes a descendible right of publicity, what standard of conduct should guide Tennessee residents endeavoring to determine whether their publicity rights are to be valued only for a lifetime or beyond? Of course, lawyers frequently have to advise clients concerning unsettled issues of law, but the exercise of diversity jurisdiction should not add to their uncertainty. Diversity jurisdiction, especially in its post-*Erie* incarnation, should not create needless diversity in the exposition of state substantive law. Even though the decision of the pertinent court of appeals may be revised by a subsequent state supreme court ruling, a state court will normally have the option of making such a ruling prospective only, thereby protecting any rights bargained for in reliance on the ruling of the pertinent court of appeals. That option would make little sense if the authoritative state court ruling came after divergent rulings had been made by several courts of appeals.

We need not and do not conclude that the state law holding of the pertinent court of appeals is automatically binding upon the federal courts of all the other circuits. The ultimate source for state law adjudication in diversity cases is the law as established by the constitution, statutes, or authoritative court decisions of the state. A federal court in another circuit would be obliged to disregard a state law holding by the pertinent court of appeals if persuaded that the holding had been superseded by a later pronouncement from state legislative or judicial sources, or that prior state court decisions had been inadvertently overlooked by the pertinent court of appeals. Neither circumstance exists in this case. Where, as here, the pertinent court of appeals has essayed its own prediction of the course of state law on a question of first impression within that state, the federal courts of other circuits should defer to that holding, perhaps always, and at least in all situations except the rare instance when it can be said with conviction that the pertinent court of appeals has disregarded clear signals emanating from the state's highest court pointing toward a different rule. However our sense of the common law might lead us to resolve the merits of this case were we judges of the Tennessee Supreme Court, as "outsiders" with respect to Tennessee law, we should defer to the views of the Sixth Circuit unless we can point to a clear basis in Tennessee law for predicting that the Tennessee courts, when confronted with a case such as this, would conclude that the Sixth Circuit's prediction was incorrect.[7] Since we are unable to find any such indication in Tennessee law, we accept *Memphis Development* as controlling authority and conclude that after Presley's death, Boxcar had no right of publicity in Presley's name and likeness to convey to Factors.

---

terest in uniformity and accept a ruling by a pertinent federal court of appeals, subject to the same qualifications we adopt for ourselves. If in some instances a state court did not do so, that might lessen but would not eliminate the appropriateness of promoting uniform exercise of diversity jurisdiction within the federal court system. And the uniformity achieved for the period after the date of the decision of the pertinent federal court of appeals is not less worthy of achievement simply because prior to that decision other federal courts or courts of other states may have made different predictions about the course of Tennessee law. The possibility of these unavoidable departures from uniformity, just like decisions of federal or other state courts rendered before an authoritative ruling by the pertinent state's highest court, is an insufficient reason to create a needless departure from uniformity during what may be an extended period beginning after a decision by the pertinent federal court of appeals and ending, if at all, only in the event of a contrary decision by the pertinent state's highest court or legislature.

7. As it happens, the author of *Memphis Development* is a distinguished member of the Tennessee bar, whose sense of what may be expected of the Tennessee Supreme Court surely surpasses our own. But since Judge Merritt's opinion so emphatically disclaims any basis for predicting how Tennessee will resolve the issue on the merits, we prefer to determine the authoritativeness of *Memphis Development* with regard to the territorial scope of the Sixth Circuit, rather than the heritage of the opinion's author.

For these reasons the judgment of the District Court is reversed.

MANSFIELD, Circuit Judge (dissenting):

I respectfully dissent. I agree with the majority that, despite the contrary assumption of all parties in *Factors I*, New York conflict of laws analysis would call for the application of Tennessee law to determine if Elvis Presley's right of publicity survived his death. However, with the utmost of respect for our distinguished and able colleagues on the Sixth Circuit, I see no warrant, if we disagree on the merits, for blindly following its decision in *Memphis Development Foundation v. Factors Etc., Inc.*, 616 F.2d 956 (6th Cir.), *cert. denied*, 449 U.S. 953 (1980), any more than we would defer to the decision of any other circuit court with which we might, as has occurred on numerous occasions, disagree or conflict. The reasoning of *Memphis Development* is not in any way derived from the local law of Tennessee. Its result is inconsistent with that of nearly every other case which has considered the issue, including the Sixth Circuit's own prior ruling on the preliminary injunction issued by the district court in *Memphis Development* and our opinion in *Factors I*. It is also contrary to all current views of scholarly commentators on the subject.

The majority starts with the proposition that deference is owed to the "interpretations" by a federal court of the law of a state within its jurisdiction, a principle with which I find no need to disagree. However, it then states that the "issue for this Court ... is whether, and under what circumstances, a ruling by a court of appeals, interpreting the common law of a state within its circuit, should be recognized as authoritative by the other federal courts of the nation." With this statement of the issue I must disagree. Here there was no interpretation of any Tennessee law by the Sixth Circuit, only a declaration of what that court thought would be a preferable general common law rule for that state. The issue before us, therefore, is whether a federal court of appeals, called upon to anticipate what general common law rule with respect to a legal question might be appropriate for a state having no law whatsoever on the subject, must adhere to the diversity decision of a sister federal court of appeals within whose boundaries the state is located. Resolution of this issue requires us to look into the reasoning behind the policy of deference which the majority would apply and decide whether it is to be applied mechanically on a geographical basis or is instead subject to any limitations.

The weight given by higher federal courts to state law rulings made by federal judges sitting in that state results from the supposed greater familiarity that such a judge will have with the local law and the methods and tendencies of the state courts. As Wright states:

> "As a general proposition, a federal court judge who sits in a particular state and has practiced before its courts may be better able to resolve complex questions about the law of that state than is some other federal judge who has no such personal acquaintance with the law of the state. For this reason federal appellate courts have frequently voiced reluctance to substitute their own view of the state law for that of the federal judge. As a matter of judicial administration, this seems defensible." C. WRIGHT, FEDERAL COURTS § 58 at 271 (3d ed. 1976) (footnote omitted).

To a lesser extent a federal court of appeals might conceivably be considered to have more familiarity with the law of a state within its boundaries than would another federal court of appeals. Even this premise is open to serious question, however, for a number of reasons. Unlike a state court or a federal district court within a single state, the court of appeals of a circuit in which several states are located, which disposes of diversity appeals as only a small percentage of its business, is not likely to gain any special familiarity with the law of one of the states within its boundaries. The Sixth Circuit, for instance, physically encompasses seven different states. Of 1,823 appeals filed with it in 1980, only 212, or 11.6% (compared with an average for all circuits of 12.5%) were diversity suits and these originated not solely from Tennessee but from all seven states. See 1980 ANNUAL REPORT OF THE DIRECTOR, ADMINISTRATIVE OFFICE OF THE UNITED STATES COURTS, Table A-12.

These facts weaken and, indeed, may even destroy the assumption that the able Sixth Circuit has some special knowledge or expertise in Tennessee law to which deference must be paid. In this case, for instance, it would be more logical to assume that, if familiarity with a particular state's law is to be the standard for deference, the United States district judge for the Western District of Tennessee, Judge Harry W. Wellford, who in a well reasoned opinion held Elvis Presley's property right in his name and image for commercial purposes to be descendible, *see* 441 F. Supp. 1323 (W.D. Tenn. 1977), had superior expertise with respect to Tennessee law....

Moreover, it is perfectly clear that the Sixth Circuit's decision in fact in no way depended on existent local law or methods. The opinion makes no effort, as is sometimes done, to determine what other states the Tennessee courts tend to look to, much less to be guided by analogous principles of Tennessee law. Instead, it expressly states at the outset that,

> "Tennessee courts have not addressed this issue directly or indirectly, and we have no way to assess their predisposition. Since the case is one of first impression, we are left to review the question in the light of practical and policy considerations, the treatment of other similar rights in our legal system, the relative weight of the conflicting interests of the parties, and certain moral presuppositions concerning death, privacy, inheritability, and economic opportunity." 616 F.2d at 958.

It then relies on John Rawls' A THEORY OF JUSTICE (1971) and the RESTATEMENT OF TORTS in evaluating these general considerations. Clearly, familiarity with Tennessee law and practice was of no consequence in the Sixth Circuit's endeavor. We, however much "outsiders", are as fully qualified effectively to "declare" Tennessee law in such fashion as our sister circuit.

If under these circumstances we were to bow to the Sixth Circuit's declaration of Tennessee law, it would have to be for reasons other than those underlying the usual deference given to federal judges who are experienced in the local law and practice of states located within their boundaries. The majority seeks to find such a basis in the overall "functioning of diversity jurisdiction". First it argues that recognizing the authoritativeness of the Sixth Circuit's ruling would enhance the "orderly development of state law." But our refusal to be bound by the Sixth Circuit here would not affect the development of Tennessee law at all. It is conceded as a matter of settled law that any Tennessee court decision or state legislation would wipe out the future significance of both *Memphis Development* and our decision. Moreover, the notion that consistency among the circuits will better "focus state legislative efforts on the appropriateness of a statutory change" is speculative at best and perhaps ill founded. If Tennessee constituents were laboring under conflicting federal court declarations of rights and duties, the legislature would be more likely to act sooner than if all decisions were consistent.

Second, while noting that lawyers must frequently advise clients concerning unsettled issues of law, the majority argues that failure to follow *Memphis Development* would promote uncertainty and "create needless diversity in the exposition of state substantive law."

This ignores the fact that our development and formation of lasting rules of common law depends heavily on healthy differences of opinion. Soundness must not be sacrificed on the altar of consistency. If two members of this panel would "probably uphold a descendible right of publicity, were (they) sitting on the Tennessee Supreme Court," and the third would certainly do so, I think we should so hold rather than retreat behind unsupportable deferential niceties.

Even the consistency achieved under the majority's rule is fortuitous and arbitrary. Had the *Memphis Development* case arisen, for example, in the Ninth Circuit and had that circuit, without reference to Tennessee law or practice, declared that Tennessee law should not allow descendibility, would we be required to follow that version unless we could prove it wrong on some local basis overlooked by the Ninth Circuit? Apparently the majority, which would "determine the authoritativeness of *Memphis Development* with regard to the territorial scope of the Sixth Circuit", would agree that such a Ninth Circuit decision would be entitled to no more weight than the usual persuasive authority of a sister circuit with which, for good reason, we might disagree. The only difference here, where the Sixth Circuit eschewed any Tennessee law basis for its declaration, is that its physical geography includes that state. In my view the lack of logic behind the majority's geographical reasoning is further demonstrated by the fact that if we had stated our holding in *Factors I* to be a declaration of our view of Tennessee law, which we would certainly have done if the parties had not at that time agreed that New York law governed, the Sixth or any other circuit would have been free to take a contrary view and thus create the very inconsistency which the majority seeks to avoid.

In the unusual situation here, where an initial court of appeals diversity declaration is in no way derived from the law or practice of the state and interprets no existing state law, we should feel free to reach a different result if sound reasons recommend it, regardless of the unpersuasive views of the sister circuit from which the initial declaration emanated. Where, as here, the Sixth Circuit itself had no Tennessee law basis for its choice and we are persuaded that other reasons dictate a contrary decision (or prediction), there is no logical justification for a rule that would permit us to depart from the Sixth Circuit's views only upon a showing of "a clear basis in Tennessee law for predicting that the Tennessee courts ... would conclude that the Sixth Circuit's prediction was incorrect."

Turning to the merits, sound principles commend a different result from that reached in *Memphis Development* on the issue of whether Elvis Presley's right of publicity survived his death. Because the issue was fully addressed in *Factors I* and because the discussion there is consistent with the vast majority of other authorities considering the problem, I will not rehash at length the elements supporting the *Factors I* result....

For the reasons outlined I believe Factors did have a valid and enforceable property right in the commercialization of Presley's persona and would therefore affirm the judgment of the district court granting it relief.

Cairns v. Franklin Mint Co.

292 F.3d 1139 (9th Cir. 2002)

Before: PREGERSON, RYMER, and T.G. NELSON, Circuit Judges.

PREGERSON, Circuit Judge:

Plaintiffs-Appellants are the trustees of the Diana Princess of Wales Memorial Fund ("the Fund") and the executors of the Estate of Diana, Princess of Wales ("the Estate"). We will refer to them collectively as "the Fund." The Fund brought several state and federal claims against Defendant-Appellee Franklin Mint. The Fund based these claims on Franklin Mint's use of the name and likeness of the late Princess Diana on commercially sold jewelry, plates, and dolls, and in advertisements for these products. The Fund appeals three holdings by the District Court: (1) the District Court's denial of the Fund's motion to reinstate its dismissed post-mortem right of publicity claim under California Civil Code § 3344.1(a)(1); (2) the District Court's grant of summary judgment in favor of Franklin Mint on the Fund's Lanham Act claim for false endorsement under 15 U.S.C. § 1125(a)(1); and (3) the District Court's award of attorneys' fees to Franklin Mint.... [W]e affirm.

I. FACTUAL AND PROCEDURAL BACKGROUND

Since 1981, when Princess Diana married Prince Charles, Franklin Mint has produced, advertised, and sold collectibles—jewelry, plates, and dolls—bearing her name and likeness. Similar products bearing Princess Diana's name and likeness were sold by other companies. Princess Diana neither authorized nor objected to any of these products.

The Fund was established in 1997 after Princess Diana's death to accept donations to be given to various charities with which Princess Diana was associated during her lifetime. The Estate exclusively authorized the Fund to use Princess Diana's name and likeness for this purpose. The Fund in turn authorized about twenty parties—but not Franklin Mint—to use the name and likeness of Princess Diana in conjunction with products sold in the United States. Franklin Mint continued to market unauthorized Diana-related products.

On May 18, 1998, the Fund brought suit against Franklin Mint in the United States District Court for the Central District of California. The complaint alleged violations of the Lanham Act for false endorsement and false advertisement under 15 U.S.C. § 1125(a)(1), and dilution of trademark under 15 U.S.C. § 1125(c)(1). The complaint also alleged violations of California's post-mortem right of publicity statute, California Civil Code § 990(a) (now California Civil Code § 3344.1(a)).....

On October 16, 1998, the District Court granted Franklin Mint's motion to dismiss the Fund's post-mortem right of publicity claim under California Civil Code § 990. *Cairns v. Franklin Mint Co.*, 24 F. Supp. 2d 1013, 1022 (C.D. Cal. 1998) ["*Cairns I*"]. The District Court reasoned that California's default personal property choice of law provision, California Civil Code § 946, applied to the Fund's post-mortem right of publicity claim and required application of the law of Great Britain, which does not recognize a post-mortem right of publicity. *Cairns I*, 24 F. Supp. 2d at 1023–29. The District Court denied Franklin Mint's motion to dismiss the Fund's Lanham Act claims for false endorsement, false advertisement, and dilution of trademark. *Id.* at 1022–23. The District Court also denied the Fund's motion for a preliminary injunction on these Lanham Act claims. *Id.* at 1023.... [The Ninth Circuit affirmed these rulings on interlocutory appeal in an unpublished decision *See Diana Princess of Wales Memorial Fund v. Franklin Mint Co.*, 1999 WL 1278044 (9th Cir. 2000).]

After the District Court dismissed the Fund's post-mortem right of publicity claim, the California Legislature renumbered the post-mortem right of publicity statute from § 990 to § 3344.1 and amended it to "apply to the adjudication of liability and the imposition of any damages or other remedies in cases in which the liability, damages, and other remedies arise from acts occurring directly in this state." Cal. Civ. Code § 3344.1(n). Based on this amendment, the Fund filed a motion to reinstate its dismissed post-mortem right of publicity claim. The Fund argued that § 3344.1(n) is a choice of law provision that requires application of California law, which recognizes a post-mortem right of publicity.

On June 22, 2000, the District Court denied the Fund's motion to reinstate its post-mortem right of publicity claim and motion for a preliminary injunction. *Cairns v. Franklin Mint Co.,* 120 F. Supp. 2d 880, 887 (C.D. Cal. 2000) [*"Cairns II"*]. The District Court concluded, based on the plain language of § 3344.1(n) and its legislative history, that this section is *not* a choice of law provision. *Id.* at 883–85. The District Court further concluded that California's default personal property choice of law provision, California Civil Code § 946, continues to apply to the Fund's post-mortem right of publicity claim and requires application of the law of Great Britain, which does not recognize a post-mortem right of publicity. *Cairns II,* 120 F. Supp. 2d at 881–82.

On June 27, 2000, the District Court granted Franklin Mint's motion for summary judgment on the Fund's Lanham Act false endorsement claim. *Cairns v. Franklin Mint Co.,* 107 F. Supp. 2d 1212, 1223 (C.D. Cal. 2000) [*"Cairns III"*]. The District Court concluded that Franklin Mint's use of Princess Diana's name and likeness did not implicate the source identification purpose of trademark protection. *Id.* at 1214–16. The District Court also … concluded that there was no likelihood of consumer confusion as to the origin of Franklin Mint's Diana-related products. *Cairns III,* 107 F. Supp. 2d at 1216–21.[4]

The Fund timely appealed the District Court's denial of its motion to reinstate the post-mortem right of publicity claim and the District Court's grant of Franklin Mint's motion for summary judgment on the Lanham Act claim for false endorsement.…

II. POST-MORTEM RIGHT OF PUBLICITY CLAIM

A. Introduction

California's post-mortem right of publicity statute, in both its former version, California Civil Code § 990(a) (West 1998), and its current version, California Civil Code § 3344.1(a) (West 2002), provides in part that "[a]ny person who uses a deceased personality's name, voice, signature, photograph, or likeness, in any manner, on or in products, merchandise, or goods, or for purposes of advertising or selling, or soliciting purchases of, products, merchandise, goods, or services, without prior consent from the [decedent's successor or successors in interest], shall be liable for any damages sustained by the person or persons injured as a result thereof." It further provides that "[t]he rights recognized under this section are [personal] property rights." Cal. Civ. Code § 990(b) (West 1998); Cal. Civ. Code § 3344.1(b) (West 2002).

As enacted in 1984 and amended in 1988, California's post-mortem right of publicity statute did not contain a choice of law provision. *See* Cal. Civ. Code § 990 (West 1998). The District Court concluded that California's default personal property choice of law provision in California Civil Code § 946 applied to the Fund's post-mortem right of publicity claim and required application of the law of the decedent's domicile.[5] The law of Great Britain, where Princess Diana was domiciled, does not recognize post-mortem right of publicity claims. *See Bi-Rite Enters. v. Bruce Miner Co.,* 757 F.2d 440, 442 (1st Cir. 1985) (citing *Tolley v. Fry,* 1 K.B. 467 (1930)); J. Thomas McCarthy, *Rights of Publicity & Privacy,* § 6.21 (1998). Accordingly, the District Court dismissed the claim. On interlocu-

---

4. The District Court also granted Franklin Mint's motion for summary judgment on the Fund's Lanham Act dilution of trademark and false advertisement claims.… The Fund does not appeal these decisions.

5. California Civil Code § 946 states: "If there is no law to the contrary, in the place where personal property is situated, it is deemed to follow the person of its owner, and is governed by the law of his domicile." The Fund argues, and we assume *arguendo,* that its alleged post-mortem right of publicity would be "situated" in California.

tory appeal of this dismissal and the accompanying denial of a preliminary injunction, we affirmed by memorandum disposition.

Effective January 1, 2000, the Legislature renumbered California's post-mortem right of publicity statute from §990 to §3344.1 and amended it to "apply to the adjudication of liability and the imposition of any damages or other remedies in cases in which the liability, damages, and other remedies arise from acts occurring directly in this state." Cal. Civ. Code §3344.1(n) (West 2002). The former version of the statute contained no comparable provision. *See* Cal. Civ. Code §990 (West 1998). Following this amendment, the Fund moved to reinstate its post-mortem right of publicity claim, arguing that §3344.1(n) is a choice of law provision that requires application of California law. The District Court denied the motion, concluding that §3344.1(n) is not a choice of law provision. The District Court further concluded that California's default personal property choice of law provision in California Civil Code §946 applies to the current version of the post-mortem right of publicity in §3344.1—as it did to the former version of that right in §990— and requires the application of the law of the decedent's domicile, Great Britain, which does not recognize a post-mortem right of publicity.

The Fund argues before us—as it did before the District Court—that §3344.1(n) is a choice of law provision requiring application of California law to its post-mortem right of publicity claim. We review questions of statutory interpretation *de novo. See In re Mac-Intyre,* 74 F.3d 186, 187 (9th Cir. 1996). We conclude that the plain language of §3344.1(n), as well as its legislative history, supports the District Court's decision not to reinstate the Fund's post-mortem right of publicity claim.

B. Plain Language of the Statute

Courts "must interpret a ... statute according to its plain meaning, except in the rare cases [in which] the literal application of a statute will produce a result demonstrably at odds with the intentions of its drafters." *In re Arden,* 176 F.3d 1226, 1229 (9th Cir. 1999).... Section 3344.1(n) limits the application of California's post-mortem right of publicity statute to "cases in which the liability, damages, and other remedies arise from acts occurring directly in this state." The District Court concluded that by the plain meaning of its language, this provision is not a choice of law provision, but "simply addresses the reach of the statute's coverage." *Cairns II,* 120 F. Supp. 2d at 883.

We agree. Section 3344.1(b) provides that the post-mortem right of publicity is a (personal) property right. Section 3344.1(n) states that California's post-mortem right of publicity statute "shall apply to cases ... aris[ing] from acts occurring directly in [California]." Section 3344.1(n) does *not* state that California's post-mortem right of publicity statute applies to such cases *regardless of the domicile* of the owner of the right. Section 946 provides that personal property is governed by the law of the domicile of its owner unless there is law to the contrary in the place where the personal property is situated, *i.e.,* California. *See supra* note 5. The statement in §3344.1(n) that California's post-mortem right of publicity statute "shall apply to cases ... aris[ing] from acts occurring directly in [California]" is compatible with the post-mortem right of publicity being governed by the law of the domicile of its owner, because the statute does not state by its plain language that such cases are *not* governed by the law of the domicile of the owner. Thus, there is no "law to the contrary" to prevent application of the default choice of law provision in §946 to the post-mortem right of publicity statute in §3344.1. Accordingly, unless the "literal application" of the statute will produce "a result demonstrably at odds with the intentions of its drafters," *Arden,* 176 F.3d at 1229, §946 applies to §3344.1, and the Fund's post-mortem right of publicity claim is foreclosed.

The Fund argues that "[t]here is nothing in [§ 3344.1] to suggest that a court should look to Cal. Civil Code § 946 ... to determine whether the post-mortem right of publicity applies to a particular plaintiff or her heirs." Section 946, however, is a *default* choice of law provision that applies "[i]f there is no law to the contrary," and no explicit reference to this default provision should be expected in § 3344.1 — let alone required — for § 946 to apply.

C. Legislative History

The legislative history of § 3344.1 further supports our conclusion that § 3344.1(n) is not a choice of law provision. On January 20, 1999, Senator Burton introduced Senate Bill 209 seeking to amend the former version of the post-mortem right of publicity statute in § 990. The proposed amendment initially contained a subsection (o) that stated: "[A] plaintiff has standing to bring an action pursuant to this section if any of the acts giving rise to the action occurred in this state, *whether or not the plaintiff is a domiciliary of this state.*" *Cairns II,* 120 F. Supp. 2d at 884 (emphasis added). The "domiciliary of this state" language was later deleted from the proposed amendment. The amendment was ultimately adopted without this language as § 3344.1(n), which reads as follows: "This section shall apply to the adjudication of liability and the imposition of any damages or other remedies in cases in which the liability, damages, and other remedies arise from acts occurring directly in this state." Cal. Civ. Code § 3344.1(n) (West 2002).

The California Assembly Judiciary Committee Hearing of June 22, 1999 provides evidence that the Legislature did *not* intend § 3344.1(n), as adopted, to prevent application of § 946 to the post-mortem right of publicity. During that hearing, Senator Burton attempted to re-introduce the "domiciliary of this state" language. Assembly Member and Committee Vice-Chair Pacheco asked whether such an addition was necessary and whether there was "any law that says you have to be domiciled in the state at the time of death." Mark Lee, counsel for the Fund in this case before the District Court and present at the hearing on behalf of the Fund as a proponent of Senate Bill 209, answered that the District Court in *Cairns I* had "held that domicile was required."[6] After further discussion, Senator Burton withdrew his proposed amendment to add the "domiciliary of the state" language to what became § 3344.1(n).

We have observed that "California courts give substantial weight to the deletion of a provision during the drafting stage. 'The rejection by the Legislature of a specific provision contained in an act as originally introduced is most persuasive to the conclusion that the act should not be construed to include the omitted provision.'" *Jimeno v. Mobil Oil Corp.,* 66 F.3d 1514, 1530 (9th Cir. 1995) (quoting *Rich v. State Bd. of Optometry,* 235 Cal. App. 2d 591, 45 Cal. Rptr. 512, 522 (1965)). Here, the Committee deleted the "domiciliary of this state" language and resisted Senator Burton's attempt to reinsert this language. The Legislature ultimately passed § 3344.1(n) without the "domiciliary of this state" language. Under *Jimeno,* this "rejection by the Legislature" of the "domiciliary of this state" language is "most persuasive to the conclusion that [§ 3344.1(n)] should not be

---

6. Similarly, the Senate Rules Committee Report on Senate Bill No. 209, as amended March 3, 1999, states:

> SB 209 would state that "pursuant to the jurisdiction provided under Code of Civil Procedure 410.10, a plaintiff has standing to bring an action pursuant to this section if any of the acts giving rise to the action occurred in this state, *whether or not the decedent was a domiciliary of this state at the time of death.*" ... The author [*i.e.,* Senator Burton] asserts that *this clarification of law is necessary in light of a recent decision, Lord Simon Cairns v. Franklin Mint.*

Senate Rules Com. Rep. Cal. S.B. 209 (as amended Mar. 3, 1999) (emphasis added).

construed to include the omitted ['domiciliary of this state' language]." 66 F.3d at 1530. The rejection of the "domiciliary of this state" language is made more persuasive by the California Assembly Judiciary Committee's insistence on deleting this language although the Committee was made aware that the District Court's decision in *Cairns I* required domicile in California in the absence of such language.

Taken together, the legislative history strongly indicates that the Legislature did *not* intend to statutorily overrule the District Court's requirement of California domicile in *Cairns I*. Thus, a "literal application" of § 3344.1(n) will not produce "a result demonstrably at odds with the intentions of its drafters." *Arden,* 176 F.3d at 1229. Accordingly, the Fund's post-mortem right of publicity claim must fail because the law of Princess Diana's domicile, Great Britain, governs and that law does not recognize a post-mortem right of publicity....

For the foregoing reasons, we affirm the District Court's denial of the Fund's motion to reinstate its post-mortem right of publicity claim. We also affirm the District Court's grant of Franklin Mint's motion for summary judgment on the Fund's false endorsement claim. We finally affirm the District Court's award of $2,308,000 in attorneys' fees to Franklin Mint.

AFFIRMED.

Notes and Questions

1. What choice-of-law principle is implicit in the complaint and opinion in *Schumann*? Does it make sense to litigate the existence of a right of publicity on a jurisdiction-by-jurisdiction basis? If you had to choose only one law to apply to the claims in *Schumann*, which state's or country's law would you choose?

2. *Schumann* introduces us to another principle: the "presumption of identity of the laws." In many countries, a court will presume that the law of a foreign country is the same as the law of the forum unless and until one of the parties proves otherwise. Thus, a party seeking to have the court apply foreign law bears the burden of proving the existence and content of foreign law.

The presumption arose from the curious practice in common-law countries of treating foreign law as a question of fact. The presumption is less important in the United States after the adoption in 1966 of Federal Rule of Civil Procedure 44.1, which states: "In determining foreign law, the court may consider any relevant material or source, including testimony, whether or not submitted by a party or admissible under the Federal Rules of Evidence." This allows the court to take judicial notice of the content of foreign law, the same way as it would the law of another state in the United States. However, the presumption is still sometimes used in federal and state courts if the court cannot determine what foreign law provides.

In *Schumann*, the presumption plays an important role in dismissing the causes of action for seventeen states and all of the foreign countries except "the British Isles." Although the court only formally applies the presumption to common-law jurisdictions, it effectively applies it to civil-law countries as well, absent any claim in the pleading that those countries recognize a right of privacy under their own law.

3. *Schumann* arose and was decided one year after the Second Circuit in *Haelan Laboratories* predicted under the *Erie* doctrine that New York common law would recognize

a "right of publicity"; but the decision does not cite to or discuss *Haelan*. This omission is probably explained by the fact that the complaint was filed well before the decision in *Haelan*. Of course, a state court would not be bound by the decision of the Second Circuit in any event; and, as discussed previously, the Second Circuit's prediction turned out to be wrong.

4. What choice-of-law principle does the court apply in *Factors II*? Why does the court conclude that New York would apply Tennessee law to the issue of whether a post-mortem right of publicity exists? Should the existence of a post-mortem right of publicity be determined by a single state for all jurisdictions, or should each jurisdiction decide for itself whether to recognize a post-mortem right of publicity for both residents and non-residents?

5. Does the court in *Factors II* apply Tennessee law to all issues in the case? If not, why not? Is there a persuasive reason to distinguish the issue of whether a post-mortem right of publicity exists from any other issues in the case?

6. Having decided that Tennessee law applies to the issue of the existence of a post-mortem right, the court was then faced with the problem of ascertaining what Tennessee law was. The only relevant authority was the decision of the U.S. Court of Appeals for the Sixth Circuit, predicting under the *Erie* doctrine (without any guidance from Tennessee state courts) that Tennessee would not recognize a post-mortem right. The question the panel faced was whether to defer to the Sixth Circuit's ruling, or to decide the issue anew.

Do you agree with the majority's resolution of this issue? Does it make sense for one Circuit to defer to the decision of another Circuit without independently examining the issue? Are you persuaded that doing so helps avoid a split in authority and achieve uniformity? Is not the dissent correct that a lack of uniformity could arise in a variety of other ways? Is there reason to believe that the judges of the Sixth Circuit are more familiar with Tennessee law than the district judge in Tennessee whom the Sixth Circuit reversed?

7. The decision in *Factors II* was issued on June 29, 1981. Subsequently, on October 2, 1981, a judge of the Tennessee Chancery Court held (in an unpublished decision) that Tennessee *would* recognize a post-mortem right of publicity. *See Commerce Union Bank v. Coors of the Cumberland, Inc.*, 7 Media L. Rptr. 2204 (Tenn. Chan. Ct. 1981). The district court issued a stay and permitted the plaintiff to petition the Second Circuit to recall its mandate and rehear the case. Before the Second Circuit could rule, however, a different judge of the Tennessee Chancery Court held that Tennessee did *not* recognize a post-mortem right of publicity. *See Lancaster v. Factors Etc., Inc.*, 9 Media L. Rptr. 1109 (Tenn. Chan. Ct. 1982). In view of the conflicting opinions, the majority of the Second Circuit panel denied the petition for rehearing. *See Factors Etc., Inc. v. Pro Arts, Inc.*, 701 F.2d 11 (2d Cir. 1983).

Ultimately, of course, the Tennessee Court of Appeal ruled that Tennessee common law *does* recognize a post-mortem right of publicity, and the Tennessee legislature enacted a statutory post-mortem right. *See* Chapter IV. Does this subsequent history have any bearing on whether the panel in *Factors II* should or should not have deferred to the Sixth Circuit's prediction concerning Tennessee law?

8. In *Cairns*, the choice-of-law issue was governed by statute. Do you agree with the court that California Civil Code § 946 applied to the dispute? That statute specifies that personal property is governed by the law of the owner's domicile, "[i]f there is no law to the contrary, in the place where personal property is situated." Where should the right of publicity be deemed to be "situated" for purposes of this statute?

9. The decision points out that, after *Cairns I*, the Legislature amended California Civil Code § 3344.1 to add subsection (n). The court avoids quoting the first sentence of that subsection in full. It states:

> This section shall apply to the adjudication of liability and the imposition of any damages or other remedies in cases in which the liability, damages, and other remedies arise from acts occurring directly in this state.

Cal. Civ. Code § 3344.1(n). Do you agree with the court that the "plain language" indicates that this section is *not* a choice of law provision? What other purpose could the language serve?

10. On the other hand, the court's interpretation of subsection (n) is harmless error if one concedes that the language is, at least, ambiguous enough to warrant consulting the legislative history. As the opinion makes clear, there was an *express* choice of law provision in the bill as introduced that specified the statute would apply "whether or not the plaintiff is a domiciliary of this state." That language was taken out of the bill; and when Senator Burton proposed that it be restored, the amendment was defeated. This history strongly indicates that the Legislature did *not* intend to overrule *Cairns I*, regardless of whatever ambiguity remains in subsection (n).

C. Jurisdiction and Choice of Law in the European Union

1. Jurisdiction

In the European Union, relations between the courts of its member nations are governed by Council Regulation 44/2001/EC on Jurisdiction and Enforcement of Judgments in Civil and Commercial Matters (the so-called Brussels Regulation, because it is a revision of the Brussels Convention of 1968). The Brussels Regulation provides for both general and specific jurisdiction.

Under Article 2 of the Regulation, "persons domiciled in a Member State shall, whatever their nationality, be sued in the courts of that Member State." This Article confers general jurisdiction on the courts of the defendant's domicile for all causes of action, regardless of where the cause of action arose (or at least for causes of action arising within the E.U.).

Specific jurisdiction is governed by Articles 5 through 7. Article 5 provides in relevant part:

> A person domiciled in a Member State may, in another Member State, be sued
>
> 1. (a) in matters relating to a contract, in the courts for the place of performance of the obligation in question; ...
>
> 3. in matters relating to tort, delict or quasi-delict, in the courts for the place where the harmful event occurred or may occur ...

Thus, for most actions based on personality rights, specific jurisdiction will exist in the Member State in which the alleged infringement occurs (or is threatened to occur). This may allow the plaintiff to sue in the courts of his or her home country, at least if the offending material was distributed there. However, if jurisdiction in a Member State is based on Article 5(3), the plaintiff likely will only be able to recover damages for the territory of that Member State:

> [Under] Article 5(3) of the Convention, the victim of a libel by a newspaper article distributed in several Contracting States may bring an action for damages against the publisher either before the courts of the Contracting State of the place where the publisher of the defamatory publication is established, which have jurisdiction to award damages for all the harm caused by the defamation, or before the courts of each Contracting State in which the publication was distributed and where the victim claims to have suffered injury to his reputation, which have jurisdiction to rule solely in respect of the harm caused in the State of the court seised

Shevill v. Presse-Alliance SA, Case No. C-68/93 (ECJ 1995), ¶ 33. Thus, if the plaintiff wants to recover damages for all Member States in a single action, he or she typically will have to sue the defendant in the courts of the defendant's domicile.

It bears repeating that these rules are only binding for defendants residing with the European Union. Article 4(1) of the Regulation specifies that "[i]f the defendant is *not* domiciled in a Member State, the jurisdiction of the courts of each Member State shall ... be determined by the law of that Member State" (emphasis added). In the United Kingdom, for example, jurisdiction over libel actions has been based on as few as 23 copies distributed in that country. This tendency of British courts to assert jurisdiction based on very few contacts has encouraged many non-residents to sue American authors and publishers for libel in the U.K. *See, e.g.,* Adam Cohen, *'Libel Tourism': When Freedom of Speech Takes a Holiday*, New York Times, Sept. 14, 2008. As to whether U.S. courts would enforce a judgment obtained under such circumstances, see Chapter XIV.B.3.

In addition to the Brussels Regulation in the European Union, you may also wish to consider the jurisdiction of the European Court of Human Rights, which is governed by Articles 32 through 37 of the Convention for the Protection of Human Rights and Fundamental Freedoms. The basic provision is that "[t]he Court may receive applications from any person ... claiming to be the victim of a violation of by one of the High Contracting Parties of the rights set forth in the Convention or the protocols thereto." Article 34. However, "[t]he Court may only deal with the matter after all domestic remedies have been exhausted." Article 35(1).

---

2. Choice of Law

Choice of law within the European Union is governed by a different set of Regulations: Regulation 593/2008/EC on the Law Applicable to Contractual Obligations (Rome I) and Regulation 864/2007/EC on the Law Applicable to Non-Contractual Obligations (Rome II). The relevant provision for harm to personality rights is contained in Article 4 of the Rome II Regulation:

> 1. Unless otherwise provided for in this Regulation, the law applicable to non-contractual obligation arising out of a tort/delict shall be the law of the country in which the damage occurs irrespective of the country in which the event giving rise to the damage occurred and irrespective of the country or countries in which the indirect consequences of that event occur.

2. However, where the person claimed to be liable and the person sustaining damage both have their habitual residence in the same country at the time when the damage occurs, the law of that country shall apply.

3. Where it is clear from all the circumstances of the case that the tort/delict is manifestly more closely connected with a country other than that indicated in paragraphs 1 or 2, the law of that other country shall apply. A manifestly closer connection with another country might be based in particular on a pre-existing relationship between the parties, such as a contract, that is closely connected with the tort/delict in question.

Similarly, Article 8(1) provides that "the law applicable to a non-contractual obligation arising from an infringement of an intellectual property right shall be the law of the country for which protection is claimed" (which is typically the law of the country in which infringement occurs). However, unlike in the United States, it is unlikely that the personality rights we have studied in various European countries would be considered to be "intellectual property" rights.

In *Douglas v. Hello! Ltd.*, [2005] EWCA Civ. 595, [2005] 4 All ER 128 (Ct. App. 2005), Michael Douglas and Catherine Zeta-Jones brought suit in the United Kingdom, claiming violations of their right to exploit private information relating to them — in this case, photographs of their wedding, which was held in New York City. Among other things, the defendant argued that New York law applied (and it claimed that New York would not recognize a claim under those circumstances). The British Court of Appeal disagreed:

We do not consider that the law of New York has any direct application on the facts of this case. The cause of action is based on the publication in this jurisdiction and the complaint is that private information was conveyed to readers in this jurisdiction. The test of whether the information was private so as to attract the protection of English law must be governed by English law. That test, as established by *Campbell v. MGN*, is whether Hello! knew or ought to have known that the Douglases had a reasonable expectation that the information would remain private. Where the events to which the information relates take place outside England — in this instance in New York — the law of the place where they take place may nonetheless be relevant to the question of whether there is a reasonable expectation that the events will remain private. [¶ 100]

The court did sound one note of caution, however:

If, in the present case, the law of New York had provided that any member of the public had a right to be present at a wedding taking place in a hotel and to take and publish photographs of that wedding, then photographs of the wedding would be unlikely to have satisfied the test of privacy [under British law]. That was not the case, however. The law of New York clearly entitled the Douglases to arrange for their wedding to take place in circumstances designed to ensure that events at the wedding remained private, at least so far as photographic detail was concerned. The fact that photographs taken in violation of that privacy might have been published with impunity in New York has no direct bearing on whether the information fell to be treated as private and confidential in England. The question of whether, if unauthorised photographs of the wedding had actually been published in New York, privacy and confidentiality in England would have been destroyed is a different question, and one relevant to the next question that we have to address. [¶ 101]

Under these principles, how do you think a British court would resolve the choice-of-law problem in the *Schumann* case? How about the choice-of-law problem in *Cairns*? What if the estate of a celebrity who was domiciled in California at the time of her death sued a seller of celebrity merchandise in the United Kingdom?

Chapter XIII

Remedies for Violations of Rights of Publicity

A. Injunctive Relief

The most common form of relief awarded in rights of publicity cases is an injunction. Injunctive relief may be awarded both at the end of the lawsuit and on an interim basis prior to a final judgment (a temporary restraining order and/or a preliminary injunction). Many state statutes expressly provide for injunctive relief in cases of violations of rights of publicity. *See, e.g.* RCW § 63.60.060(1). Both U.S. and foreign courts will issue injunctions in proper cases.

In the United States and the U.K., injunctions are considered equitable remedies and their issuance is regulated by the principles of equity. (In the U.K., *see Douglas v. Hello! Ltd.*, [2005] EWCA Civ. 595, [2005] 4 All ER 128 (Ct. App. 2005) (excerpted below regarding damages).) Therefore, even if a court finds that a defendant infringed a plaintiff's right of publicity, an injunction does not issue as a matter of course. For example, in *Comedy III Productions, Inc. v. Saderup* (Chapter VIII), the Court of Appeals vacated the trial court's injunction on the grounds that it was unlikely that the defendant would violate plaintiffs' right of publicity in the future.

In *eBay, Inc. v. MercExchange, LLC*, 547 U.S. 388 (2006), the U.S. Supreme Court held that courts in patent cases (and, by implication, in other intellectual property cases) cannot automatically assume that an injunction is proper in all cases of liability. *eBay* tells courts to consider the traditional requirements of equity before issuing an injunction:

> (1) that [plaintiff] has suffered an irreparable injury; (2) that remedies available at law, such as monetary damages, are inadequate to compensate for that injury; (3) that, considering the balance of hardships between the plaintiff and defendant, a remedy in equity is warranted; and (4) that the public interest would not be disserved by a permanent injunction

Id. at 390.

On a proper showing, a court also may enter a preliminary injunction, pending the final disposition of the case. In *Winter v. Natural Resources Defense Council, Inc.*, 129 S. Ct. 365 (2008), the Supreme Court stated:

> A plaintiff seeking a preliminary injunction must establish that he is likely to succeed on the merits, that he is likely to suffer irreparable harm in the absence of preliminary relief, that the balance of equities tips in his favor, and that an injunction is in the public interest.

Id. at 374. The Court further stated:

A preliminary injunction is an extraordinary remedy never awarded as of right. In each case, courts must balance the competing claims of injury and must consider the effect on each party of the granting or withholding of the requested relief.

Id. at 376 (internal citations and quotations omitted). As you may recall, in *Estate of Presley v. Russen* (Chapter III), the court denied in part a request for a preliminary injunction, despite finding likelihood of success on the merits, because it did not believe plaintiff had shown irreparable harm.

B. Damages

Waits v. Frito-Lay, Inc.
978 F.2d 1093 (9th Cir. 1992)

BOOCHEVER, Circuit Judge:

Defendants Frito-Lay, Inc., and Tracy-Locke, Inc., appeal a jury verdict and award of $2.6 million in compensatory damages, punitive damages, and attorney's fees, in favor of singer Tom Waits. Waits sued the snack food manufacturer and its advertising agency for voice misappropriation and false endorsement following the broadcast of a radio commercial for SalsaRio Doritos which featured a vocal performance imitating Waits' raspy singing voice....

BACKGROUND

Tom Waits is a professional singer, songwriter, and actor of some reknown.... Since the early 1970s, when his professional singing career began, Waits has recorded more than seventeen albums and has toured extensively, playing to sold-out audiences throughout the United States, Canada, Europe, Japan, and Australia.... Tom Waits does not, however, do commercials. He has maintained this policy consistently during the past ten years, rejecting numerous lucrative offers to endorse major products. Moreover, Waits' policy is a public one: in magazine, radio, and newspaper interviews he has expressed his philosophy that musical artists should not do commercials because it detracts from their artistic integrity....

[The court recited the facts in detail, including the fact that Frito-Lay was aware of possible legal problems with imitating Waits' voice, based on the Ninth Circuit's ruling in *Midler v. Ford Motor Co.* (reprinted in Chapter II) and its knowledge that Waits did not do commercials.]

DISCUSSION

I. *Voice Misappropriation*

[The court upheld the continuing viability of *Midler*, and affirmed the jury's finding that Waits' voice had been misappropriated. It then turned to the damage award.]

C. *Compensatory Damage Award*

The jury awarded Waits the following compensatory damages for voice misappropriation: $100,000 for the fair market value of his services; $200,000 for injury to his peace, happiness and feelings; and $75,000 for injury to his goodwill, professional standing and future publicity value. The defendants contest the latter two awards, disputing both the availability of such damages in a voice misappropriation action and the sufficiency of the evidence supporting the awards.

1. Injury to Peace, Happiness and Feelings

The defendants argue that in right of publicity actions, only damages to compensate for economic injury are available. We disagree. Although the injury stemming from violation of the right of publicity "may be largely, or even wholly, of an economic or material nature," we have recognized that "it is quite possible that the appropriation of the identity of a celebrity may induce humiliation, embarrassment, and mental distress." *Motschenbacher* [*v. R.J. Reynolds Tobacco Co.*], 498 F.2d [821,] 824 & n. 11 [(9th Cir. 1974)]. Contrary to the defendants' assertions, *Midler* neither discussed nor limited the damages recoverable in a voice misappropriation action. *Midler* makes reference to the market value of Midler's voice solely to support its conclusion that her voice has economic value and, therefore, is a protectable property right.

In assessing the propriety of mental distress damages, our focus is properly directed to the nature of the infringement and its embarrassing impact on the plaintiff. *Publicity and Privacy* § 4.2[A]. Often the objectionable nature of the use will cause mental distress. *Id.* § 4.2[B], [C], [D] (discussing cases). In *Grant v. Esquire, Inc.*, 367 F. Supp. 876 (S.D.N.Y. 1973), for example, the court found that the mere use of a celebrity's identity could cause embarrassment for which mental distress damages would be available. The case involved a suit by Cary Grant against *Esquire* magazine for publishing a photograph in which Grant's head was superimposed on a clothing model's torso. Like Waits, Grant had taken a public position against reaping commercial profits from the publicity value of his identity. *Id.* at 880. The court, after finding that Grant had a protectable right of publicity, noted that "[i]f the jury decides in plaintiff Grant's favor he will of course be entitled to recover for any lacerations to his feelings that he may be able to establish" in addition to the fair market value of use of his identity. *Id.* at 881. Given the evidence that the commercial use of his voice was particularly offensive to Waits, we conclude that Waits' prayer for mental distress damages was properly submitted to the jury.

The defendants argue, however, that merely taking offense is an insufficient basis for awarding mental distress damages, and that under California law the evidence was insufficient to support the award. In California, mental distress damages may be recovered for "shame, humiliation, embarrassment, [and] anger." *Young v. Bank of America*, 141 Cal. App. 3d 108, 114, 190 Cal. Rptr. 122 (1983).... Waits testified that when he heard the Doritos commercial, "this corn chip sermon," he was shocked and very angry. These feelings "grew and grew over a period of a couple of days" because of his strong public opposition to doing commercials. Waits testified, "[I]t embarrassed me. I had to call all my friends, that if they hear this thing, please be informed this is not me. I was on the phone for days. I also had people calling me saying, 'Gee, Tom, I heard the new Doritos ad.'" Added to this evidence of Waits' shock, anger, and embarrassment is the strong inference that, because of his outspoken public stance against doing commercial endorsements, the Doritos commercial humiliated Waits by making him an apparent hypocrite. This evidence was sufficient both to allow the jury to consider mental distress damages and to support their eventual award.

2. Injury to Goodwill and Future Publicity Value

The defendants next argue that reputational damages are available only in defamation actions and that since Waits did not allege or prove defamation, they were unavailable here. Further, they argue, there was no evidence to support the award of such damages because Waits did not show that his career had suffered. Again, we reject these contentions.

We have no doubt, in light of general tort liability principles, that where the misappropriation of identity causes injury to reputation, compensation for such injury is appropriate. Reputational damages, moreover, have been awarded in right of publicity cases. The central issue is not whether these damages were available, but whether the evidence was sufficient to establish injury to Waits' reputation. As we noted above, the jury could have inferred from the evidence that the commercial created a public impression that Waits was a hypocrite for endorsing Doritos. Moreover, it also could have inferred damage to his artistic reputation, for Waits had testified that "part of my character and personality and image that I have cultivated is that I do not endorse products." Finally, from the testimony of Waits' expert witness, the jury could have inferred that if Waits ever wanted to do a commercial in the future, the fee he could command would be lowered by $50,000 to $150,000 because of the Doritos commercial. This evidence was sufficient to support the jury's award of $75,000 for injury to Waits' goodwill and future publicity value.

D. *Punitive Damage Award*

The jury awarded Waits a total of $2 million in punitive damages for voice misappropriation: $1.5 million against Tracy-Locke and $500,000 against Frito-Lay. The defendants ask that we vacate this award, arguing that punitive damages are unavailable as a matter of law, and alternatively, that the evidence was insufficient to support their award.

In California, exemplary or punitive damages are available "where it is proven by clear and convincing evidence that the defendant has been guilty of oppression, fraud, or malice." Cal. Civ. Code § 3294(a) (West Supp. 1992). The statute defines "malice" in pertinent part as "despicable conduct which is carried on by the defendant with a *willful and conscious disregard of the rights* or safety of others." *Id.* § 3294(c)(1) (emphasis added). The defendants contend that because *Midler* was so recently decided and so imprecise in the scope of its holding, they could not have been aware of the rights they were infringing upon in broadcasting the commercial. Thus, they reason, their conduct was not in "conscious disregard" of Waits' property right in his voice.

Where an issue is one of first impression or where a right has not been clearly established, punitive damages are generally unavailable. The right of a well-known professional singer to control the commercial use of a distinctive voice, however, was not an "issue of first impression" in this case. The right had been established clearly by *Midler*. The evidence was unequivocal that, although *Midler* was decided just three months before the conduct at issue, Tracy-Locke personnel responsible for making the Doritos commercial were familiar with the *Midler* decision. Tracy-Locke was concerned enough that the commercial could result in voice misappropriation liability that it cautioned Frito-Lay of the legal risks in choosing the Carter version. At the same time, however, Tracy-Locke stated its readiness to indemnify Frito-Lay against damages. Frito-Lay, reassured by the indemnification, chose to proceed with the Carter version. In going forward with the commercial, the defendants knowingly took a calculated risk, thereby consciously disregarding the effect of these actions on Waits' legally recognized rights.

The defendants argue, however, that although they may have been aware that legal risks were involved, they had a good faith belief that Waits' rights would not be infringed because they read the legal precedents differently. This argument leaves us unpersuaded. Good faith cannot be manufactured by looking to the law of other jurisdictions to define the rights of California residents. *Midler* could not be more clear that, in California at least, a well-known singer with a distinctive voice has a property right in that voice. Waits is a California resident, a fact of which Tracy-Locke personnel were aware. The defendants made a conscious decision to broadcast a vocal performance imitating Waits in markets across the country, including San Francisco and Los Angeles. This evidence is sufficient to raise at least a *prima facie* showing that defendants acted in conscious disregard of rights recognized in California.

Even if punitive damages are available, the defendants argue, the award must be vacated because it is not supported by clear and convincing evidence, as required by California law. Clear and convincing evidence means evidence sufficient to support a finding of "high probability." *Mock v. Michigan Millers Mutual Ins. Co.*, 4 Cal. App. 4th 306, 5 Cal. Rptr. 2d 594, 610 (1992). On appeal, we must determine whether, viewing the evidence in the light most favorable to Waits, any rational jury could have found a high probability that the defendants acted with malice, *i.e.*, despicably and with willful and conscious disregard of Waits' rights.

The evidence the jury heard included testimony that Carter, the Waits' impersonator, told Brenner that Waits had a policy against doing commercials and would not like this one. Brenner knew of Waits' policy because he had tried unsuccessfully to hire him for another commercial. In the face of Brenner's warnings that the commercial sounded too much like Waits and presented serious legal concerns, Grossman called a lawyer. Although the lawyer thought the scenario Grossman painted him did not present a colorable legal problem, Grossman had not told the lawyer that the commercial featured a voice that sounded like Waits—only that the "feeling" of the music was the same. Grossman urged Frito-Lay to choose the Carter version over one that did not sound like Waits. Moreover, at the same time Grossman disclosed the legal risk involved with the Carter version, he stated that Tracy-Locke would indemnify Frito-Lay in the event of a lawsuit. The responsible Frito-Lay executive, who was also familiar with Waits and his background, chose to go with the Carter version. The effect of their actions on Waits, according to his testimony, was to tarnish the artistic integrity which he had striven to achieve.

We believe that, viewed most favorably to Waits, this evidence was adequate to support a finding of high probability that Tracy-Locke and Frito-Lay acted with malice. Despicability reflects a moral judgment, "conscious disregard" a state of mind. A rational jury could have found the defendants' conduct despicable because they knowingly impugned Waits' integrity in the public eye. A rational jury also could have found that the defendants, in spite of their awareness of Waits' legal right to control the commercial use of his voice, acted in conscious disregard of that right by broadcasting the commercial. We therefore affirm the award of punitive damages.

II. *Lanham Act Claim*

Section 43(a) of the Lanham Act, prohibits the use of false designations of origin, false descriptions, and false representations in the advertising and sale of goods and services. Waits' claim under section 43(a) is premised on the theory that by using an imitation of his distinctive voice in an admitted parody of a Tom Waits song, the defendants misrepresented his association with and endorsement of SalsaRio Doritos. The jury found in Waits' favor and awarded him $100,000 in damages. The district court also awarded him attorneys' fees under section 35 of the Lanham Act. On appeal, the defendants argue that Waits lacks standing to bring a Lanham Act claim, that Waits' false endorsement claim fails on its merits, that the damage award is duplicative, and that attorneys' fees are improper. Before we address these contentions, however, we turn to the threshold issue of whether false endorsement claims are properly cognizable under section 43(a) of the Lanham Act,[5] a question of first impression in this circuit....

[The court upheld the application of §43(a) to a claim for false endorsement.]

D. *Damages*

The defendants urge us to vacate the damage award on Waits' Lanham Act claim as duplicative of those damages awarded for voice misappropriation representing the fair market value of Waits' services. Waits does not contest this point. Standing by the representations he made to the jury at trial that he was not seeking a double recovery, he asserts on appeal that he "does not oppose a reduction of the final judgment in the amount of $100,000 based on the overlapping Lanham Act award."

In instructing the jury on Waits' Lanham Act claim, the court stated that it could award damages for the fair market value of Waits' services. The jury awarded Waits $100,000 on this claim. It also awarded Waits $100,000 for the fair market value of his services on his voice misappropriation claim. The damages awarded under the Lanham Act, therefore, are duplicative. Accordingly, we vacate this portion of the judgment.

E. *Attorneys' Fees*

Section 35 of the Lanham Act authorizes attorneys' fee awards for prevailing plaintiffs in "exceptional cases." 15 U.S.C. § 1117. Exceptional cases include those in which the defendants' conduct is "malicious, fraudulent, deliberate, or wilful." *Sealy, Inc. v. Easy Living, Inc.*, 743 F.2d 1378, 1384 (9th Cir. 1984) (*citing* S. Rep. No. 1400, 93rd Cong., 2d Sess. (1974), *reprinted in* 1974 U.S.C.C.A.N. 7132); *see Transgo*, 768 F.2d at 1026. We review attorneys' fee awards under the Lanham Act for abuse of discretion.

In awarding punitive damages on Waits' voice misappropriation claim, the jury specifically found that the defendants had acted with oppression, fraud, or malice. That finding qualifies this case as an exceptional one within the meaning of section 35. The district court was therefore within its discretion in awarding Waits reasonable attorneys' fees....

Notes and Questions

1. The jury awarded Waits compensatory damages under four separate theories: (1) the value of his services (*i.e.*, as an endorser); (2) injury to his peace and happiness—essentially, mental distress over the use of an imitation of his voice; (3) injury to his goodwill and reputation; and (4) false endorsement. The court found that (1) and (4) were duplicative and struck the latter. But it upheld all of the other damage awards. Should the court have also considered the problem that awarding damages for the value of his services was incongruous, given Waits' assertion that he did not want to have his voice used to promote products *and* given the award of damages for his mental anguish?

2. The California statutes that confer causes of action for violations of rights of publicity specifically authorize punitive damages. Cal. Civ. Code §§ 3344(a), 3344.1(a). *See also* Nev. Rev. Stat. Ann. § 597.810(1)(b)(2) (punitive damages may be awarded if defendant "knowingly" used defendant's name, voice, or likeness). Other states have specific

---

5. Although we agree with the defendants that the damage award is duplicative and vacate it, the underlying issues of the cognizability of false endorsement actions, Waits' standing to sue, and the merits of his Lanham Act claim are not moot, inasmuch as the judgment on this claim also supports an award of attorneys' fees.

provisions authorizing treble damages in cases of knowing violations, but do not specifically authorize punitive damages. *See, e.g.,* R.I. Gen. L. §9-1-28; 214 Mass. Gen. L. Ann. §3A. Punitive damages are not available for Lanham Act claims (though punitive damages can be combined with Lanham Act awards when there is a state-law basis for punitive damages). Section 35(a) of the Lanham Act permits courts to increase damage awards up to three times the compensatory damages, but such adjustments are "subject to the principles of equity," and they must be "compensation and not a penalty." 15 U.S.C. §1117(a).

3. In this case, the court upheld the award of punitive damages, finding defendants' conduct "despicable," and finding that defendants knew not only that Waits would object to the use of his voice, but that he refused to endorse any products on principle. Short of such knowledge, when would it be reasonable to permit an award of punitive damages in such cases? For example, consider the commemorative busts of Dr. Martin Luther King, Jr. that were at issue in *Martin Luther King Jr. Center for Social Change, Inc. v. American Heritage Products, Inc.* (Chapter IV). Was that an appropriate case for punitive damages?

4. In *White v. Samsung Electronics* (Chapters III and VIII), a jury ultimately awarded Vanna White $400,000. Unlike Tom Waits, White was willing to endorse products and services (although perhaps not in the manner portrayed in that case). Should that affect the theories under which she can recover damages?

5. In the *Tony Twist* case in Chapter VIII (*Doe v. Cablevision*), the plaintiff received an award of $15 million, for "endorsement value." Do you think that award was justified under the circumstances of that case?

Andretti v. Borla Performance Industries, Inc.
426 F.3d 824 (6th Cir. 2005)

RALPH B. GUY, JR., Circuit Judge:

This case involves a dispute over Mario Andretti's right of publicity. Mario Andretti and Car Sound Exhaust System, Inc. (Car Sound) entered into a contract in which Andretti agreed to be Car Sound's corporate spokesperson. During the contract period, defendant Borla Performance Industries, Inc. (Borla) advertised a statement Andretti had made about Borla's product. Andretti had no prior knowledge and did not give Borla permission to use his name or quotation. Andretti and M.A. 500, Inc. (collectively, "Andretti") sued Borla, seeking a permanent injunction and damages for violating Andretti's right to publicity, tortiously interfering with a business relationship, violating the Michigan Consumer Protection Act, *quantum meruit*, violating the Lanham Act §§1125(a) and 1125(c), and unfair competition. The district court granted summary judgment to Borla on all the damage claims, but issued the permanent injunction against Borla sought by Andretti. The court then awarded Rule 11 sanctions against Andretti, ordered Andretti to pay the costs incurred by Borla after it made an unsuccessful Rule 68 offer of judgment, denied Borla's other requests for costs and fees, and denied Andretti's request for costs. We affirm the district court's rulings on every issue.

I.

The facts underlying this case are undisputed and uncomplicated. Mario Andretti was a successful and well known race-car driver before he retired from automobile racing. Andretti is now a corporate spokesman for companies that contract with Andretti for the exclusive right to utilize his name, image, likeness, and personal services. On November

1, 2001, Andretti and Car Sound, a manufacturer of after-market exhaust systems and catalytic converters, entered into a contract that provided Car Sound with the exclusive right for four years to utilize Andretti's rights of publicity with regard to exhaust systems. Borla, Car Sound's largest direct competitor, began an advertisement campaign in the spring of 2003 that included a quote from Andretti in which he praised a Borla product. Borla received permission to use the quotation from the publication in which the quote originally appeared, but it did not seek or receive Andretti's permission.

Andretti filed a five-count complaint and a motion for a preliminary injunction against Borla in Oakland County Circuit Court, Michigan, on March 20, 2003. Borla removed the complaint to federal court. To demonstrate that the amount in controversy exceeded the federal diversity jurisdiction requirement of $75,000, Borla's attorney attached his own declaration to the notice of removal stating that Andretti's pre-suit demands to Borla were about $200,000. The parties stipulated to a preliminary injunction order on April 30, 2003. In June, Andretti filed an eight-count First Amended Complaint.... Borla made an offer of judgment pursuant to Federal Rule of Civil Procedure 68 on December 22, 2003. Borla's offer included $15,000 for costs, expenses, fees, and damages and a permanent injunction "forever barring, enjoining, and restraining Defendant from using or disseminating any advertisement or promotional material that contains the quotation given by Plaintiff, Mario Andretti, on page 17 of the Summer 2001 edition of the C5 Registry." Andretti rejected the Rule 68 offer of judgment....

II.

...

C. Borla's Motion for Summary Judgment

We review *de novo* the district court's grant of summary judgment....

The district court decided that Andretti did not produce any evidence of damages and therefore, in light of Borla's offer to enter a permanent injunction, Andretti's claims were moot. Andretti argues that there was a genuine issue of material fact as to his damages because he had submitted evidence of damages in his supplementation of document requests and in his interrogatory responses, because Borla failed to elicit evidence concerning damages when it deposed Andretti, and because Borla's attorney admitted the fact of Andretti's damages in his declaration supporting removal from state court to federal court. Andretti's arguments are without merit for the reasons explained below.

1. Andretti did not present evidence of damages to the district court

Andretti argues that he did provide evidence of his damages to the district court because his supplemental responses to Borla's document requests were submitted as evidence. The supplemental responses consisted of Andretti's identification of documents that responded to each document request. The documents were identified by Bates Stamp numbers. The actual documents were not presented as evidence by either party. According to plaintiffs' representations in the briefs, some of the documents identified in the response were contracts between Andretti and various corporations in which Andretti agreed to be a corporate spokesperson for considerable compensation. One of the contracts was Andretti's agreement with Car Sound, which revealed that Car Sound paid Andretti $500,000 annually for the use of his rights of publicity. Plaintiffs argue that the reference to certain Bates Stamp numbers that correlate with the contracts "demonstrates there is a host of evidence as to both the nature and amount of Andretti's damages in this case." We disagree. Even though plaintiffs had the documents when they responded to the motion, plaintiffs admit that neither they nor Borla presented the documents to the district court. Moreover, the supplemental response listed only Bates Stamp numbers, not a description of the documents that were provided. The district court could not consider the evidentiary value of documents of which it was not aware.[5]

2. The response to interrogatory did not create genuine issue of damages

Andretti claims that one of his interrogatory responses provides sufficient evidence of damages. Interrogatory No. 22 asked: "Please describe in detail how Plaintiff alleges that his good will and reputation has been damaged by Borla's advertisement at issue in this litigation, including but not limited to specific examples of how Borla's advertisement has affected Plaintiff's good will and reputation." Andretti replied:

> Andretti objects to this interrogatory as overly broad, unduly burdensome, requests confidential and proprietary information, and not reasonably calculated to lead to the discovery of admissible evidence. Without waiving this objection, Borla's advertisement has damaged Andretti's goodwill and reputation in the sense that the automotive after-market industry is well aware of Andretti's exclusive, long-term engagement with Car Sound. Andretti's occupation, now that his racing career is over, is that of a corporate spokesperson. His rights of publicity are his largest and greatest asset. It would be very easy for folks in the highly competitive automotive industry, given Borla's actions, to consider Andretti one who provides his services purely for the money and without any allegiance or loyalty to the relationships he has worked diligently to establish over the years. All of his hard work and dedication could be erased by the one selfish move of a competitor like Borla.

This response merely states a category of damages that Andretti might incur, but he does not claim that he has actually suffered any damages in this case. Possible damage to his reputation as a corporate spokesperson is purely hypothetical and is far too speculative to create a genuine issue of damages. *See, e.g., Johnson v. Jones,* 149 F.3d 494, 507 (6th Cir. 1998) (holding that a court should not award damages that are "wholly speculative").

3. Defendant's failure to ask about damages is irrelevant

According to Andretti, Borla should be estopped from arguing that there is no evidence of damages because Borla either knew of Andretti's damages or failed to elicit evidence concerning damages during discovery. This line of reasoning is without merit because once the movant of a summary judgment motion satisfies its burden by demonstrating the absence of a genuine issue of material fact, the nonmoving party "must produce specific facts demonstrating a genuine issue of fact for trial if it is to withstand summary judgment." *Leadbetter v. Gilley,* 385 F.3d 683, 690 (6th Cir. 2004) (citing *Anderson v. Liberty Lobby, Inc.,* 477 U.S. 242, 247–48 (1986)). It was not Borla's burden to discover or produce evidence of Andretti's damages, especially when the evidence was exclusively within Andretti's control. Moreover, Andretti implies that Borla misled the district court because the contracts demonstrated Andretti's damages and Borla was familiar with the contracts, but Borla represented to the district court that no evidence of damages existed. The contracts standing alone did not provide evidence of Andretti's damages. They helped establish the value of corporate sponsorship contracts, but did not show that any current

---

5. Furthermore, Andretti has not presented the documents to this court on appeal. Even if he did, we would be unable to review them because we generally decline to review evidence not presented to the district court.

contract or future contract opportunity was impaired. Therefore, Borla did not mislead the court by arguing that Andretti had no evidence of actual damages.

4. Attorney's declaration is not evidence of damages

Andretti contends that Borla's attorney's declaration contains an admission that Andretti incurred damages. Borla's attorney, Melvin Raznick, attached his own declaration to the notice of removal of Andretti's complaint to federal court based on diversity. Raznick declared that Andretti, through his attorney, demanded $200,000 in monetary damages in addition to a retraction of Borla's advertisement and Borla's promise not to run the ad in the future. Raznick also declared that

> based upon the Plaintiff's own claims of stated damages in the amount of $200,000.00, plus the additional costs that would clearly be incurred by BORLA if Plaintiff received his requested relief ... it is my good faith belief that the amount in controversy in the present action at the time of this Notice [o]f Removal exceeds the $75,000.00 jurisdictional limit required under federal diversity jurisdiction.

Raznick's recounting of Andretti's demand for $200,000 is not the equivalent of declaring that he believed Andretti had indeed incurred damages of $200,000. Raznik's declaration necessarily implied that the amount in controversy was $200,000 *if proven*. Andretti's contention that the declaration creates a question of fact as to his damages is unavailing....

G. Rule 68 Costs

Rule 68 provides that anytime more than ten days before trial, a defendant may present a plaintiff with an offer of judgment against the defendant "for the money or property or to the effect specified in the offer." If the plaintiff rejects the offer of judgment, and "the judgment finally obtained by the offeree is not more favorable than the offer, the offeree must pay the costs incurred after the making of the offer." Fed. R. Civ. P. 68. Although this circuit apparently has not set forth the standard of review for Rule 68 rulings, we join the other circuits that review *de novo* the legal interpretations of Rule 68, and review for clear error the factual findings concerning the circumstances under which Rule 68 offers were made....

The district court awarded Borla its costs incurred after December 22, 2003, the date Andretti rejected Borla's Rule 68 offer of judgment. Andretti appeals that ruling, arguing that the final judgment was more favorable than Borla's Rule 68 offer of judgment for two reasons: the permanent injunction is more valuable to Andretti than monetary damages, and the specific wording of the Rule 68 offer's injunction was less favorable than the wording of the permanent injunction.

In support of his argument that a judgment in his favor and an injunction is more valuable than monetary damages, Andretti relies on *Lish v. Harper's Magazine Foundation*, 148 F.R.D. 516 (S.D.N.Y. 1993), which held that money damages are not the only measure of whether a plaintiff has obtained a "more favorable" judgment under Rule 68. We agree with the *Lish* court that a favorable judgment and an injunction can be more valuable to a plaintiff than damages. Unfortunately for Andretti, Borla's Rule 68 offer included damages and a permanent injunction, but the final judgment awarded Andretti an injunction only. Even though comparing the value of damages to an injunction is like comparing apples and oranges, in this case we must compare the value of an apple plus an orange versus only an apple. Andretti's argument that the injunction is worth more than the offer of an injunction plus damages is unpersuasive.

Andretti also argues that the injunction in the judgment is more valuable than the injunction in Borla's Rule 68 offer because the judgment's injunction is worded more favorably.... [The court rejected that argument.]

AFFIRMED.

Notes and Questions

1. Rule 26(a)(1)(A)(iii) of the Federal Rules of Civil Procedure provides as follows:

a party must, without awaiting a discovery request, provide to the other parties:

(iii) a computation of each category of damages claimed by the disclosing party—who must also make available for inspection and copying ... the documents or other evidentiary material, unless privileged or protected from disclosure, on which each computation is based, including materials bearing on the nature and extent of injuries suffered ...

Had this material been provided by Andretti, and had he introduced it in response to the summary judgment motion, he likely would have avoided summary judgment on the issue of damages.

2. This case demonstrates that courts are not always willing to allow fuzzy damage claims to be presented to a jury in the hopes that they will award a large sum as compensatory damages. Rather, courts may scrutinize such claims before presenting them to a jury to insure that any award will not be made out of sympathy or other improper sentiment. In this case, the defendant did not really contest that it had improperly used Andretti's statement as an endorsement (it offered to stipulate to an injunction), but it did contest whether there were any damages. While Andretti likely could have proven damages had he made more of an effort, his failure to do so rendered him vulnerable to summary judgment.

3. Why couldn't Andretti demonstrate the kind of mental distress damages shown by Tom Waits? To what extent was the court's reaction to the damage question in *Andretti* influenced by its estimation of the impropriety of defendant's conduct? How was defendant's conduct in *Andretti* different from the conduct of defendants in *Waits*?

4. *Andretti* also illustrates a rather seldom-used procedural device—the Offer of Judgment. Under Federal Rule of Civil Procedure 68, a "defending" party can offer to settle the matter formally with the other side by presenting an offer of judgment. If the other side rejects the offer, and the result is not more favorable to the rejecting party than the offer, the rejecting party is liable for the costs of the action after the offer is made.

Douglas v. Hello!, Ltd.

[2005] EWCA Civ. 595, [2005] 4 All ER 128,
[2005] E.M.L.R. 28 (Ct. App. 2005),
aff'd on other grounds, [2007] UKHL 21, [2007] E.M.L.R. 12 (H.L. 2007)

[Michael Douglas and Catherine Zeta-Jones gave the exclusive rights to publish photographs of their wedding to OK! Magazine. However, an uninvited guest managed to get into the wedding and took pictures, which were sold to and published in Hello! Magazine. Douglas and Zeta-Jones sued Hello! for "breach of confidence," a theory which the U.K. courts approved in this case. After upholding the finding of liability, the U.K. Court of Appeal discussed damages claimed by Douglas and Zeta-Jones.]

The Douglases' claim for a notional licence fee

243. When it came to the assessment of damages, the Douglases were awarded £3,750 [roughly $7500] each as general damages for mental distress, plus a further £7000 between them for additional expenses and disruption in respect of selecting photographs for publication. Given that they are entitled to damages and that OK! are not entitled to damages, it is contended on behalf of the Douglases that they should be entitled to more substantial damages, namely a sum equal to the notional licence they would have charged Hello! to permit them to publish the unauthorised photographs. The Douglases also contend that the judge's assessment of that fee at £125,000 was significantly too low. We observe at the outset that it is not easy to understand why the Douglases' appeal in this connection should be contingent upon Hello!'s appeal succeeding against OK!. This anomaly raises an immediate question mark over the validity of this claim.

244. It is well established that damages in a case involving unauthorised use of, or unauthorised benefiting from, intellectual property and similar rights can be assessed in a number of different ways. In *General Tire & Rubber Co v. Firestone Tyre and Rubber Co Ltd.* [1975] 1 WLR 819 at pp 824 to 827, Lord Wilberforce identified the normal categories at least in patent cases. They are the profit, or the royalty, which was or would have been achieved (*e.g.* where the defendant manufactures, or licences the manufacture of, goods covered by the patent), and the licence fee which would reasonably have been charged (*e.g.* where it is not possible to assess the level of profit). The present case is far from normal, and in our view none of these normal methods of assessment would be appropriate.

245. This is not a case where a profit was made by the defendant: bearing in mind the payment they made, £125,000, for the unauthorised photographs, Hello! actually made a loss on the whole exercise. This is not a case where a royalty, or its equivalent, would be appropriate, partly for the same reason, and partly because Hello! effected no licensing, or its equivalent, in relation to the use of the unauthorised photographs.

246. There are obvious problems with assessing the Douglases' damages on a notional licence fee basis. First, the whole basis of their (as opposed to OK!'s) complaint about Hello!'s publication of the unauthorised photographs is upset and affront at invasion of privacy, not loss of the opportunity to earn money. Indeed, they have already claimed and been paid, damages assessed on that former basis. That factor alone would not prevent an assessment on a notional licence fee basis, but it is not a good start. Secondly, the Douglases would never have agreed to any of the unauthorised photographs being published. The licence fee approach will normally involve a fictional negotiation, but the unreality of the fictional negotiation in this case is palpable.

247. Thirdly, and most importantly, having sold the exclusive right to publish photographs of the reception to OK!, the Douglases would not have been in a position to grant a licence to Hello!. In this connection, we do not consider that, in light of the terms of the OK! contract, especially clause 10, the Douglases could claim to be required to account for the notional licence fee to OK!. Accordingly, an award of a notional licence fee would involve the Douglases being unjustly enriched: they have already been paid £1m[il-lion] for the exclusive right to publish photographs of the reception. As was said in argument, they have thereby exhausted their relevant commercial interest.

248. Quite apart from these factors, while it is not a sufficient reason for rejecting the notional licence fee approach, there is the difficulty of assessing a fee. The Douglases would have been very unwilling to agree to publication of the unauthorised photographs in light of the terms of the OK! contract, the quality of the photographs, and the circumstances in which they were taken. Hello! would presumably have been prepared to pay at least £125,000, as that is what they actually paid for them, but Mr Browne made it clear that the Douglases would have wanted a lot more. The worse the quality of the photographs, the less they would have been worth to Hello! and the more the Douglases would have wanted for their publication.

249. In all these circumstances, we are of the view that a notional licence fee would not be the right basis on which to assess the Douglases' damages, even given that they, but not OK!, are entitled to claim against Hello!. If, however, Hello! had made a profit on the publication, we would have had no hesitation in accepting that the Douglases would have been entitled to seek an account of that profit. Such an approach would not run into the difficulties of principle which their notional licence fee argument faces. Such an approach may also serve to discourage any wrongful publication, at least where it is motivated by money.

250. Finally, if it had been right to award damages to the Douglases on the basis of a notional licence fee, we would not, in any event, have thought it right to interfere with the judge's assessment of £125,000. Various factors to which we have made reference render it impossible to contend that the figure adopted by the judge was one which he could not properly have reached. We have in mind the fact that the assessment was a matter of valuation opinion, the difficulties inherent in this particular assessment, the fact that Hello! actually paid £150,000 for the unauthorised photographs, and the fact that Hello! made a loss on the whole exercise.

Problem 8

In *Christoff v. Nestlé USA* (reprinted in Chapter XI) the defendant used plaintiff's face on the label of its "Taster's Choice" instant coffee. Plaintiff was not a celebrity and was not the first "face" of Taster's Choice. When plaintiff won his case at trial, damages became an issue. How should one measure damages in this kind of case? Should the plaintiff be entitled to defendant's profits from the product? If not, how would you value plaintiff's contribution toward defendant's business? Is there a difference between having an ordinary picture and having a particular picture on a jar of coffee? Who should bear the burden of demonstrating that? What other possible measures of damages can you imagine?

C. Attorney's Fees and Other Relief

1. Attorney's Fees

As a general rule, in the United States litigants bear their own attorneys' fees, win or lose. (This is often called the "American rule.") However, this rule can be altered by contract (which is seldom at issue in rights of publicity cases), or by statute. Several state right of publicity statutes have altered the American rule. In California, the relevant statutes (one for living celebrities and one for deceased celebrities) each expressly state that "The prevailing party in any action under this section shall also be entitled to attorney's fees and costs." Cal. Civ. Code §§ 3344(a), 3344.1(a). *Accord* 12 Okla. Stat. Ann. § 1449(A); RCW § 63.60.060(5). But other statutes, such as the one in Wisconsin, only allow attorneys fees to be recovered by a successful plaintiff (not "the prevailing party"), except in unusual cases. *See, e.g.,* Wis. Stat. Ann. § 995.50(1)(c), (6)(a) (the latter section permits an award of "fees and costs" to the defendant only if the action was "frivolous"). Still other statutes are silent on the issue of attorney's fees. *See, e.g.,* Va. Code Ann. § 8.01-40.

Kirby v. Sega of America, Inc.
144 Cal. App. 4th 47, 50 Cal. Rptr. 3d 607 (2006)

[Plaintiff, the lead singer in a band, sued a video game distributor, claiming that one of the characters of the video game constituted a violation of her rights of publicity under California statutory and common law, and the Lanham Act. The trial court granted summary judgment for defendant, on First Amendment grounds, and the Court of Appeal affirmed this ruling. The court then turned to the claim for attorney's fees.]

[California Civil Code] Section 3344, subdivision (a) clearly states that "[t]he prevailing party in any action under this section shall ... be entitled to attorney's fees and costs." Under this provision, respondents sought approximately $763,000 in attorney's fees and costs, and ultimately received an award of approximately $608,000. Kirby concedes section 3344's directive that fees "shall" be awarded to the prevailing party in a statutory appropriation action is clearly mandatory. Nevertheless, she argues the statute should be applied permissively and only in cases in which the suit is deemed frivolous or brought in bad faith or without substantial justification. Otherwise, she insists, the statute "presents a clear disincentive for plaintiffs to enforce...." Her argument is misdirected. The mandatory fee provision of section 3344, subdivision (a) leaves no room for ambiguity. Whether the course is sound is not for us to say. This is the course the Legislature has chosen and, until that body changes course, we must enforce the rule. The fee award was proper....

As *Kirby* demonstrates, a mandatory attorney's fees provision such as that contained in the California statute may become a significant disincentive for one side or the other to pursue or defend vigorously a claim under the statute. Such a provision may also provide the parties with a considerable incentive to settle the case to avoid the imposition of attorney's fees.

Determining the proper amount of a fee award is also a difficult problem. Many plaintiffs' attorneys handle cases on a contingency fee basis, as opposed to charging an hourly rate. Moreover, a court is obliged to review the submission of the prevailing party to determine whether it is "reasonable." Obviously, this will involve not only the hourly rate, but the reasonableness of the hours spent.

The Lanham Act and Attorney's Fees

In *Waits,* the court awarded attorney's fees under the Lanham Act, rather than California law. (Although the *Waits* court found a violation of California common law, there was no statutory violation because the defendant did not use Waits' actual voice. *See Midler v. Ford Motor Co.* in Chapter II.) Section 35 of the Lanham Act, 15 U.S.C. §1117, permits a court to award attorneys fees "in exceptional cases." Thus, unlike the California statutory claims, claims under the Lanham Act do not automatically — or even ordinarily — result in an award of attorneys' fees. The *Waits* court determined that the facts of that case, where "the jury specifically found that the defendants had acted with oppression, fraud, or malice," qualified as an exceptional case. In *Kirby*, the defendant, as prevailing party, also requested attorneys' fees on the claim brought by plaintiff under the Lanham Act. The Court of Appeal responded in a footnote:

> As to the claim for violation of the Lanham Act, the trial court denied respondents attorney's fees, concluding Kirby's action was neither unreasonable or groundless. (*See Stephen W. Boney, Inc. v. Boney Services, Inc.* (9th Cir. 1997) 127 F.3d 821, 825, 827 [prevailing defendant may be awarded fees in an "exceptional case," *i.e.*, one in which plaintiff's claims are groundless, unreasonable, vexatious or pursued in bad faith].) The amount of the fees awarded was reduced after the trial court concluded the amount sought by respondents was not reasonable. However, the court found all of Kirby's state statutory and common law claims "inextricably intertwined," and refused to further apportion the fee award. (*Akins v. Enterprise Rent-a-Car Co.* (2000) 79 Cal. App. 4th 1127, 1133, 94 Cal. Rptr. 2d 448 [When statutory claims providing for fees are combined with claims for which attorney's fees are not available, prevailing party may recover fees only on statutory claim unless claims are so intertwined or pertain to issues common to claims in which fees are properly allowed].) Kirby does not take issue with these rulings.

Kirby v. Sega of America, Inc., 144 Cal. App. 4th 47, 62 n.7, 50 Cal. Rptr. 3d 607, 618 n.7 (2006). As you can see, when the prevailing party is the defendant, showing that the case is "exceptional" requires more than simply showing that the plaintiff's claim could not withstand a summary judgment motion, or even a motion to dismiss at the pleading stage. Rather, there must be some element of bad faith involved on the part of the plaintiff before a court will award attorneys' fees to a prevailing defendant. *Kirby* was able to sidestep another complication: what to do when there are claims under state law, for which attorneys' fees are mandatory, and federal law, where they are not. The trial court ruled that the state and federal claims were "inextricably intertwined," and thus did not separate the fees to be awarded for each claim. This ruling was not appealed by plaintiff. However, the appellate court's language clearly indicates that such a separation should be made in most cases.

---

2. Other Relief

Some state statutes go beyond monetary and injunctive relief and permit courts to order forfeiture of the offending goods. *See, e.g.,* Tenn. Code Ann. §47-25-1105(d); RCW §63.60.060(4).

Chapter XIV

Extraterritorial Enforcement of Rights of Publicity

A. Introduction

One of the traditional hallmarks of international agreements concerning intellectual property protection has been the principle of territoriality, under which the enforcement of intellectual property rights is subject to the laws and, ordinarily, the courts of the country where the infringement of those rights occurs. The concept of territoriality underlies the major international treaties relating to intellectual property rights, such as the Paris Convention for the Protection of Industrial Property, the Berne Convention for the Protection of Literary and Artistic Works, and the Agreement on Trade Related Aspects of Intellectual Property Rights, or TRIPS (which is part of the Marrakesh Agreement Establishing the World Trade Organization).

Territoriality is a function of international comity; it is generally considered inappropriate for one country to attempt to dictate the proper intellectual property standards to be applied to conduct occurring outside of that country. However, the concept of territoriality is not a rigid, absolute limit on extraterritorial enforcement. On occasion, the courts of one country will enforce their standards against actions occurring outside of that country. Usually, this requires that the extraterritorial acts have a significant effect on the enforcing country.

For example, if a French actress's image is being used in Portugal without her authorization, one would not expect a United States court to step in and attempt to enforce the actress's rights under U.S. law. Instead, she would be expected to use Portuguese courts and Portuguese law. The United States would not have any interest in the alleged violation of her rights. However, one might ask whether and under what circumstances French courts could or would attempt to adjudicate the dispute.

In this Chapter, we shall examine the circumstances in which one country's courts might be persuaded to apply that country's law to actions taking place outside of the country.

B. Domestic Courts

1. Injunctions Acting Internationally

Ali v. Playgirl, Inc.
447 F. Supp. 723 (S.D.N.Y. 1978)

GAGLIARDI, District Judge:

Plaintiff Muhammad Ali, a citizen of Illinois and until recently the heavyweight boxing champion of the world, has brought this diversity action for injunctive relief and damages against defendants Playgirl, Inc., a California corporation, Independent News Company ("Independent"), a New York corporation, and Tony Yamada, a California citizen, for their alleged unauthorized printing, publication and distribution of an objectionable portrait of Ali in the February, 1978 issue of Playgirl Magazine ("Playgirl"), a monthly magazine published by Playgirl, Inc., and distributed in New York State by Independent. The portrait complained of depicts a nude black man seated in the corner of a boxing ring and is claimed to be unmistakably recognizable as plaintiff Ali. Alleging that the publication of this picture constitutes, inter alia, a violation of his rights under Section 51 of the New York Civil Rights Law (McKinney 1976) and of his related common law "right of publicity", Ali now moves for a preliminary injunction ... directing defendants Playgirl, Inc. and Independent to cease distribution and dissemination of the February, 1978 issue of Playgirl Magazine, ... and to surrender to plaintiff any printing plates or devices used to reproduce the portrait complained of. For the reasons which follow and to the extent indicated below, plaintiff's motion for a preliminary injunction is granted....

DISCUSSION

...

Liability on the Merits

... Defendants do not, and indeed cannot, seriously dispute the assertion that the offensive drawing is in fact Ali's "portrait or picture." This phrase, as used in § 51, is not restricted to photographs, but generally comprises those representations which are recognizable as likenesses of the complaining individual. Even a cursory inspection of the picture which is the subject of this action strongly suggests that the facial characteristics of the black male portrayed are those of Muhammad Ali. The cheekbones, broad nose and wideset brown eyes, together with the distinctive smile and close cropped black hair are recognizable as the features of the plaintiff, one of the most widely known athletes of our time. In addition, the figure depicted is seated on a stool in the corner of a boxing ring with both hands taped and outstretched resting on the ropes on either side. Although the picture is captioned "Mystery Man," the identification of the individual as Ali is further implied by an accompanying verse which refers to the figure as "the Greatest". This court may take judicial notice that plaintiff Ali has regularly claimed that appellation for himself and that his efforts to identify himself in the public mind as "the Greatest" have been so successful that he is regularly identified as such in the news media....

[The court found violations of New York statutory and common law right of publicity.]

Remaining Issues

Defendant Playgirl, Inc. contends that under New York law any injunction which issues cannot extend to prohibit publication or distribution of the portrait complained of beyond the boundaries of New York State, citing *Rosemont Enterprises, Inc. v. Urban Systems, Inc.*, 42 A.D.2d 544, 345 N.Y.S.2d 17 (1st Dept. 1973). Consequently, Playgirl, Inc. takes the position that, although it is subject to the *in personam* jurisdiction of this court and has announced its intention to distribute the issue of Playgirl Magazine containing the offensive picture throughout England, the court is without authority to restrain that distribution. This court cannot agree.

Although the issue is not entirely free from question, this court agrees that, under the rule of *Erie Railroad Co. v. Tompkins*, it is to be guided by applicable state law in determining the geographical scope of any injunction it issues in aid of state law rights.... The New York case relied on by defendants for the proposition that any injunction issued by this court must not extend beyond New York, *Rosemont*, restricts the extent of §51 injunctive relief in certain circumstances due to a concern for possible conflicts between the law of New York and the applicable law of other jurisdictions. In that regard this court is clearly bound by the law of New York.

However, defendant Playgirl, Inc., misconstrues the rationale of *Rosemont* and its applicability to the facts of the instant action. That case arose from a suit brought under §51 of the Civil Rights Law by Howard Hughes. The lower court held that the defendants' unauthorized marketing and distribution of "The Howard Hughes Game," a board game based on plaintiff Hughes' career, constituted an appropriation of plaintiff's property rights in his name and career in violation of §51. *Rosemont Enterprises, Inc. v. Urban Systems, Inc.*, 72 Misc. 2d 788, 790–91, 340 N.Y.S.2d 144, 146–47 (Sup. Ct. N.Y. Co. 1973). As to equitable relief, the lower court held that with the exception of his co-plaintiff, with whom he had an assignment contract, "(p)laintiff is free to protect himself from the exploitation of his name and likeness *against all the world*," 72 Misc. 2d at 791, 340 N.Y.S.2d at 147 (emphasis added). On appeal the Appellate Division, in a three-sentence *per curiam* decision, affirmed as to liability but modified the unlimited scope of the injunction. The court's holding was that

> "the injunction should be restricted to activities, such as manufacturing, distributing, selling, etc., in the State of New York. In other jurisdictions (*see* Hofstadter and Horowitz, Right of Privacy (1964)), the law with respect to the right of privacy could have other efficacy with respect to a public figure..., both in common law interpretation and in statutes...."

Careful examination of this holding in light of the lower court injunction compels the conclusion that the Appellate Division did not intend to establish a flat prohibition against any §51 injunction extending beyond the limit of New York State.[10] Rather, reviewing an injunction which declared plaintiff's rights under §51 to be equitably protected as "against all the world," the Appellate Division recognized that, as a practical matter, such global restraint would plainly involve intrusions into unknown foreign jurisdictions of such numbers and varieties of substantive law that no conflict-of-law analysis concerning the law of privacy could be undertaken. Consequently, the reviewing court exercised its discretion under the facts before it to note simply that "(i)n other jurisdictions, the law with respect to the right of privacy *could* have other efficacy with respect to a public figure" 42

---

10. A New York court with personal jurisdiction over the parties has the power to enjoin the commission of acts in a foreign jurisdiction. [citations omitted]

A.D.2d at 544, 345 N.Y.S.2d at 18 (emphasis added; citations omitted), and to restrict application of the injunction to New York.

In the present case, by contrast, this court is not faced with factual circumstances involving the necessity of equitable relief running throughout numerous indeterminable jurisdictions. Defendant Playgirl, Inc., has represented its intention to distribute overseas only in England. For purposes of the motion for preliminary relief and compliance with the second branch of the *Sonesta* test, this court concludes that the law of England with respect to plaintiff's right of privacy, at least insofar as it includes his proprietary right of publicity and reputation, is such that under it there exist "sufficiently serious questions going to the merits to make them a fair ground for litigation." *Sonesta International Hotels v. Wellington Associates, supra,* 483 F.2d [247,] 250 [(2d Cir. 1973)]. *See generally, Roberson v. Rochester Folding Box Co.,* 171 N.Y. 538, 64 N.E. 442 (1902) (holding no common law right to protection of injured feelings and discussing and distinguishing English cases granting equitable restraint where use of plaintiff's name would injure his reputation or property); *Pavesich v. New England Life Insurance Co.,* 122 Ga. 190, 50 S.E. 68 (1905) (finding right of privacy "derived from natural law," *id.* at 70, and analyzing English cases); Brittan, *The Right of Privacy in England and the United States,* 37 Tul. L. Rev. 235 (1963). Furthermore, the balance of hardships tips decidedly toward Ali in this matter, for defendant Playgirl, Inc. is merely being restrained from further distribution and is not being affirmatively ordered to undertake new or unduly burdensome obligations. Since all the parties and legal contentions are presently before this court, to require plaintiff to commence a new action in England would subject him to unnecessary and avoidable hardship. Finally, as discussed previously, plaintiff has satisfied this court that there is a strong possibility of irreparable injury absent the issuance of a preliminary injunction. For the foregoing reasons, the preliminary injunction shall extend to restrain defendants' activities with respect to all copies of the magazine containing the disputed portrait in England as well as New York.

CONCLUSION

A hearing on the issue of a permanent injunction shall be scheduled promptly. Among the issues there to be determined is whether or not the privacy or publicity law of England does in fact "have other efficacy with respect to a public figure." *Rosemont Enterprises v. Urban Systems, Inc., supra,* 42 A.D.2d at 544, 345 N.Y.S.2d 18. *See* Rule 44.1, Fed.R.Civ.P....

So Ordered.

Notes and Questions

1. The court here indicates that if it has personal jurisdiction over the defendant, it is empowered to issue an extraterritorial injunction. Is that an appropriate rule, even if Great Britain would *not* permit such an injunction? If the defendant violates the injunction, but only in Britain, would you expect British courts to be willing to enforce the injunction? If not, who would enforce the injunction?

2. On what basis did the court distinguish the *Rosemont* case, which it claims is binding authority? Does the court say that an extraterritorial injunction will issue as a matter of course in cases like this? If not, what factors will guide the court's use of its authority?

3. Now that you have read several cases regarding British rights of publicity, you should be able to evaluate whether Ali would have been able to recover in a British court for this use of his image. Do you think a British court would have been willing to issue the injunction?

4. The remedy sought in this case was a preliminary injunction. That would not accord final relief, although in many cases such preliminary relief effectively ends the litigation. What do you expect would happen next? Suppose that Ali went to trial and sought monetary damages. Should the New York court award damages based on activities in both the U.S. and Britain? In the copyright sphere, the Ninth Circuit has held that damage awards under U.S. law cannot reflect acts of infringement that take place entirely abroad. *See Subafilms, Ltd. v. MGM-Pathe Communications Co.*, 24 F.3d 1088 (9th Cir. 1994); *see also Los Angeles News Service v. Reuters Television International, Ltd.*, 340 F.3d 926 (9th Cir. 1998) (where a complete act of infringement takes place in the U.S., plaintiff may recover defendant's profits, but not actual damages, resulting from further exploitation of the infringing material in other countries).

5. The issue of extraterritorial enforcement actually has two dimensions: national and international. Because rights of publicity are primarily creatures of state law, one may reasonably ask whether it is appropriate for the courts of State A to apply State A law to activities occurring in State B, particularly when injunctive relief is requested. Under some circumstances, it may not matter. If State B law is essentially the same as State A law, then it should not be a problem. However, if State B law is not the same as State A law (for example, if the plaintiff is the heir of the celebrity and State B either does not permit post-mortem rights of publicity, or its term has expired), then there is a problem. Obviously, there is a conflicts of law dimension to this problem as well. (See Chapter XII.) Does this court indicate how it would deal with that situation? This issue is explored further below.

6. In *Chang v. Virgin Mobile USA, LLC*, 2009 WL 111570 (N.D. Tex. 2009) (reprinted in Chapter XII), the court dismissed a right of publicity claim brought against Virgin Australia, the Australian subsidiary of Virgin Mobile, because the court lacked personal jurisdiction over the defendant. (Claims against the other defendants were dismissed for other reasons.) The claim arose when Virgin Australia used pictures of the plaintiff that had been posted on Flickr (on the Internet) as part of an advertising campaign in Australia. But suppose the court *had* asserted personal jurisdiction over Virgin Australia. Assuming that plaintiff's rights under Texas law had been violated, should the court issue an injunction against the Australian advertising campaign? Alternatively, if the court chose to apply Australian law, should it issue the injunction?

7. *Extraterritoriality and the Lanham Act.* In Chapter V, we discussed the use of the Lanham Act—the federal trademark statute—to protect rights of publicity. In some cases, celebrities may bring claims of false endorsement; in other cases, they may assert that their names and/or likenesses have become actual trademarks. In any event, the issue here is whether an American court can issue an injunction (and/or award damages) based on a violation of the Lanham Act that occurs outside the country. Unlike the situation in copyright and patent (*see, e.g.*, Note 4, above), courts have permitted the Lanham Act to extend to acts occurring outside the U.S. The authority for this traces to a Supreme Court opinion over a half century ago: *Steele v. Bulova Watch Co.*, 344 U.S. 280, 285–86 (1952), in which the Court upheld use of the Lanham Act against a U.S. citizen whose sales of infringing goods took place in Mexico, but where some of the parts apparently came from the U.S. More recently, the Fifth Circuit upheld the use of the Lanham Act in a case where defendant's infringing sales took place entirely in Saudi Arabia, but where packaging and

other preliminary activities occurred in the United States. *American Rice, Inc. v. Producers Rice Mill, Inc.*, 518 F.3d 321 (5th Cir. 2008). The court cited three elements to test the validity of extraterritorial jurisdiction: the citizenship of the defendant (in this case, a U.S. citizen), the effect on United States commerce, and possible affront to the foreign nation. 518 F.3d at 327.

In a case more relevant to the celebrity rights issue, a jazz musician sued a Japanese company "that adopted the name 'Cecil McBee' [plaintiff's name] for its adolescent female clothing line." *McBee v. Delica Co., Ltd.*, 417 F.3d 107, 111 (1st Cir. 2005). Although *McBee*, like *American Rice*, asserts that Congress has broad power to reach the conduct of American citizens acting abroad, in this case the activities were those of a foreign citizen. In such cases, the *McBee* court stated as follows:

> We hold that the Lanham Act grants subject matter jurisdiction over extraterritorial conduct by foreign defendants only where the conduct has a substantial effect on United States commerce.

417 F.3d at 120. Finding no "substantial effect on United States commerce," the court denied relief in this case. Significantly, however, the court "disaggregated" the elements cited in *American Rice* (which are found in an early Second Circuit opinion, *Vanity Fair Mills v. T. Eaton Co.*, 234 F.2d 633, 642 (2d Cir.1956)) and was, in theory, willing to find extraterritorial jurisdiction even where the defendant was not an American citizen. An equally significant corollary of the disaggregation is that, where the defendant *is* an American citizen, one may not need to show as significant an effect on U.S. commerce in order to assert authority under the Lanham Act. *McBee*, 417 F.3d at 118.

Cases like *McBee* and *American Rice* demonstrate that the Lanham Act may be a significant tool for celebrities, even where the offending activity takes place in another country. This is particularly true where the defendant is an American citizen, a situation cited by both courts as one in which the extraterritorial power of the Lanham Act was strongest. Do these cases suggest a possible basis for recovery in the *Chang* hypothetical in Note 6 above? Of course, the issue of personal jurisdiction, which was so prominent in the actual *Chang* case, will be a significant deterrent in many cases. *See Pebble Beach Co. v. Caddy*, 453 F.3d 1151, 1153 (9th Cir. 2006) (no personal jurisdiction in Lanham Act case against U.K. bed and breakfast owner calling its establishment "Pebble Beach").

---

2. Injunctions Crossing State Lines

Carson v. Here's Johnny Portable Toilets, Inc.
810 F.2d 104 (6th Cir. 1987) (*per curiam*)

[This was a follow-up to the case excerpted in Chapter II. In this opinion, the court focused on the propriety of the relief granted to Carson, in particular the breadth of the injunction:]

In an earlier published opinion, *Carson v. Here's Johnny Portable Toilets, Inc.*, 698 F.2d 831 (6th Cir. 1983), this court held that under Michigan law Johnny Carson, one of the plaintiffs herein, has a "right of publicity" in the phrase "Here's Johnny." This case was remanded to the district court, for a determination of appropriate relief.... Upon remand the district court enjoined the defendant from using the phrase anywhere in the country and awarded $31,661.96 in damages.... On appeal the defendant challenges the damage award and asks that we limit the geographical scope of the injunction to the State of Michigan.

One cannot be sure how most jurisdictions other than Michigan would have ruled on the merits of this case. Many states have never considered whether a right of publicity exists, and even fewer have considered whether that right protects not only an entertainer's name or picture but also a phrase or nickname or other symbol associated with the entertainer. . . .

Because there are indications that other states would hold as we have predicted Michigan would, and because the defendant is uncertain, at this point, whether it wants to use the phrase "Here's Johnny" in any state where the substantive law arguably differs from Michigan's, we see no harm in letting the injunction stand in its present form for the time being, at least. If the defendant should hereafter decide that it wants to use the phrase in a state (other than Michigan) where it believes such use would be legal but for the injunction, it will be free to seek a modification of the injunction from the district court at that time. As we see the equities, in the light of the parties' conduct to date and the probable trend of the law nationally, it would be fairer to require the defendant to take the litigation initiative in such a situation than to require the plaintiffs to do so. . . .

The judgment of the district court is affirmed, without prejudice to the defendant's right to seek future modification of the injunction in the event of changed conditions that might make modification appropriate.

Herman Miller, Inc. v. Palazzetti Imports & Exports, Inc.
270 F.3d 298 (6th Cir. 2001)

[Like the *Carson* case, this case also involved a nationwide injunction against a violation of the right of publicity. However, in this case, the Sixth Circuit stated that:] The district court abused its discretion. Courts should exercise caution in extending the right of publicity to states that do not recognize that right [citing the RESTATEMENT (THIRD) OF UNFAIR COMPETITION, §48, cmt. c. (1995)]. . . .

The facts of *Here's Johnny II* are distinguishable from the facts of this case. In *Here's Johnny II*, the defendant challenged the imposition of a nationwide injunction, arguing that it be limited to the state of Michigan. The court specifically noted the fact that "the defendant is uncertain, at this point, whether it wants to use the phrase 'Here's Johnny' in any state where the substantive law arguably differs from Michigan's." . . .

Unlike in *Here's Johnny II*, Palazzetti is *already* operating in a state that does not recognize a post-mortem right of publicity. Moreover, its principal place of business is in that state. It would be unjust to impose Michigan law on Palazzetti's operations in New York and other states that have explicitly refused to recognize a post-mortem right of publicity. Therefore, we hold that the portion of the district court's injunction relating to Herman Miller's right of publicity claims shall be modified to exclude those states that explicitly do not recognize a post-mortem right of publicity.[16]

---

16. The injunction shall continue to apply in all states that explicitly recognize a post-mortem right of publicity as well as those states that have not addressed the issue. Palazzetti has not requested that the latter states be excluded from the injunction. If a state subsequently makes an explicit pronouncement refusing to recognize a post-mortem right of publicity, Palazzetti is permitted to request a modification of the injunction upon a showing that its conduct is lawful under the law of that state.

Notes and Questions

1. As a result of *Carson II*, the defendant would have to make a motion to modify the injunction if it wants to use the "Here's Johnny" trademark outside of Michigan. Is the court's decision reasonable (especially considering the equitable nature of the relief)? Is the court's decision consistent with the *Ali* decision? Does the distinction drawn in the *Herman Miller* case between that case and *Carson* make sense? Is the situation in *Carson* really different from that in *Herman Miller*?

2. Should courts treat an injunction that acts extraterritorially but *within* the United States differently than an injunction that reaches beyond the United States? Why or why not?

3. On the issue of extraterritorial injunctions, *see generally* David S. Welkowitz, *Preemption, Extraterritoriality, and the Problem of State Antidilution Laws,* 67 Tul. L. Rev. 1 (1992) (discussing the constitutionality of using state dilution laws to enjoin activity in states without such laws).

---

3. Enforcing Foreign Judgments in the United States

The flip side of applying one state's or one country's law extraterritorially is enforcing a judgment from one jurisdiction in another jurisdiction. Within the United States, judgments from one state court are made enforceable in another state by the Full Faith and Credit Clause of the Constitution. *See* U.S. Const. Art. IV, § 1. However, foreign judgments are subject to a different set of considerations. One mechanism for enforcement is the Uniform Foreign Money Judgment Recognition Act. As its name implies, it only applies to judgments for monetary damages, not injunctions.

In *Sarl Louis Feraud Int'l v. Viewfinder, Inc.,* 489 F.3d 474 (2d Cir. 2007), the Second Circuit analyzed the Uniform Act in a case in which a French court had granted relief against the defendant's posting of photographs of a fashion show where the plaintiff's fashion designs were displayed. Defendant claimed a First Amendment right that would trump the enforcement of the French judgment. (Although fashion designs are protected in France under French copyright and design laws, fashion designs are not protectable under U.S. law.) The New York statute in question contained the following exception to enforcement: "A foreign country judgment need not be recognized if ... the cause of action on which the judgment is based is repugnant to the public policy of this state." N.Y. C.P.L.R. § 5304(b)(4). The Second Circuit agreed that "Laws that are antithetical to the First Amendment will create such a situation. Foreign judgments that impinge on First Amendment rights will be found to be 'repugnant' to public policy." However, it went on to say:

> Intellectual property laws co-exist with the First Amendment in this country, and the fact that an entity is a news publication engaging in speech activity does not, standing alone, relieve such entities of their obligation to obey intellectual property laws. While an entity's status as a news publication may be highly probative on certain relevant inquiries, such as whether that entity has a fair use defense to copyright infringement, it does not render that entity immune from liability under intellectual property laws....

Rather, because Section 5304(b) requires courts to examine the cause of action on which the foreign judgment was based, the district court should have analyzed whether the intellectual property regime upon which the French Judgments were based impinged on rights protected by the First Amendment....

Because the fair use doctrine balances the competing interests of the copyright laws and the First Amendment, some analysis of that doctrine is generally needed before a court can conclude that a foreign copyright judgment is repugnant to public policy.

489 F.3d at 480, 481, 482. The Second Circuit remanded the case to the District Court with the following admonition:

If the publication of photographs of copyrighted material in the same manner as Viewfinder has done in this case would not be fair use under United States law, then the French intellectual property regime sanctioning the same conduct certainly would not be repugnant to public policy. Similarly, if the sole reason that [defendant] Viewfinder's conduct would be permitted under United States copyright law is that plaintiffs' dress designs are not copyrightable in the United States, the French Judgment would not appear to be repugnant. However, without further development of the record, we cannot reach any conclusions as to whether Viewfinder's conduct would fall within the protection of the fair use doctrine.

Id. at 483. The court also instructed the District Court to determine whether French law provided comparable protection (defendant had defaulted in the French action and thus forfeited its right to defend on such a basis in the French courts). On remand, plaintiff moved for summary judgment, claiming that defendant's use was not fair use under U.S. law and, therefore, it did not matter whether French law provided comparable protection. However, the District Court denied the motion, holding that there were issues of fact to be decided. 2008 WL 5272770 (S.D.N.Y. 2008).

As we have seen, free speech protections in Europe are not as robust as they are in the United States. In the area of defamation, for example, Britain's libel laws are notoriously more plaintiff-friendly than those in the U.S. This fact has led some plaintiffs in defamation cases to sue for libel in Britain and then to try to enforce the resulting judgment in the U.S., a practice some commentators have labeled "libel tourism." *See, e.g.,* Adam Cohen, *'Libel Tourism': When Freedom of Speech Takes a Holiday,* New York Times, September 14, 2008. In New York, a bill to prevent enforcement of such judgments was enacted in 2008. *See* N.Y. Civ. Prac. L. § 5304(b)(8). A similar bill (H.R. 2765) was passed by the U.S. House of Representatives in June 2009, and is currently pending in the Senate. The bill would allow defendants who successfully resist enforcement of such judgments to recover their attorneys' fees.

C. Foreign Courts

Although the following case does not deal with rights of publicity, it does deal with an intellectual property problem (cybersquatting), and the difficulty of enforcing an injunction against such activity when the defendant is outside of the country.

Australian Competition and Consumer Commission v. Chen

2003 FCA 897, 201 A.L.R. 40 (Fed. Ct. Australia 2003)

SACKVILLE J.:

The proceedings

1. The applicant (the ACCC) seeks declaratory and injunctive relief against the respondent in respect of conduct that is said to be misleading and deceptive, in contravention of § 52 and other provisions of the Trade Practices Act 1974 (Cth) (the TP Act). The proceedings, which were commenced on 3 October 2002, have been undefended.

2. The ACCC complains that the respondent, who is a resident of the United States, has engaged in misleading and deceptive conduct over the Internet, to the detriment of Australian consumers. One question in the proceedings is whether the court should grant an injunction to restrain the respondent's conduct, having regard to the conceded fact that there is no mechanism available for the registration or enforcement of any such injunction in the courts of the United States, federal or state....

[The Australian Competition and Consumer Commisssion, or ACCC, charged that defendant had registered several domain names that were confusingly similar to the official domain names used by the Sydney Opera House.]

5. The ACCC, despite extensive investigations, has never succeeded in serving the respondent personally with any documents or, indeed, definitively ascertaining his whereabouts at any particular time. However, the evidence indicates that he is a resident of the United States....

6. It also appears from recent inquiries undertaken by the ACCC that, although the [defendant's registered] sites continue to exist and to be accessible from Australia, they no longer contain any information or make any representations relating to the trust or to events at the Sydney Opera House.... The likelihood is that the change came about, partly at least, because the ACCC vigorously pursued the matter with United States service providers that host the sites and also with its regulatory counterpart in that country, the Federal Trade Commission (the FTC).... The [defendant's] registration of the domain name "sydneyopera.org", appears to have expired on 17 January 2003. A new registration record was created on 25 February 2003, with a new registrar and registrant. The evidence suggests that the new registrant is not connected to the respondent, although the possibility of a connection cannot be ruled out.

7. The ACCC seeks declarations that the respondent, in connection with the imitation site [and other sites]:

- engaged in conduct that was misleading or deceptive or was likely to mislead or deceive, in contravention of § 52 of the TP Act;

- made false or misleading representations in contravention of § 53(c) and (d) of the TP Act; and

- engaged in conduct that was liable to mislead the public in relation to services in contravention of § 55A of the TP Act.

8. The ACCC also seeks injunctions pursuant to § 80 of the TP Act:

- requiring the respondent to take all steps to remove and prevent access to the sites by persons or computers within Australia (whether or not that requires the entire removal of the sites);

• restraining the respondent from publishing, operating or maintaining the sites or any similar Internet website in circumstances where the sites are accessible by persons or computers within Australia; and

• restraining the respondent from publishing, operating or maintaining the sites or any similar Internet website so as to engage in misleading or deceptive conduct in contravention of the TP Act....

10. On 8 October 2002, Conti J made an order pursuant to Federal Court Rules ... that the ACCC be granted leave to serve the originating process outside the Commonwealth on terms and conditions that the ACCC employ private agents in the United States to effect personal service.... His Honour made orders requiring the respondent to take all steps to remove the sites from the World Wide Web so that they cease to be and until further order remain inaccessible to persons or computers within Australia. His Honour also restrained the respondent, until further order, from publishing, operating or maintaining the sites in circumstances where they are accessible to persons or computers within Australia.

11. The ACCC was unable to serve the originating process on the respondent personally.

12. On 8 November 2002, on the application of the ACCC, I made an order pursuant to the Rules ... for substituted service of the initiating process on the respondent. I did so on the basis that the ACCC had shown that it was "impracticable to serve [the process] in the manner set out in the Rules". The orders required a variety of steps to be taken, both in relation to hard copies and electronic versions of the originating process, in order to bring the proceedings to the respondent's attention. The ACCC duly complied with those orders.

13. As I have noted, the respondent has played no part in the proceedings. Nonetheless, I am prepared to infer from the evidence relating to the respondent's involvement in the sites and the many steps taken, particularly by electronic means, to bring the proceedings to his attention that he has been made aware of these proceedings and of the relief sought against him in this court.

The legislation

14. Section 52(1) of the TP Act provides that a corporation shall not, in trade or commerce, engage in conduct that is misleading or deceptive or is likely to mislead or deceive....

Findings

30. I am satisfied, on the balance of probabilities, that the respondent, by operating and maintaining the sites, made the [mis]representations alleged by the ACCC.

31. I accept the ACCC's submission that representations (h) and (i) [that the website would furnish tickets to events at the Sydney Opera House] were representations as to future matters within §51A of the TP Act and that the respondent had no reasonable grounds for making those representations. I also accept the ACCC's submission that, having regard to the evidence to which I have referred, the other representations were misleading and deceptive, in so far as they were made to members of the public in Australia.

32.... Accordingly, in my view, the ACCC has established that the respondent contravened §§52, 53(c) and 55A of the TP Act by reason of his activities in relation to the sites....

Relief

The ACCC's submissions

33. Mr McClintock acknowledged that the respondent is resident in the United States and that he has no known connection with Australia, other than through the sites. Mr Mc-

Clintock also acknowledged that there is no mechanism for the registration or enforcement in the United States of an injunction granted against a United States resident by an Australian court under the TP Act. He accepted that the strong likelihood is that no injunction could be enforced against the respondent through the United States courts if he chose simply to ignore the orders. Mr McClintock also accepted that this court should take into account, in determining what relief is appropriate, the fact that the sites have ceased to refer to the Sydney Opera House and no longer purport to offer a facility for purchasing tickets to events at the Opera House.

34. Nonetheless, Mr McClintock submitted that in the circumstances of the case it is appropriate to grant both declaratory and injunctive relief. He pointed to evidence showing the prevalence of cross-border consumer fraud or deception and the need to protect the public from exploitation. He contended that there is a utility in making declarations or orders which mark the court's disapproval of the conduct and vindicate the public interest in taking all available measures to curtail misleading or deceptive conduct. He also relied on evidence suggesting that regulatory authorities in the United States, particularly the FTC, are more likely to cooperate in protecting Australian consumers from cross-border fraud if an Australian court has made formal orders restraining the offending conduct or requiring remedial action.

The principles

…

Injunctive relief

… 40. Mr McClintock submitted that the court has power under § 80 of the TP Act to grant an injunction requiring a person to do or refrain from doing something outside Australia. He supported that contention by reference to the well-established proposition that, apart from a few exceptional cases such as those relating to title to foreign land:

> "… a court of equity will not consider itself to be debarred from interceding, if it is otherwise appropriate to do so, merely because it appears that the property to which the claims of the plaintiff relate is situate abroad or that the acts he seeks to have performed or enjoined, as the case may be, will, if they take place at all, take place outside the jurisdiction."

As was said by Brooking J in *National Australia Bank Ltd. v. Dessau* [1988] VR 521 at 522:

> "… the jurisdiction is grounded not on any pretension to the exercise of judicial power abroad but on the circumstance that the defendant, being amenable to the court's jurisdiction, can be personally directed to act or not to act."

41. The issue, however, is not the scope of the jurisdiction of a court of equity acting in personam, but the extent of the power conferred on the court by § 80 of the TP Act. The language of § 80(1) is broad: once the court is satisfied that one of the preconditions has been met, it "may grant an injunction in such terms as the court determines to be appropriate". There is nothing in this language that imposes an implied territorial limitation on the power of the court. On the contrary, not only is the language of § 80(1) broad enough to permit the court to prohibit or mandate acts abroad, but there is good reason to interpret it in this way.

42. Section 6(2) of the TP Act extends the application of Pt V (and other provisions) to conduct in trade or commerce between Australia and places outside Australia. In enacting this provision, parliament has relied on the trade and commerce power conferred by § 51(i) of the Constitution. The extended application of the TP Act has the effect that a person outside Australia (but subject to the jurisdiction of the court …) might well con-

travene provisions of the Act and thereby enliven the power conferred on the court by §80(1). In these circumstances, in my opinion, §80 should be read as contemplating that an injunction may be granted prohibiting or requiring the performance of acts outside Australia. I should add that the court may have a similar power pursuant to §23 of the Federal Court of Australia Act 1976 (Cth), but it is not necessary to pursue that possibility in the present case.

43. Of course, the fact that the respondent is outside Australia and, for that reason, any order might be difficult or impossible to enforce, may be a relevant consideration in determining whether a court should grant injunctive relief. In this respect, courts of equity have expressed divergent views. Some courts have taken the robust approach that:

> ... [i]t is not the habit of this Court in considering whether or not it will make an order to contemplate the possibility that it will not be obeyed. [*Re Liddell's Settlement Trusts* [1936] Ch 365 at 374; [1936] 1 All ER 239 per Romer LJ, cited with approval by Lord Scarman (with whom Lords Wilberforce, Diplock, Keith and Bridge agreed) in *Castanho v. Brown & Root (UK) Ltd.* [1981] AC 557 at 574; [1981] 1 All ER 143 at 150]

Other authorities suggest that a court should not put itself in the position of making an order that it cannot enforce.

44. I think that Dr Spry is correct to suggest that the preferable position, as a matter of principle, is that:

> "... the precise probability that the particular order in question will be obeyed has more or less weight according to the other circumstances and is taken by the court into account in exercising its discretion, together with such other matters as the degree of injury or inconvenience that will be suffered by the plaintiff if he does not obtain relief."

45. It seems to me that this approach is also appropriate in determining whether or not to grant an injunction pursuant to §80 of the TP Act. The fact that an order is likely to prove difficult or even impossible to enforce is not necessarily a bar to the grant of relief, although it is a material consideration to be weighed against other circumstances relevant to the exercise of the court's discretion....

Should an injunction be granted?

49. The question of injunctive relief is more difficult. I have explained the obstacles in the path of enforcing in the United States any injunction granted by the court. In general, a court will be loath to make orders affecting conduct outside Australia in circumstances where direct enforcement of those orders is difficult or impossible. It is also true that the offending conduct has ceased and that the respondent no longer appears to be associated with the domain name "sydneyopera.org". These are powerful considerations militating against the grant of an injunction.

50. I have, however, formed the view that, in the special circumstances of the present case, it is appropriate to grant an injunction, although I think any injunction should be framed more narrowly than the ACCC proposes. There are three factors which suggest to me that an injunction should be granted notwithstanding cogent considerations pointing to a different conclusion.

51. First, for the reasons I have given, this is not a case where it can be definitively concluded that the respondent does not intend to resume misleading and deceptive conduct aimed (among others) at Australian consumers. There is a risk that the respondent

may resume the misleading and deceptive conduct that has characterised his operations in the past, although I cannot say that it is probable that he will.

52. Secondly, the ACCC adduced evidence showing that cross-border fraud and misleading conduct, particularly through the Internet, is a growing problem for the international community. The problem has prompted consumer protection and law enforcement agencies from many countries, as well as international agencies, to establish mechanisms for international cooperation to protect consumers. For example:

- On 11 June 2003, the Council of the Organisation for Economic Cooperation and Development (OECD) adopted Guidelines for Protecting Consumers from Fraudulent and Deceptive Commercial Practices Across Borders that had been developed by the OECD's Committee on Consumer Policy.

- The ACCC, the FTC and agencies from 30 other countries are parties to the Memorandum on the Establishment and Operation of the International Consumer Protection and Enforcement Network (the ICPEN memorandum). The main "common objective" of ICPEN is "to encourage practical action to prevent cross-border marketing Malpractice" and its long-term goals include taking action to combat cross-border breaches of consumer protection laws and to facilitate effective cross-border remedies.

- In July 2000, the ACCC and the FTC entered into an Agreement on the Mutual Enforcement Assistance in Consumer Protection (the cooperation agreement). The cooperation agreement recognises "the challenge posed by cross-border Internet fraud and deception" and records that:

"... the Parties intend to assist one another and to cooperate on a reciprocal basis in providing or obtaining Evidence that could assist in determining whether a person has violated or is about to violate their respective Consumer Protection Laws, or in facilitating the administration or enforcement of such Consumer Protection Laws.

The assistance contemplated by the cooperative agreement includes, in appropriate cases, "co-ordinating enforcement against transborder violations of the Parties' respective Consumer Protection Laws".

53. This evidence suggests that the court should take into account, in determining what relief should be granted in respect of cross-border misleading conduct, the growing scale of the problem, particularly over the Internet, and the desirability of fashioning remedies that can reasonably be expected to discourage, if not entirely prevent such activities.

54. Thirdly, evidence was given by Mr Sitesh Bhojani, a member of the ACCC and Chair of its Enforcement Committee, that the ACCC would bring any orders made in these proceedings to the attention of the FTC and request its assistance in relation thereto pursuant to the cooperation agreement and in accordance with the ICPEN memorandum. As I pointed out in argument, Mr Bhojani's affidavit might have been more specific in detailing the assistance that would be sought from the FTC and the terms on which it is likely to be provided. Nonetheless, I am prepared to infer that the FTC is more likely to institute action against the respondent to curtail misleading or deceptive conduct in the United States which affects Australian consumers (should such conduct be repeated) if an Australian court grants injunctive relief than if it does not.

55. The extraterritorial enforcement of federal orders is ordinarily a matter for the domestic law of the country in which the orders are sought to be enforced. At common law,

four conditions must be satisfied if a foreign judgment is to be recognised by an Australian court (P E Nygh and M Davies, *Conflict of Laws in Australia*, 7th ed, 2002, p 169):

> "(a) the foreign court must have exercised a jurisdiction which Australian courts will recognise; (b) the foreign judgment must be final and conclusive; (c) there must be an identity of parties; and (d) if based on a judgment in personam, the judgment must be for a fixed debt." ...

56. The Foreign Judgments Act 1991 (Cth) now provides a mechanism for the registration and enforcement of overseas judgments, on the basis of "substantial reciprocity of treatment": § 5(1). The legislation follows the patterns of the Foreign Judgments (Reciprocal Enforcement) Act 1933 (UK) and similar state and territory legislation. To date the legislative scheme applies only to an "enforceable money judgment", although there is provision for the scheme to be extended by regulation to non-money judgments of a reciprocating country: § 5(6).

57. If the Australian rules governing the enforcement of foreign judgments are similar to those in force in other countries, there will rarely be a direct mechanism available for the extraterritorial enforcement of an injunction granted by an Australian court. This might suggest that an order requiring or prohibiting conduct in a foreign country can be seen as an act of futility. But the emergence of international cooperation to curb fraudulent or misleading transnational conduct gives rise to alternative possibilities. In assessing whether the grant of injunction is futile, it seems to me to be appropriate to take into account not only formal enforcement mechanisms, but the likely response of administrative agencies in the foreign country. If, for example, an agency such as the FTC in the United States is likely to initiate measures designed to curb misleading and deceptive conduct affecting Australian consumers because that conduct is the subject of a prohibitory injunction issued by an Australian court, I would not characterise the grant of such relief as an act of futility, notwithstanding that the injunction itself cannot be directly enforced through the courts of the United States.

58. In the present case, an injunction granted by this court restraining the respondent from resuming his misleading and deceptive conduct is likely to improve materially the chances of the ACCC obtaining the support of the FTC to take measures under the law of the United States to curb that conduct (should it recur). As I have said, I do not think it likely that the respondent will resume his activities to the detriment of Australian consumers, but there is a risk that he may do so. If he does, Australian consumers are likely to be adversely affected. In these circumstances, in my opinion, the making of an appropriately framed injunction against the respondent cannot be characterised as futile.

59. For the reasons I have given, an injunction should be granted against the respondent, but in more limited terms than the relief sought by the ACCC. The application seeks orders, in effect, requiring the respondent to prevent access to the sites by persons or computers within Australia, even if that requires removal of the sites. But there is no evidence that the material on the sites, other than that material relating to the Sydney Opera House, was or is misleading or deceptive. Nor does the evidence allow me to infer that the FTC would be prepared to take action to close down the sites, as distinct from responding favourably to a request to take measures under United States law to prevent the respondent publishing misleading or deceptive material relating to the Sydney Opera House.

60. Accordingly, I think that any injunction should be limited to restraining the respondent (by himself, his servants or agents) from publishing on the sites, or any similar Internet site accessible in Australia, information or material relating to the Sydney Opera House, or events at the Sydney Opera House, that is misleading or deceptive or is

likely to mislead or deceive consumers in Australia. I shall direct the ACCC to bring in short minutes of order to that effect.

61. I add this comment. While domestic courts can, to a limited extent, adapt their procedures and remedies to meet the challenges posed by cross-border transactions in the Internet age, an effective response requires international cooperation of a high order. As the evidence in this case shows, some steps have been taken to secure that cooperation. Clearly enough, much more needs to be done if Australian consumers are to be adequately protected against fraud or misleading conduct perpetrated over the Internet.

Conclusion

62. The ACCC has made out its claim to declaratory and injunctive relief by reason of the respondent's contraventions of the TP Act, although the form of the injunction I propose to grant is narrower than that sought by the ACCC. I shall direct the ACCC to bring in short minutes of order consistent with these reasons.

Notes and Questions

1. The Australian court admits that it is unlikely that its order will be enforceable. Why, then, does it bother to issue an injunction?

2. This lawsuit was brought by a government entity. Do you think that had any effect on the court's willingness to issue an injunction? Suppose this had been a purely private lawsuit to restrain the use of a confusingly similar domain name, or a lawsuit relating to keyword advertising that could be viewed in Australia (where the advertising could be accessed by Australian consumers via the Internet), but which was otherwise essentially the same — *i.e.*, the injunction would be unenforceable. Would that have made this a different case?

3. Do you think a U.S. court would issue an injunction under the circumstances of this case?

4. Can you envision countries cooperating to allow cross-border relief in right of publicity cases? What obstacles do you foresee to such cooperation?

Recognition and Enforcement of Judgments in the European Union

As noted in Chapter XII, the European Union has adopted a regulation on Jurisdiction and Enforcement of Judgments in Civil and Commercial Matters. *See* Council Regulation 44/2001/EC of 22 December 2000 (the successor to the Brussels Convention of 1968). That regulation provides in Article 33 that "A judgment given in a Member State shall be recognised in the other Member States without any special procedure being required." Article 34 provides for several exceptions: if "such recognition is manifestly contrary to public policy in the Member State in which recognition is sought"; if the defendant defaulted and was not properly served, "unless the defendant failed to commence proceedings to challenge the judgment when it was possible for him to do so"; and when the judgment is irreconcilable with a previous judgment between the parties. Article 35 provides that a judgment shall not be recognised if it conflicts with the rules on jurisdiction set forth in the regulation.

Article 38 of the regulation provides that "A judgment given in a Member State and enforceable in that State shall be enforced in another Member State when, on the application of any interested party, it has been declared enforceable there." In addition, Article 41 provides that "the judgment shall be declared enforceable immediately on completion of the formalities in Article 53, without any review under Articles 34 and 35," and without giving the defendant any opportunity to be heard. Only on appeal from a declaration of enforceability may a party raise the exceptions provided for in Articles 34 and 35. Moreover, under Article 45, "[u]nder no circumstances may the foreign judgment be reviewed as to its substance."

The regulation, of course, applies only to judgments issued by the 27 member states of the European Union. When it comes to judgments from other countries, such as the United States, enforcement is governed by national law in the country in which enforcement is sought.

Appendix

New York Civil Rights Law § 50

A person, firm or corporation that uses for advertising purposes, or for the purposes of trade, the name, portrait or picture of any living person without having first obtained the written consent of such person, or if a minor of his or her parent or guardian, is guilty of a misdemeanor.

New York Civil Rights Law § 51

Any person whose name, portrait, picture or voice is used within this state for advertising purposes or for the purposes of trade without the written consent first obtained as above provided may maintain an equitable action in the supreme court of this state against the person, firm or corporation so using his name, portrait, picture or voice, to prevent and restrain the use thereof; and may also sue and recover damages for any injuries sustained by reason of such use and if the defendant shall have knowingly used such person's name, portrait, picture or voice in such manner as is forbidden or declared to be unlawful by section fifty of this article, the jury, in its discretion, may award exemplary damages. But nothing contained in this article shall be so construed as to prevent any person, firm or corporation from selling or otherwise transferring any material containing such name, portrait, picture or voice in whatever medium to any user of such name, portrait, picture or voice, or to any third party for sale or transfer directly or indirectly to such a user, for use in a manner lawful under this article; nothing contained in this article shall be so construed as to prevent any person, firm or corporation, practicing the profession of photography, from exhibiting in or about his or its establishment specimens of the work of such establishment, unless the same is continued by such person, firm or corporation after written notice objecting thereto has been given by the person portrayed; and nothing contained in this article shall be so construed as to prevent any person, firm or corporation from using the name, portrait, picture or voice of any manufacturer or dealer in connection with the goods, wares and merchandise manufactured, produced or dealt in by him which he has sold or disposed of with such name, portrait, picture or voice used in connection therewith; or from using the name, portrait, picture or voice of any author, composer or artist in connection with his literary, musical or artistic productions which he has sold or disposed of with such name, portrait, picture or voice used in connection therewith. Nothing contained in this section shall be construed to prohibit the copyright owner of a sound recording from disposing of, dealing in, licensing or selling that sound recording to any party, if the right to dispose of, deal in, license or sell such sound recording has been conferred by contract or other written document by such living person or the holder of such right. Nothing contained in the foregoing sentence shall be deemed to abrogate or otherwise limit any rights or remedies otherwise conferred by federal law or state law.

[Derived from L. 1903, ch. 132, §§ 1–2. Codified in L. 1909, ch. 14; amended L. 1911, ch. 226; L. 1921, ch. 501; L. 1979, ch. 656, § 2; L. 1983, ch. 280, § 1; L. 1995, ch. 674, § 1.]

California Civil Code § 3344

(a) Any person who knowingly uses another's name, voice, signature, photograph, or likeness, in any manner, on or in products, merchandise, or goods, or for purposes of advertising or selling, or soliciting purchases of, products, merchandise, goods or services, without such person's prior consent, or, in the case of a minor, the prior consent of his parent or legal guardian, shall be liable for any damages sustained by the person or persons injured as a result thereof. In addition, in any action brought under this section, the person who violated the section shall be liable to the injured party or parties in an amount equal to the greater of seven hundred fifty dollars ($750) or the actual damages suffered by him or her as a result of the unauthorized use, and any profits from the unauthorized use that are attributable to the use and are not taken into account in computing the actual damages. In establishing such profits, the injured party or parties are required to present proof only of the gross revenue attributable to such use, and the person who violated this section is required to prove his or her deductible expenses. Punitive damages may also be awarded to the injured party or parties. The prevailing party in any action under this section shall also be entitled to attorney's fees and costs.

(b) As used in this section, "photograph" means any photograph or photographic reproduction, still or moving, or any videotape or live television transmission, of any person, such that the person is readily identifiable.

(1) A person shall be deemed to be readily identifiable from a photograph when one who views the photograph with the naked eye can reasonably determine that the person depicted in the photograph is the same person who is complaining of its unauthorized use.

(2) If the photograph includes more than one person so identifiable, then the person or persons complaining of the use shall be represented as individuals rather than solely as members of a definable group represented in the photograph. A definable group includes, but is not limited to, the following examples: a crowd at any sporting event, a crowd in any street or public building, the audience at any theatrical or stage production, a glee club, or a baseball team.

(3) A person or persons shall be considered to be represented as members of a definable group if they are represented in the photograph solely as a result of being present at the time the photograph was taken and have not been singled out as individuals in any manner.

(c) Where a photograph or likeness of an employee of the person using the photograph or likeness appearing in the advertisement or other publication prepared by or in behalf of the user is only incidental, and not essential, to the purpose of the publication in which it appears, there shall arise a rebuttable presumption affecting the burden of producing evidence that the failure to obtain the consent of the employee was not a knowing use of the employee's photograph or likeness.

(d) For purposes of this section, a use of a name, voice, signature, photograph, or likeness in connection with any news, public affairs, or sports broadcast or account, or any political campaign, shall not constitute a use for which consent is required under subdivision (a).

(e) The use of a name, voice, signature, photograph, or likeness in a commercial medium shall not constitute a use for which consent is required under subdivision (a) solely because the material containing such use is commercially sponsored or contains paid advertising. Rather it shall be a question of fact whether or not the use of the person's name, voice, signature, photograph, or likeness was so directly connected with the commercial sponsorship or with the paid advertising as to constitute a use for which consent is required under subdivision (a).

(f) Nothing in this section shall apply to the owners or employees of any medium used for advertising, including, but not limited to, newspapers, magazines, radio and television networks and stations, cable television systems, billboards, and transit ads, by whom any advertisement or solicitation in violation of this section is published or disseminated, unless it is established that such owners or employees had knowledge of the unauthorized use of the person's name, voice, signature, photograph, or likeness as prohibited by this section.

(g) The remedies provided for in this section are cumulative and shall be in addition to any others provided for by law.

[Added by Stats. 1971, ch. 1595, § 1; amended by Stats. 1984, ch. 1704, § 2.]

California Civil Code § 3344.1

(a)(1) Any person who uses a deceased personality's name, voice, signature, photograph, or likeness, in any manner, on or in products, merchandise, or goods, or for purposes of advertising or selling, or soliciting purchases of, products, merchandise, goods, or services, without prior consent from the person or persons specified in subdivision (c), shall be liable for any damages sustained by the person or persons injured as a result thereof. In addition, in any action brought under this section, the person who violated the section shall be liable to the injured party or parties in an amount equal to the greater of seven hundred fifty dollars ($750) or the actual damages suffered by the injured party or parties, as a result of the unauthorized use, and any profits from the unauthorized use that are attributable to the use and are not taken into account in computing the actual damages. In establishing these profits, the injured party or parties shall be required to present proof only of the gross revenue attributable to the use and the person who violated the section is required to prove his or her deductible expenses. Punitive damages may also be awarded to the injured party or parties. The prevailing party or parties in any action under this section shall also be entitled to attorney's fees and costs.

(2) For purposes of this subdivision, a play, book, magazine, newspaper, musical composition, audiovisual work, radio or television program, single and original work of art, work of political or newsworthy value, or an advertisement or commercial announcement for any of these works, shall not be considered a product, article of merchandise, good, or service if it is fictional or nonfictional entertainment, or a dramatic, literary, or musical work.

(3) If a work that is protected under paragraph (2) includes within it a use in connection with a product, article of merchandise, good, or service, this use

shall not be exempt under this subdivision, notwithstanding the unprotected use's inclusion in a work otherwise exempt under this subdivision, if the claimant proves that this use is so directly connected with a product, article of merchandise, good, or service as to constitute an act of advertising, selling, or soliciting purchases of that product, article of merchandise, good, or service by the deceased personality without prior consent from the person or persons specified in subdivision (c).

(b) The rights recognized under this section are property rights, freely transferable or descendible, in whole or in part, by contract or by means of any trust or any other testamentary instrument, executed before or after January 1, 1985. The rights recognized under this section shall be deemed to have existed at the time of death of any deceased personality who died prior to January 1, 1985, and, except as provided in subdivision (o), shall vest in the persons entitled to these property rights under the testamentary instrument of the deceased personality effective as of the date of his or her death. In the absence of an express transfer in a testamentary instrument of the deceased personality's rights in his or her name, voice, signature, photograph, or likeness, a provision in the testamentary instrument that provides for the disposition of the residue of the deceased personality's assets shall be effective to transfer the rights recognized under this section in accordance with the terms of that provision. The rights established by this section shall also be freely transferable or descendible by contract, trust, or any other testamentary instrument by any subsequent owner of the deceased personality's rights as recognized by this section. Nothing in this section shall be construed to render invalid or unenforceable any contract entered into by a deceased personality during his or her lifetime by which the deceased personality assigned the rights, in whole or in part, to use his or her name, voice, signature, photograph or likeness, regardless of whether the contract was entered into before or after January 1, 1985.

(c) The consent required by this section shall be exercisable by the person or persons to whom the right of consent, or portion thereof, has been transferred in accordance with subdivision (b), or if no transfer has occurred, then by the person or persons to whom the right of consent, or portion thereof, has passed in accordance with subdivision (d).

(d) Subject to subdivisions (b) and (c), after the death of any person, the rights under this section shall belong to the following person or persons and may be exercised, on behalf of and for the benefit of all of those persons, by those persons who, in the aggregate, are entitled to more than a one-half interest in the rights:

(1) The entire interest in those rights belong to the surviving spouse of the deceased personality unless there are any surviving children or grandchildren of the deceased personality, in which case one-half of the entire interest in those rights belong to the surviving spouse.

(2) The entire interest in those rights belong to the surviving children of the deceased personality and to the surviving children of any dead child of the deceased personality unless the deceased personality has a surviving spouse, in which case the ownership of a one-half interest in rights is divided among the surviving children and grandchildren.

(3) If there is no surviving spouse, and no surviving children or grandchildren, then the entire interest in those rights belong to the surviving parent or parents of the deceased personality.

(4) The rights of the deceased personality's children and grandchildren are in all cases divided among them and exercisable in the manner provided in Section

240 of the Probate Code according to the number of the deceased personality's children represented. The share of the children of a dead child of a deceased personality can be exercised only by the action of a majority of them.

(e) If any deceased personality does not transfer his or her rights under this section by contract, or by means of a trust or testamentary instrument, and there are no surviving persons as described in subdivision (d), then the rights set forth in subdivision (a) shall terminate.

(f)(1) A successor in interest to the rights of a deceased personality under this section or a licensee thereof may not recover damages for a use prohibited by this section that occurs before the successor in interest or licensee registers a claim of the rights under paragraph (2).

(2) Any person claiming to be a successor in interest to the rights of a deceased personality under this section or a licensee thereof may register that claim with the Secretary of State on a form prescribed by the Secretary of State and upon payment of a fee as set forth in subdivision (d) of Section 12195 of the Government Code. The form shall be verified and shall include the name and date of death of the deceased personality, the name and address of the claimant, the basis of the claim, and the rights claimed.

(3) Upon receipt and after filing of any document under this section, the Secretary of State shall post the document along with the entire registry of persons claiming to be a successor in interest to the rights of a deceased personality or a registered licensee under this section upon the World Wide Web, also known as the Internet. The Secretary of State may microfilm or reproduce by other techniques any of the filings or documents and destroy the original filing or document. The microfilm or other reproduction of any document under the provisions of this section shall be admissible in any court of law. The microfilm or other reproduction of any document may be destroyed by the Secretary of State 70 years after the death of the personality named therein.

(4) Claims registered under this subdivision shall be public records.

(g) No action shall be brought under this section by reason of any use of a deceased personality's name, voice, signature, photograph, or likeness occurring after the expiration of 70 years after the death of the deceased personality.

(h) As used in this section, "deceased personality" means any natural person whose name, voice, signature, photograph, or likeness has commercial value at the time of his or her death, whether or not during the lifetime of that natural person the person used his or her name, voice, signature, photograph, or likeness on or in products, merchandise or goods, or for purposes of advertising or selling, or solicitation of purchase of, products, merchandise, goods, or services. A "deceased personality" shall include, without limitation, any such natural person who has died within 70 years prior to January 1, 1985.

(i) As used in this section, "photograph" means any photograph or photographic reproduction, still or moving, or any video tape or live television transmission, of any person, such that the deceased personality is readily identifiable. A deceased personality shall be deemed to be readily identifiable from a photograph when one who views the photograph with the naked eye can reasonably determine who the person depicted in the photograph is.

(j) For purposes of this section, a use of a name, voice, signature, photograph, or likeness in connection with any news, public affairs, or sports broadcast or account, or any political campaign, shall not constitute a use for which consent is required under subdivision (a).

(k) The use of a name, voice, signature, photograph, or likeness in a commercial medium shall not constitute a use for which consent is required under subdivision (a) solely because the material containing the use is commercially sponsored or contains paid advertising. Rather, it shall be a question of fact whether or not the use of the deceased personality's name, voice, signature, photograph, or likeness was so directly connected with the commercial sponsorship or with the paid advertising as to constitute a use for which consent is required under subdivision (a).

(l) Nothing in this section shall apply to the owners or employees of any medium used for advertising, including, but not limited to, newspapers, magazines, radio and television networks and stations, cable television systems, billboards, and transit ads, by whom any advertisement or solicitation in violation of this section is published or disseminated, unless it is established that the owners or employees had knowledge of the unauthorized use of the deceased personality's name, voice, signature, photograph, or likeness as prohibited by this section.

(m) The remedies provided for in this section are cumulative and shall be in addition to any others provided for by law.

(n) This section shall apply to the adjudication of liability and the imposition of any damages or other remedies in cases in which the liability, damages, and other remedies arise from acts occurring directly in this state. For purposes of this section, acts giving rise to liability shall be limited to the use, on or in products, merchandise, goods, or services, or the advertising or selling, or soliciting purchases of, products, merchandise, goods, or services prohibited by this section.

(o) Notwithstanding any provision of this section to the contrary, if an action was taken prior to May 1, 2007, to exercise rights recognized under this section relating to a deceased personality who died prior to January 1, 1985, by a person described in subdivision (d), other than a person who was disinherited by the deceased personality in a testamentary instrument, and the exercise of those rights was not challenged successfully in a court action by a person described in subdivision (b), that exercise shall not be affected by subdivision (b). In such a case, the rights that would otherwise vest in one or more persons described in subdivision (b) shall vest solely in the person or persons described in subdivision (d), other than a person disinherited by the deceased personality in a testamentary instrument, for all future purposes.

(p) The rights recognized by this section are expressly made retroactive, including to those deceased personalities who died before January 1, 1985.

[Former § 990, added by Stats. 1984, ch. 1704, § 1; amended by Stats. 1988, ch. 113, § 2; amended and renumbered by Stats. 1999, ch. 998, § 1; amended by Stats. 1999, ch. 1000, § 9.5; Stats. 2007, ch. 439, § 1.]

Index

Case names and ship names are in *italic* font. Pages numbers with images are in **bold** font.